Achieve for *Principles of Macroeconomics*

Engaging Every Student. Supporting Every Instructor. Proven Success. Continued Enhancement.

Achieve for Economics sets the standard for integrating **activities, assessments, and analytics** into your teaching. It brings together all of the features that instructors and students need—an e-book with interactive graphing, LearningCurve adaptive quizzing, and other instructional and application activities, assessments, and extensive instructor resources—in a powerful platform that offers:

- A clean, intuitive, **mobile-friendly** interface.
- Powerful analytics.
- Self-regulated learning and goal-setting surveys.
- A fully integrated iClicker classroom response system.
- Exciting, enhanced, interactive graphing tools.

Our resources were **co-designed with instructors and students**, using a foundation of **learning research** and rigorous testing. The result is pedagogically superior content, organization, and functionality. Achieve's pre-built assignments engage students both *inside* and *outside* of class. And Achieve is effective for students of *all levels* of motivation and preparedness, whether they are high achievers or need extra support.

Macmillan Learning offers **deep platform integration** of Achieve with all LMS providers, including Blackboard, Brightspace, Canvas, and Moodle. With integration, students can access course content and their grades through one sign-in. And you can pair Achieve with course tools from your LMS, such as discussion boards and chat and Gradebook functionality. LMS integration is also available with Inclusive Access. For more information, visit MacmillanLearning.com/College/US/Solutions/LMS-Integration or talk to your local sales representative.

Achieve was built with **accessibility** in mind. Macmillan Learning strives to create products that are usable by all learners and meet universally applied accessibility standards. In addition to addressing product compatibility with assistive technologies such as screen reader software, alternative keyboard devices, and voice recognition products, we are working to ensure that the content and platforms we provide are fully accessible. For more information visit https://www.macmillan-learning.com/college/us/our-story/accessibility

◄ **LearningCurve Adaptive Quizzing** With a game-like interface, this popular and effective quizzing engine offers students a low-stakes way to brush up on concepts and help identify knowledge gaps. Questions are linked to relevant e-book sections, providing both the incentive to read and a framework for an efficient reading experience.

← Back to Study Plan	Score: 0/150	Question Value: 35 points

Lisa has a stand at the local farmer's market where she sells honey from her farm. Every week, Lisa sells out of honey while still having people waiting in line to buy some. What is happening in the market for Lisa's honey?

- ○ Quantity demanded exceeds quantity supplied, creating a shortage.
- ○ Quantity demanded exceeds quantity supplied, creating a surplus.
- ○ Quantity supplied exceeds quantity demanded, creating a surplus.
- ○ Quantity supplied exceeds quantity demanded, creating a shortage.

Need help on this question?

Read about this topic (no penalty)	Get a hint (fewer points)	Show answer (no points)

▶ **Enhanced E-Book with Interactive Graphs and an Integrated Podcast** The Achieve e-book offers highlighting, bookmarking, and note-taking. Students can download the e-book to read offline or to have it read aloud to them. Achieve allows instructors to assign chapter sections as homework.

The second edition e-book also includes embedded **Think Like an Economist podcast** episodes. Stevenson and Wolfers have created this engaging podcast that extends the themes of the text. The podcast is also paired with assignable questions within Achieve.

Figure 5b | A Decrease in Supply

Ⓐ A **decrease in supply** causes the supply curve to **shift left.**
Ⓑ This leads to a new supply-equals-demand **equilibrium.**
Ⓒ Leading to an **increase in the price.**
Ⓓ And a **decrease in the quantity.**

Click on the icon to make the graph fully interactive.

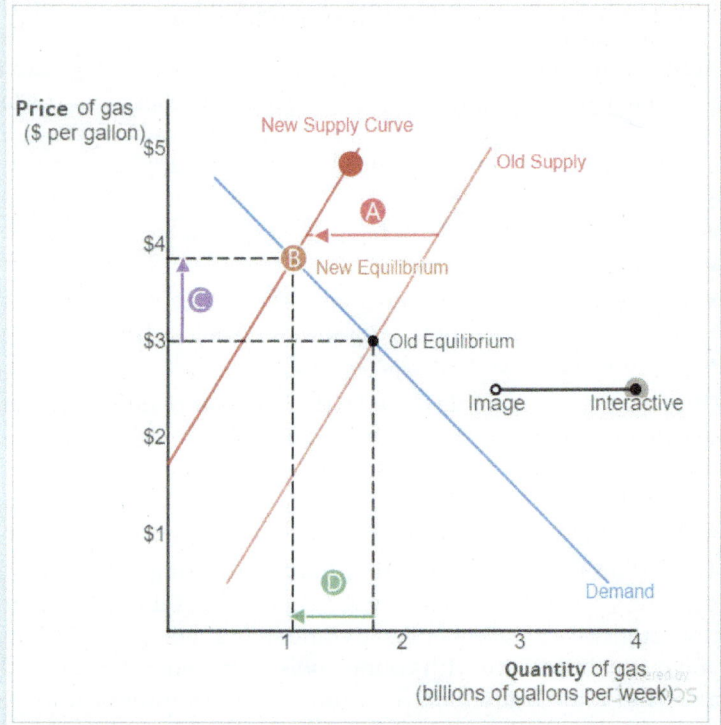

Figure 1

Imports and **exports** are a rising share of the U.S. economy

Share of GDP

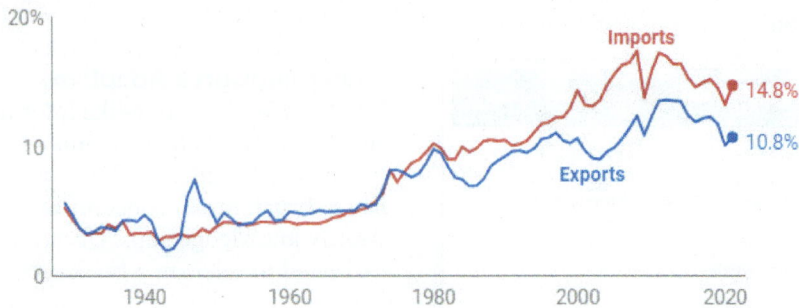

Chart: © Worth Publishers • Source: U.S. Bureau of Economic Analysis • Get the data • Download image

▲ The Achieve e-book now features interactive graphs. Students can now engage with economic models to see how components of the graph change as market dynamics change. Every data graph in the text is now interactive, so students can explore live visualizations and improve their data literacy.

ACTIVITIES

▶ **Decision Points** Decision Points activities allow students to explore their own decision-making process and how economic principles and thinking can inform their decisions. Students work step-by-step through decision-making scenarios, receiving feedback about how economic principles did (or did not) play into their choices. Decisions Points help students apply economic insights to their everyday lives.

Class Discussion, Remote Learning Activity

Instructor Activity Guide: Experimental Derivation of a Demand Curve

👥 **Best For**	⏱ **Class Time**	📊 **Implementation Effort**	⚠ **Bloom's Taxonomy**
Small Classes; Remote Instruction	40 minutes	Moderate	Apply

Activity Summary

In this activity, the instructor conducts a live auction for two drinks. Student responses are recorded to create a demand schedule and demand curve. The class then discusses factors that may shift the demand curve.

For video conferencing lectures (synchronous learning):

1. Use iClicker Cloud to record answers in real time. Prior to the lecture, set up a series of questions in iClicker Cloud which emulates the same responses you would expect to receive from a face-to-face class. Go over the instructions for the game, and then have students respond using the iClicker app. Some games may be more interesting if you repeat them a few times to see how students change their answers as they learn how their peers respond.
2. Some games only work if student answers are hidden from the class so have students submit their answers via a private chat to you or email. Then, reveal to the class how everyone responded.

Resources for this Activity

🖥 Clicker Questions for Experimental Derivation of a Demand Curve

⬇ Download

Recommended Tools

Ⓘ iClicker Cloud

Two drinks (such as Coke or coffee)

◀ **Instructor Activity Guides** The guides provide instructors with a structured plan to facilitate an activity that encourages student engagement in both face-to-face and remote learning courses. Each guide is based on a single topic and allows students to participate through questions, group work, presentations, and/or simulations. The guide displays the activity type, estimated prep and class time, implementation instructions, suggestions for remote implementation where applicable, and Learning Objectives and Bloom's level for ease of use. Our Instructor Activity Guides encourage engagement from a Pre-Class Reflection question to prime student interest and offer follow-up iClicker questions to measure comprehension.

▶ **Work It Out** These skill-building activities pair sample end-of-chapter problems with targeted feedback and video explanations to help students solve problems step-by-step. This approach allows students to work independently, tests their comprehension of concepts, and prepares them for class and exams.

News Analysis Macmillan Learning has partnered with leading news organizations to bring incisive analysis of current economic and policy trends into the economics classroom. In Achieve, instructors can access and assign activities on each video and memo that starts with basic reading comprehension and builds up to applying the analytical tools students have learned in their course to the economic or policy issue covered in the media.

ASSESSMENTS

▶ **End-of-Chapter Questions**
Developed by economists active in the classroom, these multistep problems are paired with rich feedback for incorrect and correct responses that guide students through the process of problem solving. These questions also feature our user-friendly graphing tool, designed so students focus entirely on economics and not on how to use the application.

Homework Curated homework problems feature randomly sampled variables and our user-friendly graphing tool. These problems are multistep with a variety of answer inputs—each with detailed and targeted feedback specific to that answer.

Practice Quizzes Designed to be used as a study tool, these quizzes feature multiple-choice questions and allow for multiple attempts as students familiarize themselves with content.

ANALYTICS

▶ **Learning Objectives, Reports, and Insights** Every asset you can assign in Achieve is tagged to specific Learning Objectives. Reporting within Achieve helps students see how they are performing against objectives, and it helps instructors determine if any student, group of students, or the class as a whole needs extra help in specific areas. This enables more efficient and effective instructor interventions.

Achieve provides reports on student activities, assignments, and assessments at the course level, unit level, subunit level, and individual student level, so instructors can identify trouble spots and adjust their efforts accordingly. Within Reports, the Insights section offers snapshots with high-level data on student performance and behavior, to answer such questions as:

- What are the top Learning Objectives to review in this unit?
- What are the top assignments to review?
- What's the range of performance on a particular assignment?
- How many students aren't logging in?

Achieve offers surveys that help students self-direct, and develop confidence in, their own learning:

- The **Goal-Setting Survey** asks students to consider their goals for the class and how they plan to manage their time and learning strategies.
- **Reflection surveys** ask students to reflect on what's been working and where they need to make changes.
- **Each completed survey generates a report** that reveals how each student is doing, beyond the course grade.

These tools help instructors engage their students in a discussion on soft skills, such as metacognition, effective learning and time management strategies, and other noncognitive skills that impact student success.

Powerful Support for Instructors

Test Bank This comprehensive Test Bank contains multiple-choice and short-answer questions to help instructors assess students' comprehension, interpretation, and ability to synthesize.

Lecture Slides These brief, interactive, and visually interesting slides are designed to hold students' attention in class with graphics and animations demonstrating key concepts and real-world examples.

Clicker Slides These slides contain questions to incorporate active learning in the classroom. Students can participate by using the iClicker app on their smartphone or laptop.

iClicker Integration With Achieve's seamless integration with iClicker, you can help any student participate—in the classroom or virtually. iClicker's attendance feature gets students in class, then instructors can choose from flexible polling and quizzing options to engage, check understanding, and get feedback from students in real time. iClicker also allows students to participate using laptops, mobile devices, or iClicker remotes— whichever each student prefers. Additionally, we offer Instructor Activity Guides and book-specific iClicker question slides within Achieve to make the most out of your class time. It's no surprise that over a decade after being founded by educators, iClicker still leads the market. And thousands of instructors continue to give every student a voice with our simple, award-winning student engagement solutions.

Instructor's Resource Manual The Instructor's Resource Manual offers instructors teaching materials and tips to enhance the classroom experience, along with chapter objectives, outlines, and suggestions for further reading.

Gradebook Assignment scores are collected into a comprehensive Gradebook providing instructors reporting on individuals and overall course performance.

Customer Support Our Achieve Client Success Specialist Team—dedicated platform experts—provides collaboration, software expertise, and consulting to tailor each course to fit your instructional goals and student needs. Start with a demo at a time that works for you to learn more about how to set up your custom-ized course. Talk to your sales representative or visit https://www .macmillanlearning.com/college/us /contact-us/training-and-demos for more information.

Powerful, Continued Input from the Faculty Advisory Board

We are delighted to partner with the following faculty members who provide us with feedback, insight, and ideas to continually improve Achieve for both students and instructors:

Annette Chamberlain, *Virginia Western Community College*

Christopher Clarke, *Washington State University*

Thomas Flesher, *Suffolk County Community College*

Sherry Jensen, *Salt Lake Community College*

Erika Martinez, *University of South Florida*

Susan McCoy, *Des Moines Area Community College*

Eric Parsons, *University of Missouri*

Aisling Winston, *University of Buffalo*

> **Pricing and bundling options are available at the Macmillan student store: store.macmillanlearning.com/**

WHAT'S NEW IN THE SECOND EDITION?

The overwhelming majority of instructors and students use Achieve online courseware for *Principles of Macroeconomics*. The new edition offers significant improvements to Achieve. New digital assets in every chapter include:

- **"Think Like an Economist" podcast.** Betsey Stevenson and Justin Wolfers have created this engaging podcast that extends the themes of their text and is linked to virtually every chapter in the text. Episodes are available in Achieve, are assignable with assessment questions, and are linked in the text.
- **Interactive graphs.** To help students improve data literacy and understand economic models, Achieve now offers interactive graphs throughout the e-book. Students can manipulate graphs to simulate market dynamics and to explore historical data, providing a more engaging reading and learning experience.
- **New homework assignments available in Achieve.** Reimagined assessment offers targeted feedback for use in class and as homework assignments. Designed so that students learn by doing the economics, these problems contain multiple question types, including our innovative and intuitive graphing tool that assesses students' understanding of economics and not their use of graphing software. Each chapter offers a new set of assignable, multi-step problems that complement online, auto-graded versions of the end-of-chapter problems.

The second edition of the text has new coverage and updates throughout. In particular:

- **Chapter 1** offers a stronger emphasis on the theme Every Decision Is an Economic Decision. New coverage of the coronavirus pandemic, including female workplace participation and consumer decisions around work, family, attending school, and starting a business.
- **Chapter 2** includes coverage of pandemic-related demand shifters (baking supplies, gym equipment, bikes, puzzles, workout apps), shutdown-related examples of which retailers did well in the recession, and revised sections on using economic thinking to change behavior and save money.
- **Chapter 4** includes a new chapter-opening story about an applicant entering the job market, an improved three-step recipe for predicting market changes, and new examples of equilibrium during

the pandemic, such as the markets for clothing and child care.

- **Chapter 5** includes a new analysis of the consumer surplus derived from childhood Covid-19 vaccinations.
- **Chapter 6** includes a new discussion of the peer-to-peer marketplace, and revised discussions of on how prices help coordinate better outcomes between suppliers and consumers and act as incentives for suppliers. New examples illuminate the concepts of comparative advantage and specialization.
- **Chapter 7** includes a revised discussion of the arguments for and against limiting international trade, and a fresh look at U.S. policy on free trade.
- **Chapter 9** includes GDP data updates throughout.
- **Chapter 10** includes an expanded discussion of North and South Korea, the latest coverage of technological progress, and updates on Baby Boomer retirement and its effect on the workforce.
- **Chapter 11** analyzes unemployment during the pandemic, updated minimum wage coverage, and discussion of supply-equals-demand equilibrium wage.
- **Chapter 12** has expanded coverage of inflation undermining, advice on how to beat money illusion by negotiating for a real wage, and more on the costs of expected inflation.
- **Chapter 13** covers the pandemic's effect on saving and consumption, and a discussion on high interest rates and their effect on borrowing.
- **Chapter 14** includes clarified presentation of investment tools: compounding and discounting, new coverage of investment decisions related to environmental concerns, and a new interactive table showing research

on return to investment for nearly every college in the United States.

- **Chapter 15** includes more coverage on student loans, monitoring your FICO score, and new coverage on how the toilet paper panic of 2020 was like a bank run.
- **Chapter 16** includes analysis of Covid-19's effect on supply chains and disruption on investment.
- **Chapter 17** clarifies booms, expansions and recessions, and includes new coverage of the Covid recession throughout.
- **Chapter 18** analyzes Peloton during the pandemic, revamped coverage of how interest rates boost consumption, and new content on policy decisions during the pandemic.
- **Chapter 19** discusses the effects of Covid-19 and related restrictions on the restaurant industry.
- **Chapter 20** expands coverage on imports prices and their effect on the Phillips Curve, and includes a new Interpreting the Data on global supply chains.
- **Chapter 21** has a new opening story on Philip Jefferson, recently appointed Federal Reserve Governor, a feature on how a virus is like a tax, and new analysis on macroeconomic shocks and policy responses in the wake of Covid-19.
- **Chapter 22** includes coverage of the Fed's response to the pandemic, including negative interest rate policy, suspension of the reserve requirement, the discount window, and quantitative easing.
- **Chapter 23** covers the government's response to the pandemic, including social insurance, and stimulus payments and their effect on households and the overall macroeconomy.

PRINCIPLES of
MACROECONOMICS

PRINCIPLES of MACROECONOMICS

Second Edition

Betsey Stevenson

University of Michigan

Justin Wolfers

University of Michigan

worth publishers
Macmillan Learning

New York

Executive Vice President and General Manager: Charles Linsmeier
Vice President, Social Sciences and High School: Shani Fisher
Senior Executive Program Manager: Carolyn Merrill
Executive Development Editor: Lukia Kliossis
Senior Development Editor: Ann Kirby-Payne
Executive Marketing Manager: Scott Guile
Marketing Assistant: Claudia Cruz
Market Development Manager: Stephanie Ellis
Executive Director, Digital Workflow Strategy: Noel Hohnstine
Senior Lead Content Developer: Joshua Hill
Media Editor: Stephanie Sosa
Media Project Manager: Andrew Vaccaro
Editorial Assistant: Amanda Nava
Senior Director, Content Management Enhancement: Tracey Kuehn
Senior Managing Editor: Lisa Kinne
Senior Content Project Manager: Martha Emry
Senior Workflow Manager: Jennifer Wetzel
Production Supervisor: Brianna Lester
Associate Director of Content Standards: Betsy Granger
Director of Design, Content Management: Diana Blume
Senior Design Services Manager: Natasha A. S. Wolfe
Interior Design: Kevin Kall and Dirk Kaufman
Senior Cover Design Manager: John Callahan
Cover Design: Dirk Kaufman
Art Manager: Matthew McAdams
Illustration Coordinator: Janice Donnola
Illustrations: Network Graphics
Executive Permissions Editor: Robin Fadool
Photo Researcher: Cheryl Dubois, Lumina Datamatics, Inc.
Composition: Lumina Datamatics, Inc.
Printing and Binding: King Printing Co., Inc.

ISBN-13: 978-1-319-33017-0 / ISBN-10: 1-319-33017-7

Loose-leaf Edition
ISBN-13: 978-1-319-43335-2 / ISBN-10: 1-319-43335-9

International Edition
ISBN-13: 978-1-319-49855-9 / ISBN-10: 1-319-49855-8

Library of Congress Control Number: 2022942492

Worth Publishers
120 Broadway
New York, NY 10271
www.macmillanlearning.com

Dedication

With thanks to those in previous generations who inspired, educated, and raised us.

In awe of those in the next generation—you are better, faster, and smarter.

And with inspiration from introductory students who are about to learn that economics will give you superpowers—our hope is that you'll use those superpowers to create a more joyful world.

About the Authors

Betsey Stevenson is a professor of economics and public policy at the University of Michigan. Her research focuses on public policy and the labor market. She is an expert on women's labor market experiences, the economic forces shaping the modern family, and the role of subjective well-being data for public policy. She frequently testifies before Congress on the state of the labor market, its impact on the broad macroeconomy, and the impact of public policy on the labor market and the macroeconomy. She is a research associate with the National Bureau of Economic Research, a fellow of the Institute for Economic Research in Munich, a visiting associate professor of economics at the University of Sydney, and a research Fellow with the Centre for Economic Policy Research in London. She served as the chief economist of the U.S. Department of Labor from 2010 to 2011 and as a member of the Council of Economic Advisers from 2013 to 2015, where she advised President Obama on social policy, labor market, and trade issues. In 2020, she served as a member of the Biden-Harris transition team for the U.S. Treasury. Betsey is a trusted presence in the public debate about economics and public policy and she frequently writes policy-focused columns and provides commentary on television, radio, and to newspapers. She earned a BA in economics and mathematics from Wellesley College and an AM and PhD in economics from Harvard University.

Justin Wolfers is a professor of economics and public policy at the University of Michigan. He does research in both macroeconomics and applied microeconomics topics, and has explored unemployment and inflation, the power of prediction markets, the economic forces shaping the modern family, discrimination, and happiness. He is a research associate with the National Bureau for Economic Research, a fellow of the Brookings Institution, a fellow of the Peterson Institute for International Economics, a research fellow with the Centre for Economic Policy Research in London, a fellow of the Institute for Economic Research in Munich, a visiting professor of economics at the University of Sydney, and an international research fellow at the Kiel Institute for the World Economy in Germany. He has been an editor of the Brookings Papers on Economic Activity, a board member on the Committee on the Status of Women in Economics, a member of the Panel of Advisors of the U.S. Congressional Budget Office, among many other board and advisory positions. He is currently a contributing columnist for the *New York Times*, and has written about economic issues in numerous other outlets. He is frequently quoted in the media on economic policy and relied upon to provide unbiased assessments of the current state of the macroeconomy. Justin earned a BA in economics from the University of Sydney and an AM and PhD in economics from Harvard University.

One of them was once described by *Jezebel.com* as the "hippest-economist-ever." The other was not.

Betsey and Justin live in Ann Arbor, Michigan, with their children Matilda and Oliver, their lovable mutt, Max, and their playful cat, Bela.

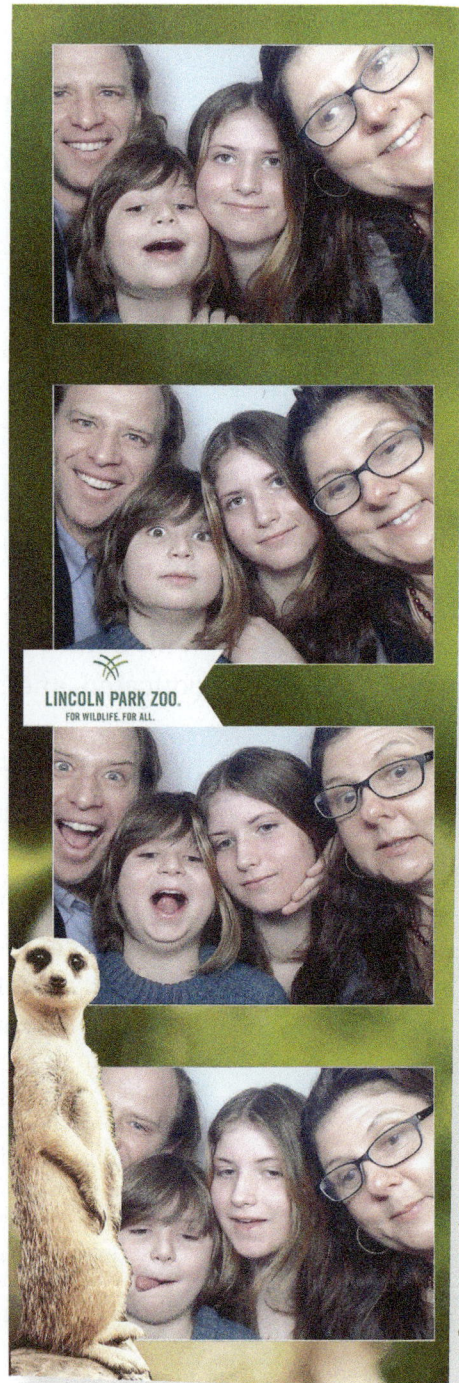

LINCOLN PARK ZOO.
FOR WILDLIFE. FOR ALL.

Betsey Stevenson and Justin Wolfers

A Fresh Perspective on Economics

A slow-motion revolution has transformed economics. We've moved beyond the widget factory—the standardized set of business interactions involving inputs, outputs, and pricing decisions—toward a social science that can speak to the decisions we make in every aspect of our lives. Successive cohorts of economists have transformed the field so that it has greater relevance and a closer relationship to actual human behavior, making it more meaningful to more people. This is no longer your parents' economics.

This transformation presents a once-in-a-generation teaching opportunity. More than ever before, we have the capacity to deliver a compelling introductory economics class that will deliver an extraordinary return on our students' investment in the field.

This opportunity requires a textbook that works with instructors to showcase how economics has become *broader,* and we show that it is more relevant to a larger, more diverse population of students. It has to show that economics has become more *useful* for the ordinary business of life, and our students delight in seeing the relevance of economic tools to the real-world decisions they face. We believe that by focusing on *intuition,* we can reorient students to seeing themselves as economic actors poised to apply the lessons they're learning throughout their lives.

Our fresh perspective gives us an opportunity to write in a voice that students actually want to read. If you've ever had the pleasure of reading one of those popular economics books that takes readers on a joyous romp through our field, you quickly understand why millions of people spend their weekends reading them. Podcast rankings and best-seller lists reveal a latent demand for an approach that supplies some of the same magic. We aim to bring that sense of delight and discovery to your introductory economics class.

Economics can provide students with a toolkit of extraordinary breadth, usefulness, and insight. It's a toolkit they can use to better understand and navigate their world, empowering them to make better decisions in the many different roles they'll play in the economy, their communities, and their careers—indeed, in every aspect of their lives.

For economics instructors, the opportunity is larger still, giving us the capacity to transform individual lives and entire communities. Our goal is for every single student who turns the page to do more than remember—to use(!)—what they've learned, every day, for the rest of their lives. We aim to show them the power and transformative potential in the lessons they're about to absorb.

We each have that one class that we remember from college. It's the class you look back on as having somehow caused your synapses to fire differently, that sparked new neural connections, and provided a clarity that felt like it allowed you to see beyond the horizon. It might have been the class that inspired you to study economics—or maybe it was an elective that, though it seemed tangential to your studies at the time, you've found yourself drawing on every day since. We want principles of economics to be *that class* for each of our students, and for each of yours.

Betsey Stevenson

Justin Wolfers

How to Think Like an Economist

Many students don't realize—and instructors sometimes forget—that economics is, in its simplest form, the study of "the ordinary business of everyday life." Learning to think like an economist can profoundly change the way we all go about that business, informing decisions ranging from how we manage our own time to how governments allocate budgets. We've built *Principles of Economics* with the goal of teaching students to see the world through an economic lens and make informed decisions that benefit them and reflect their values.

Recognize that *every decision is an economic decision*

Should you get a job, or go to grad school? Do it yourself, or delegate? Spend your extra money, or save it? Economists know that economic principles can be applied broadly, to just about any decision. Our goal is for *every single student* to walk out of the principles course with a consistent toolkit for economic decision making.

Learn the four core principles of economics

In Chapter 1, we introduce students to four core principles that form a simple but powerful framework for making even the most mundane decisions:

- The marginal principle: Should you study for one more hour?
- The cost-benefit principle: Should you devote the hour to economics, or to another course?
- The opportunity cost principle: What else could you do with that hour?
- The interdependence principle: How will it affect your grade? Your cumulative GPA? Your options for future courses? Your social life? Your sleep? Your roommates' sleep?

By starting small, we lay a solid foundation for the study of economics. We then return to these four core principles throughout the book, to show students how these basic tools scale up to larger decisions, with higher stakes.

Lay a solid foundation with supply and demand

The four core principles are the foundation upon which we build our understanding of supply, demand, and equilibrium. We walk students patiently through these crucial topics, dedicating a full chapter to each, and providing ample support with concrete, familiar examples, and plenty of opportunities to practice drawing and shifting curves. We've seen how this patient and deliberate approach helps students to build a deeper and more intuitive understanding of the ideas behind the curves and a thorough understanding of the way these economic forces affect decisions across the economy. By the time students get through the first few chapters, the urge to find an equilibrium is practically a reflex.

Build up from there

Armed with the core principles and well versed in applying the supply-and-demand framework, students arrive at later chapters ready to apply their economic intuition to new markets and more advanced topics. In each case, we follow a familiar recipe, starting with individual choices, then aggregating them to yield demand and supply curves, and ultimately market outcomes. We work through the core principles to discover a series of Rational Rules, such as producing until marginal revenue equals marginal cost, or consuming until the marginal benefit of a dollar of spending today is equal to the marginal benefit of spending a dollar-plus-interest tomorrow.

Learn "one economics"

The core principles of economics are the same whether students are studying micro-economics or macroeconomics. In *Principles of Microeconomics,* for example, we take a broad approach to externalities, applying it not only to governments looking to mini-mize environmental harm, but also to managers looking to fix misaligned incentives in the workplace. In *Principles of Macroeconomics,* the framework we introduce to forecast consumption yields concrete advice about when to save, how to form a saving plan, and how to stick to it. No matter which course they take, students become nimble users of the economic approach, applying it to problems big and small.

Use economics every day

Few students will become professional economists—*but every single one of them is an economic decision maker.* They'll manage their own time, finances, and families. They'll work in businesses, nonprofits, or in the public sector. They'll all be affected by economic policy. We want them to see how economics can make them more effective decision makers in each of these roles. For example, we introduce comparative advantage as a framework for efficiently allocating household tasks, and show how it can be used to orga-nize teams, businesses, and other organizations before finally discussing it as a driver of international trade. Our analysis of the relative efficiency of markets demonstrates how managers and nonprofits can harness market forces. This broad reach makes economics more inviting to more students, whether they want to be economists or educators, engi-neers or entrepreneurs.

A Modern Approach to Macroeconomics

Our approach integrates the current economic insights into the principles curriculum, reflecting both the realities that students experience and the problems that modern economists are focused on.

Micro Foundations of Macroeconomics

Whether economists are looking at microeconomic or macroeconomic topics, our method is the same: Focus on individual decisions, explore the factors that shape those decisions, and aggregate them to illustrate market outcomes. This sharp focus on micro foundations puts the student front and center, confronting them with the decisions they face—or will face—in their own lives. Students analyze decisions related to consumption and saving (Chapter 13) and investment (Chapter 14) to see the interaction between their personal choices and broader economic trends. They'll explore the role of the financial sector (Chapter 15), learn some basic rules of personal finance, and consider the influence of the global economy (Chapter 16). By highlighting the connections between individual decisions and the economy at large, we make broad economic concepts personal—and therefore memorable and useful.

GDP equals total spending on final goods

which embodies the value created at earlier stages

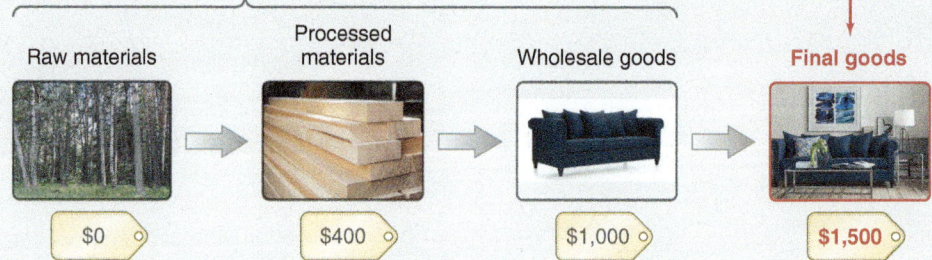

Raw materials	Processed materials	Wholesale goods	**Final goods**
$0	$400	$1,000	**$1,500**

Photo left to right: Alalal/Shutterstock; Vasily Gamayunov/Shutterstock © Worth Publishers

A Flexible Approach to Business Cycle Models

Students may feel they are at the mercy of the business cycle. We teach them to distinguish short-term fluctuations from long-term trends, to recognize what happens during recessions and expansions, and to understand how it all affects them. We introduce them to the indicators that they can use to assess where the economy is—and where it might be going—at any given time.

Of course, any economist knows that there's more than one way to analyze the business cycle, and we want instructors to be able to choose the approach that works best for them. We start with what we call The Fed View, our analysis of business cycles follows the approach and language that policymakers use to analyze macroeconomic fluctuations. We start students off with a thorough examination of the nature of business cycles (Chapter 17). From there, we move on to show them a stylized version of the basic framework that Federal Reserve policymakers use to interpret the business cycle. Students learn how to use the *IS* curve to explain spending decisions, together with an *MP* curve that describes monetary policy and the influence of the financial sector (Chapter 18). We then add a modern Phillips curve to explain inflation (Chapter 19). Finally, we bring these pieces together into a complete general equilibrium model (Chapter 20). This approach echoes media reports of ongoing policy debates, and will remain relevant to students long after they leave the classroom.

Of course, we also recognize that many instructors prefer to teach using the more traditional Aggregate Demand and Aggregate Supply model, and so we provide full coverage of The *AD-AS* View in a single chapter (Chapter 21). An appendix (A Closer Look at Aggregate Expenditure and the Multiplier) offers a more detailed treatment into aggregate expenditure and the multiplier for instructors who wish to engage more deeply with that content.

Instructors are invited to choose the approach that works best for them. Either path will lead students to the same conclusion—a clear understanding of business cycles—and prepare them for a thorough understanding of how monetary and fiscal policy can be used to counter the effects of the business cycle.

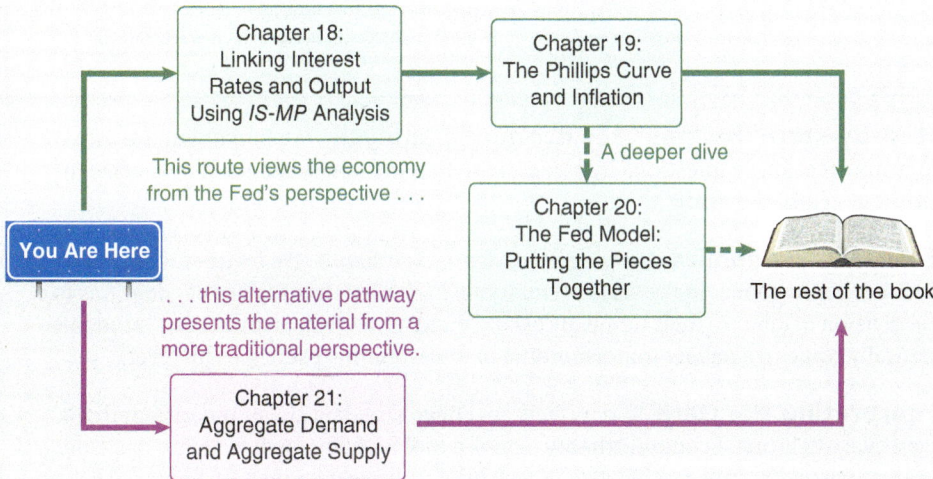

Organizational note: *As discussed in this part's opener, different economists analyze business cycles from slightly different perspectives. Much like viewing a concert, you can see things differently depending on where you sit. Now that you've been introduced to business cycles, it's time for you—or more likely, your instructor—to choose your seat for the macroeconomic show. If your instructor wants you to see the economy from the same perspective as the Fed does, they'll direct you to head on to read Chapters 18 and 19 (perhaps with Chapter 20 as a capstone). If your instructor recommends a more traditional view, then they'll have you read Chapter 21. And if they want you to really appreciate the role of aggregate expenditure, they might recommend you start with the appendix. Remember that you'll still be able to see the whole show, no matter where you sit.*

```
Chapter 18:          Chapter 19:
Linking Interest     The Phillips Curve
Rates and Output     and Inflation
Using IS-MP Analysis

This route views the economy        A deeper dive
from the Fed's perspective . . .
                                 Chapter 20:
You Are Here                     The Fed Model:
                                 Putting the Pieces
                                 Together            The rest of the book
. . . this alternative pathway
presents the material from a
more traditional perspective.

Chapter 21:
Aggregate Demand
and Aggregate Supply
```

A Real-World Look at Economic Policy

Macroeconomic policy is where students' lives and the economy at large intersect, and every student can benefit from understanding how it is made and implemented, and what policy decisions mean for them. We begin by stepping inside a Federal Reserve meeting to learn how it sets monetary policy, before exploring its goals and the tools it uses to keep the economy running smoothly (Chapter 22). We then take a look at how the government shapes economic policy through taxing and spending decisions, and how it uses fiscal policy to smooth business cycle (Chapter 23). Throughout both chapters, we provide tangible connections between policy and personal decisions, so students can use what they've learned to develop their own ideas about how the country should manage its economy—and how they should manage their own.

Applications That Keep It Real

Benjamin Franklin famously observed, "Tell me and I forget; Teach me and I remember; Involve me and I learn." As instructors, we know that he was right—the best way for students to learn is to involve them with the content, and we've worked hard to demonstrate that students' lives already involve—and will always involve—real economic decisions.

A Three-Step Recipe for Predicting Market Outcomes

Congratulations! You have now built the foundations of a powerful framework for predicting market outcomes. The study of buyers that you began in Chapter 2 tells you which factors shape and shift the demand curve. Likewise, your study of sellers that you began in Chapter 3 tells you about the supply side. When you put these together, you can predict how markets will respond to changing economic conditions. This simple supply-and-demand framework is the most powerful predictive device I know.

Okay, let's practice actually applying the supply-and-demand approach by analyzing a few real-world business questions. When you work through these examples, you should use the following three-step recipe that will help you predict real-world market outcomes.

Step 1: Determine which curve is shifting (supply, demand, or both). Remember that any change affecting buyers or their marginal benefits will shift the demand curve, while any change affecting sellers or their marginal costs will shift the supply curve.

Step 2: Determine if it's an increase, shifting the curve to the right, or a decrease, shifting the curve to the left. An increase in marginal benefit is an increase in demand, while an increase in marginal cost creates a decrease in supply.

Step 3: Determine how prices and quantities will change in the new equilibrium. Compare the old equilibrium with the new equilibrium.

Step-by-step "recipes" for economic analysis We boil down the most common economic questions into basic instructions that students, like chefs, can return to again and again.

Everyday Economics No widgets, no lemonade stands. We invite students to apply their economic toolkit to the sorts of situations they face—from salary negotiations to the division of labor in their home. By asking themselves "what would I do?" students naturally come to a deeper understanding of the economic principles involved.

Interpreting the Data Today, facts are cheap and data are abundant—perhaps even overwhelming. Economic theory—once a tool for filling in data gaps—has emerged as a framework for interpreting data. These brief features demonstrate how to use it, and help students learn to transform data into insight.

Do the Economics

Answers: a. Don't let yesterday's $35 sunk cost lead you to go to a party you won't enjoy. b. Walk out. You've already paid for the ticket and can't get the money back, so the $13 is a sunk cost you should ignore. c. The problem says that you would prefer to be with your friends, so go to Miami already! The $700 nonrefundable ticket is a sunk cost.

It is easy to fall for the sunk-cost fallacy. Think about the following scenarios:

a. Yesterday you bought a Halloween costume for $35 to wear to a friend's Halloween party. But today you're feeling sick, and as you're getting dressed to go to the party, you realize that you won't enjoy it. Do you head to the party?

b. You paid $13 for movie tickets. But 30 minutes into the film, you've seen enough: The acting is terrible, the plot is predictable, and the jokes are cringe-worthy. Do you stay for the last hour?

c. You found a great deal for spring break: a $700 package deal to Puerto Rico. You immediately buy the package and tell your friends about it. Unfortunately, by the time they call, tickets are sold out. Instead, your friends decide to drive to Miami, where you can all stay for free with your best friend's uncle. You would prefer to be with your friends, but the $700 ticket is nonrefundable. Do you go to Puerto Rico? ∎

Do the Economics Embedded directly into the text narrative, these brief exercises confront students with real-life scenarios and challenge them to "do economics," by analyzing the underlying logic of specific scenarios and working through the solutions. With practice, students begin to see economics as a verb—an active process of applying economics to understand the world and inform their choices.

Tools for Efficient Learning

We've worked hard to think like students. Integrated study tools prepare students for the road ahead, support students while they read, and provide practical tools for review.

A Textbook Navigation System

It can be all too be easy for students to get lost in the economic woods, focusing only on the trees right in front of them. We provide tools to help students both see the road ahead and pan back to see the bigger picture so that they can synthesize what they're learning as they move through the course.

A Quick Review of Graphs Introductory economics should be inviting, not intimidating. So we start off the course by reminding students of what they already know, and prime them for what's ahead with a simplified preview.

Part I: Foundations of Economics

The Big Picture

We'll start our adventure by introducing you to the **four core principles** that provide the foundation of all economic analysis. Taken together, they form a **decision-making framework** that you can apply to make better decisions. Your goal here is to **develop your economic intuition** so that you can apply these principles to real decisions that you'll face in your personal and professional life.

Next, we'll put that economic intuition to work by applying the core principles to understand how people decide what to buy and what to sell. We'll build your understanding of the building blocks of economic analysis: **demand** and **supply.** You'll learn to analyze how these market forces lead to an **equilibrium** that determines the price and quantity of nearly everything.

As you progress through these four chapters, you'll begin to sense the supply and demand forces at play in your everyday life—from the things you buy to the attention you supply to different endeavors. Building a solid foundation in economics will provide you with an **economic toolkit** that will serve you well long after you have finished this course.

1 The Four Core Principles of Economics

Learn the four core principles that provide the foundation of all economic analysis, and use them to analyze choices and make better decisions.
- Why is it useful to learn to think like an economist?
- How do you evaluate costs and benefits?
- Which costs should you look at when evaluating a choice?
- Why should you learn to think on the margin?
- How do all our decisions interact?

2 Demand and Consumer Choice

Understand people's buying (or demand) decisions.
- What is the shape of *your* individual demand curve?
- How can you apply the core principles of economics to make good buying decisions?
- How does individual demand add up to market demand?
- Which factors shift demand curves?

3 Supply and Producer Choice

Learn how businesses make supply decisions.
- What is the shape of *your* individual supply curve?
- How can you apply the core principles to make good supply decisions?
- How does individual supply add up to market supply?
- Which factors shift supply curves?

4 Equilibrium: Where Supply Meets Demand

Analyze how supply and demand determine the equilibrium price and quantity.
- How do markets determine what is produced and how it is allocated?
- How do markets bring supply and demand into balance?
- What happens when demand and supply shift?
- What do changes in prices and quantity reveal?

◄ **Content roadmaps**
Simple graphic organizers lay out content for each set of chapters. Students never wander into "uncharted territory," but instead arrive at each new topic fully prepared, with a broad view of the terrain and a plan for navigating it.

Supply and Producer Choice

CHAPTER 3

While you might not think of yourself as a seller if you aren't managing a business, you are already managing one very important small business: Your Own Undertaking (or YOU, for short). YOU are already making very important supply decisions. You may have sold concert tickets on StubHub; perhaps you have sold collectibles on eBay or a piece of furniture on Facebook Marketplace. You may hold a part-time job, where you sell your labor in return for an hourly wage.

How much would you sell your seat for?

You also supply things in transactions that don't involve money. Your household is like a small business, and you might produce cooking or cleaning services in return for similar services from your family or housemates. You probably supply child care, transport, and advice to those you love. You also supply camaraderie to your friends, an audience to online advertisers, and your attention to this important chapter on supply.

In this chapter, we'll dig into *supply*—the decisions that we make as sellers. The structure of this chapter largely parallels our analysis of demand. We'll start with individual decisions and apply the core principles of economics to help guide you to make good supply decisions. Next, we'll pan back and assess total market supply, which is the sum of these individual decisions. We'll then explore how changing market conditions shift supply.

There's a lot to cover with supply—the global economy consists of millions of businesses producing and selling a dazzling array of goods. But the same logic underpins every business decision. Let's start by putting ourselves into the shoes of a seller trying to decide how much to produce and sell.

Chapter Objective

Understand how sellers make supply decisions.

3.1 Individual Supply: What You Sell, at Each Price
Discover the shape of your business's individual supply curve.

3.2 Your Decisions and Your Individual Supply Curve
Apply the core principles to make good supply decisions.

3.3 Market Supply: What the Market Sells
Add up individual supply to discover market supply.

3.4 What Shifts Supply Curves?
Understand what factors shift supply curves.

3.5 Shifts versus Movements Along Supply Curves
Distinguish between movements along a supply curve and shifts of supply curves.

🎙 **Podcast**
Supply
Getting the Best Out of What You Sell

Five factors shift the market supply curve:
1. Input prices
2. Productivity and technology
3. Prices of related outputs
4. Expectations
5. The type and number of sellers
. . . and not a change in price.

3.2 Your Decisions and Your Individual Supply Curve

Learning Objective *Apply the core principles to make good supply decisions.*

Don't Summarize . . . Synthesize

Effective studying requires more than just repeating and reviewing. We've developed study tools that encourage students to unpack what they've learned, repackage it with what they already knew, and test themselves on how well they understand it all.

3.6 Tying It Together

The Principles That Guide Demand Also Guide Supply

I bet you've noticed some similarities between this chapter, which analyzed supply and seller's decisions, and the previous chapter, which analyzed demand and buyer's decisions. There's a good reason for this — the forces that drive supply and demand are very closely related. This is best illustrated by a simple thought experiment involving a brief detour to Mars.

But let's start on Earth. Think about a simple transaction, such as when you pull into my gas station and buy 10 gallons of gas for $30. (I don't actually own a gas station, but let's pretend for a moment that I do.) If you're like most economics students, you'll analyze this by noting that you are buying gas and I am selling gas. Consequently, we can analyze this transaction by exploring your demand for gas and my supply of gas.

Now consider how a Martian — who understands neither money nor gas — might view the same transaction. They might think that I am trying to buy your dollar bills and you are willing to sell them to me. How will I pay for your dollar bills? Why, with gas, of course. Viewed this way, I am the buyer who has a demand for your dollar bills, and you are the seller who is willing to supply them to me if I'm willing to pay you enough gallons of gas.

◀ Tying It Together Each chapter concludes with thoughtfully composed sections that show students how to synthesize new information with prior knowledge—a crucial component of understanding and retention.

Producer Surplus

Consumer surplus tells us about the gains that buyers get from a trade. But buyers aren't the only ones who benefit from a transaction; sellers also gain something. When you gain economic surplus from *selling* something, economists refer to it as **producer surplus,** because you're earning that surplus in your role as a producer. You gain producer surplus when you sell something at a higher price than the marginal costs you incur.

Producer surplus is the price, less the marginal cost. Let's analyze what happens when you buy a pair of Levi's for $50, but this time, we'll focus on the producer's perspective. For Levi Strauss, the company that makes those jeans, the marginal benefit of selling you those jeans is the $50 price you paid for them. And the marginal cost is the $35 worth of extra denim, thread, and labor it took to make that extra pair of jeans. Levi's is thrilled to get $50 in return for $35 worth of denim, thread and labor. It's thrilled because producing and selling those jeans made the company $15 better off. This $15 is the producer surplus that Levi's gains from this transaction.

Producer surplus describes the gain a producer gets from selling something at a higher price than necessary for them to want to supply the item, which is its marginal cost. More generally, the producer surplus a seller gains from a transaction is the price they receive less the marginal cost. And so, you can measure it as:

$$\text{Producer surplus} = \text{Price} - \text{Marginal cost}$$

Producer surplus is the area above the supply curve and below the price. So far, we've figured out the producer surplus from Levi's selling you one pair of jeans. What about the total producer surplus from all the jeans sold by all producers? The producer surplus from any individual transaction is the price less marginal cost. This leads to a simple graphical representation: Total producer surplus in a market is *the area below the price and above the supply curve, out to the quantity sold,* as shown in Figure 2.

To see why, recall from Chapter 3 that the supply curve is also the seller's marginal cost curve. This means that each point on the supply curve reveals a seller's marginal cost. And so for any given sale, a seller gains producer surplus equal to the price, less their marginal cost, and the marginal cost is the height of the supply curve. Add up this producer surplus across all jeans sold, and you'll end up adding the entire area above the supply curve and below the price, out to the quantity sold.

You earn producer surplus on all but your last sale. As a seller, your producer surplus is the difference between the price and your marginal costs. But the Rational Rule

◀ Integrated study guide We've built a simple but effective study tool right into the reading experience. Glance at the colored and boldfaced headings before reading the chapter for a useful preview; reread them afterward to thoroughly review and check your understanding of each topic.

Producer surplus is the price, less the marginal cost.

Producer surplus is the area above the supply curve and below the price.

You earn producer surplus on all but your last sale.

◀ Chapter at
a Glance
Innovative visual
summaries provide a
clear overview of the
key concepts in each
chapter.

Chapter 3 Review

Chapter at a Glance

An Individual Supply Curve
Shows the quantity supplied at each price

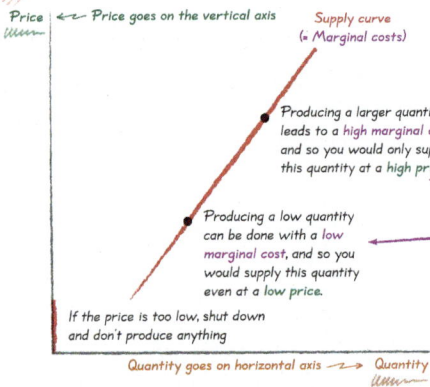

Price ← Price goes on the vertical axis

Supply curve
(= Marginal costs)

Producing a larger quantity
leads to a high marginal cost,
and so you would only supply
this quantity at a high price.

Producing a low quantity
can be done with a low
marginal cost, and so you
would supply this quantity
even at a low price.

If the price is too low, shut down
and don't produce anything

Quantity goes on horizontal axis —→ Quantity

The Rational Rule for Sellers

Sell more of an item if its price is greater
than (or equal to) marginal cost

Price = Marginal cost

Your supply curve is your marginal cost curve.

Your supply curve is upward-sloping because of
increasing marginal costs.

Market Supply Curves
Add up individual supply curves to get the market supply curve. Remember to account for not only current
businesses in the market, but also to consider whether new businesses may enter the market when the price rises,
or whether existing business may exit the market when the price falls. The same factors that shape individual
supply shape market supply.

When the Price Changes:
Movement Along the Supply Curve

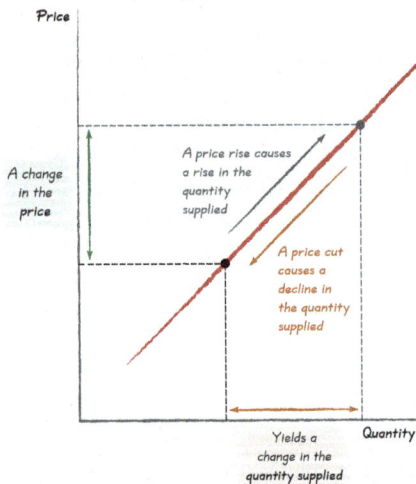

Price

A change
in the
price

A price rise causes
a rise in the
quantity
supplied

A price cut
causes a
decline in
the quantity
supplied

Yields a
change in the
quantity supplied

Quantity

When Other Factors Change:
Shifts in the Supply Curve

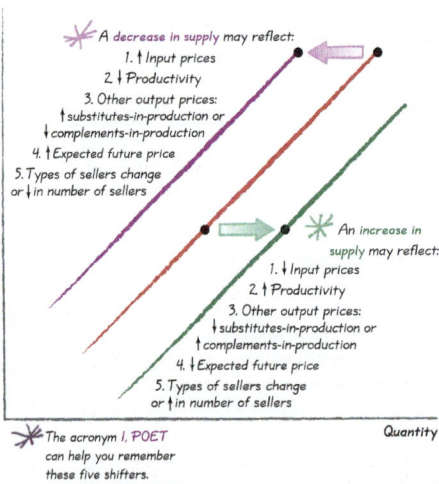

Price

A decrease in supply may reflect:
1. ↑ Input prices
2. ↓ Productivity
3. Other output prices:
   ↑ substitutes-in-production or
   ↓ complements-in-production
4. ↑ Expected future price
5. Types of sellers change
   or ↓ in number of sellers

An increase in
supply may reflect:
1. ↓ Input prices
2. ↑ Productivity
3. Other output prices:
   ↓ substitutes-in-production or
   ↑ complements-in-production
4. ↓ Expected future price
5. Types of sellers change
   or ↑ in number of sellers

The acronym I, POET
can help you remember
these five shifters.

Quantity

▶ Study
Problems Each
chapter ends with a
full set of problems,
aligned to chapter
learning objectives.

Study Problems

Learning Objective 2.1 *Discover the shape of your individual
demand curve.*

1. You just took an Uber from home to campus for the first
   time and were willing to pay $13 for the trip. It was so
   much easier than driving yourself that you are willing to
   pay $21 for the same trip tomorrow. Have you violated the
   law of demand? Why or why not?

2. DoorDash, a food delivery service, has recently expanded
   to your area. The accompanying table contains the number of deliveries per month that you demand at various
   delivery prices. Use this information to plot your individual demand curve. Describe the shape of your individual
   demand curve.

Hours of after-school child care	Marginal benefit (per hour)
1	$32
2	$30
3	$20
4	$14

5. Nicole is attending school in Philadelphia. Each year she
   returns home to visit her family and friends in New York
   City. Kathy's annual demand curve for train tickets from
   Philadelphia to New York is provided in the accompanying graph. How much benefit does Kathy receive from
   each trip home? If the price of a round-trip ticket is $230,
   how many trips should Kathy take?

An Active Approach to Graphing

An economics graph is not a static object for students to look at and memorize; it's something students need to *work through*. That's why we've reimagined these graphs in a way that emphasizes the *process* of graphing.

Figure 3 | **The Consequences of Imports**

If there is no international trade:

No-trade equilibrium occurs where quantity demanded by domestic buyers equals quantity supplied by domestic sellers, resulting in 100 million shirts sold at a price of $20.

When we allow imports:

Step **1** The price of imported goods declines to the world price.

Step **2** At this new price, check the domestic supply curve to find that the quantity supplied by domestic sellers declines, and check the domestic demand curve to find the quantity demanded by domestic buyers rises.

Step **3** Imports make up the difference between domestic demand and domestic supply.

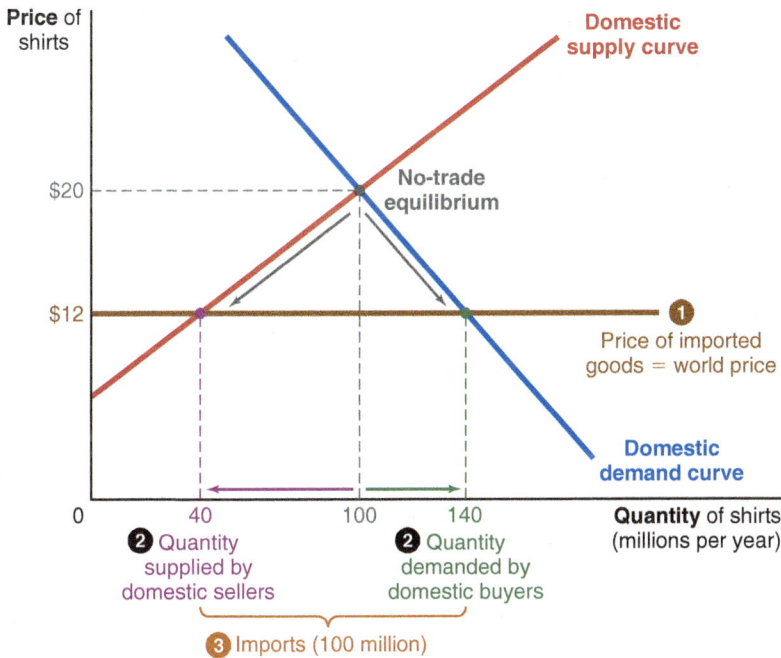

When we allow imports:

Step **1** : The price of imports = the world price of $12, *a price cut*.

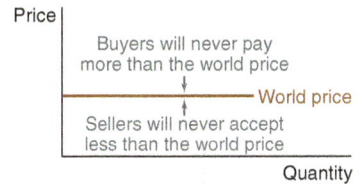

Price

Buyers will never pay more than the world price

World price

Sellers will never accept less than the world price

Quantity

Step **2** : At this new price:
a) The quantity supplied by domestic sellers *declines* (to 40 million shirts)
b) The quantity demanded by domestic buyers *rises* (to 140 million shirts)

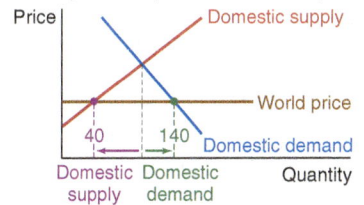

Price
Domestic supply
World price
40   140
Domestic demand
Domestic   Domestic   Quantity
supply   demand

Step **3** : The difference is made up by imports (= 140m − 40m = 100 million shirts)

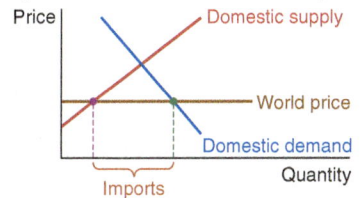

Price
Domestic supply
World price
Domestic demand
Quantity
Imports

Price of shirts

Domestic supply curve

No-trade equilibrium

$20

$12

1
Price of imported goods = world price

Domestic demand curve

0   40   100   140   **Quantity** of shirts (millions per year)

2 Quantity supplied by domestic sellers

2 Quantity demanded by domestic buyers

3 Imports (100 million)

▲ **Step-by-step graphs** We crack the curves open by breaking key economics graphs down into carefully formulated steps.

Exports Help Producers
Extra producer surplus = B + D

Exports Hurt Consumers
Lost consumer surplus = B

Net Gains Exceed Losses
Increased economic surplus = D

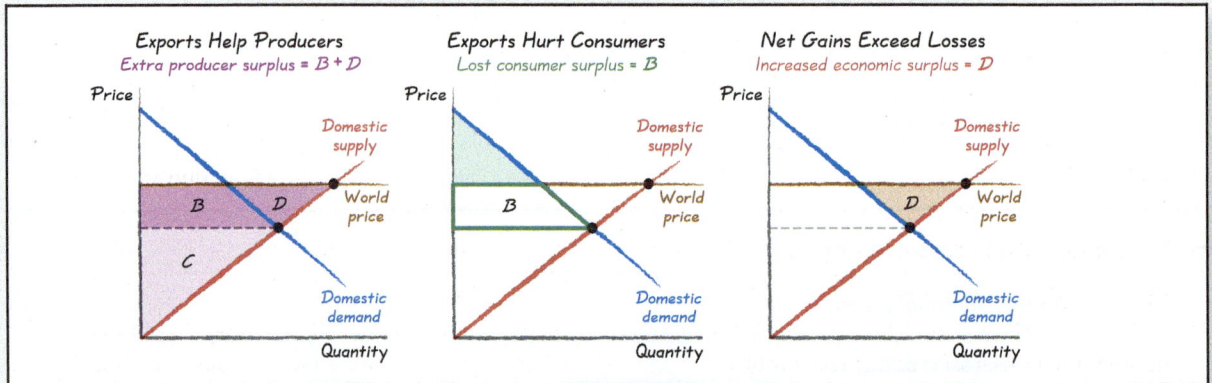

▲ **Casual graphs model good economics habits** We encourage students to interact with economics by sketching thumbnail graphs in the margins, on the backs of envelopes, or wherever they prefer to thoughtfully doodle. These casual graphs model the process of translating economic phenomena into visual representations.

If some U.S. states lower the legal drinking age, what will be the effect on the market for beer?

More consumers

→ An increase in demand

Result: Higher price, higher quantity.

During the coronavirus pandemic, retailers needed to take additional precautions such as purchasing hand sanitizer, providing employees with masks, and sanitizing surfaces more. What effect does this have on the market for the goods that they sell?

Higher cost of inputs

→ A decrease in supply

Result: Higher price, lower quantity.

How did the increase in work from home during the coronavirus pandemic affect the market for gasoline?

Lower price of a substitute (it's effectively cheaper to work from home since the boss now encourages it)

→ A decrease in demand

Result: Lower price, lower quantity.

▲ **Practice, practice, practice** Constant repetition encourages students to think graphically whenever they encounter new economic questions.

Acknowledgments

The journey from being passionate about communicating economics to writing a successful Principles of Economics textbook is long and involves a large cast of characters, each of whom has played a crucial role in getting to this point. It starts with the family who nurtured our curiosity about the world and a lifelong love of learning. And from there we have grown through the guidance of a cast of teachers and scholars who encouraged, taught, and mentored us along the way. Our journey has introduced us to policymakers committed to understanding economics in order to make the world a better place. We have both now had decades of students whose questions, curiosity, and passion have inspired us.

The textbook project itself has introduced us to a family within academic publishing, and each of them is dedicated to ensuring that students get all that they can out of their education. We are in awe of their dedication and talents. None of this would be possible without these folks, so let's start naming some of them.

As every parent knows, the starting point is those who brought us here. Justin wouldn't be here without Roslyn Wolfers's passion, work ethic, and commitment to excellence. Betsey was nurtured and supported in all her endeavors by her parents, Helen and Gordon Stevenson. They have also been heroes throughout this project by stepping into any new role as needed, from emergency house maintenance to beloved grandparent (and caregiver). Our children Matilda and Oliver are now 12 and 9. They have never known life without their parents working on this textbook. We are grateful to them for their forgiveness for the weekends and late nights spent working and the inevitable dinner conversation that turned to economics. They fuel us every day with the joy of being their parents. Of course, two working parents also need the love, support, and understanding of a team of people who can step in to help us in the domestic domain. We are eternally grateful to have the love, support and understanding of Patricia Gruber, Sean Manuel, Cherith Harkness, Jill Benevides, and Ellen Goodman.

We have been blessed to have worked with literally hundreds of academic colleagues who shared their vision for the field. Greg Mankiw has been a supporter of our textbook work from the beginning, providing invaluable advice and experience. Justin cut his teeth on textbook work as a graduate student working for Greg, and over the ensuing years we have remained in awe of Greg's ability to dig into complex economic questions using the simple insights and algebra from introductory economics.

There have been dozens of teaching assistants who added their expertise, and thousands of students at the University of Michigan who have shared their experiences. We can't thank you all by name, but are grateful for your input, and we hope that you see your influence in the DNA of this book. We are particularly grateful to colleagues Ron Caldwell and Scott Cunningham, who have debated every pedagogic choice we've made. Anna Paulson and Cindy Ivanac-Lillig of the Federal Reserve Bank of Chicago gave us detailed feedback to ensure we caught the nuances of monetary policy practices. Dozens of reviewers whose names appear on the following pages challenged us to think harder and be clearer. Our colleague Alan Deardorff gave us detailed and useful feedback on all things trade related. And we want to thank our magnificent research assistants—Adam Bressler, Jack Bryan, Saskia DeVries, Emily Fletcher, Callie Furmaniuk, Nick Guisinger, Joshua Ravichandran, Noah Rich, Torin Rittenberg, and Jan Zilinsky—who have researched everything from the GDP of South Korea to the box office take of *Star Wars*. Joanne Moore spent years working late hours and using her insights as a student and instructor to help craft the Chapters at a Glance, and spot errors in the work. Bonnie Kavoussi worked with us tirelessly as we strove to complete our first draft, and we benefited tremendously from her research assistance, but more generally her creativity, excellent writing skills, and passion for economics.

The team at Macmillan who has brought this project from an idea to a second edition is large and each person has played a crucial role. Bruce Kaplan was our first development editor. One of the great joys of being a teacher is knowing that some part of your work will live on after you—in the knowledge, practice, and good deeds of your students. And while Bruce was formally our editor, he was really our teacher. Bruce passed away in 2021, but his work lives on. Every time one of us writes a clear sentence, it is because of the lessons he taught us. We hope to continue to honor his legacy by continuing to occasionally find that clear sentence which opens our students' minds.

Ann Kirby-Payne and Lukia Kliossis took over as our development editors. Throughout the first edition they improved every word in this book and made every figure and picture shine. By the time we began the second edition they had become a perfectly in sync team. They know our vision perhaps better than we do and are certainly better at executing on it. They aren't just editors, but also educators, which is the highest compliment we can give. The second edition reflects their tenacity, dedication, humor, and talent. They are literally the best (and they also ensure we don't misuse words like "literally.") We wish that we could bottle their positivity, generosity, and enormous talent and sprinkle it like fairy dust over the whole world.

Joshua Hill is that rare talent who is both a master of economics (actually, a doctor) and of pedagogy, and in his wizardlike ways has conjured up much of the ecosystem within which this book lies. We wanted the best resources for instructors in the business and he made it happen. He has sweated every question, every PowerPoint slide, and every supplement that students and their instructors rely on to translate the words on the page to doing economics.

We are grateful for the wise counsel, big-picture leadership, and the inspiring values provided by Carolyn Merrill, Shani Fisher, and Chuck Linsmeier. A dedicated sales team has helped get the textbook and learning materials into the hands of students all over the country. We are grateful to everything Clay Bolton and Scott Guile have done to ensure that our book has met instructors and students around the country (and the world).

Sharon Balbos helped us in our early days, teaching us what this textbook caper is all about. Sarah Keeling Dorger saw our potential and encouraged us to embark down the road of economic education. Craig Bleyer and Liz Widdicombe made a bet that changed our lives forever.

Noel Hohnstine leads the media and assessment team and has helped to bring the idea of a textbook into a twenty-first century learning experience. We are fortunate to have had such a talented production and design group for our book, and owe a debt of gratitude to Tracey Kuehn, Betsy Granger, Lisa Kinne, Robin Fadool, Jennifer Wetzel, Brianna Lester, Andrew Vaccaro, Diana Blume, Natasha Wolfe, Matt McAdams, Janice Donnola, John Callahan, Dirk Kaufman, Kevin Kall, and Cheryl DuBois. The entire mind-boggling process of production and scheduling was masterfully coordinated by Martha Emry. Amanda Gaglione, Allison Curley, and Amanda Nava coordinated an extraordinary quantity of virtual paper flow during the turn-over process. In many ways, we've all grown up together, and it has been a great joy watching the members of our textbook family be promoted to bigger and better assignments. Like the families we grew up in, our textbook family pushes us to do our best, provides us room to grow, and lifts us up. And much like the families we grew up in, our textbook family is driven by a sense of purpose and a commitment to educating the next generation. We are grateful for them and draw inspiration from them every day.

We express our deep appreciation to the many reviewers* who provided invaluable feedback as we developed this project.

Sindy Abadie, *Southwest Tennessee Community College*

Dorian Abreu, *Hunter College*

Seemi Ahmad, *Dutchess Community College*

Jason Aimone, *Baylor University*

Haydory Akbar Ahmed, *Missouri State University*

Basil Al-Hashimi, *Mesa Community College, Red Mountain Campus*

Samuel Allen, *Virginia Military Institute*

Shahina Amin, *The University of Northern Iowa*

Lian An, *University of North Florida*

Giuliana Campanelli Andreopoulos, *William Paterson University*

Elena Antoniadou, *Auburn University*

Anna Antus, *North Hennepin Community College*

Hannah Apps, *Kalamazoo College*

Ramses Armendariz, *Indiana University, Kelley School of Business*

Luke Armstrong, *Lee College*

Becca Arnold, *San Diego Mesa College*

Sonia Asare, *Capital Community*

Daniel Asfaw, *Indiana University and Purdue University Indianapolis*

Ioanna Avgeri, *ONCAMPUS Amsterdam*

Collins Ayoo, *Carleton University*

Sahar Bahmani, *University of Wisconsin at Parkside*

Diana Bajrami, *College of Alameda*

Gyanendra Baral, *Oklahoma City Community College*

Leah Barnhard, *Wichita State University*

Hamid Bastin, *Shippensburg University*

James E. Bathgate, *Western Nevada College*

Clare Battista, *California Polytechnic State University–San Luis Obispo*

Leon Battista, *Bronx Community College*

Klaus G. Becker, *Texas Tech University*

Christina Beers, *Ohio University*

Susan M. Bell, *Seminole State College of Florida*

Audrey Benavidez, *Del Mar College*

Cynthia Benelli, *Santa Barbara City College*

Janine Bergeron, *Southern New Hampshire University*

Prasun Bhattacharjee, *East Tennessee State University*

Amrita Bhattacharya, *Southern Illinois University, Carbondale*

David Black, *University of Toledo*

Lane Boyte-Eckis, *Troy University*

Amanda Bradbury, *University of Central Missouri*

Elizabeth Breitbach, *University of South Carolina*

Joseph Brignone, *Brigham Young University*

Stacey Brook, *University of Iowa*

Bruce Brown, *Cal Poly Pomona*

Dave Brown, *Penn State University*

Joseph Bucci, *Chestnut Hill College*

David Burk, *Georgetown University*

Bill Burrows, *Lane Community College*

Names in bold in the list above have provided feedback to inform this second edition.

Randall Campbell, *Mississippi State University*

James Carden, *University of Mississippi*

Valbona Cela, *Tri-County Technical College*

Stephanie Cellini, *George Washington University*

Rik Chakraborti, *University of Wyoming*

Jieun Chang, *Southwestern Oklahoma State University*

David Chaplin, *Northwest Nazarene University*

June Charles, *North Lake College*

Anoshua Chaudhuri, *San Francisco State University*

Adam Check, *University of St. Thomas*

Nan-Ting Chou, *University of Louisville*

Shih-Hsien Chuang, *Northwest Missouri State University*

Dmitry Chulkov, *Indiana University Kokomo*

Christopher Clarke, *Washington State University*

Marcelo Clerici-Arias, *Stanford University*

Kevin Cochrane, *Colorado Mesa University*

Bradley Collins, *Blue Ridge Community College*

Gregory Colson, *University of Georgia*

Larry Cook, *University of Toledo*

Jeremy Cook, *Wheaton College*

Kevin Crimmins, *University of North Carolina at Charlotte*

Patrick Crowley, *Texas A&M University, Corpus Christi*

Berg Cui, *Indiana University*

John Cullis, *Iowa State University*

Mark Cullivan, *San Diego State University*

Scott Cunningham, *Baylor University*

Chifeng Dai, *Southern Illinois University*

Sonia Dalmia, *Grand Valley State University*

Manabendra Dasgupta, *University of Alabama at Birmingham*

Andrew Davis, *Acadia University*

Stephen Davis, *Southwest Minnesota State University*

Dale R. DeBoer, *University of Colorado, Colorado Springs*

Juan DelaCruz, *Lehman College*

Cornelia Denvir, *Ulster County Community College*

Brooks Depro, *Elon University*

Michael Derry, *Polk State Lakeland Gateway to College*

Satis Devkota, *University of Minnesota, Morris*

Paramita Dhar, *Central Connecticut State University*

Liang Ding, *Macalester College*

Veronika Dolar, *Suny College at Old Westbury*

David Dupuis, *Université de Sherbrooke*

Carmen Dybwad, *University of Regina*

Eva Dziadula, *University of Notre Dame*

Finley Edwards, *Baylor University*

Renee Edwards, *Houston Community College*

Sherine El Hag, *California State University, Dominguez Hills*

Harold W. Elder, *University of Alabama*

Scott Elliott, *Hocking College*

Harry Ellis Jr., *University of North Texas*

Tisha L. N. Emerson, *Baylor University*

Michael Enz, *Roanoke College*

Jonathan Ernest, *Clemson University*

Mark Evers, *Southern Utah University and University of Denver*

Terry Eyland, *Bishop's University*

Elena Falcettoni, *University of Minnesota*

Mohammadmahdi Farsiabi, *Wayne State University*

Irene R. Foster, *The George Washington University*

Jennifer Fowler, *Belmont University*

Gerald Fox, *High Point University*

Melanie Fox, *Virginia Tech*

David Franck, *Francis Marion University*

Tracey Freiberg, *St. John's University*

Matthew Friedman, *University of Wisconsin, Madison*

Florencia Gabriele, *Emmanuel College*

Mary N. Gade, *Oklahoma State University*

Cynthia L. Gamez, *El Paso Community College*

Guanlin Gao, *Chaminade University of Honolulu*

Phillip Garner, *Dixie State University*

Karl Geisler, *Idaho State University*

Pedro Gete, *Georgetown University*

Linda Ghent, *Eastern Illinois University*

Shankar Ghimire, *Western Illinois University*

Alex Gialanella, *New England College*

Otis Gilley, *Louisiana Tech University*

Rob Girtz, *Black Hills State University*

Gregory Givens, *University of Alabama*

Christian G. Glupker, *Grand Valley State University*

Malcolm Gold, *Avila University*

Tao Gong, *University of Maryland Eastern Shore*

Terri Gonzales-Kreisman, *Delgado Community College*

Richard Gosselin, *Houston Community College*

David Gray, *University of Ottawa*

Natalia Gray, *Southeast Missouri State University*

Joanne Guo, *University of Bridgeport*

Jason Gurtovoy, *Embry-Riddle Aeronautical University*

Jamie Haischer, *Polk State Lakeland Gateway to College*

David Harris, *Benedictine College*

Darcy Hartman, *The Ohio State University*

William Hawkins, *Yale University*

Megharanji Hazra, *Towson University*

Jessica Hennessey, *Furman University*

Ryan Herzog, *Gonzaga University*

Joshua Hess, *University of South Carolina*

Wayne R. Hickenbottom, *University of Texas at Austin*

Paul M. Holmes, *Ashland University*

Jim Hornsten, *Northwestern University*

Indrit Hoxha, *Penn State University, Harrisburg*

Yu Hsing, *Southeastern Louisiana University*

Kuang-Chung Hsu, *University of Central Oklahoma*

Brian Hurst, *San Jose State University*

Taurean Hutchinson, *Susquehanna University*

Jennifer Imazeki, *San Diego State University*

Maksim Isakin, *Cleveland State University*

Nuria Quella Isla, *Stony Brook University*

Miren Ivankovic, *Anderson University and Clemson University*

Jesse Jacobs, *Fort Hays State University*

Michael Jones, *University of Cincinnati*

George Jones, *University of Wisconsin Rock County*

Troy Joseph, *Carleton University*

George A. Jouganatos, *California State University, Sacramento*

Steve Kaifa, *County College of Morris*

Serkan Kalman, *The College of New Jersey*

Lillian Kamal, *University of Hartford*

Alice Louise Kassens, *Roanoke College*

Nargess Kayhani, *Mount Saint Vincent University*

Hossein S. Kazemi, *Stonehill College*

Sukanya Kemp, *University of Akron*

Zafar Dad Khan, *University of Virginia's College at Wise*

Frank W. Kim, *Point Loma Nazarene University*

Hyeongwoo Kim, *Auburn University*

Jongsung Kim, *Bryant University*

Janice Rye Kinghorn, *Miami University*

Richard Kirk, *Georgia State University Perimeter College*

Audrey Kline, *University of Louisville*

Colin Knapp, *Penn State University*

Mikhail Kouliavtsev, *Stephen F. Austin State University*

Catherine S. Krause, *University of New Mexico*

Santosh Kumar, *Sam Houston State University*

Dan LaFave, *Colby College*

Ghislaine Lang, *San Jose State University*

Susan Laury, *Georgia State University*

Daniel Lawson, *Oakland Community College*

Nhan Le, *Alma College*

Tuan Viet Le, *West Virginia Wesleyan College*

Jim Lee, *Texas A&M University, Corpus Christi*

Michael Leonard, *Kwantlen Polytechnic University*

Amy Leung, Folsom Lake College

Hank Lewis, *Lone Star College, University Park*

Willis Lewis, *Winthrop University*

Zhen Li, *Albion College*

Carlos Liard, *Central Connecticut State University*

Sung Soo Lim, *Calvin College*

Bo Liu, Southern New Hampshire University

Haiyong Liu, *East Carolina University*

Ira T. Lovitch, *Mount Saint Mary's University, Los Angeles*

Heather Luea, Vanderbilt University

Jo Lugovsky, University of Kansas

Rotua Lumbantobing, *Western Connecticut State University*

Gennady Lyakir, *Fashion Institute of Technology*

Rita Madarassy, *Santa Clara University*

Mark Maier, *Glendale Community College*

Svitlana Maksymenko, *University of Pittsburgh*

C. Lucy Malakar, *Lorain County Community College*

Khawaja Mamun, *Sacred Heart University*

Abir Mandal, *University of Kansas*

Emily Marshall, *Dickinson College*

Ladan Masoudie, *University of Southern California*

Robert McComb, *Texas Tech University*

Clinton McCully, *Northern Virginia Community College*

Eric McDermott, *University of Illinois, Urbana-Champaign*

Steven McMullen, *Hope College*

Lois McWhorter, *University of the Cumberlands*

Shah Mehrabi, Montgomery College

Saul Mekies, *Kirkwood Community College and University of Iowa*

Diego Mendez-Carbajo, *Illinois Wesleyan University*

Gretchen Mester, Anne Arundel Community College

Lewis Metcalf, *Parkland College*

Charles Meyrick, *Housatonic Community College*

Meghan Hennessy Mihal, *St. Thomas Aquinas College*

Garrett Milam, University of Puget Sound

Jeanette Milius, *Iowa Western Community College*

Edward Millner, *Virginia Commonwealth University*

Joshua Mitton, Irvine Valley College

Phillip Mixon, *Troy University*

Lavinia Moldovan, *Mount Royal University*

Mark Monsky, *Wake Technical Community College*

Shelby Moore, Amarillo College

Sucharita Mukherjee, *College of Saint Benedict*

Yolunda Nabors, *Tennessee Technological University*

Lindsey Nagy, *Muhlenberg College*

ABM Nasir, *North Carolina Central University*

Ronald C. Necoechea, *Roberts Wesleyan College*

Augustine C. Nelson, *University of Miami*

Nicolas Nervo, *Tarrant County College*

Charles Newton, *Houston Community College*

Chau Nguyen, Mesa Community College

Mihai Nica, *University of Central Oklahoma*

Alexandra Nica, University of Iowa

Jelena Nikolic, *Northeastern University*

Dmitri Nizovtsev, *Washburn University*

Lindsay Noble Calkins, *John Carroll University*

Claudette Nyang'oro, *Miami Dade College*

Scott Ogawa, *Northwestern University*

Gokcen G. Ogruk-Maz, *Texas Wesleyan University*

Jinhwan Oh, *Ewha Womans University*

David J. O'Hara, *Metropolitan State University*

Sheyi Oladipo, *SUNY College at Old Westbury*

Grace Onodipe, *Georgia Gwinnett College*

Nur M. Onvural, *Pfeiffer University*

Wafa Hakim Orman, *University of Alabama in Huntsville*

Catherine R. Pakaluk, *The Catholic University of America*

Debashis Pal, *University of Cincinnati*

Maria Papapavlou, *San Jacinto College*

Jason Patalinghug, Southern Connecticut State University

Darshak Patel, *University of Kentucky*

Lourenco Paz, *Baylor University*

Nicholas D. Peppes, *St. Louis Community College*

Timothy Perri, *Appalachian State University*

Matthew Pham, *The Ohio State University*

Josh Phillips, Iowa Central Community College

Paul Pieper, University of Illinois at Chicago

Julien Picault, *UBC Okanagan*

Brennan Platt, *Brigham Young University*

Sanela Porca, *University of South Carolina Aiken*

Joseph Price, Brigham Young University, Provo

Ashley Provencher, *Siena College*

Sarah Quintanar, *University of Arkansas at Little Rock*

Reza M. Ramazani, Saint Michael's College

Surekha K. B. Rao, *Indiana University Northwest*

Christian Raschke, *Sam Houston State University*

Jack Reardon, *University of Wisconsin, Eau Claire*

Megan Regan, Wake Forest University

Tracy L. Regan, *Boston College*

Agne Reizgeviciute, *California State University, Chico*

Tim Reynolds, Alvin Community College

Sam Richardson, *Boston College*

Christopher Roark, *University of Chicago*

Amanda Ross, *University of Alabama*

Wes Routon, *Georgia Gwinnett College*

Moumita Roy, *Bloomsburg University*

Marina Rubenkov, Milwaukee Area Technical College, Downtown

Jeffrey Rubin, *Rutgers University*

Stefan Ruediger, *Arizona State University*

Melissa M. Rueterbusch, *Mott Community College*

Malkiat Sandhu, *University of California, Silicon Valley Extension*

Chandini Sankaran, *Boston College*

Naveen Sarna, *Northern Virginia Community College*

George Sarraf, *University of California Irvine*

Edward Sayre, *University of Southern Mississippi*

Edward Scahill, *University of Scranton*

Mark Scanlan, Stephen F. Austin State University

Helen Schneider, *University of Texas at Austin*

Heather A. Schumacker, Salt Lake Community College

Armine Shahoyan, *Tulane University*

Alexandra Shiu Nicolay, *McLennan Community College*

Jonathan Silberman, *Oakland University*

Joe Silverman, *San Diego State University*

Harmeet Singh, *Texas A&M University, Kingsville*

Catherine Skura, *Sandhills Community College*

Anastasia Smith, *Pfeiffer University*

Deanna Smith, *Missouri State University, West Plains*

Joseph Sobieralski, *Southwestern Illinois College*

Katherine Sobota, *Bowling Green State University*

Mario Solis-Garcia, *Macalester College*

Robert Sonora, *Fort Lewis College*

Carolyne Soper, *Central Connecticut State University*

Nicole Soto, *Southern New Hampshire University*

Forrest Spence, *University of Notre Dame*

Richard Stahnke, *University of Maryland*

Kalina Staub, *University of North Carolina, Chapel Hill*

Josh Staveley-O'Carroll, *Babson College*

Andrew Stephenson, *Georgia Gwinnett College*

Jeffrey Stewart, *University of Dayton*

Edward Strafaci, *Wagner College*

Jacqueline Strenio, *Southern Oregon University*

Carolyn Fabian Stumph, *Purdue University Fort Wayne*

Peter Summers, *High Point University*

Meiping (Aggie) Sun, *Fordham University*

Timothy Sweeney, *Metropolitan Community College, Omaha*

Andre Switala, *Boston University*

Philip Szmedra, *Georgia Southwestern State University*

Vera Tabakova, *East Carolina University*

Raul Tadle, *California State University, Sacramento*

Ariuntungalag Taivan, *University of Minnesota Duluth*

Shelley Tapp, *Wayland Baptist University*

Michael Tasto, *Southern New Hampshire University*

Eric Taylor, *Central Piedmont Community College*

Mark L. Tendall, *Stanford University*

Vitaly Terekhov, *Marianopolis College*

Deborah Thorsen, *Palm Beach State College, Palm Beach Gardens*

William Thralls, *Johnson & Wales University, North Miami*

Angela K. Thurman, *Tarrant County College*

James Tierney, *Penn State University*

Edward J. Timmons, *Saint Francis University*

Trevor Tombe, *University of Calgary*

Susanne Toney, *Savannah State University*

Richard Tontz, *California State University, Northridge*

Jill A. Trask, *Tarrant County College, Southeast Campus*

Carey Treado, *University of Pittsburgh*

Yulya Truskinovsky, *Wayne State University*

Phillip Tussing, *Houston Community College*

Tate Twinam, *University of Washington, Bothell*

Nathaniel Udall, *Wharton County Junior College*

Veronica Udeogalanya, *Medgar Evers College*

Don Joseph Paredes Uy-Barreta, *Hult International Business School*

Vicar S. Valencia, *Indiana University South Bend*

Ross S vanWassenhove, *University of Houston*

Sam Vegter, *Western Piedmont Community College*

Angelino Viceisza, *Spelman College*

Norma Vite-Leon, *Marianopolis College*

Rubina Vohra, *New Jersey City University*

Lucia Vojtassak, *University of Calgary*

Annie Voy, *Gonzaga University*

Cheryl Wachenheim, *North Dakota State University*

William A. Walsh, *University of Alabama*

Qingbin Wang, *Johnson & Wales University*

Yaqin Wang, *Youngstown State University*

Yongqing Wang, *University of Wisconsin–Milwaukee at Waukesha*

Kaycee Chandler Washington, *Collin College*

Wendy Wasnich, *Ashland University*

Don Weimer, *Milwaukee Area Technical College, Downtown*

Kristine West, *St. Catherine University*

Elizabeth M. Wheaton, *Southern Methodist University*

Katie Wick, *Abilene Christian University*

A. Williams, *Gateway Community College*

Amanda L. Wilsker, *Georgia Gwinnett College*

Allison Witman, *University of North Carolina Wilmington*

Jim R. Wollscheid, *University of Arkansas, Fort Smith*

Kelvin Wong, *Arizona State University*

Jadrian Wooten, *Penn State University*

Sonia Worrell Asare, *Capital Community College*

Deborah Amelia Wright, *Southeastern Community College*

Sheng Xiao, *Westminster College*

Travis Yates, *Penn State University*

Janice Yee, *Worcester State University*

Kuzey Yilmaz, *Cleveland State University*

James Yoo, *California Baptist University*

Anthony Zambelli, *Cuyamaca College*

George Zestos, *Christopher Newport University*

Fang Zhang, *California State University, Fullerton*

Hong Zhuang, *Indiana State University, South Bend*

Oleksandr (Alex) Zhylyevskyy, *Iowa State University*

Organization of This Book

Learn the four principles of economics that create a decision making framework to help you better understand demand, supply, and equilibrium and build a solid foundation for economic analysis.

PART I Foundations of Economics

Use supply and demand analysis to evaluate welfare, understand the gains from trade, explore the consequences of global trade, and to assess inequality and poverty.

PART II Analyzing Markets

Learn how economists measure economic activity and economic growth, what causes unemployment (and what it costs), and how to evaluate inflation and its consequences.

PART III Macroeconomic Foundations and the Long Run

See how individual decisions produce macroeconomic outcomes, and learn to make good choices no matter what economic conditions you face.

PART IV Micro Foundations of Macroeconomics

Learn about business cycles, then analyze them by applying the same tools that policymakers use (Chapters 18–20) or by taking a more traditional approach (Chapter 21). Your instructor will guide you on which path to take.

PART V The Business Cycle

Get an insider's view of how macroeconomic policy is made and implemented, and how it affects your life and the broader economy.

PART VI Macroeconomic Policy

Take a deeper dive into some more traditional material.

Appendix:

Contents

A Quick Review of Graphs

You'll see a lot of graphs in the pages ahead—don't let it scare you. You encounter graphs every time you scroll through your news feed: charts for election results, opinion polls, sales figures, health outcomes, and just about anything else. Apps on your phone might supply you with graphs to show how many steps you took last week, how much you spent over the past month on different types of goods, or how many books you read last year. When you were applying to college, you probably consulted graphs that showed the range of entrance exam scores for first-year students at schools you were eyeing to see how you measured up.

We live in a time when data is cheap and plentiful, and so many aspects of our lives are quantified. Graphs make sifting through all of it a lot easier. Economics can make you a more effective user of all of that data. To start, here's a quick refresher to walk you through some familiar graphs, with useful tips on how to read them. Along the way, we'll remind you of some of the basic tools and language you'll use to work through them.

Graphs That Break Down Numbers

Figure 1 | Breaking Down Average Household Spending

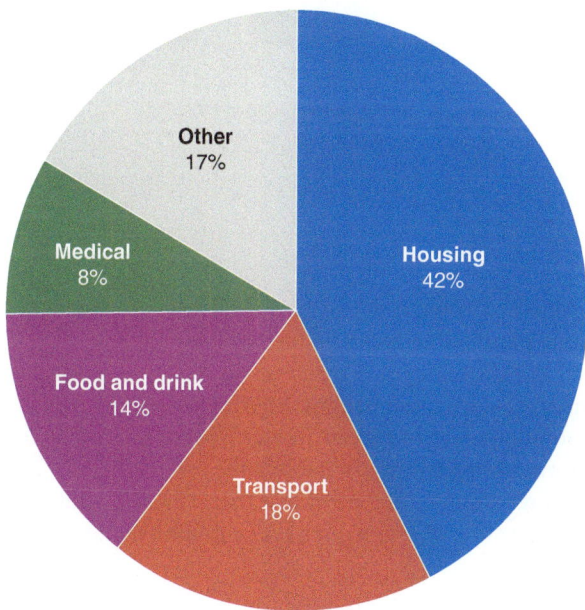

*Because a pie chart is designed to show the whole, the numbers must add to 100. But occasionally you'll get a total that isn't quite 100% because of rounded numbers

Source: Bureau of Labor Statistics

▲ **Pie Charts** When you want to break down a total into its component slices, **pie charts** can provide an easy way to show each of the parts that comprise the whole.

Figure 2 | The Distribution of Income in the United States

Average annual family income in 2019 before tax

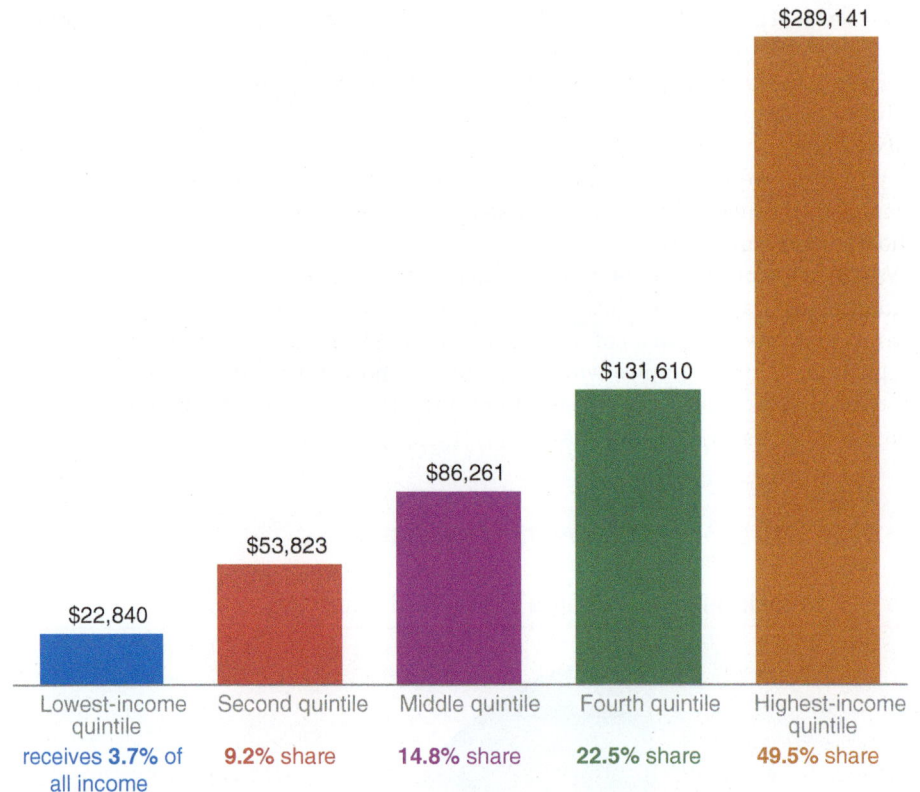

Lowest-income quintile	Second quintile	Middle quintile	Fourth quintile	Highest-income quintile
$22,840	$53,823	$86,261	$131,610	$289,141
receives **3.7%** of all income	**9.2%** share	**14.8%** share	**22.5%** share	**49.5%** share

* Remember, a **quintile** is one fifth

Source: U.S. Census Bureau

▲ **Analyzing Distributions** When you want to see how an economic statistic—say, income—is distributed across the population, it can be helpful to divide the data up into smaller, equal-sized segments. In economics you'll come across lots of data that has been broken down into fifths, segments that we call **quintiles.** This breakdown reveals the dispersion in outcomes across the population—a fact often obscured by measures like the median or mean. Bar charts like this one use quintiles to show that the lowest-income fifth of the population get by with an average annual income of less than $25,000, while the highest-income fifth enjoys an average income of over a quarter of a million dollars.

Graphs That Show Comparisons

Most of the graphs you encounter are designed to *visualize* numbers, give them scale, and provide opportunities to make *comparisons*.

Figure 3 | **Workers with More Education Have Higher Average Annual Earnings**

Average earnings in 2020

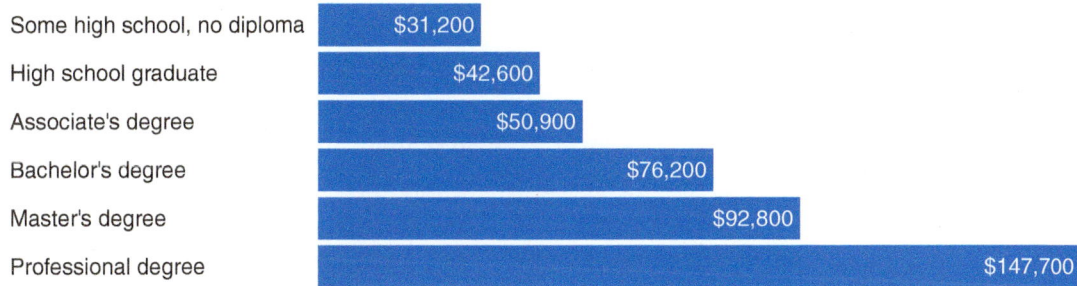

Some high school, no diploma	$31,200
High school graduate	$42,600
Associate's degree	$50,900
Bachelor's degree	$76,200
Master's degree	$92,800
Professional degree	$147,700

* Data are only as good as their source.
 Be sure to l••k below find out where the numbers come from.

Source: U.S. Census Bureau

▲ **Bar Chart and Dot Plot** Sometimes you'll want to compare data for different categories. One of the most common ways to visualize and compare data across different categories is with a bar chart. For example, a **bar chart** can show you, for particular levels of education, the median earnings of the person with that amount of education. Each bar represents a category of education—like college graduate—and the height of the bar shows the median earnings of a person with that level of education. It's easy to see that people with more education generally have higher earnings.

▼ Time-Series Graphs Often, you'll want to look at how a certain indicator or data point changes over time. Plot time on the horizontal axis and your data (in this case, the percentage of the population who complete high school and college) along the vertical axis, and voila:

A boring spreadsheet of numbers like this:

	A	B	C
		Share who completed	Share with a Bachelor's
1	Year	high school	degree
2	1910	13.5%	2.7%
3	1920	16.4%	3.3%
4	1930	19.1%	3.9%
5	1940	24.5%	4.6%

. . . becomes a clear **time-series graph.** The years become the horizontal axis, now for each column B and C, plot the data along the vertical axis for each year and connect the dots. Voila! You have a pretty graph that makes it much easier to take in the big finding— educational attainment has risen over time.

Figure 4 | **High School and College Graduation Rates Have Risen**

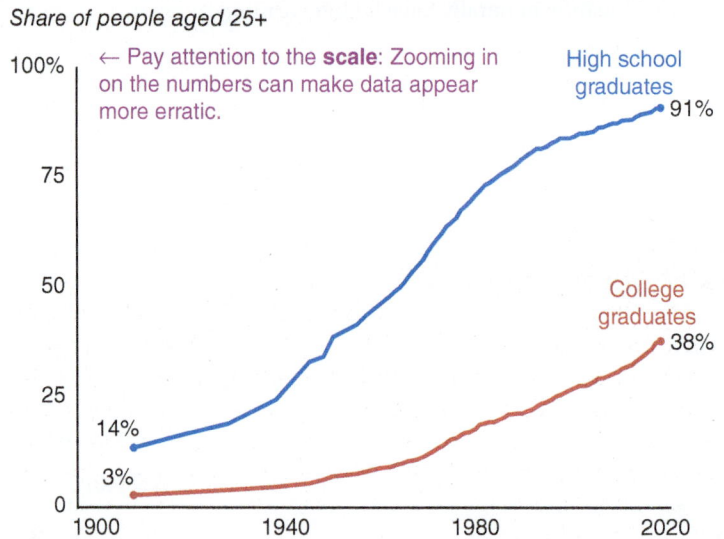

Share of people aged 25+

← Pay attention to the **scale**: Zooming in on the numbers can make data appear more erratic.

High school graduates 91%

College graduates 38%

14%

3%

Check the **date range** ▫ to make sure you're getting the big picture, not just a blip of the data.

Source: U.S. Census Bureau and NCES

Graphs That Show Relationships

In economics, we are concerned not just with numbers describing different outcomes, but with *relationships* between different outcomes. The **coordinate system** enables you to display two sets of data on a single graph. This simple setup forms the skeleton of many of the graphs you will encounter in economics; it's also one that you're probably familiar with from middle school math class. You can plot one measure on the horizontal axis, and a second measure on the vertical, so each data point shows a pair of outcomes for an individual person, state, or country.

Figure 5 | **Higher GDP per Person Is Associated with Higher Life Satisfaction**

↑ *Average life satisfaction score in a country (0-10 scale)*

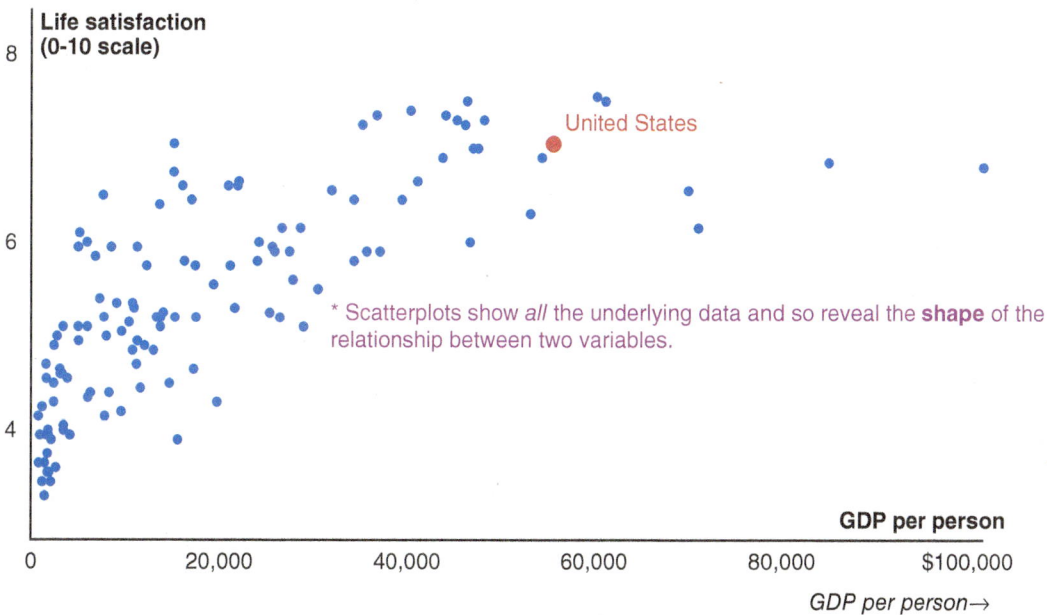

Source: Gallup World Poll and World Bank

▲ Scatterplot You can plot individual data points on a coordinate graph to create a **scatterplot.** This simple graph helps you to see the range of responses and see if any patterns emerge. For example, we can plot the average happiness of people in a country and each country's average income. Americans rated their level of life satisfaction on average to be about 7 on a scale of 1–10; and their average annual income is about $56,000 per person. The red dot represents those two numbers—it shows the average level of happiness *and* income for people in the United States. The other dots represents another country's averages. Looking at all the dots, you can see that richer countries are generally happier countries. There's a relationship there.

Figure 6 | Lukia's Demand for Avocados Depends on the Price

How many avocados does Lukia plan to buy each week?

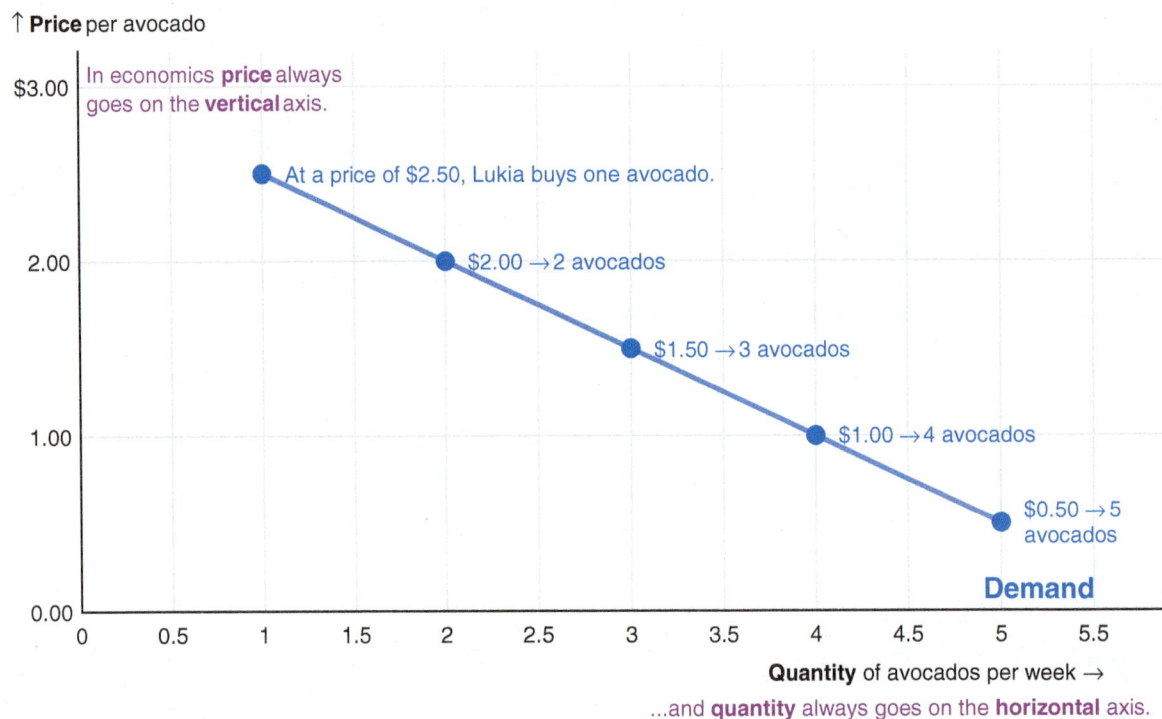

↑ **Price** per avocado

In economics **price** always goes on the **vertical** axis.

At a price of $2.50, Lukia buys one avocado.

$2.00 → 2 avocados

$1.50 → 3 avocados

$1.00 → 4 avocados

$0.50 → 5 avocados

Demand

Quantity of avocados per week →

...and **quantity** always goes on the **horizontal** axis.

▲ **The stylized graphs of economics** One thing you'll graph a lot in economics is the relationship between the price of stuff and the quantity of stuff people will buy or sell at different prices. The **demand curve,** a fundamental tool in economics, shows the quantity of stuff that people will buy at different prices. The demand curve always shows price on the vertical axis and quantity on the horizontal axis.

The demand curve will almost always slope down from top left to bottom right, reflecting the idea that when something becomes cheaper, people buy more of it. For example, when avocados are priced at $2.50 each, Lukia will only buy one. But when they are on sale for $0.50, she'll buy five, and eat avocado toast all week long.

This graph demonstrates a **negative relationship** between quantity and price—you can see this because the line tilts downward as you look from left to right. If the line tilted upward from left to right, you'd be looking at a **positive relationship.**

In economics you'll want to look at not just the direction of the line, but the steepness of it. This is called the **slope.** You calculate the slope along a straight line by looking at two points on the line, and dividing the vertical change by the horizontal change. In simple terms, it's *rise over run.* In mathematical terms, it's

Hint: The little triangle (Δ) is the Greek symbol delta. It's used as a shorthand for "change" – in this case, a change in value.

$$\text{Slope} = \frac{\text{Change in the value on the vertical axis}}{\text{Change in value on the horizontal axis}} = \frac{\Delta y}{\Delta x} = \frac{\text{rise}}{\text{run}}$$

In the chapters ahead, you'll see lots of stylized graphs like this. We'll take the time to walk you through each one, and provide a quick refresher on how to do all the calculations that come up in this book as we get to them.

A Relationship Is Not The Same Thing as Cause and Effect

Sometimes you'll look at a graph, and you'll see a very clear relationship between two variables. For example, if you compare the volume of ice cream produced in the United States over time with the number of airline miles flown in the same time period, you'll see a clear relationship:

Figure 7 | Ice Cream Production Rises and Falls with Air Travel

Change since January 2016

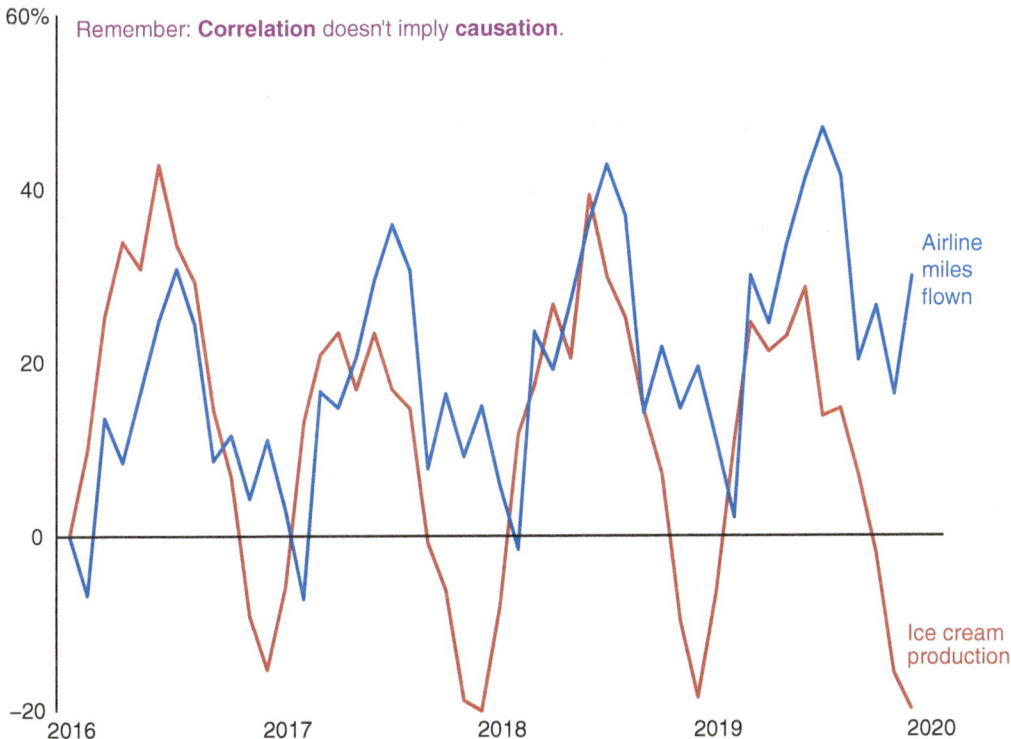

Source: St Louis Federal Reserve

You probably wouldn't infer that the presence of airplanes flying overhead leads people to eat more ice cream. Lots of variables are related, but that doesn't mean that one causes the other. There are other **omitted variables**—like the fact that people tend to go on vacation in the summer, and also eat more ice cream in the summer—that are related to both of these outcomes.

It's also possible to think you've identified a cause-and-effect relationship, but to get it backward. If you compared airline miles flown with, say, time students spend in school, you would probably conclude that families tend to schedule vacations during school breaks. But if you conclude that kids don't go to school in the summer or during the winter holidays because they're traveling, you've **reversed the causality.**

Both cases should make you wary about drawing conclusions whenever you look at data, be it in a textbook like this one or a news story: The fact that two things are related, or correlated, doesn't mean one causes the other. As the saying goes, "correlation does not imply causation."

PART I:
Foundations of Economics

Part I: Foundations of Economics

The Big Picture

We'll start our adventure by introducing you to the **four core principles** that provide the foundation of all economic analysis. Taken together, they form a **decision-making framework** that you can apply to make better decisions. Your goal here is to **develop your economic intuition** so that you can apply these principles to real decisions that you'll face in your personal and professional life.

Next, we'll put that economic intuition to work by applying the core principles to understand how people decide what to buy and what to sell. We'll build your understanding of the building blocks of economic analysis: **demand** and **supply**. You'll learn to analyze how these market forces lead to an **equilibrium** that determines the price and quantity of nearly everything.

As you progress through these four chapters, you'll begin to sense the supply and demand forces at play in your everyday life—from the things you buy to the attention you supply to different endeavors. Building a solid foundation in economics will provide you with an **economic toolkit** that will serve you well long after you have finished this course.

1 The Four Core Principles of Economics

Learn the four core principles that provide the foundation of all economic analysis, and use them to analyze choices and make better decisions.

- Why is it useful to learn to think like an economist?
- How do you evaluate costs and benefits?
- Which costs should you look at when evaluating a choice?
- Why should you learn to think on the margin?
- How do all our decisions interact?

2 Demand and Consumer Choice

Understand people's buying (or demand) decisions.

- What is the shape of *your* individual demand curve?
- How can you apply the core principles of economics to make good buying decisions?
- How does individual demand add up to market demand?
- Which factors shift demand curves?

3 Supply and Producer Choice

Learn how businesses make supply decisions.

- What is the shape of *your* individual supply curve?
- How can you apply the core principles to make good supply decisions?
- How does individual supply add up to market supply?
- Which factors shift supply curves?

4 Equilibrium: Where Supply Meets Demand

Analyze how supply and demand determine the equilibrium price and quantity.

- How do markets determine what is produced and how it is allocated?
- How do markets bring supply and demand into balance?
- What happens when demand and supply shift?
- What do changes in prices and quantity reveal?

The Four Core Principles of Economics

I remember sitting where you're sitting—in an introductory economics class—a few years back. (OK, quite a few.) I didn't exactly know what to think about the subject, or where it would lead me. I felt one part excitement, and two parts trepidation. Ultimately that class changed my life. It provided me with an *approach* to thinking that is both broad and powerful. It gave me a new *lens* through which I could understand the world. It provided clarity and *insight*. And above all, it was *useful.* I'm not exaggerating when I say that not a day goes by when I don't use the tools I learned in that introductory class. It was the best investment I ever made.

Every economist starts out right where you are.

While some parts of that class came naturally, other parts seemed unnecessarily complicated. I kept studying economics in order to master these complexities. But a funny thing happened along the way: The more I studied the subject, the more I came to understand that, in fact, economics isn't all that complicated. Sometimes economists just make it sound complicated.

I learned that economics is just a small set of ideas—or *principles*—that you can apply over and over. It took me a decade to fully understand the power and reach of these principles—but it needn't take you that long. That's why I wrote the book that you're reading right now: I want to teach you these powerful principles, and I want you to learn how to use them. I believe that everyone can benefit from the clarity that economic tools bring. I hope that by the end of this chapter, you'll have mastered what it took me so long to learn: That economics is built upon four core principles that can be used to provide insight into just about any problem.

I invested much of my adult life learning this, and it was worth it. For you, it's just one chapter, so it's a much better investment. Let's dig in.

Chapter Objective

Learn the four core principles that provide the foundation of all economic analysis, and use them to analyze choices and make better decisions.

1.1 A Principled Approach to Economics
Understand economics as a way of thinking, grounded in a set of broadly applicable principles that you'll find useful "in the ordinary business of life."

1.2 The Cost-Benefit Principle
Costs and benefits are the incentives that shape decisions. You should evaluate the full set of costs and benefits of any choice, and pursue only those whose benefits are at least as large as their costs.

1.3 The Opportunity Cost Principle
The true cost of something is the next best alternative you must give up to get it. Your decisions should reflect this opportunity cost, rather than just the out-of-pocket financial costs.

1.4 The Marginal Principle
Decisions about quantities are best made incrementally. You should break "how many" decisions down into a series of smaller, or marginal, decisions.

1.5 The Interdependence Principle
Your best choice depends on your other choices, the choices others make, developments in other markets, and expectations about the future. When any of these factors change, your best choice might change.

🎙 Podcast
Think Like an Economist
Why Should You Think Like an Economist?

1.1 A Principled Approach to Economics

Learning Objective *Understand economics as a way of thinking, grounded in a set of broadly applicable principles that you'll find useful "in the ordinary business of life."*

Economics is not just about money, nor is it just about business or even government policy — though it can be helpful for understanding each of these. Rather, it's a way of thinking. The economic approach can also help you understand politics, families, careers, and just about every aspect of your life. The economic toolkit that will help you better manage your money, your employees, and your business will also help you better manage your time, your energy, and your relationships. It will provide you with guidance as you make small decisions, such as whether to walk out of a bad concert (you should), and big ones, such as whether to buy a car (it depends). Once you start thinking like an economist, you'll find yourself constantly discovering new ways in which it can be useful.

Ultimately all of economics is built on a small set of principles that together define what it means to "think like an economist." If you learn these core principles, you'll be able to do this too. Following this principled approach means that rather than memorizing facts about the economy, you'll learn a systematic approach to thinking about the world.

The Economic Approach

One famous definition of economics describes it as the study of people "in the ordinary business of life." I like this definition because it hints at the idea that the same principles that you might use to analyze business decisions will also be useful for analyzing the decisions that arise in everyday life. In fact, I hope that you will come to see that every decision is an economic decision. But rather than memorizing this specific definition, I want you to learn to *do* economics. Economics is a toolkit, and this chapter is an introduction to actively using it.

We're going to start with the four core principles that comprise the foundation upon which all economic reasoning is based. Wrap your head around these ideas and connect them to the difficult choices you confront, and you'll be *doing economics.* You'll be translating basic economic principles into carefully considered actions. As you learn to employ the tools of the economist's trade, you'll quickly see how these principles can help you make better choices in both your personal life and your professional life. Internalize these principles, and you'll find yourself *doing economics* every single day.

In this chapter, you'll learn the four core principles of economics. The rest of your study of economics will be about applying them. This approach will guide you through both *microeconomics,* in which you will study individual decisions and their implications for specific markets, as well as *macroeconomics,* in which you will trace through the broader implications of individual decisions across the whole economy.

A Systematic Framework for Making Decisions

The atom is the basic unit of matter, and so physicists begin by trying to understand the atom, and from that, build their insights into the functioning of our physical world. For economists, individual decisions — choices — are the foundation of all economic forces. Your decisions, and those of others, collectively determine what's made, who gets it, and whether it yields fair outcomes. Because these broad economic outcomes are the product of many individual choices, economic analysis always begins by focusing on individual decisions.

Should you stream one more episode? It's an economic decision.

Nicolas Maderna/Shutterstock

This is where the four core principles come in. Together, they provide a systematic framework for analyzing individual decisions. In particular, through the rest of this chapter, we'll see that whenever economists evaluate a decision:

- We consider the costs and benefits of a choice. (The cost-benefit principle.)
- Before making a choice, we consider the alternatives, asking: "Or what?" (The opportunity cost principle.)
- We think at the margin, always asking whether a bit more or a bit less of something would be an improvement. (The marginal principle.)
- And we are particularly attuned to understanding how different decisions depend on each other. (The interdependence principle.)

Sounds straightforward, right? The challenge is applying these ideas — which we'll analyze through the rest of this chapter — to the wide array of decisions you'll face in your life.

If you get in the habit of thinking about economics through the core principles, you'll develop a sharper understanding and make better decisions. Speaking of which, you now face an important decision: You have to decide whether to keep reading, or not. Thousands of my past students can attest that the benefit of learning to think like an economist far exceeds the cost. And as you're about to discover, when the benefits exceed the costs, the first of these principles tells you that it's a choice worth making.

1.2 The Cost-Benefit Principle

Learning Objective *Costs and benefits are the incentives that shape decisions. You should evaluate the full set of costs and benefits of any choice, and pursue only those whose benefits are at least as large as their costs.*

🎙 Podcast
Think Like an Economist
**The Cost-Benefit
Principle: Pros and Cons**

Nerida Kyle is a 23-year-old economics graduate who is about to start her first full-time job, working as a human resources manager in Houston. She likes her new apartment, but it's too far from work to bike or walk, and there's no reliable public transportation option. Nerida figures that she'll need to buy a car to get to work because the only viable alternative is a costly Uber ride each way. But is buying a car really her best choice?

The **cost-benefit principle** says that costs and benefits are the *incentives* that shape decisions. This principle suggests that before you make any decision, you should:

- Evaluate the full set of costs and benefits associated with that choice.
- Pursue that choice only if the benefits are at least as large as the costs.

This principle says that Nerida should buy a car only if it yields benefits that are at least as large as the cost. Because the balance of costs and benefits define Nerida's incentive to buy the car, this principle is sometimes best remembered by its conclusion: *incentives matter.*

The cost-benefit principle isn't just relevant when deciding whether to purchase a car — it is relevant for literally any choice that you might consider. Look around, and you'll see that decisions people make — where to buy groceries, whether to study economics, and what career to pursue — reflect their incentives, as they weigh the balance of costs and benefits.

Although it may seem obvious to do something only if the benefits exceed the costs, following the cost-benefit principle can be more challenging than it sounds. The trick is to think broadly about what constitutes a cost or benefit.

cost-benefit principle Costs and benefits are the incentives that shape decisions. You should evaluate the full set of costs and benefits of any choice, and pursue only those whose benefits are at least as large as their costs.

Quantifying Costs and Benefits

The hardest part of analyzing costs and benefits can be figuring out how to compare very different aspects of a decision. Let's think about a simpler choice: You walk into a coffee shop and have to decide whether to buy a coffee. The chalkboard above the counter says that the price of coffee is $3.

The **cost-benefit principle** says that you should buy the coffee if the benefit is at least as large as the cost. The cost is pretty easy to quantify: It's the $3 you'll have to fork over. The benefits, however, are harder to measure: How can you quantify the rich aroma of freshly ground coffee, the earthy richness of the first sip, and the caffeine-fueled jolt that follows?

And how do you compare these benefits with three dollar bills? There's an old expression that says you can't compare apples and oranges. But actually, you can.

Convert costs and benefits into dollars by evaluating your willingness to pay.

There's a trick that economists use: We convert each cost and benefit into its money equivalent. It's easier than you may think: Simply assess your **willingness to pay** by asking yourself what is the most that you would be willing to pay in order to obtain a particular benefit or to avoid a particular cost.

Let's use this approach to quantify the benefits of coffee. Are you willing to pay $5 for it? If not, how about $4? Maybe $3? How about just $2? Maybe only $1? If you don't like coffee, you probably aren't willing to pay anything. If the most you are willing to pay is $4, then this is the dollar value of the benefits you receive from that coffee.

You should always ask yourself about your willingness to pay before you look at the price. After all, you are trying to quantify the benefit you get from buying a cup of coffee, and that benefit depends on how delicious it is to you, not the price on the menu.

Let's say that you are willing to pay up to $4 for a good cup of coffee. This doesn't mean that you actually want to pay $4 — of course you would prefer to pay a lower price, and you're happy to see that it only costs $3.

Now that you've answered the willingness-to-pay question, you have quantified both the benefit ($4) and the cost ($3) of coffee in the same units (money). With costs and benefits in the same unit, it's easy to apply the **cost-benefit principle**. In this case, the benefit exceeds the cost, so you should buy that coffee. Yum.

Money is the measuring stick, not the objective.

Some people worry that converting costs and benefits into their monetary equivalents reflects an unhealthy obsession among economists with money, or a belief that money is the only thing that matters. But that's wrong. Money is simply a common measuring stick that allows you to compare a wide variety of costs and benefits, taking account of *both* financial *and* nonfinancial aspects of a decision. Economists are no more obsessed with money than architects are obsessed with inches; these are just how we take our measurements.

Converting costs and benefits into their monetary equivalents will allow you to take account of a wide variety of nonfinancial issues. For example, you can factor in the degree of satisfaction you get from a cup of coffee, the value of your time or effort in getting to the café, and the happiness you get from supporting a local small business. Any consequence of your choices can be a cost or benefit, as long as it has meaning to you.

willingness to pay The maximum amount a buyer would be willing to pay for something. To convert costs or benefits into their monetary equivalent, ask yourself: "What is the most I am willing to pay to get this benefit (or avoid that cost)?"

pixprovider AB/E+/Getty Images

Money is just a tool for measuring value.

Interpreting the DATA   **What's the benefit you get from Google Search?**

Imagine life without Google search. How would you settle trivia debates with friends? Do research for class projects? Find a scholarship, internship, or apartment? Using Google costs $0, but the benefit you get from having all of the world's information at your fingertips is much larger.

One way to consider how much benefit you get from Google's search engine is to imagine living without it. Instead of Googling for answers, you would have to head to the library to answer most questions. Researchers have found that students can answer a typical question ("What scholarships are offered in the state of Washington?") in about 7 minutes if they use Google, but it takes about 22 minutes to find the answer at the library. Once you factor in the number of searches people do, and put a value on the time saved, Google's chief economist has calculated that the benefits from using Google to search for information adds up to around $500 per year in value for the average American. The fact that searching on Google is free, but people clearly value it illustrates an important point: The benefit you get from something can be unrelated to the price you pay. ∎

The cost-benefit principle isn't selfish — if you aren't. At first glance, it may seem like the cost-benefit principle encourages selfish decisions. By this view, doing something nice — such as buying your friend a coffee — is all cost and no benefit. But this reasoning is wrong, because it defines costs and benefits too narrowly.

A careful cost-benefit analysis takes into account both the financial and nonfinancial aspects of a decision. Your innate generosity is an important nonfinancial aspect to consider. If you enjoy buying your friend a coffee — perhaps you like seeing them happy, or maybe you enjoy their company — then this is an important nonfinancial benefit that you need to account for.

How can you quantify this benefit? As with other nonfinancial benefits, you should think in terms of your willingness to pay: How much are you willing to pay so that your friend can enjoy a coffee? The more you enjoy doing nice things like this, the more you are willing to pay for it. Similarly, the benefit of donating time or money to a nonprofit will be higher the more the cause means to you. You need to include these unselfish motivations in your cost-benefit calculations.

The key to using the cost-benefit principle properly is to think broadly about the full set of costs and benefits involved in your choices. When you account for your unselfish motivations, the cost-benefit principle will lead you to make unselfish choices.

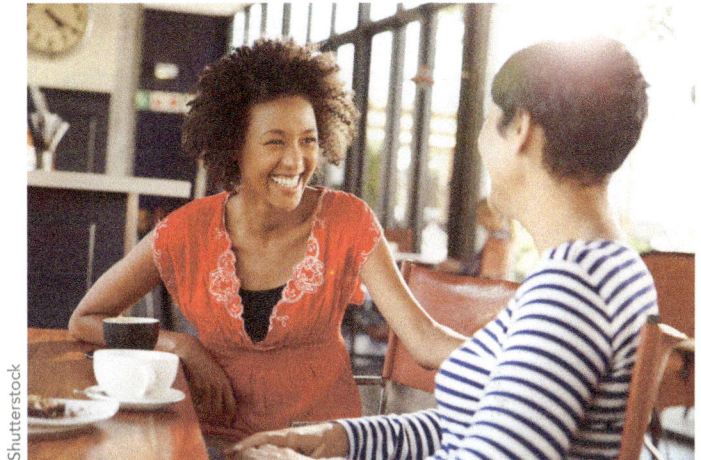

The cost-benefit principle isn't just about you.

Maximize Your Economic Surplus

When you follow the cost-benefit principle, every decision you make will yield larger benefits than costs. The difference between the benefits you enjoy and the costs you incur is called your **economic surplus,** and it is a measure of how much your decision has improved your well-being. Making good decisions is all about maximizing your economic surplus.

Follow the cost-benefit principle, and your choices will increase your economic surplus. You generate economic surplus every time you make a decision in accord with the cost-benefit principle. Consider again what happened when you bought a cup of coffee: As a buyer, you gained something worth $4 to you (remember, that's your willingness to pay for it), and in exchange, you transferred something worth only $3 (your money). This simple act of exchange generated an extra $1 worth of benefits for you! That's your economic surplus.

Now think about the same transaction from the perspective of the seller — the entrepreneur who owns the café. If a cup of coffee costs $1 to make, then she has exchanged something worth $1 to her (some coffee beans, perhaps some milk and sugar, and a few minutes of a barista's time) for something worth $3 (your money), generating $2 of economic surplus for her. Both buyer and seller are better off.

economic surplus The total benefits minus total costs flowing from a decision. It measures how much a decision has improved your well-being.

Let's consider a more important example: Sony Music might offer you a job paying $45,000 per year, but you love the music industry so much that you would have accepted the job even if it paid $35,000. If so, your new job yields you an economic surplus of $10,000. Of course, if Sony's managers are following the cost-benefit principle, they offered you the job because they believe that you will generate benefits for them that exceed the $45,000 per year that they are offering to pay you. Perhaps by finding some great new artists, you are expected to generate an extra $75,000 per year in new revenue, generating $30,000 in economic surplus for them. The cost-benefit principle ensures that both you and Sony Music make choices that generate additional economic surplus, and avoid those that reduce your economic surplus.

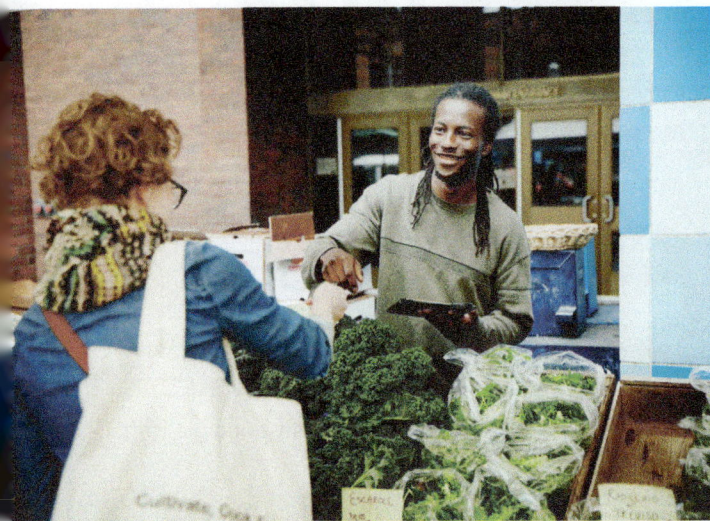

Sellers get money, buyers get the stuff they want. Both are better off.

Thomas Barwick/DigitalVision/Getty Images

Both buyers and sellers benefit from voluntary exchange. In each of the above examples, both the buyer and seller benefited from the transaction, with each earning an economic surplus. If buyers and sellers always follow the cost-benefit principle, then each will choose to trade only if the benefits to them are at least as large as their costs. This ensures that all transactions will yield economic surplus. This idea — that both sides benefit from a voluntary exchange — lies at the heart of all economic transactions.

This insight should shape how you think about economic transactions. Often noneconomists think about the economy as a sporting competition in which one person wins and the other loses. It's a colorful analogy — but it is false.

It's more useful to think of economic transactions as being more like cooperation than competition. The café owner has something you really want (coffee), and you have something they really want (money). By cooperating, you can make each other better off. Similarly, you may have something Sony Music really wants (the ability to identify great bands) and they have something you want (a fun job and a good salary). Both buyers and sellers benefit from voluntary exchange, as long as they each follow the cost-benefit principle.

Focus on Costs and Benefits, Not How They're Framed

The cost-benefit principle says that you should make choices based on the underlying costs and benefits of the choice you face, rather than how they are described or *framed*. For example, you've probably seen price tags that show an "original price" and a "sale price." The store is trying to suggest that you are getting a great deal and therefore should be willing to pay their asking price. You need to ask yourself: Do the benefits of the item on sale outweigh the sale price? The original price doesn't help you answer this question.

Sellers might also try to influence your willingness to pay by showing you higher-priced alternatives. For example, many restaurants list one outrageously expensive item on the menu expecting few people to actually order it. The goal is to frame everything else on the menu as cheap by comparison. Again, your choice should depend on your costs and benefits, and not on something irrelevant like a higher-priced option that you'd never choose!

Following the advice of the cost-benefit principle can be harder than it sounds. For instance, how would you respond to the following scenario?

Do the Economics

You're the CEO of a large but struggling insurance company. Sales have fallen, and you need to cut costs in order to avoid losing money this year. You anticipate needing to fire

6,000 of your employees. Your management team has been exploring alternatives to this drastic action. During your Monday morning meeting, they suggest two possible plans:

- *Plan A:*   Saves 2,000 jobs.
- *Plan B:*   Has a one-in-three chance of saving all 6,000 jobs, but a two-in-three chance of saving no jobs at all.

Which plan would you choose?

Plan A ☐   Plan B ☐

You arrive back at work on Tuesday, and your management team tells you that they have figured out a new set of alternatives to consider. They present the following two different alternatives:

- *Plan 1:*   Will result in the certain loss of 4,000 jobs.
- *Plan 2:*   Has a two-in-three chance of losing all 6,000 jobs, but a one-in-three chance of losing no jobs.

Which plan would you choose?

Plan 1 ☐   Plan 2 ☐

Let's now turn from using your gut to make decisions, to rigorously applying the cost-benefit principle. If you compare the choices you were offered on Monday with those offered on Tuesday, you will soon realize: They are identical! They were simply framed differently. That's right: Since the total number of jobs at stake is 6,000, Plan A, which saves 2,000 jobs, is the same as Plan 1, which loses 4,000 jobs. Similarly, a one-in-three chance of saving 6,000 jobs in Plan B is the same as a one-in-three chance of losing no jobs in Plan 2.

So, if you chose Plan A on Monday, you also should have chosen Plan 1 on Tuesday, and if you chose Plan B on Monday, you also should have chosen Plan 2 on Tuesday. However, it's possible that your choices between Monday and Tuesday were not consistent. If so, you're not alone.

In fact, around 80% of people choose Plan A when offered a choice between Plans A and B, and about 80% of people choose Plan 2 when offered a choice between Plans 1 and 2. This means that most people change their decision depending on how it is described. And that's a mistake that someone applying the cost-benefit principle wouldn't make. ∎

Framing effects can lead you astray.   This is an example of a broader problem. Psychologists have documented that small differences in how alternatives are described, or framed, can lead people to make different choices. This phenomenon is known as the **framing effect.** Although the framing effect is common, it is not rational. If you want to make good decisions that aren't affected by how your choices are described, you should follow the cost-benefit principle. That is, you should evaluate the full set of costs and benefits of each alternative and pursue only those whose benefits are at least as large as their costs.

If you rigorously followed the cost-benefit principle, laying out the pros and cons of each plan, you would've ended up with an analysis like that in Figure 1.

framing effect When a decision is affected by how a choice is described, or framed. You should avoid framing effects altering your own decisions.

Figure 1 | Costs and Benefits of Each Plan

	Monday's alternatives		Tuesday's alternatives	
	Plan A	**Plan B**	**Plan 1**	**Plan 2**
Benefit	Save 2,000 jobs	One-in-three chance to save 6,000 jobs	Save 2,000 jobs*	One-in-three chance to save 6,000 jobs*
Cost	Lose 4,000 jobs*	Two-in-three chance to lose 6,000 jobs*	Lose 4,000 jobs	Two-in-three chance to lose 6,000 jobs

*Remember: If you do nothing, your firm will lose 6,000 jobs.

When you articulate your costs and benefits this clearly, you're less likely to fall prey to framing effects.

Applying the Cost-Benefit Principle

Let's return to the decision we started with: Should Nerida buy a car or simply take an Uber to work every day? Since she's trying to decide what to do over the next year, she should consider the costs and benefits that accrue over that year. Here are the costs she came up with:

- She can buy her brother's 5-year-old Ford Focus for $10,000, and she expects that she can sell it for $8,000 after using it for the year.
- She plans to drive 5 miles to and from work, 5 days a week, for 50 weeks per year (she takes 2 weeks off for vacation), and she anticipates getting 25 miles per gallon. Gas currently sells for $3 per gallon.
- Insurance costs $1,500 per year.
- She anticipates spending another $500 per year on repairs.
- Parking costs $5 per day.

The benefit of buying a car will be the Uber fares that she doesn't have to pay. Each time she avoids taking an Uber to or from work, she'll save $10 in fares. Over the course of a year, this will add up to $5,000. (For now, let's say that this is the only benefit she gets from owning a car, because she can borrow her roommate's car on the weekends.)

Figure 2 tallies up the costs and benefits. This is a useful exercise, highlighting just how expensive the total costs of driving are. Once Nerida considers all the hidden costs, the total of cost owning a car for one year adds up to $5,550! This annual cost is larger than the $5,000 benefit of not having to pay for an Uber each day. So while it feels decadent, Nerida takes an Uber to and from work every day. And this earns $550 worth of economic surplus — not a bad return for doing a few quick calculations!

Figure 2 | The Costs and Benefits of Car Ownership

Costs (Costs associated with buying and maintaining a car and driving to and from work for a year)		Benefits (Savings from not taking an Uber)	
Cost of the car: $10,000 purchase price minus $8,000 resale value	$2,000	Uber fare savings: $10 per trip × 2 trips per day × 5 days per week × 50 weeks per year	$5,000
Gas costs: 5 miles × 2 trips per day × 5 days per week × 50 weeks = 2,500 miles. Because she gets 25 miles per gallon, she'll need 2,500 miles / 25 miles per gallon = 100 gallons, which cost a total of $3 per gallon × 100 gallons.	$300		
Parking costs: $5 per day × 5 days per week × 50 weeks per year	$1,250		
Insurance	$1,500		
Repairs	$500		
Total annual costs	$5,550	Total annual benefits	$5,000

The true cost of car ownership

Are you surprised by how expensive car ownership is? In fact, for many people, it's even more costly than this. Sure, you might be wondering about whether you would have benefits like being able to drive to the store or to see friends or to get away for the weekend. Or maybe you are worried about catching a virus on public transportation or in a rideshare. You can add these benefits into your calculation. You might make the wrong decision about whether to buy a car unless you account for the full set of costs and benefits associated with owning a car. To help you, the American Automobile Association (AAA) publishes a worksheet to help people figure out the true cost of car ownership. The typical person driving a small sedan spends over $7,000 a year to own and operate their car. Click through to https://exchange.aaa.com/automotive/aaas-your-driving-costs/ and calculate what it will cost you. The results might surprise you. ■

Calculate costs and benefits, relative to your next best alternative. Let's pause to notice something important about how Nerida calculated her costs and benefits. She's comparing buying a car with relying on ride-sharing apps like Uber. That is, she's comparing one possibility — driving to work — with its *next best alternative,* which is taking an Uber. In fact, this is exactly the type of thinking that lies at the heart of our next principle: the opportunity cost principle. It's an important principle because it will help you count your costs and benefits properly.

1.3 The Opportunity Cost Principle

Learning Objective *The true cost of something is the next best alternative you must give up to get it. Your decisions should reflect this opportunity cost, rather than just the out-of-pocket financial costs.*

🎙 Podcast
Think Like an Economist
The Opportunity Cost Principle: Or What?

Nerida's career has stalled out a bit due to the Covid pandemic. She managed to hang onto her job, but she hasn't gotten a raise or promotion in a while and she feels stuck. Some of her mentors have suggested that she consider going back to school to get a Master of Business Administration (MBA). But is it worth it? The cost-benefit principle tells her that a good decision requires comparing the relevant benefits and costs. The benefits of an MBA are better career prospects. Indeed, careful studies show that MBAs earn around 10% more than comparable college graduates, and a more advanced degree often opens up opportunities for more interesting and enjoyable work. But what are the costs?

Opportunity Costs Reflect Scarcity

The most obvious cost of an MBA is tuition, which is about $60,000 per year for two years. But this isn't the only cost. For instance, if Nerida pursues an MBA full time, she'll have to quit her job. The more Nerida thinks about it, the more she realizes that some costs aren't always obvious. And so she is left wondering: How can she be sure that her decisions reflect her true costs and benefits?

The opportunity cost of something is the next best alternative you have to give up. Your decisions should reflect your **opportunity cost,** rather than just out-of-pocket costs, because the true cost of something is what you must give up to get it. This principle reminds you that whether you are deciding how to spend your money, your time, or anything else, you should think about its alternative uses. It tells you to assess the consequences of your choice relative to the *best* of your alternatives. The principle forces

opportunity cost The true cost of something is the next best alternative you have to give up to get it.

you to focus on the real *trade-offs* you face, and in doing so you will make better decisions. The opportunity cost principle is such a fundamental part of economic thinking that when economists say "costs," we really mean opportunity costs.

Let's now see how thinking about opportunity costs might lead you to assess your decisions differently.

People who haven't studied economics tend to think about the cost of something as the out-of-pocket financial cost—how much money they must spend to pay for it. But this can be very misleading.

For instance, studying economics in the library until closing time every day doesn't lead to any extra out-of-pocket costs. If this were the right way to think about costs, then you would be in the library studying economics whenever it's open, since the benefit (learning more economics, which helps you make better decisions) surely offsets the out-of-pocket cost of zero. But it ignores other important costs. Your time is scarce, and so each hour spent studying economics has an opportunity cost, because it's an hour that you can't spend studying psychology, marketing, history, or math. It's also an hour you can't spend sleeping, working, or just enjoying life. You should study another hour of economics only if it yields benefits that are at least as large as those of the best of these alternatives.

The opportunity cost principle leads you to focus on the true trade-offs you face. If you make one choice (studying economics until 3 A.M.), what is the best alternative that you're forced to give up? Just as the opportunity cost principle can help you better allocate your time (as in this example), it can help you better allocate your scarce money, attention, and resources.

The opportunity cost principle highlights the problem of scarcity. If you ever think that a choice involves no costs, think again. Even if there's no out-of-pocket cost, there's always an opportunity cost. The logic is simple: Whenever you choose to do something, you are implicitly choosing not to do something else. Deciding to watch a movie? That's a decision not to spend two hours preparing for class. The forgone opportunity to pursue an activity is the opportunity cost that you need to consider.

scarcity Resources are limited, therefore any resource you spend pursuing one activity leaves fewer resources to pursue others. Scarcity implies that you always face a trade-off.

This opportunity cost arises because of a fundamental economic problem: **scarcity.** Your resources are limited—that is, they're scarce. It's not just that you have limited income, but you also have limited time (only 24 hours in a day), limited attention, and limited willpower. Any resources you spend pursuing one activity leaves fewer resources to pursue others. Scarcity implies that you always face a trade-off. Whenever you use any scarce resource—your time, money, attention, willpower, or other resources—there's an opportunity cost.

> **EVERYDAY Economics** The opportunity cost is the road not taken

The opportunity cost principle even informs some poetry. Consider the last stanza of the poem "The Road Not Taken," by the great American poet Robert Frost:

> *I shall be telling this with a sigh*
> *Somewhere ages and ages hence:*
> *Two roads diverged in a wood, and I—*
> *I took the one less traveled by,*
> *And that has made all the difference.*

Frost's traveler has come to a fork in the road, and faces a stark choice: which path to take. What is the opportunity cost of taking one path? The opportunity cost is the road not taken. Frost's traveler takes "the one less traveled by," and when he says that this "has made all the difference," he is comparing it to his next best alternative. You can think of the opportunity cost principle as asking you to consider "the road not taken." ∎

Calculating Your Opportunity Costs

Remember, the opportunity cost of something is what you give up to get it. So, if you want to make sure that you are evaluating your opportunity cost correctly, you should ask yourself two questions:

1. What happens if you pursue your choice?

2. What happens under your next best alternative?

That's it. Now, let's apply this principle to figuring out the true opportunity cost of pursuing an MBA.

1. *What happens if Nerida pursues an MBA?*
    If Nerida pursues an MBA, she'll quit her job, pay tuition, pay for room and board, and spend a lot of time studying. These consequences are listed in the first column of Figure 3.

2. *What happens if Nerida pursues her next best alternative?*
    Nerida's next best alternative is to keep working in her current job. If she chooses this route, she won't have to pay tuition, she'll earn $70,000 per year, she'll still have to pay for rent and meals, and she'll spend her days working. These consequences are listed in the second column of Figure 3.

Figure 3 | **The Opportunity Costs of Pursuing an MBA (per year)**

Costs of her choice —	Costs of her next best alternative =	Opportunity cost
If Nerida pursues an MBA	*If she continues to work full time instead*	*The cost of an MBA, relative to working full time*
Tuition costs $60,000	She won't pay tuition	$60,000 tuition
She quits her job	She earns $70,000 from her job	**+** $70,000 in forgone income
Room and board cost $24,000	Rent and meals cost $24,000	**+** No opportunity cost (She has to pay for housing and food whether or not she pursues an MBA)
10 hours per day studying	10 hours per day at work	**+** No opportunity cost (She works 10 hours per day either way)

= $130,000 per year in total opportunity cost

If the opportunity cost of something is what you must give up to get it, then it's the difference between the consequences of making that choice and the consequences of the next best alternative. So the opportunity cost of pursuing an MBA — shown in the final column of Figure 3 — is equal to the first column minus the second column. We've found that the opportunity cost of pursuing an MBA is $130,000 per year, and so a two-year program comes at a cost of $260,000. This analysis reveals that Nerida should pursue an MBA only if the benefit exceeds the total opportunity cost of $260,000.

Your analysis has revealed four important lessons about opportunity costs:

Lesson 1: Some out-of-pocket costs are opportunity costs. The first cost that Nerida thought about was the $60,000 per year cost of tuition. Obviously, this is an out-of-pocket cost. It is also an opportunity cost — she has to pay tuition if she pursues an MBA, but she wouldn't incur this expense if she pursued her next best alternative, which is continuing in her current job.

Lesson 2: Opportunity costs need not involve out-of-pocket financial costs. But focusing too much on out-of-pocket financial costs might lead you to miss important opportunity costs. For instance, one of the biggest costs of pursuing an MBA is the salary that you forgo when you leave your job. Nerida is currently earning $70,000 per year, so going without this paycheck is a substantial opportunity cost!

Lesson 3: Not all out-of-pocket costs are real opportunity costs. Paying too much attention to out-of-pocket financial costs can also lead you to think about factors that aren't actually relevant opportunity costs. For instance, if Nerida pursues an MBA, she'll have to pay $24,000 per year for room and board. But room and board isn't a cost that should be associated with getting an MBA: you have to pay for food and housing whether you get an MBA or not. If the expense is the same, and if you have to pay for it under either alternative, then it's not an opportunity cost. However, if your next best alternative involves cheaper food and housing costs then you would count the difference in the cost for room and board.

Lesson 4: Some nonfinancial costs are not opportunity costs. There are also nonfinancial costs of pursuing an MBA. For instance, Nerida will have to work hard, studying 10 hours per day. But Nerida already works hard for 10 hours per day in her current job. Thus, relative to her next best alternative, the hard work demanded by an MBA program isn't an opportunity cost.

> Four lessons about opportunity costs:
> 1. Some out-of-pocket costs are opportunity costs.
> 2. Opportunity costs need not involve out-of-pocket costs.
> 3. Not all out-of-pocket costs are opportunity costs.
> 4. Some nonfinancial costs are not opportunity costs.

EVERYDAY Economics   The true cost of college

You now have the tools you need to assess the true cost of your own college experience. I bet you thought about the cost of college before applying, and you probably looked up the numbers on your college's website. But you may have been thinking about it wrong. That website probably listed the cost of things such as tuition, housing, meals, books, and health insurance — a list that is surprisingly unhelpful for evaluating the true opportunity cost of attending college.

For that, you need to know: If you weren't attending college, what would be different? It's true that you wouldn't be paying tuition, so that's an opportunity cost. But you would surely continue to eat, so most if not all of the cost of food isn't an opportunity cost (it counts only if you could eat cheaper elsewhere). The same goes for the cost of rent and health insurance. College websites always manage to omit the biggest cost of going to college, which is that if you weren't studying, you would probably be employed and earning tens of thousands of dollars. Those forgone earnings are an important opportunity cost that you need to consider.

In fact, many students attended college during the pandemic even though classes were online, and they didn't get the benefit of meeting in person with professors and socializing with classmates. But while the benefits of college were lower during the pandemic, so were the opportunity costs. Jobs became pretty scarce, so students weren't necessarily forgoing earnings to attend school.

Going to college always involves opportunity costs, and so you should apply the opportunity cost principle to your decision. That way you can make sure that the benefit of your college education exceeds the cost. ∎

In order to make a good decision, you always have to ask "Or what?," comparing your choice to its next best alternative.

andresr/E+/Getty Images

The "Or What?" Trick

To apply the opportunity cost principle correctly, just make sure that whenever you pose a question, the word *OR* appears in the middle of it. For example, when Nerida asks, "Should I get an MBA?" she needs to add: "OR keep working?" The "OR" forces you to consider your alternatives, which is at the heart of the opportunity cost principle. So remember, always ask: "Or what?"

Sometimes you'll find that you can list more than one alternative. When this happens, remember that the opportunity cost is the *best* of these alternatives. So you have a choice: Ask yourself "Or what?" . . ., OR sometimes make bad choices.

Do the Economics

Consider the opportunity costs of each of the following choices:

- *Should you hang out with your friends on Saturday afternoon?*
  Or what? Or should you study for Tuesday's exam?

- *Should you devote a lot of time to an extracurricular activity and aim for a top leadership position?*
  Or what? Or should you study a lot more and aim for straight A's?

- *Should you do an unpaid internship this summer?*
  Or what? Or should you continue waiting tables?

- *Should you hire your best friend to work in your family business?*
  Or what? Or should you hire someone else?

- *Should you put your savings in the stock market, where it could grow a lot in value over the long run, but where it can also fall in value?*
  Or what? Or should you put your savings in the bank, where the value of your savings will stay roughly the same?

- *Should your online store export its goods, selling them to people in other countries?*
  Or what? Or sell them only to people domestically?

- *Should you spend all of your current earnings?*
  Or what? Or should you save some of your earnings to spend in the future?

Your actual answers to these questions are unique to you, but they still make up some of the biggest costs you'll face. That's why you're learning the tools of economics, so that you can make better decisions for your own unique life. ■

How Entrepreneurs Think About Opportunity Cost

The opportunity cost principle is also critical to how entrepreneurs evaluate whether or not to start a business. Just as you shouldn't be overly focused on out-of-pocket costs, entrepreneurs know to look beyond their business revenues and financial costs. They also understand that starting a new business imposes some hard-to-see opportunity costs. The "or what" approach makes these costs clearer. Starting a new business requires confronting the following two questions:

- *Should you start a new business or stay in your current job?*
  Starting a new business means quitting your job and, thus, giving up the steady income and benefits paid by your employer. These *forgone earnings* are the opportunity cost of an entrepreneur's time.

- *Should you invest your money in the new business or leave it in the bank?*
  Investing your money in your business means not keeping it in the bank, and so not earning interest. This *forgone interest* is your opportunity cost.

So when you are thinking about starting a new business, it isn't enough just to figure out whether you'll earn a financial profit. Starting a business is only a good idea if the benefit it yields — those financial profits — are large enough to offset the opportunity cost of the income you forgo by investing both your time and your money into this business, rather than your next best alternative.

You Should Ignore Sunk Costs

Sometimes when you've spent a lot of time or money on a project, you may think: "I can't stop now; I've already put so much into this project." But this is a mistake. When the time, effort, and other costs you put into the project cannot be reversed, they are referred to as **sunk costs.** And good decision makers ignore sunk costs. Why? The opportunity cost principle asks you to compare the consequences of your choice with the consequences of the next best alternative. Since sunk costs can't be reversed, you'll incur those costs under either scenario, which means that they are not opportunity costs. Thus, you should ignore sunk costs.

    Unfortunately, many of us find it hard to ignore sunk costs in our everyday lives. Have you ever seen anyone stay in an unhappy relationship because they've already spent so much time working on it? Or perhaps you've seen someone stay in a college major, job, or career that they hate, figuring that it's the right thing to do, given how much time and effort they have put into it. Sometimes corporate executives make similar mistakes, throwing good money after bad, in the hope that an investment project will eventually pay off.

sunk cost A cost that has been incurred and cannot be reversed. A sunk cost exists in whatever choice you make, and hence it is not an opportunity cost. Good decisions ignore sunk costs.

Do the Economics

It is easy to fall for the sunk-cost fallacy. Think about the following scenarios:

a. Yesterday you bought a Halloween costume for $35 to wear to a friend's Halloween party. But today you're feeling sick, and as you're getting dressed to go to the party, you realize that you won't enjoy it. Do you head to the party?

b. You paid $10 for premium access to a new movie. But 30 minutes into the film, you've seen enough: The acting is terrible, the plot is predictable, and the jokes are cringeworthy. Do you keep watching? What if you had paid to see it in a theater instead?

c. You accepted a summer internship in another city, and signed a three-month lease on an apartment there. But at the last moment you're offered a different internship at a company close to home. The pay is the same, but it is better aligned with your career plans and you have always wanted to work there. You can live at home for free if you take the second internship, but you won't get back the $3,000 you've paid for the apartment near the first internship. Should the apartment you've rented factor into your decision? ∎

Answers: a. Don't let yesterday's $35 sunk cost lead you to go to a party you won't enjoy. b. Stop watching. You've already paid for access and can't get the money back, but you can still save the value of the time you haven't yet spent watching it. If you went to the theater, walk out. Money spent on premium access or movie theater tickets is a sunk cost you should ignore in deciding whether to keep watching something. c. If living at home and taking the better internship is better than taking the worse internship and living for "free" near it, then take the better internship. Of course you wouldn't be living for free, but the $3,000 is a sunk cost and you should ignore it when making your decision.

Applying the Opportunity Cost Principle

The opportunity cost principle is an incredibly powerful tool that can help you better understand all sorts of decisions. The following examples illustrate just how important it is in explaining the decisions that people make.

The economy went bust in 2020, but with premium films like *Mulan* debuting online, Disney+ boomed.

Why do people watch more movies during an economic downturn? During the 2008 recession, the movie business boomed. And during the pandemic, streaming services enjoyed record profits. Why? The most important cost of seeing a movie isn't the price of the ticket or the streaming service. Instead, it's the opportunity cost of your time. The movie takes two hours, and you could spend this time doing something else. Perhaps you could be working instead of seeing the movie. But when the economy is weak, there are fewer jobs, and there is often less work to do, and so the opportunity cost of your time is lower. Or perhaps the alternative to the movie is going to a party. But fewer people throw parties when the economy is weak and even fewer threw them during the pandemic when parties were both dangerous and often prohibited by local laws. So your alternative to watching a movie during a recession might be a night watching television. Because the opportunity cost of time is lower during an economic downturn (especially one caused by a pandemic!), people choose to watch more movies. In fact, a weak economy is often good news for the movie industry.

Why do most people end up waiting until they are in their late 20s or 30s to marry? Many high school students get involved in romantic relationships, but very few get married. Why? The choice you face is: Should I get married or keep searching for a better match? As a teenager or young adult, you may have had only a couple of romantic entanglements, and so the possibility that later on you'll meet someone who's an even better match is pretty high. That is, the opportunity cost of marriage — the opportunity to search for an even better partner — is high. By your twenties and thirties, you have more life experience and have met people from many spheres of life. While there's always the possibility that you'll find someone even better later on, the opportunity cost of getting married falls as you get older.

Distribution of Age at First Marriage

Share of first marriages in 2019 occurring at each age

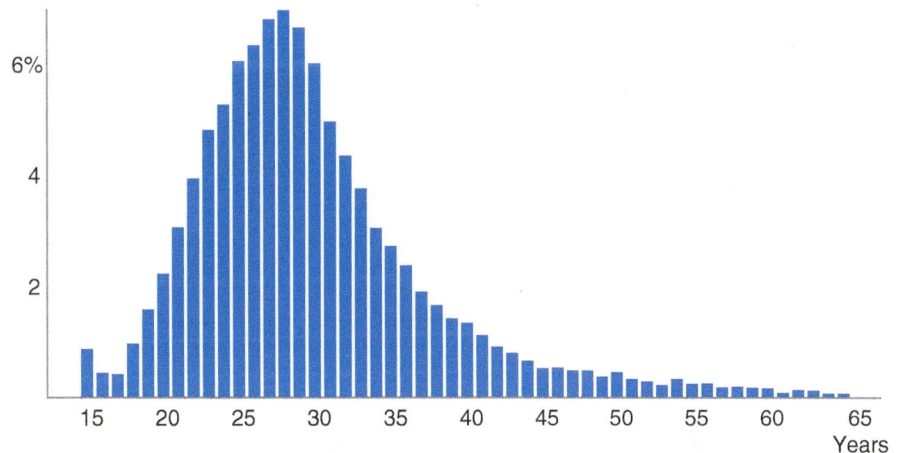

Data from: U.S. Census Bureau.

Why do people with terminal illnesses want unproven experimental drugs? Most people are unwilling to take unproven experimental drugs, because they fear that the drugs will do more harm than good. But people with terminal illnesses sometimes plead with their doctors to be allowed to be part of a new medical trial. Why? For healthy people, the choice they face is between taking part in a risky experiment and continuing with their healthy, happy lives. For those with terminal illnesses, the alternative to the risky experiment is continued illness and probable death. Due to this lower opportunity cost, people with severe illnesses are willing to take risks that others are not.

There's no such thing as a free doughnut. Early morning meetings often include a tray of doughnuts on the conference table. These doughnuts are delicious, and you don't have to pay for them. But they aren't free once you consider their opportunity cost. That's why I never eat them. Like most people, I try to stay healthy by limiting the treats I eat each day. So when I see a tray of doughnuts, I ask myself: Should I eat the doughnut now, or enjoy a bowl of ice cream later? The price of the doughnut is $0, but it's not free because the opportunity cost of a doughnut for me is a bowl of ice cream. Since I love ice cream more than doughnut, it's a price that's usually too high for me to pay.

Interpreting the DATA   **Why have mothers joined—and recently left—the workforce?**

In 1975, more than half of all mothers stayed out of the labor force. By 2019, nearly three-quarters of mothers with kids under age 18 worked outside of the home or were actively trying to find a job. But the trend shifted dramatically in 2020: During the pandemic, women's employment fell back to levels last seen in the late 1980s. Changing opportunity costs explain both why women entered the labor force in the decades before the pandemic, and partly why they were disproportionately hurt when the pandemic hit.

Proportion of Mothers Neither Working Nor Looking for Work

Among women with kids aged under 18

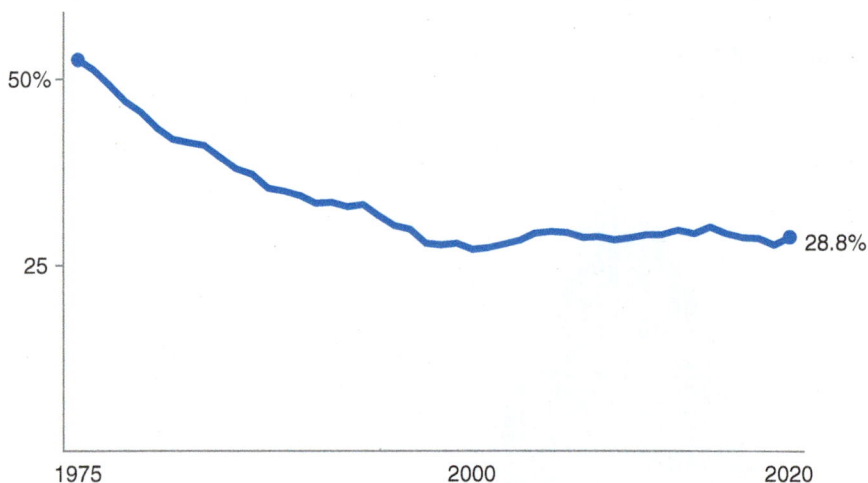

Data from: Bureau of Labor Statistics

People face a trade-off between making things for themselves and working for pay that allows them to buy things made by others. So parents need to divide their time between home production — making meals, cleaning, taking care of and educating children, growing food in the garden — and market work, which enables them to buy things like food, cleaning products and services, child care, housing, and other goods and services they want or need.

The opportunity cost of women staying home to focus on home production rose as women's wages rose over time because staying home means giving up more income (and therefore more purchased goods and services) as earnings opportunities rise. As this opportunity cost rose, more women chose to develop careers before having children, and many also decided to stay in the workforce after having children.

But the opportunity cost of working for pay was upended in 2020, when schools and day-care providers were shut down to prevent the spread of Covid-19. Suddenly, the opportunity cost of work for pay rose, and many families needed to have someone cut back on paid work in order to do the unpaid labor at home. ■

The Production Possibility Frontier

production possibility frontier
Shows the different sets of output that are attainable with your scarce resources.

Sometimes you'll find it useful to visualize your opportunity costs. That's what the **production possibility frontier (PPF)** is for — it maps out the different sets of output that are attainable with your scarce resources. It illustrates the trade-offs — that is, the opportunity costs — you confront when deciding how best to allocate scarce resources like your time, money, raw inputs, or production capacity.

The production possibility frontier illustrates your alternative outputs.

Let's see how this applies to your study time. If you have three hours per night to study, you can allocate that time between studying economics and studying psychology. Perhaps each extra hour per night you devote to studying economics will raise your econ grade by 8 points, while allocating that time to studying psychology instead will improve your psych grade by only 4 points.

Effectively you're the CEO of a grades-producing factory whose inputs are study time and whose outputs are grades. You can devote your factory's resources to boosting your econ or psych scores to varying degrees. At one extreme, you could spend all three hours studying economics, which would raise your econ grade by 24 points (and psych by nothing). At the other extreme, you could spend all three hours studying psychology, which would improve your psych grade by 12 points (and econ by nothing). In between there's a bunch of other possibilities for allocating your study time, each of which corresponds to a point on your production possibility frontier. Together, these points form a frontier, shown in Figure 4 as a straight line (although in many other cases, your production possibilities frontier may be a bowed-out curve). We call this a *frontier,* because it describes the most that you can produce given your current circumstances. If you waste your resources, or use them inefficiently, you won't even hit this frontier, and you'll end up producing less of each output than you otherwise could.

Figure 4 | The Production Possibility Frontier

You have 3 hours per night to devote to studying either economics (where each hour will boost your grade by 8 points) or psychology (where each hour will boost your grade by 4 points). The **production possibility frontier** shows what you can produce with alternative allocations of your time.

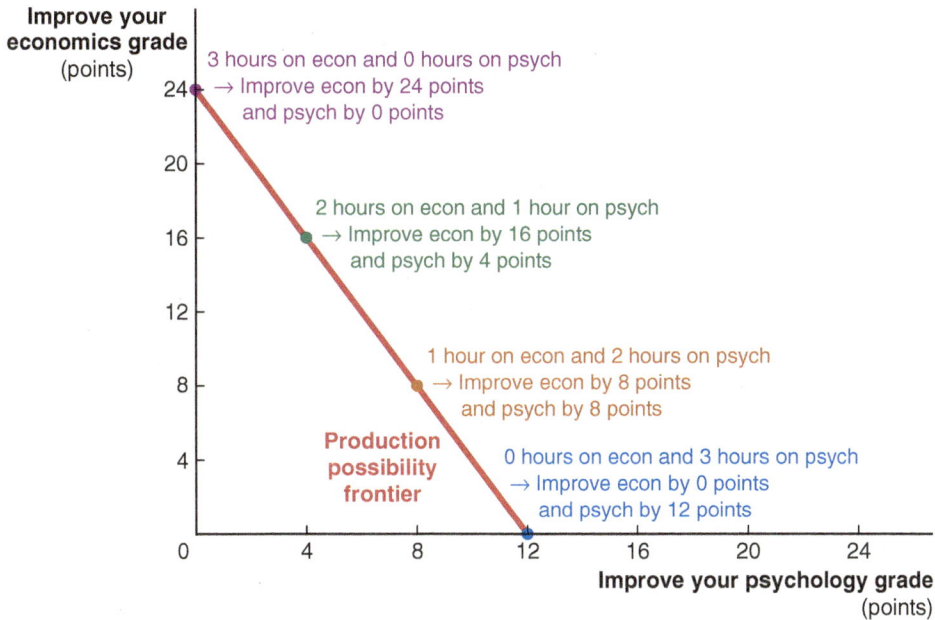

Improve your economics grade (points)

3 hours on econ and 0 hours on psych
→ Improve econ by 24 points
and psych by 0 points

2 hours on econ and 1 hour on psych
→ Improve econ by 16 points
and psych by 4 points

1 hour on econ and 2 hours on psych
→ Improve econ by 8 points
and psych by 8 points

Production possibility frontier

0 hours on econ and 3 hours on psych
→ Improve econ by 0 points
and psych by 12 points

Improve your psychology grade (points)

Moving along your production possibility frontier reveals your opportunity costs. When you're on your production possibility frontier, you can't produce more of one output unless you produce less of the other. Moving along your production possibility frontier highlights this opportunity cost: Every hour you devote to studying psychology (which increases your psych grade by 4 points) is one less hour you can devote to economics (which would have boosted your econ grade by 8 points). As a result, the opportunity cost of adding 4 more points to your psych grade is earning 8 fewer points on econ.

Productivity gains shift your production possibility frontier outward. So, what if you want to produce more than is possible with your production possibility frontier? Well, you'll have to change something. One way to do that is to discover new production techniques that allow you to do more with the same amount of inputs. For example, if you uncover more effective study habits (my advice: reading the text and

It's a frontier.

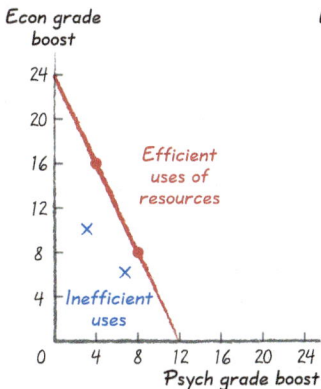

Econ grade boost

Efficient uses of resources

Inefficient uses

Psych grade boost

It illustrates your opportunity costs.

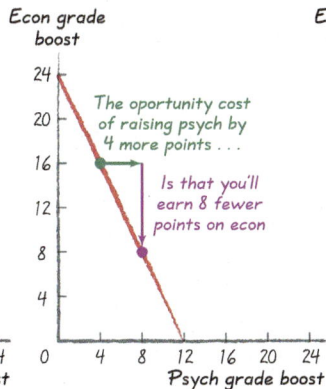

Econ grade boost

The opportunity cost of raising psych by 4 more points . . .

Is that you'll earn 8 fewer points on econ

Psych grade boost

Greater productivity pushes out the frontier.

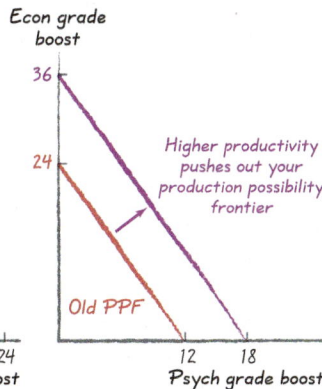

Econ grade boost

Higher productivity pushes out your production possibility frontier

Old PPF

Psych grade boost

doing some practice quizzes before class is much more productive than cramming weeks later), you might be able to increase the grade boost that comes from each hour you spend studying. This increase in productivity shifts out your production possibility frontier. But even if you get better at studying psych and econ, your resources are still limited, and so there's still an opportunity cost to your time.

Evaluating Either/Or Decisions

Let's take stock. The two principles that we have studied so far provide useful guidance whenever you are trying to decide whether or not to do something — such as whether to get an MBA, whether to get married, whether to go to a movie, and whether to look for a job. Since you either choose to do these things or not, we call these "either/or" choices. The cost-benefit principle says: Do it if the benefits are at least as large as the costs. But what are the costs? The opportunity cost principle says that the true cost of something is the best alternative you give up to get it. Taken together, these principles say: You should pursue your choice if it yields benefits that are at least as large as the opportunity cost, which is your next best alternative.

But not every decision is an "either/or" choice. How many classes should you take? How many workers should you hire? How many children should you have? In the next section, we'll show you how to simplify even incredibly complicated "how many" choices into a series of much simpler "either/or" choices using our third core principle.

🎙️ **Podcast**

Think Like an Economist

The Marginal Principle: Just One More?

1.4 The Marginal Principle

Learning Objective *Decisions about quantities are best made incrementally. You should break "how many" decisions down into a series of smaller, or marginal, decisions.*

Let's revisit Nerida, a few years after business school. She has decided to combine her entrepreneurial savvy with her love of food by opening her own restaurant. She has already chosen a location and remodeled it. Next, she needs to decide how many workers to hire. The benefit of hiring a larger staff is that she'll serve more meals, leading to higher revenue. But this also means higher costs — because more staff means a higher wage bill, and selling more meals means buying more fresh ingredients. As with so many things, there's a trade-off. So, Nerida wonders just how many workers she should hire.

The **marginal principle** says that decisions about quantities are best made incrementally. Whenever you face a decision about how many of something to choose (such as, "How many workers should I hire?"), break it into a series of smaller, or marginal, decisions (such as, "Should I hire one more worker?").

This suggests that you evaluate whether the extra benefit from hiring one more worker exceeds the extra cost of that extra worker. We call the extra benefit you get from one more worker the **marginal benefit;** the extra cost of that worker is called the **marginal cost.** Applying the cost-benefit principle to this marginal choice, you should hire one more worker only if the marginal benefit is at least as large as the marginal cost.

As Figure 5 illustrates, this is a process that you should apply iteratively: After you've decided to hire that extra worker, you should compare the marginal cost and benefit of hiring *another* worker. Again, if the marginal benefit exceeds the marginal cost, you should hire that person, too. Then you should ask whether it is worth hiring yet another worker. And so it continues, as you work your way through a series of straightforward "either/or" choices, until eventually you decide against hiring any more workers.

marginal principle Decisions about quantities are best made incrementally. You should break "how many" questions into a series of smaller, or marginal decisions, weighing marginal benefits and marginal costs.

marginal benefit The extra benefit from one extra unit (of goods purchased, hours studied, etc.).

marginal cost The extra cost from one extra unit.

When Is the Marginal Principle Useful?

Whenever you have to decide "how many" of something to choose, you should use the marginal principle to break your decision into a series of smaller marginal choices. And while the marginal principle isn't always relevant, you'll find that some "either/or" choices have "how many" questions lurking within. For instance, Nerida was deciding not just whether to open a restaurant (an "either/or" decision), but also how big it should be, and so she found the marginal principle useful when she decided how many square feet of retail space to lease.

The bottom line: First, determine what type of choice you face. If you face a "how many" choice, you should break it down into a series of smaller marginal decisions. You know that you have broken a decision into its smallest components when you are left with only "either/or" choices to make. Then, apply the cost-benefit principle and the opportunity cost principle to each of these simpler "either/or" choices.

Figure 5 | Applying the Marginal Principle

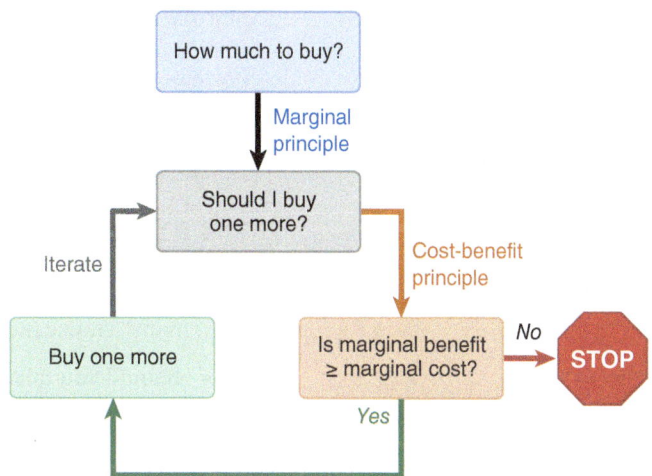

Do the Economics

Apply the marginal principle to simplify the following decisions:

- *How many workers should I hire?*
  Simplifies to: *Should I hire one more worker?*

- *How many pairs of shoes should I buy?*
  Simplifies to: *Should I buy one more pair of shoes?*

- *How many classes should I take?*
  Simplifies to: *Should I take one more class this semester?*

- *How many children should I have?*
  Simplifies to: *Should I have one (more) child?*

- *How many hours per week should I work?*
  If you are in a job where you can change your hours of work, then you should ask: *Should I work one more hour?*
  If you are in a job where you work per shift then you should ask: *Should I work one more shift?* If you can't change the number of hours you work, then this is an either-or question (*should I get a second job?*) and can't be further simplified. ∎

Now we have figured out how to restate any "how many" choice as an "either/or" marginal choice. But remember, deciding "how many" actually requires answering a *series* of these marginal "either/or" questions. Every time you ask one of these marginal questions and the answer is yes, you should ask it again. And if the answer is yes, ask it yet again. You should keep asking until the answer is no. In fact, that is the essence of the most powerful application of the marginal principle, as we will learn in the next section.

> Applying the marginal principle: Once you have broken a problem into a series of marginal choices, apply the cost-benefit principle. The marginal principle is useful for "how many" decisions, but not for "either/or" choices.

Using the Rational Rule to Maximize Your Economic Surplus

The marginal principle provides a simple rule of thumb that will help you maximize your economic surplus (the difference between your total benefits and total costs). Here's the rule:

The **Rational Rule:** *If something is worth doing, keep doing it until your marginal benefits equal your marginal costs.*

The logic of this rule is straightforward. You know from the cost-benefit principle that whenever the benefits of a choice exceed the costs, it is a good choice. When you apply the

> **Rational Rule** If something is worth doing, keep doing it until your marginal benefits equal your marginal costs.

marginal principle, you don't analyze the "how many" choice all at once ("How many workers should I hire?"). Instead, you analyze a series of simpler "either/or" choices ("Should I hire one more worker?"). The marginal principle tells you to keep hiring, as long as the marginal benefit of each worker exceeds the marginal cost. But you should stop hiring just before the marginal cost becomes larger than the marginal benefit. When does this occur? In most cases, this crossing point occurs right when the marginal benefit is equal to the marginal cost. (In the remaining cases — when the marginal benefit and marginal cost are never exactly equal — you should keep hiring for as long as the marginal benefit exceeds the marginal cost.)

The Rational Rule says to keep going until marginal benefit equals marginal cost. Let's apply this reasoning to a decision you face at the start of each semester: how many classes to take. The marginal principle says to break up this "how many" choice into a series of "either/or" choices.

- Should you take one class? The benefit of the first class is surely greater than the cost. So you should definitely take that class.

- Given that you are taking one class this semester, should you take a second? If the marginal benefit of this extra class exceeds the marginal cost, you should.

- The same logic holds for a third class and a fourth (and possibly more). In fact, you should keep increasing your course load as long as the marginal benefit of each extra class is at least as large as the marginal cost.

- But at some point — usually when you are thinking about whether to take a fifth or a sixth class — the marginal benefit of an extra class will be too low or the marginal cost too high (perhaps because the opportunity cost of one more class is constant sleep deprivation). If the marginal cost of that extra class is greater than the marginal benefit, you shouldn't take that extra class.

The Rational Rule leads to good decisions. Why would you want to set your marginal benefits equal to your marginal costs? After all, don't you simply want to maximize your economic surplus — the difference between the benefits you enjoy and the costs you incur? It turns out that if you follow the Rational Rule, you will maximize your economic surplus. Why? Let's try to provide Nerida with some insight as she tries to figure out how many workers to hire.

If the marginal benefit of hiring one more worker exceeds the marginal cost, then hiring that worker will increase your economic surplus. Since the marginal benefit of this extra worker exceeds their marginal cost, hiring them will increase your total benefit by more than it increases your total cost. Thus, hiring this extra worker will raise your economic surplus. If you always hire an additional worker when the marginal benefit is greater than the marginal cost, you will increase your economic surplus, which moves you ever closer to the point at which your economic surplus is at its highest possible level.

If the marginal benefit of hiring one more worker is less than the marginal cost, then hiring that worker will lower your economic surplus. If you hire this worker, they would raise your total costs by more than they would raise your total benefits, and so hiring them would lower your economic surplus. Hiring (or keeping) a worker whose marginal benefit is less than their marginal cost will move you further away from the point at which your economic surplus is maximized.

You maximize your economic surplus right at the point where the marginal cost of hiring the last worker equals the marginal benefit. So, hiring more workers will increase your economic surplus as long as the marginal benefit exceeds the marginal cost. But at some point, the marginal benefit of an additional worker will be less than the marginal cost. When this happens, hiring that worker would reduce your economic surplus. So, at what point do you stop hiring? Right when the marginal benefit equals the marginal cost. At this point, you have increased your economic surplus as much as possible, right up to the point where hiring another worker would reduce your economic surplus.

Do the Economics

Let's now apply the Rational Rule to help Nerida decide how many workers to hire. In each row of Figure 6, she has written down her projections of her total costs and total benefits at different staffing levels. She considers as few as two staff (in the first row), to as many as seven (in the final row). Each staffing level is noted in the first column. The second column shows the number of meals that Nerida anticipates selling, which increases as she hires more staff.

Figure 6 | **Nerida's Weekly Costs and Benefits Depend on the Number of Staff**

Number of workers	Meals served	Total benefits (Revenue = $25 × number of meals)	Marginal benefit (Change in total benefit from hiring an extra worker)	Total costs ($10 per meal food costs + $300 per worker + $500 rent + $1,000 for Nerida's time)	Marginal cost (Change in total cost from hiring an extra worker)	Profit or economic surplus (Total benefits less total costs)
2	160	$4,000		$3,700		$300
3	210	$5,250	$1,250	$4,500	$800	$750
4	250	$6,250	$1,000	$5,200	$700	$1,050
5	280	$7,000	$750	$5,800	$600	$1,200
6	300	$7,500	$500	$6,300	$500	$1,200
7	310	$7,750	$250	$6,700	$400	$1,050

Profit is maximized when marginal benefit = marginal cost

Maximum profit

Marginal benefit equals marginal cost

On the benefit side, the more meals Nerida sells each week, the greater the revenue she earns. On average, each meal sells for about $25, and so her weekly revenue will be $25, multiplied by the number of meals served. This *total revenue,* which is her total benefit, is shown in the third column. On the cost side, running a restaurant is an expensive business. She pays $500 per week in rent. Each worker she hires costs $300 per week, and each extra meal that is prepared costs $10 in raw ingredients. Also, as an entrepreneur, she has to consider the opportunity cost of her own time, which is $1,000 per week. The sum of these costs is her total cost, and the total costs associated with each staffing level are shown in the fifth column.

But the marginal principle suggests that we focus on Nerida's marginal benefits, rather than her total benefits. The marginal benefit of hiring an additional worker, shown in the fourth column, is the extra revenue that she will earn from that worker. For example, the marginal benefit of hiring the third worker is simply the total benefit from hiring three workers, minus the total benefit from hiring two workers, or $5,250 − $4,000 = $1,250 per week. We can do similar calculations for each extra staff member, and these marginal benefit calculations are shown in the fourth column.

We also need to work out Nerida's marginal costs, which are the extra costs that come with hiring each extra worker (and from making the extra meals they serve). For instance, adding a third worker and increasing the number of meals Nerida serves causes her total costs to rise from $3,700 per week in the first row, to $4,500 per week in the next row, for a marginal cost of $800. When we do similar marginal cost calculations for each additional staff member, we arrive at the numbers shown in the sixth column.

Now, let's apply the Rational Rule. Notice that hiring that third worker brings an additional (or marginal) benefit of $1,250 per week, and an additional (or marginal) cost of $800 per week. Because the marginal benefits exceed the marginal costs, Nerida is definitely better off hiring that third worker. But should she also hire a fourth worker? And what about a fifth worker after that? The Rational Rule says to keep hiring workers until the marginal benefits are equal to the marginal costs. In this case, Nerida's marginal benefits and costs are equal when she hires six workers. And so the rule says: Hire six workers.

Does this make sense? You can check the final column, which calculates her economic surplus, which in this case is her economic profit — her total benefits less total costs. Looking down this column, the highest profit Nerida can earn is $1,200. She can earn this profit if she hires either five or six workers. The Rational Rule led Nerida to hire six workers, which is the choice that yields the (equal) highest profits. Great news!

You might notice that the Rational Rule recommends that you keep hiring until the marginal benefit is equal to the marginal cost, which occurred when she hired six workers. But hiring that sixth worker whose marginal benefit was exactly equal to their marginal cost neither raised nor lowered her economic surplus. So while the rule told Nerida to hire six workers, she would have earned the same profit had she hired only five people. In practice, the important point is to stop hiring just before your marginal cost becomes larger than your marginal benefit. ■

Applying the Rational Rule

As you study economics, you will see that the Rational Rule is applicable to many different kinds of decisions. Indeed, it describes how people like Nerida actually run their businesses. While this information can be hard to know in advance, the Rational Rule is still practically useful. Let's look at how it can be applied even in the face of uncertainty about costs and benefits.

Experiment at the margin to learn your marginal costs and benefits. Nerida has worked out potential scenarios to help her decide how many workers to hire. But in reality, she isn't sure whether she would be better off hiring two workers or three. So she experiments with different staffing decisions. She starts by hiring two workers. And then, as an experiment, she tries hiring one more person to see if that increases her benefits by more than it increases her costs. If it does — that is, if the marginal benefit exceeds the marginal cost — she'll declare that experiment a success, and keep that extra person on payroll permanently. If the marginal costs exceed the marginal benefits, she'll eventually reduce her staff by one employee.

Nerida finds that hiring the third worker yields additional revenue which more than offsets the extra costs. She continues her experimenting, hiring a fourth person; if that also raises her profits, she'll experiment further. With each experiment, she focuses on the changes in costs and benefits that occur; these are her marginal costs and marginal benefits. When she tries adding a seventh worker, she finds that her costs rise by more than her revenue (and hence that the seventh person reduces her total profit). She declares that experiment a failure and won't keep a seventh worker on permanently.

Notice that in this process of judging her experiments as successes or failures, Nerida is following the Rational Rule: If increasing staff is worth doing, she'll keep doing it until her marginal benefits equal her marginal costs. By using this rule, she experiments her way to the point where her profits are maximized.

Do the Economics

Now, it's your turn to apply the Rational Rule to make decisions. Remember to think about the relevant marginal costs and marginal benefits. Consider yourself in the following roles:

- As a consumer: *How many cups of coffee should you buy today?*
  Keep buying coffee until the marginal benefit (your willingness to pay for that last cup of coffee) is equal to the marginal cost (the price, the time it takes to get it, and the sleep you might lose if you are over-caffeinated).

- As a producer: *How many tons of coffee should you produce?*
  Keep producing coffee until the marginal benefit of producing an extra ton (the wholesale price you can sell it for) is equal to the marginal cost of producing another ton.

- As a worker: *How many hours should you work as a barista?*
  Keep working until the marginal benefit (your hourly wage) is equal to the marginal cost of working (the value of the marginal hour of leisure or study time that you are missing).

- As an investor: *How much should you invest in a new chain of specialty coffee shops?*
  Keep investing until the marginal benefit (your return on the last dollar invested) is equal to the marginal cost. (This includes the opportunity cost of that last dollar: How else could you invest that dollar, and how could you spend it now?)

- As an export company: *How many tons of coffee should you export?*
  Keep exporting until the marginal benefit (the price you can get for the coffee overseas) is equal to the marginal cost (the price at which domestic producers will sell you one more ton, plus the price of shipping it overseas).

- As a job-seeker: *How many coffee shops should you send your résumé to?*
  Keep sending job applications until the marginal benefit (the value of the increased chance of finding a job) is equal to the marginal cost of an application (the time and hassle of filling out one more application).

- As an employer: *How many baristas should you hire?*
  Keep hiring until the marginal benefit of an extra barista (the rise in revenues you get from selling more coffee) is equal to the marginal cost (the wages of that last worker and the cost of that extra coffee). ∎

The marginal principle creates a structure to simplify complicated "how many" questions. The power of the marginal principle is that it creates a common structure in all decisions in which you choose "how many," and it simplifies an otherwise complicated decision. The best choices — the ones that maximize your economic surplus — all follow the same pattern, as described by the Rational Rule: Choose the quantity where the marginal benefit equals the marginal cost. That way, you will maximize your economic surplus.

Thinking like an economist is all about learning to identify the key issues underpinning any choice. The cost-benefit principle asks you to identify the relevant costs and benefits of a decision. The opportunity cost principle asks you to identify your true cost — the cost of not pursuing your next best alternative. And the marginal principle asks you to identify the marginal choices that make up any "how many" decision. Now, let's turn to the final principle, which involves identifying the many different ways that your decisions affect and are affected by other decisions.

They may all look the same, but that doesn't mean that the marginal benefit of each bean is the same.

1.5 The Interdependence Principle

Learning Objective *Your best choice depends on your other choices, the choices others make, developments in other markets, and expectations about the future. When any of these factors change, your best choice might change.*

🎙 Podcast
Think Like an Economist
The Interdependence Principle: No Decision Is an Island

Nerida's restaurant is doing well, and she's thinking about expanding her hours to include lunch service. She's aware that the likely success of the lunch shift — and hence whether it's worth pursuing — depends on a range of other factors. First of all, it depends on *her other decisions.* Nerida has also been thinking about offering cooking classes, but she doesn't have enough bandwidth to succeed at both new projects. Second, it depends on the *decisions made by others within her market.* If a nearby competitor opens for lunch, there may not be enough customers for her to break even serving lunch. As such, her best choice depends on the choices of her rivals. It also depends on how many people continue to work from home, rather than working from the nearby office complex. But if more people eat out rather than bringing lunch from home, then perhaps it will be profitable. So her best choice also depends on the choices her potential customers make. Third, it depends on *developments in other markets.* If Amazon opens a new regional headquarters nearby, that will mean more foot traffic, and more potential lunchtime customers. But she'll have to compete with Amazon for workers, and so it might also mean that she'll have to pay higher wages. Fourth, it depends on her *expectations about the future.* Nerida expects the economy to grow next year, and for her customers to have more money in their pockets, which could potentially make her lunch service very profitable.

As Nerida thinks harder about all of this, she sees that the economy — and indeed, her life — is filled with interdependencies. Her best decision depends on many factors, and as these other factors change, so does her best course of action. In fact, prior to the pandemic she was pretty sure she would open for lunch. But so many people are continuing to work from home that she has decided that cooking classes are more likely to be the best use of her resources.

All choices are interdependent, and they both shape — and are shaped by — the choices that you and others make, both now and in the future.

interdependence principle Your best choice depends on your other choices, the choices others make, developments in other markets, and expectations about the future. When any of these factors changes, your best choice might change.

This is the **interdependence principle,** which recognizes that your best choice depends on your other choices, the choices others make, developments in other markets, and expectations about the future. When any of these factors changes, your best choice might change. There are four types of interdependencies you'll need to think about:

1. Dependencies between each of your individual choices
2. Dependencies between people or businesses in the same market
3. Dependencies between markets
4. Dependencies through time

The **interdependence principle** is not just for businesses like Nerida's. For example, think about how you choose your classes. First, if you take an economics class, you won't be able to take some other class that is scheduled at the same time.

Second, if another student takes the last spot in a popular class, then you will have to take a different class. That is, your decisions about which classes to take also depend on the choices of others in the same "market."

Third, if you believe (as I do!) that the falling cost and increasing capacity of data-crunching computers means that the skills you learn in introductory economics — which include how to interpret those data — have become more valuable, then your best decision in one market (which class to take) depends on outcomes in other markets (the growing availability of data).

And fourth, your decision to study economics today changes the set of classes you have met the prerequisites for, affecting the courses you can take next year. For example, completing introductory economics will enable you to take more advanced economics courses in the future, whereas those classes wouldn't be an option if you didn't take this class. Thus, the best course to take this year depends on what classes you expect to take in the future.

The broader point is that the best choice for you — such as which classes you take this semester — will depend on many other factors. If any of these other factors change, then your best choice might change, too. Let's explore these four different types of dependencies in greater detail.

Interdependency 1: Dependencies Between Your Own Choices

Since you have limited resources, every choice you make affects the resources available for every other decision. This interdependence follows from the many different constraints you face. Consider the following examples:

How you spend your limited attention will affect your grades.

- You have a budget constraint due to *limited income,* and so the amount of money available to spend on entertainment depends on how much you spend on food.

- You have *limited time* because there are only 24 hours in a day, and so the amount of time available to study for economics depends on how much time you spend studying psychology.

- You have *limited attention,* so the amount of attention you give your economics lecture depends on whether you allow yourself to be distracted by your smartphone.

- You have *limited production capacity* because you have only one oven, and so your ability to bake a pie for dessert depends on how many main and side dishes are planned for the oven.

- You have *limited wealth* to invest, and so the amount you invest in a new startup depends on how much you invest in stocks and bonds.

In these cases, the interdependence follows from limited income, time, attention, production capacity, and wealth. Before moving on, ponder how other constraints, such as limited energy, limited cognitive capacity, and limited willpower will create other interdependencies between your choices.

Interdependency 2: Dependencies Between Economic Actors

The choices made by other economic actors — people, businesses, governments, or other groups — shape the choices available to you. In many cases, this arises because you're competing for society's scarce resources. The more others get, the less that's left over for you. Consequently, your best choice depends on the choices that others make.

You can easily see these interdependencies by focusing on how buyers or sellers compete in a market. For instance, if Microsoft hires the best computer programmers in Seattle, it will be hard for a Seattle-based startup to find talented employees. And so a startup's hiring outcomes depend on those made by Microsoft, because they're competing buyers in the labor market. Alternatively, if your classmate is hired by Microsoft, that's one less job for you to get. In this case, your outcome depends on your classmate's because you're competing sellers in the labor market.

To get a sense of these interdependencies, it's useful to start by identifying the relevant market. It's an approach that applies well beyond traditional markets, as the following examples show:

- Your ability to date the most interesting person in your class depends on the other people they might date in your class.
  You're competing buyers in the dating market.

- Whether your vote sways the next election depends on whether my vote offsets yours.
  We're competing sellers in the market for votes.

- Whether your parents attend your younger brother's Tuesday evening choir recital depends on whether they're attending your sister's Tuesday evening soccer game.
  Your siblings are competing buyers in the market for parental attention.

- Whether the school board adopts your new policy proposal depends on whether they prefer my alternative proposal.
  We're competing sellers in the marketplace of ideas.

Understanding these interdependencies between competitors in a market is a critical first step. In the chapters that follow, we'll push these ideas further, analyzing the forces of supply and demand in greater detail.

Interdependency 3: Dependencies Between Markets

Choices are also interdependent across *different markets.* In particular, changes in prices and opportunities in one market affect the choices you might make in other markets. For instance:

- Declining interest rates in the credit market make it less expensive to get a mortgage, which might lead you to buy a home.
  Your choice in the housing market depends on the credit market.
- When demand for housing falls, entrepreneurs often convert existing homes into something else, such as child care centers, making it easier for you to find child care.
  Your choice in the child care market depends on the housing market.
- If you live in an area with many high-quality, low-cost child care options, you may be more likely to return to work soon after becoming a parent.
  Your choice in the labor market depends on the market for child care.
- When more than one family member has a job, households are more likely to need two cars.
  Your choice in the car market depends on the labor market.

So you can see that there are dependencies running all the way from the credit market to the housing market, to the child care market, to the labor market. If you ignore the interdependence principle, you could be tempted to just consider each market in isolation. But as these examples demonstrate, this can risk missing a large part of the story, because changes in these other markets shape your costs and benefits and can thereby change which option is your best choice.

Interdependency 4: Dependencies Over Time

As a consumer, you always face the option of buying something tomorrow, rather than buying it today. Similarly, executives get to choose when to produce goods and when to bring them to market, while investors, employers, and workers get to decide when to invest, hire, and work. These alternatives mean that your choices always reflect a trade-off across time: Is it better to act today, or tomorrow? As expectations about the future change, the terms of this trade-off change, and so your best choice might change.

Your choices are also linked through time by the investments you make. If you invest in a new factory, in your education, or in getting fit, this expands your choices in the future, as these investments give you the opportunity to produce more, get a better job, or enjoy better health, respectively. Because your future depends so heavily on the choices you make today, you need to be sure to consider these connections. And so the investment choices you'll want to make today depend on your expectations about the future.

What Else?

The big idea behind the interdependence principle is to ask, "What else?" *What else* might my decision affect? *What else* might affect my decision? Your answers will help you figure out all the ways in which your costs and benefits — and hence your best choice — might change if other factors change.

1.6 | Tying It Together

Make Better Decisions—and Understand the Decisions of Others

That's it: the economic method, boiled down to four core principles. Think I'm kidding? I'm not. Thinking like an economist is simply a matter of applying the core principles to the world around you. That's why it is so important that you understand these core principles.

Put the four core principles to work. I presented the four core principles of economics in the order that is easiest to learn. But when you confront a problem, you should think through the principles in a different order. Here's the four-step recipe you should apply:

Step 1: First, use the marginal principle by breaking "how many" choices down into simpler marginal choices. Ask yourself whether you would be better off doing a bit more of something, or a bit less.

Step 2: Then apply the cost-benefit principle by assessing the relevant costs and benefits. Since you're analyzing a marginal question, this says you need to assess whether the marginal benefit exceeds the marginal cost.

Step 3: To evaluate all the relevant costs and benefits, you'll need to apply the opportunity cost principle and ask, "Or what?" This ensures that you take full account of what you give up when you make a choice. Remember to focus on the relevant opportunity costs, not just financial out-of-pocket costs.

Step 4: The interdependence principle helps you identify how changes in other factors—in your own choices, other people, other markets, and expectations about the future—might lead you to make a different decision.

The rest of your study of economics is really about applying this framework to a range of interesting social and economic contexts. In the chapters ahead, we'll study the decisions that you'll make in your various roles as an economic actor—as a buyer, a seller, a worker, a boss, an entrepreneur, an investor, an importer, or an exporter. In each chapter the method will be the same, and it will quickly become familiar: I'll ask you to put yourself in the shoes of that economic actor and apply the core principles of economics so that you can figure out how to make the best decisions possible. With some practice, you'll be able to use the core principles to ensure that you make good decisions in every sphere of your life.

Imagine walking in someone else's shoes.

To predict what others will do, put yourself in their shoes. The core principles of economics that we've outlined in this chapter aren't just useful for helping you make good decisions. They can also be used for the equally important task of understanding and even predicting the decisions of others: your customers, competitors, employees, suppliers, and even friends and family.

The key to forecasting how they'll respond is a little exercise that I like to call the **someone else's shoes technique.** The idea behind putting yourself in someone else's shoes is to allow yourself to have an empathetic understanding of how someone else views the world. In movies like *Freaky Friday,* mother and daughter have to switch bodies to learn to understand each other, but you can do it by mentally putting yourself in someone else's shoes.

someone else's shoes technique
Imagine yourself in someone else's position in order to understand their objectives and constraints, and forecast the decisions they will make.

Now that you're at the end of your first chapter, let me give you a study tip that you can use throughout this book. If you've only got 10 minutes and want to review the key ideas from a chapter, go back, quickly flip through it, and you'll discover that **the bold headings that look like this are a built-in study guide.** If you re-read only those headings, you'll get all the key points. Or if you want my "cheat sheet," turn the page.

That's the essence of the someone else's shoes technique. If you want to forecast the decisions that someone else will make, imagine yourself in their situation, and try to figure out what decision you would make if you were them. Putting yourself in someone else's shoes is all about empathy, and it's important to account for that person's preferences and the constraints that they face. It's likely that they are trying to make good decisions, and so these four core principles can help you better understand and predict the decisions that they will make.

Principles in short. If you find it hard to remember all the detail that you've read in this chapter, relax. It all boils down to asking four questions that are so simple you need just a few words. Always ask:

- One more? (*The* marginal principle)
- Does the benefit beat the cost? (*The* cost-benefit principle)
- Or what? (*The* opportunity cost principle)
- What else? (*The* interdependence principle)

Chapter 1 Review

Chapter at a Glance

The Cost-Benefit Principle

Costs and benefits are the incentives that shape decisions. You should evaluate the full set of costs and benefits of any choice you face, and only pursue those whose benefits are at least as large as their costs.

✳ **That is, incentives matter!**

The difference between benefits and costs is your economic surplus. If your costs and benefits cannot be directly compared, evaluate them in terms of your willingness to pay for them.

Don't let the framing of a choice—that is, how it's described—affect your cost-benefit analysis.

The Opportunity Cost Principle

The true cost of something is the next best alternative you must give up to get it. Your decisions should reflect this opportunity cost, rather than just the out-of-pocket financial costs.

✳ **Good decisions focus on opportunity cost, rather than direct financial costs.**

Make sure that whenever you consider a decision, you ask, "Or what?" For example: "Should I get an MBA?" Or what? "Or stay in my current job?" The "or" part highlights your opportunity cost.

Sunk costs are not opportunity costs, and so they should be ignored.

The Marginal Principle

Decisions about quantities are best made incrementally.

✳ **Break "how many" decisions down into a series of smaller, or marginal, decisions.**

For example, instead of asking: "How many workers should I hire?" ask: "Should I hire one more person?" Answering this requires comparing the "extra" or marginal benefits of that extra person with the "extra" or marginal costs incurred.

Following the Rational Rule will maximize your economic surplus: *If something is worth doing, keep doing it until your marginal benefits equal your marginal costs.*

The Interdependence Principle

Your best choice depends on your other choices, the choices others make, developments in other markets, and expectations about the future. When any of these factors change, your best choice might change.

✳ **Consider four kinds of interdependence:**

1. Dependencies between your own choices
2. Dependencies between people/firms in a market
3. Dependencies between markets
4. Dependencies through time

Apply the core principles, in this order:

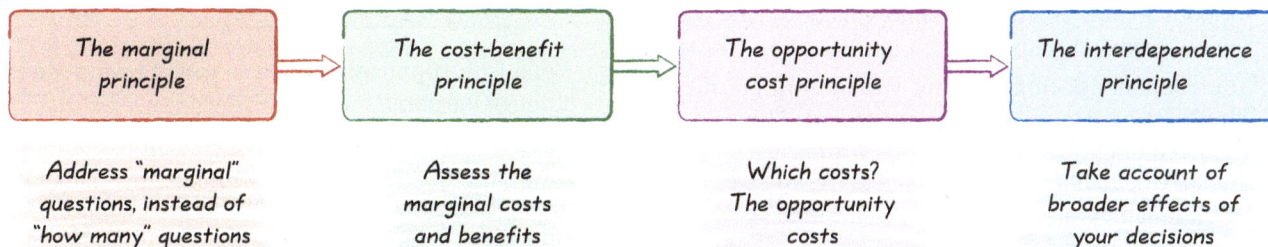

The marginal principle	→	The cost-benefit principle	→	The opportunity cost principle	→	The interdependence principle
Address "marginal" questions, instead of "how many" questions		Assess the marginal costs and benefits		Which costs? The opportunity costs		Take account of broader effects of your decisions

To forecast the decisions others make, put yourself in their shoes. If you had their objectives and constraints, what decision would you make?

Key Terms

cost-benefit principle, 5

economic surplus, 7

framing effect, 9

interdependence principle, 26

marginal benefit, 20

marginal cost, 20

marginal principle, 20

opportunity cost, 11

production possibility frontier, 18

Rational Rule, 21

scarcity, 12

someone else's shoes technique, 29

sunk cost, 16

willingness to pay, 6

Study Problems

Learning Objective 1.2 *Costs and benefits are the incentives that shape decisions. You should evaluate the full set of costs and benefits of any choice, and pursue only those whose benefits are at least as large as their costs.*

1. Consider the following statement: "Economists always put things into monetary terms; as a result, economics can most appropriately be called the study of money."

   Is this true or false? Briefly explain your reasoning.

2. Use the cost-benefit principle to evaluate the following:

   a. You are about to buy a calculator for $10, and the salesperson tells you that the model you want to buy is on sale for $5 at the store's other branch, which is a 20-minute drive away. Would you make the trip?

   b. You are about to buy a laptop for $1,000 and the salesperson tells you that the model you want to buy is on sale for $995 at the store's other branch, which is a 20-minute drive away. Would you make the trip?

   c. Did you make the same choice in both cases? Should you have? Do you think this is how people actually choose?

3. Ivan has inherited his grandmother's 1963 Chevrolet Corvette, which he values at $45,000. He decides that he might be willing to sell it, so he posts it on Craigslist for $55,000. Samantha is interested and willing to pay up to $72,000. Would Ivan and Samantha want to voluntarily engage in trade? How much economic surplus is created for both of them as a result of this exchange? What is the total economic surplus?

4. You are considering whether you should go out to dinner at a restaurant with your friend. The meal is expected to cost you $40, you typically leave a 20% tip, and an Uber will cost you $5 to get there. You value the restaurant meal at $20. You enjoy your friend's company and are willing to pay $30 just to spend an evening with her. If you did not go out to the restaurant, you would eat at home using groceries that cost you $8. How much are the benefits and costs associated with going out to dinner with your friend? Should you go out to dinner with your friend?

Learning Objective 1.3 *The true cost of something is the next best alternative you must give up to get it. Your decisions should reflect this opportunity cost, rather than just the out-of-pocket financial costs.*

5. During the economic downturn of 2008–2009, the unemployment rate increased to nearly 10%. At the same time, the price of college tuition and the number of college enrollees increased. Using the opportunity cost principle, explain why more people would enroll in college during this time period even as the price of college increased.

6. A friend once remarked that longer movies were a better deal than shorter movies because the ticket price was the same in both cases. Therefore, the longer movie provided more benefit for the same cost as a shorter movie. Using the opportunity cost principle, evaluate your friend's statement.

7. It is a beautiful afternoon and you are considering taking a leisurely stroll through the park. There are several other activities you had considered doing instead. The value you would have received from each of the activities is provided in the table below.

Alternative activities	Value
Streaming a movie	$5
Taking a nap	$8
Chatting with your best friend	$13
Reading a new book	$15

What is the opportunity cost to you of taking the stroll through the park?

8. Suppose you have midterms in economics and astronomy tomorrow, and you have only four hours left to study. The accompanying table provides the combinations of time spent studying economics and astronomy and your expected exam scores.

   a. Draw a production possibilities frontier to illustrate your study options. What is the opportunity cost, in terms of your grades, of studying one extra hour for economics or one extra hour for astronomy?

b. If your goal is to maximize your combined exam scores, how many hours should you spend studying each subject?

c. Your laptop dies and refuses to start up. All your notes and class materials are saved on its hard drive. How do your production possibilities change? Illustrate in your graph from part (a).

d.

Hours spent studying economics	Economics exam score	Hours spent studying astronomy	Astronomy exam score
0	60	0	70
1	80	1	83
2	90	2	87
3	95	3	90
4	98	4	92

9. Your niece is deciding whether or not to open a lemonade stand. She expects to sell 20 cups of lemonade for $1 per cup. She already made a sign that cost her $10 and will have $15 worth of additional costs for cups and lemonade mix if she decides to open the stand. If your niece decides to open the lemonade stand, how much profit will she earn? Should she open the lemonade stand? What kind of cost is the $10 spent on the lemonade stand sign?

Learning Objective 1.4 *Decisions about quantities are best made incrementally. You should break "how many" decisions down into a series of smaller, or marginal, decisions.*

10. In 2016, the top-selling pharmaceutical drug in the world was AbbVie's Humira, which is used for the treatment of several common, chronic conditions. The majority of its profits are derived from treatment of the most common diseases, so why does AbbVie develop drugs for rare diseases instead of investing all of its resources toward drugs for common diseases? Use the marginal principle to briefly explain your answer.

11. Aliyah is preparing to expand her IT consulting company. The current market rate for IT professionals is $58,000 per year. Each employee she hires will also require a computer and equipment that costs $6,000 per employee annually. Hiring more employees means that Aliyah can provide consulting services to more clients each year. Each client Aliyah has will pay her $15,000 per year.

The number of clients Aliyah can take on depends on the number of workers she hires, as shown in the accompanying table. What is the marginal cost and marginal benefit of hiring each worker? Using the Rational Rule to maximize her economic surplus, how many workers should Aliyah hire?

Number of workers	Clients per year
0	0
1	11
2	20
3	27
4	32

12. Neal is a coffee drinker. At the local coffee shop, the price of a cup of coffee is $3. Neal's total benefits from drinking coffee is provided in the accompanying table. What is Neal's marginal benefit of consuming each cup of coffee? How many cups should he consume each day?

Quantity of coffee	Total benefits
1	$8
2	$14
3	$18
4	$20
5	$21

Learning Objective 1.5 *Your best choice depends on your other choices, the choices others make, developments in other markets, and expectations about the future. When any of these factors change, your best choice might change.*

13. You are a preschool teacher working at a public school, but are considering quitting your job to start a day-care facility of your own. Describe four types of dependencies that will affect your decision, with at least one example for each.

14. Consider your decision to read this textbook on economics. Identify which of the four core principles of economics is most relevant for the following aspects of that decision.

a. Reading this textbook will help establish a solid foundation for understanding concepts you will learn in more advanced economics courses.

b. Reading this textbook will require time and effort, but doing so will help you improve your grade in this course.

c. The time you will spend reading this textbook could instead be used to study for your chemistry exam.

d. Each extra page that you read and each practice problem that you complete will help you increase your understanding of the material.

15. For each of the following, indicate how you might apply the four core principles of economics.

a. You are considering whether you should vote in the next election.

b. You watch a beautiful sunset from the back porch of your home.

c. Should you major in economics or philosophy?

d. Should you and your spouse purchase a second vehicle?

Demand and Consumer Choice

There's a part of your brain that fires up every time you evaluate a possible buying decision. Every time you look at a menu, a price tag, or an advertisement, it springs into action, asking: Is this a good deal? Should I buy? If so, how many? Sometimes the answer is no, and you'll decide not to buy. Sometimes the answer is yes, and you'll make a small purchase — perhaps a $1 cookie. And sometimes you'll make a life-changing decision such as choosing to buy a car

Chang W. Lee/The New York Times/Redux Pictures

Some decisions are sweeter than others.

or a house. Collectively, even those small decisions add up to a big deal—they're a large chunk of the millions of dollars you will probably spend over your lifetime.

In this chapter, we'll examine the decisions that we make as buyers. We'll start by studying individual demand, zooming in on the decisions that you make as an individual consumer trying to decide how much of a product to buy. We'll apply the core principles of economics that we developed in Chapter 1 to guide you toward making better buying decisions.

Next, we'll analyze market demand, which managers use to project how much of a product the market as a whole will buy at each price. We'll then explore how changing market conditions shift market demand.

By the end of this chapter, you'll understand the key factors that drive the millions of purchasing decisions that underpin much of our economy. Let's get started.

Chapter Objective

Understand people's buying, or demand, decisions.

2.1 Individual Demand: What You Want, at Each Price
Discover the shape of your individual demand curve.

2.2 Your Decisions and Your Demand Curve
Apply the core principles of economics to make good demand decisions.

2.3 Market Demand: What the Market Wants
Add up individual demand to discover market demand.

2.4 What Shifts Demand Curves?
Understand what factors shift demand curves.

2.5 Shifts versus Movements Along Demand Curves
Distinguish between movements along a demand curve and shifts of demand curves.

🎙 **Podcast**
Think Like an Economist
The Law of Demand: How You Choose to Buy

Individual Demand: What You Want, at Each Price

Learning Objective *Discover the shape of your individual demand curve.*

It's Monday morning, and Darren is driving to work when he notices his gas tank is nearly empty. The nearby gas station typically offers the best prices, and right now, its sign says $3 per gallon. So Darren faces a decision: How much gas should he buy?

You face decisions like this every day. When you see a deal on your favorite jeans, you have to decide whether to click through and buy another pair at the discounted price, or to make do with what you already have. Before class, you probably had to decide whether to buy a cup of coffee or save your money for other uses. Every time you see a price tag, you face the same question: At this price, what quantity should you buy?

Darren faces similar questions when he heads to the gas station. He was recently surveyed about his consumption of gas; Figure 1 shows the survey form, with Darren's responses in purple.

Each row of Figure 1 asks Darren how much gas on average he would buy per week, at different prices. Of course, Darren won't just put a gallon or two in his tank each week; rather, he's thinking about how the gas price changes how much he'll drive, and hence how often he'll need to fill his tank. His answers reflect the amount of gas he thinks he'll buy over the course of the year, averaged out per week. The first row shows that when the price of gas is $5 per gallon, he is willing to buy only 1 gallon of gas per week, on average. The last row shows that when the price is as low as $1 per gallon, he plans to buy 7 gallons per week.

Figure 1 | **A Survey of an Individual's Gasoline Demand**

Name:	*Darren*

We are interested in understanding next year's demand for gas. What quantity of gas do you expect to purchase per week next year:

If the price is $5 per gallon?	*1 gallon*
If the price is $4 per gallon?	*2 gallons*
If the price is $3 per gallon?	*3 gallons*
If the price is $2 per gallon?	*5 gallons*
If the price is $1 per gallon?	*7 gallons*

An Individual Demand Curve

You know the old saying: "A picture is worth a thousand words"? Well, you can plot Darren's survey responses on a graph to create a picture that summarizes his buying plans. This graph is called his **individual demand curve,** and it plots the quantity that he plans to buy at each price. If your graphing skills are a bit rusty, don't worry; we'll proceed slowly (we've provided "A Quick Review of Graphs" at the beginning of this book for anyone who wants a refresher).

The line in Figure 2 illustrates Darren's individual demand curve for gas. Each dot corresponds with one of Darren's responses to the gas survey shown in Figure 1.

For instance, Darren said that if the price of gas is $5 per gallon, he plans to buy 1 gallon per week. This point is plotted in the top left of Figure 2; simply look across from the price of $5 (on the vertical axis) to the quantity of 1 gallon of gas (on the horizontal axis), and you can see this first response, graphed as the first point. Likewise, Darren said that if the price of gas is $4 per gallon, he plans to buy 2 gallons of gas per week, and this is the next point plotted on Figure 2. You can see each of his responses plotted as a point in Figure 2.

There are also many different prices that Darren wasn't asked about. For instance, he wasn't asked how he would respond to a gas price of $2.50. A straight line between the $2 and $3 dots provides a reasonable estimate, suggesting that he would buy 4 gallons. This line connecting the dots is Darren's individual demand curve, showing the quantity he will demand at each price.

To remember what an individual demand curve is, just break down the name: "Individual" means we are referring to one person; "demand" means it's about buying decisions; and "curve" means we are graphing it (and sometimes these curves are straight lines). That's it: Your individual demand curve is a graph summarizing your buying plans, and how they vary with the price.

individual demand curve A graph that plots the quantity of an item that an individual buyer plans to purchase at each price.

Figure 2 | Graphing an Individual Demand Curve

Darren's Individual Demand Curve

How much gasoline is he willing to buy at each price?

(A) Price is on the vertical axis, and quantity demanded is on the horizontal axis.

(B) When the price is **$5 per gallon**, Darren will purchase just **1 gallon** of gas per week. An individual demand curve also illustrates how the quantity demanded changes as the price changes. If the price falls to **$4 per gallon**, the quantity he demands will rise to **2 gallons** per week. At a price of **$3**, he will buy **3 gallons**, and so on.

(C) The **individual demand curve** shows the quantity of gas per week that Darren is willing to buy, at each price. The individual demand curve is downward sloping: The lower the price, the higher the quantity demanded.

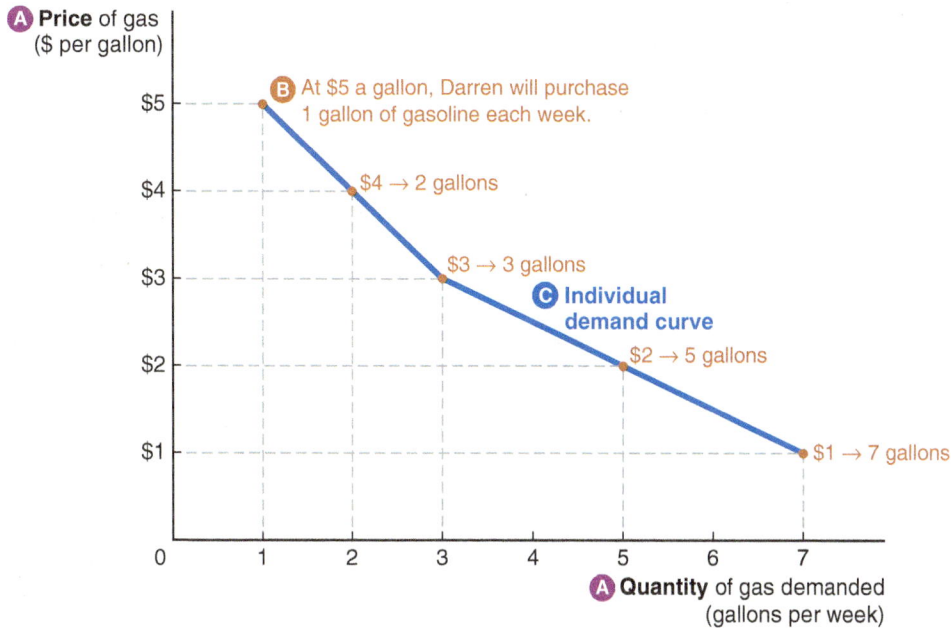

(A) Price of gas ($ per gallon)

(B) At $5 a gallon, Darren will purchase 1 gallon of gasoline each week.

$4 → 2 gallons

$3 → 3 gallons

(C) Individual demand curve

$2 → 5 gallons

$1 → 7 gallons

(A) Quantity of gas demanded (gallons per week)

Economists use consistent graphing conventions. Be careful to always use the same conventions when graphing demand curves. Price always goes on the vertical axis, and the quantity demanded goes on the horizontal axis. (I remember this as "Ps before Qs," so that as I look from left to right, or from top to bottom, I label Ps — the price — before labeling Qs — the quantity.)

Don't forget to label the units on both axes. In this case, the price of gas is measured in dollars per gallon. The quantity of gas demanded is measured in gallons per week.

Some students ask why price goes on the vertical axis and quantity goes on the horizontal axis. There's no good answer — it's because economists have graphed demand curves in this way for so long that it's now a convention that everyone follows. By following these established conventions, we can all speak the same, consistent language.

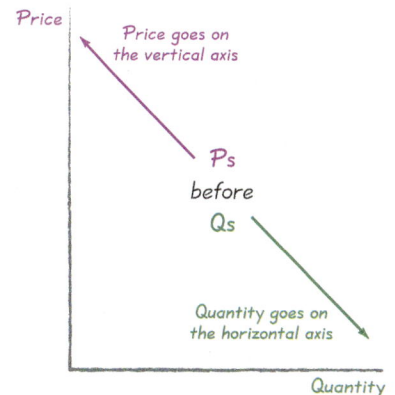

Price goes on the vertical axis

Ps before Qs

Quantity goes on the horizontal axis

An individual demand curve holds other things constant. The demand curve shown in Figure 2 plots Darren's buying plans, given current economic conditions. But if something important were to change — say, if he lost his job — then his buying plans would change, and so his individual demand curve would change, too. In order to acknowledge this, economists say that a particular demand curve is graphed, **"holding other things constant."**

Economists know that things other than price can influence demand — in fact, the **interdependence principle** reminds us not to forget these connections! But first, we want to consider what happens when the price — and only the price — changes. When we "hold other things constant," we're really just pushing aside changes in those other factors for now, so that we can focus on understanding how demand is affected by the price.

"holding other things constant" A commonly used qualifier noting that your conclusions may change if some factor that you haven't analyzed changes. (In Latin, it's *ceteris paribus*.)

The individual demand curve is downward-sloping. Notice that Darren's individual demand curve is downward-sloping: It starts high on the left, and as you move to the right it heads downward. Downward-sloping demand means that as the price falls the quantity demanded rises. When gas costs less, people buy more of it. Or you think about it the other way around: If gas costs more, people buy less of it.

Discover your individual demand curve. Whenever you see a price and pause to decide whether to make a purchase and, if so, how many of an item to buy, you are considering the quantity you will demand at that price. If you graphed these thoughts, you would plot your individual demand curve. Let's delve into this idea in a bit more detail, and explore your individual demand curve for jeans.

> Remember: Your individual demand curve is a graph summarizing your buying plans, and how they vary with the price.

Do the Economics

Executives at Levi's want to understand their customers better. So they've asked their marketing team to figure out the individual demand curve for jeans of customers like you.

Marketing executives often run surveys to learn about demand for their product, and the Levi's jeans survey, in Panel A of Figure 3, is an example. Go ahead and take the survey. Next, turn to Panel B below and plot your responses.

Figure 3 | Discover Your Individual Demand Curve

Panel A:

Levi's is interested in understanding how many pairs of jeans you will buy over the next five years. Holding other things constant, how many pairs of jeans do you expect to purchase:

Price of jeans ($ per pair)	Quantity of jeans
If jeans cost $150?	
If jeans cost $125?	
If jeans cost $100?	
If jeans cost $75?	
If jeans cost $50?	
If jeans cost $25?	

Panel B: Your Individual Demand Curve

How many pairs of jeans do you expect to purchase at each price?

To graph your individual demand curve, plot the data from your responses to the Levi's jeans survey.

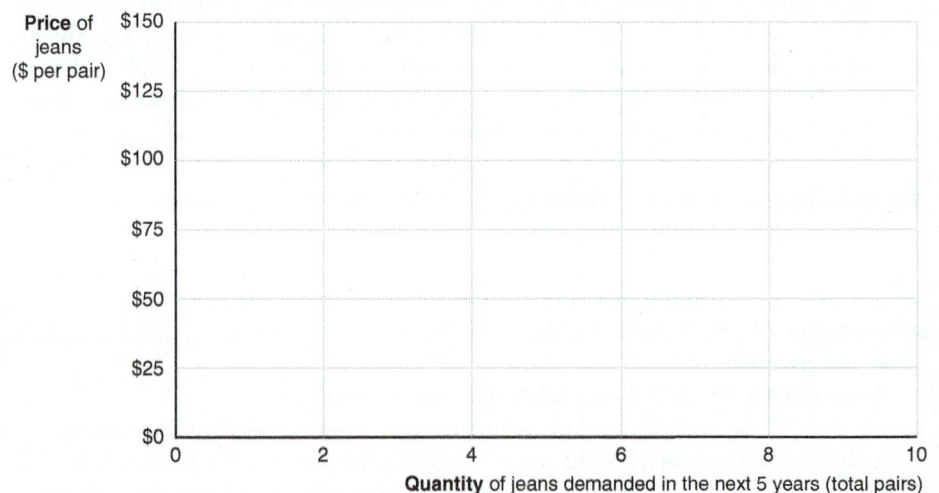

Quantity of jeans demanded in the next 5 years (total pairs)

Done? Great — you've just plotted your individual demand curve for jeans. And I'm willing to bet that you plotted a downward-sloping demand curve. ■

The Law of Demand

Okay, we've figured out your individual demand curve and Darren's individual demand curve for gasoline. Darren's demand curve was downward-sloping just like I bet your demand for jeans was downward-sloping. If you repeat the same exercise for other goods, you'll quickly discover that your individual demand curve for gas, ice cream, concert tickets — or just about anything else — is also downward-sloping.

Economists have asked similar questions about thousands of goods over hundreds of years, and we keep seeing the same pattern: The quantity demanded is higher when the price is lower. It's such a pervasive pattern that economists call the tendency for the quantity demanded to be higher when the price is lower the **law of demand.**

Your individual demand curve is simply a graph that describes the quantity you will demand at each price. It's useful, because it allows businesses to forecast how customers like you will respond to different prices. And since the law of demand suggests that you'll demand a larger quantity when the price is low, businesses will forecast that your demand curve is downward-sloping.

Now that you know how to construct your individual demand curve, let's explore how you can apply the core principles of economics to make better demand decisions.

law of demand The tendency for quantity demanded to be higher when the price is lower.

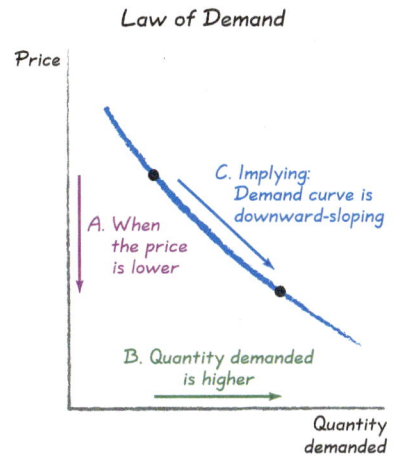

Law of Demand

2.2 Your Decisions and Your Demand Curve

Learning Objective *Apply the core principles of economics to make good demand decisions.*

So far, we've focused on the actual buying decisions that people make. Let's turn to the harder question: What are the best buying choices you can make? The core principles of economics can provide useful guidance. As we go through each principle, you'll get a deeper sense of the various factors that shape individual demand curves.

Choosing the Best Quantity to Buy

Let's start with individual demand curve. In a follow-up interview, Darren provided some insight into his preferences. He starts by thinking about all of the possible uses he has for each additional gallon of gas. He then prioritizes them by thinking about the benefits he gets from each use. Because money is the measuring stick by which we assess benefits, he puts a dollar value on these benefits that summarizes how much he's willing to pay for each possible use of a gallon of gas. Figure 4 gives his explanations for how he'll use each gallon of gas and the benefit each use has for him.

Focus on your marginal benefits. Each row shows one of Darren's uses for each additional gallon of gas. He's listed them in order of his priority — from the uses that deliver the largest benefit to him, to those that deliver the least benefit. When he thinks about these benefits, he's not just thinking about the dollars involved. He's thinking about his benefits broadly, such as the benefits of saving time, of seeing his parents, or of taking a relaxing drive to unwind. In each case, he's comparing them to his next best alternative.

When Darren thinks about the different ways he can use an extra gallon of gas, he's really thinking about the additional benefit of one more gallon of gas. That's his marginal benefit, and it is shown in the final column of Figure 4.

Remember: The additional benefit you get from buying one additional unit of a particular item is called its *marginal benefit*.

Figure 4 | Darren's Uses for Gas

Priority	Darren's thoughts	Marginal benefit
1 (Highest Priority)	If I buy only one gallon of gas per week, I'll use it to do my weekly shopping at the Walmart two towns over. The alternative is to shop at my neighborhood supermarket, which is more expensive. Going to Walmart instead saves me $5 each week.	$5.00
2	If I buy a second gallon of gas, I'll also drive two miles to work every day. I prefer this to catching the bus. The time and money saved add up to a $4 benefit.	$4.00
3	A third gallon of gas allows me to visit my parents more often. I could call them instead, but I prefer seeing them. There's no financial benefit to this, but there's a benefit nonetheless, because I love my parents. Putting a number on this is hard, but I'm willing to pay up to $3 for the gallon of gas required for this visit.	$3.00
4	With a fourth gallon of gas, I can drive to hang out with my friends during the weekend. I could get a ride instead, since all of my buddies live nearby, but it's nice to have the flexibility that driving gives me. I get about $2.50 in benefit from this.	$2.50
5	A fifth gallon allows me to drive to the gym twice a week. But I could jog there instead, which is a good warm-up. Saving time is useful, but given that I have to warm up anyway, the benefit of driving to the gym is worth only $2.	$2.00
6	If I buy a sixth gallon of gas, I'll use it to do my weekly errands. But I'm nearly as happy just walking around town to do these errands. The benefit of driving to do errands is only $1.50.	$1.50
7 (Lowest Priority)	If I buy a seventh gallon, I'll use it to take a scenic drive when I need some quiet time. But I'm nearly as happy taking quiet time at home, so the benefit of this option is pretty low. Perhaps this gallon yields a benefit as small as $1.	$1.00

Do the Economics

Let's return to Darren as he was driving toward the gas station. He noticed that gas is selling for $3 per gallon (well, actually for $2.99 $\%_{10}$) and he's trying to decide how much to buy. What is your advice?

- *Should he buy a first gallon of gas?*

  Yes. According to Figure 4, Darren will use this gallon to shop at Walmart, which yields him a marginal benefit of $5, which is greater than the $3 it will cost him.

- *Should he buy a second gallon of gas at $3? (Hint: You should ask: What are the benefits? What will this cost?)*

  The second gallon of gas yields a $4 marginal benefit, which is greater than the marginal cost of $3. Sounds like a good deal.

- *And should he buy a third gallon?*

  The third gallon is a close call. It yields $3 of marginal benefits, which is slightly more than the marginal cost (which is actually $2.99 $\%_{10}$). But the marginal benefit exceeds the marginal cost, so Darren should buy this third gallon.

- *What about a fourth gallon?*

  The fourth gallons yields a $2.50 marginal benefit, and spending $3 to get a $2.50 marginal benefit is a bad idea since you come out behind.

- *And a fifth? A sixth?*

  Similar logic suggests that Darren shouldn't buy a fifth or sixth gallon either: In each case they yield a marginal benefit less than the $3 marginal cost of a gallon of gas.

- *Bottom line: What quantity of gas should he buy at $2.99 $\%_{10}$?*

  Darren should buy three gallons of gas.

Notice that your advice is based solely on comparing the price of a gallon of gas with the *marginal benefit* that Darren gets from it. In fact, whenever you need to figure out

OK, so gas is never *exactly* $3 per gallon.

your demand for any good, you should follow the same logic, comparing the price with your marginal benefit. This is why economists say that understanding demand is all about understanding marginal benefits. ∎

Apply the core principles to make good buying decisions. Darren's approach to buying gas seems pretty sensible. In fact, he's implicitly relying on the core principles of economics. You'll want to apply the same logic when you're making your own demand decisions, whether you're deciding how many pairs of jeans to purchase, how many streaming services to subscribe to or how many workers to hire. Let's see how.

The marginal principle says that you should break "how many" questions into a series of smaller marginal choices. Darren's clearly thinking this way, considering each additional, or marginal, gallon of gas separately, and how he would use it. It means that he's ready to analyze the simpler question of whether to buy just one more gallon of gas. Indeed, we just evaluated whether to buy a first, then a second, then a third and a fourth gallon of gas when the price was $3.

For each of these marginal decisions, Darren's best choice depends on the cost-benefit principle, which says: Yes, he should buy that additional gallon of gas if its benefit exceeds the cost. The cost of an additional gallon of gas is simply its price. The benefit of an additional gallon is called its marginal benefit.

Notice that when Darren evaluates his marginal benefits, he applies the opportunity cost principle, asking: "Or what?" He doesn't just ask about the benefits of driving to Walmart; he compares it to the next best alternative, which for him is to do his shopping nearby. It's only by comparing driving to Walmart with the next best alternative that he figured out that the marginal benefit of the first gallon of gas is $5. He does something similar in each row of Figure 4.

Here's a chance to test yourself: Go back and underline the "Or what?" — the next best alternative that Darren identifies on each row. (Answer: It's the second sentence of each row.)

The Rational Rule for Buyers

Working systematically through the core principles — as shown in Figure 5 — leads to the conclusion that Darren should keep buying additional gallons of gas as long as the marginal benefit is greater than or equal to the price.

Figure 5 | Rational Rule for Buyers

Marginal principle	Cost-benefit principle	Opportunity cost principle	Implies	Rational Rule for Buyers
How many gallons of gas should I buy? →	Should I buy one more gallon? →	Depends on: *Marginal benefit* v. *Price* →	Assess *marginal benefit* of driving, relative to next best alternative →	Buy one more gallon if: *Marginal benefit ≥ Price*

We've uncovered a pretty powerful rule, which you can apply to *any* buying decision:

The **Rational Rule for Buyers**: *Buy more of an item if the marginal benefit of one more is greater than or equal to the price.*

The Rational Rule for Buyers puts together the advice from three of the four core principles in one sentence. You should think at the margin, comparing the marginal benefit of one more unit with the marginal cost (in this case, the price), and evaluate these costs and benefits relative to your next best alternative. You can apply this rule to your real-world buying decisions. For instance, it says to Darren: You should buy another gallon of gas if it yields a marginal benefit greater than or equal to its price.

Rational Rule for Buyers Buy more of an item if the marginal benefit of one more is greater than or equal to the price.

For now, we're focusing only on the effects of different prices, holding these other things constant. But notice that Darren's decisions depend on the availability of the bus, his desire to go to the gym, and even his love for his parents! When we return to the interdependence principle later in this chapter, we'll see that if these other things were to change, so would his plans.

Follow the Rational Rule for Buyers to maximize your economic surplus.

The Rational Rule for Buyers is good advice. Why? If buying one more gallon of gas yields marginal benefits for Darren that exceed the price he pays, then he is better off. That is, he'll enjoy greater economic surplus — which is the difference between his total benefits and total costs — because this purchase will boost his total benefits by more than it boosts his total costs. And that's the reason why you'll want to follow this rule in your own life.

In fact, you want to take *every* opportunity to make those purchases that will make you better off, and pass on any purchases that will make you worse off. If you relentlessly follow the Rational Rule for Buyers and buy more gas (and more food, more clothes, and so on) for as long as the marginal benefits are at least as large as the price, then by taking every opportunity to boost your economic surplus, you'll succeed at maximizing your economic surplus.

You might wonder why this rule says its marginal benefit is *exactly equal* to the price. The truth is that this decision doesn't make a difference, because buying that last unit will make you neither better off nor worse off. Still, you should continue to buy up to, *and including,* the point when marginal benefit equals price, because it will make the rest of your analysis a bit simpler.

> To maximize your economic surplus, keep applying the Rational Rule for Buyers, continuing to buy until:
>
> Price = Marginal benefit

Keep buying until price equals marginal benefit.

If you follow the Rational Rule for Buyers, you'll keep buying more gas until the marginal benefit of the last gallon you buy is *equal* to the price. Why? The rule suggests you keep buying gallons of gas as long as the marginal benefit of each gallon is at least as high as the price. Consequently, you will stop buying more gas just before the marginal benefit of the next gallon falls below the price — which occurs when the *marginal benefit equals the price.*

You might recognize this insight. Recall the Rational Rule from Chapter 1, which said: "If something is worth doing, keep doing it until your marginal benefits equal your marginal costs." We're simply adapting this rule to when you're buying stuff, and so the marginal cost of an extra gallon of gas or pair of jeans is simply the price. As such, adapting the *Rational Rule* to your role as a buyer says you should keep buying until:

$$\text{Price} = \text{Marginal benefit}$$

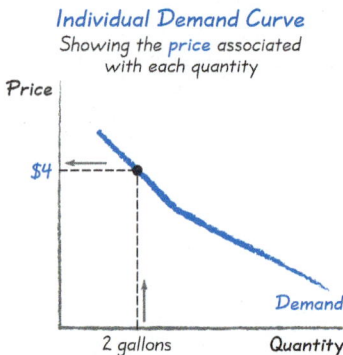

Individual Demand Curve
Showing the price associated with each quantity

Your demand curve is also your marginal benefit curve.

Hopefully you can now see why economists say that understanding demand requires remembering just one phrase: *Price equals marginal benefit.*

This reveals a new perspective for thinking about demand: Your demand curve is also your marginal benefit curve. Your demand curve illustrates the price at which you will buy each quantity of gas. If you keep buying until price equals marginal benefit, then the same curve illustrates the marginal benefit of each gallon of gas.

Price = *Marginal benefit*

↓

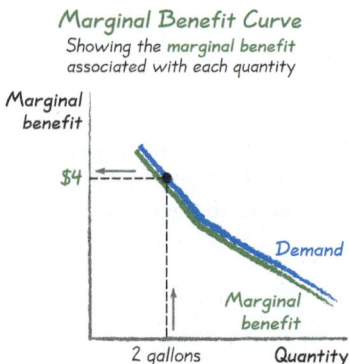

Marginal Benefit Curve
Showing the marginal benefit associated with each quantity

Your demand curve reveals your marginal benefits.

This yields an important insight for managers. It's likely that you'll want to know how much your customers benefit from your products. You could commission an expensive survey to find out. But there's a cheaper way to do this: Your customers' demand curves are also their marginal benefit curves, and so you can also learn about their marginal benefits by just observing their buying patterns. For instance, if Darren buys two gallons of gas when the price is $4 per gallon, then you can infer that the marginal benefit to Darren of that second gallon is $4.

Diminishing marginal benefit explains why your demand curve is downward-sloping. Economists have studied the marginal benefits of many different items and discovered a general tendency toward **diminishing marginal benefit.** That is, the marginal benefit of each additional unit is smaller than the marginal benefit of the previous unit.

Think about ice cream (yum!). One or two scoops are scrumptious. A third scoop still tastes pretty good. By the fourth, you're getting tired of all that sugar. And a fifth scoop will probably make you feel sick. As you eat more ice cream, the marginal benefit of another scoop keeps getting smaller.

A similar pattern follows for other goods. Take Darren's demand for gas. He planned to use his first gallon of gas for his high marginal benefit activities (shopping), his second gallon would go to a slightly lower-benefit activity (driving to work), and each successive gallon would be used for a lower-priority trip. As a result, each extra gallon yields a successively lower marginal benefit.

If you think about most of the things you buy in a year, I bet you'll agree that you get diminishing marginal benefits from not just extra scoops of ice cream, or gallons of gas, but also jeans, concert tickets, game downloads and just about everything you buy.

Diminishing marginal benefits is an important phenomenon because it means that each extra purchase yields a lower marginal benefit, and hence your marginal benefit curve is downward-sloping. Since your marginal benefit curve is also your demand curve, this means that your demand curve is downward-sloping. That is, if extra scoops of ice cream, gallons of gas, or pairs of jeans yield a lower marginal benefit, you'll buy them only if the price is lower. And that's why your individual demand curve is downward-sloping.

diminishing marginal benefit
Each additional unit yields a smaller marginal benefit than the previous unit.

How Realistic Is This Theory of Demand?

By this point you might be thinking: Is this realistic? Does anyone really act this way? And maybe it is a bit unrealistic to say that when you're shopping, you're actually thinking deeply about your marginal benefits. Good point. But these are still important ideas, for two reasons.

Thinking through the core principles provides useful advice and helpful forecasts. First, the Rational Rule for Buyers provides useful advice to *you*. As you learn to apply this rule to your everyday buying decisions, you'll find yourself making better decisions.

Second, these rules will often provide a useful way for you to understand, and even predict, how other people will act. As we discussed in Chapter 1, if you want to know how someone else will act, put yourself in their shoes and ask: What would you do if you were them? Presumably, you would try to make the best decisions possible, so you would try to follow the Rational Rule for Buyers. In fact, retailers have long known that diminishing marginal benefits is an important factor in determining sales — that is one reason you often see specials like: "Buy one, get the second half-off."

As buyers experiment, they come to act as if they follow the core principles. Of course, people don't always act exactly as this theory suggests, but they generally do (and should!) buy more of those goods with higher marginal benefits and lower prices. And even though most people aren't thinking through the exact calculations that we've outlined, they may follow a different process to the same outcome.

People move closer and closer to making their very best decisions as they gain more experience. Perhaps you got overexcited when you visited Sam's Club for the first time and bought a 40-pound bag of rice, only to realize it would take you years to get through it, and it would take up too much of your kitchen to store it. But next time you hit the store, you'll make savvier choices. Through the process of experimenting — buying different goods and different amounts of goods — people find out what works best for them. As a result, people will often end up making choices as if they made the calculations that our theories predict they should make. This is going to be a really useful insight, as we now turn to analyzing how buyers — as a group — combine to make up market demand.

2.3 Market Demand: What the Market Wants

Learning Objective *Add up individual demand to discover market demand.*

We've focused so far on the buying decisions of individuals. Now it's time to pan back and take a broad view, analyzing *market demand* — the purchasing decisions of all buyers taken as a whole. As a manager, you'll find this broad view useful because total market demand tells you how much business is up for grabs. But not just businesses need to know market demand: Nonprofits seeking donations, universities seeking applicants, and YouTube wanna-be stars seeking subscribers all benefit from being able to estimate market demand for what they're selling. In each case, you're interested in assessing the total quantity demanded — across the entire market — at each price. The **market demand curve** provides exactly this information: It plots the total quantity of a good demanded by the market — that is, across all potential buyers — at each price.

market demand curve A graph plotting the total quantity of an item demanded by the entire market, at each price.

From Individual Demand to Market Demand

Let's explore how real-world managers estimate the market demand curve for their products. As we'll see, individual demand curves are the building blocks of market demand.

Market demand is the sum of the quantity demanded by each person. For each price, the market demand curve illustrates the total quantity demanded by the market. This means you'll need to figure out the total quantity demanded when the price is $1, then $2, then $3, and so on. At each specific price, the total quantity demanded is simply the sum of the quantity that each potential consumer will demand at that price.

Follow a four-step recipe to figure out market demand curves. One way to get this information is to survey potential customers. In fact, there's a simple four-step recipe that many managers follow to estimate the market demand curve for their products.

Step 1: Survey your customers, asking each person the quantity they will buy at each price. When Darren was surveyed about his gas-purchasing behavior (in Figure 1), it was as part of a broader survey that was sent to a representative sample of 300 potential customers, asking each of them about the quantity of gas they plan to buy at each price. Their responses are shown in Panel A, on the left of Figure 6, with each person's response shown in a different column. I've only shown you the responses of the first two people to respond — Darren and Brooklyn — but in the full spreadsheet, there are another 298 columns.

Figure 6 | From Individual Demand to Total Market Demand

Panel A: Individual Demand

Step 1: Run a survey						
Price ($ per gallon)	Darren's demand		Brooklyn's demand		... 298 other people ...	
$1	7	+	4	+	...	=
$2	5	+	3	+	...	=
$3	3	+	2	+	...	=
$4	2	+	1	+	...	=
$5	1	+	0	+	...	=

Panel B: Total Market Demand

Step 2	Step 3	Projection
Total demand across 300 people	Scale up to represent 300 million people	Total market demand
2,800 gallons	× one million	= 2.8 billion gallons
2,400 gallons	× one million	= 2.4 billion gallons
2,000 gallons	× one million	= 2.0 billion gallons
1,600 gallons	× one million	= 1.6 billion gallons
1,200 gallons	× one million	= 1.2 billion gallons

Step 2: For each price, add up the total quantity demanded by your customers. *For each price,* you should add up the quantity demanded by each person in the survey. The

top row shows that when the price is $1 per gallon, Darren demands 7 gallons, Brooklyn demands 4 gallons, and you also need to add up the quantities demanded by each of the other 298 potential customers who were surveyed. This is calculated on the full spreadsheet, and it adds up to 2,800 gallons.

I repeated these calculations for each price from $1 to $5 — once for each row — and the results are shown in the first column of Panel B, presented on the right of Figure 6. This is where you can see that at a price of $1 per gallon, the survey respondents would collectively buy 2,800 gallons of gas, and at $2 per gallon, this would fall to 2,400 gallons.

> To add up demand, you add the quantity demanded by each individual at that price (and not the price each individual pays at each quantity).

Step 3: Scale up the quantities demanded by the survey respondents so that they represent the whole market. If the total market for gas consisted of just the 300 people we surveyed, then these numbers would represent the market demand. But in reality, there are around 300 million potential customers in the United States. The idea of market research is that our survey of 300 people is intended to be representative of those 300 million potential customers. This means that the total quantity demanded by the entire population will be one million times larger than the total quantity demanded by the 300 survey respondents. Thus, you need to scale up the quantities so that they represent the whole market. This works only if the 300 people in your survey are representative of the broader population of 300 million Americans.

In practice, this means that when the price of gas is $1 per gallon, and the 300 people surveyed collectively say that they would buy a total of 2,800 gallons of gas, you can project that the entire market of 300 million consumers would buy 2,800 million gallons of gas (that is, 2.8 billion gallons) per week. Consequently, the projected market demand at each price, shown in the final column of Figure 6, is one million times the total quantity demanded by our survey respondents.

Step 4: Plot the total quantity demanded by the market at each price to draw the market demand curve. The graphing conventions for *market* demand curves are the same as when graphing *individual* demand curves: Price is on the vertical axis, and quantity on the horizontal axis. For each price listed in the first column in Figure 6, you plot the corresponding total quantity demanded by the market, which is listed in the last column. Each row in the table is represented by a purple dot in Figure 7. We then connect these dots to

---

Figure 7 | Estimating Market Demand

To calculate the market demand curve for the entire United States:

Step ❶: Survey a representative sample of the market, asking each person **the quantity they will buy at each price**. (Shown in Figure 6).
Step ❷: For each price, add up the **total quantity demanded by the people surveyed**.
Step ❸: To make projections about the **total quantity demanded by the entire market**, scale up the quantities demanded by the survey respondents so that they represent the whole market. We have 300 survey respondents representing 300 million consumers, and so we project that the quantity demanded by the entire population will be **one million times larger**.
Step ❹: Plot the **total quantity demanded by the entire market** at each price to get the **market demand curve**.

❶ Price	❷ Total quantity demanded by 300 survey respondents	❸ Projection: Total market demand by 300 million consumers
($ per gallon)	(gallons per week)	(gallons per week)
$5	1,200	× one million = 1.2 billion
$4	1,600	× one million = 1.6 billion
$3	2,000	× one million = 2.0 billion
$2	2,400	× one million = 2.4 billion
$1	2,800	× one million = 2.8 billion

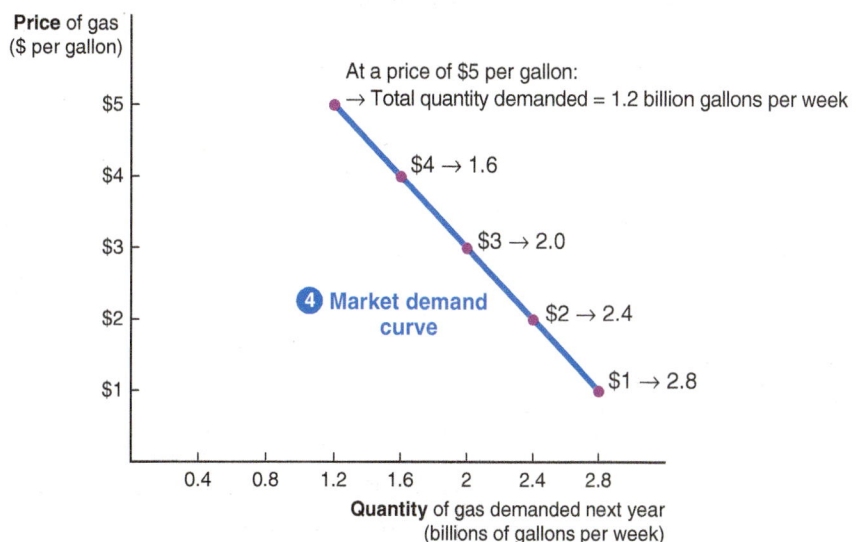

At a price of $5 per gallon:
→ Total quantity demanded = 1.2 billion gallons per week
$4 → 1.6
$3 → 2.0
❹ Market demand curve
$2 → 2.4
$1 → 2.8

Price of gas ($ per gallon)

Quantity of gas demanded next year (billions of gallons per week)

arrive at our estimate of the market demand curve for gasoline in the United States. In fact, this figure is quite similar to the statistical estimates of demand curves that major gasoline executives actually rely on.

The Market Demand Curve Is Downward-Sloping

We've seen (in Figure 7) that the market demand curve for gas is downward-sloping. Executives in virtually every industry have used similar methods to find the market demand curves for their products, and time and again, they have found that the total quantity demanded by the market tends to be higher when the price is lower. That is, market demand curves obey the law of demand: The total quantity demanded is higher when the price is lower.

Your understanding of this *market*-wide phenomenon follows directly from your understanding of *individual* demand curves. The market demand curve is built by adding up individual demand at each price, and so it inherits many of the characteristics of those individual demand curves. In particular, since lower gas prices induce most people to increase the quantity of gas they demand, lower prices lead the total quantity demanded by the market — that is, the sum of the quantities demanded across all people — to increase.

Prices change the quantity demanded for both new and old customers.
Gas station owners report that there are two reasons why lower prices yield an increase in the quantity demanded by the market. First, when prices are low, their current customers buy more gas. Second, gas station owners report that lower prices help them get new customers, as the lower cost of driving encourages some people to buy a car. These two aspects of demand — increasing the quantity demanded among existing customers and an increase in quantity demanded from new customers — are important parts of market demand for most goods.

This is why you have to consider the demand of all *potential* customers when estimating your demand curve, rather than just looking at current customers, since changes in price can change who your customers are.

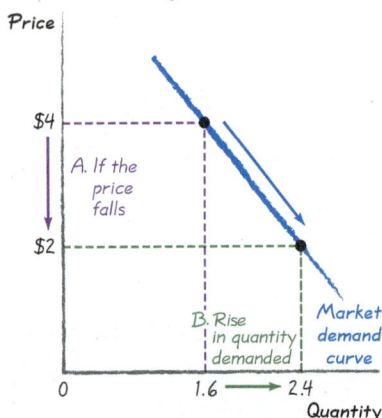

Movement Along the Demand Curve

Movements Along the Demand Curve

Managers find the market demand curve to be useful, because it shows them how the market price shapes the total quantity demanded across all buyers. To forecast the total quantity demanded, simply locate the price on the vertical axis, look straight across until you hit the demand curve, and then look straight down to the quantity on the horizontal axis for your answer. Figure 7 shows that at a price of $4, the total quantity of gas demanded by the market is 1.6 billion gallons per week. To figure out what will happen if the price falls to $2, find the new price on the vertical axis, this time looking across from a price of $2 until you hit a new point on the demand curve. Then look down to the quantity on the horizontal axis, which says that the new quantity of gas demanded is 2.4 billion gallons of gas. Just as the law of demand suggests, a fall in price led to a rise in the quantity demanded, from 1.6 billion to 2.4 billion gallons per week.

Did you notice that the price change led the market to move from one point on the demand curve to another point along the same curve? In fact, whenever you're assessing the consequences of a price change — when nothing else is changing (recall we are holding other things constant) — you'll always compare different points along the same demand curve. That is, price changes cause movement along a fixed demand curve. After all, the demand curve summarizes the entire relationship between price and the quantity demanded.

We will use very specific language to make what we are talking about clear: A change in price causes a **movement along the demand curve,** yielding a **change in the quantity demanded.** Yes, I know this sounds unwieldy, but it will help keep things straight. Trust me.

movement along the demand curve A price change causes movement from one point on a fixed demand curve to another point on the same curve.

change in the quantity demanded The change in quantity associated with movement along a fixed demand curve.

2.4 What Shifts Demand Curves?

Learning Objective *Understand what factors shift demand curves.*

So far, we've analyzed how the quantity demanded varies with the price of a good, *holding other things constant.* We've used three of the four core principles — the opportunity cost principle, the cost-benefit principle, and the marginal principle — to uncover some powerful ideas about demand, such as the Rational Rule for Buyers.

But what happens when other things aren't constant — that is, when factors other than the price change? For that, we're going to need to bring in the fourth principle.

The Interdependence Principle and Shifting Demand Curves

The interdependence principle reminds you that a buyer's best choice also depends on many other factors beyond price, and if any of these other factors change, so might their demand decisions. For instance, the quantity of gas you'll buy (at any given price) might change when you get a pay raise, the amount of traffic decreases, or the price of alternatives such as catching the bus falls. When you're no longer holding these other things constant, the demand curve may shift. When the demand curve itself moves, we refer to it as a **shift in the demand curve.** Because your demand curve is also your marginal benefit curve, any factor that changes your marginal benefits will shift your demand curve.

As Figure 8 illustrates, a rightward shift is an **increase in demand,** because at each and every price, the quantity demanded is higher. A leftward shift is a **decrease in demand,** because the quantity demanded is lower at each and every price.

shift in the demand curve A movement of the demand curve itself.

increase in demand A shift of the demand curve to the right.

decrease in demand A shift of the demand curve to the left.

Figure 8 | Shifts in the Demand Curve

Panel A: An Increase in Demand

A An increase in demand shifts the demand curve to the right, leading to a higher quantity demanded at each and every price.

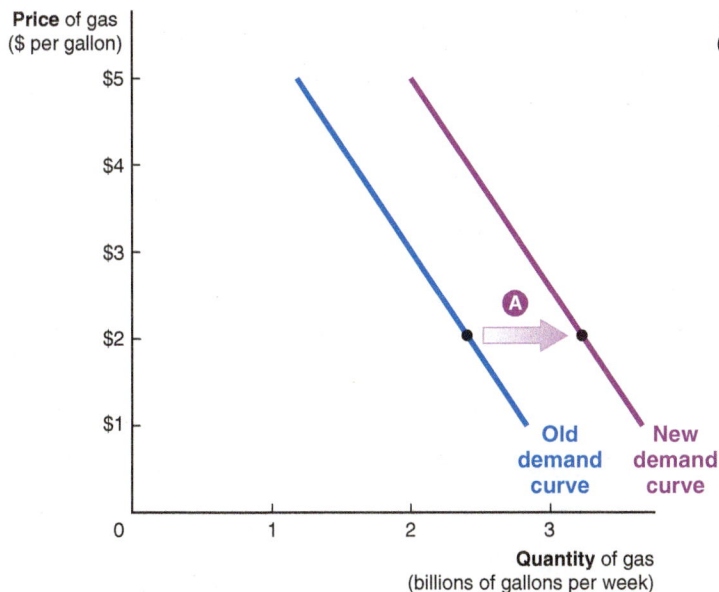

Panel B: A Decrease in Demand

B A decrease in demand shifts the demand curve to the left, leading to a lower quantity demanded at each and every price.

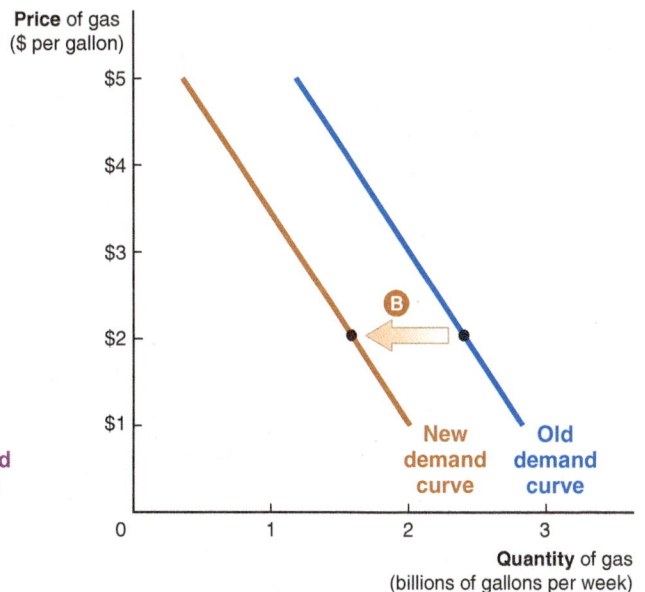

Six Factors That Shift the Demand Curve

The interdependence principle reminds you that buying choices depend on many other factors. When those other factors shift, so will people's buying plans, thereby shifting the demand curve. The key factors that cause the demand curve to shift are:

1. Income
2. Preferences
3. Prices of related goods
4. Expectations
5. Congestion and network effects
6. The type and number of buyers

Changes in any of the first five of these factors shift individual demand curves, and because the market demand curve is built up from individual demand curves, they shift the market demand curve. The final factor — the type and number of buyers — only shifts market demand curves.

Demand shifter 1: Income. All of your individual choices are interdependent, since you have only a limited amount of income to spend. Money you spend on gas is money that you can't spend on clothes. But when your income is higher, you can afford to buy a larger quantity of both. Thus, at each and every price level, you can buy a larger quantity of gas (and clothes), causing your demand curve to shift to the right — which we call an increase in demand. If your income were to fall, then you would probably choose to buy less gas at each and every price, shifting your demand curve to the left — and that's called a decrease in demand.

normal good A good for which higher income causes an increase in demand.

inferior good A good for which higher income causes a decrease in demand.

If your demand for a good or service increases when your income is higher, we call it a **normal good.** Most goods are normal goods. For example, when your income is higher, you'll likely spend more money on housing, clothes, and entertainment than you do when your income is lower.

But for some goods, demand decreases when income rises. Economists refer to these goods as **inferior goods.** This term doesn't refer to the quality of the goods (or of the people who buy them); it simply describes goods for which demand decreases as income increases. For instance, when you're in college and struggling with a limited income, you might take the bus a lot, but when you get your first full-time job, you might buy a car or take more Ubers. Since the higher income in your first job reduced your demand for bus rides, we conclude that bus rides are an inferior good.

Here's a quick exercise to get them straight: If you've fantasized about some purchase you will make when you get your first job after graduation — it could be something big (like a car) or a small indulgence (like a weekly manicure) — that good is, for you, a normal good. If there's anything you plan to *stop* buying when you start earning more money — instant soup, do-it-yourself manicure supplies, bus fare — then that good is an inferior good for you. Alternatively, you might spend more on similar goods as your income increases. For example, a college student who loves hoodies may head to Uniqlo, where they can get a nice hoodie for about 30 bucks. A software engineer making $100K per year might spring for a $112 hoodie from American Giant. And somewhere on the income scale is a person wealthy enough to spend $2,000 on a designer cashmere hoodie. The point is not that hoodies are great (although they objectively are) but that people's incomes affect how much they are willing to spend on them. Designer clothes tend to be normal goods, while modestly priced brands tend to be inferior goods.

xiaorui/Shutterstock

An inferior good that provides superior comfort.

Interpreting the DATA   Why Walmart beat Target during the 2007–09 recession

The distinction between normal and inferior goods can be pretty useful in practice. For instance, economists studying retail stores have found that rising income led to more purchases at Target and fewer at Walmart. Somewhat cheekily (but entirely accurately), they concluded that "shopping at Target is perfectly normal."

Walmart has always focused on offering low prices, and that pays off particularly well when people's incomes are hurting. During 2008–2009, average income fell, and Walmart saw demand for its products rise. This is the definition of inferior goods in the economics sense — stuff people buy more of when they have less money. From an economy-wide perspective, it means that bad times for the economy are good times for Walmart. In comparison, Target, which sells mainly normal goods, experienced a decrease in demand. Figure 9 shows that the recession, which increased the demand for Walmart's goods, led its stock price to rise, while the decrease in demand for Target's goods led the value of its stock to fall by about 40%. ∎

Figure 9 | Normal and Inferior Goods

The 2008 recession caused Walmart's stock price to rise, even though other retailers like Target fell.

Ⓐ In 2007, Target's stock price was much higher than Walmart's.
Ⓑ The U.S. economy entered a recession in December 2007, and average incomes fell.
Ⓒ Walmart sells inferior goods, so a *decline* in average income led to an *increase in demand*, and so its stock price rose.
Ⓓ Target sells normal goods, so falling average income led to a *decrease in demand*, and so its stock price fell.

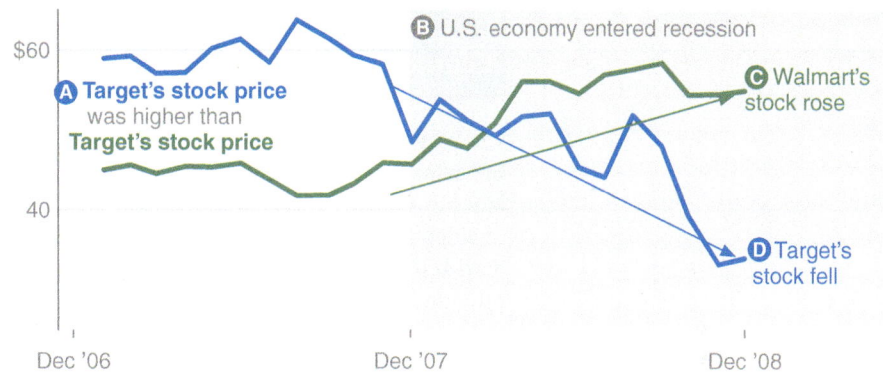

Data from: New York Stock Exchange.

Demand shifter 2: Your preferences. Changes in your preferences can shift your demand curve. What if Darren becomes a parent? His entire spending plan might change as he considers his new needs. Would he want to drive more, perhaps to have easier access to day care? Or would he take the bus more so that he could enjoy a few minutes of rest? In fact, there are large numbers of marketers trying to figure out how to take advantage of the changes in people's demand due to life events like getting married or becoming a parent.

Companies spend billions of dollars each year attempting to influence our preferences through advertising. If Pepsi somehow convinces you that it's better than Coke, this will increase your demand for Pepsi and decrease your demand for Coke. *Social pressure* can also shift your demand curve. For instance, rising environmental awareness has increased demand for electric vehicles, shifting the demand curve to the right. Preferences are also affected by fashion cycles. For example, the pandemic led to a surge in demand for comfy clothes like sweatpants and athleisure, shifting their demand curves to the right. But the return to in-person activities saw those fads fade away, and the demand curve for sweatpants shifted back to the left.

Demand shifter 3: Prices of related goods. Your choices are also interdependent across different goods. For instance, your demand for hot dogs is closely related to your demand for hot dog buns. If the price of hot dog buns rises, you'll buy fewer hot dog buns *and* fewer hot dogs. That means that the higher cost of hot dog buns causes a decrease in your demand for hot dogs, shifting your demand curve for hot dogs to the left. When the higher price of one good decreases your demand for another good or the lower price of one good increases your demand for another good, we call them **complementary goods.**

Typically, complementary goods "go well together." That is, a hot dog bun is a complement to a hot dog, just like a new case is a complement to your new smartphone. Similarly, cars are a complement to gas because gas and a car are used together to drive, and

New phone? You're probably going to buy a new case, too.

complementary goods Goods that go together. Your demand for a good will decrease if the price of a complementary good rises and will increase if the price of a complementary good falls.

substitute goods Goods that replace each other. Your demand for a good will increase if the price of a substitute good rises, and it will fall if the price of a substitute good falls.

so cheaper gas leads more people to drive, and this increases the demand for cars shifting the demand curve to the right.

While complementary goods go together, **substitute goods** replace each other. For example, walking, cycling, ride-sharing, and catching the bus are all substitutes for driving. If the price of bus tickets doubles, you might start driving to work instead of catching the bus, increasing your demand for gas. Your demand for any good will increase if the price of its substitutes rises. Conversely, your demand will decrease if the price of substitutes falls.

EVERYDAY Economics   How to use economic thinking to change behavior

You may not realize it, but we use substitutes and complements all the time to change the behavior of others — and sometimes even our own. For instance, parents might help their kids pay for textbooks, laptops, and desk chairs (complements to studying), but not parties or video games (which are substitutes for studying) in order to encourage their kids to work hard at school. Likewise, employers want their workers to focus at work, so they strategically provide free coffee, which is a complement to focused work, and they often block access to Facebook, which is a substitute. If you've ever treated yourself to new workout clothes to motivate you to go to the gym — or replaced the junk food in your fridge with healthier options — you've used the magic of economic thinking to change your own behavior. ■

Demand shifter 4: Expectations. As a consumer, you get to choose not only what to buy, but also when to buy it. Your choices are linked through time. This simple insight can help you save money and, along the way, shift your demand curves. Think about your reaction when you drive past a gas station charging exorbitantly high prices. If you believe that this high price is only temporary, you might put off filling your tank for a few days, decreasing today's demand for gas. Conversely, if you believe gas prices are going to rise further, you should probably fill up right away, increasing today's demand. That is, your expectations about future gas prices can shift your demand curve to the left or to the right.

This insight is really an example of the logic of substitutes: Gas purchased tomorrow is a substitute for gas purchased today, and a higher price for this substitute increases demand for gas purchased today, while a lower price decreases it.

EVERYDAY Economics   How to save money by thinking ahead

Uber's surge-pricing feature automatically boosts the price of a ride so that it will be two or three times higher during peak hours, as an incentive to get more drivers on the road. As a rider, you can save some money by planning trips a bit more strategically. Instead of calling for a ride during a peak period — say, just after a concert gets out — you could hang out with your friends for a bit and get a ride home an hour later, when the rush is over and the price has returned to normal.

Notice what's happening here: Your expectations about a lower price later tonight leads to a decline in your demand for Ubers right now. That's because a ride home later tonight is a substitute for a ride home right now, and a lower price of the substitute decreases your demand. It's an example of a more general idea: You can save a few bucks by making sure you think about future prices before you buy. ■

Demand shifter 5: Congestion and network effects. The usefulness of some products — and hence your demand for them — is also shaped by the choices that other people make. For example, millions of U.S. college students use Facebook,

Instagram, or Snapchat. But college students in China are more likely to use WeChat, which is by far the most popular social media platform in Asia. This is an example of a **network effect** — where a product or service becomes more useful to you as more people use it. As it becomes more useful, it yields greater marginal benefits, increasing your demand.

Network effects can have important business implications in some markets: Signing up a few early adopters can make some products more valuable to other customers, increasing the demand for the product, leading more customers to adopt the product, and making it even more valuable again. In these markets, winning the early rounds of competition is critical to your business's long-run success.

By contrast, some products become less valuable when more people use them. This reverse case is called a **congestion effect.** For example, your demand for driving on a particular road declines if many others are also using that road, since more cars create congestion and traffic. Likewise, your demand for a particular formal dress might decrease if someone else is wearing it.

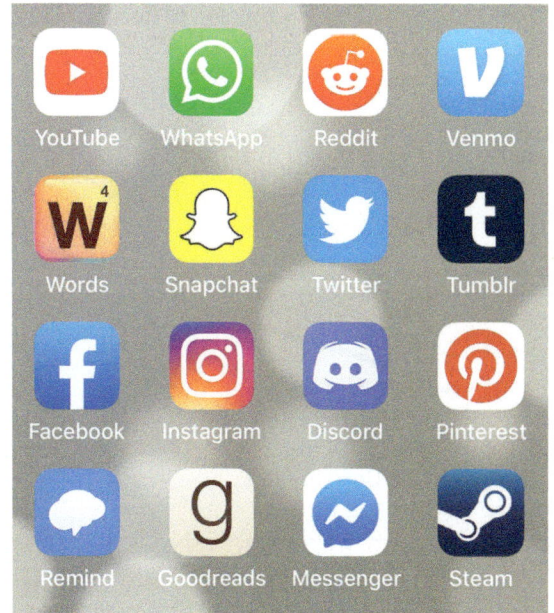

Love it or hate it? Depends on who else is using it.

network effect When a good becomes more useful because other people use it. If more people buy such a good, your demand for it will also increase.

congestion effect When a good becomes less valuable because other people use it. If more people buy such a product, your demand for it will decrease.

	EVERYDAY Economics

What determines the language we speak, the computer programs we use, and the cars we drive?

Network and congestion effects are everywhere. Most U.S. schools teach English rather than Portuguese. This isn't because English is the more beautiful language; it is simply the most useful language, given that most people in the United States speak English. In Brazil, the reverse occurs.

The types of cars that people buy are also interdependent. City-dwellers sometimes buy SUVs, but not because they plan to go off-road driving. Instead, they worry that because there are so many other large cars on the road, they now need to drive a large car to stand a reasonable chance of surviving an accident. Thus, the choices made by other people in the United States affect your demand for Google Drive, Zoom, Slack, large cars, and learning English. ∎

Demand shifter 6: Type and number of buyers. So far, we have analyzed the five factors that shift individual demand curves. Because market demand is the sum of individual demand, the factors that shift individual demand also shift market demand. If the size or the composition of the market changes through demographic composition or type of buyers in the market, then market demand will also change.

Additionally, market demand is shaped by the number of buyers. If the number of potential buyers rises, then there are more individual demand curves to add up when calculating market demand. Thus, an increase in the number of potential buyers shifts the market demand curve to the right. Over short periods of time, increases in population are relatively unimportant, as the U.S. population grows by only about 1% each year. But over longer periods, this can add up. The U.S. population has more than doubled since 1950, and this alone has doubled the quantity demanded in most markets. The U.S. population is expected to increase by nearly a third between 2016 and 2060. The dependence of demand curves on market size partly explains why many business owners are in favor of increased immigration: More people means increased demand for their firm's products.

For instance, the baby boom that followed World War II initially led to an increase in the demand for baby clothes. As this huge cohort progressed through their lives, there was an increase in the demand for schoolbooks, then for college education, and subsequently for houses, cars, and child care. Over the next decade, these aging baby boomers will cause demand for health care and nursing homes to rise. But there's

The U.S. population is expected to keep growing

Population in millions

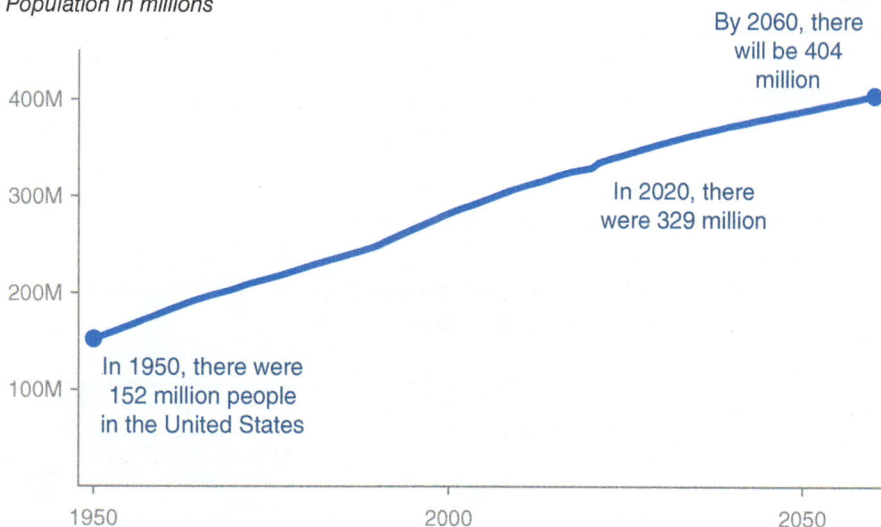

Data from: U.S. Census Bureau.

Six factors shift the market demand curve:

1. Income
2. Preferences
3. Prices of related goods
4. Expectations
5. Congestion and network effects
6. The type and number of buyers

. . . but not a change in price.

also another sizable cohort — the Millennials, born between 1981 and 1996 — and their preferences and life stages will shape market demand in the United States.

Another critical factor increasing market size is international trade and the opening of new foreign markets. For instance, the opening of the Chinese economy means that there are now more than one billion Chinese consumers for exporters to serve, which potentially represents an enormous shift in demand.

When things other than price change, your demand curve may shift. As we've seen, changes in market conditions affect your demand decisions. These changes reflect the interdependence principle at work: Your best choices depend on many factors, and when these factors change, so will your best buying decisions. The five factors that shift individual demand curves — your income, your preferences, the prices of other goods, your expectations, and network and congestion effects — are all factors that can change your marginal benefit. Because your marginal benefit curve is your demand curve, shifts in these factors can shift your demand curve. Keep these factors in mind as we now turn to the distinction between movements along the demand curve versus shifts of the demand curve.

2.5 Shifts versus Movements Along Demand Curves

Learning Objective *Distinguish between movements along a demand curve and shifts of demand curves.*

It can be tricky to figure out when to look for movements along the demand curve versus shifts in that curve. But it's essential if you are going to correctly forecast the consequences of changing economic conditions. Here's a simple rule of thumb: If the only thing that's changing is the price, then you're thinking about a movement along the demand curve. But when other market conditions change, you need to think about shifts of the demand curve.

Movements Along the Demand Curve

When the price changes, you are analyzing a movement along the demand curve. When other factors change, the demand curve may shift.

To see why changes in price are different from changes in other factors, let's revisit Darren after the price of gas changes. This price change won't lead Darren to change his answers to the survey in Figure 1. That survey already described his plans to change the quantity of gas he uses if the price changes. Likewise, his individual demand curve — which simply plotted his answers to that survey — will be unchanged. And if individual demand curves don't shift following a price change, then neither will the market demand curve. The logic is this: A demand curve is a plan for how to respond to different prices, and if buyers' plans haven't shifted, then the market demand curve hasn't shifted.

Indeed, managers find the demand curve to be useful precisely because they can use it to assess the consequences of a price change. For instance, Panel A in Figure 10 shows that when the price of gas is $4, the total quantity demanded will be 1.6 billion gallons per week, and when the price of gas falls to $2, the quantity demanded will rise to 2.4 billion gallons. As you can see, this price change leads to a movement along the demand curve. And this analysis shows that a lower price leads to an increase in the quantity demanded.

Figure 10 | Movement Along the Demand Curve versus Shifts in the Demand Curve

Panel A—When the Price Changes:
Movement Along the Demand Curve

Ⓐ A **change in price**, from $4 to $2 per gallon,
Ⓑ Causes a **movement along the demand curve**,
Ⓒ Leading to a **change in the quantity demanded**, raising the quantity demanded from 1.6 to 2.4 billion gallons per week.

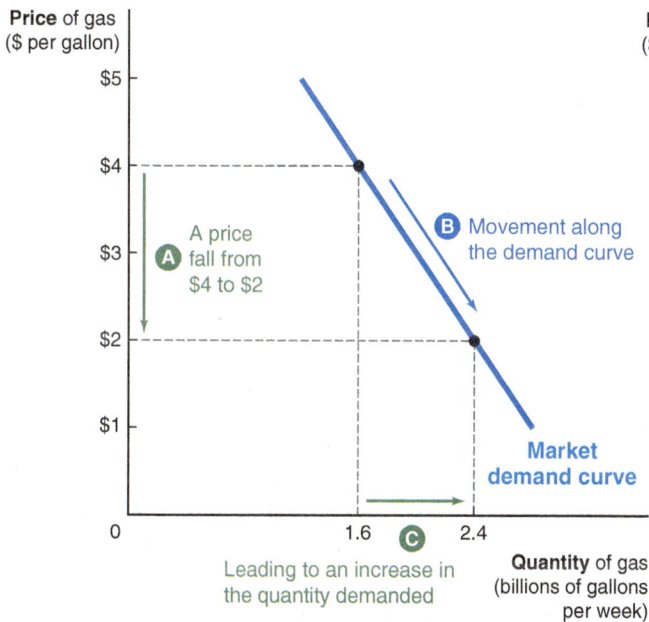

Panel B—When Other Factors Change:
Shifts in the Demand Curve

Ⓐ A **decrease in demand** shifts the demand curve to the left, decreasing the quantity demanded at each and every price.

Ⓑ An **increase in demand** shifts the demand curve to the right, increasing the quantity demanded at each and every price.

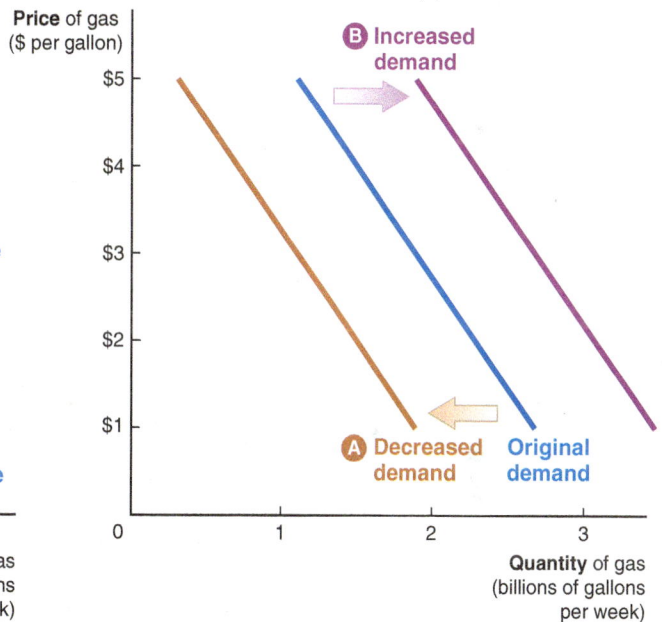

Shifts in Demand

But if other factors change — factors other than the price — then Darren might revise his buying plans. For instance, changes in things like Darren's income, his preference for driving, the price of alternatives such as Uber, his expectations about future gas prices, or the number of other drivers creating traffic could all lead him to decide to change how much gas he'll buy even if the price doesn't change. When these factors change the quantity that Darren demands at a given price, they lead to a shift in his demand curve.

To figure out whether a change in market conditions will shift the demand curve, ask yourself: Has something changed that would cause you to give different answers to a survey about the quantity you'll demand at each price? If so, then this will shift your demand curve. The right-hand panel of Figure 10 illustrates an increase in demand, which causes the demand curve to shift to the right, and also a decrease in demand, which causes it to shift to the left.

Of course, not every change in market conditions will cause the demand curve to shift. If those changes don't change your answers to the survey about your demand plans, then your demand hasn't shifted. But if they do change, then it is connected, and this dependence may change things. This is the **interdependence principle** in action — when your

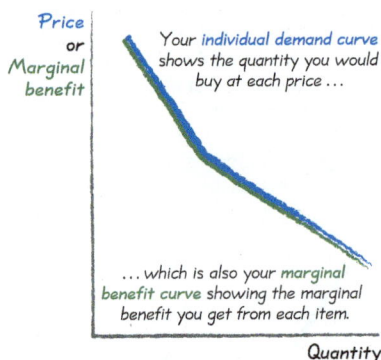

best choice changes because of changes in your other choices, the choices others make, developments in other markets, or expectations about the future, your demand curve shifts. To make it easy to think about what could shift the demand curve, remember the six demand shifters: Income, Preferences, Prices of related goods, Expectations, Congestion and network effects, and the Type and number of buyers. Finally, let me give you a hint that will help you memorize these six factors: Rearrange the first letter of each of them, and it will spell out PEPTIC, which should make this lesson a bit easier to digest.

2.6 Tying It Together

Individual Decisions Drive Market Demand

We have studied demand from two perspectives. We started with the individual demand decisions that you make, and then considered total market demand for a product, across all buyers. Both perspectives are important. Managers want to know how much people will buy at each price. This is exactly what the market demand curve reveals. Consumers want to know how to make the best choices given their limited income, and this is what our study of individual demand addresses. Because these individual demand curves are the building blocks of the market demand curve, these questions are fundamentally intertwined.

How much should I buy? The Rational Rule for Buyers distills the core economic principles down to one simple piece of advice: *Buy more of an item if the marginal benefit of one more is greater than (or equal to) the price.* Follow this advice consistently, and you'll keep buying until your marginal benefit equals the price. In turn, your individual demand curve is your marginal benefit curve. And the tendency toward diminishing marginal benefits means that your marginal benefit curve — and hence your demand curve — is downward-sloping. You can see why economists say that understanding demand is all about understanding marginal benefits.

There's also a more general idea at work here. In Chapter 1, we introduced the Rational Rule, which simply says: *If something is worth doing, keep doing it until the marginal benefit equals the marginal cost.* The Rational Rule for Buyers is just the application of this rule to your buying decisions, where the marginal cost of buying something is the price. Throughout your study of economics, we'll discover that whenever you are trying to figure out how to make optimal choices — whether in your role as a buyer, seller, worker, boss, entrepreneur, investor, or anything else — the relevant rule will turn out to be an application of the Rational Rule. That's the advantage of our principles-based approach: It highlights the similarities of good decision making across very different contexts. Stay tuned; we'll see more of this in future chapters.

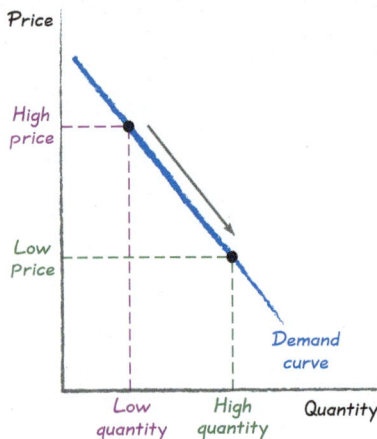

How can managers forecast the total quantity they will sell? Managers find the market demand curve to be useful because it allows them to forecast how changing economic conditions will affect the quantity they will sell. When the price changes, this causes *a movement along the market demand curve,* and hence changes in the total *quantity demanded.* Because the demand curve is downward-sloping, a lower price will raise the total quantity demanded, and a higher price will reduce the total quantity demanded.

But there are also several factors that shift your demand curve. An *increase* in demand is a rightward shift of the demand curve at each and every price, while a *decrease* in demand is a leftward shift.

The **interdependence principle** leads us to six key factors that shift demand curves. These include changes in:

- *Income*: Higher income increases the demand for normal goods but decreases the demand for inferior goods.
- *Preferences*: Demand for particular goods can increase or decrease as your desire for those goods change. Preferences can be changed by trends, advertising, changing lifestyles, and countless other factors. Advertisers will try to increase your demand for their products. Social pressure can also shift demand curves.
- *Prices of related goods*: Demand will increase if the price of substitute goods rises, or the price of complementary goods falls. Demand will decrease if the price of substitute goods falls, or the price of complementary goods rises.
- *Expectations*: If prices are expected to rise, today's demand will increase; if prices are expected to fall, today's demand will decrease.
- *Congestion and network effects*: If a good with network effects becomes more popular, demand will increase. If a good with congestion effects becomes more popular, demand will decrease.
- *Type and number of buyers*: Demand will increase due to population growth, immigration, or access to new international markets. Demographic change can also shift demand. This factor only affects market demand curves, not individual demand.

This chapter focused on consumers and how marginal benefits shape demand. In the next chapter, we'll turn our focus to businesses and how the marginal costs of production affect supply.

An increase in demand

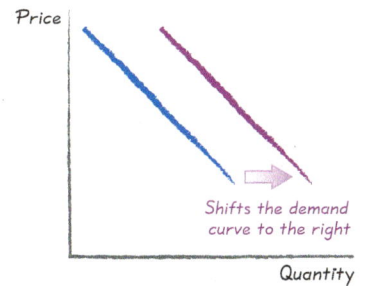

Shifts the demand curve to the right

A decrease in demand

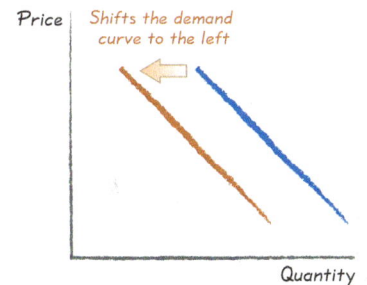

Shifts the demand curve to the left

Chapter 2 Review

Chapter at a Glance

An Individual Demand Curve
Shows the quantity demanded at each price.

Price ← Price goes on the vertical axis

The first few items yield a high marginal benefit, and so you would buy even at a high price.

But at a higher quantity, each extra item yields a low marginal benefit, and so you would only buy at a low price.

Demand curve (= Marginal benefits)

Quantity goes on horizontal axis → Quantity

The Rational Rule for Buyers
Buy more of an item if its marginal benefit is greater than (or equal to) the price

↓

Price = Marginal benefit

↓

Your demand curve is your marginal benefit curve.

↓

Your demand curve is downward-sloping because of diminishing marginal benefits.

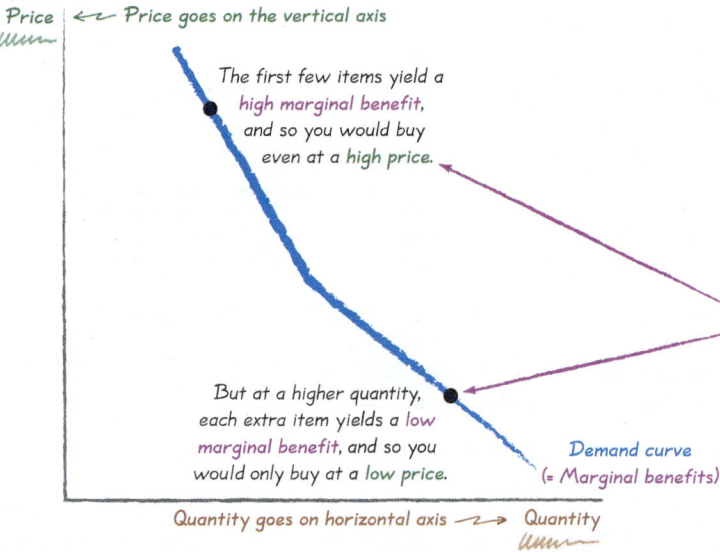

Market Demand Curves
1. Survey a representative sample of the market, asking people the quantity they will buy at each price.
2. For each price, add up the total quantity demanded by the people surveyed.
3. Scale up the quantities demanded by the people surveyed, so that they represent the entire market.
4. Plot the total quantity demanded by the market, against price.

When the Price Changes:
Movement Along the Demand Curve

Price

A change in the price

A price rise causes a decline in quantity demanded

A price cut causes a rise in quantity demanded.

Yields a change in the quantity demanded.

Quantity

When Other Factors Change:
Shifts in the Demand Curve

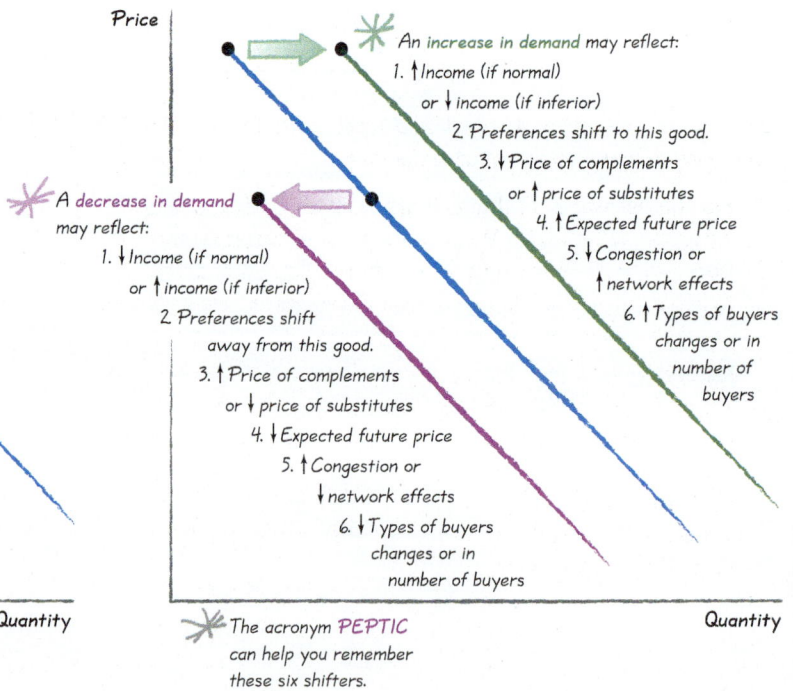

Price

An increase in demand may reflect:
1. ↑Income (if normal) or ↓income (if inferior)
2. Preferences shift to this good.
3. ↓Price of complements or ↑price of substitutes
4. ↑Expected future price
5. ↓Congestion or ↑network effects
6. ↑Types of buyers changes or in number of buyers

A decrease in demand may reflect:
1. ↓Income (if normal) or ↑income (if inferior)
2. Preferences shift away from this good.
3. ↑Price of complements or ↓price of substitutes
4. ↓Expected future price
5. ↑Congestion or ↓network effects
6. ↓Types of buyers changes or in number of buyers

Quantity

The acronym PEPTIC can help you remember these six shifters.

Key Terms

Study Problems

Learning Objective 2.1 *Discover the shape of your individual demand curve.*

1. You just took an Uber from home to campus for the first time and were willing to pay $13 for the trip. It was so much easier than driving yourself that you are willing to pay $21 for the same trip tomorrow. Have you violated the law of demand? Why or why not?

2. DoorDash, a food delivery service, has recently expanded to your area. The accompanying table contains the number of deliveries per month that you demand at various delivery prices. Use this information to plot your individual demand curve. Describe the shape of your individual demand curve.

Price	Deliveries
$10	2
$7	4
$5	6
$4	8
$2	10
$1	12

Learning Objective 2.2 *Apply the core principles of economics to make good demand decisions.*

3. Do you use water for things that are beyond what is necessary to sustain life? What if the price of water in your home tripled? How would you respond? Are there activities that you would change or stop doing? Briefly explain. Does your demand for water obey the law of demand?

4. Consider Ron's demand for after-school care for his children. The marginal benefit Ron receives for every hour of child care is provided in the accompanying table. Using the Rational Rule for Buyers, if an hour of child care costs $24, how many hours would Ron purchase each day? What about for $18 per hour? Draw Ron's marginal benefit curve and his demand curve.

Hours of after-school child care	Marginal benefit (per hour)
1	$32
2	$30
3	$20
4	$14

5. Nicole is attending school in Philadelphia. Each year she returns home to visit her family and friends in New York City. Kathy's annual demand curve for train tickets from Philadelphia to New York is provided in the accompanying graph. How much benefit does Kathy receive from each trip home? If the price of a round-trip ticket is $230, how many trips should Kathy take?

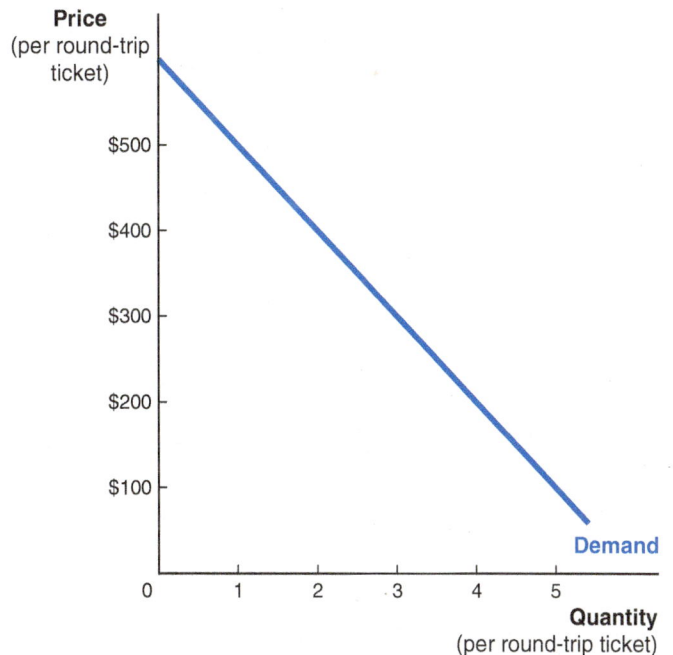

6. A team of analysts at Amazon is researching the viability of producing a smart watch. How might they estimate potential demand for their smart watch? What kinds of factors would the analysts want to keep in mind to create the most accurate estimates?

7. The marginal benefit received for each gallon of gasoline consumed per week for Ang, Tony, and Gianna is provided in the accompanying table. On the same graph, plot each of their individual demand curves. Assuming these are the only people in the market, graph the market demand curve for gasoline.

Gallons consumed per week	Ang's marginal benefit	Tony's marginal benefit	Gianna's marginal benefit
1	$7	$4	$8
2	$5	$3	$6
3	$3	$2	$4
4	$1	$1	$2

8. You own the only pharmacy in the small town of Jackson City, which has 40,000 residents. You would like to get a sense of what the local demand is for seasonal allergy medicine so you can determine how many packages to keep in stock and what price to charge. You conduct a survey of four residents of Jackson City, asking them about the quantity of allergy medicine they would buy each allergy season at various prices. Their responses are shown in the accompanying table. Estimate and graph the demand for the *entire* town of Jackson City.

Price	Lee	June	Carlotta	Eric
$8	8	5	6	9
$10	6	4	5	5
$12	4	3	4	3
$14	2	2	2	1
$18	0	1	1	0

9. For each of the following goods or services, indicate whether you think they are normal or inferior goods for most consumers. Briefly explain your reasoning.

   a. The newest iPhone

   b. 10-year-old used cars

   c. Dental services

10. When Sony released the PlayStation 5, it was reported that it was taking a loss of $50 on every console. However, Sony expected to make this up with sales of online play subscriptions (PS+) and increased royalties from video games. Use the concepts described in this chapter to help explain this strategy.

11. For each of the following pairs of goods or services, identify if they are substitutes or complements and use a graph to illustrate how the change described impacts the markets for both goods or services.

    a. Gasoline and sport utility vehicles: The price of gasoline increases.

    b. Taking a train or plane between New York City and Washington, DC: The price of airfare increases.

    c. A smartphone and a Verizon data plan: The price of a monthly data plan increases.

12. Consider the market demand curve for the Samsung Galaxy smartphone. For each of the following, assess whether it would cause a rightward shift in the demand curve, a leftward shift in the demand curve, or no change in the demand curve.

    a. Batteries in Samsung smartphones begin to spontaneously combust.

    b. Apple decides to increase the price of the newest iPhone by 10%.

    c. Samsung increases the price of the Galaxy by 10%.

13. Recent tariffs on imported steel could cause the price to consumers of new cars to increase by as much as $300. Use a graph to illustrate the impact of this on the current demand curve for new cars in the United States.

14. As part of the marketing team at Delta Air Lines you must develop a strategy to increase demand for flights between Kansas City and Detroit. You examine the data from previous flights and determine that the existing demand for flights between the two cities is as given in the following table.

Price per flight	Quantity demanded per day
$200	1,200
$300	1,100
$400	1,000
$500	900
$600	800
$700	700

a. However, your team launches a viral advertising campaign that is so successful that all existing consumers increase their willingness to pay by $100, and 50 new customers demand flights at every price. Fill in the following table to show the new quantity demanded at each price following the advertising campaign.

Price per flight	Quantity demanded per day after the advertising campaign
$200	1,350
$300	
$400	
$500	
$600	
$700	

b. Use a graph to illustrate both the initial demand curve and the new demand curve from part (a).

Learning Objective 2.5 *Distinguish between movements along a demand curve and shifts of demand curves.*

15. Find the flaw in reasoning in the following statement: "An increase in the cost of oil will cause the price of a plane ticket to increase. This increase in price will cause a decrease in demand for airline travel and a leftward shift in the demand curve."

16. Illustrate graphically how each of the following events will impact the demand for cups of coffee and explain why demand changes.

   a. Average hourly wages increase in the United States.

   b. The state of California requires all coffee houses to post warnings to consumers of the cancer-causing components of coffee.

   c. Coffee houses increase the price of coffee in order to pay their baristas more.

Supply and Producer Choice

While you might not think of yourself as a seller if you aren't managing a business, you are already managing one very important small business: Your Own Undertaking (or YOU, for short). YOU are already making very important supply decisions. You may have sold concert tickets on StubHub; perhaps you have sold collectibles on eBay or a piece of furniture on Facebook Marketplace. You may hold a part-time job, where you sell your labor in return for an hourly wage.

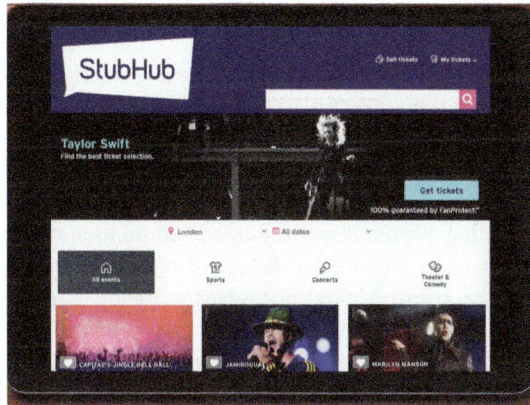

How much would you sell your seat for?

M4OS Photos/Alamy

You also supply things in transactions that don't involve money. Your household is like a small business, and you might produce cooking or cleaning services in return for similar services from your family or housemates. You probably supply child care, transport, and advice to those you love. You also supply camaraderie to your friends, an audience to online advertisers, and your attention to this important chapter on supply.

In this chapter, we'll dig into *supply*—the decisions that we make as sellers. The structure of this chapter largely parallels our analysis of demand. We'll start with individual decisions and apply the core principles of economics to help guide you to make good supply decisions. Next, we'll pan back and assess total market supply, which is the sum of these individual decisions. We'll then explore how changing market conditions shift supply.

There's a lot to cover with supply—the global economy consists of millions of businesses producing and selling a dazzling array of goods. But the same logic underpins every business decision. Let's start by putting ourselves into the shoes of a seller trying to decide how much to produce and sell.

Chapter Objective

Understand how sellers make supply decisions.

3.1 Individual Supply: What You Sell, at Each Price
Discover the shape of your business's individual supply curve.

3.2 Your Decisions and Your Individual Supply Curve
Apply the core principles to make good supply decisions.

3.3 Market Supply: What the Market Sells
Add up individual supply to discover market supply.

3.4 What Shifts Supply Curves?
Understand what factors shift supply curves.

3.5 Shifts versus Movements Along Supply Curves
Distinguish between movements along a supply curve and shifts of supply curves.

🎙 **Podcast**
Think Like An Economist
Supply: Getting the Best Out of What You Sell

3.1 Individual Supply: What You Sell, at Each Price

Learning Objective *Discover the shape of your business's individual supply curve.*

Shannon is preparing for her company's annual planning summit. She joined BP's management training program straight out of college and has spent the past few years working as a business analyst in the strategy division. BP is a major producer and seller of gasoline, and the planning summit brings together the heads of every major business unit to formulate production and sales plans for the next year. Shannon impressed her boss enough that she's been picked to present the division's analysis.

Shannon knows that the decisions made at the planning summit will ripple throughout the company. The head of the retail division will use these plans to coordinate sales targets across thousands of gas stations. The engineers who lead the refinery division—the large plants that transform crude oil into gasoline—will use these decisions to determine their production schedules. And the logistics division—which buys the crude oil needed by the refineries—will start making purchasing plans based on the details Shannon provides.

The question Shannon is addressing is one that is central to all businesses: *Given the price of our product, what quantity should we supply?* The stakes are high, because the right decision can be the difference between a healthy profit and a big loss.

At the summit, Shannon gives a presentation outlining how the company should respond if the price of gas increases next year. Because a higher gas price would make selling more gas profitable, she recommends that the company ramp up production. Her presentation is quite specific, outlining exactly how much BP should increase production, depending on how much prices rise.

She then turns to more pessimistic scenarios, assessing how the company should respond to lower gas prices. If the price of gas falls next year, she recommends cutting back the quantity of gas BP produces and sells. Her presentation makes clear that the lower the gas price falls, the greater the cutbacks required, and hence the lower the quantity they would supply. Finally, she concludes that if the gas price is sufficiently low, the best way to minimize losses would be to halt production entirely and produce no gas. While this would be a hard decision to make, it would help BP survive until gas prices rose again.

Shannon's presentation details how the ideal quantity to produce and sell varies depending on the price. Because price is a critical factor in determining any company's profitability, businesses often find it useful to plan for a variety of different scenarios. Figure 1 shows the memo that Shannon distributed after the meeting, describing her company's supply plans for next year. Each bullet point in Shannon's memo shows the quantity of gasoline she recommends that BP supply at each price.

A refinery transforms crude oil into gasoline.

Figure 1 | **BP's Supply Plan**

Memo

TO: All department heads—Refining, Retail, and Logistics units
FROM: Shannon David, Business Planning Division
SUBJECT: Gasoline Supply Plans

This memo summarizes the production and sales plans that we agreed upon in last week's planning summit. Specifically, we decided:

- If the gas price is $1 per gallon, we will produce 10 million gallons per week.
- If the gas price is $2 per gallon, we will produce 15 million gallons per week.
- If the gas price is $3 per gallon, we will produce 20 million gallons per week.
- If the gas price is $4 per gallon, we will produce 25 million gallons per week.
- If the gas price is $5 per gallon, we will produce 30 million gallons per week.
- If the gas price is below $1 per gallon, all production will shut down, so we will produce zero gallons per week.

Please use these numbers as the basis for setting next year's plans for your division. These production and sales plans are based on our current understanding of market conditions, which may change; if so, we will revisit these numbers.

An Individual Supply Curve

individual supply curve A graph plotting the quantity of an item that a business plans to sell at each price.

While Shannon has written the plan as a memo, economists prefer to visualize these plans in a graph. An **individual supply curve** is a graph that shows the quantity that a business plans to sell at each price; it summarizes a business's selling plans. You can graph an individual supply curve for anything that you might sell—space in your garage, the use of your electric scooter, your tutoring services—you just need to think about the quantity you'd sell at each price.

An individual supply curve graphs your selling plans. Figure 2 graphs the individual supply curve for Shannon's company, plotting the supply plans she outlined point by point in her memo. The graphing conventions for supply curves are the same as for demand curves: Price goes on the vertical axis, and quantity is on the horizontal axis. (Remember: Ps before Qs.)

Figure 2 | An Individual Supply Curve

BP's Individual Supply Curve:

How much gasoline is it willing to supply at each price?

Ⓐ When the price is **$1 per gallon**, BP plans to sell just **10 million gallons** per week. An individual supply curve also illustrates how the quantity a business will supply changes as the price changes. If the price rises to **$2 per gallon**, the quantity supplied will rise to **15 million gallons** per week; at a price of **$3 per gallon**, it will rise to **20 million gallons**; and so on.

Ⓑ At very **low prices—below $1 per gallon**—BP will stop producing gas, and so the quantity supplied is zero.

Ⓒ The **individual supply curve** shows the quantity of gas that BP is willing to sell, at each price. It is an upward-sloping curve: the higher the price, the higher the quantity supplied.

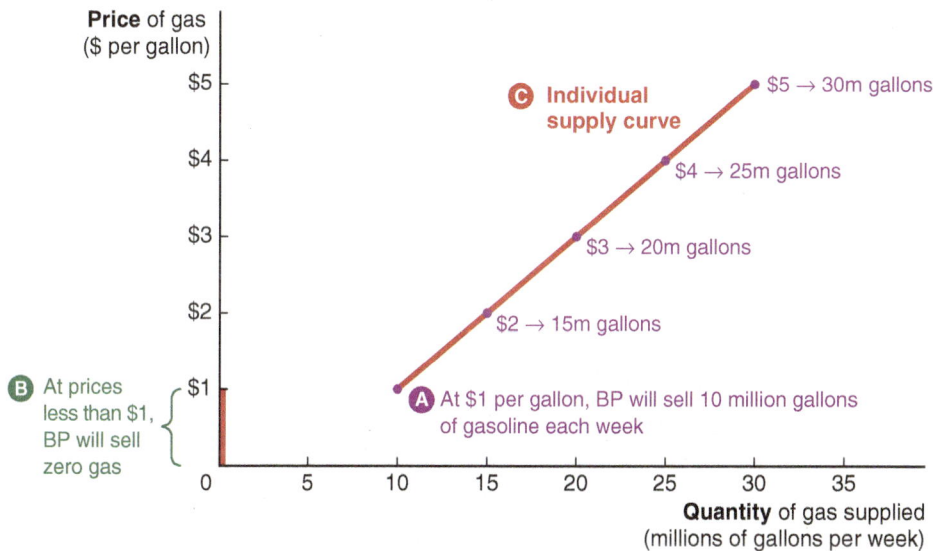

Each bullet point in Shannon's memo represents a separate point on her company's individual supply curve. The first bullet point says that at a price of $1 per gallon, BP plans to produce 10 million gallons of gas per week. This point is plotted at the lower left of Figure 2 — simply look across from the price of $1 (on the vertical axis) to the quantity of 10 million gallons of gas (on the horizontal axis), and you'll find it graphed as the first point. The next bullet point in the memo is plotted as the next point to the right: When the price rises to $2 per gallon, BP plans to increase the quantity supplied to 15 million gallons of gas per week. Each subsequent point shows that as the price rises, the quantity BP plans to supply also rises, all the way up to the final point, where a price of $5 per gallon leads Shannon to recommend that BP supply 30 million gallons of gas per week. Finally, we connect these dots in order to estimate the quantity supplied at prices in between those mentioned in Shannon's memo. This line is BP's individual supply curve, and it illustrates the quantity the company will supply, at each price.

Notice the final bullet point in Shannon's memo: It says that when the price falls below $1, the company should supply zero gas. Why? For any company, there's a point where the price is sufficiently low that your best choice is to minimize your losses by temporarily shutting down operations until the price rises again. This is illustrated by the vertical red line on the far left of Figure 2, which shows that if the price is between $0 and $0.99, BP plans to supply zero gallons of gas.

An individual supply curve holds other things constant. The supply curve shown in Figure 2 plots the amount of gas BP will supply at different prices, given current

Which should you keep, and which should you sell?

economic conditions. But if something important were to change — say, the price of crude oil rose, or the wages of refinery workers fell — BP would change its plans, and those new plans would result in a new supply curve. This is why we say that an individual supply curve shows the quantity of gas that her company is willing to sell at each price, *holding other things constant*. Of course, the interdependence principle reminds us that things other than price can influence supply. But for now, we're "holding other things constant," so that we can focus on what happens when the price — and only the price — changes. Stay tuned, though, because later in this chapter we'll analyze how shifts in these other factors can cause the supply curve to shift.

The individual supply curve is upward-sloping. Notice that the individual supply curve in Figure 2 rises upward as you look from left to right. It is *upward-sloping* because at higher gas prices, BP plans to supply a larger quantity. This makes sense — if each gallon brings a higher price, selling extra gallons of gas will be more profitable, and so BP should do more of it. (I'll call this supply curve "upward-sloping" even though it's vertical for prices below $1, because eventually higher prices led to a larger quantity supplied.)

Not all businesses go through the careful planning process that BP does. But even so, each of them still has an individual supply curve. After all, every business must choose what quantity to supply when the price changes. When you graph these choices, the resulting individual supply curve illustrates the extent to which a higher price leads to a larger quantity supplied.

Do the Economics

Just as BP is making supply decisions, you are also making important supply decisions in your everyday life. Let's work through an example, and discover the shape of your individual supply curve.

At the end of this year, you'll probably have several used college textbooks. And once you've passed your exams, you'll have to choose which books to keep and which to sell to next year's students. As such, you are a supplier in the market for college textbooks. For each book, you'll have to decide whether it is worth selling, given the price. If the book is uninteresting, or if it is for a class that's not relevant for your future work, you are likely to sell it, even if you can only get a few dollars for it. But if it's a book that you'll need to refer to

---

Figure 3 | Discover Your Individual Supply Curve

Panel A: Amazon Textbook Buyback Survey

Amazon is interested in understanding how many of your used textbooks you will sell at the end of the year. Other things being equal, how many of your current textbooks do you expect to sell?

Price of used textbooks	Quantity of used textbooks you will sell this year
If the price is $5 per book	
If the price is $10 per book	
If the price is $20 per book	
If the price is $40 per book	
If the price is $60 per book	
If the price is $80 per book	
If the price is $100 per book	

Panel B: Your Individual Supply Curve

How many used textbooks are you willing to sell at each price?

To graph your individual supply curve, plot the data from your responses to the Amazon Textbook Buyback Survey.

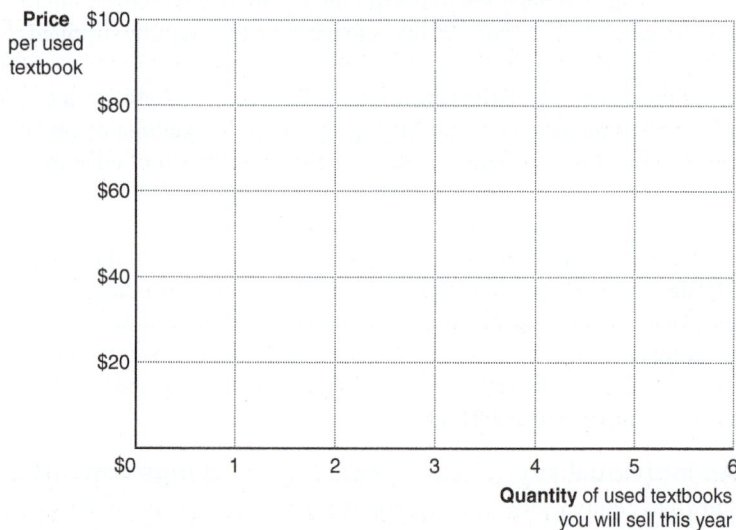

Price per used textbook: $0, $20, $40, $60, $80, $100

Quantity of used textbooks you will sell this year: 0, 1, 2, 3, 4, 5, 6

for next year's classes or later in your career, then you will be more reluctant to sell it. In fact, you may be happy to keep many of your books. But if you can get a high enough price, you'll go ahead and sell them. So the quantity of used textbooks you supply depends on the price.

Amazon launched a textbook buyback scheme, and their senior executives are trying to figure out what price they will need to offer sellers like you. One way for them to assess market conditions is to run a simple survey, like the one shown in Panel A of Figure 3.

Go ahead and fill in your answers, describing your supply plans: How many second-hand textbooks will you re-sell at the end of the year, if you're offered a price of $5 per book? What if the price is $10, $20, $30, $40, or even higher? Now, take the data from Panel A and plot your responses in Panel B of Figure 3. You have discovered your individual supply curve for textbooks. When Amazon's executives analyze your individual supply curve, they will notice that the higher the price they offer, the larger the quantity that you will supply. That is, they'll discover that individual supply curves for used textbooks are upward-sloping. ∎

The Law of Supply

You've now seen that BP will supply more gas when the price of gas is high. Likewise, you will supply more used textbooks when their price is high. In fact, economists have studied supply decisions in thousands of different markets, and they have found that there's a general tendency for the quantity supplied to be higher when the price is higher. It's an intuitive idea: If you can sell something for a higher price, you'll sell more of it (holding other things constant). This is such a general principle that economists call it the **law of supply.** This law means that supply curves are upward-sloping, because higher prices are associated with larger quantities.

You are a supplier. Let's continue thinking about the supply decisions of our favorite business, YOU, Incorporated. It turns out that YOU are making supply decisions every day. You are a supplier whenever you offer something in exchange for something else. And so figuring out your role as a supplier means answering two simple questions: What are you supplying? And in exchange for what?

If you are selling your old cell phone, then you are a supplier of cell phones. If you sold T-shirts at your band's last show, you are a supplier of merchandise. You are also a supplier when you offer services, instead of "stuff." If you have a job, you are a supplier of labor to your employer. Your economics professor is a supplier of educational services.

Asking, "In exchange for what?" tells us about the price. Sometimes the price is some amount of cash — say, if you sold the Lego minifigures you collected in middle school for $8 each on eBay, or your on-campus job pays $10 per hour. But the price isn't always measured in dollars. For instance, you might offer to help your friend with their Spanish homework, on the understanding that they will help you with your calculus. Here, you are supplying your services as an Spanish tutor. And there is a price attached to your help, even though it's not measured in dollars: You are hoping for a certain amount of calculus tutoring in return.

When you start to think like this, you'll see that you are making important supply decisions every day of your life. Even though many of these don't look like standard business decisions, you can learn to make better decisions by following the same logic that managers use when figuring out how to make good supply choices. Let's now turn to exploring that logic, working through Shannon's thoughts as she analyzed the best supply decisions for BP.

law of supply The tendency for the quantity supplied to be higher when the price is higher.

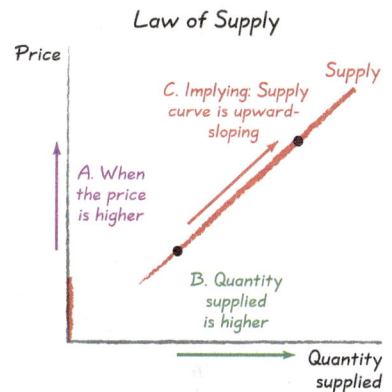

If you're willing to part with them, you, too, can be a supplier.

3.2 Your Decisions and Your Individual Supply Curve

Learning Objective *Apply the core principles to make good supply decisions.*

We've learned how to summarize your supply plans using an individual supply curve. But where do these plans come from? Let's step back to see how Shannon prepared her analysis. We'll start by digging into the best pricing decisions for BP, and then turn to how to use the core principles to guide the choice of what quantity to produce at each price.

Setting Prices in Competitive Markets

A key part of Shannon's role is understanding the competitive environment, and she has analyzed BP's position carefully. It operates in a fiercely competitive market in which dozens and dozens of refineries are producing gasoline. Those refineries are all trying to sell their gas through thousands of gas stations around the nation, and the main product they sell — gasoline — is pretty much identical. Consumers are just as happy purchasing gas refined by BP as they are purchasing gas refined by any other firm, because BP gas is neither better nor worse than gas from Exxon, Shell, or Chevron.

perfect competition Markets in which (1) all firms in an industry sell an identical good; and (2) there are many buyers and sellers, each of whom is small relative to the size of the market.

Shannon has discovered that BP operates in a market characterized by **perfect competition,** which is the special case in which

1. all businesses are selling an identical good
2. there are many sellers and many buyers, each of whom is small relative to the size of the market.

This has important implications for BP's price-setting strategy.

Perfectly competitive firms are price-takers, following the market price. When you're operating in a perfectly competitive market, your best strategy is to charge a price that is pretty much identical to whatever your competitors are charging. So, when the prevailing market price of gas is $3 per gallon, Shannon recommends that BP follow along, also selling its gas for $3.

Here's why. BP could try charging a bit more than the market price, but if it charges $3.10 when its competitors sell an identical product for $3, it will quickly lose all its customers. Alternatively, BP could try to undercut its competitors, selling its gas for $2.90 per gallon instead. But this doesn't make sense either. Because BP is small relative to the entire refinery industry, it can expand production and still continue to sell a higher quantity of gas at the market price of $3 per gallon. So the only effect of charging a price below the market price will be to reduce the profits BP will earn on each gallon of gas it produces.

price-taker Someone who decides to charge the prevailing price and whose actions do not affect the prevailing price.

Consequently, sellers in perfectly competitive markets don't spend a lot of time strategizing about price, because their best price is the market price. This makes them **price-takers,** which means they take the market price as given and just follow along. Likewise, when you're a buyer in a perfectly competitive market — say, when you're buying gas — you're acting as a price-taker, because you take the price as given and decide what quantity to buy.

Not all markets are perfectly competitive. For the rest of this chapter — indeed, throughout our analysis of supply, demand, and equilibrium — we'll focus on perfectly competitive markets in which buyers and sellers are price-takers. But I have a confession to make: Perfect competition doesn't describe most markets. Most markets involve some degree of imperfection. Perhaps they have only a handful of buyers or a handful of sellers. Or maybe they are selling a unique product, or a product with a lot of loyal fans. In these situations, buyers and sellers may no longer be price-takers.

So why are we asking you to focus on perfectly competitive markets, when the real world is usually not perfectly competitive? Partly this is because nearly all markets involve some degree of competition, and so this is a natural foundation on which to build your understanding. We'll learn how perfectly competitive markets work, and along the way we'll build the analytical foundation you'll need when you later turn to focusing on imperfectly competitive markets. Focusing on perfect competition will also help simplify your introduction to economics. Once you've learned one extreme situation — perfect competition — you'll find it easier to consider what happens in the fuzzy real world, where even though competition isn't perfect, it's still pretty fierce.

Choosing the Best Quantity to Supply

Since BP operates in a perfectly competitive market, Shannon focuses her attention on the question of what quantity to supply at any given price. She has a vast spreadsheet listing information about BP's cost of production. But how can she transform this information into a concrete plan?

Apply the core principles to your supply decisions. It's time to put yourself in Shannon's shoes and apply the core principles, so that you can figure out the plan that will yield the largest possible profit for BP. We'll start by figuring out what quantity to supply when the price of gas is $3 per gallon. If you repeat this step for the whole range of prices, you will have mapped out BP's whole supply curve.

So let's start by analyzing how many gallons of gas BP should produce when the price is $3. I've included the core principles in Figure 4 below, to remind you of how they might help you here.

Figure 4 | Applying the Core Economic Principles to Your Supply Decisions

Principle	The Idea	Applying the Principle
The marginal principle	Decisions about quantities are best made incrementally. Break "how many" questions into a series of smaller, or marginal, decisions.	Should I supply one more gallon of gas?
The cost-benefit principle	Costs and benefits are the incentives that shape decisions. You should evaluate the full set of costs and benefits of any choice, and only pursue those whose benefits are at least as large as their costs.	Is the price you can sell the extra gallon of gas for at least as much as it costs to make (its marginal cost)? If so, then yes, you want to supply it.
The opportunity cost principle	The true cost of something is the next best alternative you must give up to get it. Your decisions should reflect this opportunity cost, rather than just the out-of-pocket financial costs.	Ask, "Or what?" If my business doesn't produce this gallon of gas, how else could we use our resources? This principle helps you figure out what to count as marginal costs.
The interdependence principle	Your best choice depends on your other choices, the choices others make, developments in other markets, and expectations about the future. When any of these factors change, your best choice might change.	"Holding other things constant" means we'll put aside these other factors for now and will return to them later.

Thinking at the margin means asking: Should you produce one more? The marginal principle says that decisions about quantities are best made incrementally, and that you should break "how many" questions into a series of smaller marginal choices. Instead of asking "how many" gallons of gas to produce, ask: *Should I produce one more gallon of gas?*

Compare marginal benefit and marginal cost. The answer depends on the cost-benefit principle, which says: Yes, you should produce that additional gallon of gas if the benefit of that extra gallon exceeds the cost. That is, your decision *depends on the balance of marginal benefits and marginal costs.*

Of course, a refinery manager who's responsible for making millions of gallons of gas per day probably does not analyze her production gallon by gallon. She might think instead in terms of whether to expand annual production of gas by a million extra gallons. But we'll persist in asking whether to produce just one more gallon because the unit of measure is not all that important when you are making supply decisions. The point is that smart supply decisions focus on marginal benefits and marginal costs. This insight — that it is the marginal costs of production and the marginal benefit from selling goods (that's the price in perfectly competitive markets) that drive production decisions — is followed by most businesses that you know.

The *marginal benefit* to your firm of producing an additional gallon of gas is simply the amount of money you'll get for it. If the price of gas is $3, then the marginal benefit to

Someday, you will learn to love spreadsheets.

BP of producing another gallon of gas is $3. That is, in a perfectly competitive market, your marginal benefit is the market price.

What about the *marginal cost* — that is, the extra cost from producing one extra gallon of gas? Returning to her spreadsheets, Shannon sees that she has detailed data on the quantities of crude oil and other inputs, such as chemical additives, that will be needed in order to expand production, as well as the additional hours that BP workers will have to put in.

Your marginal costs include variable costs but exclude fixed costs. As you think about what expenses to include in your calculation of marginal cost, you should apply the opportunity cost principle, asking, "Or what?" You shouldn't just calculate the cost of producing another gallon of gas; you should compare it to the next best alternative, which is not expanding production.

variable costs Those costs — like labor and raw materials — that vary with the quantity of output you produce.

If BP expands production, it will have to buy more crude oil, buy more chemical additives, and pay its workers to work overtime. In the next best alternative — in which BP doesn't expand production — it won't need to buy this extra oil and extra chemicals, or pay these extra wages. As such, these are all opportunity costs — they're costs that BP incurs when it expands production, but wouldn't incur otherwise. These are called **variable costs,** because they *vary* with the quantity of output you produce. Your marginal costs are your additional variable costs.

Shannon's spreadsheets also show that BP incurs a range of other costs. For instance, there's the cost of the refinery structures and equipment. But these pose no opportunity cost, because BP would have to pay for its building and equipment even if it pursued its next best alternative of not expanding production. The same is true for the land that it uses and the money BP pays its top managers, because producing another gallon of gas doesn't require more land or another CEO. These are all examples of **fixed costs** that don't change when you vary the quantity of output you produce. Because you have to pay your fixed costs whether or not you expand your production, they're not part of the opportunity cost of producing more gas. Your fixed costs are irrelevant to your marginal cost.

fixed cost Those costs that don't vary when you change the quantity of output you produce.

Bottom line: As you calculate your marginal cost, make sure that it reflects only the variable costs that you'll incur from producing extra gas, and that you're excluding all fixed costs.

The Rational Rule for Sellers in Competitive Markets

It's time to put all of this advice together. We've worked through the core principles — as summarized in the flowchart below — and that led us to the conclusion that BP should keep selling additional gallons of gas as long as the price is greater than (or equal to) the marginal cost.

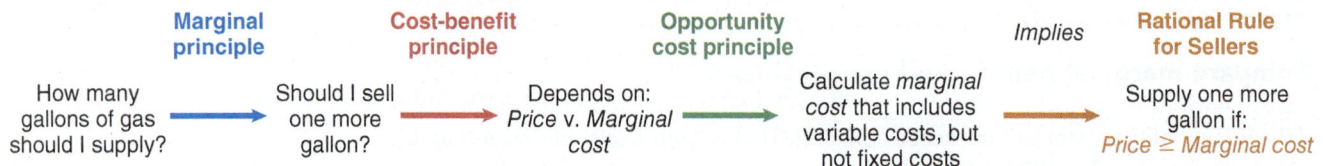

Marginal principle	**Cost-benefit principle**	**Opportunity cost principle**	*Implies*	**Rational Rule for Sellers**
How many gallons of gas should I supply?	Should I sell one more gallon?	Depends on: *Price* v. *Marginal cost*		Calculate *marginal cost* that includes variable costs, but not fixed costs	Supply one more gallon if: *Price ≥ Marginal cost*

In fact you've uncovered a pretty powerful rule, which you can apply to *any* selling decision (in perfectly competitive markets):

Rational Rule for Sellers in Competitive Markets Sell one more unit if the price is greater than (or is equal to) the marginal cost.

The **Rational Rule for Sellers in Competitive Markets:** *Sell one more unit if the price is greater than (or equal to) the marginal cost.*

The Rational Rule for Sellers puts together the advice from three of the four principles in one sentence. It takes the big question facing managers about what quantity to sell and reminds you to think at the margin, assessing whether to sell one more unit by comparing your marginal benefit (in this case, the price you'll get) with the marginal cost, recognizing that you should tally up your additional variable costs because they're the only true opportunity cost of expanding production.

Sellers in competitive markets apply this rule to their real-world supply decisions. For instance, it says to Shannon that BP should expand production if the price of gas exceeds marginal cost. Indeed, BP should keep expanding production for as long as the price continues to be at least as large as marginal cost.

Follow the Rational Rule for Sellers to maximize your profits. The Rational Rule for Sellers is good advice because it will lead you to expand production whenever it will boost your profits. After all, if the price of that extra gallon of gas exceeds the marginal cost, then producing and selling that extra gallon will lead BP's revenues to rise by at least as much as their costs. As a result, BP's profit — which is its revenues minus its costs — will rise. Indeed, if you relentlessly follow the Rational Rule for Sellers — so that you take every opportunity to supply goods when the price is at least as high as your marginal cost — you'll produce the quantity that earns your firm the largest possible profit. It's the fact that this rule maximizes your profits that makes it good advice for aspiring managers to follow.

(And if you're wondering why the Rational Rule for Sellers says to still sell an additional unit even when its price is *exactly equal* to it marginal cost, realize that doing so will neither increase nor decrease your profits. It says to continue to sell up to, *and including*, the point when price equals marginal cost, only because it will make the rest of your analysis a bit simpler.)

Keep selling until price equals marginal cost. If you follow this rule consistently, you'll continue to raise the quantity you supply until the point at which the marginal cost of the last gallon is equal to the price. Why? Just as the Rational Rule for Buyers tells you to keep buying until your marginal benefit is equal to your marginal cost (which is the price), the Rational Rule for Sellers tells you to keep selling gallons of gas until your marginal benefit (the price) is equal to your marginal cost. That means you raise the quantity of gas supplied as long as the price of each additional gallon is at least as high as the marginal cost. Consequently, you should stop increasing the quantity of gas you supply just before the marginal cost exceeds the price — which occurs in competitive markets when *price equals marginal cost.*

You might recognize this insight as applying the Rational Rule from Chapter 1, which said: "If something is worth doing, keep doing it until your marginal benefits equal your marginal costs." When you're a supplier in a competitive market, the marginal benefit of selling an additional unit is the price. As such, adapting the rule to your role as a supplier in a competitive market says you should expand production until:

$$Price = Marginal\ cost$$

Your supply curve is also your marginal cost curve. At this point, it should be clear why economists say that understanding supply is all about understanding marginal costs.

Indeed, this reveals a new perspective for thinking about supply: Your firm's individual supply curve is also its marginal cost curve. After all, your individual supply curve plots the *price* associated with each specific quantity of gas you might supply. If you keep selling until *price equals marginal cost,* then the same curve illustrates the *marginal cost* associated with each gallon of gas.

Your supply curve reveals your marginal costs. As an executive, you might want to compare your company's marginal costs to those of your rivals. Or perhaps, as an analyst tracking the industry, you might be interested in understanding a business's cost structure. Or, as a policymaker, you might need to better understand the costs of certain activities. You could try asking, but most companies will refuse to divulge this proprietary information, particularly if they're worried that doing so will put them at a competitive disadvantage. But don't let that stop you. As long as a company follows the Rational Rule for Sellers, its individual supply curve is also its marginal cost curve. This means that you can also learn about its marginal costs just by observing its selling patterns. For instance, if a refinery supplies exactly 20 million gallons of gas when the price is $3, then you can infer that the marginal cost of producing that final gallon must be roughly $3.

To maximize your profits, keep applying the Rational Rule for Sellers, continuing to produce until:

$$Price = Marginal\ cost$$

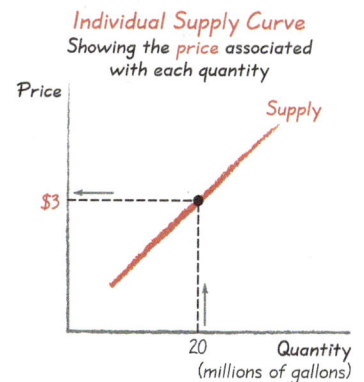

Individual Supply Curve
Showing the price associated with each quantity

+

Price = Marginal cost

↓

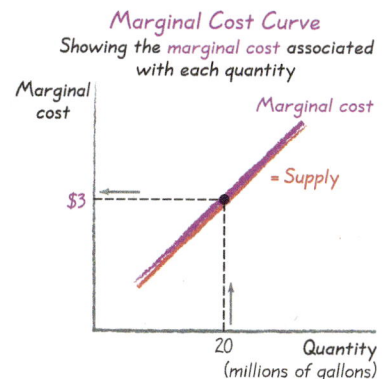

Marginal Cost Curve
Showing the marginal cost associated with each quantity

The important insight is that supply is all about marginal costs. Because a supply curve is a marginal cost curve, understanding supply is really about understanding marginal costs.

Rising Marginal Cost Explains Why Your Supply Curve Is Upward-Sloping

Recall that the law of supply says that the quantity supplied tends to be higher when the price is higher. That is, it says the supply curve is upward-sloping. But what makes the supply curve upward-sloping?

For companies that follow the Rational Rule for Sellers, the supply curve is also their marginal cost curve. This implies that the supply curve must be upward-sloping because the marginal cost curve is upward-sloping. And why is that? Because, at some point as you increase the quantity you produce, the marginal cost of producing an extra gallon of gas rises. This increasing marginal cost reflects bottlenecks that arise when you try to expand production.

Diminishing marginal product leads to rising marginal costs. Expanding your production requires increasing your use of inputs, like labor. The extra output you get from an additional unit of input — like hiring one more worker — is called the **marginal product** of that input. Most firms find that at some point, hiring additional workers yields smaller and smaller increases in output. That is, they experience **diminishing marginal product,** which occurs when the marginal product of an input declines as you use more of it. (Note that diminishing marginal product doesn't mean that extra inputs will *reduce* your output. Rather, it says that the extra output produced by the next worker you hire won't be quite *as large* as the extra output produced by the previous worker you hired.)

In the short run, diminishing marginal product can occur when some of your inputs are fixed. Extra workers around a fixed office space can make it crowded and noisy, making it hard for anyone to get anything done. In a factory, extra workers might spend more time waiting for others to finish using equipment. A farmer can sow more seed, but with a fixed plot of land, that will lead the plants to become overcrowded, and many won't survive.

In the longer run, you can expand production by increasing all your inputs — hiring more workers and buying more equipment and land. But the new workers you hire will have less experience and so will take longer to get things done. It will be hard to find new land that's as fertile or well-located as your existing land. Expanding your company's research and development team won't boost your output by much if new ideas become harder to find. And managing a large workforce can become more unwieldy, creating coordination problems as your company's top management is stretched thin. Whatever the cause, the result is that at some point, adding extra inputs won't produce as much extra output, and so your marginal costs will rise.

> **marginal product** The increase in output that arises from an additional unit of an input, like labor.
>
> **diminishing marginal product** The marginal product of an input declines as you use more of that input.

EVERYDAY Economics   **The diminishing marginal product of homework**

You've probably experienced diminishing marginal product while writing a paper for a class. The first day's work might be super-productive; you gather your research, put your notes together, and start on a rough draft. On the second day, you expand on a few sections, improve your draft, and work out the inconsistencies. On the third day, you're starting with a pretty good paper, and while you can find ways to improve it, you're not making it much better. You could keep working on it forever, and each day you could probably find another small way to improve it. But you're experiencing diminishing marginal product as the amount that each successive day's work will boost your grade gets smaller and smaller. At some point the marginal product of an additional day's work on the paper is so low that you're better off just handing it in and catching up on your other subjects. ∎

Rising input costs also lead to rising marginal costs. There's a second reason your marginal costs might rise as you increase production: The cost of your inputs might rise. As you buy more of an input, its opportunity cost — what the input could be used for instead — rises. You may be required to pay time and a half in order to get your staff to work overtime. Or perhaps you'll need to offer higher wages to attract more workers. It may also become harder to find workers or other inputs, raising search costs. Or perhaps inputs can be found only farther away, raising transportation costs. The result is that at some point, the rising costs of your inputs might lead your marginal costs to rise.

Supply curves are upward-sloping because of rising marginal costs due to:
1. diminishing marginal product.
2. rising input costs.

🔗 **See the Connections**

Follow the Rational Rule for Sellers in Competitive Markets ➡️ *Price = Marginal cost* (the Rational Rule, applied to sellers) ➡️ Your supply curve is your marginal cost curve ➡️ Your supply curve is upward-sloping because of rising marginal costs

How Realistic Is This Theory of Supply?

By now, you may be scratching your head and asking: Do managers really behave this way? At a large firm like BP, they probably do — graduates with skills like Shannon's are in high demand, particularly by larger and more sophisticated businesses. But what about other companies?

As sellers experiment, they may come to act as if they follow the core principles. Many sellers — particularly smaller businesses — can't or won't engage in the kind of deep analytics used by companies like BP. But chances are they do something simpler instead: They experiment with quantity, producing a bit more or a bit less each week to see how it affects their profits. This process of experimentation leads their managers to continue to make better decisions, until they've eventually discovered the quantity that maximizes their profits. The Rational Rule for Sellers is valuable, because it provides a more direct path to figuring out the quantity that will maximize profits in a competitive market. But ultimately, the managers who experiment their way to the profit-maximizing outcome will end up making exactly the same supply choices as if they were following this rule. So if you need to figure out what choices a manager will make, the Rational Rule for Sellers will provide a pretty good forecast.

Survival of the fittest will weed out bad managers. There's also an evolutionary force that leads most businesses to ultimately follow the Rational Rule for Sellers. Because it leads businesses to maximize profits, those who follow the Rational Rule for Sellers will be the most successful. Other business decisions that lead to lower profitability will likely ultimately go out of business. You can think of this as a version of "survival of the fittest": Businesses that make decisions that yield outcomes similar to the Rational Rule for Sellers — that is, that get closer to maximizing their profits — will survive. Businesses that make worse decisions are more likely to fail. And so whether intentionally or by accident, the businesses that survive make decisions *as if* they were following the Rational Rule for Sellers.

Thinking through the principles provides useful advice and helpful forecasts. The Rational Rule for Sellers is important for two reasons. First, it provides useful advice to sellers, guiding them toward decisions that will earn their businesses the largest possible profit. Read up on companies that you admire, and you'll discover that they keep a laser-like focus on their marginal costs when making supply decisions, just as the rule suggests.

It's also useful for a second reason: If you need to forecast the supply decisions of a savvy manager, it's a good bet that they are thinking through the Rational Rule for Sellers and focusing on marginal costs. And if your competitors or suppliers don't want to reveal their marginal costs to you, you can still infer what those costs are by analyzing their supply decisions. Since their individual supply curve is their marginal cost curve, their supply decisions reveal their marginal costs. This will be a useful insight as we turn to analyzing how sellers as a group combine to shape market supply.

3.3 # Market Supply: What the Market Sells

Learning Objective *Add up individual supply to discover market supply.*

So far, we've focused on the supply decisions of an individual firm. Now it's time to analyze *market supply* — the total quantity of an item supplied across all firms in the market. Just as your company's individual supply curve illustrates the quantity that an individual business will supply at each price, the **market supply curve** plots the total quantity that the entire market — including all producers — will supply, at each price.

market supply curve A graph plotting the total quantity of an item supplied by the entire market, at each price.

From Individual Supply to Market Supply

Just as we built market demand curves by adding up individual demand, we build market supply curves by adding up the individual supply curves of all potential suppliers.

Market supply is the sum of the quantity supplied by each seller. For each price, the market supply curve illustrates the total quantity supplied by the market. This means that you'll need to figure out the total quantity supplied when the price is $1, then $2, then $3, and so on. To find the total quantity supplied at a given price, simply add up the quantity supplied by each individual supplier.

There's a shortcut you can use if all the suppliers are quite similar. For example, if 100 refineries are making the same supply decisions as BP, then at any given price, the quantity supplied will be 100 times the quantity BP supplies. This relationship between individual and market supply is shown in Figure 5. Because the market supply curve is built

---

Figure 5 | **The Market Supply Curve for Gasoline in the United States**

Market supply plots the total quantity supplied across all sellers, at each price.

Ⓐ **Individual supply** refers to the quantity an individual business will supply at each price. Plotting these numbers yields the **individual supply curve**.
Ⓑ The market consists of **100 similar suppliers,** and so the total quantity supplied by the market at any given price will be 100 times larger.
Ⓒ Plotting the **market supply** at each price yields the **market supply curve**.

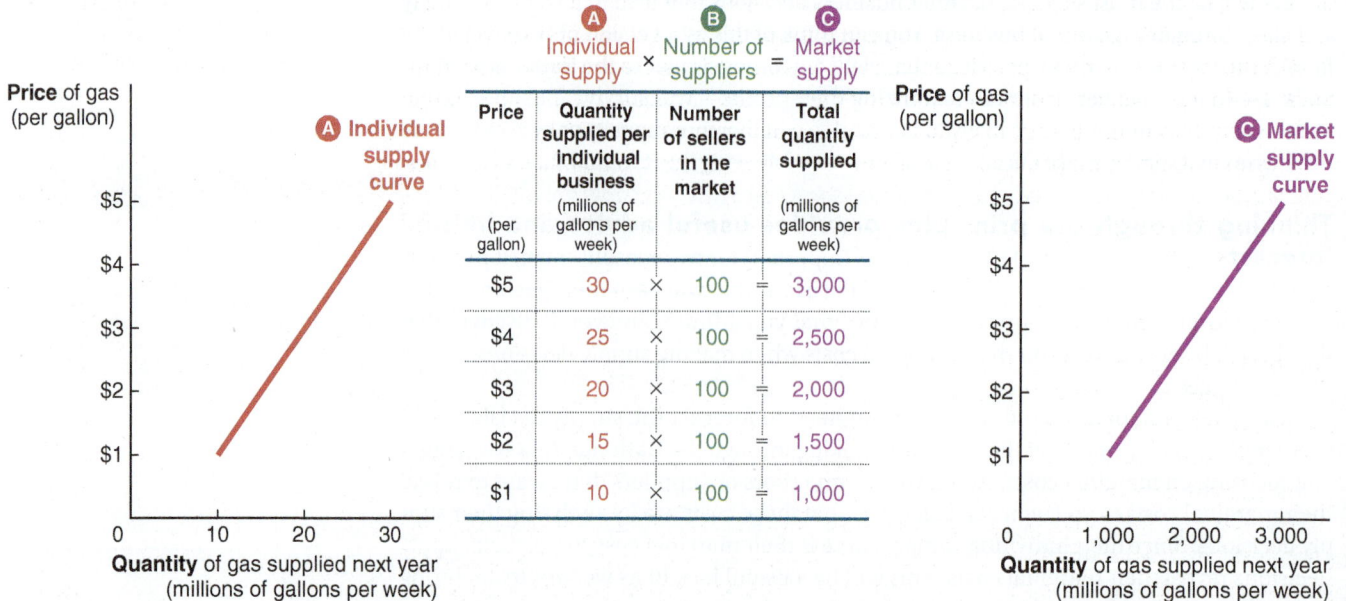

| Ⓐ Individual supply | × | Ⓑ Number of suppliers | = | Ⓒ Market supply |

Price (per gallon)	Quantity supplied per individual business (millions of gallons per week)	Number of sellers in the market	Total quantity supplied (millions of gallons per week)
$5	30 ×	100 =	3,000
$4	25 ×	100 =	2,500
$3	20 ×	100 =	2,000
$2	15 ×	100 =	1,500
$1	10 ×	100 =	1,000

Price of gas (per gallon) — Ⓐ **Individual supply curve**

Quantity of gas supplied next year (millions of gallons per week)

Price of gas (per gallon) — Ⓒ **Market supply curve**

Quantity of gas supplied next year (millions of gallons per week)

from individual supply curves, the same factors that shape individual supply (such as rising marginal costs) also shape market supply.

How market analysts estimate supply curves. Estimating market supply curves in the real world is somewhat more complicated, as suppliers are not typically identical to each other. As such, when you want to assess market supply, you'll need to figure out how much each potential supplier will supply at any given price.

For example, we already know that BP produces 20 million gallons of gas when the price of gas is $3. But how many other businesses are also producing gas? And how much will they each supply when the price is $3? Just as you can get a sense of market demand from surveying a subset of potential buyers, you can estimate market supply by surveying a sample of businesses, asking how much they will each supply at any given price. A comprehensive survey can illustrate how different segments of the market will increase the quantity supplied as the price changes. The tricky part is that you have to survey not only those businesses that are currently supplying gas, but also those businesses that might enter the market when the price is high.

The Market Supply Curve Is Upward-Sloping

The market supply curve in Figure 5 shows that a higher price of gas leads to a higher total quantity of gas to be supplied, and hence the market supply curve is upward-sloping. Economists have found that in virtually every market, the higher the price, the greater the quantity supplied. That is, the market supply curve obeys the law of supply.

There are two reasons why a higher price leads to a larger quantity supplied to the market:

Reason 1: A higher price leads individual businesses to supply a larger quantity. When the price of the good your business sells is higher, you'll supply a larger quantity. Indeed, this is exactly what the individual supply curve shows. And because the market supply curve is built by adding up individual supply at each price, it inherits many of the characteristics of those individual supply curves, including their upward slope.

Reason 2: A higher price means more businesses are supplying their goods and services; a lower price means fewer businesses are doing so. There's a second dynamic to consider: A higher price means that it's more profitable to be a supplier in your industry. That's the sort of signal that leads existing firms to expand into your market, or new entrepreneurs to start new businesses. As a result, a higher price leads to more suppliers, leading to a larger quantity supplied.

On the flip side, a lower price means fewer businesses will be profitable, and thus fewer businesses will be willing to supply their goods and services. That, in turn, helps explain why a lower price leads to a smaller total quantity being supplied.

As you evaluate market supply, make sure that your analysis accounts for both the choices that existing businesses make and also for whether new businesses will enter the market or existing businesses will exit.

> Why the market supply curve is upward-sloping:
> 1. A higher price leads individual sellers to increase supply.
> 2. A higher price means it's more profitable to be a supplier; a lower price means it's less profitable.

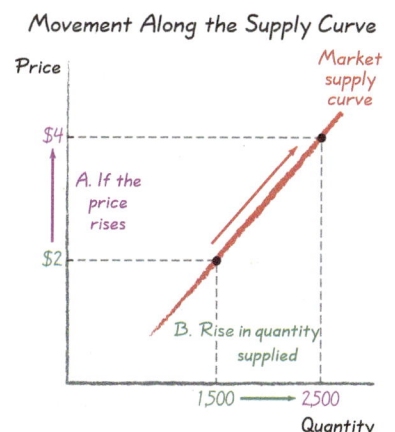

Movements Along the Supply Curve

The market supply curve is useful because it aggregates and summarizes the behavior of their competitors, showing the total quantity supplied across all sellers. To forecast the total quantity supplied in your market, simply locate the price on the vertical axis, then look across until you hit the supply curve, and finally look straight down to the quantity on the horizontal axis for your answer.

For example, the market supply curve shown on the right of Figure 5 shows that at $2 per gallon, the market supplies 1,500 million gallons of gas. To figure out what happens when the price rises to $4, find $4 on the vertical axis, look across to where it hits the market

Movement Along the Supply Curve

supply curve, and then look down at the horizontal axis to see that the new quantity of gas supplied is 2,500 million gallons. Just as the law of supply suggests, a higher price led to a rise in the quantity supplied from 1,500 million to 2,500 million gallons per week.

Notice that a price change led to a movement from one point on the market supply curve to another point along the same curve. That is, a price change causes movement from one point on a fixed supply curve to another point on the same curve. We use very specific terminology to keep this clear: A change in prices causes **movement along the supply curve,** yielding a **change in the quantity supplied.** (This is just like demand, where a change in price causes movement along the demand curve, yielding a change in the quantity demanded.)

movement along the supply curve A price change causes movement from one point on a fixed supply curve to another point on the same curve.

change in the quantity supplied The change in quantity associated with movement along a fixed supply curve.

3.4 What Shifts Supply Curves?

Learning Objective *Understand what factors shift supply curves.*

So far we've considered how the quantity supplied varies with the price of a good, *holding other things constant*. We applied the opportunity cost principle, the cost-benefit principle, and the marginal principle, and learned how the quantity supplied varies with the price. Now it's time to bring in the interdependence principle and ask: What happens when factors other than price change?

The Interdependence Principle and Shifting Supply Curves

The interdependence principle reminds you that your best choice as a seller depends on many other factors beyond price, and when these other factors change, so might your supply decisions. For instance, if the price of crude oil — which is an input into gasoline — rises, Shannon would recommend that BP revise its supply plans. She would also revise BP's supply plans if the engineering division discovers more efficient production processes, or if it becomes more profitable to shift to a different line of business.

In each case, the quantity that BP is willing to supply at any given price would change. They're all examples of changing conditions leading sellers to revise their supply plans, and their new plans create a new supply curve. When the supply curve moves, we refer to it as a **shift in the supply curve.** Because your supply curve is also your marginal cost curve, any factor that changes your marginal costs will shift your supply curve.

As Figure 6 illustrates, a rightward shift is an **increase in supply,** because at each and every price, the quantity supplied is higher. A leftward shift is a **decrease in supply,** because the quantity supplied is lower at each and every price.

shift in the supply curve A movement of the supply curve itself.

increase in supply A shift of the supply curve to the right.

decrease in supply A shift of the supply curve to the left.

Five Factors That Shift the Supply Curve

The interdependence principle tells us that suppliers' choices depend on many other factors, and when those other factors shift, so will their selling plans, thereby shifting the supply curve. The key factors that cause the supply curve to shift are:

1. Input prices
2. Productivity and technology
3. Prices of related outputs ⎫ Shift individual supply and hence
4. Expectations ⎭ market supply
5. The type and number of sellers ⟶ Only shifts market supply

Changes in any of the first four of these factors shift individual supply curves, and because the market supply curve is built up from individual supply curves, these factors

Figure 6 | Shifts of the Supply Curve

Panel A: An Increase in Supply

Ⓐ An **increase in supply shifts the supply curve to the right**, leading to a higher quantity supplied at each and every price.

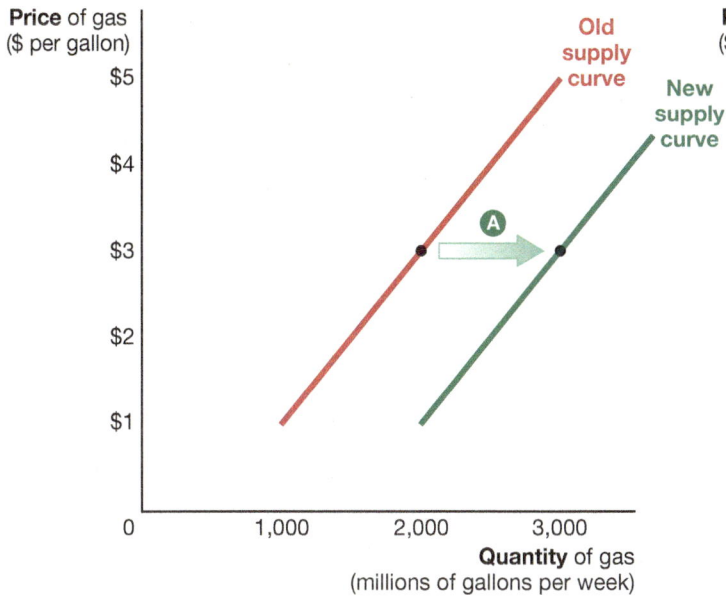

Panel B: A Decrease in Supply

Ⓑ A **decrease in supply shifts the supply curve to the left**, leading to a lower quantity supplied at each and every price.

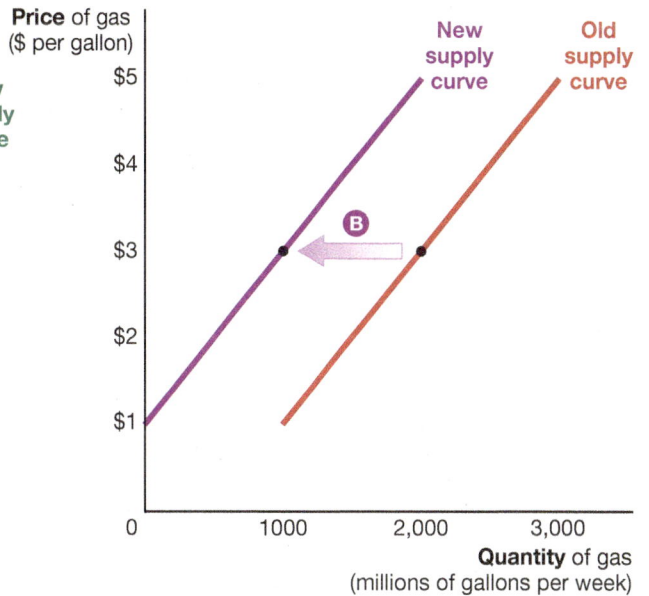

shift the market supply curve, too. The fifth and final factor — the type and number of sellers — only shifts the market supply curve.

As we now turn to analyzing how each of these factors leads to a shift in supply, a recurrent theme will be that any factor that changes marginal costs — including opportunity costs — will cause a shift in supply.

Supply shifter 1: Input prices. The interdependence principle reminds us that the choices other businesses make affect your decisions. When your suppliers change the prices of your inputs, they change your marginal costs, and this will shift your supply curve.

For instance, refineries have two key inputs: crude oil and labor. If the price of either of these inputs rises, then so will BP's marginal cost of producing each additional gallon. And that in turn lowers the quantity BP is willing to supply at any given price. Another way to say this is that a rise in marginal costs causes the price associated with any point on the supply curve to rise, because the marginal cost curve is the supply curve. This change is a leftward shift in BP's supply curve. Likewise, a decline in input costs will shift BP's supply curve to the right.

More generally, changes in any input price will cause your supply curve to shift — whether it's a change in the price of an input like crude oil or a change in the hourly wage you pay your workers. There's also a global dimension to this: If your inputs are purchased internationally, then changes in the foreign exchange rate will also affect your costs, shifting your supply curve.

Supply shifter 2: Productivity and technology. Productivity growth — producing more output with fewer inputs — is a key force reducing marginal costs through time. And because your supply curve is also your marginal cost curve, higher productivity leads to an increase in supply, shifting the supply curve to the right.

For instance, if BP adopts new refinery processes that allow it to produce the same amount of gasoline with fewer workers or less crude oil, this will reduce its marginal costs. Because new production techniques will be adopted only if they reduce costs, this process of ongoing improvement generally lowers costs, shifting the supply curve to the right.

Productivity growth is often driven by technological change, including the invention and adoption of new types of machinery, processes, or management techniques.

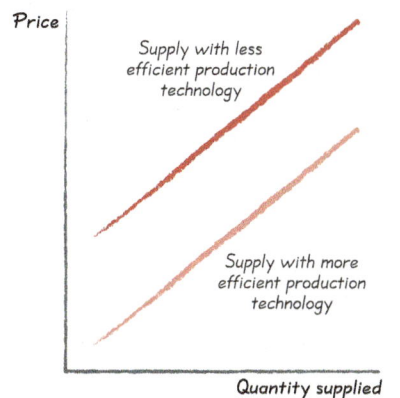

The **interdependence principle** is critical to these shifts, because disruptive technological change in one industry is often due to developments in other industries. For instance, the internet was first developed as a military communications network, but it has since revolutionized production, sales, and distribution in industries as diverse as music, media, travel, and manufacturing. Productivity gains may also reflect your business's investments in research and development.

There's also a natural tendency for productivity to rise through time due to learning by doing, as managers learn what does and doesn't work, thereby discovering further efficiencies. This is one reason businesses grow over time: As they become more efficient, their supply curve shifts to the right.

Supply shifter 3: Other opportunities (prices of related outputs).

The **interdependence principle** also emphasizes the connections between different markets. As a supplier, your decisions are interdependent because there are many different lines of business you could engage in. For instance, BP can use its oil refineries to produce gasoline or to produce alternative products such as diesel fuel. If the price of diesel fuel rises enough, it will be more profitable for BP to produce diesel than to produce gasoline. This will lead BP to switch some production from gasoline to diesel, shifting its gasoline supply curve to the left. When the price increase of one good (like diesel) decreases your supply of another (like gasoline), we call them **substitutes-in-production.**

Typically, substitutes-in-production arise when you can use your resources to produce alternative goods (like gasoline versus diesel). This is the **opportunity cost principle** at work, as a higher price of diesel raises the opportunity cost of producing gasoline. This higher marginal cost of producing gasoline (remember: marginal cost includes opportunity costs, and not just out-of-pocket costs) causes BP to decrease its supply of gasoline.

By contrast, goods that are **complements-in-production** are usually produced together. For instance, asphalt — the surface used to make our roads — is a natural byproduct of refineries. So if the price of asphalt rises, it becomes more profitable to operate a refinery, even if the price of gasoline remains unchanged. As a result, an increase in the price of complements-in-production (like asphalt) leads BP to increase its supply of gasoline. You can think of the extra revenues from asphalt as effectively lowering the marginal cost of producing gasoline, shifting the supply curve to the right.

A warning: Don't confuse the complements (products that you might consume together, such as a hot dog and a hot dog bun), that shift demand curves with complements-in-production (products you might produce together, such as gasoline and asphalt), which shift supply curves. Likewise, don't confuse the substitutes (goods you might consume as a substitute for each other, like buying pizza instead of a hot dog) that shift demand curves with substitutes-in-production (alternative uses of resources you use for production, like producing diesel instead of gasoline), which shift supply curves.

Bottom line: Supply will increase (shift to the right) if the prices of goods that are substitutes-in-production fall or if the prices of complements-in-production rise. And, supply will decrease (shift to the left) if the prices of substitutes-in-production rise or the prices of complements-in-production fall.

Supply shifter 4: Expectations.

Recall from the **interdependence principle** that your decisions are linked through time. In the short run, if you expect the price of your product to rise next year, you can increase your profits by storing it and selling it next year. This will decrease your supply this year (shifting your supply curve to the left) and increase your supply next year (shifting next year's supply curve to the right). You can see this as an application of the **opportunity cost principle**, as the opportunity cost of selling your goods this year is selling them next year. And so expectations of higher gas prices in the future raises the opportunity cost of supplying gas this year, leading to a decrease in this year's supply.

Of course, this matters only for goods that can be stored for later use. For example, future price changes will cause a shift in the supply of gasoline (which is storable), but not fresh fish (which isn't). When goods are storable, your decisions about how much to *produce* this year can be separated from your decisions about the quantity to *supply* for sale. This distinction is particularly important when you expect prices to change. For instance,

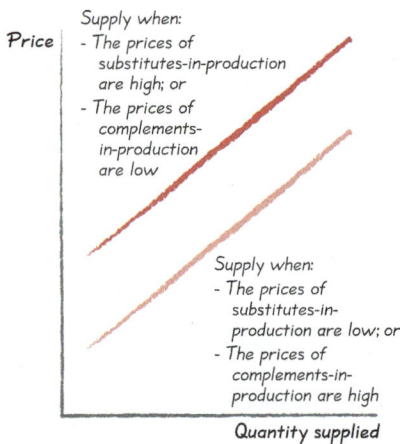

substitutes-in-production
Alternative uses of your resources. Your supply of a good will decrease if the price of a substitute-in-production rises.

complements-in-production
Goods that are made together. Your supply of a good will increase if the price of a complement-in-production rises.

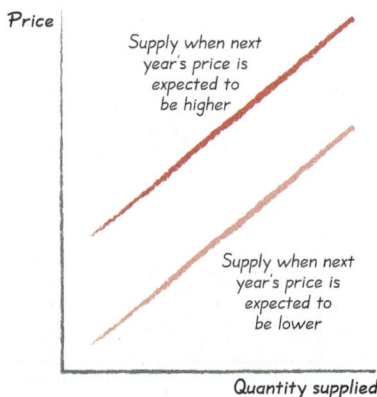

when BP expects a higher gas price next year, it will increase production this year but decrease its supply this year, storing unsold gasoline to sell later at a higher price. Next year, when the higher price arrives, it will increase both its production and supply.

If BP expects higher prices to persist in the long run, it will buy more equipment and hire more workers, which will increase both its production and its supply. Thus, the expectation of higher prices will decrease supply only in the short term; in the long run, businesses will invest in expanding capacity, increasing supply.

Supply shifter 5: The type and number of sellers. The final supply shift to consider is the type and number of sellers. Let's start by looking at what happens when the number of sellers changes. If new sellers enter the market, then the supply from these new sellers needs to be added to the market supply. As new sellers enter the market, they increase the total quantity supplied at each price, shifting the supply curve to the right. Similarly, if sellers shut their doors, exiting the market, the supply curve will shift to the left. Because the entry and exit decisions of businesses are driven by expected future profits, any factor that changes expected future profits will change the number of suppliers in the market and thereby shift the market supply curve.

The type of sellers matters too. Because the market supply adds up the total amount supplied by all the sellers in a market, if those sellers change, so will the market supply curve. If the market is composed of different types of businesses, then the composition of market supply will change.

It's worth noting that the first four supply shifters impact market supply because they shift individual supply curves. Each factor that leads your business to increase supply will likely also lead your competitors to increase supply. Because the market supply curve is simply the sum of individual supply curves, each of these factors will also shift the market supply curve. However, the fifth shifter — the type and number of sellers — doesn't involve shifts of individual supply curves. Changes in the type and number of sellers shift only the market supply curve.

When things other than price change, your supply curve may shift. Your individual supply curve is your marginal cost curve, so anything that shifts your marginal costs will shift your supply curve. Indeed, each of the four factors that shift individual supply curves are relevant because they change your marginal costs. Changes in the prices of your inputs and your business's productivity both directly change your marginal costs. Changes in the prices of alternative outputs (that is, of substitutes-in-production and complements-in-production) and expectations about future prices also shift your marginal costs, by changing the opportunity cost of what you're producing and when you sell it.

Because the market supply curve is built from individual supply curves, these four factors shift the market supply curve, too. You can usually figure out the direction of the shift by remembering that any increase in marginal costs leads to a decrease in supply (shifting the curve to the left), while a decrease in marginal costs leads to an increase in supply (shifting the curve to the right). The fifth and final factor — the type and number of sellers — also shifts the market supply curve, but not individual supply curves. Keep these factors in mind as we now return to exploring the distinction between movements along the supply curve versus shifts of the supply curve.

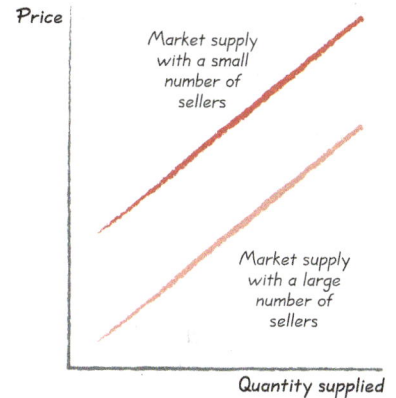

Five factors shift the market supply curve:
1. Input prices
2. Productivity and technology
3. Prices of related outputs
4. Expectations
5. The type and number of sellers
. . . and not a change in price.

3.5 Shifts versus Movements Along Supply Curves

Learning Objective *Distinguish between movements along a supply curve and shifts of supply curves.*

Supply curves are useful tools for analyzing how changing market conditions shape the quantity that businesses supply. But it's important to distinguish between *movements along* a supply curve and *shifts of* a supply curve. Here's a simple rule of thumb: *If the only thing that's change is the price, then you're thinking about a movement along the supply curve. But when other market conditions change, you need to think about shifts of the supply curve.*

Movements Along the Supply Curve

The supply curve doesn't shift following a price change because the supply curve already summarizes how much a business will change the quantity it supplies if the price changes. Think back to Shannon's memo (way back in Figure 1), in which she laid out the quantity she recommends BP supply at each price. A price change won't lead her to revise her memo — after all, the point of that memo was to lay out a plan for how BP should respond to different prices. And because BP's individual supply curve simply plots the plans outlined in Shannon's memo, if these plans don't shift, neither will its individual supply curve.

If individual supply curves don't shift following a price change, then neither will the market supply curve. The point is that a market supply curve summarizes how all potential suppliers plan to respond to different prices; if none of their individual plans shift, then the market supply curve won't shift.

The supply curve is useful precisely because you can use it to assess the consequences of a price change. For instance, Panel A in Figure 7 shows that when the price of gas is $2, the total quantity supplied by the market is 1.5 billion gallons per week. It also shows that when the price of gas is $4, the quantity supplied rises to 2.5 billion gallons per week. As you can see, this price change leads to a movement along the supply curve. This analysis shows that a higher price leads to a rise in the quantity supplied.

Figure 7 | Movement Along a Supply Curve versus Shifts of the Supply Curve

Panel A: When the Price Changes:

Movement Along the Supply Curve

Ⓐ A **change in price**, from $2 to $4 per gallon.
Ⓑ Causes a **movement along the supply curve**.
Ⓒ Leading to a **change in the quantity supplied**, raising the quantity supplied from 1.5 to 2.5 billion gallons per week.

Panel B: When Other Factors Change:

Shifts of the Supply Curve

Ⓐ A **decrease in supply** shifts the supply curve to the left, decreasing the quantity supplied at each and every price.
Ⓑ An **increase in supply** shifts the supply curve to the right, increasing the quantity supplied at each and every price.

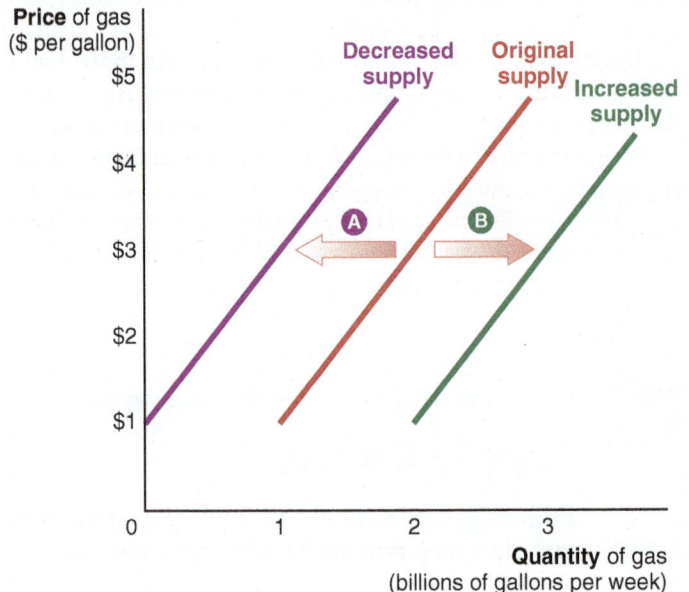

Shifts in Supply

When other factors change — factors other than price — you should revisit your plans about the quantity you'll supply at each price. For example, a change in the price of BP's inputs, its productivity, its other options for production, or its expectations about future prices would lead Shannon to revise BP's supply plans. These factors will change the quantity that BP supplies at any given price, and as a result, they'll shift the supply curve. In order for a specific change in market conditions to shift your supply curve, it has to change your supply plans.

Remember that your supply curve is also your marginal cost curve, and so anything that changes your marginal costs will shift your supply curve. As you think about whether your costs have changed, make sure to think about both your out-of-pocket costs and your opportunity costs. If your marginal costs and hence your supply plans shift, then your supply curve will shift, as shown in Panel B of Figure 7. Lower marginal costs make it profitable to sell a larger quantity at any given price and so will lead to an increase in supply, shifting the supply curve to the right. By contrast, higher marginal costs mean that it's no longer profitable to produce as large a quantity at any given price and so will lead to a decrease in supply, shifting the supply curve to the left.

Shifts in supply are all about the interdependence principle: Your best supply decisions depend on many other factors, and when those factors change, so will your supply curve. The easy way to assess which factors cause the supply curve to shift is to remember the five supply shifters described in the last section: Input prices; Productivity and technology; Other opportunities and the price of related outputs; Expectations; and Type and number of sellers. And here's a hint that will help you remember all five of these: Their first letters spell out I, POET. So when it comes to memorizing the five factors that shift the supply curve, just remember you're a poet and then you'll know it.

3.6 Tying It Together

The Principles That Guide Demand Also Guide Supply

I bet you've noticed some similarities between this chapter, which analyzed supply and seller's decisions, and the previous chapter, which analyzed demand and buyer's decisions. There's a good reason for this — the forces that drive supply and demand are very closely related. This is best illustrated by a simple thought experiment involving a brief detour to Mars.

But let's start on Earth. Think about a simple transaction, such as when you pull into my gas station and buy 10 gallons of gas for $30. (I don't actually own a gas station, but let's pretend for a moment that I do.) If you're like most economics students, you'll analyze this by noting that you are buying gas and I am selling gas. Consequently, we can analyze this transaction by exploring your demand for gas and my supply of gas.

Now consider how a Martian — who understands neither money nor gas — might view the same transaction. They might think that I am trying to buy your dollar bills and you are willing to sell them to me. How will I pay for your dollar bills? Why, with gas, of course. Viewed this way, I am the buyer who has a demand for your dollar bills, and you are the seller who is willing to supply them to me if I'm willing to pay you enough gallons of gas.

Neither the Martian's nor the Earthling's interpretation is wrong. You are just as much a buyer of gas as you are a seller of dollar bills. And I am just as much a seller of gas as a buyer of dollar bills. When you think about it this way, it's no surprise that the same principles that animate our study of demand are also essential to understanding supply.

This similarity makes learning supply and demand a lot easier. In reality, only one set of principles governs the decisions you make as both a buyer and a seller. In our analysis of both supply and demand decisions, we used the same four core principles of economics to analyze how to make good decisions. Figure 8 highlights how these same foundations lead to some striking parallels between making good decisions as a seller and making good decisions as a buyer. It also highlights crucial differences, the most important of which is that we usually consider demand to be motivated by a desire by consumers to maximize economic surplus, while businesses on the supply side are trying to maximize profits.

Figure 8 | The Parallels Between Demand and Supply

	Demand	Supply
Your objective	Maximize economic surplus, which is the difference between the benefit you get and the price you pay.	Maximize profits, which is the difference between your revenues and your costs.
To decide on your quantity, follow the:	Rational Rule for Buyers: Buy one more item if the marginal benefit exceeds (or is equal to) the price.	Rational Rule for Sellers in Competitive Markets: Sell one more item if the price exceeds (or is equal to) the marginal cost.
Implying that:	Your demand curve is your marginal benefit curve.	Your supply curve is your marginal cost curve.
Curve slopes	Demand curves slope down. Because of diminishing marginal benefit.	Supply curves slope up. Because of increasing marginal cost.
The market	The market demand curve is the sum of the quantity each individual consumer demands, at each particular price.	The market supply curve is the sum of the quantity each individual business supplies, at each particular price.
A rise in price causes	A movement along the demand curve, reducing the quantity demanded.	A movement along the supply curve, raising the quantity supplied.
A fall in price causes	A movement along the demand curve, raising the quantity demanded.	A movement along the supply curve, reducing the quantity supplied.
Curves are shifted by	Shifts of demand curves are caused by changes in: • Income • Preferences • Prices of substitutes or complements • Expectations • Congestion or network effects • The type and number of consumers (shifts market demand only) . . . and not by a change in market price.	Shifts of supply curves are caused by changes in: • Input prices • Productivity and technology • Prices of substitutes-in-production and complements-in-production • Expectations • The type and number of sellers (shifts market supply only) . . . and not by a change in market price.

Chapter 3 Review
Chapter at a Glance

An Individual Supply Curve
Shows the quantity supplied at each price

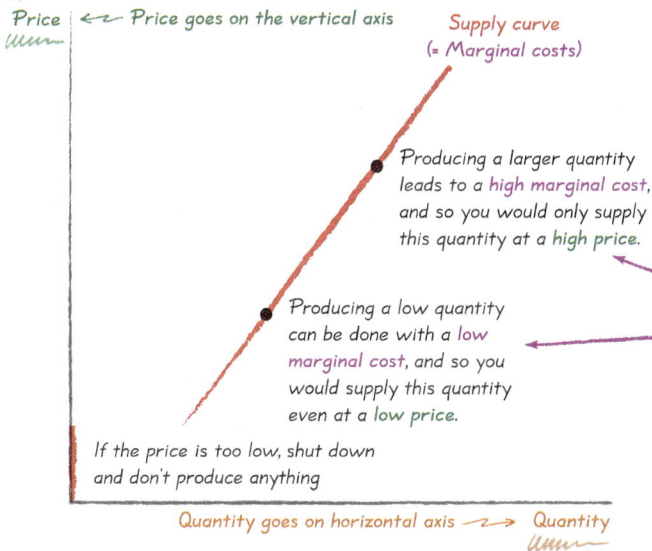

Price ← Price goes on the vertical axis

Supply curve (= Marginal costs)

Producing a larger quantity leads to a high marginal cost, and so you would only supply this quantity at a high price.

Producing a low quantity can be done with a low marginal cost, and so you would supply this quantity even at a low price.

If the price is too low, shut down and don't produce anything

Quantity goes on horizontal axis → Quantity

The Rational Rule for Sellers

Sell more of an item if its price is greater than (or equal to) marginal cost

Price = Marginal cost

Your supply curve is your marginal cost curve.

Your supply curve is upward-sloping because of increasing marginal costs.

Market Supply Curves
Add up individual supply curves to get the market supply curve. Remember to account for not only current businesses in the market, but also to consider whether new businesses may enter the market when the price rises, or whether existing business may exit the market when the price falls. The same factors that shape individual supply shape market supply.

When the Price Changes:
Movement Along the Supply Curve

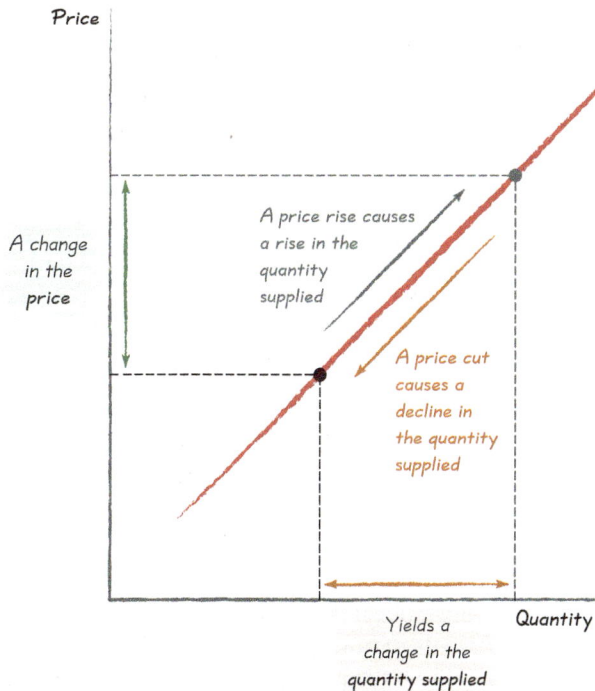

A change in the price

A price rise causes a rise in the quantity supplied

A price cut causes a decline in the quantity supplied

Yields a change in the quantity supplied

When Other Factors Change:
Shifts in the Supply Curve

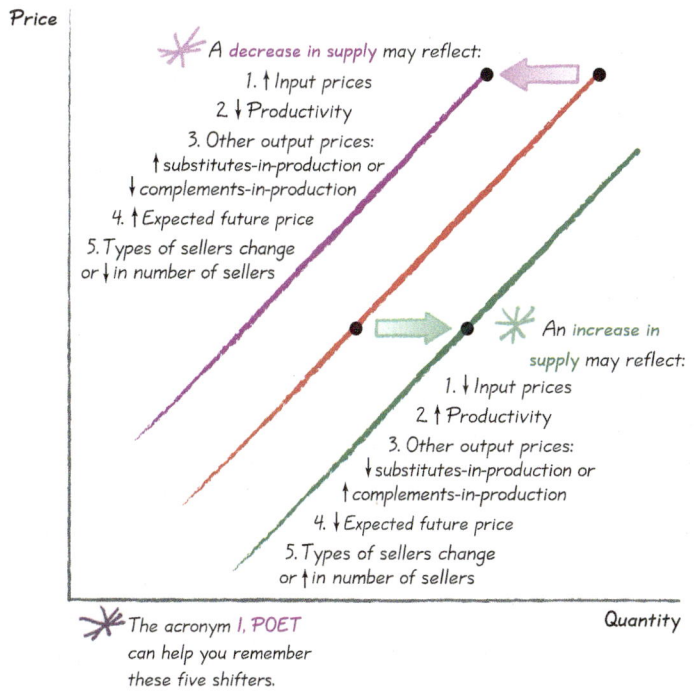

A decrease in supply may reflect:
1. ↑ Input prices
2. ↓ Productivity
3. Other output prices: ↑ substitutes-in-production or ↓ complements-in-production
4. ↑ Expected future price
5. Types of sellers change or ↓ in number of sellers

An increase in supply may reflect:
1. ↓ Input prices
2. ↑ Productivity
3. Other output prices: ↓ substitutes-in-production or ↑ complements-in-production
4. ↓ Expected future price
5. Types of sellers change or ↑ in number of sellers

The acronym I, POET can help you remember these five shifters.

Key Terms

change in the quantity supplied, 74

complements-in-production, 76

decrease in supply, 74

diminishing marginal product, 70

fixed costs, 68

increase in supply, 74

individual supply curve, 62

law of supply, 65

marginal product, 70

market supply curve, 72

movement along the supply curve, 74

perfect competition, 66

price-taker, 66

Rational Rule for Sellers in Competitive Markets, 68

shift in the supply curve, 74

substitutes-in-production, 76

variable costs, 68

Study Problems

Learning Objective 3.1 *Discover the shape of your business's individual supply curve.*

1. Most people don't manage a business, but nearly everyone acts as a seller in some context. Give some examples of how you operate as a seller in your everyday life.

2. Workers act as sellers of their time in the labor market in return for some wage. Let's discover your individual supply curve for labor. For each hourly wage rate provided in the accompanying table, determine how many hours you would be willing to work each week. Then, plot your individual supply curve for labor. Are there wage rates at which you would not be willing to work at all? Use the concept of opportunity cost to briefly explain your reasoning.

Hourly wage rate	Hours willing to work each week
$10	
$20	
$30	
$40	

3. You've probably come across locations along the highway where there's a Exxon-Mobil gas station on one side of the street and a Shell gas station on the other. The two gas stations are often selling us gasoline at exactly the same price. Why is this occurring?

4. You have landed a job as an analyst for a company that is selling a new environmentally friendly single-serve coffee maker. Using the accompanying supply plan, draw your company's individual supply curve. Does your company's supply curve follow the law of supply?

Price	Quantity supplied (thousands)
$100	0
$150	500
$200	1,000
$250	1,500
$300	2,000
$350	2,500
$400	3,000

5. Tomas is the general manager for a local automated car wash. The market he operates is perfectly competitive: Every car wash in the area is charging $7 for a car wash, which is also the marginal cost per wash. What will happen to Tomas's profits if he changes his price to $8. Why? What about a price of $5? What is his profit-maximizing price?

6. Lina is the owner and manager of a small coffee shop that employs three workers who use the shop's one coffee machine to brew coffee for paying customers. Business has begun to pick up; lines are getting longer every day in her shop. On a busy morning, Lina sees her employees scrambling to take orders, get cups, fill coffee from the coffee machine, add cream and sugar, and serve customers in a timely manner. She figures if she hires three more employees, she'll be able to sell twice as much coffee. Do you think she's likely to be right? Why or why not?

Learning Objective 3.2 *Apply the core principles to make good supply decisions.*

7. Determine which of the four core principles should be applied in the following decisions and explain how to apply them.

   a. Your boss has offered to pay you for up to five hours of overtime today. You've already been working for 10 hours and are deciding if you want to stay another hour.

   b. A local UPS manager is trying to decide if they should pay for a new truck and driver to supply a larger quantity of package deliveries each day.

8. Boeing is a producer of aircraft. Determine whether each of the following are fixed costs or variable costs for Boeing. Then, determine if they should be included in the marginal cost of producing an additional plane.

   a. The manufacturing plant used to produce the aircraft

   b. The labor used to produce the aircraft

   c. The seats that are installed in each aircraft

9. Miker, a manufacturer of generic medications, is deciding how much to charge retailers for their generic acetaminophen. The marginal cost for each bottle is provided in the accompanying table. If the price of a bottle is $7.75, how many thousands of bottles would Miker produce each day? What about if the price is $9.00 per bottle? Use the

Rational Rule for Sellers in Competitive Markets to help explain why the values are different. Finally, draw Miker's individual supply curve.

Quantity of acetaminophen (thousands of bottles)	Marginal cost (per bottle)
1	$6.00
2	$7.00
3	$7.75
4	$8.25
5	$9.00
6	$9.50

Learning Objective 3.3 *Add up individual supply to discover market supply.*

10. What is wrong with the following statement?

The market supply for natural gas is the sum of all prices that natural gas producers are willing and able to sell at for every quantity.

11. Suppose there are four gas stations in your town. The quantity of gas that each one is willing to supply per week at various prices is provided in the accompanying table. Determine the quantity supplied for the entire market at each price, and graph the market supply curve. Illustrate on your graph what happens to the supply curve when the price rises from $3 to $5.

Price per gallon	Station A	Station B	Station C	Station D
$5	8,000	5,000	6,000	9,000
$4	6,000	4,000	5,000	5,000
$3	4,000	3,000	4,000	3,000
$2	2,000	2,000	2,000	1,000
$1	0	1,000	1,000	0

Learning Objective 3.4 *Understand what factors shift supply curves.*

12. Maria is an industrial engineer at a Nissan plant. Using the interdependence principle, explain why and how she should change production plans if one of her engine suppliers cuts the price they charge Nissan by 50%. What about if workers unionize and demand a 12% across-the-board pay raise?

13. You have recently been hired by Delta Air Lines to work in its strategy division. For each of the following, illustrate how Delta's supply curve for airline flights will be affected by drawing a graph showing any changes.

a. A global pandemic increases the risk from air travel.

b. Innovative new software allows Delta to more efficiently allocate its aircraft.

c. Delta has just signed a new labor contract that raises the hourly wage it pays to its employees.

14. When Dell adopted a "lean production" process — a management tool that reduces inefficiencies without reducing production — it became one of the world's largest computer manufacturers. What impact did the adoption of lean production techniques have on Dell's individual supply curve for computers? Use a graph to help illustrate your answer.

Learning Objective 3.5 *Distinguish between movements along a supply curve and shifts of supply curves.*

15. What impact does the decision to enroll in college have on your individual supply curve for labor while you are in college? Does it cause a shift in the supply curve or a movement along the supply curve? Draw a graph to illustrate your decision.

16. Briefly explain whether each of the following represents a shift in supply or a change in quantity supplied. Use a graph to illustrate your answer.

a. An increase in the use of corn in the production of ethanol has raised the cost of corn to farmers who use it as livestock feed.

b. Speculators in world steel markets push the price of steel up, leading U.S. steel companies to expand production.

Equilibrium: Where Supply Meets Demand

Scene one: You've spent weeks polishing your resume and read dozens of job ads. After learning as much as you can about the various positions, you've found a posting for what you hope will be your dream job. You take a deep breath, upload your application, and hit "send."

Scene two: The campus coffee shop. The deep sofas look inviting. This looks like a nice place to relax and enjoy a latte or herbal tea, and so you walk in. The barista greets you with a warm smile and asks: "What will it be?"

Scene three: It's 2 A.M., and you're still awake. You've been searching for hours, and the web pages are starting to blur. But you know that if you persist, you'll find an online store offering a great deal on the television you want.

Scene four: Justin Bieber's right Yeezy sneaker, tossed into the audience during a concert, is up for auction on eBay. The first bid comes in around $7,000. There are five days left before the bidding ends, and the shoe will go to the highest bidder. That's five days for you to consider how much of a "belieber" you are and whether you'd give your right leg to own his right shoe.

These stories are all about the same thing: markets, the interaction of supply and demand. Buyers and sellers come together in a market, and your job in this chapter is to analyze how the forces of supply and demand interact in markets. The last two chapters provided a solid foundation for assessing the choices that both buyers and sellers make. Our task now is to bring both sides together within a complete supply-and-demand framework. It's a valuable framework that's essential for understanding the business world, and a lot more. You'll use it to forecast what gets bought and sold, what the prices of various products will be, and how these outcomes change when economic conditions change. Indeed, it's such a powerful framework that it will guide much of the rest of your study of economics.

After studying economics for a while, you will start to see supply and demand curves everywhere.

Joelle Icard/Getty Images

Chapter Objective

Analyze how supply and demand determine the equilibrium price and quantity.

4.1 Understanding Markets
Survey the central role that markets play in our society, determining what is produced, how, by whom, and who gets it.

4.2 Equilibrium
Analyze how markets bring supply and demand into balance.

4.3 Predicting Market Changes
Assess the consequences of shifts in demand and supply, and how changes in prices and quantities reveal whether demand or supply changed.

🎙 Podcast
Think Like an Economist
Equilibrium—Balance in a Busy World

4.1 Understanding Markets

Learning Objective *Survey the central role that markets play in our society, determining what is produced, how, by whom, and who gets it.*

Imagine that it's your job to organize society. It's much harder than you might think. For instance, you have to decide which goods get produced. Given that a typical grocery store stocks around 40,000 items, and Amazon sells more than 10 million different items, this might take forever. That's only the beginning.

You also have to decide who will produce each of these goods, where to produce them, and how they'll be made. You'll need to buy enough raw materials and make sure you've hired workers with the right skills, each equipped with the right tools. Somehow, you also need to ensure that each good is produced in the most efficient way possible by the lowest-cost supplier.

Once you've made these production decisions, you still need to decide how to allocate these goods, figuring out who gets what. Making good allocation decisions requires understanding who would really value which goods. There's no point, for instance, in giving a steak to a vegetarian.

planned economy Centralized decisions are made about what and how goods and services are produced and allocated.

market economy Each individual makes their own production and consumption decisions, buying and selling in markets.

Thankfully, this isn't how we organize our society. There's no central planner telling each of us what to make, or what we each get. Instead, we rely on markets to organize what is produced, how it's produced, and how it's allocated. In place of the central plans used in **planned economies** like Cuba and the former Soviet Union (and, to a lesser degree, China), the **market economies** of North America, Europe, and Australia are organized around markets. Instead of central plans, market economies use prices and the incentives they create to allocate goods. For instance, if you really want an electric car, you'll be willing to pay a higher price for one. In turn, the prospect of selling hybrid cars for more money than a nonhybrid alternative provides an incentive for Toyota to produce more hybrid cars.

What Is a Market?

market A setting bringing together potential buyers and sellers.

A **market** is any setting that brings together potential buyers (demanders) and sellers (suppliers). Armed with this definition, you'll see that markets are everywhere, organizing most of what we do. When you send your resume in response to a job posting, you are a seller (supplier) in the labor market. When you buy a cup of coffee, you're a buyer (demander) in the coffee market. Similarly, when you place an online order for a television or bid on an auction for Bieber's Yeezy, you are a demander in the markets for televisions and memorabilia. Indeed, whenever you spend money buying something, there's a good chance that you're acting as a demander of consumer goods or services. And whenever you get paid something, there's a good chance you're acting as a supplier of consumer goods and services.

Markets are everywhere. But there are many other economic roles that you'll also play. You also have likely been or will be a buyer in the labor market, buying the hard work of babysitters, tutors, or even the employees of your own business. When you take out an auto loan, you're on the demand side in the market for credit. If you have savings in the bank, you're a supplier of credit, as the bank will lend your money to other borrowers. You're also embedded in a global market: Your purchase of an imported laptop from China sets off a chain of transactions in which the retailer selling the computer trades U.S. dollars for Chinese yuan in the foreign exchange market, and then uses those yuan to purchase the laptop in China.

Each of these transactions involves a buyer and a seller meeting in a market. And in each case, there's a price that plays a central role, whether it's the price of a cup of coffee, the wage earned by a worker, the interest rate on a loan or a savings account, or a foreign exchange rate.

Take an expansive view of markets. Modern economists believe that markets play a role in your life beyond simply what you buy and sell. This expansive view of economics requires a creative understanding of what the relevant "prices" are. For instance, as a voter, you're a supplier in the market for votes. These votes aren't literally bought and sold, but you're more likely to vote for the politician who promises the policies you want. And so the price in the market for votes is the work that the politician does to develop and campaign on their policies. The higher this price — that is, the politician who develops the best policies and runs the best campaign — then the more likely it is that you'll supply your vote to that politician.

Someday you may also be in the marriage market, open to the possibility that the right person will become your spouse. In this market, the price is the promise you make about how much love and support you'll offer, and the effort you'll put into helping run your joint household. The higher the price you offer — that is, the more you appear to be a terrific catch — the more likely your demand for a spouse will be met by a willing supplier. But as much as the market metaphor may help you understand dating markets, I still suggest calling your partner "sweetie" rather than "supplier."

There's also a market for grades. I don't mean to suggest that your professor is corrupt. Instead, students are on the demand side for grades, and professors are on the supply side. The price for good grades is good performance on quizzes, papers, and exams. Even when there isn't an explicit curve, performance is often relative. That means that when there's a lot of demand in a market, prices tend to be higher. When there are a lot of students trying to earn an A (that is, demand is high), it will require more hard work (that is, the price will be high).

When you think creatively, you'll start to see markets everywhere. Your introduction to economics will involve close study of the markets for consumer products, labor, machinery, land, financing, government bonds, foreign currencies, and more. But there are also markets for information, health, education, friends, influence, attention, and even love. Armed with this broader notion of markets, you'll come to see just how pervasive market forces are. That's why the core principles of economics can help you make better decisions across nearly all domains in your life.

A long-dead philosopher once said, "Teach a parrot the terms 'supply and demand' and you've got an economist." He was only half-joking.

How Markets Are Organized

There are many different ways in which buyers and sellers meet, and each of them counts as a market. A few examples are illustrated in Figure 1. In some cases, like in a coffee shop, prices are posted, and you simply pay the price, grab your latte, and go. Alternatively, perhaps you've participated in an auction, where the price you pay depends on how much the other bidders forced you to raise your bid on Justin Bieber's right shoe.

Increasingly, markets are migrating online, and so your shopping has probably increasingly meant comparing prices across dozens of websites. When you search for a job, you may also be searching online but the price might not be posted. The wage they are hoping to pay may be listed by the buyer, you may put your desired wage on your application, or the wage may be the result of a negotiation once you have a job offer. While each of these settings seems very different — brick-and-mortar stores versus internet stores, bidding versus posted prices versus negotiated prices — they're all markets because they bring buyers and sellers together. And in each case, the price is determined by the forces of supply and demand.

In each of these markets, outcomes are determined by the forces of supply and demand, so we can use the same economic framework to understand all of them. Indeed, the power of economic analysis is that supply and demand are the key forces shaping outcomes in many different kinds of markets. But there's also an important qualification: The supply and demand curves that we've studied so far are most appropriate for analyzing markets that are characterized by *perfect competition*.

Recall that perfect competition involves many buyers and many sellers of an identical good, and each of these buyers is small relative to the whole market. In reality, many markets are not perfectly competitive. And so in later chapters, we'll see how some of our

Figure 1 | **Various Markets**

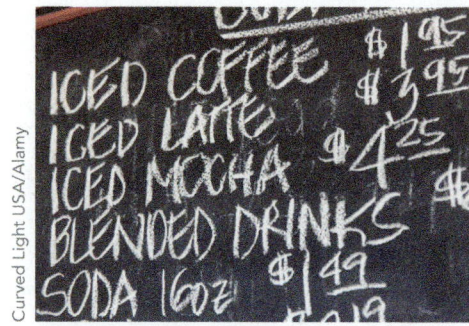

Posted prices at a café

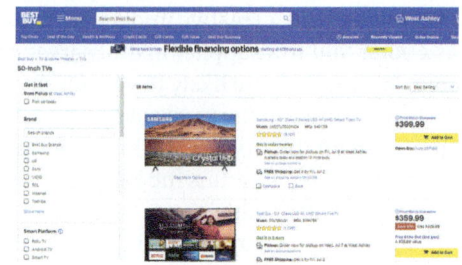

Online prices for a new TV

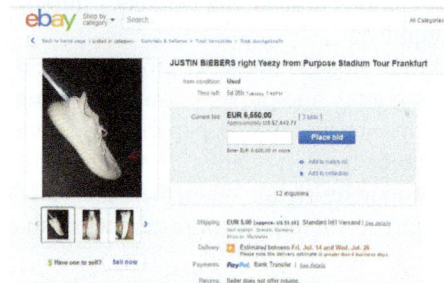

Justin's right shoe, selling at auction

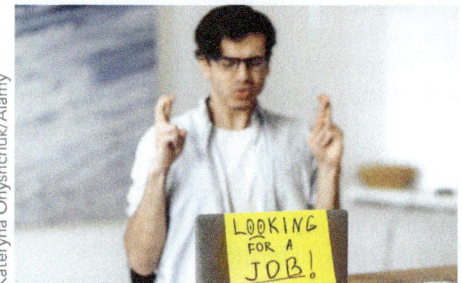

Applying for jobs posted online

conclusions can change depending on the degree of competition in the market. But in this chapter, we'll work toward an understanding of how supply and demand interact in perfectly competitive markets.

4.2 Equilibrium

Learning Objective *Analyze how markets bring supply and demand into balance.*

equilibrium The point at which there is no tendency for change. A market is in equilibrium when the quantity supplied equals the quantity demanded.

You may have encountered the term **equilibrium** in your science classes. Scientists refer to equilibrium as a stable situation with no tendency to change; this occurs when competing forces balance each other. The same idea applies in economics. A market is in equilibrium when the quantity supplied is equal to the quantity demanded.

In equilibrium, every seller who wants to sell an item at the current price can find a buyer, and every buyer who wants to buy at the current price can find a willing seller. Because of this balancing, there's no tendency for the market price to change when a market is in supply-equals-demand equilibrium. There's only one price at which the quantity supplied equals the quantity demanded. This is referred to as the **equilibrium price.** The resulting quantity is called the **equilibrium quantity.**

equilibrium price The price at which the market is in equilibrium.

equilibrium quantity The quantity demanded and supplied when the market is in equilibrium.

Supply Equals Demand

The building blocks of our analysis will be market demand and supply curves. As you know, market demand and supply curves summarize the purchasing and producing decisions of all the participants in the market. The equilibrium occurs at the point at which the market supply and demand curves cross, because this is the point at which the quantity supplied equals the quantity demanded.

Figure 2 | Supply and Demand

The Market for Gas in the United States

Equilibrium occurs where the supply curve cuts the demand curve.

Ⓐ The **quantity of gas demanded at each price** is listed in the table, and graphed as the downward-sloping **demand curve**.
Ⓑ The **quantity of gas supplied at each price** is listed in the next column of the table, and graphed as the upward-sloping **supply curve**.
Ⓒ Supply-equals-demand **equilibrium** occurs where the supply and demand curves meet. This yields an **equilibrium price** of $3, and an **equilibrium quantity** of 2 billion gallons of gas that's produced and purchased each week. There is no shortage or surplus in equilibrium.
Ⓓ At **any price below the equilibrium price**, such as $2, the quantity demanded exceeds the quantity supplied, yielding a **shortage**.
Ⓔ At **any price higher than the equilibrium price**, such as $4, the quantity supplied exceeds the quantity demanded, yielding a **surplus**.

Price	Ⓐ Quantity demanded	Ⓑ Quantity supplied	Quantity supplied minus quantity demanded
$2	2.4	1.5	Ⓓ −0.9 (a shortage)
$3	2.0	2.0	Ⓒ Equilibrium: No shortage or surplus
$4	1.6	2.5	Ⓔ +0.9 (a surplus)

Note: All quantities are billions of gallons per week.

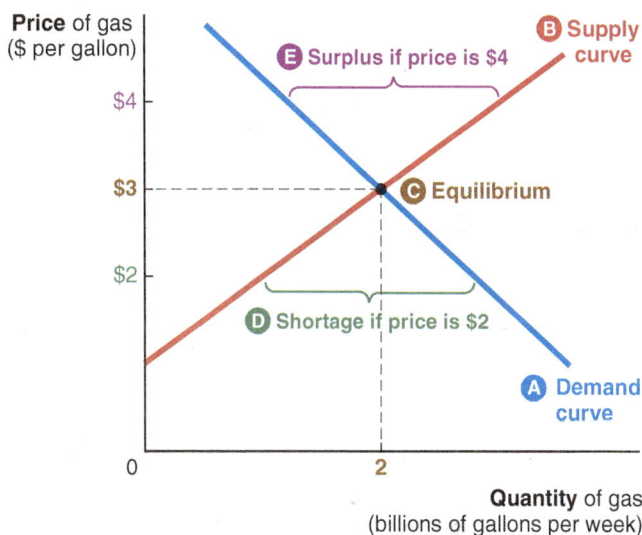

You will see this most clearly by working through an example, and Figure 2 reintroduces the data on the market demand for gasoline (which should be familiar from Chapter 2) and data on the market supply (from Chapter 3). The table lists both the quantity demanded at each price and the quantity supplied at each price. Graphing the price against the quantity demanded yields the downward-sloping market demand curve shown on the right. Likewise, graphing the price against the quantity supplied yields the upward-sloping market supply curve.

Now that we've graphed the relevant data, it's time to figure out the equilibrium. Equilibrium occurs at the point where the quantity demanded is equal to the quantity supplied, and this occurs where the curves cross. Check both the graph and the table, and you'll see that when the price is $3 per gallon, then 2 billion gallons of gas are demanded each week, and 2 billion gallons are supplied. Consequently, the equilibrium price of gas is $3 per gallon, and at that price, the equilibrium quantity of gas produced each week is 2 billion gallons. Markets have a tendency to move toward equilibrium, and once they find it, prices and quantities stop changing—at least until something disturbs the market.

EVERYDAY Economics   **Why is water cheap, while diamonds are expensive?**

Water is essential for human survival. Not only is it delicious and refreshing, but it also sustains all life. If you don't drink enough water, you'll die. And yet water is extremely cheap. Contrast this with diamonds, which are inessential for human survival and yet incredibly expensive. What gives? Your analysis of supply and demand yields two important lessons that are at the core of resolving this paradox.

AlmarinaStudio/Shutterstock

Rashid Valitov/Shutterstock

Diamonds or water: Which is more valuable?

shortage When the quantity demanded exceeds the quantity supplied.

surplus When the quantity demanded is less than the quantity supplied.

Prices are determined by both supply and demand. If you think it's surprising that water can be both essential and cheap, you're probably only thinking about the demand (or marginal benefit) side: You figure that if something is essential, people must be willing to pay a lot for it. But prices are determined by *both* supply and demand. When you think about the supply (or marginal cost) side, you'll notice that water is also plentiful and costs little to produce, while diamonds are scarce and expensive to mine.

Prices are determined at the margin. Now recall that your demand curve is your *marginal* benefit curve, while the supply curve is your *marginal* cost curve. That is, when you think about your demand for water, you need to think about your marginal benefit, not total benefit.

The total benefit of all your water consumption is extraordinarily high — it sustains your life. If the price of water rose, you probably wouldn't drink less — but you might take shorter showers or water your lawn less often. The "marginal" gallon of water you buy is quite inessential, thus your willingness to pay for a gallon of water is low, because the marginal gallon brings little marginal benefit. But if water ever were to become so scarce that the marginal gallon would save you from dehydration, your willingness to pay for one more gallon of water may be so high as to make water more valuable than diamonds. ■

Getting to Equilibrium

So far, we've focused on equilibrium as the point at which there's no tendency for change. It's also important because markets tend to move toward the point of supply-equals-demand equilibrium. As a result, you can use your analysis of equilibrium to predict whether prices are likely to rise or fall.

Shortages cause the price to rise. Let's begin by thinking about what happens when the price is below the equilibrium level. Figure 2 demonstrates that when gas is only $2 per gallon, a **shortage** will result: The quantity of gas demanded (2.4 billion gallons per week) far exceeds the quantity supplied (1.5 billion gallons). There are too many people chasing too little gas, leading to shortages. As a result, individual gas stations find themselves selling out of gas, or facing long queues of desperate customers. How will suppliers and demanders respond to this shortage?

Start by putting yourself in the shoes of your local gas station owner. You know that at a price of $2, you will sell out of gas. You also know that if you raise your price to $2.10, you'll still sell all your gas (check Figure 3; there's still a shortage), and so raising your price means raising your profits. Raising your price to $2.20 will raise your profits even further, and you will still sell all your gas. As long as the shortage persists, you'll keep marking up your price.

Gas customers are also a critical part of the process of pushing the price toward equilibrium. If you're a customer who's worried about a gas shortage, you might tell a gas station owner that you're willing to pay 10 cents per gallon above her posted price of $2.20 to avoid missing out, and so the price rises to $2.30. As this process continues, the price will keep rising until the gas shortage is eliminated, which occurs when the price is $3.

Surpluses cause the price to fall. A similar process operates in the reverse direction when the price is above its equilibrium. Figure 2 shows that when gas is $4 per gallon, a **surplus** results as the quantity of gas supplied far exceeds the quantity demanded. Gas station owners, trying to sell off their unsold gas, will charge lower prices in the hopes of attracting more customers. With enough competition, repeated rounds of discounting will push the price down to $3 per gallon, eliminating this surplus.

Figure 3 illustrates that when supply and demand are out of step, the forces of competition push markets toward the equilibrium price, thereby eliminating any shortages or surpluses. Economists emphasize this equilibrium point because it can help you figure out whether prices are headed up or down. It's only when a market reaches equilibrium that supply and demand will be in balance, and so there will be no tendency for the price to change.

Figure 3 | How Markets Approach Equilibrium

There are two forces pushing markets toward equilibrium:

A When **the price is above the equilibrium price**: A **surplus** leads to discounts, which **push the price down**.

B When **the price is below the equilibrium price**: A **shortage** leads to markups, which **push the price up**.

C Only when **supply equals demand** is the price stable and the market is in equilibrium.

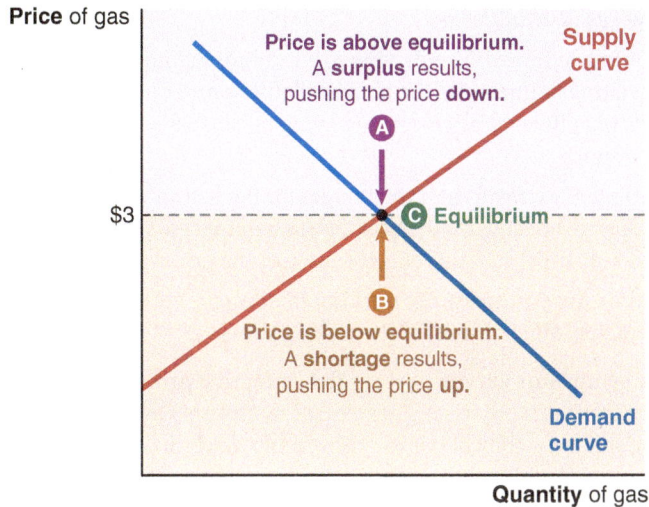

Price of gas

Price is above equilibrium.
A **surplus** results,
pushing the price **down.**

Supply curve

A

$3 - - - **C** Equilibrium - - - - -

B

Price is below equilibrium.
A **shortage** results,
pushing the price **up.**

Demand curve

Quantity of gas

Figuring Out Whether Markets Are in Equilibrium

How can you tell whether a market is in a supply-equals-demand equilibrium? A simple diagnostic is to check whether prices are changing. Whenever the price is rising, that's a sign that at the current price, the quantity demanded exceeds the quantity supplied. And if the price is falling, it's likely that the quantity supplied exceeds the quantity demanded. If prices are free to adjust, then eventually these markets will be drawn to their equilibrium.

But sometimes, this process of price adjustment might be slow, or the price isn't free to change. And so this excess demand or supply will spill over into other domains. Let's examine what happens when a market is not in equilibrium.

EVERYDAY Economics   Smart parking meters

Have you ever driven around for what seemed like hours, looking for a place to park? The problem is that the number of parking spaces is relatively fixed, and during busy times, the quantity of spots demanded exceeds this fixed supply. What you're experiencing is a parking market that's stuck out of equilibrium. And the price can't rise to eliminate this shortage, because that would require reprogramming all the parking meters.

People respond in different ways to this problem. You might keep circling the block, effectively queuing for the next spot that comes up. Another possibility is to alter your plans for the evening by starting your night with dinner at a restaurant that offers valet parking. Yet another alternative — one that's quite common in neighborhoods where parking is scarce — is that you'll find someone who will let you park in their driveway for $20. But these are costly fixes — and they don't really solve the problem. When the price can't change, the shortage of parking spots can persist.

Is there a better solution? The city of San Francisco thinks so, and it has experimented with one possibility: "smart" parking meters that respond to market conditions. These meters charge higher prices to park in the most overcrowded areas during busy times, and lower prices during less popular times. Known as "demand-responsive pricing," it seems to have worked: Since it began, the number of people "cruising" for a spot fell by about 30%. ∎

There are three symptoms of a market in disequilibrium. The problem of insufficient parking spaces highlights the three symptoms of a market out of equilibrium, which is also known as *disequilibrium*:

Symptom 1: Queuing. When you're driving around looking for a spot, you're effectively queuing—waiting in line—for the next available spot. The extra time you spend in the queue raises the effective price you're paying because it will cost you both time and money to get a spot.

Symptom 2: Bundling of extras. When you bought dinner just so you could get the valet to park your car, you were effectively buying extras (that dinner) so you could get the thing you wanted (the parking spot), and this effectively raises the price you're paying to park.

Symptom 3: A secondary market. By parking in someone else's driveway, you've found a way around the "official" market for parking spots.

Each of these symptoms serves to raise the "effective price," even when the price charged by sellers can't directly rise. These three symptoms of disequilibrium are not just about parking spaces — they occur in many markets when prices can't freely adjust. For instance, when a new videogame console is released, you'll often see gamers queuing to snag a scarce console. You'll find videogame stores that will sell you a console only if you also buy a bunch of extra games that they bundle with it. And you'll find people reselling their consoles at a hefty markup on secondary markets like eBay or Craigslist.

If the problem is a surplus instead of a shortage, you'll observe similar symptoms, although in reverse — in a way that lowers the "effective price." For instance, sellers may queue to meet buyers — such as when the unemployed (who are potential sellers of labor) queue for a chance at a job interview. Buyers may demand "extras" be bundled for free, such as when savvy car buyers can get the dealership to throw in an upgrade. And prices will be lower on the secondary market, such as when tickets to unpopular events sell below face value on StubHub.

> Three symptoms of a market in disequilibrium:
> 1. Queuing
> 2. Bundling of extras
> 3. A secondary market

4.3 Predicting Market Changes

Learning Objective *Assess the consequences of shifts in demand and supply, and how changes in prices and quantities reveal whether demand or supply changed.*

So far, we've seen that the intersection of market supply and demand curves determines the equilibrium price and quantity. We're now going to harness this powerful insight to predict how prices will change when economic conditions change.

Shifts in Demand

We will start by considering what happens to the equilibrium price and quantity when economic conditions cause the demand curve to shift. Remember that the market demand curve summarizes people's current buying plans, but if those plans shift, then so will the market demand curve. There are several factors that shift demand, but remember that a change in the price will not cause a shift in demand.

Any change that leads you (or others) to buy a larger quantity at each price is an increase in demand, shifting the demand curve to the right. If the change leads people to buy a smaller quantity at each price, it's a decrease in demand, shifting the demand curve to the left. Again, don't confuse these shifts in the demand curve with a movement along the demand curve due to a change in price, which leads to a change in the quantity demanded. (Head back to Chapter 2 if you need more of a review of shifts versus movements along the demand curve.)

Figure 4 illustrates how the market equilibrium changes when the demand curve shifts. The original or old equilibrium in this market — shown as the black dot — occurs when gas sells for $3 per gallon, and 2 billion gallons of gas are sold each week. But following a shift in demand, the market will move to a new equilibrium.

Figure 4 | Shifts in the Demand Curve

Shifts in demand cause price and quantity to move in the same direction.

Panel A: An Increase in Demand

Ⓐ An increase in demand causes the demand curve to shift right.
Ⓑ This leads to a new supply-equals-demand equilibrium.
Ⓒ Leading to an increase in the price.
Ⓓ And an increase in quantity.

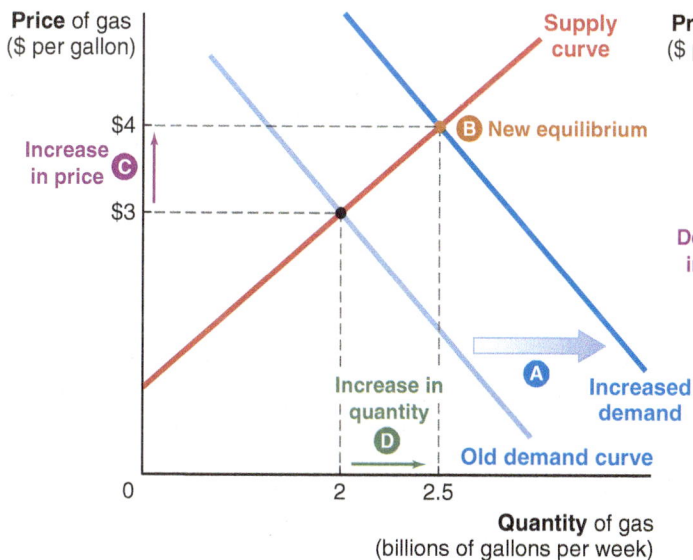

Panel B: A Decrease in Demand

Ⓐ A decrease in demand causes the demand curve to shift left.
Ⓑ This leads to a new supply-equals-demand equilibrium.
Ⓒ Leading to a decrease in the price.
Ⓓ And a decrease in quantity.

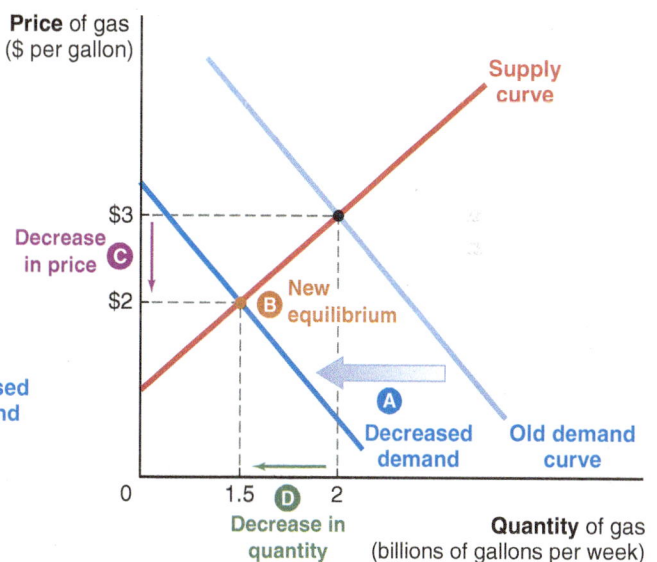

An increase in demand leads to a higher price and a larger quantity.

Panel A in Figure 4 shows the consequences of an increase in demand, which is a shift of the demand curve to the right and a movement along the supply curve. The new equilibrium occurs at the point where this new demand curve intersects the supply curve, and you can read off the new equilibrium price ($4) and quantity (2.5 billion gallons). This new equilibrium price is higher than in the old equilibrium ($4, compared with $3), as is the new equilibrium quantity (2.5 billion gallons, compared with 2 billion).

What's causing this change? An increase in demand means that buyers want to buy more at the old price of $3, but sellers don't want to supply any more. If the price didn't change, a shortage would result. But the prospect of a shortage leads the price to be bid up to $4, and that higher price is the incentive that leads suppliers to increase the quantity they supply as they move along their supply curve. The end result is that an increase in demand causes an increase in both the price and quantity.

A decrease in demand leads to a lower price and a smaller quantity. Panel B in Figure 4 shows that the opposite shift has the opposite effect. It shows a decrease in demand, which shifts the demand curve to the left, moving the market to a new equilibrium where this new demand curve cuts the supply curve. Comparing the new equilibrium to the old one, you'll see that this decrease in demand causes a reduction in both the equilibrium price (to $2 per gallon) and quantity (to 1.5 billion gallons).

Again, pause to reflect on why this happens. There's decreased demand, but at the old price of $3, no change in supply. If the price didn't change, a surplus would result. The prospect of a surplus leads the price to be bid down to $2, and that lower price is the incentive that leads suppliers to decrease the quantity they supply as they move along their supply curve. The end result is that a decrease in demand causes a decrease in both the price and quantity.

Demand shifts lead price and quantity to move in the same direction. Notice that the equilibrium price and quantity both increase following an increase in demand, and they both decrease following a decrease in demand. So in both cases, shifts in demand cause price and quantity to change in the same direction. As we're about to see, that's not true for shifts in supply.

Shifts in Supply

Now let's consider what happens when economic conditions cause supply to change. Recall that the market supply curve summarizes sellers current selling plans, and if those plans shift, then so will the market supply curve. There are several factors that shift supply, but remember: A change in the price will not cause a shift in supply.

A shift that increases the quantity suppliers plan to sell at each price is an increase in supply, and it shifts the supply curve to the right. The opposite — a decrease in supply — shifts the curve to the left. As we explore the consequences of shifts in the supply curve, be sure not to confuse them with movements along the supply curve, which occur when businesses change their quantity supplied in response to a change in price. (Head back to Chapter 3 if you need more of a review of shifts versus movements along the supply curve.)

A shift in *supply* causes price and quantity to move in opposite directions. A shift in *demand* causes price and quantity to move in the same direction.

Figure 5 illustrates the consequences of shifts in supply. Once again, the original or old equilibrium in this market occurs when gas sells for $3 per gallon and 2 billion gallons of gas are produced. But if there's a shift in supply, the market will move to a new equilibrium.

An increase in supply leads to a lower price and a larger quantity. Panel A in Figure 5 shows an increase in supply, when the supply curve shifts to the right. The new equilibrium occurs at the point where this new supply curve cuts the demand curve. At this point, there is a new equilibrium price (of $2) and quantity (of 2.4 billion gallons). This new equilibrium price is lower than in the old equilibrium ($2, compared with $3), and the new quantity is larger (2.4 billion gallons, compared with 2 billion).

To see what's going on, realize that an increase in supply means that managers want to sell more at the old price of $3, but buyers don't want to demand any more. If the price didn't change, this increase in supply would lead to a surplus. And this is what causes the price to be bid down to $2. That lower price incentivizes buyers to increase the quantity they demand as they move along their demand curve. The end result is that an increase in supply causes a decrease in price and an increase in quantity.

Figure 5 | Shifts in the Supply Curve

Shifts in supply cause price and quantity to move in opposite directions.

Panel A: An Increase in Supply

Ⓐ An **increase in supply** causes the supply curve to **shift right**.
Ⓑ This leads to a new supply-equals-demand **equilibrium**.
Ⓒ Leading to a **decrease in the price**.
Ⓓ And an **increase in quantity**.

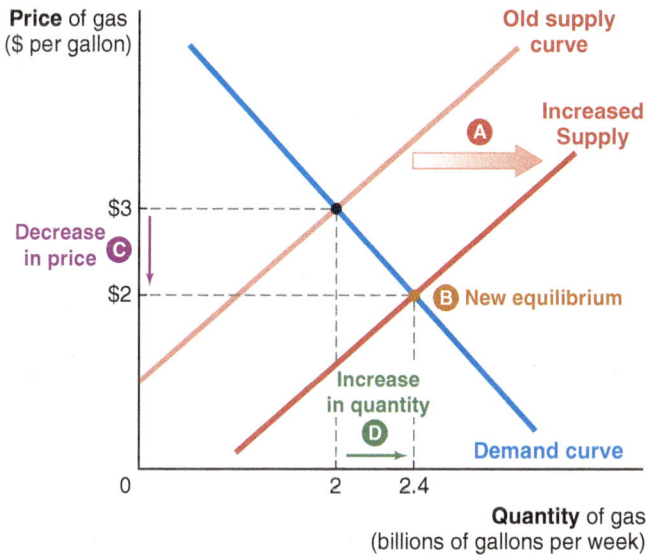

Panel B: A Decrease in Supply

Ⓐ A **decrease in supply** causes the supply curve to **shift left**.
Ⓑ This leads to a new supply-equals-demand **equilibrium**.
Ⓒ Leading to an **increase in the price**.
Ⓓ And a **decrease in quantity**.

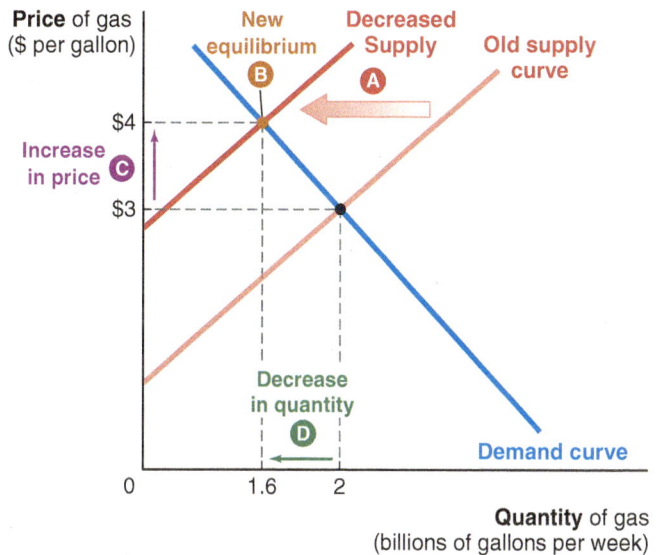

A decrease in supply leads to a higher price and a smaller quantity.

Panel B in Figure 5 shows that the opposite shift has the opposite effect. It shows a decrease in supply, which shifts the supply curve to the left, moving the market to a new equilibrium where this new supply curve cuts the demand curve. Comparing the new equilibrium to the old one, you'll see that this decrease in supply causes an increase in the equilibrium price (to $4 per gallon) and a decrease in the quantity (to 1.6 billion gallons).

Let's think through why this happens. There's decreased supply, but no change in demand. If the price didn't change from $3, this decreased supply would lead to a shortage. The prospect of this shortage leads the price to be bid up to $4, and that higher price incentivizes buyers to decrease the quantity they demand as they move along their demand curve.

Supply shifts lead price and quantity to move in opposite directions.

Notice that an increase in supply causes the price to fall and the quantity to rise, while a decrease in supply causes the price to rise and the quantity to fall. That is, *a shift in supply causes price and quantity to move in opposite directions.* By contrast, your analysis of demand shifts revealed that *a shift in demand causes price and quantity to move in the same direction.* As you work through further examples, you can use these rules to check your analysis.

A shift in *supply* causes price and quantity to move in opposite directions. A shift in *demand* causes price and quantity to move in the same direction.

A Three-Step Recipe for Predicting Market Outcomes

Congratulations! You have now built the foundations of a powerful framework for predicting market outcomes. The study of buyers that you began in Chapter 2 tells you which factors shape and shift the demand curve. Likewise, your study of sellers that you began in Chapter 3 tells you about the supply side. When you put these together, you can predict how markets will respond to changing economic conditions. This simple supply-and-demand framework is the most powerful predictive device I know.

Okay, let's practice actually applying the supply-and-demand approach by analyzing a few real-world business questions. When you work through these examples, you should use the following three-step recipe that will help you predict real-world market outcomes.

Step 1: Determine which curve is shifting (supply, demand, or both). Remember that any change affecting buyers or their marginal benefits will shift the demand curve, while any change affecting sellers or their marginal costs will shift the supply curve.

Step 2: Determine if it's an increase, shifting the curve to the right, or a decrease, shifting the curve to the left. An increase in marginal benefit is an increase in demand, while an increase in marginal cost creates a decrease in supply.

Step 3: Determine how prices and quantities will change in the new equilibrium. Compare the old equilibrium with the new equilibrium.

Let's see how the three-step recipe works, using a few simple examples.

Example 1: *A major retailer announces plans to install charging stations for electric cars in 400 parking spaces in 120 cities. How will this affect the demand for electric cars?*

Step 1: Because *buyers* of electric cars will have greater access to charging stations while running errands, the convenience — and therefore marginal benefit — of owning an electric car will be higher, so this will *shift the demand curve.*

Step 2: The increased convenience will *increase* demand for electric cars, *shifting the demand curve to the right.*

Step 3: At the new equilibrium, this increased demand will *raise both the price and quantity* of electric vehicles. This is good news for electric car manufacturers.

Example 2: *Amazon announces that it is developing technology to deliver orders to customers within 30 minutes. Owners of local brick-and-mortar stores want to know how this will affect their company's sales.*

Step 1: Since the people who normally buy from their local stores will have a closer substitute for buying goods that they want quickly, this will *shift the demand curve.*

Step 2: These buyers will find buying from Amazon to be more attractive, making them less likely to buy from local brick-and-mortar stores. This is a *decrease* in demand for goods from local stores, *shifting the demand curve to the left.*

Step 3: Reduced demand will lead to a new equilibrium with both a *lower price and a lower quantity.* This is bad news for local stores.

Example 3: *The federal government announces a plan to fund research that will eventually lower the cost of the batteries used in electric cars. The head of General Motors' electric vehicle division wants to know how these innovations will affect the electric car market.*

Step 1: Since the new manufacturing technologies will affect the *seller's* marginal cost of producing each electric car, this will *shift the supply curve.*

Step 2: Because these cheaper batteries will reduce the cost of an important input into making electric cars, it will lower their marginal costs. Lower marginal costs lead to an *increase* in supply, *shifting the supply curve to the right.*

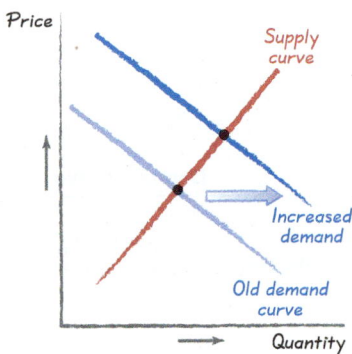

Price / Supply curve / Increased demand / Old demand curve / Quantity

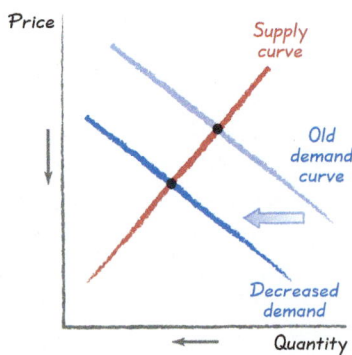

Price / Supply curve / Old demand curve / Decreased demand / Quantity

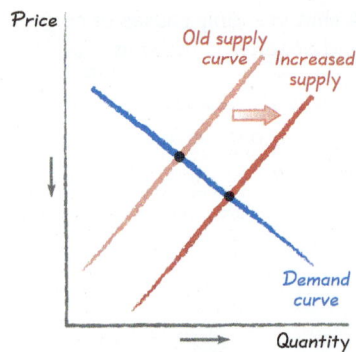

Price / Old supply curve / Increased supply / Demand curve / Quantity

Step 3: This increased supply will mean a *lower price* and *higher quantity* of electric cars sold — a welcome development for those who would like to see more "green" vehicles on the roads.

Example 4: *Due to a drought in California, farmers face rising costs for water. Almond farming is a water-intensive process. How will the drought affect the market for almonds?*

Step 1: Since water is an input into almond farming, the scarcity of the input will increase the *seller's* marginal cost of producing almonds, which will *shift the supply curve.*

Step 2: Because the marginal cost of producing almonds will rise, supply will *decrease, shifting the supply curve to the left.*

Step 3: This decrease in supply will lead to a new equilibrium involving a *higher price and lower quantity* of almonds.

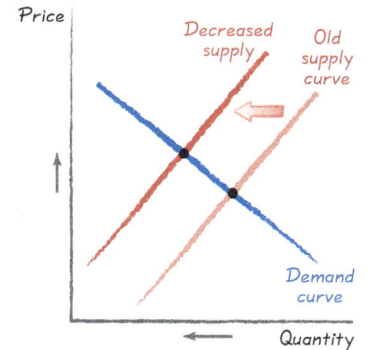

Summary of the consequences of shifting supply and demand. Let's summarize where we are so far. Figure 6 sums up what we've learned from analyzing shifts in supply and demand.

Figure 6 | Consequences of Shifts in Demand or Supply

	Effect on equilibrium quantity	Effect on equilibrium price	
Increase in demand (Example: The effect of a new contagious virus on hand sanitizer)	Rises	Rises	*Shifts in demand cause price and quantity to move in the same direction*
Decrease in demand (Example: The effect of a new contagious virus on air travel)	Falls	Falls	
Increase in supply (Example: The effect of more efficient battery production on electric cars)	Rises	Falls	*Shifts in supply cause price and quantity to move in opposite directions*
Decrease in supply (Example: The effect of higher oil prices on the gasoline market)	Falls	Rises	

Do the Economics

Think you've got this business of predicting outcomes all figured out? Here's your chance to check, as you work through a dozen more examples.

If some U.S. states lower the legal drinking age, what will be the effect on the market for beer?

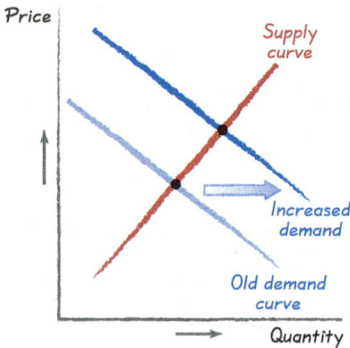

More consumers

→ An increase in demand

Result: Higher price, higher quantity.

During the coronavirus pandemic, retailers needed to take additional precautions such as purchasing hand sanitizer, providing employees with masks, and sanitizing surfaces more. What effect does this have on the market for the goods that they sell?

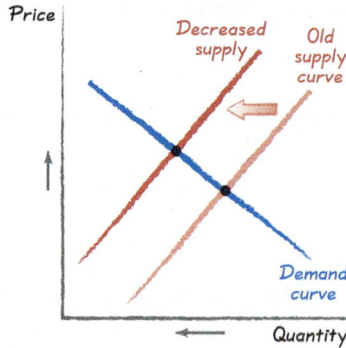

Higher cost of inputs

→ A decrease in supply

Result: Higher price, lower quantity.

How did the increase in work from home during the coronavirus pandemic affect the market for gasoline?

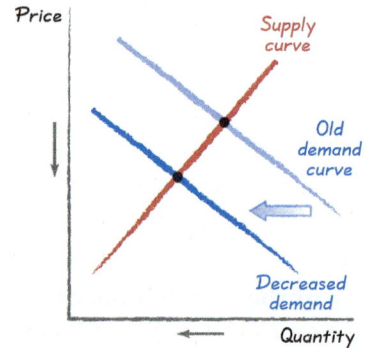

Lower price of a substitute (it's effectively cheaper to work from home since the boss now encourages it)

→ A decrease in demand

Result: Lower price, lower quantity.

Fishers can now use a "fishfinder" to locate schools of fish in the ocean. How might this affect the market for fish?

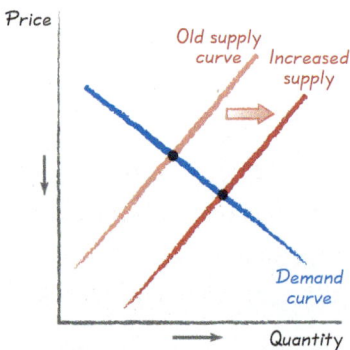

Greater productive efficiency

→ An increase in supply

Result: Lower price, higher quantity.

Before a hurricane, people stock up on essential supplies such as food and water. How will this affect the market for groceries?

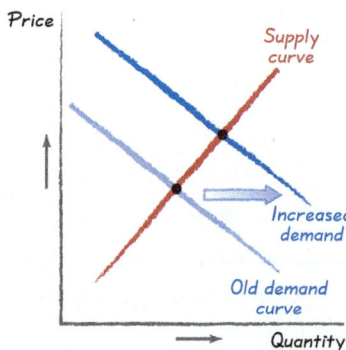

Consumers prefer greater quantities

→ An increase in demand

Result: Higher price, higher quantity.

Increasingly, corn is being turned into biofuel instead of being used as food. What has this done to the market for corn as a food?

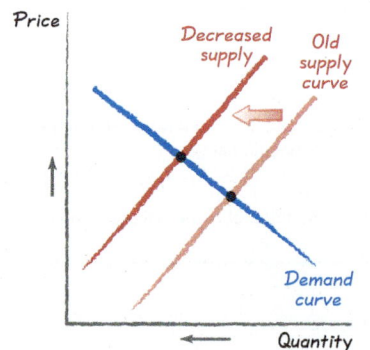

Biofuel and feed corn are substitutes-in-production

→ A decrease in supply

Result: Higher price, lower quantity.

Sony reduced the price of its latest PlayStation videogame console. What effect will this have on the market for competing consoles such as the Xbox?

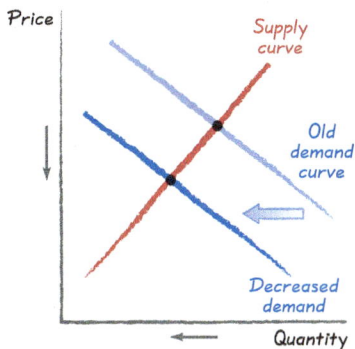

Lower price of substitute goods
→ A decrease in demand
Result: Lower price, lower quantity.

Coal is burned to produce electricity. What happens in the market for electricity when the price of coal decreases?

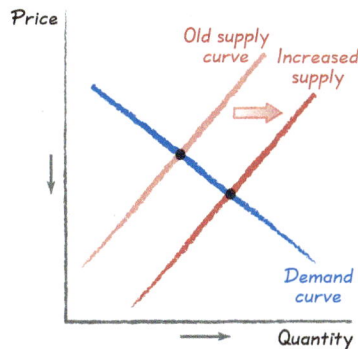

Lower cost of input
→ An increase in supply
Result: Lower price, higher quantity.

An Indian car company plans to sell cars in the United States. What will be the effect on the market for cars in the United States?

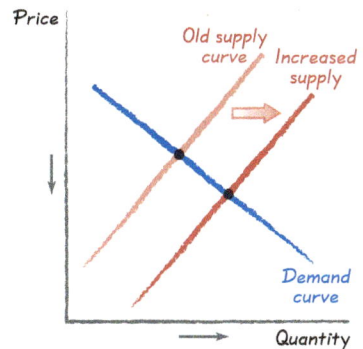

More sellers in the market
→ An increase in supply
Result: Lower price, higher quantity.

Incomes fell during the last recession. How did this affect the market for clothing?

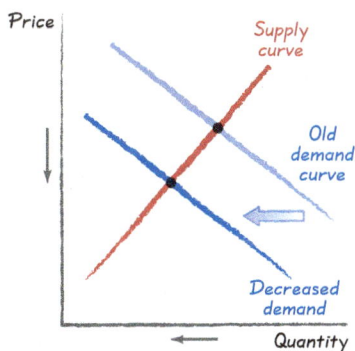

Lower incomes
→ A decrease in demand (since clothing is a normal good)
Result: Lower price, lower quantity.

It was found that certain types of plastic water bottles release harmful chemicals. What happened in the market for metal water bottles?

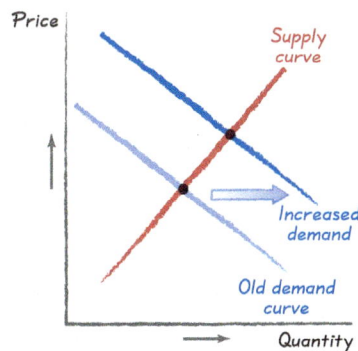

Consumer preferences shifted
→ An increase in demand
Result: Higher price, higher quantity.

Researchers have found that climate change is having a negative impact on rice crops, reducing global rice yields. What is the effect on the market for rice?

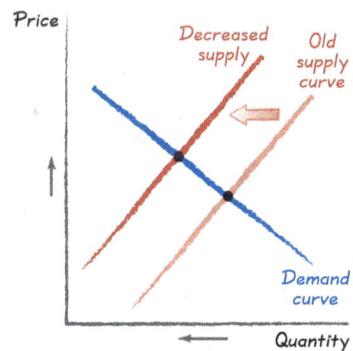

Decreased productivity of farms
→ A decrease in supply
Result: Higher price, lower quantity. ∎

When Both Supply and Demand Shift

So far, we've analyzed what happens when *either* supply or demand shifts. But what happens when *both* curves shift at the same time? Fortunately, the same rules still hold, and when more than one curve shifts, you can simply add up the effects. Let's see how with an example.

In 2008 the gasoline market was hit by two sharp changes: The U.S. economy entered a severe recession, and the price of crude oil (which is a crucial input for gasoline) rose sharply. A recession reduces the incomes of gas consumers, which causes a decrease in their demand for gas. Higher oil prices raise costs for gasoline suppliers, decreasing supply. What's the likely impact of these simultaneous shifts on the market for gasoline?

Let's begin by considering each of these shifts separately. When you have more than one shock, you can start by looking at each shift separately and then adding up the effects.

Let's start by considering the recession. A recession reduces the incomes of gas consumers, which causes a decrease in their demand for gas. This decrease in demand lowers the equilibrium quantity and price. (You can check this with a quick supply-and-demand sketch, or by looking up at the second row of Figure 6.)

Now let's think through the rise in the price of oil. Higher oil prices raise input costs for gasoline suppliers, causing a decrease in supply. This shift lowers the equilibrium quantity but raises the equilibrium price. (Again, confirm this with a quick sketch.)

Finally, add up each of these effects. Both of these shifts lower the equilibrium quantity. The effect on the price is a bit trickier: While the first shift (the decrease in demand) suggests the price will fall, the second shift (the decrease in supply) suggests it will rise. The total change in the price is therefore unclear. Thus, the combined effect of these two shifts is that quantity will fall, but the price could either rise or fall.

In fact, when supply and demand both shift, your conclusion will often be "it depends." That's because a change in supply might cause the price or quantity to move in one direction, and then the change in demand can cause it to move in the opposite direction. The total effect depends on which shift has the biggest impact.

The effect of two shifts can depend on which curve shifts the most.

Figure 7 illustrates this point, by showing two extreme cases. Case 1 shows what happens when the demand shift is much bigger than the shift in supply. Case 2 shows the opposite extreme, with a small shift in demand and a much bigger shift in supply. Just as we predicted, the equilibrium quantity declines in both cases. But in Case 1, the price of gas falls, while in Case 2, the price of gas rises. This follows the prediction that the price can either rise or fall, and it shows that the outcome depends on whether the shift in demand or shift in supply dominates. (In fact, the price might even stay the same if the two effects exactly offset each other.)

Figure 7 | Shifts in Supply and Demand

When Both Supply and Demand Curves Shift

*Analyze two extreme cases: Case 1—A **big** demand shift with a **small** supply shift.*

*Case 2—A **small** demand shift with a **big** supply shift.*

Ⓐ A **decrease** in <u>both</u> supply and demand causes **both curves to shift left**.

Ⓑ This leads to a new supply-equals-demand **equilibrium**.

Implications depend on whether it's a big shift in supply and a small shift in demand, or a small shift in supply and a big shift in demand.

Ⓒ The **price could rise or fall**: It falls in Case 1, but rises in Case 2.

Ⓓ And a **decrease in quantity** occurs in either scenario.

Case 1: A Big Shift in Demand and a Small Shift in Supply

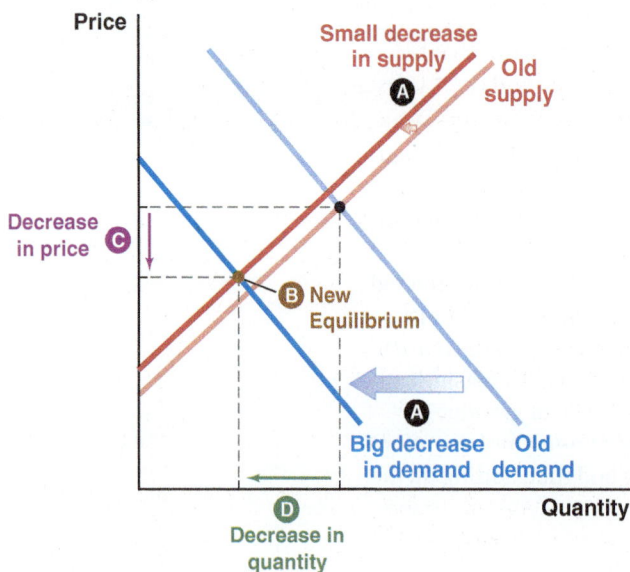

Case 2: A Small Shift in Demand and a Big Shift in Supply

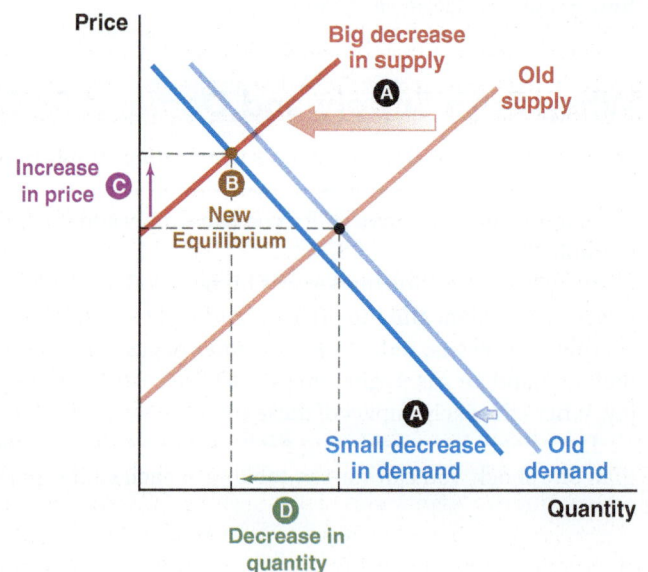

Use the morning-evening method to work out the effects of two curves shifting. So far we've analyzed what happens when demand and supply both decrease. You're now in a position to analyze all the different cases in which there are simultaneous shifts that lead both supply and demand to either increase or decrease. Figure 8 shows how to work through each possibility and introduces a shortcut you might find helpful, which we call the *morning-evening method*.

Figure 8 | When Both Supply and Demand Curves Shift

	Morning	*Evening*	Total effect (*Morning* + *Evening*)	
	Effect of demand shock	Effect of supply shock	Effect on equilibrium price	Effect on equilibrium quantity
Increase in demand and increase in supply	↑P, ↑Q	↓P, ↑Q	It depends (↑P + ↓P)	Rises (↑Q + ↑Q)
Increase in demand and decrease in supply	↑P, ↑Q	↑P, ↓Q	Rises (↑P + ↑P)	It depends (↑Q + ↓Q)
Decrease in demand and increase in supply	↓P, ↓Q	↓P, ↑Q	Falls (↓P + ↓P)	It depends (↓Q + ↑Q)
Decrease in demand and decrease in supply	↓P, ↓Q	↑P, ↓Q	It depends (↓P + ↑P)	Falls (↓Q + ↓Q)

Here's the idea. Analyzing two curves shifting at the same time can get confusing. It's much simpler to think about it *as if* the demand curve shifts in the morning and the supply curve shifts in the evening. (The order doesn't really matter.) This way you can just think about one shift at a time. To find out the total change over the course of the day, simply add up the morning effect and the evening effect.

Let's try it, starting with the first row of Figure 8: What happens when there's an increase in both demand and supply? To be concrete, think about the market for lifeguards in the summer, which is flooded with new buyers as pools and beaches open for the season (increasing demand) and new suppliers as students become available to work as lifeguards (increasing supply).

Start with the morning, when the increase in demand leads to an increase in the quantity of lifeguards hired, and an increase in the price they're paid (that is, their wage). Next, evaluate the changes that occur in the evening. An increase in supply will lead to an increase in quantity, and a decrease in price.

Finally, to evaluate what happened over the day as a whole, simply add up what happened in the morning and the evening. The quantity rose in the morning and rose again in the evening, so it must have risen over the day as a whole. But the effect on the price is a bit thornier: It rose in the morning and fell in the evening. Over the whole day, the change in the price is unclear — it might have risen or fallen, depending on whether the demand shift had a bigger or smaller effect than the supply shift. In fact, this analysis provides an accurate diagnosis of how the market for lifeguards changes in the summer: The quantity rises, while the price can either rise or fall.

The second row of Figure 8 asks you to work through the implications of an increase in demand, combined with a decrease in supply, while the third row asks you to work out what happens when demand decreases but supply increases. You should work through each of these examples for yourself, following the logic discussed above. The fourth row shows the final possibility — a decrease in demand and a decrease in supply — which is exactly what happened in the gasoline example we discussed above (and illustrated in Figure 7).

Bottom line: When more than one curve shifts, you can consider the implications first of one shift and then of the other, and then add them together. And don't be surprised if your prediction for changes in price or quantity is, "It depends."

Summertime means overtime; wintertime means out of work.

Spencer Platt/Getty Images

Interpreting Market Data

So far, we've used supply and demand to help you *predict* the consequences of changing market conditions. Let's now turn to an alternative way of thinking, in which supply and demand are diagnostic tools to help you *diagnose* what is happening in the economy. In order to do this, you need to remember two key rules:

Rule 1: If prices and quantities move in the same direction, then the demand curve has definitely shifted. (It's possible that the supply curve may also have shifted.)

Rule 2: If prices and quantities move in opposite directions, then the supply curve has definitely shifted. (It's possible that the demand curve may also have shifted.)

Armed with these rules, let's work through some examples of how changes in prices and quantities are important clues that will help you figure out what's driving changing market conditions.

Interpreting the DATA   How did e-books change the publishing industry?

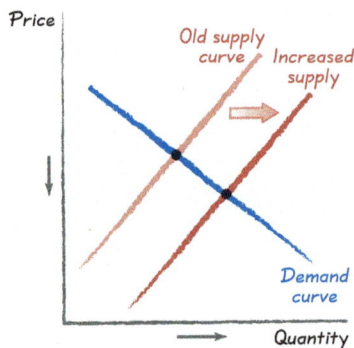

Electronic book readers, such as the Amazon Kindle, have given consumers the choice to buy the latest bestseller either as a printed book or as an e-book. In response, the quantity of most bestsellers sold rose (summing across electronic and paper editions), while the average price paid per book fell. What do these price and quantity changes tell us?

Because price and quantity moved in opposite directions, we can infer that this reflects a shift in the supply curve, and the fact that the quantity rose implies that supply increased. Why? An e-book can be produced at a much lower marginal cost (there's no expensive paper or binding or warehousing or shipping), and a decline in marginal costs will increase supply. ■

Interpreting the DATA   Why do house sales boom during the summer, but house prices don't?

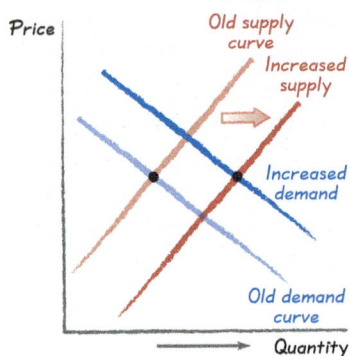

Every summer, the quantity of houses sold rises dramatically, but the price of housing doesn't change much. What do these market movements tell us?

It's easy to see why many buyers want to move in the summer — work is typically slower, and their kids won't have to change schools during the school year. Consequently, the demand for housing increases.

But if this were the whole story, then housing prices would typically rise in the summer, when in reality they're usually flat. This suggests that there is also an increase in supply. In fact, this makes sense: Many people trying to buy a new house are also trying to sell their old house. Consequently, both supply and demand increase in the summer. Both of these forces lead to an increase in the quantity sold. And because the increase in supply is roughly equal to the increase in demand, the pressure on housing prices to rise (due to increasing demand) is offset by pressure on them to fall (due to increasing supply). ■

Interpreting the DATA   How did the coronavirus pandemic affect the market for child care?

The coronavirus pandemic prompted many child care centers to close as they faced increased costs related to new health and safety protocols. One study found that child care providers faced a nearly 50 percent increase in operating costs. If this were all that happened, we would expect the decline in the supply of child care services to lead the price of child care to rise and the quantity to fall. But while child care centers were facing rising costs of providing care, demand for child care services also fell. Parents lost work due to the pandemic, reducing their need for child care. And many parents were hesitant to use child care services due to the increased risk that their child would either get sick or bring Covid home. Again, if this were all that had happened, a decline in demand would lead the price to fall and the quantity to fall. Both forces led to an enormous decline in the quantity of child care used in early 2021 compared to 2020. However, the price for child care changed little, which allows us to infer that the impacts on price of the decreases in supply and in demand roughly offset each other. ■

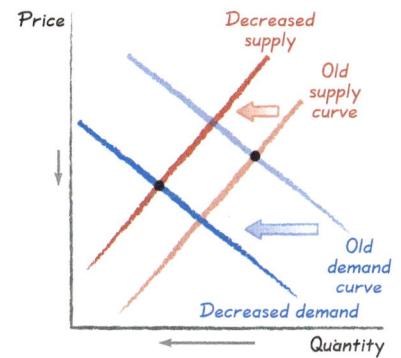

4.4 Tying It Together

The Supply-and-Demand Framework Is a Multitasker

You've now covered an enormous amount of ground. In particular, you've developed a complete framework that you can use to analyze any competitive market, whether it's the market for gas, food, shelter, or indeed anything else.

In Chapter 1, you learned about four core principles of economics, and we made the promise that these principles would be the key ingredients of any economic analysis. Since then, we've applied these principles to a key market, the market for gasoline.

We began in Chapter 2 by considering the demand side — focusing on potential buyers of gasoline. It turns out the amount of gas that any individual is willing to buy depends on the price of gas, and this relationship is summarized by their individual demand curve. By adding up the demand of many consumers, we arrived at the market demand curve, which summarizes the total quantity of gas demanded by the market at each potential price.

In Chapter 3, we turned to the supply side, analyzing potential sellers of gasoline. The quantity of gas that a seller is willing to sell depends on the price of gas, and this relationship is also neatly summarized, this time by their supply curves. Adding up supply across different sellers yields the market supply curve.

Finally, in this chapter, we've seen how these market demand and supply curves reveal the market equilibrium, and how the market will tend to move toward producing the equilibrium quantity at the equilibrium price. This price acts as the signal for some people to buy and others to sell, and hence determines what gets made, by whom, and to whom it is sold.

This supply-and-demand framework is very important. In fact, it is the basis of almost all economic analysis. The rest of economics comes down to developing these ideas in two directions. First, we'll apply these insights to other important markets, such as the markets for labor, capital, and housing. And second, we'll refine our analysis so that you can gain greater insight into the real world, where markets are not always perfectly competitive. You'll be using this framework a lot — in fact we think you'll use it for the rest of your life. So if you feel unsure about it, come back and read these chapters again.

Chapter 4 Review

Chapter at a Glance

Getting to Equilibrium

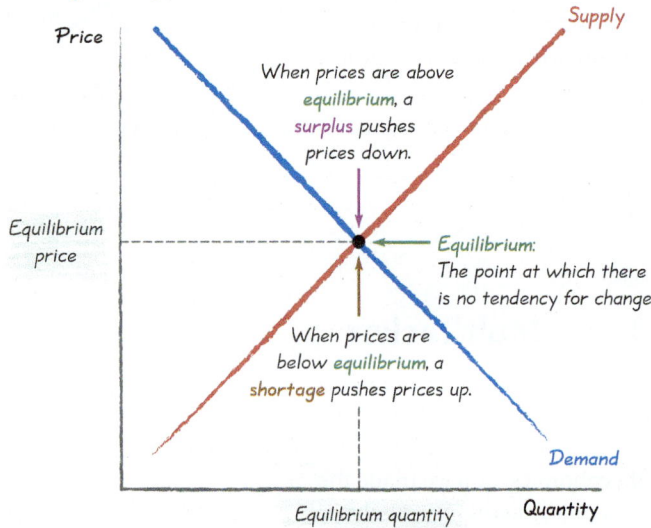

Price

Supply

When prices are above **equilibrium**, a **surplus** pushes prices down.

Equilibrium price

Equilibrium: The point at which there is no tendency for change

When prices are below **equilibrium**, a **shortage** pushes prices up.

Demand

Equilibrium quantity   Quantity

Is it a shortage or a surplus?

With a **surplus**: Prices are falling, discounting may occur, sellers may queue to find buyers, and sometimes extras get bundled for "free."

With a **shortage**: Prices are rising, buyers may queue to meet sellers, and sometimes there are secondary markets and/or "bundling" of unnecessary costly extras.

Three-step recipe when market conditions change

Step 1: Is the **supply** or **demand** curve shifting (or both)?
Step 2:. Is that shift an **increase** (shifting the curve to the right) or a **decrease** (shifting the curve to the left)?
Step 3: How will prices and quantities change in the new equilibrium?

Shifts in Demand

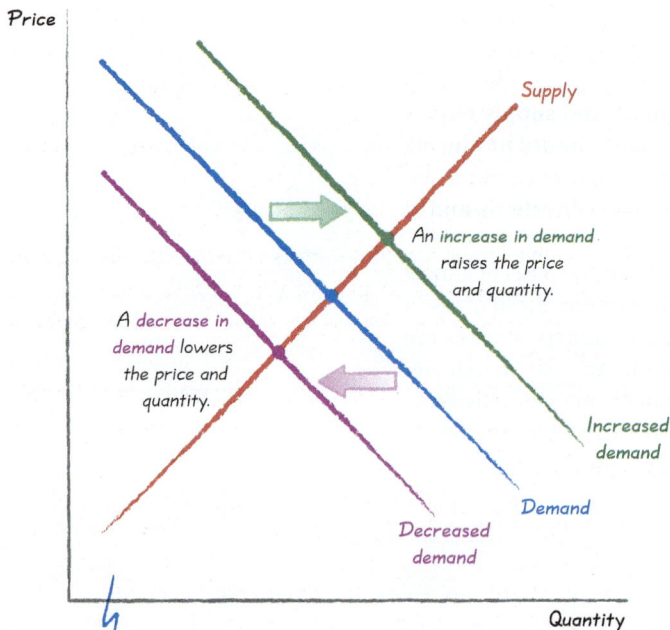

Price

Supply

An **increase in demand** raises the price and quantity.

A **decrease in demand** lowers the price and quantity.

Increased demand

Demand

Decreased demand

Quantity

If the price and quantity move in the **same** direction, then you know that the **demand curve** has shifted.
(Beware: The **supply curve** may have also shifted.)

Shifts in Supply

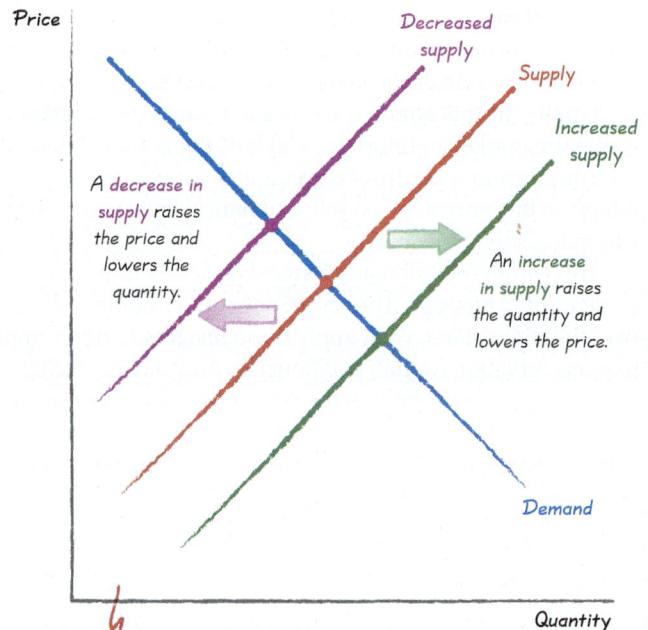

Price

Decreased supply

Supply

Increased supply

A **decrease in supply** raises the price and lowers the quantity.

An **increase in supply** raises the quantity and lowers the price.

Demand

Quantity

If the price and quantity move in **opposite** directions, then you know that the **supply curve** has shifted.
(Beware: The **demand curve** may have also shifted.)

Key Terms

equilibrium, 88

equilibrium price, 88

equilibrium quantity, 88

market, 86

market economies, 86

planned economies, 86

shortage, 90

surplus, 90

Study Problems

Learning Objective 4.1 *Survey the central role that markets play in our society, determining what is produced, how, by whom, and who gets it.*

1. Provide some examples of markets in which you participated, or will participate in, today. How often were you a buyer/demander? How often were you the seller/supplier? How would a change in price have affected your choices?

2. Provide some examples of markets that don't use currency to pay for goods and services.

3. Explain how looking for someone to marry is like a market. How is a marriage market similar to a labor market?

4. You are the coordinator of a nonprofit that distributes donated items to three local homeless shelters. What is the most efficient way to allocate your supplies to meet demand at different locations? Which of these best represent a planned approach and which best represent a market approach?

   a. Divide the donations evenly among the three shelters.

   b. Ask shelters to submit their requests, and decide what to send where based on their answers.

   c. Offer each shelter a virtual "budget" and have them bid on different items.

5. You purchased a ticket to the musical *Hamilton* through a verified reseller for $457.00. When your ticket arrives, you see the face value printed on it is $259.00. Based on this transaction, is the face value price being charged by the show's producers above, below, or equal to the equilibrium price? How do you know?

Learning Objective 4.2 *Analyze how markets bring supply and demand into balance.*

6. If the average price of gasoline is $3.25 per gallon in your town, and gasoline is a perfectly competitive market, explain what might happen and why in your town if the price of gas dropped to $0.50 overnight? What if it jumped up to $10 per gallon overnight?

7. Movie stars such as Salma Hayek, Samuel L. Jackson, Dwayne Johnson, and Jennifer Lawrence are paid millions of dollars per movie, which can take as much as six months of full-time work for an actor, while doctors and nurses earn considerably less over the same time period. Briefly explain why.

8. Consider the following data from the market demand and supply for apartments.

Rent	Quantity demanded	Quantity supplied
$2,000	5,000	23,000
$1,800	8,000	20,000
$1,600	11,000	17,000
$1,400	14,000	14,000
$1,200	17,000	11,000
$1,000	20,000	8,000

The average monthly rent for apartments is currently $1,200. At this price, how many apartments will be rented in this market? Is the market currently in equilibrium, experiencing a shortage, or experiencing a surplus? What do you expect to happen to the average rent? What is the equilibrium rent and quantity in the market?

9. When you arrive at the gas station, there is a line of cars wrapped around the block waiting for gas, so you go to the gas station down the road, only to find another line of cars! You get in line and end up waiting over an hour just to get to the pump and then are told that they've run out of gas. Is this market in equilibrium? Why or why not?

Learning Objective 4.3 *Assess the consequences of shifts in demand and supply, and how changes in prices and quantities reveal whether demand or supply changed.*

10. Higher average incomes increase the demand for preventative dental visits. Explain why this will lead the quantity supplied of dental visits to increase, but supply will not increase.

11. Suppose the supply of green tea increases; why is it that equilibrium price and equilibrium quantity move in opposite directions?

12. When British regulators were forced to suspend the license of a flu vaccine plant in Liverpool operated by the Chiron Corporation due to concerns over bacterial contamination, the number of flu vaccines available in the U.S. market decreased by 48 million doses. This was nearly half of the total supply of vaccines in the market. Use a supply-and-demand diagram to illustrate the impact of this event on the market for flu vaccines in the United States. What impact will this have on the equilibrium price and equilibrium quantity in the U.S. vaccine market?

13. In each of the following examples, determine how supply or demand shift and how the equilibrium price and quantity change.

    a. Smartphones: Microchips used in smartphones have become more powerful and less costly to produce.

    b. ALS medical research funds: The ALS ice bucket challenge goes viral, leading to greater awareness around the benefits and needs of ALS research.

14. According to a 2016 article in the *Wall Street Journal*, "After years of relative equilibrium, the job market for nurses is heating up in many markets, driving up wages and sign-on bonuses for the nation's fifth-largest occupation." Many nurses who previously delayed their retirement due to the 2008 recession had begun to retire, resulting in a retirement wave that caused nurses to exit the workforce in greater numbers than new nurses were entering. At the same time, demand for nurses had increased due to the additional health care coverage associated with job growth over the previous decade since the recession and the Affordable Care Act.

    a. Draw a demand and supply graph illustrating these developments in the market for nurses.

    b. Based on your diagram, forecast what will happen to the equilibrium wage for nurses as a result of the shift(s)? Is this consistent with what we actually observed?

    c. Briefly discuss whether this problem provides enough information to determine whether the equilibrium quantity of nurses increased or decreased.

    Source: Melanie Evans, "Nurses Are Again in Demand," *Wall Street Journal*, November 7, 2016, https://www.wsj.com/articles/nurses-are-again-in-demand-1478514622.

15. Show in a diagram the effect on the demand curve, the supply curve, the equilibrium price, and the equilibrium quantity of each of the following events.

    a. The market for steel in the United States: Fuel efficiency regulations have reduced the use of steel in automobile production and increased the use of lighter materials such as aluminum AND import restrictions limit the amount of steel that can be imported into the United States.

    b. The market for international airline tickets: Incomes decline due to a recession AND Norwegian Airlines adds more U.S. cities to its list of international flight destinations.

16. In each of the following scenarios, explain the changes in either supply or demand that would result. If the initial equilibrium price were yet to change, indicate whether a surplus or a shortage would result. Given this, what do you expect will subsequently happen to the price of the good?

    a. *In the market for paper:* New advances in recycling technology reduce the cost of producing paper made from recycled materials.

    b. *In the market for light bulbs:* Recently General Electric, one of the largest suppliers of light bulbs, decided to discontinue producing light bulbs.

    c. *In the market for Las Vegas hotels:* A heat wave in Las Vegas causes tourists to cancel their hotel room reservations and vacation elsewhere.

17. For each of the following observations, determine whether supply, demand, or both shifted and how.

    a. Over the last decade, the price of hybrid electric vehicles decreased, while the number of hybrid vehicles sold increased.

    b. During winter, the number of daily air routes between Denver and Aspen, Colorado, increases, as does the price of a ticket.

    c. From January through April in the United States, personal certified public accountants (CPAs) see a dramatic increase in their number of billable hours, but the average hourly rate of a CPA remains the same.

PART II:
Analyzing Markets

The Big Picture

You've mastered the basic tools of demand, supply, and equilibrium—now it's time to put them to work. In the chapters ahead, we'll use them to **analyze markets.**

We'll start by learning how to use supply and demand curves to **evaluate welfare,** illustrating how they can help policymakers figure out which policies will do the most to improve people's well-being. We'll also evaluate when supply and demand will lead to **efficient** outcomes and when they will lead to **market failure.**

Next, we'll bring everything together to demonstrate how market forces help reallocate stuff to better uses, and how prices help coordinate economic activity. We'll also see how you can get more done when you focus on your **comparative advantage** and do the activities for which you have the lowest opportunity cost. The result is that trade between buyers and sellers makes them both better off, generating **gains from trade.**

We'll then explore how **international trade** reshapes the domestic economy, and debate about whether **trade policy** should encourage freer trade or try to protect Americans from foreign competition. Finally, we'll shift to assessing the broader issues of **income inequality,** the incidence of **poverty,** and the government's role in income **redistribution.**

5 Welfare Economics: Evaluating Market Efficiency and Market Failure

Analyze how markets affect economic welfare.

- How do economists evaluate welfare and economic efficiency?
- How can you measure the gains to buyers and the gains to sellers?
- How efficient are competitive markets?
- What are the costs of market failure?
- What are the limitations of economic efficiency in policy analysis?

6 Comparative Advantage and Gains from Trade

Examine how markets generate gains from trade.

- What do markets do?
- How can you best allocate tasks to ensure they're done with the lowest opportunity cost?
- What is comparative advantage and why does it allow more to be produced?
- What role do prices play in coordinating economic activity?
- How can you harness market forces in your own life?

7 International Trade

Understand the consequences of global trade.

- Why do we trade with people in other countries?
- Who gains from international trade? Who loses?
- What are arguments for and against international trade?
- What are the effects of trade policy?
- How does globalization shape your life?

8 Inequality, Poverty, and Social Insurance

Understand inequality, poverty, the tools government uses to address them.

- How much economic inequality is there in the United States?
- How prevalent is poverty, and what are its implications?
- How does the government affect inequality and poverty?
- What are the arguments for and against income redistribution?

Welfare Economics: Evaluating Market Efficiency and Market Failure

If your parents are at all like mine, they probably warned you never to get in a stranger's car. They likely warned you not to meet up with random strangers from the internet, too. Yet every time you open your Uber app, you literally summon strangers from the internet, and then get in their car. This now-common transaction shows just how much change rideshare apps like Uber have wrought.

Ride-sharing changed more than just transportation.

Onfokus-/iStock/Getty Images

Drivers must pay all their own expenses from owning and maintaining their cars to filling them with gas. By using their own cars, they are essentially providing their own workplace. They get all the freedoms of being their own boss, such as deciding when, where, and for how long they want to work. But this freedom comes with a cost, as drivers aren't covered by the federal laws that protect most other workers, including minimum-wage laws, unemployment insurance, and worker's compensation.

Uber is disruptive. It has led to a huge decline in business for taxi drivers. Existing taxi companies are finding it hard to recruit new drivers, and they're losing customers. For people looking for a ride, it is easier than ever to get one. When Uber enters a city, it tends to dramatically increase the number of available drivers compared to the number of taxi drivers that had been available.

All of this has led to a fierce policy debate about whether Uber is a good thing. Not everyone is convinced that it is, and at various points, local governments in many countries have restricted or even outright banned ride-sharing.

It's a debate in which economic arguments loom large. But how can we tell whether allowing rideshare services like Uber is good for a community? How do economists weigh the gains to riders and rideshare drivers against the cost to taxi drivers? Should we just trust that the market is delivering what people want?

This chapter introduces the tools of welfare economics, which you'll use to assess how different outcomes affect economic well-being. We'll start with an overview of how economists evaluate public policies. We'll calculate economic surplus, and use this to assess the efficiency of markets. Then we'll take a look at how markets can fail, and use these tools to assess the costs of market failure. Finally, we'll join the debate about the appropriate role of economic efficiency in policy analysis.

Chapter Objective

Analyze how markets affect economic welfare.

5.1 Evaluating Public Policies
Learn how to evaluate welfare and economic efficiency.

5.2 Measuring Economic Surplus
Measure the economic surplus generated in a market.

5.3 Market Efficiency
Assess the efficiency of markets.

5.4 Market Failure and Deadweight Loss
Measure the costs of market failure.

5.5 Beyond Economic Efficiency
Evaluate the limitations of economic efficiency in policy analysis.

🎙️ Podcast
Think Like an Economist
Economic Surplus—Getting the Most Out of Life

5.1 Evaluating Public Policies

Learning Objective *Learn how to evaluate welfare and economic efficiency.*

Should we raise the minimum wage? Should carbon be taxed? Should college be free? Should cities require mask-wearing during outbreaks of airborne diseases? Should the speed limit be higher? Should we reduce barriers to trading with China? Each of these questions brings intense political debate. As a voter, a taxpayer, a community activist, or a business stakeholder — and possibly even as a policy adviser, policymaker, or politician — you're going to play a key role in that debate.

Positive and Normative Policy Analysis

Your contribution will be most valuable if it's based on careful analysis. Typically, this means that you should conduct your analysis in two distinct stages.

Stage 1: Positive analysis describes what *will* happen. The first stage of analysis is to ask: *What will happen if we adopt this policy?* This calls for a purely objective analysis, describing and forecasting the effects of the policy. For instance, you can use the supply-and-demand framework to predict the likely consequences of increasing the minimum wage. You can use it to forecast the number of people who'll get a pay raise, to estimate how much their pay will increase, to assess the effects on the profitability of employers, and to predict how many jobs businesses will eliminate due to these higher wages. An in-depth analysis might even detail the characteristics of those who will gain and those who will lose from such a policy. This type of inquiry, an assessment that describes what is happening or predicts what will happen, is called **positive analysis.**

positive analysis Describes what *is* happening, explaining why, or predicting what will happen.

Stage 2: Normative analysis assesses what *should* happen. The second step is to ask: *Which is the better outcome, and what policy should the government adopt?* Answering this question requires a value judgment about which outcome is better. In the first step, positive analysis, economists merely describe likely effects. But this second step requires you to make a judgment about what *should* happen, or what *ought* to be done. Whenever you use words like *should* or *ought*, you're doing **normative analysis,** because your conclusions rest on normative, or value judgments.

normative analysis Prescribes what *should* happen, which involves value judgments.

Think about the minimum wage: Should it be raised or not? Positive analysis is helpful, because it lays out the likely consequences of the policy, outlining who'll gain, who'll lose, and what the stakes are for all concerned. But to assess whether the policy is worth pursuing, you need to evaluate whether the gains to some people outweigh the losses to others, and that requires a value judgment. It depends on how you weigh the benefits of higher wages for low-wage workers against the costs of lower profits for employers and the pain of unemployment for those who lose their jobs. Whatever view you hold, I bet that at least one of your classmates has a different set of values and so comes to a different conclusion.

Do the Economics

Which of the following claims involve positive analysis, and which reflect normative analysis?

a. Lower college tuition will lead to more children from low-income families attending college.

b. College tuition should be lower so that students from low-income families can afford it.

c. The average American taxpayer pays around 15% of their income in federal income taxes.

d. Income taxes are too high and the federal government should cut them.

e. A leading forecaster expects Americans to import more than $500 billion worth of goods from China next year.

f. The United States should renegotiate trade agreements with China. ∎

Answer: a, c, and e are positive analysis, and b, d, and f involve normative analysis.

Efficiency and Equity

If you're going to take a position in policy debates advocating what the government should do, then you're going to need a way to judge which policy yields better outcomes. That is, we need a way to evaluate how a policy affects how well people are doing in terms of happiness, well-being, or prosperity—in other words, their *welfare*. Fortunately, you've already developed the building blocks that can be helpful for this kind of normative analysis.

The outcome that yields the most economic surplus is the most efficient outcome. Economists often evaluate policies using the criterion of **economic efficiency,** which says that the more economic surplus that's generated, the better the outcome. Recall that **economic surplus** measures the benefits that follow from a decision, less the costs you incur. It measures the gains generated whenever something is bought or sold. When economists describe an outcome as more efficient, they mean that it yields more economic surplus. At the extreme, the **efficient outcome** yields the largest possible economic surplus. The underlying logic is that economic surplus measures the size of the economic pie, and more pie is always better. Mmmm, pie . . .

economic efficiency An outcome is more economically efficient if it yields more economic surplus.

economic surplus The total benefits minus total costs flowing from a decision; it measures how much a decision has improved your well-being.

efficient outcome The efficient outcome yields the largest possible economic surplus.

Efficient outcomes won't make everyone happy. Increasing economic efficiency rarely makes everyone happy, because most policies help some people but harm others. Economic efficiency simply assesses whether economic surplus rises, which can occur only if the gains in economic surplus to those who are helped are larger than the declines in surplus among those who are harmed. But even if a policy is efficient, some people might be harmed, and those who are harmed aren't going to be happy.

For instance, the laws that allow Uber to operate in your city probably raise economic surplus, even as they harm taxi drivers who now face more competition. Economic surplus is higher because, overall, the benefits to Uber drivers and passengers outweigh the harm suffered by taxi drivers. But that argument is little solace to those taxi drivers who lose their livelihood.

Efficient outcomes hold the potential to make everyone better off. Relying on economic efficiency implicitly involves some difficult value judgments. In this case, it embeds the judgment that the harm done to taxi drivers is a reasonable price to pay for the benefits to Uber's drivers and customers. Perhaps you agree with this judgment, and perhaps you don't.

One argument for focusing on efficiency is that whenever economic surplus rises, it's *possible* for those who benefit to compensate those who were harmed, and to do so in a way that ensures everyone's better off. That's because with a bigger pie it's always possible to slice it in a way that ensures everyone gets a bigger slice. In practice, this might mean levying a small tax on Uber's drivers and customers, and sending the proceeds to the taxi drivers who were hurt by this policy.

Equity is also important (but ignored by efficiency). In reality, it's rare for new policies to compensate the people they harm. Thus, the argument that it's possible to make everyone better off is just that — a possibility. The reality is that policies change both the level of economic surplus and the distribution of that surplus.

Consequently, real-world policy debates are rarely about efficiency alone. They are also about **equity,** which means they are concerned with whether a policy will yield a fair distribution of economic benefits. When you evaluate both efficiency and equity, you'll account for both the size of the pie, and how it's sliced.

equity A measure of fairness. An outcome yields greater equity if it results in a fairer distribution of economic benefits.

5.2 Measuring Economic Surplus

Learning Objective *Measure the economic surplus generated in a market.*

We've just seen that economic surplus plays an important role in economic policy debates. So, if you want to influence these debates, you'll need to know how to measure economic surplus. That's our next task.

Consumer Surplus

consumer surplus The economic surplus you get from buying something. Consumer surplus = Marginal benefit – Price.

When you gain economic surplus from buying something, economists refer to it as **consumer surplus,** because you're earning that surplus in your role as a consumer. You gain consumer surplus when you buy something for a cheaper price than the marginal benefit you get from it.

Consumer surplus is your marginal benefit, less the price. Let's take a familiar example. You're in the fitting room at your favorite store, and you've just tried on the perfect pair of Levi's. But the price tag is missing. Looking in the mirror, you decide you're willing to pay up to $80 for them. You ask the clerk to look up the price and learn some good news: The price is only $50. You were willing to pay up to $80 for the jeans, but you can buy them for only $50 — it's like you're $30 ahead! That $30 gain is the consumer surplus you get when you buy those jeans.

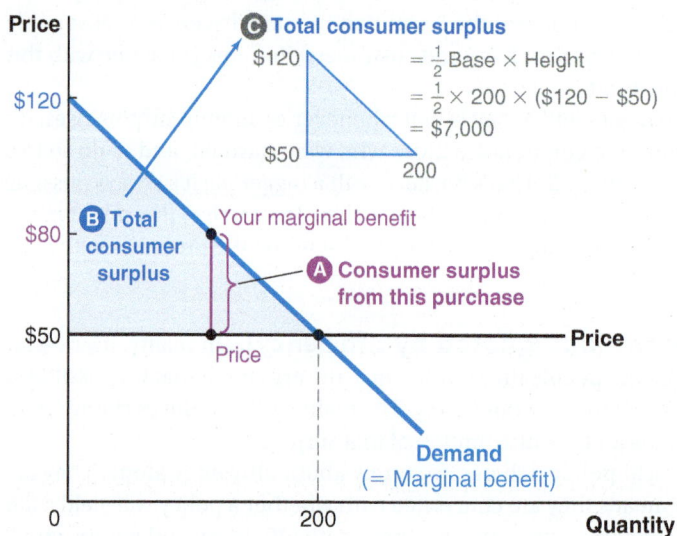

Your marginal benefit is your willingness to pay for these jeans.

Consumer surplus describes the gain from buying something at a price below the highest price you were willing to pay, which is your marginal benefit. Therefore, it's the marginal benefit you'll get from those jeans, less the price you pay. You can see it graphically in Figure 1, and you can measure it as:

$$\text{Consumer surplus} = \text{Marginal benefit} - \text{Price}$$

Figure 1 | **Consumer Surplus**

Ⓐ Your consumer surplus from *a single purchase* is the difference between your marginal benefit and the price.

Ⓑ The total consumer surplus *across all buyers* is the area under the demand curve above the price.

Ⓒ This is the **area of a triangle** $= \frac{1}{2}$ **Base × Height**.

Ⓒ Total consumer surplus
$= \frac{1}{2}$ Base × Height
$= \frac{1}{2} \times 200 \times (\$120 - \$50)$
$= \$7,000$

Consumer surplus is the area below the demand curve and above the price. So far, we've analyzed the consumer surplus of a single transaction — it's the marginal benefit you get, less the price you pay. What about the consumer surplus of all purchases in a market? Let's take a look at the market demand curve.

Recall from Chapter 2 that the demand curve is the marginal benefit curve. This means that each point on the demand curve reveals an individual buyer's marginal benefit. And so for any individual purchase, the consumer surplus gained is the marginal benefit (which is given by the height of the demand curve) less the price. You can see the consumer surplus from your single purchase shown as the difference between the point on the demand curve where the marginal benefit is equal to $80 minus the price of $50. Add up this gain for each pair of jeans sold, and you'll end up with the entire area under the market demand curve and above the price, out to the quantity purchased. This reveals that total consumer surplus in a market is *the area under the market demand curve and above the price, out to the quantity sold.*

The area of a triangle is half the base, times the height. When the demand curve is a straight line, consumer surplus is a right triangle. Figuring out total consumer surplus means figuring out the area of that triangle, which is half the base, times the height. (And you thought high school geometry wasn't useful!)

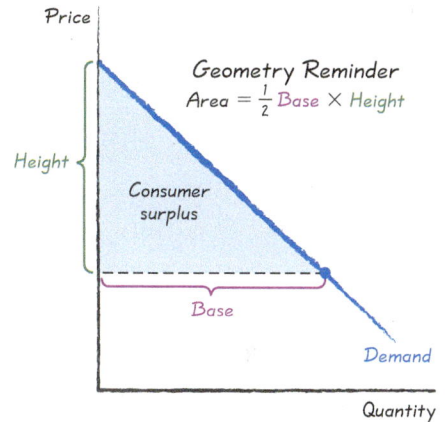

Do the Economics

What's the consumer surplus of a song? Let's try to work it out. Take Rihanna's song "Work," which she performed with Drake. Rihanna sold 10 million copies of this song for roughly $1.29 a copy. If half the people who bought this song said in a survey that they would have been willing to pay at least $2.29 for it, then we have two points on the demand curve for this song. If we connect these two points to get an estimate of the demand curve for this song, we'll discover that the demand curve cuts the vertical axis at $3.29.

Consumer surplus is the area under the demand curve and above the price, out to the quantity sold. Zoom in on that triangle:

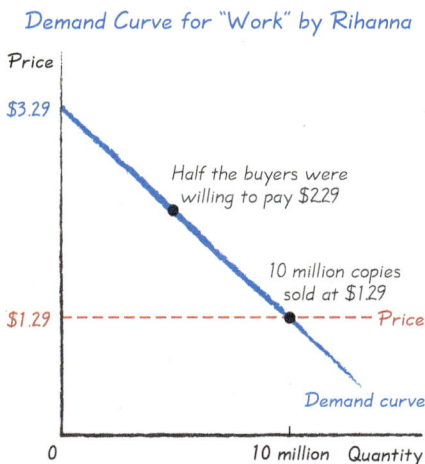

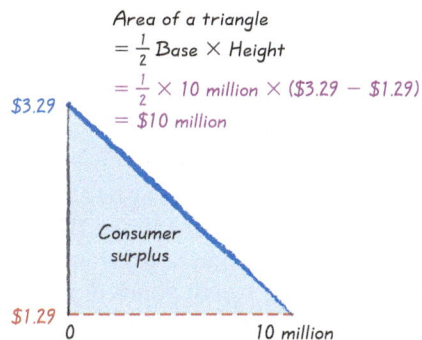

That's it. Rihanna's song created around $10 million in consumer surplus for her fans. Thanks, Rihanna! ■

You earn consumer surplus on all but your last purchase. Some students are puzzled by the idea that consumer surplus is the difference between their marginal benefit and the price, while the Rational Rule for Buyers (introduced in Chapter 2) says to keep buying until price equals marginal benefit. But there's no contradiction. The Rational Rule tells you to keep buying jeans until the marginal benefit *of the last pair* is equal to the price.

If you bought four pairs, then your fourth and last pair yields a marginal benefit equal to their $50 price tag. That means you won't earn any consumer surplus on that last pair. But the marginal benefit from your first pair is likely much higher — you don't have to wear shorts! Perhaps your marginal benefit was $80 for that first pair, exceeding the $50 price, and therefore, yielding a healthy consumer surplus. Likewise, you also may earn consumer surplus on the second and third pair you buy. The point is, even if you earn no consumer surplus on the last item you purchase, you'll likely earn consumer surplus from all of your preceding purchases.

You enjoy a lot of consumer surplus in your life. Consumer surplus is important because the price you pay for something is often a poor indicator of the benefits you get from it. Consider water. Because it's so cheap, your marginal gallon of water is probably used for something pretty unnecessary, like running the faucet while brushing your teeth.

Not every use of water saves your life.

But how much would you be willing to pay for the half-gallon a day you need to stay alive? Thousands of dollars, right? Yet your water bill shows that you pay only pennies for it. The fact that water is cheap doesn't mean that it's not valuable; rather, it means that you're enjoying thousands of dollars of water-related consumer surplus.

The same idea applies to health care. Antibiotics that sell for only a few dollars can prevent a simple infection from becoming life threatening. Vaccinations protect you from Covid-19, polio, hepatitis and more, helping both you and those who could potentially catch something from you, yet they cost very little. And if you've ever had a friend or relative survive a life-saving operation, you've probably enjoyed a lot of surgery-related consumer surplus. Even if the surgery costs thousands, that price is small relative to the benefit of saving a loved one.

Each of these examples shows that you'll enjoy a lot of consumer surplus in your life. Indeed, that's a theme we'll continue to explore in the next case study.

Interpreting the DATA   **Consumer surplus of the internet**

Perhaps you started your day by checking your e-mail. Maybe you skimmed Instagram, Facebook, Snapchat, or Twitter. Hopefully you looked up the weather forecast before heading out. You might have listened to a podcast on the way to class. While you (hopefully!) didn't look at your phone during class, when it ended you may have used Google to look up a troubling concept. And later in the evening, you might have used Yelp to choose where to get dinner, and checked Google Maps for directions. Or maybe it's a quiet night, so you headed home to browse Reddit, read the news, and then watch videos on YouTube. How much did you pay to use each of these sites?

Nothing. Nada. $0.

If you used the price to measure the economic importance of your favorite websites, you'd infer that they're worth nothing. But that would be a mistake. It's a mistake, because it fails to account for the enormous consumer surplus that a good website generates.

To measure this consumer surplus, think about how much you would pay each year to have access to Google. Likewise, you can evaluate your willingness to pay for

Wikipedia, TikTok, and all the other internet services to figure out the marginal benefit you get from your favorite websites. The consumer surplus you get from these services is your marginal benefit since the price — which you subtract from marginal benefit to get consumer surplus — is zero.

Economists have made such calculations, considering different ways of measuring the marginal benefit people get from these services. They've looked at how much people used to spend on internet access when it was a newer, more expensive technology; at how much people used to pay for non-internet-based substitutes like encyclopedias; at how much time people spend on the internet; and at what people say they would have to be paid to give up access to internet services. While estimates vary, one reasonable estimate is that access to the internet collectively brings the average person around $2,600 per year worth of consumer surplus. Consumer surplus reveals that these websites are extremely valuable, even though most of this value isn't reflected in their low or nonexistent price. ■

Producer Surplus

Consumer surplus tells us about the gains that buyers get from a trade. But buyers aren't the only ones who benefit from a transaction; sellers also gain something. When you gain economic surplus from *selling* something, economists refer to it as **producer surplus**, because you're earning that surplus in your role as a producer. You gain producer surplus when you sell something at a higher price than the marginal costs you incur.

producer surplus The economic surplus you get from selling something. Producer surplus = Price – Marginal cost.

Producer surplus is the price, less the marginal cost. Let's analyze what happens when you buy a pair of Levi's for $50, but this time, we'll focus on the producer's perspective. For Levi Strauss, the company that makes those jeans, the marginal benefit of selling you those jeans is the $50 price you paid for them. And the marginal cost is the $35 worth of extra denim, thread, and labor it took to make that extra pair of jeans. Levi's is thrilled to get $50 in return for $35 worth of denim, thread, and labor. It's thrilled because producing and selling those jeans made the company $15 better off. This $15 is the producer surplus that Levi's gains from this transaction.

Producer surplus describes the gain a producer gets from selling something at a higher price than necessary for them to want to supply the item, which is its marginal cost. More generally, the producer surplus a seller gains from a transaction is the price they receive less the marginal cost. And so, you can measure it as:

$$\text{Producer surplus} = \text{Price} - \text{Marginal cost}$$

Producer surplus is the area above the supply curve and below the price. So far, we've figured out the producer surplus from Levi's selling you one pair of jeans. What about the total producer surplus from all the jeans sold by all producers? The producer surplus from any individual transaction is the price less marginal cost. This leads to a simple graphical representation: Total producer surplus in a market is *the area below the price and above the supply curve, out to the quantity sold,* as shown in Figure 2.

To see why, recall from Chapter 3 that the supply curve is also the seller's marginal cost curve. This means that each point on the supply curve reveals a seller's marginal cost. And so for any given sale, a seller gains producer surplus equal to the price, less their marginal cost, and the marginal cost is the height of the supply curve. Add up this producer surplus across all jeans sold, and you'll end up adding the entire area above the supply curve and below the price, out to the quantity sold.

You earn producer surplus on all but your last sale. As a seller, your producer surplus is the difference between the price and your marginal costs. But the Rational Rule for Sellers in Competitive Markets (in Chapter 3) says to keep selling until price equals marginal cost. At first glance, this might confuse you into thinking that you won't earn any producer surplus if you follow this rule. But that's not right. Remember that the Rational Rule says to keep selling *until* price equals marginal cost. This means that price is equal to

Figure 2 | **Producer Surplus**

Ⓐ **Producer surplus** from a *single sale* is the difference between the price the seller receives and the marginal cost.

Ⓑ The **total producer surplus** *across all sellers* is the area above the supply curve below the price out to the quantity sold.

Ⓒ This is the **area of a triangle** $= \frac{1}{2}$ **Base × Height**.

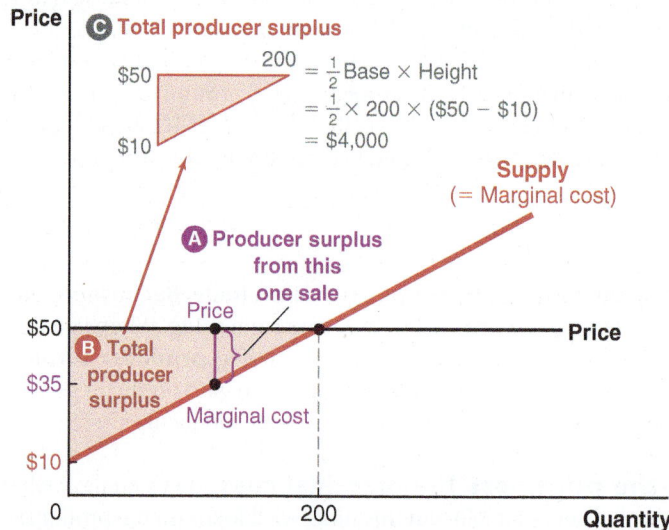

marginal cost only for the last (or marginal) pair of jeans you sell. With an upward-sloping marginal cost curve, the marginal cost of every other pair of jeans you make is lower, and so you'll earn a healthy producer surplus on all but the last pair of jeans you sell.

EVERYDAY Economics   **The producer surplus of work**

My first job was babysitting, and I loved it. I got to eat the family's snack food, have fun playing with the kids, then watch TV after they went to bed. The pay was also great. Here's what I never told the parents who hired me — I would have done it for half the pay.

Have you ever had a job where you would have done it for less than you were actually paid? If so, then you earned producer surplus at your job.

Here's the logic: As a worker, you're a supplier. The product you are supplying (or selling) is your labor, and your hourly wage is the price you're selling it at. What's the relevant marginal cost? Applying the opportunity cost principle, it's the value of your next best use of that hour. If the wage exceeds how much you value this alternative use of your time, then you're earning producer surplus.

In one survey, around one-third of American workers said they would stay in their job even if their salary were cut by 25%. A typical economics graduate with a few years of work experience earns about $60,000 per year, and so this would mean sticking with your employer even if you were paid $15,000 per year less. So we can infer that many folks are earning at least $15,000 per year in producer surplus! ∎

Voluntary Exchange and Gains from Trade

Next time you go shopping, pay attention to how polite everyone is. When I last made a purchase, I handed over my payment and said thank you, and the seller thanked me back. We now understand why. I thanked the seller because the store gave me something that I valued more than what I paid for it. I was grateful to gain some consumer surplus.

And the seller thanked me because I gave them money that they value more than the item they were handing over. They were grateful to gain some producer surplus.

This is more than mere politeness — it reveals a deeper economic truth: Voluntary transactions create both consumer and producer surplus. This means both the buyer and the seller gain from trade. The big idea here is that buying or selling goods and services isn't a zero-sum game in which one person wins at the other person's expense. Instead, trade is a win-win situation, creating gains for both the buyer and the seller. That's what economists mean when they talk about *gains from trade*. (We'll explore gains from trade further in the next chapter.)

Voluntary exchange ensures both buyer and seller enjoy gains from trade. Trade generates gains for both the buyer and the seller because it's based on **voluntary exchange,** where buyers and sellers exchange money for goods only if they both want to. And you want to buy or sell stuff only if it will make you better off.

Think about it: As a buyer following the cost-benefit principle, you'll buy a pair of jeans only if the marginal benefit you receive is at least as large as the price you pay. That is, you'll buy something only if it yields consumer surplus. Likewise, a supplier following the cost-benefit principle will sell jeans only if the price is at least as large as their marginal cost. That is, suppliers produce stuff only if they expect it will generate producer surplus. So voluntary exchange ensures that both buyer and seller enjoy gains from trade (or at least that neither is made worse off).

voluntary exchange Buyers and sellers exchange money for goods only if they both want to.

Markets are about competition *and* cooperation. This leads to an underappreciated perspective. You might be used to thinking about markets as being driven by competition. But voluntary exchange generates economic surplus for both buyers and sellers, and so perhaps it's more useful to think about markets as facilitating *cooperation*. Just as your purchase of Levi's jeans helps boost its bottom line, Levi's production of jeans has also helped you line your bottom.

This doesn't mean that consumers and producers share equally in the gains from trade. But even if the gains are unequal, as long as both buyers and sellers are well-informed and follow the cost-benefit principle, neither will engage in a trade that makes them worse off.

Economic surplus is marginal benefit less marginal cost. Let's put the pieces together. The economic surplus generated by a transaction is the sum of consumer surplus enjoyed by the buyer (the marginal benefit, less the price) and the producer surplus accruing to the seller (the price, less the marginal cost). Add them up, and the economic surplus generated by a transaction is the marginal benefit less the marginal cost:

$$\text{Economic surplus} = \underbrace{\text{Consumer surplus}}_{\text{Marginal benefit} - \text{Price}} + \underbrace{\text{Producer surplus}}_{\text{Price} - \text{Marginal cost}}$$
$$= \text{Marginal benefit} - \text{Marginal cost}$$

For instance, when you buy a pair of jeans that brings you $80 worth of benefit, and it cost Levi's only $35 worth of denim, cotton, and labor, the transaction creates $45 in economic surplus.

Economic surplus is the area between the demand and supply curves. Total economic surplus, or gains from trade, across a whole market is the consumer surplus triangle (the area below the demand curve and above the price) plus the producer surplus triangle (the area above the supply curve and below the price). Add them up and you'll discover that *economic surplus is the area between the demand and supply curves, to the left of the quantity bought and sold,* as shown in Figure 3.

Alternatively, you can think of the economic surplus from a single transaction as being the marginal benefit less the marginal cost. Add this up across all items purchased, and it's the difference between marginal benefits (the demand curve) and marginal cost (the supply curve) across all items bought and sold. That's why economic surplus is the area

Figure 3 | Economic Surplus

Ⓐ Economic surplus of a *single transaction* is the marginal benefit, less the marginal cost.
Ⓑ Economic surplus is the area between the demand and supply curves out to the quantity bought and sold.
Ⓒ Economic surplus gained from all transactions:
= ***Consumer surplus*** + ***Producer surplus***.
= ***Marginal benefit*** − ***Marginal cost***.

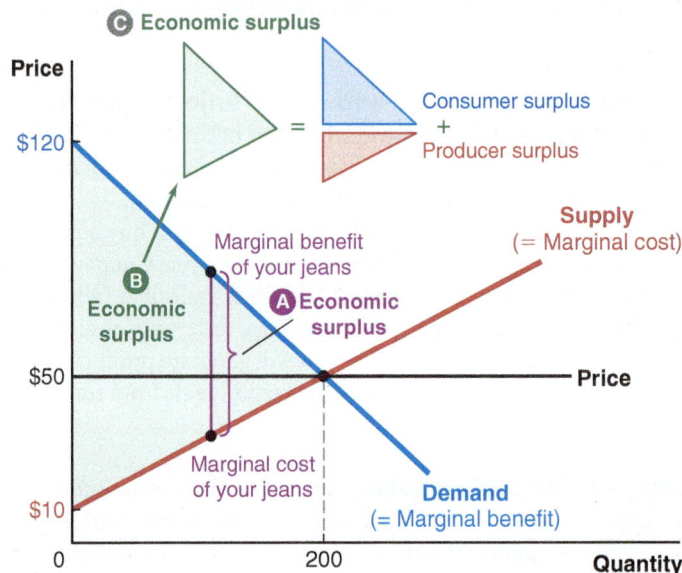

between the demand (or marginal benefit) curve and the supply (or marginal cost) curve, out to the total quantity.

By now you should have a good sense of how to measure economic surplus — it's the marginal benefit to the buyer less the marginal cost to the seller. This means that on a graph, it's the area between the demand and supply curves, to the left of the quantity sold.

Now let's use these tools to assess the efficiency of markets.

5.3 Market Efficiency

Learning Objective *Assess the efficiency of markets.*

Markets are the central organizing institution of our lives. They determine what products are made, how much is produced, who makes what, who gets what, and what the price will be. Markets determine your income and what you can afford to buy. It isn't always this way. In centrally planned economies like Cuba, North Korea, and to an extent China, the government decides what gets made, and who gets what.

Most countries — and most economists — prefer market-based economies because markets yield more efficient outcomes. That is, markets create the largest possible amount of economic surplus. They do so by providing efficient answers to three central questions: (1) who makes what; (2) who gets what; and (3) how much gets bought and sold? Let's explore how markets answer each of these questions.

Question 1: Who Makes What?

Think about the supply side of the economy: Millions of businesses produce a dizzying array of products. How do we know which businesses should produce which products? Which firms should produce a lot, and which should produce only a little? Who should be in business, and who should go kaput? While it's nearly impossible for any individual to find the best answers, a well-functioning market can figure it all out. Let's explore how.

Efficient production minimizes costs. **Efficient production** occurs when we produce a given level of output at the lowest possible cost. This requires allocating production so that each item is produced at the lowest marginal cost.

Consider two important suppliers in the market for tomatoes. Harris Sisters is a small family farm in North Carolina, while Big Red is a large industrial farm in California. The marginal cost curve of each farm is shown in Figure 4, along with the current price of tomatoes, which is $2 per pound.

efficient production Producing a given quantity of output at the lowest possible cost, which requires producing each good at the lowest marginal cost.

Figure 4 | **Which Firm Should Supply How Much?**

Ⓐ When the price is $2, **Harris Sisters supplies 3 million pounds** and **Big Red supplies 7 million pounds**.

Ⓑ If Harris Sisters produces a larger share, **total costs will rise** because **Harris Sisters will produce these extra tomatoes at a marginal cost > $2**, even as Big Red's marginal costs are < $2.

Ⓒ If Big Red produces a larger share, **total costs will rise**, because **Big Red will produce those extra tomatoes at a marginal cost > $2**, even as Harris Sisters' marginal cost is < $2.

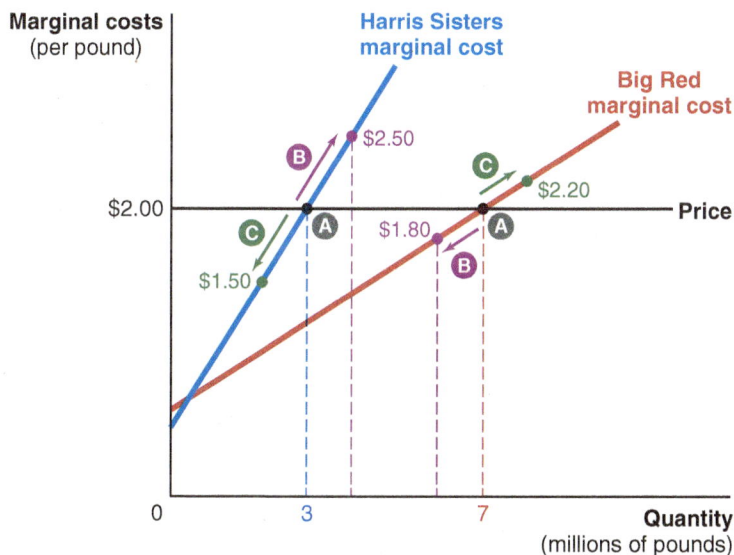

A business's marginal cost curve is also its individual supply curve, so when the price is $2 per pound, Big Red supplies 7 million pounds of tomatoes, and Harris Sisters supplies 3 million pounds. This is efficient production, because there's no way to produce 10 million pounds of tomatoes at a lower cost. That is, supply and demand lead to efficient production.

To see this, consider the alternatives.

What if you ask Harris Sisters to produce a greater number of tomatoes and Big Red to produce fewer? The total cost of producing those 10 million tomatoes will rise. It will cost Harris Sisters more than $2 per pound to produce those extra tomatoes (perhaps as much as $2.50 per pound) even though Big Red had previously produced those extra tomatoes at a marginal cost less than $2 per pound (perhaps as low as $1.80). So this alternative is inefficient, because it raises the total cost of producing these 10 million pounds of tomatoes.

Alternatively, what if you ask Harris Sisters to produce fewer tomatoes and Big Red to produce more? That's also inefficient. The problem is that when Big Red produces more tomatoes, its marginal cost exceeds $2 per pound (perhaps it's as high as $2.20), while Harris Sisters could have produced those extra tomatoes at a marginal cost below $2 (perhaps as low as $1.50). And so this alternative plan is also costlier.

Putting the pieces together, we've discovered that any production plan other than the one caused by the forces of supply and demand would raise costs. Amazingly enough, supply and demand lead Harris Sisters and Big Red to divvy up total production in such a way as to ensure that it occurs at the lowest possible cost! This is how competitive markets lead to efficient production in which each item is produced at the lowest possible cost.

Markets distribute production across firms in a way that minimizes costs. It's worth pausing to think about how amazing this is. The farmers at Big Red and Harris Sisters don't know each other, and indeed, they've never even been in touch. Neither has an interest in ensuring that 10 million pounds of tomatoes is produced as cheaply as possible. Instead, each of them pursues their own self-interest, choosing the production levels that maximize their own profits. Yet this self-interest leads these businesses to split production in a way that ensures that together they produce the industry's total output at the lowest possible cost.

In sum, competition leads to overall efficient production. In the extreme, perfectly competitive markets ensure that every good is produced by the supplier who can do so at the lowest possible marginal cost.

Question 2: Who Gets What?

Let's now turn to the demand side of the economy. There are millions of people who all want to consume the myriad products the economy produces. Who should get what? To take just one example: Who should get a lot of tomatoes, and who should get only a few? Intuitively, we want the tomatoes to go to people who will really value them. After all, there's no point in sending tomatoes to folks like my uncle who despises them.

efficient allocation Allocating goods to create the largest economic surplus, which requires that each good goes to the person who'll get the highest marginal benefit from it.

Efficient allocation maximizes benefits. An **efficient allocation** occurs when goods are allocated to create the largest economic surplus from the allocation, which requires that each good goes to the person who gets the highest marginal benefit from it (at least as measured by how much they are willing to pay).

Consider two tomato buyers, Camila and Peter. Their marginal benefit curves are shown in Figure 5. Remember, these marginal benefit curves are also their individual demand curves, and so when the price is $2, Peter will buy 7 pounds of tomatoes, and Camila will buy 3 pounds.

Figure 5 | Who Should Get How Much?

A When the price is $2, **Peter buys 7 pounds of tomatoes**, and **Camila buys 3 pounds**.
B Giving Peter fewer and Camila more is a bad idea because **Peter forgoes tomatoes with a marginal benefit > $2**, but **Camila only gets < $2 marginal benefit** from extra tomatoes.
C Giving Peter more and Camila fewer is also a bad idea, because **Peter gets < $2 marginal benefit** from extra tomatoes, but **Camila forgoes tomatoes yielding > $2 marginal benefit**.

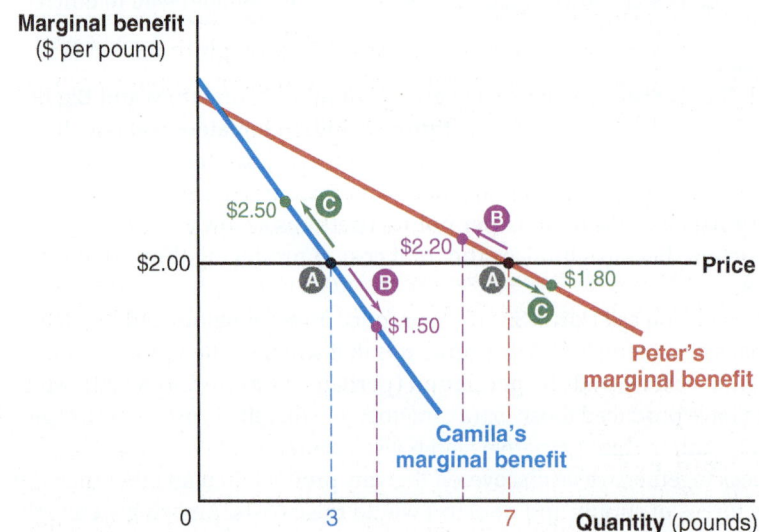

This is an efficient allocation, because each tomato is going to the person with the highest marginal benefit, ensuring that they generate the largest economic surplus. That is, supply and demand leads to an efficient allocation.

To see this, consider alternative allocations.

You could give Camila some of Peter's tomatoes. But that will decrease economic surplus, because the extra benefit to Camila is less than the forgone benefit to Peter. The reason is that Camila's marginal benefit from extra tomatoes is less than $2 (perhaps as low as $1.50), while Peter is forgoing tomatoes from which he would get a marginal benefit that's greater than $2 (perhaps as high as $2.20).

Alternatively, you could try to give Peter some of Camila's tomatoes, but this will also decrease economic surplus, because Peter's marginal benefit from getting extra tomatoes is less than $2 (say, $1.80), while Camila will forgo tomatoes from which she would get a marginal benefit that's greater than $2 (perhaps $2.50).

We've discovered that the forces of supply and demand lead Camila and Peter to divvy up these tomatoes in a way that ensures each tomato goes to the person who'll get the highest marginal benefit from it (at least as measured in terms of willingness to pay). Any other allocation would reduce the total amount of economic surplus. It follows that competitive markets lead to an efficient allocation of goods in which each item winds up being sold to the person who'll get the highest marginal benefit from it.

Markets allocate goods to those with the highest marginal benefit. This is an extraordinary outcome. Neither Camila nor Peter know each other, and indeed, they've never even spoken. But by each pursuing their self-interest, they've ensured that each tomato is allocated to the person who would enjoy the highest marginal benefit from it. This same logic applies to how markets allocate billions of tomatoes (and countless other items) across millions of buyers — the competitive market will allocate them to the folks with the highest marginal benefit. As each buyer pursues their own self-interest, the market allots each tomato to the person who gets the largest marginal benefit, at least as measured by their willingness to pay.

Question 3: How Much Gets Bought and Sold?

Our final step is to analyze the quantity of goods that is bought and sold. We'll assess whether the forces of supply and demand lead to the **efficient quantity,** which is the quantity that produces the largest possible economic surplus.

efficient quantity The quantity that produces the largest possible economic surplus.

The Rational Rule for Markets says to produce until marginal benefit equals marginal cost. Let's start by figuring out the efficient quantity of tomatoes: How many tomatoes will produce the largest possible economic surplus for society as a whole? Since this is a "how many" question, the marginal principle says to focus on the simpler question: "Should we produce one more tomato?" Next, apply the cost-benefit principle, which says that yes, an extra tomato will increase economic surplus, as long as the marginal benefit is at least as large as the marginal cost.

Put the pieces together, and we get the following very helpful rule.

The **Rational Rule for Markets:** *To increase economic surplus, produce more of an item if the marginal benefit of one more is greater than (or equal to) its marginal cost.*

Rational Rule for Markets Produce more of a good if its marginal benefit is greater than (or equal to) the marginal cost.

It follows that we'll get the largest possible economic surplus if the market keeps producing until marginal benefit equals marginal cost. That is, the efficient quantity occurs where:

$$\text{Marginal benefit} = \text{Marginal cost}$$

Supply and demand produce the surplus-maximizing quantity. There is no one in charge of the market; somehow, the forces of supply and demand naturally produce this surplus-maximizing quantity. Recall that equilibrium occurs where supply equals demand. In a well-functioning market, the supply curve is also the marginal cost curve, and the demand curve is also the marginal benefit curve. So supply-equals-demand equilibrium occurs at the point where marginal benefit equals marginal cost. As Figure 6 illustrates, this is the point that creates the largest possible economic surplus.

Figure 6 | **What Quantity Yields the Most Surplus**

Ⓐ At quantities less than the equilibrium, the **marginal benefit to buyers** of another unit **exceeds the marginal cost to sellers**.
Ⓑ At quantities greater than the equilibrium, the **marginal cost to sellers exceeds the marginal benefit to buyers**.
Ⓒ Therefore, the **equilibrium quantity** creates the **largest possible economic surplus**.

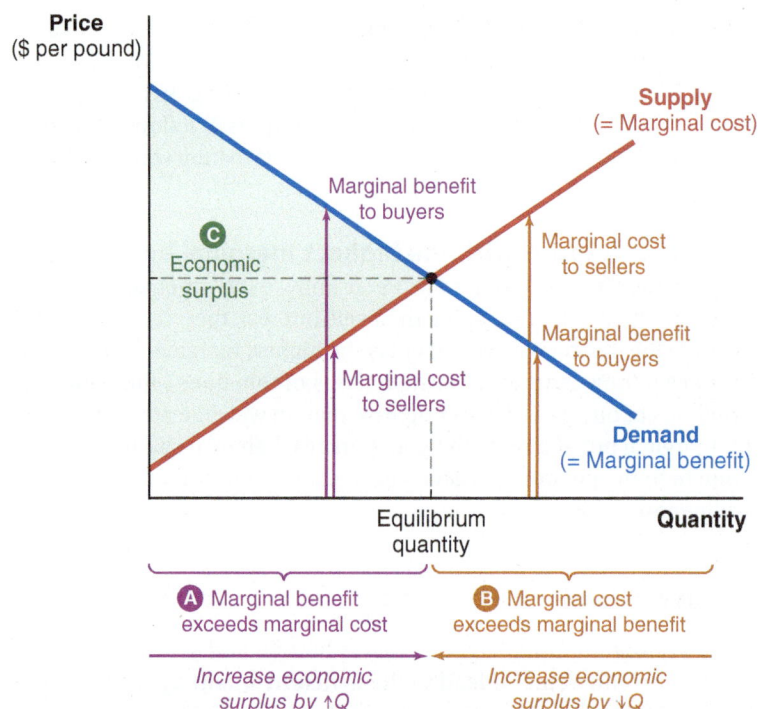

To see why, realize that if sellers produce less than the equilibrium quantity, the marginal benefit to buyers exceeds the marginal cost to sellers, and so we could increase economic surplus by increasing production. On the flip side, if sellers produce more than the equilibrium quantity, the marginal cost to sellers exceeds the marginal benefit to buyers, and so we could increase economic surplus by decreasing production.

It follows that the quantity that maximizes economic surplus is also the equilibrium quantity that results from the forces of supply and demand. That is, competitive markets lead to the *efficient quantity* of any good.

It's as if all economic activity is being directed by "an invisible hand." Let's put all of this together, because it's a pretty extraordinary finding. Organizing our economy — deciding who makes what, who gets what, and how much to make of each good — is a task of astonishing difficulty. It's so difficult that no committee of expert economists could ever figure out how to do all of this efficiently.

Yet millions of buyers and sellers, guided by nothing but their own self-interest, end up doing what an expert committee cannot. They produce the quantity that maximizes the total amount of economic surplus. They ensure that this quantity is produced at the lowest marginal cost. And they ensure that each good goes to the person who draws the largest marginal benefit from it, as revealed by their willingness to pay. The market achieves an efficient outcome, despite the fact that no market participant is trying to achieve that goal. Instead, as each person pursues their independent self-interest, they guide the market toward an efficient outcome. As Adam Smith, the eighteenth-century philosopher who is widely regarded as one of the founders of economics, noted, it is as if all economic activity is guided by an "invisible hand."

5.4 Market Failure and Deadweight Loss

Learning Objective *Measure the costs of market failure.*

So far we've seen that whatever quantity of goods is produced, competitive markets lead to *efficient production*, which means those goods are produced at the lowest overall cost. Competitive markets also lead to *efficient allocation*, which means those goods are allocated to the people who get the largest marginal benefit from them. And competitive markets lead to the efficient quantity. In short, competitive markets yield efficient outcomes, which means they generate the largest possible economic surplus. It sounds like markets are amazing and never get things wrong. Not so fast. There's a critically important caveat: Our supply and demand curves represent well-informed buyers and sellers interacting in a well-functioning market with perfect competition. But the world doesn't typically work this perfectly.

Market Failure

In reality, supply and demand don't always work as smoothly as we'd like. **Market failure** occurs when the forces of supply and demand lead to an inefficient outcome. Market failures are common, and their frequency and severity should temper your enthusiasm for market forces.

market failure When the forces of supply and demand lead to an inefficient outcome.

There are five main sources of market failure. Let's explore why they arise and how they change market outcomes.

Market failure 1: Market power undermines competitive pressures. The problem of *market power* arises when markets don't meet the perfectly competitive ideal of many sellers selling identical products. Instead, most markets are dominated by only a handful of companies. For instance, nearly every major breakfast cereal in the United States is made either by General Mills, Kellogg's, Quaker, or Post. The cereals they sell all differ to some degree. Sellers exploit this limited competition by charging higher prices, and this leads consumers to buy a smaller quantity. The result is that market power leads to underproduction as businesses with market power tend to produce less than the efficient quantity. How much less depends on how much market power they have.

Market failure 2: Externalities create side effects. The problem of *externalities* arises whenever the choices that buyers and sellers make have side effects on others.

For instance, many utilities produce electricity by burning coal, which has side effects including smog, acid rain, and greenhouse gases. You (and many others) are affected by these side effects even if you don't buy or sell coal, or electricity produced from coal. When suppliers don't take sufficient account of these side effects, they'll produce more coal and hence more pollution than is in society's best interests. More generally, businesses tend to produce more than the efficient quantity of products with negative side effects.

Externalities aren't always negative. Some activities have side effects that help other people — such as when your flu shot not only protects you from getting sick but also prevents others from getting sick because you won't infect them with the virus. If people don't take account of these positive side effects, they'll do fewer of these helpful activities than are in society's best interests.

Whether externalities are good or bad, they interfere with the ability of markets to produce the efficient quantity.

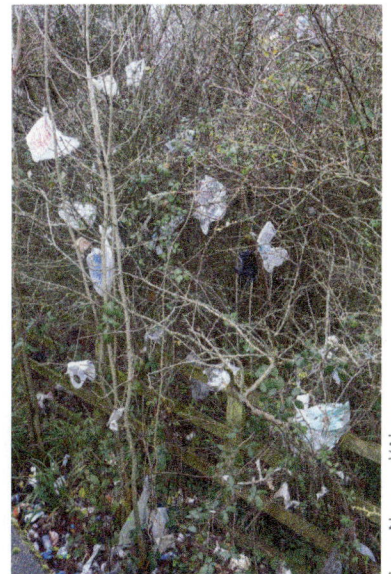

Even if you don't litter, you feel the side effects of it.

Market failure 3: Information problems undermine trust. The problem of private information can arise when you're worried that the folks you're doing business with know something you don't. For instance, if a seller knows more about the quality of the used car they're selling than you do, you might wonder why they're selling it. Your fears about what they're hiding might lead you not to buy that second-hand car. It's an example of how *private information* (that is, information that one party has but the other does not) can undermine trust, leading people to buy or sell less than the efficient quantity.

Market failure 4: Irrationality leads to bad decisions. Sometimes people make decisions that aren't in their best interests. If buyers don't systematically follow the Rational Rule for Buyers, their demand decisions may no longer reflect their marginal benefits, and so an efficient allocation is unlikely. And if suppliers don't systematically follow the Rational Rule for Sellers, their supply decisions may not be driven by their marginal costs, and so efficient production is unlikely.

In fact, psychologists and behavioral economists have documented many ways in which people systematically make mistakes. In the chapters ahead, you'll see how individual behaviors add up to affect the economy as a whole.

Market failure 5: Government can impede market forces. Government regulations and taxes can impede market forces. Taxes on buying or selling stuff leads a lower quantity to be bought or sold. Likewise, regulating the price sellers can charge or limiting the quantity they can sell also changes the quantity sold. Sometimes these government regulations exist to combat the market failures listed above, such as environmental regulations that try to prevent overpollution. But sometimes government regulations create their own distortions, pushing the market away from the efficient quantity.

> Five sources of market failure:
> 1. Market power
> 2. Externalities
> 3. Private information
> 4. Irrationality
> 5. Government regulations

Deadweight Loss

deadweight loss How far economic surplus falls below the efficient outcome; Deadweight loss = Economic surplus at the efficient quantity − Actual economic surplus.

The costs of market failure can be measured by calculating how much it reduces economic surplus. That's the idea behind **deadweight loss,** which is the difference between the largest possible economic surplus (which occurs at the efficient quantity), and the actual level of economic surplus:

Deadweight loss = Economic surplus at efficient quantity − Actual economic surplus

Economic surplus and deadweight loss focus on marginal benefits and marginal costs. Calculating deadweight loss requires you to measure economic surplus at two points — at the efficient quantity and at the actual quantity. Remember that the economic surplus in any given transaction is:

Economic surplus = Marginal benefit − Marginal cost

Often when we measure economic surplus, we use a shortcut: We look at the demand and supply curves. When there is no market failure, the demand curve corresponds with marginal benefits, and the supply curve corresponds with marginal costs. In this situation economic surplus is the area between the demand and supply curves. Market failure can make the demand curve a poor measure of marginal benefits, or it can make the supply curve a poor measure of marginal costs, or both. That's why we'll avoid the shortcut of looking at demand and supply curves and instead focus directly on the marginal benefit and marginal cost curves. And because the economic surplus of any individual transaction is the difference between marginal benefit and marginal cost curves, the *economic surplus in the entire market is the area between the marginal benefit and marginal cost curves, out to the quantity.*

Producing less than the efficient quantity creates deadweight loss. Figure 7 returns to the tomato market, but this time, there's a market failure,

Figure 7 | **Underproduction Creates Deadweight Loss**

Ⓐ Market failure leads the **actual quantity** produced to be less than the efficient quantity.

Ⓑ This yields **actual economic surplus** equal to the area below the marginal benefit curve and above marginal cost curve, out to this actual quantity.

Ⓒ **Deadweight loss** shows how much greater economic surplus could have been, if the efficient quantity were produced.

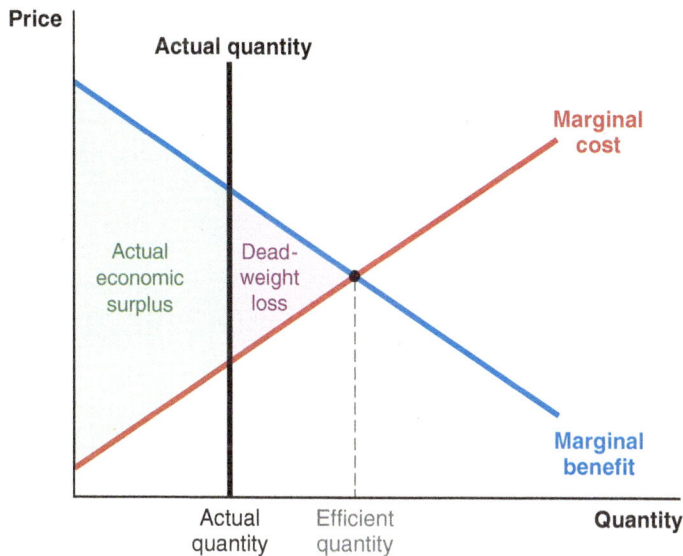

which means that the actual quantity of tomatoes bought or sold — shown as the vertical line — is less than the efficient quantity. For now, we'll put aside the reason for this market failure — what matters is figuring out the consequences for economic surplus.

Start by measuring the economic surplus at the efficient quantity. To find the efficient quantity, follow the **Rational Rule for Markets**, which says to keep increasing the quantity until marginal cost equals marginal benefit. That is, the efficient quantity is where the marginal cost and marginal benefit curves intersect. The corresponding economic surplus is the area between these curves, out to the efficient quantity. In Figure 7, it's the entire triangle — including both the green and purple parts — shaped like this one: ▷. Because this is the efficient quantity, this is the largest possible economic surplus for this market.

Next, evaluate the economic surplus when market failure leads a smaller actual quantity to be sold. The corresponding economic surplus is the area between the marginal benefit and marginal cost curves, out to this smaller actual quantity. In Figure 7, it's the green trapezoid shaped like this one: ▷.

Deadweight loss measures economic surplus lost due to this market failure and so measures how far this actual economic surplus falls short of the larger economic surplus that occurs at the efficient quantity. As such, it's the lost economic surplus due to the actual quantity falling short of the efficient quantity — and this is shown as the smaller purple triangle shaped like this: ▷. This deadweight loss triangle reflects the failure to execute potentially advantageous transactions, as increasing the quantity would yield marginal benefits that exceed marginal costs.

Finally, notice that the deadweight loss from underproduction is shaped like an arrowhead, pointing toward the efficient quantity.

Producing more than the efficient quantity also creates deadweight loss.

Next, consider the possibility that a market failure leads to overproduction, with the actual quantity exceeding the efficient quantity. Again, we'll put aside the question of precisely what market failure causes this, but just note that the actual quantity is shown as a vertical line in Figure 8.

Figure 8 | Overproduction Creates Deadweight Loss

Ⓐ Market failure leads the **actual quantity** produced to be greater than efficient quantity.

Ⓑ The largest possible economic surplus is the area below the marginal benefit curve and above the marginal cost curve, out to the efficient quantity.

Ⓒ Deadweight loss shows how much economic surplus is destroyed by producing more than the efficient quantity.

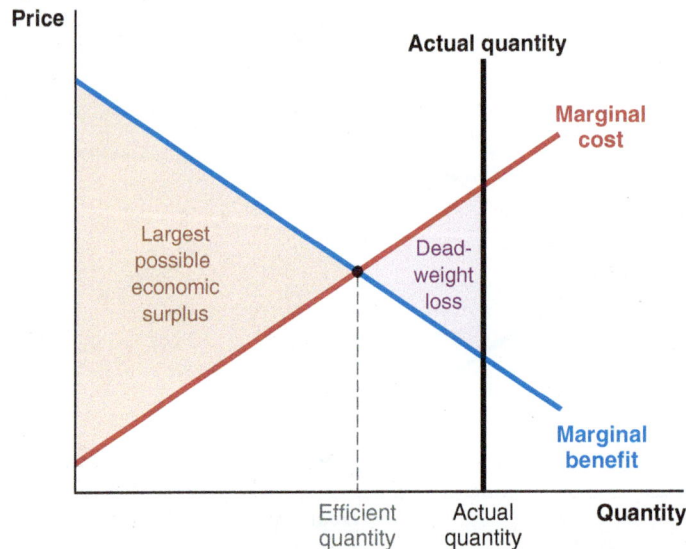

The efficient quantity, as before, is the quantity at which marginal cost and marginal benefit are equal. The corresponding economic surplus — which is the largest possible economic surplus — is shaded in orange and looks like this triangle: ▶.

In this case, market failure leads a larger quantity to be produced. Notice that once production exceeds the efficient quantity, the marginal benefit of these extra tomatoes is *less* than the marginal cost. That is, this extra production actually reduces economic surplus. It's not that these tomatoes are bad, it's that the extra cost to produce them exceeds the marginal benefits people derive from them.

These extra goods reduce economic surplus by an amount equal to the difference between their marginal costs and marginal benefits. Thus, the deadweight loss due to overproduction is the area between the marginal cost and marginal benefit curves, from the efficient quantity out to the actual quantity. It's the purple triangle shaped like this one: ◀.

Deadweight loss looks like an arrowhead pointed at the efficient quantity. Notice that when there's underproduction (as in Figure 7), the deadweight loss — which looks like this ▶ — appears to be an arrowhead pointing at the efficient quantity. And when there's overproduction (as in Figure 8), the deadweight loss — which looks like this ◀ — also appears to be an arrowhead pointing at the efficient quantity. In both cases, it appears as the arrowhead is pointing from the actual quantity to the efficient quantity. It's like the graph is trying to give you advice: The economy will do better if we move this way.

Quantities rather than prices are essential to measuring deadweight loss. Notice that we calculated deadweight loss based on the marginal cost and benefit curves, and the actual quantity produced. None of our calculations depended on what happened to the price. That is because deadweight loss measures the consequences of producing a quantity that's larger or smaller than the efficient quantity.

Once the quantity has been determined, the price only redistributes economic surplus. For instance, a higher price for tomatoes means that tomato buyers pay more — which reduces their consumer surplus — but in equal measure, tomato sellers receive more, which increases their producer surplus. The buyer's loss is the seller's gain, and the net effect is that total amount of economic surplus, which is shared by buyers and sellers, remains unchanged.

Bottom line: It's the quantity that determines the total amount of economic surplus, and hence the deadweight loss. You need to analyze the price only if you want to figure out whether buyers or sellers enjoy more of that economic surplus.

Market Failure versus Government Failure

It's time to step back, to analyze what all this means for some of the biggest economic, political, and, indeed, philosophical debates of our time: How much of a role should market forces play in our society? And how much of a role is there for the government?

The efficiency of well-functioning markets points to the importance of market forces. We discovered that well-functioning competitive markets can do extraordinary things: They ensure that each good or service is produced by the business that can do so at the lowest possible marginal cost (that's the idea of *productive efficiency*), that each good goes to the person who'll get the highest marginal benefit from it (that's the idea of *allocative efficiency*), and that we'll produce the quantity of each good that yields the largest possible economic surplus (that is, the *efficient quantity*). All told, perfectly functioning markets lead to the *efficient outcome,* which means they produce the largest possible economic surplus. This finding is the most persuasive case for organizing our society around markets.

Market failure points to an important role for government. While this sounds good in theory, the reality is that market failure is common. And that means that markets will typically produce somewhat worse outcomes than in the ideal case, yielding at least some costly deadweight loss. That, in turn, provides a powerful argument for the government to play a role, because well-designed policies can limit market failure, yielding more efficient outcomes that reduce deadweight loss.

There's a lot of debate about how big that role should be. In some cases, government can improve things by helping organize and regulate markets. For example, food safety standards ensure that no one sells peanut butter tainted with salmonella. In others, it will use taxes, subsidies, and quantity regulations to correct market failures. For example, the government taxes smoking and subsidizes flu shots for the elderly. And sometimes the government will provide what the market can't — such as when the government provides national security and social welfare programs.

Government failure limits the extent to which we should rely on government. The existence of market failure doesn't necessarily suggest that government will do a better job. That's because of another problem, **government failure,** which exists when government policies lead to worse outcomes. Often this arises because politicians and bureaucrats make choices that aren't in the public interest.

government failure When government policies lead to worse outcomes.

Politicians can be motivated to make the choices that will improve their reelection chances, rather than those that will improve efficiency or equity. That leads them to be overly responsive to voters who are politically organized and not to those who stay quiet. They're more responsive to those who give big campaign donations than to those who don't. And they'll often choose what is popular rather than what is right. The result is that government responses to existing market failures can actually make things worse.

The problem of government failure may be even worse in nondemocratic countries, where a monarch or a dictator doesn't need to worry that bad policies will be punished by voters. As such, they're free to focus on enriching themselves and their cronies without facing any electoral consequences.

Government failure isn't only about politicians. Government bureaucrats also face incentives that may lead them to do things that are not in the public's interest. Agency heads seeking to increase their power may create a sprawling and bloated bureaucracy that fails to provide efficient services. Some bureaucrats become too friendly with the folks they regulate and start to act in the best interests of that industry, rather than the broader public. Similarly, some bureaucrats focus on the narrow interests of a few rather than the more complicated and mixed interests of the overall society.

The point is that just as market failure is pervasive, so is government failure. The question of whether our society would be better off with a greater emphasis on market forces versus a more forceful government comes down to whether the losses caused by market failure exceed those caused by government failure. Your judgment likely varies across different policies, on different issues, in different markets, with different branches of government, and in different times and places.

5.5 Beyond Economic Efficiency

Learning Objective *Evaluate the limitations of economic efficiency in policy analysis.*

When you get involved in economic policy debates — advocating for one position or another — your arguments will move beyond purely positive analysis, to normative analysis. And that means that you need to figure out a way to assess whether one outcome is better than another.

As we learned, one criteria that many economists use is economic efficiency. By this view, we should choose the outcome that yields the larger economic surplus. Even though this approach is common in economics, you may not find it entirely satisfying. (I hope you're not hungry, because we're going to talk about pie again.)

Critiques of Economic Efficiency

Focusing on economic efficiency can sound like a version of the argument that we should always choose the largest possible pie. While that might sound like it's a good idea, realize that it implicitly embeds some very strong value judgments that have led many people to criticize the focus given to economic efficiency. So, before you decide whether to evaluate an economic policy on efficiency grounds alone, you should consider the following three critiques.

Critique 1: Distribution matters, and so it's also important to account for equity. First, a focus on economic efficiency means trying to obtain the largest possible economic surplus, irrespective of who it goes to. But most people believe the *distribution* of economic benefits also matters. That's why in reality, most economists look beyond efficiency and also consider equity. That means they also analyze the **distributional consequences** of new policies — meaning who gets what — and assess whether that outcome seems fair or equitable. This critique says that it's not just the size of the pie that matters, but also how it's sliced.

distributional consequences
Who gets what.

Critique 2: Willingness to pay reflects ability to pay, not just marginal benefit. Recall that economic surplus is the marginal benefit of a decision, less the marginal cost. Maximizing economic surplus requires ensuring that each good goes to the person with the largest possible marginal benefit. So far, so good.

But realize that economists often equate marginal benefits with your willingness to pay. That means economic surplus is built on the idea that if you're willing to pay more for a slice of pie than I am, then we can infer that you derive a greater marginal benefit from that slice, and so you should get it.

But this raises what I call the Kim Kardashian problem. There's one slice of pie left, and you really want it — you love pie! Given that you love pie, you argue that it makes sense for you to get it. But Kim counters that it would be more efficient for her to get it.

Let's do the math: You love pie, and so you're willing to pay up to $12 for that last slice, which is a lot of money for you. Kardashian is incredibly wealthy. Even though she won't enjoy eating pie as much as you will, she's willing to pay $50 for the last slice — after all, she has so much money, why not spend it on pie?

Chris Weeks/Wirelmage/Getty Images

This is why she has a greater willingness to pay.

Economic surplus is built on the idea that Kardashian is right — the fact that she's willing to pay more than you are means that there's a greater economic surplus from her getting that last slice. The problem here is that how much you are willing to pay for pie partly reflects how much you like pie, and partly reflects your ability to pay.

Critique 3: The means matter, not just the ends. Economic efficiency is all about *outcomes*. But there are other ways to evaluate distribution.

Some people think that what matters more is the *process*. For instance, if you made the pie, perhaps you deserve a bigger slice.

Others focus on equality of opportunity rather than outcomes. If everyone had a chance to make a pie, why should those who actually made pie be forced to share with others?

Or you might care about the process that was used to decide how to cut the pie. Was it democratic or dictatorial? Finally, you might believe that everyone has a right to have some pie regardless of all the other criteria.

Whatever your beliefs, the point is that people don't always judge the desirability of an approach purely by the outcomes it creates — often, the process matters, too. But judgments based on economic efficiency focus only on the consequences of a policy, and not on the process that led to that outcome.

Use economic efficiency cautiously. None of this is to say that you should ignore economic efficiency. Rather, you should use it carefully, aided by a clear sense of its precise meaning. Your normative analysis may involve analyzing economic efficiency, but you might also choose to emphasize other ethical considerations, too.

Indeed, real-world policy debates typically reflect not only a technical evaluation of economic efficiency and deadweight loss, but also analysis of distributional and equity consequences, as well as broader notions of fairness. Few arguments are won by describing only what will happen to economic surplus.

5.6 | Tying It Together

Efficiency, Equity, and the Challenge of Evaluating Policy

It's time to pull all these threads together and return to the debate about whether the government should allow ride-sharing companies like Uber to operate. You'll see that the tools you've developed in this chapter provide a powerful lens for analyzing public policies.

The first stage of our analysis involves positive analysis, asking: What *is* going to happen when we ban (or when we allow) Uber? That means analyzing what will happen to the employment and wages of both taxi drivers and of Uber drivers; assessing whether Uber has increased the total quantity of rides; evaluating how much people have to pay for a ride; and accounting for nonfinancial costs and benefits such as whether Uber has reduced the typical wait time to get a ride home. Careful analysis found that wages and employment of taxi drivers fell when Uber entered the market; employment of Uber drivers rose, and those Uber drivers enjoy more flexible work hours. The overall number of rides rose, and passenger wait times fell. Your positive analysis tells you who gains from ride-sharing (Uber drivers and their customers), and who loses (taxi drivers), and by how much.

Balancing these competing interests requires a normative analysis, which assesses which outcome is better and what policy the government should adopt. You might start by asking whether economic surplus increased. You know the quantity of rides went up, but in order to assess whether total economic surplus rose or fell, you'll need to know why.

The answer is that market failure, government failure, and technological change have all played a role in this rapidly shifting market.

Let's start with market failure. When taxis first started out, passengers didn't know whether their driver would be safe or reckless. Government responded by regulating taxis to ensure that only qualified drivers could offer rides. That made taxi licenses valuable.

That sparked a form of government failure to develop over time. Here's the problem: Existing taxis earn more when they face fewer competitors. And so taxi owners pressured the government to limit the number of new taxi drivers and new taxi companies from entering the market. Government officials relented, restricting the supply of taxis. This artificial restriction on supply led the quantity of rides to be less than the efficient quantity, creating deadweight loss. For example, Boston had fewer than 2,000 taxi drivers allowed under their regulations when Uber entered the market. Uber quickly grew to more than 20,000 drivers in the city.

Sometimes market forces work to undo the inefficiencies created by government failure. And that is exactly what Uber did. Because it's not technically a taxi company, it tried to skirt these regulations. As a result, the entry of Uber increased the quantity of rides toward the efficient quantity, thereby raising economic surplus. Of course, Uber also adds congestion on the road and pollution in the air, so it's possible that there are now too many rides! In that case, economic surplus would be higher with some limitations on Uber.

Technological change also played an important role. Ride-sharing apps provide efficient routing using GPS, they allow drivers to use a car that might otherwise sit in their driveway, and they permit drivers to flexibly schedule their shifts for when their opportunity costs are lowest. These changes all reduce the marginal cost of producing a ride.

Lower marginal costs lead to a rise in the efficient quantity of rides. If there were no increase in the quantity supplied, this would have led to an even larger gap between the actual quantity and the efficient quantity of rides, creating even more deadweight loss.

All told, Uber likely increased the total amount of economic surplus, and that's why economists tend to view ride-sharing as a good outcome. However, economic surplus doesn't have to be your only criteria in a normative analysis. You might have concern about distributional effects of Uber or concerns about the fairness of undercutting the full-time profession of taxi drivers.

Ultimately, your opinion will depend on how you value the gains to the winners relative to the losses for the losers. Reasonable people might bring different values to this discussion, weighing these costs and benefits differently. However, analysis of economic surplus provides you with an important tool with which to begin crafting your own personal view.

Chapter 5 Review
Chapter at a Glance

Evaluating Public Policies

Positive Analysis: Describes what **is** happening, explaining why, or predicting what will happen.
Normative Analysis: Prescribes what **should** happen, which involves value judgments.

Policies can be evaluated using the criteria of:

Economic Efficiency: An outcome is more economically efficient if it yields more Economic Surplus.

Equity: An outcome yields greater equity if it results in a fairer distribution of economic benefits.

Measuring Economic Surplus

Economic Surplus: The benefit of an action, less the cost. Economic surplus = Marginal benefit – Marginal cost	=	Consumer Surplus: The economic surplus you get from buying something. Consumer surplus = Marginal benefit – Price	+	Producer Surplus: The economic surplus you get from selling something. Producer surplus = Price – Marginal cost

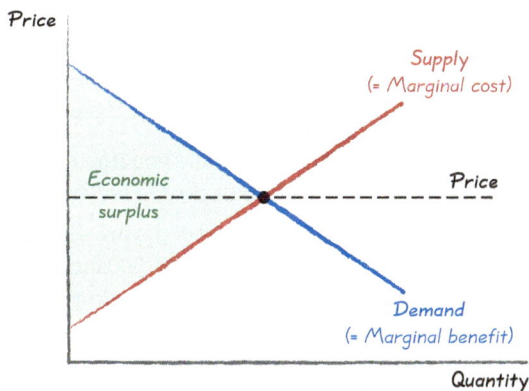

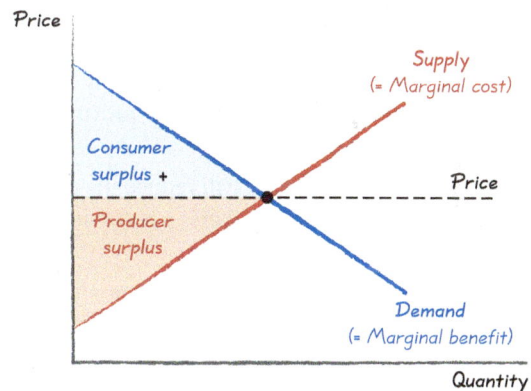

Market Efficiency

Efficient Outcome: The efficient outcome yields the largest possible Economic Surplus. Markets create efficient outcomes by:

1. Efficient Production Producing a given quantity of output at the lowest possible cost, which requires producing each good at the lowest marginal cost.	2. Efficient Allocation Allocating goods to create the largest Economic Surplus, which requires that each good goes to the person who'll get the highest marginal benefit from it.	3. Efficient Quantity The quantity that produces the largest possible Economic Surplus. **The Rational Rule for Markets:** Produce more of a good if its marginal benefit is greater than (or equal to) the marginal cost.

Measuring the Costs of Market Failure

Market failure: When the forces of supply and demand lead to an inefficient outcome.
Deadweight loss: How far Economic Surplus falls below the Efficient Outcome.
Deadweight loss = Economic surplus at efficient quantity – Actual economic surplus
Government failure: When government policies lead to worse outcomes.

Key Terms

Study Problems

Learning Objective 5.1 *Learn how to evaluate welfare and economic efficiency.*

1. Think of an important policy issue and provide an example of both a positive economic statement and a normative economic statement related to that policy.

2. If an outcome is economically efficient, does this mean that everybody involved benefits? Provide an example to briefly explain your reasoning.

3. Identify each of the following statements as either a positive statement or a normative statement:

   a. Raising taxes on pollution emissions will result in some factories closing.

   b. The federal government should tax pollution to address climate change.

   c. An increase in the gasoline tax will reduce the amount that people drive and therefore cause a reduction in air pollution.

   d. If the federal income tax is increased, workers will decide to increase the number of hours they work each year.

4. Sean is a community college student and has been saving his tips from his job waiting tables at a restaurant for months to see *Hamilton*. He is willing to pay $705 for a ticket. Anca has seen *Hamilton* five times already, but wants to see it again before heading to Europe for a month. She is willing to pay $1,250 for a ticket. There is one ticket left, and the seller is charging $700. Does Sean or Anca buying the ticket lead to a more economically efficient outcome?

Learning Objective 5.2 *Measure the economic surplus generated in a market.*

5. Think of something you've purchased in the last few days. How much consumer surplus did you get from the purchase? Use the Rational Rule for Buyers to explain why you purchased that quantity. How much producer surplus do you think the seller got, and what is total economic surplus? Use the Rational Rule for Sellers to explain why the seller sold the item to you.

6. You are planning a move across town. Doing your research, you find that the average rate of a moving company is $250 per hour for two movers (moving truck included). The marginal benefit you receive from each hour of the two movers' time (and truck) is listed in the accompanying table.

Hours of movers' time	Marginal benefit
1 hour	$850
2 hours	$620
3 hours	$500
4 hours	$250
5 hours	$150
6 hours	$100
7 hours	$0

   a. For how many hours should you hire the movers? How much consumer surplus do you receive?

   b. Now suppose that instead of paying per hour, a moving company offers a flat rate of $1,500 for two movers plus a truck for an eight-hour day. Would you hire the movers? How has your consumer surplus changed?

7. If the daily demand curve for gasoline is as provided in the following graph, then how much consumer surplus would consumers receive if the market price for gasoline was $3.50 per gallon? What about for a price of $2.50 per gallon?

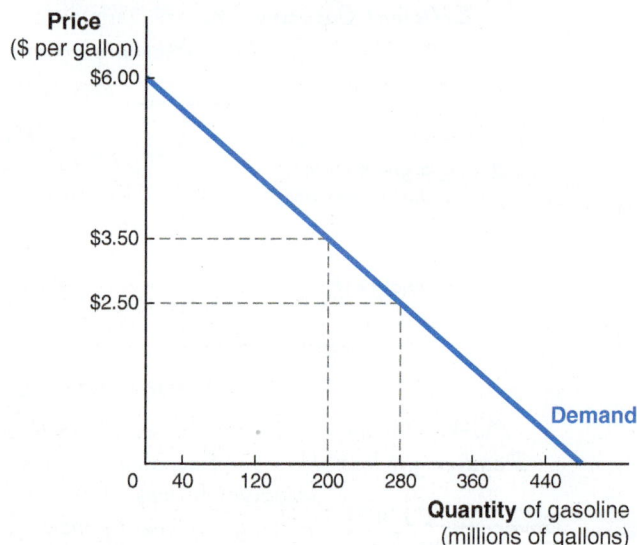

8. Last year the average price for an airline ticket was $400, but the average price dropped to $350 this year due to a decrease in the demand for airplane travel. The accompanying table contains information on the supply of air travel.

Airfare (price per ticket)	Quantity supplied (millions of seats)
$0	0
$175	350
$350	700
$400	800
$575	1,150
$750	1,500

Draw the supply curve and use it to calculate producer surplus last year and producer surplus this year. How did producer surplus change?

Learning Objective 5.3 *Assess the efficiency of markets.*

9. There are dozens of laptop manufacturers around the world. Does the idea of efficient production mean that there should only be one laptop manufacturer making laptops at the lowest marginal cost?

10. Use the Rational Rule for Markets to explain why the equilibrium quantity in a market maximizes the market's total economic surplus.

11. Consider the market for tilapia. Ripple Rock Fish Farms, a small family fish farm in Ohio, and The Fishin' Company, a large corporate supplier, are both producers of tilapia. The marginal cost curves for both firms are shown in the accompanying graph.

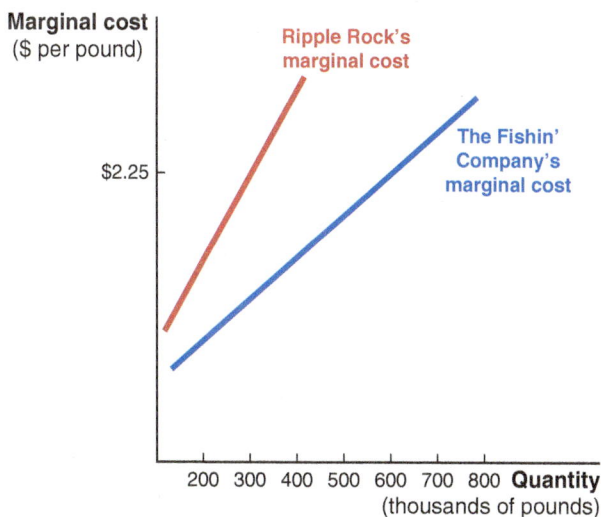

If the market price is $2.25 per pound of tilapia, how many pounds of tilapia would Ripple Rock supply? What about The Fishin' Company? How many total pounds would they collectively supply? Is this allocation the most productively efficient way to produce this quantity of tilapia?

12. Now, consider two people in the market for tilapia, Reagan and Cassidy. The marginal benefit curves for both individuals are shown in the accompanying graph.

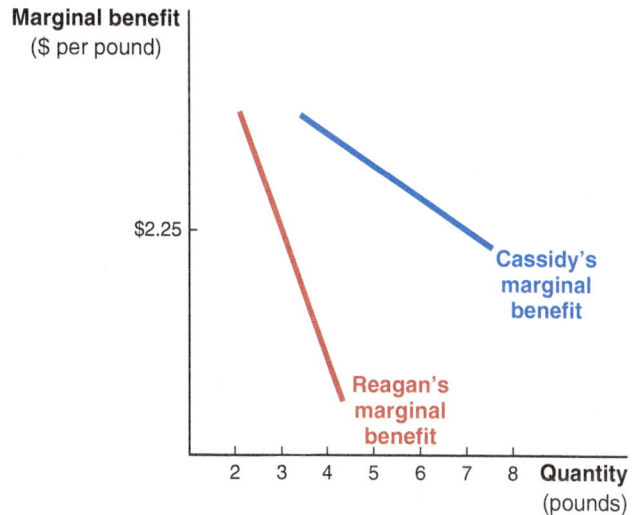

If the market price of tilapia is $2.25 per pound, how many pounds would Reagan purchase? How many pounds would Cassidy purchase? How many total pounds will they collectively purchase? Is this allocation the most allocatively efficient way to distribute this quantity of tilapia?

13. Fei, Morgan, and Lakesha are all in the market for new Levi's jeans. The marginal benefit for each pair of jeans per year for each of them is provided in the following table:

Quantity	Fei	Morgan	Lakesha
1	$85	$40	$90
2	$60	$32	$75
3	$32	$24	$55
4	$20	$16	$32
5	$15	$8	$25

If the price of a pair of Levi's jeans is $32, how many pairs of jeans will each person purchase? How much consumer surplus does each of them receive from the last pair of jeans purchased? How much consumer surplus will each of them receive for each of the pairs they buy at a price of $32? How much do they receive collectively?

Learning Objective 5.4 *Measure the costs of market failure.*

14. Why do markets sometimes fail to generate efficient outcomes?

15. Can you think of any examples of markets that fail? Explain why that market failure does not mean that government control will necessarily lead to a better outcome.

16. A study done by University of Minnesota economist Joel Waldfogel estimated the difference in the actual monetary value of gifts received and how much the recipient would have been willing to pay to buy them on their own.

The results suggested that the average receiver's valuation was approximately 90% of the actual purchase price.

a. In 2017, it was estimated that the average amount spent on winter holiday gifts in the United States was $906. Based on the estimate from the Waldfogel study, how much of this would be considered a deadweight loss?

b. In 2017, there were approximately 250 million people in the United States above the age of 18. Assuming that each individual purchased $906 worth of gifts, what is the size of the total deadweight loss associated with gift giving in the United States?

17. Consider the national market for in-home child care in the accompanying graph.

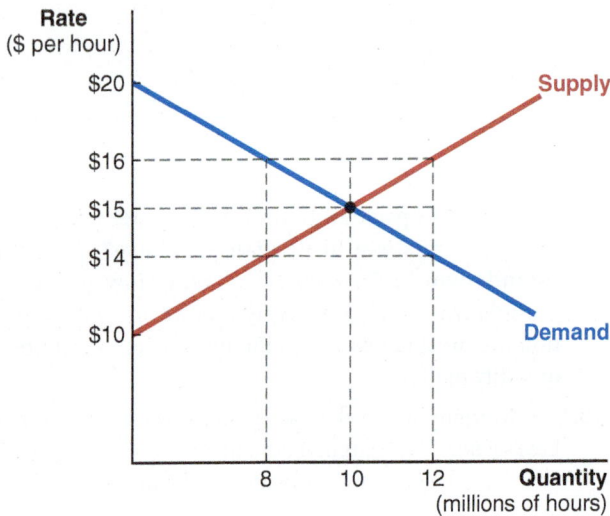

a. At 10 million hours, what is the size of total economic surplus in this market? Label the area representing total economic surplus on the graph.

b. At 8 million hours, what is the size of total economic surplus in this market? Label the area representing total economic surplus on the graph.

c. Is total economic surplus at 8 million hours larger or smaller than at 10 million hours? Label the area on the graph representing the difference in economic surplus. What is this area called?

d. Between 8 million hours and 10 million hours, which of the following is true? The marginal benefit to households exceeds the marginal cost to child care providers, or the marginal cost to child care providers exceeds the marginal benefit to households.

e. Repeat parts b–d for 12 million hours instead of 8 million hours.

f. What is the efficient quantity of hours in this market?

Comparative Advantage and Gains from Trade

Airbnb did something extraordinary: it revolutionized the short-term accommodation market by persuading homeowners, and even some renters, to become suppliers. There have always been people with spare rooms or empty houses, and there have always been travelers looking for places to stay. But it was hard for them to connect with each other. Airbnb persuaded those with empty beds to make them available to strangers on the internet. Similarly, Airbnb persuaded travelers that rather than staying in a hotel, they should rent a room or apartment (or yurt, or castle, or just about any kind of accommodation you can imagine) from strangers on the internet.

Why stay in a hotel when you can rent someone's treehouse for the weekend?

Luciana Rinaldi/Shutterstock

Airbnb was an early inventor of the *peer-to-peer marketplace*, which created new possibilities by connecting people who might benefit from trading with each other. As a result, there are students staying with two aspiring actors in Los Angeles, honeymooners staying in an Airstream on the Washington coast, tourists living in a clocktower in London, and a family enjoying a week in a yurt in Montana. None of these folks know each other, yet they're sending each other money and staying in each other's homes. And they're all enjoying gains from trade: The travelers gain an interesting place to stay, and their hosts gain a welcome boost to their incomes.

The true star of this story is not Airbnb's management, but the market that Airbnb helped create. It brings together different people, in different places, each with different needs and different assets. The market coordinates all of this activity, allocating the family to the yurt and the students to a room in an apartment in Los Angeles. This new peer-to-peer marketplace was revolutionary when Airbnb started out, but there are now many other companies playing a similar role—helping people rent out their RVs, boats, docks, cars, and surfboards.

The story of the development of peer-to-peer markets reminds us of the magic of markets. Markets are everywhere. You interact with them so often that sometimes you forget how pervasive they are. Indeed, markets are arguably the dominant force organizing our lives today. Airbnb and other peer-to-peer marketplace platforms help remind us of the value that the market can generate.

In this chapter, we take a closer look at what markets do for us. The key idea is that markets are all about harvesting the gains from trade that make each of us better off. We'll begin by describing gains from trade. Then we'll see how comparative advantage generates these gains. Finally, we'll explore the key role that prices play in coordinating economic activity, and how managers can harness market forces to make better choices. Let's get started.

🎙 Podcast
Think Like an Economist
Gains from Trade—Why Ringo Played the Drums

6.1   Gains from Trade

Learning Objective *Understand the role of markets in reallocating resources to better uses.*

gains from trade The benefits that come from reallocating resources, goods, and services to better uses.

What exactly is it that markets do? Here's the big idea. You have some stuff. Other people have other stuff. They want some of your stuff more than you do. You want some of their stuff more than they do. So you swap some of your stuff for some of their stuff. Hey, presto! You're both better off, because now you both have stuff you want more. These benefits you get from reallocating stuff to its better uses are called the **gains from trade.**

That's what markets do: They reallocate stuff — resources, goods, and services — to better uses, generating gains from trade. That's it. It's a simple yet powerful concept.

Obviously I've simplified, so let's connect the dots a bit more. Usually, you don't directly trade your stuff for someone else's. Instead, you buy and sell goods and services using money. Money is just a convenience that allows you to engage in more complicated trades; the idea is the same as if you were trading for other stuff. And when I say that markets allocate "stuff," think about that idea broadly — they allocate all sorts of resources, goods, and services, including time.

When you sell an hour of your labor to your employer for $15, and then use that $15 to buy food, you've effectively traded your time for food. You gain from this trade because you want that food more than you want another hour of time to do something else. In fact, everyone gains. Your employer gains because the work you did for them boosted their profits and now they can buy more stuff. The grocer who sold you the food also gains, because they can spend your $15 to buy goods that they value more highly.

When people buy and sell their labor, they're using markets to allocate people to tasks and tasks to people. Let's explore this idea a bit further, as we turn our attention to how markets create gains from trade by effectively allocating tasks. We'll start with a simple but delicious task: cooking dinner.

6.2   Comparative Advantage

Learning Objective *Use comparative advantage to allocate tasks to those with the lowest opportunity cost.*

Should you cook dinner tonight, or should your roommate? It's a seemingly small decision, and the stakes are pretty low. But you'll have to make this decision at dinner time for a lot of the days in your life. That makes the stakes seem a bit higher. And you don't just have to figure out who'll cook. Every day, you make dozens of other decisions, deciding who should clean the house, shop for groceries, or pay the bills. The underlying question in each case is the same: How best to allocate these tasks?

If you've ever been in a management position — at work, in a club or volunteer organization, or on a sports team — you've likely faced similar questions. How do you divide tasks among team members? Who should be in charge of organizing meetings and ensuring the team meets deadlines? Who determines how team members should spend their time, or how the organization should spend its budget? These management questions are the same ones you face as a household manager: How best to allocate these tasks?

Now think about the whole economy. Literally billions of tasks are performed in all sorts of organizations across the United States. Each task could be performed by any one of millions of workers who each have different skills, and in some instances, the task could also be completed by a machine. The economic management question facing the country is similar to the question you confront as the manager of your company or your household: How best to allocate these tasks?

Whether you're responsible for running your household, a student organization, a nonprofit, a business, or the whole economy, you'll need to figure out how best to allocate different tasks. Whatever task you're thinking about, your goal should be to allocate each task to whoever can produce the same quality work at the lowest cost. Allocating to the lowest-cost producer allows tasks to be produced at the lowest cost. The one big idea that can help you do this is comparative advantage. This idea is so big that it is at the center of a lot of economic thinking. Perhaps even more importantly, it's at the center of how economists tend to organize their own lives and the lives of their families.

Introducing Comparative Advantage

Let's start with a simple case, analyzing how two roommates, Helen and Jamie, should allocate tasks around their home. It's a pretty stylized example, but stick with me, because it will yield an insight that applies equally well whether you're the manager of your household, your company, or the economy.

Helen and Jamie want to figure out how best to assign their household tasks. For now, we'll focus on just two tasks, cooking and vacuuming. Like good economists, they start with the data:

- Helen says that she can vacuum their house in four hours, or she can make a meal in two hours.
- Jamie says that vacuuming their house also takes him four hours, but it takes him only one hour to make a meal.

So how should they assign these tasks?

Absolute advantage tells you who's best at a task, but not who should do the task. Helen argues that Jamie should do all the household tasks because he is better at all household chores than her. After all, Jamie can make meals in less time than she can, and she's no faster at vacuuming. *If* we measured costs in terms of time spent, she's got a point — each chore costs Jamie less or equal time than it costs Helen. Helen's argument is based on the idea that economists call **absolute advantage,** which is the ability of one person to do a task using fewer inputs than someone else.

But Helen's argument is dead wrong because she's not thinking about opportunity costs. In fact, lots of people make this error.

absolute advantage The ability to do a task using fewer inputs.

Comparative advantage is all about opportunity cost. The opportunity cost principle reminds you that the true cost of something is what you must give up to get it. To figure out the true cost of Helen or Jamie vacuuming the house, you need to ask, "Or what?" Jamie can vacuum the house, *or* spend that time making meals. That's why the opportunity cost of Jamie vacuuming is the number of meals he could have otherwise cooked. Likewise, if Helen vacuums the house, the opportunity cost is the number of meals she could otherwise have made. You should focus on opportunity cost because you want to minimize what you have to give up to get the task done — which is what opportunity cost measures.

To get the most output with your given inputs, you should allocate each task to the person with the lowest opportunity cost. That's such an important point that I'll say it again: You should allocate each task to the person who can do it at the lowest opportunity cost. This seemingly straightforward idea is so important that economists have a specific term for it: The person with the lower opportunity cost of completing a particular task has a **comparative advantage** at that task. It's *comparative* because opportunity cost compares what you can produce if assigned one task with what you would produce if you spent that time on another task. And it's an *advantage* because a lower opportunity cost means that you give up less to get a task done, and so it's more efficient for you to do that task.

comparative advantage The ability to do a task at a lower opportunity cost.

When each person in a group — a household, a business, an organization, or the economy — focuses on the task for which they have a comparative advantage, the group will produce more. This larger economic pie is due to the gains from trade from reallocating or trading tasks. If Helen and Jamie want to produce more — or if they want more free time — they should assign the vacuuming to whoever has a comparative advantage in vacuuming, and whoever has a comparative advantage in cooking should cook. So, we now turn to asking: Who has a comparative advantage in each task?

Calculate the opportunity cost of each task. The top panel of Figure 1 shows how long it takes Jamie or Helen to vacuum the house, or produce one meal. But to find out who has a comparative advantage in vacuuming, you'll need to focus instead on *opportunity costs*. The opportunity cost of doing a task is the output you could produce in your next best alternative task. You can calculate it as follows:

$$\text{Opportunity cost of a task} = \frac{\text{Hours this task takes}}{\text{Hours required to produce alternative output}}$$

You can see this formula in action, as follows:

- Jamie takes four hours to vacuum the house, but if he spent that time cooking instead, he would have four more hours to devote to cooking, during which he would produce one meal per hour. And so for Jamie, vacuuming the house comes at an opportunity cost of 4 hours/1 hour per meal = 4 meals.

- Helen takes four hours to vacuum the house, but if she spent that time cooking instead, she would have four more hours to devote to cooking, during which she would produce a meal every two hours. Thus, for Helen, vacuuming the house comes at an opportunity cost of 4 hours/2 hours per meal = 2 meals.

The lower panel of Figure 1 shifts the focus from the rate of production to opportunity costs. The left column shows the opportunity cost for each person of vacuuming the house in terms of meals they could make instead. Comparing Helen's and Jamie's opportunity costs reveals that Helen has a comparative advantage at vacuuming, because vacuuming the house costs her fewer forgone meals than if Jamie were to do the job. (The opportunity cost of vacuuming the house is only two meals for Helen, versus four meals for Jamie.)

Okay, so now let's figure out who has a comparative advantage in cooking, by seeing who can make a meal at the lowest opportunity cost:

- Jamie takes only an hour to make a meal, but if he spent that time cleaning instead, he would have one more hour to vacuum at a rate of one house every four hours. Thus for Jamie, one meal comes at an opportunity cost of vacuuming 1 hour/4 hours per house = $\frac{1}{4}$ of the house.

- Helen takes two hours to make a meal, but if she spent that time cleaning instead, she would have two more hours to vacuum at a rate of one house every four hours. Thus, for Helen, one meal comes at an opportunity cost of vacuuming 2 hours/4 hours per house = $\frac{1}{2}$ of the house.

Figure 1 | **Evaluating Opportunity Costs**

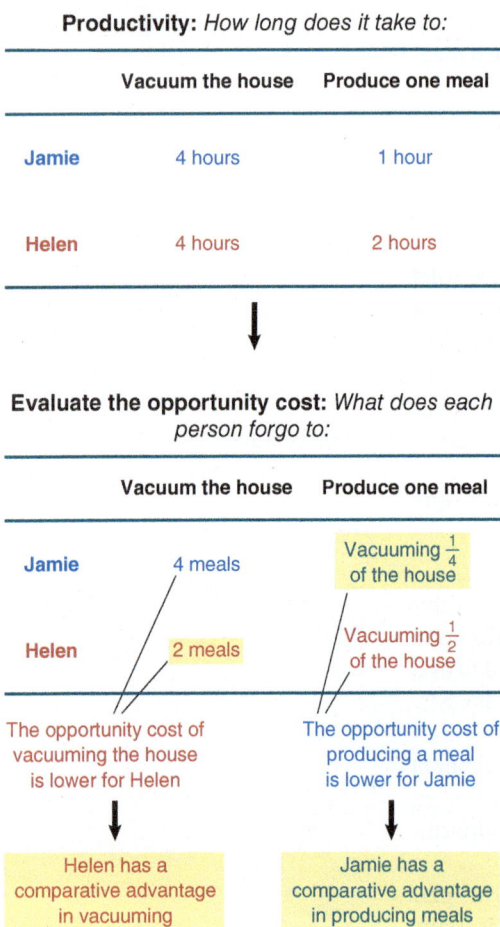

Productivity: *How long does it take to:*

	Vacuum the house	Produce one meal
Jamie	4 hours	1 hour
Helen	4 hours	2 hours

↓

Evaluate the opportunity cost: *What does each person forgo to:*

	Vacuum the house	Produce one meal
Jamie	4 meals	Vacuuming $\frac{1}{4}$ of the house
Helen	2 meals	Vacuuming $\frac{1}{2}$ of the house

The opportunity cost of vacuuming the house is lower for Helen

The opportunity cost of producing a meal is lower for Jamie

↓

Helen has a comparative advantage in vacuuming

↓

Jamie has a comparative advantage in producing meals

Comparing these (in the right column) reveals that Jamie has a comparative advantage at producing meals because each meal costs him less forgone vacuuming than it costs Helen (the opportunity cost of producing another meal is that he won't vacuum only one-quarter of the house for Jamie, compared with half the house for Helen).

Everyone has a comparative advantage. Notice that, in an absolute sense, Helen is better at neither cooking nor vacuuming than Jamie is. That is, Helen lacks an absolute advantage at any task. But even though Helen isn't better at any household task, she can still help her household produce more. After all, her household is better off assigning her to some task than to nothing at all. That's why the opportunity cost principle is so central here—it ensures that you think about all of the possible uses of Helen's time. And it shows that Helen will make the biggest contribution if she's assigned to the task that she's least bad at relative to Jamie.

It's often most intuitive to think of comparative advantage in exactly these terms: You have a comparative advantage in the task that you're least bad at. Everyone has a comparative advantage in something, even if they don't have an absolute advantage in anything, because everyone must be least bad at something as long as people have different opportunity costs.

A three-step recipe identifies who has a comparative advantage in each task. You're going to want to identify who has a comparative advantage in other situations, so let's take a step back and walk through the three steps we've followed:

Step 1: Determine how long each task would take each person (as in the top panel of Figure 1). This measures the cost of producing each good, in hours.

Step 2: Convert this into a measure of opportunity cost by calculating how much of the alternative good you could have produced in that time.

Step 3: Evaluate who has a comparative advantage at each task by assessing who can produce each good at the lowest opportunity cost.

You can use this three-step recipe to identify comparative advantage in any domain.

Do the Economics

Akilah and Zara are partners in a small suburban law office. They have to decide how to assign the work that they're getting. Akilah can write a will in three hours, or an employment contract in six hours. Zara is slower, and it takes her nine hours to write a will, and nine hours to write an employment contract.

Step 1: Measure the cost of producing each good *in hours*.

Productivity: *How long does it take to:*

	Write a will	Write an employment contract
Akilah	3 hours	6 hours
Zara	9 hours	9 hours

Step 2: Calculate the *opportunity cost* of producing each good.

  a. Evaluate the opportunity cost for Akilah and Zara to produce a will. (Hint: You're making comparisons *across* tasks, so you compute it by comparing numbers *across* a row.)

  b. Evaluate the opportunity cost for Akilah and Zara to produce an employment contract.

Evaluate the opportunity cost: *What does each forgo to:*

	Write a will	Write an employment contract
Akilah	A will takes Akilah 3 hours, and in that time she could otherwise write ___ employment contract(s)	An employment contract takes Akilah 6 hours, and in that time she could otherwise write ___ will(s)
Zara	A will takes Zara 9 hours, and in that time she could otherwise write ___ employment contract(s)	An employment contract takes Zara 9 hours, and in that time she could otherwise write ___ will(s)

Step 3: Evaluate who has a *comparative advantage* by assessing who has the lowest opportunity cost for each task.

c. Who has a comparative advantage in writing wills? (Hint: You're trying to figure out who's *down* for the task, so look *down* that column to find who has the lowest opportunity cost.)

d. Who has a comparative advantage in writing employment contracts? ■

Answers: a. Akilah: ½, Zara: 1;
b. Akilah: 2, Zara: 1; c. Akilah; d. Zara

Rearranging who does what increases output. There's a big payoff from thinking in terms of comparative advantage: Simply by rearranging who does what, you can produce more with the same inputs. All you need to do is reallocate the tasks so that we each do more of those tasks where we each hold a comparative advantage, and less of the other tasks.

This logic says that Jamie should reallocate time from vacuuming to cooking, and Helen should reallocate time from cooking to vacuuming. Figure 2 illustrates what'll happen if they follow this advice.

Figure 2 | Gains from Trade Due to Comparative Advantage

Reallocate *tasks* according to comparative advantage to increase output

If Helen and Jamie each reallocate four more hours per week to their comparative advantage (and four fewer hours to the other task) . . .

	Vacuuming	Meals produced
Jamie	*4 fewer hours vacuuming* → House gets vacuumed 1 fewer time	*4 more hours cooking* → 4 more meals
Helen	*4 more hours vacuuming* → House gets vacuumed 1 more time	*4 fewer hours cooking* → 2 fewer meals
Total	House still gets vacuumed as often	2 more meals each week

In this example, Jamie reallocates four hours each week from vacuuming to cooking, which will mean the house gets vacuumed one fewer time, but he'll make four more meals per week. And if Helen reallocates four hours each week from making meals to vacuuming, she'll produce two fewer meals per week but make sure the house gets vacuumed one more time. Add it up, and as the bottom row shows, their household now produces two extra meals each week and the house still gets vacuumed. Specializing according to comparative advantage has made both Helen and Jamie better off — there are two more nights each week when they'll eat at home, rather than having to pay for takeout.

Where do these extra meals come from? It's not from working harder — Helen and Jamie are simply reallocating the tasks each does around the house, so neither of them is working longer hours on household chores. And they're not necessarily getting better at doing the tasks they've been assigned (although that could also happen). Rather, this extra output is the dividend from rearranging their household tasks according to comparative advantage. That's the power of comparative advantage: By ensuring each task is done at the lowest opportunity cost, you produce more in the same amount of time.

This extra output is called the *gains from trade,* because Helen can get her meals made at the lowest opportunity cost only by trading tasks with Jamie, and Jamie can get the vacuuming done at the lowest opportunity cost only by trading tasks with Helen.

Trading allows people to reallocate tasks so that more output is produced with a lower opportunity cost. This leads to **specialization** in which people focus on specific tasks, spending more of their time on what they're relatively good at, and less of their time doing other things.

specialization Focusing on specific tasks.

Comparative Advantage in Action

The big idea here is that you can produce more if you use comparative advantage to assign tasks. You should assign each task to the person who can do it at the lowest opportunity cost. This is an idea that you can apply well beyond the simple example we've explored so far.

Use comparative advantage to assign workers to tasks. Good managers use comparative advantage to figure out how to assign their team members to different jobs:

- Your dentist probably doesn't clean your teeth or take your X-rays. Instead, most dentists allocate these tasks to their hygienist, which frees them up to do more complicated (and expensive!) procedures on another patient.
- Veterinarians usually focus their time on medical exams and treatment, and leave tasks like nail trimming to veterinary assistants.
- Senior lawyers rarely draft legal motions. Instead, they assign those tasks to junior lawyers or paralegals, which frees up the senior lawyer to do the more profitable work of meeting with clients and strategically planning their legal approach to a case.
- Your hairdresser probably doesn't wash your hair. Instead, hairdressers typically allocate that task to an assistant, so that they can do more high-paying tints, highlights, or coloring jobs.
- Chef Alice Waters is the best cook in her kitchen at the famed Chez Panisse in Berkeley, California — but that doesn't mean she does the cooking. A restaurateur and executive chef, Waters' time is best spent overseeing her business: working with local vendors, planning menus, creating new dishes, and training staff on how to prepare them.

In each case, the idea is that you should delegate tasks whenever you can delegate them to someone with a lower opportunity cost. And the upside is that it'll free you up to spend more time on those tasks where you hold a comparative advantage.

While both your vet and their assistant know how to trim your puppy's nails, only one of them has a comparative advantage.

EVERYDAY Economics   **Should the best drummer play the drums?**

It's been reported that when John Lennon was asked "Is Ringo Starr the best drummer in the world?" he responded that "he's not the best drummer in the Beatles!" He may be right because their bassist, Paul McCartney, was also a superb drummer. And this makes me think that the Beatles were also savvy economists, using comparative advantage to assign tasks. After all, if the opportunity cost of having McCartney play drums was losing him as a bass guitarist, that's too high a price to pay. Comparative advantage says that you don't necessarily want the best drummer playing drums, because you also need to think about their opportunity cost. ■

Markets Facilitate Gains from Trade

So far we've found that Helen and Jamie are both better off — they produce more — if they hold a household meeting and divvy up their household tasks according to comparative advantage. But this simple story points to a broader lesson that extends well beyond assigning tasks to your roommates.

Markets offer the opportunity to specialize according to comparative advantage. What if Helen and Jamie live in two separate houses? The logic of comparative advantage still applies. This logic says that they'll both be better off if each task

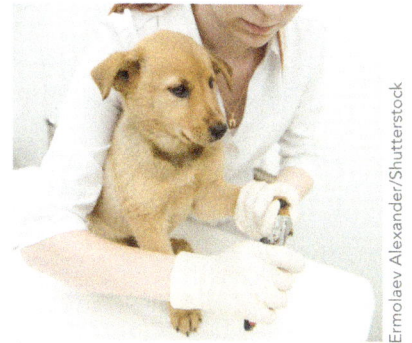

"He's not the best drummer in the Beatles."

is assigned to the person who can do it at the lowest opportunity cost. That might mean that Helen occasionally drops by Jamie's house to vacuum, and Jamie repays the favor by sending Helen home with some of his pre-prepared meals. As we've seen, trading tasks like this makes them both better off.

Okay, but what if Helen and Jamie don't even know each other? The logic still works. This is where markets come in: Markets help strangers exploit the gains from trade that come from specializing according to comparative advantage. The logic of comparative advantage tells Helen to do more of the tasks where her opportunity cost is low, and to rely on others for tasks where she has a higher opportunity cost. That logic will lead her to start a company that'll vacuum people's living rooms for them. And when she's hungry, she'll use some of her profits to buy meals from someone who can make them at a lower opportunity cost than she can. Who knows, she may even buy meals made by some guy called Jamie.

Likewise, the logic of comparative advantage tells Jamie to do more of those tasks where his opportunity cost is low, and rely on others for tasks where he has a high opportunity cost. That's why he'll partner with a delivery network to sell meal kits to folks too busy to do elaborate food prep. And when his floors get dirty, he'll see if there's a business that can get his vacuuming done. He might even become a customer of his old friend Helen.

The gains from trade are just as great in this market-based exchange as they are when Helen and Jamie are roommates. And the incentive to do this is just as great, because when Helen and Jamie each focus on those tasks where they hold a comparative advantage, together they get more done. That is, there are gains from trade.

Comparative advantage explains why there are gains from trade in markets. Indeed, our simple story is an abridged version of a real-world business success story, in which Helen is Helen Greiner. As an undergraduate student she was so inspired by R2-D2 in *Star Wars* that she focused her studies on robotics and artificial intelligence. It led her to start the company iRobot, which makes little robots that vacuum or mop your home for you. Helen's robots are so efficient that they can vacuum at a lower opportunity cost than you can. And even though you don't know Helen Greiner, you can still trade with her. Pay her company $200, and in return the robot she helped invent will do your vacuuming, allowing you to spend the hours you save on those tasks where you have a comparative advantage.

Helen Greiner, co-founder of iRobot Corp.

Likewise, Jamie is a stand-in for Jamie Oliver, the British celebrity cook. He, too, is specializing in tasks where he holds a comparative advantage. He recently partnered with HelloFresh, a service that delivers recipes and all necessary ingredients directly to your door, so you can enjoy preparing delicious meals without having to do the work of meal planning and food shopping. Even though you don't know Jamie, for a reasonable weekly fee, he'll send you his meal kits, saving you time that you can spend on activities where you hold a comparative advantage.

The beauty of all this is that markets allow you to trade tasks with both Helen and Jamie, so that you can spend less time on tasks like cleaning and cooking where your opportunity cost is high, and more time on tasks where you hold a comparative advantage. And because each task — vacuuming the house, making dinner, and studying economics — is being done at its lowest possible opportunity cost, you're each better off. The big idea here is that people following their comparative advantage creates gains from trade.

Comparative advantage explains why people specialize. This simple story about Helen and Jamie is not just about two happy roommates. Rather, it's a metaphor for the entire economy. It explains why each of us specializes in the specific tasks for which we hold a comparative advantage — those with leadership skills work as managers, number-crunchers work as analysts, and empathetic folks work in health and human services. Each of us uses the money we make to buy goods and services from folks who have a comparative advantage producing them — we buy cars designed by skilled engineers, meals from efficient cooks, and education from professional teachers.

Jamie Oliver, celebrity chef.

In turn, all of this comparative advantage–driven specialization ensures that each product is made at the lowest opportunity cost, which ensures there are gains from all this trade.

Do more of what you're relatively good at, and less of the other stuff.
Comparative advantage boils down to one key piece of advice: Do more of what you're *relatively* good at, and less of the other stuff. This simple advice explains why:

- TaskRabbit is so successful: If you're busy, you can't afford the time to assemble your new Ikea furniture. But through TaskRabbit, you can find someone who has a comparative advantage in building furniture, and hire them to do it for you.
- It can pay to take an Uber to work: Not only will you save the expense of driving your car, but you can spend your commuting time getting a head start on responding to office email or planning your weekend.
- Few executives make their own lunch: The opportunity cost of spending 10 minutes making a sandwich is simply too high when you have an empire to run.
- Busy families buy pre-cut vegetables: The opportunity cost of chopping vegetables is time busy parents could spend helping their kids with their homework.
- Politicians let lobbyists draft bills for them: The opportunity cost of drafting legislation is time that an elected representative can spend meeting with their constituents.
- Actors don't do their own stunts: Even though no one is tougher than Dwayne "The Rock" Johnson, he doesn't do his own stunts, because the opportunity cost of The Rock breaking a bone is much greater than it is for his cousin, Tanoai Reed, who works as his stunt double.

Only one of them is Dwayne Johnson. The other has a lower opportunity cost of stunt work.

In each of these cases, the market plays an important role in helping people focus on the tasks for which they have a comparative advantage. The time and energy you save on tasks other people do is time you can allocate to tasks for which you do have a comparative advantage.

Interpreting the DATA | How shifting comparative advantage explains changes in family life

Comparative advantage can explain some of the most important social changes of the past century, including the changing nature of work, families, and relationships. Let me explain.

Most households have two broad sets of tasks to manage: the task of earning money to purchase goods and services, and the tasks of providing goods and services for the household directly such as child care and housekeeping. Economists often refer to these two groups of tasks as market-based work and home production. Historically, home production was a full-time job, and the opportunity cost of doing this work was the forgone earnings from not working for pay. Comparative advantage suggests that home production should be assigned to the person who can do it at the lowest opportunity cost.

Back in your grandparents' day, discrimination kept women's wages well below those of men. As a result, each hour of home production came with a lower opportunity cost for your grandmother than for your grandfather, because it meant forgoing an hour of lower-paid work. That's why so many women of that era were homemakers, while their husbands pursued paid work.

As the twentieth century progressed, social and economic changes led more women to go to college. More education led to higher potential wages for women, increasing the opportunity cost of staying home. As the logic of comparative advantage suggests, this led more women to enter the workforce.

What happened to housework, then? A parallel development — the invention of new household appliances — led families to reorganize their domestic priorities. Here's why: Appliances like washing machines, dishwashers, and vacuuming robots are labor-saving tools that reduced the amount of human time needed to get clean clothes, dishes, and floors. And the technology that allowed prepackaged foods meant that industrial kitchens could churn out easily reheated meals at a lower opportunity cost than any homemaker. As a result, your parents' generation spends a lot less time on housework than their parents did. Your generation will do even less, as online services make it easier for you to outsource and automate chores like paying your bills and doing the grocery shopping.

In turn, this technological change means that the opportunity cost of working for pay has fallen — the housework will still get done! — and so in many more households today, both parents work. They're following the dictates of comparative advantage, doing what they're relatively good at — working in their job — and relying on others (including domestic robots!) to do some of the other stuff. ■

Comparative Advantage Drives International Trade

Comparative advantage explains how you benefit from specializing in some tasks and trading with others. This also means that comparative advantage explains why we trade with people who live in other countries, and hence it explains *international trade*.

To see why, let's return to the story of Helen and Jamie. As we discovered, they're both better off when Helen takes more responsibility for vacuuming the house, and Jamie does more of the cooking. The same logic applies to the real-world Helen Greiner and Jamie Oliver. In the real world it means that Helen will buy tasty meals designed by Jamie, by purchasing them from HelloFresh. And Jamie will buy a Roomba designed by Helen, to vacuum his house. These choices are driven by the now-familiar logic that says trading — either trading tasks in a household, or trading meals for robots in the market — enables Helen and Jamie to get their cooking and cleaning done at the lowest opportunity cost.

We trade with foreigners for the same reason we trade with locals. Now let's add one more wrinkle: Helen Greiner is American, while Jamie Oliver is British. When Jamie buys a Roomba, it's an export from an American seller to a British buyer. And if Helen buys one of Jamie's meal kits, it's an export from a British-German partnership (Jamie is British; HelloFresh is German) to an American. This international trade between an American and a Brit makes them both better off, creating gains from trade.

By this telling, the gains from trade created by comparative advantage are the reason for international trade. Those gains from trade are an incentive for people all around the world to focus on what they're best at and rely on others for the other stuff. And as a result, tasks will be allocated to the people who can do them at the lowest opportunity cost — even when that person happens to live overseas.

We'll study international trade in greater depth in Chapter 7. But even now, it should be clear that when comparative advantage drives you to trade with someone — and even if that person is living overseas — you'll both end up better off.

Oleksiy Maksymenko Photography/Alamy

Invented in the United States and helping people worldwide focus on their comparative advantage.

| EVERYDAY Economics | Trading across the borders of Dan's lawn |

Dan grew up mowing lawns and raking leaves. His parents gave him a summer allowance to do that work for his family. He also took on other families' yard work for pay. By the end of high school, he was filling his summer days with yard work. He kept at it while he trained as a plumber. But once he started his own business, and as demand for his plumbing services grew, he found that it no longer made sense for him to mow his own lawn. The time he spent mowing his lawn was time he could spend working on clients' bathroom renovations or fixing broken water heaters. So Dan hired a local teenager, Karla, to take care of his lawn. Financially, he was better off, because he paid Karla less to mow his lawn than he was paid for his time as a plumber. And Karla was happy to have an additional client since yard work paid better than other part-time jobs and offered greater flexibility. This is comparative advantage creating gains from trade: Both Dan and Karla are made better off from trading.

Comparative advantage doesn't depend on whether the borders of Dan's lawn represent just his property or a whole new country. To see this, think about it as if Dan's property was his kingdom. We can call it Republic of Danrovia, population four (Dan has a partner and two small kids).

Critics of international trade will argue that trade has wrought extraordinary havoc upon Danrovia. This once-proud republic used to have a thriving agricultural sector (his yardwork), but this traditional way of life has collapsed. It was destroyed by an influx of cheap foreign labor (workers from the Kingdom of Karla). All Danrovia has to show for it is a huge bilateral trade deficit with the Kingdom of Karla (the deficit that arises because Dan pays Karla every weekend, but Karla buys nothing from Dan).

Every word of this argument makes trade sound terrible, and every word is true (although exaggerated for effect). But I still think this trade was worthwhile, and Dan and Karla agree. The critics have overlooked two untold stories that are central to the logic of comparative advantage. First, Danrovia's profitable plumbing industry has grown even stronger. And second, too often the trade debate focuses only on the production side of the economy, effectively asking who's doing the yard work. But this misses the consumption side, which is where the gains are. Dan consumes and enjoys the fruits of the yard work every time he sits in his yard and enjoys his beautiful lawn. He also enjoys a few extra purchases with some of the gains from trade — the extra money he makes plumbing instead of doing yard work. And Karla also gets a boost in consumption from the spending that her gains from trade allow. ■

Do it yourself, or delegate? It depends on your comparative advantage.

Comparative advantage is about reallocating resources to their better uses. You've come a long way in uncovering what markets are all about. The economy largely consists of folks selling stuff they've made (or services they provide), and other folks buying it. We now see why they do this — they're reallocating tasks according to comparative advantage. And all this trade generates gains from trade, which make both buyer and seller better off.

This should lead you to think differently about markets. Rather than thinking about them as a zero-sum competition in which your gain is my loss, the logic of comparative advantage shows how they can enable a win-win outcome for both buyer and seller.

If that now seems obvious, then you're well on your way to thinking like an economist. You won't meet an economist who doesn't believe in the power of comparative advantage. But it just might be the hardest idea for noneconomists to believe.

6.3 The Power of Prices

Learning Objective *Understand the role that prices play in coordinating economic activity.*

Markets help allocate tasks in a way that gets the most out of the gains from trade. To do that, everyone needs to be able to focus on tasks for which they hold a comparative advantage, which requires knowing where each resource — such as your time — has the most relative value. That is where prices come in.

You've already learned how the quantity supplied and quantity demanded respond to changes in the price, but it's worth pausing to think about the many roles that prices play in coordinating economic activity. Prices convey information and create incentives.

Organizing all the tasks that are done in our economy is a colossal logistical challenge. Each business needs access to the right inputs. Those inputs need to arrive at the right time. They need to be combined in just the right way to be transformed into useful products. And those products need to go to the right people. Markets do an extraordinary job of organizing all of this. But how?

The answer is prices. They play three central roles. First, a price is a message that is heard around the globe. Second, a price is an incentive, inducing people to make better choices. And third, prices aggregate information, incorporating the judgments that motivate thousands of buying and selling decisions. Prices guide nearly every decision we make, helping to organize and coordinate economic activity.

Role 1: A Price Is a Message

It's pronounced "keen-wah," and it's delicious.

Quinoa has been called the "miracle grain of the Andes." Its small, rice-like seeds are grown almost exclusively on the plains of the Andes mountains in Peru and Bolivia, and it's so nutritious that NASA feeds it to astronauts. While quinoa is an ancient grain, it was largely ignored by consumers outside of the six countries that grew it until early in the twenty-first century. The high protein content and other health benefits of quinoa led to a surge of interest in quinoa around the globe — in fact, 2013 was declared "the year of quinoa" by the United Nations. Today, you can stop by just about any grocery store and find quinoa salads, quinoa breakfast cereals, quinoa granola bars, quinoa crackers, and even quinoa-based mac and cheese.

The quinoa fad took place far away from the farmers who are high in the Andes mountains, cut off from news about the rest of the world. How do they learn about food trends in the United States? And how do American gourmands communicate their new love for quinoa to the farmers in Peru and Bolivia?

The price acts as a messenger communicating the sharp increase in demand. A skyrocketing price is sending important messages, creating a line of communication between buyers and sellers.

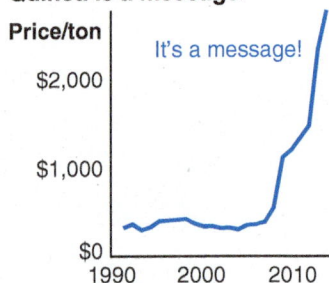

The rising price of Peruvian Quinoa is a message.

The price is a message to potential suppliers. Potential suppliers may not otherwise know much about what's happening on the demand side of the market. Peruvian and Bolivian farmers may know little about American food trends, but they know the price of quinoa. When the price skyrockets, it sends these farmers a very clear message: "Quinoa is now more valuable — grow more quinoa!" More generally, a price tells potential suppliers how much buyers value their products, because it reveals the buyer's marginal benefit, or willingness to pay.

The price is a message to potential buyers. Potential buyers may not otherwise know what is happening on the supply side of the market. Few Americans pay much attention to agricultural developments in the Andes, and so you're probably unaware of how difficult it is for Peruvian farmers to expand quinoa production. But you do look at the prices when you're at a restaurant or grocery store. When the price of quinoa rises, it sends potential buyers like you a clear message: "Quinoa is scarce — buy less of it!" More generally, the price tells potential buyers about how expensive it is for sellers to produce more of a product, as it reveals the seller's marginal cost.

These messages help coordinate better outcomes. Price messages help coordinate the extraordinary chain of events that puts quinoa on your plate. Some of your quinoa might come from a Peruvian farmer who expands his production. And some might come from a Bolivian family that cuts back and eats more Argentinian-grown wheat instead. That quinoa might get to you on a Norwegian container ship that'll transport it to the United States. All of this occurs even if you don't know anyone in Peru, Bolivia, Argentina, or Norway.

It takes an extraordinary degree of coordination to get that quinoa to you. Prices are what make this miracle of global coordination possible. Price allows for the rapid-fire transmission of messages that are equally well understood in English, Spanish, Norwegian, and Quechua (the language spoken in the Andes).

Role 2: A Price Is an Incentive

So far I've described prices as providing a valuable line of communication between buyers and sellers. People respond to these messages because prices serve another role: A price is an *incentive*. The incentive is straightforward: A high price is an incentive for buyers to cut back a bit, just as it's an incentive for suppliers to expand production. A low price provides the opposite incentive.

A price is an incentive for suppliers. A high price is an incentive for suppliers to increase production, because it creates new profit opportunities. A high price for quinoa is an incentive for farmers in the Andes to switch from growing corn to growing quinoa, which is what spurred them to quadruple their production of quinoa. This high price is an incentive for Bolivians to leave their mining jobs to return to their rural villages to farm quinoa. It's also an incentive stimulating innovation, and scientists at a Peruvian university have developed a variety of quinoa that will grow in coastal areas.

A high price is an incentive with global influence, and it led farmers in dozens of countries around the globe to experiment with growing quinoa. American geneticists are hard at work mapping the quinoa genome that will help them genetically engineer new high-yielding varieties. This extraordinary mobilization occurs because the high price is an incentive for producers to increase the quantity they supply. A low price does the opposite — it is an incentive for suppliers to reduce production, because other opportunities start to look better.

A price is an incentive for buyers. For potential buyers, a high price raises the opportunity cost of consuming quinoa, creating an incentive to consume less. This incentive has far-reaching effects. It led many Peruvian and Bolivian families to switch from eating quinoa to alternative grains like wheat, which became relatively more affordable when the price of quinoa rose. South American farmers no longer use quinoa as chicken food. And if you've been in an American salad shop lately, the scoop of quinoa that you get may have gotten a little smaller. Each of these folks is conserving quinoa because the high price is an incentive for potential buyers to decrease the quantity they demand. The opposite is true when the price falls: In that case there is an incentive for buyers to consume more because quinoa has become cheaper relative to its substitutes.

A price provides an incentive for strangers to cooperate. When the price of quinoa rose, quinoa farmers received a message that they should start selling it. The end result is that the quinoa that was once reserved for a South American chicken started showing up on supermarket shelves in the United States. This occurs even though South American chickens neither know you nor particularly care about you. Rather, the South American chicken farmer is moved to consume less, allowing your local salad shop to sell you that quinoa as part of a salad. This all happens due to the incentives embedded in the price of quinoa.

Mark J. Barrett/Alamy

No quinoa for you.

Role 3: A Price Aggregates Information

A price also aggregates information. Learn how to interpret what it's saying, and you'll make better decisions. The clearest example of this involves **prediction markets,** in which people trade contracts whose payoffs are linked to whether an uncertain event occurs. For instance, there are prediction markets where you can buy a share that'll be worth $1 if a Democrat wins the next election (and nothing otherwise). They're called prediction markets, because their price effectively communicates a prediction. For instance, if the price of that Democratic stock is $0.60, you can think of this as the market forecasting that the Democrat has (roughly) a 60 percent chance of winning.

prediction markets Markets whose payoffs are linked to whether an uncertain event occurs.

The process of buying and selling aggregates information. Prediction markets yield useful forecasts because prices aggregate information. For instance, someone in Wisconsin who sees a lot of yard signs and bumper stickers supporting the Democrat might buy stock, while someone in New Mexico who saw the candidate give a bad speech might sell it. Good polling numbers might lead more people to buy the stock, while rising unpopularity might lead others to sell it. And so it goes on.

Through this process, the price will come to reflect — or aggregate — all of this information. Careful studies have shown that prediction markets yield more accurate forecasts than public opinion polls, statistical models, or televised experts. This means that you can quickly become an expert on politics simply by following political prediction markets online.

Market prices broadcast useful information. The same idea applies in other markets, and there are many financial prices that yield valuable business intelligence. The price of financial contracts linked to Federal Reserve decisions reveals the odds that interest rates will rise. The price of a futures contract — where a buyer agrees to purchase a commodity like oil, wheat, or natural gas at a specific time in the future — is effectively a bet on the future price of these commodities. Tracking the price of these contracts can provide useful intel about future disruptions to your input costs.

While some of these financial products might seem a bit obscure, the broader idea is that because prices aggregate information, they provide you with useful business intelligence.

> A price is:
> 1. A message
> 2. An incentive
> 3. A bundle of information

EVERYDAY Economics   Use markets to pick a better tournament bracket

Hannah Foslien/Getty Images

Surprised? The prediction markets weren't.

Sports-betting markets are effectively prediction markets, because a bet on your favorite team is the same as buying a security that'll pay off only if your team wins. The prices in these markets — the betting odds — aggregate information from thousands of bettors, who have studied just about every conceivable detail about each team. As a result, studies have shown them to be incredibly accurate. And that's your opportunity: You can use these prices as an aid while filling out your March Madness bracket, and you'll effectively be drawing on the expertise of thousands of sports-mad bettors. My co-workers will tell you this works — I've won the workplace bracket a few times even though I don't actually follow basketball closely. So even if you're not a big sports fan, you can quickly get up to speed to be able to fill out a bracket or in small talk by looking at sports-betting markets. ∎

6.4 How Managers Can Harness Market Forces

Learning Objective *Be ready to harness market forces in your own life.*

When Japanese troops in Korea surrendered at the end of World War II, it set in motion a remarkable natural experiment to see the effects of organizing a society based on markets. The country was effectively divided into two: half of the region came to be known as North Korea and the other half is now known as South Korea. The North Korean side was aligned with the Soviet Union, which helped to set up a centrally planned economy in which government officials decided who made what, who got what, and how much was made. By contrast, the United States helped set up a market economy in South Korea, and instead of a centralized government bureaucracy directing economic activity, it was left to market forces.

Economists have pointed to this as a natural experiment that highlights the benefits of activity being driven by market forces. Both Koreas were equally poor in the immediate aftermath of the war. Today, the average annual income in market-oriented South Korea is about $43,000 per year. That's about 20 times greater than in centrally planned North Korea, where average income is about $1,700 per person and people are often hungry. Market forces have allowed South Koreans to explore and make the most of gains from trade, and this has made them enormously better off.

There's no more striking way to see this difference than the photos that NASA takes from space. As satellite photos show, South Korea is brightly lit and pulsating with activity, while North Korea is dark, as if nothing is happening.

This isn't just a lesson about running a country. The point of this story is to see the success that market forces can have in allocating scarce resources to their most beneficial use. While many people extol the virtues of market economies, when it comes to running their business, they act more like North Korea — using centralized managers to make decisions — rather than South Korea — using market forces to allocate your scarce resources.

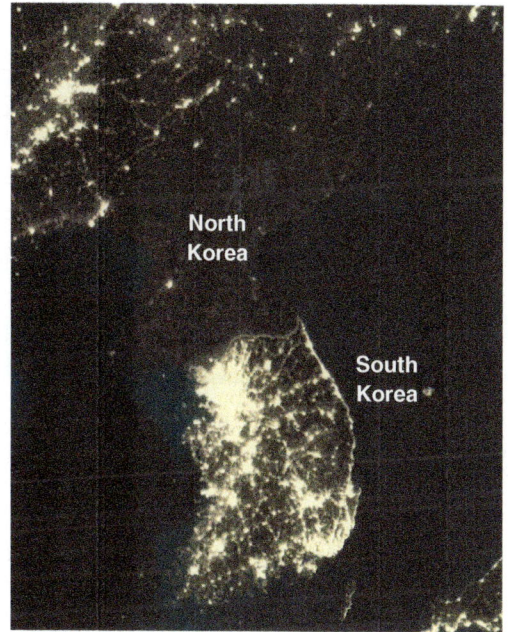

Satellite images of North and South Korea illustrate the power of market forces.

Internal Markets Allocate Resources

Internal markets are markets that managers set up *within* their organization so that different divisions can buy and sell scarce resources. The idea is to harness more of the power of market forces to help businesses grow and become more profitable. Just as market economies efficiently allocate scarce resources to better uses within a society, internal markets can allocate scarce resources to better uses within a company, nonprofit, or government agency.

internal markets Markets within a company to buy and sell scarce resources.

A typical CEO — much like the leader of North Korea — holds an enormous amount of centralized power, and uses that power to direct activity within a company. A CEO — again, much like North Korea's supreme leader — heads a vast bureaucracy, and, together with their deputies, formulates long-term plans that guide the broader enterprise and decide how best to deploy workers and machinery among their alternative uses. But savvy CEOs are learning to become more efficient by harnessing the power of markets. Let's dig into some examples.

The knowledge problem means that managers can't get the information they need. Feeding America is a nonprofit — the largest network of food banks in the United States. It solicits food donations from large companies like Kraft or Walmart, and then allocates that food to 210 regional food banks around the country. Their good work means that thousands of families will be able to eat tonight.

The logistics of getting this right are complicated. To see why, put yourself in the shoes of an executive at Feeding America's Chicago headquarters. You've just been sent a truckload of fruit to distribute, and you want to send it to the region that'll get the largest benefit from it. To figure out where this is, you'll need to know the marginal benefit of a truckload of fruit for each of your 210 regional food banks. Calling all 210 regional food banks would take forever, and even then, you've got no guarantee they'll provide accurate information.

This is an example of the **knowledge problem,** which is that the knowledge or information you need to make a good decision may be so broadly dispersed that it's not available to any individual decision maker. Think of this knowledge as being like a treasure map. The problem is that many people have a few small shreds of the map — the food bank in Houston may know the marginal benefit *it* would get from another truckload of fruit, just as the food bank in Jacksonville knows *its* marginal benefit. But no one has access to the whole map — what each food bank's marginal benefit is — making it impossible

knowledge problem When knowledge needed to make a good decision is not available to the decision maker.

An internal market determines what food they're serving at this food bank.

to navigate a path to the best outcome. Without access to this dispersed information, the executives at headquarters have no way to identify the best use for that truckload of fruit.

Markets solve the knowledge problem. The folks running Feeding America realized that they could harness market forces to help them. After all, if markets allocate stuff to its better uses, they figured that an internal market can help them allocate food to where it'll be most useful. They set up an internal market for allocating donated food. Here's how it works: When a new truckload of food arrives, all food banks can bid for it in an internal eBay-style auction. This means that the food banks that really need fruit can bid more for fruit. Because the highest bidder wins the auction, each truckload of donated food goes to a food bank that really needs it. To ensure that all food banks can compete for the food on a level playing field, they don't bid using real money, but rather an artificial currency issued by Feeding America.

This internal market avoids the knowledge problem, because it doesn't rely on a centralized decision maker knowing what's best, or on personal relationships that may lead some regional food banks to do better than others. Instead, it relies on each regional food bank knowing its own marginal benefit and bidding accordingly. To continue the treasure map analogy: You don't need the whole map if there's someone at each navigation point telling you where to go next. Feeding America has discovered that the forces of supply and demand can allocate the donated food more efficiently than their managers can. The result is that less food is wasted, more people get fed, and because donors know their food is finding families in need, they're more willing to donate.

Use internal markets to allocate scarce resources. Feeding America's success points to a lesson that you should remember when you're a manager: You might be able to harness the power of markets to help you do a better job.

For instance, at Google, when computer resources were scarce, the executive team didn't ask managers to decide whether the Gmail team was more deserving than the YouTube or Chrome teams. Instead, managers allocated computer processing time, disk space, and memory by setting up an internal market so that the different product teams could compete to buy the space they needed. NASA has tried something similar. When NASA sent a spacecraft to Saturn, it had to figure out how to allocate the scarce resources of weight, electric power, data transmission, and budget across the different teams conducting scientific experiments. Rather than rely on the judgment of managers, it set up an internal market in which the scientists could trade the resources they needed.

EVERYDAY Economics   Getting into the classes you want

Many college students have experienced the frustration of wanting to take a particular class, only to discover that it is full. Can you think of a way to use internal markets to make sure that you get into the classes you value the most? Several leading business and law schools have devised a solution: They allocate scarce slots in popular classes with an internal market. Each student is given the same amount of fake money to use to buy and sell spots in popular classes. The more you want to be in a particular class, the more you'll bid, leading each spot to be allocated to the student who values it most. ∎

Internal prediction markets can improve your forecasts. Another type of internal market — an internal prediction market — can be helpful whenever you need an accurate forecast. For instance, managers at Ford need accurate forecasts of the number of each type of vehicle they'll sell each week. Traditionally they relied on forecasts put together by their internal analysts. But when Ford set up a prediction market and allowed its employees to bet on the outcome, the market yielded forecasts that were 25% more accurate.

Likewise, Google's managers need to forecast things like how many people will use Gmail, whether a project will be completed on time, and what its competitors will do. When Google set up its own prediction markets, the prices yielded remarkably accurate forecasts about these critically important business issues. Experiments at other companies such as HP, Intel, Nokia, and Siemens yielded similar findings.

6.5 Tying It Together

The Magic of Markets and Comparative Advantage

This chapter is about understanding what markets do. And what they do best is reallocate resources to better uses. That reallocation generates gains from trade. What's the source of these gains from trade? We make more stuff when we use comparative advantage to reallocate tasks to their lowest-cost producer. The result is an extraordinary degree of specialization, in which prices play a central role in coordinating economic activity.

A miracle of the market economy.

We can see all of this by following the story of a particular good through the economy, from start to finish. Here's what happened when Nobel laureate Milton Friedman gazed with wonder upon a single pencil, musing about the extraordinary economic journey it took to your desk:

> Look at this lead pencil. There's not a single person in the world who could make this pencil . . .

> The wood . . . comes from a tree . . . To cut down that tree, it took a saw. To make the saw, it took steel. To make steel, it took iron ore. This black center . . . comes from some mines in South America. This red top up here, this eraser, a bit of rubber, probably comes from Malaya, where the rubber tree isn't even native! It was imported from South America by some businessmen with the help of the British government. This brass ferrule? I haven't the slightest idea where it came from. Or the yellow paint! Or the paint that made the black lines. Or the glue that holds it together.

> Literally thousands of people cooperated to make this pencil. People who don't speak the same language, who practice different religions, who might hate one another if they ever met!

Next time you pick up a pencil, you really should marvel at the extraordinary path that it has taken to you. And marvel also at the incredibly low price: If you buy a few dozen pencils, they'll cost you only about 10 cents each.

These two marvels are linked. The pencil follows an extraordinary path because every single part of the pencil is produced by folks who specialize in the narrow task for which they hold a comparative advantage. Markets reallocate stuff to better uses, and in this case, they reallocate the tasks that go into making a pencil to those who can do them at the lowest opportunity cost.

The extraordinary symphony of productive effort that led to the production of Milton Friedman's pencil was conducted by the price system, which sends a message about what is needed, provides an incentive to act, and aggregates the information needed to decide how to act.

So if you're ever stuck in an exam trying to remember what markets do, just look at the pencil you're writing with.

Chapter 6 Review

Chapter at a Glance

Gains from Trade: The benefits that come from reallocating resources, goods, and services to better uses.

Comparative Advantage: The ability to do a task at a lower **opportunity cost**. Use comparative advantage to allocate tasks to those with the lowest opportunity cost.
(*Absolute Advantage:* The ability to do a task using fewer inputs.)

A three step recipe identifies who has a comparative advantage in each task:

#1. Determine how long the task would take each person. This measures the cost of producing each good, **in hours**.

Productivity: *How long does it take to complete:*

	Task A	Task B
Person 1	___ hours	___ hours
Person 2	___ hours	___ hours

#2. Convert this into a measure of **opportunity cost**, by calculating how much of the alternative good you could have produced in that time.

Evaluate the opportunity cost: *What does each forego to complete:*

	Task A	Task B
Person 1	Task A takes **Person 1** ___ hours, and in that time they could otherwise complete ___ of **Task B**	Task B takes **Person 1** ___ hours, and in that time they could otherwise complete ___ of **Task A**
Person 2	Task A takes **Person 2** ___ hours, and in that time they could otherwise complete ___ of **Task B**	Task B takes **Person 2** ___ hours, and in that time they could otherwise complete ___ of **Task A**

#3. Evaluate who has a **comparative advantage** at each task by assessing who can do each task or produce each good at the lowest opportunity cost.

Prices play three central roles

1. **A price is a message**, providing a valuable line of communication between buyers and sellers.
2. **A price is an incentive**, inducing people to make better choices.
3. **A price aggregates information**, incorporating the judgments that motivate the thousands of buying and selling decisions that push the price up or down.

Harnessing Market Forces

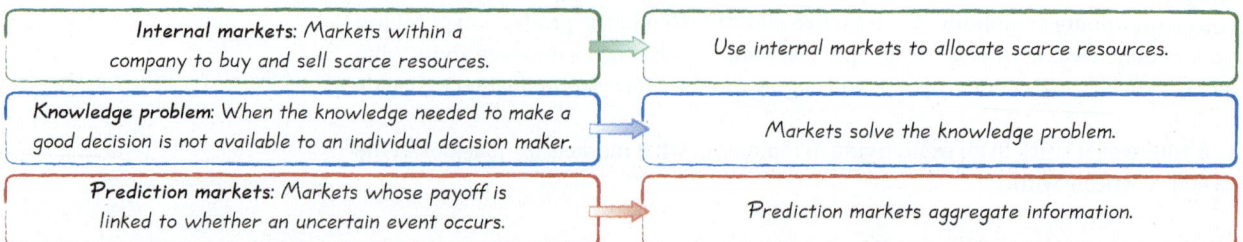

Internal markets: Markets within a company to buy and sell scarce resources.	→ Use internal markets to allocate scarce resources.
Knowledge problem: When the knowledge needed to make a good decision is not available to an individual decision maker.	→ Markets solve the knowledge problem.
Prediction markets: Markets whose payoff is linked to whether an uncertain event occurs.	→ Prediction markets aggregate information.

Key Terms

absolute advantage, 137

comparative advantage, 137

gains from trade, 136

internal markets, 149

knowledge problem, 149

prediction market, 147

specialization, 140

Study Problems

Learning Objective 6.1 *Understand the role of markets in reallocating resources to better uses.*

1. How has the emergence of ride-sharing apps like Lyft and Uber created gains from trade that didn't exist before?

2. Explain the gains from trade that arise for both buyers and sellers in the following transactions:

   a. Neighbors Jordan and Chelsea are both working parents. They are able to hire a single babysitter to care for both of their toddlers for 75% of what they would collectively have to pay two separate babysitters.

   b. Elijah decides that his family should eat more healthy meals, but they are short on time. He buys a subscription that sends healthy preplanned meals to his home three times a week.

   c. Callie accepts an extra shift at work and hires a cleaning service to clean her apartment.

Learning Objective 6.2 *Use comparative advantage to allocate tasks to those with the lowest opportunity cost.*

3. Think of your current roommate(s) or people you have lived with in the past, and provide an example of a household task that you have an absolute advantage completing and a household task you have a comparative advantage completing. Would it be better for your household if you specialized in the task for which you have an absolute advantage, or the task for which you have a comparative advantage? Explain your reasoning.

4. Explain how you can apply the three-step recipe of identifying comparative advantages to completing a group project.

5. Use comparative advantage to explain why you don't produce everything you consume. For example, why do you buy a T-shirt from Target instead of making it yourself? Or why do you buy groceries instead of growing your own food?

6. Use the opportunity cost principle to describe what you gain from specializing in your chosen (or to be chosen) profession.

7. Use the ideas of comparative advantage and specialization to explain why, over the last several decades, the number of manufacturing jobs have decreased in the United States and increased in other countries such as Mexico.

8. You and your friend Olivia both volunteer at a cat rescue. The shelter supervisor asks the two of you to clean out crates and haul bags of cat food from the donation area to storage. You know from your last time volunteering that you can clean out 10 crates in an hour or move 5 bags of cat food. Olivia can clean out 6 crates in an hour or move 6 bags of cat food. Olivia suggests that you split the tasks equally. Answer the following questions to determine if Olivia is making the best decision.

   a. Who has an absolute advantage in doing each task?

   b. What are Olivia's opportunity costs of doing each task?

   c. What are your opportunity costs of doing each task?

   d. Who has a comparative advantage in doing each task?

   e. Who should do each task to minimize the amount of time you both spend?

   f. Was Olivia's suggestion the best possible way to allocate your time? Why or why not?

9. You're working on a homework assignment with a partner, Deidre, that consists of an essay and graphing questions. You can write an essay in 15 minutes, while Deidre takes 20 minutes to write an essay of similar quality. You can answer a graphing question in 30 minutes, and it also takes Deidre 30 minutes.

   a. What are you and your partner's opportunity cost of writing an essay and of answering graphing questions?

   b. Use the opportunity cost principle to determine each of your comparative advantages.

   c. If you each agree to spend one more hour on the task for which you hold a comparative advantage, and one less hour on the other task, what will happen to your joint output?

10. As the manager at a local florist, you supervise two employees, Anita and Jerome. There are two tasks that need to be completed: floral arrangements and flower delivery. It takes Anita 30 minutes to finish one floral arrangement, and it takes her 40 minutes to make one delivery. It takes Jerome 10 minutes to finish one floral arrangement and it takes him 30 minutes to make one delivery.

    a. Who has an absolute advantage in each task?

    b. What are Anita and Jerome's opportunity costs of making floral arrangements? What is each of their opportunity costs of making one delivery?

c. Who has a comparative advantage in floral arrangements? What about deliveries?

d. Suppose, initially, Jerome and Anita each spent 4 hours daily creating floral arrangements and 2 hours daily making deliveries. If you changed their tasks so that each individual did nothing but the task for which they had a comparative advantage, how many more floral arrangements would your store make, and how many more deliveries?

11. Imagine that it takes an average Australian miner 10 hours to mine a metric ton of coal and 20 hours to mine a metric ton of manganese. It takes the average South African miner 4 hours to mine a metric ton of coal and 12 hours to mine a metric ton of manganese.

a. Create a table to show how productive each miner is in a day.

b. For each miner, calculate the opportunity cost of mining a ton of coal and a ton of manganese.

c. In what task does each miner have a comparative advantage?

d. Which resource will each country import? How about export?

e. Explain how markets provide the opportunity for the mining companies to specialize and earn gains from trade.

12. In 2017, Ecuador's biggest export was crude (unprocessed) petroleum, 63% of which it exported to the United States, and Ecuador's biggest import was refined (processed) petroleum, of which 70% was imported from the United States. What does this tell you about the countries' comparative advantages in extracting petroleum and refining petroleum?

Learning Objective 6.3 *Understand the role that prices play in coordinating economic activity.*

13. You manage a farm equipment supply store in Iowa. Explain how you could use the price of soybean futures as a message, an incentive, and as a source of information to help make better business decisions. For example, what does the future price of soybeans tell you about whether you should increase your supply of soybean equipment or shift your stock toward corn equipment?

14. Go to an online predictions market (searching online should find you a number of them quickly) and make a prediction based on the prices you find. What information

does the price tell you? How confident are you in this prediction and why?

15. Over a six-month period in 2007, the price of corn increased by almost 70% as a result of increased demand for ethanol biofuel.

a. What message does the dramatic price increase send to buyers and farmers?

b. How does the price change impact buyers' and farmers' incentives?

c. How do you think buyers and farmers responded to the dramatic price increase?

16. Between 2016 and 2017, Nintendo produced 2.3 million NES Classic Edition mini consoles that sold out in stores almost immediately. The retail price of the mini console was $59.99. However, if you were to check eBay at the time, you would see that people were buying the units for $250 each from resellers. Describe what message this price sends to both resellers and people buying the consoles to play them. How does the high price change their incentives?

17. Large airlines sometimes engage in fuel hedging as a way to avoid wild changes in jet fuel prices. To fuel hedge, an airline purchases a futures contract from an oil company that states they will purchase a set quantity of jet fuel at a specific price in the future regardless of what the actual market price is in the future. What do you expect to happen to the price of jet fuel in the future if the price of a fuel hedge decreases? Why?

Learning Objective 6.4 *Be ready to harness market forces in your own life.*

18. Provide an example of a knowledge problem that has impacted a company or an organization. Describe how setting up an internal market would help better allocate resources to solve the knowledge problem.

19. You are a director at a game studio. The CEO emailed you asking for the most accurate chances of the game making its release date. How could you use a predictions market to answer the CEO's question?

20. You're working as a paid intern on a small team of four software developers: Each member of the team faces different deadlines and requires your support at different times. You work only 40 hours per week. How could the company set up an internal market to ensure that your time is best allocated among the four team members each month?

International Trade

Turn your shirt inside out and look at the tag. No, not the washing instructions—look at the tag that tells you where it was made. Most likely it says, "Made in China," or perhaps Vietnam, Mexico, or Indonesia. Now try your jeans. Even if they're Levi's—what could be more American?—they're probably not made in the United States. Your smartphone might have been designed in America, but it was likely assembled in China. Keep looking around you: at your laptop, your bike, or the food you'll eat tonight. You'll quickly discover that much of it is made in another country.

You're probably wearing the world on your back.

Now fast forward to your future career. If you're an accountant, you might work for a company with offices all around the globe. If you're a programmer, your app will be sold in dozens of countries. If you're in advertising, your best clients might be multinationals, and your slogan will be heard worldwide. If you go into finance, you might buy and sell foreign companies. And if you're running a business, you'll be more successful if you think about the whole world as your market, rather than just the United States.

The point is that economic opportunities extend across national borders. Trade barriers have fallen, transportation has improved, and electronic networks make communication easier. The world is now more interconnected than ever, and globalization will transform the opportunities available to you. It's time to explore the implications. Why do we do all this international trade? Who's gaining? Who's getting hurt? There's a lot of fear about international trade, but as you read on, hopefully you'll also see it as a source of opportunity.

Chapter Objective

Understand the consequences of global trade.

7.1 Comparative Advantage Is the Foundation of International Trade
Discover why we trade with people in other countries.

7.2 How International Trade Shapes Your Market
Use supply and demand to assess the consequences of international trade.

7.3 The Debate About International Trade
Evaluate the arguments for and against international trade.

7.4 International Trade Policy
Understand how and why governments regulate international trade.

7.5 Effects of Globalization
Explore how globalization shapes your life.

🎙 **Podcast**
Think Like an Economist
International Trade—Cars from Corn

7.1   Comparative Advantage Is the Foundation of International Trade

Learning Objective *Discover why we trade with people in other countries.*

import To buy goods or services from foreign sellers.

export To sell goods or services to foreign buyers.

What drives people in different countries to trade with each other? The most obvious reason to buy goods from abroad is that you can get a better deal. You will choose to **import**—that is, buy goods or services from foreign sellers—when foreign products are a better deal than their U.S.-made equivalents.

Likewise, American businesses choose to **export**—that is, sell their goods or services to foreign buyers—when they can make more money than they would if they just sold them in the United States. Indeed, many businesses find more customers willing to pay a high price for their products when they supply them to all 8 billion people on the planet, rather than just the 330 million Americans in their domestic market.

Comparative Advantage and International Trade

You can get a better deal by trading with foreigners for the same reason that you get a better deal by trading with people within your country. The reason is *comparative advantage*. (This should all be familiar from the first half of Chapter 6. If it's not, go back and read it right now. The idea of comparative advantage is so important to international trade that I'll wait here until you're done.)

You have a comparative advantage in a task if you can complete it at a lower opportunity cost than someone else. Instead of making everything yourself, you should specialize in those activities where you have a comparative advantage, because this means your opportunity cost is lower than that of others. And you should rely on your trading partners for the other stuff, where their opportunity costs are lower.

When we each specialize according to our comparative advantage, we're each doing more of what we're relatively good at, and trading with others so we're buying the things they're relatively good at. The result is that we can both end up better off. Specializing according to comparative advantage means that we can produce more together than we can apart.

Borders are irrelevant to the logic of comparative advantage. This idea of assigning tasks to those with the lowest opportunity cost is no less persuasive if the folks with the lowest opportunity cost happen to live in another country. After all, an international border is just an arbitrary invisible line. The same logic and calculations that suggest you'll be better off if you trade with other Americans also suggest that you'll be better off if you trade with foreigners who happen to be on the other side of that invisible line.

Comparative advantage drives international trade. This logic says that we choose to import and export for the same reasons we do business with other Americans: Specializing according to comparative advantage can give us both more of the stuff we want. The only thing that's different about international trade is the scope and scale of specialization that's possible when there are 8 billion people to trade with.

Comparative advantage leads Americans to produce and export those goods where their opportunity costs are low and to import those goods where their opportunity costs are high. This is why computer scientists and engineers in the United States design the iPhone, while factory workers in China manufacture them. Both sides gain when trade is driven by comparative advantage, as this division of labor leads to lower iPhone prices for Americans and better-designed smartphones for the Chinese.

Does comparative advantage really drive international trade? Some of this might seem far-fetched. After all, do people really make the sort of comparative advantage calculations we outlined in Chapter 6 before deciding whether to import or export goods?

They do, but in a much simpler way: They just look at the price tag. When you shop for T-shirts, the cost-benefit principle tells you to pay careful attention to the price. And in a competitive market, the price is equal to marginal cost. (Yep, that's the marginal principle at work again.) This means that when you compare the price of an imported T-shirt with the price of the domestically produced one, you're effectively comparing their marginal costs. The opportunity cost principle reminds you that marginal cost should include all relevant opportunity costs. By looking for the lower-priced T-shirt, you're effectively evaluating which was made at the lowest opportunity cost. This is exactly what the idea of comparative advantage suggests you should do. And when you buy that cheaper T-shirt, you're buying from the manufacturer who has a comparative advantage in shirt-making.

The price tag will tell you a lot about your comparative advantage.

What Gets Traded?

Comparative advantage yields a pretty stark piece of advice: Produce what you're good at and buy what you aren't. Applied to international trade, this says to export the stuff you can produce at the lowest opportunity cost, and import the other stuff. In reality, that advice is a bit too stark, because there's one more factor to consider: trade costs.

Trade costs determine whether it's worth buying or selling internationally. **Trade costs** are the extra costs — aside from the price — incurred as a result of buying or selling your goods internationally rather than domestically. For instance, buying a car from Japan involves shipping costs. You might also have to pay an extra tax to the U.S. government on imports, or a tax to a foreign government for exports. The opportunity cost principle reminds you to consider the full set of costs — not just the out-of-pocket financial expenses. And so trade costs also include shipping delays, the hassle of working across language barriers and time zones, dealing with foreign laws, and adapting to different ways of doing business.

The cost-benefit principle says that trade is only worthwhile if the benefit exceeds the cost. This means that you should only import a good if the foreign price is enough of a discount to offset the associated trade costs. Likewise, you should export a good only if the price you'll get exceeds the local price by enough to offset the export-related trade costs.

Trade costs limit how important international trade is in your sector. If a product has high trade costs, then it's unlikely that importing or exporting the good will pass the cost-benefit test. But if trade costs are low, then international trade will be worthwhile. (You might recognize similar ideas from shopping online, which is worth it only if shipping costs are low.)

It follows that trade costs determine whether international trade will be a big factor in your market. For example, trade costs associated with digital music are virtually zero — Spotify simply exports bits and bytes — and so there's a huge amount of international trade in music. Clothes are more expensive to trade, but they're still easily transported in massive container ships, which explains why your shirt was probably imported. However, it's prohibitively expensive to get a cavity filled in another country (think of the flight costs), and it's virtually impossible to transport a house. Consequently, there's almost no international trade in dental services, and no international trade in houses.

Remember: We learned in the previous chapter that comparative advantage is the ability to do a task at a lower opportunity cost. If this feels unfamiliar, go back and read it again — it's really important!

trade costs The extra costs incurred as a result of buying or selling internationally, rather than domestically.

Do the Economics

Which of the following goods or services are traded internationally? (Hint: Think about the relevant trade costs.)

☐ Land   ☐ Wheat   ☐ Flowers
☐ Coffee beans   ☐ A hot cup of coffee ☐ Sandwiches
☐ Laptops   ☐ Cloud computing   ☐ Surveillance equipment
☐ A haircut   ☐ Hair gel   ☐ Hairdressing scissors
☐ Cars   ☐ Bikes   ☐ Taxi rides
☐ Bowling shoes   ☐ Bowling alleys   ☐ An afternoon bowling   ■

Answer: Coffee beans, laptops, cars, bowling shoes, wheat, cloud computing, hair gel, bikes, flowers, surveillance equipment, hairdressing scissors

Trade costs don't just determine what is traded. As the next case study shows, they also determine how much stuff is imported and exported. Indeed, declining trade costs are responsible for one of the most important economic trends of your lifetime.

Interpreting the DATA **Global trade is rising because of declining trade costs**

International trade — both exports and imports — has been a growing share of the U.S. economy throughout the entire postwar period (Figure 1). This trend — sometimes called "globalization" — has transformed the economy. And it's largely due to declining trade costs.

Figure 1 | Imports and Exports Are a Rising Share of the U.S. Economy

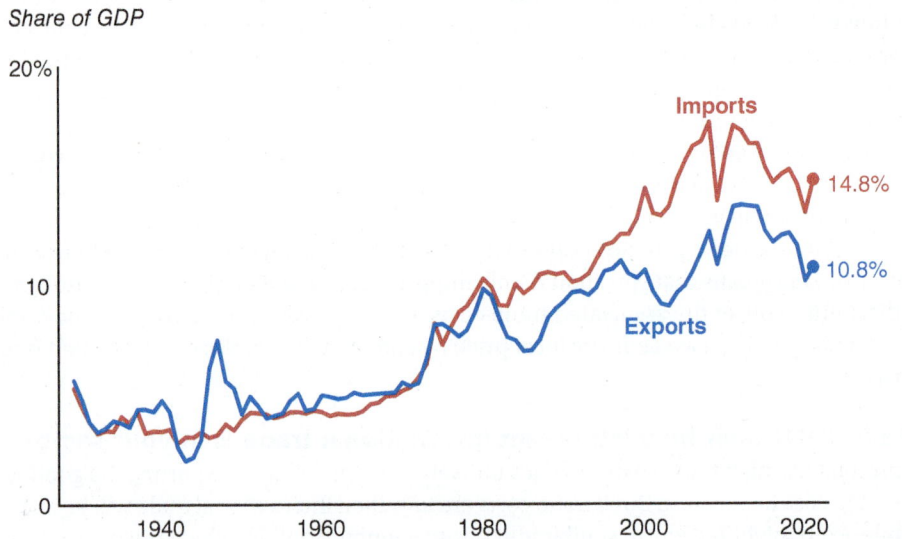

Data from: U.S. Bureau of Economic Analysis.

The United States has brokered trade agreements with a number of countries that have eliminated extra taxes (called *tariffs*) imposed on trading with them. Some of these agreements have also reduced the red tape that often hinders trade.

The standardization of shipping containers dramatically decreased the cost of shipping goods overseas, and ongoing improvements in air travel reduced transport costs. As more people around the world have learned to speak English, it has emerged as the language of international business, making it easier to work across borders.

The internet has revolutionized global trade in the service sector. For instance, the financial industry links banks and financial networks, which make international transactions at lightning speed. Even some health care has gone global: It's now easy for foreign radiologists to read X-rays taken in the United States, or for an American specialist to consult on cases abroad.

As trade costs fall, companies trade more intermediate inputs, creating global supply chains. For instance, Barbie is produced by a global supply chain. Her plastic limbs and hair are made by workers in Taiwan and Japan; she's assembled in Indonesia, Malaysia, and China; and she was designed and marketed in the United States. International trade allows Barbie to be manufactured and sold more inexpensively, while allowing workers in each country to contribute what they can do at the lowest opportunity cost. ■

They have seen the world.

Choosing Your Trading Partners: Sources of Comparative Advantage

It's a good bet that trade costs will continue to fall, making international trade an even more important force through your career. This more integrated global marketplace will create new opportunities for you to exploit your comparative advantage. Which raises the question: What *is* your comparative advantage, and what strategic choices can you make to enhance it?

Economists have identified three factors that shape your comparative advantage: relatively abundant inputs, specialized skills, and the benefits of mass production. Let's examine each in detail.

Source 1: Abundant inputs—Take advantage of what you have, to get what you want.
New Zealand has lots of land, and so New Zealand farmers can raise sheep and to export wool at a relatively low cost. Canada has ample forests, and so Canadian foresters export wood and related products like paper. The United States has thousands of scientists, and so American pharmaceutical companies export new medicines. Each of these examples reflects a comparative advantage that is due to the relative abundance of the necessary inputs compared to their trading partners.

Some of this relative abundance of inputs is simply a matter of climate, geography, and natural resources. But people, businesses, and countries can shape their advantages through strategic investments. For instance, the United States created an abundance of colleges and universities that employ scholars who do scientific research and that turn out a relative abundance of highly educated workers. The result is that the United States has a comparative advantage in scientific fields.

This focus on abundant inputs suggests that international trade is about exporting products made with resources you have a lot of, and importing products made with resources that are scarce. Importantly, it is *relative* abundance of inputs that matters — whether you have more or less labor, capital, land, or sunshine relative to your trading partners.

The more your trading partner differs from you, the larger the gains from trade will be. If your trading partner has very different resources, it's likely they'll also have very different opportunity costs — leading to greater gains from trade. So even if the old saying that "opposites attract" might not be great advice for choosing romantic partners, it's great advice for choosing trading partners.

Interpreting the DATA What inputs are relatively abundant in the United States?

As a savvy manager, you should specialize in making and exporting products that rely on inputs that are relatively abundant for you. And you'll find likely customers in areas where those inputs are relatively scarce.

Compared to countries like Australia and Canada, the United States doesn't have particularly abundant land (Canada is physically bigger than the United States, but its population is smaller than that of California!). And compared to countries such as China, India, and Brazil, the United States doesn't have particularly abundant labor. This might leave you thinking that because our businesses use state-of-the-art machinery, the United

The United States has abundant skilled labor

Share of people aged 15–64 who have completed tertiary education

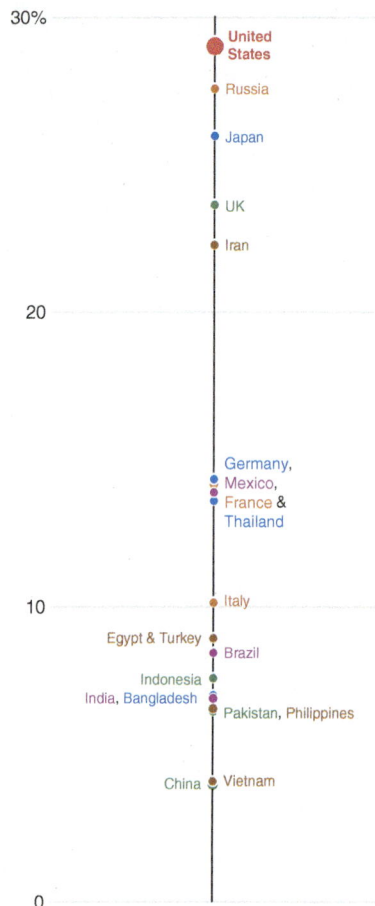

Data from: Barro and Lee data for 20 most populous countries.

Billy the bookcase and his creator, Rita the robot.

Sources of comparative advantage:
1. Abundant inputs
2. Specialized skills
3. Mass production

States has relatively abundant capital. But studies have found that the United States exports goods that are slightly *less* capital intensive than its imports. So what abundant inputs drive our comparative advantage?

The answer is a specific category of labor: *highly educated* workers. Compared to other countries, the United States has an abundance of workers who have attained highly specialized skills through higher education. In turn, this means that our comparative advantage is in producing skill-intensive goods, such as scientific and medical instruments, airplanes, and computer software. This is good news for college students: You're our comparative advantage!

This also means that less-educated workers are *relatively* scarce in the United States, and so we have a comparative disadvantage in producing goods that rely on more manual labor. This explains why Americans import toys, footwear, and clothing from businesses in China and Mexico. In these countries, there are fewer highly educated workers and relatively more workers whose comparative advantage is in factory work. So when you think about your comparative advantage, just look around at your classmates and realize that relative to your international competitors, you have access to a large number of highly educated and creative workers. ■

Source 2: Develop a specialized skill. Businesses in Switzerland, France, and the United States have roughly similar access to capital and skilled workers. Yet the Swiss are the world's best watchmakers, the French produce the greatest cheese (sorry, Wisconsin!), and Americans make terrific movies (usually). In each case, skilled artisans produce watches, cheese, or movies in a way that their foreign counterparts can't match. Your unique skills, production methods, or expertise can be an important source of comparative advantage.

As they say, practice makes perfect: If you — or your business or your country — focus on a specific product for a long time, you'll likely discover new production techniques that will lower your costs. This comparative advantage gets stronger over time, as you produce more and learn more. Economists refer to this as "learning by doing," and it explains how a long-term investment in a specific industry can pay off. No matter what you are selling, you'll discover that the more you produce, the more efficient you'll become, which will lead you to sell more and hence produce more, creating more opportunities to learn, further reinforcing your comparative advantage.

Source 3: Exploit the benefits of mass production. Ikea sells millions of Billy bookcases each year to buyers all around the world. It sells so many of them because the Billy bookcase is so inexpensive. And the Billy bookcase is so inexpensive because Ikea sells so many of them. This virtuous cycle arises because of the benefits of mass production (which are sometimes called *economies of scale*).

When you're producing millions of bookcases, you can invest in creating highly specialized production lines that are much more efficient. For instance, rather than hiring skilled woodworkers to make the Billy, Ikea has specialized robots that can work 24 hours a day, 7 days a week. The automated production line is so efficient that it makes a new bookcase every five seconds. (Sadly, it'll take you a lot longer to construct it from the cryptic instructions.) In addition, Ikea is one of the world's largest purchasers of wood, and it uses this bargaining power to negotiate cheaper wood prices, further lowering its input costs. Put it all together, and the opportunity cost of producing another bookcase is lower for Ikea than for any other business. These lower opportunity costs due to the benefits of mass production can be another enduring source of comparative advantage, particularly for large producers.

EVERYDAY Economics   Using comparative advantage at home

The same big idea that drives international trade — comparative advantage — also explains why you trade tasks with people you live with to make your household run more efficiently. It's simple: You want to allocate each task to the person who has a comparative advantage. And thinking about the sources of comparative advantage can help.

Who should do the weekly shopping? The idea that *abundant inputs* create comparative advantage suggests assigning that task to the housemate who owns a car, because they have a relative abundance of the necessary capital equipment. Who should be responsible for tech suport around the house — making sure the Wi-Fi works, and that the stereo can pair with everyone's phones? Assign that task to whoever has developed a *specialized skill* in computer networking. As they get used to troubleshooting, they'll develop even more expertise. And what about cooking dinner? Perhaps everyone in your home is equally capable of making a pot of spaghetti — so nobody has a comparative advantage. However, since it's just as easy to make spaghetti for four as it is for one, the *benefits of mass production* create a comparative advantage for whoever is already cooking for themselves to cook for the whole household.

The same ideas about comparative advantage that guide global businesses can also spur your household to greater efficiency, ensuring that you'll deal with your shopping, technology, and meals at the lowest possible opportunity cost. ∎

Now that we've explored how comparative advantage drives international trade, it's time to explore how international trade reshapes supply and demand.

7.2 How International Trade Shapes Your Market

Learning Objective *Use supply and demand to assess the consequences of international trade.*

International trade reshapes the forces of supply and demand in the United States, and so our next task is to assess how it changes outcomes in the various markets in which you'll do business.

The World Market

Let's start with the shirt you're wearing right now. Chances are that it began life in a foreign factory, probably in a country with a lot of low-wage workers. Your shirt then joined millions of others for the journey to the United States in one of the huge container ships that links the shirt market in the United States with those in China, Vietnam, Indonesia, and the rest of the world.

World supply and world demand determine the world price. The market for T-shirts is a truly global market. Thousands of manufacturers around the world compete to sell their T-shirts to billions of potential buyers located in just about every country on Earth. When T-shirts are traded internationally, the price is determined by the interactions of all the buyers and sellers around the world. That is, the price is determined in the *world market* by the intersection of world supply and world demand. *World supply* describes the total quantity of shirts produced by all manufacturers in the world at each price. Similarly, *world demand* describes the total quantity of shirts demanded across all shirt buyers in the world, at each price. Figure 2 illustrates how world demand and world supply jointly determine

Figure 2 | The World Market

Ⓐ **World supply** is the total quantity of shirts supplied by all sellers around the world.
Ⓑ **World demand** is the total quantity of shirts demanded by all buyers around the world.
Ⓒ **Equilibrium** occurs in the world market when world supply equals world demand.
Ⓓ The **world price** is the price that shirts are bought and sold for on the world market.

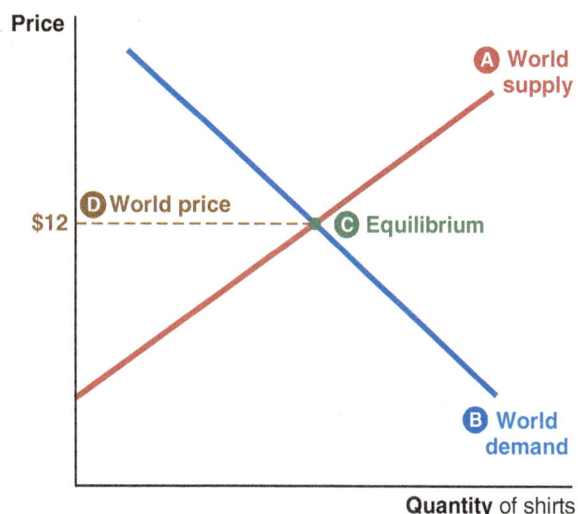

world price The price that a product sells for in the global market.

the **world price**, which is the price that a traded good sells at in the world market. This world price is the price that consumers pay to buy imported shirts, and the price that producers can get for exporting their shirts.

When the United States is a small player, take the world price as given. Realize that the United States is only a relatively small player in the global shirt market. This means that the actions of U.S. importers and exporters barely affect the world price. That is, in the world market, U.S. buyers and sellers are *price-takers,* which means that they can take the world price as given. (Only those who are big players relative to world supply or world demand need to think about how their decisions change the world price.)

How Imports Change Your Market

domestic demand curve Shows the quantity of a product that all domestic consumers added together plan to buy, at each price.

domestic supply curve Shows the quantity of a product that all domestic suppliers added together plan to sell, at each price.

Let's now explore how international trade shapes the domestic market. We'll need some new terminology to do this. The **domestic demand curve** illustrates the quantity of goods that domestic buyers — that is, all Americans taken together — plan to buy at each price. Likewise, the **domestic supply curve** illustrates the quantity of goods that domestic producers plan to sell at each price. These curves, which are shown in Figure 3, will be familiar from our earlier study of supply and demand. But we now need to be clear that these curves refer only to U.S. buyers and U.S. sellers.

Figure 3 | The Consequences of Imports

If there is no international trade:
No-trade equilibrium occurs where quantity demanded by domestic buyers equals quantity supplied by domestic sellers, resulting in 100 million shirts sold at a price of $20.

When we allow imports:
Step ❶ The price of imported goods declines to the world price.
Step ❷ At this new price, check the domestic supply curve to find that the quantity supplied by domestic sellers declines, and check the domestic demand curve to find the quantity demanded by domestic buyers rises.
Step ❸ Imports make up the difference between domestic demand and domestic supply.

When we allow imports:
Step ❶ : The price of imports = the world price of $12, *a price cut.*

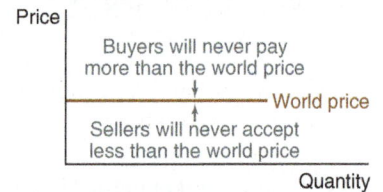

Step ❷ : At this new price:
a) The quantity supplied by domestic sellers *declines* (to 40 million shirts)
b) The quantity demanded by domestic buyers *rises* (to 140 million shirts)

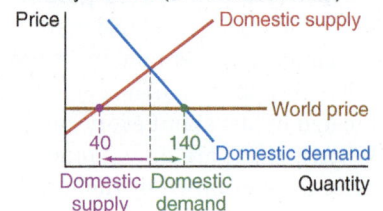

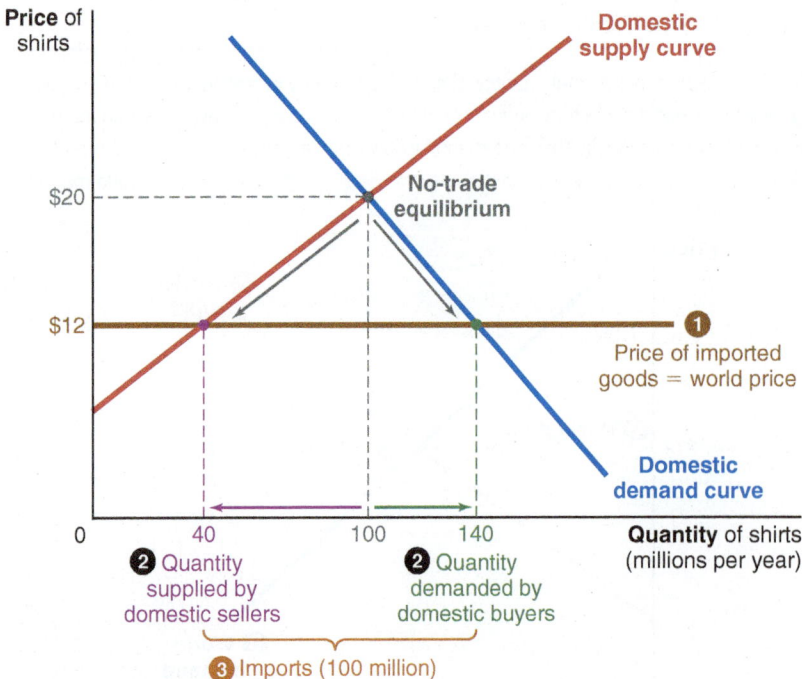

Step ❸ : The difference is made up by imports (= 140m − 40m = 100 million shirts)

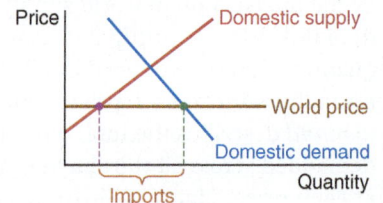

Evaluate the equilibrium when there's no trade. To set a baseline for comparison, we'll start by assessing the likely outcomes if there were no trade. As before, it's all about where supply meets demand. In the absence of international trade, the equilibrium price is determined by the intersection of the domestic demand and supply curves. In Figure 3, these curves intersect when shirts sell for $20.

Use a three-step recipe to evaluate how imports shape domestic markets. To see what happens when we allow for the possibility of international trade, we'll follow a simple three-step recipe:

Step 1: Figure out the new price.

When you can buy goods from abroad, you have new options to consider. For instance, international trade gives buyers the option to import shirts at the world price of $12. As a result, no U.S. buyer will ever pay a seller more than $12 for a shirt. Likewise, international trade means that sellers always have the option to export their shirts at the world price of $12. This means U.S. sellers will never accept less than $12 per shirt. And so if buyers never pay more than $12, and sellers never sell for less than $12, the equilibrium price must be $12. *For traded goods, the price is equal to the world price.*

Step 2: Determine the quantities demanded and supplied by domestic buyers and sellers at this new price.

To find the responses of Americans to this new lower price, consult their domestic demand and domestic supply curves. Begin by locating the new price, $12, on the vertical axis in Figure 3, and then look across until you hit the domestic supply curve. Look down, and you'll see that domestic sellers will supply 40 million shirts when they can get $12 per shirt. And when you look across from the $12 price until you hit the domestic demand curve and look down, you'll see that domestic buyers will demand 140 million shirts.

Step 3: Assess the quantity that will be traded.

International trade makes up the gap between the quantity demanded by domestic buyers and the quantity supplied by domestic sellers. In this case, Americans want to buy more shirts than American producers supply, and so imports make up the difference.

Imports lead to lower prices, less domestic production, and more domestic consumption. Putting the pieces together, we've found that when buyers import goods:

- The price declines to the world price.
- This lower price leads to a lower quantity supplied by domestic sellers, but a higher quantity demanded by domestic buyers.
- Imports fill the gap between the quantity demanded and the quantity supplied.

Our simple three-step recipe gives you a useful forecast about what's likely to happen as a result of importing foreign shirts. But do imports make you better off? As we'll see, the answer depends on whether you're a consumer or producer of shirts.

David McNew/Getty Images

Your shirt is arriving.

A three-step recipe for evaluating the effects of trade:
1. Figure out the new price.
2. Determine the quantities demanded and supplied by domestic buyers and sellers at this new price.
3. Assess the quantity that will be traded.

🔗 **See the Connections**

| What are the effects of imports? | → | The price is lower (= world price). | → | *At this lower price:* The quantity demanded by domestic buyers is higher. And the quantity supplied by domestic sellers is lower. | → | Imports make up the difference between the quantity demanded by domestic buyers and the quantity supplied by domestic sellers. |

Imports Raise Economic Surplus

U.S. consumers gain when they import their shirts, because they get lower prices. But U.S. producers lose, because foreign competition forces them to lower their prices or lose customers. The cost-benefit principle suggests that policy makers should make decisions about trade policy based on whether the gains exceed the losses.

To assess the balance of these competing effects, we'll compare how much consumer surplus buyers gain with how much producer surplus suppliers lose. That's the exercise we perform in Figure 4. This figure may look complicated at first glance, but by proceeding slowly, you'll see that it's actually pretty intuitive.

Figure 4 | The Welfare Consequences of Allowing Imports

Effects of Imports on Economic Surplus

	No trade	Free trade	Difference
Consumer surplus	A	$A + B + D$	$B + D$
Producer surplus	$B + C$	C	$-B$
Total surplus	$A + B + C$	$A + B + C + D$	$+D$

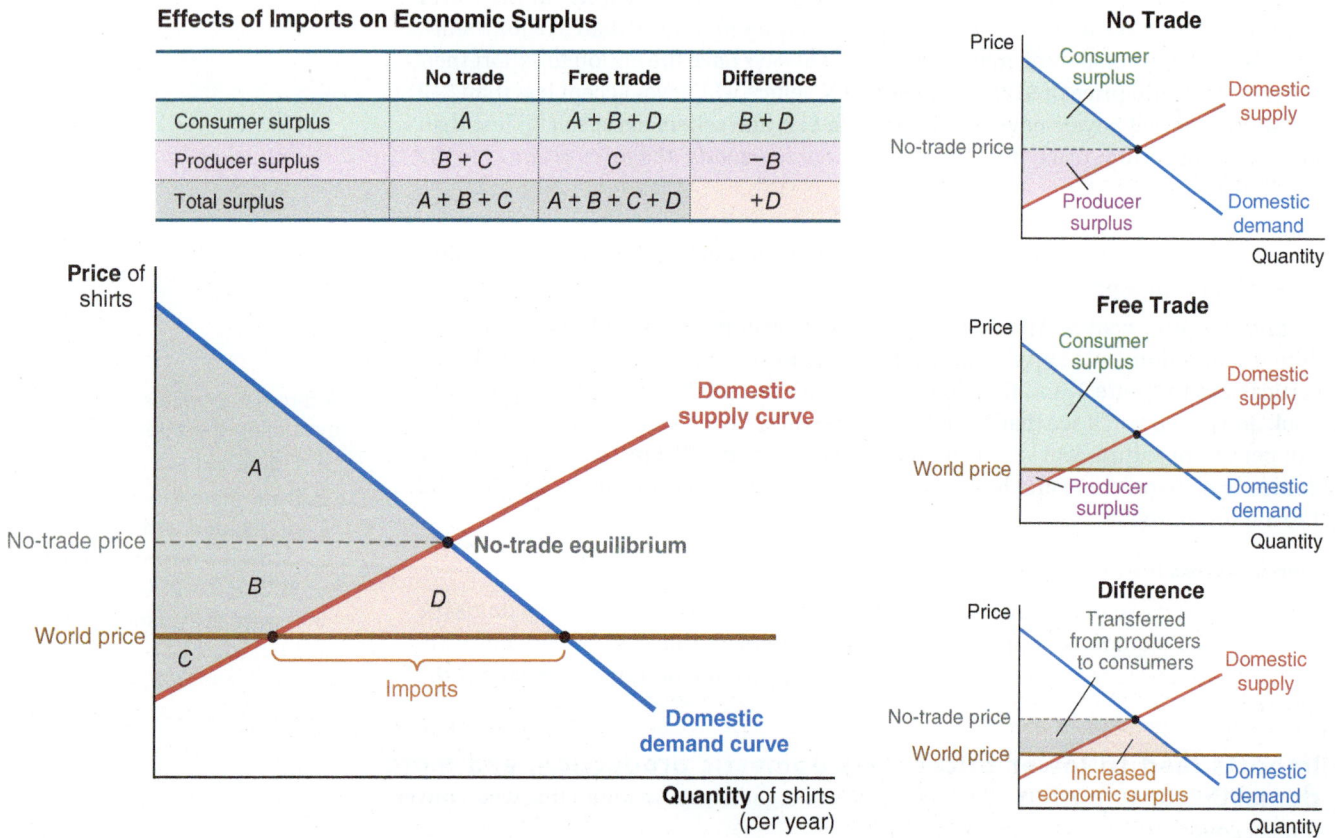

Start by assessing economic surplus when there's no international trade to set a baseline. In this case, the no-trade equilibrium occurs where the domestic supply and demand curves cross. Remember that domestic buyers earn consumer surplus when they get to buy a shirt at a price that is lower than their marginal benefit. Because the domestic demand curve shows these marginal benefits, their consumer surplus is the area below the domestic demand curve, but above the price. This is the triangle labeled area A in Figure 4. Domestic suppliers earn producer surplus when the price is above their marginal cost. Because the domestic supply curve reflects each producer's marginal costs, their producer surplus is the area that's above the domestic supply curve and below the price. This is the large triangle of area $B + C$.

So the total economic surplus with no trade is the area $A + B + C$. That's the baseline. What happens when we allow imports?

Lower-priced imports raise consumer surplus. Allowing imports leads domestic buyers to pay a lower price, and at this lower price they buy a larger quantity of these low-priced shirts. As a result, domestic buyers enjoy more consumer surplus. Graphically, consumer surplus is now the area below the demand curve but above the price buyers pay, which is now the world price, and so consumer surplus is now the large triangle $A + B + D$. You can see why domestic consumers are happier: The lower price of shirt imports raises their consumer surplus — from area A to the larger area, $A + B + D$.

Domestic producers lose producer surplus due to foreign competition.

Domestic producers are worse off because a lower world price means that they have to sell their shirts at a lower price, and as a result, they no longer find it profitable to sell as many shirts. Graphically, producer surplus is the area above their domestic supply curve but below the price they charge, which is now the lower world price. You can now see why producers are less happy: The lower price of shirts reduces their producer surplus — from area $B + C$ to the smaller area C.

The benefits exceed the costs, and imports raise total economic surplus.

So far, we've seen that imports raise the consumer surplus enjoyed by U.S. consumers and lower the producer surplus of U.S. producers. What's the net effect?

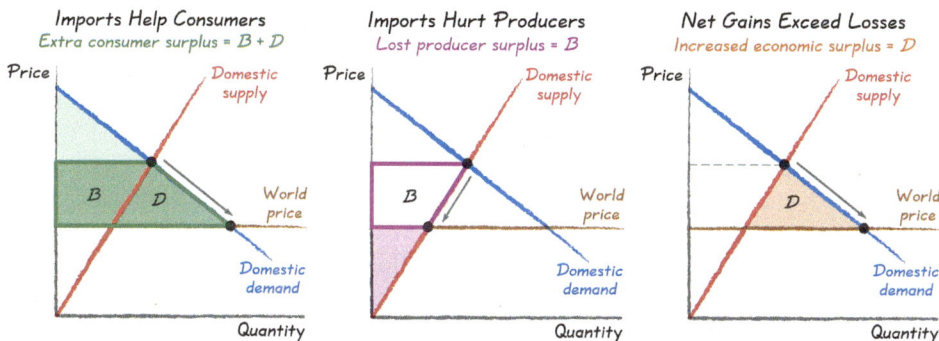

We've figured out that consumers gain [B/D], while producers lose a smaller amount, [B]. This means that taken together, Americans — when we take account of their roles as both consumers and producers — gain economic surplus from importing, and this net gain is the area [D].

Many people are surprised to hear economists say that imports are good for Americans. Often, this is because when people think about "the economy," they think about producers — the factories, businesses, and workers who lose some economic surplus. But it's important not to forget consumers, who derive an even larger benefit from lower prices.

The gains to buyers from allowing imports exceed the losses to sellers. There's a neat intuition underlying all of this. The initial effect of imports is to lower the price of shirts, and we've seen that Americans respond to this lower price by changing the number of shirts they buy and sell. But nothing forces them to do so. Indeed, if Americans didn't change the quantity of shirts they bought and sold, this price cut would lead U.S. buyers to gain exactly as much economic surplus as U.S. sellers would lose. (After all, cutting the price by a dollar makes the buyer a buck better off and the seller a buck worse off.) In reality, U.S. buyers lean into a good deal by buying more of those inexpensive shirts (often from abroad) which *amplifies their gains*. And U.S. sellers lean away from unprofitable production and so *minimize their losses* by supplying fewer inexpensive shirts. The net effect is that the amplified gains to buyers outweigh the minimized losses to sellers, and so imports lead Americans as a whole to enjoy more economic surplus.

Recap: The consequences of allowing imports.
Let's summarize what we've learned about imports. It's always best to start with what happens to the price. Competition from foreign sellers causes the price of goods we import to fall. Buyers respond by raising the quantity they demand, while sellers respond by reducing the quantity they supply, with imports filling the difference.

The lower price increases the consumer surplus of buyers and decreases the producer surplus of sellers. And because buyers amplify their gains and sellers minimize their losses, the net effect is to boost total economic surplus. That is, taken as a whole, people in the United States gain economic surplus from importing stuff from abroad. Finally, notice that this conclusion holds irrespective the amount of U.S. exports that are purchased by foreigners.

Imports ⟶ ↓Price

Domestic Buyers: ↑Quantity demanded

Consumers buy more at a lower price ⟶ ↑Consumer surplus (amplified gains)

Domestic Sellers: ↓Quantity supplied

Producers sell less at a lower price ⟶ ↓Producer surplus (minimized losses)

\>

↑Economic surplus

Okay, that's the effect of imports. Now it's time to apply the same approach to analyzing the market for exports.

How Exports Change Your Market

Snowmobiles aren't just a lot of fun, they're also an engineering marvel, built using technologies first developed in the automobile and aviation manufacturing sectors. This is why the United States is a global leader in developing, manufacturing, and exporting snowmobiles. Figure 5 shows the domestic demand and supply curves for snowmobiles. If there were no trade, equilibrium would occur where these curves cross. At a price of $9,000, the quantity of snowmobiles demanded by domestic buyers (50,000) exactly matches the quantity supplied by domestic sellers. But what happens when U.S. manufacturers like Arctic Cat and Polaris also export their snowmobiles?

Use the three-step recipe to evaluate how exports shape domestic markets. We're going to run through the same three-step recipe we used to evaluate imports, but this time to assess the effects of exports.

Step 1: Figure out the new price.

Internationally, there's a lot of demand for snowmobiles, and the world price is $12,000. This means that suppliers won't sell snowmobiles to domestic U.S. buyers for less than the $12,000 they can get by selling in the world market. Likewise, buyers have the option to import snowmobiles from foreign sellers such as the Canadian company Bombardier for $12,000, and so they'll never pay domestic sellers more than $12,000. If suppliers never sell for less than $12,000, and buyers never pay more than $12,000, the equilibrium price must be $12,000. *For traded goods, the price is equal to the world price.*

Step 2: Determine the quantities demanded and supplied by domestic buyers and sellers at this new price.

Begin by locating the new $12,000 price on the vertical axis, and then look across until you hit the domestic demand curve. Look down, and you'll see that domestic buyers will demand 40,000 snowmobiles. To find the quantity domestic producers will supply, look across from the $12,000 price until you hit the domestic supply curve, then look down, and you'll see that they'll supply 70,000 snowmobiles.

Step 3: Assess the quantity that will be traded.

Exports make up the gap between the quantity supplied by domestic sellers and the quantity demanded by domestic buyers. In this case, domestic suppliers produce

Figure 5 | The Consequences of Exports

If there is no international trade:

No-trade equilibrium occurs where quantity demanded by domestic buyers equals quantity supplied by domestic sellers, resulting in 50,000 snowmobiles sold at a price of $9,000.

When we allow exports:

Step ❶ The price of exported goods **rises to the world price**.

Step ❷ At this new price, check the **domestic demand curve** to find the **quantity demanded by domestic buyers falls**, and check the **domestic supply curve** to find that the **quantity supplied by domestic sellers rises**.

Step ❸ **Exports** make up the difference between domestic supply and domestic demand.

When we allow exports:

Step ❶ : The price of exports = the world price of $12,000, *a price rise.*

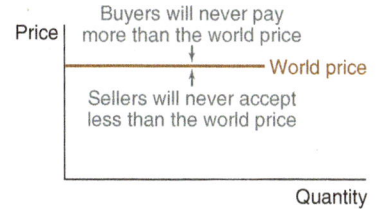

Step ❷ : At this new price:
   a) The quantity supplied by domestic sellers *rises* (to 70,000 snowmobiles)
   b) The quantity demanded by domestic buyers *declines* (to 40,000 snowmobiles)

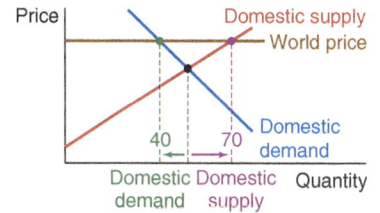

Step ❸ : The difference is made up by exports (= 70,000 − 40,000 = 30,000 snowmobiles)

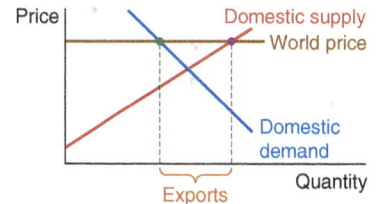

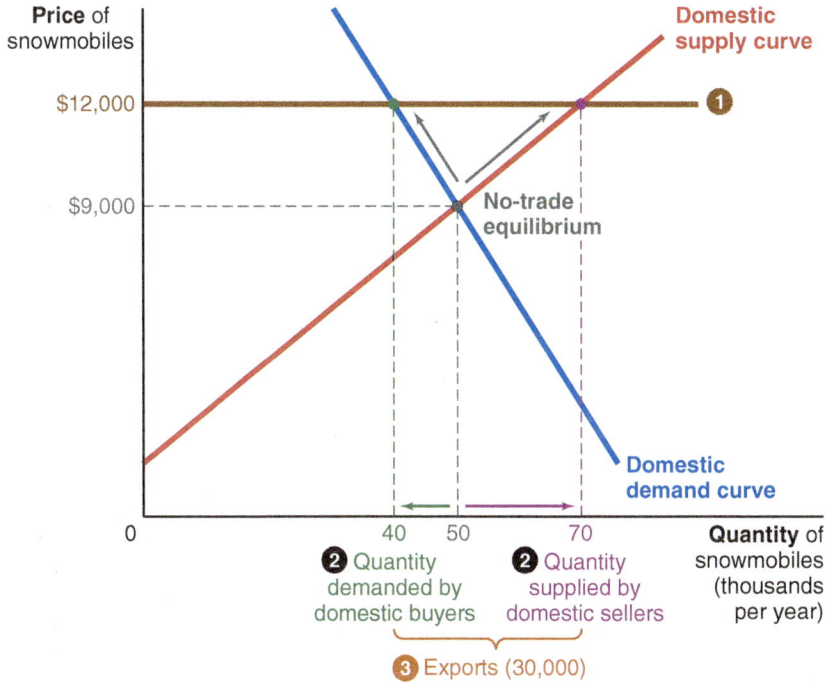

70,000 snowmobiles and domestic buyers purchase only 40,000 of them, and so the remaining 30,000 snowmobiles are exported to be sold to foreign buyers.

🔗 See the Connections

What are the effects of exports? → The price is higher (= world price). → *At this higher price:* The quantity demanded by domestic buyers is lower. And the quantity supplied by domestic sellers is higher. → Exports make up the difference between the quantity demanded by domestic buyers and the quantity supplied by domestic sellers.

Exports lead to higher prices, more domestic production, and less domestic consumption.

We've now figured out the effects of exports. When domestic sellers export their goods:

- The price rises to the world price.
- This higher price leads to a higher quantity supplied by domestic sellers but a lower quantity demanded by domestic buyers.
- Exports fill the gap between the quantity supplied and the quantity demanded.

This tells us how exports reshape the forces of supply and demand. But do exports make you better off? Your view likely depends on whether you're a buyer or seller of snowmobiles.

Exports Raise Economic Surplus

Previously, we worked out that imports raise Americans' total economic surplus. What about exports? It turns out that they also raise Americans' economic surplus. To see why, let's keep working our way through the market for snowmobiles, in Figure 6.

Figure 6 | **The Welfare Consequences of Allowing Exports**

Effects of Exports on Economic Surplus

	No trade	Free trade	Difference
Consumer surplus	$A + B$	A	$-B$
Producer surplus	C	$B + C + D$	$B + D$
Total surplus	$A + B + C$	$A + B + C + D$	$+D$

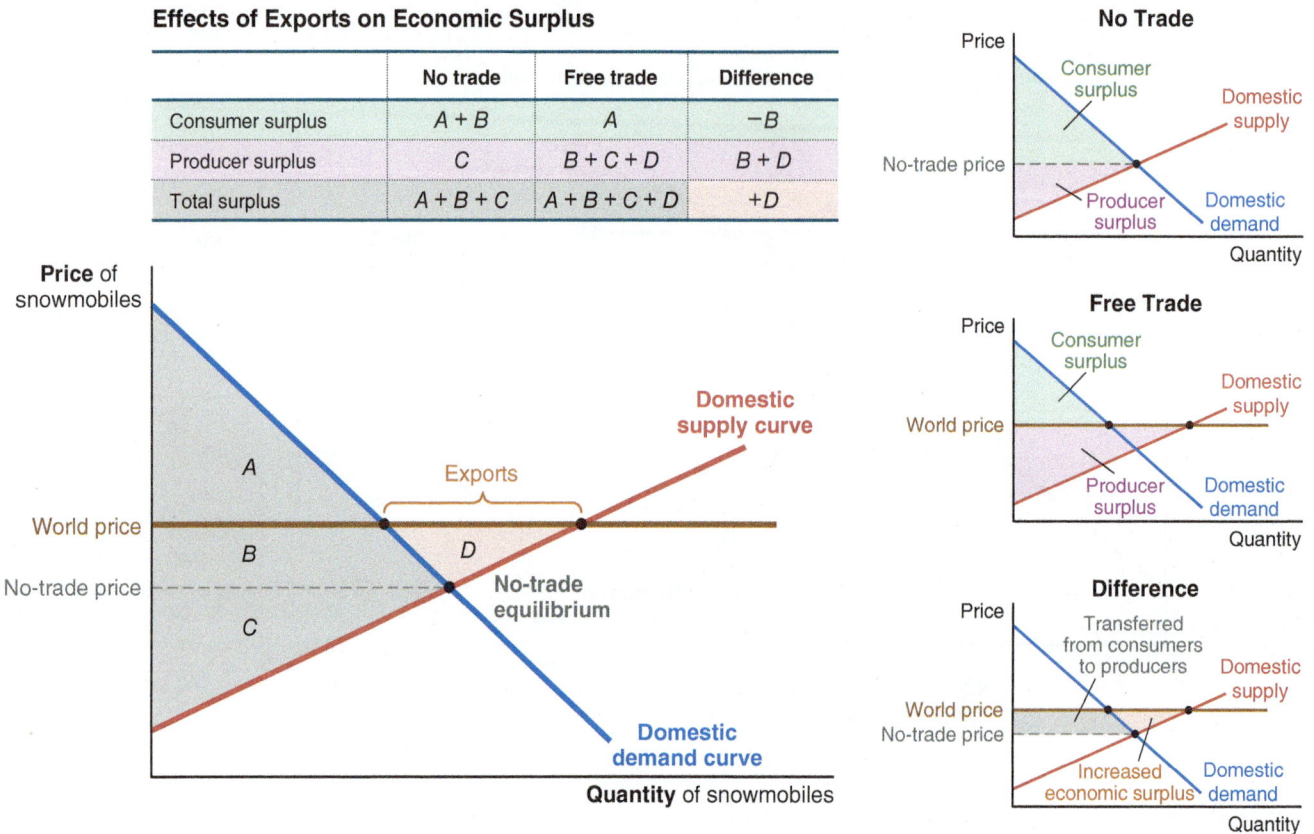

Start by assessing economic surplus when there's no international trade to set a baseline. With no international trade in snowmobiles, equilibrium occurs where the domestic supply and demand curves cross. At this no-trade price, buyers earn consumer surplus equal to area $A + B$, while domestic sellers earn a producer surplus equal to area C. So the total economic surplus with no trade is equal to area $A + B + C$. How does it change when we allow exports?

More expensive exports raise producer surplus. Allowing domestic producers to export their snowmobiles raises the price they can get for them, because foreign buyers are willing to pay more. This higher price leads domestic producers to produce a larger quantity. As a result, producer surplus rises. Graphically, producer surplus is the area above the domestic supply curve but below the new higher price, which is now the world price, and so it is area $B + C + D$. Domestic producers are happy to have the opportunity to export because the greater demand for their product raises their producer surplus — from area C to the larger area $B + C + D$.

Domestic consumers lose consumer surplus due to foreign competition. Domestic buyers are worse off because they now have to compete with buyers in other countries to get a snowmobile, and so the price they pay rises to the higher world price. This higher price causes them to reduce the quantity they demand. Graphically, consumer surplus is the area below the demand curve, but above this higher price, and so it is area *A*. Exports make domestic consumers less happy because the higher price of snow-mobiles reduces their consumer surplus — from area *A* + *B*, when there is no trade, to the smaller area *A*.

The benefits exceed the costs, and exports raise total economic surplus. So far we've seen that exports raise the producer surplus enjoyed by U.S. suppliers and reduce the consumer surplus of U.S. consumers. What's the net effect?

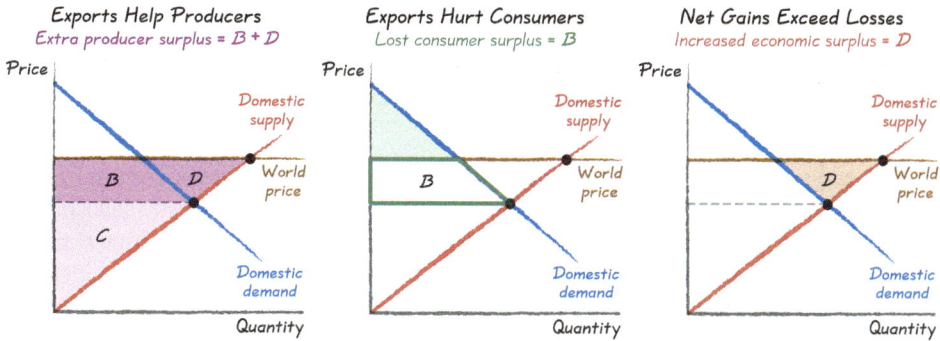

We've figured out that domestic producers gain [*B + D*] , while domestic consumers lose a smaller amount, [*B*] . This means that Americans — when we take account of their roles as producers and consumers — gain economic surplus from exporting, and this net gain is shown as area [*D*] .

Recap: The consequences of allowing exports. Let's summarize what we've learned about exports. First, we analyze what happens to the price. We export those goods that foreign buyers are willing to pay a lot more for, and this leads the price of goods that we export to rise. That higher price leads domestic sellers to supply a larger quantity, while domestic buyers reduce the quantity they demand. Exports fill the gap between domestic supply and domestic demand.

The higher price increases the producer surplus of domestic sellers, and decreases the consumer surplus of domestic buyers. Remember, sellers amplify their gains by selling more snowmobiles at the higher price, while buyers minimize their losses by purchasing a smaller quantity. As a result, the net effect is that exports boost the total economic surplus that Americans enjoy.

Who Wins, and Who Loses? The Politics of International Trade

We've covered a lot of ground, but now you're well positioned to forecast how changing trade patterns will affect your market. I've summarized our key findings in Figure 7.

Figure 7 | The Effects of International Trade

Effects on:	Effects of allowing	
	Imports	Exports
Domestic price	↓	↑
Quantity supplied by domestic businesses	↓	↑
Quantity demanded by domestic consumers	↑	↓
Consumer surplus (of U.S. consumers)	↑ (a lot)	↓ (a bit)
Producer surplus (of U.S. producers)	↓ (a bit)	↑ (a lot)
Total economic surplus (in the United States)	↑	↑

You don't need to memorize this whole table. Just remember that you import to get a lower price on stuff you buy, and you export to get a higher price on stuff you sell. Get this right, and the rest will follow. Supply-and-demand analysis tells you that higher prices lead domestic buyers to reduce the quantity they demand and domestic sellers to increase the quantity they supply. (Lower prices lead to the opposite.) The consequences for consumer and producer surplus make sense if you simply remember that consumers like low prices while producers prefer high prices.

International trade increases economic surplus, but not everyone wins.
We've seen that trade increases the economic surplus enjoyed by Americans. That's the argument in support of trade. We've analyzed imports and exports. In both cases, the free flow of goods and services across national borders raises the total economic surplus enjoyed by Americans. We'd see the same thing if we performed the analysis for any other country. The implication is that international trade raises the living standards of *both* Americans *and* our trading partners. And it does so both when we are the exporters and when we are the importers.

But trade doesn't just expand the pie; it also redistributes it. That means not everyone gains from international trade, and it likely makes some people worse off. Whether you will personally gain or lose from lower prices for shirts (or higher prices for snowmobiles) depends on whether you're a buyer or a seller of shirts (or snowmobiles). This mix of positive and negative effects is critical to understanding the political debate about trade, because people often advocate for what's in their personal interest, rather than what's in the best interest of the country as a whole.

Import-competing businesses oppose international trade. The folks who argue most vehemently against international trade are typically those who stand to lose from it. This is why business leaders in industries that compete with imports — such as U.S. clothing manufacturers — often lobby for fewer imports. Workers in these businesses might be worried about their jobs, and so they also argue against free trade.

Beyond import-competing businesses, there are also folks harmed by competing with foreign buyers to purchase American-made products. For instance, when U.S. businesses export their snowmobiles, it raises the price, which hurts domestic buyers of snowmobiles. So folks in Alaska who don't want to pay higher prices for snowmobiles might oppose free trade of snowmobiles.

Exporters and import-dependent businesses support international trade. Similar logic says that the groups most likely to favor free trade are those who gain from the ability to compete in foreign markets. This is why export-oriented businesses like Arctic Cat and Polaris snowmobiles support efforts to open up new markets in Canada, France, and Finland. The other big supporters of trade are U.S. businesses that import cheaper raw materials such as oil, steel, and machinery.

Consumers are rarely an active voice in this debate, but perhaps they should be. After all, it's likely that you also benefit from trade in the form of less expensive shirts, cell phones, and laptop computers. But consumers often don't realize that these gains are the result of international trade. Even if they did realize this, they aren't organized into effective lobby groups, and so their voice is often missing from the political debate.

Do the Economics

For each of the following developments, figure out the effect on the price, and hence whether they help or hurt American buyers and American sellers:

   a. The United States resumes importing sugar from Cuba.

   b. Sweden refuses to buy lobsters exported from Maine.

   c. A trade deal makes it easier for U.S. farmers to sell beef in Japan.

   d. China commits to importing a larger quantity of U.S. soybeans.

   e. Technology makes it possible for Indian radiologists to read the X-rays of U.S. patients. ∎

Answers: a. ↓P, helps buyers, hurts sellers; b. ↓P, helps buyers, hurts sellers; c. ↑P, hurts buyers, helps sellers; d. ↑P, hurts buyers, helps sellers; e. ↓P, helps buyers, hurts sellers.

7.3 The Debate About International Trade

Learning Objective *Evaluate the arguments for and against international trade.*

Let's consider the arguments that are most frequently used in the often-heated debates about whether international trade is good or bad for poeple in the United States.

Five Arguments for Limiting International Trade (and Five Counterarguments)

Our supply-and-demand analysis showed that both imports and exports raise the economic surplus for Americans. But it left out some important details that sometimes lead people to argue for restraining international trade. The proponents of trade restraints raise five major arguments, and while these arguments can be used to argue against all international trade, they're more often used to argue for restraints in specific sectors or circumstances. We'll evaluate each one, and then turn to the counterarguments. It's up to you to judge when and where you find each argument or counterargument to be most persuasive.

Argument 1: National security requires that we produce strategically important goods ourselves. When some countries limited the export of masks and vaccines during the coronavirus pandemic, their trading partners were forced to do without. It was a difficult reminder that relying on international trade can make you uncomfortably reliant on foreign governments. And so it may be critical to our national security to produce our own supply of those strategically important goods that are critical to our health and safety.

   A similar argument has often been made that an effective national defense requires the United States to produce its own weapons systems. Some extend this idea to include tech products with security implications. An even broader interpretation suggests that we also need to avoid relying on foreign sources of food, so that we can still eat even if we are cut off from our trading partners.

   The counterargument is that these concerns are often overstated. For example, our food supply remained reliable during the pandemic, even as many trading routes were disrupted. The national security argument is often cited by industries — such as the

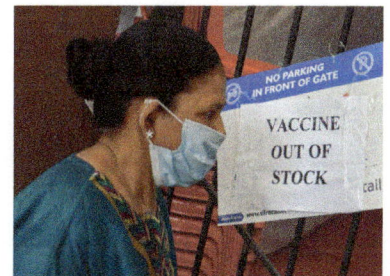

Global vaccine shortages arose when top vaccine makers in the United States and Europe were pressured not to export their scarce doses.

U.S. watchmaking industry! — with only a tenuous connection to our actual safety and security. Moreover, trade restraints can undermine our national security, such as when limits on U.S. exports of encryption software reduced competition enough that it became profitable for foreign competitors to develop their own encryption technology.

Argument 2: Protection can help infant industries develop. The infant industry argument suggests that governments can help create new industries by shielding fledgling businesses from international competition. For instance, Brazil banned imports of computers for many years, hoping that new Brazilian businesses — infants — would spring up to meet demand, and over time develop efficient production methods. Brazil hoped that once these businesses had learned enough to be globally competitive, they could allow international trade to resume.

But infant industries often fail to grow up. Brazil's computer makers never became as efficient as U.S. businesses like Dell. All that Brazil got for its efforts was high computer prices and some inefficient computer businesses that eventually went bust. This example illustrates the critique that it can be difficult for governments to identify which industries are likely to mature well if shielded from competition. A related problem is that infant industries often acquire enough political power to pressure governments to keep renewing their "temporary" assistance.

Argument 3: Anti-dumping laws prevent unfair competition. Another argument suggests that sometimes trade policy should be used to shield domestic businesses from unfair competition. For instance, sometimes a foreign company will try to drive their U.S. rivals out of business by temporarily charging extremely low prices — effectively "dumping" their goods on the U.S. market. If they succeed, they'll reduce competition, allowing them to later raise their prices, which would be bad for American consumers. Anti-dumping laws try to prevent this.

Opponents argue that in practice it's hard to figure out if foreign businesses are dumping their goods to drive out U.S. competitors, or if they're efficient producers offering great prices. Whatever the reality, local businesses will try to convince the government that cheap imports represent unfair competition. Sometimes those local businesses are right, and anti-dumping laws serve their purpose. But frequently, these foreign businesses simply hold a comparative advantage that allows them to produce at a lower cost.

Argument 4: Trade shouldn't be a way to skirt regulations. Voters in the United States have agreed, through the laws passed by their elected officials, that businesses must meet certain minimum standards. For example, U.S. factories can't employ children, they must pay a minimum wage, they have to comply with environmental standards, and they must meet safety standards.

These standards drive costs up, but we get something in return — namely, safer products, a cleaner environment, and a marketplace that treats people fairly. Trade provides a way to get around these social agreements. For instance, we strictly regulate how U.S. factories dispose of environmentally sensitive waste. But if foreign factories don't dispose of waste properly, buying goods produced by them is just as bad for the environment. By this view, it makes sense to restrict some kinds of trade to preserve the rules society has agreed upon. The argument is that if we prevent unsafe or unethical practices at home, we often want to also hold foreign businesses to the same standards.

Opponents argue that the labor or environmental standards that are appropriate for a high-income country like the United States are not appropriate for low-income countries. They argue that working in a low-paid job beats having no job, therefore refusing to trade with countries that do not have the labor standards of the United States will lead to more poverty. Similarly, lower-income countries may find some of the environmental standards of higher-income countries prohibitively costly. Trading with these countries facilitates economic development that will make stricter labor and environmental standards more feasible in the long run.

Argument 5: Foreign competition may lead to job losses. Possibly the most common argument against free trade comes from workers who worry that foreign competition will cost them their jobs. Our earlier analysis suggests that workers in import-competing sectors are right to be concerned, because greater openness to trade leads uncompetitive American businesses to shrink and lay off workers.

While restraining foreign trade can preserve some jobs in import-competing sectors, it will destroy jobs in businesses that rely on imported inputs. For instance, U.S. restrictions on sugar imports preserve jobs in the domestic sugar industry, but the high price of sugar in the United States (nearly double that of the rest of the world) has pushed candy manufacturing to other countries. Trade typically also causes export-oriented sectors to expand, and retaliatory trade restrictions often prevent these jobs — which typically offer higher wages — from being created.

Many of those workers who lose their jobs due to trade eventually retrain and find new jobs. This suggests that opening up to international trade might temporarily raise unemployment, but it'll have no effect in the long run. Indeed, Figure 8 shows that there is no long-term relationship between how much a country imports and its unemployment rate.

However, it's important to note that the "temporary" adjustments caused by trade may last for a long time. For example, the tremendous growth in Chinese exports over recent decades led many American manufacturing plants to close, and in the hardest-hit towns, few of these lost jobs have been replaced by new jobs, even many years later. So while trade might only have a temporary effect on unemployment, this "temporary" effect may last long enough to be virtually permanent for some people and communities.

An Intuitive Approach to the International Trade Debate

As you've probably noticed, the economic argument in favor of international trade — which is based on comparative advantage boosting economic surplus — can be pretty technical. This has led economists to try to find better ways to explain their ideas. The following two parables provide a different perspective, highlighting the logical errors that sometimes creep into political debates about trade.

Harvesting an Iowa car crop? There are at least two ways to make cars. The first involves assembly lines in Detroit, where skilled manufacturing workers — assisted by plenty of robots — transform steel into General Motors cars. The second way is less well known: You can grow cars in Iowa.

Here's how. Buy corn seeds, sow them, and water them. With enough care, you'll soon have a field full of corn. Harvest this corn, and put it on a boat headed onto the Pacific Ocean. Wait a few months, and the ship will return with Toyotas. Now just drive those cars off the boat. Voila! You've harvested a crop of cars that you grew from seeds. The fact that this happened because the cargo ship stopped in Japan to trade corn for cars is beside the point. The cars were the direct result of the efforts of farmers in Iowa.

Both of these methods of making cars employ plenty of American workers — in one case, it's manufacturing workers in Detroit; in the other, it's farm workers in Iowa. And they each produce high-quality cars. So why would we prefer one approach to the other? This question is central to the trade debate, because when people argue for protecting American industries from international competition, they're effectively arguing that we should build cars in Detroit, and stop growing them in Iowa. But that's inefficient. When there are different ways to make something, we typically encourage different producers to compete with each other, and buyers choose which

Figure 8 | **Unemployment Is Not Related to Imports**

Each point shows imports and unemployment for a separate country.

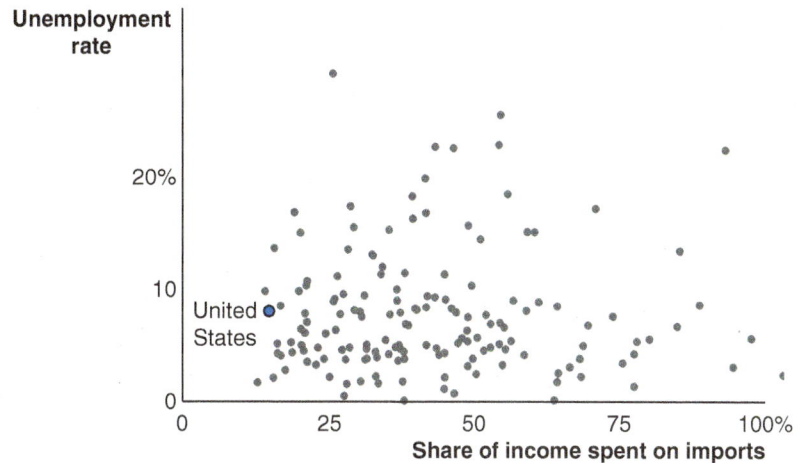

Data from: World Bank.

Arguments for restraining international trade . . . *and counterarguments against trade restraints:*

1. Protecting national security . . . *but this is relevant only to a few industries*

2. Helping infant industries . . . *but many infant industries never grow up*

3. Preventing unfair competition . . . *but is it unfair competition, or fierce competition?*

4. Enforcing minimum standards . . . *but do rich-country standards help poor countries?*

5. Saving jobs . . . *but trade changes what workers do, not how many people work*

This is one way to make cars.

This is another: You can grow corn and export it overseas, in return for new cars.

offers better value for their money. But if we force Americans to buy Detroit-made cars, even if it's more cost-effective to grow them in Iowa, then we'll end up paying more for our cars. This efficiency loss is a major reason not to restrict international trade, and it arises because restricting trade limits the reach of comparative advantage.

Free trade in the solar system? Despite this, many people still argue that international trade is "unfair." The Alliance for American Manufacturing made this argument in a letter to *The New York Times,* shown in the left column, below.

One way to assess the validity of an argument is to consider its implications in an analogous setting. The right column shows an imaginary but otherwise similar letter that the American light-bulb manufacturers might write, complaining about the cheap imports of light, not from another country, but from even further away — from the Sun!

The Alliance for American Manufacturing is hoping that its arguments will convince the government to ban or tax imports from China. Do you find its argument convincing? If so, why shouldn't the (fake) Alliance for Light-Bulb Manufacturing also get similar protection? It's easy to do — we could just require that buildings eliminate their windows to protect light-bulb manufacturers from the Sun's "unfair" competition! That sounds absurd, but that's sort of the point of this story.

The New York Times	The Universal Times
To the Editor:	To the Editor:
No thoughtful discussion about the impact of trade on workers, consumers, and America's economic future can take place without recognition of the role that China plays in today's global marketplace.	No thoughtful discussion about the impact of trade on workers, consumers, and America's economic future can take place without recognition of the role that the Sun plays in today's global marketplace for light.
While many factors affect employment and wages in the United States, it's wrong to minimize or dismiss the role of trade, especially with China. Our lopsided trade deficit with Beijing — $256 billion last year alone — highlights its market-distorting practices, including subsidies, dumping, currency manipulation, counterfeiting, and lax labor and environmental standards.	While many factors affect employment and wages in the United States, it's wrong to minimize or dismiss the role of trade, especially with the Sun. Our lopsided trade deficit with the Sun is a big problem: We import all of our natural light from the Sun, while the Sun buys none of our products. The problem is market-distorting practices that allow the Sun to export light at an unfair price of $0. Also, the Sun has lax labor and environmental standards. (It has none.)
These unfair trade practices have cost 1.8 million American jobs since 2001, according to an Economic Policy Institute study. American consumers pay in other ways: unsafe and uninspected food, toys, and medication, and higher local taxes when factories close. Until we insist that China honor its commitments, American workers will continue to lose.	These unfair trade practices have cost American light-bulb manufacturers dearly. If we all used artificial light during the day instead of just at night, it would double employment in the industry. American consumers pay for sunlight in other ways: The sun causes cancer, it makes us hot during the summer, and it causes higher local taxes when light-bulb factories close.
Scott Paul, Executive Director Alliance for American Manufacturing	Paul Scott, Executive Director Alliance for Light-Bulb Manufacturing

Let's now turn to examining international trade policy in more detail.

7.4 | International Trade Policy

Learning Objective *Understand how and why governments regulate international trade.*

Your company's success in winning international business will depend on navigating the complex maze of government policies that foreign governments put in place to help protect their domestic businesses — your rivals! — from competition. So it's time to explore how countries regulate trade and how those regulations will affect your market conditions. We'll then turn to examining global trade agreements, which limit the ways that individual countries can protect their industries.

Tools of Trade Policy

Managers of international businesses quickly learn that they need to compete in two domains. The first is the market, where you'll compete to produce the best goods at the lowest price. The second is the political marketplace, where your foreign rivals lobby their governments to adopt policies that will protect them from having to compete with you. That's why our next task is to evaluate how international trade policies can affect your market.

Tariffs are a tax on imported goods. As **tariffs** are taxes on imported goods, they increase trade costs. We can use our domestic demand and supply curves to figure out the consequences of this higher trade cost.

tariff A tax on imported products.

For instance, what happens if the government imposes a $4 tariff on T-shirts? We already know what happens without the tariff: The equilibrium price will be equal to the world price of $12. This outcome is shown by the gray line in Figure 9.

Figure 9 | The Effects of an Import Tariff

1 Initially, the price of imported T-shirts is $12. A $4 tariff raises trade costs by $4, causing the **price to rise** to $16.

2 Due to this higher price: Domestic buyers **demand a lower quantity**. Domestic sellers **supply a higher quantity**.

3 Which means that with a tariff, **imports are lower**.

4 The tariff leads to: A **decrease in consumer surplus**, and a **smaller increase in producer surplus** and **government revenue**, thereby **decreasing total economic surplus**.

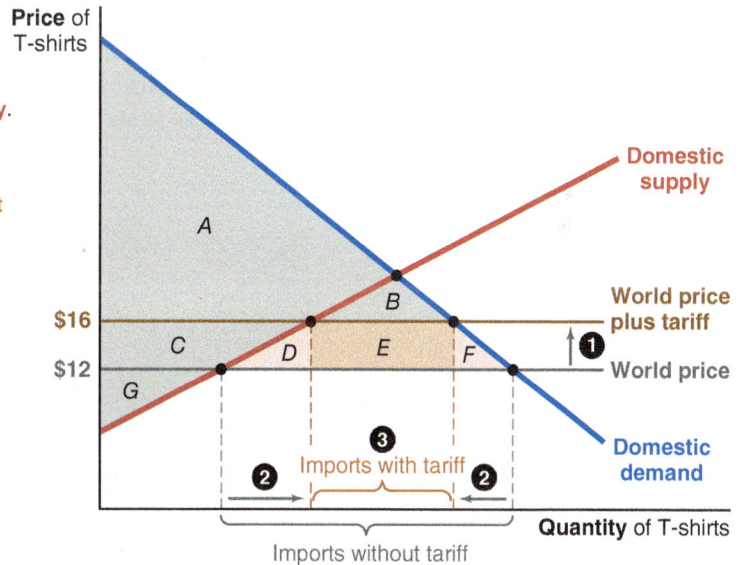

Welfare Effects of an Import Tariff

		No tariff	With tariff	Difference
Consumer surplus	Area below demand curve and above price	$A + B + C + D + E + F$	$A + B$	$-(C + D + E + F)$
Producer surplus	Area above supply curve and below price	G	$C + G$	$+C$
Government surplus	$4 per T-shirt times the number of T-shirts imported	None	E	$+E$
Total surplus	Sum of above	$A + B + C + D + E + F + G$	$A + B + C + E + G$	$-(D + F)$

Let's use our three-step recipe to see the effects of adding a $4 tariff:

Step 1: Find out the new price. This tariff adds $4 to the trade costs of importers. Because the world price of $12 is fixed, importers have to pay the world price of $12 plus the tariff of $4. Therefore, the price of T-shirts rises by $4, to $16.

Step 2: Determine the quantities demanded and supplied by domestic buyers and sellers at this new price. Consult the domestic supply and demand curves to discover that at the new higher price, the quantity demanded by domestic buyers is lower, while the quantity supplied by domestic suppliers is higher.

Step 3: Assess the quantity that will be traded. Recall that imports make up the gap between the quantities demanded and supplied. Because this gap shrinks, imports fall.

OK, so given these effects, who wins and who loses from a tariff?

Domestic buyers are unhappy because the higher price means they pay an extra $4 per T-shirt. Their consumer surplus is the area under the demand curve and above the price. Before the tariff, this was equal to the triangle made up of the areas $A + B + C + D + E + F$. After the tariff, this falls to area $A + B$. Thus, tariffs cause consumer surplus to fall by area $C + D + E + F$.

Domestic suppliers are happy because the higher price means higher profit margins on each shirt sold, and they also sell an increased quantity. Producer surplus is the area above the supply curve and below the price. Without a tariff, this was area G. After the tariff, it is area $C + G$. Thus, tariffs cause producer surplus to rise by an amount equal to area C.

The government also gains because it collects $4 of revenue for each T-shirt imported. This total tax revenue is equal to the $4 tax (which is the height of rectangle E) times the total number of imports (the width of rectangle E). So the tariff yields tax revenue equal to the height times width — that is, the area of rectangle E.

Adding all this up, consumers lose $C + D + E + F$; producers gain C; and the government gains E. Hence, in total, a tariff will decrease U.S. economic surplus by an amount equal to area $D + F$.

If you're worried that Figure 9 looks complicated, don't be. The graphs below show how we built it. We started by analyzing outcomes without a tariff. Then we analyzed the case with a tariff, tracking consumer surplus, producer surplus, and government revenue. Finally, we looked to see what changed.

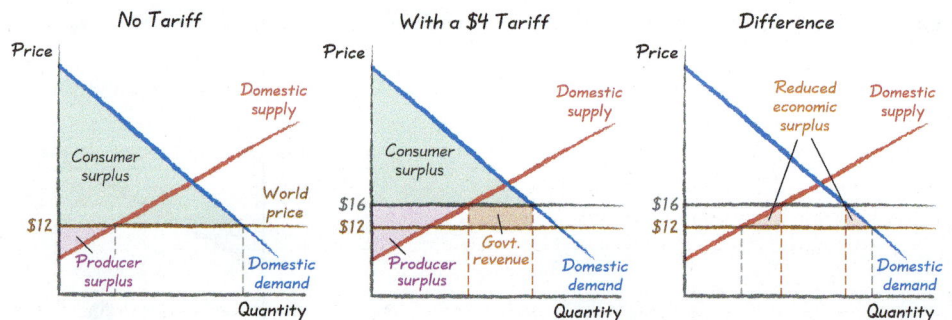

And the end result is worth all this work: We've found that imposing tariffs on foreign goods actually reduces the total economic surplus enjoyed by Americans! That might sound surprising until you dig into who's really paying the tariff. While the $4 tariff raises government revenue from foreign sellers, this extra cost leads those sellers to raise the price they charge U.S. buyers by $4, and so it's U.S. consumers who ultimately pay the $4 tariff. The tariff revenue is effectively paid by one group of Americans (consumers) to another (the government). The more important consequence is that the tariff-induced price hike distorts both how many shirts U.S. consumers buy (they cut back, not buying shirts they might have otherwise enjoyed), and how many shirts U.S. producers will supply (they'll keep producing beyond the point where foreign producers are more efficient). These distortions reduce total economic surplus.

Red tape raises costs like a tariff, but it doesn't raise revenue. Tariffs aren't the only tool that governments use to restrain international trade. Consider what it takes to export a bicycle to Bujumbura, a city in Burundi where bikes are often used as taxis. After you've shipped that bike to the nearest port in Tanzania, it will wait for 50 days of pre-arrival approvals, 8 days of port handling, and 15 days to go through customs.

It then takes a month to transport the bike to the border of Burundi, where it will take another 12 days to get through customs again, be loaded on a barge, and be transported to the Bujumbura port, where it will have to go through customs again. The 124 days, 19 documents, and 55 signatures required to get a bike to Bujumbura aren't just a headache; they add a lot to your trading costs.

These bureaucratic hurdles — commonly referred to as *red tape* — ultimately have the same effect as a tariff — they increase trade costs and so raise the price of U.S.-made bikes to foreign buyers. The effect of this higher price is the same, whether it's caused by tariffs or red tape: It reduces the quantity demanded, raises the quantity supplied by local Burundi an sellers, and therefore reduces international trade. But red tape is more inefficient than a tariff, because unlike a tariff, it doesn't raise revenue for the government.

Given all the red tape, it's a miracle this bicycle ever made it to Burundi!

Import quotas have similar effects to tariffs, but don't raise revenue.

Tariffs and red tape affect trade because they raise the price of foreign goods, reducing the quantity of international trade. Setting an **import quota** — which limits the quantity of a good that can be imported — can have the same effect. For instance, the $4 tariff on shirts in Figure 9 reduces imports to a quantity equal to the width of rectangle *E*. The government could achieve the exact same outcome — the same price and the same quantity demanded, supplied, and imported — if instead it imposed a quota limiting imports to this quantity. However with a quota, the government wouldn't raise revenue the way it does with tariffs (unless it auctioned off a limited number of import licenses).

import quota A limit on the quantity of a good that can be imported.

Exchange rate manipulation changes the price of your goods in foreign markets.

Foreign governments also can give their companies a leg up by manipulating their exchange rate. Think about how this affects an American exporter, such as Boeing. If a Boeing 737 typically sells for US$60 million (the "US$" symbol means "in U.S. dollars"), and it takes six Chinese yuan (China's currency) to buy one U.S. dollar, then each plane will cost a Chinese buyer 360 million yuan. But if the Chinese government sets the exchange rate so that it takes seven yuan to buy one U.S. dollar, then the price of Boeing's plane for a Chinese buyer rises to US$60 million × 7 yuan per dollar = 420 million yuan. In effect, China's exchange rate movement adds 60 million yuan to the cost of each American-made Boeing plane, making it less likely that a Chinese airline will buy one. Artificially depressing the value of the yuan so that it takes more yuan to buy a dollar makes U.S. products more expensive for Chinese buyers.

The cheaper yuan also makes it cheaper for Americans to import goods from China. Consider a shirt that a business in China will sell for 84 yuan. When the exchange rate is 6 yuan per dollar, this sells for 84/6 = US$14. But when value of the yuan is pushed down to 7 yuan per dollar, it sells for US$12 instead. Thus, U.S. producers in both exporting and import-competing industries lose business when China artificially lowers the value of its currency. On the flip side, U.S. consumers gain from buying Chinese goods at lower prices. In the past, China's government has intervened to devalue its currency to increase its exports and reduce its imports, and this policy has been a subject of some controversy.

Current Trade Policy

We've come a long way in understanding the many ways that government policy can shape trade. Let's take a look at the current state of play.

U.S. trade policy largely embraces free trade.

While trade policy is still hotly debated, the United States still broadly encourages international trade. Figure 10 shows that the average tariff charged on imports into the United States was only 2.8% in 2020, which is down from rates as high as 29% over a century ago. It also shows a small rise starting under President Trump in 2018, although average tariff rates remained relatively low despite his pro-tariff rhetoric. The United States has as few or fewer trade barriers than nearly all of our trading partners.

Figure 10 | Average Tariff Rate Levied by the United States

Tariffs collected as a share of total imports

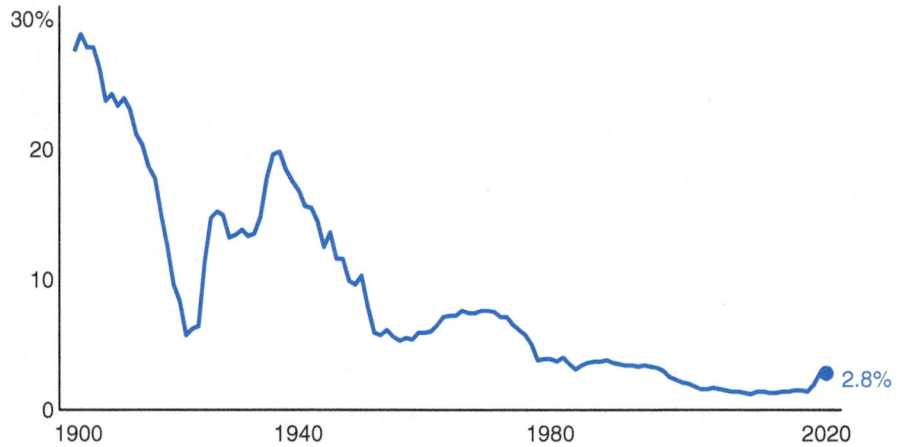

Data from: U.S. International Trade Commission.

Figure 11 | Average Tariff Rates

The United States has low tariff rates, as do many of its trading partners
Average tariff rates charged on imports

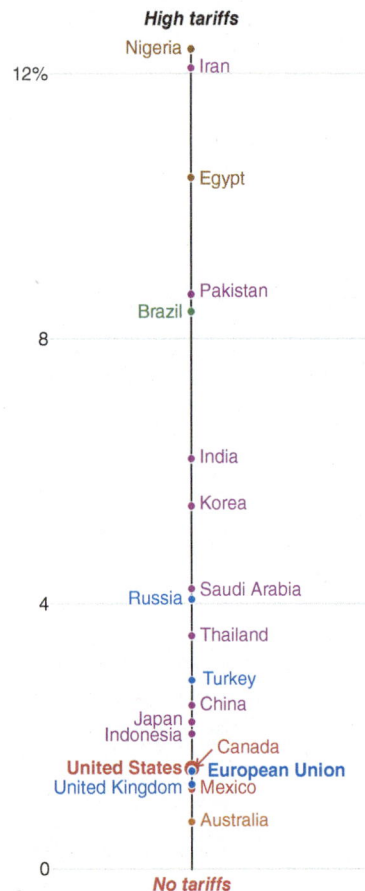

Data from: World Bank.

However, the United States still protects a few specific industries from foreign trade. Most notably, the farm lobby has been successful in persuading the government to maintain high tariffs, particularly on dairy products, tobacco, and sugar. President Trump also imposed new tariffs on steel and other products. Even so, when government economists analyzed all significant import restrictions in 2017, they found that in total they reduce total economic surplus by about $3.3 billion, which sounds like a lot until you realize that it amounts to about $10 per person.

The bottom line is that even as trade disputes frequently hit the headlines, the United States has largely embraced free trade in most (though not all) sectors of the economy.

The United States has signed many free trade agreements. Your fate as an exporter will depend partly on the trade policies in the United States and the countries you're exporting to. Tariffs vary across products and across countries. The average tariff rates in the world's major economies, shown in Figure 11, are typically pretty low.

In many cases, you'll actually face lower tariffs than shown here, because the United States has negotiated free trade agreements with various neighbors. The most important agreement is the United States-Mexico-Canada Agreement (USMCA), which updates (and renames) the previous North American Free Trade Agreement (commonly called NAFTA). This agreement ensures that there are few barriers to trade and investment between the three members, effectively making North America a free trade zone. The United States is also a member of the Dominican Republic–Central America Free Trade Agreement, which includes Costa Rica, the Dominican Republic, El Salvador, Guatemala, Honduras, and Nicaragua. The United States has also negotiated bilateral (that is, two-way) trade deals with Australia, Bahrain, Chile, Colombia, Israel, Jordan, Morocco, Oman, Panama, Peru, Singapore, and South Korea. While these are often called "free trade agreements," it's more accurate to call them free-*er* trade agreements, since they typically reduce rather than eliminate trade barriers.

The World Trade Organization facilitates global agreements to reduce trade barriers. Negotiating these trade agreements country by country is time-consuming. That's why large-scale multilateral (that is, many-country) trade agreements often make more sense. Today, nearly all countries are members of the World Trade Organization (or WTO to its friends), which provides a forum for countries to jointly negotiate to reduce or eliminate trade barriers. It has played a major role in reducing trade barriers throughout the world.

WTO rules include two important principles intended to limit trading barriers. The first, called *most-favored-nation status*, requires member nations to treat all members equally — at least as well as the most favored nation. (There is an exception for free trade agreements.) And second, the *national treatment principle* means that imported goods and locally produced goods must be treated equally once they've entered a country. If your business is hurt by trade barriers that violate these principles, the WTO will help settle your dispute.

Because tariffs are now quite low, trade negotiations have shifted from cutting tariffs to facilitating trade in services, reducing red tape, safeguarding intellectual property, and addressing environmental standards. Continuing progress will lead your life to become even more tightly integrated with global developments, a trend we'll turn to next.

7.5 Effects of Globalization

Learning Objective *Illustrate how globalization shapes your life.*

The interdependence principle reminds us that your economic life depends on decisions made by others, including people all around the world. The increasing global integration of economies, cultures, political institutions, and ideas is called **globalization.** As trade costs have declined because of lower trade barriers, closer political integration, improved telecommunications, electronic banking, the internet, and improved rail, sea, and air transportation, our lives have become increasingly connected with those of folks in other countries. But as much as globalization is a trendy buzzword today, it's not actually new: International trade has been with us, and growing, for centuries. In fact, Christopher Columbus first bumped into America while trying to find a trade route from Portugal to Asia.

globalization The increasing economic, political, and cultural integration of different countries.

Globalization and the Labor Market

Imagine that you work for Boeing, building airplanes. Each plane from the production line embodies some of your labor. And so every time one of these planes is exported to China, so is some of your labor. Effectively, you are selling some of your labor in China. Likewise, each shirt that you import from China embodies the labor of workers in China. So, even though *laborers* don't directly compete with each other (they're in different national labor markets), their *labor* does compete — it's just embodied in the goods and services that are traded between countries.

Productivity determines average wages. This leads some to worry that globalization may force U.S. wages down to the low levels seen in countries like China, India, or Mexico. If all workers were similar, this might be a long-run consequence of international trade — and it would be disastrous for American workers. On average, U.S. manufacturing workers earn $39 per hour, compared to $1.69 in India, $4.11 in China, $2.06 in the Philippines, and $3.91 in Mexico. (The comparable wages in Japan are $26, and in Germany, $43 per hour.)

However, wages aren't going to be equalized anytime soon, because workers are not all the same. The productivity of an average manufacturing worker in the United States is 12 times higher than that of a similar worker in China. This means that businesses are willing to pay American workers 12 times more. Figure 12 shows that countries with higher productivity tend to enjoy higher average wages.

International trade is raising income inequality within the United States. Not all workers in a country benefit from international trade, as it raises some wages while lowering others. In particular, recall that the United States exports skill-intensive goods such as computer software. As trade costs fall, foreign demand for these

Figure 12 | Countries with Higher Wages Have Higher Productivity

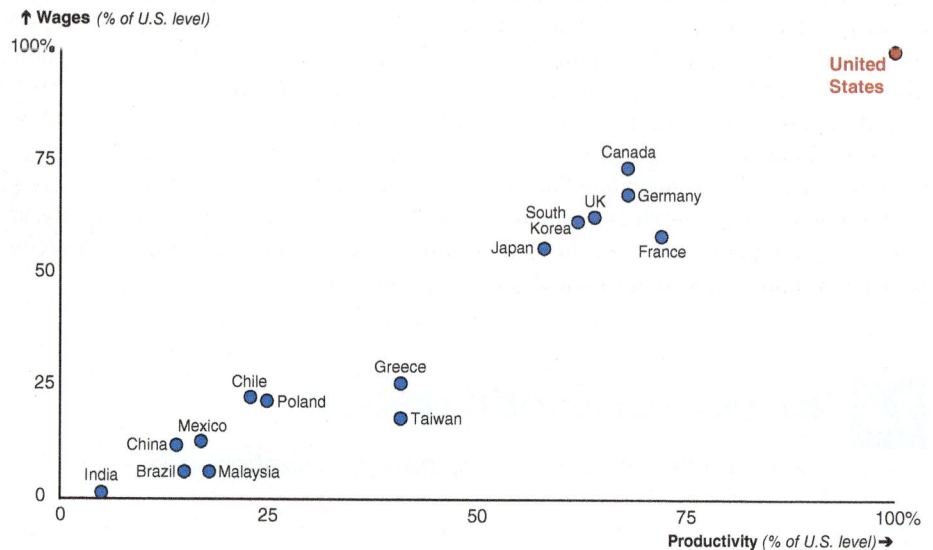

Data from: Ceglowski and Golub, "Does China Still Have a Labor Cost Advantage?" *Global Economy Journal* 12, no. 3 (2012).

goods increases. This also increases the demand for workers who can perform this skill-intensive work. Consequently, globalization has raised the incomes of highly educated workers in the United States, because it increased the demand for the goods and services they create.

Conversely, many of our trading partners have abundant workers with only a few years of education. And so, they have successfully exported goods like clothing that use more manual labor. As these countries engaged in more trade, Americans imported more clothing, which decreased the demand for domestically produced clothing. In turn, this decreased the demand for less-educated workers in the United States, leading to lower wages for those workers.

More generally, globalization reduced the wages of workers in import-competing sectors, and in the United States, these sectors tend to employ a lot workers who have less education. Consequently, international trade likely explains some of the rise in income inequality in the United States over recent decades.

International trade can have the same effect as immigration. There's an interesting implication of all this for immigration policy. The government currently restricts the number of foreigners immigrating to the United States, partly to shield domestic workers from foreign competition. But even though foreign *laborers* can't enter the United States at will, foreign *labor* can — at least to the extent that it is embodied in imports produced by foreign workers. And so trade in goods can have the exact same effects that immigration otherwise might, serving as a source of competition for American labor.

Are foreign workers being exploited or offered opportunity? When you buy a shirt from China, it was probably made by someone earning less than $2 per hour, often in grim conditions — certainly far worse than would be legal in the United States. Opponents of globalization often argue that it's immoral and exploitative to buy cheap shirts made under such bad conditions. Do you agree?

Before answering, consider the counterargument, which invokes the **opportunity cost principle**, to ask: "Or what?" We could keep buying these shirts, or stop, but what would this mean for foreign workers? For many workers in China, it's likely that their next best alternative involves working for an even lower wage. While $2 per hour is a low wage for an American, for many people in rural China, it represents a big improvement in their quality of life.

This debate is especially relevant to debates about "fair trade" versus "free trade." Both sides argue that Americans should continue to trade with people in poor countries. But "fair trade" advocates argue that we should pay higher prices for imports — high enough to ensure a reasonable standard of living for the workers involved. They also argue that U.S. negotiators should insist on including minimum labor standards as a part of new trade agreements. They claim fair trade would yield better working conditions and higher incomes for foreign workers, albeit at the cost of higher prices in the United States.

But it's likely that the higher prices for fair-trade shirts would reduce the quantity demanded. And so these policies might destroy the jobs of the very people they aim to help. What are your thoughts on fair trade?

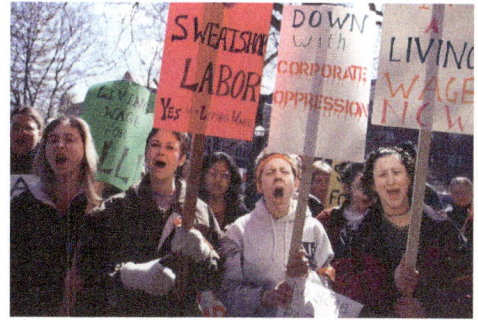

College students protesting against sweatshop labor have pressured many universities to adopt fair-trade buying policies.

7.6 Tying It Together

How Economists View Trade

Your life is more closely integrated with the rest of the globe than at any time in human history. This chapter has given you the tools to understand how international trade is reshaping your markets and your life. You're now equipped to recognize both the opportunities and the threats from globalization.

There are some subtle but important differences in how these economic tools might lead you to view trade, compared to the general public. Here are some of the key insights from the economic perspective:

Trade is about cooperation, not competition. Trade is like a good friendship, as both friends and trading partners find ways to enrich each other's lives. The magic of voluntary exchange is that it makes both the buyer and the seller better off, no matter which country they're living in. But trade is often described in very different terms — as if it's a competition, and every time China wins, the United States loses.

This view of trade as a competition makes the mistake of viewing global business as a fight over a fixed pie. But trade is about reallocating tasks so that they're done more efficiently. Ultimately, it's about cooperation so that everyone gets more of what they want. The beauty of international trade is that if we can import apples at a lower cost than growing them ourselves, we can bake a bigger apple pie.

People trade. Countries don't. When economists talk about trade, they talk about people, rather than countries. That's because people trade; countries don't. The United States doesn't buy shirts; individual consumers in the United States do. Focus on the choices that each of those people make, and you'll see more clearly that international trade involves millions of people cooperating with strangers they've never met, to get a better deal.

Trade is not just about business. Consumers matter too. When noneconomists think about "the economy," they tend to focus on businesses, such as the auto plant that was relocated to another country. They're right to be concerned, as many businesses are threatened by low-cost imports. But when economists analyze the economy, they think about buyers as well as sellers. Cheap imports may threaten some jobs, but they also offer American workers a way to make their paychecks go further, which raises their living standards. When you replace your laptop or your cell phone, or buy a nice piece of clothing at a good price, you're reaping the benefits of global trade.

Trade is an opportunity, and not just a threat. For the workers who might lose their jobs at the auto plant, the threat posed by international trade is very real. But just as some auto plants are closing, dozens of new office buildings are opening.

Even as some businesses shrink, others find ways to profit from the opportunity to sell to a global marketplace of 8 billion people.

However, just as economic thinking about trade can provide clarity, there are also blind spots.

Trade is a threat, and not just an opportunity. Sometimes, the logic of the cost-benefit principle leads economists to focus too much on the bottom line. The bottom line is that trade expands the pie, but this misses the equally important fact that trade also redistributes it. If someone else gets your slice of pie, you're likely to think that an economist who reminds you that it's a bigger pie just doesn't get it.

Trade causes disruption in the short run. While trade may increase the size of the pie in the long run, reassigning people to different pie-making roles causes a lot of disruption in the short run. Economists often focus on the long run effects of things, but they may need to pay more attention to these short-run disruptions. After all, these temporary effects can last long enough — sometimes many years — that they're nearly permanent for the people involved.

Trade is not just about economics. The closure of an auto plant doesn't just destroy jobs; it can devastate a city, wreck a particular way of life, and wipe out local traditions. As the world becomes more integrated, local and national cultures are becoming more similar. And so globalization is not just about the size of the pie, or even how we slice it, but also about the flavor of the pie.

Global integration will continue to be a major force throughout your life. And so my advice is that you think how best to position yourself to benefit from the enormous opportunities it will bring.

Chapter 7 Review

Chapter at a Glance

Comparative advantage drives international trade.

Sources of comparative advantage: | Abundant inputs | | Specialized skills | | Mass production |

Consequences of Imports

| No Trade | Step 1: Figure out the new price (Domestic price = World price) | Step 2: Determine the quantities demanded and supplied | Step 3: Assess the quantity that will be traded (Imports fill the gap) |

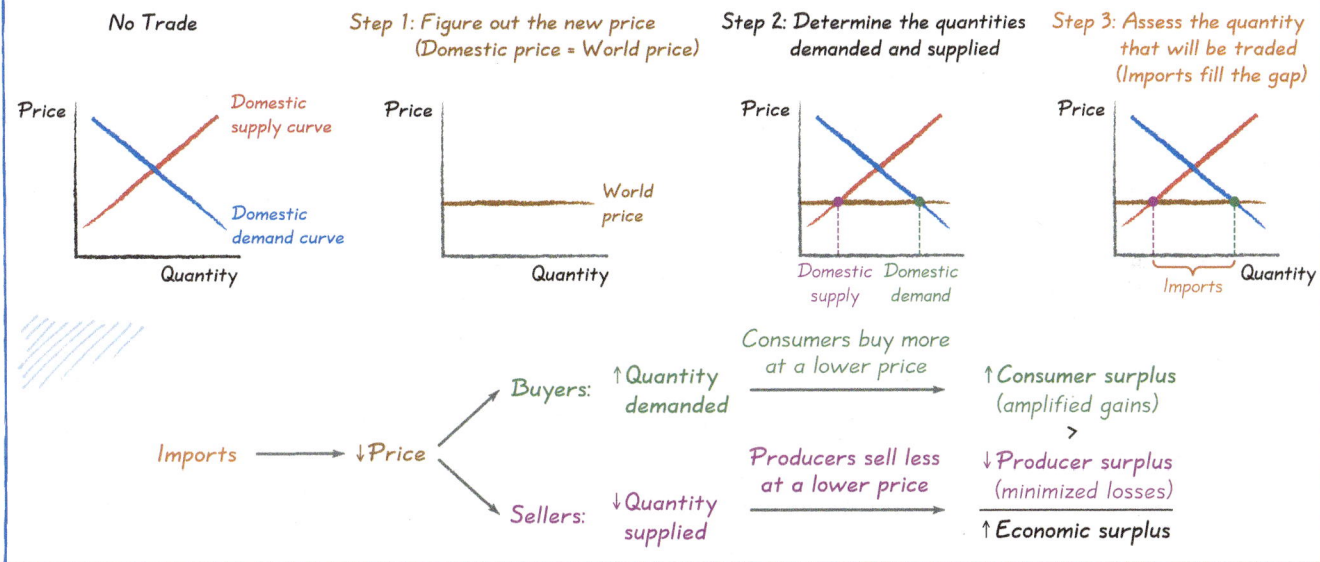

Imports ⟶ ↓Price

Buyers: ↑Quantity demanded ⟶ Consumers buy more at a lower price ⟶ ↑Consumer surplus (amplified gains)

Sellers: ↓Quantity supplied ⟶ Producers sell less at a lower price ⟶ ↓Producer surplus (minimized losses)

↑Economic surplus

Consequences of Exports

| No Trade | Step 1: Figure out the new price (Domestic price = World price) | Step 2: Determine the quantities demanded and supplied | Step 3: Assess the quantity that will be traded (Exports fill the gap) |

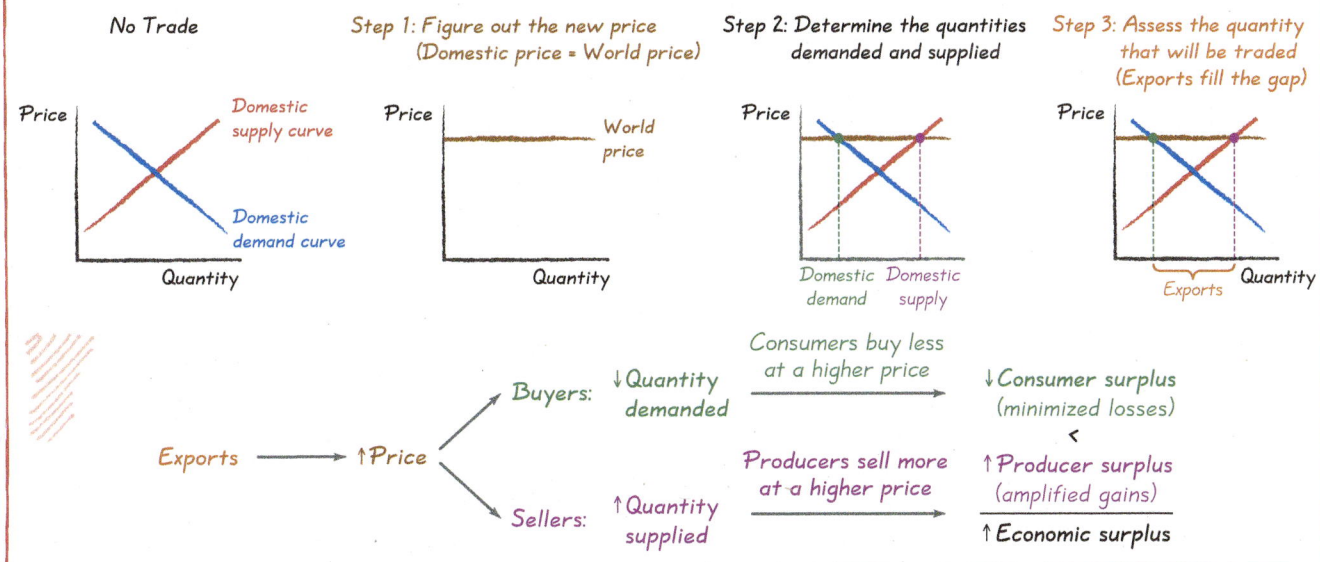

Exports ⟶ ↑Price

Buyers: ↓Quantity demanded ⟶ Consumers buy less at a higher price ⟶ ↓Consumer surplus (minimized losses)

Sellers: ↑Quantity supplied ⟶ Producers sell more at a higher price ⟶ ↑Producer surplus (amplified gains)

↑Economic surplus

Arguments for Limiting Trade

1. National security
2. Infant industry
3. Preventing unfair competition
4. Enforcing minimum standards
5. Saving jobs

Trade Policy Tools

1. Tariffs: a tax on imported products
2. Import quotas
3. Red tape
4. Exchange rate manipulation
5. Free-trade agreements (and the WTO)

Globalization: The increasing economic, political, and cultural integration of different countries.

Key Terms

Study Problems

Learning Objective 7.1 *Discover why we trade with people in other countries.*

1. Meagan, a contractor, is hired to install cabinets in a new home and has to decide whether to build the cabinets herself or purchase them from a local cabinet shop. What role does comparative advantage play in her decision? Will your answer change if she has to purchase the cabinets from a foreign supplier?

2. Why do you think Colombia's key exports include coffee, flowers, bananas, and tropical fruits?

3. For each of the following, explain how it can be a source of comparative advantage and provide an example.

   a. Abundant inputs   **c.** Mass production

   b. Specialized skills

4. For each of the following goods that are imported into the United States, identify which of the three sources of comparative advantage (abundant inputs, specialized skills, or mass production) accounts for that country's comparative advantage.

   a. The United States imported $32.4 billion worth of passenger cars from Japan in 2020.

   b. The United States imported $3 billion worth of watches and jewelry from Switzerland in 2020.

   c. The United States imported $4.1 billion worth of woven apparel items from Bangladesh in 2020.

Learning Objective 7.2 *Use supply and demand to assess the consequences of international trade.*

5. The proponents of the free trade agreement between the United States, Mexico, and Canada argued that it would raise the average living standards of people in the United States. Briefly explain why this could occur.

6. Both Democratic and Republican opponents of this free trade agreement have argued that it harms many people in the United States. Identify some of the groups likely to be harmed by this trade agreement.

7. Improved transportation and storage technologies has made it easier for people in the United States to source their fresh fruit from abroad, and the majority of fruit is now imported, with much it coming from Mexico, Chile, Guatemala, and Costa Rica.

Use a supply-and-demand graph, together with our three-step recipe, to describe the consequences of fruit imports on the American fruit market, illustrating the effects on the price, on the production of American fruit farmers, on the amount of fruit Americans consume.

Illustrate the changes in consumer and producer surplus to assess who gains from this trade and who loses.

8. In 2020, the United States imported approximately 6 million barrels of crude oil per day at an average price of $42 per barrel. The domestic demand and supply of crude oil in the United States is given by the graph below.

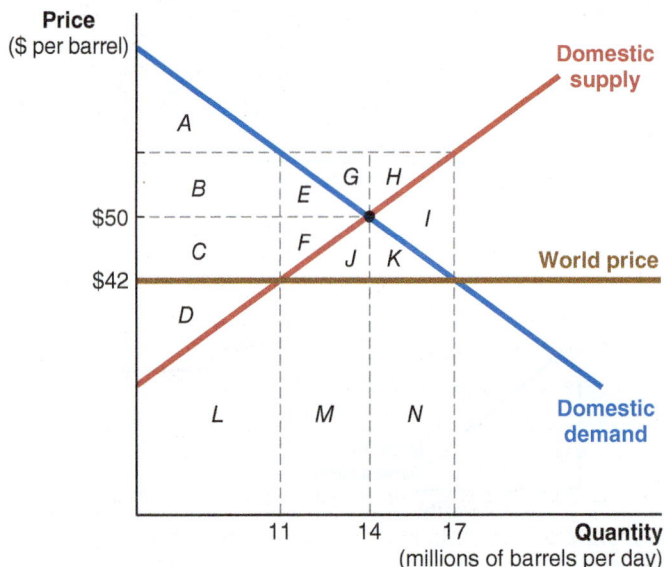

Use the letters and values in the graph to fill in the following table.

	Without trade	With trade
Price in the United States		
Quantity supplied domestically		
Quantity demanded domestically		
Quantity imported		
Area of consumer surplus		
Area of producer surplus		

9. Draw a domestic demand and domestic supply curve for apples in the United States using data given in the table below.

Price (per apple)	Quantity demanded domestically (millions of pounds per year)	Quantity supplied domestically (millions of pounds per year)
$ 0.15	9,300	7,580
$ 0.30	8,440	8,440
$ 0.45	7,580	9,300
$ 0.60	6,720	10,160

a. Identify the equilibrium price and quantity without trade.

b. If the price at which apples are traded in the world market is $0.15 per apple higher than the domestic price, what is the world price?

c. If the United States allows international trade, how many apples will be produced domestically in the United States, and how many apples will be purchased in the United States?

d. Will the United States import or export apples? How many?

e. Will consumer surplus rise or fall? What about producer surplus? And total economic surplus?

Learning Objective 7.3 *Evaluate the arguments for and against international trade.*

10. For each of the following cases, briefly explain the rationale for limiting trade and provide a possible counterargument.

a. National security requires we produce strategically important goods ourselves.

b. Temporary trade restraints can help infant industries develop.

c. Anti-dumping laws prevent unfair competition.

d. Trade shouldn't be a way to skirt regulations.

e. Foreign competition leads to job losses.

11. Which of these arguments or counterarguments do you find most persuasive when considering trade restraints concerning:

a. Face masks and other medical necessities

b. Breakfast cereals

c. Semiconductors used to build 5th generation ("5G") data networks

d. T-shirts

e. Soybeans

12. The United States imports a lot of cars, despite having its own auto industry. Each of the following statements are arguments some people could make for restricting imports of cars into the United States. For each statement,

identify the threat to the U.S. industry that the argument is trying to counter, and identify the opportunities that would be given up if the argument wins.

a. "Foreign manufacturers are offloading cars made with cheap foreign labor operating in unsafe and unhealthy factories. We must pass a law to prevent this exploitation."

b. "We need to foster the innovation of companies like Tesla that can truly change the auto industry. Allowing foreign electric vehicle manufacturers to sell cars in the U.S. will squander any chance of creating those cars domestically."

c. "You shouldn't buy a car from Nissan or BMW! You're putting people here out of a job."

Learning Objective 7.4 *Understand how and why governments regulate international trade.*

13. a. In 2018, the United States imposed tariffs of 20% to 50% on imported home washing machines. Explain how these tariffs affect the price that Whirlpool (a U.S. manufacturer) charges for washing machines, how it will affect the quantity it supplies, and the number of workers it hires.

b. Shortly after, the United States imposed a 25% tariff on imports of steel, which is an important raw material used in making washing machines. Explain how these tariffs will affect Whirlpool's price, its profitability, the number of washers it sells, and how this will affect Whirlpool's hiring plans.

14. The U.S. sugar industry has enjoyed trade protection since 1789 when Congress enacted the first tariff against foreign-produced sugar.

The world price for sugar was around $0.12 per pound at the start of 2019. Using the table below, figure out how much sugar would be demanded and supplied domestically at the world price. How much sugar would be imported into the United States?

Illustrate using a graph.

Price ($ per pound)	Quantity demanded domestically (millions of pounds per year)	Quantity supplied domestically (millions of pounds per year)
$ 0.06	36,000	4,500
$ 0.12	30,000	9,000
$ 0.18	24,000	13,500
$ 0.24	18,000	18,000

Show graphically how the price of sugar in the United States, imports, domestic consumer surplus, domestic producer surplus, and government revenue would change if the United States imposes a 6-cent tariff per pound of sugar.

15. The United States has historically imposed import tariffs on tobacco. The domestic supply and domestic demand for tobacco are illustrated by the graph below.

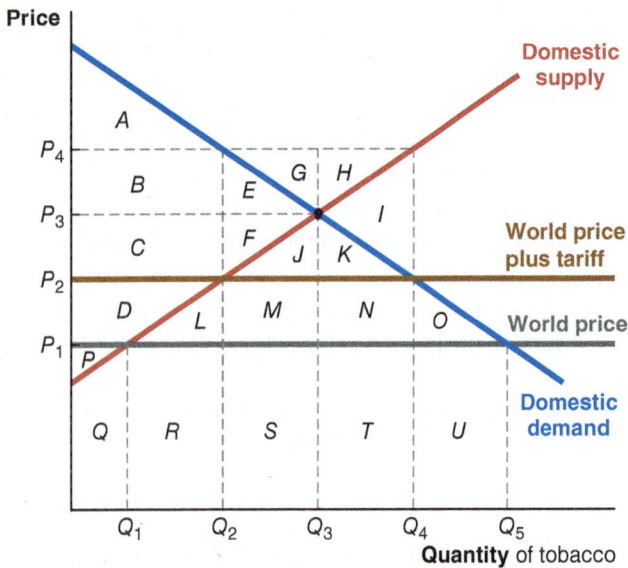

a. Use the letters and values in the graph to fill in the following table, comparing the outcomes of free trade and restricted trade.

	Without tariff	With import tariff	Difference
Price in the United States			
Quantity of domestic demand			
Quantity of domestic supply			
Imports			
Area of consumer surplus			
Area of producer surplus			
Area of government revenue			
Area of total economic surplus (including government)			

b. If the government decides to replace the tariff with a quota that will have the same effect on the market as the tariff, the quota should restrict imports to what quantity?

Learning Objective 7.5 *Illustrate how globalization shapes your life.*

16. Kemala is a factory worker in Indonesia, where she earns the equivalent of roughly US$1 per hour producing T-shirts to export to the United States. Some people argue that this wage is exploitative and unfair, while others argue that she is a great example of the benefits of free trade. Explain the economic reasoning behind both sides of this argument.

17. You are thinking of purchasing a new shirt for $5 that has a "Made in Indonesia" tag on it. You're shopping with a friend who mentions how terrible working conditions are for textile workers in Indonesia and says, "If they'd only charge $10 for their shirts, then all the sweatshop workers would be so much better off." Describe a possible counterargument.

Inequality, Poverty, and Social Insurance

Jamil and Alexis are sophomores at the University of Illinois, where they are both double majoring in economics and psychology. They each dream of running their own company someday; they both love video games, and they are both looking to gain work experience during the summer that will help build their resumes.

In many ways, Jamil and Alexis are similar. But there's an important difference. Jamil's parents are successful physicians. He never experienced financial struggles growing up, and while his parents repeatedly tell him that college is a big investment, they are paying for his education. He hasn't had to take out any student loans, and when he considers options for summer employment, he is able to focus on the long-term benefits for his career.

Does where you started affect how you finish?

Alexis is the child of a single mother who works two jobs to make ends meet. One of her worst childhood memories is being evicted. While financial aid has made college possible for her, she's anxious about the amount of debt she is accumulating from her student loans. When she considers summer employment, how much the job pays is an important factor. An unpaid internship is simply out of the question.

In many respects, Jamil and Alexis have equal educational opportunities, but economic inequality shapes and constrains their choices. Different views about inequality underpin some of our most contentious public policy debates. The same issues underlie disagreements about choices within our universities, workplaces, and communities.

This chapter will arm you with some important facts about inequality. We'll also develop a framework for thinking about inequality and take a look at the tools the government uses to reduce inequality and poverty. Understanding inequality and poverty is also central to making sound financial decisions. Sure, the average income of college graduates is pretty good, but few people earn the average. Instead, the income distribution of college students is varied—some of you will earn much more than average, while others will struggle. It's also likely that your life will involve both periods of plenty and periods of deprivation, so arming yourself with knowledge about inequality and poverty will help you better prepare.

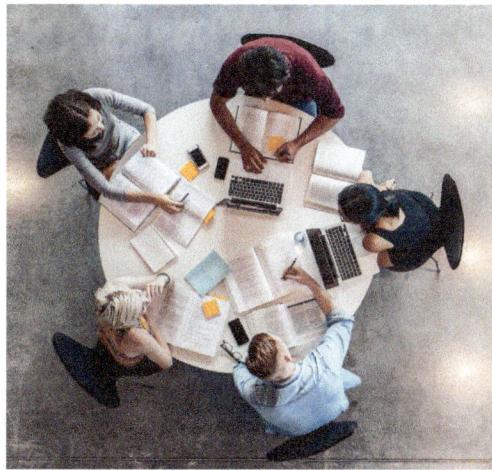

Chapter Objective

Understand inequality, poverty, the tools government uses to address them, and the trade-off between efficiency and equity.

8.1 Measuring Inequality
Measure the extent of economic inequality in the United States.

8.2 Poverty
Assess the prevalence and implications of poverty.

8.3 The Social Safety Net, Social Insurance, and Redistributive Taxation
Discover the ways in which government redistributes.

8.4 The Debate About Income Redistribution
Be prepared to join the debate about income redistribution.

🎙 **Podcast**
Think Like an Economist
Inequality—Understanding the Gap between Rich and Poor

Measuring Inequality

Learning Objective *Measure the extent of economic inequality in the United States.*

Many political debates boil down to disagreements about how much inequality and poverty there is, and what to do about it. In order to have an informed opinion, you need to understand the facts. And so our next task is to survey the data. As we dig into the numbers, we'll discover that there are many different ways to assess the extent of inequality and poverty, each of which yields different insights. Our goal is to present an array of different measures, so that you can see the full picture and form your own judgments.

Figure 1 | The Distribution of Income in the United States

Average annual family income in 2020 before tax

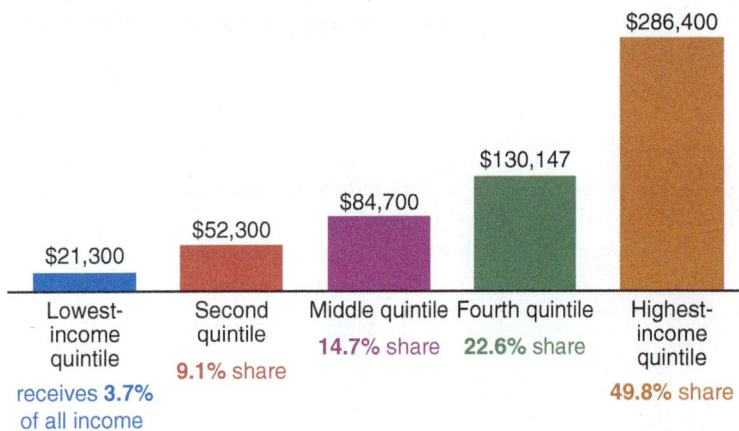

A quintile refers to one fifth of American families.

Data from: U.S. Census Bureau.

Figure 2 | Changes in the Distribution of Income Over Time

Share of total income

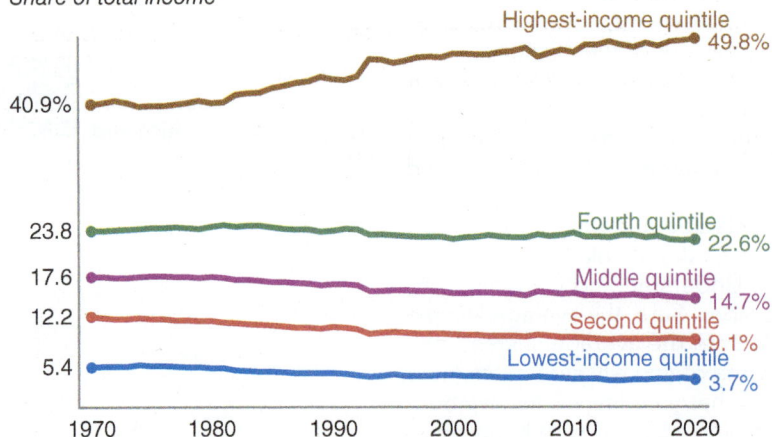

Data from: U.S. Census Bureau.

Income Inequality

Let's start with income — which is the money you receive in a period of time, such as a year. We'll look at U.S. data to see how much income inequality there is in the United States and how it's been changing. Then we'll turn to international data to examine inequality around the world.

Income is distributed unequally. To analyze the distribution of income, we sort families from low to high income, and then divide them into five equal-sized groups, called *quintiles*. The leftmost bar in Figure 1 shows that the average family income of the lowest-income quintile of families is $21,300 per year. Taking these folks together, the bottom fifth receives 3.7% of total income. At the other extreme, the right-most bar shows that the highest-income quintile has an average family income of $286,400. Taking all their income together, the highest-income quintile earns nearly half (49.8%) of all income in the United States.

Income inequality is rising. Figure 2 shows how the income share of each quintile has changed since 1970. The largest shift is at the top: The highest-income quintile has increased their share of income from 40.9% in 1970 to 49.8% in 2020. The share of income accruing to each of the other quintiles has declined. However, this doesn't necessarily mean that their income fell. Even though they're getting smaller slices, the size of the pie grew. Incomes grew for many families over this period, but incomes grew fastest for those at the top of the income distribution, which means that their share of all income earned in the United States also grew.

The bottom quintile doesn't look like it has changed much, but don't let the compressed scale fool you — their share has fallen by nearly a third, from 5.4% to 3.7%.

The rich are getting richer. While the rich are a small proportion of the population, they account for a remarkably large share of total income. The top 5% of families receive more than one-third of all income (34.6%, to be exact). The richest 1% receive nearly one-fifth, and the very richest 0.1% of families earn over one-tenth of all income.

Figure 3 broadens the historical lens and tracks the income shares of those at the top of the distribution over the last century. While current levels of inequality are high relative to historical norms, we saw similar levels of inequality in the 1920s. Inequality subsequently fell through the 1950s before starting its long recent rise in the 1980s.

The United States is more unequal than most developed countries. Let's compare the income distribution in the United States with that in other developed nations. Each bar in Figure 4 runs from the income held by those at the 10th percentile — meaning that only 10% of people in the country have less income — to the income held by the 90th percentile — meaning that only 10% of the people in the country have more income than them. Among these countries, the gap between the two ends is largest for the United States. The United States stands out because its rich are richer than those in other countries.

The distribution of income around the world is even more unequal. So far we've focused on differences between high-income and low-income families within one country — the United States. But the differences between high-income and low-income countries are much larger. As a result, the level of income inequality across the whole world is much larger than it is in any individual country. Figure 5 shows the global income distribution, plotting the share of the global population at each level of annual income. Be careful as you read this figure to note that the horizontal axis shows a ratio (or logarithmic) scale. Notice that much of the world's population gets by on an annual income that's less than $1,000 per year. Indeed, many earn an annual income of only a few hundred dollars, or just a dollar or two per day. This global context suggests that even the very poor in the United States are well off compared to the billions of people scraping to get by in India, China, and elsewhere in the developing world.

Alternative Measures of Inequality

So far we've examined inequality in annual income. But annual income is by no means the single best indicator of your living standards, your purchasing power, or your opportunities. Income varies from year to year for many people, and people differ in both the amount of their

Figure 3 | A Rising Share of Income Is Going to the Top

Share of pre-tax income going to highest income taxpayers

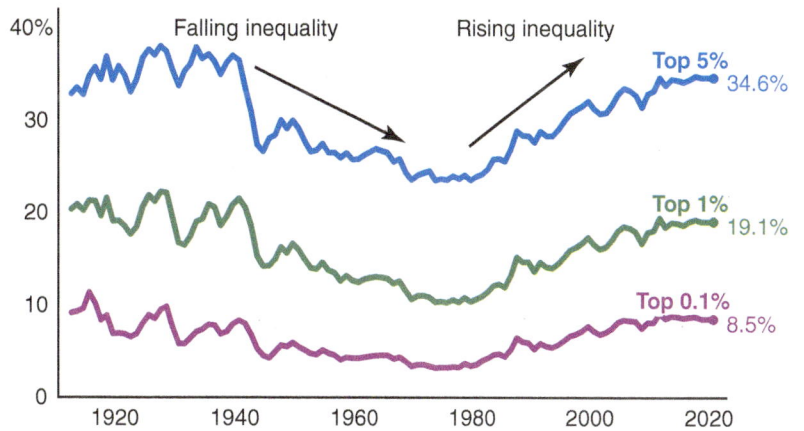

Data from: World Inequality Database.

Figure 4 | The United States Has a Larger Income Gap Between Rich and Poor Than Other Countries

Bars show the inequality of income between the poorest and the richest tenth in each country.

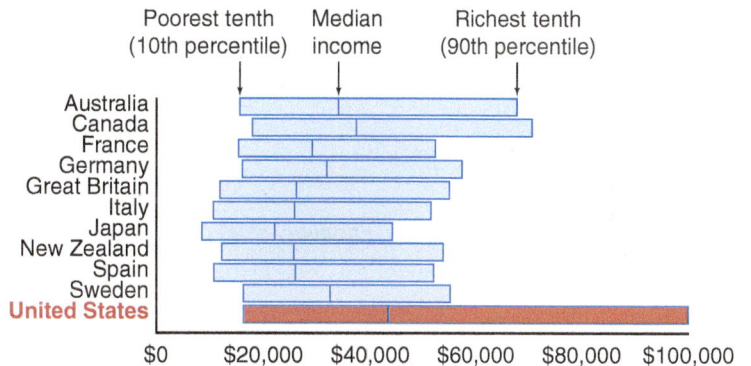

Income is disposable household income, adjusted for household size, and differences in the cost of living.

Data from: OECD income distribution database for around 2019.

Figure 5 | The Distribution of Income Across the Entire World

Share of global population at each annual income level

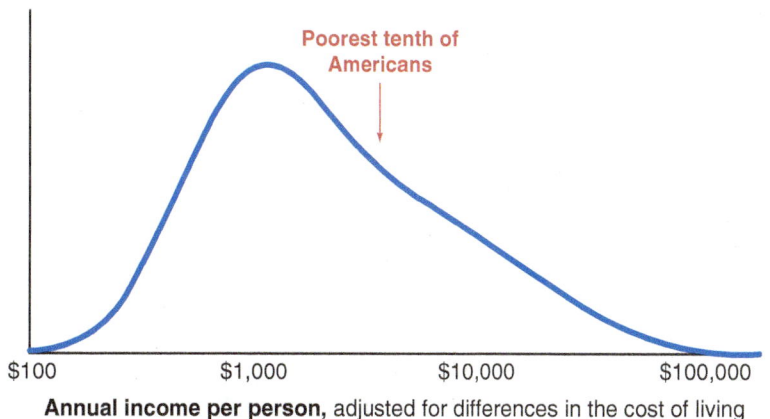

Annual income per person, adjusted for differences in the cost of living

Note: Ratio (or logarithmic) scale on horizontal axis.

Data from: Branko Milanovic, *Global Inequality: A New Approach for the Age of Globalization*, 2016.

savings and their ability to earn more in the future. For instance, if you're like most students, you probably have a small amount of savings and have a low annual income. But five years from now, you'll probably be earning a lot more than you are today. Today, as a student, you're focusing on building your skill set precisely because you expect to earn more down the road. You might also be young, without a lot of work experience. Imagine meeting a 50-year-old who's worked full time since they were 18. If they have the same annual earnings that you have this year, do you think that there is any inequality between the two of you? What if they earn nothing, but have an investment portfolio and savings worth $2 million?

There are no right answers to these questions — they simply represent different ways to think about inequality. Let's explore them.

There is much more inequality of wealth than income. Your total purchasing power and your economic resources may be better represented by your wealth than your income. **Wealth** refers to all the assets — including savings, cars, a home — that you currently have. Wealth is considered a stock, which is something that is measured at one specific time and represents the amount of assets you have at that time. In contrast, income is a flow, since the money flows in over time.

Wealth is much more unequally distributed than income. Figure 6 shows that the poorest half of all U.S. households holds a tiny share of all wealth — only 1%. (Many of these households are in debt, so they actually hold a negative share.) At the opposite extreme, millionaires — who make up the wealthiest tenth — collectively hold 76% of all wealth. And even within this select group, wealth is still extremely unequally distributed. In fact, the wealthiest 1% — folks who have more than $11 million in wealth — holds 37% of all wealth. Wealth is much more unequally distributed than income. This inequality partly reflects the fact that wealth accumulates and is passed from generation to generation.

wealth All the assets — including savings, cars, a home — that you currently have.

Figure 6 | Wealth Is Heavily Concentrated Among the Very Rich

For every $100 of wealth in the United States...

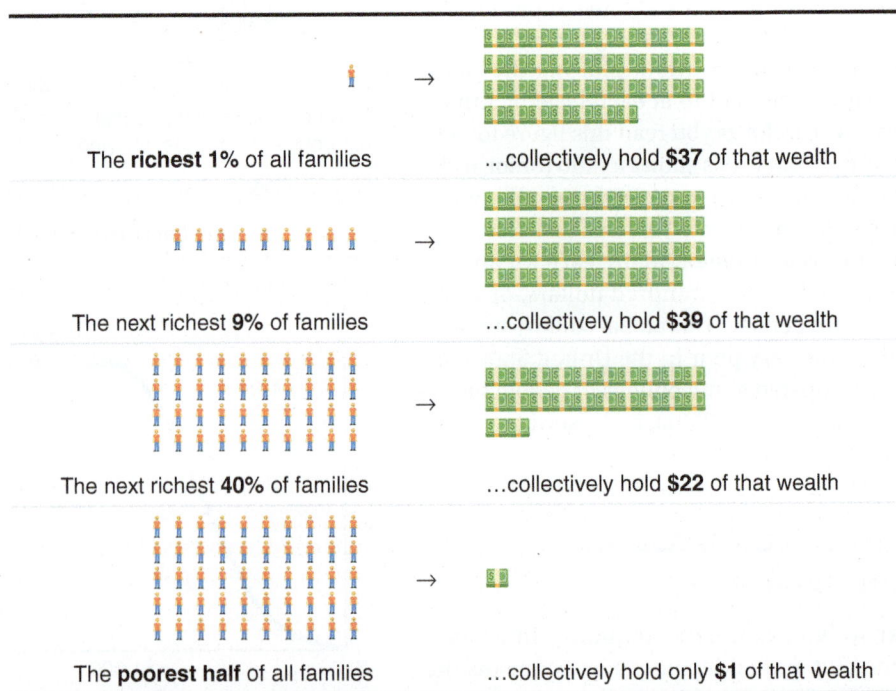

The **richest 1%** of all families → ...collectively hold **$37** of that wealth

The next richest **9%** of families → ...collectively hold **$39** of that wealth

The next richest **40%** of families → ...collectively hold **$22** of that wealth

The **poorest half** of all families → ...collectively hold only **$1** of that wealth

Data from: Survey of Consumer Finances, 2019.

Permanent income may be a better measure of living standards. Economists believe that your living standards largely reflect your **permanent income** — which is your average lifetime income — rather than your income in a given year. There is less inequality in permanent income than in measured annual income because some of the annual income inequality reflects temporary ups and downs that don't reflect your long-run economic situation. There are also clear patterns as you age: People earn less when they are young and tend to earn more as they get older and become more experienced. So some inequality reflects differences between younger and older people.

Because people can borrow and save, permanent income is a better predictor of what you can afford to consume than annual income. For instance, it makes more sense for you as a college student to borrow money than it would for someone in their 50s with the same earnings as you because your highest-earning years are ahead of you. That means that you can consume more today by borrowing from your future, while still having higher future consumption. Similarly, you should always save when you are doing well financially because you'll need your savings when you hit the inevitable bumps in the road that we all face. And you'll want to save during your working years to prepare for later in life when you're likely to retire.

permanent income Your average lifetime income.

There is less inequality in spending than in income. An alternative approach suggests that because your living standards are largely determined by the goods and services you actually buy and consume, inequality in living standards may be better measured by focusing on what people spend, rather than on what they earn. In Figure 1 we saw that the top quintile of the population receives around 13 times as much *income* as the bottom quintile. But differences in *spending* are much less stark. The top quintile spends only around four times as much as the bottom quintile. You're probably thinking that's because the highest-income families save more, and you're right. But people whose incomes are temporarily high or low drive much of the measured inequality in income. Those with temporarily high incomes *are saving* because they know that their good times won't last. Those with temporarily low incomes, on the other hand, often dip into their savings or borrow money to prevent their consumption from falling as much as their income. These patterns mean that there is less consumption inequality.

Intergenerational mobility and inequality of opportunity. Inequality in current income, wealth, permanent income, and consumption are all examples of inequality in *outcomes*. How might we measure inequality of *opportunity*? Many people believe that regardless of whether the socioeconomic status you are born into, you should have the same opportunity to succeed. This suggests focusing on **intergenerational mobility** — the extent to which your economic circumstances are independent of those of your parents. Careful studies show that around half of the economic advantage or disadvantage enjoyed by your parents will be transmitted to you. For instance, if your household earns about 80% more than the typical household, on average, kids like you will earn about 40% more than the typical child. Economic disadvantage is similarly transmitted from parents to children. So your parents matter, but your own hard work, your investments, and luck also matter.

intergenerational mobility The extent to which the economic status of children is independent of the economic status of their parents.

You've probably heard the United States described as the "land of opportunity." Yet despite this self-image, the United States has less intergenerational mobility than Australia, Canada, France, Germany, or Sweden, and is at a level roughly comparable with the United Kingdom. But even across the United States there are large differences in intergenerational mobility. Researchers have shown that the chances that a child raised in a low-income household makes it to the top quintile of the income distribution varies substantially across U.S. cities, even among neighborhoods within cities. This research shows that the neighborhood that you grow up in can have a big impact on your outcomes as an adult. To find out about the intergenerational mobility of the neighborhood you grew up in, you can visit opportunityatlas.org.

Figure 7 | Distribution of Wealth

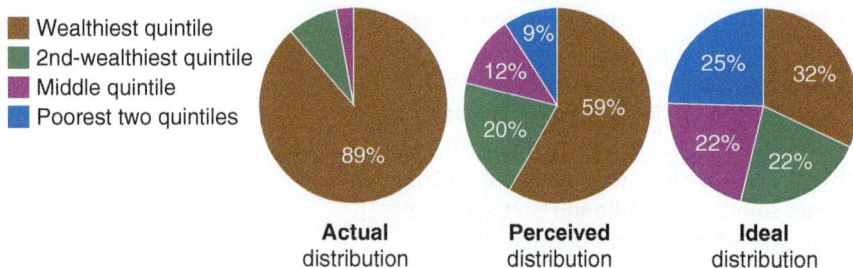

- Wealthiest quintile
- 2nd-wealthiest quintile
- Middle quintile
- Poorest two quintiles

Actual distribution — 89%

Perceived distribution — 59%, 20%, 12%, 9%

Ideal distribution — 32%, 22%, 22%, 25%

Data from: "Building a Better America—One Wealth Quintile at a Time," by Michael A. Norton and Dan Ariely, 2011 and "Household wealth trends in the United States, 1962 to 2019" by Edward N. Wolff.

You now have a robust understanding about the degree of economic inequality in the United States. This understanding is crucial to resolving some of our fiercest political debates.

The left pie in Figure 7 shows the actual distribution of wealth, while the next pie shows the results of a survey asking people what they think the distribution of wealth is. Comparing these pies, we learn that people don't accurately perceive the extent of wealth inequality. They know that the rich have a large share of total wealth, but they underestimate just how lopsided that share is.

The same survey also asked about what they think the ideal distribution would be, and the pie on the right suggests that people would prefer wealth to be more equally distributed. Taken together, we see that while some of the debate about inequality is driven by differences about what people want, some of it is driven by a lack of knowledge of the facts. ∎

A guide to learning more about almost anything. At this point, it should be clear that measuring inequality is no easy task. People can easily be misled if they hear only one statistic. In fact, if you want to persuade someone of your view, you'll likely find that some statistics are better for your position than others. It's not uncommon for those with a particular interest or point of view to cherry-pick their favorite statistics, which is why you can't always trust what you read or hear.

Notice that you were able to get a useful understanding of inequality by following the process that economists often use when trying to learn more about a new area:

- You examined the *current levels* of inequality.
- You dug deeper to see *who* was more or less affected by inequality.
- You analyzed how inequality has *changed* over time.
- You compared inequality *across countries*.
- You reexamined the *robustness* of our conclusions to alternative ways of conceptualizing, defining, and measuring inequality.

This is a guide that you'll find tremendously helpful throughout your career. Simply replace the word "inequality" in these bullet points with wages, international trade, taxes, bicycle commuting, vegetarianism, or whatever issue you are trying to learn about, and you'll quickly become an expert.

8.2 Poverty

Learning Objective *Assess the prevalence and implications of poverty.*

So far we've been analyzing inequality. But inequality reflects two phenomena: the abundance of the rich and the poverty of the poor. Many people argue that poverty is the more important phenomenon, so let's now apply our recipe to understanding the key facts about poverty.

Defining Poverty

If we are going to measure poverty, we have to start by defining it. But defining poverty is not a simple task — in fact, it can be surprisingly controversial. Every country defines poverty somewhat differently, and even within the United States, there is more than one definition. However, the U.S. government has designated one measure the official measure of poverty, so that's a good place to start.

In the United States you are officially in poverty if your family income is below the **poverty line** (also called a poverty threshold). The poverty line is a somewhat arbitrary threshold. It was originally set in 1963, using data on family purchases in 1955. Back then, families spent about a third of their incomes on food, so the poverty line was set at three times the cost of a low-cost food plan. The poverty line has been updated for inflation ever since. In 2021, the official poverty line for a family of four was a family income of $27,500, and it was $18,700 for a family of two. The line varies to reflect the costs of supporting different-sized families.

poverty line An income level set by the government below which a family is defined to be in poverty; also called a poverty threshold.

How many people are in poverty? The official **poverty rate** is the share of people whose family income falls below the poverty line. The poverty rate in 2020 was 11.4% of the population, meaning that roughly one in nine people were in poverty.

poverty rate The percentage of people whose family income is below the poverty line.

The official poverty rate has not changed much over time. Figure 8 shows that the share of people whose income is less than the official poverty line has been largely stable at around one in eight over the past five decades, even though the average income of the population as a whole has more than doubled. This suggests that those at the bottom of the income distribution have not shared in the rising prosperity of the past five decades.

The official poverty rate is calculated using a measure of income that reflects money income. That means that it counts everything you earn or is paid to you. This includes direct cash benefits such as unemployment insurance and Social Security insurance payments. However, the official poverty rate fails to account for the tax credits and many noncash benefits provided by government programs designed to help those in poverty. As a result, the official poverty rate doesn't adequately capture the resources available to those living in poverty. However, it highlights the success of unemployment insurance during the Covid recession in preventing poverty from spiking during a period of widespread unemployment.

Figure 8 | The Official Poverty Rate Has Been Quite Stable over Many Decades

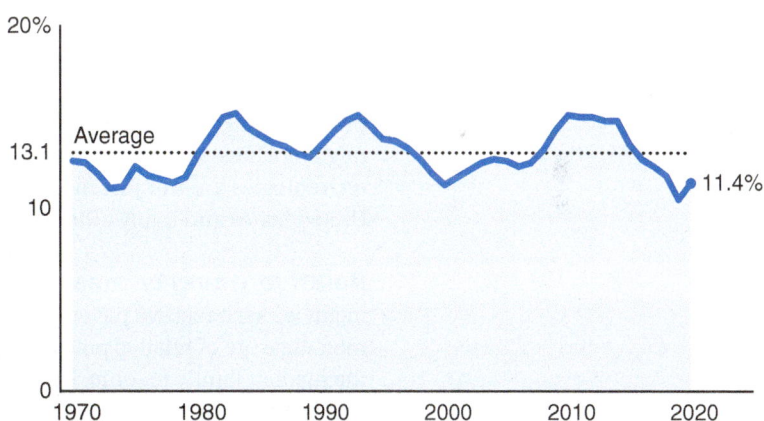

Share of Americans in poverty

Data from: U.S. Census Bureau.

Absolute versus Relative Poverty

The official U.S. poverty rate compares people's incomes today with living standards from the 1950s. To understand what this means for making comparisons across time, let's take a look at two different ways of measuring poverty. **Absolute poverty** is a measure of the adequacy of resources relative to an absolute or unchanging standard.

The alternative view is **relative poverty**, which is a measure that compares resources relative to the material living standards of your contemporary society. Absolute poverty is a universal standard for assessing whether basic needs are met that does not change over time. If the poverty line is set using absolute poverty, then it is the same in the United States as in Zambia, and the same today as in prehistoric times. In contrast, relative poverty considers whether you have the resources to participate in your society. What's considered essential depends on what everyone else in the community has, so relative poverty is a measure of poverty which takes into account the living standards of those around you.

absolute poverty A measure of the adequacy of resources relative to an absolute standard of living.

relative poverty A measure of the adequacy of resources relative to the material living standards of your contemporary society.

Most measures of poverty are neither purely absolute nor purely relative. In reality, most people consider something between absolute and relative as a reasonable way to measure poverty, but where to draw the line between the two is the subject of heated debates.

Figure 9 | Different Approaches to Measuring Poverty Yield Different Poverty Lines

Annual income required to avoid poverty, adjusted for inflation

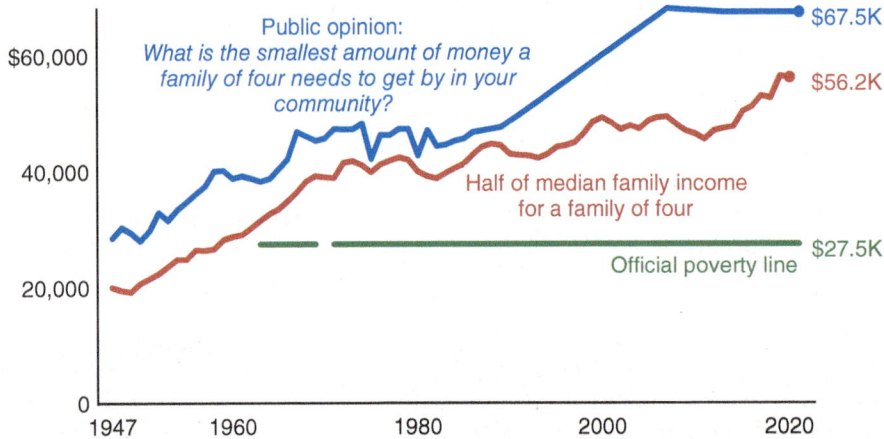

Data from: Census Bureau and Gallup.

The U.S. poverty line is neither a purely absolute nor purely relative standard. The official U.S. poverty line has features of both a relative and an absolute standard. The measure is relative in that it was developed to be at a level that reflects the fact that the United States is a high-income country. But technically, the measure is absolute, because — as Figure 9 shows — it was set at an absolute level more than 50 years ago. Since the poverty line was set in 1963, it has been adjusted only for inflation — which means that it can buy the same bundle of goods it could buy in 1963. The advantage of this approach is that the poverty line in the United States tracks through time how many people are below an unchanging standard. The disadvantage is that living standards have risen over time, and so the official poverty line has become decreasingly relevant as our society has become increasingly prosperous. For instance, in the 1960s, some who had incomes above the poverty line might not have had access to a phone or even running water in their home. These modern technologies are not just more common, but are central to a life without poverty in the United States and many other developed nations today.

Relative poverty measures show higher levels of poverty. How, then, might we set a relative poverty line that will keep up with our rising prosperity? One common measure of relative poverty says that you are poor if your family income is below half the median family income. Indeed, as Figure 9 shows, when the official poverty line for a family of four was established in 1963, it was roughly equal to half of median family earnings. The rise in median family income since then means that half of the median family income has risen to $56,000. The fact that the U.S. official poverty rate was equal to half the median income of a family in the mid-1960s is what makes it a relative measure. The fact that it is stuck at that level while U.S. incomes — including the median income — have grown is what makes it an absolute measure.

Another approach to measuring relative poverty involves surveying the public about what they think is an adequate income to "get by." Figure 9 shows that the average responses to this question have risen as our society has gotten richer. This suggests that most people think about minimal income needs as being relative to the contemporary standards of their society.

Which of these alternative poverty lines do you think makes most sense?

Do the Economics

If you believed that the poverty line should be based on public opinion about what is required to "get by," would this lead you to think that there are more or fewer people in poverty than is measured by the official statistics? ∎

Absolute poverty in a global perspective. The United Nations and the World Bank focus on absolute poverty, setting *a global poverty line* of $1.90 per day. They calculate that this is the minimum needed for human survival in modern times. Globally, 896 million people — including 15% of people in the developing world — are living below this poverty line. Under an alternative poverty line of $3.10 per day, the global ranks of the poor rise to 2.1 billion people, or about one-third of all people.

Think about what it means to get by on this.

Interpreting the DATA   What is it like to live on $1.90 per day?

What does it mean to live in poverty? Let's investigate the economic lives of Anuperna and Raja, a couple who are roughly representative of an impoverished family in Udaipur, India. Both Anuperna and Raja work cultivating their land. Raja also works as a laborer; when there's no work nearby, he will migrate for a few months and send his meager wages home. Anuperna is also an entrepreneur, making and selling saris. Neither of them are literate. They live with their three kids and Raja's mother in a small two-room house with no electricity, toilets, or tap water. Food accounts for two-thirds of their household spending, leaving little for anything else. They own a bed, but no chairs or tables. While their better-off neighbors have a radio or a bicycle, they do without. Hunger is a key concern, and when income is scarce, they will do without food for an entire day. More often, they make do by eating less in a day than they need to stave off hunger. Of all the deprivations of poverty, this is the hardest, and Anuperna says that she finds it hard to stay in good spirits when she's hungry. Like most of her neighbors, Anuperna is underweight and also anemic. She, Raja, and the kids are also frequently sick, or weak, but they rarely seek treatment because it is expensive. Instead of complaining, Anuperna is grateful for the health of her children as around one-eighth of all children in her village die before the age of five. ∎

She works hard, but has little.

The U.S. poor are not members of the global poor. The global poverty line of $1.90 per day is a measure of extreme poverty. This measure is also a useful benchmark for the United States. Researchers have shown that such extreme poverty in the United States has risen in recent decades. Yet, most American families in extreme poverty will receive some kind of assistance or only spend a few months in such extreme poverty.

For the most part, people struggling with poverty in the United States and other developed countries are better off than those struggling in the developing world. In fact, more than 95% of people in the developing world get by on less than the U.S. official poverty line. Moreover, throughout most of human history, nearly everyone — even those in rich countries — lived on less than the official U.S. poverty line. When considered in either a global or historical context, even those at the bottom of American income distribution have a lot. This suggests that in the United States, it makes more sense to focus on relative poverty.

The Incidence of Poverty in the United States

While there is disagreement about how to measure poverty in the United States, there are a few facts about poverty that turn out to be true regardless of whether one measures poverty using the official U.S. poverty rate or alternative measures. First, the majority of people who are in poverty will spend much of their lives in poverty. However, most people will spend some time in poverty during their lifetime. Second, children and single moms are the most likely to be in poverty. Third, people of color are more likely to experience poverty. Let's take a closer look at each of these facts.

Most poverty spells are short, but most low-income people are in long-term poverty. Millions of people both enter and escape poverty each year. Some people spend much of their lives in poverty. Others fall on hard times briefly or even choose to make sacrifices in the short term, for instance, forgoing income to pursue more education. (College students living in dorms are automatically excluded from the official poverty rate, but roughly half of college students living on their own have incomes below the U.S. official poverty line.)

There are big differences between experiencing a spell of poverty and a lifetime of poverty. Most *spells* of poverty are temporary, with around half lasting less than a year. But at any point in time, long-term poverty is an important problem: More than half of all people whose incomes are currently below the U.S. official poverty rate are in the midst of a spell of poverty that will last eight years or more. That is, people in long-term poverty are both a small proportion of those who enter poverty, and a large share of the poor at any point in time. The distinction between temporary and long-term poverty is further complicated by the fact that poverty is often recurrent, and over half of all people who escape poverty will return to poverty within five years.

Figure 10 | Who Is in Poverty?

Proportion of each people in each group below the poverty line in 2020

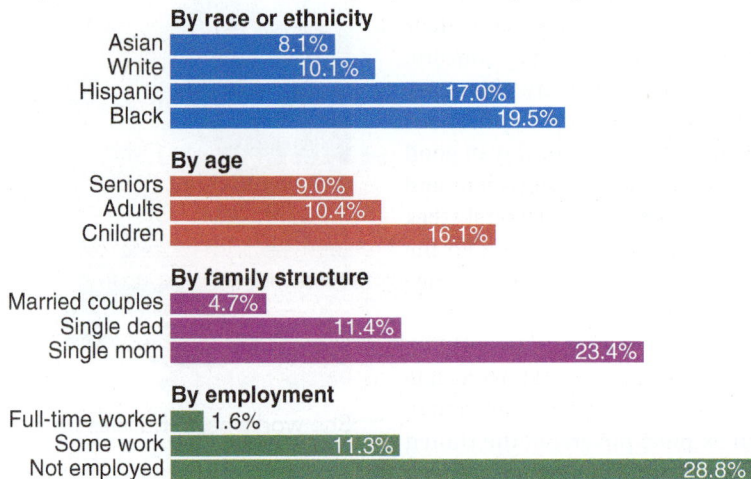

By race or ethnicity
- Asian: 8.1%
- White: 10.1%
- Hispanic: 17.0%
- Black: 19.5%

By age
- Seniors: 9.0%
- Adults: 10.4%
- Children: 16.1%

By family structure
- Married couples: 4.7%
- Single dad: 11.4%
- Single mom: 23.4%

By employment
- Full-time worker: 1.6%
- Some work: 11.3%
- Not employed: 28.8%

Data from: U.S. Census Bureau.

Some groups are more likely to experience poverty than others. Figure 10 shows that while all racial groups are afflicted by poverty, those in some groups are more likely to experience poverty. The top cluster of bars shows people who are Black or Hispanic are about twice as likely to be in poverty compared to those who are White or Asian. Even so, three-fifths of those in poverty are people who are non-Hispanic White.

The next cluster of bars in Figure 10 shows that poverty varies by age. Seniors aged 65 years and older have low poverty rates, largely because Social Security income payments provide most retirees with an income above the poverty line. By contrast, child poverty is quite common — one in six kids are in poverty. That means that you or someone you know likely grew up in poverty. Even though many people keep it hidden, the fact that a large number of children are in poverty is a reality in most communities.

The third cluster of bars shows another factor that is closely aligned with child poverty. Single parents — particularly single mothers — experience extremely high poverty rates. It's not just a matter of having only one income; single parents also face logistical difficulties juggling work with their child care responsibilities, and income-based government assistance for single-parent families isn't generous enough to lift them out of poverty. The concentration of poverty among the racial, ethnic, age, and family structures shown in Figure 10 is a long-standing pattern. Moreover, these disadvantages cumulate, so that nearly half of the children of Black or Hispanic single parents live in poverty.

The deeper cause of poverty is a lack of full-time employment. The bottom cluster of bars in Figure 10 shows that only 2% of adults with full-time year-round jobs are in poverty. Those who aren't employed, or who work part-time or part-year, are much more likely to be in poverty.

Household and employment changes can trigger a spell of poverty. What precipitates a spell of poverty? The biggest risk is losing a job. Another significant trigger is divorce or separation, which leads family income to be spread across two households. Other changes in the household can also be trigger points for poverty, such as the birth of a child, the death of a breadwinner, or a young adult trying to set up on their own.

All of this reveals a sobering insight: All of us are susceptible to the risks that lead to poverty, including joblessness and changes in family structure. These risks can strike without much warning. In fact, more than half of all Americans will experience poverty at some point in their lives. Social insurance is designed to help reduce some of the hardship associated with a spell of very little income. Let's turn to exploring what social insurance is and how it works.

8.3 The Social Safety Net, Social Insurance, and Redistributive Taxation

Learning Objective *Discover the ways in which government redistributes.*

The numbers you have seen so far are data on people's incomes before taxes. Once we take taxes and *transfers* — meaning the cash, goods, and services the government provides some people — into account, there is less inequality and less poverty. That's because most governments take actions that help reduce the inequality and poverty that would occur without government.

There are several ways in which government reduces inequality and poverty. Government funds the social safety net, which is the cash assistance, goods, and services provided by the government to improve the lives of those living in or near poverty. There are also government programs that insure you against bad outcomes such as unemployment, illness, developing a work-limiting disability, or outliving your savings. These programs are called **social insurance** because it's insurance, but it's provided socially by everyone in society rather than by a private insurance company.

Government raises the money for the safety net (and everything else it does!) through taxes — which themselves are an equalizing force, since our overall system of taxation is progressive. A **progressive tax** is a tax in which those with more income tend to pay a higher share of their income in taxes. A country can be described as having a progressive tax system when the sum of taxes people pay are on average progressive.

Let's explore how the safety net, social insurance, and taxes equalize incomes in the United States.

social insurance Government-provided insurance against bad outcomes such as unemployment, illness, disability, or outliving your savings.

progressive tax A tax where those with more income tend to pay a higher share of their income in taxes.

The Social Safety Net for Those in or Near Poverty

To help ensure a minimum material standard of living for those at the bottom of the income distribution, the government does more explicit redistribution to those at the bottom through social safety-net programs. The major programs are described in Figure 11.

Safety net programs designed to help those with low incomes are means-tested. In order to ensure that benefits only reach those truly in need, many social safety net programs are **means-tested,** which means that your eligibility depends on your income. In addition, some programs also have asset tests to ensure that the idle wealthy don't get benefits.

The elderly and the disabled are protected by Supplemental Security Income; working families are helped by the Earned Income Tax Credit; single parents often rely on cash assistance; and many of the jobless get by with the help of the Supplemental Nutrition Assistance Program (lots of people still refer to it as "food stamps"). Medicaid helps each of these groups. In theory, many of those in poverty qualify for housing assistance, but in reality, long waiting lists mean that few actually receive it.

This patchwork of programs means that some people fall through the cracks and don't receive any assistance, while others are eligible for several programs.

means-tested programs Programs for which eligibility is based on income and sometimes wealth.

Figure 11 | Major U.S. Government Redistribution Programs

Program	Provides	Target population	Recipients (millions)	Monthly spending per recipient
Medicaid	Health care	Poor families with dependent children, disabled, elderly	80	$456
Earned Income Tax Credit (EITC)	Tax rebates	Working families with children	27	$256
Supplemental Nutrition Assistance Program (SNAP)	An ATM-like card that can be used to buy food.	All low-income people	46	$125
Supplemental Security Income (SSI)	Money	Low-income elderly or disabled	8.4	$539
Housing assistance	Subsidized rent	Low-income people, particularly families, elderly and disabled	5.1	$529
"Temporary Assistance to Needy Families (TANF)"	Money	Temporary help for low-income families with children	4.1	$172

Note: Data on recipients and costs are from 2014–2015. Programs are listed in order of total expenditures.

The safety net helps support a lot of families. Once we account for the overlap across programs, somewhere between one in three and one in four people live in a household currently receiving some form of assistance. An even larger proportion will need this assistance at some point in their lives. Thus, the social safety net provides support for much of the population. This may surprise you if you have never received benefits or you think you don't know anyone who has. But perhaps this is because many people who find themselves in need of benefits don't tell friends or family about it.

Safety net programs provide minimal support. Notice that the typical monthly payments in Figure 11 aren't particularly generous. But these safety net programs often provide enough to raise low-income families with children above the poverty line. Recall that the poverty rate is calculated excluding most of these benefits — direct cash assistance like TANF and Supplement Security Income is included, but the other benefits are not. Including the value of all benefits helps lift about a third of the people living in poverty above the poverty line.

Safety net programs include cash assistance, tax breaks, and in-kind transfers. While some safety net programs provide income or tax breaks, others provide specific goods, which are sometimes called *in-kind transfers*. For instance, the food support program known as SNAP provides an ATM-style card that can be used only to buy food; housing vouchers can be spent only on housing. But many economists are puzzled by this: Why help people with in-kind benefits, rather than just giving an equivalent benefit as cash? After all, recipients can use cash to buy whatever they most need — food or housing.

There are four key reasons why government provides in-kind benefits rather than cash benefits. First, giving goods rather than cash prevents recipients from making bad choices, such as gambling the money away. Second, taxpayers may care more about reducing homelessness or hunger, rather than about what will make the recipient happiest. Third, providing an in-kind benefit that only the poor will value — such as public housing — makes it more likely that only those who truly need the assistance will get it. And fourth, some in-kind benefits — such as child care — are a complement to work, which helps offset the incentive for recipients to rely on the safety net rather than work.

Why parents often prefer in-kind support to cash

Many parents are a bit like governments, preferring to give their kids specific help or gifts rather than cash, despite the fact you could use cash to buy exactly what you need. Their reasons are often similar to those advocating for in-kind government benefits. Your parents may worry that you'll make bad choices, spending cash on things that they don't think are important or valuable. They often choose gifts that they see as an investment in your future — such as helping to finance your college tuition, or helping you buy a car so you can get to your new job. After all, your success means that you won't need to rely on them for support when you are older. ■

Social Insurance Programs

Some safety net programs are not means-tested but rather are insurance programs that cover everyone, regardless of income. You probably know about renters insurance, homeowners insurance, and car insurance: You pay a small amount each month to the insurance company, and if misfortune strikes, your stolen laptop will be replaced, your destroyed home will be rebuilt, or your crumpled car will be fixed. Buying insurance is a good way to protect yourself against these risks.

The same logic says that it's also a good idea to insure against financial risks involved with losing your job, becoming disabled, incurring huge medical bills, or outliving your savings. The problem is that many of the things we want to insure against are difficult for private insurance companies to provide profitably. And so the government steps in to make sure that everyone can get access to certain forms of insurance. It is known as "social" insurance because it is provided "socially" — by your fellow taxpayers — rather than by private insurance firms. Figure 12 outlines the most important social insurance programs in the United States.

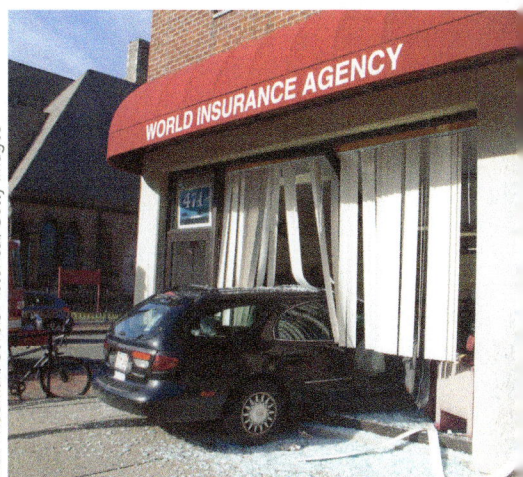

Don't worry. It's insured.

Figure 12 | The Largest U.S. Social Insurance Programs

Program	Insurance against	Paid for by	Beneficiaries (millions)	Average monthly benefit
Social Security	Outliving your savings, dying before your kids are grown	A tax on workers and employers	52	$1,337
Unemployment Insurance	Losing your job through no fault of your own	A tax on employers	2.9	$300
Disability Insurance	Developing a work-limiting disability	A tax on workers and employers	10	$1,060
Workers' Compensation	Getting injured at work	Employers are required to buy it	3.0	$2,067
Medicare	Health insurance for people 65 and older	A tax on workers and employers	55	$857

Note: The average benefit amount for workers' compensation is the amount spent by employers on total benefits divided by the number of claims in 2015.

Benefits are based on certain bad outcomes. Social insurance — like private insurance — pays you when you experience a bad outcome. Unemployment insurance exists to provide protection against temporary spells of unemployment. Workers' compensation provides payments and medical benefits if you are injured at work. And disability insurance provides payments if you develop a work-limiting disability. Social Security provides income in retirement and therefore insures people against outliving their savings. The outcome you are being insured against is living longer than you expect or having inadequate savings due to stock market declines or higher-than-expected inflation (which means your money doesn't buy as many things as you were expecting). Social Security provides a stream of income to the elderly for the rest of their lives to ensure that they don't outlive their savings. Social Security also provides benefits to certain survivors when people die. A child who loses a parent, for example, will receive Social Security benefits to help support them until they turn 18. In this way, Social Security also provides life insurance to parents. Finally, Medicare provides health insurance to people age 65 or older and therefore covers some of the costs of medical care when they develop health problems.

People pay into social insurance programs. Just like you pay your insurance company a monthly payment to provide you with car insurance, people make regular payments into social insurance programs. Sometimes the money is withheld from workers' paychecks, and sometimes employers pay. For example, for Social Security, disability insurance, and Medicare, you pay 7.65% of your wages to the program, and your employer also kicks in the same amount. Employers pay employment insurance taxes on workers' wages and are asked to pay a certain amount per worker to ensure that their workers are covered by workers' compensation insurance.

> Want to figure out what Social Security benefits you'll get when you retire? It's a complicated formula, accounting for your 35 highest-earning years of earnings, your retirement age, and the inflation rate. These online calculators provide a good estimate: www.ssa.gov /planners/calculators

EVERYDAY Economics How to insure against bad decisions

Social Security serves three purposes as a social safety net. The first is ensuring that people who earn very little during their working years are not destitute in old age. The second is providing longevity insurance. If you are lucky enough to live well past typical life expectancy, then you need a lot more in retirement savings, yet that money is often better spent during the earlier part of your life. After all, if you die at a typical age, you will have been able to spend everything you earned. So it makes sense to be insured against living a long time. Finally, Social Security provides insurance against making a bad decision. People who aren't good planners will spend their income having fun today, rather than saving for old age. They discover what a bad idea this is only when it's too late. Social Security insures against the risk of making such myopic decisions by forcing contributions to the Social Security system. But Social Security doesn't guarantee a comfortable retirement — so it's important that workers who can afford to do it begin planning for their old age early. When you start your first job, find out about the retirement plan, and start saving right away. And for those with student loans or car payments, a handy trick can be to keep making those loan payments after you've paid off the loans — just make the payments into your retirement account instead. After all, you've gotten used to that money flowing out of your account each month. You won't feel any poorer, but you'll be making your future self a lot richer. ∎

Benefits are based on your past earnings. Social Security, unemployment insurance, workers' compensation, and disability insurance payments are all partially a function of your past earnings. Those who have earned more have paid more in, and are eligible to receive more benefits. Social insurance programs are explicitly not means-tested. That means that you don't need to have a financial need to get access to these benefits. Every once in a while Congress complains about someone whose tax return shows an income for the previous year of more than a million dollars, yet they are receiving unemployment insurance benefits. But the point of social insurance is that everyone pays for the insurance and is covered by it, regardless of how much money they have.

How marriage provides insurance

Here's an important benefit of marriage: It provides something akin to social insurance. Think about traditional wedding vows: Spouses promise to look after each other "for better, for worse, for richer, for poorer, in sickness and in health." That sounds like a promise to provide unemployment insurance, disability insurance, and health insurance. Just as unemployment insurance ensures that you'll still be able to get by when you lose your job, a working spouse effectively provides the same insurance. In both cases, someone — your spouse or the government — will help you pay for groceries if you lose your job. Your spouse can do a better job of insuring you if they don't face the same risks as you do, which is one reason to marry someone who works in a different occupation or at least for a different employer — you're less likely to both experience unemployment if you aren't both working in the same field or at the same company.

But marriage provides imperfect insurance, because there remains the risk that your spouse will also lose their job. Divorce also provides an escape hatch in which one spouse can fail to provide the other with the promised coverage when a bad event happens. ◼

You may have a lot in common, but you'll get less insurance marrying someone just like you.

So far, we've examined the redistributive effects of government spending. Let's now turn to analyzing the redistributive role played by taxes.

The Tax System

All the goods and services, social insurance, and safety net programs funded by the government are paid for by taxpayers. You've seen so far how spending by the government is used to fight poverty and reduce inequality. Tax dollars fund all of that, but because we don't all pay the same amount in taxes, the tax system itself reduces inequality.

Federal income taxes are progressive. **Income taxes** are taxes collected on all income, regardless of its source. Income includes earned income from wages and unearned income — such as investment income, pensions, and gifts. The 2022 federal income tax schedule for unmarried individuals in the United States is shown in Figure 13. As you can see, the higher your income is, the higher the tax rate that you pay on each additional dollar you earn.

While this suggests that the tax system is designed to make sure higher-income people pay a higher share of their income in taxes (that it's a progressive tax system), it isn't the whole story. Billionaire investor Warren Buffett is often described as the most successful investor in the world. But he's also known for pointing out that he pays a lower tax rate than his receptionist. He calculated that he had paid only around 18% of his income in federal income tax, while his receptionist paid around 30%. Is this a widespread problem? Buffett thinks it is, especially amongst the Forbes 400 (the 400 wealthiest people in America). He said:

> I'll bet a million dollars against any member of the Forbes 400 who challenges me that the average federal tax rate including income and payroll taxes for the Forbes 400 will be less than the average of their receptionists.

No one has taken him up on this bet. Let's explore why.

Some investment gains are excluded from income taxes. If you buy an asset for $2,000 and then sell it for $3,000 a year later, the $1,000 gain you make is treated differently from other income. Taxes on such gains are complicated. In 2020, capital gains tax rates were either 0%, 15%, or 20% depending on how long you held the asset before selling, as well as your taxable and nontaxable income. But here's the problem: Super high-income folks can often find legal ways to pay the lower rate despite having a high

income taxes Taxes collected on all income, regardless of its source.

Figure 13 | Federal Income Tax Rates, 2022

For each dollar of income between	Your tax rate is
$0 and $10,275	10%
$10,276 and $41,775	12%
$41,776 and $89,075	22%
$89,076 and $170,050	24%
$170,051 and $215,950	32%
$215,951 and $539,900	35%
More than $539,901	37%

income. And because, even at the top rate, capital gains tax rates are lower than income tax rates, people who earn much of their income from investment gains end up paying a lower average tax rate than people who earn most of their income in wages. In 2021, President Biden proposed a new higher capital gains tax bracket of 39.6% for those with incomes over a million dollars.

Higher income people get bigger tax breaks.   It's important to remember that the federal income tax scale shown in Figure 13 applies only to your "taxable income." There are lots of special exemptions that reduce how much of your income counts as taxable income. If you save for retirement, the government rewards you by excluding what you save from taxable income. If you buy a house, the government rewards you by letting you subtract the interest you pay on your home loan from your taxable income. If you're a student, you may get to subtract some of the tuition you paid from your taxable income.

These exclusions reduce the taxable income of the highest earners the most because they spend more of their money on the types of things for which there are special exemptions. That means that exclusions reduce the progressivity of the tax system.

Many other taxes aren't progressive.   Beyond income taxes, there are a raft of other taxes, which taken together are largely regressive. A **regressive tax** is a tax where those with lower incomes pay a higher share of their income on the tax compared to people with higher incomes. Taxes based on the things you buy, rather than the money you earn, tend to be regressive. The reason is that the rich tend to spend a smaller share of their income. Because state and local governments tax more of what people buy, these taxes are, on average, regressive. The poorest fifth of households pay nearly 11% of their income on state and local taxes, while the richest fifth of households pay around 7%.

regressive tax A tax where those with less income tend to pay a higher share of their income on the tax.

Taxes that fund most social insurance programs are not progressive.   The taxes that fund social insurance programs do not contribute to the progressivity of our tax system. Mostly they are proportional taxes in which we all pay the same percentage of our income regardless of whether we earn a little or a lot. They actually become regressive at the top, because many of these programs cap the amount of income subject to the tax. For example, Social Security taxes are applied only to roughly the first $150,000 of wages. Anything earned over that is not subject to Social Security taxes.

Overall, the tax system is progressive.   Let's put the pieces together. The basic federal income tax scale shown in Figure 13 is progressive, taxing the rich at a higher rate than the poor. Most of the taxes people pay are not federal income taxes, and many of those other taxes tend to favor the rich. However, taken together, the tax system still remains progressive. Overall, the poorest fifth of all households pay around 16% of their income as tax, while the richest one-fifth pay closer to 30%, although the richest 1% pay slightly lower taxes than the rest of this group.

8.4   The Debate About Income Redistribution

Learning Objective   *Be prepared to join the debate about income redistribution.*

Given everything you've read so far, do you think that the government needs to redistribute more to combat inequality and poverty, or do you think that it redistributes too much? This question is at the root of many of our fiercest political debates, and it separates left-wing or progressive politicians, who typically advocate more redistribution, from right-wing or conservative politicians, who usually advocate less.

The Economic Logic of Redistribution

Let's begin with the simple logic of redistribution and explore how it can raise total benefits, or well-being. Money is a means to an end, so when we consider whether redistribution of money is a good idea, it's useful to ask how money affects people's well-being. Economists refer to your *well-being* as your **utility.** The marginal principle reminds you to think at the margin, and the idea of diminishing marginal benefit also applies to money. That is, your 50,000th dollar—which you might use to pay for entertainment—yields a smaller boost in your utility than your 10,000th dollar—which you will likely spend on food or shelter. To be precise, **marginal utility** is the boost in utility you get from an extra dollar. And because each additional dollar yields a smaller boost to your well-being, you have **diminishing marginal utility.** This means that your marginal utility may be large when you have a low income, but it gets smaller as you get richer.

To be concrete, consider Alison, a single mother in Ohio who struggles to pay for her and her son's allergy and asthma medicine. If she had another $100, she could afford to purchase another asthma inhaler. Now imagine instead what billionaire Michael Jordan might do with an extra $100. He likes fine cigars, so perhaps he'll buy another $100 cigar. Who do you think has higher marginal utility from the extra $100?

Redistribution can increase total well-being. To find out the role of money in shaping well-being, researchers have asked thousands of Americans to rate their well-being on a 0–10 scale. Figure 14 shows a line of best fit illustrating the average level of well-being reported (on the vertical axis) at each level of income (on the horizontal axis). The fact that the line is upward-sloping shows

utility A measure of well-being.

marginal utility The additional utility you get from one more dollar.

diminishing marginal utility Each additional dollar yields a smaller boost to your utility—that is, less marginal utility—than the previous dollar.

Who would benefit the most from an extra $100? Billionaire Michael Jordan? Or this family?

Figure 14 | Income and Well-Being

How does income redistribution affect well-being?

A The well-being curve shows the average level of satisfaction at each level of income. The slope gets flatter as income increases, reflecting diminishing marginal benefits.

B If we **redistribute** $25,000 to the low-income person, from the high-income person:

C The income of the low-income person rises from $20,000 to $45,000, and their well-being rises a lot (from 5.7 to 6.5).

D The income of the high-income person falls from $200,000 to $175,000, and their well-being falls a little (from 7.45 to 7.40).

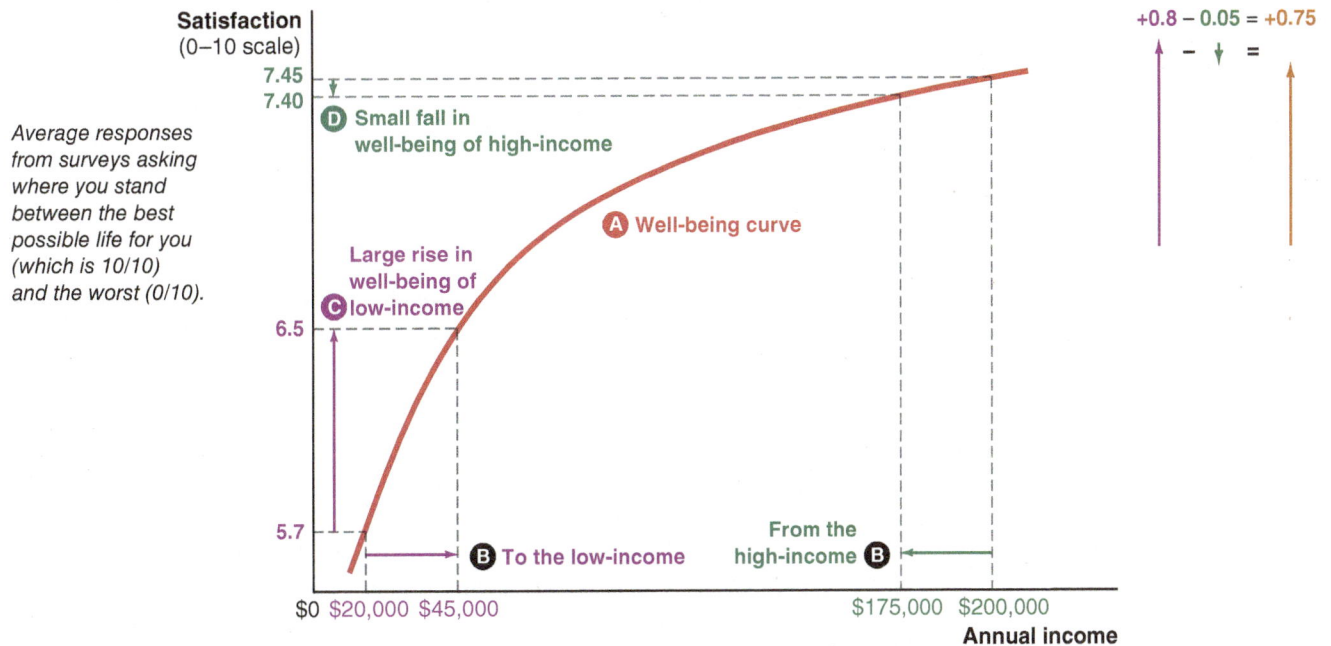

that people with more income are happier than those with less income. More importantly, focus on the slope of this curve. The slope illustrates the change in well-being associated with a change in income — the extra benefit from extra income. This curve flattens out as income rises — the slope gets smaller and smaller — which means that the extra benefit of an extra dollar is higher the poorer you are (the slope is larger at low incomes but is smaller at high incomes). That is, these data illustrate a pattern of diminishing marginal benefit from extra dollars.

Now that we've measured the extent of diminishing marginal benefits, we can use Figure 14 to analyze the gains from redistribution. Consider someone in the top fifth of the income distribution earning $200,000, and someone from the bottom fifth, earning $20,000. The well-being curve suggests that we might expect their well-being scores to be 7.45 and 5.7 respectively, which adds up to 13.15. If you redistribute $25,000 from the high-income person to the low-income person, the well-being of the high-income person will fall by 0.05, while the well-being of the low-income person will rise by 0.8. Consequently, this redistribution causes total well-being to rise by 0.75 (from 13.15 to 6.5 + 7.4 = 13.9).

The idea of maximizing total well-being comes from utilitarianism. The political philosophy that government should try to maximize total utility in society is known as **utilitarianism.** This belief holds that government redistribution is beneficial because transferring $100 from someone with a lot of resources — like Michael Jordan — to someone with fewer resources — like Alison — will lead to a society with a higher level of well-being, or utility. That gain arises because taxing $100 of Michael Jordan's income reduces his utility by only a little compared to the utility gain that Alison would enjoy from receiving that $100. As such, government can raise total utility by redistributing resources from the rich to the poor.

utilitarianism The political philosophy that government should try to maximize total utility in society.

The Costs of Redistribution: The Leaky Bucket

Even if you consider yourself a utilitarian, you face a problem: There's no easy way to redistribute money from the rich to the poor. Redistribution can be like moving money using a leaky bucket — some of the money gets lost along the way. Let's turn to examining the costs of redistribution to see why some of the money gets lost.

Administrative costs subtract from what you can redistribute. The first cost is the bucket itself. There's overhead involved in running social insurance and safety net programs. New applications for benefits must be processed; auditors make sure that no improper payments are made; policies must be enforced; and payments must be made. All of this is done by government workers, who must be paid. While these administrative costs are the most obvious financial costs of redistribution programs, they're relatively small. As we'll see in a moment, the more important costs arise from how the social safety net distorts work incentives.

A leaky bucket makes redistribution less effective.

Taxes and means-tested programs reduce the incentive to work. Some of the leakage is actually money lost before it is even collected. The problem is that we raise the money to pay for redistribution through income taxes. Higher income taxes reduce the rewards from working. When you get a smaller reward for working, you might choose to work less. That's why when the government tries to redistribute money by taxing high earners, those high earners might respond by working less, leaving less money available to be redistributed.

The presence of a social safety net also reduces the incentive to work. The opportunity cost principle reminds you that an important cost of working is what you must give up in order to work. Your opportunity cost of work is the benefits you get from whatever you would be doing instead — studying, socializing, taking care of kids or an adult who needs care. The benefit of work is the wage you earn from working. The safety net means that when you work, the relevant opportunity cost is not only your time, but also the potential that you might lose cash or in-kind benefits. If you use the cost-benefit principle to

decide whether to take a job, the presence of the safety net will make you more likely to turn down a job.

The safety net can also reduce the incentives for people to seek higher-paying work. The problem is that means-tested benefits are reduced as people earn more. That means that recipients not only pay taxes from every extra dollar earned, but they also lose benefits. The sum of higher taxes and reduced benefits accruing from each dollar you earn is called your **effective marginal tax rate.** As the following example shows, those with low incomes can face such high effective marginal tax rates that even though they are earning more through work, their living standards hardly improve at all.

effective marginal tax rate The amount of each extra dollar you earn that you lose to higher taxes and lower government benefits.

EVERYDAY Economics   Why earning more might mean taking home less

One economist tells the story of meeting a low-income woman who taught him about the problems of high effective marginal tax rates:

> She had moved from a $25,000 a year job to a $35,000 a year job, and suddenly she couldn't make ends meet any more. She showed me all her pay stubs. She really did come out behind by several hundred dollars a month. She lost free health insurance and instead had to pay $230 a month for her employer-provided health insurance. Her rent associated with her Section 8 voucher [housing assistance] went up by 30% of the income gain (which is the rule). She lost the ($280 a month) subsidized child-care voucher she had for after-school care for her child. She lost around $1,600 a year of the EITC [Earned Income Tax Credit]. She paid payroll tax on the additional income. Finally, the new job was in Boston, and she lived in a suburb. So now she has $300 a month of additional gas and parking charges.

This woman lost more than $10,000 in benefits by earning $10,000 more! With her payroll taxes also factored in, her effective marginal tax rate was well above 100%. The fact that she was better off earning $25,000 a year than $35,000 is known as a *poverty trap*. It's a trap because neither earning a higher nor a lower income will improve her situation by much. ■

Higher taxes mean more tax avoidance, tax evasion, and fraud. Because safety net payments are based on your income, there's an incentive to try to make your income appear as low as possible. Likewise, the higher taxes required to fund redistribution provide a strong incentive to engage in complicated accounting tricks to lower your tax bill. These incentives lead to both legal but wasteful *tax avoidance* (doing things explicitly to try to reduce the taxes you owe by taking advantage of loopholes in the tax system), and illegal *tax evasion* (which means not honestly reporting all your income, such as being paid "off the books" and not reporting it to the IRS). With any benefit program, there will always be someone who tries to take advantage of it. Perhaps it's claiming benefits for kids you don't actually have or pretending you have a health issue or disability that you don't actually have (or that isn't severe enough to qualify). Whenever there's a rule limiting who gets benefits, someone will try to break the rule, even if most people don't. To continue the leaky bucket analogy, the problem isn't just that the bucket leaks, it's that some people are actively trying to punch holes in it.

Redistribution is costly, because of:
1. Administrative costs
2. Higher taxes and benefit reductions, both of which can reduce the incentive to work
3. Tax avoidance, evasion, and fraud
. . . which all lead to a leaky bucket.

How leaky is the bucket?   We've detailed three ways in which redistribution programs are costly. The first — administrative costs — is fairly small. The remaining two costs are more important. And they are all linked by a common theme: They arise because redistribution distorts incentives. The more that people respond to these incentives, the greater the cost of redistribution. Thus much of the debate about redistribution is between those who believe the costs are high because people are strongly influenced by these financial incentives, and those who believe that the costs are low because people respond only a little to these incentives.

The Trade-off Between Efficiency and Equality

Let's take stock. Efforts to equalize the distribution of income may help put dollars in the hands of those who value the dollars most, which raises total well-being. But tax and redistribution programs are costly because they distort incentives, thereby reducing work effort. As such, more equal incomes may come at the cost of lower average incomes. Economists refer to this as the *equality-efficiency trade-off*.

To understand the trade-offs, consider the extremes. What would happen if the government redistributed until we all got the same income no matter what? There would be no incentive to work hard, start a new business, or even bother to work since none of your efforts would be rewarded with a higher income. As a result, total production in the economy would plummet. Ultimately, we would all be entitled to an equal-sized slice of a pretty small pie.

At the other extreme, imagine a world with no income redistribution. With no safety net programs to finance, taxes would fall, increasing your incentive to work hard, invest, or start new businesses. The size of the pie would grow, but with no redistribution, but with no redistribution many people who are sick, elderly, unemployed, or have work-limiting disabilities would be destitute. And the size of the pie may not grow by very much as some people may avoid starting new businesses, making investments, or even trying to obtain new jobs, if there is no safety net to help them if they fail. A larger pie is little solace to those surviving on the crumbs.

Extreme efficiency comes at a cost of terrible inequality, while perfect equality comes at a cost of terrible inefficiency. In reality, no one thinks either extreme makes sense. Instead, political debates are typically about how much pie to trade off in order to give everyone a fairer share.

Greater equality doesn't always mean less efficiency. This trade-off isn't a hard and fast rule, and there are cases where there's no efficiency cost to increasing equality. For instance, studies show that societies with greater income inequality typically exhibit less trust, tolerance, and community involvement and more crime. The resulting violence and political unrest can be costly to manage, diverting resources to public safety, prisons, security systems, and other unproductive pursuits.

Income inequality also concentrates political power, which can lead to policies that further increase inequality, such as tax cuts for the rich. These forces may make it difficult for the government to make good policy because they undermine public support for public investment in education, infrastructure, and a clean environment. These adverse outcomes may ultimately lead to weaker economic growth.

There are also instances where social benefits can encourage long-term investment among individuals. For instance, paid maternity leave has been shown to increase women's labor force participation by giving women a much needed break after the birth of a child then facilitates an easy transition back to work after the leave. Closing racial gaps in learning can increase long-term economic growth by encouraging further investment in education among a wider group of people. More generally, government investment in both early childhood education and education through college increases worker productivity.

While it is possible in some cases to make our economy both more equal and more efficient, these cases present the easy choices. But after we exhaust these easy choices, we'll then be stuck with the difficult trade-offs. How do you feel about these trade-offs?

Do the Economics

Let's return to our earlier thought experiment to help you sort out your views about income inequality. Recall that in Figure 14 we evaluated a policy that redistributed $25,000 from each family in the top quintile (earning $200,000) to a family in the bottom quintile (who earned only $20,000). But we didn't account for the leaky bucket. In reality, low-income families will receive less than $25,000, and so greater equality comes at a cost.

Would you choose a bigger pie? Or more equal slices?

canbedone/Shutterstock

- Suppose that 20% leaks out; this would leave a $20,000 grant to the low-income families. Do you think society as a whole would be better off?
- What if 40% leaks out, so each low-income family receives only an extra $15,000?
- What if 60% leaks out, so each low-income family receives only an extra $10,000?
- What if 80% leaks out? Does an extra $5,000 benefit a low-income family more than $25,000 benefits a high-income family?
- Where would you draw the line?

It's an interesting thought experiment. If you were to follow the utilitarian logic of maximizing total well-being as in Figure 14, even 90% leakage would increase total utility in society. What's your answer? Compare the answer you gave with that of your friends, and it will give you a sense of just how different people's views are about inequality. ■

Fairness and Redistribution

As much as economists like to talk about total costs and benefits, the debate about redistribution is also a debate about fairness. In fact, economists have long been concerned about the trade-off between equity — what's fair or just — and efficiency. But that debate requires settling on a notion of fairness, and there are many competing notions of fairness.

Your sense of fairness is likely shaped by many different intuitions. It's important to understand these intuitions, because they guide the real-life decisions that you confront every day. As we investigate these different ideas, try to recognize how each of them shapes your own choices. Bear in mind that these different ideas can coexist, and each may be important to you, to a greater or lesser degree, or in some settings more than others.

Is fairness about equality of outcomes? One common belief is that *more equal outcomes* are fairer. The following simple experiment demonstrates this. Imagine that I give your friend $10, and I tell them to split it with you in whatever way they see fit. But there's one condition: If you don't agree to the deal they offer, neither of you will get anything. What will you do if they offer you only $1? Go ahead, and think about it before reading the next paragraph. Have you decided how to respond? Okay, read on.

Your accountant would urge you to accept the offer of $1 — after all, it's more than the $0 you'll get if you reject the offer. But if you're like most people, you will reject the offer. Experiments repeatedly show that many people reject offers that are below what they regard as a fair share. For most people, this idea of fairness is so important that they'll give up what they view as too small a share, rather than accept an outcome they regard as too unequal. What about you? Would you accept $1? $2? $3? The higher your cutoff, the greater is your willingness-to-pay for fairness. The same reasoning you use in this experiment might lead you to advocate for policies that help create a less unequal distribution of income.

DedMityay/Shutterstock

Are they offering you a fair share?

Is fairness about equality of opportunity? An alternative view of fairness emphasizes equality of *opportunity,* rather than equality of *outcomes.* The basic idea is that fairness requires a level playing field that ensures that people with the same native talents and ambition can compete on equal terms for higher incomes. Consequently, fairness requires eliminating discrimination on the basis of race, gender, or ethnicity. It also requires ensuring that children from low-income families and disadvantaged communities can compete on equal terms with children whose families provide them with private schools, tutors, and family connections. Typically, this requires redistributing resources — such as through support of public schools — to ensure that all kids get a fair shot.

Is fairness about the process? Your sense of fairness may also depend on how fair you find the *process* by which inequalities are generated. For instance, think about grading. Most students argue that if the process is fair — the exams are clear, the grading is consistent, and no one cheats — then it's fair that those who did well earn higher grades than those who didn't. These differences are okay when they are the result of a fair process. If you have this sense of fairness, you may think that income differences are okay, unless an unfair process — such as when someone gets rich by stealing — generates them.

Is fairness about what you deserve? Some people think of fairness in terms of what you *deserve,* or what you contribute to society. Unfortunately, the most highly rewarded people are not always the most deserving. For instance, let's consider the stories of two millionaires. Paris Hilton is a high school dropout with a criminal record. She's rich, because her great-grandfather founded Hilton hotels, and she inherited some of that wealth.

By contrast, Alexa von Tobel took a very different path to financial success. After graduating from Harvard in 2006, she worked in investment banking for two years, working long hours. While in business school she won a prestigious business plan competition for young entrepreneurs. Her idea was a website to provide personal finance advice targeted at young women. She invested her savings in founding her new firm, and put in long hours. She still works long hours, but she's now CEO of a successful startup called LearnVest.

Do both Paris Hilton and Alexa von Tobel "deserve" their riches in equal measure? The big difference between them is the role of luck versus hard work in determining their success. If most people with a lot of money get their money from luck, how much do you think we should redistribute from the rich to the poor? Would you feel differently if Alexa von Tobel were more representative of those with a lot of money?

Is Paris Hilton a deserving millionaire?

What about Alexa von Tobel?

Interpreting the DATA   What explains differences in social spending?

Figure 15 | **Beliefs Determine Social Spending**

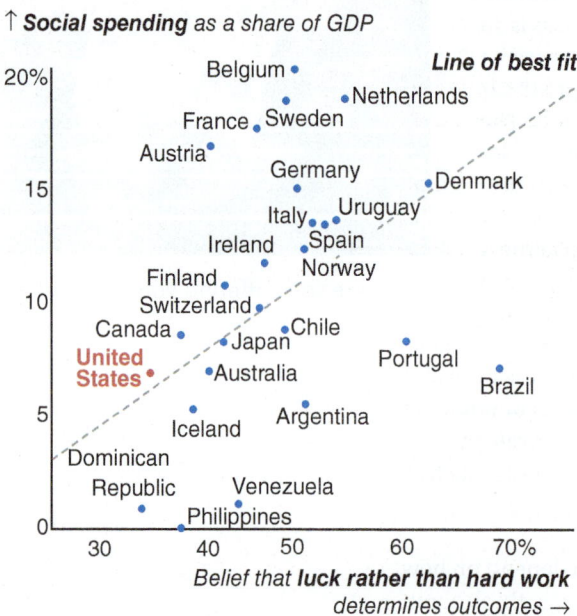

↑ *Social spending* as a share of GDP

Data from: Alberto Alesina and George-Marios Angeletos (2005), "Fairness and Redistribution."

What determines success: Hard work, or luck? If you are an American, chances are you think hard work plays a more significant role than luck. But folks in other wealthy countries are more likely to believe that luck plays an important role in determining income. As shown in Figure 15, researchers have found a clear relationship between social spending and the proportion of the population that believes that luck determines income. The more people believe in luck, the more the country tends to redistribute. ∎

Is fairness best judged behind the veil of ignorance? As remarkable as Alexa von Tobel's success is, perhaps it is due to a different kind of luck. She was lucky to be born with intelligence, drive, and entrepreneurial spirit; to be born into a family and community who helped her develop those talents; and in a time and place where her particular skills are highly rewarded. Without this luck, she might have had a very different life. Despite her skills and effort, her life might have had much worse outcomes. The billionaire investor Warren Buffett says his great wealth is due to his own lucky circumstances: He was lucky to be born a male at a time when men had far more opportunities than women, in a country that provided ample education opportunities, in a family and a country that helped him develop his particular talents, and in a society that rewards them.

Most people believe that before you are born, you haven't done anything to deserve a good or a bad life. You don't know what life circumstances you'll be born into, and if you could choose, many of you would choose to be born with fortunate circumstances. But you don't get to choose. One way to think about whether society should be more or less equal is to ignore the circumstances you happen to have been born into. Instead, ask yourself what you would want if you didn't know what circumstances you would be born into. Philosophers call this technique the veil of ignorance. It's a powerful way of thinking clearly about what makes for a just society. Behind the veil of ignorance, what kind of redistribution would you choose?

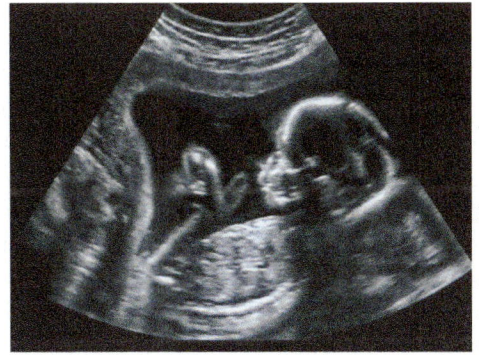

There's no telling what your circumstances will be.

Is fairness about power and class differences? While economists tend to focus on individuals, sociologists broaden the lens to consider class, group, and other social structures. This permits them to analyze how power may reside in particular groups, and how inequalities in the distribution of power both cause and result from income inequality. By this view, the privileged class — the wealthy, the well-connected, those in positions of power — have a lot of control over the political process, and they use this to further their own interests. Even if you don't have much power, your choices and your sense of fairness are likely shaped by your identification with your socioeconomic class, race, ethnicity, religion, gender, or where you are from.

So, of these different perspectives on fairness, which are "right" or "wrong"? Unfortunately, there's no simple answer, and philosophers and others still debate these issues. So it's up to you to decide how much emphasis to put on different notions of fairness.

8.5 | Tying It Together

Three Tools to Form Your Own Views on Redistribution

There's an old story about a person who died crossing a stream with an *average* depth of only six inches. Sure, most of the stream was shallow, but parts of it were deep enough to drown in. Just as the depth of the river varies, so do incomes: You can drown crossing a river that is on average shallow, and you can be deeply in poverty even in a country in which average incomes are high. Understanding the economic risks we face requires understanding income inequality and poverty. As we've seen, high average incomes mask large differences in income, wealth, well-being, and opportunities. Moreover, these inequalities have been rising.

Inequality, poverty, and redistribution are central issues underlying many of our public debates. You are and will continue to be an important participant in these debates in your roles as a voter, an employer, and a community member. This chapter has isolated three key factors that may shape your views about redistribution:

1. Redistribution can raise total well-being by redistributing money to the folks who can benefit most from it. While nearly everyone agrees on this basic logic, there's a spectrum of views about how important it is. If you think people at the bottom of the income distribution are barely getting by, and so are likely to benefit a lot from an extra dollar, then this provides a powerful argument for redistribution. But perhaps you think this argument isn't so convincing. After all, the bottom of the U.S. income distribution still has a high material living standard compared to much of the world. And remember, any dollar we redistribute to a family in need comes out of some other family's budget. The higher the marginal utility of an extra dollar to the families being asked to give up income, the weaker the case for redistribution. You're now an informed player in this debate: You've seen the actual data on the distribution of income. So where are your views along this spectrum?

2. Redistribution occurs via a leaky bucket. The costs of redistribution — the leakage — exists because redistribution also distorts incentives, reducing work effort. Again, there's a spectrum of views about how leaky the bucket is. If people respond strongly to these distorted incentives, then the bucket is extremely leaky. But perhaps people are only vaguely aware of these disincentives, or financial incentives aren't the key factor motivating people to work hard. If so, the bucket may not be that leaky. So far empirical studies haven't fully resolved this debate.

3. Your views about redistribution will depend on your values. It will be affected not only by just how much you value fairness, but also by which concepts of fairness are most important to you. Some perspectives on fairness lead to a greater emphasis on redistribution, and others suggest less. How much weight would you put on equality of outcomes, versus equality of opportunity? Even if you subscribe to equality of opportunity, there's a spectrum of views about what that means. Are we all born with an equal opportunity to succeed, or do income disparities create unequal opportunities, which need to be redressed? How much do income disparities reflect luck — the inherited privilege of the rich, and the bad luck of the poor — versus hard work? Are the processes that lead to economic disparities fair?

There are differences of opinion on whether or how to address issues of poverty and inequality. But nearly everyone agrees that the right analytic framework for analyzing redistribution involves asking three key questions:

1. How large are the benefits of redistributing income to those who most benefit from it?

2. How large are the costs due to the leaky bucket?

3. How fair is this redistribution?

Now that you're equipped with this analytic framework, and also a good sense of the data, it's time to draw your own conclusions. Think hard — these issues shape important choices that you'll face in your family, your work life, and your community.

Chapter 8 Review

Chapter at a Glance

Income Inequality: The differences in annual income between people.

Alternative measures of inequality:

- Permanent income: Your average lifetime income
- Inequality of opportunity: Lack of intergenerational mobility
- Wealth
- Consumption

Poverty

Poverty line: An income level, below which a family is defined to be in poverty.

Absolute poverty: Judges the adequacy of resources relative to an absolute standard of living.

Relative poverty: Judges poverty relative to the material living standards of your contemporary society.

Spells vs. People: Even though a large share of people will experience a short spell of poverty, most of those currently in poverty are in a long-term spell of poverty.

The Ways in Which Government Redistributes

Social safety net: The cash assistance, goods, and services given to those at the bottom of the income distribution.

- Means-tested → Eligibility is based on income and sometimes wealth.
- Minimal support → lifts about a third of people living in poverty out of poverty.

Social insurance: Government-provided insurance against bad outcomes such as unemployment, illness, disability, or outliving your savings.

- Benefits are based on uncertain outcomes
- Everyone pays into social insurance
- Benefits are based on past earnings

Taxes: Pay for the safety net and social insurance.

Progressive tax: A tax where those with more income tend to pay a higher share of their income in taxes.

Federal income taxes are progressive, however some things reduce overall progressivity in the tax system:

- Investment gains are taxed at a lower rate
- Higher-income people get bigger tax breaks
- Many other taxes aren't progressive

Analyzing Redistribution

Question 1: How large are the benefits of redistributing income to those who most benefit from it?

A. The slope of the well-being curve gets flatter as income increases, reflecting *diminishing marginal benefits*.

B. If we redistribute *to the poor, from the rich*:

C. The well-being of the *rich falls a little*.

D. The well-being of *the poor rises a lot*.

Question 2: How large are the costs due to the leaky bucket? Consider:

- Administrative costs
- Higher taxes ↓ work incentive
- Benefits reduction
- Tax avoidance, evasion, and fraud

Question 3: How fair is this redistribution? Consider:

- Equality of outcomes
- Equality of opportunity
- Fair processes
- What you deserve
- Veil of ignorance
- Power and class

The Benefits of Redistribution

Satisfaction

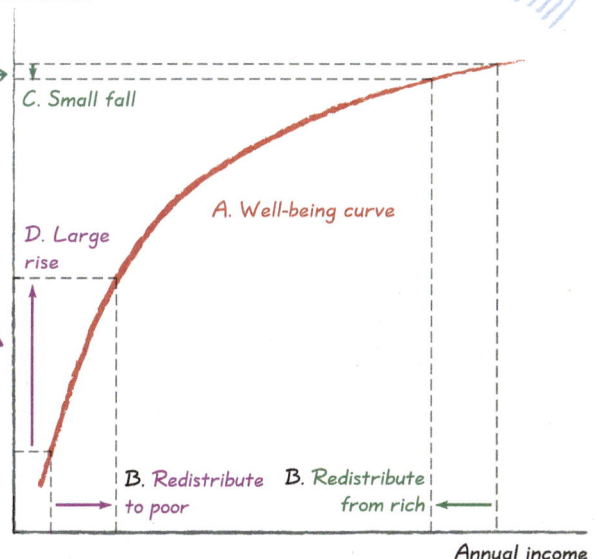

C. Small fall

A. Well-being curve

D. Large rise

B. Redistribute to poor

B. Redistribute from rich

Annual income

Key Terms

absolute poverty, 193

diminishing marginal utility, 203

effective marginal tax rate, 205

income taxes, 201

intergenerational mobility, 191

marginal utility, 203

means-tested programs, 197

permanent income, 191

poverty line, 193

poverty rate, 193

progressive tax, 197

regressive tax, 202

relative poverty, 193

social insurance, 197

utilitarianism, 204

utility, 203

wealth, 190

Study Problems

Learning Objective 8.1 *Measure the extent of economic inequality in the United States.*

1. Discussions of inequality often focus on income inequality. What are two other measures of inequality—and why is it important to consider more than one measure?

2. In the United States, the richest quintile of the population receives 13 times as much income as the poorest quintile. However, the richest quintile spends only four times as much as the poorest quintile. What are some of the reasons that there is such a stark difference between income inequality and consumption inequality?

3. Given your experience and what you've learned from the chapter, what factors lead to a high income? Which are under your control, and which are not?

4. The accompanying table contains data on the income distribution of five states. Pick one and sketch out its income distribution similar to Figure 1. What percentage of all income does the highest-income quintile earn? Using what you learned in the text, if current trends continue, how do you expect the share of income going to the highest-income quintile to change in the next 20 years?

Average Annual Family Income

State	Lowest-income quintile	Second quintile	Middle quintile	Fourth quintile	Highest-income quintile
CA	$14,300	$39,000	$67,700	$109,100	$250,400
FL	$11,900	$30,900	$51,100	$80,600	$190,500
NY	$12,200	$35,100	$63,300	$103,500	$253,100
MN	$15,900	$40,300	$66,100	$100,100	$211,600
TX	$12,900	$34,100	$57,600	$91,700	$208,100

5. Johanna's parents earn about 30% more than the average household. What does this tell you about Johanna's likely income as an adult given the estimates of U.S. intergenerational income mobility discussed in the chapter? What would it tell you about her income if the United States had perfect income mobility?

6. In the United States, we are inundated with statistical claims and information daily—in politics, in media, and in advertising. How do you determine whether a statistic is useful or misleading? Explain your reasoning.

Learning Objective 8.2 *Assess the prevalence and implications of poverty.*

7. Explain whether the U.S. poverty line is an absolute or relative measure.

8. When the original poverty line was created, not everyone who was in poverty had access to a phone or running water in their homes. What are some things you think are necessary to enjoy a reasonable standard of living today? How much do you think it would cost to achieve that reasonable standard of living?

9. Your classmate David tells you that you don't need to worry about people in poverty because most spells of poverty are short. Explain his possible misunderstanding of poverty.

10. Renika has $60,000 in wealth, but the official poverty statistics count her as being in poverty. Explain why this is. If Renika has quit her job in order to go to graduate school, and $60,000 reflects her cash savings, do you agree that she is in poverty? What if Renika is elderly and the $60,000 reflects the value of her rural home?

Learning Objective 8.3 *Discover the ways in which government redistributes.*

11. Two of your friends are in a heated debate. Elena says that the rich pay higher taxes, and Warren argues the rich pay lower taxes by cheating the system. Which of them is correct? Are there ways in which both of them are partially correct? Discuss.

12. At Thanksgiving, your uncle complains that he pays taxes for no reason because the government just hands cash out to people who don't truly deserve or need it. He then says, "The system would work if they made sure people who receive help are the ones who really need it." What tools does the government use to help ensure aid goes to those in need? How can you explain the safety net system to him in an objective way?

13. Your friends, knowing you have studied economics, have started asking you for some advice. Briefly explain

a government assistance option that may be available to them in each of the following scenarios.

a. Your friend Carla has been employed by the same company for two years but was recently laid off.

b. Your cousin Simon always pays his rent on time, but he earns so little that he often doesn't have enough food at the end of the month.

c. Your roommate Chelsea fell while at work and broke her leg. She won't be able to return to work and do her job properly until the injury fully heals.

d. Your friends Jaden and Sandy were doing fine, but since the birth of their new child, their income is strained. They worry about providing medical care for their baby.

14. One way to levy a tax on the things people buy is through a sales tax — a tax on purchases that is typically a percentage of the purchase price. For example, in Michigan everyone, regardless of their income, pays a 6% sales tax on their purchases. Do you think that this tax is progressive, regressive, or neither? Do you think that it has the same impact on low-income and high-income families? Why or why not?

Learning Objective 8.4 *Be prepared to join the debate about income redistribution.*

15. Several studies suggest that the availability of free or low-cost child care increases labor force participation, particularly for mothers. In other words, redistributing to low-income mothers by giving them access to low-cost child care leads them to work more hours. What does this insight say about whether greater equality always comes at a cost of lower efficiency?

16. Imagine that you are preparing your will and are trying to decide how to divide your assets between your two grown children. Your daughter Tonya is a chemical engineer who earns a high income. Your son Terry opted out of college and went to work straight out of high school. Now Terry works in construction; he works just as hard as Tanya, but he is less affluent than she is. Elaborate on each of the following concepts about fairness and distribution illustrated in the chapter.

a. Split your wealth evenly between Terry and Tonya, because you always treat them equally.

b. Leave Terry your wealth to offset the income gap between him and his sister.

c. Leave your money to the child who you think deserves more money.

d. Tell your kids you'll leave your money to whoever does the most to take care of you in your old age.

e. Leave your money to charity instead.

17. At a classroom holiday party, there is a slight shortage of lemonade, so that three people will not have any if everyone at the front of the line fills their cups.

a. One parent tells students to fill their glasses only two-thirds, so that everyone can have some lemonade. Under what notion(s) of fairness is this a fair outcome?

b. A student at the front of the line says that everyone had the same chance to line up, and therefore, those who were goofing around and ended up at the back of the line should lose out and have tap water instead. Under what notion(s) of fairness is this a fair outcome?

c. What do you think a utilitarian would do?

18. Using the figure below, calculate the gain from redistributing $25,000 from those earning $100,000 to those earning $50,000. Why do you think that this gain in well-being is smaller than the redistribution in the example in the chapter, which redistributed from someone earning $200,000 to someone earning $20,000? What are some potential problems with this redistribution plan?

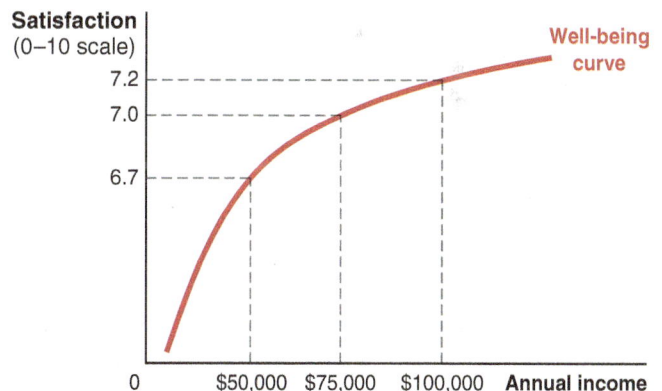

19. Your friend Burrell says that the government should hire fewer social workers in order to reduce the cost of federal assistance programs. He says reducing administrative costs will allow people to pay much lower taxes. Identify the possible flaw in his argument.

PART III:

Macroeconomic Foundations and the Long Run

The Big Picture

It's time to shift focus from *your economy* (microeconomics) to *the economy* (macroeconomics). As we'll discover, there's a close link, because macroeconomic outcomes reflect millions of individual microeconomic decisions. Macro builds on micro and sharpens our focus on the interdependence between all of these decisions.

In the chapters ahead, we'll examine the key measures used to assess an economy's health. We'll start by exploring what **gross domestic product** is, and why it's a closely watched measure of economic health. We'll then ask what drives **economic growth,** analyzing why some countries have become rich, while others remain poor. It matters, because the factors that raise the growth rate can potentially raise billions of people from poverty. We'll then turn to **unemployment,** analyzing what causes joblessness, who it affects, and how costly it can be for society. Finally, we'll examine **inflation** and how **changes in the overall price level** are measured, and what they mean for individuals, for businesses, and for the economy overall.

9 Sizing Up the Economy Using GDP

Measure and analyze total economic activity.

- What is macroeconomics all about?
- What is gross domestic product, and how is it measured?
- How effectively can economists measure living standards?
- How can you compare output and income over time when prices are always changing?
- Are there tricks you can use to help make sense of unimaginably big numbers?

10 Economic Growth

Understand what determines the rate of economic growth.

- How has economic growth shaped modern life?
- What are the ingredients that determine total output?
- Can the economy continue to grow forever?
- Where do new ideas come from, and how do they shape economic growth?
- What role do government institutions play in economic growth?

11 Unemployment

Assess the causes and costs of unemployment.

- Who is unemployed, and who isn't?
- Why are there always some people who are unemployed?
- What causes unemployment?
- What are the social and economic consequences of unemployment?
- How can you protect yourself from the harmful effects of unemployment?

12 Inflation and Money

Evaluate the rate of inflation and its consequences.

- What is inflation, and how is it measured?
- How can you adjust dollar amounts to account for the effect of inflation?
- What is money, what does it do, and how is it affected by inflation?
- What are the consequences of inflation?
- How does inflation trick people into making bad decisions? (And how can you avoid this?)

Sizing Up the Economy Using GDP

Inga Koster was a business student enjoying a semester abroad in Scotland when she tasted her first smoothie. She'd never encountered this delicious blend of fresh fruit and vegetable juices in her native Germany. It was cool and refreshing, and the extra vitamins provided a welcome boost in the face of the bleak Scottish weather.

Six months later she was back in Germany, trying to figure out what to do with the rest of her life. Her attention soon returned to that smoothie. She couldn't find a similar product in nearby supermarkets, which gave her an idea. She teamed up with two friends to write a business plan, and they founded True Fruits, which today is a successful smoothie company with over $50 million in annual sales.

GDP data can help Inga Koster figure out which markets are ripe for smoothies.

Katja Kuhl

True Fruits has now grown to the point that Koster and her team are looking to expand internationally. But where? True Fruits smoothies are a small everyday luxury, so they're most likely to sell well in countries with high incomes. That sets Koster's team searching for data that can tell them which countries have high incomes. This is where GDP comes in.

Our task in this chapter is to figure out how to measure the size of the entire economy. We'll focus on a measure of the size of a country's economy called *gross domestic product—GDP* for short. GDP provides valuable insight into how much is being produced, spent, and earned. It is the most closely tracked measure of macroeconomic performance. The information it provides can help policymakers, investors, and entrepreneurs like Inga Koster make good decisions. You can also use GDP to track how an economy is changing over time. In the next chapter, we'll dig into the determinants of those changes. Our first step is learning how to measure the size of an economy.

You'll also need to know how to interpret what these numbers are telling you. We'll evaluate what GDP counts, what it misses, and how useful it is as a measure of what really matters, which is our living standards. Finally, because this chapter is about how best to size up an economy, we'll develop a few tricks that will help you make better sense of economic numbers.

Chapter Objective

Measure and analyze total economic activity.

9.1 GDP and the Macroeconomy
Learn how to measure the size of an economy using gross domestic product.

9.2 GDP Measures Total Spending, Output, and Income
Analyze GDP as a measure of total spending, output, and income.

9.3 What GDP Captures and What It Misses
Assess GDP as a measure of living standards.

9.4 Real and Nominal GDP
Distinguish between real changes in quantities and the effects of changing prices.

9.5 Millions, Billions, and Trillions
Scale large numbers into something more manageable.

🎙 Podcast
Think Like an Economist
Gross Domestic Product—Adding Up Everything We Do

9.1 GDP and the Macroeconomy

Learning Objective *Learn how to measure the size of an economy using gross domestic product.*

Imagine yourself in six years. You're working in a job you love, living in an apartment you love, and you've decided that it's finally time to upgrade your second-hand couch for a brand-new one. As we'll see in this chapter, this very personal decision will have ripple effects throughout the economy. This is where we shift our attention from *microeconomics* — the study of individual decisions in specific markets — toward *macroeconomics*, which examines the economy as a whole.

From Microeconomics to Macroeconomics

Don't think about micro- and macroeconomics as distinct halves of economics. Rather, think about macroeconomics as being built upon your understanding of microeconomics. The tools you've developed so far — the core principles of economics, a framework for analyzing supply, demand, and equilibrium, and an awareness of market failure — will continue to be useful as you study macroeconomics.

What shifts is our focus, from *individual* income, output, or spending decisions and the implications for individual markets, to the *total* amount of income, output, or spending across all the households, businesses, and levels of government that collectively make up the economy, as shown in Figure 1.

Figure 1 | **Shifting from a Microeconomic to a Macroeconomic Perspective**

	Microeconomics	Macroeconomics
Income	Your individual income.	Total income in the whole country.
Output	The output your business produces.	Total output produced by all businesses in a country.
Spending	Your spending, or the spending of your family or your company.	Total spending across all people, businesses, and the government in a country.

Our task in this chapter is to figure out how to *measure* three things: total income, total output, and total spending within a country. Each of these paths of inquiry lead to the same destination: gross domestic product, or GDP. I'll tell you more about what GDP is in just a moment. But first, we're going to need to dig a bit deeper to see how this one key statistic can measure three different things.

The Circular Flow

Macroeconomics is a lot like traffic. An individual driver who slows down to gawk at a fender-bender will also cause the car behind them to brake, causing the car behind that one to slow as well, and so on. The effects of that one brief slowdown ripple throughout an interdependent system.

The circular flow illustrates interdependence in the macroeconomy. In macroeconomics, as in traffic, your choices depend on what others do, and what others do depends on what people like you do. It's the interdependence principle at work: Your household income depends on how many people businesses hire, which depends on how much output they want to produce, which depends on how much households want to spend, which depends, in turn, on how much income households earn. While your

A microeconomic decision ...

... with macroeconomic consequences.

income might seem like an output of the system, it's also an input in an interdependent cycle, both impacting and impacted by macroeconomic conditions.

The **circular flow diagram** provides a conceptual framework for analyzing these macroeconomic interdependencies. This diagram, shown in Figure 2, illustrates the flow of money and resources through the economy, highlighting the linkages between households — like yours! — and businesses. (To keep things manageable, for now we'll omit the government, the financial sector, and the rest of the world.)

circular flow diagram A simple model of the economy that illustrates how households and businesses are linked.

Figure 2 | The Circular Flow of Income and Resources

The circular flow shows that the **market value of output = spending on output = income received = wages + profits**. **GDP** is defined as the value of these flows.

The **green arrows** show that each **flow of goods or services in one direction** is matched by **a flow of money in the other direction**, shown by the **purple arrows**.

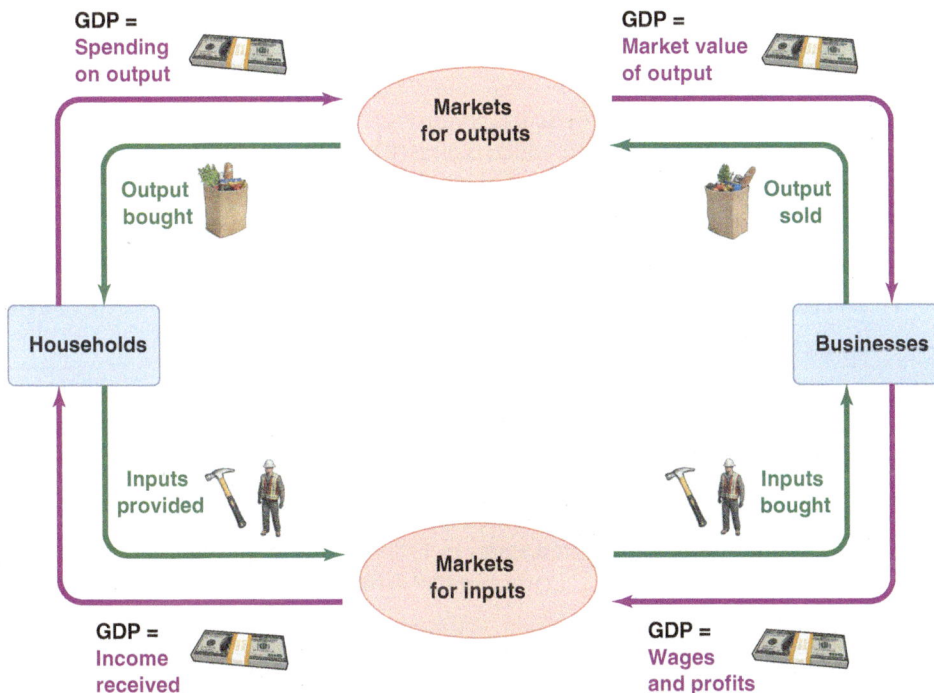

Businesses and households interact in the markets for both inputs and outputs. The circular flow diagram highlights two types of interactions. The top of the diagram shows the market for outputs, where consumers like you demand food, cars, haircuts, and other finished products, and businesses supply them. Your spending — and that of others — pays for this output. The bottom of the diagram shows the market for inputs, where businesses demand labor and capital, and households provide them in return for wages and profits.

All flows of resources are matched by flows of money. The circular flow shows that there are two ways to track what's going on in the economy. First, the green arrows show the flow of *real resources* — the flow of actual inputs like the labor that households sell to businesses, and the flow of actual outputs like the goods and services that businesses sell to households. Second, the purple arrows represent the flow of *money* exchanged for resources and show us the market value of these resource flows. Each flow of real resources is matched by an equal and opposite flow of money.

Total income, total output, and total spending are all equal. The flow of money is a measure of the market value of the resources that are bought, sold, produced, and earned. This reveals that:

- All output produced gets sold at some market price, and so the *market value of total output must be equal to total spending.*
- Every dollar that someone spends is a dollar of income for someone else, and so *total spending must be equal to total income.*

It follows that total output, total spending, and total income in an economy all have the same value. That value is an economy's GDP.

Digging into the Definition of GDP

gross domestic product (GDP) The market value of all final goods and services produced within a country in a year.

GDP, which stands for **gross domestic product (GDP),** is a key measure of economic activity. Specifically, it's the *market value of all final goods and services produced within a country in a year.* Conceptually, you can think about all the things that people get paid to do in a year in the United States. If you tally up the value of all the goods and services they produce, you'll know what our collective output is. Add up all the apples, oranges, haircuts, hot dogs, Hollywood movies, education, housing, cars, shoes, and everything else that was produced, and in 2021, it came to a grand total of $23 trillion.

GDP per person Total GDP divided by the population; also referred to as *GDP per capita.*

A number this big can be hard to wrap your mind around and can be of limited use when comparing GDP over time or across countries. That's why we'll focus on **GDP per person** (also called *GDP per capita*), which is total GDP divided by the population. Dividing $23 trillion per year by 332.2 million people reveals that GDP per person was $69,200 in the United States in 2021. This means that:

- average income per person was $69,200;
- average output per person was $69,200; and
- average spending per person was $69,200.

So what, specifically, do these dollar values capture? The definition of GDP is: The market value of all final goods and services produced within a country in a year. That's a bit of a mouthful, so let's unpack it, piece by piece.

"The market value ..." The grand total of $23 trillion is the *market value* of everything that was produced in the United States in 2021. Getting to this grand total requires adding up the value of everything that was produced, from thousands of armchairs to millions of zippers.

If this sounds a bit like comparing apples and oranges, realize that the old expression is wrong. In fact, you *can* compare apples and oranges — and armchairs and zippers, too — as long as you find a common unit. And for GDP, as with many measures in economics, that common unit is the dollar. GDP adds the total dollars spent on armchairs to the total dollars spent on zippers, and everything in between. This means that GDP values each good according to its market price — valuing each $300 armchair as if it's 100 times as valuable as a $3 zipper. In a competitive market, the price of a product is equal to its marginal benefit, so valuing goods at their market prices effectively values them the same way consumers do.

"... of all ..." GDP aims to be as comprehensive a measure as possible, and thus it attempts to include everything that's produced and sold in markets. This includes both goods (such as armchairs and zippers) and services (such as accounting services and zoo visits). It's not just the stuff that you buy for yourself, but also the things that the government purchases for you, such as public education, vaccine research, and national defense.

As much as GDP tries to be comprehensive, it doesn't include economic activity that occurs outside of markets. This means that the vacuum that you purchased at Walmart is part of GDP, but the cleaning services you provide your household when you use it are not. Paradoxically, if you hire someone to use your vacuum to clean your floors, their work is counted as GDP, but if you do it yourself, your work isn't.

final goods and services Finished goods or services.

"... final goods and services ..." GDP only counts **final goods and services,** which are *finished* goods or services, meaning that they are ready to be consumed by someone. Let's go shopping to understand exactly what we mean by finished goods and services.

You've found your perfect couch at Crate & Barrel. It is considered a final product because you're the final user, so the $1,500 price of the couch gets added to GDP. That $1,500 price includes the value of all the contributions that created your couch, from the tree that's now your couch frame, the lumberjack who felled that tree, the manufacturer who assembled the couch, the driver who trucked it to the store, and the salesperson who sold it to you. Because the price of a final good incorporates all the contributions of the prior stages of production, it's sufficient to just count the final goods produced.

Importantly, this means that GDP doesn't separately include **intermediate goods and services,** which are those goods and services used as *inputs* in the production of other products. You don't want to count both the value of the couch and the value of the wood that went into it, because that would effectively count the cost of the wood twice. That's why when you're trying to figure out how much is produced in the economy, you should focus on *final* goods and services, such as the couch you might buy at Crate & Barrel.

intermediate goods and services Goods or services used as inputs in the production of other products.

Intermediate Good: Wood waiting to be used to build your couch.

"... produced ..." Because GDP measures production, it doesn't count *resale* of existing finished goods. If you buy a new couch from Crate & Barrel, that sale adds to GDP because that couch was just produced. But when you bought your old second-hand couch on Craigslist, your purchase did not add to GDP because it doesn't involve any new production. Second-hand sales merely change the ownership of goods that have already been produced and were previously counted in GDP.

"... within a country ..." GDP measures what we're collectively *producing* domestically, meaning *within the United States.* It includes everything produced in workplaces in the United States — even if they're made by a foreign-owned business, and even if the goods are sold to people outside the United States. It excludes any goods produced in other countries, so it doesn't count goods produced in American-owned factories in other countries and goods produced overseas that will be shipped to U.S. consumers.

Final Good: The couch on the showroom floor, waiting for you to buy it.

"... in a year." When you measure GDP, you add up all the activity that's occurred during a given time period. Most countries add up all the activity that occurs within a year. In order to stay up to date, we typically take four measurements a year (one every three months, which is called a quarter). We add up the production over the four quarters of the year to find out what was produced during the full year. (When the government reports GDP for just one quarter, it usually multiplies it by four, so that it's reporting GDP at an annual rate.)

Notice that GDP is a *flow,* measuring the new output that's produced within a year. Alternatively phrased, it's the new spending you do this year, or the new income you earn this year. Make sure not to confuse the flow of income with wealth, which is the *stock* of assets — everything you own — measured at a specific point in time.

To summarize, GDP is . . .

the market value	→	*Value each product at its market price*
of all	→	*Include all goods and services*
final goods and services	→	*Count only final goods and services, omitting intermediate goods*
produced	→	*Omit resale of already-produced goods*
within a country	→	*Include all goods produced within the United States (even by foreign-owned businesses), but exclude goods produced overseas (even by American-owned businesses)*
in a year.	→	*Add up the flow of output over a year*

9.2 GDP Measures Total Spending, Output, and Income

Learning Objective *Analyze GDP as a measure of total spending, output, and income.*

The fact that GDP is three things at once — total spending, total output, and total income — is not just a surprising insight; it's also useful. It means that there are three different ways to measure GDP:

- by adding up every dollar of *spending*;
- by adding up every dollar's worth of *output* produced; or
- by adding up every dollar of *income* earned.

In order to get a good estimate of the state of the economy, the government does all three. That's why our next task is to explore how each of these measures is compiled and to investigate the useful business intelligence that each reveals. The simplest way to do this is to follow a single item on its path through the economy, which brings us back to your future couch.

Your couch's story begins with Bennett Lumber, a family-owned lumber company in Washington. Bennett Lumber chops down and transforms trees into lumber that can be used to make furniture. The company might sell $400 worth of lumber to McCreary Modern, a furniture manufacturer in North Carolina. McCreary Modern turns that lumber into a couch that it will sell to a retailer, such as Crate & Barrel, for $1,000. (While couches also need other inputs like fabric, cushion fillings, nails, and glue, we'll put these aside for now to keep things simple.) Crate & Barrel markets the couch and sells it to you for $1,500.

As we're about to discover, there are three different ways to figure out how much GDP this little story just created, and they all lead to the same answer.

Perspective 1: GDP Measures Total Spending

The first perspective on GDP comes from viewing it as the sum of total spending in the economy. Tracking spending is useful, because you can figure out who's doing all that spending — whether it's businesses, households, governments, or foreigners — and what they're buying.

GDP is total spending on final goods. This method of measuring GDP simply adds up total spending in the economy. But remember: GDP includes only spending on final goods, so the key transaction occurs when the *final user* buys the couch at Crate & Barrel. We focus on the final good — the Crate & Barrel couch — because its price embodies the productive efforts of the earlier stages of production at Bennett Lumber and McCreary Modern. Consequently, total spending on final goods — and hence the GDP created by this chain of production — is $1,500.

GDP equals total spending on final goods

which embodies the value created at earlier stages

Raw materials	Processed materials	Wholesale goods	Final goods
$0	$400	$1,000	$1,500

Photo left to right: Alalal/Shutterstock.com; Vasily Gamayunov/Shutterstock

GDP includes new inventories. Because GDP is a measure of production (that's the "P" in "GDP"), it counts goods in the year they're *made,* regardless of the year in which they're *sold.* This means that it's important to also count new inventories — goods that have been produced but not yet sold — as part of GDP. And so when more unsold couches sit in Crate & Barrel's showrooms or warehouses, they're included in GDP, because they've been produced. You can think of this as a form of spending — imagine that Crate & Barrel's inventory division bought those couches from its couch division. Because everything that's produced will either be bought this year or stored as inventories, the inclusion of inventories in GDP ensures that total spending equals total output.

GDP is the sum of consumption, investment, government purchases, and net exports. Now here's the big payoff to measuring GDP by tracking spending: You can track who's doing all that spending and what they're buying. Indeed, total GDP is calculated by adding up the value of different types of spending.

Economists often use abbreviations to describe each type of spending: $\underline{C}$onsumption is denoted C; $\underline{I}$nvestment is I, $\underline{G}$overnment purchases are G, and $\underline{N}$et e$\underline{X}$ports are NX. Finally, GDP is denoted Y. (Why Y? Y not.)

Because GDP is the sum of each type of spending, it's calculated as follows:

$$\underbrace{Y}_{\text{GDP}} = \underbrace{C}_{\text{Consumption}} + \underbrace{I}_{\text{Investment}} + \underbrace{G}_{\substack{\text{Government} \\ \text{purchases}}} + \underbrace{NX}_{\text{Net exports}}$$

This equation is an identity, which means that it's always true because it describes the definition of GDP. That's because consumption, investment (including investment in inventories), government purchases, and net exports collectively define all the goods and services produced in the economy.

As a result, we measure GDP by adding total spending on consumption, investment, government purchases, and net exports. Figure 3 illustrates these calculations.

Okay, that's the big picture. Now, let's take a look at the details of each of these types of spending.

Household purchases are typically called consumption. When your household buys goods and services, it's counted in GDP as **consumption.** Your consumption includes goods such as food, clothes, and gas, as well as services such as doctor visits, bus fares, and your cell phone bill. It also includes *durable goods,* which are long-lasting goods such as cars, couches, and washing machines. Even though durable goods take many years to fully use, they're counted as consumption in the year that they're purchased.

The money people spend on rent is also counted in GDP as a form of consumption. This raises a tricky issue, because homeowners enjoy a similar stream of benefits in terms of shelter and comfort, but they don't pay any rent. In order to treat all housing services equally, GDP also counts an *imputed rent* — an estimate of the rental value of your home — that you (the consumer of housing services) effectively pay to yourself (the homeowner). We'll dig deeper into consumption in Chapter 13.

> In macroeconomics:
> **Y** stands for **GDP**
> **C** is for **Consumption**
> **I** is for **Investment**
> **G** refers to **Government purchases**
> **NX** stands for **Net exports**

Figure 3 | **GDP Is the Sum of All Spending on Final Goods and Services**

= *Consumption* + *Investment* + *Government purchases* + *Net exports*

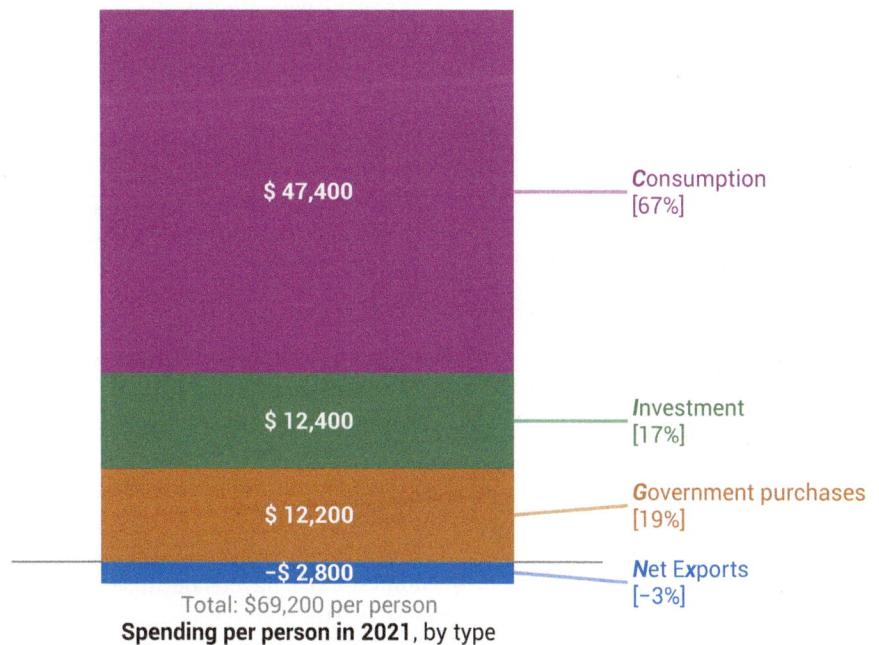

$47,400 — Consumption [67%]

$12,400 — Investment [17%]

$12,200 — Government purchases [19%]

–$2,800 — Net Exports [–3%]

Total: $69,200 per person

Spending per person in 2021, by type

Data from: Bureau of Economic Analysis.

consumption Household spending on final goods and services.

investment Spending on new capital assets that increase the economy's productive capacity.

This is an investment.

government purchases Government purchases of goods and services.

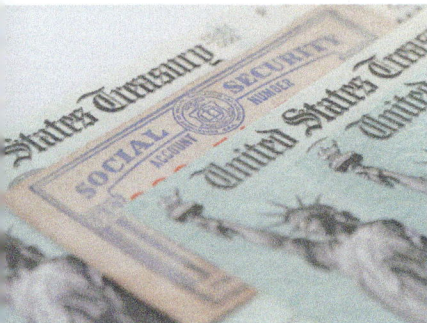

Social Security payments transfer income and so they don't count toward GDP.

transfer payments Payments that transfer income from one person to another.

exports Goods or services produced domestically and purchased by foreign buyers.

imports Goods or services produced overseas and purchased by domestic buyers.

net exports Spending on exports minus spending on imports.

Business purchases are typically called investment. Economists use the word **investment** to refer to spending on new capital assets that increase the economy's productive capacity. It includes both the *purchase* and the *production* of long-lived assets that contribute to future production. Building a factory is an investment because it will produce goods for many years. Office furniture, equipment, airplanes, and just about any long-lasting good used in a business is an investment. It is an investment because those goods will be used to produce more goods and services. Business investment also includes spending on research and development. New inventories are counted as a form of investment because they'll lead to future sales.

But be careful, because this macroeconomic definition of the word *investment* is very different from its everyday usage. Remember, GDP is about production, so a macroeconomist says that investment occurs only when something new — such as a newly constructed office building — is *produced*. By contrast, casual conversations about "investing," are often about depositing your money in the bank, buying stocks, or purchasing a block of land. But when you put your money in the bank, you're not actually buying anything — you're saving it to spend later. When you buy stocks, you're usually buying a share of an *existing* business from someone else. And when you buy a block of land, you're buying an existing asset. Because GDP measures what's produced, it doesn't count the storage of your savings, the resale of stock in existing companies, or the resale of real estate as investment.

While most investment is done by businesses, when your household buys a newly built home, it counts as investment, because it increases the economy's capacity to provide housing services. And so newly built houses are added to GDP as residential investment. But if you buy an existing house, you're simply changing who owns an existing asset, so your purchase isn't included in GDP. We'll take a deep dive into investment in Chapter 14.

Government purchases are called ... government purchases. Whenever the government buys stuff — goods and services — it's counted as **government purchases.** This includes local government spending on schools, state government expenditures on highways, and federal government outlays on the military.

When the government pays the salary of a teacher or a corporal in the Marines, it's paying them to produce educational or defense services, so their salaries are counted in GDP as government purchases. But a lot of government spending doesn't count as government purchases. For instance, the government sends out billions of dollars in Social Security and unemployment insurance checks. These are examples of **transfer payments,** which transfer income from one entity (the government) to another (an individual). Because transfer payments involve no new production of goods or services, they're not counted in GDP. The term *government purchases* might sound a bit clunky, but the word *purchases* is there to remind you that it's all about the stuff the government buys (and so excludes transfers). We'll take a closer look at government spending in Chapter 23.

Foreign purchases of our goods less our purchases of foreign goods is called net exports. Finally, we need to account for linkages with the global economy, while remembering that GDP measures *domestic production*. **Exports** are goods and services that we produce domestically in the United States and sell to people and businesses in other countries. Because exports are *produced* domestically, this spending is included in GDP.

Imports are goods and services that are produced in other countries and purchased by domestic U.S. buyers. Because imports aren't produced domestically, they're *excluded* from GDP. This means that the money you spend on Canadian maple syrup isn't included in U.S. GDP. This gets a bit tricky because that syrup was purchased by a household and so was already counted as consumption. Indeed, all imports of final goods and services are already counted as either consumption, investment, or government purchases (depending on who bought them). So to exclude any influence of foreign-produced goods and services from GDP, we need to subtract spending on imports from total spending.

As a result, GDP adds in exports and subtracts imports. This is why it counts **net exports,** which is spending on exports minus spending on imports. But don't let this confuse you into thinking that imports subtract from GDP. They don't. They're simply *excluded* from GDP — they're neither a positive nor a negative. But in *calculating* GDP, we need to subtract spending on imports to offset the fact that spending on imports has already been counted in the other categories.

We'll explore imports and exports further in Chapter 16.

Perspective 2: GDP Is Total Output

An alternative perspective views GDP as the sum of total output. It's a useful perspective because it highlights what's being made and by whom. It provides an economy-wide benchmark against which you can compare your company's size and productivity. And by tracking goods through the production process, this perspective maps the structure of production, so that you can assess which sectors are large (Hint: the services sector), which are growing, and how interdependent they are.

GDP is the sum of value added at each stage of production. So far, we've seen that GDP is equal to total *spending*. Because every dollar that is spent buys someone else's output, it's also a measure of the market value of total *output*. This in turn implies that we can measure GDP by adding up total output across all businesses.

Economists have devised a clever way to measure the output of each business involved in a complicated production process. It's based on the idea that at each step of the production process, a company uses materials prepared by others, and then transforms them into something more valuable. The amount by which your company increases the value of an item is called its **value added,** and it's a measure of your contribution toward producing that item. This means that your company's value added is your total sales minus the cost of the intermediate goods and services you bought from other firms.

value added The amount by which the value of an item is increased at each stage of production.

= Total sales – Cost of intermediate inputs

Each stage of the production process before the final sale adds value. Let's return to your couch to really explore these issues. The production process began when Bennett Lumber took raw material (a tree) and turned it into lumber that it sold to McCreary Modern for $400. That tree cost Bennett Lumber nothing (we'll come back later to the problems of valuing natural resources as if they're free). And so the work it did — felling the tree, sawing it into planks, and drying and finishing it into commercial-grade lumber that sold for $400 — created $400 of value. Next, McCreary Modern used that $400 worth of lumber and turned it into a couch that it sold to a retailer for $1,000, which means that transforming raw lumber into a couch added $600 of value (again, for simplicity, we're ignoring fabric, cushion fillings, etc.). The couch then went to Crate & Barrel, which advertised it and sold it to you. Crate & Barrel bought the couch for $1,000 and sold it for $1,500, which means that its efforts — online ads, the sales staff, and its retail location — added $500 of value.

GDP equals total output
which is measured as the sum of value added at each stage

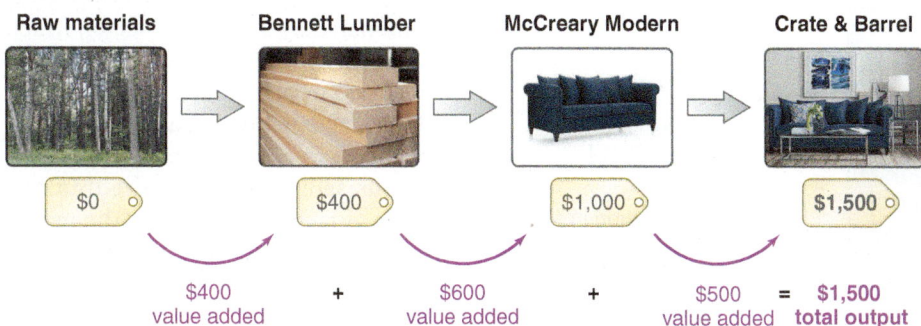

Raw materials	Bennett Lumber	McCreary Modern	Crate & Barrel
$0	$400	$1,000	$1,500

$400 value added + $600 value added + $500 value added = **$1,500 total output**

Photo left to right: Alalal/Shutterstock; Vasily Gamayunov/Shutterstock

Add the output of each firm in this production chain — $400 of value added by Bennett Lumber plus $600 from McCreary Modern plus $500 by Crate & Barrel — and you'll discover that this production process added $1,500 to GDP. Now, think about all the couches — and cars and coffees and cab rides — sold every day. Total GDP is the sum of the value added across all businesses in the economy.

Total output and total spending are equal (and they both equal GDP). This calculation of total output yields the exact same answer as calculating GDP based on spending on final goods. Both suggest the couch adds $1,500 to GDP.

I didn't "fix" the numbers to work this way. Rather, it always works out this way because of a deeper truth. The spending-based measure of GDP focuses on the value of the couch once it emerges from the final stage of production. The output-based measure takes a different perspective, adding up the value created at each stage along the way. But these are just two different perspectives on the same couch, and they must yield the same answer because whatever value that couch has at the end of the process (that's the spending-based measure) must have accrued somewhere along the way (which is what the sum of value added measures).

Do the Economics

Let's work through the value added of one particular business. In 2021, Harley Davidson reported revenue of $4.5 billion from sales of motorcycles and related products. It used $3.2 billion in intermediate inputs to make this output. What was its value added?

$$Value\ added = \$4.9\ billion - \$3.2\ billion = \$1.7\ billion$$

As a result, Harley Davidson's motorcycles added $1.3 billion to GDP in the United States.

Output of Harley Davidson Motorcycles	
Total sales	$4.5 billion
less intermediate inputs	−$3.2 billion
equals value added	*= $1.3 billion added to GDP*

2021 Data from: Harley Davidson annual report.

You can use the idea of value added to calculate the total GDP created by your favorite business. Many companies release data on their sales and costs, and a quick Google search will turn up annual reports that provide you the data you need. ∎

Production of services dominates goods. Once you've measured the value added by businesses in different sectors of the economy, measuring total output simply requires adding up the output across each of these sectors, as shown in Figure 4. These data are particularly valuable because they reveal the structure of production. They show that the modern U.S. economy is dominated by the service sector, which accounts for 82% of output. By contrast, goods account for only 17% of the economy. Make sure that your mental image of a modern economy matches this service-based reality. If you're thinking about a factory, you've got the wrong image. It's far more realistic to picture banks, hospitals, schools, restaurants, wholesalers, and retailers, as well as consulting, legal, and accounting firms.

While Figure 4 shows total output broken down into a handful of broad

Figure 4 | **GDP Is the Sum of All Output Produced**

= *Sum of value-added produced by firms in each industry*
= *Goods produced* + *Services produced*

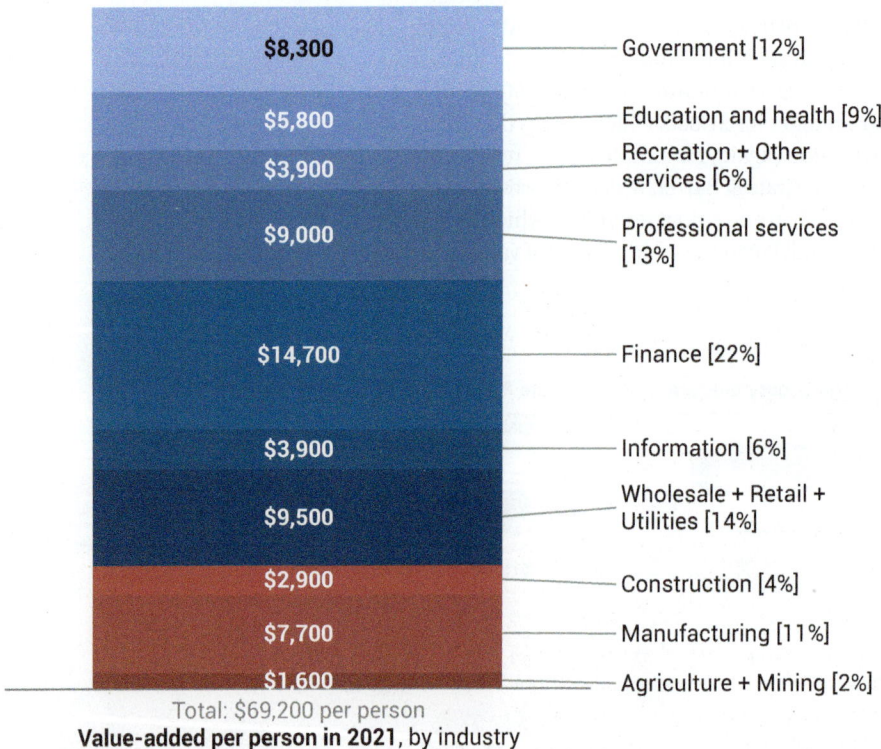

Value	Industry
$8,300	Government [12%]
$5,800	Education and health [9%]
$3,900	Recreation + Other services [6%]
$9,000	Professional services [13%]
$14,700	Finance [22%]
$3,900	Information [6%]
$9,500	Wholesale + Retail + Utilities [14%]
$2,900	Construction [4%]
$7,700	Manufacturing [11%]
$1,600	Agriculture + Mining [2%]

Total: $69,200 per person
Value-added per person in 2021, by industry

Data from: Bureau of Economic Analysis.

industries, you can dive into the numbers and drill down into dozens of subsectors, comparing output of, say, paper products to water transportation.

Perspective 3: GDP Measures Total Income

Our final perspective views GDP as the sum of all incomes. It's a particularly useful perspective, because GDP per person measures average income, which you can use to assess the material living standards in a country and whether they're improving. And by tracking whether this income is going to workers as wages or to business owners as profits, this perspective tells you who is enjoying the fruits of all this economic activity.

GDP is total income, which is the sum of total wages and total profits. There are two sides to every transaction — a buyer and a seller — and so every dollar that a buyer spends also registers as a dollar of income to a seller. This means that we can also measure GDP by adding up the *total income* earned in productive activities. That means adding up all of the wages earned by workers, as well as the profits that shareholders and business owners earn.

Let's return to the couch to see how this plays out. Bennett Lumber started with raw materials that cost it nothing, and ended up with $400 of revenue. In terms of income flows, it paid $300 in wages to its workers, leaving it with a $100 profit. McCreary Modern got $1,000 of revenue from selling its couch, paid $400 to Bennett Lumber, and spent an additional $500 on wages, so the company was left with $100 in profit. Finally, Crate & Barrel got $1,500 from selling you a couch it bought for $1,000. It paid $200 in wages and salaries, which left it with $300 in profit. Across all three firms, total wages add up to $1,000 and total profits add up to $500.

GDP equals the sum of all income = total wages + total profits

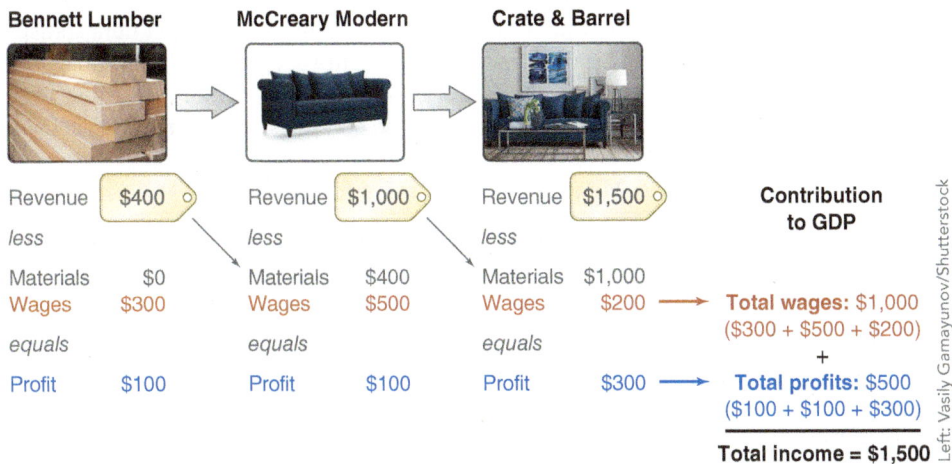

Bennett Lumber		McCreary Modern		Crate & Barrel		
Revenue	$400	Revenue	$1,000	Revenue	$1,500	**Contribution to GDP**
less		*less*		*less*		
Materials	$0	Materials	$400	Materials	$1,000	
Wages	$300	Wages	$500	Wages	$200	**Total wages: $1,000** ($300 + $500 + $200)
equals		*equals*		*equals*		+
Profit	$100	Profit	$100	Profit	$300	**Total profits: $500** ($100 + $100 + $300)
						Total income = $1,500

Left: Vasily Gamayunov/Shutterstock

Total income is the sum of wages and profits, so measuring GDP as total income suggests that this couch added $1,000 + $500 = $1,500 to GDP. More generally, GDP can be calculated as the sum of all wages earned by workers plus profits earned by the owners of capital.

Capital gains and losses aren't counted as new income. Just as your purchase of an existing asset isn't counted as new investment, your earnings from selling an existing asset (such as shares, land, or other financial assets) doesn't count as new income. Capital gains don't count as GDP even when you sell assets at a higher price than you paid for them, because they're simply the resale of existing assets rather than income earned from productive activity. Nothing is gained from speculative transactions, because a seller's gain from getting a higher price is offset by the buyer's loss at having to pay that higher price.

Figure 5 | Labor's Share of GDP Fell over Recent Decades

Share of GDP paid to workers

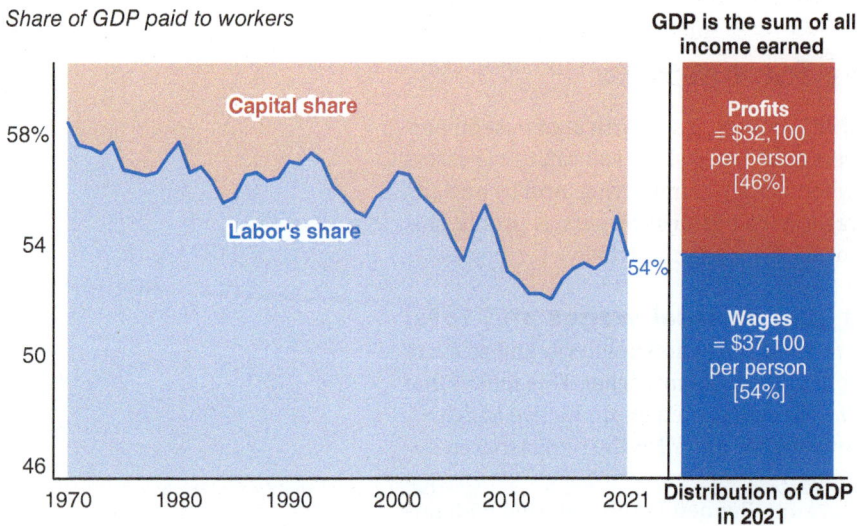

Data from: Bureau of Economic Analysis.

Labor's share of total income is declining. These income-based data are useful, because they describe how we divide the economic pie between workers and the owners of capital. As such, they reveal the extent to which GDP boosts the purchasing power of households, versus the financial status of businesses.

The *labor share* describes the share of total income that goes to workers as wages, salaries, and benefits. Historically, workers received nearly two-thirds of all income, but as Figure 5 illustrates, the labor share has declined over recent decades. In turn, the *capital share*—the share of income that goes to the owners of capital—has risen. Because capital is owned by a smaller and higher income group of Americans, this rising capital share has led to rising income inequality.

Putting It All Together

Okay, it's time to take a breath and look at the big picture to see how far we've come. We started by *defining* GDP as "the market value of all final goods and services produced within a country in a year." Next came the *conceptual insight* that GDP is a measure of total spending, of total output, and of total income. Finally, we've dug into the practical implication that we can *measure* GDP by adding total spending, total output, or total income.

Even though these each measure the same thing—GDP—U.S. government statisticians give them different names, which are listed in Figure 6. While total spending, total output, and total income are the same in *theory,* they get different names because real-world *measurements* can differ because each relies on different sources of imperfect data.

Figure 6 | Three Ways to Measure the Same Thing

GDP is . . .	. . . it can be measured as . . .	. . . that measurement is called
Total spending	$Y = C + I + G + NX$	"Gross Domestic Product"
Total output	Sum of value added	"Value Added"
Total income	Total wages + Total profits	"Gross Domestic Income"

> GDP measures:
> 1. Total spending
> 2. Total output
> 3. Total income

You're now equipped to make sense of all these data. If you want to dig in deeper, point your browser to www.bea.gov/national/index.htm#gdp.

9.3 What GDP Captures and What It Misses

Learning Objective *Assess GDP as a measure of living standards.*

There's an old saying in business that "what gets measured gets managed." Measuring an activity helps you understand it and provides insight into how to improve it. Managers focus on the stuff that's measured because those are the outcomes for which they are held accountable. This idea has implications for macroeconomics, too, because it suggests that policymakers tend to focus on outcomes that are well measured.

And that in turn raises important questions: Is GDP an adequate gauge of economic conditions? Does it provide a reliable measure of living standards or, more ambitiously, the quality of life?

Limitations of GDP

Former U.S. Senator Robert F. Kennedy famously argued that GDP misses much of what's important to a good society. He said:

> [GDP] does not allow for the health of our children, the quality of their education, or the joy of their play. It does not include the beauty of our poetry or the strength of our marriages, the intelligence of our public debate or the integrity of our public officials. It measures neither our courage, nor our wisdom, nor our devotion to our country. It measures everything, in short, except that which makes life worthwhile.

Kennedy was right that GDP misses a lot of what's important. Let's explore some of the most important limitations of GDP.

Limitation 1: Prices are not values. Oscar Wilde once wrote that the definition of a cynic is one who "knows the price of everything but the value of nothing." He might have said the same about GDP. That's because GDP is the *market value* of all goods and services, so it effectively assigns each item a *value* equal to its *market price.*

But our values are not the same as market prices. The paperback edition of Maya Angelou's novel *I Know Why the Caged Bird Sings* — a classic work of American fiction — sells for $7.99. That's about half the price of *This Book Loves You*, by popular YouTuber PewDiePie, which is priced at $15.99 and includes such profound advice as "Don't be yourself. Be a pizza. Everyone loves pizza." Most people would say that Angelou's work is more valuable, but at these prices, each copy of PewDiePie's book adds more to GDP.

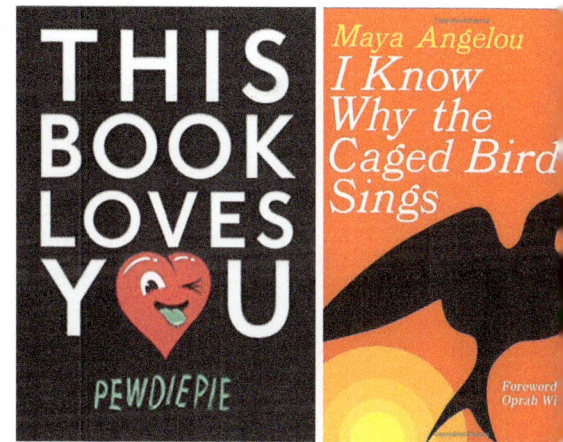

Which is worth more? Meme-ish wisdom for $15.99, or a literary classic for $7.99?

The argument for valuing goods at their market prices is that in a perfectly competitive market, the price is equal to the marginal benefit of the last good or service purchased. But this still misses a lot. Consider the value of clean water. When the price of water is low, you keep buying it until the last gallon has a pretty low marginal benefit, perhaps using it to wash your car. So the price reflects the pretty low marginal benefit of the last gallon. But the earlier gallons — the gallons of drinking water necessary to prevent you from dying of dehydration — are much more valuable. The problem is that GDP counts only your spending on a good, but your benefit is often much larger if you enjoy *consumer surplus.* This is a particularly pressing problem when it comes to analyzing the value of internet services such as Google, Snapchat, or Wikipedia, each of which is sold at a price of zero, and so counts very little toward GDP. Additionally, market failures can mean that the price of a good or service may not be equal to a consumer's marginal benefit.

Limitation 2: Nonmarket activities — including household production — are excluded. GDP measures only goods and services that are sold in markets, which misses a lot of productive activity. You probably do your own laundry, clean your own apartment, and cook your own meals. If you have kids or pets, you likely spend a lot of time taking care of them. All of this activity is productive — you're creating valuable goods and services — but none of it is counted in GDP. One recent estimate suggests that the value of all the uncounted housework, cooking, odd jobs, yard work, shopping, and child care that we do for ourselves over the course of a year adds up to roughly $9,000 per person.

The omission of nonmarket activities can lead to some weird results. If instead of doing these tasks for ourselves, we paid others to do them, they would suddenly be considered market activities that are counted toward GDP. As a result, measured GDP per person would suddenly be $9,000 higher, even though the total amount of productive activity would be exactly the same.

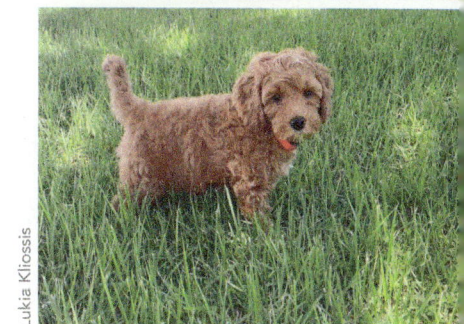

Taking care of your babies won't count toward GDP.

The $60 you earned babysitting is probably not in GDP.

Limitation 3: The shadow economy is missing. A large amount of economic activity occurs "in the shadows," purposely conducted out of view of the government, because it involves illegal products such as drugs, banned services such as gambling, businesses operating without necessary licenses, workplaces that flout labor standards, or the use of cash to avoid paying taxes. Together, these activities are called the *shadow economy*. Many of these activities occur deep enough in the shadows that they're unmeasured, and thus they're effectively excluded from GDP. The shadow economy includes organized crime, the guitarist performing for tips on a street corner, and the plumber who repaired your sink and asked for cash payment. It may even include the $60 you were paid to babysit last weekend, if neither you nor the family plan to report that payment in government surveys.

Interpreting the DATA   Measuring the shadow economy

Most transactions in the shadow economy occur in cash, and so excessively strong demand for currency for transactions is an indicator of a thriving shadow economy. Indeed, it's a bit suspicious that in 2017 there was $1,571 billion of U.S. dollars in circulation, of which $1,252 billion was in $100 bills. That's roughly 38 Benjamin Franklins per American, even though they're rarely used in everyday transactions. While many of these high-value bills are held by people outside the United States, it's likely that many of them are used in the shadow economy to avoid an incriminating paper trail.

Economists have used insights like this to guesstimate the size of the shadow economy. The results, shown in Figure 7, suggest that it's quite large. Counting the shadow economy would boost GDP in the United States by about 8%. It's even bigger in many other countries, partly because their higher taxes and more restrictive regulations provide a greater incentive to push economic activity into the shadows.

Figure 7 | How Much Larger Would GDP Be if It Counted the Shadow Economy?

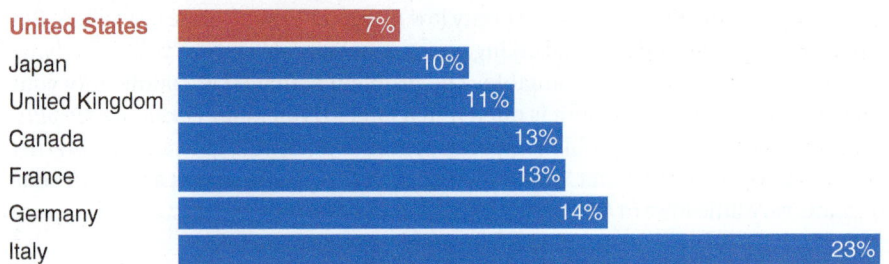

Country	Percentage
United States	7%
Japan	10%
United Kingdom	11%
Canada	13%
France	13%
Germany	14%
Italy	23%

Data from: Enste, Dominik H., "The Shadow Economy in Industrial Countries." ■

Destruction or production?

Limitation 4: Environmental degradation isn't counted. When Bennett Lumber cuts down trees and sells the lumber for $400, this is counted as adding $400 to GDP. Effectively, GDP treats natural resources as if they have no value until they're transformed into something else. What you might see as *destruction* — the clear-cutting of an old-growth forest — GDP counts as *production,* because it only sees new lumber being produced. Because GDP treats nature as if it's free, it ignores the costs of environmental degradation, fails to account for biodiversity, and takes no account of global warming, even as it counts the output of polluting factories as positive contributions.

Limitation 5: Leisure doesn't count. One way to produce more is to work more. If your company doesn't offer paid vacation time, you might choose to clock more hours at work rather than take unpaid leave. You'll earn more income, but your quality of life might suffer. Similarly, if everyone worked more, GDP would get a boost. But that extra output comes with a cost that GDP ignores. To understand the cost of working, you can apply the opportunity cost principle, which reminds you to ask, "Or what?" If you weren't working, what would you be doing? Would you be spending time with your friends or family? Baking your own bread? Watching a movie? Whatever you choose, a day of work means a day less of leisure. The problem is that GDP counts the benefit of work — more income! — but omits the cost, which is less leisure.

Boosting happiness, but not GDP.

EVERYDAY Economics   **Would you rather live in the United States or in France?**

France has instituted a 35-hour workweek, requiring employers to pay overtime or offer "rest days" to compensate for any extra hours worked. By contrast, in the United States the typical workweek is 40 hours. France also requires that workers have access to substantial paid vacation time, paid sick leave, and paid parental leave. None of these are required in the United States. Add it all up, and over the course of a year, a typical French employee works 300–400 fewer hours than their American counterpart. That's the equivalent of ten fewer workweeks! But this comes at a cost. The average income in France — that is, GDP per person — is 28% lower than it is in the United States. Which would you prefer: more money, or more time off? ■

The French have more time to sit in cafés than Americans do, but less money to spend in them.

Limitation 6: GDP ignores distribution. You can think of GDP as measuring the size of our economic pie, with GDP per person measuring the size of the average slice. But what really matters to people is their *actual* slice, not the average slice. And so the distribution of income matters, too. This point has become particularly salient over recent decades, because much of the income growth since the 1980s has accrued to the very richest households. Figure 8 shows that even as the living standards of the *average* American adult have risen rapidly, the living standards of those in the bottom half of the income distribution have barely risen.

Limitations of GDP:
1. Prices are not values.
2. Nonmarket activities — including household production — are excluded.
3. The shadow economy is missing.
4. Environmental degradation isn't counted.
5. Leisure doesn't count.
6. GDP ignores distribution.

Figure 8 | **Average Income Has Risen but Not for the Poorest Half**

Real national income per adult (before tax)

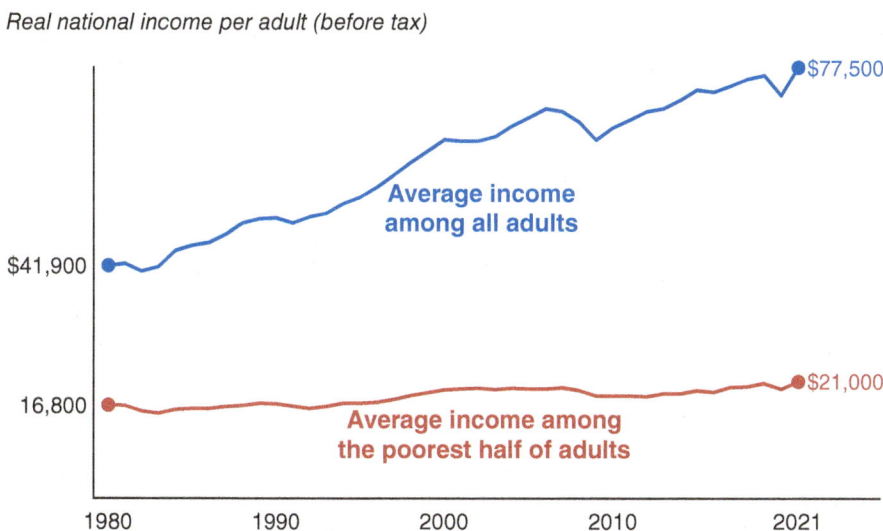

Data from: World Inequality Database.

GDP as a Measure of Living Standards

While GDP leaves out a lot, it remains a useful indicator of national well-being. That's because the higher GDP per person is, the easier it is to invest in children's health, in education, in creating beautiful art and poetry, and in taking the time to invest in your personal relationships. By this argument, it's not that GDP measures what matters, but rather that it measures the *resources* that a society has available to pursue what matters. If we use those resources well, then people who live in countries with high GDP per person will live happier, more fulfilling lives.

Indeed, Figure 9 illustrates that people who live in countries with higher GDP per person tend to enjoy better life outcomes. The top left panel shows the results of surveys asking people to rate how satisfied they are with their lives on a 0–10 scale. The average score is much higher in countries with high GDP. Other surveys reveal that people in countries with high GDP are more likely to rate themselves as being happy, they're more likely to smile or laugh a lot, and they're more likely to feel that they're treated with respect. They're also less likely to experience pain and less likely to feel depressed.

Figure 9 | Higher GDP Is Correlated with Better Life Outcomes

Higher GDP is associated with greater life satisfaction

↑ *Average life satisfaction (0-10 scale)*

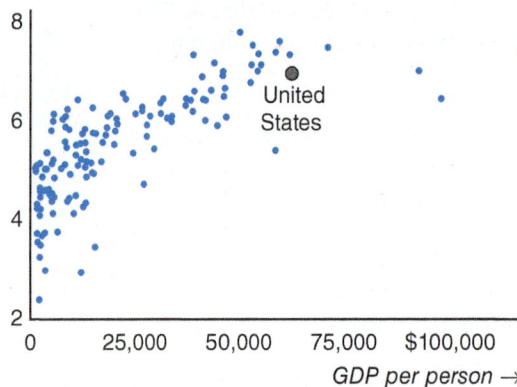

Higher GDP is associated with more education

↑ *Average years of schooling*

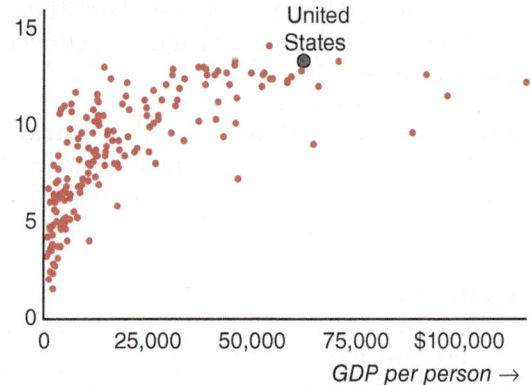

Higher GDP is associated with less infant mortality

↑ *Infant deaths per thousand live births*

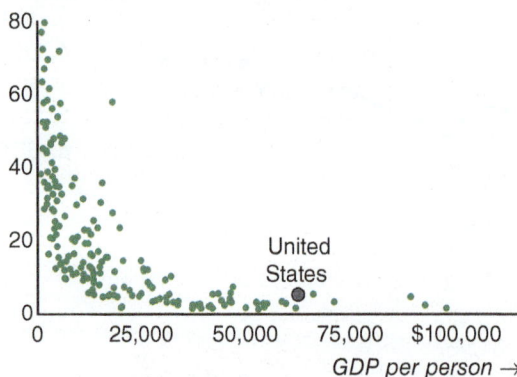

Higher GDP is associated with longer life expectancy

↑ *Life expectancy at birth, in years*

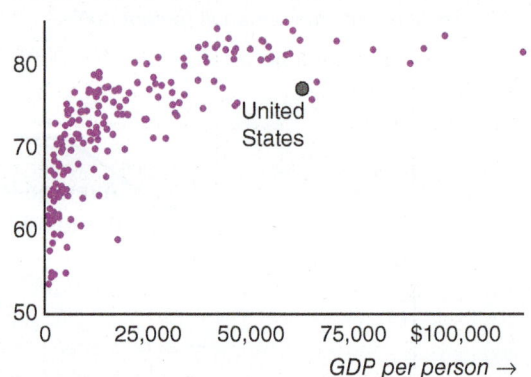

Data from: World Bank and World Happiness Report; World Bank and United Nations; World Bank.

The other three panels turn to more objective indicators and show that in countries with higher GDP per person, people get more education, live to older ages on average, and have fewer babies die before their first birthday. This is partly because higher GDP is associated with better access to a variety of necessities — including water, sanitation, food, shelter, medical care, and education. People in countries with high GDP also tend to enjoy more rights and personal freedoms and to live in more inclusive societies. For all of its shortcomings, GDP appears to be quite closely related to many other indicators of quality of life.

EVERYDAY Economics **Picturing GDP: Three countries, three families**

Ann Rosling Rönnlung started the website Dollar Street to help people visualize everyday life in countries at different levels of economic development. You can see differences in the houses people live in, what they're about to purchase, and the things they aspire to buy one day. Let's take a look at three typical families in countries with very different levels of GDP per person:

The Pingol family lives in the Philippines, where GDP per person is $8,900.

Abraham works as a truck driver. His wife, Evelyn, works as an accountant.

They have four children and live in this two-bedroom house.

Their next big purchase will be food, but they dream of one day buying a car.

The Zhao family lives in China, where GDP per person is $18,200.

Tiecai works as a taxi driver. His wife, Yanqing, works in a grocery store.

They have one child and their home is in the same area where they grew up.

Their next big purchase will be a TV, but they dream of buying a car.

The Howard family lives in United States, where GDP per person is $69,200.

Bryan works as a sales director for a wine company. His wife, Christina, is a stay-at-home mom.

They have two children and live in this four-bedroom house.

Their next big purchase will be a car for their daughter. They dream of purchasing a vacation home. ■

Pingol family: Luc Forsyth for Dollar Street; Zhao family: Benikhlef Abdelhak for Dollar Street; Howard family: Zoriah Miller for Dollar Street

9.4 Real and Nominal GDP

Learning Objective *Distinguish between real changes in quantities and the effects of changing prices.*

U.S. GDP has more than doubled since the end of the last century. In 2021, it was $23 trillion, compared to 2000, when it was $10.25 trillion. But total economic activity didn't double over this period. The problem is that the *market value* of total production can double because we're making twice the *quantity* of stuff, or because we're making the same quantity of stuff but *market prices* are twice as high. Or, as in this case, it can reflect some combination of rising prices and rising quantities. This distinction matters, because an increase in the quantity of stuff we produce raises living standards, while a change in the price tags attached to that stuff doesn't change anyone's quality of life.

Real and Nominal GDP

nominal GDP GDP measured in today's prices.

Nominal GDP is GDP measured in today's prices. To calculate nominal GDP, you add up the market value of total production in a year using the *current prices* prevailing in that year. Nominal GDP is useful if you want to know what GDP is right now, based on the prices that you face right now. However, nominal GDP is not very useful for making comparisons over time. The problem is that when prices rise over time — a process known as inflation (which we'll explore in Chapter 12) — nominal GDP will rise even when actual production is unchanged. For instance, nominal GDP values last year's apple crop at last year's price (say, $1 per pound), while this year's nominal GDP will value apples at this year's price of $2 per pound. If we produce the same number of apples but count this year's apples as if they're twice as valuable, it appears that apples' contribution to GDP has doubled even though actual apple production is unchanged.

real GDP GDP measured in constant prices.

When you're evaluating changes in economic activity over time, you should analyze real GDP instead. **Real GDP** is GDP measured in constant prices, so that it excludes the effects of price changes. By focusing only on changes in GDP due to changes in the *quantity* of output produced, real GDP isolates growth in output. It's calculated by adding up GDP as if no prices changed between last year and this year. It's called *real* GDP to remind you that it measures the *real* change in production, rather than changes in the price tags attached to each product.

When economists talk about GDP growth, they nearly always mean "growth in real GDP." In fact, most people who talk about changes in GDP are referring to changes in real GDP. So when you see a CNN report that says the "U.S. economy grew 2.3% last year," you can safely assume it's describing real GDP.

How to Calculate Real GDP

You'll better understand the distinction between real and nominal GDP by seeing how they're calculated. In order to make the numbers as simple as possible, we'll calculate GDP growth as if Crate & Barrel were the only business in the whole economy, and Crate & Barrel sells only couches. (Expanding this example to include the rest of the economy won't change anything beyond making the calculations more complicated.)

Figure 10 gives the key inputs to our calculations, for both "last year" when 100 couches were sold at a price of $1,500 each, and "this year," when 103 couches were sold at a price of $1,530 each. Over these two years, the average price, $\bar{P}$, is $1,515.

Figure 10 | Calculating Real and Nominal GDP

	Quantity sold (Q)	Calculating Nominal GDP			Calculating Real GDP	
		Actual price (P)	Nominal GDP = P × Q		Average price $\overline{P} = \dfrac{P_t + P_{t-1}}{2}$	Real GDP = $\overline{P}$ × Q
Last year	100 couches	$1,500	$1,500 × 100 = $150,000		$1,515	$1,515 × 100 = $151,500
This year	103 couches	$1,530	$1,530 × 103 = $157,590		$1,515	$1,515 × 103 = $156,045
Growth rate	+3%	+2%	+5%		+0%	+3%

Calculate nominal GDP using current prices. Nominal GDP is calculated as the market value of total output in each year, where each year's output is valued based on the market price in the year it was produced. So in this example, nominal GDP grew from $150,000 (= 100 couches × $1,500) last year, to $157,590 (= 103 couches × $1,530) this year. This is an increase of 5%, and this rise reflects an increase in both the price of couches and the quantity produced. Because nominal GDP in each year is calculated using the current price for that year, it's sometimes referred to as *GDP at current prices.*

Calculate real GDP using constant prices. Real GDP is calculated by computing growth in the value of output between this year and last year, where that output is valued using an unchanging, or constant, set of prices. As a result, it's sometimes referred to as *GDP at constant prices.* To be precise, GDP growth between any pair of adjacent years is calculated using the *average* price level over those two years. (This is part of a procedure known as *chain-weighting,* which calculates the growth in real GDP over time by first calculating growth between pairs of adjoining years using the average price in that specific pair of years, and then chaining together or accumulating these year-to-year growth rates to estimate growth over longer periods.)

So in our example, we calculate real GDP as if the price were constant at its average level of $1,515 over these two years. As a result, we compute that real GDP grew from $151,500 (=100 couches × $1,515) to $156,045 (=103 couches × $1,515). This is an increase of 3%, which is the same growth rate as the quantity of couches sold.

Do the Economics

Last year, Dell sold 100 laptops at $1,000 each, and this year, it sold 104 laptops at $1,060 each. Calculate (a) the growth rate of prices; (b) the growth rate of Dell's contribution to nominal GDP; and (c) the growth rate of Dell's contribution to real GDP. ∎

Answers: a. Prices grew by 6%. b. Nominal GDP rose from 100 × $1,000 = $100,000 to 104 × $1,060 = $110,240. This is a growth rate of (110,240 − 100,000)/100,000 × 100 = 10%. c. The average price is ($1,000 + $1,060)/2 = $1,030. Thus, real GDP rose from 100 × $1,030 = $103,000 to 104 × $1,030 = $107,120, a growth rate of (107,120 − 103,000)/103,000 × 100 = 4%.

There's a trick for moving quickly between real and nominal GDP growth. This simple method makes the math a lot easier. For changes over short periods of time (perhaps a few years):

% Change in nominal GDP ≈ % Change in real GDP + % Change in prices

The ≈ symbol means it's *approximately equal* to. So it's not perfect, but it's a really good estimate. In Figure 10, real GDP rose by 3%, and the price of couches rose by 2%, and so this formula correctly predicts that nominal GDP rose by approximately 5%.

If you rearrange a bit, this also gives you a way to calculate growth in real GDP:

% Change in real GDP ≈ % Change in nominal GDP − % Change in prices

Thus, the growth rate of real GDP is simply the growth rate of nominal GDP, less the average growth rate of prices. (We'll dive deeper into this subject in Chapter 12, where we'll learn that *inflation* is a general rise in prices, and the specific measure of inflation used to estimate real GDP is called the *GDP deflator*.)

Do the Economics

a. In 2021, nominal GDP grew 5.2%, and prices rose by 2.3%. Calculate the growth rate of real GDP.
b. Head to https://fred.stlouisfed.org and find the growth rate of nominal GDP last year, as well as the growth rate of the GDP deflator. Calculate growth in real GDP. ■

Finally, I bet you've noticed that macroeconomics often involves unimaginably large numbers — such as the $23 trillion worth of U.S. GDP. Our last task is to develop some strategies you can use to make sense of these huge sums.

9.5 Millions, Billions, and Trillions

Learning Objective *Scale large numbers into something more manageable.*

If you've seen the classic movie *Austin Powers: International Man of Mystery,* you'll know one of my favorite lines. Austin Powers's nemesis, Dr. Evil, wakes up from a 30-year sleep with a dastardly plan — he wants to steal a nuclear warhead and "hold the world ransom for... ONE MILLION DOLLARS." The joke is that what sounds like a lot to Dr. Evil is a pittance in the grand scheme of things. It's less than the U.S. military spends per minute.

The Problem of Big Numbers

It turns out that Dr. Evil is in good company. I have worked with many policymakers, and it's stunning how often they confuse millions, billions, and trillions, even though they're tasked with voting on legislation costing millions, billions, and trillions of dollars! The problem is that everyday life gives our brains plenty of practice at making sense of small numbers. But we have very little experience with much larger numbers, so it can be hard to wrap your mind around them. It's no surprise, then, that psychologists have found that people often have faulty intuitions about large numbers, noting that once numbers get beyond a certain point, they start to lose meaning to people. That's why people sometimes just give up and say, "a gazillion." So we'll spend some time now making sure that you think clearly about these differences, since they're critically important for understanding the macroeconomy.

Start by visualizing the difference. Close your eyes and picture a single $100 bill. It is thin, small, and can easily fit in your pocket. $10,000 is a tidy bundle of Benjamin Franklins. Figure 11 shows that 100 of those stacks — which adds up to a million dollars — fills a briefcase. Next, realize $1 billion is 1,000 of these briefcases of cash. You can probably jam 1,000 briefcases of cash into a school bus (but only just), and so a billion dollars is roughly a busload of $100 bills. In order to get to a trillion dollars, you'll need to get 1,000 busloads of cash together, and you can probably fit this into a football field if you double-stack them. So a trillion dollars is a football field stacked with $100 bills to a bit above your head.

Holding the world ransom ... for one million dollars.

Figure 11 | Millions, Billions, and Trillions

Let's start with $100

$10,000 is a tidy bundle

$1 million fills a briefcase

$1 billion is a busload of cash

There you are!

$1 trillion is a football field of cash, stacked taller than a typical person

Want to picture the total amount of annual GDP for the United States? It's around $23 trillion, about 23 times larger. This time, imagine your favorite football stadium, and fill it with $100 bills from ground level all the way up to the nosebleed seats. That's roughly annual U.S. GDP.

Four Strategies for Scaling Big Numbers

I've got a confession: Big numbers can trip me up, too. So how do I make sure that I don't get confused? I scale big numbers so that they're easier to manage. Here are a few strategies you can use to make sure that you don't get confused.

Strategy 1: Evaluate what it means per person. The size of the U.S. economy is almost unimaginably large. What does it even mean to produce a football stadium full of $100 bills each year? Instead of trying to imagine this, try reducing this number to more human terms by thinking about it in terms of what it means per person. Total GDP in 2021 was $23 trillion, but it's far more intuitive to think of this as $69,200 per person.

Keeping a few baseline numbers in the back of your mind will help you apply this strategy as you encounter more macroeconomic data:

- The world population is nearly 8 billion.
- The United States population is about 330 million.
- There are around 100 million households in the United States.

When you encounter other large numbers, you'll better comprehend their scale if you bring them down to size by converting them to a per person or per household measure. This means that if I tell you that the United States spends $100 million per year on research to develop self-driving cars, you realize this means roughly 30 cents per person. Or, if you learn that the household furniture sector spends $900 million per year on advertising, it's $9 per household. These are easier numbers to evaluate.

Strategy 2: Compare big numbers to the size of the economy. An alternative approach scales big numbers by comparing them to the size of the total economy. This is why macroeconomists often compare big numbers to total GDP. For example, in 2021, the federal government's budget deficit — its outlays less its revenue from taxes and other sources — was $2.8 trillion. Without further context, it can be hard to make sense of a number this big. But compare it to total GDP, and you'll discover that the budget deficit was equal to 12.4% of GDP, which gives you a better sense of the scale of the problem.

Strategy 3: Compare big numbers to their own history. Another way to scale big numbers is to evaluate their size relative to their previous values. This is what percentage changes do. For instance, 6 million Americans were unemployed in 2021, which sounds like a lot. But when you scale it relative to past numbers, you discover that it's fewer than half of the number of people who were unemployed in 2010, which is a useful context for understanding the scope of the problem.

Strategy 4: Use the Rule of 70 to evaluate long-run growth rates. Sometimes small differences in percentage changes can have bigger implications than you might think, and you can help sort these out by using a simple rule of thumb. The **Rule of 70** says that you can figure out approximately how many years it will take something to double if you divide 70 by its annual growth rate:

Rule of 70 Divide 70 by the annual growth rate to approximately get the number of years until the original amount doubles.

$$\text{Years it takes something to double} \approx \frac{70}{\text{Annual growth rate}}$$

For instance, between 1971 and 2021, real GDP per person in the United States grew at an average rate of 1.75% per year. At that rate, it would take $\approx 70/1.75 = 40$ years for average income to double. (Note that you divide by 1.75, not 0.0175.) Over the 50-year period, income doubled and got about a quarter of the way to doubling again. By comparison, in Singapore, real GDP per person grew at an average annual rate of 5.1%, which means that it doubled every $\approx 70/5.1 = 13$ years. And indeed, over the 50-year period, Singapore's average income doubled four times.

You can use this approximation to figure out how long it will take you to double your savings, how long it will take a country to double its average income, and how long it will take your business to double your number of customers. As you'll discover — and as Figure 12 shows — relatively small differences in annual growth rates lead to big differences over many years because growth tends to compound over time.

To scale big numbers:
1. Use "per person" figures
2. Compare to total GDP
3. Track the same number over time
4. Use the Rule of 70

Figure 12 | The Rule of 70 Tells You (Approximately) How Long it Takes Something to Double

The number of years it takes something to double ≈ 70/annual growth rate
↑ *Time to double*

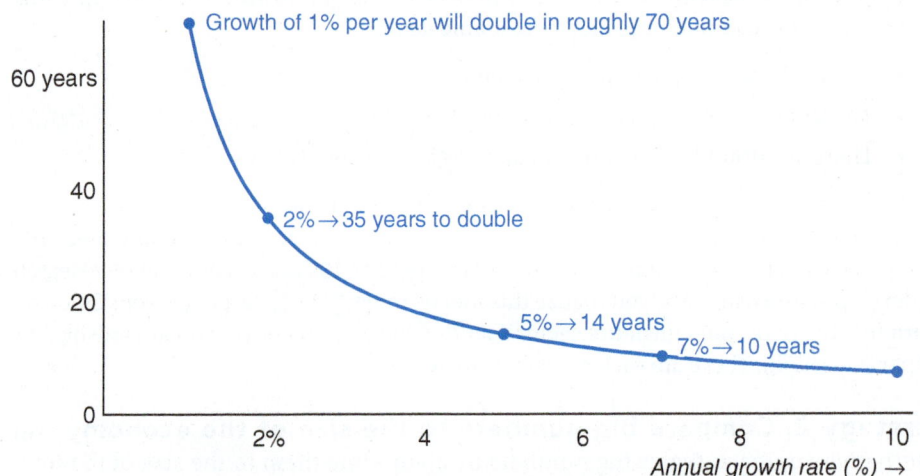

Growth of 1% per year will double in roughly 70 years

60 years

40

2% → 35 years to double

20

5% → 14 years

7% → 10 years

0

2%   4   6   8   10

Annual growth rate (%) →

Be careful: The rule of 70 is an approximation that becomes inaccurate for larger growth rates.

Do the Economics

The ability to convert big numbers into more manageable terms is a valuable skill beyond macroeconomics. Indeed, if you ever interview for a job in consulting, it's likely they'll test you on these abilities. So it's worth practicing:

a. Does Walmart employ roughly a thousand, a million, or a billion Americans?

b. Is the total amount paid in wages and salaries in the United States each year several millions, billions or trillions of dollars?

c. McDonald's boasts that it sells "billions and billions of burgers" each year. Is this really plausible?

d. Does Amazon Prime have 200 thousand members, 200 million, or 200 billion?

e. In 100 years do you expect the price of a cup of coffee to be $2, $20, or $200?

It's worth building your skill in working with big numbers like this, because it will prove to be a valuable asset that you'll use every time you confront new economic data. So keep practicing! ■

9.6 Tying It Together

What Gets Measured Gets Managed

You now know quite precisely what GDP is, how it's measured, and how to interpret it. This is a vital skill, because GDP will be a consistent theme through the rest of your study of macroeconomics. GDP is a useful measure of material living standards, and a key goal of macroeconomics is to find ways for people to live better lives.

You can use GDP per person to assess differences in average income across countries. Figure 13 reveals some striking disparities. GDP per person is $69,200 in the United States compared to only $1,100 per person in the Democratic Republic of the Congo. Much of the world's population lives in India, where GDP per person is $7,300, or in China, where it's $19,300. These differences in GDP per person have enormous implications for child mortality, life expectancy, and happiness. Finding a way to raise these countries' GDP per capita to the level of the United States would have astounding consequences for human welfare. That's why the next chapter analyzes the long-run determinants of economic growth, providing a framework that you can use to assess why GDP per person is so much lower in the Congo than in the United States, and the types of institutions and policies that can spur greater economic development.

We'll then move on to two other important macroeconomic indicators, unemployment and inflation. Unemployment and GDP are intricately linked because when people aren't working, they're not producing, earning income, or spending much. Unemployment not only robs many people of their purpose, it also leads the economy to produce less GDP than it potentially could. When we get to the chapter on inflation, we'll build upon what you've already learned about the distinction between real and nominal GDP. And we'll assess the extent to which higher rates of inflation can disrupt the economy, reducing GDP.

The subsequent set of chapters dig into the "microfoundations" of macroeconomics, analyzing the individual choices that add up to GDP. If you remember that $Y = C + I + G + NX$, you'll have a roadmap for the path ahead. We'll devote a chapter to study each of these components of GDP, beginning with consumption, then investment, and then international finance which will lead into an exploration of how imports and exports affect and are affected by exchange rates. We'll come back to studying G — that is, government purchases — in a later chapter on fiscal policy.

Figure 13 | **The United States Is One of the World's Richest Countries**

GDP per person in the world's 20 most populous countries, adjusted for difference in the cost of living

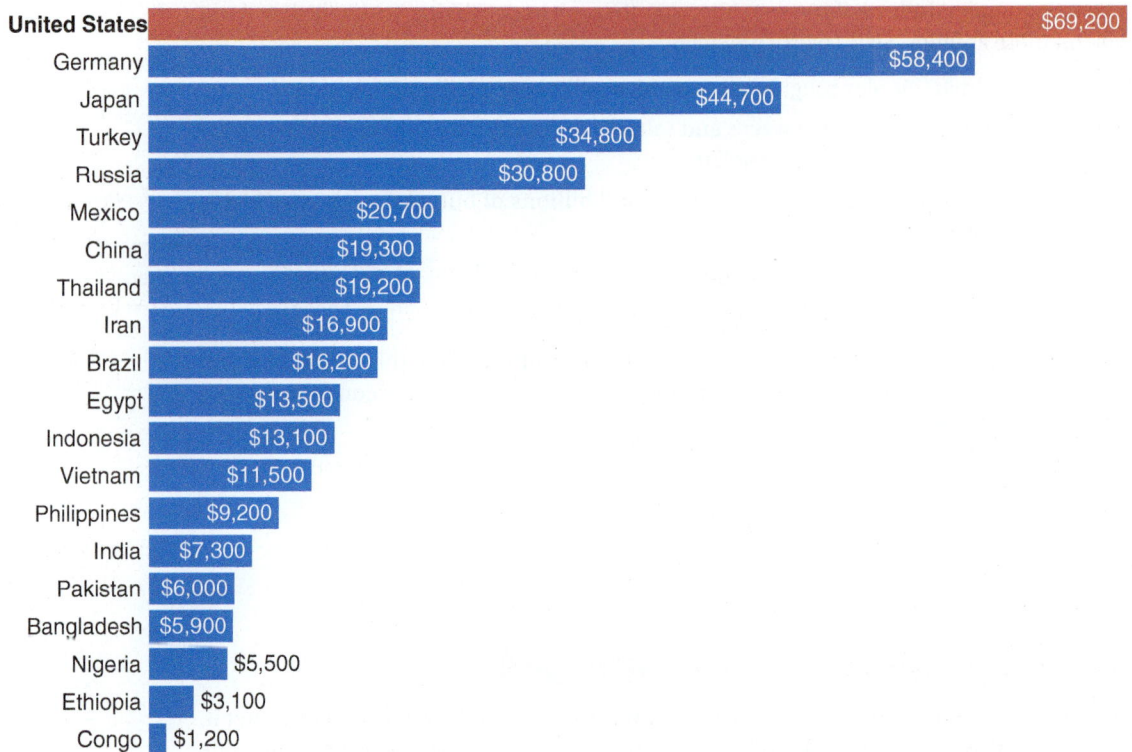

Country	GDP per person
United States	$69,200
Germany	$58,400
Japan	$44,700
Turkey	$34,800
Russia	$30,800
Mexico	$20,700
China	$19,300
Thailand	$19,200
Iran	$16,900
Brazil	$16,200
Egypt	$13,500
Indonesia	$13,100
Vietnam	$11,500
Philippines	$9,200
India	$7,300
Pakistan	$6,000
Bangladesh	$5,900
Nigeria	$5,500
Ethiopia	$3,100
Congo	$1,200

Data from: IMF data for 2021.

The next group of chapters focuses on the year-to-year fluctuations in GDP and other economic indicators. These short-term fluctuations are called the business cycle, and they can be incredibly disruptive as output, unemployment, and inflation rise and fall. Over a series of several chapters, we'll explore the role of spending, financial, and supply shocks in creating these fluctuations.

Finally, we'll spend the last two chapters examining the macroeconomic policies that governments pursue both to boost GDP and to reduce its year-to-year fluctuations. The chapter on monetary policy explores how the Federal Reserve adjusts interest rates in order to influence economic activity, while the chapter on fiscal policy assesses how the government shapes the economy through its tax and spending decisions.

At the end of all this, you might think that economists are obsessed with GDP. We're not. Economists and policymakers focus on GDP because it is a useful measure of material living standards. When you boost GDP, you boost the resources that a society has to pursue what's important to its citizens, and often that means that they are able to live richer, fuller, and happier lives. That's what really matters.

Chapter 9 Review

Chapter at a Glance

Gross Domestic Product (GDP): The market value of all final goods and services produced within a country in a year.

The market value ⟶ Value each product at its market price

of all ⟶ Include all goods and services

final goods and services ⟶ Count only final goods and services, omitting intermediate goods

produced ⟶ Omit resale of already-produced goods

within a country ⟶ Include all goods produced within the United States (even by foreign-owned businesses), but exclude goods produced overseas (even by American-owned businesses).

in a year. ⟶ Add up the flow of output over a year

$$Y = C + I + G + NX$$

GDP   Consumption   Investment   Government purchases   Net exports

GDP is . . .	. . . It can be measured as...	. . . That measurement is called
Total spending	$Y = C + I + G + NX$	"Gross Domestic Product"
Total output	Sum of value added = Total sales – cost of intermediate inputs	"Value Added"
Total income	Total wages + Total profits	"Gross Domestic Income"

These measurements of GDP get different names because even though they are the same in theory, real-world measurements of each can differ because each relies on different sources of imperfect data.

Limitations of GDP

1. Prices are not values
2. Nonmarket activities are excluded
3. The shadow economy is missing

4. Environmental degradation isn't counted
5. Leisure doesn't count
6. GDP ignores distribution

Real and Nominal Variables

Nominal GDP: Adds up the market value of total production in a year using the current prices prevailing in that year.

Real GDP: Excludes the effects of price changes, so it isolates economic growth that's due to changes in the quantity of output produced.

% Change in real GDP ≈ % Change in nominal GDP – % Change in prices

Four Strategies for Scaling Big Numbers

1. Evaluate what it means per person	2. Compare big numbers to the size of the economy	3. Compare big numbers to their own history	4. Use the Rule of 70 to evaluate long-run growth rates

✳ The Rule of 70: Years it takes something to double ≈ $\dfrac{70}{\text{Annual growth rate}}$

Key Terms

circular flow diagram, 219

consumption, 223

exports, 224

final goods and services, 220

GDP per person, 220

government purchases, 224

gross domestic product (GDP), 220

imports, 224

intermediate goods and services, 221

investment, 224

net exports, 224

nominal GDP, 234

real GDP, 234

Rule of 70, 238

transfer payments, 224

value added, 225

Study Problems

Learning Objective 9.1 *Learn how to measure the size of an economy using gross domestic product.*

1. You have decided to open a salad shop. Use the interdependence principle to describe how this impacts the economy by drawing a circular flow diagram. Make sure you draw and explain the flows of resources and money between your salad shop, your employees, the output market, and the input market. How does your salad shop impact total spending, total output, and total income in the economy?

2. You bought an old car a couple years ago for $1,000 and put about $5,000 of parts and labor into improving it. You sold it yesterday for $3,000. How does this sale affect GDP? Explain.

3. For each of the following transactions, determine if it takes place in the market for outputs or the market for inputs. Then, determine the direction of the flow of goods and services and the flow of money between households and businesses. Finally, determine how GDP as measured by the market value of output, spending on output, income received, or wages and profits changes.

   a. Labanya purchases a robotic vacuum cleaner on Amazon for $375.

   b. Matt gets paid $3,000 to teach a creative writing class at his local community college.

   c. Dollar General hires 10 new workers at the federal minimum wage to staff a new store.

   d. 96 million people purchased a monthly Spotify premium subscription for $10 last month.

4. In 2020, GDP in Switzerland was $752 billion and GDP in the United States was $21 trillion. Does this indicate that the standard of living in Switzerland must be well below that of the United States? Switzerland has a population of 8.6 million people, while the United States has a population of 332 million people. How could you better scale the numbers to compare their standards of living?

Learning Objective 9.2 *Analyze GDP as a measure of total spending, output, and income.*

5. After reading a report that says that around 70% of U.S. GDP is consumption, your friend Alex states, "Spending 70% of GDP on consumption is a lot. All people care about is buying stuff, consuming stuff, and accumulating stuff. We would be much better off if we spent our money on services or experiences." Identify Alex's misunderstanding of GDP.

6. Think of a good or service you've purchased in the last month. Explain how your purchase changed GDP by using each of the three ways to measure GDP: adding up every dollar spent, adding up every dollar's worth of output produced by detailing the value added at every stage of production, and adding up every dollar of income earned. How should GDP differ based on the way it is measured?

7. Explain how total spending and total income for an economy must be equal.

8. From your own experiences, provide an example of each: consumption, investment, government purchases, and net exports.

9. Determine whether each of the following transactions contributes to the calculation of GDP as total spending. If it does contribute to GDP, then identify the relevant component of GDP (*C*, *I*, *G*, or *NX*).

   a. Michelin sells tires to Nissan to install on their 2022 Sentras that are produced and sold in the United States.

   b. Molly Maid provides house cleaning services across the United States.

   c. U.S. consumers import $3.5 billion of woven apparel from Bangladesh.

   d. The U.S. government spent $523.1 billion on national defense.

   e. Entrepreneur and *Shark Tank* investor Barbara Corcoran purchases 15% of Cousins Maine Lobster food truck company for $55,000.

10. Use the data to calculate nominal U.S. GDP using the spending approach in 2020 and 2021.

	2020 (billions of dollars)	2021 (billions of dollars)
Consumption	$14,000	$15,700
Investment	$3,600	$4,100
Exports	$2,100	$2,500
Imports	$2,800	$3,400
Government spending	$3,900	$4,100

11. Consider an economy which produces and sells, among a host of other things, 100 million T-shirts a year. The average T-shirt begins life when a farmer plants seeds she put away last year, waters them, harvests the cotton, then sells the cotton to a mill for $0.75, which sells the fabric to a T-shirt factory for $1.50, which sells the T-shirt to a wholesaler for $5, who sells it to Nordstrom for $10, which finally sells it to you for $17. Determine the impact of T-shirts on annual GDP by calculating the total output of the entire production process. Then compare it to total spending on final T-shirts. What do you notice about the two?

12. Explain why total spending on T-shirts in the previous problem is also equal to the total incomes earned in the economy. Hint: there are two sides to every transaction.

Learning Objective 9.3 *Assess GDP as a measure of living standards.*

13. Jeremiah expressed his disdain for the economic reports he heard on the news. "All economists care about is increasing GDP," he said. "I wish economists cared about living conditions and well-being instead of just some economic indicator." How could you acknowledge the shortcomings of GDP to Jeremiah, while also showing him how GDP functions as both an economic indicator and a measure of well-being?

14. In 2010, 4.9 million barrels of oil spilled into the Gulf of Mexico due to an explosion on an oil rig. Describe both the negative and positive impact this disaster had on GDP. Explain how this example highlights the limitations of GDP.

15. Between 2000 and 2021, real GDP per person grew, on average, 1.1% per year in the United States. Did this GDP growth benefit all Americans? What does this tell us about the limitations of GDP as a measure of living standards?

16. Vinny and Sandra have just had their first baby and need to make a decision about how to handle work and child care responsibilities. Explain how each of the options below will affect measured GDP, relative to when they both worked full time and had no child care responsibilities.

a. Both Vinny and Sandra will return to work and pay a child care provider $600 per week to care for their child.

b. Both Vinny and Sandra will return to work, while Sandra's mother takes care of their child without financial compensation.

c. Both Vinny and Sandra will return to work, while Vinny's brother takes care of their baby. They'll pay him $600 a week to care for their child, but neither they nor Vinny's brother will report those payments to the IRS or on any government surveys.

d. Vinny and Sandra will each return to work part time and split child care responsibilities.

e. Vinny will stay home to care for the baby, while Sandra returns to work full time.

17. The following graph plots GDP per person and life expectancy of countries around the world. Identify possible reasons for the relationship shown by the graph.

Higher GDP is associated with longer life expectancy

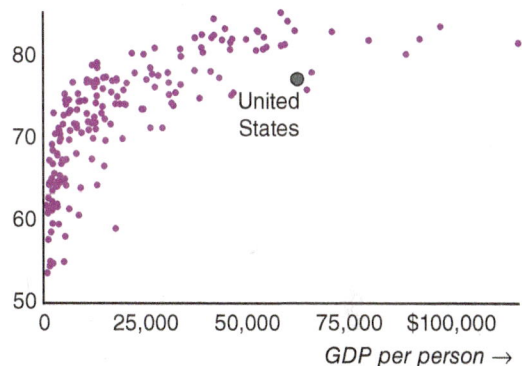

Data from: World Bank.

18. Identify the limitation of GDP relevant to each scenario.

a. The U.S. Department of Commerce reports that a "dead zone" of low oxygen that can kill fish and marine life in the Gulf of Mexico has grown as large as the state of New Jersey. It is the result of agricultural and developed land runoff in the Mississippi River watershed.

b. The World Bank reports that in 2015 the income share held by the bottom 10% of the U.S. income distribution was 1.7%. The income share held by highest 10% of the U.S. income distribution was 30.6%.

c. Data from the Pew Research Center shows that one in five U.S. parents and caregivers stay at home.

d. U.S. GDP per person is around 7% higher than Netherlands GDP per person. However, American workers typically work about 26% more hours per year than Dutch workers.

e. Most internet searches (86.5%) occur via Google, Google Maps, or Google Images, all of which provide search results for free.

Learning Objective 9.4 *Distinguish between real changes in quantities and the effects of changing prices.*

19. You read two articles online. The first says GDP grew by 5% last quarter, but the second states that the economy grew by 3.4% over the same time period. What do you think explains the difference in the two measures?

20. If nominal GDP rose, does that mean that production had to increase as well? Why or why not? What about if real GDP increased? Why is it important to use real GDP when comparing changes over time?

21. The table contains price and quantity information for two vehicle models produced by Ford Motor Company, the F-series trucks and Escape SUVs.

	2016		2017	
	Price	**Quantity**	**Price**	**Quantity**
Escape SUVs	$24,485	307,069	$24,645	308,296
F-series trucks	$44,400	820,799	$47,800	896,764

a. Calculate the amount contributed by Ford to U.S. GDP (real and nominal) from the sales of the two models in 2016 and 2017.

b. Determine the growth rate of nominal GDP (if Ford were the entire economy).

c. Determine the growth rate of real GDP (if Ford were the entire economy).

d. Use the shortcut you learned to convert between real and nominal growth rates to determine the growth rate of prices.

e. Is the increase in nominal GDP due to a change in quantity, a change in prices, or both?

22. In Iceland, nominal GDP grew by 10.4% in 2021, while real GDP grew by 4.3%. Approximately what was the percentage change in average prices?

Learning Objective 9.5 *Scale large numbers into something more manageable.*

23. In 2018, the White House proposed a 33% cut in the United States Agency for International Development (USAID) budget for the upcoming fiscal year, which would have reduced USAID spending in 2019 to $16.8 billion. The total proposed budget for the U.S. federal government was $4.4 trillion. How could you explain the magnitude of foreign aid spending by developing a sense of scale?

24. In 2020, India was the world's third largest economy, with a $9 trillion GDP (as measured in U.S. dollars). India was also one of the world's fastest-growing economies, and over the previous decade, real GDP grew at an average rate of 5% per year.

a. If the country maintains the same growth rate, how many years will it take for India's GDP to double?

b. Bangladesh's GDP was $286.27 billion, but its growth rate was equal to India's. How many years will it take for Bangladesh's economy to double?

c. Although Bangladesh and India have the same annual growth rate, their economies are much different in size. How can you explain the size difference to someone who is unfamiliar with scaling large numbers? Which strategies would you use?

Economic Growth

You live a life that is extraordinarily luxurious compared to most of human history. It's not just that you have the modern conveniences of computers, cell phones, and the internet. A hundred years ago only one-third of households had electricity, and many lacked indoor plumbing. Many people didn't have enough to eat.

Since it was harder to keep things sanitary, people got sick a lot more often. Much of modern medicine hadn't been invented yet, including antibiotics and most major vaccines. A bad case of the flu, a stomach bug, or a bout of diphtheria would kill you. Without antibiotics, surgery was unsafe. Famines and outbreaks of communicable diseases killed millions of people. The average American could expect to live only to age 55.

In 1920, real GDP per person was the equivalent of about $9,000. By 2021, GDP per person was more than six times higher, having risen to $69,200. This means that you'll likely earn more in the first decade of your career than your great-grandparents did in their entire lifetimes. This higher income means that most Americans have enough to eat, a comfortable place to live, good health care, instant communication, reliable transportation, and almost unlimited information at our fingertips. Today, the average American can expect to live to age 78. Economic growth has improved both the quantity and the quality of our lives.

But life remains hard in much of the rest of the world. Today, the average income of Americans is more than triple that of people in China, eight times that of Indians, and sixteen times the average in sub-Saharan Africa. Many aspects of daily life in the United States are the result of more than a century of robust economic growth. Not all countries have experienced as much growth. In places like Ethiopia and Congo, life isn't much different from 100 years ago. A large share of the population spends their days focused on activities necessary for survival, like subsistence farming, seeking clean water, and building adequate shelter. In this chapter, we'll explore how economic growth got the United States to where it is today, why some countries are still so far behind, and what countries can do to grow faster.

Understanding the drivers of economic growth gives you a new way of looking at the world.

Mark Wallinger's The World Turned Upside Down at LSE/Photo by Maltida Wolfers

Chapter Objective

Understand what determines the rate of economic growth.

10.1 Economic Growth Facts
Learn how economies have grown over time.

10.2 The Ingredients of Economic Growth
Uncover the ingredients for economic growth.

10.3 The Analytics of Economic Growth
Understand how workers, capital accumulation, and technological progress work together to create economic growth.

10.4 Public Policy: Why Institutions Matter for Growth
Find out why government institutions matter for economic growth.

🎙 Podcast
Think Like an Economist
Economic Growth—
Improving Our Lives

Before there was a written record, there was art.

TAHA JAWASHI/AFP/Getty Images

10.1   Economic Growth Facts

Learning Objective *Learn how economies have grown over time.*

To understand economic growth today, it's useful to start by understanding how much people struggled and how little progress there was for most of human history. So let's step way back in time to more than a million years ago.

Economic Growth Since 1 Million B.C.E.

There aren't a lot of records dating back to 1 million B.C.E., but the clues we do have all paint a bleak picture. People lived hand-to-mouth, first as hunters and gatherers. The transition from hunting and gathering to farming allowed people to settle down into communities and form societies. While they no longer had to roam to find food, most people toiled daily in agriculture. Even so, they did not produce enough food to feed everyone adequately. People were so poor that starvation and malnutrition were common. Skeletal remains show severe deficiencies in vitamins and minerals, and widespread disease. Men were six inches shorter, on average, compared to today, reflecting the malnutrition they faced as children. While there were some bright spots, such as ancient Greece, and there were rulers who amassed riches, most people from 1 million B.C.E. through 1200 C.E. lived in grinding poverty. And each successive generation was as poor as the previous one.

Economists estimate that from around 1 million B.C.E. until around 1200 C.E., GDP per person was only around $200 per year in today's dollars. While it's hard to know the exact amount for sure, it was roughly the minimum needed to sustain life. What is clear is that real GDP per person didn't change much until around 1200 C.E., when it started to rise, albeit very gradually. In fact, growth was so slow that it took roughly 600 years for real GDP per person to double. At the start of the 1800s, world real GDP per person was roughly $400. That's adjusted for inflation, so that means $400 worth of goods and services at prices similar to those you face today. Imagine trying to get by a whole year on only $400!

Agricultural advances meant more food and less hunger. For much of human history, most people's primary job was securing enough food to avoid starvation. But as agricultural techniques improved over the centuries, people could produce more food with less work. The benefits of these changes became most apparent in the

Technological advances transformed agriculture.

PHAS/Universal Images Group/ Getty Images

1800s, with advances in farming such as better crop rotation, the use of farm enclosures, switching to higher-yielding crops, and new farm equipment. Markets to distribute food became more sophisticated, thanks to better transportation infrastructure. The expansion of inland waterways and roads reduced the cost of selling what farmers produced. Taken together, these developments meant less hunger and fewer people needed to work on farms. By 1850, less than a quarter of the British workforce worked in agriculture; these benefits were also seen in much of Europe and North America.

The Industrial Revolution created an engine of economic growth. Because fewer resources were needed to grow food, increased agricultural production also sowed the seeds for the Industrial Revolution — a revolution that brought machine power to our efforts to make and transport food and goods. As meeting their nutritional needs became less burdensome, people had more time to pursue other activities, and intellectual life thrived. Inventors pioneered revolutionary new products such as the steam engine, sewing machine, telephone, and light bulb. Prior to these inventions, most work was powered by humans or animals. It can be hard to comprehend the magnitude of this change, but take a minute to imagine what your life would be like if you had nothing but your own energy and that of animals to help you get through your day.

The invention of machines that could substitute for human or animal labor, and the subsequent investment in making these machines available, brought enormous growth in what people could produce. Workers moved from farms to factories, and their ability to produce output increased at a rapid pace. This was the real beginning of increasing income and living standards. After taking nearly 600 years for global real GDP per person to double, it more than doubled between the early 1800s and the early 1900s. Economic growth then exploded: Worldwide real GDP per person doubled again by the 1950s, and then again by 1975, again by the early 2000s, and again by 2020.

A century of growth transformed Austin, Texas.

Economic growth means rising living standards and longer lives. When people produce more, they can consume more. That means fewer people go hungry, and more people have a comfortable place to live, sanitary conditions, and more resources to invest in their health and education. Growth doesn't just mean you consume more stuff; it's what enables you to live and thrive. Economic growth led the world population to grow and life expectancy — the average number of years that a person may expect to live — to rise. In 1800, there were a billion people in the world; today, there are more than 8 billion. In 1800, average life expectancy in every country was below age 50. Today, the average person in many of the richest countries in the world can expect to live well into their 80s. (While the United States is among the richest countries, it has a lower average life expectancy than many other rich countries.)

Yet even today, average life expectancy in many of the world's poorest countries is not much above age 50. The problem is that the agricultural and industrial revolutions didn't lead to economic growth everywhere. Some countries thrived, while others stagnated. And some countries started down the right path, but got lost along the way. Let's zoom in on the past 200 years to take a closer look.

Economic Growth over the Past Two Centuries

When economic growth was proceeding at a glacial pace, there wasn't much of a difference in GDP per person between countries. Figure 1 shows real GDP per person in various parts of the world, first in 1820 and then in 2020. In 1820, annual real GDP per person averaged around $700 in Africa, $900 in Asia, and roughly $1,000 in Latin America and Eastern Europe. In the wealthiest parts of the world — Western Europe and the United States (and also Canada and Australia) — real GDP per person was a bit more than $2,000. While that was more than double than much of the rest of the world, it was low enough that hunger was still never too far from people's minds.

Figure 1 | Small Differences in Growth Rates Have Big Consequences

Real GDP per person in 1820 and 2018

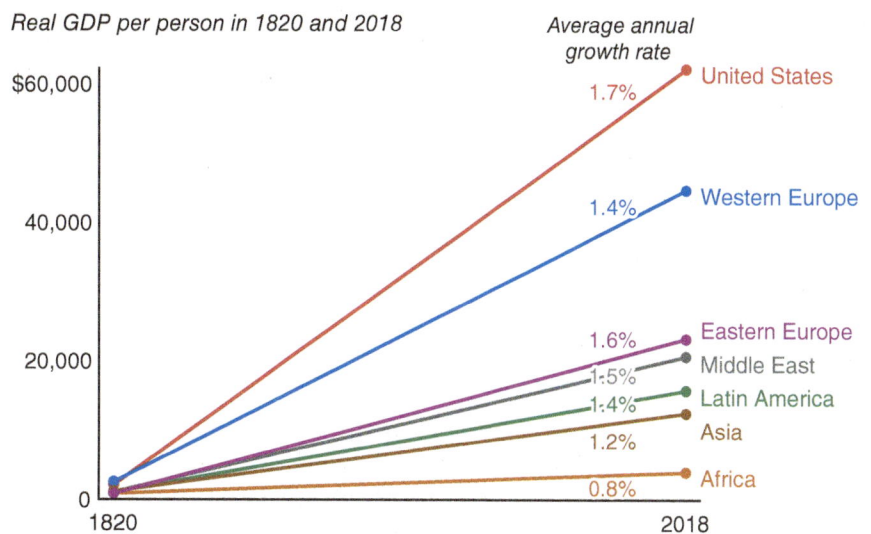

Data from: Maddison Project Database 2020.

Small differences in growth rates can have big effects. The Industrial Revolution fueled more economic growth in some parts of the world than others. As Figure 1 illustrates, what may seem like small differences in growth rates lead to enormous differences over time. Only a few tenths of a percentage point in annual growth rates differentiate today's economically developed countries from less-developed countries — but those small differences in growth rates were compounded over hundreds of years.

In the United States, real GDP per person was nearly $50,000 in 2010 — more than 20 times greater than it had been roughly 200 years earlier. In Western Europe, real GDP per person was nearly $35,000 in 2010. The growth in Western Europe and North America left the rest of the world far behind. In 2020, there was a clear distinction between the "rich" West and the rest of the world, where real GDP per person grew, but at much slower rates. In Africa, output per person grew at roughly half the rate as in the West, which meant that by the time it doubled in Africa, it had quadrupled in the West.

There have been growth successes and disasters. In the 16th century, Spain was a great power, sending explorers around the world, fostering international trade, and establishing an enormous empire. But between 1600 and 1850, its economy barely grew, while income per person in Great Britain more than doubled. Spanish real GDP per person grew so slowly that by 1900, it was only roughly double what it had been back in the 1600s. Even in 1950, when some of today's older Spaniards were born, incomes were only about two and half times what they were 400 years earlier. The second half of the twentieth century was more successful for Spain; income per person in 2020 was roughly seven times what it was in 1950.

Argentina provides another example of what happens when growth stalls. Just before the turn of the twentieth century, Argentina was one of the richest countries in the world, and its economy was growing rapidly. Figure 2 shows that around 1900 its real GDP per person was comparable to that in the United States and United Kingdom. But growth sputtered in the early 1900s, and it made little progress for decades. A country that had once been richer than Spain, Japan, and South Korea fell behind those countries' economies. In 2021, its average income was about one-fifth of the average income of the United States.

Figure 2 also shows the success stories of Japan and South Korea. Japan had little growth through the mid-1900s. The second half of the twentieth century, however, was a time of robust GDP growth. South Korea also had explosive growth in the second half of the twentieth century after separating from North Korea in the 1940s. Japan and South Korea now have GDP per person on par with many affluent Western nations.

Countries like India and China stagnated for centuries before taking off during the past few decades. In 2021, India's average income adjusted for inflation was more than three times higher than it had been in 1990, and China's average income had grown tenfold. In comparison, the average income in the United States only rose by about half during that same time period. Recent rapid growth in poorer countries has helped decrease inequality between nations around the world.

The facts about economic growth are astonishing. Over the past 200 years the global economy has grown enormously, transforming our quality of life. But this development has been uneven, creating remarkable disparities with average income in some countries many times larger than in others. Now let's turn to figuring out why.

Figure 2 | **There Have Been Growth Disasters and Miracles**

Real GDP per person, relative to the United States

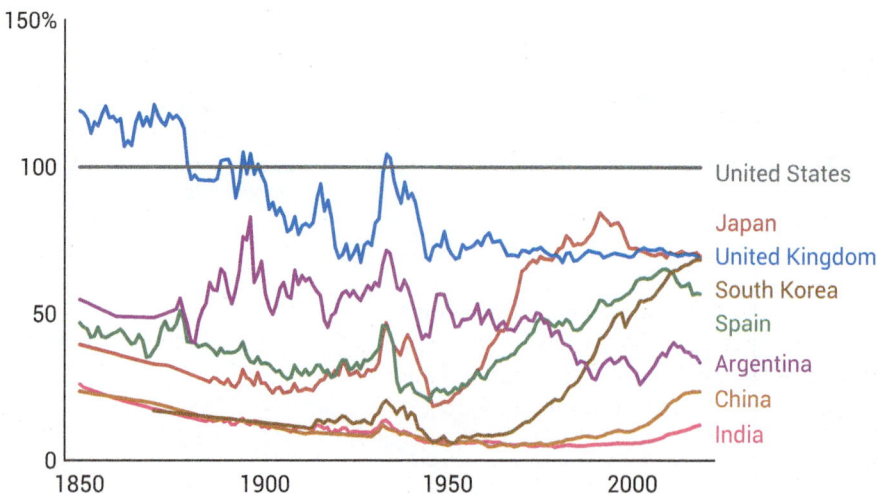

Data from: Maddison Project Database 2020.

10.2 The Ingredients of Economic Growth

Learning Objective *Uncover the ingredients for economic growth.*

Why are some countries rich, while others are so poor that they barely produce enough for people to survive? And what makes some countries grow richer over time, while others stagnate? Perhaps no other question in economics — indeed, in all of the social sciences — has such far-reaching implications for human well-being. An answer might provide a roadmap that poor countries could use to become rich, helping billions of people escape poverty and hunger. And so we turn to asking: What determines how much output each country produces?

The Production Function

Whether you're analyzing how much your household, your business, or a whole country produces, you'll find it useful to organize your thoughts around the idea of a production function. A **production function** describes the methods by which inputs are transformed into outputs, and so it determines the total production that's possible with a given set of ingredients.

production function The methods by which inputs are transformed into output which determines the total production that's possible with a given set of ingredients.

A production function is like a cookbook. If you've ever baked a cake, then you've got some experience with a production function. You probably looked in a cookbook and found a recipe that relied on ingredients that you had available. Then you followed the instructions on how to combine flour, sugar, milk, and eggs in order to produce your cake. That cookbook told you how much cake you'd produce, given the quantity of ingredients you used.

Production function
Methods for transforming inputs into output

In this example, think of the production function as the whole cookbook, rather than an individual recipe. A recipe describes a particular production technique that relies on a specific quantity of milk, flour, and eggs. A cookbook is a collection of the most important recipes, and each page lists a different production technique you might choose, depending on the ingredients you have available. A cookbook and a production function both describe how different mixtures of inputs can be combined to produce valuable output.

A production function describes how a business transforms inputs into outputs. The same ideas apply to any productive activity. Your company's production function is the cookbook of management techniques you can use to transform your inputs into output. By this view, running a business is a lot like baking a cake, and your job as a manager is to acquire the right ingredients — the right people, skills, and machinery — and mix them in the appropriate proportions to produce valuable output.

For instance, if you're running a cake shop, you'll mix together the hard work and skills of pastry chefs, cake decorators, and cashiers with retail space, display cases, commercial mixers, and ovens, along with raw ingredients like flour, butter, and sugar. Your bakery's production function describes how the quantity of cake you'll produce varies according to the amount of each ingredient you add to the mixture.

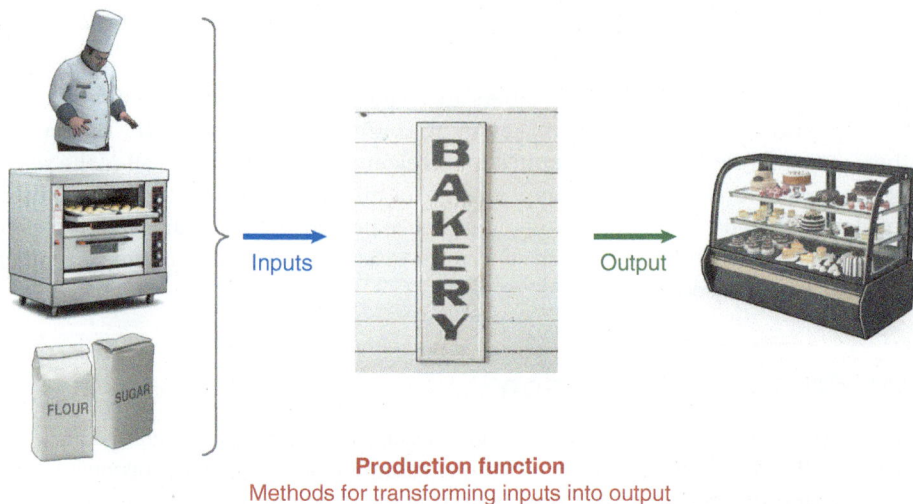

Production function
Methods for transforming inputs into output

Just as a cake shop has a production function, so too does a consulting firm, a hotel, a law firm, a hospital, or a high school. In each case, managers play the role of chef, mixing together workers, specialized skills, and equipment, to bake consulting services, a restful night, legal victories, healthy patients, or educated students. Your company's production function describes the total quantity of output your business can produce depending on the quantities of each input you employ.

The aggregate production function links GDP to labor, human capital, and physical capital. The same idea can be applied at the level of the whole economy where the *aggregate production function* relates total output — that is, GDP — to the quantity of inputs employed. As with individual businesses, the key ingredients are *Labor* (denoted L), **human capital,** which describes the knowledge and skills that workers bring to the job (denoted H), and **physical capital,** which describes the tools, machinery, and structures we work with (the letter C was taken, so economists follow the German spelling of Kapital and label physical capital as K). The aggregate production function doesn't include a separate role for intermediate inputs such as the flour used by a pastry chef, because intermediate inputs are typically produced by other businesses within the economy. Flour, for instance, is produced by mills that process the wheat grown by farmers, and so it's already the result of combining labor, skills, and capital.

human capital The accumulated knowledge and skills that make a worker more productive.

physical capital The tools, machinery, and structures that are inputs in the production process.

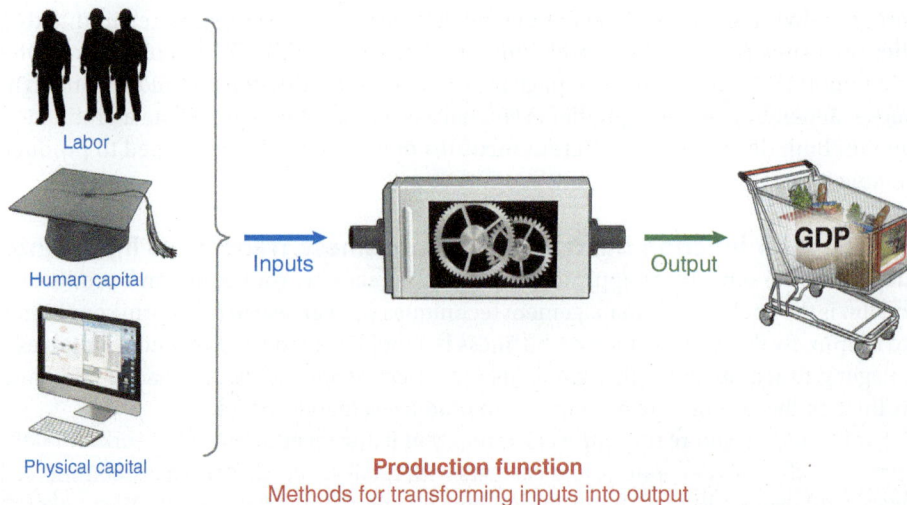

Production function
Methods for transforming inputs into output

A production function describes how output varies with inputs. The aggregate production function captures the idea that when you use more ingredients — more labor, more human capital, and more physical capital — you'll get more output. It quantifies this relationship, telling you how much extra output businesses will produce as they add more labor, human capital, or physical capital. It can be useful to represent this idea mathematically, and the following equation simply says that the quantity of output a country will produce (denoted Y) depends on the quantity of each of these inputs:

Output is a function of inputs

$$Y = f(L, H, K)$$

Labor Human Physical
       capital capital

The aggregate production function illustrates that a country will produce more output if:

- It employs more labor
- Its workers become more highly skilled, accumulating human capital
- It accumulates more physical capital

Finally, a production function reflects the production techniques — or recipes — that are known at a specific point in time. Finding new and more efficient recipes will shift the production function, creating an additional engine of growth:

- Discovering new and more efficient recipes makes it possible to transform a given quantity of ingredients into a greater quantity of output.

Let's dig into each of these ingredients in turn.

> A country's output depends on . . .
> *Available inputs:*
> 1. Labor input
> 2. Human capital
> 3. Physical capital
> *And also:*
> 4. Recipes for transforming inputs into output

Ingredient 1: Labor and Total Hours Worked

As you know from personal experience, the more hours you work, the more you get done. The same thing applies to the whole economy: The more labor that workers do, the more output gets produced. The total quantity of labor input is measured as the sum of all hours worked across the whole economy. It reflects four factors: the size of the population, the fraction of the population that is of working age, the share of those working-age people who choose to work, and how many hours each worker puts in. Let's consider each of these, in turn.

Population boosts total GDP, but not GDP per person. The total population of a country provides the upper limit to how much labor it can supply, which explains why the countries with the largest populations tend to produce the most GDP. Rapid population growth — more births, fewer deaths, and more immigration — leads to rapid economic growth. But that doesn't mean that a larger population will yield higher living standards, because that larger GDP gets shared over more people. Population is a key determinant of GDP, but not GDP per person.

As we analyze material living standards, we'll focus on the determinants of GDP per person. That in turn will lead us to focus on other per-person variables: hours worked per person, human capital per person, and physical capital per person.

Unfavorable demographics can slow economic growth. The demographic structure of the population matters, because children and the elderly rarely work. The *dependency ratio* measures the number of people either too young (under 18) or too old (65 or older) to work, per 100 people of working age. Figure 3 shows that the dependency ratio rose sharply in the United States due to the baby boom that followed World War II. The dependency ratio then fell as many of those babies grew up and became workers.

sirtravelalot/Shutterstock

More babies means more workers, eventually.

Figure 3 | The Dependency Ratio Is Projected to Rise

Number of people too young (under 18) or too old (65+) to work per 100 working-age people

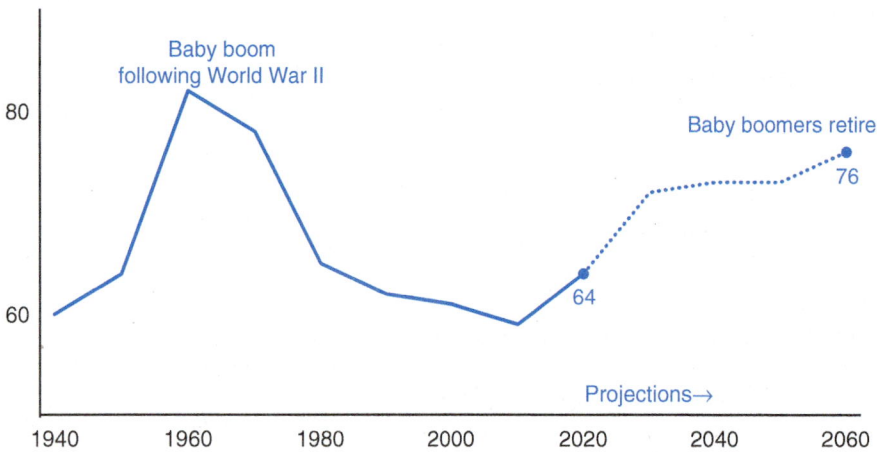

Data from: U.S. Census Bureau.

Figure 4 | Women's Employment Rose Dramatically During the 20th Century

Share of adult women who are employed

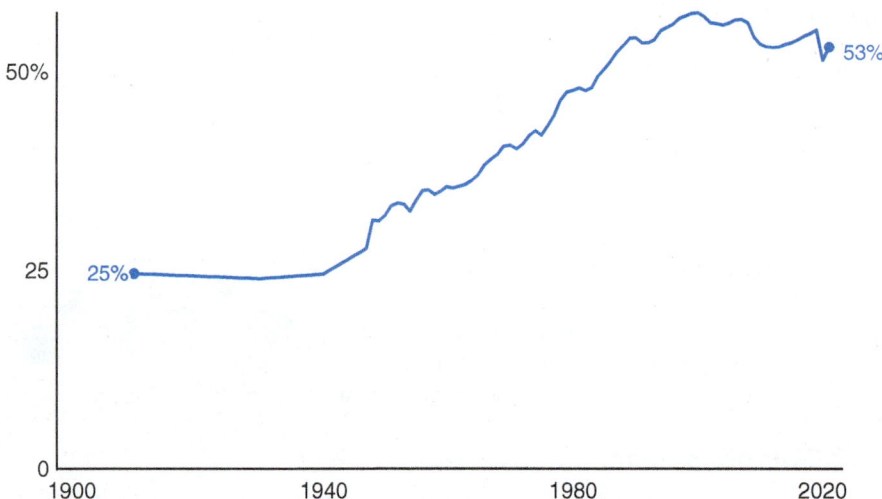

Data from: BLS and Census.

By 2020, for every 100 people of working age, there were 61 people either too young or too old to work. This dependency ratio is projected to rise sharply over the next few decades, as those born in the postwar baby boom retire, and it will remain high due to increased life expectancy. The dependency ratio has risen throughout richer countries more generally as economic growth has led to longer lives. The rising share of dependents is likely to slow economic growth in richer countries over the coming decades.

Women's increased employment created economic growth. The labor pool grows when a larger share of the working-age population works. The main driver of the rising labor force participation in many countries over the past century has been an extraordinary transformation in attitudes toward women in the workplace. In the early 1900s few women worked outside the home, particularly once they married. By the early 2000s in the United States, that share had almost tripled. Much of this change occurred in the 1960s, 1970s, and 1980s. This shift of women from the home into the market was responsible for a substantial share of the rise in U.S. GDP per person through this period. Female labor force participation continued to grow in most rich countries in the 21st century. The United States has been an outlier, with growth in women's labor force participation stalling at the start of the 21st century.

Shorter workweeks reduce GDP but may raise well-being. Total labor input reflects not only the number of workers, but also how many hours each person works, on average. The more hours that people work, the more GDP they'll produce.

But that doesn't mean we should work all the time! As we discussed in Chapter 9, one limitation of GDP is that it doesn't capture the benefit of the leisure you enjoy when you're not working. As countries get richer, people tend to choose more leisure over work time. The reduction in the average work week has slowed GDP growth but probably improved well-being.

Ingredient 2: Human Capital

labor productivity The quantity of goods and services that each person produces per hour of work.

While hours of work reflect the quantity of labor used, output also reflects how productive people are while at work. The more each worker produces per hour, the higher GDP will be. Economists refer to output per hour of work as **labor productivity.**

Your labor productivity depends critically on your human capital, which describes the skills and knowledge that you develop through education, training, and practice. As you learn economics, you are building your human capital: You're acquiring new analytic tools that will help you make better decisions, developing frameworks you'll use to transform data into insight, and building the intellectual muscles that you'll apply to better understand, analyze, and predict human behavior. This human capital is a key reason why economics graduates are so highly paid. Your ability to learn economics (as well as everything else you're studying) builds on a foundation you laid many years ago, all of which combine to form your human capital.

Primary education develops literacy, which is a key tool for further learning. Literacy is such a foundational skill that you probably take it for granted. Yet it's essential for economic life: You need to be able to read to follow written instructions, communicate with co-workers, execute written contracts, look things up online, read a newspaper, or evaluate political candidates. That's why you probably spent your first few years of elementary school learning to read and write.

Figure 5 shows that while literacy is nearly universal among industrialized countries, it remains a substantial barrier in many poorer countries. This is important because literacy is the foundation of all later learning, empowering people to acquire further specialized knowledge. Indeed, right now it's empowering you to learn about the economic impact of literacy!

Figure 5 | **Adult Literacy Rates Vary Across Regions**

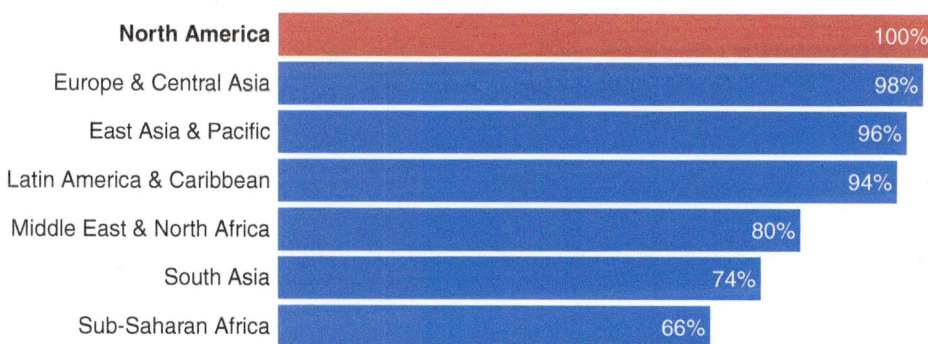

Region	Rate
North America	100%
Europe & Central Asia	98%
East Asia & Pacific	96%
Latin America & Caribbean	94%
Middle East & North Africa	80%
South Asia	74%
Sub-Saharan Africa	66%

Data from: World Bank.

Secondary education promotes greater productivity in a range of jobs. One of the key reasons the United States was one of the fastest-growing economies in the twentieth century is that it invested more in the education of its citizens than other countries did. A century ago, many mocked the idea of making high school free and available to everyone, arguing that there remained a great need for physical labor and that laborers wouldn't benefit from having a high school education. Despite these arguments, support for high school education grew rapidly in the United States. Figure 6 shows that high school diplomas went from being a rarity in the United States in 1900 to being nearly universal today. The claim that this education wouldn't be useful turned

Figure 6 | **High School and College Graduation Rates Have Risen**

Share of people aged 25+

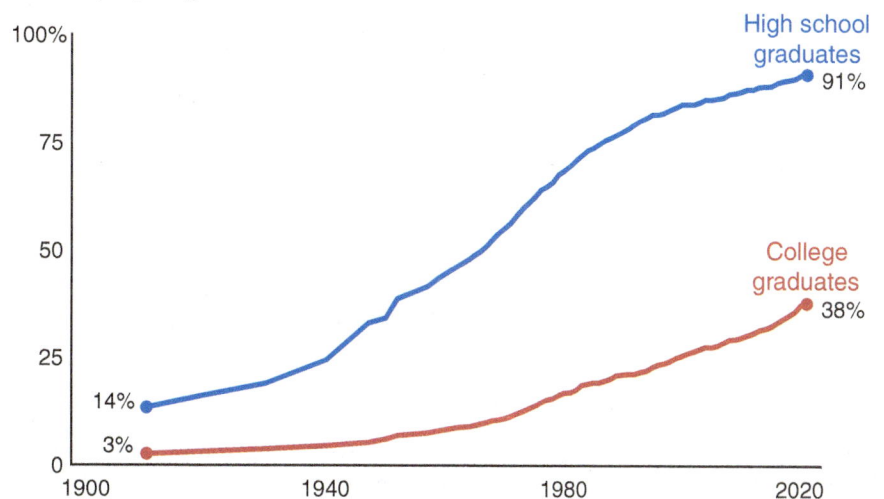

High school graduates 91%

College graduates 38%

14%

3%

Data from: U.S. Census Bureau and NCES.

out to be wrong, as it enabled blue-collar workers to work with increasingly sophisticated machinery, boosting their productivity.

Further gains in human capital will come from expanding college education. Figure 7 shows that most countries lag behind the United States in terms of primary and secondary education. But now that both are nearly universal in the United States, further gains in human capital accumulation will come from more people completing a college education.

Figure 7 | The United States Leads the World in the *Quantity* of Education Gained

Each dot shows the share of a country's working-age population that has attended that level of education

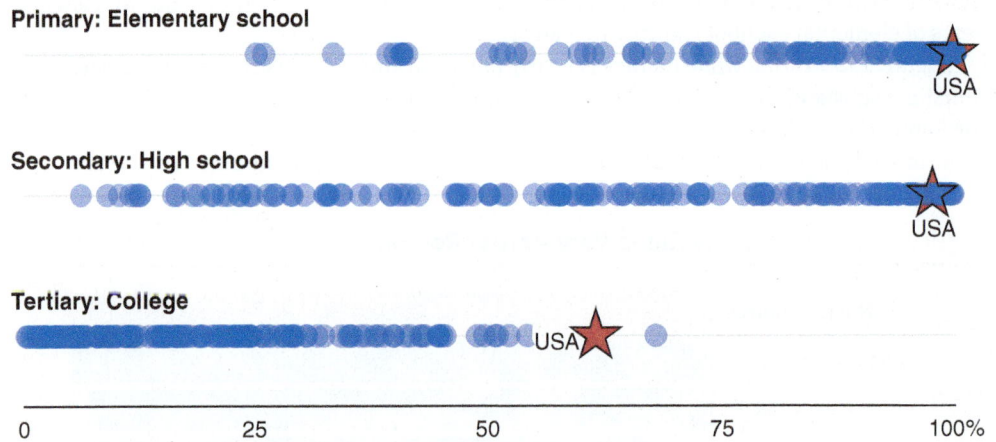

Data from: Barro-Lee Educational Attainment Database.

The rate of return to making these investments is high: Each year of college raises your earnings by around 8%, and employers pay this premium because the skills you learn in college tend to make workers more productive. Those who complete a college degree enjoy more than $1 million higher lifetime earnings on average, suggesting that a college degree leads you to produce at least a million dollars more in output. (The boost is even larger for economics students!)

So far we've measured human capital mainly in terms of the quantity of education you get, but it also depends on the quality of that education. Figure 8 shows that when common international exams are given across countries, the United States is no longer a world leader. This explains why so many education policy debates are focused on improving the quality of education.

Figure 8 | The *Quality* of American Educational Outcomes Is Unexceptional

Each dot shows the average test score of 15-year-old students in each country on a common international exam

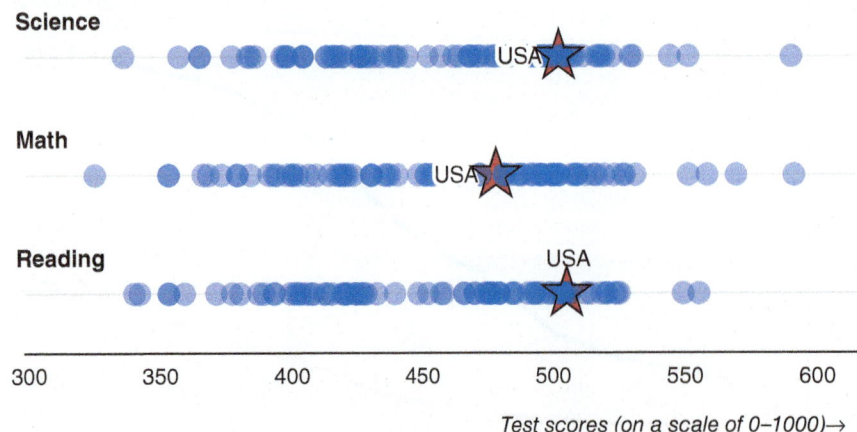

Out of 78 countries, the United States ranks 18th in science, 37th in math, and 13th in reading.
Data from: Program for International Student Assessment.

Ingredient 3: Capital Accumulation

The third factor that determines how much you can produce per hour is the equipment you'll work with. For instance, a pastry chef working with commercial-grade mixers, large ovens, and other kitchen equipment is more productive than one without access to all that equipment. The **capital stock** is the total quantity of physical capital, and it includes all equipment and structures that can be used in the production of goods and services. It includes privately owned tools, machines, and factories, as well as government-provided infrastructure, such as roads, electricity networks, and telecommunications.

capital stock The total quantity of physical capital that can be used in the production of goods and services.

Physical capital is a complement to labor.

Workers produce more when they have the right tools available to them, so physical capital is best viewed as a *complement* to labor. As such, the quantity of capital per worker is an important determinant of labor productivity. While some people worry that machines are a *substitute* for labor, the reality is that they help workers get more done. After all, a pastry chef equipped with a commercial mixer doesn't have to mix batter by hand, which enables them to produce more cakes in the same amount of time. Indeed, the Industrial Revolution — during which workers went from working with hand tools to harnessing machine power — marked a turning point in history as it sparked a productivity boom that led economic growth to take off.

Investment depends on the savings rate.

Companies grow their capital stock by investing in new equipment and structures. This process is so important that we'll spend all of Chapter 14 on investment and all of Chapter 15 exploring the role that financial markets play in this process. For now, the key point is that investment occurs out of resources that are saved rather than consumed. And so, the savings rate is a critical determinant of investment, which ultimately determines the amount of capital each worker has to work with.

Foreign investment builds the capital stock.

The other way to grow the American capital stock is through *foreign investment*. For instance, in 2018, Toyota and Mazda partnered to build a new car production plant in Huntsville, Alabama, that produced its first vehicle in 2022. This more than $2 million foreign investment added to the U.S. capital stock, and it employs U.S. workers who will work with that capital. The cars that recently started rolling off that production line are made in the United States, and therefore count toward U.S. GDP. The wages will go to the United States, but the profits will go to the Japanese owners of the plant.

New Recipes for Combining Ingredients: Technological Progress

Recall that a production function is like a cookbook, listing the most important recipes for mixing labor, human capital, and physical capital together to produce output. This points to the final source of economic growth: New ideas, recipes, or production techniques. Economists refer to new methods for using existing resources as **technological progress.** It is important because these new methods create ways to produce more valuable output from your existing inputs.

technological progress New methods for using existing resources.

Technological progress is like a new recipe for combining ingredients.

Technological progress can involve new production techniques that build on scientific discoveries to allow more output from existing inputs. For instance, the discovery of how to rotate crops to replenish the soil led to a massive boost in crop yields. It's effectively a new recipe for farmers, telling them how to combine their land, labor, and capital in a way that produces more output. Technological progress can also result from new and better management techniques. For instance, the Japanese auto industry is famously efficient due to ingenious management techniques its automakers use to run streamlined production lines. Their recipe for combining workers and capital has since spread around the world.

Sometimes technological progress literally is just a new recipe. Oral rehydration therapy might be the most important medical advance in a generation. It's a blend of sugar, salt, and water, which if mixed in just the right proportions, will revive a child dying from cholera-induced diarrhea. Since this recipe was discovered in the 1960s, it has saved tens of millions of lives.

Computers embody technological progress.   The technological progress that sparked the computer revolution is also a new recipe. The key ingredient of computers is sand (or silicone dioxide), and it has existed for thousands of years, but we typically used it in other recipes: Kids at the beach built castles out of it, builders used it as an ingredient in their cement mixes, and artisans in Venice melted it to create glass. What's new is the understanding that silica can both conduct and block electricity, which means that it's a semiconductor. That understanding created new recipes in which sand can be combined with other ingredients to create the sophisticated chips that power modern computers.

This highlights an important distinction. Technological progress doesn't refer to computers, or even the silicone chips that power them. Those are items of physical capital that *embody* technological progress. The underlying technological change is the idea or recipe for combining these ingredients to create a computer.

We had the ingredients the whole time.

Johannes Kornelius/ Shutterstock

Interpreting the DATA   The falling cost of light

Technological progress is responsible for one of the most transformative changes you've probably never thought about: The increased production of light. The bulb that's shining above your head right now is providing what was once an extraordinary luxury. New recipes for producing light have made it plentiful and cheap today.

Go back far enough in human history, and the only recipe to create light involved gathering wood, rubbing two rocks or sticks together, and using the resulting spark to light a fire. It would take a solid 60-hour week of work to gather enough firewood to produce 1,000 lumen-hours of light, which is probably less than your overhead light will give off over the next hour. Thousands of years later, a new recipe was developed, in which wicks were dipped into molten animal fat to create candles. George Washington calculated that burning one candle for five hours each night would cost him £8 per year, which took about 120 hours of work to either earn the money or make the candles. Many families lived in darkness, instead.

All that changed when Thomas Edison created an extraordinary new method for producing light by inventing the electric light bulb. Your great-great-grandparents could work a 60-hour week to get five months of continuous light. Today, we have LED lights, and that same amount of labor will buy you all the light you'll need for the rest of your life, plus some. Figure 9 shows just how much the price of light has fallen due to these new recipes for producing light. The declining cost has transformed modern life, so that we can spend our evenings reading, studying, or socializing. It's a story that illuminates just how important technological progress can be. ■

Figure 9 | **The Declining Price of Light**

Hours of work to produce 1,000 lumen-hours ratio (or logarithmic) scale

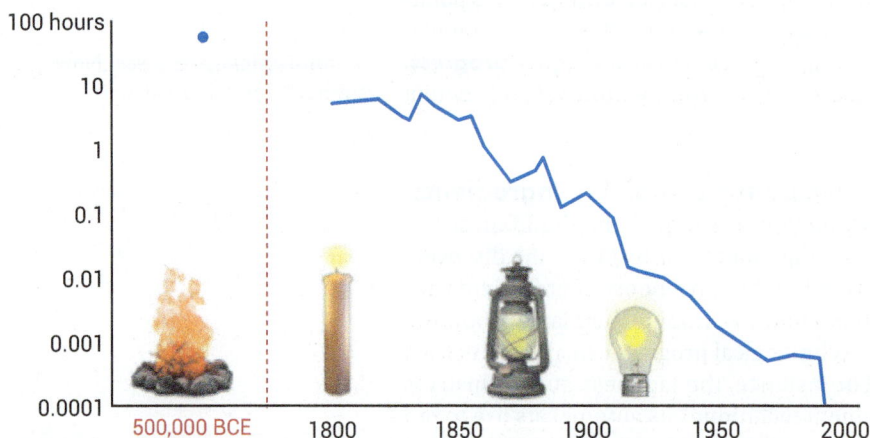

Data from: William D. Nordhaus, "Do real-output and real-wage measures capture reality? The history of lighting suggests not."

The Analytics of Economic Growth

Learning Objective *Understand how workers, capital accumulation, and technological progress work together to create economic growth.*

So far we've explored the ingredients that determine how much a country produces at a given point in time. Now it's time to see what happens when we put these ingredients together to answer the question: Where does economic growth come from, and will it continue?

Analyzing the Production Function

We'll return to the production function, because it determines the roles that new ideas, labor, human capital, and physical capital play in determining output. This framework generates a number of important insights into the process of economic growth.

Insight 1: Constant returns to scale means doubling inputs will double output.   Most economists believe that doubling all of the inputs to the aggregate production function — the labor, physical capital, and human capital used — will lead to twice the output. This implies that the production function has **constant returns to scale,** which means that increasing all inputs by some proportion will cause output to rise by the same proportion. The *replication argument* explains why. If you want to double the output of your factory, you can simply replicate everything you're already doing — opening a second, identical factory that will produce just as much as your first, using just as much labor, human capital, and physical capital. In total, then, you'll be using twice the inputs — twice the labor, human capital, and physical capital — to produce twice the output.

You can also apply this argument at the level of the whole economy, so that replicating each individual business would yield an economy that is twice as big and that uses twice the inputs to produce twice the output.

This means that if the United States grows, and the capital stock grows enough that capital per person stays the same, and investment in education also rises in proportion so that human capital per person is unchanged, then GDP per person will stay the same.

Insight 2: There are diminishing returns to capital. Now you know that if you double all your inputs, then you'll double all your outputs. But what happens if you just double your physical capital and don't change the number of workers? You'll produce more, but you won't produce twice as much. Increasing only physical capital will produce a less than proportionate increase in output. Precisely how much extra it produces depends on how much capital you have to begin with.

The **law of diminishing returns** says that when one input is held constant, increases in the other inputs will, at some point, yield smaller and smaller increases in output. In this case, if there's a fixed number of workers and technology isn't changing, successive increments of physical capital will yield smaller and smaller boosts to what each worker produces. Similarly, with a fixed physical capital stock, adding more workers will yield smaller boosts to production. This doesn't mean that more capital or more workers aren't helpful, but that each additional investment is less helpful than the previous one when at least one factor of production is held constant.

Figure 10 shows the relationship between the amount of physical capital per worker and the output they produce — in other words, GDP per worker. When workers don't have many tools to work with, the marginal benefit of adding one more unit of capital per person will lead to large gains in output. But once each worker has a lot of capital, adding more capital has a smaller effect. The idea is that more tools are helpful, but at some point, extra tools won't make that much of a difference.

constant returns to scale Increasing all inputs by some proportion will cause output to rise by the same proportion.

law of diminishing returns When one input is held constant, increases in the other inputs will, at some point, begin to yield smaller and smaller increases in output.

Figure 10 | **Diminishing Returns to Capital**

A given increase in physical capital per person raises GDP per worker, but at a diminishing rate.

Ⓐ A given **change in the capital stock** will increase GDP per worker, but by how much depends on how much capital you start with.

Ⓑ When capital per worker is low to begin with, GDP per worker **increases by a lot**.

Ⓒ When capital per worker is high to begin with, GDP per worker **increases by less**.

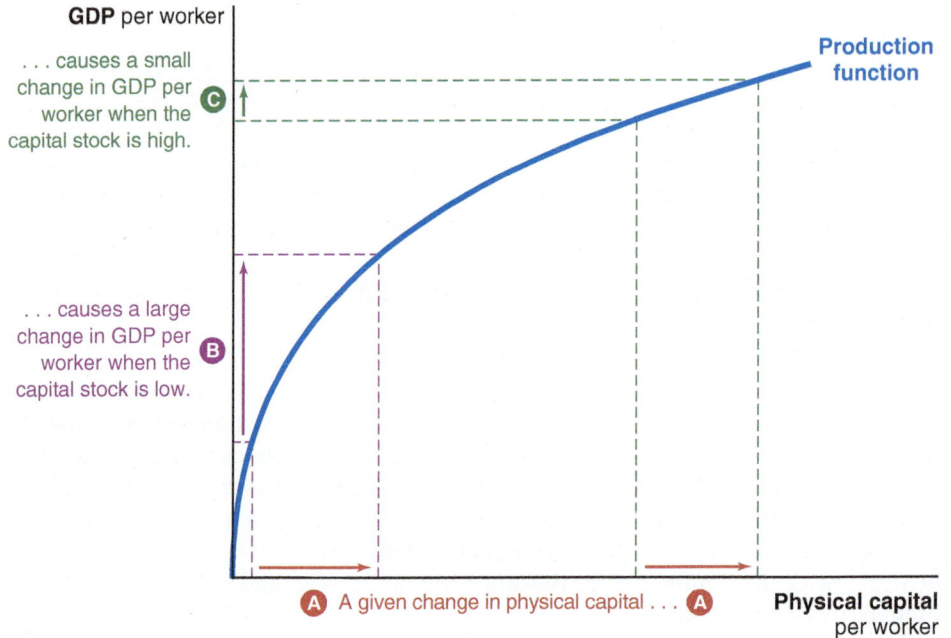

GDP per worker

. . . causes a small change in GDP per worker when the capital stock is high. Ⓒ

. . . causes a large change in GDP per worker when the capital stock is low. Ⓑ

Production function

Ⓐ A given change in physical capital . . . Ⓐ **Physical capital** per worker

South Korea is no longer a poor country, thanks to catch-up growth.

catch-up growth The rapid growth that occurs when a relatively poor country invests in its physical capital.

Insight 3: Poor countries can enjoy catch-up growth. Diminishing returns means that in rich countries with lots of physical capital, additional investment in capital won't cause much of a boost in output. But it can lead to a much bigger gain in output for poor countries that have very little capital to start with. So if a relatively poor country starts investing in machines, factories, and other equipment, it will experience relatively rapid output growth.

Indeed, this is the story of South Korea's extraordinary growth that rocketed it from a poor country to a rich one. In 1970, South Korea had very low levels of physical capital per person. Over the next 30 years, GDP grew by a factor of 12, fueled by a 27-fold increase in the quantity of physical capital. A comparison with the United States makes the point clearly. Physical capital per person increased by roughly $65,000 in both South Korea and the United States, but because the United States already had abundant physical capital, it didn't generate growth anywhere near as impressive.

The rapid growth that occurs when a relatively poor country invests in physical capital is known as **catch-up growth.** It raises the possibility that if poor countries make similar investments to rich countries, the gap between poor and rich countries will narrow.

Capital Accumulation and the Solow Model

Our analysis so far suggests that capital accumulation can play an important role in boosting output. But can capital accumulation, by itself, serve as an engine for *ongoing* growth in output per person? To answer this question, we'll need to consider *both* the production function (which describes how more capital creates more output) and the process of capital accumulation (in which more output leads to more investment in physical capital). The set of insights that we'll gain from simultaneously analyzing the production function, investment, capital accumulation, and economic growth is some-times called the *Solow model*.

Insight 4: The capital stock will grow as long as investment outpaces depreciation.

A country's capital stock evolves over time as a result of investment and depreciation. Investments in new equipment and structures boost the capital stock and, therefore the economy's capacity to produce output. But over time, machines break down, factories crumble, and roads get potholes. So each year some proportion of the existing capital stock is destroyed by **depreciation.**

This means that the capital stock will grow — that is, capital will continue to accumulate — as long as investment exceeds depreciation. And the production function tells you that as long as capital per person is growing, then so is output per person, which means living standards are rising. Taken together, this means that the economy will keep growing as long as investment exceeds depreciation.

depreciation The decline in capital due to wear and tear, obsolescence, accidental damage, and aging.

Insight 5: Physical capital per worker will eventually stop growing.

Unfortunately, this won't continue forever. First, there's the problem of rising depreciation: As the capital stock grows, there are more machines, and if a fixed fraction of them fail each year, total depreciation will grow. That means the economy will need to generate larger and larger amounts of investment merely to replace the capital lost to depreciation. Second, there's the problem of diminishing returns: Each increment of additional capital creates a smaller and smaller addition to output. If businesses devote some share of their output to investment, then these smaller boosts to output will yield successively smaller boosts to investment.

This combination of diminishing returns and depreciation means that at some point the amount of new investment the economy generates will no longer exceed the amount of capital lost to depreciation. When investment and depreciation are equal, the capital stock stops growing.

This machine makes them more productive, but how many can they use at once?

Insight 6: Capital accumulation can't sustain long-term economic growth.

The key question the Solow model asks is whether capital accumulation can generate sustained economic growth. Will a burst of investment set in motion a virtuous cycle, in which the increase in capital leads to more output, and that output is used to fund more investment, which will further increase the capital stock, which in turn will further boost output, and so on?

That virtuous cycle exists, but we've discovered that eventually this process peters out. Each successive cycle of increased capital yields successively smaller boosts in output, and so smaller boosts in investment. But on each successive cycle, the economy's depreciation bill keeps rising. Eventually the process stalls because the economy grows to the point where new investment in capital merely offsets depreciation. The capital stock remains at a rest point that we call the *steady state*. And when the capital stock stops growing, then — in the absence of technological progress or other factors changing the number of workers or their skills — output will stop growing too. Economic growth has stalled, and the economy has come to rest.

We've discovered that while capital accumulation alone can't support *sustained* economic growth, it can explain why poor countries will experience rapid growth as they catch up or converge to rich countries. But capital accumulation can't explain why rich countries such as the United States and much of Europe have enjoyed sustained economic growth. That means we're going to need to look elsewhere to figure out what's driving the ongoing rise in output per person in advanced economies.

Technological Progress

The key to sustained economic growth is technological progress. The development of new production methods creates new ways to combine existing resources to produce more valuable output. Businesses can use these new and improved recipes to produce more output from any given set of inputs.

Figure 11 | Technological Progress Shifts the Production Function

Ⓐ Technological progress leads to an **increase in the output produced with a given set of inputs**.

Ⓑ An economy with a given amount of capital per worker can now **produce more output** per person than before.

Ⓒ Technological progress also boosts the **extra output** that each extra machine produces, making investment more productive and valuable.

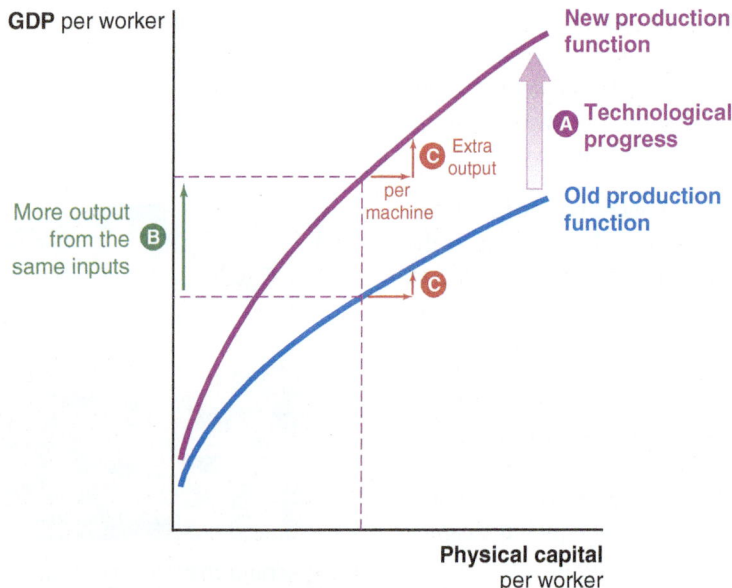

Technological progress shifts the production function. That means it increases the output that's produced from any given level of inputs. As Figure 11 illustrates, this shifts the production function upward, boosting the amount of output each person produces, for a given level of capital per person.

Technological progress can make investing in capital more productive and more valuable. Specifically, notice that the new production function in Figure 11 is steeper. That means that the extra output you get from investing in one more machine has risen. A burst of technological progress will also spur a burst of new investment, and the economy will grow toward a new and higher steady-state level of capital. So technological progress both leads to more output from existing inputs and also spurs capital accumulation, raising the level of inputs.

Figure 11 illustrates that one burst of technological progress can push the production function up, which will raise the level of GDP. And so it follows that sustained and continual bursts of technological progress will lead to sustained growth in GDP. By this view, the key to sustained economic growth is sustained technological progress, continually pushing the production function up.

Technological progress relies on new ideas. Now that you know how important technological progress is to economic growth, a natural question is: How do we get it? New technology is fundamentally about new ideas. It is new ideas that create new ways to transform existing physical inputs into more valuable outputs. But where do new ideas come from, and how do they power economic growth?

Two things drive technological progress: how quickly new ideas are created, and how many resources are devoted to generating new ideas. Workers can produce either goods and services or new ideas. So the number of workers focused on new ideas can rise both from a rising population, and also by allocating resources away from producing goods and services toward producing new ideas. There's a trade-off here: In the short run, if everyone produced goods and services, our economy would produce more goods and services. But in the long run, with no one investing in technological progress, there would be no economic growth. Only if enough resources are devoted to ongoing research and development will the economy yield a steady stream of new ideas, powering ongoing economic growth.

Marie Curie's ideas about radiation led to discoveries, and eventually treatments that could cure cancer.

The absence of technological progress explains why growth took so long to occur. The insight that technological progress requires resources can help explain why the world went millennia without generating economic growth: When people were in a battle to survive, there were no spare resources to devote to generating new ideas. And so subsistence living begat subsistence living.

This insight also explains why the agricultural revolution was the catalyst that sparked the modern era of sustained economic growth. Improvements in agriculture allowed societies to produce more food with less labor. With more time to think, people started generating new ideas. And those ideas spurred the Industrial Revolution, which led to the modern era of sustained economic growth. It's a process that builds on itself: The more an economy is already producing, the easier it is to sacrifice production today in order to invest in generating the ideas that will power future economic growth. You can think about all this through the lens of the **opportunity cost principle**. Back when humans weren't producing enough food to prevent starvation, the opportunity cost of producing new ideas instead of farming was producing less food, which translated to starvation and death. Today, the opportunity cost of having people work on innovation is lower, and so we do more of it.

Technological progress allowed us to break the cycle of poverty.

Thomas Malthus, an eighteenth-century economist, feared that living standards could never truly improve because as more food was produced, the population would grow, which would require more food production. He believed that food production would never successfully outpace population growth, so the world was forever doomed to subsistence living. Malthus was wrong about the future, but he was right about the past. Remember that for more than a million years, there was so little economic growth that GDP per person remained near the minimum necessary to sustain life. The reason for this is that for most of history, there was little technological progress.

Malthus was wrong about the future because technological progress in agriculture vastly outpaced population growth. The earth's ability "to produce subsistence for humanity" was much greater than he ever thought possible, and that change occurred because of new ideas about how to produce more with less. We now grow food using a small fraction of the resources that were required in Malthus's time.

There are no limits to technological progress.

Some wonder if there are any limits to how fast the economy can grow. They worry that if the economy grows too quickly, we may run out of the things we need, such as oil, land, and other natural resources. You already learned that such concerns in the eighteenth century focused on population growth. Modern-day concerns about the limits of economic growth have often focused on energy consumption. Not only might greenhouse gases warm the planet, but energy use gives off waste heat, and so the more energy we use, the hotter the planet will become. But it turns out that even as countries like the United States have continued to grow, we haven't increased our energy consumption much. Indeed, the consumption of fossil fuels in the United States declined over the past two decades. On a per-person basis, U.S. energy consumption peaked in the 1970s. This doesn't mean that you shouldn't worry about pollution; it just means that you can't conclude that our energy consumption means economic growth is limited.

If new ideas are the engine of economic growth, then our ability to combine existing resources in ever more productive and valuable ways is limited only by our imagination. As long as we keep coming up with new ways to do more with less, the economy can keep growing. As a result, most economists expect that we will enjoy ongoing economic growth and continually rising living standards for the foreseeable future.

Ideas can generate unlimited growth.

Society's ability to continually produce new ideas is the key to unlocking long-run growth. And idea-driven, rather than capital-driven, economic growth can be sustained because ideas are different from physical capital in three ways:

- *Ideas can be freely shared.* My use of a new idea doesn't make it harder for you to use that idea. Economists refer to this as *nonrival*, which means that one person's use of an idea doesn't subtract from another's.

- *Ideas do not depreciate with use.* An idea doesn't wear out the way a factory does.

- *Ideas may promote other ideas.* Ideas can beget new ideas through spillover effects. For example, Apple's invention of the iPhone spurred app creators to invent new applications for smartphones. Ideas can also beget new ideas by lowering the opportunity cost of producing new ideas. This means that ideas can create a virtuous cycle of more ideas, more growth, and then even more ideas.

> Remember:
> - Ideas can be freely shared
> - Ideas do not depreciate with use
> - Ideas may promote other ideas

The fact that ideas can be *freely shared* means that any new idea can be deployed across thousands or even millions of producers, making the entire economy more productive.

Because ideas *don't depreciate* with use, we don't need ongoing annual investments to be able to keep using an idea. This means that unlike investment in physical capital, all new investment in ideas will boost the stock of ideas, which generates higher levels of output. As long we continue investing in the research and development that generates the ideas that fuel technological progress, the economy will continue to grow. And the insight that ideas may *promote other ideas* means that the process of discovering new ideas can be self-sustaining, leading economic growth *to be self-reinforcing.*

EVERYDAY Economics   Innovative companies make time for new ideas

Successful managers know that new ideas are the key not just to economic growth, but to the growth of their own business. Google founders Larry Page and Sergey Brin recognized the trade-off workers face between producing goods and services and producing new ideas — and they wanted to ensure that their employees spent time working on new ideas. That's why Google embraces the "20% rule," which empowers all employees to spend up to 20% of their workweek dreaming up and developing their own ideas for new products. Google argues that this option helps keep their highly creative employees engaged in generating new ideas. It also ensures that workers maintain control over their creative energy and some of their work time. Does it work? It sure seems to: Gmail, Google Maps, and Google News all started as projects that employees pursued in their 20% time.

Lots of companies implement similar tactics to ensure that their employees devote some time to developing new ideas. For example, the CEO of Bosch Group asked its entire workforce to form into teams that were tasked with trying to come up with ways to compete against Bosch. They took the best ideas these teams came up with and gave a selected group of people eight weeks' leave from their regular duties to see if they could turn the idea into a new or improved product for Bosch.

The bottom line is that it takes time to come up with new ideas, and smart managers make sure that their workers have time to innovate. ■

You may think it's just a washing machine, but it started with an idea.

The problem with ideas is that they are often *nonexcludable,* which means that it's hard for you to prevent others from using — and profiting off — your idea. It's a problem that can lead people to underinvest in coming up with new ideas, creating innovations, and bringing them to the market. Here's why: If you invent a safe self-driving car, you can sell those cars and potentially make a nice profit. But the faster others can copy your idea and get their competing cars ready to sell, the smaller your profits will be. You might be better off copying someone else's idea, rather than spending a lot of your time and resources coming up with a new idea. And so the nonexcludability of ideas creates an incentive to imitate rather than innovate.

As a result, businesses will devote fewer resources to innovation than is in society's best interests. To see this, let's apply the core principles of good decision making to the question of how much your business will invest in research and development. Apply the **marginal principle**, which says to break the question of how much to invest down to: Should I invest one more dollar? Next, apply the **cost-benefit principle** and conclude that you should if the marginal benefits *to your business* of the additional dollar invested exceed the marginal costs *you pay.* This leads to the right decision for you, but the wrong decision for society if others benefit from your research and development. Because ideas can be copied and innovations have spillover effects, others benefit from your investments in generating new ideas. Yet those benefits are not included in your personal cost-benefit calculation. That's why market forces tend to lead businesses to invest too little in generating new ideas.

But well-designed intellectual property laws can help ensure that more innovation occurs. Indeed, institutions — the "rules of the game" — play an important role in fostering economic growth, and so our next task is to explore their effects.

10.4 Public Policy: Why Institutions Matter for Growth

Learning Objective *Find out why government institutions matter for economic growth.*

So far we've focused on the proximate causes of economic growth: It's the result of new ideas, as well as investing in human capital and accumulating physical capital. But that just pushes the question one level deeper: What factors determine whether people will invent new ideas and invest in human or physical capital? That's our next task. To preview, the key is *incentives*, which depend on *institutions*.

The **cost-benefit principle** provides a useful reminder of the importance of incentives. What's the benefit of investing in research and development if your competitors can steal your ideas? Why work hard if the government can seize your output? Why work to develop new products if there aren't roads and networks that will allow you to distribute them? The government, and institutions more generally, provide the framework that creates the right incentives for people to come up with new ideas and bring them to the marketplace. The institutional environment created by the government determines the rules that people follow, and the incentives for their work. That environment is a crucial determinant of people's willingness to invest in education, capital, and ideas.

The most common reasons that countries fail to grow are related to their institutions and government. Two countries may have the same amount of physical and human capital, but what they produce depends on how efficiently workers, workers' skills, and physical capital are allocated across the economy. And that allocation has a lot to do with the "rules of the game," or the institutional structure in a country. Do property rights protect people's investments? Can you count on the government to enforce the laws so everyone is playing by the same, agreed-upon rules? Can you trust the government? Is it stable? The answers to these questions should guide your choices, and they determine how fast your country's economy will grow. The government also plays an important role in encouraging investment in physical and human capital and funding research into new ideas. Let's explore some of the important ways a country's institutions and government determine its outcomes.

Property Rights

Property rights determine who controls a tangible or intangible resource. When property rights are well defined, the rules are clear, and people can spend less time fighting over a particular resource. This is also what provides the incentives for you to work hard to be able to get a resource like money, land, or an ownership stake in a company — since you know that once you have it, that right will be respected.

If you grew up with siblings, you probably have a good sense of the importance of property rights. Perhaps a parent ("the government" in your household) helped enforce whose turn it was to use a shared household resource like a computer. Without clear rules and enforcement, you might have wasted a lot of time fighting with a sibling to claim your right to a resource instead of actually spending time with that resource. Or perhaps you got a part-time job to be able to afford your own laptop. Would you have worked as hard if your sibling could simply take it from you without asking?

To have well-defined property rights requires having a clear set of laws that establish your rights, and a stable, trusted system of enforcing those laws. If you decide to invest in a friend's new designer clothing rental business, you have to trust that you'll receive and be able to keep your share of the business and profits. Without property rights and a trusted enforcement system that protects your rights, no one creates wealth because they fear that they will simply lose it. That means that trusted and efficient enforcement institutions play an important role in creating the right environment for economic growth.

People are reluctant to make investments when they worry that their business partners or others will successfully take off with their money, or when they fear that contracts

property rights Control over a tangible or intangible resource.

Property rights matter.

are unlikely to be enforced. Sometimes the government does too little to enforce property rights and the rule of law, and sometimes the government itself becomes part of the problem. In corrupt countries and political systems, people fear that government will strip them of their wealth.

Government Stability

Corruption and political instability can discourage investment and innovation. Turmoil at home creates incentives for political leaders to extract resources for their personal gain. And it discourages investment since political uncertainty means people can't count on receiving the returns on their investment.

Think back to Argentina's history of stalled economic growth in the twentieth century. After several decades as the world's fastest-growing economy, Argentina suffered military coups in 1930, 1943, 1955, 1962, 1966, and 1976. Needless to say, generations of Argentinians lived with political instability throughout their lives, and it shaped the choices they made. The problem wasn't only political instability, but also a periodic overhauling of the Supreme Court, a perception that property rights were insecure, and a lack of confidence in the central bank to control inflation. These were all important reasons why Argentina failed to thrive over the past century.

Efficiency of Regulation

In the United States, the typical business is up and running in just a handful of days. And if you want to start selling your uniquely designed jewelry on Etsy, you can start your business in just a few minutes. In some cases, it's essential to have regulators to ensure that your new business is going to do good rather than harm. For instance, it's better for society if a new restaurant is following health standards, or a new manufacturing plant isn't dumping harmful chemicals into the local water supply. Sometimes it even helps get your business going when potential customers know that they can trust that your product won't hurt them, since government regulations provide some basic assurances.

In general, regulatory oversight in the United States is lighter than in most of the rest of the world. The World Bank estimates that it takes 6 days to start a business in the United States. Compare that with Argentina, where it takes 25 days to open a business (and even this reflects a substantial improvement from the 66 days it took in 2003). Political instability often goes hand in hand with excessive bureaucratic obstacles. For example, in Venezuela, it took 230 days to open a business in 2016. In the time it takes you to get through the red tape in Venezuela to open a business, you could have opened nearly 40 businesses in the United States.

You may find it surprising that, on average, it's harder to open a business in poorer countries than in richer countries. After all, the poorer the country, the more it could benefit from entrepreneurship. Yet this is the trap a lot of countries are in — it's hard to invest or innovate because of excessive red tape. These bureaucratic obstacles are often compounded by government corruption and insufficient enforcement of property rights. Together, this creates few incentives to invest and innovate, which is an important reason why some countries are poor. Regulation and rules are essential to a well-functioning market economy, but they can also be inefficient or excessive. Sometimes they create more problems than they solve.

Government Policy to Encourage Innovation

Government policy plays a particularly important role when it comes to innovation. A trusted government, with clear property rights, a well-functioning legal framework, and regulations that effectively balance protecting the public with encouraging entrepreneurship are all part of the institutional structure that economists have shown is crucial for economic success. Government policy is also important for helping to create incentives and

If you don't trust the government, you probably won't start a new business.

It isn't hard to set up your own business in the United States.

support the development of new ideas. One way it does that is by protecting investments in new ideas to ensure those who invest in them are able to profit off their investment. Another way is by directly paying for research and development. Let's explore these ideas a little further.

Innovation strategy 1: Create incentives through intellectual property laws. Discovering new ideas, coming up with new inventions, or designing innovative business processes can be an expensive endeavor, costing you millions of dollars in research and development. The cost-benefit principle suggests that entrepreneurs will make this investment only if the benefits to them exceed the costs. But if other businesses can simply copy your ideas, then some of the benefits that your idea creates will end up benefiting them rather than you. And if enough rivals copy your invention, competitive forces will push the price down, meaning that customers benefit at the expense of your bottom line. This undermines the incentive for businesses to invest in innovation. The government uses intellectual property laws to protect the value of your innovation. These laws typically give you an exclusive right to use your idea, ensuring that other businesses that want to use it will have to pay you for the right to do so. One form of intellectual property right is copyright, which gives authors and artists exclusive rights to their work. Trademarks protect firms from competitors who want to use their brand names. And patents grant people and companies exclusive rights to inventions, whether it's the design for the iPhone or how to make a new pharmaceutical drug.

If you invent something new, patents give you the right to be the only seller, typically for a period of several decades, giving you an effective monopoly. This gives you the power to charge a high price and hence enjoy large profits. The prospect of these large profits represents a large benefit to innovating, leading businesses to do more of it. The difficult policy question is to figure out how long of a period an inventor should be given the right to be a monopolist. Since the government is trying to balance the benefit of providing a strong incentive for innovation against the cost to consumers of allowing a monopolist to charge high prices, protections make sense, but only up to a point. For instance, a country might want to let a drug company be the only seller of a new drug for a few decades, but it wouldn't want to protect that drug from competition forever.

Innovation strategy 2: Subsidize research and development. While intellectual property laws aim to boost the benefit of innovation, an alternative approach focuses on reducing the cost of innovating. In particular, governments can directly subsidize research into new ideas. When the government helps lower the cost of innovation, businesses do more of it. In the United States, research and development subsidies go to companies, the government, research centers, nonprofits, and universities.

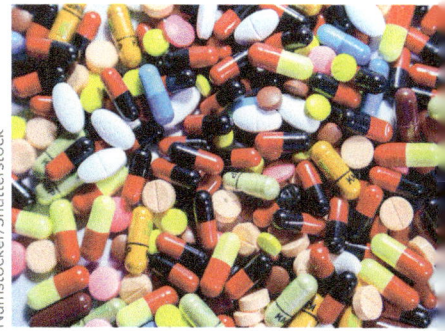
Patents encourage innovation in areas ranging from iPhones to pharmaceutical drugs.

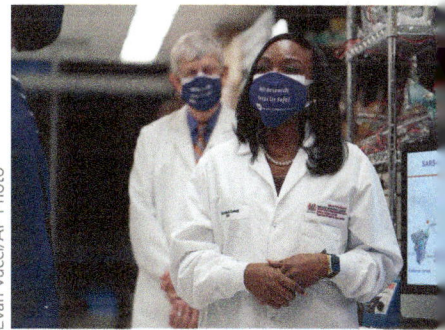
The government subsidizes important research.

Institutions that promote economic growth:
1. Property rights
2. Government stability
3. Efficient regulation
4. Government policy encouraging innovation

How the government encourages innovation:
1. Intellectual property laws
2. Research and development subsidies

Interpreting the DATA How did the United States get so rich?

Economists credit the success of the United States to a combination of factors. The United States has strong institutions like the rule of law, competitive markets, and a democratic system of government. It also has a strong base of both physical capital and human capital, as well as highly developed technology, norms, and institutions that transform capital and labor into products and services that people want to buy. The United States industrialized before many other countries, and it was a center of innovation, manufacturing, and trade. It grew enormously, from a GDP per person of roughly $2,000 in 1800 to over $69,200 in 2021.

In contrast, many other countries are not so lucky. They suffer from political instability or from governments that seize property or run on bribes. This can lead to inadequate investment in physical and human capital, little technological development, and a lack of institutions promoting growth. Poor countries tend to stay poor until their institutions improve. ∎

10.5 | Tying It Together

Growth Matters

If you compressed the last million years of human history into 24 hours, then it's only in the last one minute that humanity has moved beyond grinding poverty and subsistence. That makes that last minute seem rather miraculous: Something unleashed the forces of economic growth, and as a result, today you live in one of the richest countries in the world, at the richest moment in the history of humanity.

Perhaps that inspires a feeling of gratitude. For me, it also inspires a sense of wonder: What caused this growth, and will it continue? While some countries have enjoyed the good fortune that economic growth brings, others have experienced slower growth, and as a result, billions of people remain poor. What explains this?

As we've seen, small differences in economic growth rates, once they've compounded for hundreds of years, can have massive effects. This means that the insights that might yield even a small change in the rate of economic growth have staggering consequences for human well-being.

This chapter draws together the key insights from generations of economists trying to uncover the drivers of economic growth. The result is a basic framework that identifies the key ingredients of output as labor, human capital, and physical capital, along with the recipes or technology we use to combine them. More inputs lead to more output. An earlier generation of economists had hoped that the process of physical capital accumulation — boosting the quantity of machinery available to workers — would be enough to sustain ongoing growth. But the Solow model dashes that hope: It delivers the good news that boosting the rate at which we invest in capital will boost output, which in turn will generate more investment in capital, and hence a further boost in output. That means greater investment can lead the rate of economic growth to rise for a few decades as the economy transitions toward a new high-output steady state. But the Solow model also delivers bad news, explaining why capital accumulation is not a strong enough force to generate sustained economic growth. The problem is that eventually diminishing returns kick in, and extra machines won't generate enough extra output to pay for the extra maintenance they require. When the economy hits its new steady state, this force no longer propels the economy forward.

What, then, drives long-term economic growth? New ideas — in the form of ingenious inventions, advanced business processes, and innovative management techniques — provide new recipes for combining labor, physical capital, and human capital. These new recipes allow us to create more output with the same resources. Ideas don't depreciate, and so if we keep generating new ideas, the economy can keep growing. As long as ideas help us use our existing resources more effectively, there are no limits to growth.

What economic settings will lead to more investment in new ideas, supplemented by investments in physical capital that embodies these new ideas, and in the human capital needed to take advantage of new technologies? What really matters are the incentives and institutions that spur more of these investments. Careful studies of the varied growth paths of different countries over many periods of history reveal that property rights, government stability, effective regulation, and research and development policies all encourage the investments that will cause growth. Together, these insights provide a roadmap that poor countries might be able to use to ignite economic growth.

As important as these findings are, economists have yet to discover the perfect recipe for generating new ideas. This is why economics is engaged in a search for new ideas about how to generate . . . new ideas. Yes, that sounds a bit meta. But it also explains just why economics is so important: If ideas are important drivers of growth, then ideas about how to motivate businesses to invest in creating more ideas are the most important ideas of all. If economists can figure out which rules and incentives will generate the most new ideas, we may catalyze an era of even faster economic growth. The possibilities are extraordinary. A new idea about new ideas could turn out to be the most transformative idea in the history of humanity.

Economic growth can continue as long as we keep coming up with new ideas.

RichVintage/Getty Images

Chapter 10 Review
Chapter at a Glance

Ingredients of Economic Growth

Labor input: Number of workers to transform raw materials into products and services that people want to buy.

Human capital: The accumulated knowledge and skills that make a worker more productive.

Physical capital: The total amount of tools, machinery, and structures that can be used in the production of goods and services.

Technological progress: New methods for using existing resources to produce more valuable output.

How the Components Work Together

Production function: The methods for transforming *labor input*, *human capital*, and *physical capital* into goods and services (outputs).

Constant returns to scale: Doubling *all* inputs (*labor input*, *human capital*, and *physical capital*) leads to a doubling of all the outputs.

Diminishing returns: When *one* input (*labor input*, *human capital*, or *physical capital*) is held constant, increases in the other inputs will, at some point, begin to yield smaller and smaller increases in output.

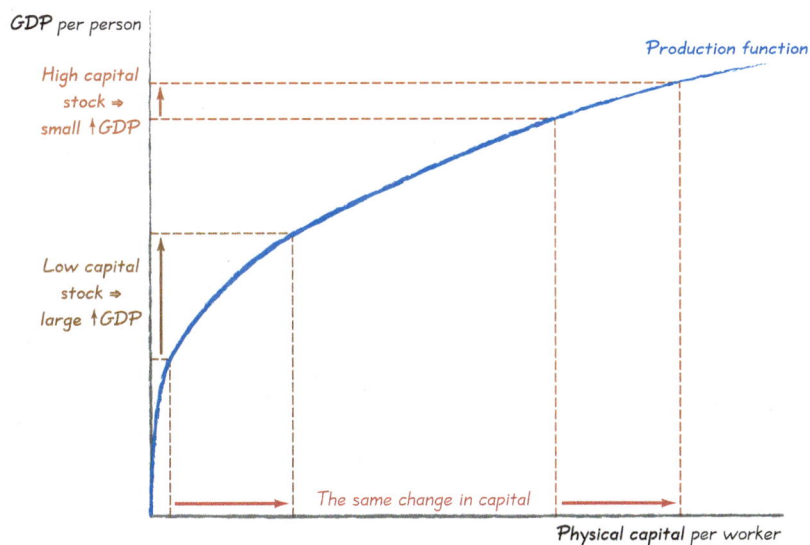

Technological change increases GDP per person for any level of capital per person.

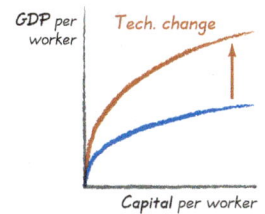

Technological progress relies on new ideas.

Ideas can generate unlimited growth because they:

1. Can be freely shared
2. Don't depreciate with use
3. May promote other ideas

Diminishing returns and **depreciation** mean that investment in *physical capital* is a **limited source of growth**.

Catch-up growth: The rapid growth that occurs when a relatively poor country (with low capital stock) invests in its *physical capital*.

Why institutions matter for economic growth: They provide the framework that creates the right incentives for people to invest in *physical* and *human* capital and generate **new ideas and products**.

Property rights	Without property rights and a trusted enforcement system, no one creates wealth.
Government stability	Corruption and political instability discourage investment and innovation by reducing the potential benefits from such investments.
Efficiency of regulation	Excessive red tape can make it hard to invest or innovate.
Government policy to encourage innovation	Government policy can support development of new ideas by: 1. Increasing the marginal benefit through intellectual property laws 2. Decreasing the marginal cost by subsidizing research and development

Key Terms

capital stock, 255

catch-up growth, 258

constant returns to scale, 257

depreciation (capital), 259

human capital, 250

labor productivity, 252

law of diminishing returns, 257

physical capital, 250

production function, 249

property rights, 263

technological progress, 255

Study Problems

Learning Objective 10.1 *Learn how economies have grown over time.*

1. Since the Industrial Revolution, economic growth has increased tremendously. Discuss some of the outcomes of that economic growth.

2. Consider the history of the world from 1 million B.C. until now. Although limited data exists from early history, we still have some information about how people lived and how much they consumed.

   a. Has the global rate of economic growth remained constant throughout history?

   b. Which of the following time periods experienced the highest *average annual growth rate*?

   • 1 million B.C. to 1200 A.D.

   • 1200 to 1800 A.D.

   • 1800 to 1950 A.D.

   • 1950 to 1975 A.D.

Learning Objective 10.2 *Uncover the ingredients for economic growth.*

3. All U.S. states require children to attend school. Mandatory school attendance ends at ages 16–18, depending on the state. The adult literacy rate in North America was 100% in 2020. Discuss how compulsory education impacts labor productivity, the aggregate production function, and overall economic growth.

4. An example of U.K. foreign investment is the aerospace manufacturing plant in Austin, Texas, that is owned by the U.K.-owned BAE Systems. Describe how this investment affects the three inputs into the aggregate production function and GDP growth.

5. Discuss an example of technological progress not mentioned in the chapter and how it impacted economic growth.

6. For each of the following, identify which inputs into the production function changed and their effects on economic growth.

   a. The government passes a new program that encourages more employers to provide on-the-job training.

   b. Improvements to health care cause an increasing share of older people to work instead of retiring.

   c. The federal government increases annual spending on national infrastructure.

   d. A large baby boom occurred two decades ago.

7. The U.S. savings rate has fallen from an annual rate of around 13% in the mid-1970s to 6% at the end of 2018. What are the consequences of a declining savings rate for economic growth?

Learning Objective 10.3 *Understand how workers, capital accumulation, and technological progress work together to create economic growth.*

8. Your friend Owen is a bit of a pessimist. "The world already has 8 billion people," he says. "The population is growing too fast. Soon, there will be a food shortage — especially for people in undeveloped countries. They are too far behind modern times." Using what you've learned about economic growth, why might Owen be wrong?

9. One analyst predicts that self-driving cars will ultimately reduce the number of cars that are produced. She argues that because self-driving cars can drive other people rather than sitting in people's driveways and garages, the United States will need to produce fewer cars. She argues that growth will slow because we are producing a decreasing number of cars each year. Do you agree? Why or why not?

10. What can you tell about an aggregate production function if real GDP per worker increases by 10% in response to all of the inputs increasing by 10%? What would you expect to happen if you doubled all the inputs? Explain your answer.

11. In the movie *Avengers: Infinity War*, antagonist Thanos believes that he can limit suffering and starvation by erasing half the population from existence. You've just watched the film with your pessimistic pal Owen. "Thanos did the right thing," Owen tells you, again claiming that humanity would be better off if the population were smaller. Use the aggregate production function presented in the chapter to show Owen how an economist would analyze Thanos's decision.

12. Technological advancements in the restaurant industry are increasing the output that can be produced by chefs and their equipment. For example, Spyce is a Boston

restaurant with robotic chefs that enable each human worker to produce and serve more meals. How will this technological progress impact the U.S. economy? Use a graph of the production function to explain the impact and clearly label the effect.

13. In Uganda, GDP per person is $2,280 per year, and in Japan it is $42,338. What do you think is likely to happen to each country's GDP per person if they both increase their physical capital per person by 20%? Which country do you expect to have a larger relative change in its output per person? Explain your answer.

14. In the debate over the Tax Cuts and Job Act of 2018, Republicans argued that businesses needed an incentive to invest more in physical capital in order for the United States to see much faster economic growth. In a rich country like the United States, why is investing in physical capital both important and yet unlikely to lead to a large increase in economic growth?

15. The International Monetary Fund (IMF) publishes World Economic Outlook Updates biannually. According to the July 2018 Update, the expected annual growth rate of advanced countries was 2.2% for 2019. On the other hand, expected annual growth for developing countries was 5.1%. Explain why developing countries might be growing so much faster than developed countries.

Learning Objective 10.4 *Find out why government institutions matter for economic growth.*

16. In 2019, Venezuelan real GDP was only a third of what it had been in 2013. This erased more than four decades of economic growth. During the same time period, charges of bribery and corruption were piling up on members of the Venezuelan government, including president Nicolás Maduro, whose 2019 reelection was widely perceived as illegitimate. Using what you learned in the chapter, discuss how bribery and corruption in the Venezuelan government could lead to declines in GDP. What are some of the crucial elements that governments must provide to encourage innovation and growth?

17. You've started developing an app that examines students' personalities and other characteristics, and sorts them into highly effective study groups. Using the cost-benefit principle, compare your incentives to innovate and develop the software if (1) anyone could just copy your code and sell it, or (2) the government allowed you to patent your code. How do your marginal benefits differ with and without intellectual property laws?

18. For each of the following institutions, provide a real-world example and explain how it promotes economic growth.

a. Enforceable property rights

b. Predictable and stable government

c. Efficient regulation

19. For years, Invisalign faced no direct competitors and was an industry leader within its niche in the orthodontics appliances market, earning $231 million profit in 2017. Invisalign pioneered the creation of clear dental trays that straighten teeth without the use of metal braces. What type of government policy fostered Invisalign's innovation and provided protection from competition? Why does the government provide protection to companies like Invisalign who can dominate a market? What do you expect to happen when the government protection expires?

Unemployment

Mary left a lucrative job at Google to work as a product manager at a tech startup. But her new company has not been as successful as expected, and she — along with half the staff — just got laid off. Two weeks into unemployment, she runs into a former colleague who is gushing about a new promotion. Mary would rather avoid telling her that things at the startup did not go well, but she summons her courage and admits that she's been laid off because she knows that any conversation can be a job lead.

Unemployment can happen to anyone.

skaman306/Moment/Getty Images

🎙 **Podcast**
Think Like an Economist
Unemployment—Does Joblessness Have to Mean Hopelessness?

Mary is a diligent job-seeker. She works hard each day to find and follow up on leads. After two months, she lands a position at a technology company where a friend works. She's thrilled to have a paycheck, but she also knows that she'll have to pinch pennies for a while: She went a few months without her usual salary and had to dip into savings to cover expenses. She wants to build her savings back up quickly, as she now knows just how important it is to have savings when facing unemployment.

Searching for a job is time-consuming and hard, both financially and emotionally. Yet jobs end as businesses fail, work becomes automated or outsourced, and factories close. And people leave jobs to pursue other opportunities, to meet personal obligations, and sometimes to take a break from a job they hate. Most people transition jobs at least ten times before they turn 50. Some job transitions may involve a period of unemployment—a time when you're ready to work, but don't have a job. No matter what the reason, when you're unemployed, you'll spend your days looking for work instead of doing work.

Some unemployment is inevitable, but that doesn't make it any less miserable when it happens. Thankfully, unemployment doesn't always last long, and understanding it will help you better manage those transitions for yourself. In this chapter, we'll learn more about unemployment and its causes. First, we'll delve into the different ways unemployment is measured to get a better understanding of the labor market. Then, we'll investigate the causes of unemployment. Finally, we'll examine the costs of unemployment, which go far beyond lost wages. The job market is a critical institution for millions of Americans, and it will be for you, too, when you graduate. So let's get started.

11.1 Employment and Unemployment

Learning Objective *Understand what unemployment is and how it's measured.*

The unemployment rate is one of the most followed economic statistics. Why? It's a good indicator of the state of the economy. But it also matters for you. Your job prospects will depend on the unemployment rate when you graduate. You or someone you love will probably be unemployed at some point. The desire to understand unemployment drives many people's interest in macroeconomics. You probably already have a sense that the unemployment rate measures the percentage of people who can't find work, but it has a formal definition and measurement approach. When the U.S. Bureau of Labor Statistics began to systematically collect data on unemployment, it worked with governments around the world to agree on a definition that would enable them to track data on unemployment over time and across countries. Let's start by first considering how governments define the employed and the unemployed.

The Employed and the Unemployed

Before we can begin to count who among us doesn't have a job, we need to figure out who to include in the group of people we are considering. After all, we don't expect toddlers to have a job, so we can't consider them unemployed! So whom should we count?

The Bureau of Labor Statistics (BLS), which has been charged by the U.S. Congress to measure the employed and the unemployed, considers everyone age 16 and older to be of *working age*. They start at 16 because that's the age at which you get to decide whether to go to school or work. (Perhaps you didn't know it was a choice!) Other countries follow a similar definition — starting the measure at their legal school-leaving age. Notice that there isn't an upper age cutoff: If you're still kicking around your own home at age 100, you'll be counted among the working-age population. The BLS focuses on the civilian, noninstitutionalized population. Therefore they measure the **working-age population** as those 16 and older who are not in the military or institutionalized.

Now that you know who's in the working-age population, it's easy to define the **employed:** They are simply people in the working-age population who are working. "Employed" doesn't necessarily mean that you have an employer; working-age adults who are self-employed are also counted as employed. For example, Uber drivers are self-employed, rather than employees of Uber. Many people work in all sorts of jobs in which they aren't considered employees — but as long as they work at least one hour during the week for pay of some kind, they are considered employed. Additionally, people who have jobs but are temporarily absent from them are considered employed whether or not they are paid for the time they are taking off.

The **unemployed** are people in the working-age population without jobs who are trying to get jobs. To be counted among the unemployed, you must be

- part of the working-age population;
- not currently working;
- actively searching for work; and
- able to accept a job if it were offered.

Notice that to be unemployed, you have to do more than want a job: You must be actually trying to get a job and available to work if you find one. This is the standard definition that has been consistently used all over the world for decades, which allows us to compare unemployment rates over time and across countries.

The employed plus the unemployed are the labor force. The **labor force** is the part of the working-age population that is employed or unemployed — they're the people who are available to produce goods and services.

---

working-age population Those age 16 or older who are not in the military or institutionalized.

employed Working-age people who are working.

unemployed Working-age people without jobs who are trying to get jobs.

labor force The employed plus the unemployed.

Everyone in the working-age population falls into one of three categories: employed, unemployed, or a third category called **not in the labor force.** Those who are not in the labor force are working-age people who are neither employed nor unemployed. There are nearly 100 million working-age adults who are not in the labor force. Some are retired, in school, taking care of a child or other family member, or too unwell to work. Others may have decided that it's too hard to find a job and have given up on trying to find one.

To get a sense of the magnitudes, Figure 1 shows the entire working-age population divided into the employed, the unemployed, and those not in the labor force. Most working-age adults are employed, and only a small sliver are unemployed. The unemployed and the employed form the labor force, and together they are just under two-thirds of the working-age population. The remaining third are those not in the labor force.

The Bureau of Labor Statistics collects monthly data on who's employed, unemployed, and not in the labor force. You can see the latest data yourself by looking up the BLS's monthly employment situation report.

Figure 1 | U.S. Working-Age Population

Labor force = Employed + Unemployed

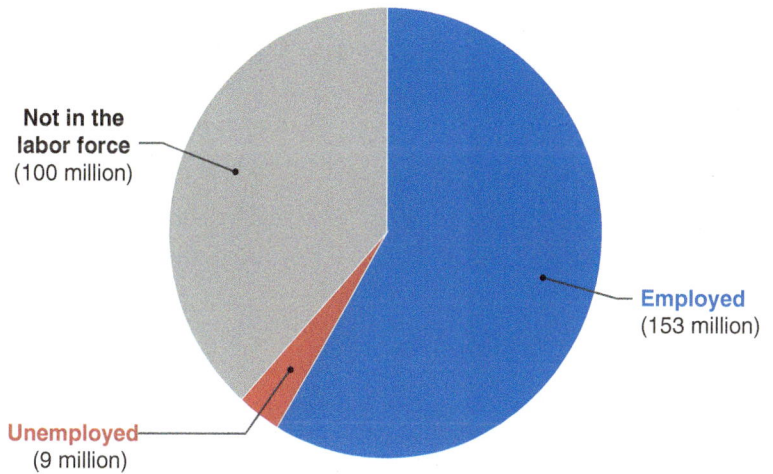

Not in the labor force (100 million)

Employed (153 million)

Unemployed (9 million)

Data from: Bureau of Labor Statistics data for 2021.

not in the labor force Those in the working-age population who are neither employed nor unemployed.

Do the Economics

Identify whether each of these people are employed, unemployed, or not in the labor force.

a. Taylor recently graduated from college and is not currently working. They plan to start searching for a job next month after they are moved back to their family's house and had time to catch up with their friends.

b. Zari is working 40 hours a week in a salaried position as an administrative assistant. She is searching for a new job where she can better use her skills and earn more money.

c. Stephanie just finished a degree in elementary education and is hoping to find a teaching job. In the meantime, she works 10 hours a week as an after-school nanny for one family. She also works one day a week as a housekeeper for another family.

d. Gita is a current full-time student. She's excited to graduate, but she has another semester to go. She scours online job listings at night to get a sense of the jobs that are available and to see if she can secure a job offer before she graduates.

e. Wei was a manager at a Walmart store that closed. When he heard he was being laid off, he immediately applied to drive for Uber. He's now driving for Uber part-time while he searches for a new position as a retail manager.

f. Malik was recently laid off. He is actively looking for a job and has several promising interviews lined up. ∎

Answers: a. Taylor is not in the labor force because they aren't actively looking for work. b. Zari is employed—the fact that she is currently searching for a new job doesn't change her employment status. c. Stephanie is employed because she is getting a few hours of paid work each week. d. Gita is not in the labor force because she is a full-time student and therefore not currently available to start a job. e. Wei is employed because he is earning money driving. f. Malik is unemployed.

Labor Force Participation

The **labor force participation rate** is the percentage of the working-age population that is either employed or unemployed:

$$\text{Labor force participation rate} = \frac{\text{Employed} + \text{Unemployed}}{\text{Working-age population}} \times 100$$

labor force participation rate The percentage of the working-age population that is either employed or unemployed.

Figure 2 | **The Labor Force Participation Rate Rose Through the 20th Century and Declined in Recent Decades**

Share of the working age population that is either employed or unemployed

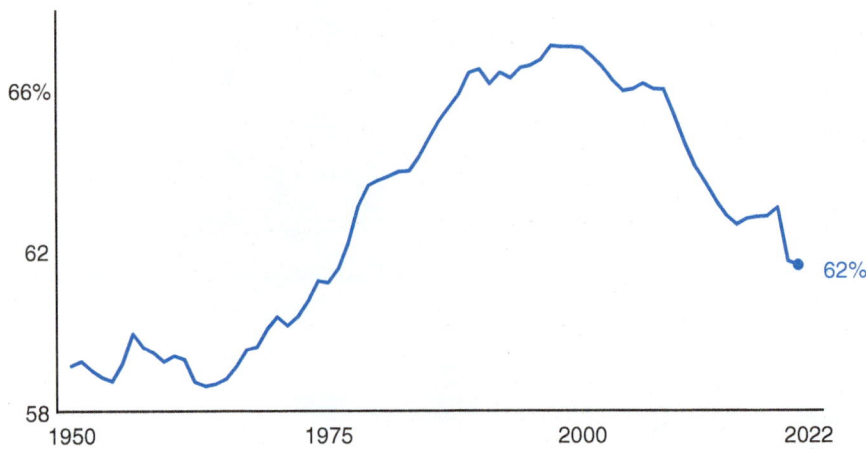

Data from: Bureau of Labor Statistics.

Figure 3 | **Men's Labor Force Participation Has Declined as Women's Participation Has Risen**

Labor force participation rate

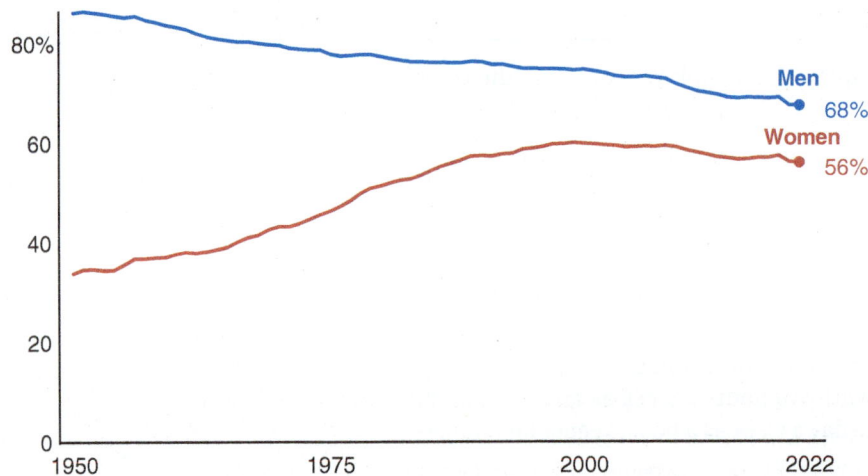

Data from: Bureau of Labor Statistics.

Figure 2 shows that the labor force participation rate grew throughout the twentieth century as an increasing share of adults worked outside the home. This growth in the labor force was an important source of GDP growth. In contrast, the labor force participation rate has declined from its peak rate of 67.1% last reached in 2000.

The labor force participation rate patterns differ for men and women. There were two strong trends in the labor force participation rate during the twentieth century: growth in women's participation and decline in men's. Figure 3 shows labor force participation rates separately for men and women. In the 1950s, men were more than twice as likely as women to be in the labor force. Women's labor force participation grew throughout the twentieth century, with particularly rapid growth in the 1970s and 1980s. In contrast, male participation in the labor force has fallen over much of the past 70 years. The growth in women's labor force participation more than offset the decline in male participation for most of the twentieth century, but this is no longer true as women's participation peaked in 1999.

In recent decades some of the decline in labor force participation reflects an increase in the number of people retired as a large generation known as the "baby boomers" started to reach retirement age in 2008. However, even if you look at people ages 25 to 54 — what economists call "prime age" — the trend of declining male labor force participation has continued through much of the twenty-first century. Labor force participation among prime-age women has been more turbulent in the twenty-first century with periods of both decline and growth.

Interpreting the DATA Why did women's labor force participation rise in the twentieth century while men's declined?

In the 1950s, only about a third of women worked outside the home. Back then, it was legal to refuse to hire women, to fire them once they married, and to pay them less than men were paid for doing the exact same work. As their husbands' incomes from paid work grew, middle- and upper-class married women chose to focus on providing their families with household tasks like cooking, cleaning, and taking care of children. These tasks, while providing valuable services to the family, are not included in measures of employment or GDP.

But things began to change in the 1960s. A wave of technological, legal, and cultural shifts led women's labor force participation to surge in the 1970s and 1980s.

New technology like electric washing machines and dishwashers, along with prepackaged foods, made home production more efficient, lessening the need for a full-time home-maker. New access to control over fertility enabled women to invest in their education and career more reliably, which fueled an increase in women's educational attainment and work experience. Laws forbidding gender discrimination opened new doors for women, and the Equal Pay Act of 1963 required equal pay for equal work (although this has proven difficult to enforce). Finally, cultural attitudes against working mothers slowly broke down: By 2012, the General Social Survey found that only 5% of Americans thought that mothers should stay home to care for school-age kids. All of these changes helped lead the women's labor force participation rate to grow dramatically, as shown in Figure 3.

In contrast, male labor force participation has declined in every decade for the past 70 years. Much of the dramatic decline seen in the graph reflects more young men staying out of the labor force to focus on education, like completing high school and college, and more older men enjoying retirement. So we want to focus instead on prime-age men (25–54) who we typically expect to be working. In the 1950s, 98% of prime-age men worked; in 2018, only 89% of them did. That decline means more than 7 million men who are in what many consider to be their prime working years are neither working nor looking for work. This long-standing decline in prime-age male labor force participation reflects many social changes, and the truth is that economists don't fully understand what is causing it.

Likely drivers of recent declines in labor demand — such as automation and globalization — don't explain early decades of decline. Other factors, such as men staying home to care for children or aging parents, or going back to school at older ages, explain only a very small amount of the decline.

Recent research has pointed to a decrease in the share of men with family responsibilities: Fewer men are marrying and having children than in the past, and without a family to help support, some men choose to work less. Other research has found that some men are choosing not to work because an increase in the quality of video games has increased the opportunity cost of work! In sum, many social and labor market changes have led fewer men to seek and find employment. This is an ongoing societal challenge with consequences that go well beyond the labor market. ■

An invention that helped spur the rise in women's labor force participation.

The Unemployment Rate

The **unemployment rate** is the percentage of the labor force that's unemployed:

$$\text{Unemployment rate} = \frac{\text{Unemployed}}{\text{Labor force}} \times 100$$

Because the unemployment rate is designed to tell us what percentage of people who are trying to find work have failed to do so, it's measured as a percentage of the labor force. By measuring the unemployed as a share of the labor force, we can compare unemployment rates across states and countries that have different labor force participation rates. (If it were measured as a share of the working-age population, countries with lower labor force participation rates would have lower unemployment rates on average.)

Unemployment rates vary for different groups. Figure 4 shows that some groups experience higher unemployment rates than others. The top set of bars shows that the unemployment rate is lower for those with more education. The unemployment rate among people who have no more education beyond high school is roughly twice that of those who have gone on to graduate from college. Now you see why people have been telling you your whole life to stay in school!

The unemployment rate also differs by race and ethnicity. Black and Hispanic Americans persistently have unemployment rates that are well above rates experienced by White and Asian Americans. This difference remains even when efforts are made to compare people with similar educational backgrounds and work experience.

Figure 4 also shows that unemployment is much more common when you're young.

Finally, the lowest panel shows that unemployment rates don't really differ much between men and women.

unemployment rate The percentage of the labor force that is unemployed.

Figure 4 | Unemployment Rates Vary Across Demographic Groups

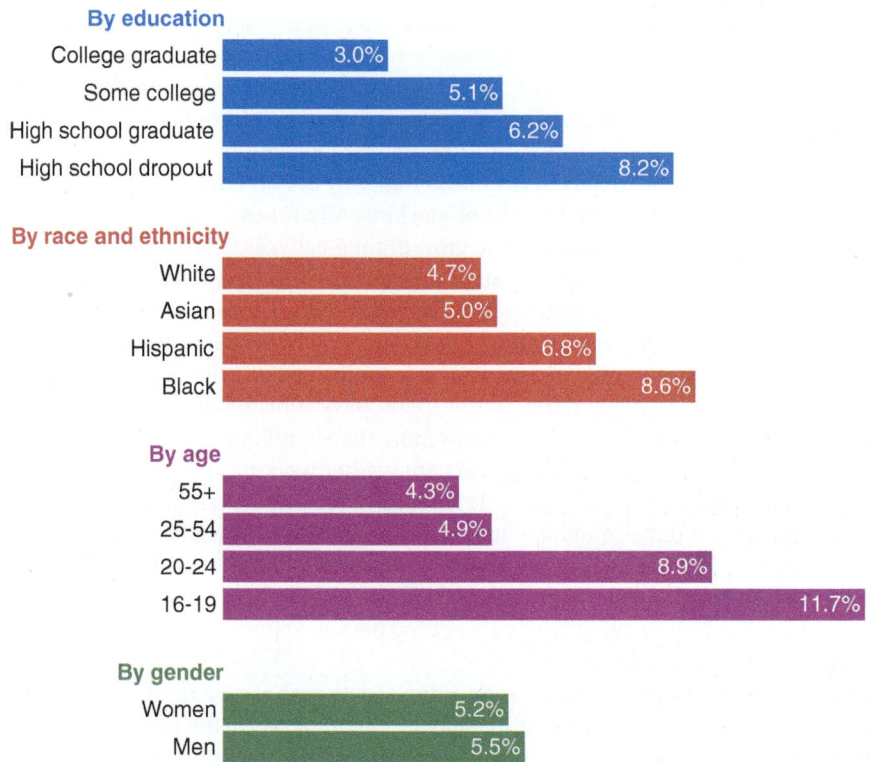

By education

College graduate	3.0%
Some college	5.1%
High school graduate	6.2%
High school dropout	8.2%

By race and ethnicity

White	4.7%
Asian	5.0%
Hispanic	6.8%
Black	8.6%

By age

55+	4.3%
25-54	4.9%
20-24	8.9%
16-19	11.7%

By gender

Women	5.2%
Men	5.5%

Data from: Bureau of Labor Statistics data for 2021 by education, race, age, and gender.

Do the Economics

Let's figure out the unemployment rate in the United States. In 2021, there were 262 million adults in the United States. Of these people, 9 million were unemployed, 153 million were employed, and 100 million were not in the labor force.

What was the unemployment rate?

$$\text{Unemployment rate} = \frac{\text{Unemployed}}{\text{Labor force}} \times 100 = \frac{9 \text{ million}}{153 \text{ million} + 9 \text{ million}} \times 100 = 5.5\%$$

So, the unemployment rate was 5.5%. ∎

Figure 5 | Unemployment Rates Vary Across Countries

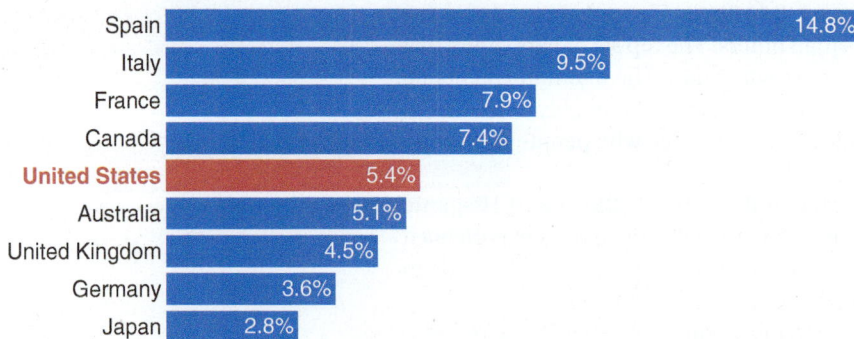

Spain	14.8%
Italy	9.5%
France	7.9%
Canada	7.4%
United States	5.4%
Australia	5.1%
United Kingdom	4.5%
Germany	3.6%
Japan	2.8%

Data from: OECD Harmonized Unemployment data for 2021.

Unemployment rates differ around the world. The United States has a lower unemployment rate than many other countries. Figure 5 shows that there were a handful of countries with lower unemployment rates than the United States in 2021. While each of these countries had different experiences with the Covid pandemic and its impact on the labor market, these basic patterns have been seen for decades. Spain, Italy, and France all tend to have unemployment rates that are higher than those experienced in the United States. In contrast, Germany and Japan historically have low unemployment rates compared to the United States.

The unemployment rate fluctuates over time, but it's never zero.
The unemployment rate also varies over time as the economy strengthens and weakens. When the economy is growing fast, the unemployment rate tends to fall, and when the economy is slowing down, it tends to rise. Figure 6 shows that the U.S. unemployment rate moves up and down, with the most dramatic rise and subsequent fall occurring in 2020. During the Covid pandemic, a lot of people became unemployed at least temporarily as people stayed home to avoid getting sick. As the economy reopened, a lot of people went back to their same jobs and the unemployment rate came down quickly. Figure 6 shows that while the unemployment rate can rise and fall, it typically returns to a rate between 4% and 5%. The **equilibrium unemployment rate** is the long-run unemployment rate to which the economy tends to return. The unemployment rate tends to fluctuate around this level, as you see in Figure 6. Some economists call this the "natural rate of unemployment," but there isn't anything natural about it. Instead, you should think of it as the unemployment rate that can persist in equilibrium.

So why does the unemployment rate stay above zero in equilibrium? After all, no one really wants to be unemployed. The causes of unemployment are varied, but before we turn to the causes of unemployment, let's explore the mechanics of how people flow into and out of jobs. The speed of that process is part of what determines unemployment.

Figure 6 | The Unemployment Rate Fluctuates Over Time

Unemployment as a share of the labor force

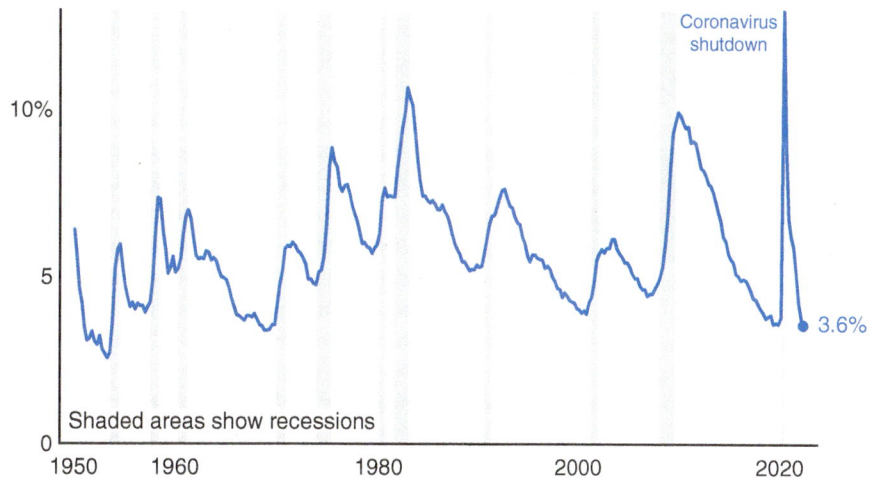

Data from: Bureau of Labor Statistics.

equilibrium unemployment rate
The long-run unemployment rate to which the economy tends to return.

11.2 The Dynamics of the Labor Market

Learning Objective *Learn how people move in and out of jobs and in and out of the labor market.*

Picture a busy restaurant: As customers leave, new customers are seated. Tables are always turning over, so arriving customers can usually find a table without much of a wait. Sometimes, though, the restaurant gets backed up and there are more customers than available tables.

The labor market is in many ways like a crowded restaurant, where jobs are like tables and workers are like hungry diners. Every day, hundreds of thousands of people leave and start jobs. People leave jobs for all sorts of reasons — they may get laid off or fired, they may quit for a better job, or they may quit to exit the labor force. Just like a dynamic restaurant, where a large number of tables turning over regularly makes it easy for new people to arrive and find a table quickly, a dynamic labor market makes it easy for new people to enter the labor market and find a job quickly.

But, like a restaurant, the labor market can also get backed up. Potential workers may not be well matched to the jobs available. If many people become unemployed at once, there may not be enough job openings for everyone. There may be barriers to employers eliminating inefficient jobs or workers, which slows down the process of creating new jobs or hiring new workers. Let's take a closer look at the dynamics of the U.S. labor market.

As some customers leave, others take their place.

Jobs come and go.

Labor Market Flows

The dynamics of the U.S. labor market are staggering. In any given month, more than 6 million people in the United States start a new job and over 6 million people leave jobs. Entrepreneurs hire people for their new businesses, and existing businesses fill positions as people leave and create new jobs as they expand. Businesses eliminate jobs, fire workers, and even close their doors completely when the market no longer wants their products. Entire sectors of the economy shrink or expand.

Shifts in specific sectors of the economy often capture a lot of attention — especially when a sector is shrinking. Manufacturing, coal, and retail stores are examples of sectors that have shrunk in recent decades in the United States. These sectors have lost jobs, partially due to labor-saving technological change. But there are also expanding sectors that are adding even more jobs. For example, the United States has seen rapid growth in health care, education, and information technology. But these sectoral shifts are just a tiny slice of what happens every day.

A dynamic labor market makes it easier for people to find new jobs. Open up an online job board and look at the postings today. You'll see jobs in expanding sectors, like new media managers, but you'll also see plenty of manufacturing jobs and retail jobs despite the fact that those sectors are shrinking. The largest source of job openings comes from people leaving existing jobs, and even declining sectors continue to have a lot of people leaving jobs and new people being hired. All that turnover makes it easier for workers and jobs to find each other.

There can be a lot of hiring even in a declining sector. Over the past two decades, more than 60 million people were hired into manufacturing jobs even though the sector shrank by 5 million jobs. How did that happen? More than 65 million people quit or lost manufacturing jobs. Because it's a declining sector, some people won't find jobs and others will have a long wait for a new job. A declining sector is like a restaurant in which finished diners keep creating open tables for new diners, but management keeps taking away some of the tables, so there are more people seeking tables than there are tables available. In contrast, it's easier to find a job in an expanding sector because the number of jobs being created exceeds the number of people leaving jobs, making it easier for everyone to find a job. It's like a busy restaurant that was able to open its outdoor seating area; despite the crowds, lots of people get a seat quickly.

Most job-seekers are employed. One aspect of a dynamic labor market is that most people seeking new jobs are already employed. This makes finding a job harder for the unemployed because they are competing not just against other people without jobs, but also people with current jobs. Research shows that employers tend to prefer people with jobs, so it's easier to find work when you already have a job.

Most unemployment spells are short. The typical person who becomes unemployed will be back in a job within 10 weeks, and most of them will be back in a job within a month. But not everyone is so lucky. Some find themselves unemployed for a long time. This is more likely to happen when there are fewer job openings, such as during and in the aftermath of the 2007–2009 recession. By mid-2010, nearly half the unemployed had been unemployed for more than six months.

Even when there are many openings, a few people will get unlucky, and none of the jobs they apply for will work out. Anyone who spends more than six consecutive months unemployed is **long-term unemployed.** In 2022, about one in four people who were unemployed were long-term unemployed.

long-term unemployed People who have been unemployed for six consecutive months or longer.

Discrimination and skill loss make it hard for the long-term unemployed to find work. Studies show that those who experience long-term unemployment are discriminated against by potential employers. Workers who have similar skills but have a long spell of unemployment on their resume are less likely to be given an interview and less likely to be hired. In addition to discrimination, the long-term unemployed may lose skills and connections the longer they are out of work. For both of these reasons, the number of opportunities the long-term unemployed get dwindles over time, and some lose hope and stop searching altogether.

Alternative Measures of Unemployment

When people lose hope and stop searching, should we count those people as unemployed? There are also millions of people who have jobs but want more hours, or would prefer a job that used more of their skills. Are these folks a bit unemployed? Let's consider broader measures of unemployment, looking beyond those who are actively seeking and available for work and are yet without any work. There are two groups of people we need to consider: those who are not in the labor force but who would work under the right conditions, and those who want more work.

Some people not in the labor force would work under the right conditions. In addition to counting the unemployed, the United States also measures the number of people who say they want to work. If they aren't currently searching for a job, but they have searched for a job within the past year, they are called **marginally attached** to the labor force. These folks aren't in the labor force and aren't counted among the unemployed. However, a broader measure of unemployment includes the unemployed plus the marginally attached, shown in the second column of Figure 7 (the BLS calls this measure "U-5"). This broader measure leads to a slightly higher measure of unemployment. Roughly a quarter of those who are marginally attached are called *discouraged workers*. They are called "discouraged" because the reason they give for not looking for work is that they don't believe there are jobs available for them. Other marginally attached workers say they aren't looking because they have family responsibilities, transportation problems, health problems, or they are getting job training. Some of these folks might be discouraged in the ordinary sense of the word as well.

marginally attached Someone who wants a job and who has looked for a job within the past year, but who isn't counted as unemployed because they aren't currently searching for work.

Figure 7 | Broader Measures Suggest That Joblessness Is More Common

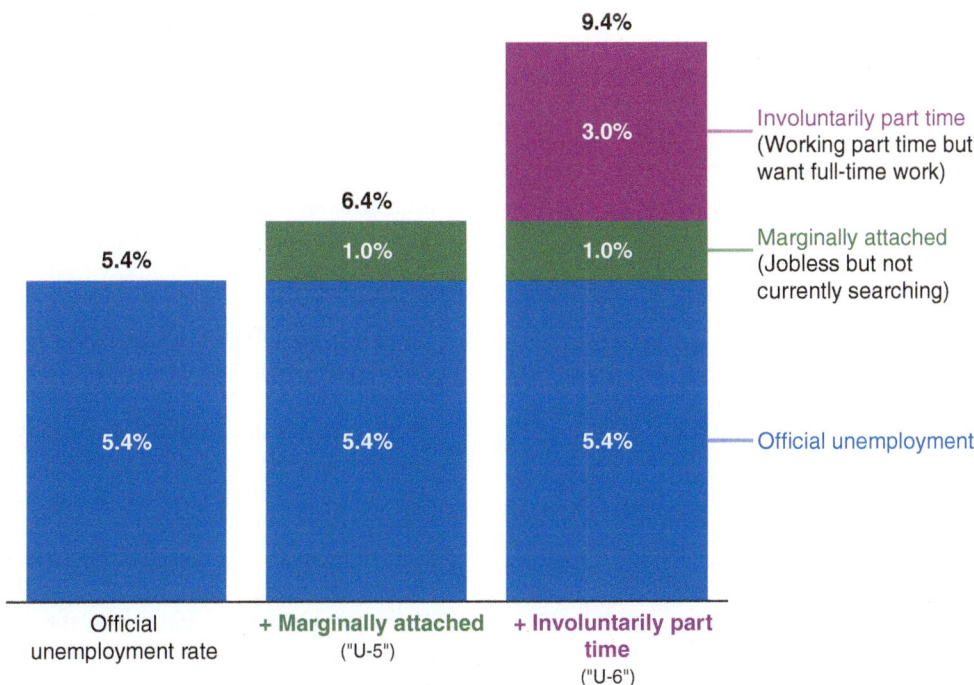

Data from: Bureau of Labor Statistics data for 2021.

There are many other people outside the labor force who aren't among the marginally attached, but might enter the labor force if the right job came along. For example, a parent who quit a job to take care of young kids might be thinking about going back to work. But it can be hard to reliably assess how many of these people there are because their decision hinges on whether or not they happen to hear about the right job. Millions of people reenter the labor force each month, and most people who leave the labor force don't plan to do so permanently.

Some people who are employed would prefer better jobs. Other broader measures of unemployment consider people who are **underemployed**. There are two ways to be underemployed. The first is that you want a full-time job, but aren't getting full-time hours. The second is that your job isn't adequately using your skills. Both versions of underemployment are important for thinking about how people are being utilized. But for measuring that underutilization, it's easier to count the people who want more hours. Let's see why.

underemployed Someone who has some work but wants more hours, or whose job isn't adequately using their skills.

Imagine that you've just graduated and are working part time as a server at a restaurant while you are looking for a full-time job in market research. You will be counted among the employed. But you didn't go to college to wait tables 12 hours a week. Because you have a part-time job and you want a full-time job, you would be considered **involuntarily part time.** The third column of Figure 7 shows this category of worker added to the unemployment rate and the share of marginally attached workers. This is the broadest measure of unemployment (referred to by the BLS as "U-6") and it is a substantially higher share of the labor force. In 2021, 3% of the labor force was involuntarily part time. Put together, this broadest measure of unemployment was 9.4% in 2021.

involuntarily part time Someone who wants full-time work and is working part time because they haven't found a full-time job.

What if the restaurant offers you full-time work? You'll probably still consider yourself underemployed even if you take the hours to help pay the bills. It might seem obvious that a college graduate waiting tables is underemployed, but how about a fiction writer who works full time waiting tables to pay the bills while working on their first novel? Or an aspiring entrepreneur who is waiting tables in order to make connections that will help them open their own restaurant? While it's easy to measure whether you're getting enough hours, it's hard to develop a set of criteria that successfully measures whether your skills are being used as effectively as possible.

Alternative measures of unemployment tend to follow movements in unemployment. Figure 8 shows the measures of unemployment seen in Figure 7 over many years. You can see that the difference between the unemployment rate and alternative measures of unemployment is roughly stable over time as these measures tend to move together. Typically, when the unemployment rate goes down, so does the share of people who've recently given up searching for a job or are involuntarily part time.

Alternative measures of unemployment are important if you want to know how many people are potentially available to work as businesses create more jobs. But since the relationship between alternative measures and the unemployment rate is fairly stable over time, a good guess is that the broadest measure of unemployment is roughly twice the unemployment rate.

Figure 8 | Alternative Measures of Unemployment Move Together

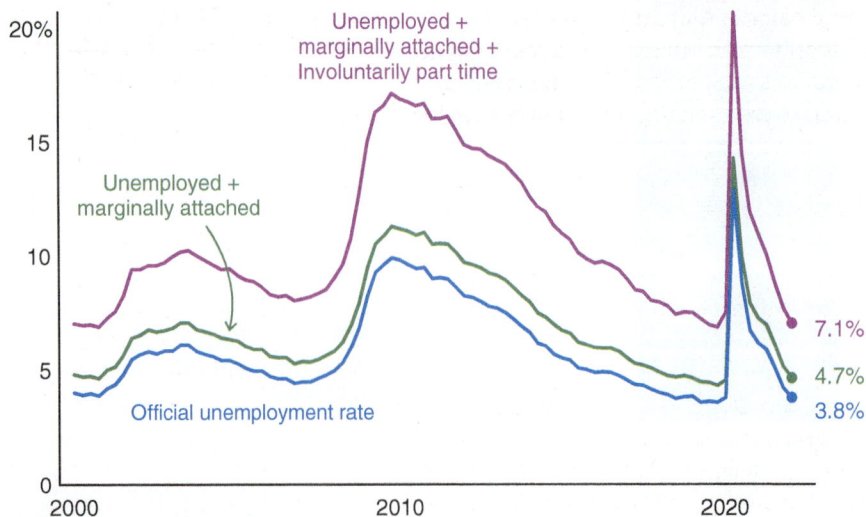

Data from: Bureau of Labor Statistics.

Understanding Unemployment

Learning Objective *Analyze the causes of unemployment.*

Now that we've explored the labor market and discovered how to measure unemployment, it's time to dig into what causes unemployment. The starting point is supply and demand in the market for labor. Workers supply their labor, selling it for a price (their wage). Like other markets, supply is upward-sloping, meaning that workers supply more labor when wages are high. Employers — buyers of labor — demand less when the price of labor is high, so they hire fewer people when wages are high.

If market forces worked perfectly, wages would adjust to the point where the quantity of labor demanded is equal to the quantity of labor supplied, as shown in Figure 9. The forces of supply and demand would ensure that everyone who wanted to work at wages that employers were willing to pay would find jobs. That's because workers who wanted a job but couldn't find one would be willing to work for a bit less, pushing wages down so that employers would hire more people, and fewer people would want jobs. Nobody would be unemployed — anyone willing to work for the market wage would be able to find a job. Unfortunately, market forces don't usually work perfectly.

Figure 9 | Labor Demand Equals Labor Supply

In equilibrium, no one is unemployed

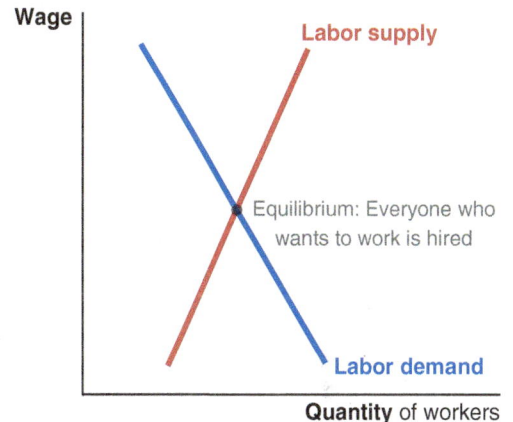

Equilibrium: Everyone who wants to work is hired

Quantity of workers

Types of Unemployment

Unemployment reflects the failure of the market to bring the demand for labor in balance with its supply. Why does this happen? There are three categories of reasons why people experience unemployment. Let's start by learning what the three categories are.

Unemployment type 1: Frictional unemployment. Frictional unemployment occurs because it takes time for employers to search for workers and for workers to search for jobs. Labor demand and labor supply might be in balance — in other words, there might be enough jobs for all the people who want them — but the process of matching workers and jobs isn't instantaneous. When you graduate from college, you'll spend a lot of time talking to employers, going on interviews, and trying to figure out which job has the right mix of tasks, co-workers, benefits, and perks that will make it the best fit for you. You may even need to relocate to where your skills are most in demand by employers.

frictional unemployment
Unemployment due to the time it takes for employers to search for workers and for workers to search for jobs.

Unemployment type 2: Structural unemployment. Structural unemployment occurs when there are structural barriers that prevent wages from falling to the point where labor demand and labor supply are in equilibrium. Because wages remain higher than the equilibrium level, more workers want to work, but employers offer fewer jobs. There are many reasons for this: Employers sometimes want to pay higher wages to get more effort out of workers; unions may push for higher wages; and governments may enact policies that make it hard for labor demand and labor supply to be in equilibrium. These features of the labor market can lead to unemployment, and we'll explore why in this section.

structural unemployment
Unemployment that occurs because wages don't fall to bring labor demand and supply into equilibrium.

Unemployment type 3: Cyclical unemployment. Cyclical unemployment occurs when there is a temporary downturn in the economy. It explains why the unemployment rate was so high during the 2020 recession and why it came down as the economy recovered. Cyclical unemployment reflects the fact that during a downturn there are lots of unused resources in the economy — unfortunately, that includes workers. Cyclical unemployment can be caused by many different kinds of problems. In 2020, the economic downturn and high unemployment was caused by the Covid pandemic. The downturn before that was triggered by problems in the financial sector. In later chapters, we'll

cyclical unemployment
Unemployment that is due to a temporary downturn in the economy.

explore why there are temporary ups and downs in the economy and how they lead to unemployment.

Frictional and structural unemployment explain why the equilibrium unemployment rate is above zero. In contrast, cyclical unemployment explains why unemployment rises and falls around the equilibrium unemployment rate. In this chapter, we'll examine the unemployment that can persist even when the economy is doing well. So we'll focus on better understanding what causes frictional and structural unemployment and how these types of unemployment can be reduced.

> Three types of unemployment:
> 1. Frictional
> 2. Structural
> 3. Cyclical

Frictional Unemployment: It Takes Time to Find a Job

Frictional unemployment occurs when there are enough jobs for everyone, but the process of matching workers to jobs isn't instantaneous. Searching for a job reflects an information problem—there's a good job out there for you, but you don't know where it is. You have particular training, interests, and experiences for a job that would be a great fit for you, but a terrible fit for someone else, and vice versa. The longer it takes for workers and employers to find each other, the higher frictional unemployment will be.

Three major factors determine how much time it takes for workers and employers to find each other, and thus, how much frictional unemployment there is. The first is the efficiency of all the technology, networks, and other resources that help workers and employers find each other. The second is the distribution of skills among workers, compared to the distribution of skills needed by employers. Finally, there is workers' access to financial support when they're looking for work. Let's go through each of these.

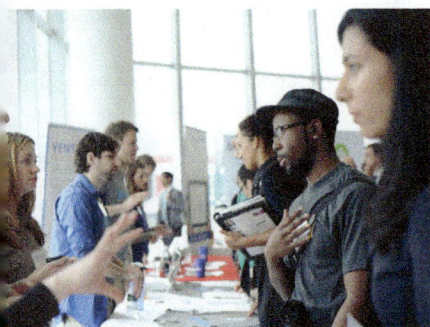

Frictional unemployment includes time spent looking for the right job.

Frances Roberts/Alamy

Factor #1: The efficiency of the resources employers and workers use to find each other. Employers and workers have to find each other. They may rely on word of mouth, online job postings, recruiting firms, or career centers on college campuses. Since frictional unemployment reflects an information problem, anything that affects the information that's available can affect the amount of frictional unemployment. The better workers are at identifying jobs that are a good fit for them, the less time they need to spend searching. Similarly, when managers can use technologies to screen applications effectively, it typically takes less time for them to identify a worker who will be a good fit for them.

The more efficient the resources available for workers and managers to find each other, the lower frictional unemployment is likely to be. Many of these tools are provided by the private sector—job postings, informational interviews, online job boards, employment agencies, and job placement services. But there's also a role for public policy, since better job matching can reduce frictional unemployment. That's why governments often run job-search centers to help businesses find the right workers, and to help job-seekers find the right jobs. Research shows that when workers get access to job-search assistance, they are reemployed faster.

Factor #2: The alignment of the skills workers have and the skills employers desire. If all workers had the same skills and all jobs used the same skills, then it wouldn't take very long for workers and jobs to match. Imagine you have to sort a basket full of socks into pairs. If all the socks are the same, it's a breeze.

But if you're like me, you have lots of different socks, and sorting them into pairs can be frustrating. Similarly, when workers all differ in their skills and personalities, and jobs differ in their attributes and the skills that they need, it becomes harder for workers and businesses to find each other. So the more diverse workers and jobs are, the more difficult it is for workers and employers to find the right match.

There can also be *skills mismatch,* meaning that the skills workers have are not the skills that employers want. Technological change and international trade lead to changes in the mix of industries and occupations in which jobs are available, and this can lead

It may take time to find a match.

David Malan/Stone/Getty Images

to skills mismatch. In fact, the labor market is constantly adapting, with some sectors growing more slowly or disappearing altogether, while other sectors grow rapidly. The United States has become increasingly service-oriented — consulting, other professional services, and health services have grown by millions of jobs since 2000. Meanwhile, goods-producing sectors such as manufacturing have been in decline as technological change has led many workers to be replaced by machines.

When sectors are in decline, it can be hard for workers to find a new job in the industry in which they previously worked. While there are still typically millions of jobs available, they are increasingly more competitive, as there are more workers than jobs. Millions of workers change occupations each month, but it can take time for people to realize that their skills are not in as much demand and to seek retraining. As a result, shifts in the skills needed by employers can lead to increases in frictional unemployment as workers take longer to find jobs.

Some people call the changing mix of occupations and industries structural unemployment, but they mean the word differently from how we use it. They are referring to structural changes in the labor market that reduce the number of jobs that are a match for the skills and experiences of some workers. But the reality is that throughout your lifetime, you'll likely need to adapt your skills to the changing needs of the labor market — you'll probably change your occupation (most people do!), and you'll need to learn to use new technology. Perhaps the most important set of skills you are developing right now is the ability to take in new information and adapt based on what you are learning.

Public policy can respond by helping workers learn what jobs do fit their skills, helping them identify regions where job growth is occurring, and offering job-retraining programs. Retraining programs can reduce frictional unemployment by helping workers develop the skills that are in demand by employers.

Factor #3: Unemployment insurance and other income support during unemployment. When the government supports people financially during unemployment, unemployment is likely to last longer. Unemployment insurance is a program through which the government provides financial assistance to workers who've lost their job through no fault of their own. The program pays a modest amount — no more than half of a worker's previous wages and typically much less — usually for up to six months. The program's goal is to reduce the hardships people face as they struggle to pay for housing, food, and other necessities while unemployed.

To understand why unemployment insurance can lead to longer unemployment durations, apply the opportunity cost principle. When you are unemployed, you can choose to focus on the jobs that are a best fit for your skills; if you do that, you'll be more likely to land a higher-paying job that you'll want to stay in. Alternatively, if you are desperate for cash, you might walk into the corner store that has posted a help wanted sign and take their minimum-wage job. The opportunity cost of staying unemployed to focus on searching for a better job is the wage you could earn by taking that corner store job, or whatever would be the easiest job for you to get.

Unemployment insurance reduces the opportunity cost of another day spent searching because if you took the job, you'd get the wage but lose the unemployment insurance check. So if you could have earned $100 working, but would lose $50 in unemployment insurance, your opportunity cost is only $50. Not surprisingly, when people have unemployment insurance, they tend to spend more days searching and focus their search more on the jobs that are the best fit for them.

Studies show that countries offering more financial support to people when they're unemployed tend to have higher unemployment rates. But studies also show that people without access to unemployment insurance suffer from bigger declines in consumption and greater hardship. Moreover, without sufficient savings or unemployment insurance, some people end up settling for worse jobs because continuing to search means not having enough to eat or losing their housing. In these situations, income support during a job search can lead workers to better long-term outcomes.

Sources of frictional unemployment:
1. Job-search resources
2. Skills mismatch
3. Unemployment insurance and other income support

Personal referrals help—so start building your network now.

EVERYDAY Economics   Why it matters who you know

Studies show that if you have a personal referral when you apply for a job, you're more likely to get a job interview — and if you get an interview, you're more likely to get a job offer, which is also likely to come with a bigger pay package. No wonder people who get job offers through referrals are more likely to accept the offer.

Why is it so great to have a referral? Referrals contain information that's hard to get elsewhere. It can be hard for employers to credibly learn whether you're likely to fit in with your co-workers, and whether you're a hard worker with the right skills for the job. If someone who works at the company vouches for you, they are providing valuable information that the hiring manager can't easily see in a resume or learn in an interview. And they're likely to tell the truth — after all, if you get hired, they'll have to work with you. Similarly, your friend has information about the job you want. They can tell you if workers are happy, if the company is well managed, and whether hard work is likely to lead to a promotion. While you can ask about those things in an interview, it might be hard for a manager to credibly tell you the answers. After all, who's going to admit to unhappy workers, poor management, and no career path?

Roughly half of available jobs are filled using a personal referral to help make the connection, and about two-thirds of companies have a program to encourage referrals. Some companies will even pay you a bonus if they hire someone you refer.

People worry that referrals are unfair. But employers don't ask for them because they want to do anyone a favor — they like referrals because they lead to better matches. Referred truck drivers have fewer accidents than those hired without a referral. Referred high-tech workers generate more patents. And referred workers overall are much less likely to quit. All this means that referred workers are more profitable. Referrals are a win-win situation for job-seekers and employers, but they do mean that people who know more people get a leg up. It's a good idea to try to get to know — and stay in touch with — people who are in the line of work you want to be in so that you can build your network of potential referrers. ■

Structural Unemployment: When Wages Are Stuck Above the Supply-Equals-Demand Equilibrium Wage

Structural unemployment occurs because there simply aren't enough jobs for everyone who wants to work at the prevailing market wage. In other words, there are structural impediments preventing wages from falling to the point where the quantity of labor supplied is equal to the quantity of labor demanded.

Figure 10 shows that in a well-functioning labor market, equilibrium occurs at the intersection of the labor supply and labor demand curves. At that point, there is no structural unemployment — there are just as many jobs as there are workers. But sometimes wages are prevented from falling to the supply-equals-demand equilibrium point. Employers demand fewer workers when the prevailing market wage is above the supply-equals-demand equilibrium wage. Yet, the quantity of labor supplied is higher because more people want to work at higher wages. As shown in Figure 10, when the prevailing market wage is above the supply-equals-demand equilibrium wage, there's a gap between the number of jobs available and the number of available workers. This gap is structural unemployment. The number of people unemployed is equal to the difference between the quantity of labor supplied at the prevailing market wage and the quantity of labor demanded.

The prevailing market wage can persist above the supply-equals-demand equilibrium wage for several reasons. Employers might choose to pay higher wages in order to get employees to work harder, employees might use their bargaining power to demand higher wages, and there might be institutional barriers to lowering wages. Let's start by considering why employers might choose to pay higher wages, and then we'll turn to other factors.

Figure 10 | Structural Unemployment

Structural unemployment occurs when wages are unable to fall to the supply equals demand wage.

Ⓐ When wages can easily adjust to market conditions, equilibrium occurs at the supply equals demand wage, where the labor supply curve meets the labor demand curve and there is no unemployment.

Ⓑ Sometimes, the prevailing market wage gets stuck above the equilibrium wage.

Ⓒ As a result, there's a persistent gap between the supply of labor and the demand for it. This causes structural unemployment.

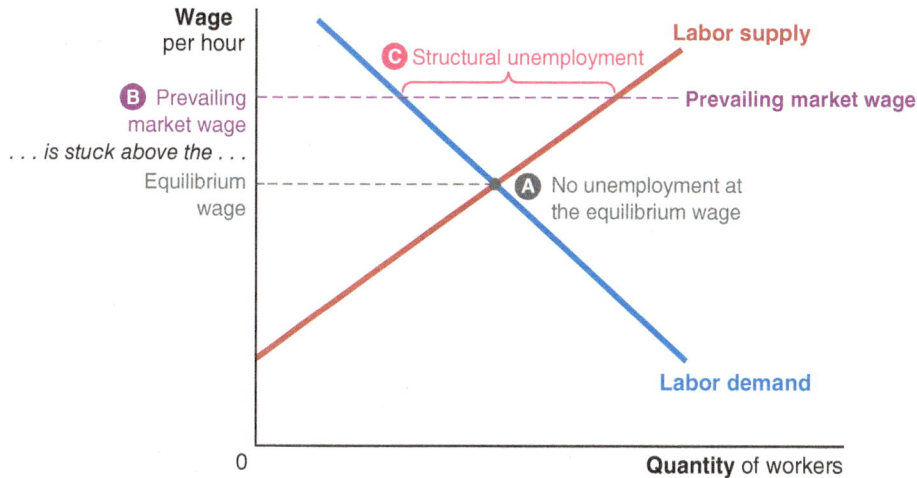

Wage per hour

Ⓒ Structural unemployment

Labor supply

Ⓑ Prevailing market wage

Prevailing market wage

... is stuck above the ...

Equilibrium wage

Ⓐ No unemployment at the equilibrium wage

Labor demand

0   Quantity of workers

Efficiency wages: One cause of structural unemployment.

In 1913, Henry Ford made history with the introduction of the moving assembly line in auto production. Workers would stand in place and focus on a single simple task—such as screwing in a particular nut over and over again. This innovation allowed Ford to more than double his production. But he quickly ran into a problem: The work was painfully, mind-numbingly dull. Similar low-skill factory jobs were plentiful in Detroit, so when workers couldn't take the monotony any longer, they quit. The average worker stayed only a few months, which meant Ford was constantly hiring and training new workers.

So in 1914, Ford made history again—this time by more than doubling wages to what has famously become known as the $5 day. That doesn't sound like much today, but back when the prevailing market wage was $2.25, it was a big deal. Applicants flooded his factory gates looking for work. To get a job with Ford in 1914, you had to be two things: a good worker, and lucky. If you came in drunk, failed to show up, or couldn't keep up with the work, you were fired. But even if you were a hard worker, there were more workers hoping to land a $5-a-day job than there were positions at Ford. That's why you also had to be lucky. Persistence also helped, so people would line up day after day, hoping to get hired.

Efficiency wages make it unprofitable for employers to lower wages.

Not only did Henry Ford pioneer the assembly line, but he helped pioneer a new cause of unemployment. Paying higher than the equilibrium wage meant that not everyone who wanted to work at that wage was able to get a job. Those who waited hopefully at the factory gate could have been working elsewhere at the prevailing market wage; instead, they were unemployed, taking their chances at getting a higher-paying Ford job.

Economists refer to Ford's higher-than-market wage as an **efficiency wage**—a wage above the prevailing market wage, paid to encourage greater worker productivity. When you're paid a wage that's higher than what you would get elsewhere, you're more careful not to lose it, meaning you don't slack off, skip work, or antagonize co-workers or managers. Highly paid workers are also more likely to feel valued, inspiring them to give back to their employer in the form of greater effort.

Workers would line up for a chance to work on the Ford assembly line.

Hulton Archive/Getty Images

efficiency wage A higher wage paid to encourage greater worker productivity.

When searching for a job meant waiting for a chance at a job, lots of folks were willing to wait for a job at Ford.

Efficiency wages can lower total labor costs. Ford's problem of rapid turnover ended with the $5 wage. And his workers became even more productive. Any worker who was feeling frustrated simply had to glance out the window at the queue of hopeful workers ready to take their job to be reminded of how good they had it. Workers who quit knew that their next job would probably only pay $2.25. Since the marginal benefit of a new job offer was low compared to what they currently had, Ford's workers stayed focused on their tasks to avoid being fired. Ford later referred to the $5 wage as one of his greatest cost-saving moves.

Efficiency wages create unemployment. Ford was able to hire all the workers he wanted at $5 a day because he was paying more than other employers. The higher wage increased labor supply to the Ford plant by encouraging people to try to get a job at his plant. To understand why labor supply increases, apply the marginal benefit principle: the marginal benefit of each day spent waiting outside the factory rises due to the higher efficiency wage. But not everyone can get hired at the higher wage. Some accept jobs at a lower wage at another auto plant — for them, the marginal benefit of standing outside the Ford factory (the chance at getting the Ford wage premium) isn't as big as the marginal cost of the forgone wage they would earn working at another plant. But for some workers, that marginal benefit will be big enough that they'll give up working elsewhere, or they'll enter the labor market, in order to stand in line and hope to get their lucky break at the Ford plant.

When you search for a job today, you don't usually line up at a factory gate. But a job search still takes effort and sometimes people are so busy searching that they are unable to work. And if some companies pay more, it might make sense to spend a few extra days or weeks unemployed in order to seek out and apply for those jobs. Efficiency wages can also cause unemployment because some people might also decide that they will work if they can get a good high-paying job, but it isn't worth working if they can't. These folks will be unemployed until they can land a job with a high-paying employer. And remember, employers who are paying an efficiency wage don't want to hire all the people who want to work for them.

Institutions: Additional Causes of Structural Unemployment

Efficiency wages are not the only reason why wages don't fall to bring labor supply and labor demand into balance. The labor market has many unique institutional features that can keep the wage above its supply-equals-demand equilibrium wage. These causes of structural unemployment make workers with jobs better off, but the higher wages and compensation and greater job security make jobs scarce for others.

Three institutional factors tend to be primary causes of structural unemployment around the world: unions, job protection regulations, and minimum wage laws. Let's find out more about how each of these can contribute to structural unemployment.

Unions can keep wages high for some workers. Unions are organizations representing workers who band together to negotiate jointly with their employers. Unionized workers earn about 15% more than a comparable worker in a non-union job and often receive better benefits.

There are lots of reasons why unions are effective. Unions give greater bargaining power to workers, allowing them to extract some of the profits that might otherwise go to management or investors. They might have different information from that of management, allowing businesses to make better decisions because they have an effective way to gather input from workers. Regardless of the reason, union wages mean that more workers want union jobs than there are union jobs available, and employers might demand fewer workers at the higher wage. The result is structural unemployment.

Unions are no longer a big part of most industries in the United States. Only around 7% of private-sector workers are unionized. But unions play a much larger role in education

Thousands of people will apply for this well-paying, unionized job.

and other public-sector jobs. In other countries, for example Belgium, Norway, and Germany, unions play a large role in the labor market.

Job protection regulations make it hard to fire workers.

If you want to reduce the number of people unemployed, why not just make it harder for businesses to fire people? Many countries have tried this strategy. So, put yourself in the shoes of a manager in such a country. If you hire a person and they don't work out, you'll either have to keep paying them, or pay a large price to let them go. That should cause you to think twice before making someone a job offer. You should be confident that they'll generate enough additional revenue to justify their wage, because if they don't, you can't fire them.

Think back to the reasons employers pay efficiency wages: Workers are more productive when they really want to keep their jobs. So what do you think happens to worker productivity if employers can't fire workers? Some workers may slack off, knowing that it's hard for them to be fired. Because workers are less productive, on average, employers want to hire fewer of them.

While job protection policies succeed in reducing the number of people who lose their job, they also reduce the number of workers businesses want to hire at any given wage. Such policies reduce labor demand, and thus employment is lower than what would occur without these policies. They can result in lower wages, or they can exacerbate structural unemployment if other factors are making it hard for wages to fall. Such policies can also increase frictional unemployment by encouraging employers to search longer to find a good match. Fewer workers will be willing to leave jobs because they know it will be hard to find another job. Thus, job protection regulations make for a less dynamic and less flexible labor market.

The challenges of high firing costs are apparent in France and Italy, where employers are required to provide a government-approved reason to fire a worker, and there are obstacles to laying off many workers at once. Such policies are good for people who are already employed and want to stay in their current jobs. But they're not good for the unemployed workers and those who want to change jobs or employers.

The minimum wage keeps wages from falling below the set minimum wage.

The federal minimum wage law requires your employer to pay you at least $7.25 per hour. Some states have their own higher minimum wages. If the minimum wage is higher than the equilibrium wage, businesses want to hire fewer workers. Yet more workers want to work at the higher wage. The resulting gap between the labor supplied and labor demanded is structural unemployment.

The minimum wage is a hotly contested issue. Opponents focus on the unemployment that's created by the minimum wage. They argue that setting the minimum wage too high will lead to fewer jobs. For many, unemployment is even worse than a low-wage job. Proponents argue that the poor earn low wages because they lack bargaining power relative to employers, and a slightly higher wage won't lead to much of a change in the labor market. Essentially, they argue that neither supply nor demand for labor changes vary much with the wage.

Economists who've studied the effects of raising the minimum wage suggest that raising the minimum wage leads to a negligible change in overall unemployment. Most workers earn wages well above the minimum wage, so the minimum wage applies only to a small subgroup of workers. Many studies show that raising the minimum wage results in only small changes in the number of such workers hired, although economists disagree about just how big or small the effect is. The change in unemployment also depends on just how high the minimum wage is relative to the supply-equals-demand wage: the higher it is, the more structural unemployment there will be.

The biggest impact of minimum wage laws is on the unemployment rate of teenagers. Lots of them want to work when the minimum wage is high, but fewer of them are desired by employers. Instead, slightly more experienced or older workers get the jobs.

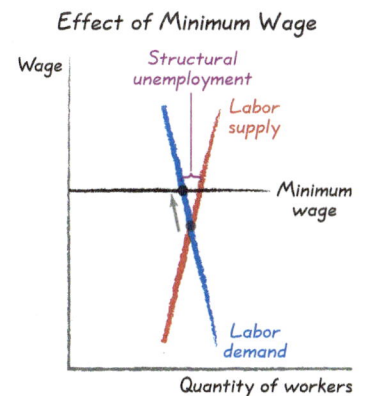

Effect of Minimum Wage

Institutional causes of structural unemployment:

1. Unions
2. Job protection regulations
3. Minimum wage laws

Understanding Frictional and Structural Unemployment

Frictional and structural unemployment explain why the equilibrium unemployment rate is above zero. Frictional unemployment occurs because looking for a good job takes time. Structural unemployment occurs when more people want to work at the prevailing wage than there are employers desiring workers. You've also seen that there are things government can do to reduce frictional and structural unemployment, but there are other things government does that can increase these types of unemployment. Sometimes these choices involve trade-offs — like helping people get through unemployment with less hardship versus encouraging them to take a job right away. To better understand these trade-offs, we'll next turn to the costs of unemployment for individuals and society.

11.4   The Costs of Unemployment

Learning Objective *Learn about the economic and social costs of unemployment.*

When workers are unemployed, everyone loses: workers, their families, and the communities in which they live. When more people are unemployed, more people suffer.

The Economic Costs of Unemployment

Instead of earning an income, the unemployed have to spend their time looking for work. The process can take weeks and often months, and some may give up and drop out of the labor force entirely. This has serious economic costs — both for the unemployed and for society more generally.

The unemployed often end up with lower wages and worse career opportunities. The unemployed don't just have to worry about lost wages while they're looking for work — they also have to worry about lower pay in the future. Even when someone finds work again, they often receive lower pay for decades. This earnings loss is especially acute if they lost their job during a recession. Research shows that men who are laid off as part of a mass layoff lose an average of 1.4 years of earnings when the overall unemployment rate is low. But when the unemployment rate is high, researchers found that such men lose 2.8 years of earnings.

Permanent unemployment can arise from periods of high unemployment. When unemployment rates are high, it becomes even harder to find work. It can take years, so some workers lose hope and stop trying to find work. They may also lose skills or important contacts, or be unable to keep up with changing technology and other developments. The loss of skills and hope, as well as discrimination against the long-term unemployed, all contribute to lower lifetime earnings for those who experience long-term unemployment.

If long durations of joblessness shake workers' desire to search for work, then labor force participation rates may fall in response. When long durations of unemployment make it harder for the unemployed to find work, a phenomenon known as **hysteresis** may occur. You might have heard of this term in other contexts — it refers to any system that depends on its past. In the context of unemployment, hysteresis occurs when a period of high unemployment leads to a higher equilibrium unemployment rate. In other words, the temporarily bad economy makes it harder for people to find jobs, even after the economy recovers. So even when enough jobs are finally available, it takes people longer to find them. As a result, a temporary period of high unemployment permanently creates

hysteresis When a period of high unemployment leads to a higher equilibrium unemployment rate.

more frictional unemployment. That happened following the 2020 recession, which saw record rates of job openings, and yet employment had yet to fully recover by early 2022. Sometimes the rises in frictional unemployment following a recession can last a very long time. For example, research shows that the large rise in long-term unemployment in Europe in the early 1980s was to blame for the chronically high unemployment rates that occurred in the decades afterward.

High unemployment means that the government receives lower tax revenues but spends more. When fewer people have jobs, the government takes in less tax revenue. When fewer people are working and paying income and payroll taxes, they're not only unable to provide for themselves, but they're also contributing less to public goods such as infrastructure, the military, and scientific research. Meanwhile, higher unemployment can strain government budgets, as more people need to use the social safety net. This can divert government spending from other priorities and cause tax rates to rise.

The Social Costs of Unemployment

The costs of unemployment are greater than lost wages and output. There are also costs in terms of health, well-being, crime, and children's outcomes — all of which affect more than just those who are unemployed. Work is one of society's most important institutions, and it's a key source of identity and social ties as well as income. When people lose their jobs, they often lose much more than just income.

Unemployment can be isolating and painful. Unemployment is very disruptive. Your day may be less structured and seem endless. You may find yourself more isolated, more stressed, and unable to spend money on the things that used to be part of the everyday rhythm of your life.

Surveys reveal that the unemployed are more dissatisfied with their lives than the employed. They're more likely to experience depression, anxiety, poverty, and divorce. All of these negative outcomes also come with a higher risk of death, including suicide. Unemployment can lead to social isolation and a loss of self-confidence and meaning in life.

Long-term unemployment is associated with worse outcomes. You've seen that those who are long-term unemployed lose skills and face discrimination when looking for work. Studies also show that long-term unemployment leads to greater permanent earnings losses, as the wages that long-term unemployed workers get when they do find work are often much lower than what they were previously earning. The long-term unemployed also are more likely to have health problems. A job loss nearly doubles their chances of dying a year later, and their death rates are higher for decades later.

Children whose parents experience unemployment suffer. It's probably no surprise that the families of the unemployed also suffer. Layoffs lead to higher divorce rates. The children of laid-off workers suffer from the lost household income and from the stress that the family goes through. These children end up with worse academic outcomes, worse mental health outcomes, and worse employment outcomes, making less money as adults. When a parent loses a job while a child is in high school, that child is less likely to go to college. More generally, when job losses in a state go up, children's outcomes at school go down.

Unemployment can be miserable.

Protecting Yourself from the Harmful Effects of Unemployment

Unemployment can be terrible. But there are some things you can do to help protect yourself from the harmful effects of unemployment.

Do more job searching than you really want to do. Job searching when you're unemployed is a miserable experience. Too often people procrastinate finding a job, doing too little search until their savings start to run out or their unemployment insurance is about to end. But remember the core principles of economics and apply for any job for which the marginal benefit of applying (the probability of getting a job offer times the wage) exceeds the marginal cost of applying (and remember that the emotional pain of applying is short-lived!).

Build up a nest egg. We've seen that half of those who lose their job end up unemployed for more than 10 weeks, and it's not unusual for it to take six months to find work. That's why financial advisers tell you to have three to six months of expenses saved up. You should save up more if you are not eligible for unemployment insurance or if the unemployment rate is high. Remember that anyone can end up finding themselves unemployed. But the experience is not as bad if you have some money in the bank.

Build new skills. The economy is constantly adapting, and you must too. Continuing to learn and build your skills is necessary not only to advance your career, but to stay employed — and to land on your feet if you find yourself unemployed.

Keep an eye out for better opportunities when you're employed. Many employed people keep searching for other opportunities. Keeping an eye out for better opportunities when you're employed can help you advance in your career by identifying jobs that use recent skills you've built, but it can also help if things start to get rocky in your current position. Many people who think their job is likely to come to an end begin searching long before a pink slip arrives. Such searching increases the chance that you'll avoid unemployment by being able to start a new job right away.

Build a strong professional network and tap into it if you become unemployed. Your professional network can help you learn about new opportunities and promote you for them when you are employed. It can also help provide those resources when you're unemployed. In fact, you're more likely to get hired if you have a referral. So if you find yourself unemployed, it's time to call on everyone you know to tell them that you're looking. It takes courage to tell your friends you're looking for work, or to broadcast your job search through social media, but letting people know that you're looking for a new opportunity can pay off.

Avoid long-term unemployment. Sometimes you're offered a job that's not quite as good as you think is possible. If it's your first week searching, you might want to turn it down, but don't keep turning jobs down forever. You've learned about the scarring effects of long-term unemployment — that means that you want to avoid it even if it means settling for Mr. Not-So-Right Job. The good news is that, unlike marriage, you can keep searching for a better job even while you're employed.

It's always a good idea to save for a rainy day.

Rob Hyrons/Shutterstock

11.5 | Tying It Together

The Unemployment Rate Shapes Your Opportunities

During your lifetime you'll be both a seller and a buyer in the labor market. You'll be a buyer as a manager hiring employees or in your personal life hiring people to fix your pipes or look after your pets or children. You'll be a seller any time you work to generate income, either working for yourself or for an employer.

As both a buyer and seller of labor, unemployment will be an important factor in your life, and not just when you yourself are unemployed. As a worker, the opportunity cost of quitting your current job or spending time out of the labor market will depend on how easy it is to find work when you want it. That in turn affects how easy it is to get a promotion, how much you earn, and sometimes even how hard you work. Likewise, the ease with which employers can find and retain good workers can have a profound effect on their bottom line.

It's easier to find or fill a job in a labor market in which workers and jobs match easily — that is, when frictional unemployment is low. But high frictional unemployment means that if you're an employer, it's hard to find the right workers for your needs. You're spending resources — time, energy, and money — looking for employees instead of concentrating on your business. If a job opening takes two months to fill, that's two months that you don't have someone in the job helping you to increase revenue. As a worker, high frictional unemployment means spending your time and energy searching for work instead of bringing home a paycheck. Thus, both workers and employers benefit from technologies and policies that help match workers with employers.

But sometimes the problem is not that workers and employers can't find each other — it's that there simply aren't enough jobs to go around. Labor market institutions, such as unions and regulations, can offer protections and improve conditions for workers on the job. But because they affect employers' ability to hire, fire, and determine the pay of their workers, they have an impact on businesses' hiring decisions and can contribute to structural unemployment. How you feel about the trade-off of better working conditions and more unemployment should inform your decisions about which policies to support, whether you are a voter or a policymaker.

This chapter focused on frictional and structural unemployment, the two types of unemployment that can persist even when the economy is doing well. We also touched briefly on cyclical unemployment, which is the result of economic shocks that reduce the use of resources in the economy. During periods of cyclical unemployment, factories sit idle, machines go unused, and unfortunately, workers get pushed to the sidelines. We'll focus on why that happens when we turn to business cycles in Chapter 17.

Whatever the cause, unemployment is never fun. It can have devastating consequences for workers, their families, and their communities. We all work and hire people in the shadow of the unemployment rate. That's why unemployment is the macroeconomic issue you've probably heard the most about, and it's why we'll continue to examine unemployment throughout our study of macroeconomics.

Chapter 11 Review

Chapter at a Glance

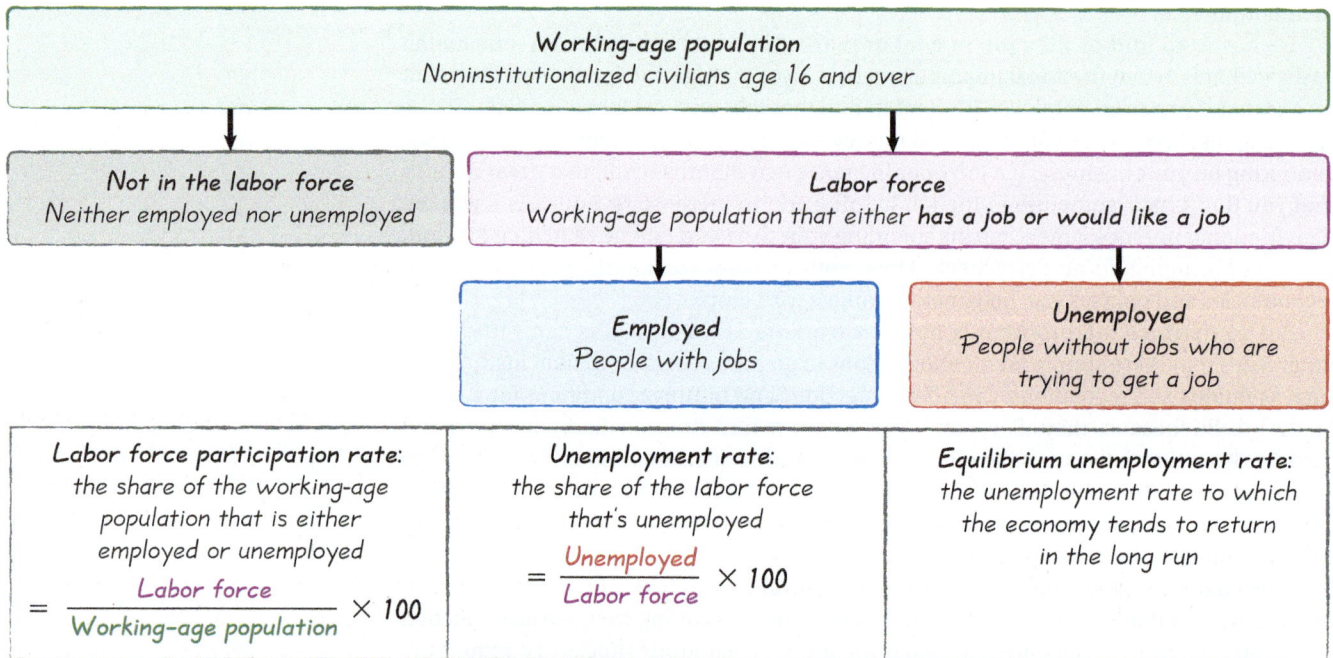

Working-age population
Noninstitutionalized civilians age 16 and over

Not in the labor force
Neither employed nor unemployed

Labor force
Working-age population that either **has a job or would like a job**

Employed
People with jobs

Unemployed
People without jobs who are trying to get a job

Labor force participation rate: the share of the working-age population that is either employed or unemployed

$$= \frac{\text{Labor force}}{\text{Working-age population}} \times 100$$

Unemployment rate: the share of the labor force that's unemployed

$$= \frac{\text{Unemployed}}{\text{Labor force}} \times 100$$

Equilibrium unemployment rate: the unemployment rate to which the economy tends to return in the long run

Alternative Measures of Unemployment Might Also Include

Underemployed: Someone who has some work but wants more hours or whose job isn't adequately using their skills.

Marginally attached: Someone who wants a job, and who has looked for a job within the past year, but who isn't counted as unemployed because they aren't currently searching for work.

Involuntarily part time: Someone who wants full-time work and is working part time because they haven't found a full-time job.

Causes of Unemployment

	Frictional unemployment	Structural unemployment	Cyclical unemployment
Definition	Unemployment due to the time it takes for employers to search for workers and for workers to search for jobs.	Unemployment that occurs because wages don't fall to bring labor demand and supply into equilibrium.	Unemployment that is due to a temporary downturn in the economy.
Sources	1. Job search resources 2. Skills mismatch 3. Unemployment Insurance and other income support	1. Efficiency wages: Higher wages paid to encourage greater worker productivity 2. Institutional causes: • Unions • Job protection regulations • Minimum wage laws	You'll learn more about how unemployment rises and falls later, in the chapter on Business Cycles.

Costs of Unemployment

- Lower wages and worse career opportunities
- Permanent joblessness can arise from periods of high unemployment
- Lower tax revenue and higher government spending
- Unemployment is isolating and painful
- Long-term unemployment is associated with worse outcomes
- Children whose parents experience unemployment suffer

Key Terms

cyclical unemployment, 281

efficiency wage, 285

employed, 272

equilibrium unemployment rate, 277

frictional unemployment, 281

hysteresis, 288

involuntarily part time, 280

labor force, 272

labor force participation rate, 273

long-term unemployed, 278

marginally attached, 279

not in the labor force, 273

structural unemployment, 281

underemployed, 280

unemployed, 272

unemployment rate, 275

working-age population, 272

Study Problems

Learning Objective 11.1 *Understand what unemployment is and how it's measured.*

1. Think of three people from your own life (or even from popular TV shows and films) who are or were unemployed, employed, and not in the labor force. What events and choices led to their employment situation?

2. Describe three economic or social changes that have contributed to the trends in labor force participation rates for men and women since the 1950s. How have these changes impacted the trade-offs people face between home production and the labor market?

3. Sarah, Alicia, and Philip all lost their jobs when the medical billing firm they worked for was acquired by another company. After a few weeks of searching for another full-time job, Sarah decided to go back to school to get an LPN certification. In order to finish as fast as possible, Sarah chooses not to work while finishing the certification. Alicia took a part-time job in retail shortly after losing her job, but she continues to search diligently for full-time work. Philip searched for a job for the first five weeks after being laid off, but as bills began piling up, he found himself moving into his parents' basement. He recently gave up looking for work because he figures that jobs just aren't available right now, so there is no point in looking. Are Sarah, Alicia, and Philip unemployed, employed, or not in the labor force? Would any of the three be considered a discouraged worker? How would each contribute to the unemployment rate?

4. Using the following data from the U.S. Bureau of Labor Statistics, calculate the size of the labor force, the unemployment rate, and the labor force participation rate for 2009 and 2018.

Type of worker	Number of individuals in 2009	Number of individuals in 2018
Working-age population	236 million	258 million
Unemployed	14.3 million	6.3 million
Employed	140 million	156 million

Learning Objective 11.2 *Learn how people move in and out of jobs and in and out of the labor market.*

5. From the perspective of workers and employers, discuss the benefits and the costs of a dynamic labor market.

6. Explain why it is possible to find many job openings in shrinking industries such as newspaper publishing or brick-and-mortar retail.

7. Should the official unemployment rate include people who have searched for work in the last year but are not currently searching? Would such a measure be better or worse than the official measure of the unemployment rate?

8. Determine the labor market status of each of the following people. If they are unemployed, can they be considered long-term unemployed?

   a. Demetrius is a voice-over actor. He has a gig this week, but next week he'll have to start auditioning for new roles.

   b. Alejandra is laid off and has to take a part-time retail job because she can't find a full-time job. She is spending her extra time learning how to code.

   c. Kathryn quit her job when it was relocated too far away from her family. She has been looking for work for eight months, but so far she hasn't been called in for an interview.

9. Use the table below from the U.S. Bureau of Labor Statistics to answer the following questions.

Category	May 2022
Civilian labor force	164.4 million
Employed	158.4 million
Unemployed	5.9 million
Not in labor force	93 million
Marginally attached to the labor force	0.7 million
Involuntarily part time	4.2 million

   a. What was the unemployment rate in May 2022?

   b. If we were to count marginally attached workers as unemployed, what would the unemployment rate have been in May 2022?

   c. If we were to count all of those who are working part time involuntarily as unemployed, what would the unemployment rate have been in May 2022?

   d. If you repeated this calculation for all time periods for the United States and graphed the data, do you think the changes in the unemployment rates would all look similar or different? Why?

10. Consider the following scenarios and explain for each what the effect is on the official unemployment rate.

   a. Unemployed people become discouraged and stop searching for work.

   b. Previously unemployed people find part-time jobs, even though they need full-time work.

   c. Formerly discouraged workers find work.

   d. People who were previously discouraged workers begin looking for work again.

Learning Objective 11.3 *Analyze the causes of unemployment.*

11. What is the equilibrium unemployment rate and why isn't it equal to zero? Explain.

12. Why would a company want to pay its workers more than the prevailing market wage? What is the impact on employers, workers, and the overall labor market?

13. Classify the following scenarios as examples of frictional, structural, or cyclical unemployment, and explain your answer.

   a. Nava just finished a computer science degree and wants to live in Austin. There are lots of openings for people with her skills, but she wants to be sure to find a job that's a good fit. She moves to Austin without a job and crashes on a friend's couch while interviewing.

   b. A food-processing factory decides to increase its wages by 50% above what its competitors are paying. They find that fewer workers quit or call in sick, and that they have lower spoilage rates as a result of the more consistent, productive workforce. Its competitors respond by raising wages as well. The quantity of labor supplied to the industry increases to try to take advantage of the higher wages and is higher than the quantity demanded by employers at the new wage.

   c. Li Wei owns a homebuilding company. During a severe downturn in the housing market, he has to fire many of his subcontractors.

   d. Which of the three types of unemployment (frictional, structural, or cyclical) will persist even if the wage is at the equilibrium wage? Explain your answer.

14. Consider whether each of the following would increase or decrease frictional unemployment.

   a. LinkedIn improves its algorithms, enabling it to more efficiently connect employers with workers who have the experience and skills they need.

   b. Rapid innovation in the tech sector means that the skills required to develop, manage, and service new products are constantly changing.

   c. Unemployment insurance programs become less generous.

15. Janel is the general manager at a new café and wants to hire a few baristas. The going rate for baristas in the area is $9.55 per hour. Janel has heard that many of the local coffee shops have high turnover with baristas "ghosting" them — simply not showing up for their shift and never coming back. Janel starts to put together an advertisement to hire baristas for $9.55 per hour, but changes her mind and lists the wage at $11 per hour. Why would Janel pay $9.55 per hour? What's the rationale for paying $11 (or any wage higher than $9.55)?

16. Suppose the graph depicts the labor market for retail associates in Nashville.

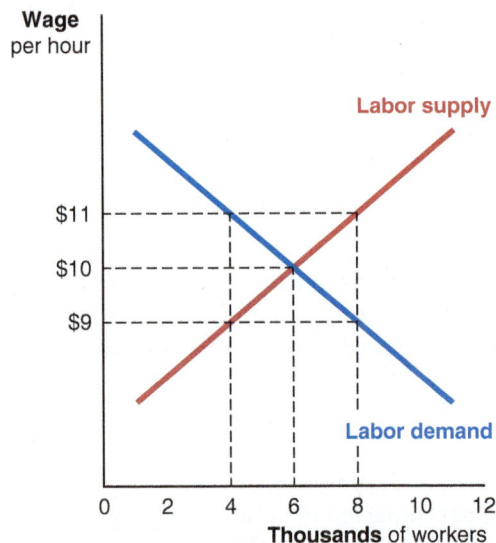

   a. What is the equilibrium wage for retail associates? How many associates are employed at the equilibrium wage, and what is the unemployment rate?

   b. The Tennessee state government enacts a minimum wage of $9 per hour. How many associates are employed at $9 per hour? Is there any unemployment?

   c. Workers successfully lobby the state legislature, and the minimum wage is raised to $11 per hour. How many associates are employed at $11 per hour? Is there any unemployment? If so, are these workers frictionally, structurally, or cyclically unemployed?

Learning Objective 11.4 *Learn about the economic and social costs of unemployment.*

17. Jaivan has two children and is an auto worker who became unemployed, along with most of his co-workers, when the plant where he worked closed. Describe and discuss the economic costs of unemployment to Jaivan, his family, and his community.

18. Your friend talks to you about how the company she works for is having a terrible year. She's terrified of getting laid off and the impact it would have on her family. What advice would you give her to prepare for the possibility of unemployment?

19. An economic downturn throws millions of people out of work. In some industries, workers who remain employed, or "insiders," continue to develop their skills, enabling them to push wages above the level at which less-skilled "outsiders" could be employed. What do you expect to happen to the equilibrium unemployment rate due to hysteresis? Explain your reasoning.

Inflation and Money

Inflation nearly destroyed Coca-Cola. It's a story that begins over a century ago, when Coke was a fledgling company selling most of its product through soda fountains. A couple of sharp Tennessee lawyers thought that they could make money selling Coke in bottles, instead. The owner of Coca-Cola wasn't interested in bottling Coke, but he was willing to let them do it as long as they bought the Coke syrup from him. He wrote a contract committing Coke to sell them this secret syrup at 92 cents per gallon, which at the time included a hefty profit margin. Coke committed to sell the bottlers syrup at this price *forever*.

Timeless advertising and inflation don't always get along.

That commitment was a costly mistake. Over time, prices tend to rise on average, a process known as inflation. And over time the price of sugar, rent, transportation, labor, and all the other stuff that goes into making Coke rose. That meant the cost of producing the syrup kept rising, even as Coke had to keep selling it for 92 cents a gallon. By 1920, Coca-Cola was losing $29,000 per day.

Faced with these financial pressures, Coca-Cola found a way to renegotiate its syrup contract. But Coke's executives quickly forgot the broader lesson—that it's important to pay attention to inflation. A few decades later, Coke took another financial beating due to its failure to consider inflation. This time the problem was that vending machines would only accept one coin (a nickel) and could not give change. And so, while production costs increased and the prices of competing beverages rose with inflation, the price of a Coke remained stuck at 5 cents. Things got so dire that the head of Coke wrote to his hunting pal, President Eisenhower, asking the government to mint a 7½ cent coin. (Eisenhower refused.)

Coke misjudged the influence of inflation, and it led to two very costly mistakes. They're mistakes you can learn from, which is why the rest of this chapter will analyze inflation. We'll explore how inflation is measured, how it affects you, and the problems it can cause. And hopefully along the way, you'll gain some insights that will help you make better choices than Coke's executives did.

Chapter Objective

Evaluate the rate of inflation and its consequences.

12.1 Measuring Inflation
Understand what inflation is and how to measure it.

12.2 Different Measures of Inflation
Pick the right inflation measure for the task at hand.

12.3 Adjusting for the Effects of Inflation
Learn to account for the influence of inflation before making big decisions.

12.4 The Role of Money and the Costs of Inflation
Analyze the role of money so that you can assess the costs of inflation.

🎙 Podcast

Think Like an Economist
Inflation—When Money Loses Its Value

12.1 # 12.1 Measuring Inflation

Learning Objective *Understand what inflation is and how to measure it.*

I bet you've heard people, particularly older people, complain about rising prices. They complain that nearly everything is more expensive than it used to be. They worry that prices will keep rising, making it hard for them to save, send their kids to college, or prepare for retirement.

They'll tell stories about how cheap things used to be. Like how in 1990, the average price of a movie ticket was only $4.23, a gallon of regular gas was $1.16, and bananas were a mere $0.46 a pound. Today you'll pay more for those things. In mid-2021, a movie ticket cost $9.16, a gallon of regular gas was $3.01, and bananas were $0.62 a pound.

inflation A generalized rise in the overall level of prices.

They're describing **inflation,** which is *a generalized rise in the overall level of prices.* Inflation can also be described as *a rise in the cost of living.* As a result, inflation is also *a decline in the purchasing power of money,* because it means that a $20 bill buys fewer movie tickets, less gas, and fewer bananas than it did in 1990. When there's been inflation, it means that you'll be spending more to buy the same stuff you bought the year before. The good news is that wages rise on average too. But that means you have to pay attention to inflation in order to know whether *your* wages are rising enough for you to be able to continue to afford all the things you buy. Let's take a deeper look at inflation and how to measure it.

The Price of a Basket of Goods and Services

consumer price index (CPI) An index that tracks the average price consumers pay over time for a representative "basket" of goods and services.

There is more than one measure of inflation, but the inflation measure that's most relevant to your life as a consumer is calculated using the **consumer price index** (or **CPI** for short). The CPI is a measure of the average prices people pay over time for the goods and services they buy. More formally, it is an index that tracks the *average price* consumers pay over time for a representative basket of goods and services. Statisticians refer to the lists they compile of the goods and services people typically buy as a *basket.* It's a metaphor — after all, a haircut can't go into a basket! The CPI is a closely watched indicator, and headlines like "Inflation ticks up" or "Inflation falling" are typically about the CPI.

Romariolen/Shutterstock

The CPI basket includes groceries — but also shelter, education, haircuts, and streaming services.

inflation rate The annual percentage increase in the average price level.

The inflation rate is the percentage change in the price of a fixed basket of goods. The CPI measures how much prices change on average. But not all prices rise by the same amount; some prices will rise more than others, and some prices will even fall. To know how much inflation is occurring, we need to tally up all these price changes. Government statisticians effectively create a shopping list of the things that a typical consumer would buy, and then send people to grocery stores and other retailers to track the price of each of those items.

The price of that basket of goods is a measure of the average *price level* in the economy. The **inflation rate** is the annual percentage increase in the average price level, and it's calculated as the percentage change in the price of this basket of goods and services:

$$\text{Inflation rate} = \frac{\text{Price level this year} - \text{Price level last year}}{\text{Price level last year}} \times 100$$

So if the price of that basket rose from $100 last year to $102 this year, this calculation says that inflation was 2%. That means that:

- On average, prices are 2% higher this year than last year;
- The cost of living is 2% higher than it was last year; and
- A dollar buys roughly 2% less than it did last year.

Not every price change is a sign of inflation. You should distinguish the macroeconomic phenomena of inflation, which is a *generalized rise in prices,* from the microeconomic phenomena of *relative price adjustment,* in which the price of individual goods rises or falls relative to other prices as their specific supply and demand ebbs and flows. In reality, when there is inflation, there are also often relative price changes that are happening at the same time. For example, 2021 saw higher-than-normal inflation, and there were also relative price changes. For example, meat prices rose relative to the price of meat substitutes.

Constructing the Consumer Price Index and Measuring Inflation

Now that you know what the CPI is, let's dig into understanding how it's constructed and used to measure inflation. The government agency in charge of measuring consumer prices is the Bureau of Labor Statistics (the BLS for short). In order to measure inflation using the CPI, it needs to know what people buy and the prices they pay. Government statisticians then tally up the cost of the typical basket of goods and services and compare to how this cost changes over time to calculate the inflation rate. Let's take a closer look at each of these four steps.

Step 1: Find out what people typically buy. The first challenge is figuring out what to put into the basket — and how much of each item to put into it — to represent the goods and services that the average consumer buys. To do that, the BLS surveys thousands of people, asking them how much they spend on bread, haircuts, medical expenses, cellular service, rent, and so on. Statisticians use these surveys to construct a basket of goods and services that represents the average household's purchases.

Figure 1 reveals that people spend most of their money on housing, food, and transport. While your spending patterns may differ, this basket matches the average American's purchases pretty closely.

Figure 1 | The CPI Basket

What do people typically buy?

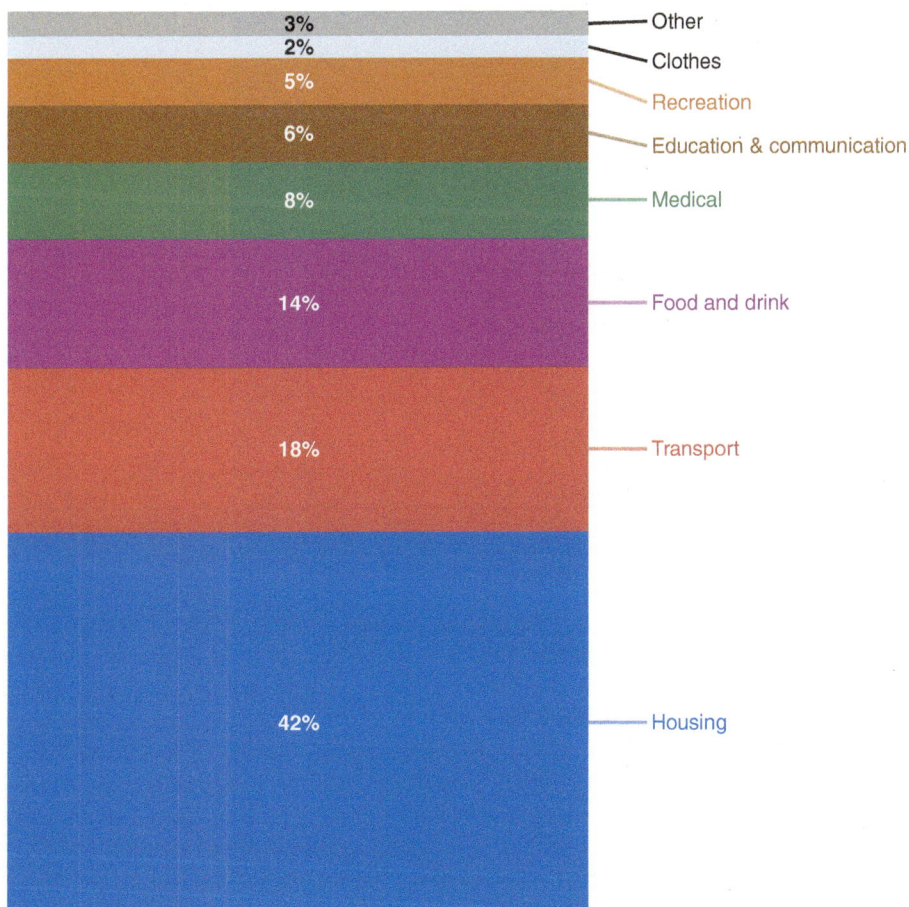

3%	Other
2%	Clothes
5%	Recreation
6%	Education & communication
8%	Medical
14%	Food and drink
18%	Transport
42%	Housing

Share of a typical household's spending

Data from: Bureau of Labor Statistics.

Each of these categories contains many different goods and services. Housing includes spending on rent, as well as all the associated costs like electricity, fuel, water, and household goods. Food includes groceries and restaurant meals. Transport includes new and used cars, gas, subway, bus, and airfares. The basket includes just about everything that you spend money on, so it includes not only physical stuff you buy (and could put in an actual basket) but also services like doctors visits, streaming subscriptions, and college tuition.

Step 2: Collect prices from the stores where people do their shopping.
Once you've assembled a representative basket of goods and services, you need to track how much it costs to buy everything in it. And that means tracking the price of thousands of goods and services. Surveyors visit thousands of retailers around the country from Walmart Supercenters to local mom-and-pop stores. They click through online stores, call doctors' offices, and collect rental prices on real estate. Altogether, the government keeps track of the prices of thousands of goods and services.

Step 3: Tally up the price of the basket of goods and services.
Now, add up all the prices, accounting for the fact that this basket includes more of some items than others. The totals, shown in Figure 2, aren't a simple average of every price. Rather, the CPI puts more weight on products you buy more of, so that if on average people buy five times as much coffee as tea, then the basket includes five times as much coffee as tea.

Figure 2 | The Consumer Price Index Measures the Price of a Basket of Goods Over Time

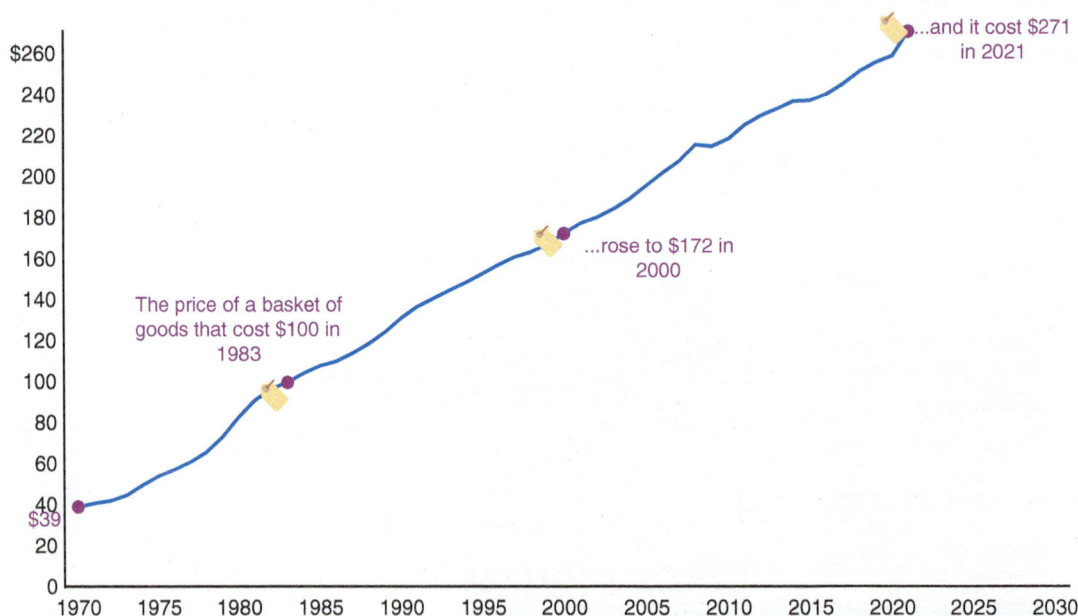

...and it cost $271 in 2021

...rose to $172 in 2000

The price of a basket of goods that cost $100 in 1983

$39

Data from: Bureau of Labor Statistics.

The total cost in dollars of this representative basket of stuff is scaled to create a price index. The idea is to pick an arbitrary year (called the base year) and track changes in the cost of that basket of goods and services over time. To make it easy, economists tend to scale the cost of the basket in the base year to $100. You might be thinking, why not use the amount the average person spends in the base year? But the CPI is focused on how much prices are changing, not how big the average person's basket is. And the math is a lot easier to manage if we start with a $100 basket! Take a look at Figure 2, which shows how the cost of this basket has changed over time. Scaling the price level to $100 in a base year makes it easy for you to see that prices have roughly tripled since the early 1980s.

Step 4: Calculate the inflation rate. You've already done all the hard work. The final step is to calculate the inflation rate, remembering that it's the percentage change in the price of that fixed basket of goods over a year.

Figure 3 shows the inflation rate for each year since 1970. In the late 1970s inflation was much higher than in subsequent decades, sometimes above 10%. In 2009, when the economy was in a deep downturn, average prices actually fell. A generalized decrease in the overall price level is known as **deflation.** More recently, inflation rose rapidly in 2021 and 2022 as the economy recovered from the Covid recession.

deflation A generalized decrease in the overall level of prices.

Figure 3 | **The Inflation Rate**

Annual change in the price of a basket of goods and services (CPI)

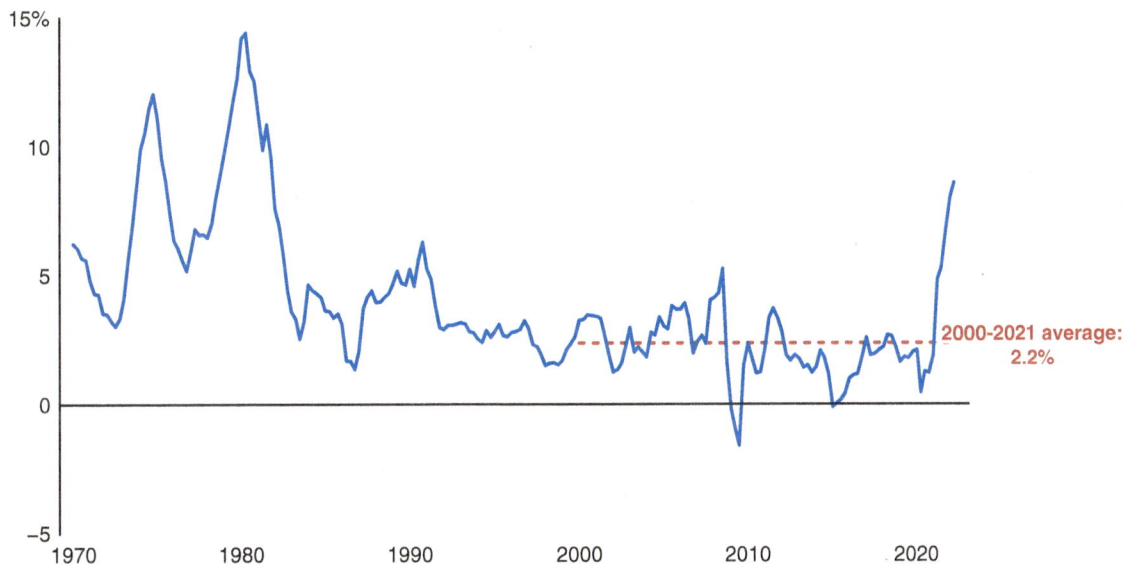

Data from: Bureau of Labor Statistics.

Deflation may sound good, but it actually can cause big problems in the economy because some people stop buying goods and services in order to wait for them to become cheaper. We'll discuss the problems of deflation and the tools the government uses to fight it in Chapter 22.

Do the Economics

Let's put your new skills to the test and calculate an inflation rate. To do this for the average American consumer requires enormous amounts of data because people buy a lot of different goods and services. To keep it simple, let's calculate the inflation rate experienced by one really simple consumer: my dog Max. Max is your average American dog — as a mutt, he's an average of many breeds — and he has average tastes.

Step 1: Find out what Max typically buys.

Max eats a small can of dog food each morning and another in the evening, which means that he goes through 730 cans per year. He also gets a few scoops of kibble each day, which adds up to six 30-pound bags per year. He visits the vet twice per year on average, and he gets a couple of new chew toys on his birthday. This list describes Max's basket of goods and services, and it's recorded in the first column of Figure 4.

To measure inflation:
1. Find out what people buy
2. Collect prices
3. Tally up the cost of the basket
4. Calculate inflation as the percentage change in the price of the basket

Figure 4 | Calculating Inflation

Step 1: What do dogs buy?	Step 2: Collect prices		Step 3: Tally up the costs	
Max's basket of goods and services	Price in 2021	Price in 2022	Cost in 2021 (= Price in 2021 × Quantity)	Cost in 2022 (= Price in 2022 × Quantity)
730 cans of dog food	$1.80 per can	$1.85 per can	$1.80 × 730 = $1,314	$1.85 × 730 = $1,351
6 bags of kibble	$40 per bag	$41 per bag	$40 × 6 = $240	$41 × 6 = $246
2 vet visits	$60 per visit	$65 per visit	$60 × 2 = $120	$65 × 2 = $130
2 chew toys	$10 per toy	$11 per toy	$10 × 2 = $20	$11 × 2 = $22
Cost of Max's basket			$1,694	$1,749

Step 4: Calculate the inflation rate $= \dfrac{\$1,749 - \$1,694}{\$1,694} \times 100 = \mathbf{3.2\%}$

Meet Max the wonder dog.

Step 2: Collect prices.

You need to find the prices of dog food, vet visits, and dog toys. I've listed what I paid for each of these throughout the year in 2021 (shown in the second column) and 2022 (in the third column) of Figure 4.

Step 3: Tally up the cost of a fixed basket of goods and services.

Next, add up the total cost of Max's basket of goods and services each year. Since Max purchased the same quantity of good and services in both years, this is just the total spending on canned food plus spending on kibble, vet visits, and chew toys. Because he eats a lot more cans of canned food than bags of kibble, the price of canned food gets a much higher weight in this total cost. As the bottom row of Figure 4 shows, the cost of this basket of goods rose from $1,694 in 2021 (yes, dogs are expensive!), to $1,749 in 2022.

Step 4: Calculate the inflation rate.

A representative and fixed basket of dog consumption cost $1,694 in 2021, and $1,749 in 2022, so the inflation rate for dogs was $\dfrac{\$1,749 - \$1,694}{\$1,694} \times 100 = 3.2\%$. Woof!

   Max had a lower inflation rate than humans because the prices of the stuff he consumes went up by less than the stuff most people consume. If you want to see how much inflation you experience, keep a record of what you buy and track the corresponding prices over time. ■

The Challenges of Measuring the True Cost of Living

One goal of the CPI is to measure changes in the cost of living — how much your spending has to rise to maintain a given quality of life. But the CPI is an imperfect measure of the cost of living. The problem is that it tracks the changing price of a *fixed* basket of goods, while in reality, consumers' buying patterns change often. As new products are developed and as the availability and price of goods and services change relative to other options, people adjust the items in their basket in order to maintain (or improve) their quality of life. Failing to account for these changing buying patterns tends to overstate changes in the cost of living. There are three related biases to the way the CPI is measured, and they all suggest that the CPI overstates changes in the cost of living.

Quality improvements can hide price decreases. Businesses are constantly introducing new and improved products. How should we think about price changes that come with quality changes? A 128 GB iPhone 13 Pro cost $999 in 2022, a price increase of 66% over the first iPhone. But the first iPhone had a maximum of 8 GB of storage. Storage isn't the only difference: The processor speed is much faster on the iPhone 13 Pro, the screen is bigger, and the battery life is longer. The original iPhone did have a camera, but it was pretty bad: low resolution, no low-light capabilities, and no front-facing "selfie" features. If you're getting something better, then how should you think about the price change?

This is an issue that the people who measure inflation confront on a daily basis. To truly measure inflation, we need to compare price changes on a quality-adjusted basis. But it's impossible to account for every quality improvement, and so some part of the measured rise in prices is likely due to unmeasured quality improvements, rather than to a true rise in the cost of living. That means that the CPI overstates inflation because quality improvements are not fully accounted for in adjustments.

New products can make you better off, thereby reducing your cost of living. The CPI ignores the fact that the price of an iPhone fell from infinity in 2006 (you couldn't buy one at any price!), to $599 when it was released in 2007. It's an invention that reduced the cost of living, because it replaced many goods and services that people previously spent a lot of money on: landline phone service and answering machines; watches and calculators; cameras, film, and photo processing; GPS devices and music players; and newspapers and magazines. Because the CPI tracks only the changing prices of *existing* goods, it doesn't account for the reduction in the cost of living due to the introduction of new products.

Even if they didn't buy these things before, people who buy smartphones today are better off because they now have access to this technology. When the iPhone was introduced, people shifted their budget from other things toward the iPhone. Why? Because their marginal benefit from spending $599 on an iPhone was higher than whatever else they could have spent that $599 on (or else the cost-benefit principle tells us they wouldn't have bought the iPhone).

The BLS doesn't attempt to compare new products to the products being replaced in the basket. Over time, the BLS adds new products to the basket and removes others, but it doesn't compare the price of new products (like iPhones) to the products being replaced (like cameras). Once new products become part of the typical person's basket of goods and services, changes in their prices will contribute to changes in the overall price level. But because the CPI tracks only the changing prices of *existing* goods and services, it doesn't account for the savings and improved quality of life that follow from the invention of new products.

You can save money by changing the things you buy. When prices rise, people adapt and change the products in their actual shopping baskets. For instance, when the price of bananas rises, you might buy oranges or apples instead. You *substitute* what's in your shopping basket to find cheaper ways to achieve the same quality of life.

Substituting low-inflation goods and services for high-inflation ones is a good strategy. But the CPI measures the prices of a *fixed* basket of goods, so it effectively assumes that people keep buying the same number of bananas no matter how expensive they get. It doesn't capture substitution across items. This leads measured inflation to outpace changes in people's actual cost of living. This is called **substitution bias** — the overestimate of the cost of living that occurs because people substitute toward goods and services whose prices rise by less.

It's hard to know for sure how much substitution bias there is. Even though you substituted an orange for a banana to minimize the negative effect of more expensive bananas on your well-being, there's still a negative effect. How big is it? That depends on how much worse off you are from the switch, which depends on your personal preferences.

How much does the CPI overstate inflation? Economists continue to debate how big these measurement problems are. Careful studies suggest that the bias due to the unmeasured quality improvements, new products, and substitution together lead the CPI to

giedre vaitekune/Shutterstock

It used to cost a lot more to take a picture.

substitution bias The overestimate of the cost of living that occurs because people substitute toward goods whose prices rise by less.

Patti McConville/Alamy Stock Photo

What will you do when their price goes up?

Three things the CPI misses:
1. Quality improvements
2. New products
3. Substitutions

overstate the rising cost of living by nearly 1% per year. Most of this is due to new products and unmeasured quality improvements. The *chained CPI* is an alternative inflation measure that is designed to update the basket of goods each month to correct for substitution bias. This alternative measure of inflation tends to be about a quarter of a percentage point lower than the CPI, and many economists argue that it's a truer measure of changes in the cost of living.

12.2 Different Measures of Inflation

Learning Objective *Pick the right inflation measure for the task at hand.*

Inflation data are used for many different tasks: They're a guideline for cost-of-living adjustments, an input to adjusting financial and economic indicators, a guidepost for Federal Reserve policymakers, and an indicator that forecasters use to project where the economy is going. Each role is best served by slightly different measures of inflation. While the CPI remains the most popular measure of inflation, different measures of inflation consider different baskets of goods and services and can be more relevant for different tasks.

Consumer Prices

So far we've been focusing on the prices that consumers pay when they buy goods and services. Let's take a look at how various measures of inflation in consumer prices differ, and what each is useful for.

The CPI is used for cost-of-living adjustments. The CPI is the most widely accepted measure of the change in cost of living. That's why workers who want to protect themselves from the effects of the rising cost of living insist that their employment contracts include **indexation** clauses, which automatically adjust their wages in line with the CPI. The government indexes Social Security and other payments so that they're automatically adjusted to keep pace with the rising cost of living. And the income cutoffs to qualify for many government programs are automatically adjusted each year to account for inflation.

indexation Automatically adjusting wages, benefits, tax brackets, and the like to compensate for inflation.

Monetary policy focuses on the personal consumption expenditure deflator. One key goal of the Federal Reserve is to achieve low and stable inflation. As we'll discuss in Chapter 22, its target inflation rate is 2%. But rather than focus on the CPI, the Fed sets this target in terms of the *personal consumption expenditure deflator* (or the PCE deflator, to its friends). This alternative measure of inflation is based on a slightly different basket of goods and services that also includes items that you consume but don't pay for directly, like medical care paid for you by your employer or the government. The goods and services in the PCE basket are continually updated, so (much like the chained CPI), it accounts for changing patterns of spending. This means that the PCE deflator does not have the problem of substitution bias that the CPI has. As Figure 5 shows, the Fed's preferred measure of PCE inflation moves in lockstep with CPI inflation, though it is often lower due to the correction for substitution bias.

Figure 5 | Alternative Measures of Inflation Move Together

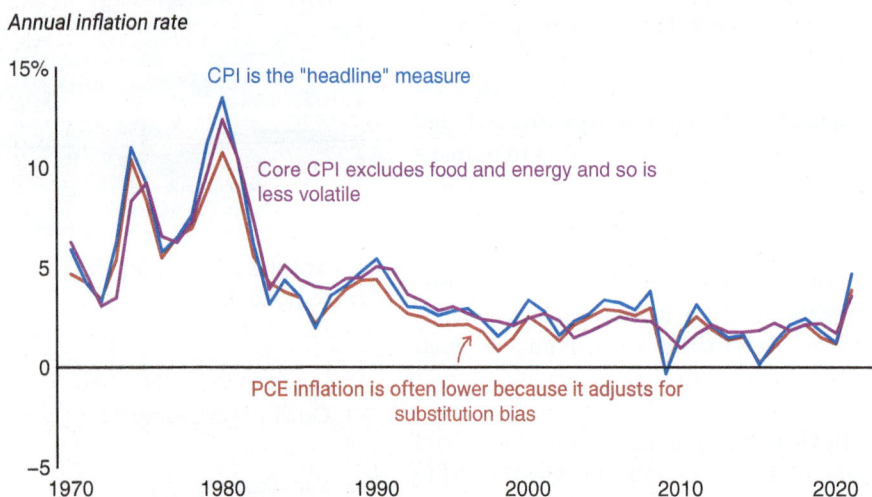

Annual inflation rate

CPI is the "headline" measure

Core CPI excludes food and energy and so is less volatile

PCE inflation is often lower because it adjusts for substitution bias

Data from: Bureau of Labor Statistics and Bureau of Economic Analysis.

When forecasters look for the underlying trend in inflation, they consult an alternative measure of inflation that excludes food and energy. This measure is called *core inflation*. Sometimes people think this is odd because food and energy are two of the most critical purchases people make. They are excluded not because they aren't important, but because their prices are often volatile and they don't track broader inflation trends. Food prices rise and fall with agricultural harvests, and oil prices fluctuate with geopolitical tensions. Excluding these volatile prices often provides a clearer reading of underlying inflation trends. As Figure 5 illustrates, core inflation tends to be similar to the headline measure, but it bounces around less.

Business Prices

The CPI is designed to measure inflation as experienced by people in their day-to-day lives. But if you're running a business, you care about the prices of inputs into your production process or the price at which you can sell your output. Similarly, if you want to know if a country is producing more output or just charging higher prices, you need to account for inflation in the prices of all the goods and services that are produced.

Inflation experienced by businesses is measured by the producer price index. The **producer price index** (or PPI for short) measures the price of inputs into the production process. It's useful because it helps businesses see how the prices that matter to them are changing. It's also useful because it can help you keep tabs on what's likely happening to your competitors' costs. From a macroeconomic perspective, it's worth tracking the inflation that businesses face because rising input prices eventually cause them to raise their prices.

producer price index (PPI) A price index that tracks the prices of inputs into the production process.

The GDP deflator tells us about the changing prices of all goods and services produced. When you're adjusting dollar amounts describing what the economy produces, you should focus on the **GDP deflator,** which is an alternative price index that's calculated based on a basket of goods and services that represents everything the U.S. economy *produces.* That means it accounts for the prices of everything we make — from sandwiches to submarines — and that unlike the CPI, it includes capital goods but excludes imported goods. The GDP deflator is particularly important because it can be used to convert nominal GDP into real GDP. Recall from Chapter 9 that real GDP is measured using a fixed price level so that it isolates changes in the amount of stuff being produced from changes in the price level. That means we can compare real and nominal GDP to compute the GDP deflator:

GDP deflator A price index that tracks the price of all goods and services produced domestically.

$$\text{GDP deflator} = \frac{\text{Nominal GDP}}{\text{Real GDP}} \times 100$$

Now that you know many different measures of inflation, let's turn to ways you might use them, as you make adjustments for the effects of inflation. That's going to require a quick trip to a galaxy far, far away . . .

12.3 Adjusting for the Effects of Inflation

Learning Objective *Learn to account for the influence of inflation before making big decisions.*

When *Variety* magazine held a poll asking readers which was the best Star Wars film of all time, few voted for episode seven, *Star Wars: The Force Awakens.* Yet in dollar terms it appears — at least at first glance — to be the most successful Star Wars film ever. When it was released in the United States in 2015, its box office revenues added up to $937 million, making it one of the top grossing movies of all time. By this measure, *The Force Awakens* was more than three times as successful as the original Star Wars, which took in only $307 million when it was first released in 1977.

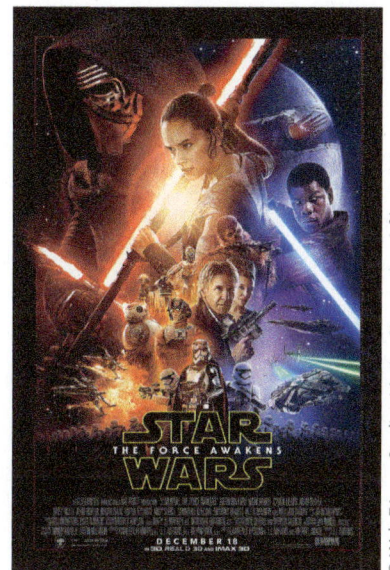

© Walt Disney Studios Motion Pictures/Lucasfilm Ltd./ Courtesy Everett Collection

The force of inflation made this appear to be the most popular Star Wars movie.

Figure 6 | The Consumer Price Index

Year	CPI
1977	60.6
1978	65.2
1979	72.6
1980	82.4
1981	90.9
1982	96.5
1983	99.6
1984	103.9
1985	107.6
1986	109.6
1987	113.6
1988	118.3
1989	124.0
1990	130.7
1991	136.2
1992	140.3
1993	144.5
1994	148.2
1995	152.4
1996	156.9
1997	160.5
1998	163.0
1999	166.6
2000	172.2
2001	177.1
2002	179.9
2003	184.0
2004	188.9
2005	195.3
2006	201.6
2007	207.3
2008	215.3
2009	214.5
2010	218.1
2011	224.9
2012	229.6
2013	233.0
2014	236.7
2015	237.0
2016	240.0
2017	245.1
2018	251.1
2019	255.7
2020	258.8
2021	271.0

Data from: Bureau of Labor Statistics.

But fans, critics, and economists agree that the original Star Wars (that's *Episode IV: A New Hope* to you youngsters) was a much better film. The problem is that the dark side has distorted these numbers.

Comparing Dollars over Time

The dark side here is inflation. Rising prices effectively mean that the value of a dollar has declined over time. And that makes it difficult to compare dollar amounts from different time periods, because past amounts are measured in dollars that were more valuable than today's dollars.

Use the inflation adjustment formula to adjust for changing prices. You'll make better judgments if you compare dollar amounts from different eras using a common metric. This is where you'll find the CPI to be useful. The CPI tracks the average price level over time, so you can use it to convert dollar amounts from the past into their equivalent purchasing power in today's dollars.

To do this, multiply the dollar amount from another time by the ratio of today's price level to the price level at that time:

$$\text{Today's dollars} = \text{Another time's dollars} \times \frac{\text{Price level today}}{\text{Price level in another time}}$$

Do the Economics

You can see how this formula works by converting the box office take from different eras into today's dollars (and to help you, Figure 6 shows you the price level for each year):

- *The Force Awakens* was released in 2015, and it grossed $937 million in 2015 dollars, when the CPI was 237.0. Today (in 2021) the CPI is 271.0. Therefore:

$$\text{Revenue in 2021 dollars} = \$937 \text{ million} \times \frac{271.0}{237.0} = \$1,071 \text{ million}$$

Movie	Release year	CPI in release year	Box office total (for original U.S. release)	
			In release year's dollars	**In 2021 dollars**
Original trilogy				
Star Wars "A New Hope"	1977	60.6	$307m	
The Empire Strikes Back	1980	82.4	$209m	
Return of the Jedi	1983	99.6	$253m	
Prequel trilogy				
The Phantom Menace	1999	166.6	$431m	
Attack of the Clones	2002	179.9	$302m	
Revenge of the Sith	2005	195.3	$380m	
Sequel trilogy				
The Force Awakens	2015	237.0	$937m	
The Last Jedi	2017	245.1	$620m	
The Rise of Skywalker	2019	255.7	$515m	

Note: CPI in 2021 was 271.0.

Data from: Box Office Mojo.

The original Star Wars release grossed $307 million in 1977 dollars, when the CPI was 60.6. Therefore:

$$\text{Revenue in 2021 dollars} = \$307 \text{ million} \times \frac{271.1}{60.6} = \$1,373 \text{ million}$$

Once you account for the influence of inflation, the truth emerges: The original Star Wars had the larger inflation-adjusted revenue, which makes sense, because it was a much more popular film. Now try some on your own: Convert the box office take for the original release of all nine of the main Star Wars movies into 2021 dollars. ∎

Answers: $1,373m; $687m; $688m; $701m; $455m; $527m; $1,071m; $686m; $546m.

Real and Nominal Variables

The broader idea is that when you're comparing dollar amounts from different time periods, inflation can distort your comparisons. This insight applies well beyond box office receipts, to GDP, wages, your income, revenues, costs — indeed, any variable measured in dollars.

Real variables adjust for inflation. This is why economists distinguish between two types of measures. A **nominal variable** is measured in dollars (or some other currency) whose values may fluctuate over time. As a result, nominal variables can rise or fall due to either changing quantities (the number of people seeing a movie) or inflation (which changes the price of movie tickets).

nominal variable A variable measured in dollars (whose value may fluctuate over time).

By contrast, a **real variable** has been adjusted to account for the influence of inflation. You can convert nominal variables into real variables by converting dollar amounts from different time periods into the equivalent number of today's dollars.

real variable A variable that has been adjusted to account for inflation.

As you saw when we looked at how the CPI is calculated, macroeconomists often adjust variables into dollars from a specific year, and that year is called the *base year*. For instance, real GDP data are published in 2012 dollars. There is nothing special about 2012; you could pick any year to be the base year. With 2012 as the base year, you can calculate real GDP as follows:

$$\text{Real value in 2012 dollars} = \text{Nominal value in year } t \text{ dollars} \times \frac{\text{Price level in 2012}}{\text{Price level in year } t}$$

By analyzing dollar amounts once they've been converted into dollars from some fixed year — whether it's 2012 or some other base year — you're effectively holding the average price level constant, which means that you've stripped out the effects of inflation. Because real variables aren't affected by changing prices, they change only in response to changes in physical quantities.

Focus on real variables. Real variables give you a better sense of the underlying trade-offs, particularly when you're making comparisons over time. To give a few examples:

- To analyze whether your purchasing power is rising, you should analyze your *real income,* which adjusts for the effects of inflation, rather than your nominal income in dollars.

- To assess whether your stocks have become more valuable, focus on the *real wealth* in your portfolio, rather than its nominal value.

- To evaluate whether your sales staff are performing better, focus on your company's *real revenues,* rather than nominal revenues, which rise with inflation. Let's see how this works.

Do the Economics

In 2020 (when the CPI was 258.8), Walmart's annual revenue was $559 billion. By 2021, Walmart's annual report boasted that revenue had grown to $573 billion (and the CPI rose to 271). Calculate the growth in Walmart's real revenue, using 2012 as the base year (when the CPI was 229.6). ∎

Answers:
- Revenue from 2020 in 2012 dollars = $559 billion × 229.6/258.8 = $496 billion.
- Revenue from 2021 in 2012 dollars = $573 billion × 229.6/271 = $485 billion.
- Therefore real revenue fell from $496b to $485b, a decline of −2.2%.

You can calculate real growth as nominal growth minus inflation. This calculation took a fair bit of work. Fortunately, you already learned a shortcut in Chapter 9 that will make it easier to calculate real growth rates. Recall that for relatively small percentage changes (say, changes of less than 10%):

Percent change in real value ≈ Percent change in nominal value − Percent change in prices

For instance, between 2020 and 2021, Walmart's nominal revenue rose by 2.5%, and over the same period, the CPI grew 4.7%. Thus, Walmart's real revenue fell by 2.5% − 4.7% = −2.2%.

Do the Economics

Answer: Percent change in real wage = Percent change nominal wage − Percent change in prices = 4.2% − 4.7% = −0.5%.

The average nominal wage grew 4.2% in 2021, and the CPI grew 4.7%. How much did real wages grow? ■

Real and Nominal Interest Rates

Let's see how all this applies to the benefits and costs of saving or borrowing money. Typically, you receive interest payments when you save, and you pay interest when you borrow. If you put $100 in the bank at the start of the year and your bank adds $5 in interest you'll have $105 at the end of the year. But does this really measure the benefit to you?

The nominal interest rate measures the return in dollars. That extra 5% you receive is the **nominal interest rate,** which is the stated interest rate without a correction for the effects of inflation. It reflects the return, *measured in dollars,* for the use of $100 for a year. How much better off you are depends on *what you can buy* with that $105. If inflation has led prices to rise by 3% so that it now takes $103 to buy what would have cost $100 last year, then you're only $2 better off.

nominal interest rate The stated interest rate without a correction for the effects of inflation.

real interest rate The interest rate in terms of changes in your purchasing power; ≈ Nominal interest rate − Inflation rate

The real interest rate measures what you can buy with those dollars. If you want to accurately measure the benefit you'll get from saving $100 for a year — or the cost of borrowing $100 for a year — you'll need to account for the influence of inflation. That's what the **real interest rate** does: It measures the interest rate in terms of changes in your *purchasing power*. It's useful because it shifts your focus from how many extra dollar bills you'll receive, to what you can buy with those dollar bills. It's called the real interest rate because it focuses on the real benefit you'll get from saving. For low rates of inflation, there's a simple shortcut you can use to calculate the real interest rate:

Real interest rate ≈ Nominal interest rate − Inflation rate

So in this example, where the nominal interest rate was 5% and the inflation rate was 3%, the real interest rate is (approximately) 5% − 3% = 2%. That's why we said that in this example, saving $100 for a year makes you $2 better off.

Overcoming Money Illusion

money illusion The (mistaken) tendency to focus on nominal dollar amounts instead of inflation-adjusted amounts.

When *The Force Awakens* smashed box office records, the press trumpeted it as the most successful movie ever made. This is an example of **money illusion** — the (mistaken) tendency to focus on nominal dollar amounts — and it can lead you to be fooled by inflation. People can make very costly mistakes when they focus on nominal rather than real variables. If you learn to recognize money illusion, you can avoid being suckered into making bad decisions.

Money illusion can distort decisions. A survey asked people to consider what choices they would make if all prices throughout the economy — including their income — were to rise by 25%. In particular, it asked them to imagine that the price of a leather chair that they had planned to buy had increased from $400 to $500. Apply the opportunity cost principle, and you'll see that the opportunity cost of buying the chair remains unchanged because anything else you could spend that money on has also become 25% more expensive. Yet nearly two-fifths of the respondents said they would be less likely to buy the chair at this increased price. Money illusion led people to focus instead on the higher dollar cost, rather than the unchanged opportunity cost. Don't let money illusion fool you into focusing on the price in dollar terms; pay attention to the real opportunity cost instead.

Money illusion can lead to mis-pricing. When listing a home for sale, many homeowners start by thinking about how much they bought it for. But money illusion leads them to think about the price they paid in nominal dollars, without adjusting for inflation. That can be a disastrously bad guide if you purchased your home decades earlier, when average prices were a lot lower. Failing to account for inflation can lead homeowners to sell their houses at prices that are tens of thousands of dollars too low. If you are ever selling — or buying — real estate, don't make the same mistake. The best guide to the value of a home isn't the price it sold for years ago — it's the prices that similar houses in your neighborhood have sold for recently.

Money illusion creates nominal wage rigidity. People hate it when their employer cuts their wage. It feels unfair, and they resent it. Smart managers understand this, so even when their business is struggling, they'll try to get by without ever cutting nominal wages, a pattern known as **nominal wage rigidity.** You can see this in Figure 7, which shows the distribution of pay raises for U.S. workers. There's a big pile-up at 0%, which shows that the boss often chooses to stick with last year's wage rather than to cut anyone's pay. But notice that this pile-up occurs at a zero percent *nominal* wage rise. Money illusion led workers to feel okay because their wage — *measured in dollars* — wasn't being cut. But the reality is that inflation that year was 2%, and so their real wages were cut by 2%.

nominal wage rigidity Reluctance to cut nominal wages.

Figure 7 | The Distribution of Nominal Wage Changes Show That Few Workers Receive Nominal Wage Cuts and Many Workers "Pile Up" at a Zero Percent Nominal Wage Change

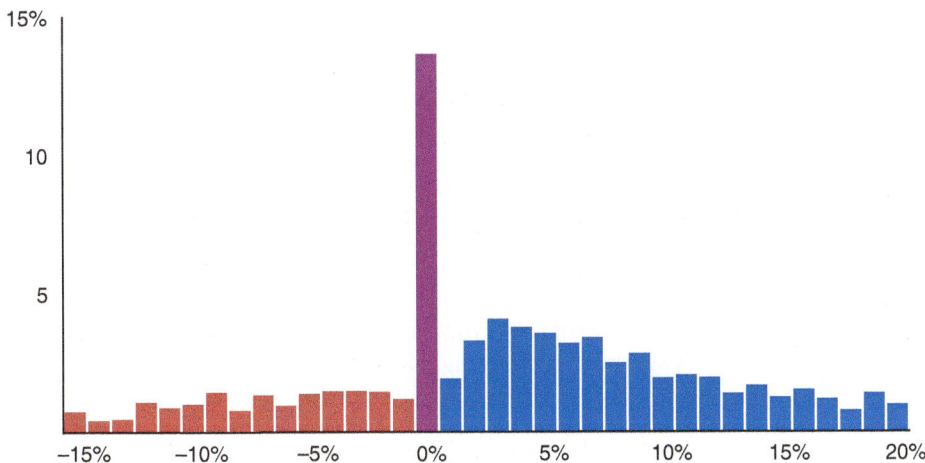

Share of workers

Data from: Federal Reserve Bank of San Francisco Wage Rigidity Meter Data for 2021.

Everyday Economics   Beat money illusion by negotiating for a real raise

A few years back a friend of mine was negotiating a raise with his boss and reached out to me for advice. He was earning $100,000 per year and his boss offered him a contract that would see his wage rise by 5% over the five-year term of the contract. My friend wanted

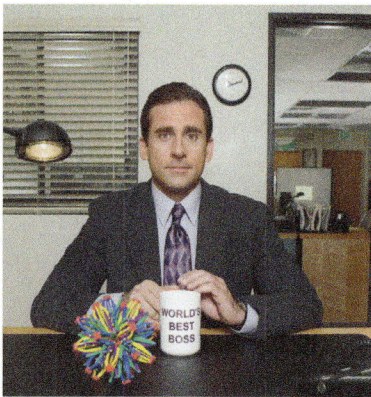

He doesn't want to give you a raise.

more, but he understood his boss had limited funds, and he was pleased to see his hard work rewarded with a pay increase.

But he wasn't getting a real pay raise. Inflation was running at about 2% per year, so over five years, the average price level would rise by about 10% while his wages would only grow at half that rate. If your nominal wage rises by 5% over a period when prices rise by 10%, then your boss is actually cutting your real wage by about 5%.

My friend's mistake was to think about his current nominal wage as the baseline in his wage negotiations. Relative to that reference point, any boost to his nominal wage was framed as good news. Instead, you want to make your current *real* wage the starting point.

So when you next negotiate over your pay, begin the conversation with your boss by pointing out that inflation has reduced the value of your wage. Lay out the latest numbers and suggest that you expect an inflation-based adjustment to offset the rising cost of living. There's not really a good counterargument, so it's likely they'll agree. Now that you've set your real wage as the baseline, turn the conversation to what sort of *real* wage boost you deserve for your hard work over the past year. If you've performed well, this conversation should also go well. How well? When I advised my friend to follow this script in his negotiation, he ended up with a much bigger raise than his boss originally offered — more than enough to offset inflation. If his experience is any guide, it will work for you, too. ∎

12.4 The Role of Money and the Costs of Inflation

Learning Objective *Analyze the role of money so that you can assess the costs of inflation.*

People dislike inflation. In one survey — taken when inflation was well below 2% — more than half of Americans described rising prices as a "very big problem," while another third called it a "moderately big problem." Economists tend to be less concerned about low rates of inflation than the general public. In fact, most economists think that we should aim for inflation of around 2% a year. When the rate of inflation gets a bit higher, however, problems can emerge.

Indeed, when inflation spiked to over 8% in mid-2022, nearly all Americans surveyed described inflation as a problem. This time economists tended to agree, but for different reasons. To understand both the real and perceived costs of inflation, it is useful to start with the topic of money.

The Functions of Money

You've probably spent much of your life thinking about money, worrying about money, or dreaming about money. But have you ever just sat down and thought hard about what money *is?* It's not just the pieces of paper in your wallet; it's also the deposit in your checking account and the bits and bytes in your digital wallet (such as your Venmo or Apple cash balance). **Money** is any asset that's regularly used in transactions.

money Any asset regularly used in transactions.

More importantly, think about what money *does.* It's an essential component of our modern economy because it serves three key functions: It's a medium of exchange, a unit of account, and a store of value. Let's explore each of these in turn.

Function 1: Money is a medium of exchange. You're using money as a medium of exchange whenever you hand it over to buy stuff, or alternatively, when you accept it from your employer in exchange for your hard work. If there were no such thing as money, you would either have to make everything you need for yourself, or barter for it. But barter constrains you to doing business only when there's a *double coincidence of wants:* You can trade your extra milk for bread only if you can find someone who wants milk and coincidentally has extra bread.

Money eliminates this constraint, creating opportunities for you to *specialize.* You can focus on the narrow set of tasks where your skills are most valuable, knowing that you can spend the money you earn to buy fresh bread from a professional baker, a smartphone manufactured in Chinese factories, and shares in Amazon. Without a widely used medium of exchange, bartering small slices of your workday for some bread, a smartphone made on the other side of the world, and part ownership of an online company would be a logistical nightmare. With money, it's an everyday convenience.

But money can be an effective medium of exchange only if it's widely accepted. And that depends on sellers maintaining faith that when they accept money, they'll subsequently be able to use it to buy stuff they want. When you agree to sell something, you are implicitly thinking about what else you will be able to buy with that money.

Function 2: Money is a unit of account. Money is also a unit of account, which means that it's a *common unit* that people use to measure economic value. Indeed, just as architects use yards to measure distance, we all use dollars as the common unit to describe prices, record debts, and write financial contracts. Using a common unit is useful because it makes it easier to apply the opportunity cost principle and ask, "Or what?" If apples cost $1 a pound and oranges cost $1.25 a pound, then you know you have to give up more apples to get a pound of oranges.

It's important that our common unit be a *stable unit* of account for measuring economic value for the same reason that it's useful to have a stable unit of account to measure distance — it simplifies comparisons and eases communication. If your architect's measuring tape were to shrink or expand each day, it would no longer be very useful. The same is true for money: The value of a dollar needs to be relatively stable for it to be a reliable unit of account.

A common unit of account makes these comparisons easier.

Function 3: Money is a store of value. When you save money for a rainy day, you're using money as a store of value, storing your purchasing power for another day. Want to ensure that you have goods and services to consume in retirement? You can do that by earning money today, saving or storing that money, and then using it in the future to buy stuff. While there are other ways of shifting wealth to the future — you could try storing gold bricks, fine art, or canned food instead — none of these is a good store of value: the price of gold fluctuates a lot, fine art is hard to store, and canned food loses its value as it reaches its expiration date.

Money successfully functions as a store of value when it's easy to store and can reliably hold its value over time.

You could store your wealth this way, but do you really want to?

Inflation undermines the productive benefit of money. Money plays a productive role in the economy similar to a lubricant that keeps the economic engine operating efficiently. When inflation is low and stable, money serves its three functions well, and the economic engine hums along.

But high or unpredictable inflation erodes the functions of money. Inflation can undermine the role of money as a medium of exchange because sellers don't know how much the money is going to be worth when they get a chance to try to convert it to the things they want. In extreme cases, it can feel more secure to barter than to accept an unknown value of money. This essentially happens because inflation can destroy money's ability to be a store of value. If prices are rising so fast that the $100 you receive today will buy only half as much next week, then it can be hard to know what payments in money are worth. Finally, when inflation is high or unpredictable, money is also a less effective *unit of account* when its value is uncertain, because a price denominated in dollars is less informative when you aren't sure what a dollar is worth. You'll be less willing to sign an employment contract that spells out future wages in dollar terms if you can't be sure those dollars will buy you a reasonable quality of life.

As we're about to see, when inflation makes money a less effective economic lubricant, it can cause the whole economic engine to seize up.

The three functions of money:
1. Medium of exchange
2. Unit of account
3. Store of value

The Costs of Hyperinflation

hyperinflation Extremely high rates of inflation.

The costs imposed by inflation become most obvious in the worst-case scenario of an extremely high rate of inflation, also called a **hyperinflation.** The point at which a high inflation rate becomes classified as hyperinflation is not precisely agreed upon, but if prices are at least doubling every few months, you're looking at hyperinflation. Fortunately, hyperinflation is rare. One of the most famous examples is the chaotic German hyperinflation of 1922–1923, when prices doubled every few days!

Unfortunately, hyperinflation continues to be a modern reality. Recently, Venezuela has struggled with hyperinflation. An annual inflation rate measured in thousands of percent per year has pushed the price of a café con leche from 450 Venezuelan bolivars in mid-2016 to 1.4 trillion bolivars just a few years later, as you can see in Figure 8.

Figure 8 | Price of a Cafe con Leche in Venezuela

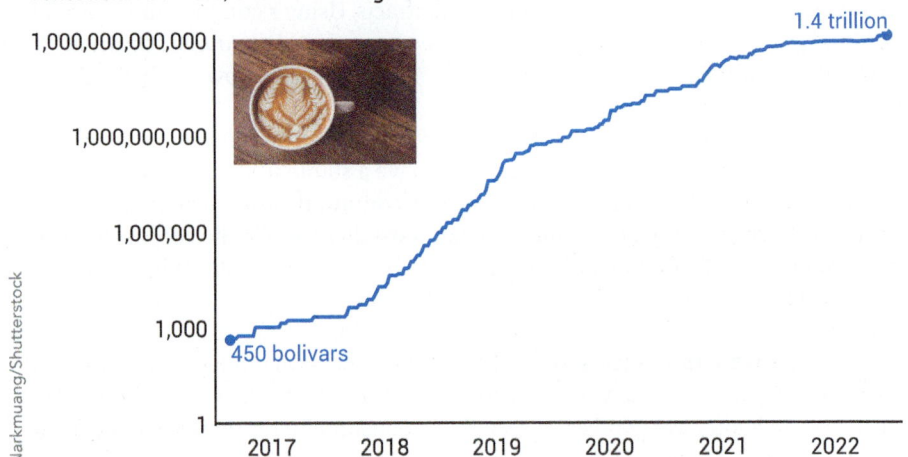

Venezuelan bolivars, shown on a log scale

Venezuela has twice re-denominated its currency (eliminating zeroes). For consistency, the price here is reported in "old" bolivars.

Data from: Bloomberg Cafe Con Leche Index.

Mutitia Narkmuang/Shutterstock

Hyperinflation can make life harder. Within a few years, a crate of bolivars that would have bought a house could no longer buy a carton of eggs. The currency became so worthless that when thieves looted a store, they left behind dozens of 20 bolivar bills because they didn't think it was worth the effort to pick them up.

Venezuela's experience illustrates how the logistical challenges of dealing with hyperinflation come to dominate everyday life. It takes heaping fistfuls of cash to buy anything. Wallets can't fit enough cash, so people have taken to stuffing bundles of notes into backpacks. One shopkeeper said that he weighs banknotes rather than counting them. Bank branches regularly run out of money. ATMs need to be refilled every three hours; the lines are long, and the withdrawal limit is so low that people can get only enough bolivars to pay for a few bus rides. Some stores responded to the shortage by selling cash to customers, who buy it with a credit card. But the markups are steep, and you might pay a 180,000 bolivar credit card charge to get a 100,000 bolivar note.

Hyperinflation erodes all the functions of money. Hyperinflation destroyed the bolivar as a *store of value*. Indeed, the bolivar lost its value so quickly that Venezuelans would race to spend their cash before it became worthless. The hassle required to get cash also made the bolivar an unattractive *medium of exchange*. Instead, people figured out workarounds. Barter became more common — taxi drivers took cigarettes in lieu of cash, a haircut could be bought for five bananas and two eggs, and Facebook pages where people could swap toothpaste, baby formula, and other essentials sprang up. Folks who were well-connected used U.S. dollars instead of Venezuelan bolivars. American Airlines refused to accept bolivars for flights out of Venezuela, insisting their customers use foreign credit cards to buy their tickets online. Amid all this chaos, there was no reliable *unit of account* in Venezuela. Even in real estate, where the law requires contracts to be written in bolivars, a group of realtors established a password-protected website that lists the prices of houses in U.S. dollars.

The Venezuelan hyperinflation aptly illustrates the problem that arises in every episode of hyperinflation: When money no longer works as it should, every facet of economic life becomes more difficult. As one Venezuelan said, "Something so simple as taking money out of a bank machine or buying a coffee or taking a taxi has become a race for survival." While hyperinflation is not the only problem in Venezuela — add in a big dose of corruption and mismanagement and stir — the result was an economic depression, widespread poverty, and a humanitarian disaster in which millions of people starved despite living in a country blessed with extraordinarily valuable oil reserves.

A huge stack of Venezuelan bolivars that's now worth less than US$2.

The Costs of Expected Inflation

While hyperinflation illustrates the costs of high rates of inflation, it's worth remembering that this is an extreme outcome. More moderate rates of inflation have more moderate costs. At the other extreme, some economists argue that the 2% inflation rate that the United States aims for is close enough to price stability that it imposes few costs. But when inflation creeps a bit higher, it can be more disruptive. Inflation can stabilize at the same rate year after year as people come to expect a certain level of inflation. But even this expected inflation can have costs. We'll explore these costs first and then turn to the extra costs that arise when inflation is unexpected. We'll explore this by first analyzing why expected inflation is costly, and then turn to the extra costs that arise when inflation is unexpected.

Cost 1: Inflation creates menu costs for sellers. Put yourself in the shoes of a manager who has to decide how many times to change their prices each year. The marginal principle reminds you that it's simpler to ask whether to raise your price one more time. The cost-benefit principle says: Yes, adjust your price today if the marginal benefit of doing so exceeds the marginal cost. The cost to a restaurant of raising prices is printing or programming new menus, which is why economists describe the marginal cost of adjusting your price as **menu costs**. The marginal benefit of adjusting your price is that you'll shift to a price that covers the rising cost of your inputs. The higher inflation is — and the faster your costs rise — the larger this marginal benefit is. As a result, higher inflation leads to more frequent price adjustment.

menu costs The marginal cost of adjusting prices.

Inflation is costly because it leads businesses to devote valuable resources to reprinting menus, adjusting price tags, and reprogramming vending machines more often. These costs arise because inflation renders money an *unstable unit of account* — prices are marked in dollars, but those dollars are worth less — and so last year's price is no longer suitable this year.

Cost 2: Inflation creates shoe-leather costs for buyers. Next, think about how inflation will affect your relationship with money. You have to decide how many dollars to leave as cash in your physical or digital wallet and how much to leave in a bank account that pays you interest. This is a "how many" question, so the marginal principle says to focus on the simpler question of whether to withdraw one extra dollar. The cost-benefit principle says yes, withdraw that extra dollar if the marginal benefit exceeds the marginal cost. The marginal benefit of withdrawing an extra dollar is the convenience of having more cash available to spend right away. The marginal cost comes from the opportunity cost principle,

People waiting to get cash in Venezuela.

which reminds you that every dollar you withdraw would otherwise stay in your savings account earning a real interest rate. Inflation adds another cost: As prices rise, the cash in your wallet comes to be worth less. This cost is a big deal in Venezuela, because the 100,000 bolivar note you have in your wallet this week might buy only half as much next week. It follows that when inflation is high, the marginal cost of holding money is high, leading people to hold less of it.

Just as inflation erodes the value of banknotes, it also eats into the value of the balance in your Venmo or checking accounts. So inflation will also lead you to hold less of these other forms of money. As many Venezuelans have discovered, that means you'll need to visit your bank more often, withdrawing money only as you need it, and rushing to spend it quickly. The time and effort this takes are called **shoe-leather costs,** because they arise from running around town, which wears down the leather on your shoes. We may not spend as much time running around town literally wearing out our shoe leather these days, but there are real costs — in terms of lost time — that come from constantly moving your money around to preserve its value. These metaphorical shoe-leather costs arise because inflation undermines money's function as a *store of value,* forcing people to take costly measures to keep their wealth in assets that better maintain their value.

shoe-leather costs The costs incurred trying to avoid holding cash.

The Costs of Unexpected Inflation

So far we've considered the costs that arise when everyone expects inflation to occur. There are additional costs that occur when inflation is unexpectedly higher or lower than anticipated.

Cost 3: Inflation confuses the signals that prices send. Prices play a key role in coordinating economic activity. An increase in the price of an individual good like quinoa is a signal from buyers that they really want quinoa; the price transmits this information to quinoa producers, who see it as an incentive to expand production. By contrast, macroeconomics teaches us that when inflation causes all prices to rise, there's no reason to expand production because the higher price of your output is matched by an equal rise in the price of your inputs.

The problem is that if the price of quinoa rises, it can be hard for producers to figure out whether that higher price is due to increased demand for quinoa or to a burst of unexpected inflation. In the resulting confusion, some managers will respond to unexpected inflation by expanding production, although they'll later discover that was a mistake because their costs have risen. At other times they'll fail to expand production when demand for their product has risen because they mistakenly guessed that the higher price reflected an unexpected burst of inflation. These mistakes occur because inflation undermines the stability of dollars as a *unit of account,* and this instability confounds the signals that price sends.

Did the price rise because demand for quinoa increased, or is it just inflation?

EVERYDAY Economics   The costs of grade inflation

Back in 1950, the average grade at Harvard was roughly a C+. Today, it's an A−. This is a representative example of the broader trend of "grade inflation," and Figure 9 shows that many colleges give increasingly generous grades.

This grade inflation is costly, for the same reasons unexpected inflation is costly — it distorts the signals that grades send. Grades are most useful when they signal your ability to potential employers. But grade inflation makes it hard for employers to know whether you have a high GPA because you're an exceptional student or because you graduated from a school that pumped up everyone's grades.

Figure 9 | Average Grades Have Risen at Nearly Every College

Grade point average

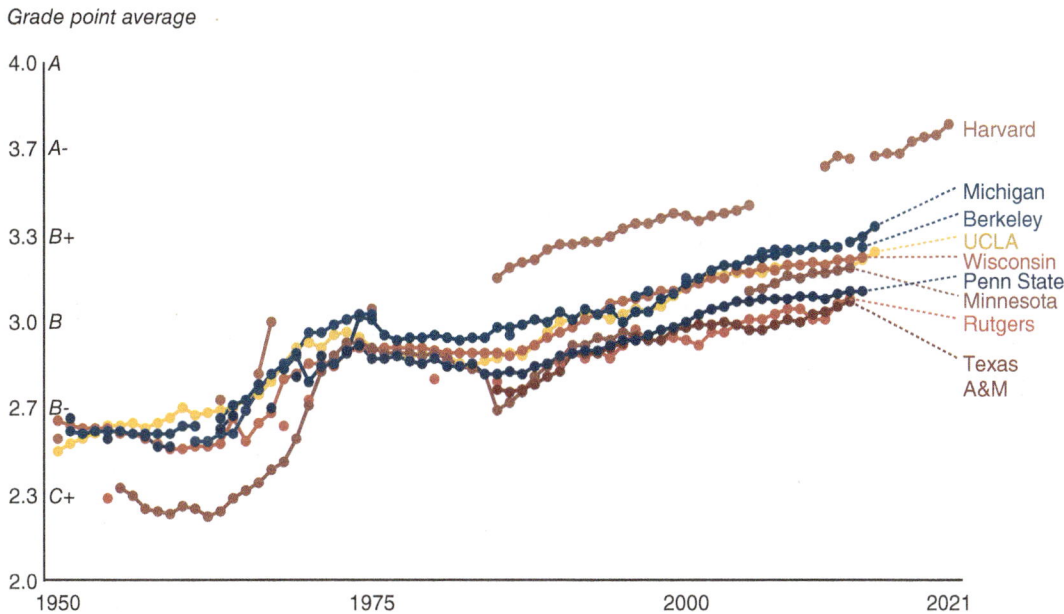

Data from: GradeInflation.com. ∎

Cost 4: Inflation redistributes. Unexpected inflation redistributes from savers and lenders toward borrowers. This occurs because most loans specify repayment schedules in nominal terms — they use dollars as the *unit of account* — and so unexpected inflation changes the real value of your repayments. For instance, if you borrow $15,000 to buy a car at a 5% nominal interest rate, the repayment schedule commits you to paying $283 per month for the next five years. Perhaps that 5% nominal interest rate reflects expectations of 2% inflation and a 3% real interest rate. But if inflation ends up being higher — say if it's 4% — then the real interest rate you'll pay will be 1%, instead. You'll gain, and your bank will lose, because even though you'll keep sending in that $283 each month, the dollars you send your bank aren't worth as much.

When this happens, lenders can go broke, as many did during the 1980s savings and loans crisis. The seeds of the crisis were sown in the 1960s, when expectations of 2% inflation led some lenders to offer 30-year mortgages at fixed nominal interest rates as low as 5%.

But inflation unexpectedly rocketed above 10% in the 1970s, and it stayed high through to the early 1980s. This unexpected inflation was good news for borrowers, because their monthly loan repayments remained fixed in dollar terms even as their nominal income rose. But for lenders, it was disastrous. In inflation-adjusted terms, borrowers repaid *less* than they borrowed. (In economic terms, this is called a *negative real interest rate*.) Many financial institutions went belly-up as a result.

When inflation is lower than anticipated, the opposite happens: The real value of your repayments rises, so lenders gain at the expense of borrowers. This happened in the United States in the 1980s, when home buyers, who expected inflation to continue at 10%, signed up for 30-year mortgages charging nominal interest rates of 15%. But the Federal Reserve brought inflation down much faster than anyone expected. Inflation nosedived — falling from 10% to below 2% within a few years. Borrowers ended up with much higher real interest rates than anticipated. This led banks to amass huge profits, at the expense of homeowners.

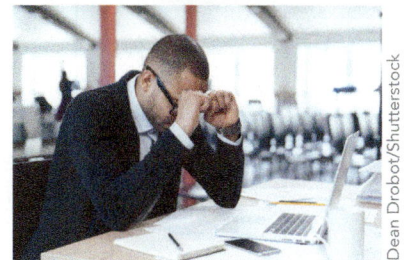

Inflation that's higher than expected is good for borrowers and bad for lenders.

The Inflation Fallacy

People worry about inflation because they go to the store and see higher prices. That sounds bad. If you have to pay more for what you're buying, then you can't buy as much as before, right? Surveys show that more than three-quarters of people agree that inflation erodes their purchasing power. But that's true only if your income stays the same, which it rarely does. Inflation means that on average, *all prices are rising* — and that usually means that wages and salaries are also rising.

inflation fallacy The mistaken belief that inflation destroys purchasing power.

The **inflation fallacy** is the mistaken belief that inflation destroys purchasing power. It's a fallacy because it tells only half the story. While a $1 price rise makes a buyer $1 poorer, it also makes the seller $1 richer. It follows that higher prices don't destroy purchasing power.

Moreover, inflation is a *generalized* rise in all prices, and so it raises the price of what you sell just as much as it raises the price of what you buy. You sell your labor, and inflation typically boosts the price of labor — meaning your wages — in lockstep with the price of the stuff you buy, as shown in Figure 10. Likewise, the price of the stocks in your portfolio and the interest you earn on your savings tend to rise with inflation, leaving your purchasing power roughly unchanged.

Figure 10 | Nominal Wages Tend to Grow in Lockstep with Inflation

Percentage change over the past year

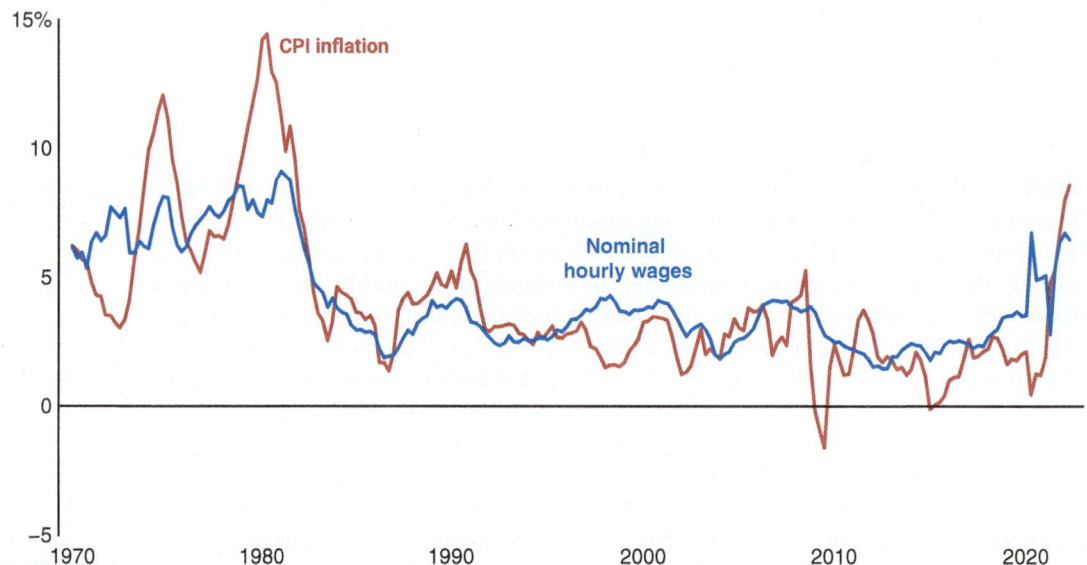

Data from: Bureau of Labor Statistics.

The inflation fallacy reflects a psychological bias. People are quick to blame inflation for the higher prices they pay, but they interpret the parallel rise in their nominal wages as an earned reward for their hard work, unrelated to inflation. While their logic is wrong, their unhappiness is real. This makes inflation a potent political issue.

It's the real stuff that matters, not how it's measured. To see the error that drives the inflation fallacy, consider the following thought experiment. Imagine that you wake up on New Year's Day, and every price tag in the economy has an extra zero on the end of it. Gumballs sell for $2.50 instead of a quarter. Trinkets at the dollar store sell for $10. And a pair of jeans sells for $500 instead of $50. It's not just the price of things you buy that changes, but the price of *everything*. Your wage rises from $12 per hour to $120. Your bank statement says that your $400 in savings is now $4,000. Everything involving a dollar sign gets multiplied by ten. It's like the dollar has shrunk and its value is one-tenth what it was before. But in another sense, nothing has changed: Everyone has ten times as many of these shrunken dollars.

Imagine how this new economy will work. Apart from all those extra zeros floating around, nothing will change. Your purchasing power won't change, because your paycheck is ten times higher to compensate for prices being ten times higher. You won't change how many gumballs, trinkets, or jeans you buy, because the opportunity cost of buying each of these items remains unchanged. More generally, you won't change what stuff you buy, what you'll produce, or how many hours you work. Indeed, no one will change the *quantities* of the stuff they buy, sell, produce, or do. Across the whole economy, this purely *nominal change* — a change in the number of zeros on each price tag — will have no effect on *real variables*. There'll be no change in the total amount of each good purchased, the quantity of production, or the purchasing power of your income.

As this thought experiment reveals, the costs of inflation aren't due to the price level being higher. Rather, it's the *process* of changing all these prices that's costly. The process of changing prices leads sellers to incur menu costs and buyers to incur shoe-leather costs, and unexpected price changes also create costly confusion and arbitrary redistribution.

What if it shrank?

12.5 Tying It Together

Five Strategies for Managing the Costs of Inflation

As we've seen in this chapter, inflation doesn't have to spell disaster. When inflation strikes, there can be a big payoff from pursuing some of the following strategies:

Strategy 1: Don't be fooled by money illusion. When people focus on dollar amounts rather than the underlying trade-offs, they make costly mistakes. Don't make that mistake. Whenever you're analyzing dollar amounts — whether its pay raises, rosy revenue numbers, or investment returns — ask yourself whether inflation-adjusted numbers would better represent the underlying trade-offs. In most cases, they will.

Strategy 2: Take opportunities to index for inflation. Savvy negotiators insist that contracts include *indexation clauses*, which means the wages or prices listed automatically rise with inflation. You'll worry less about a surprise burst of 5% inflation if you know that your contract ensures you'll automatically get a compensating 5% nominal wage rise. An added bonus is that you won't need to negotiate with your boss as often.

Strategy 3: When inflation is high, spend more time looking for cheaper alternatives. Although inflation describes a rise in the general price level, it typically reflects staggered rounds of individual price rises, as one store changes its prices this week, another changes next week, and so on. That means that when inflation is high, prices can vary. So it's worth shopping around a bit more, seeking sellers that haven't updated their prices quickly enough. When you do, you're likely to find a few bargains.

Strategy 4: When inflation is high, avoid holding cash. Inflation eats away at the value of money, so when inflation starts running above a few percent a year, you should limit the amount of cash you hold. Keep the balance in your digital wallet down, and limit your use of checking accounts that don't pay interest. You'll be better off stashing your funds in a savings account, where the nominal interest rate tends to rise with inflation, protecting the real value of your savings.

Strategy 5: Hedge against inflation risk. Do you have some money to invest, and want to mitigate the risk of inflation? The government issues inflation-indexed bonds with nominal interest payments that automatically rise with the inflation rate. These are arguably among the safest investments you can make, because there's no risk that inflation can undermine the real interest rate you earn.

Chapter 12 Review

Chapter at a Glance

Inflation: *A generalized rise in the overall level of prices.*
Inflation can also be described as *a rise in the cost of living.*
As a result, inflation is also *a decline in the purchasing power of money.*

Measuring Inflation

The inflation measure that's most relevant to your life as a consumer is calculated using the **consumer price index (CPI)**, an index that tracks the average price consumers pay over time for a representative "basket" of goods and services.

To measure inflation:
1. Find out what people buy and construct a representative basket of goods and services.
2. Collect prices from the stores where people do their shopping.
3. Tally up the cost of the basket of goods and services.
4. Calculate the inflation rate: The annual percentage increase in the average price level.

$$\text{Inflation rate} = \frac{\text{Price level this year} - \text{Price level last year}}{\text{Price level last year}} \times 100$$

Adjusting for the Effects of Inflation

Real variable: *A variable that has been adjusted to account for inflation.*

Nominal variable: *A variable measured in dollars (whose values may fluctuate over time).*

You can convert nominal variables into real variables by applying the inflation adjustment formula:

$$\text{Today's dollars} = \text{Another time's dollars} \times \frac{\text{Price level today}}{\text{Price level in another time}}$$

For relatively small percentage changes:

Percent change in real value ≈ Percent change in nominal value − Percent change in prices

Real interest rate ≈ Nominal interest rate − Inflation rate

Money illusion: The (mistaken) tendency to focus on nominal dollar amounts instead of inflation-adjusted amounts. Money illusion creates **nominal wage rigidity** (reluctance to cut nominal wages).

Different Measures of Inflation

Consumer Prices
1. Cost of living adjustments → consumer price index (CPI)
2. A target for monetary policy → personal consumption expenditure deflator
3. Forecasting underlying inflation trends → Core inflation (excluding food and energy)

Business Prices
1. Cost of inputs → producer price index (PPI)
2. Estimating the price of all output and hence real GDP → GDP deflator

Inflation Overstates the Cost of Living Because of . . .

• Unmeasured quality improvements   • New products   • Substitution bias

Money: *Any asset regularly used in transactions.*
• Medium of exchange   • Unit of account   • Store of value

The Costs of Inflation

Expected inflation
1. Menu costs for sellers
2. Shoe-leather costs for buyers

Unexpected inflation
3. Confuses the signals that prices send
4. Redistribution

The inflation fallacy: The mistaken belief that inflation destroys purchasing power.

Key Terms

consumer price index (CPI), 296

deflation, 299

GDP deflator, 303

hyperinflation, 310

indexation, 302

inflation, 296

inflation fallacy, 314

inflation rate, 296

menu costs, 311

money, 308

money illusion, 306

nominal interest rate, 306

nominal variable, 305

nominal wage rigidity, 307

producer price index (PPI), 303

real interest rate, 306

real variable, 305

shoe-leather costs, 312

substitution bias, 301

Study Problems

Learning Objective 12.1 *Understand what inflation is and how to measure it.*

1. You go to the gas station and see that the price of gasoline is unchanged. Can you use this observation to determine that the economy is not experiencing inflation? Explain your reasoning.

2. Does a change in the average price of water or a change in the average rent for housing have a bigger impact on CPI?

3. Think about constructing a CPI for students. What do you think belongs in the basket of goods and services for the average student? Do you think that the value of this basket over time has likely changed more or less than the CPI? Why?

4. Think of a good (other than smartphones) that has increased or even decreased in quality over time while the price has remained relatively constant. Explain how the change in quality could bias CPI.

5. Which of the following are signs of inflation?

   a. The price of a house in a high-demand market increased by 6% last year.

   b. CPI in the European Union was 106 in 2020 and 109 in 2021.

   c. The price of lithium-ion batteries falls as new production technologies make manufacturing cheaper.

6. CPI in the United States was 255.7 in 2019 and 258.8 in 2020. What was the inflation rate in 2020?

7. Suppose the typical college student spends money primarily on the products in the following table.

Product	Quantity	2021 price	2022 price
Soda	365	$2.25	$2.30
Pizzas	200	$10.00	$11.00
Chicken wings	165	$7.00	$7.50
Room and board	1	$10,000	$10,800
Textbooks	4	$150	$165

   a. What is the cost of the basket in 2021?

   b. What is the cost of the basket in 2022?

   c. What is the 2022 inflation rate for a college student?

   d. Has the cost of living for college students risen or fallen?

8. For each scenario, determine which challenge of measuring the true cost of living — quality improvements, new products, or substitution bias — a price index constructed 15 years ago would experience.

   a. A typical family owns more cell phones and fewer landline telephones than it did a decade ago. The average price of a cell phone plan is lower than that of a residential line.

   b. Very few households had high-speed internet connections 15 years ago. Now most households do, and the average price has fallen each year.

   c. Over the last 10 years, personal computers have gotten faster and acquired new features that enable users to perform many more tasks.

Learning Objective 12.2 *Pick the right inflation measure for the task at hand.*

9. Both CPI and the GDP deflator measure the change in the price of goods and services and tend to change in similar ways over time. In 2021, CPI rose by 4.7%, while the GDP deflator rose by 4.1%. Explain what might lead them to rise at different rates using what you know about the differences between CPI and the GDP deflator.

10. Which measure or measures of inflation should be used in the following scenarios? Explain your answers.

    a. You're a buyer at an auto factory that is facing rising input costs. Your manager asks you to determine if competitors are also experiencing rising input prices.

    b. A teachers union wants to include annual cost-of-living adjustments in their next contract.

Learning Objective 12.3 *Learn to account for the influence of inflation before making big decisions.*

11. You tell your grandmother about a car you're thinking of buying and, as expected, she tells you a story about buying her first brand new car for $1,500. You feel envious of older

generations and wish you could buy a new car for $1,500. Explain how you are falling victim to money illusion.

12. During the 2007–2009 Great Recession, many universities placed salary freezes on their faculty and staff. What happened to the real incomes of the employees, and why?

13. The average household income in the United States in 1975 was $13,800 and CPI was 53.8. Convert the average income in 1975 to 2021 dollars if CPI was 271.0 in 2021.

14. In 2003, Julia Roberts was paid a then record-shattering $25 million for her role in the film *Mona Lisa Smile*. In 2013, Sandra Bullock earned $70 million for the film *Gravity*. Use the data in Figure 6 to determine which of the two had higher real earnings.

15. In 2018, Apple's revenue was $267 billion, and it grew to $378 billion in 2021.

   a. What is the nominal growth rate of Apple's revenue from 2018 to 2021?

   b. What is the value of Apple's 2021 revenue in 2018 dollars? (In 2018, the CPI was 251.1, and in 2021, it was 271.0.)

   c. What is the real growth rate of Apple's revenue from 2018 to 2021?

16. You open a savings account with a 0.5% per year nominal interest rate, and the economy experiences 3% per year inflation. What is your nominal and real annual interest rate on the account? What will happen to the purchasing power of money you place in the account over time?

17. Behavioral economists have discovered that people view a 2% decrease in their income without inflation as unfair, but a 3% increase in their income in the presence of 5% inflation as fair. What are the nominal and real rates of change in their incomes? What tendency is leading people to feel like the pay decrease is unfair?

Learning Objective 12.4 *Analyze the role of money so that you can assess the costs of inflation.*

18. Explain how you would trade your efforts for goods or services you need if the economy did not use money of any kind? How does money make trade easier?

19. Is inflation more costly when it is expected, or unexpected?

20. For each scenario, determine which function of money is being described.

   a. Robert pays $8.00 to cross the Golden Gate Bridge.

   b. Liza considers which is the better deal: a desk lamp priced at $24.99, or a hanging lamp priced at $29.99.

   c. Gilberto deposits $1,000 in his savings account.

   d. Carmela examines a menu posted outside a restaurant, trying to determine whether a meal there would fit within her budget.

21. Identify which cost of inflation — menu costs or shoe-leather costs — is illustrated in each of the following scenarios.

   a. During the German hyperinflation of 1922–1923, some workers reportedly were paid two to three times per day. They would then rush out to spend their earnings before they became nearly worthless.

   b. A hyperinflation in Zimbabwe was so severe that, according to one observer of supermarket employees, they were "running around that store with label makers, changing the prices three, four times a day."

22. You take out student loans to help pay for your degree at a 5% annual interest rate. Assume the bank expected inflation to average 3% per year. What real interest rate did they expect to earn from your loan? What happens if inflation is actually 5% per year? Who is better off if inflation is higher than expected? What if it is lower than expected? Why?

23. The cost of the average consumer's basket of goods and services in 2022 is roughly 12 times what it was in 1950. In other words, what the average consumer bought for $100 in 1950 would cost a consumer $1,200 in 2022. Does this mean that the purchasing power of the average consumer is one-twelfth what it was in 1950? Explain your reasoning.

PART IV:
Micro Foundations of Macroeconomics

The Big Picture

The chapters ahead are all based on the same idea: The behavior of the macroeconomic whole reflects millions of individual microeconomic decisions. And so if you want to understand the big picture, you'll need to understand decisions that you — and countless people just like you — make every day.

We'll start by analyzing how people make **consumption and saving** decisions. We'll see that deciding whether to spend your money today or save it for the future is all about making trade-offs over time. Next, we'll examine how managers make **investment** decisions that involve trading off a big upfront cost for an ongoing stream of future benefits. Along the way, we'll share economic insights into how you can make better consumption, saving, and investment decisions in your own life.

We'll then apply these ideas to the **financial sector,** where we'll evaluate the different opportunities offered by stocks, bonds, and banks. We'll assess whether to trust financial experts, whether you can beat the market, and whether your money is safe. Finally, we'll turn to the **international sector,** where we'll explore the opportunities offered by globalization, as we analyze the decisions you make about whether to invest abroad, whether to buy or sell U.S. dollars, and whether to import or export goods.

13 Consumption and Saving

See the connections between your spending and savings decisions and the macroeconomy.

- Why do Americans spend more than any other country in history?
- How much should you spend and how much should you save?
- Does consumption respond differently to changes in income that are temporary or permanent? Does it respond differently to changes in income that are anticipated versus unanticipated?
- How do consumers respond to changing economic conditions?
- Why do people save, and should they save more?

14 Investment

Analyze how managers can make good investment decisions.

- Why are investment decisions so important in determining macroeconomic outcomes?
- How can investors compare the values of money they receive at different points in time?
- When is an investment worth pursuing?
- How do changing economic conditions affect whether an investment is worthwhile?
- What determines the long-run real interest rate?

15 The Financial Sector

Understand the role played by the financial sector.

- What are banks, what do they do, and is your bank really safe?
- What are bonds, and what does the bond market do?
- What are stocks, and what does the stock market do?
- How can you value stocks, and can you predict where stock prices are going?
- Are expert stock pickers any good?
- How can you make better decisions with your own investments?

16 International Finance and the Exchange Rate

Understand the linkages between the exchange rate, imports, and exports.

- How closely is the U.S. economy linked to the global economy?
- What's a dollar really worth?
- Why does the U.S. dollar rise and fall?
- How does the value of the U.S. dollar affect your company's international competitiveness?
- How can you track how money flows around the world?

Consumption and Saving

Imagine waking up and discovering that you have received $1,000 you weren't expecting. Maybe it's a check from the government, intended to stimulate the economy. Maybe your parents sold their home, and decided to share some of the proceeds with you. Maybe you received a small inheritance after a relative passed away. Whatever the reason, you are faced with the unfamiliar feeling of having more money than you thought you had. So, what are you going to do with it? You start fantasizing about a spring break trip, or a new wardrobe, or maybe a new laptop. Then you remember that you still owe $200 on your credit card from the last time you splurged on a mini-vacation. And then there's that funny sound that your car has been making, indicating it might need to be serviced soon.

How much should you spend now? How much you should you put aside so that you can spend more in the future? Each day, millions of people face spending and savings decisions like this. Sometimes they're trying to figure out how to divvy up their regular paycheck among immediate spending needs, paying off debt, and preparing for the future. And once in a while, they're thinking about what to do with an unexpected windfall of cash. There is no universally right choice—your best spending and saving choices depend on your situation, including your personal goals, your life trajectory, and the risks you face along the way. While your choices will depend on your situation, there are some general principles that tend to guide people's spending and saving decisions. We'll carefully lay out the economic logic that will give you the tools you need to figure out the best spending, borrowing, and saving decisions for you. Along the way, we'll also consider some common mistakes people make.

By learning how to apply these tools to your spending and saving decisions, you'll gain insight into how other people think about theirs, and this will help you understand the macroeconomy. The macroeconomy is simply the sum of the decisions of many individuals, and so this approach (known among economists as building from the micro foundations of macroeconomics) will give you an understanding of the broad drivers of consumption and saving across the whole economy.

We'll begin the chapter by analyzing total consumer spending, or *consumption*, across the whole economy. Then we'll zoom in on individual consumers—like you!—to assess how people tend to make consumption choices. We'll then pan back and assess what that means for the macroeconomy. Consumption and saving are linked, since what you don't spend, you save. So we'll conclude by exploring what all this means for saving—both your saving and national saving.

What will you do with your money?

Justin Sullivan/Getty Images News/Getty Images

Chapter Objective

See the connections between your spending and savings decisions and the macroeconomy.

13.1 Consumption, Saving, and Income
Understand how consumption and saving vary with income.

13.2 The Micro Foundations of Consumption
Apply the core principles of economics to consumption decisions.

13.3 The Macroeconomics of Consumption
Predict the behavior of total consumption in the economy.

13.4 What Shifts Consumption?
Assess how changing macroeconomic conditions shift consumption.

13.5 Saving
Learn how to form a smart saving plan.

🎙 **Podcast**
Think Like an Economist
Consumption and Saving — Spend Now or Save to Spend Later

13.1 Consumption, Saving, and Income

Learning Objective *Understand how consumption and saving vary with income.*

Consumption refers to household spending on final goods and services. It's by far the single largest component of GDP, and as Figure 1 shows, it accounts for more than two-thirds of total spending. Consumption is sometimes referred to as consumer spending because it includes spending on just about anything that people buy in their personal lives. Things like food, rent, clothes, electricity, medical bills, cell phones, cars, and internet service are all included in consumption.

Consumption and Income

Income is one of the key factors determining consumption, and we use the **consumption function** to show the relationship between consumption and income.

The consumption function plots the level of consumption associated with each level of income. It's a summary of household spending plans, showing how total consumption spending varies with the level of total income. Figure 2 shows the consumption function, illustrating how different levels of income (shown on the horizontal axis) lead to different levels of consumption spending (shown on the vertical axis). The consumption function is upward-sloping: It starts low on the left, and as you move to the right, it rises, illustrating that higher income leads to higher consumption. In this example, it's shown as a straight line, but it need not be — its shape depends on the actual choices that people make. The consumption function is upward-sloping because when people have more income, they tend to spend more.

Figure 1 | Consumption Is About Two-thirds of GDP

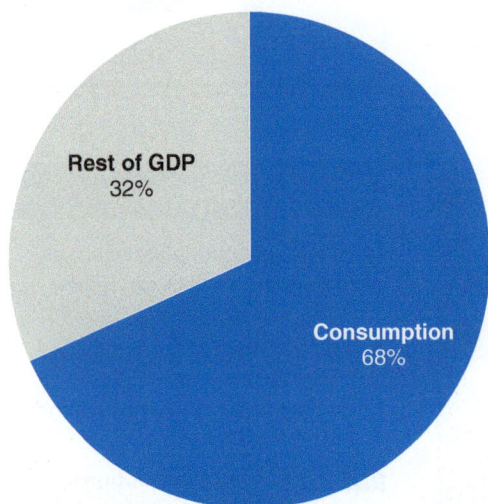

Data from: 2021 data from Bureau of Economic Analysis.

consumption Household spending on final goods and services.

consumption function A curve plotting the level of consumption associated with each level of income.

Figure 2 | The Consumption Function

Ⓐ The **consumption function** shows how **consumption varies depending on the level of income**.
Ⓑ It is **upward-sloping** because more income leads to more consumption.
Ⓒ The **slope** of the consumption function, called the **marginal propensity to consume,** describes the **extra consumption** that arises from each dollar of **extra income**.

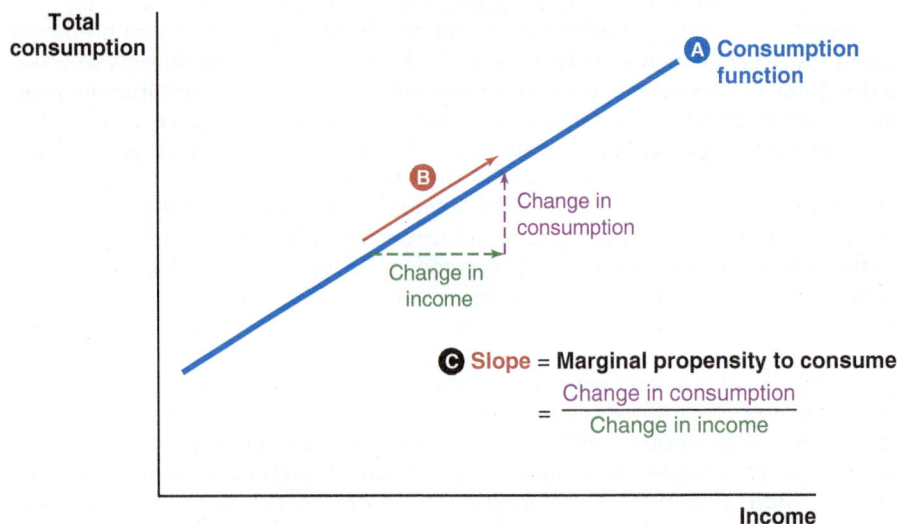

marginal propensity to consume
The fraction of each extra dollar of income that households spend on consumption.

The marginal propensity to consume tells you how much consumption rises when income rises. The fraction of each extra dollar of income that households spend on consumption is called the **marginal propensity to consume.** You can measure the marginal propensity to consume by observing how consumption responds to a change in income. It's the ratio of the change in consumption to the change in income. Your individual marginal propensity to consume is one if you immediately spend all of any extra income you receive, and it's zero if you save all of any extra income (spending none of it right away). Most people will spend some of their extra income right away, but will also typically save some of it (to spend later). And so the marginal propensity to consume, which is the proportion of each extra dollar consumed, is typically greater than zero, but less than one.

The marginal propensity to consume is an important concept in macroeconomics because it tells you how much consumption will increase when total income or GDP increases. If the average marginal propensity to consume is 0.6, then a $100 billion increase in total income will lead to a $60 billion rise in consumption.

The marginal propensity to consume determines the slope of the consumption function. To see this, remember the slope of a line is "rise over run," and so the slope of the consumption function is the ratio of the change in consumption to a change in income (which is the marginal propensity to consume!).

Interpreting the DATA — The consumption function explains why you consume way more than your great-grandparents did

Over time the United States has gotten richer, with real GDP per person more than triple what it was in 1950. The consumption function tells us that higher income leads to higher consumption. In the left panel of Figure 3, we plot average consumption and average income—that is, GDP per person—in the United States in an individual year. (In this graph, as throughout the whole chapter, all data are adjusted for inflation and thus are real GDP per person.) The dots lie along an upward-sloping line, illustrating that average consumption per person in the United States has risen as GDP per person has risen over time—just as the consumption function predicts. The most recent data are at the top right, and they show that our consumption has also more than tripled since the 1950s. By the end of 2021, just a year after the Covid pandemic, our incomes had fully recovered and hit new record highs and so had our levels of consumption. And these record levels of consumption per person are exactly what you'd expect given recent levels of GDP per person.

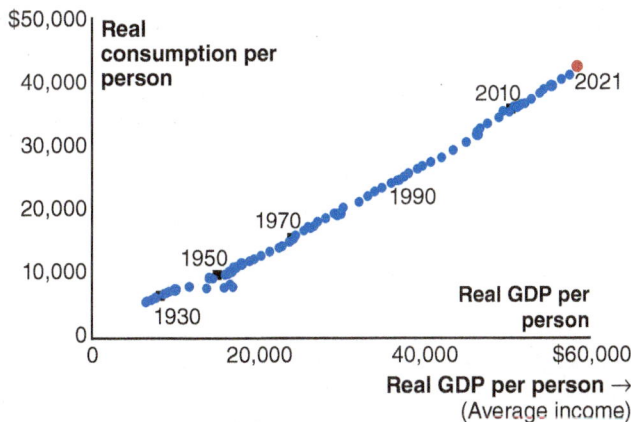

We can also look at a cross-national consumption function, plotting average consumption and GDP per person for an individual country in a particular year. The right panel

Consumption per person is higher in the United States than at any time in our history or than in any other country.

Figure 3 | Consumption and GDP

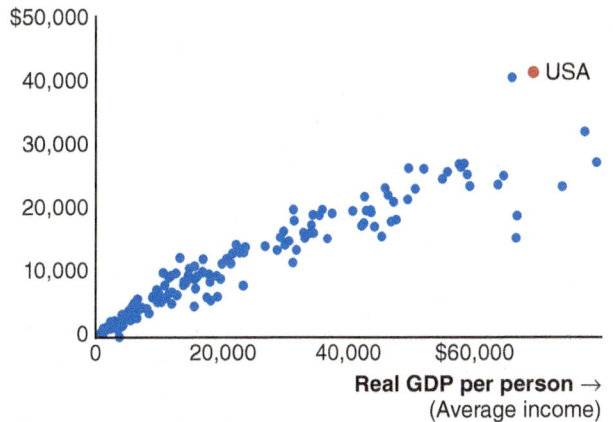

Data from: Bureau of Economic Analysis; World Bank.

of Figure 3 does just this for 2021, which is the latest comparable data. This figure shows that average consumption is higher in the United States than in other countries, largely because Americans enjoy a higher average income than most other countries. Again, the dots are clustered along an upward-sloping line, illustrating that people in countries with higher GDP per person tend to spend more on consumption. These two charts show the consumption function in real life! ■

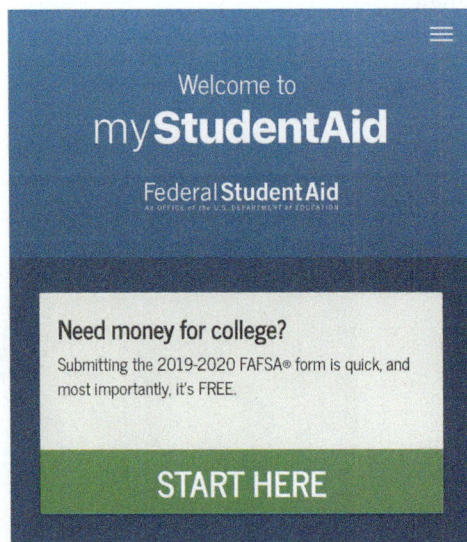

Saving and Income

Consumption rises with income, but most people don't tend to spend all of the additional income they get right away. When people consume less than their income, the remainder is saving. **Saving** is the portion of income that you don't spend on consumption in a given period. So if in a month, you earned $2,000 and spend $1,800 on everything you consume, then you'll have saved $200. Because every dollar you don't spend is saved, your consumption decisions determine your saving. Equally, every dollar you don't save is spent (by definition), and so your saving decisions determine your consumption.

$$\text{Saving} = \text{Income} - \text{Consumption}$$

Whether you sock that unspent income away in the bank or use it to pay down existing debts such as your student loans, it counts as saving. That means when you graduate and start paying your student loans out of your income, you are saving. Alternatively, when your consumption exceeds your income in a given period — as it does for many students — you are **dissaving** (sometimes referred to as negative saving). Whether you fund this gap between your spending and your income by borrowing money — say, taking on more student loans — or by withdrawing money from your savings, it counts as dissaving.

From a microeconomic perspective, saving is important because it adds to your wealth, allowing you to boost your consumption in the future. From a macroeconomic perspective, saving is important because it provides the flow of resources the financial sector uses to fund investment projects.

In all of this, we're focusing on the *flows* — new saving, consumption, and income in a specific period of time, such as a year. People often think about their stock of savings meaning all the money they have saved over time. Your stock of savings is your wealth. The amount by which your assets exceed your debts is called your **net wealth.** Saving increases your net wealth, but dissaving decreases it.

Your student debt is a form of dissaving, but your student loan payments will count as saving.

saving The portion of income that you don't spend in a given period.

dissaving The excess amount you consume above your income in a given period that you therefore must pay for by either withdrawing money from your savings or borrowing money.

net wealth The amount by which your assets exceed your debts.

Do the Economics

Let's apply these new ideas — of the consumption function and the relationship between income and savings — to your life. Let's fast-forward and imagine your economic future a few years after graduation. How much will you spend each year if your annual income is $30,000? What if your income is $45,000? Or $60,000? How much of a $75,000 income will you spend? As you answer these questions, fill in the blanks in the middle column of the table in Figure 4. Since saving and consumption are two sides of the same coin, once you've decided how much to spend at each level of income, you've also made your saving plans (or your debt payment plans if you are paying student loans). Calculate your saving in the final column of the table in Figure 4.

Finally, plot your consumption choices in the second panel of Figure 4. Connect the dots, and that's it! You've discovered your consumption function. If you're like most people, you'll discover that:

- Your consumption function is upward-sloping because more income leads you to increase your consumption.
- But for each extra dollar of income that you receive, your consumption rises by less than a dollar.

Figure 4 | Discover Your Consumption Function

Panel A: Your Consumption Function
Income includes income from all sources, but not loans.
Consumption counts all spending on goods and services.

Your income	Your consumption	Your saving (= Income − Consumption)
$30,000		
$45,000		
$60,000		
$75,000		

Panel B: Your Consumption Function
How much higher will your consumption spending be at each different income level?
To graph your consumption function, plot the results from the table on the left, and connect the dots.

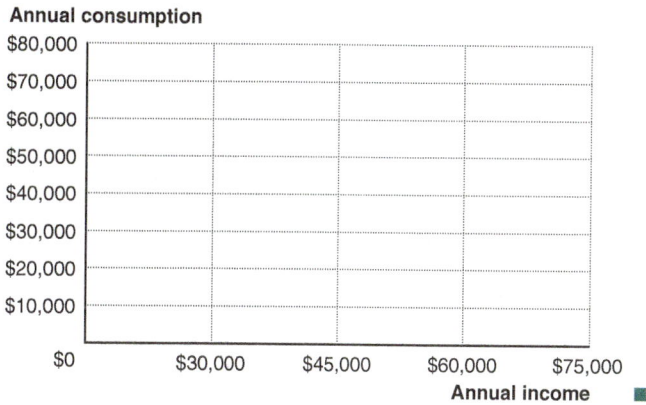

Annual consumption

(graph with y-axis from $0 to $80,000 in $10,000 increments; x-axis labeled Annual income with values $30,000, $45,000, $60,000, $75,000)

Annual income

At this point, we've used the consumption function to describe the spending (and hence saving) decisions that people make. Now it's time to analyze how people figure out how much to spend, save, and borrow. This window into consumers' thinking will help us evaluate how changing macroeconomic conditions affect total consumption across the whole economy.

13.2 The Micro Foundations of Consumption

Learning Objective *Apply the core principles of economics to consumption decisions.*

The micro foundations of consumption mean that to understand overall consumption patterns in the economy, you should start by looking at how individuals like you make consumption decisions. So let's start by considering the moment at the start of the semester when your financial aid arrives along with a reminder that it's meant to help cover your expenses through the end of the semester. If you've been in a similar situation, you'll recognize that you need to figure out how to allocate your scarce funds over the next few months, deciding how much to spend this month, versus saving for next month and the months after. It's a consequential decision. Get it wrong, and you won't have enough money for food in a few months' time.

How should you decide how much to spend now, versus save for later? This question motivates our next task, which is to develop a framework that you can use to make smart spending, saving, and borrowing choices throughout your life. This framework also yields insight into how other people make spending and saving decisions. Total consumption is the sum of consumption decisions made by millions of Americans, and so these same insights will help you understand the macroeconomics of consumption. By understanding how individual people make their consumption decisions, we'll build up an understanding of the whole.

How much should you spend?

Choosing How Much to Spend and How Much to Save

The key consumption decision you face is: *How many* dollars should you spend this month given your income? Your answer will determine not only how much you'll consume, but also how much you'll need to borrow or be able to save for next month. To make good consumption and savings decisions, start by applying the core principles of economics.

Your decision about how much to consume today is also a decision about how much to save. The interdependence principle says that the choices available to you in the future depend on the decisions you make today. This insight is particularly relevant to your consumption decisions because the spending and saving decisions you make today determine your future options. Spend too much today, and your credit card debt will create future repayment challenges. Alternatively, saving instead of spending provides a buffer you might find helpful next month. It's critical that your consumption decisions account for these future consequences.

Your decision about how many dollars to consume is a "how many" question, and the marginal principle reminds you that it's simpler to break it into a series of smaller marginal choices, asking: Should I increase my current consumption by one more dollar? If the answer is yes, then you need to ask whether to spend one more dollar, and then another dollar, and so on.

At each iteration, the cost-benefit principle says yes, you should increase your consumption by a dollar if the benefit of an extra dollar of consumption exceeds the cost. The benefit of an extra dollar of consumption is called the *marginal benefit of consumption*.

What about the cost of that extra consumption? Turn to the opportunity cost principle, which reminds you to ask, "Or what?" You could consume an extra dollar this month, *or what?* Or you could save that dollar, earn interest, and then spend that dollar-plus-interest in the future. As such, the cost of an extra dollar of consumption this year is the forgone opportunity to consume a dollar-plus-interest in the future. (When in the future? Opportunity cost is all about the next best alternative, so you should think about whenever in the future you'll get the largest marginal benefit.) Thus, the opportunity cost of an extra dollar of consumption today is the marginal benefit of consuming a dollar-plus-interest in the future.

The Rational Rule for Consumers

At this point, we've figured out that you should weigh the marginal benefit of increasing your consumption in the present against the marginal benefit of increasing your consumption by a bit more in the future. Put the pieces together, and you'll discover that we've uncovered a powerful rule that you can apply to your consumption decisions:

The **Rational Rule for Consumers:** *Consume more today if the marginal benefit of a dollar of consumption today is greater than (or equal to) the marginal benefit of spending a dollar-plus-interest in the future.*

This rule brings together all of our four core principles, in one sentence: You should think at the margin and evaluate whether to spend one more dollar (the marginal principle); compare the marginal benefit of raising consumption today with the marginal cost (the cost-benefit principle); and, in evaluating that marginal cost, account for the forgone opportunity to increase consumption in the future by a dollar-plus-interest (the opportunity cost principle). And finally, you must think about how your choices to spend today impact your future choices (the interdependence principle).

Compare the marginal benefit of spending a dollar today to the marginal benefit of spending a dollar-plus-interest in the future. Notice that the Rational Rule for Consumers effectively turns your attention from the original question of *how much* to spend today to the more helpful question of *when* to consume. It says to be *forward-looking*, so that you should spend another dollar today only if it yields a larger marginal benefit than spending a dollar-plus-interest in the future. By following this rule, you'll spend each dollar at the moment in which it yields the largest possible benefit to you. As such, it ensures that you'll get the largest possible benefit from your limited income.

You should keep spending until the marginal benefit is the same over time. The trade-off underlying the Rational Rule for Consumers is that the benefit of

Rational Rule for Consumers
Consume more today if the marginal benefit of a dollar of consumption today is greater than (or equal to) the marginal benefit of spending a dollar plus interest in the future.

delaying consumption is the interest you can earn, while the cost is that you'll have to wait to enjoy that consumption. For most people, the benefit of earning interest roughly cancels out the cost of waiting, and so we can simplify the rational rule by putting these two factors aside for now (we'll return to interest rates later in this chapter). That simplification allows the rational rule to speak more directly: It says that you should keep increasing today's consumption and decreasing future consumption until the marginal benefit of a dollar of consumption is the same today as it will be tomorrow. If you apply this rule again tomorrow, you'll make adjustments until the marginal benefit of consumption is the same tomorrow as the day after. Follow the logic further, and you'll end up making consumption plans so that the marginal benefit of the last dollar of consumption is the same in the present as in every future period.

Consumption Smoothing

When you make decisions to spend more at some times and save more at others, you're demonstrating a useful economic concept. **Consumption smoothing** describes the way people maintain a steady or smooth path for consumption spending over time, even as income fluctuates. As we're about to see, it's one of the most important implications of the Rational Rule for Consumers.

consumption smoothing
Maintaining a steady or smooth path for your consumption spending over time.

Consumption smoothing helps you avoid diminishing marginal benefits. Diminishing marginal benefit is the idea that each additional dollar of consumption yields a successively smaller marginal benefit. It says that the marginal benefit of the first few dollars of spending are high and then decline as you spend more. It's relevant because the Rational Rule for Consumers says to reallocate your spending so that the marginal benefit of the last dollar of consumption is the same in the present as in the future. And so following this rule means reallocating your spending from times when the marginal benefit is low (which is when consumption is high) to times when the marginal benefit is high (which is when consumption is low). As such, it suggests reallocating your spending from times when your consumption is high to times when it's low, leading your consumption to be relatively smooth or stable over time.

This logic says that instead of spending your financial aid check when you get it, you'll be better off distributing your spending evenly, or smoothly, throughout the semester. Figure 5 illustrates this point, showing that redistributing a dollar of consumption from a time when your spending is high (a time of plenty) to a time when it's low (a time of relative poverty) leads to an increase in your total benefits. Indeed, each move you make toward more equal consumption over time raises your well-being because you're moving your spending from times when the marginal benefit is low to times when the marginal benefit is high. Follow this logic far enough, and you'll conclude that — as long as your needs aren't changing — it's best to spend the same today as tomorrow. That is, you're best off smoothing your consumption.

It's like making a deal with your future self. Thinking about how much to spend today versus in the future can seem like a hard problem. There's another way to think about this that you might find more intuitive. It's just about making sure your decision takes account of both your current self, who enjoys this month's consumption, and your future self, who'll enjoy next month's. Put too much weight on your future self and you'll spend too little

Figure 5 | Smooth Your Consumption

Ⓐ **Diminishing marginal benefit** leads to a declining **marginal benefit curve**.

Ⓑ **Consumption smoothing** requires redistributing spending from times of **plenty (high consumption with a low marginal benefit)**, to times of **relative poverty (low consumption with a high marginal benefit)**.

Ⓒ This is beneficial because the **marginal benefit of an extra dollar during times of relative poverty** exceeds the **marginal benefit of an extra dollar during times of plenty**.

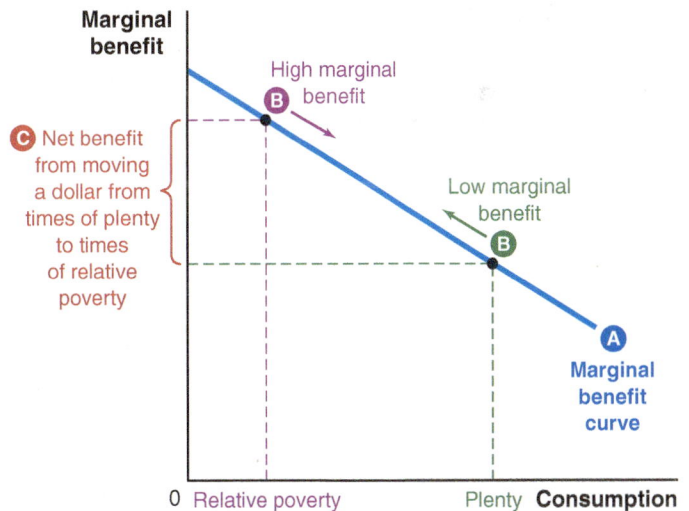

Make a deal with your future self.

today. Put too much weight on your current self and you'll spend too much. Your current and future selves have to figure out how to split your resources over time in a way that makes these two versions of you as happy as possible. If you decide that they should consume as much as the other, then you've decided that you should smooth your consumption across time.

Pace yourself.

The same advice applies: Pace yourself.

EVERYDAY Economics   How to run a marathon, enjoy a box of cookies, and survive the weekend

In fact, the idea of consumption smoothing is so intuitive that you probably already apply it to many areas of your life. It's relevant whenever you have to distribute scarce resources over time in the presence of diminishing marginal benefit.

When you toe the starting line of a marathon, you have limited energy to distribute over the next 26.2 miles. Spend too much energy in the first half, and the second half will be painful and slow. Save too much energy in the first half, and you'll fall so far behind your target pace that even the extra energy you've stored up won't be enough to make up those lost minutes. It's far better to smooth your energy consumption.

Marathon strategy is surprisingly similar to cookie strategy. If you've ever bought a box of Girl Scout cookies, you'll know the temptation to eat the whole box today, leaving none for tomorrow. That would match your cookie consumption with your cookie income. Don't do it. You'll be even happier if you smooth your cookie consumption, enjoying a delicious cookie every day until the bag runs out.

And that's the same challenge you face over the weekend. Stay up all night on Friday night, and you won't have enough energy left to enjoy Saturday's party. Pace yourself by smoothing your socializing over the weekend, and you'll enjoy it more. ■

The timing of your income is irrelevant. There's an interesting implication of all of this: The *timing* of your income — whether you receive it today or in the future — should not be relevant to your consumption choices. After all, the Rational Rule for Consumers says to allocate your consumption to whenever it'll yield the largest marginal benefit. It doesn't say anything about whether you received that income today, next month, or next year. But even if the timing of your income isn't relevant, the *level* of your income does matter. To see precisely how, we'll need to introduce one more big idea.

Permanent Income Hypothesis

permanent income Your best estimate of your long-term average income.

Your income does constrain your consumption. But when you can save or borrow money, it isn't just today's income that matters. Rather, your forward-looking spending plans are constrained by the total resources you have available to allocate to consumption over the long term. That's why instead of your *current income* (your income this week, month, or year), you should focus on your **permanent income,** which is your best estimate of your long-term average income. It measures the resources that are available for you to consume, on average, over the course of your lifetime.

The higher your permanent income, the more you can afford to consume both today and in the future. For example, before deciding how much to borrow in student loans, you should think about what you expect to earn after you graduate. If you're working toward a degree that you are confident will lead to a high-paying job after graduation, then your permanent income is high, even if your current income is low. That means that you can afford to take on more student loans and consume more in your student years, knowing that you'll find it easy to repay those loans after graduation. But if you are planning to work in a field that typically pays less, you'll want to be more cautious with your consumption (and borrowing) while you're in school.

permanent income hypothesis The idea that consumption is driven by permanent income rather than current income.

The idea that people choose how much to consume based on their permanent income (rather than their current income) is called the **permanent income hypothesis.** It has important macroeconomic implications because it says that economic fluctuations matter only to the extent that they affect permanent income. (We'll return to this idea shortly.)

Consumption smoothing requires saving *and* borrowing. If you set your consumption level based on your permanent income, then you'll need to borrow or save whenever your current income and permanent income differ. For instance, whenever your current income is below your permanent income — that is, when your income is less than you expect its long-term average to be — you'll spend more than you earn. That means that you'll need to borrow or dip into your savings to make up the difference between your consumption and your current income. But consumption smoothing also means that when your current income exceeds your permanent income, you need to build up your savings (including paying off debt from previous periods when your income fell below your permanent income). This suggests that you can gauge whether you should be saving or dissaving by comparing your current income with your permanent income.

Saving will vary over your life course. Figure 6 illustrates with a stylized illustration. The red line shows how income typically varies over the course of your life — it rises sharply as you accumulate experience and seniority, and then peaks in mid-career, before slowly declining as you get older. The blue line shows a constant (that is, smooth) level of consumption, set equal to the permanent or average income associated with the red line. Borrowing, saving, or dissaving make up the difference between current consumption and current income. This figure shows that the combination of a hump-shaped life cycle in income and relatively constant consumption explains why people tend to borrow while they're young, save during their working years, and spend down their savings during retirement.

Of course, your reality will be somewhat messier than this stylized illustration, as your consumption needs will change over your lifetime. That means your spending patterns may not be as stable as in this example. You'll also learn new information over time about your permanent income, and adjust your consumption to fit your new expectations. Even after adjusting for these issues, the basic idea of the life-cycle pattern holds. It describes the reality that the typical young person accumulates debt, while the typical retiree lives off their savings. In the middle, people pay their debt and build their retirement savings, and so they spend less than they earn.

Figure 6 | Income and Saving over the Life Cycle

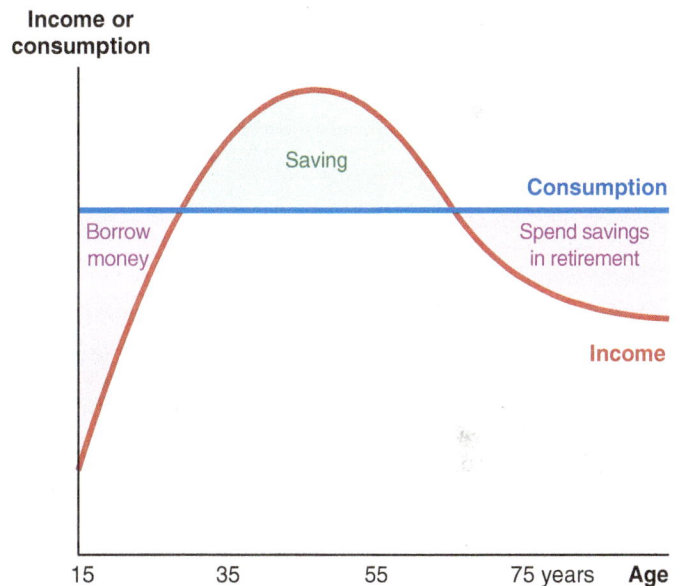

13.3 The Macroeconomics of Consumption

Learning Objective *Predict the behavior of total consumption in the economy.*

We've now uncovered the two big ideas that are the building blocks of the macroeconomics of consumption. People make decisions about how much to consume — and thus how much to save — considering their *permanent income,* and they prefer to *smooth consumption* over time. Because these forces drive individual people's consumption choices, they also drive total consumption in the economy. These two big ideas have important implications for the macroeconomic link between total income and total consumption. They'll help you see where the economy is going and better understand how total consumption will change in response to changing macroeconomic conditions.

The Relationship Between Consumption and Income

Income is an important determinant of consumption, and when income changes, consumption changes. But there are different kinds of changes in income that have different implications for consumption. We'll now dig into five important insights that will help you identify different types of income changes and how those changes will likely impact consumption.

Insight 1: A temporary change in income leads to a small change in consumption. What would you do if you won a $1 million lottery? That's a question people like to fantasize about because it would be life-changing. But let's think through exactly how it would change your life. A lottery win is a temporary boost in income because you don't expect to win it again. So how would you adjust your consumption in response? I hope you won't go out and blow the whole million bucks right away. A financial planner might advise you to spend $50,000 of it each year, so that you can enjoy higher consumption for the rest of your life.

The desire to smooth consumption over your lifetime leads to spreading a temporary spike in income out so that consumption increases very little in response. In the lottery example, a temporary increase in income (a million dollars!) leads this year's consumption to rise by only $50,000. This yields a marginal propensity to consume (or *MPC*) out of a temporary rise in income of 0.05:

$$MPC_{Temporary} = \frac{\text{Change in consumption}}{\text{Temporary change in income}} = \frac{\$50,000}{\$1,000,000} = 0.05$$

Winning a million-dollar lottery is a fun fantasy, but not something that most of us will experience. However, you might get a one-time signing bonus with a job, a gift from a relative, or even a one-time payment from the government. The same ideas apply: it's not smart to spend it all at once to boost your consumption today. If you use some of it to pay off debt, avoid taking on additional debt, or set aside some of it for emergencies, then you are spreading that consumption over time, just like in our lottery example.

Insight 2: A permanent change in income leads to a large increase in consumption. Now imagine landing a job that pays $15,000 a year more than your current job. Even better, the job puts you on a career path in which you can expect to go on to earn higher wages throughout your career. So it's not just a one-year boost; your future income is now a lot higher than you had previously anticipated. How should you respond? Unlike a temporary boost to income, this new job will mean earning more year after year. This is a much larger boost to your lifetime income than just $15,000.

Unlike a one-time gain, which you allocate over your remaining years of life, a permanent increase in your annual income means that you can enjoy increased consumption and income every year for the rest of your life. This means that the marginal propensity to consume out of permanent income is much higher than it is out of temporary income.

The marginal propensity to consume out of a rise in permanent income is typically fairly high. In fact it could be as high as 1:

$$MPC_{Permanent} = \frac{\text{Change in consumption}}{\text{Permanent change in income}} = \frac{\$15,000}{\$15,000} = 1$$

To summarize: an unanticipated change in income that's likely to continue every year for the rest of your life yields an equally large change in permanent income, and so there is a correspondingly large increase in consumption.

Don't spend it all at once.

Ringo H.W. Chiu/Getty Images News/Getty Images

Five insights about the relationship between consumption and income:
1. A temporary change in income leads to a small change in consumption.
2. A permanent change in income leads to a large change in consumption.
3. An anticipated change in income leads to no change in consumption.
4. Learning about a future income change leads to a change in consumption.
5. It's hard to forecast changes in consumption.

How to estimate your permanent income

We've seen that your level of consumption should reflect your permanent income. But what is your permanent income? A useful starting point is to analyze the lifetime earnings of people like you.

The typical college graduate will earn over a million dollars more over their lifetime compared to those with only a high school degree. But not all college graduates earn the same amount, and lifetime earnings differ dramatically across majors. People in the highest-earning majors will earn millions more over their lifetime compared to those with degrees in the lowest-earning majors. While your future earnings shouldn't be the only factor you consider when selecting a major, understanding your earnings trajectory is essential to assessing your permanent income.

Figure 7 shows the average earnings of college graduates at different points in their careers for four popular majors. These trajectories show how your earnings are likely to evolve throughout your career, so that you can estimate your permanent income.

As you can see, you are likely to experience relatively rapid income growth in the early years of your career. It follows that when you're young, your permanent income is likely much higher than your annual income. But earnings growth typically slows, and earnings may even decline, in the later years of your career.

Different careers have different trajectories, and so your field of study really matters. Economics majors tend to experience very rapid income growth as they rise through the ranks, and so while their starting salaries aren't so high, over the course of their career, they enjoy healthy average incomes. The incomes of computer scientists start higher, but don't grow quite as sharply, and indeed, their earnings actually fall later in their careers as their knowledge of specific coding languages becomes obsolete. Communications majors also follow a similar "hump shaped" trajectory, but over the course of their careers they tend to earn quite a bit less. And education majors have lower average earnings throughout their careers. While educators experience relatively slow earnings growth, seniority is typically valued in teaching careers, and so their earnings continue to grow until they retire.

Bottom line: You'll need to look beyond your starting salary to figure out your permanent income. To make fully informed consumption decisions, you'll also need to look at how your earnings are likely to evolve as you gain experience. ◼

Figure 7 | Earnings Trajectories Vary by Your College Major

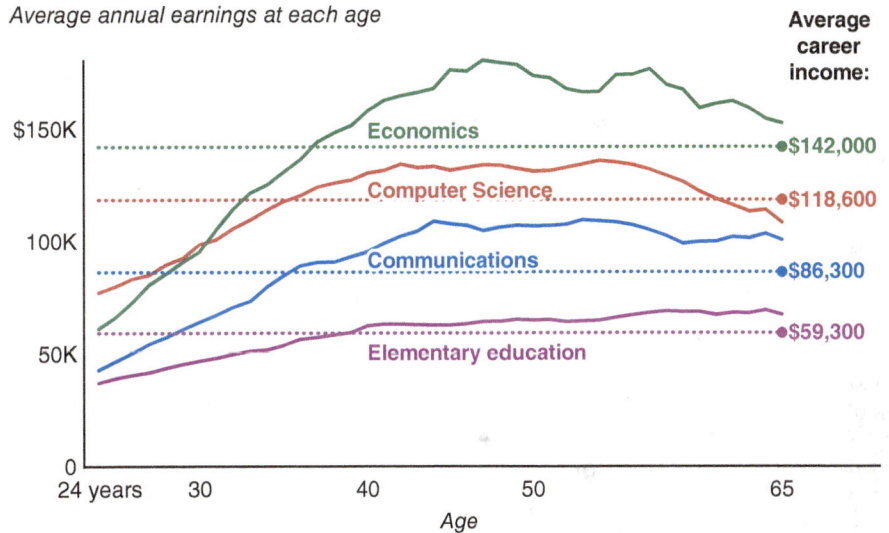

Average annual earnings at each age

Average career income:
- Economics ●$142,000
- Computer Science ●$118,600
- Communications ●$86,300
- Elementary education ●$59,300

Earnings are for full-time full-year workers with a Bachelor's degree
Data from: American Community Survey, 2016–20.

Want to learn more about the typical earnings trajectory in your field? (You should!) Point your browser to: https://www.datawrapper.de/_/LIFel/ to search for the typical trajectory for your major (or for the majors you're considering). You'll discover the data you need to make informed consumption decisions. Adjust your spending plans accordingly!

Insight 3: An anticipated change in income leads to no change in consumption.
Your permanent income is your best estimate of your long-term average income, and so it reflects your expectations about how your income will evolve over time. As such, it already factors in anticipated future changes in your income. So if you set your consumption in line with your permanent income, then anticipated changes in income won't affect your consumption. As a result, the marginal propensity to consume out of anticipated changes in income is zero.

To see this concretely, put yourself in the shoes of a political polling expert expecting to earn $60,000 in even-numbered years (when there are a lot of elections), but $40,000 in other years (when you have fewer clients). Instead of cutting your consumption spending every second year only to raise it the next, you'll be better off budgeting around earnings of $50,000 each year, which is in line with your permanent income. And so the anticipated rise in income in an election year has no effect on your consumption, just as the anticipated cut in income in odd-numbered years has no effect on what you consume.

Insight 4: Learning about a future income change leads to a change in consumption.
When does consumption respond to changes in future income? If you're basing your consumption on your permanent income, then you'll respond when you get the news about a change in your future permanent income, rather than when the money actually arrives. (By that time, it has been fully anticipated and already factored in to your spending decisions.)

For instance, if your union *unexpectedly* announces that the new contract with your employer includes higher-than-expected raises in future years, then a consumption smoother will use that information to boost their consumption right away. This also works the other way — if your company unexpectedly announces a pay freeze for the coming year such that next year's expected pay raise disappears, the permanent income hypothesis suggests that you should cut your consumption right away.

The broader point is that today's consumption can be quite sensitive to expectations about future income. This also suggests that changes in macroeconomic policy begins to have an effect on consumption when they're announced, rather than when they are implemented.

Insight 5: It's hard to forecast changes in consumption.
The final implication of all this is that changes in consumption are very difficult to forecast because changes are driven by reactions to unexpected news. After all, we've seen that consumption does not change much in response to *anticipated* changes in income. It only responds to *unanticipated* changes in income. But unanticipated changes are, by their nature, very difficult to forecast. After all, if they were easy to forecast, you would have anticipated them!

If changes in individual consumption are difficult to forecast, then it follows that changes in total consumption — the sum of the consumption decisions of millions of individual Americans who follow a similar logic — should also be difficult to forecast.

It's worth being careful about this implication. It doesn't say that the *level* of consumption is difficult to forecast. In fact, it's not: The level of consumption is usually about two-thirds of GDP. Instead, it says that future *changes* in consumption are hard to predict. Take a look at the annual changes in total U.S. consumption shown in Figure 8, and I think you'll agree that changes in consumption are hard to forecast. The change in consumption in each year appears roughly unrelated to what happened in previous years. And because consumption is a big chunk of GDP, this also means that it's awfully difficult to predict changes in GDP.

Figure 8 | Changes in Consumption Are Difficult to Forecast

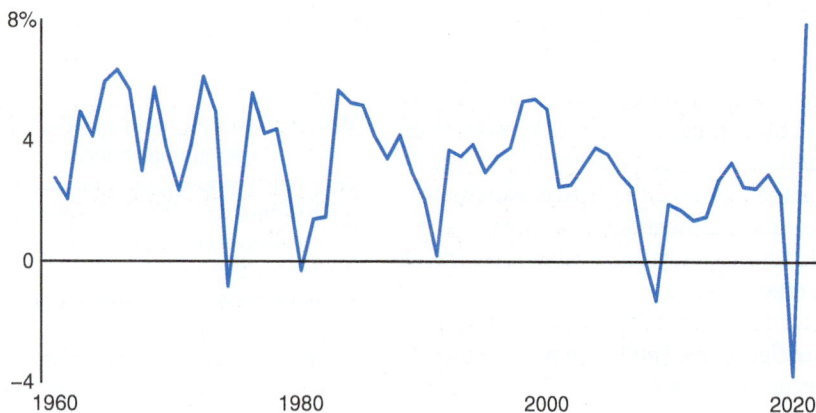

Yearly change in real consumption

Data from: Bureau of Economic Analysis.

Adding Behavioral Economics and Credit Constraints to Our Analysis

We're exploring these ideas to give you a window into the thinking that underlies the consumption choices of the millions of Americans who make up the macroeconomy. Along the way you might have wondered: Do people actually make their consumption choices like this? As you might have guessed, there are limitations to how much people can smooth their consumption. It relies on people knowing a lot about their future income and being able to both borrow and save when required. Unfortunately, borrowing and saving isn't always easy or even possible.

These practical limitations don't undermine our previous insights, but they do require us to modify them slightly. Let's start by looking at the problems people can run into, and then we'll see what this means for the insights we've developed about the relationship between income and consumption.

People can't always borrow. Some people don't follow the Rational Rule for Consumers simply because **credit constraints** limit the amount they can borrow. If you don't have savings or credit, you're constrained to spending no more than what's in your latest paycheck, and therefore you can't smooth your consumption. This is an important constraint for many Americans.

credit constraints Limits on how much you can borrow.

Credit constraints arise because banks are often reluctant to lend money to fund consumption when the loan isn't backed by *collateral* — an asset they can take over if you fall behind on your repayments. This means that you'll find it easier to borrow for certain kinds of spending, like buying a house or a new car, because the bank retains the right to foreclose on your house or repossess your car.

But it's much more difficult to find a bank willing to lend you money to buy groceries or pay rent if you don't have sufficient current income, even if you have good credit and evidence of employment. Those who are willing to make such loans often charge extremely high interest rates. It's even worse when your income is temporarily low, such as when you're unemployed. High interest rates and fees for borrowing mean that you'll have to give up a lot of future consumption in order to consume more when your income is temporarily low. That's because you'll need to use some of your future income to pay back not just what you borrowed but also the high interest and fees.

It's hard to make deliberate forward-looking plans and stick to them. Even if banks were willing to lend to you, it's hard to perfectly forecast your permanent income and make consumption plans that you stick to. Our insights into consumption come from applying a framework that's deliberate, forward-looking, and requires thinking hard about difficult trade-offs. Following the Rational Rule for Consumers requires you to constantly compare the present to the future, to make plans about when to spend and when to save, and to follow through on those plans.

The reality is that not all people can be this deliberate about their choices all the time. I bet you've occasionally made spending decisions without a careful evaluation of marginal benefits. Too many students fail to draw up a budget when their financial aid check arrives, and even if they do, temptation can thwart their plans. And all of us can face unexpected needs that disrupt even the best-laid plans. Research in behavioral economics has shown that cognitive or behavioral limitations mean that some people don't smooth their consumption. They don't save enough; they run up debt without a plan to pay it back; and they make impulse purchases.

Planning is hard work, but worth it.

Incorporating insights from psychology into our understanding of how people make economic decisions refines our understanding of the relationship between income and consumption. People tend to be impulsive, they procrastinate, and they tend to be impatient when it comes to making trade-offs between today and tomorrow. All of that means that some people won't follow the Rational Rule for Consumers and will instead simply spend what they have in the moment.

Hand-to-mouth consumers spend their current income; consumption smoothers spend permanent income. Together, these two factors — psychological limitations and credit constraints — mean that some people don't smooth their consumption, or they don't smooth it fully. Instead, they live paycheck to paycheck. As a result, their consumption reflects their current income rather than their permanent income. Economists call these folks "hand-to-mouth consumers." The term hand-to-mouth consumer is not a judgment of anyone's situation, but rather a description of their relationship between consumption and income. For many people, hand-to-mouth consumption is not so much a choice as a reality — they find it hard to borrow and difficult, if not impossible, to save; they often spend all their income on necessities. Hand-to-mouth consumers spend their income as they receive it, so their marginal propensity to consume is 1, whether the change in income is anticipated or unanticipated, temporary or permanent.

Total consumption is a mix of hand-to-mouth consumers and consumption smoothers. The macroeconomy includes all the people who smooth their consumption *and* everyone who lives hand to mouth. The five insights we developed earlier in this section describe how consumption smoothers respond to different changes in income. We've just seen that hand-to-mouth consumers tend to spend what they have, so their consumption reflects their current income. Let's take a look at how total consumption across the economy will respond to a change in income, modifying our earlier insights to account for the responses of *both* consumption smoothers and hand-to-mouth consumers.

Hybrid insight 1: *A temporary change in income* will lead to a small change in consumption for consumption smoothers and a large change in consumption for hand-to-mouth consumers. At the start of the chapter, you were asked to think about what you would do if you received an unexpected $1,000. Most people say that they would put most of it in savings or use it to pay off debt, implying that they are consumption smoothers. But others say that they would use the money right away, on any number of things ranging from health care needs to car repairs or vacations that they wouldn't have otherwise been able to purchase. Total consumption reflects the spending decisions of both groups, and so the average marginal propensity to consume out of a temporary income change will be larger when there are more hand-to-mouth consumers in a society.

Hybrid insight 2: *A permanent change in income* will lead to a large change in consumption from both consumption smoothers and hand-to-mouth consumers, leading to a large change in total consumption. Indeed, consumption will rise by about as much as permanent income. The marginal propensity to consume out of permanent changes in income remains close to 1, regardless of the mix of hand-to-mouth and consumption smoothers.

Government payments during the pandemic helped keep people working and spending from home.

Interpreting the DATA | **How much do people spend out of government payments?**

When the Covid pandemic began, one of the first actions the U.S. government took was to send households a $1,200 payment. These payments were in addition to unemployment benefits and other cash assistance given to people who had lost income. The thinking behind these payments was that higher income leads to higher consumption, and so these one-time checks would prompt people to keep consuming, which would enable businesses to keep workers on their payrolls.

The problem is that such payments are temporary and represent very small changes to permanent income. A consumption smoother might save the whole thing. However, people who are living hand to mouth might use the money immediately to purchase more food, shelter, and other necessities.

Researchers at the Federal Reserve Bank of Chicago found that people spent just under half of the checks, estimating a marginal propensity to consume of 0.46. When they dug a little further, they found that people who tend to live paycheck to paycheck had a higher *MPC* of 0.6, while those who save out of each paycheck had an *MPC* of 0.2. This tells us two things: The first is that few people are perfect consumption smoothers, and most people will spend at least a little more when they receive an unexpected windfall of money. The second is that even those living hand to mouth try to stretch an unexpected gain out as much as possible. ∎

Hybrid insight 3: *An anticipated change in income* will lead to no change in the consumption of consumption smoothers, but a large change for hand-to-mouth consumers who consume their income as it arrives. The marginal propensity to consume out of anticipated income changes will depend on the share of hand-to-mouth consumers: The larger the share of hand-to-mouth consumers, the higher the marginal propensity to consume out of an anticipated change in income.

Hybrid insight 4: *Learning about a future income change* will lead to a large change in consumption from consumption smoothers, who respond to news about future income right away, but no change from hand-to-mouth consumers, who won't respond until the extra income arrives. Once again, the marginal propensity to consume out of anticipated income changes will depend on the share of hand-to-mouth consumers. However, in this case, the larger the share of hand-to-mouth consumers, the *smaller* the marginal propensity to consume, since hand-to-mouth consumers do not increase consumption when learning about a future income change.

Hybrid insight 5: *Forecasting changes in consumption depends on the share of hand-to-mouth consumers.* Hand-to-mouth consumers spend what they have, so you can forecast changes in their consumption if you know how their income will change. Consumption smoothers, however, don't change their consumption in response to anticipated income changes, so you can't forecast changes in their consumption. Therefore, your ability to forecast changes in consumption depends on the mix of consumption smoothers and hand-to-mouth consumers.

Putting it all together, *on average* the economy shows some influence of permanent income driving consumption and some influence of current income driving consumption. Figure 9 summarizes the effect of a rise in income on consumption (labeled *C*) for consumption smoothers and for hand-to-mouth consumers. To forecast how total consumption across the economy will respond to the rise in income, you need to account for the responses of *both* consumption smoothers and hand-to-mouth consumers, as shown in the final column of Figure 9.

Figure 9 | Consequences of Changing Income for Consumption

Effect of ...	Consumption smoothers	+	Hand-to-mouth consumers	=	Total consumption
A *temporary* rise in income	Small ↑C		Large ↑C		Intermediate ↑C
A *permanent* rise in income	Large ↑C		Large ↑C		Large ↑C
An *anticipated* rise in income	No change		Large ↑C		Intermediate ↑C
News of a *future* rise in income	Large ↑C		No change		Intermediate ↑C
Forecastability of consumption changes	Hard to forecast		Forecast by looking at income changes		Difficult, but not impossible to forecast

13.4 What Shifts Consumption?

Learning Objective *Assess how changing macroeconomic conditions shift consumption.*

So far our analysis of the link between income and consumption has held other factors constant. It's time to see what happens when those other factors change. This is where the interdependence principle comes to the fore, highlighting how consumption depends on other factors, including the real interest rate, expectations, taxes, and wealth.

First, let's focus on the distinction between a shift in the consumption function and a movement along the curve. The consumption function shows how consumption depends on income. A change in income doesn't shift the consumption function; instead, it leads to a *movement along the consumption function*, as shown in Panel A of Figure 10. But other factors — including the real interest rate, expectations, taxes, and wealth — will change consumption at any given level of income. As a result, they *shift the consumption function*. Panel B of Figure 10 shows that an increase in consumption at any level of income shifts the consumption function up, while a decrease in consumption shifts it down. Our next task is to analyze the four factors that shift the consumption function.

Four consumption shifters:
1. Real interest rates
2. Expectations
3. Taxes
4. Wealth

Figure 10 | Movement Along the Consumption Function versus Shifts in the Consumption Function

Panel A—Changes in Income:
Lead to a Movement Along the Consumption Function

Ⓐ An increase in **income**
Ⓑ Leads to a **movement along the consumption function**
Ⓒ Leading to **higher consumption**

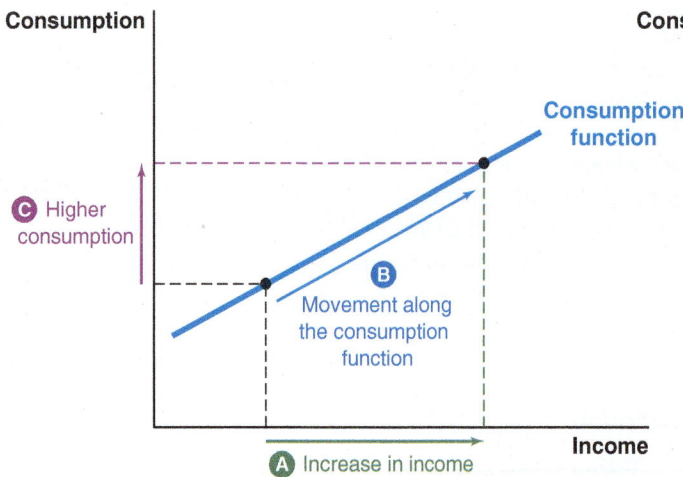

Panel B—Changes in Other Factors:
Shift the Consumption Function

Ⓐ Other factors that cause an **increase in consumption** at a given income level lead the consumption line to **shift up**.
Ⓑ Other factors that cause a **decrease in consumption** at a given income level cause the consumption line to **shift down**.

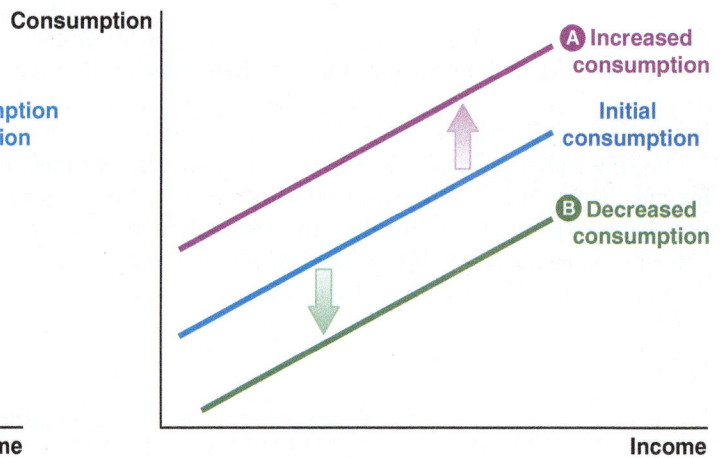

Consumption Shifter 1: Real Interest Rates

It's time to add the real interest rate to our analysis. We'll analyze its effects on saving and consumption separately.

Let's start with saving because it's the most straightforward. The benefit of saving is that you'll earn interest. A higher real interest rate raises the benefit of saving, and the **cost-benefit principle** tells you that people will respond by doing more of it. That is, a higher real interest rate leads to an increase in saving.

The effects of a higher interest rate on current consumption are a bit more complicated because there are two forces that sometimes work in opposition to each other.

First, a higher real interest rate is an incentive to substitute toward more consumption tomorrow and less today. This *substitution effect* arises because the opportunity cost of spending a dollar on consumption today is saving that dollar and spending it plus the interest earned on it in the future. The higher the real interest rate, the higher this opportunity cost, leading consumers to reduce their current consumption.

Second, a higher real interest rate boosts your income if you're a lender and decreases it if you're a borrower. That's because lenders get paid interest, while borrowers pay interest. So if you're a lender, higher interest rates boost your income, and this *income effect*

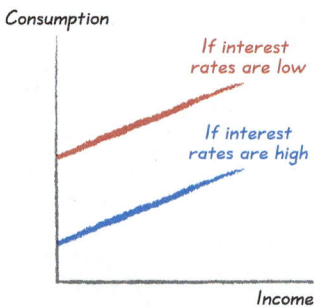

leads to higher consumption. But if you're a borrower, higher interest rates effectively reduce the income you have left after making interest payments, and this income effect reduces your consumption.

The net effect of these two sometimes-conflicting forces could go either way. But most evidence suggests that an increase in the real interest rate leads to a decrease in consumption.

Consumption Shifter 2: Expectations

Consumers' expectations about the future state of the economy can play a big role in driving consumption. Optimism about future economic growth means that people expect their future incomes will be higher. And to the extent that consumption is driven by permanent income — what consumers expect to earn in the future — optimistic expectations translate into higher consumption.

On the flip side, anxiety about the future of the economy means that people worry that their future incomes will be lower. The result is that pessimistic expectations translate into lower consumption. This is exactly what happened during the early months of the Covid pandemic, when total consumption fell by more than what would be expected from the actual decline in income. The result was what economists called "excess savings," the extra savings that U.S. households accumulated because of pessimistic expectations.

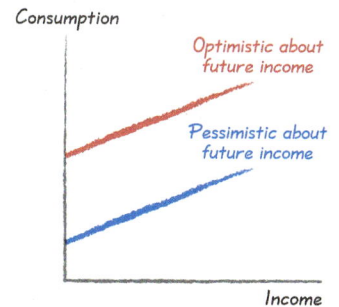

Consumption Shifter 3: Taxes

Uncle Sam taxes a chunk of your income before you even get a chance to think about whether to spend or save it. Because you can't spend that money, taxes are an important factor shaping consumption. Higher taxes reduce your **disposable income** — that is, your after-tax income — which leads to lower consumption at any given level of pre-tax income. Total pre-tax income is the same thing as GDP, so that means that high taxes lead to lower consumption for any level of GDP. That is, a tax increase will shift the consumption function downward.

On the flip side, tax cuts increase disposable income, shifting the consumption function upward, leading to higher consumption at any level of GDP. This is why governments sometimes use tax cuts to stimulate spending when the economy slows. Economists debate how effective tax cuts are as a stimulus. If consumers spend most of their tax cut — as hand-to-mouth consumers will — then it will be an effective stimulus. But consumption smoothers will recognize that a temporary tax cut doesn't boost their permanent income by much, so they'll save rather than spend most of their tax cuts. When this happens, the tax cut doesn't yield much stimulus; the government might be better off spending the money itself. We'll assess some of the evidence on this in Chapter 23 on fiscal policy.

disposable income Your after-tax income.

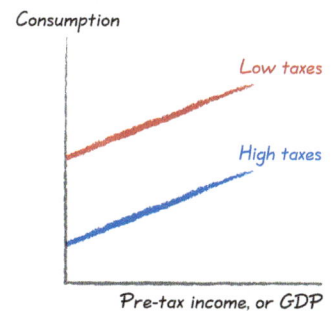

Consumption Shifter 4: Wealth

Your total resources include not just your income, but also your accumulated stock of wealth (which can be negative, if you're in debt). Greater wealth leads to an increase in consumption at any given level of income, shifting the consumption function upward.

This gives financial markets an important role in shifting consumption. For instance, rising stock prices lead the wealth of shareholders to rise, and they may choose to spend some of this extra wealth on consumption, shifting the consumption function up.

Likewise, many Americans hold most of their wealth in housing, and so an increase in house prices can also make people feel wealthier, leading them to consume more. Before spending your newfound housing wealth, realize that a broad-based rise in house prices is a double-edged sword. Higher house prices are good news because they boost your

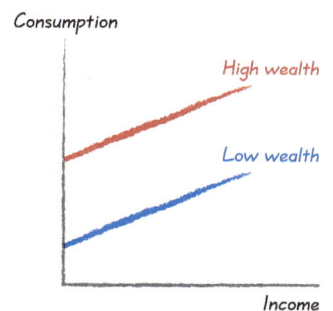

wealth. But they're also bad news because if you sell your house to realize that gain in wealth, you'll have to find somewhere else to live, and the increase in house prices will make buying another house more expensive.

You now have a good sense of how changing macroeconomic conditions shift consumption. Figure 11 summarizes what we've learned.

Figure 11 | The Macroeconomics of Consumption

Consumption Function Shifters	
The consumption function *shifts up in response to:*	↓ Real interest rates Optimistic expectations of future income ↓ Taxes ↑ Wealth
The consumption function *shifts down in response to:*	↑ Real interest rates Pessimistic expectations of future income ↑ Taxes ↓ Wealth
The consumption function *doesn't shift in response to:*	Changing income. That's a movement along the curve.

Do the Economics

For each of the following examples, figure out how the consumption function responds to changing macroeconomic conditions:

The Federal Reserve raises interest rates.

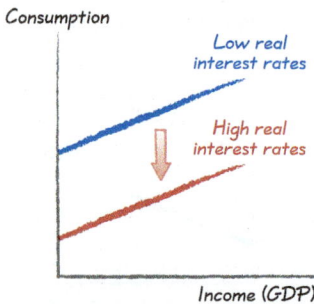

Increase in real interest rates
→ Consumption function shifts down

The stock market rises to a record high.

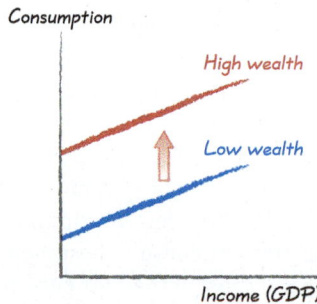

Increase in wealth
→ Consumption function shifts up

The government gives a one-time tax rebate.

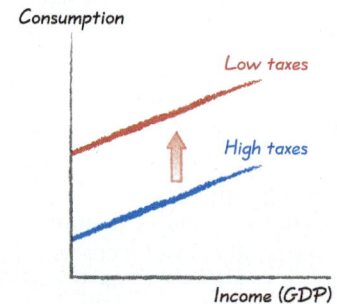

Lower taxes
→ Consumption function shifts up

People start to feel better about their financial prospects.

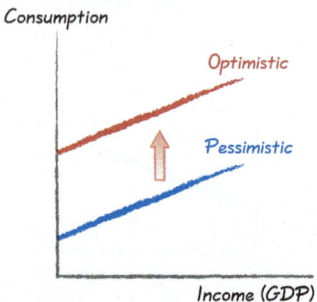

Optimistic expectations
→ Consumption function shifts up

The government raises taxes to pay off some of its debt.

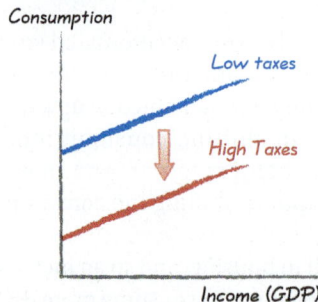

Increase in taxes
→ Consumption function shifts down

House prices plunge.

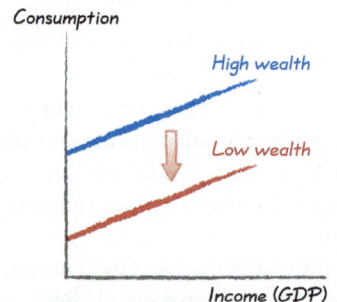

Decline in wealth
→ Consumption function shifts down ∎

Savings motives:
1. Changing income over the life cycle
2. Changing needs over the life cycle
3. Bequests
4. Precautionary saving

13.5 | Saving

Learning Objective *Learn how to form a smart saving plan.*

It's time to turn our attention from consumption to saving. Of course, this isn't a change of focus at all — how much you save depends on how much you consume, and vice versa. Don't think of this as a separate analysis of saving, but rather as a continuation of our analysis that will lead to a more complete understanding of both consumption and saving.

There are four key motives that drive saving, and it's time to explore their implications for saving, consumption, and macroeconomic outcomes.

Saving Motive 1: Changing Income over the Life Cycle

You've already seen that most people borrow when young, save in midlife, and spend down their savings in retirement. This pattern is driven by how income typically changes over the life course. Your income will probably start low and then rise over your 20s and 30s; you'll enjoy your peak earning years in your 40s, 50s, and maybe 60s; and then your income will drop off sharply when you retire. That is, your income will probably follow a hump-shaped pattern. As Figure 12 shows, it will look something like this. But your consumption shouldn't follow the same pattern. The logic of consumption smoothing is that you should save money in those phases of your life when your income will be predictably higher, so that you can spend more than your income when it's lower.

As a result, people tend to spend more than their meager incomes in their 20s and thus accumulate debt. Then as their earnings grow, they pay down their debt and accumulate savings in their 30s, 40s, and 50s. People tend to spend down their accumulated assets starting around their mid-60s, as they head into retirement.

These patterns mean that demographics have macroeconomic implications for national savings. If a large share of the population is very young or very old, then national savings will be lower than it would be if more people were middle-aged. The share of the U.S. population over age 65 — the age at which many people retire and move from saving to dissaving — has more than doubled over the past several decades. This demographic shift has helped push the national savings rate down from over 10% in the 1950s to 7% at the end of 2021.

Figure 12 | Your Income Varies over Your Life Cycle

Average income, by age

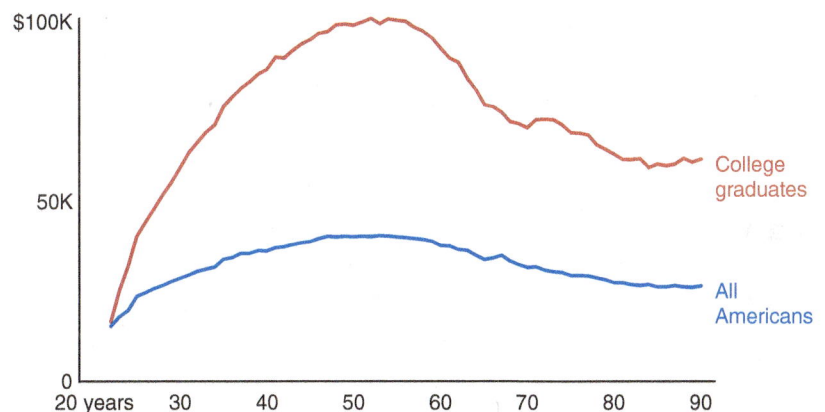

Data from: American Community Survey, 2016–2020.

Saving Motive 2: Changing Needs over the Life Cycle

Your *needs will* also vary over your life course. You should save more (and spend less) in periods when you have fewer needs, so that you'll have more to spend when there's a greater need.

Look ahead now and forecast how your needs will vary over your life course. For most college students, their most important needs are tuition, housing, and living expenses. When you graduate you won't be paying tuition any more, but you might have to start paying down your student loans. Different people follow different life paths, but for many, the next big expense comes when they get married, which might involve a costly wedding, a honeymoon, and setting up a new household. But a wedding is cheap, relative to the cost of feeding, clothing, and raising kids. If you're planning a family, be aware that those first few years with young kids involve some big expenses. It's not just diapers and toys; you'll probably need to budget for child care, and that often costs more than in-state

They're little, but they're expensive. Believe me.

Courtesy of Dustin Johnston

tuition at a public college. All of this means that for many people it's a good idea to spend modestly in your early 20s — even though your permanent income might allow higher consumption — because your needs are likely to rise as you enter your 30s.

The Rational Rule for Consumers says that if your needs are *similar* over time, then you should smooth your consumption. But if your needs are *changing,* then your consumption should also change over time. The Rational Rule for Consumers tells you to spend more when the marginal benefit of spending today is more than the marginal benefit of spending a dollar-plus-interest in the future. At certain times in your life the marginal benefit of each dollar of consumption will be higher, so you'll want to consume more. In turn, that means that you'll need to save more in those phases of your life when your needs aren't so great. The main idea here remains the same: You want to shift your spending to the times in your life when it will yield the largest marginal benefit.

Saving Motive 3: Bequests

The third motive for saving is that you might want to build up a stock of wealth that you'll pass on when you die. For some people, that means leaving an inheritance for their children. For others, it's about leaving money to a cause they care about. It's important to draw up a detailed will in order to ensure your bequest goes to help the folks you care most about.

The bequest motive helps explain why many people don't spend down all their wealth. They're hoping their money will outlive them, and that it will make a difference — for their families, their communities, or the whole world — even if they aren't around to see it.

Saving Motive 4: Precautionary Saving

The final motive for saving comes from the old saying that you should hope for the best, but prepare for the worst. This suggests that you should build up a buffer stock of saving to protect you in case financial misfortune strikes. That misfortune could be an unexpected decrease in income (losing your job, for example) or an unexpected expense (a costly health crisis, for example). Saving for a financial emergency is called **precautionary saving** because you're building up that buffer as a precaution. It's the idea that you should save for a rainy day.

precautionary saving Saving to be prepared for a financial emergency.

Save enough to weather the financial risks you face. Let's take a measure of your financial health: How would you cope if you needed to replace your car's transmission? Such a shock might set you back around $2,000. Could you come up with the money? Figure 13 shows that a survey asking Americans this question found that more than a quarter were either "probably not able" or "certainly not able" to come up with the funds. Among young adults, the numbers were even worse.

If you're in a similar situation, my advice is to build up your emergency fund. It's an urgent task because once you get into financial trouble, your problems can quickly cascade. If you can't fix your car, then you can't get to work, and if you can't get to work, you'll lose your job, and then you'll never be able to afford to fix your car.

While many people can't come up with $2,000 to fix their car, people often face even more critical risks. To evaluate how much you'll need to save, think through the sorts of financial risks you face and how much money you'll need to have on hand to weather them. One of the biggest risks you'll face is unemployment. The good news is that most people who lose their jobs find a new job within a few months; the bad news is that this still means going a few months without a paycheck. That's why financial planners typically advise that you build up a buffer stock that's equivalent to three to six months of your typical consumption.

Figure 13 | Many Americans Are Financially Unprepared

"How confident are you that you could come up with $2,000 if an unexpected need arose within the next month?"

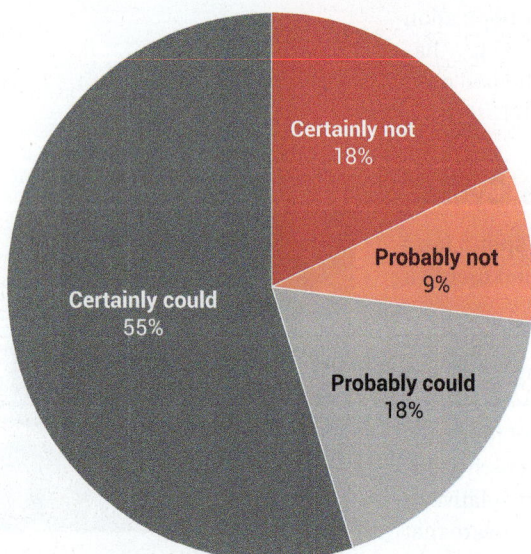

Certainly not 18%

Probably not 9%

Certainly could 55%

Probably could 18%

Data from: 2022 Personal Finance Index.

Precautionary saving is why national savings go up when economic uncertainty rises. The more uncertain your economic future looks, the larger your emergency fund should be. Whenever economic uncertainty rises, millions of people increase their precautionary saving. But remember that savings and consumption are two sides of the same coin — to save more, people have to consume less. As a result, growing uncertainty can lead to a decline in total consumption.

Figure 14 shows how the onset of the Covid pandemic in early 2020 led the personal savings rate to soar. It wasn't just that people couldn't spend their money going out to eat or shopping in person due to fear of contracting Covid. The huge increase in uncertainty led many households to cut their spending so they could be better prepared for the worst. Government financial support to households often added to savings (contributing to the savings spikes in January and March 2021). The result was a large buildup of savings by American households during the first two years of the pandemic.

Figure 14 | Saving Rose When Uncertainty Spiked Due to the Pandemic

Personal saving as a share of disposable personal income

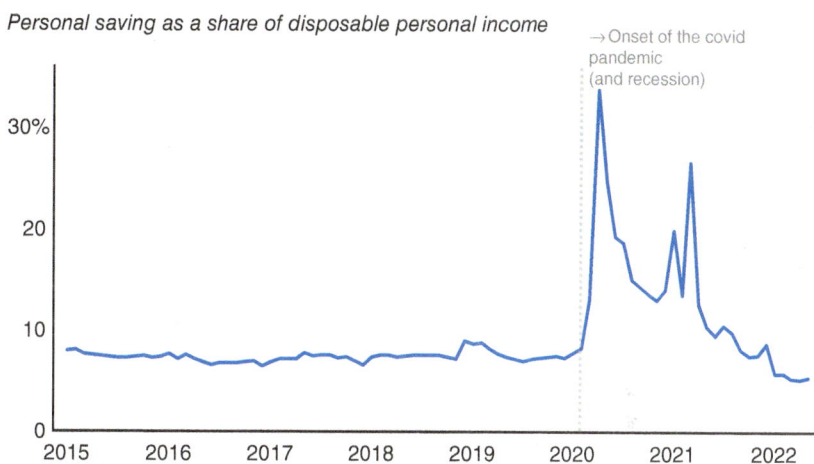

Data from: Bureau of Economic Analysis.

EVERYDAY Economics How to survive a financial emergency

If a financial emergency strikes before you've built up your emergency fund, you'll quickly discover there are no great options for borrowing money — but some options are less bad than others. The first thing to consider is whether you have a friend or family member who can loan you the money. This is often the cheapest option in dollar terms, but in personal terms it can be pretty costly, so be careful.

The rest of your options involve borrowing money through the financial sector, and it's worth evaluating the costs and benefits of each of your alternatives.

- *Credit cards:* One option is to use your credit card to cover expenses. But note that credit cards typically charge high interest rates. It's typically better to use your card to make purchases than to get a cash advance because you get a 30-day grace period to repay purchases before interest starts accruing. Borrowing cash on your credit card is worse because it typically involves fees in addition to the interest charges.

  Pay off your balance as quickly as you can (and always make minimum payments on time). If you must carry a balance, it's worth calling your credit card company to ask for a lower rate — you'll be surprised how often it works. See if they have any balance transfer offers. Be careful: Sometimes they'll offer a low introductory rate for a few months as a teaser, but plan to replace the low rate with a sky high rate later. But if you read the terms carefully and plan accordingly, you can work a balance transfer offer to your advantage.

- *Loans:* Some banks and financial service companies offer personal loans, precisely to help their customers handle a financial emergency or to pay off a high-interest credit card. Shop around for loans with low rates and good terms. If you own your car or your house, you can use them for collateral and get a lower rate — but if you don't pay them back, you risk losing your car or house.

- *Retirement accounts:* If you have a retirement plan, you might have the option of borrowing from it, and paying yourself back with interest. But ask a lot of questions

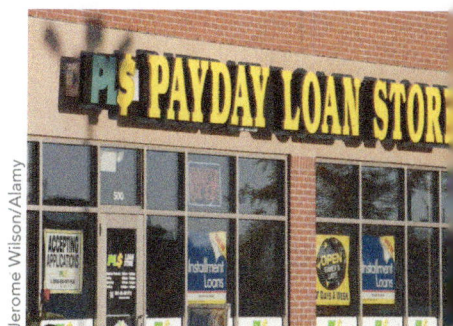

Notice that they're not advertising their interest rate.

first, because if you don't follow the rules precisely, this can lead to a significant increase in your tax obligations.

- *Payday loans:* Be very wary of payday loans. These lenders lend you small amounts of money at very high interest rates for a very short period of time. You should do everything you can to avoid these loans because they quickly get out of hand once they start to compound: The annual interest rate is often over 100% — and sometimes over 1,000%!

It's easier to get a loan at a reasonable interest rate when you've established a reputation as a responsible borrower, so it's a good idea to build up good credit before you need it. This means making all your payments on time, even when it's somewhat difficult. Your student loans are a great place to start building a good credit history. Make your minimum payments on time, and if you find yourself unable to meet your payments, take action immediately: Call and negotiate a lower payment or even a break from payments (referred to as a deferral). Good credit can help you out during times of financial stress — so don't let bad decisions ruin your credit! ∎

Smart Saving Strategies

Economists who study people's financial lives have developed smart strategies to help you manage your financial life successfully. Here are a few such strategies:

Plan ahead to avoid temptation.

Set a budget and stick to it. Research shows that people find it easier to make good decisions in advance. One famous experiment showed that people who were asked to choose a snack to eat in a week's time were more likely to choose a piece of fruit over a chocolate bar. But when offered a snack to eat right away, they were more likely to choose the chocolate. In the same way, it's much easier to save if you've planned — that is, budgeted — your spending in advance. If you're constantly deciding in the moment how much to spend, you'll find it harder to resist temptation. Instead, assess your financial situation and make a plan for how much to consume — and therefore how much to save or borrow — when you're best able to be analytic and forward-looking. Once you've made that plan, stick to it. If your plan isn't working, then go back and re-assess it.

Make sure you can handle an unexpected cost. Once you graduate, you may find yourself in a predicament in which you think you should start saving, but you have a mountain of student debt to pay. What should you do? Remember that paying off debt is a form of saving, so choosing to pay off your debt is moving your net wealth in the right direction. But unless you can borrow money easily, you also want to accumulate an emergency fund in case your car breaks down, or you have an unexpected health cost. So make the minimum payments on your loans while you build up your savings. Once you've got a solid emergency fund, start making extra payments on your student loans.

Sign up for your employer's retirement plan. Most employers will offer you some sort of retirement saving plan. Even if you have student loans or other debts, in most cases you should sign up for it. That's because most employers match your contributions to their retirement plan, usually kicking in extra money — say, a percentage of what you contribute — up to some maximum. For example, your employer might kick in 50 cents for each dollar you put into your retirement plan up to 2% of your salary. This would mean that if you saved 2% of your $50,000 income, you're putting $1,000 per year into your retirement plan, forcing your boss to kick in an extra $500. Never miss the opportunity to get free money from your boss. Don't procrastinate; sign up for your employer's retirement plan on your first day of work.

Plan to save more tomorrow. One reason people struggle to pay their student loans or to save adequately for retirement is that they get used to their current consumption spending and don't want to give anything up. Financial advisers often tell people to give up some small habit (like a daily coffee) and to save that money instead. But giving up an already established habit is hard.

What's easier is planning to save out of *future* income. One plan for building your retirement savings is to plan to keep making your student loan payments forever. Once you graduate, you'll be making regular payments to your lender. Once you've paid off your loans, keep making those payments — but make them to your retirement account. You'll never miss the money because you've never had a chance to spend it. You can do the same thing with every increase in your pay: If you get a raise of 10% with a promotion, put half of it straight into your retirement account — you'll still feel the increase in your take-home pay, while saving even more.

Keep as much of your money as you can. It sounds obvious, but there are lots of sneaky ways that money can get away from you if you're not careful. When you put your money in a retirement or investment account, you'll be charged fees, and those fees can add up. So look for the lowest fees you can find. Avoid carrying a balance on your credit card or holding on to other high-interest-rate debt for long to reduce the amount you spend on interest, and avoid late fees by paying on time, every time.

You can also hang on to more of your money if you take advantage of government programs designed to increase saving. There are many different programs — mostly geared toward saving for retirement or education — but they all boil down to the same idea: If you save into these government programs, you'll get a break on your taxes. And a break on your taxes means keeping more of your money.

13.6 | Tying It Together

Individual Decisions, Economy-Wide Effects

Our focus in this chapter on individual consumption decisions might feel like microeconomics, which is about individual decisions, rather than macroeconomics, which is about how things work at an aggregate level. In fact, any useful understanding of the macroeconomy must have micro foundations. This is the idea that the behavior of the whole is determined by the choices made by each individual. It says that the only reliable way to understand the economy-wide aggregates that are the focus of macroeconomics is to understand what drives each of the individual decisions that make up those aggregates.

This is why many leading macroeconomists describe their field as being about applying the tools of microeconomics — from the core principles on up — to build a reliable understanding of the big-picture questions that macroeconomics focuses on. This chapter has demonstrated that understanding the choices made by individual consumers can help you figure out how the economy as a whole will respond to changing conditions. The terms *microeconomics* and *macroeconomics* may not be that useful; we're just doing *economics*. Our approach has been to ignore these distinctions, in favor of using all the tools at your disposal to figure out what drives consumption.

It's an approach that we'll continue to follow throughout the rest of this book. In the next chapter, we'll focus on investment. We'll zoom in on the individual decisions that executives make about whether or not to invest in a new project. Just as we did in this chapter, we'll discover that understanding the drivers of individual choices will be incredibly helpful when it's time to work out the macroeconomic implications.

Chapter 13 Review

Chapter at a Glance

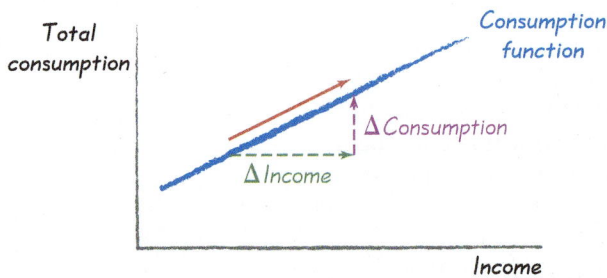

Total consumption

Consumption function

Δ Consumption

Δ Income

Income

A curve plotting the level of consumption associated with each level of income.

Marginal propensity to consume: The fraction of each extra dollar of income that households spend on consumption.

$$= Slope = \frac{\Delta Consumption}{\Delta Income}$$

Saving: The portion of income that you set aside, rather than spending on consumption.

Saving = Income − Consumption

Consumption Choices

The Rational Rule for Consumers: Consume more today if the marginal benefit of a dollar of consumption today is greater than (or equal to) the marginal benefit of spending a dollar-plus-interest in the future.

Permanent Income Hypothesis: The idea that you choose how much to consume based on your permanent income (your best estimate of your long-term average income) rather than current income.

Consumption smoothing: The idea that you should maintain a steady or smooth path for your consumption spending over time.

Real-world modifications:
• Some consumers won't follow sophisticated consumption plans.
• Credit constraints limit the amount that some people can borrow.
⇒ Hand-to-mouth consumers spend their current income.

Implications

Effect of . . .	On consumption smoothers	+	On hand-to-mouth consumers	=	Total consumption
A temporary rise in income	Small↑C		Large↑C		Intermediate↑C
A permanent rise in income	Large↑C		Large↑C		Large↑C
An anticipated rise in income	No change		Large↑C		Intermediate↑C
News of a future rise in income	Large↑C		No change		Intermediate↑C
Forecasting consumption changes	Hard to forecast		Forecast using income changes		Difficult to forecast

How Changing Economic Conditions Shift Consumption

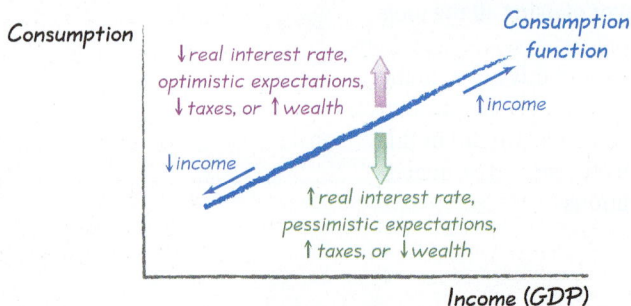

Consumption

↓real interest rate, optimistic expectations, ↓taxes, or ↑wealth

Consumption function

↑income

↓income

↑real interest rate, pessimistic expectations, ↑taxes, or ↓wealth

Income (GDP)

Is there:
• **Changing Income:** Leads to a *movement along* the consumption function.
• **Changes in Other Factors:** *Shifts* the consumption function.
  Four consumption shifters:
  1. Real interest rates
  2. Expectations of future income
  3. Taxes
  4. Wealth

Key Terms

consumption, 322

consumption function, 322

consumption smoothing, 327

credit constraints, 333

disposable income, 337

dissaving, 324

marginal propensity to consume, 322

net wealth, 324

permanent income, 328

permanent income hypothesis, 328

precautionary saving, 340

Rational Rule for Consumers, 326

saving, 324

Study Problems

Learning Objective 13.1 *Understand how consumption and saving vary with income.*

1. At your future job, you get an unexpected raise from $50,000 a year to $75,000 a year. How do your consumption and savings change? Provide a rough estimate of your marginal propensity to consume.

2. Real GDP per person falls during a devastating recession, which in turn causes consumption to fall by 5%. Would giving everyone 5% more income during the recession lead consumption to go up 5%? Why or why not?

3. Your friend just got an unexpected $1,000 tax refund. She plans to put $800 toward paying off credit card debt, put $100 toward her student loans, and use the remaining $100 to purchase a new grill for her deck. What is your friend's marginal propensity to consume? By how much has she increased her net wealth?

4. The table below contains data on per-person income and per-person consumption in the United States for several years.

Year	Real income per person (in 2012 dollars)	Real consumption per person (in 2012 dollars)
2016	$54,500	$37,500
2017	$55,300	$38,200
2018	$56,600	$39,100
2019	$57,600	$39,700
2020	$55,400	$38,100
2021	$58,500	$41,000

a. Draw the consumption function for the United States for these years.

b. What is savings at each level of income?

c. Between 2018 and 2021, how much did income rise? What about consumption? What was the marginal propensity to consume out of the increase?

Learning Objective 13.2 *Apply the core principles of economics to consumption decisions.*

5. Nicolas Cage, an award winning and prolific actor, once had a net worth of about $150 million (he earned $40 million in 2009 alone!). By 2011, he had to sell off much of his collection of homes, cars, and novelties to pay off debts and had a net worth of about $25 million. Describe how

Cage could have better applied the four core principles to get the largest benefit from his once-large income.

6. In college, most students take out loans in order to finance their education. At the same time, they still spend money on consumer goods and services: food, clothes, books, haircuts, and so on. Use the ideas of consumption smoothing and the permanent income hypothesis to explain if this is a smart decision or not.

7. Use the graph below, which illustrates the marginal benefit of consumption, to answer the following questions.

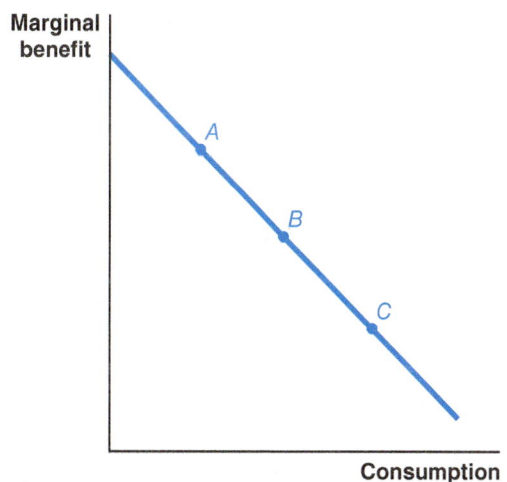

a. You became a licensed electrician last year and have been enjoying a higher income than ever before. You choose to spend the majority of your income on amenities you couldn't previously afford. Which point on the graph most likely represents your current level of consumption?

b. After many years of work as an electrician, a major economic downturn leaves you unemployed. You're finding that you must pinch pennies just to afford basic necessities. You decide to return to school, so you can pursue a career in computer programming. Which point on the graph most likely represents this level of consumption?

c. Given the two previous events, which point on the graph would help you best smooth your consumption over the long run?

8. Which of the following people are consumption smoothing and which are not? Explain your reasoning using the opportunity cost and marginal principles.

a. Sharon Tirabassi won $10 million in the Ontario lottery in 2004. By 2015, she had burnt through almost all the winnings, was riding the bus to part-time jobs, and was living in a rental property.

b. Karyn takes out modest student and personal loans to pay for living expenses while she finishes her degree. She plans to get an accounting degree and enter the workforce making about $50,000 a year, and will eventually earn close to six figures.

Learning Objective 13.3 *Predict the behavior of total consumption in the economy.*

9. Over long periods of time, the percentage of households' income spent on consumption does not change much even as income rises. Use the five insights into the relationship between income and consumption to explain this observation.

10. Describe some cognitive or behavioral limitations you have experienced when making consumption decisions and how these limitations can lead to hand-to-mouth consumption. Why is it easier to forecast the impact of an income change on consumption for hand-to-mouth consumers than for consumption smoothers?

11. What factors lead people to be credit constrained? What are the consequences? What would you expect to happen to total consumption if many people and businesses in the economy became credit constrained?

12. For each of the following scenarios, predict how consumption changes for both consumption smoothers and hand-to-mouth consumers. How does total consumption change?

a. Household incomes rise 6% this year, but income growth is expected to return to its normal growth rate of 2% next year.

b. A country with an economy based heavily on agricultural production experiences a natural disaster so severe that it will take decades for farmers to recover.

c. People expect the economy to experience a recession over the next six months.

Learning Objective 13.4 *Assess how changing macroeconomic conditions shift consumption.*

13. The American Recovery and Reinvestment Act was legislation that included temporary tax cuts designed to help pull the U.S. economy out of the Great Recession by increasing consumer spending.

a. Show graphically how a tax cut changes the consumption function.

b. Some economists argued that the tax cuts would increase consumption more if they were permanent rather than temporary. Explain why a permanent tax cut might increase consumption more than a temporary tax cut.

14. Graph the effect of an increase in the real interest rate on the consumption function for both savers and borrowers.

15. Consider the following situations. What is the effect on consumption for each scenario? Demonstrate each answer with a graph.

a. The federal government raises taxes.

b. Housing prices increase.

c. Consumer incomes rise.

d. Consumers' expectations of their future incomes plummet.

Learning Objective 13.5 *Learn how to form a smart saving plan.*

16. Explain why people tend to save more in times of economic uncertainty.

17. Paige is a supervisor at UPS. She just got a big promotion and went from working part time for $20,000 a year to full time for $55,000 a year. Her new manager tells her, "You should live like you're still making the part-time income for two years and save everything else. You'll thank me when you're my age." Should Paige follow her manager's advice?

18. The increasing cost of college has reduced how much young adults have saved for retirement. How does a higher cost of college change the life-cycle pattern of saving?

19. If parents increasingly worry about the costs their adult children and grandchildren will face because of climate change, how might that change their savings behavior?

20. Policymakers are increasingly worried that Americans are not saving enough, so one policymaker proposes increasing the amount of government support available when people experience tough times like unemployment. How would this impact savings rates?

21. Consider the following data on the personal saving rate from 1980 until today in the United States.

Personal saving as a share of disposable personal income

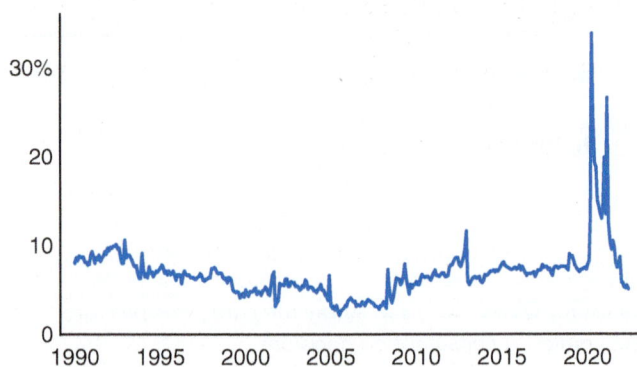

Data from: Bureau of Economic Analysis.

What patterns do you notice during and after the last four recessions? What explains these patterns?

Investment

There's a wind farm off the coast of Rhode Island, and other wind farms are springing up in Texas, Oklahoma, Maine, and California. These sleek modern wind turbines look nothing at all like the wind-mills of old. Some are twice the height of the Statue of Liberty with massive blades sweeping out over an area as large as three football fields. A single turbine can generate enough electricity for thousands of households. They're at the cutting edge of a renewable energy revolution that could power a new economy. These remarkable machines could be the start of a greener economy that saves the environment by reducing the need to burn fossil fuels.

Spinning wind into energy.

A wind farm is a massive investment. Each turbine costs millions of dollars. The owners aren't spending these sums for the environment; they're making hard-nosed investment decisions and will invest in wind only if it's profitable.

The entrepreneurs running wind farms face the same decision that confronts all managers considering whether to invest in a new piece of equipment: Is the large up-front cost worth it in order to generate a stream of future profits?

The tools that managers use to make multimillion-dollar investment decisions are the same tools that you'll want to apply in your own life whenever you're making decisions whose consequences play out over time.

Your task in this chapter is to explore the framework that executives use to eval-uate investment decisions. We'll develop some basic tools and then apply them to the sort of real-world investment decisions that you'll face in your career. We'll use the insights we gain from studying individual investment decisions to explore the drivers of broader macroeconomic patterns in investment. But first, we'll evaluate the important role that investment plays in driving macroeconomic conditions. Let's make like a turbine and get going!

Chapter Objective

Analyze how managers can make good investment decisions.

14.1 What Is Investment?
Learn what macroeconomists mean by investment and assess the role that it plays in the economy.

14.2 Tools to Analyze Investments
Master two tools for compar-ing sums of money at different points in time: compounding and discounting.

14.3 Making Investment Decisions
Evaluate whether an investment opportunity is worth pursuing.

14.4 The Macroeconomics of Investment
Assess how macroeconomic conditions drive investment.

14.5 The Market for Loanable Funds
Forecast the long-run real interest rate.

🎙 Podcast
Think Like an Economist
Investment—Upfront Costs for Future Gains

14.1 What Is Investment?

Learning Objective *Learn what macroeconomists mean by investment and assess the role that it plays in the economy.*

Investment is going to be a big part of your life. As an entrepreneur, you'll invest in starting a new business; as a manager, you'll invest in new technology; in operations, you'll invest in more efficient logistics; in accounting, you'll invest in collecting valuable information. Folks in advertising tell you to invest in your brand, while those in human resources tell you to invest in your workers. In your personal life, you'll invest in your community, in your friends, and in your romantic relationships. Right now you're investing in your education by reading about investment. And if that education lands you a job interview, you might invest in a good suit.

All of these investments involve the following proposition: You incur some *up-front cost* today in the hope of receiving *future benefits*. This trade-off between up-front costs and future benefits is critical to understanding investment.

Defining Investment

The term *investment* is a tricky one because it has a formal (and relatively narrow) definition within macroeconomics, yet the same word is often used more loosely in casual conversation where it takes on a broader meaning.

Macroeconomic investment refers to spending on new capital. Let's start by defining **capital,** which refers to assets such as equipment, structures, and intellectual property that are used repeatedly to produce output. It's relevant because when macroeconomists talk about **investment,** they mean purchases of *new* capital, which increase the economy's productive capacity. And so macroeconomic investment includes purchases of new business equipment, offices, factories, and housing, as well as inventories. Beyond physical capital, it also includes investments in research and development and other intellectual property like software.

capital Assets such as equipment, structures, and intellectual property that are used repeatedly to produce output.

investment Purchases of *new* capital, which increase the economy's productive capacity.

Macroeconomists focus on this formal definition because macroeconomic investment — that is, purchases of new capital — are an important component of total spending. It's the capital "I" in the definition of GDP (remember, Y = C + I + G + NX). Investment in new capital is also a critical ingredient in producing future output because capital tends to last a long time. Figure 1 shows that investment makes up roughly one sixth of GDP, which means that it adds up to more than $12,000 per person each year. It's a big deal.

Figure 1 | Investment Is About One-Sixth of Gross Domestic Product

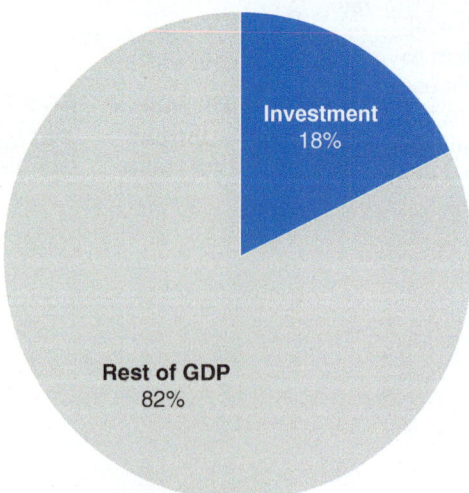

Investment 18%

Rest of GDP 82%

Data from: 2021 data from Bureau of Economic Analysis.

The word *investment* also has a (different but related) colloquial meaning. In casual conversation, people often talk about making an "investment" even when they're not buying new capital. Rather, they use the term more expansively, typically when they're incurring an up-front cost in the hope of receiving future benefits. And so people talk about investing in their brand, in their education, or in a new suit because they're hoping to reap future rewards after incurring these up-front costs. This colloquial meaning of "investment" is related to the formal definition that macroeconomists use, because investments in new capital — such as buying new machines or building new factories — also involve up-front costs and future benefits. That's why you'll find that the analytic framework that we're about to develop to understand macroeconomic investment will also help you with the broader set of choices you face that trade off up-front costs for future benefits.

Notice that the formal macroeconomic definition of investment is narrower than its colloquial meaning. Even though regular people might talk about investing in their personal brand or their education, these aren't counted as macroeconomic investments, because they don't involve purchasing new capital assets like machines. (Whenever I'm worried you might confuse the formal and colloquial meanings, I'll be sure to refer to the formal macroeconomic definition as "macroeconomic investment.")

Don't confuse investment and saving. As you've seen, the formal definition of macroeconomic investment excludes a lot of stuff that regular people often refer to as investments. The problem is that it's easy to confuse *saving* with *investment*. As we learned in Chapter 13, saving is the money you have left over after paying for your consumption spending, and you might put your savings in the bank, in a stock portfolio, or under the mattress. None of these counts as macroeconomic investment because you're not buying any new capital. (As we'll discuss later in this chapter, saving and investment are related, because if your bank lends your savings to a business that uses that money to fund a new factory, then that spending will count as investment.)

Trading existing assets doesn't count as investment. Buying shares in Google, bars of gold, or a block of land don't count as macroeconomic investment because you're simply buying an *existing* asset from someone else, without creating any new capital. For similar reasons, trading financial assets like bonds, foreign currency, or Bitcoin doesn't count. Neither does putting your money into collectibles like antiques, art, stamps, coins, rare vinyl, limited-release sneakers, trading cards, or vintage cars. Macroeconomic investment expands the economy's productive capacity, whereas trading existing assets simply re-shuffles who owns what.

He's saving, not investing.

capital stock The total quantity of capital at a point in time.

depreciation The decline in capital due to wear and tear, obsolescence, accidental damage, and aging.

Investment adds to the capital stock; depreciation subtracts from it. The total quantity of capital at a point in time is called the **capital stock.** Investment is the *flow* of new purchases of capital that add to this stock. But capital also declines over time due to **depreciation,** which includes wear and tear, obsolescence, accidental damage, and aging. As a result, this year's capital stock is equal to last year's capital stock, less depreciation, plus new investment over the past year. This means that the capital stock rises when new investment exceeds depreciation, but declines when depreciation exceeds investment.

Types of Investment

Macroeconomists break investment into three primary categories — business investment, housing, and inventories — as shown in Figure 2. Let's take a closer look at each of these types of investments.

Investment type 1: Business investment. The money that businesses spend on new capital assets is called *business investment*. Figure 2 shows that business investment accounts for the bulk of investment in the economy. It includes spending on *equipment* (new computers, machinery, and company cars), *structures* (new offices, stores, factories, and remodeling of existing facilities), and *intellectual*

Figure 2 | **The Composition of Macroeconomic Investment**

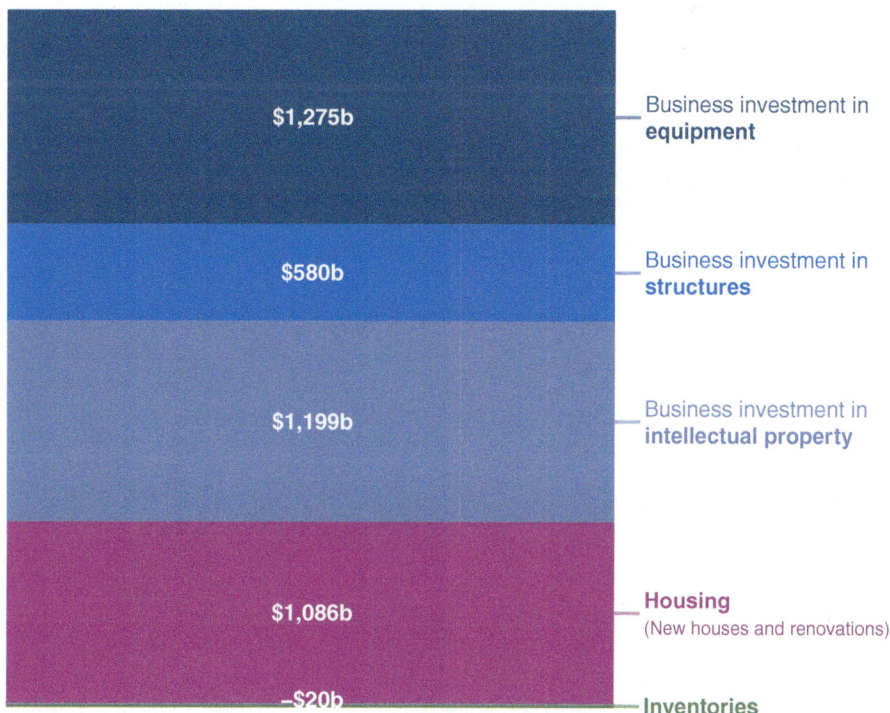

$1,275b	Business investment in **equipment**
$580b	Business investment in **structures**
$1,199b	Business investment in **intellectual property**
$1,086b	**Housing** (New houses and renovations)
−$20b	**Inventories**

Inventory investment is negative when businesses run down their inventories.

Data from: Bureau of Economic Analysis data for 2021.

CapturePB/Shutterstock

Buying a fixer-upper doesn't count as investment—but spending on renovations does.

property (spending on software; on literary, television, movie, and music production; and research and development). This spending is all categorized as business investment because it involves businesses purchasing new capital that they will use to produce future output.

Investment type 2: Housing investment. When you invest in building new houses or apartments — or in improving existing housing — it's counted as *housing investment*. It includes both homes that you plan to live in and those that you plan to rent out.

Housing investment is a bit different from business investment, because when you live in a house that you own, the house doesn't generate revenue. But the opportunity cost principle reminds you that your home *could* be used to generate rental income. Thus, building a new home counts as macroeconomic investment because it increases the stock of capital — increasing the economy's capacity to generate rent. For similar reasons, renovating your home is an investment because a renovated home could be rented for more money. But sales of existing homes simply transfer ownership from one person to another, and hence don't count as macroeconomic investment because they don't create any *new* capital.

Investment type 3: Inventories. Businesses also invest by maintaining inventories of raw materials, work-in-progress, and unsold goods. For instance, the cars you can test-drive at your local car dealership are counted as inventories. Because inventories are a critical part of the production process, they're counted as part of the capital stock. And so an increase in inventories is counted as investment.

The change in inventories is only a tiny share of total investment. But it's also volatile, because unsold goods build up quickly when sales are weak. Inventory investment can be negative when stocks of unsold goods dry up, as occurred when supply chain problems during the pandemic made it difficult to restock. Because of this volatility, changing inventories account for a big chunk of quarter-to-quarter movements in investment.

Investment Is a Key Economic Variable

Investment accounts for only around one-sixth of all spending, but economists pay close attention to it because it has an extraordinarily important impact on the economy.

Investment drives the business cycle. Investment fluctuates dramatically as business conditions change, so it plays an outsized role in driving the year-to-year economic fluctuations known as the *business cycle*. Figure 3 shows the relationship between the annual percent change in GDP and investment. A recession might lead GDP to decline by around 2% from the previous year, while investment might decline by 20%. Likewise, a strong economy might lead GDP to grow by 4%, but it could cause investment to grow by ten times as much. In short, investment changes more from year to year than GDP does.

Investment is particularly sensitive to business conditions partly because managers can easily delay or cancel expansion plans. Moreover, because investment decisions are forward-looking, they're extremely sensitive to expectations about the future state of the economy. Investment is also sensitive to interest rates and lending standards because businesses often have to get a loan to fund their investments. It's often said that once you figure out what drives investment, you've figured out much of what drives the business cycle.

Figure 3 | **Investment Drives the Business Cycle**

Percent change in GDP *and* investment *over the past year*

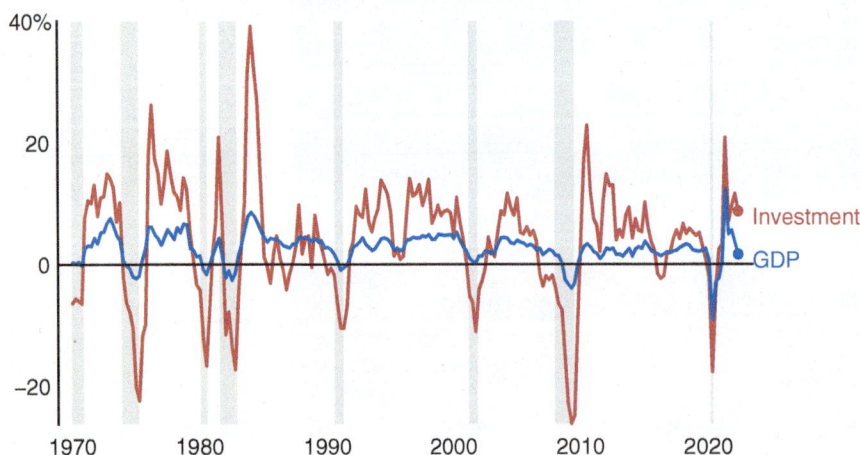

Shaded areas show recessions

Data from: Bureau of Labor Statistics.

Investment changes quickly, but the capital stock changes slowly. Today's capital stock is the accumulation of investments made over many previous years, less any depreciation that has occurred. As a result, even though investment—the *flow* of new spending on capital—often fluctuates quite dramatically, the capital stock—which is the *stock* of capital—only moves slowly. Indeed, the capital stock typically rises gradually over time, and it doesn't change much from year to year. As such, the capital stock provides a relatively stable link between last year's economy and today's economy.

Investment is a key driver of long-term prosperity. The more capital—tools, machines, and computers—your workers have to work with, the more output they'll be able to produce. Indeed, Figure 4 shows that workers in countries with more capital are typically more productive, producing more output per worker.

Education is another important driver of how much workers produce, but investments in human capital—that is, going to school and college—aren't counted in macroeconomic investment. If they were to be included, then the role of investment in making some countries more productive, and therefore more prosperous, would become even more dramatic.

Figure 4 | Countries with More Capital per Worker Produce More Output per Worker

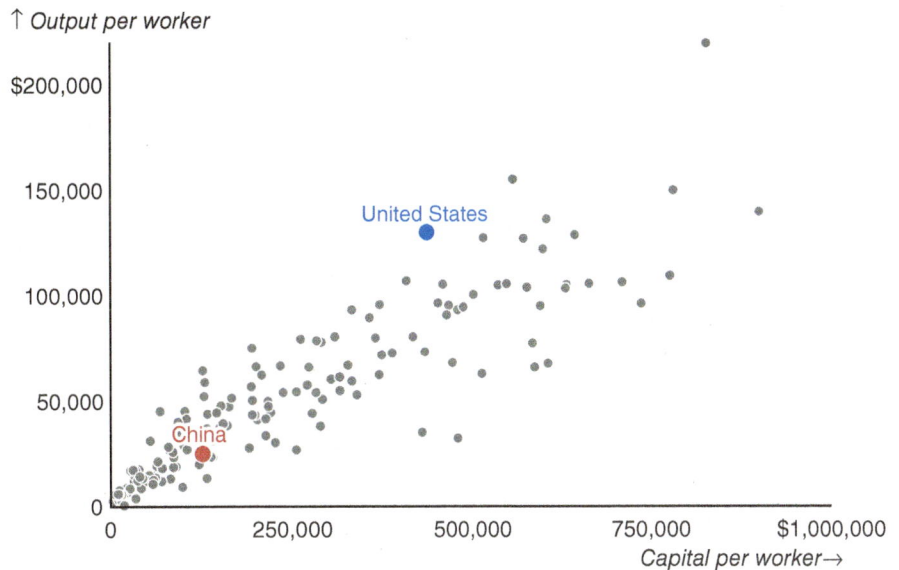

Data from: 2019 data from Penn World Tables 10.0.

Tools to Analyze Investments

Learning Objective *Master two tools for comparing sums of money at different points in time: compounding and discounting.*

Our task for the rest of this chapter is to build a framework that you can use to evaluate investment decisions. Remember, the key trade-off is typically between an up-front cost and future benefits. And so you're going to figure out how to value today's costs relative to future benefits. This requires us to develop two tools that you can use to compare costs and benefits that accrue at *different points in time*: compounding and discounting. You'll use these tools to analyze how value changes over time.

While we'll be focusing on business investments, you can use these tools any time you face a decision where at least some costs or benefits accrue in the future. That makes these tools very useful because a lot of life's big decisions are about asking whether it's worth incurring costs today in order to enjoy benefits in the future. As you learn these tools, think about applying them to questions like whether it's worth investing in your education, whether to buy a house, or even just whether to go to the gym. Indeed, right now you face a decision whether to incur the up-front cost of reading the rest of this chapter, so that you'll enjoy the benefit of making better investment decisions in the future.

Investment Tool 1: Compounding

Most investments—like starting a new company, buying a new home, or buying new equipment for your business—involve a big up-front cost that could tie your money up for years. Before you invest, the opportunity cost principle reminds you to consider the next best alternative use of your funds. Often that next best alternative will be putting your

compounding The accumulation of money over time, as you earn interest on both your principal and accrued interest.

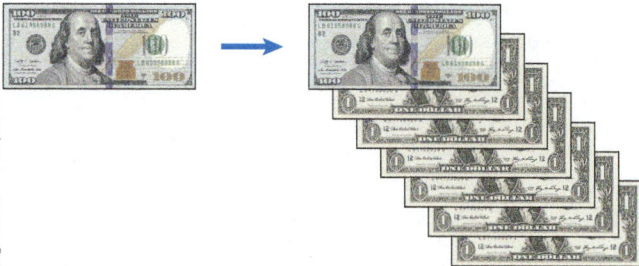

Interest transforms this into that.

money in the bank to earn interest. That's why forgone interest is an important opportunity cost of pursuing an investment project.

You can quantify this opportunity cost by asking: How much would your money grow if you put it in the bank and leave it (and the interest you earn) to accumulate over time? That's what **compounding** is all about.

Compounding helps you calculate how much money grows over time when you leave it to accumulate interest.

To see how money grows over time, let's start with a simple example: What happens when you put $100 in the bank? If the interest rate is 6%, then a year later you'll get your $100 back, plus $6 in interest.

More generally, for each dollar that you put in the bank today at an interest rate of r percent, a year later you will get your dollar back, plus interest of r cents per dollar (and so, for example, when the interest rate is 6%, r is 0.06):

$$\text{Future value in one year} = \underbrace{\text{Present value}}_{\text{You get your money back}} + \underbrace{r \times \text{Present value}}_{\text{plus } r\% \text{ interest}}$$

$$= \text{Present value} \times (1+r)$$

Each year you leave your money in the bank, it is multiplied by 1 + r.

What happens if you leave your money in the bank for more than a year and allow the interest to accumulate? Short answer: It will continue to grow, or compound. In the second year, you won't just get interest on your original deposit; you'll also get interest on the interest you earned last year. In the third year, you'll also get interest-on-interest-on-interest, and so on.

This is the magic of *compound interest:* You earn interest not only on your initial deposit but also on previously earned interest, so your wealth compounds. As we'll see, the numbers can really add up. How much? We'll need a formula to calculate how much your money will grow into by a specific future date, and we'll call this amount the **future value** of your money.

future value The amount that your money will grow into by a specific future date, as a result of accumulating interest.

The key to calculating the *future value* of a sum of money is to note that each year your total balance grows by r percent, the interest rate. This means that each year your balance is simply whatever it was the previous year, multiplied by $(1 + r)$. Figure 5 illustrates how your balance will grow:

Figure 5 | The Compounding Formula

Your money grows over time, earning interest and interest-on-interest and so on.

A Begin with an initial deposit of $P, called the **present value**.
B Each year your money will earn **interest** and grow to be $(1+r)$ times larger.
C After t years, your money has grown to be worth: **Future value = Present value** $\times (1+r)^t$.

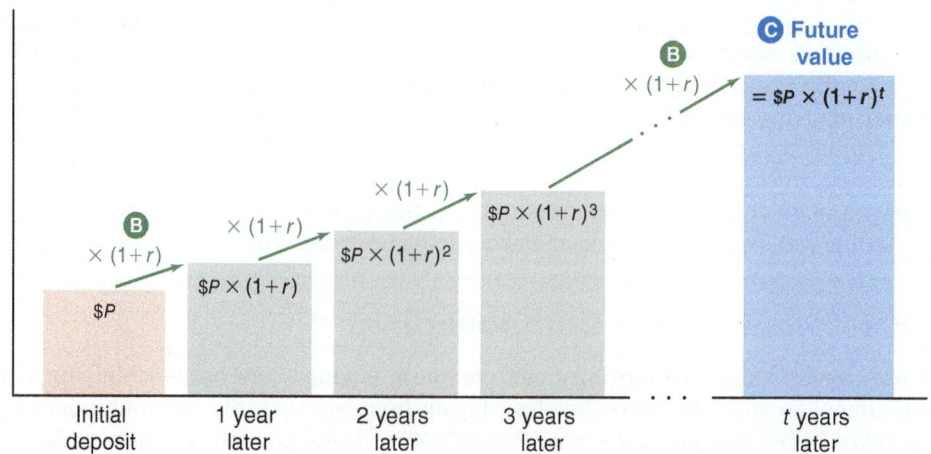

If you invest $P today, it becomes $P \times (1 + r)$ next year. The next year that balance also grows by $(1 + r)$, so after two years your balance is $P \times (1 + r) \times (1 + r)$, which can also be expressed as $P \times (1 + r)^2$. The third year it's multiplied by $(1 + r)$ again. Keep doing this for t years and the end result is the **compounding formula:**

$$\text{Future value in } t \text{ years} = \text{Present value} \times (1 + r)^t$$

compounding formula Future value in t years = Present value × $(1 + r)^t$

Use a spreadsheet to apply the compounding formula. It's even easier to figure out the future value of your money if you let a spreadsheet do the work for you. Let's see what would happen if your company invested $4 million for 30 years in a project where you expect the value of your investment to rise by 6% each year. (That is, you're effectively earning 6% interest.)

Figure 6 shows how to implement the compounding formula in a spreadsheet such as Microsoft Excel, Google Sheets, or Apple's Numbers. You need to punch the inputs into separate cells — the initial balance, which we'll call the present value since it's money you have right now; the annual interest rate; and the number of years it compounds or grows. In another cell, you can then apply the compounding formula:

$$\text{Future value in } t \text{ years} = \underbrace{\$4{,}000{,}000}_{\text{Present value}} \times \underbrace{(1 + 0.06)^{30}}_{(1 + r)^t} = \$22{,}973{,}965$$

The only real trick is to know that spreadsheets interpret the hat or caret character "^" — the one above the number 6 on your keyboard — as "to the power of," while they interpret the asterisk or star ("*" above number 8) as "multiplied by." Putting it all together, the spreadsheet shows you that over 30 years at a 6% annual interest rate, if you keep re-investing each year's gains, then $4 million grows to roughly $23 million. (To be precise, it's $22,973,965.) If that sounds like a lot, perhaps you now understand why it's called the magic of compound interest.

Figure 6 | Calculating Future Value

Punch in the present value, the annual interest rate, and the number of years, and the spreadsheet will calculate the future value your funds will grow into.

	A	B
1	**Inputs**	
2	Present (or initial) value	$4,000,000
3	Annual interest rate, r	6%
4	Years of compounding, t	30
5		
6	**Future value**	**$22,973,965**
7	= Present value × $(1 + r)^t$	$=B2*(1+B3)\text{\textasciicircum}B4$

EVERYDAY Economics

The extraordinary power of compound interest

Jonathan Holdeen was a rich New York lawyer and a bit of an oddball — a tightwad who cut his own hair, lived on a diet of prunes, milk, and shredded wheat, and cut the worn sleeves off his sweaters so he could continue to wear them as vests. He was also obsessed with compound interest. Using the compounding formula we just learned, he calculated that if he invested a penny at a 4% interest rate and allowed it to compound for a thousand years, it would grow into a thousand trillion dollars. Go ahead, check his math: $\$0.01 \times (1 + 0.04)^{1{,}000} \approx \$1{,}000{,}000{,}000{,}000{,}000$. Every penny saved, to Holdeen, was a thousand trillion dollars gained.

Holdeen wanted to use the power of compound interest to change the world. He put millions of dollars in charitable trusts and ordered that they were to compound for up to 1,000 years. He hoped that his trusts would grow into quadrillions or maybe quintillions of dollars — enough that he could abolish all taxes in Pennsylvania.

Instead, he set off a 50-year legal battle as lawyers debated whether his big idea was a good idea. The problem, according to one economist, was that the trust would grow so big that "everyone in the world would work for the Holdeens." The courts agreed that this was a bad idea, ruling that the trust had to donate each year's interest payments to charity. This ruling robbed the trust of the ability to earn interest that could compound, and so it simply stopped growing, which is why Pennsylvanians will have to keep paying taxes. ■

A thousand trillion dollars (in a thousand years).

United States Mint

Investment Tool 2: Discounting

While compounding helps you calculate how much the money you have today will grow into in the future as it accumulates interest, discounting is the flip side of the same idea: It's about figuring out how much future costs or benefits are worth today. Once again it's important because of the **opportunity cost principle**: Money that you're paid in the future rather than in the present comes with an opportunity cost — the forgone opportunity to gain from the power of compound interest. And so you have to assess: How much is money that you'll receive in the future really worth when valued relative to money in your hands today? That's what discounting is all about.

Discounting reflects the opportunity cost of benefits you receive in the future. You can evaluate the value of a future benefit in today's terms by asking: How much would you need to put in the bank today in order to grow into that sum in the future? You do this by reversing the compounding formula to convert money received in the future into the equivalent benefit that you receive in the present. The **present value** is the amount of money that you'd need to invest *today* in order to produce a specific benefit in the *future*. The process to calculate present value is called **discounting,** which means converting future values into their equivalent present values. Discounting is just the opposite of compounding — you're converting large future values into the smaller present values from which they could have grown.

To take a simple example, when the interest rate is 6%, the present value of receiving $106 in a year's time is $100, because you could get $106 next year just by putting $100 into the bank today and waiting. More generally, you can take the compounding formula — remember, it says Future value in t years = Present value $\times (1 + r)^t$ — and rearrange it to get the **discounting formula:**

$$\text{Present value} = \text{Future value in } t \text{ years} \div (1 + r)^t$$

The discounting formula shows how much money you'd need today to create a specific future value in t years' time.

present value The amount of money that you would need to invest today in order to produce a specific benefit in the future.

discounting Converting *future values* into their equivalent *present values.*

discounting formula Present value = Future value in t years $\div$ $(1 + r)^t$

Discounting converts future values into present values. Just as the compounding formula converts money you have in the present into its potential future values, the discounting formula converts potential future values into their equivalent present values.

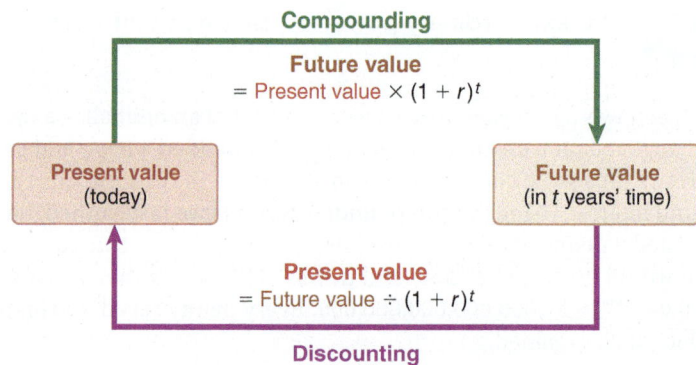

Let's apply this logic: Remember that we discovered that if your company invested $4 million for 30 years at 6% interest, then its balance will grow to be $22,973,965. We can turn that around and ask: What's the present value of receiving a payment of $22,973,965 in 30 years, if the interest rate is 6% per year? I bet you know the answer, but let's work it out using the discounting formula:

$$\text{Present value} = \underbrace{\$22,973,965}_{\text{Future value}} \div (1 + 0.06)^t = \$4,000,000$$

Just as $4 of $22,973,965 over 30 years if the interest rate is 6%, the present value of receiving $22,973,965 in 30 years' time is $4 million.

Use a spreadsheet to apply the discounting formula. Don't worry; no one expects you to do these calculations in your head! Figure 7 shows how to use a spreadsheet to work it out. This time, you enter the future value and let the spreadsheet calculate the present value by applying the *discounting formula*. (Note that spreadsheets use the forward slash "/" in place of "÷" as the symbol for division.)

This calculation suggests that you should value $23 million that your company receives in 30 years' time as much as you value receiving $4 million today. The logic of discounting is just the inverse of compounding — your company could use $4 million today to create $23 million in 30 years, simply by putting it in the bank and so that future sum is worth the equivalent of $4 million today.

Present values tell you how much you should pay for a future payoff. To see how present value calculations can be useful, let's return to Jonathan Holdeen, the oddball New York lawyer we met earlier. During the Great Depression, rich heirs and heiresses who fell on hard times found themselves in the awkward position of being poor today, but expecting a big inheritance in the future. Holdeen provided them a way out of this fix. He offered to buy up the right to their inheritance, usually at a steep discount. If they accepted, the heirs got Holdeen's cash today, and he got their inheritance when the rich relative died. Holdeen used discounting to figure out how much he'd be willing to pay for an inheritance in the future.

Figure 7 | Calculating Present Value

Punch in the future sum of money, the number of years until you receive it, and the annual interest rate, and the spreadsheet will calculate the present value, which is how much you need to invest today to get to that sum in the future.

	A	B
1	**Inputs**	
2	Future value	$22,973,965
3	Annual interest rate, r	6%
4	Years of compounding, t	30
5		
6	**Present value**	**$4,000,000**
7	= Future value ÷ $(1 + r)^t$	=B2/(1+B3)^B4

How much will you pay for her inheritance?

Do the Economics

A down-on-her-luck heiress stands to inherit $1 million from a rich aunt who's likely to die in 14 years. She offers to sell Jonathan Holdeen her inheritance rights. If you were in his shoes, what's the most you'd pay for this if the interest rate is 6%?

$$\text{Present value} = \$1{,}000{,}000 \div (1 + 0.06)^{14} = \$442{,}301$$

To see why Holdeen wouldn't want to pay more than this, realize that he could create $1 million in 14 years simply by putting $442,301 in the bank today and allowing it to compound for 14 years. ∎

Real versus Nominal Interest Rates

You can use the compounding and discounting formulas to figure out how much either the *nominal* or *real* value of your money changes through time. (Remember, nominal values refer to the number of dollars you have, while real values adjust for inflation so as to focus on your purchasing power.) The trick to figuring out how the nominal or real value of your money changes through time is picking the right interest rate:

- If you're evaluating the *nominal value* of your funds — that is, how many dollar bills you'll have in a few years' time — make sure that you plug the *nominal interest rate* into the compounding or discounting formula.

- To evaluate the *real value* of your funds — that is, your changing purchasing power, after adjusting for inflation — plug the *real interest rate* into the compounding or discounting formula.

Let's see how much this matters.

Do the Economics

Over the past century, money in the stock market grew at an average rate of 10.85% per year. If you had put $1,000 in the stock market in 1921, how much would it have compounded into by 2021?

$$\text{(Nominal) future value in 100 years} = \$1{,}000 \times (1 + 0.1085)^{100} = \$30 \text{ million!}$$

Your $1,000 would have grown over 30,000 times larger! But part of this reflects the influence of inflation, which averaged 3% per year. To evaluate what your change in purchasing power would have been, you must focus on the real interest rate. Recall that the real interest rate is (approximately) equal to the nominal interest rate (here, 10.85%) minus the inflation rate of 3% a year. Thus, funds in the stock market grew by 7.85% per year in real terms. That 7.85% represents how much more stuff you could buy each year as a result of your interest earnings.

Calculate the real growth rate of your $1,000:

$$\text{(Real) future value in 100 years} = \$1{,}000 \times (1 + 0.0785)^{100} = \$1.9 \text{ million!}$$

If you invested $1,000 in stocks in 1921, then 100 years later, it would have grown to...
• **$30 million in nominal terms**
• **$1.9 million in real (inflation-adjusted) terms**

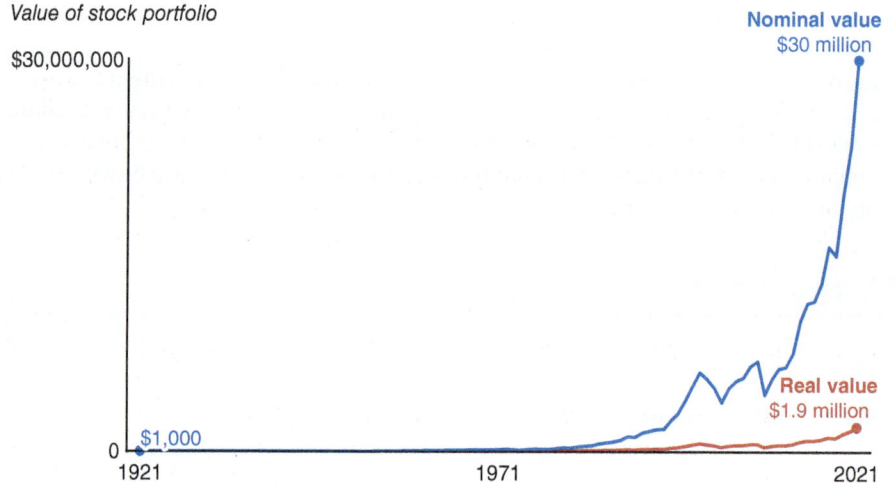

Value of stock portfolio

Data from: © SBBI Yearbook 2021.

That 3% inflation might seem small but it makes a big difference. While you'd have 30,000 times as many dollars, you wouldn't have been able to buy 30,000 times as much stuff. Instead, in real terms your purchasing power would have grown 405 times larger, meaning that you would have been able to buy 1,900 times as much stuff. While that's a lot smaller, it is still pretty awesome. The magic of compound interest is why financial advisors tell you to start saving early! ∎

14.3 Making Investment Decisions

Learning Objective *Evaluate whether an investment opportunity is worth pursuing.*

Now that you've got these tools in your analytic toolkit, it's time to put them to work. They'll be essential for our next task, which is to use them to evaluate investment opportunities.

How to Evaluate an Investment Opportunity: A Four-Step Recipe

There's no better way to illustrate this framework than to work through a real-world problem, so put yourself in the shoes of Valentina Garcia, an economics graduate now working as an energy analyst for a renewable energy company in Rhode Island. The company already operates eight wind turbines, which harness enough energy to power nearly 10,000 homes. Rapid improvements in turbine technology have made wind energy increasingly viable. The company's CEO is trying to decide whether to invest in one more turbine and has asked Valentina to crunch the numbers to see if this would be a worth-while investment.

Valentina's inner environmentalist is thrilled that wind is becoming a more main-stream energy source, but she also knows that her company can play a role in this trans-formation only if it makes good investment decisions. As a former economics student, Valentina is familiar with a simple four-step recipe for analyzing investment opportunities.

Step 1: Calculate the up-front cost. This is really just the cost part of the cost-benefit principle. Valentina makes some calls and learns that investing in a new tur-bine requires an up-front investment of $4 million.

Step 2: Predict future profits, taking account of depreciation. The bene-fits of investing in this new turbine (or any investment) are the future annual profits that it will generate. Engineers at Valentina's company have estimated the extra energy the new turbine will generate each year, and she has translated those gains into profit forecasts:

This year: Installing the turbine will take all year, so it will generate no profit.

First year profit: The turbine will generate $600,000 of new profits.

Profit in following years: As the turbine ages, it will become less productive due to *depreciation*. It will break down more often and spend more days out of service being repaired. The engineers report that, on average, a wind turbine will produce 4% less out-put each year than it did in the previous year. They're describing the **depreciation rate,** which is the proportion of an investment's remaining productive capacity you lose each year due to depreciation. We'll use the letter d to denote the depreciation rate.

Make sure that your future revenue and profit forecasts account for this depreciation. This is why Valentina forecasts that the profits this turbine generates will decline from $600,000 in the first year, to be 4% lower at $576,000 in the second year, and then another 4% lower at $552,960 in the third year. As you read down the first column of Figure 8, you'll see that in each sub-sequent year, she forecasts that the turbine will gener-ate 4% less profit than it did the previous year.

If there are other factors that might affect your future profits — such as changes in the price of your output, or of essential inputs — make sure your profit forecasts also account for these factors. This isn't rel-evant for Valentina, as she expects the price of wind energy and her variable inputs to keep up with infla-tion, and so depreciation is the only factor changing her real profits over time.

Step 3: Calculate the present value of all benefits and costs. The key challenge in evalu-ating investment projects is that the costs are usually incurred today, while the benefits will accrue in the future. Current and future dollars are not the same, and so we need to convert them both into their cur-rent equivalent so that we can compare them.

Carol Heesen/Alamy

Turbines depreciate.

depreciation rate The proportion of an investment's remaining productive capacity you lose each year due to depreciation.

Figure 8 | **Calculating the Present Value of the Stream of Future Profits**

Using a depreciation rate of d = 4% and interest rate of r = 6%

Year	Future profit = Last year's profit × (1 − d)		Present value of future profit = Future profit ÷ (1 + r)^t	
			Discounting	
0		$0		$0
1	**Depreciation**	$600,000	÷ (1 + r)^1	$566,038
2	× (1 − d)	$576,000	÷ (1 + r)^2	$512,638
3	× (1 − d)	$552,960	÷ (1 + r)^3	$464,276
4	× (1 − d)	$530,842	÷ (1 + r)^4	$420,476
...		...		...

Converting the up-front cost of the turbine into present value terms is straightforward because all of this spending occurs today (in the *present*)! As such, the present value of a $4 million up-front cost is simply $4 million.

The benefit side requires a bit more work because the turbine will generate a long-lasting flow of *future* profits. Using the discounting formula you learned earlier, Valentina calculates the *present value* of each year's profits. It's important that the interest rate you use to discount future profits reflects the next best alternative use of your funds, and so Valentina applies a 6% interest rate because that's the rate of return her company could earn on other investments. The final column of Figure 8 shows the results. It shows that the turbine will generate no profit while it's being built. In the first year it generates $600,000 of profit, but because this comes in a year's time, Valentina needs to discount it, dividing $600,000 by $(1 + 0.06)$ to calculate the present value of $566,038. As the discounting formula dictates, the $576,000 profit forecast for two years' time is discounted by dividing it by $(1 + 0.06)^2$, yielding a present value of $512,638, and so on. As you look down the final column, you can see that we need to add up the present value of each year's profit. Add it all up, and you get $566,038 + $512,638 + $464,276 + . . . and so on. A good wind turbine can last a long time, so Valentina's actual spreadsheet goes on for dozens more rows, showing the present value of each year's profit over many future years. When Valentina adds the present value of all of these future years of profits, she arrives at a total of $6 million over several decades. (You can punch the numbers into a really long spreadsheet to check this for yourself.)

A step 3 shortcut: Use the valuation formula to calculate the present value of a stream of future profits. It might look like calculating the present value of a stream of future profits takes a lot of spreadsheet work. But there's a shortcut that makes it a lot easier. The **valuation formula** says that the *present value* of a stream of payments that starts with *next year's profit* and subsequent payments decline or *depreciate* each year by d percent is:

valuation formula Present value of an ongoing stream of payments
$$= \frac{\text{Next year's profit}}{r + d}$$

$$\text{Present value of a stream of payments} = \frac{\text{Next year's profit}}{r + d}$$

It's called the *valuation formula* because it tells you how much you would value this future stream of profits in today's dollars. (This bit is in parentheses, so you can skip it. If you want some intuition for where this formula comes from, notice in the last column of Figure 8 that the present value of each year's profit is $(1 - d)/(1 + r)$ times as large as the previous year, which makes it a *geometric series*. The valuation formula follows from evaluating the infinite sum of this geometric series.) You don't need to master the intricate math of this formula to use it, but you do need to understand when to use it. Apply the valuation formula when you're evaluating the present value of a long-lasting stream of future payments that start next year and then decline at a constant proportional rate over time.

Do the Economics

Let's apply the valuation formula to Valentina's investment decision. Her turbine will generate $600,000 profit in its first year, the real interest rate is 6%, the depreciation rate is 4%, and it will keep generating profits for many decades:

$$\text{Present value of a stream of payments} = \frac{\text{Next year's profit}}{r + d} = \frac{\$600,000}{0.06 + 0.04} = \$6 \text{ million}$$

This shortcut worked perfectly, producing exactly the same answer as when we calculated each year's profits and calculated their present values. ∎

Step 4: Invest if the present value of benefits exceeds the present value of costs. Because we have now converted both the costs and benefits into present value terms, you can directly compare them. It's time to apply the **cost-benefit principle**: The total benefits of purchasing the turbine — many years of future profit that add up to a

Four steps to evaluate an investment opportunity:
1. Calculate the up-front cost.
2. Predict future profits, taking account of depreciation.
3. Calculate the present value of all benefits and costs (and don't forget the valuation formula).
4. Invest if the present value of benefits exceeds the present value of costs.

present value of $6 million — exceed the up-front cost of $4 million. As such, this looks like an extremely profitable investment, so Valentina advises her company's CEO to purchase that extra wind turbine. It's a smart decision that will add $2 million to her company's value.

The Rational Rule for Investors

Let's blow past this turbine example and look for the broader lessons from our analysis. That lesson is that you should *invest in a new project if the present value of the benefits exceeds the present value of the costs*. Such an investment will be profitable, because the benefits exceed the costs. More than that, our analysis has taken account of the opportunity cost of your funds, by discounting future profits using an interest rate that reflects the next best alternative use of your funds. And so we can conclude that this project will not only boost your profits, but also that it will boost your profits by more than investing your funds in your next best alternative.

You've now uncovered a powerful rule that you can apply to your company's investment decisions:

The **Rational Rule for Investors:** *Pursue an investment opportunity if the present value of future profits exceeds the up-front cost, C. This means you should invest when:*

$$\underbrace{\frac{\text{Next year's profit}}{r+d}}_{\substack{\text{Present value} \\ \text{of future profits}}} \geq \underbrace{C}_{\substack{\text{Up-front} \\ \text{cost}}}$$

Follow this rule, and every investment will boost your long-run profits. The Rational Rule for Investors takes the big question facing managers about how much to invest, and applies the marginal principle, focusing on the simpler question of whether you should invest in one more turbine. It relies on the cost-benefit principle to suggest that yes, you should invest if the benefits — which are the extra future profits you'll receive — exceed the up-front cost. And it embeds the opportunity cost principle, discounting future profits so as to account for what you would have to give up to get them.

The Rational Rule for Investors provides good advice because it will lead you to invest only when it will boost your long-run profitability. Let's apply it to the most important investment decision you may ever make.

Rational Rule for Investors
Pursue an investment opportunity if the present value of future profits is greater than (or perhaps equal to) the up-front cost.

EVERYDAY Economics   **Your decision to invest in education**

Your college degree is a lot like a wind turbine: It involves a big up-front cost (which you're incurring now), and it will yield a stream of benefits that will accrue over the rest of your life. (And like a turbine, there may be a lot of hot air involved.) And so, you can evaluate the benefits of investing in your intellectual machinery using the same ideas that managers use to evaluate investments in any other kind of machinery.

One big benefit of earning a degree that you'll earn a higher salary. Let's take a stab at valuing these higher earnings using the *valuation formula*. We'll need three inputs: the extra income you'll earn when you have your degree, the depreciation rate of your degree, and the real interest rate you could earn investing in your next best alternative.

Measure the extra income from earning a degree: In 2020, the average earnings of folks with a bachelor's degree (but no graduate degree) was around $76,000, compared with earnings of $43,000 for the average high school graduate. The difference is $33,000 per year. (An associate's degree boosts your earnings by a bit less than half this amount.)

The real interest rate: We'll plug in a value for the real interest rate of 2%, which is roughly the rate at which college graduates can borrow and lend. (You can experiment with other values.)

sframephoto/iStock/Getty Images

An incredibly important investment.

Measuring the depreciation rate: College graduates continue to outearn high school grad-uates throughout their lives, suggesting that whatever you learn in college sticks with you throughout your career. But your degree still depreciates, because as you age you're less likely to work. If the average career lasts for 40 years, then it follows that we can think of the depreciation rate as being around $2\frac{1}{2}\%$ per year.

Put it all together, and we get:

$$\text{Present value of a college education} = \frac{\text{Next year's "profit"}}{r+d}$$

$$= \frac{\$33,000}{0.02+0.025} = \$733,000$$

Let that sink in. A four-year college degree is so valuable that it's worth roughly three-quarters of a million dollars in present value. (And it follows that an associate's degree that provides a bit less than half this boost is worth several hundred thousand dollars.) When the benefits of earning a degree are this high, investing in your college education is likely to be a very profitable investment.

Researchers have estimated the return on your investment in your degree, crunching the numbers for students from nearly every college in the United States. Search for your college at https://cew.georgetown.edu/cew-reports/collegeroi/ to find out how students at your school typically fare. I bet you find the numbers for your school surprise you.

Given how profitable investing in your education is, I urge you to keep investing by reading the rest of this chapter about investment! ∎

An Alternative Perspective: The User Cost of Capital

Let's return to analyzing business investments. So far, we've analyzed Valentina's investment decision as if she's deciding whether to buy a wind turbine that her company will keep for-ever (or at least until it breaks down). That required assessing the full set of costs and bene-fits that accrue over the turbine's entire lifetime. You can gain an alternative perspective on the Rational Rule for Investors by pushing the marginal principle even further. Instead of asking whether to buy a machine you'll keep for many decades, you might ask: Should I buy one more machine *for one more year?* That is, should you buy a machine even if you plan on selling it in a year's time? Alternatively phrased, should you *rent* a machine for a year?

The cost-benefit principle says your answer should be yes, if the marginal benefits exceed the marginal costs. And so this alternative perspective focuses on the marginal benefit and marginal cost of using that extra machine *for one more year.* (And at the end of that year, you can evaluate what to do the following year.)

The marginal benefit is fairly straightforward: That extra machine will generate extra output and hence profit, and we'll describe this extra profit you'll earn next year as being *next year's profit.*

The user cost of capital is forgone interest plus depreciation. What is the marginal cost of buying one more wind turbine at the start of the year, and then selling it at the end? There are two costs to consider:

Depreciation: The turbine will be worth less at the end of the year because of depreci-ation. If the depreciation rate is 4%, then a $4 million turbine will sell for 4% × $4 million = $160,000 less at the end of the year because it's 4% less productive. More generally, when you buy capital equipment and sell it a year later, you can expect to lose an amount equal to the depreciation rate times the cost of the investment: $d \times C$.

Forgone interest: The opportunity cost principle reminds you that there's another cost to consider, because you're tying up your funds for a year. The opportunity cost for Valentina of investing $4 million in the wind turbine for a year is that her company could earn a 6% return on those funds, which means that she's forgoing 6% × $4 million = $240,000 in interest. More generally, this opportunity cost is equal to the forgone rate of return times the cost of the machine: $r \times C$.

Putting these two pieces together yields the **user cost of capital,** which is the extra cost associated with using one more machine next year. It's called the *user cost* because it's what you're effectively paying to "use" the machine for a year. The user cost of employing one more machine for a year is equal to the depreciation cost ($d \times C$) plus the forgone interest ($r \times C$), which adds up to:

$$\text{User cost of capital} = (r + d) \times C$$

user cost of capital The extra cost associated with using one more machine next year $= (r + d) \times C$

The user cost is also sometimes called the *rental cost* because it's the amount that a business would be willing to pay to *rent* a machine for a year.

Do the Economics

Valentina's engineers tell her that if she spends $4 million buying a new wind turbine to use next year, at the end of the year it will be worth 4% less. The real interest rate is 6% per year. Calculate the user cost of owning this turbine for one year.

$$\text{User cost} = \underbrace{(0.06 + 0.04)}_{(r+d)} \times \underbrace{\$4,000,000}_{C} = \$400,000 \;\blacksquare$$

EVERYDAY Economics   **The true cost of car ownership**

Try asking your friends what they think the annual cost of car ownership is. Chances are they'll focus on out-of-pocket costs, like gas, insurance, repairs, and registration.

But this leaves out the most important expense: The user cost of capital. Cars depreciate rapidly: If you buy a new car, you'll lose 20% almost right away, and cars typically lose around 15% of their remaining value each year after that. So if you buy a used car worth about $10,000, you can figure it will be worth only $8,500 a year from now. And you won't earn any interest on the money tied up in that car, so if the real interest rate is 3%, you'll forgo $300 in interest.

Add it up, and the user cost of capital — that is, the true cost of driving a used car next year — is $(r + d) \times C = (0.03 + 0.15) \times \$10,000 = \$1,800$. While this isn't an out-of-pocket cost, it's a real cost nonetheless because if you didn't own the car, you would be $1,800 wealthier at the end of the year. ∎

Depreciation is costly.

Compare the user cost of capital with next year's additional profit. The user cost of capital represents the marginal cost of adding one more machine for a year. The cost-benefit principle tells you to compare it to the corresponding marginal benefit of adding that extra machine, which is the extra profit you'll earn next year. Comparing these suggests that you should invest in an additional machine for next year if:

$$\underbrace{\text{Next year's profit}}_{\text{Marginal benefit}} \geq \underbrace{(r + d) \times C}_{\text{Marginal cost}}$$

Let's apply this logic to Valentina's company. The marginal benefit of investing in a turbine for a year is the extra profit it will generate next year, which you may recall is $600,000. This marginal benefit exceeds the user cost of capital we just calculated to be $400,000, so this alternative perspective also concludes that she should invest in buying the turbine.

Invest if next year's profit from adding a machine exceeds the user cost of capital.

Whether you're considering buying or renting capital, you get the same Rational Rule for Investors. Take another look at the equation above, and rearrange it by dividing both sides by $(r + d)$, and you'll see that we've rediscovered the formula for the Rational Rule for Investors we encountered a few pages back.

Buy: *Should you invest in one more machine (to keep)?*

Invest if:

Benefits > Costs
(in present value terms)

Present value of future profits > Up-front cost of buying a machine

$$\frac{\text{Next year's profit}}{r + d} > c$$

Rent: *Should you invest in a machine for one year?*

Invest if:

Benefits > Costs

Next year's profit > User cost of capital

Extra profit you'll earn in the next year > $C \times (r + d)$

$$\frac{\text{Next year's profit}}{r + d} > c$$

Both approaches yield the same
Rational Rule for Investors

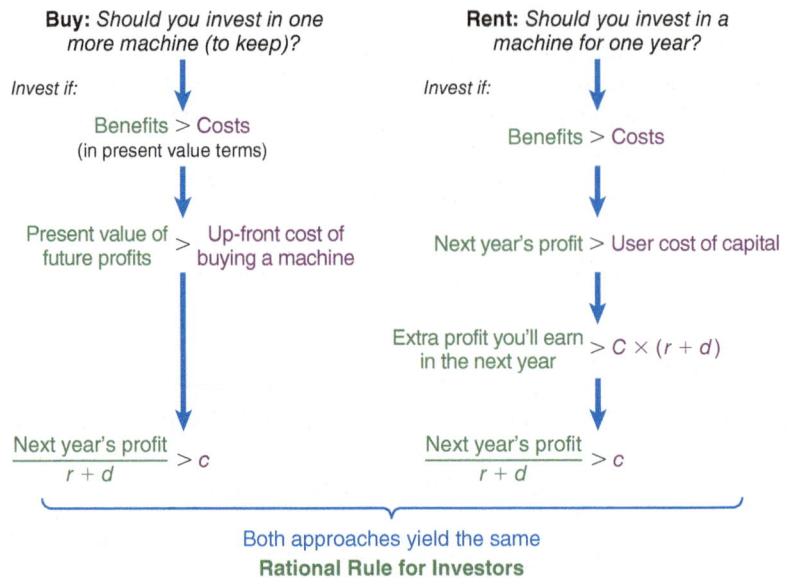

This equivalence is useful because it means that you can apply whichever approach you find most intuitive for the investment opportunity you're evaluating. For some investments you'll find it easier to evaluate the present value of future profits, while in others you'll find it simpler to compare the user cost of capital with next year's profit.

14.4 The Macroeconomics of Investment

Learning Objective *Assess how macroeconomic conditions drive investment.*

So far we've taken a largely *microeconomic* approach, analyzing when an individual business will make an individual investment. This has been quite intentional, because the *macroeconomics* of investment is built upon this microeconomic foundation. After all, total investment in the economy is simply the sum of all the individual investments that businesses make.

You might find it helpful to think of there being a list of millions of potential investment projects out there — from new turbines to factories, machines, software, and even houses — each with its own costs and benefits. In each case, executives who assess whether to proceed with the project will follow a process similar to Valentina, following the Rational Rule for Investors. And so the number of projects that proceed depend on how many will meet the test that

$$\text{Next year's profit} / (r + d) > C$$

Importantly, this investment rule focuses our attention on the key macroeconomic variables that determine investment. It says that investment will depend on expectations about future profits, the real interest rate (r), the depreciation rate (d), and the real cost of capital (C). While each of these factors are important to the macroeconomics of investment, we're going to start with the real interest rate because (as we'll soon see), it's central to both investment and saving.

The Real Interest Rate and Investment

The real interest rate plays a central role in investment decisions because of the opportunity cost principle. When managers evaluate whether to invest in new equipment, their next best alternative is often to leave their money in the bank to earn interest.

The real interest rate determines if this investment project is worthwhile.

EThamPhoto/Alamy

The higher the interest rate, the greater is this opportunity cost, and hence the less likely it is that an investment project will pass a cost-benefit test. The Rational Rule for Investors accounts for this opportunity cost by directing you to focus on present values that account for the forgone opportunity to earn bank interest. (This opportunity cost is also the reason that a higher real interest rate leads to a higher user cost of capital.)

It follows that higher real interest rates lead managers to invest less in buying new capital. The following example shows this force in action.

Do the Economics

Let's explore how the real interest rate shapes Valentina's decision. She asks you whether she should still invest in buying a $4 million turbine that's expected to generate $600,000 in profit next year — depreciating at 4% after that — if the real interest rate rises to 8%. What's your advice?

$$\text{Present value of future profits} = \frac{\$600,000}{0.08 + 0.04} = \$5 \text{ million}$$

The present value of future profits ($5 million) still exceeds the up-front costs ($4 million), so yes, she should still invest in the turbine.

Next, she asks: Should she still invest if the real interest rate rises to 12%?

$$\text{Present value of future profits} = \frac{\$600,000}{0.12 + 0.04} = \$3.75 \text{ million}$$

Now the present value of future profits ($3.75 million) is less than the present value of the costs ($4 million), so no, she should not invest. ∎

Investment declines as the real interest rate rises. As Valentina's example illustrates, whether or not an investment project will go forward depends critically on the real interest rate. More generally, the higher the real interest rate, the lower the present value of future profits, and hence, executives applying the Rational Rule for Investors will judge fewer investments to be worthwhile.

In turn, this means that high real interest rates lead to lower levels of investment across the whole economy. Or, to say it the other way, lower real interest rates lead to higher levels of investment. The **investment line** shown in Figure 9 illustrates how the quantity of investment rises as the real interest rate falls.

investment line The line that shows how lower real interest rates lead to higher levels of investment.

Factors That Shift the Investment Line

While the real interest rate is a key determinant of investment, it's not the only factor. The Rational Rule for Investors highlights that a favorable change in business conditions will lead to an increase in investment if it: increases expectations of future profits; decreases the price of capital goods (like machines); or reduces the depreciation rate. Such a change will shift the investment line to the right, as seen in Figure 10. Conversely, an unfavorable change that leads expected future profits to fall, the up-front cost of investing to rise, or depreciation to rise, will cause the investment line to shift to the left, also seen in Figure 10. Let's explore some of the key factors that can cause the investment line to shift.

Figure 9 | The Investment Line

The real interest rate determines investment.

Ⓐ A **higher real interest rate** leads to **low investment**.
Ⓑ A **lower real interest rate** leads to **high investment**.

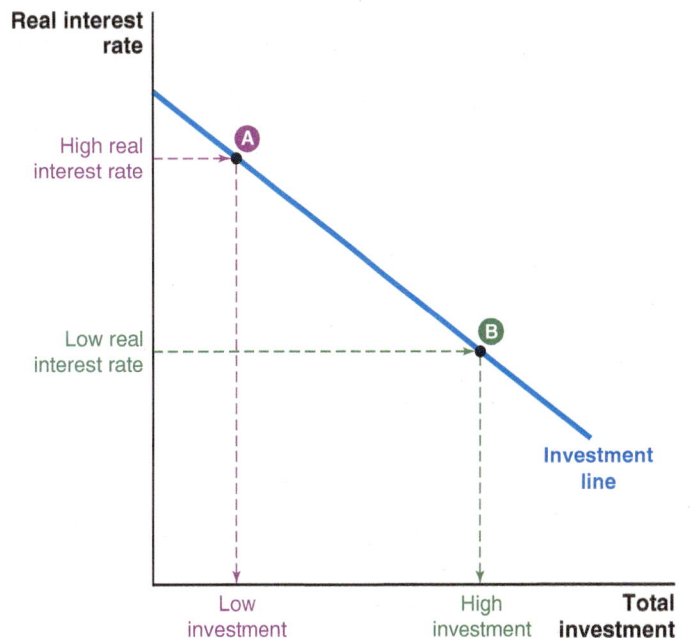

Figure 10 | Other Factors Shift the Investment Line

Changes in business conditions (other than the real interest rate) that change the profitability of investment will cause the investment line to shift.

A Any change in business conditions that makes investment more profitable will cause an **increase in investment,** which will **shift the investment line to the right.**

B Any change in business conditions that makes investment less profitable will cause a **decrease in investment,** which will **shift the investment line to the left.**

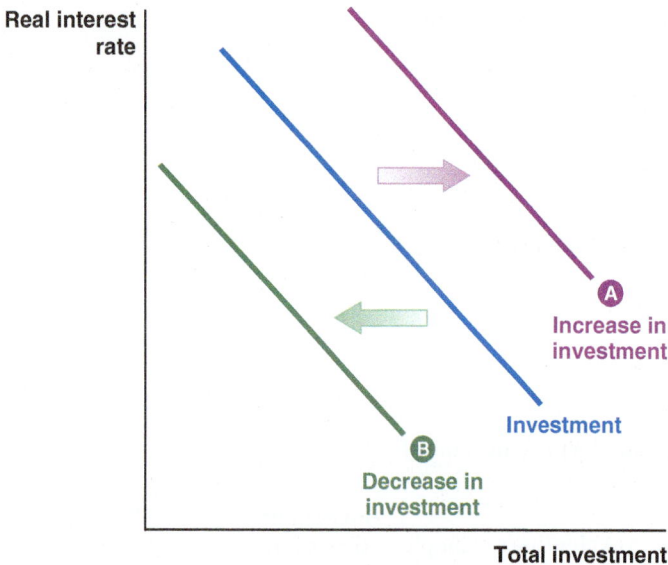

Investment shifter 1: Technological advances. Technological advances that make capital equipment more productive will boost the profits that you'll generate from buying that equipment, providing an incentive to invest more. For example, advances in wind engineering have increased the amount of electricity that an individual wind turbine generates which translates directly into larger profits. The prospect of earning larger profits makes investing in more turbines more attractive at any given interest rate. That's why technological advances shift the investment line to the right.

The development of electronic turbine monitoring technology is also expected to prevent damage to turbines due to high winds. By reducing the depreciation rate, this technology will boost future output and hence profits, thus making more investment projects profitable. Thus, advances that reduce the depreciation rate also shift the investment line to the right.

Investment shifter 2: Expectations. Investment is motivated by *expectations* about the reward of future profits. As a result, optimism and pessimism play an important role. If managers are optimistic about future economic conditions, they'll forecast that new investments are likely to yield robust profits. These optimistic expectations will lead them to invest more at a given real interest rate, shifting the investment line to the right. By contrast, pessimism about future economic conditions will lead managers to revise downward their profit forecasts. These pessimistic expectations will lead them to conclude that fewer investment projects will be profitable, shifting the investment line to the left.

The key insight is that investment isn't driven by last year's profits, but rather *expectations* about future profits. As such, the "animal spirits" of managers — their expectations, which can be colored by emotion, instinct, and behavior — drive investment to rise or fall. Indeed, Figure 11 shows that, in practice, greater optimism about future earnings translates into more investment.

Figure 11 | Expectations of Higher Earnings Lead to Increased Investment

Average expectations among chief financial officers

Data from: CFO Survey.

Investment shifter 3: Corporate taxes. The higher the corporate tax rate, the smaller the share of future profits that your company gets to keep. As such, higher corporate tax rates effectively reduce the profit that you'll get (or get to keep) from your investment. This leads to less investment at any given interest rate, shifting the investment line to the left.

On the flip side, the wind industry has benefited from tax breaks that apply specifically to wind farms. These tax breaks increase the revenue and hence profit that renewable energy companies earn from each turbine, and they've made investing in turbines in some lower-wind areas profitable. As such, lower taxes can shift the investment line to the right.

Investment shifter 4: Lending standards and cash reserves. The difficulty investment poses is that you need to pay for your new machines up front, but you'll only get the offsetting benefits in the future. This creates a financing problem: How will you finance — that is, get the up-front cash to pay for — your new investments?

For many companies, the answer is that they'll borrow the funds from a bank. But even if you're willing to pay the prevailing interest rate, it can be hard to get financing for risky projects. The problem is that banks sometimes don't want to lend for very risky projects because it's difficult for them to assess the true risk and therefore set appropriately high interest rates. When you can't get financing, you'll be able to invest only if you can pay the up-front cost out of your cash reserves. That's why investment tends to be higher — shifting the investment line to the right — when companies face less restrictive lending standards, or when they have enough cash reserves that they don't need to rely on banks.

> Four investment shifters:
> 1. Technological advances
> 2. Expectations
> 3. Corporate taxes
> 4. Lending standards and cash reserves

14.5 The Market for Loanable Funds

Learning Objective *Forecast the long-run real interest rate.*

Our analysis so far has taken the real interest rate as given. That's about to change, as we dig into the factors that shape interest rates, and hence investment.

To figure out what determines the real interest rate, we need to distinguish between two time horizons because they point to two distinct sets of forces. In the *short run,* the interest rate rises and falls from month to month as the Federal Reserve tweaks interest rates in an effort to dampen the economy's short-run ups and downs. (We'll learn more about how and why the Fed raises and lowers interest rates in Chapter 22 on monetary policy.) But the Fed's adjustments only nudge the interest rate a bit above or below its long-run level. In the *long run* — which is our focus here — the real interest rate evolves slowly over many years in response to the balance of saving and investment.

Supply and Demand of Loanable Funds

To assess the long-run drivers of the real interest rate, we'll analyze the **market for loanable funds,** which is the market for the *funds* used to buy, rent, or build capital. It brings together savers who want to lend their funds and investors who want to borrow those funds. This market determines the long-run real interest rate, and therefore the quantity of investment.

market for loanable funds The market for the funds used to buy, rent, or build capital.

Savers supply funds, and investors demand them. In this market, *savers are the suppliers,* supplying their funds to businesses who want to borrow them. *Investors are the demanders,* demanding funds to help fund their investments in new capital like wind turbines. The financial sector — banks, the bond market, and the stock market — is the *marketplace* where suppliers of funding (savers) meet demanders (investors).

The *price* of a loan is the real interest rate. It represents the real resources that a borrower must pay a lender to borrow $100 for a year. The long-run interest rate is determined by the forces of supply and demand for loanable funds, as shown in Figure 12.

The *supply curve* is upward-sloping because a higher real interest rate raises the benefits of saving (as discussed in Chapter 13), leading a larger quantity of loanable funds to be supplied. The *demand curve* is downward-sloping, because a higher real interest rate makes fewer investment projects profitable (as we established earlier in this chapter), leading a smaller quantity of loanable funds to be demanded.

The real interest rate is determined by supply and demand. *Equilibrium* in the market for loanable funds occurs at the point where the supply and demand curves cross, and it determines the equilibrium real interest rate.

Figure 12 | The Market for Loanable Funds

The long-run real interest rate is determined by supply and demand.

Ⓐ The **price** in the market for loanable funds is the long-term real interest rate.

Ⓑ The **supply** of loanable funds is upward-sloping because higher real interest rates lead to more saving.

Ⓒ The **demand** of loanable funds is downward-sloping because higher real interest rates lead to less investment.

Ⓓ **Equilibrium** occurs where supply and demand curves cross.

Ⓔ The **neutral real interest rate** is the equilibrium real interest rate when the economy operates at potential output.

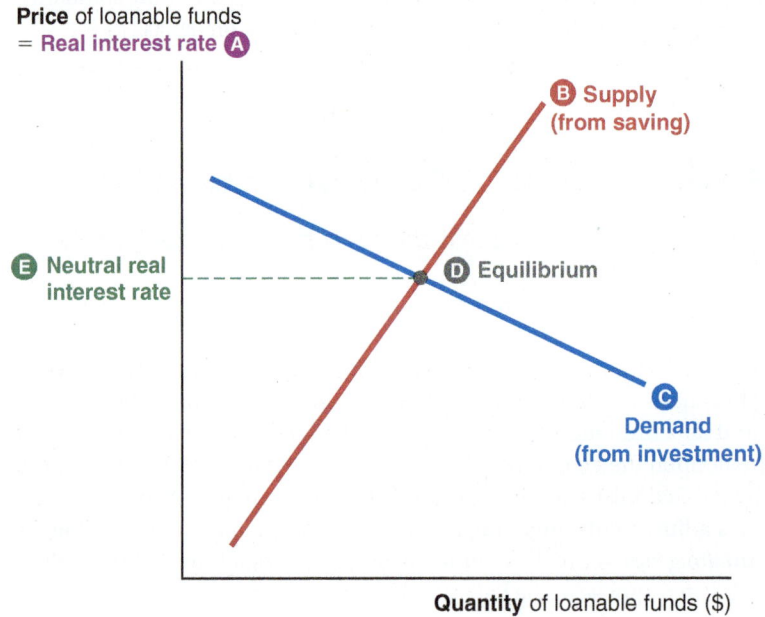

Price of loanable funds
= **Real interest rate** Ⓐ

Ⓑ **Supply (from saving)**

Ⓔ **Neutral real interest rate**

Ⓓ **Equilibrium**

Ⓒ **Demand (from investment)**

Quantity of loanable funds ($)

neutral real interest rate The interest rate that operates when the economy is in neutral—producing neither above nor below its potential.

Figure 13 | Shifts in the Supply of Loanable Funds

Ⓐ A **decrease in saving** shifts the supply of loanable funds to the left, leading to a **higher real interest rate**.

Ⓑ An **increase in saving** shifts the supply of loanable funds to the right, leading to a **lower real interest rate**.

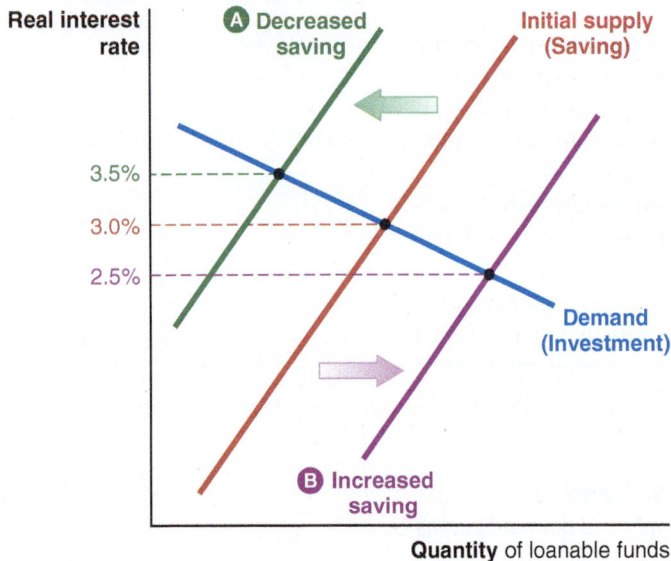

Real interest rate

Ⓐ **Decreased saving**

Initial supply (Saving)

3.5%

3.0%

2.5%

Demand (Investment)

Ⓑ **Increased saving**

Quantity of loanable funds

In order to abstract from short-run business-cycle influences, we're focusing on the supply and demand curves that apply when the economy is operating at its long-run potential. The interest rate that applies when the economy is at its long-run potential is called the **neutral real interest rate.** It's neutral because the economy is operating neither above nor below its potential — in other words, the economy is in neutral.

Our next step is to forecast how changing economic conditions change the neutral real interest rate. We'll start by analyzing factors that might shift saving and the supply of loanable funds, and then we'll turn to factors that shift investment and the demand for loanable funds.

Shifts in the Supply of Loanable Funds

A shift in saving at any given real interest rate will shift the supply of loanable funds causing the neutral real interest rate to change.

Figure 13 illustrates that a decrease in saving, which shifts the supply curve to the left (shown in green), will lead to a higher real interest rate. It also illustrates (in purple) the opposite case, in which an increase in saving shifts the supply curve to the right, which leads to a lower real interest rate.

The supply of loanable funds will shift only if there's a change in savings by one or more of the three types of economic actors who supply loanable funds: private savers, the government, and foreigners.

Supply shifter 1: Changes in personal saving by private savers. *Personal saving* refers to saving by households of whatever income they don't spend or pay as taxes. Just as putting money in the bank counts as saving, so does paying down your debt, because it frees up loanable funds for others to use. Any factor that shifts people's willingness to save will shift the supply of loanable funds.

For instance, during the coronavirus pandemic, people stayed home and cut back their spending, while the government sent out checks to support their income. The result was an increase in saving, which shifted the supply of loanable funds to the right. As vaccination rates rose, people became more comfortable venturing outside to spend money, and the resulting decrease in saving led the supply of loanable funds to shift back to the left.

Supply shifter 2: Government saving shifts due to changing budget surpluses and deficits. *Government saving* refers to saving by the government. When the government's revenues exceed its outlays, the government's budget is in surplus, and so it accumulates extra funds. It typically uses these funds to repay government debt, which frees up those funds for others to borrow, effectively increasing the supply of loanable funds available to fund investment. By contrast, a budget deficit means that the government is *dissaving* — that is, spending more than it takes in — thereby reducing the supply of loanable funds available to businesses, because the government must borrow to fund its deficit.

An increase in the budget deficit will make government saving even more negative, which shifts the supply of loanable funds to the left. As Figure 13 illustrates, a decrease in saving will lead to a new equilibrium involving both a higher real interest rate and lower investment. The decline in private investment due to a larger budget deficit is called **crowding out.** It arises because government borrowing leads to higher real interest rates, which effectively crowds out some of the firms looking for loans to fund their own investments.

crowding out The decline in private spending—and particularly investment—that follows from a rise in government borrowing.

Conversely, shifting from a budget deficit to a surplus will increase government saving, which shifts the supply of loanable funds to the right. The new equilibrium has a lower real interest rate, which makes more investment projects viable. This boost to private investment as a result of government saving is sometimes called *crowding in*. This idea motivated President Bill Clinton's macroeconomic strategy in the 1990s, as he pushed the federal budget from a large deficit into a modest surplus. As our analysis would predict, this led to a decline in long-run real interest rates, which spurred more private investment.

Supply shifter 3: Foreign saving shifts due to global shocks. The funding that comes from foreigners lending money to Americans is called *foreign saving*, or *net financial inflows*. These international financial flows are an important channel through which the global economy affects the U.S. economy. For example, in the early 2000s, an increase in saving in the rapidly growing Asian countries and the oil-producing Middle East caused a global glut of saving. Much of this increased saving was lent to American companies, so this rise in foreign saving shifted the supply of loanable funds to the right. As Figure 13 suggests, this pushed down the neutral real interest rate.

Three factors that shift the supply of loanable funds:
1. Changes in personal saving rates
2. The budget surplus (or deficit) shifts government saving
3. Global shocks shift foreign saving

Shifts in the Demand for Loanable Funds

The demand for loanable funds reflects businesses borrowing to fund their investments. This means that any factor that shifts the investment line — which describes how much

Figure 14 | Shifts in the Demand for Loanable Funds

Ⓐ An **increase in investment** shifts the demand for loanable funds to the right, leading to a **higher real interest rate**.

Ⓑ A **decrease in investment** shifts the demand for loanable funds to the left, leading to a **lower real interest rate**.

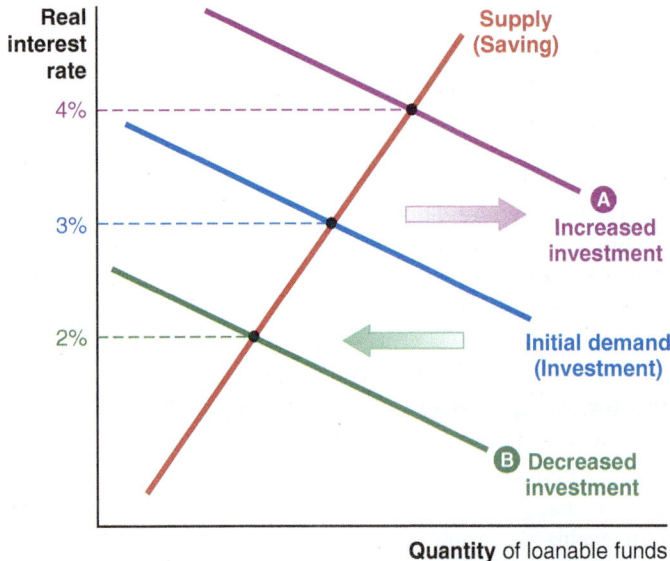

investment businesses will undertake at each real interest rate — will also shift the demand for loanable funds. And so based upon our earlier analysis, it follows that the demand for loanable funds will increase, shifting to the right in response to:

- *Technological advances* that make capital equipment more productive
- *Expectations* of stronger future profits
- *Corporate tax* cuts that mean businesses keep more of their profits
- *Easier lending standards* that allow more businesses to qualify for a loan. Alternatively, if businesses have larger *cash reserves* they won't need a loan to fund their investments.

Figure 14 illustrates (in purple) that an increase in investment will shift the demand for loanable funds to the right, leading to a higher real interest rate. If any of these factors shift in the opposite direction, it will lead to a decrease in investment, which shifts the demand for loanable funds to the left (shown in green), leading to a lower real interest rate.

Interpreting the DATA Secular stagnation and the case of the declining real interest rate

Figure 15 | The Neutral Real Interest Rate Has Declined Over Recent Decades

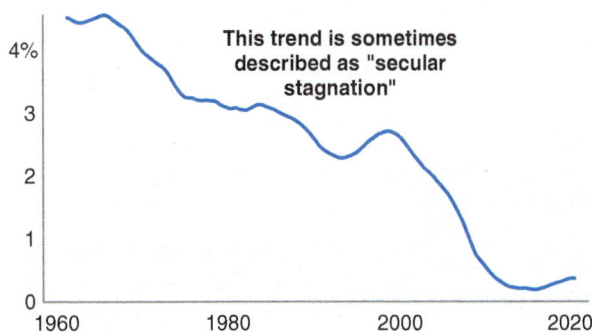

Data from: Federal Reserve Bank of New York.

Over recent decades there has been a long-term decrease in the demand for loanable funds as the structure of the economy has changed. First, population growth is slowing, and fewer new workers mean less investment is required to equip them. Second, the modern economy is increasingly powered by technology firms, which don't use much physical capital. For instance, WhatsApp grew to be worth about as much as Sony without building a single factory. And third, as capital equipment — particularly computers — becomes cheaper, businesses need fewer funds to meet their equipment needs.

Each of these factors shifts the demand for loanable funds to the left. And together, they help explain why Figure 15 shows that the neutral real interest rate has declined to very low levels since the turn of the century. This trend is sometimes called "secular stagnation." ∎

Do the Economics

Four factors that shift the demand for loanable funds:
1. Technological advances
2. Expectations
3. Corporate taxes
4. Lending standards and cash reserves

Think you've got this stuff all figured out? Okay, let's practice by predicting how the neutral real interest rate will respond to changing economic conditions. To do this, apply the same three-step recipe that you can use to predict the results of any supply-and-demand analysis:

Step 1: Will this shift saving and hence the supply of loanable funds, or will it shift investment and the demand for loanable funds?

Step 2: Is that shift an increase, shifting the curve to the right? Or is it a decrease, shifting the curve to the left?

Step 3: How will the price — that is, the neutral real interest rate — change in equilibrium? And what about the quantity of saving and investment?

Now let's apply this three-step recipe to the following scenarios:

The government cuts corporate taxes, so businesses get to keep a larger share of their profits.

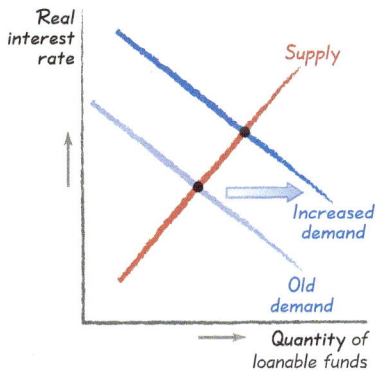

A tax cut makes investment more profitable so investment will rise.
→ Increased demand for funds

Result: Higher real interest rate, with more saving and investment.

Political strife overseas leads foreign savers to look for a "safe haven" to park their money.

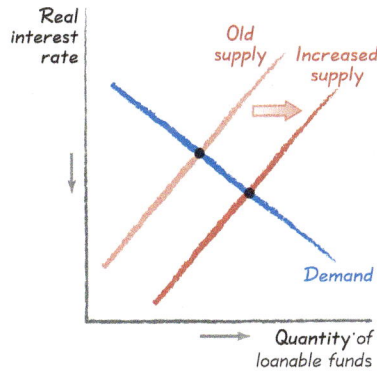

The United States is a safe haven, so foreign saving will rise.
→ Increased supply of funds

Result: Lower real interest rate with more saving and investment.

The federal government embarks on a major spending program that puts the budget into deficit.

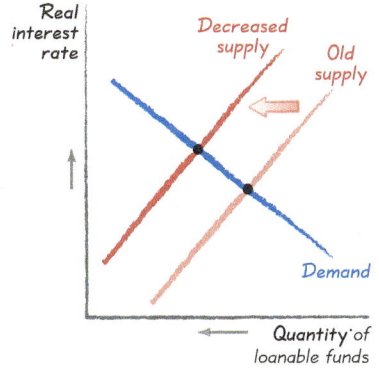

A budget deficit will decrease government saving.
→ Decrease in supply of funds

Result: Higher real interest rate with less saving and investment.

As more students go to college, an increasing share of parents open college savings accounts.

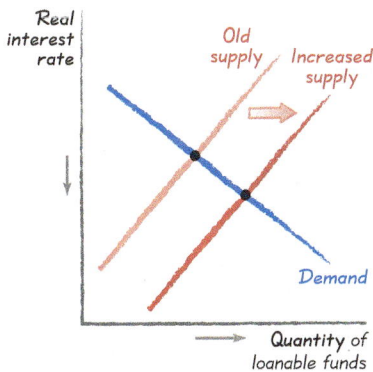

More people putting away money means private saving will rise.
→ Increased supply of funds

Result: Lower real interest rate with more saving and investment.

Business executives expect their profit margins to decline over the next decade.

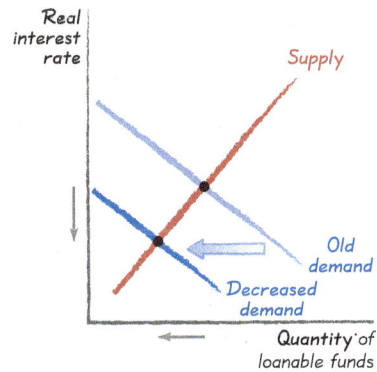

Lower future profits will reduce investment.
→ Decrease in demand for funds

Result: Lower real interest rate with less saving and investment.

The nominal interest rate rises by 2% in response to inflation rising by 2%.

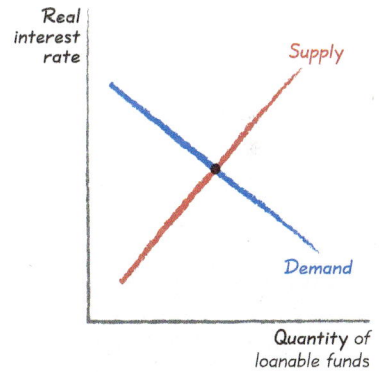

Trick question: Saving and investment respond to the real interest rate, not the nominal interest rate. An unchanged real interest rate has no effect on the supply or demand for loanable funds. ■

14.6 Tying It Together

Invest in Yourself

In this chapter, we've examined the trade-off between up-front costs and future benefits and developed a powerful framework for evaluating whether an investment is worthwhile. While we've focused on the macroeconomic implications of investment — analyzing whether a business will invest in productive capital — the same framework applies to a broad range of big and small investment decisions. Businesses use it to decide whether to open new plants, buy new equipment, or greenlight a new film or video game. And you can use it right now to make good decisions about how to invest your own money — as well as your time, energy, and attention. For example:

- As a college student, you're investing in your *human capital* now, incurring up-front costs that include the price of tuition, the time and energy you spend studying, and any income you forgo in order to attend college. In exchange, you'll enjoy a more rewarding career (and likely a more satisfying life) later.

- You can invest in your *health capital,* incurring the up-front costs of exercising and eating well now, so that you'll benefit from better health in the future.

- Even the most introverted among us can benefit from attending a few first-year mixers, joining a club, or volunteering with a like-minded group. Think of it as an investment in your *friendship capital,* exchanging the up-front cost of feeling awkward at social events now for the future benefit of lifelong friendships.

In each case, the Rational Rule for Investors provides useful advice: It's worth investing if the present value of the benefits exceeds the present value of the costs.

Good investment advice is the easy part. Following through can be harder. We've all been in that situation where we're facing a daunting task (writing a paper, reading an assigned book, or studying for an exam), but instead of following the Rational Rule for Investors, we procrastinate or allow competing options to derail us. You might intend to study tomorrow, but then tomorrow comes, and you put it off again. As a result, you underinvest in your studies.

It's a common pattern: We put off costs that we incur today — exercising, doing the laundry, applying for internships — and miss out on future benefits (like good health, clean clothes, and future employment). Sometimes the costs are small (a laundry crisis is, after all, a temporary setback). But the tendency to procrastinate can play havoc in your financial life. You may know that in the future you will want to invest in a car, in furniture for an apartment, or a down payment on a house, but it's tempting to spend your money on other things today. Research from psychologists and behavioral economists confirms that it's not just you — it's really hard to delay gratification.

Employ some simple strategies to beat procrastination. Thinking like an economist means knowing that when the benefits of investment exceed the costs, you need to follow through. You can use the following strategies to ensure you don't miss out on those future benefits.

Reward yourself. The cost-benefit principle says that if you want to do more of something, you should increase the benefits, or decrease the costs. So when you've got a big exam coming up, reward yourself for each hour you spend studying with something you enjoy (a snack, a quick chat with a friend, or 15 minutes goofing off online). Alternatively, you can make it costly *not* to study: Commit to study with a friend — and make sure it's a friend you wouldn't want to let down.

Break it up. The marginal principle reminds you that any big task can be broken up into a series of smaller, simpler steps. So don't try to write that 3,000-word essay in one sitting. Work backward from the due date, and schedule time each day of the week (or weeks) before to research, outline, write, and rewrite. On any given night, you'll have a smaller task to complete, and less reason to procrastinate.

Constrain yourself. The opportunity cost principle reminds you that the real cost of something is your next best alternative. So constrain your future choices by making that

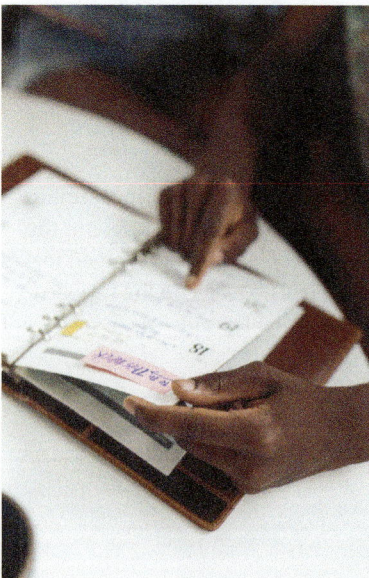

Don't leave all the decisions to your future self.

next best alternative less appealing. Block social media, have a friend change and hide your Netflix password, and lend your Xbox to a friend. Even easier: Head to the library to study and leave your phone at home so you won't have any distractions.

Make decisions in advance. If your friends ask you to go out when you should be studying, it's easy to make the wrong choice. It's the interdependence principle in action: Your choices depend upon the temptations that surround you. But if you plan ahead, it's easier to make a better choice. Decide *today* which nights next week are for socializing, and which nights are for studying. When "something comes up" next week, you'll already have made a decision, and temptation will exert less of an influence.

Use these strategies now, and I bet you'll reap benefits at the end of this term. Now that you've paid the up-front cost of reading this chapter, it's time to enjoy the future benefits of making better investment decisions for the rest of your life!

Chapter 14 Review

Chapter at a Glance

Investment: *Spending on new capital assets that increase the economy's productive capacity. Types of investment: Business investment, change in inventories, and housing investment.*

Capital Stock: *The total quantity of capital at a point in time.* Investment *is the flow of new purchases of capital that add to this stock. But capital also declines over time due to* **depreciation**, *which includes wear and tear, obsolescence, accidental damage, and aging.*

Tools to Analyze Investments

Compounding ← → Discounting

Helps you calculate how money grows over time when you leave it to accumulate interest in the bank.

You use it to figure out how much money in the future is worth today.

$$\text{Future value in } t \text{ years} = \text{Present value} \times (1 + r)^t$$

$$\text{Present value} = \text{Future value in } t \text{ years} \div (1 + r)^t$$

Interest rate (r): *The rate of r cents per dollar (use the real r for real values and nominal r for nominal values). The interest rate you use in the discounting or compounding formula should be the rate of return you could get from investing your funds in your next best alternative.*

Evaluating an Investment

Rational Rule for Investors: *Pursue an investment opportunity if:*

$$\underbrace{\frac{\text{Next year's profit}}{r + d}}_{\substack{\text{Present value} \\ \text{of future profits}}} > \underbrace{C}_{\substack{\text{Up-front} \\ \text{cost}}}$$

is the same as

Compare the **user cost of capital** *(the extra cost associated with using one more machine next year) with next year's additional profit and invest if:*

$$\underbrace{\text{Next year's profit}}_{\text{Marginal benefit}} > \underbrace{(r + d) \times C}_{\text{Marginal cost}}$$

Depreciation rate (d): *The proportion of an investment's remaining productive capacity you lose each year due to depreciation.*

Market for Loanable Funds: *The market for the funds used to buy, rent, or build capital.*

Price of loanable funds = Real interest rate

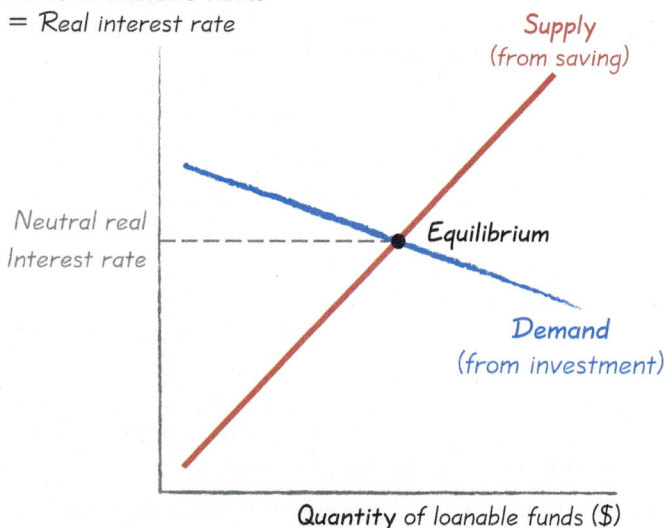

Supply (from saving)

Neutral real Interest rate

Equilibrium

Demand (from investment)

Quantity of loanable funds ($)

✱ **Predicting changes** in the neutral real interest rate:
1. Will this shift saving and hence the supply of loanable funds, or will it shift investment and the demand for loanable funds?

   Supply shifters: *changes in personal saving rates, government saving, or foreign saving.*

   Demand shifters: *Technological advances, expectations, corporate taxes, or lending standards and cash reserves.*

2. Is that shift an increase, shifting the curve to the right? Or is it a decrease, shifting the curve to the left?
3. How will the price—the neutral real interest rate—change in equilibrium? What about the quantity of saving and investment?

Key Terms

capital, 348	depreciation rate, 357	market for loanable funds, 365
capital stock, 349	discounting, 354	neutral real interest rate, 366
compounding, 352	discounting formula, 354	present value, 354
compounding formula, 353	future value, 352	Rational Rule for Investors, 359
crowding out, 367	investment, 348	user cost of capital, 361
depreciation, 349	investment line, 363	valuation formula, 358

Study Problems

Learning Objective 14.1 *Learn what macroeconomists mean by investment and assess the role that it plays in the economy.*

1. You buy $1,000 worth of Walmart stock. Why wouldn't a macroeconomist call this investment?

2. Describe how something you purchased depreciated over time and how its value changed.

3. Describe, using flows, stocks, and depreciation, why big changes in investment have relatively small impacts on the amount of capital in the economy.

4. Use the opportunity cost principle to explain why building a new house for personal use counts as investment.

5. Determine if the following scenarios are describing savings or investment. If they describe investment, which type of investment? Explain.

   a. Amazon purchases $100 million worth of products from a Chinese manufacturer to add to its warehouse inventory.

   b. SpaceX spends $5 million on writing and testing new code to improve its rocket stability.

   c. The stock market rises sharply after the Federal Reserve announces that it won't raise the interest rate.

   d. 1.2 million new homes were built in 2017 in the United States.

6. How do the following impact the capital stock? Be sure to identify depreciation and investment flows. Explain your answer.

   a. A consultant drops her laptop on the way to a big meeting and her IT department buys a replacement the next day.

   b. The *Los Angeles Times* decommissions an older printing press instead of repairing it due to a decrease in print subscriptions.

7. If GDP is confidently expected to grow at a rapid 4% rate this year, how do you predict investment spending to change? Is it likely to grow at a larger, smaller, or the same rate as GDP? Why?

8. Capital per worker in China more than doubled between 2010 and 2020. How do you expect China's output per worker to have changed over the same period? Why?

Learning Objective 14.2 *Master two tools for comparing sums of money at different points in time: compounding and discounting.*

9. Would you prefer $1 million when you retire in 40 years, or $70,000 today held in an interest-bearing account that will compound over the next 40 years?

10. Would you be better off saving for retirement early in your career or later when you're earning more? Explain.

11. Use the compounding or discounting formula to answer the following questions.

    a. Your small business has a cash reserve of about $200,000, earning 2% annual interest. How much will that be worth in 3 years?

    b. You want $1 million in your retirement account in 50 years. If your account grows at an annual rate of 4%, how much would you have to deposit today for it to grow into $1 million in 50 years?

12. If you deposit $1,200 in your retirement account in your first year of work, how much will that $1,200 be worth after 5, 10, 20, 30, 40, and 50 years at a 5% interest rate? Graph your results. What do you notice? It may be easiest to use a spreadsheet to make the calculations.

13. Nigeria's real GDP is expected to grow by about 5% per year for the next 5 years and inflation is expected to be about 12% per year. If its GDP is $480 billion, what will its nominal and real GDP be in 5 years?

Learning Objective 14.3 *Evaluate whether an investment opportunity is worth pursuing.*

14. Explain how you applied the Rational Rule for Investors to your own choice to invest in a college education, using the marginal principle, the cost-benefit principle, and the opportunity cost principle.

15. Do you think that people always follow the Rational Rule for Investors? Why or why not? Explain.

16. Think about how much you paid for your smartphone and how much it's worth today. What's the depreciation rate of your phone? Why has it lost value?

17. Management at TJX Companies is deciding whether to build a new goods distribution center. It will cost $60 million

to build, and it is likely to boost estimated additional annual profits by $5 million in its first full year of operation. Future real revenues will decline due to a depreciation rate of 5% per year. The opportunity cost of this investment is the 7% real interest rate it could otherwise earn on its funds. Should TJX build the new distribution center? Explain. What level of first-year profits would make this building profitable?

18. Consider the owner of a local boutique. She is deciding if she should upgrade the storage and display containers. The total cost would be $2,000, and the depreciation rate is 8% per year. The expected increase in next year's profits as a result of the investment is $400. Assuming a real interest rate of 5%, use the marginal principle to determine whether the owner should make this investment.

19. Martha is considering acquiring another piano for her piano academy. The cost of a new Steinway grand is around $148,000. Pianos depreciate at a rate of about 5% per year, and the academy's investment fund typically earns a return of about 10% per year. The piano is expected to boost future profits by about $30,000 per year. Should Martha acquire the piano?

Learning Objective 14.4 *Assess how macroeconomic conditions drive investment.*

20. As a manager, would you advise your company to make investments during a recession? Explain your answer.

21. Use the opportunity cost principle to explain the relationship between the real interest rate and investment spending. What does this tell you about the slope of the investment line?

22. Use the cost-benefit principle to describe how expectations change a manager's decisions to make new investments.

23. The manager of a T-shirt company is considering investing in a new embroidery machine. The machine costs $8,500, and the depreciation rate is 6.5% per year. The expected increase in next year's profit as a result of the investment would be $1,500. For what values of the interest rate should the company make this investment?

24. You are forecasting investment for a major bank. Consider what happens to investment in each of the following scenarios. Show the change graphically, using the investment line.

   a. The economy is in a recession, and firms' cash reserves are declining.

   b. Congress passes the Tax Cuts and Jobs Act (TCJA), which lowers corporate income taxes.

   c. The Federal Reserve decides to raise interest rates.

   d. A new technology is discovered that increases the productive capacity of factories.

Learning Objective 14.5 *Forecast the long-run real interest rate.*

25. Are you currently a participant in the market for loanable funds? If so, which side? What effect does your current participation (or lack thereof) have on the market?

26. Come up with a real-world example of how an increase in the budget deficit would crowd out private investment.

27. Determine if the following people are demanders, suppliers, or not involved in the market for loanable funds.

   a. Latisha wants to save up for a new laptop to use in her business, so she puts aside $100 a month until she can afford it.

   b. Gerardo borrows $30,000 from his local bank for a new addition to his warehouse.

   c. Dana puts aside $1,200 every year to buy stocks through her retirement account.

28. Evaluate the effect of each of the following events on the market for loanable funds. Explain the effects on savings, investment, and the neutral real interest rate.

   a. The government runs a government budget surplus instead of a deficit.

   b. The government decides to forgive some of the $1.6 trillion in student loan debt.

   c. Chinese investors stop sending their funds to the United States, reducing net capital inflows.

   d. The nominal interest rate rises 1% in response to a 1% rise in the inflation rate.

29. Which of the following factors could cause the neutral real interest rate to fall?

   a. Massive government budget deficits in the United States

   b. Slowing population growth

   c. A global savings glut

   d. The falling costs of capital equipment

The Financial Sector

It just may be the most famous street in the world. It runs through New York's financial district and is home to banks, the stock market, and the bond market. Fortunes are made and lost here. More money courses through this street in a minute than most of us will see in our lifetimes. It's one of the few places on Earth where account balances aren't measured in thousands or millions, but in billions or trillions of dollars.

The street is Wall Street. To some, it's a symbol of greed; to others, it's the purest distillation of market forces. Whichever your view, one thing is clear: Wall Street is the central nervous system for the whole financial system.

It's no place for the timid.

The financial sector touches every aspect of your life. Perhaps you're funding your education with student loans, or you're driving a car financed by an auto loan. Perhaps you occasionally make purchases on a credit card. Or maybe you have already purchased stocks, putting your savings into the stock market. Even if you haven't yet touched the financial sector, you likely use public goods that depend on the financial sector. For example, the roads you drive on were likely funded by the government issuing bonds.

When you finish college and start working, you'll hopefully get to enroll in a retirement plan that puts your weekly contributions into the stock market. Or perhaps you'll be an entrepreneur whose success hinges on getting your big idea funded. At some point, you'll probably buy a home, funded with a home loan that could get bought and sold dozens of times on Wall Street. And your quality of life when you retire will depend on how well your financial portfolio performed.

There are three key pillars of the financial sector: banks, the bond market, and the stock market. We'll explore each of these in turn. Along the way, you'll learn how to get the best deal you can when managing your finances.

Chapter Objective

Understand the role played by the financial sector.

15.1 Banks
Assess the role that banks play in funneling money from savers to investors.

15.2 The Bond Market
Understand how companies and governments raise money by issuing bonds.

15.3 The Stock Market
Learn how companies raise money by issuing stock.

15.4 What Drives Financial Prices?
Discover what drives financial prices.

15.5 Personal Finance
Make better decisions in financial markets.

🎙 Podcast
Think Like an Economist
The Financial Sector—Bonds, Stocks, and Shares—Should You or Shouldn't You

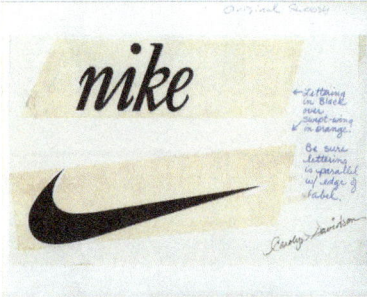

The original Nike logo design.

15.1 Banks

Learning Objective *Assess the role that banks play in funneling money from savers to investors.*

Phil Knight was a track enthusiast who ran for the legendary University of Oregon Ducks. He was also a business student with a paper to write for an entrepreneurship course. So he wrote about what he knew: running shoes. At the time, Japanese camera companies were just starting to take market share from the once-dominant German camera companies. With this in mind, he argued in his paper that the time was ripe for Japanese-made shoes to challenge the German athletic giants such as Adidas and Puma. When he presented the paper in class, his fellow students were bored. No one asked any questions, but at least he got an A.

Knight couldn't stop thinking about his big idea. After graduation, he decided to give it a try. He visited a Japanese shoe factory, presenting himself as an American tycoon. His ruse worked, and he landed a deal to sell Japanese athletic shoes in the United States. When his old track coach saw the shoes, he was so impressed that he asked to become Knight's business partner. Initially they called the company Blue Ribbon Sports. Later on, they changed it to Nike.

Knight did what many other small businesses do: He turned to his bank for a loan. The First National Bank of Oregon lent him enough money to buy 900 pairs of shoes.

Banks are an important funding source for many of life's major investments. Banks provide car loans to fund your car purchase, home loans to help you buy a home, and small business loans to help you start or expand your business. And so our first task in this chapter is to explore just what it is that banks do.

What Do Banks Do?

This is not how banks work.

When you put your money in a bank, your bank takes your money and puts it to work by lending it out. It might provide a loan to a student, a home loan to a young couple, or short-term funding for Nike. Putting your money to work is how the bank earns a profit.

Banks make money by charging higher interest rates than they pay. When you deposit your money in the bank, the bank is not storing your money for you. Instead, it's borrowing money from you. This changes how you think about your relationship with your bank: As a saver, you're the lender, and the bank is the borrower. Your bank borrows from you so that it can then lend that money to others, and in the process both you and the bank make money.

The price your bank pays to borrow your money is the interest you receive. If you earn 2% per year interest, then depositing $100 in the bank now means that a year from now, you'll have $102 in your account. Your bank makes money by lending your deposits out to someone else at a higher interest rate. If it charges 6% per year interest on its loans, then someone who borrows $100 will owe them $106 a year later. At that point, the bank owes you $102, but borrowers owe it $106, meaning that the bank made $4.

Your bank is just a middleman. It buys and then sells a somewhat unusual product: the right to use $100 for the next year. Just like the middleman in any other business, it buys its products at a low price (the 2% interest rate), and then sells it at a higher price (the 6% interest rate).

People willingly pay for this because banks provide valuable services. There are five important functions that banks provide. Let's look at them one by one.

Function 1: Banks pool savings from many savers. Your bank pools the savings of many savers and lends that pool of savings to a specific borrower. This is a valuable service for savers because even if you have only a small amount of savings, you can earn interest on it, even if the amount is too small for you to efficiently find someone who needs to borrow it. It's also easier for borrowers to go to one bank than it is for them to try to borrow from dozens of individual lenders.

Function 2: Banks spread the risk of lending money across many borrowers. Your bank doesn't lend all your savings to Nike or any one borrower. Instead, your bank pools money from thousands of savers and lends that money to thousands of borrowers. Effectively, you're lending a dollar of your money to Nike, a nickel to a local small business, a dime to your neighbor's home loan, and so on. Banks also make lending your money much less risky because they lend to a diverse array of borrowers. The more diverse this portfolio of loans is, the less risky it is.

Function 3: Banks solve information problems. Your bank is also an important information intermediary. It doesn't lend your money out to just anyone. Before a borrower can get a loan, your bank will delve into their credit history, check on their assets, and examine their debts. Banks are particularly effective at figuring out who to lend to because they're privy to the financial histories of their customers. They use this information to identify which borrowers will be able to repay their loans.

EVERYDAY Economics   How to improve your financial GPA

Whether you know it or not, banks are already gathering information about you that will affect your life for years to come. Your *credit score* (sometimes called your FICO score) is like a GPA for your financial life. It summarizes everything that credit bureaus know about what you earn, what you spend, how much you save, and how much you owe. Banks will use your credit scores to decide whether or not to loan money to you in the future — and what interest rate to charge you. So it's a wise idea to take care of your credit score by following these good practices:

- Pay your bills on time. A missed payment will stay on your credit report for seven years. If you miss a payment, catch up as soon as possible.
- After college, stay on top of your student loans. If you lose your job (or go back to school), apply for a deferral immediately.
- Develop a history of using credit responsibly. Ironically, not having a credit card doesn't help — you need to show that you can be responsible when you have credit.
- If you have a credit card, pay off the full balance every month.
- If it looks like you might fall behind on payments, call your lender. Often, they will be willing to work with you to negotiate an arrangement.
- Monitor your FICO score. Your score used to be an industry secret, but today many major banks share your score with you right on your banking app.
- You have the right to see the data that goes into your credit report and to demand corrections. You can check it for free at www.annualcreditreport.com. ∎

Function 4: Banks provide payment services. The other reason that you want a bank account — beyond earning interest — is that it makes your economic life a lot simpler. It's easier and safer to have your pay deposited directly into a bank account than to go and collect cash. Similarly, you might find it convenient to pay your rent electronically, pay your bills online, send money overseas with a bank transfer, and shop online using your credit card. Digital payment apps like Venmo and PayPal depend on banks as well. In each case, your bank is providing you with payment services that are often more convenient than using cash.

Function 5: Banks create long-term loans from short-term deposits. There's an interesting tension at the heart of banking: Your bank borrows money from savers who expect to be able to withdraw their funds whenever they want. It then lends this money to borrowers who don't have to repay their loan on demand. Instead, borrowers tend to repay over a fixed (and long) period of time. For example, homeowners might take out a loan in which they agree to a 30-year repayment plan.

maturity transformation Using short-term loans to make long-term loans.

What banks do:
1. Pool savings from many savers
2. Spread the risk of lending money across many borrowers
3. Solve information problems
4. Provide payment services
5. Create long-term loans from short-term deposits

bank run When many bank customers try to withdraw their savings at the same time.

Jeff Cameron Collingwood/Shutterstock

When there's a bank run, run.

Let's say you have some money in the bank. You put it there with the expectation that you can wake up any day and take your money out of the bank. This means that effectively, *you loan the bank money overnight.* If you don't withdraw it on any given day, then you are loaning it for another night (and thus giving yourself the option of withdrawing the money the next day). In other words, by making your funds available to you on demand, your bank effectively gets its money from taking short-term (overnight) loans from people like you. But it needs to use those funds to make longer-term loans. What it's doing is called **maturity transformation** — using short-term loans to make long-term loans. Maturity transformation ensures that investors can fund long-term projects, even when no individual savers are willing to make a long-term loan.

While banks typically successfully engage in maturity transformation, it can cause problems. In fact, it creates a risk that can lead the whole system to come crashing down. Let's see how.

Bank Runs

If your bank doesn't just store your money in its vault and leave it waiting for you, how do you know that your money will be there when you want it? The answer: You don't.

Your bank makes money by lending money. That means that it doesn't keep your money in a bank vault waiting for you. Of course, your bank knows that some people will withdraw their cash, so it keeps enough cash on hand to meet a typical level of withdrawals, plus a bit extra just in case. But it can't keep it all, because if it did, it wouldn't be able to pay you interest or pay its employees.

A **bank run** occurs when a much larger number of customers than usual try to withdraw their savings at the same time. If that happens, a bank might not have enough money on hand and therefore will not be able to give you your money. A bank run can put even a well-managed bank at risk.

Bank runs can cause a bank to collapse. On a typical day, few savers will make a withdrawal and banks have plenty of money on hand to give them when they request it. But what makes a day typical? Well, it turns out that a day is typical if most people believe that it is a typical day.

If you believe that tomorrow will be a typical day, then you can go to bed confident that if you need your money, your bank will be able to pay you since your bank can pay everyone who withdraws their money on a typical day. Given this, you're happy keeping your savings in the bank if you don't need the cash.

*If you believe that tomorrow will **not** be a typical day* — meaning you expect more people than normal will try to withdraw their money — then you shouldn't feel so reassured. Perhaps you've heard that some people are so worried about your bank's financial health that they're planning to withdraw their savings tomorrow. You realize that an abnormally large number of withdrawals might clean your bank out of cash, and so you can't afford to wait to withdraw your money. Your best response is to run — don't walk! — to the bank and withdraw your savings before other customers beat you there. If other customers follow similar logic — and I believe they will — then they'll also run to the bank.

In fact, this was the story of Washington Mutual. The bank had made a large number of home loans to borrowers who were struggling to pay them back. In September 2008, customers got wind of the bank's financial trouble, and many ran to the bank to withdraw their money. Others followed their lead, making panicked withdrawals. Within 10 days customers had withdrawn a total of $16.7 billion from their checking and savings accounts. These demands left Washington Mutual unable to conduct day-to-day business, and the bank was taken over by the government.

A bank run is likely whenever people believe that a bank run is likely. While Washington Mutual was suffering from poor financial health, the challenge for banks is that a bank run can happen even when they are financially healthy. In fact, almost anything can trigger a bank run. For example, more than 10,000 Latvians rushed to withdraw their money after a false rumor spread on Twitter that Swedish-owned banks were planning on shutting down operations in Latvia. In this sort of panic, it can be rational for you to pull your money out of the bank even if you know the rumor is untrue.

If you believe that others are going to run to withdraw their savings, then your best response is to try to get there first — before the bank runs out of money. And this is your best response whether they're doing this for good reasons (the bank is in financial trouble) or crazy reasons (it's a lunar eclipse) or even for a Twitter-fueled rumor that you know is false. And if other people believe that you're going to run to the bank, their best response is to try to get there first, no matter the reason.

This is the **interdependence principle** at work — your best choice depends on what others will do, and their best choice depends on what you will do. In normal times, this interdependence means that you're happy keeping your money in the bank, as long as others are happy keeping their money in the bank. But it also means that there's the possibility of a self-fulfilling panic: You'll panic because you're worried that others will panic, and they'll panic because they're worried you'll panic. Bank runs can be caused by anything that increases people's concerns that they will lose their money.

Bank runs can be contagious.   Because you panic if someone else panics, it's also easy to see how bank runs can be contagious across banks. Indeed, a run on one bank can potentially threaten the entire banking system. For example, on September 15, 2008, a financial institution called Lehman Brothers collapsed. The collapse of Lehman Brothers increased concern about Washington Mutual, fueling a bank run that led to Washington Mutual's collapse on September 25. As a result, depositors at other banks started looking hard at their banks, wondering if they could be next. Wachovia Bank found itself in this position as depositors withdrew deposits over the weekend following the collapse of Washington Mutual. Wachovia was forced into a *fire sale* — a quick sale due to financial distress — selling itself to Wells Fargo over the weekend to ensure its branches could open on Monday with enough funding to meet depositors' demands. As the CEO of Wachovia put it: "You could go from being OK . . . to in trouble in a matter of days. I don't think people understand how quickly events unfolded."

EVERYDAY Economics   How the toilet paper panic of 2020 was like a bank run

Stores manage their inventory the same way that banks manage their cash reserves: They want to keep enough on hand to meet the demands of customers each day. But if there's a sudden and unexpected spike in demand, they can come up short. This is exactly what happened in early 2020, as cities around the country began "locking down" to prevent the spread of Covid-19. Some people worried that stores would shut down, or that going shopping would become dangerous (or even illegal). So they started stockpiling essentials, like toilet paper. Even those who weren't worried about the pandemic began to worry that they would be left paperless — so they, too, started stockpiling toilet paper, to avoid being shut out by others. They bought more than usual not because they thought they'd need more toilet paper than usual, but because they feared (correctly) that others were buying more than they'd need, leaving none for them. Fear of a run on toilet paper — like a run on banks — can be a self-fulfilling prophecy: When enough people expect a paper shortage, that can create the reality of an actual shortage. ■

Calm down, there's plenty of road — and toilet paper — for everyone.

Deposit insurance makes bank runs much less likely.   While the United States experienced a few bank runs in 2008, they have been quite rare throughout your lifetime. But this wasn't always true. Bank runs were such a big problem in the Great Depression that in the early 1930s, over one-third of all existing banks failed. In response, the federal government introduced **deposit insurance,** which effectively guarantees that you'll always get your savings back, even if your bank collapses. This ensures that you won't lose the money you deposit in the bank. This insurance covers up to $250,000 per account.

deposit insurance A guarantee that you won't lose the money you deposit in the bank.

Figure 1 | The Introduction of Deposit Insurance Led the Number of Bank Failures to Plummet

Number of bank failures each year

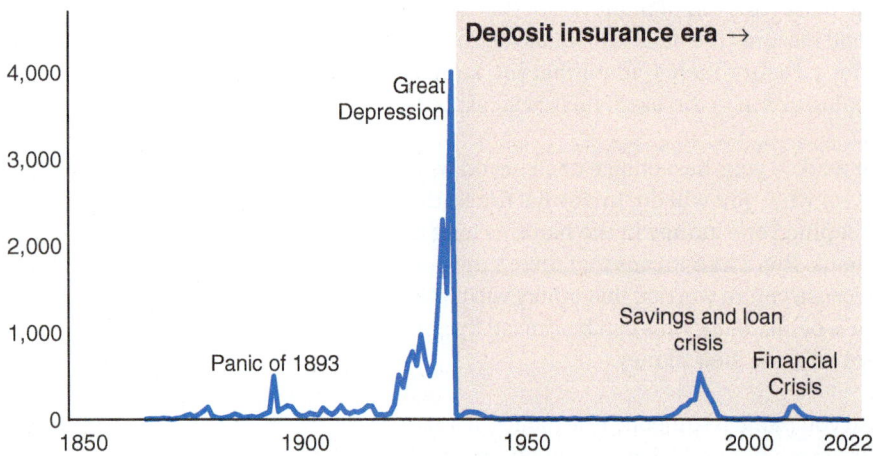

Data from: Historical Statistics of the United States and FDIC.

Deposit insurance is designed to break the interdependence that leads to self-fulfilling panics. When you have deposit insurance, you know that your savings are safe, no matter what other people do. Even if others withdraw their money from the bank, you don't need to try to beat them to the bank, since you know that you'll ultimately get your money back. Deposit insurance is a simple idea, but it really works. Figure 1 shows that since the government created deposit insurance in 1934, U.S. bank failures have become incredibly rare.

Shadow Banks

Regulating the banking system and offering deposit insurance helped to promote financial stability and prevent a financial crisis. So how did the 2008 financial crisis happen? One explanation is that regulators had overlooked the potential risk to the financial system from financial firms that are not banks, but that act in many ways like banks. In 2007, a name was coined for these types of financial firms: Shadow banks.

shadow banks Financial firms that act like banks but, since they are not actually banks, do not have to follow the same rules as banks.

A **shadow bank** refers to any financial firm that acts like a bank but, since it is not actually a bank, does not have to follow the same rules as a bank. Investment banks, insurance companies, payday lenders, private equity funds, and mortgage lenders are all examples of shadow banks. They don't take deposits like a bank, nor do they make the same kind of loans that banks do. But they do take in funds from investors who might want their money back at any time, and they use these funds to make longer-term investments. That's maturity transformation, and whenever someone is involved in maturity transformation, they run the risk of too many people wanting their money back at once. Let's take a closer look at the role shadow banks play in the financial system.

Shadow banks are susceptible to bank runs. The big idea is that shadow banks just aren't that different from banks. Shadow banks are typically engaged in activities that involve greater risk to those that put their money in them, but those depositors are also typically rewarded for taking on that extra risk with the promise of higher returns on their deposits. There doesn't have to be anything shadowy about shadow banks. Most people understand that their money is at greater risk when it's in a shadow bank, particularly since there's no deposit insurance. The problem is with no deposit insurance, they are vulnerable to bank runs. That's the short-story version of what happened in 2008 — many people withdrew their funds from these shadow banks, and they ran into serious trouble, nearly bringing the entire financial system down with them.

Bear Stearns was a shadow bank that failed in 2008. When their depositors lost faith in them, they withdrew their money, causing a (shadow) bank run and ultimately their collapse. What regulators had failed to appreciate prior to the 2008 financial crisis was that these shadow banks pose the same kind of risk that banks pose. People might want their money back at a time when the shadow bank simply does not have enough available cash. The result can be bank-run dynamics that can spill across both the entire shadow and regular banking system.

Fire sales can cause shadow bank runs to spread. A shadow bank facing a bank run has to sell its assets quickly in order to repay its depositors. Putting billions of dollars of financial assets up for sale at once floods the market, pushing the price of those assets down. Then the interdependence principle kicks in: Because other shadow banks hold similar assets, a fire sale of assets by one shadow bank in trouble reduces the market value of other shadow banks' assets. And that reduction in market value makes the customers of other shadow banks more nervous, leading to further bank runs. As more shadow banks go belly-up, there are more fire sales, and the problem spreads like a virus.

Shadow banks are opaque. There's another problem in all of this: The shadow banking system is incredibly opaque, and so when one financial institution can't pay its debts, it's hard to know who will be hurt. Unknown interdependencies can make small problems balloon into big ones. It's a bit like knowing that a small share of the meat supply is infected with illness-inducing bacteria, but not knowing which particular shipments or suppliers are affected. When this happens, millions of people stop eating meat rather than risking illness.

Bad loans are the financial equivalent of food-borne bacteria. Depositing money with a shadow bank infected with bad loans means you could lose your money. If you don't know which shadow banks are infected and there is no deposit insurance, you won't want to lend money to any of them. That's how a relatively small number of bad loans in 2008 caused lending to decline sharply, which then sparked a major recession. The result of the 2008 financial crisis was increased regulation of shadow banks to help ensure their stability during the next crisis. Shadow banks continue to play an important role in the financial system, but with greater regulation, the risk of a shadow bank run has been lowered.

Okay, that completes our tour of banks and shadow banks. Let's now turn our attention to another way to borrow money: the bond market.

15.2 The Bond Market

Learning Objective *Understand how companies and governments raise money by issuing bonds.*

Fast-forward from Nike's humble beginnings to today, and you'll find that it's grown to become one of the world's largest companies. Buoyed by their success, senior management decided they had to invest more, particularly in improving Nike's computing infrastructure and global distribution network. It's an investment worth making, but it's also expensive. Nike's financial team crunched the numbers and figured they needed another $1 billion to fund this new investment.

A bond certificate.

What Does the Bond Market Do?

If you want to borrow money, you will probably go to a bank. But what if you're Nike, looking for a cool billion? I'm afraid your local bank (indeed, most banks!) aren't prepared to deal with a loan that big. Instead, Nike does what many other corporations do — and also what the government does when looking for a loan. It turns to the bond market. The simplest way to think of the bond market is that it's where the big dogs go to borrow the big bucks.

A **bond** is basically an IOU. When Nike issues a billion dollars in bonds, it is borrowing a billion dollars and promising to pay it back in the future, with interest. The bond is just the piece of paper recording the terms of the IOU. When you buy a bond, you give Nike cash, and it gives you a piece of paper, promising to pay you back.

That piece of paper is important, though, because it spells out the terms of the loan. It records the borrower (called the *issuer,* which in this case is Nike), how much Nike has to repay at the end (the *principal,* which is $1 billion), when the loan must be repaid (the *maturity date,* which is March 27, 2027), and the interest it has promised to pay along the way (these are called *coupons*, and Nike promised to pay 2.75% interest per year).

bond An IOU. Specifically, a promise to pay back a loan with interest.

What the bond market does:
1. Channels funds from savers to borrowers
2. Funds government debt
3. Spreads risk
4. Creates liquidity

The bond market is a big deal. As of 2022, the total quantity of outstanding bonds issued in the United States was $46 trillion, or a bit more than $140,000 per person in the United States. Many students believe that they don't own any bonds. Perhaps that's true, at least while you're a student. But you'll probably go on to a career that includes a retirement plan, and your retirement plan will likely put some of your money into bonds. This means that even if you aren't right now, in a few years you're going to be a player in the bond market, albeit somewhat indirectly.

So what purpose does the bond market serve? The bond market performs four key functions.

Function 1: The bond market channels funds from savers to borrowers.
The bond market provides an alternative to banks; it's an alternative market where companies can borrow the large sums of money they need to fund their investments, and savers can lend the funds they aren't using. As such, it channels unused resources from savers (like you) to borrowers (like Nike).

While the stock market tends to hog the headlines, in fact bonds are a much bigger source of corporate financing. In 2021, companies raised more than four times as much through issuing bonds than issuing new stock: $2 trillion from issuing bonds, compared to nearly $450 billion by issuing new stock.

Function 2: The bond market funds government debt.
It's not just companies like Nike that borrow by issuing bonds — so do governments. In fact, the U.S. federal government is the biggest player in the bond market: It has borrowed over $15 trillion by issuing bonds. Whenever you hear about government debt, realize that it borrowed all that money by issuing bonds. Beyond the federal government, state and local governments (and even school districts) also borrow money by issuing bonds. Foreign governments also borrow money by issuing bonds.

Function 3: The bond market spreads risk.
Instead of issuing just one $1 billion bond to one person, Nike issues thousands of bonds in denominations as small as $1,000. This way, even if no one individual has a spare billion to lend to Nike, thousands of individuals may be willing to each make a smaller loan. By making it easy to spread borrowing across many lenders, bonds spread the risk that Nike won't repay its loan across many lenders.

Even if you had a billion dollars, you probably wouldn't want to lend it all to Nike. Instead, you should diversify your portfolio, buying a variety of bonds issued by many different companies. By not holding all your eggs in one basket, you'll make sure that if Nike collapses, you won't lose all your savings.

Function 4: The bond market creates liquidity.
The problem with lending someone money for 10 years is that you might suddenly discover you need the cash before the loan is due. Fortunately, you can sell your bond. Because there are many buyers in the bond market, you'll usually get something close to a fair price. That is, the bond market creates **liquidity**, which is the ability to quickly and easily convert your bonds into cash, with little or no loss in value.

In this way, the bond market — like banks — creates long-term loans from short-term loans. This *maturity transformation* is done through the ability to resell bonds in the bond market. When you sell your bond to someone else, you get your money back — the cash value of your bond — and they take over the loan, getting the future interest payments and the principle repayment on the maturity date.

Gorodenkoff/Shutterstock

Trading bonds creates liquidity.

liquidity The ability to quickly and easily convert your investments into cash, with little or no loss in value.

Evaluating Risks

Bonds have the advantage of clear terms: You know the interest rate you'll be paid, the date at which you'll be paid back in full, and that these promises will be honored as long as the company doesn't go bust. But there are some specific risks that you face. The first is the chance that the company goes bust: *default risk.* The second is *term risk,* and the third is *liquidity risk.* Let's explore each in turn.

Risk 1: Default risk is the risk of not getting paid. One risk of lending people money is that they won't repay their loans, and this risk also exists for bonds. If Nike goes bust, it may not have enough money to repay people who bought Nike bonds. The risk that you won't be repaid (or won't be repaid in a timely fashion) is called **default risk**. Companies like Fitch, Standard and Poor's, or Moody's evaluate companies and assign *credit ratings,* which are like credit scores for businesses and governments. Because it's difficult for each investor to assess Nike's chances of default, investors rely on these credit ratings to assess default risk.

default risk The risk that your loan won't be repaid.

A rating of "AAA" is the highest possible rating, meaning the company has an *extremely* strong capacity to repay its debt. Nike's $1 billion bond issue earned a rating of "AA–," which is not quite perfect but still good enough to suggest it has a very strong capacity to repay its debt. Figure 2 shows that the worse the rating, the higher the interest rate: as the default risk rises, lenders demand a higher return in order to take on the additional risk that the loan won't be paid back.

Figure 2 | Interest Rates Rise with Default Risk

Interest rate on corporate bonds

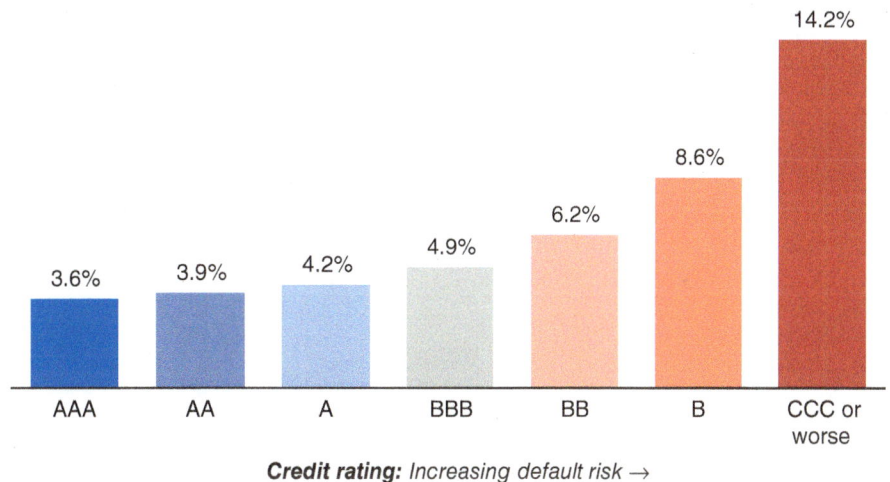

AAA	AA	A	BBB	BB	B	CCC or worse
3.6%	3.9%	4.2%	4.9%	6.2%	8.6%	14.2%

Credit rating: *Increasing default risk* →

Data from: July 2022 data from ICE BofA Indices.

Risk 2: Term risk arises when there's uncertainty about future interest rates. The opportunity cost principle reminds you that tying up your money comes with an opportunity cost — you could put that money in the bank and earn interest on it. The problem is that when you buy a bond, you don't know what future interest rates will be, so you are taking a risk as to what the opportunity cost will be over the term of the bond. The bondholders who agreed to loan Nike money for a term of 10 years at 2.375% per year were hoping that the opportunity cost over the next 10 years would be less than 2.375%. If interest rates shoot up to 4%, they are stuck earning only 2.375%, and the forgone opportunity to earn a bigger return can be an expensive opportunity cost.

Bond risks:
1. Default risk
2. Term risk
3. Liquidity risk

The risk that arises from uncertainty about future interest rates is called **term risk** because the risk is connected to the length, or term, of the loan. The more uncertain you are about future interest rates, the greater this risk is. The longer the term, the more interest rates might change, and so the higher the term risk. Nike borrowed $500 million over 30 years and faced a higher interest rate (3.375%) than it had when it borrowed $1 billion over 7 years (2.75%). Term risk explains why it had to pay this higher rate.

term risk The risk that arises from uncertainty about future interest rates.

Risk 3: Liquidity risk arises when your bond will be hard to sell. Another risk in lending out your money is that you might end up needing those funds yourself. If your money is in the bank, you solve this by simply making a withdrawal. But to "withdraw" your money from a bond, you have to sell it. While the bond market creates liquidity, there is a risk that you won't be able to quickly find a buyer for your bonds. The solution is to lower the price. At a low enough price you should be able to find a buyer, but you will have lost a lot of your funds in the process. **Liquidity risk** refers to the risk that if you need to sell an asset quickly, you may not be able to get a good price for it.

liquidity risk The risk that if you need to sell an asset quickly, you may not be able to get a good price for it.

Billions of dollars of federal government bonds are traded each day, and so these involve very little liquidity risk. But it can be harder to quickly find a buyer for a bond issued by a small company, making liquidity risk a much bigger deal.

U.S. government bonds are the safest investment. Putting all of this together, you'll discover that the safest thing you can do with your savings is to buy bonds issued by the U.S. government, which are often called *Treasuries*. They're considered safe because the U.S. government can always pay its debts simply by printing more money. (However, there remains a political risk that Congress might choose not to make debt payments in a timely fashion.) U.S. government bonds are also the most heavily traded bonds in the world — around $600 billion in Treasuries are traded each day! — and so they carry basically no liquidity risk. And a short-term loan carries almost no term risk, which is why the interest rate on short-term loans to the federal government is often described as a risk-free interest rate.

The cost of all of this safety is that lower risk comes with a lower reward, and so the interest rate on U.S. government bonds is lower than the interest rate on other bonds. That's why the U.S. government can borrow money at a lower interest rate than any other organization. Of course, it doesn't have to be this way: When investors became concerned that Greece might not be able to repay its debts in 2012, the interest rate on Greek government bonds rose to over 25%.

If you're a company looking to raise money, you don't have to turn to banks or the bond market — you also have the option of issuing stock instead. So let's turn our attention to the stock market.

15.3 The Stock Market

Learning Objective *Learn how companies raise money by issuing stock.*

In a bit more than 15 years, Phil Knight had gone from selling shoes out of the back of a van to being the CEO of a company selling nearly half of all running shoes in the United States. But Nike's impact beyond the United States was more limited, and that bugged Knight, who had global ambitions for his company. It would take a lot of money to aggressively expand worldwide — more money than Nike had. So Knight decided to sell Nike stock to the public, using the money raised to fund his ambitious global expansion plans. Let's see what this entails.

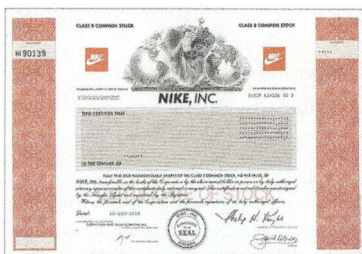

This stock certificate represents partial ownership in Nike.

What Do Stocks Do?

A stock represents partial ownership in a firm. When you own stock in a company, you own a share of the company, which is why a stock is sometimes called a share and the owners of stock are called shareholders. At the beginning of 2022, there were roughly 1,600,000,000 shares in Nike, each worth roughly $150 each. That means for $150 you can own 1/1,600,000,000 of Nike. As a partial owner of Nike, you'll make money if it makes money, and you'll lose money if it loses money. Think of your Nike stock as a claim to a (very small!) share of Nike's assets and its future profits.

A stock entitles you to a share of future profits. You stand to benefit from your ownership in two ways.

First, there are **dividends.** At the end of each year, Nike's management tallies up its profits and may pay some of it out to shareholders as a dividend. Nike usually pays a dividend every three months, and over the course of the year, the dividend adds up to an annual return equal to the value of about 1% or 2% of the value of the stock. The profits that Nike elects not to send out as dividends are called **retained earnings,** and Nike reinvests these remaining profits into the company.

This brings us to the second way you can profit from owning stock: The value of your shares can rise. As the outlook for Nike's future profitability grows, so will the value of the

dividends A share of profits that a company pays to its shareholders.

retained earnings The profits that a company chooses not to give as dividends to shareholders.

company, and hence so will the price of your stock. Figure 3 shows that Nike's stock price has gone "swoosh": If you had purchased $1,000 in Nike stock in 1980, your shares would have been worth over $1,500,000 at the end of 2021!!!

Stocks perform three key functions, which we'll review here.

Function 1: Stocks channel funds from savers to investors.
The primary reason that businesses issue stock is to raise money to fund their investments. When a business issues stock, it is essentially expanding by taking on new partners who will each own part of the company. When Nike first issued stock, it offered 2.7 million shares for sale to the general public at $11 per share, which raised $30 million, and it used this money to fund its expansion plans. Thus, stocks provide a similar function to banks and bonds, channeling unused funds from savers to investors.

When companies raise money by issuing new stock, they usually sell those shares directly to the public through what's known as an **initial public offering** (or "IPO," for short). IPOs aren't sold through the stock market. Typically IPO shares are handled by an investment bank or broker dealer, who sells the shares, typically to big institutional investors.

Function 2: Stocks spread risk.
Issuing stock is like taking on new business partners. The new stockholder provides additional cash that will allow the business to grow. In return, the new stockholder gets a share of whatever the company produces. If the company has a great year, shareholders have a great year. They may receive more in dividend payments, or they may see the value of the stock go up. In short, they gain when the company gains. But when the company has a bad year, shareholders have a bad year. Poor performance might mean that smaller dividends are paid and the value of the stock might decline. Stocks therefore spread the risk of business performance across many shareholders, reducing the risk that any one person faces.

Function 3: Stocks reallocate control.
As a shareholder who owns part of Nike, you also get a chance to have a say in how the company is run. Not directly — being a shareholder doesn't make you a manager. But shareholders get to vote in shareholder meetings. Nike's management reports to a board of directors that's elected by the shareholders. Shareholders also get to vote on major issues like whether to merge with another company, and what to pay senior management. Each share buys you one vote, and all shareholders — no matter how small their stake in the company — are entitled to turn up to the annual meeting to ask questions.

The stock market creates liquidity and makes it easier to own stocks.
The **stock market** is a market for second-hand stock, where people buy and sell existing stocks. This means that when you go to the stock market to buy Nike stock, your funds aren't going to Nike to help it open a new factory; you're simply buying from an existing shareholder who owns some Nike stock they want to sell. Just as Toyota gets nothing when you buy a pre-owned car, Nike gets nothing when you buy pre-owned stock.

A rising stock price does not directly help a company expand or become more profitable. The main role the stock market plays is to create liquidity that encourages people to invest in companies in the first place. Around $500 million worth of stock in Nike is bought and sold *each day*. All of this trading creates liquidity, meaning that if you need access to your cash, it will be easy to sell your Nike stock at something close to a fair price. Part of the reason that people were willing to buy Nike stock in their initial public offering is that they knew that if they wanted their cash back, they could easily sell their stock on the stock market. Liquidity makes investing in Nike a less risky bet.

Figure 3 | Nike's Stock Goes Swoosh

Value of $1,000 invested in 1980

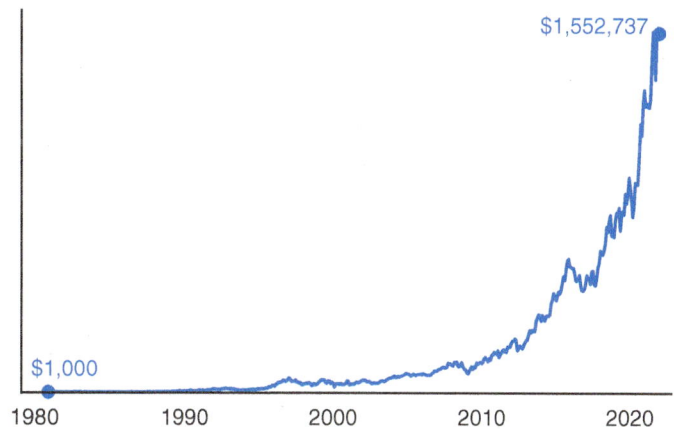

$1,552,737

$1,000

1980 1990 2000 2010 2020

Data from: Yahoo! Finance.

initial public offering When a company first sells stock directly to the public.

What stocks do:
1. Channel funds from savers to investors
2. Spread risk
3. Reallocate control

stock market The market where people buy and sell existing stocks.

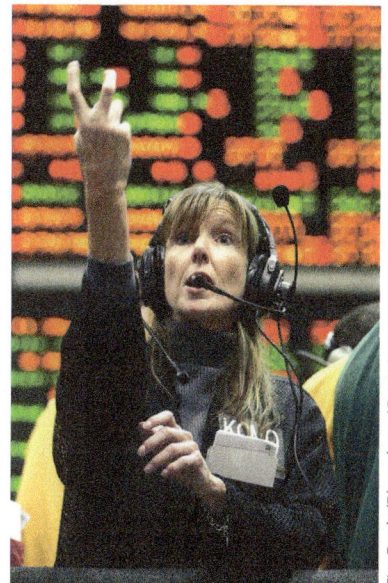

She's buying used goods.

Tim Boyle/Bloomberg/Getty Images

Comparing Stocks and Bonds

Let's step back to compare bonds and stocks more systematically so that you can choose which works best for you. It's a decision that you will someday face when you are choosing where to put your savings, or perhaps as an entrepreneur deciding how to fund your next big expansion.

Bonds pay certain annual interest payments, while stocks pay uncertain dividends. Companies can raise money by issuing bonds and by issuing new stock. In both cases, a company gets money to fund its investments, and is committed to make future payments to whoever provides that funding. Borrowing by issuing bonds commits the company to a known set of future payments: A bond specifies exactly what interest payments (the coupon payments) will be made each year. In contrast, a stock pays a dividend that depends on how the company is doing. If Nike has a bad year, it might not pay a dividend to its stockholders, but it will still have to make the specified interest payments to its bondholders. If Nike has a good year, it may issue a really big dividend to stockholders, but it will give bondholders nothing more than the promised interest payment. For a person deciding where to put their savings, bonds are a safer bet than stocks. But for a company looking to fund a big expansion, getting funding from stocks instead of bonds is less risky because it means offloading some of your risk onto your shareholders.

Bondholders get paid before stockholders if a company declares bankruptcy. When a company declares bankruptcy, its assets are sold and used to pay off its debts. Because a bond is a debt, bondholders get paid out of the proceeds of this sell-off. If there's not enough money to fully repay the bondholders, they'll get partial payment. But the stockholders get nothing unless there's money left over after the company pays all its debts. This makes bankruptcy a much greater financial risk for stockholders than it is for bondholders.

Stockholders help control how a company is run. A bondholder has no say in how a company is managed, while a stockholder is a partial owner, and hence has some say in how it's run. Corporate raiders will often use this power to try to force a company to make changes that they believe will enhance their profits. And this can make many entrepreneurs — particularly those who value total control over their company — nervous about issuing stock. In some cases, shareholders have voted in a corporate board that then fired the founder of a company from their own firm!

Figure 4 summarizes the major differences between bonds and stocks. As you'll see, it's all about the difference between lending money to a company and owning part of that company.

Figure 4 | Bonds versus Stocks

Bonds	Stocks
• Specified future interest payments	• Uncertain future dividends; depending on how well the company is doing
• First in line to get paid if the company goes bankrupt	• Last in line to get paid if the company goes bust
• No rights to help control the company	• Shareholders have a vote in how the company is run

Understanding Stock Market Data

Okay, let's dig into a bit of the jargon surrounding stocks and the stock market. Figure 5 shows you a snapshot of the stock market downloaded from Google Finance. I'm going to make it easy to interpret.

Figure 5 | What Do All Those Numbers on Google Finance Mean?

Interpreting Nike's stock market numbers

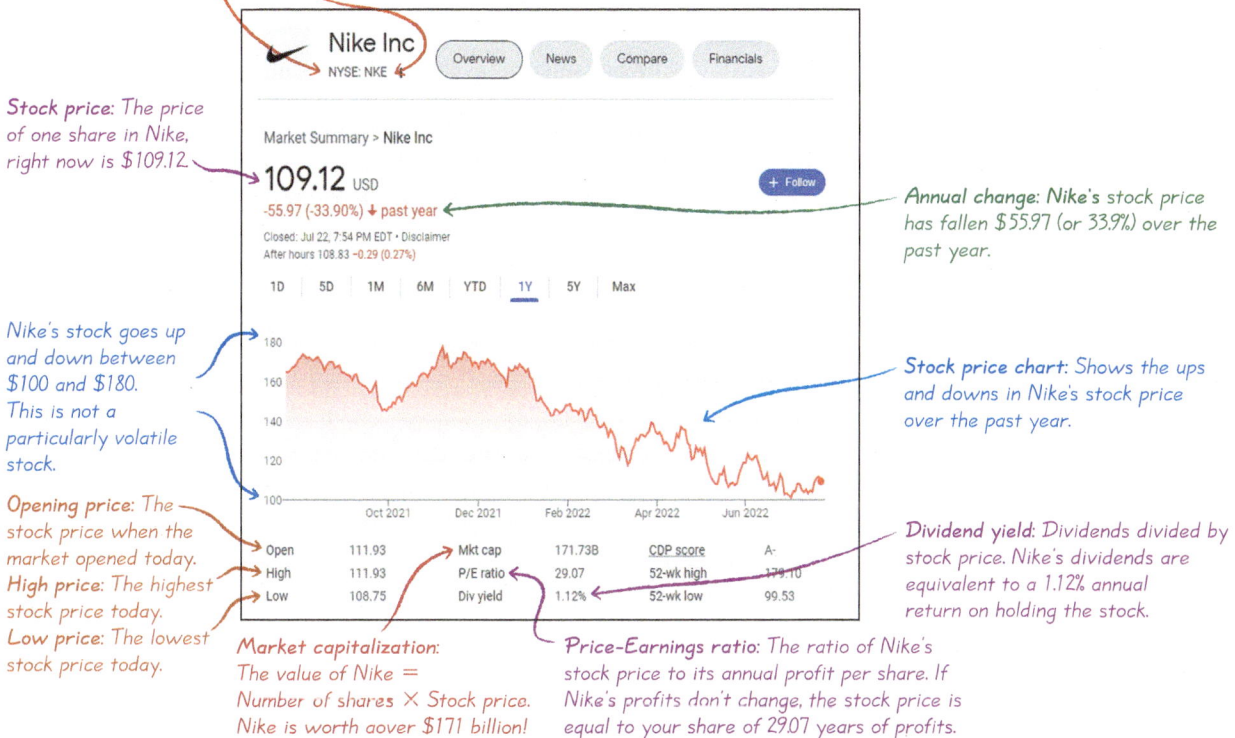

Exchange: Nike's stock is traded on the NYSE, the New York Stock Exchange.
Ticker: Every stock has an official nickname, called its ticker. Nike's is NKE.

Nike Inc
NYSE: NKE
Overview   News   Compare   Financials

Market Summary > Nike Inc

109.12 USD
-55.97 (-33.90%) ↓ past year
Closed: Jul 22, 7:54 PM EDT • Disclaimer
After hours 108.83 -0.29 (0.27%)

+ Follow

1D   5D   1M   6M   YTD   1Y   5Y   Max

Stock price: The price of one share in Nike, right now is $109.12

Annual change: Nike's stock price has fallen $55.97 (or 33.9%) over the past year.

Nike's stock goes up and down between $100 and $180. This is not a particularly volatile stock.

Stock price chart: Shows the ups and downs in Nike's stock price over the past year.

Open	111.93	Mkt cap	171.73B	CDP score	A-
High	111.93	P/E ratio	29.07	52-wk high	179.10
Low	108.75	Div yield	1.12%	52-wk low	99.53

Opening price: The stock price when the market opened today.
High price: The highest stock price today.
Low price: The lowest stock price today.

Market capitalization: The value of Nike = Number of shares × Stock price. Nike is worth aover $171 billion!

Price-Earnings ratio: The ratio of Nike's stock price to its annual profit per share. If Nike's profits don't change, the stock price is equal to your share of 29.07 years of profits.

Dividend yield: Dividends divided by stock price. Nike's dividends are equivalent to a 1.12% annual return on holding the stock.

- The current *stock price* tells you how much your stock is worth.
- The *opening price, high price,* and *low price* summarize what has happened to the stock price during today's trading session: what it traded for at the start of the day, the highest price it sold for today, and the lowest price it sold for today.
- You can get a better sense of how risky a stock is by evaluating its ups and downs over a period of several months or years. This is what a *stock price chart* can show you.
- *Market capitalization* tells you the value of the entire company. It's the number of stocks, multiplied by the stock price.
- Figure 5 also shows some important ratios like the *price-earnings ratio,* which we'll turn to in the next section.
- To get the latest data for yourself, just type "Nike Stock" into Google.

15.4 What Drives Financial Prices?

Learning Objective *Discover what drives financial prices.*

Our next task is to ask: What drives financial prices? We'll focus most of our discussion on what drives stock prices, but as you read, you'll find this material even more useful if you think about how similar ideas apply to the price of other investments. After all, many of the same motivations that lead people to buy and sell stocks lead them to buy and sell other assets such as real estate, fine art, and even truly unusual assets such as alpacas. In each case, you're buying an asset with a limited intrinsic value — perhaps the possibility of a stream of

Figure 6 | The Market for Nike Stock

A The **demand curve** shows how many stocks investors will buy at each price.

B The **supply curve** describes how many stocks investors will sell at each price.

C The **equilibrium price** is determined where supply equals demand.

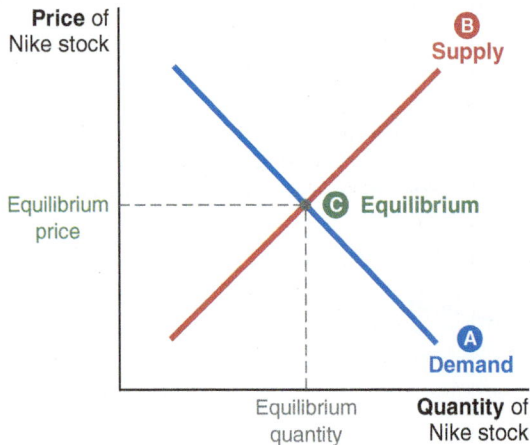

payments if your stock pays a dividend or someone rents your house — and also the potential for big profits or losses if their prices shift sharply.

Valuing Stocks

What determines the price of a stock — or indeed, any other financial asset? As with just about everything else, it's all about supply and demand. Figure 6 shows that the price of a stock reflects the same forces as in any other market. There's a demand curve for Nike stocks describing how many shares investors will buy at each price, just as there's a supply curve describing how many shares investors will sell at each price. As in other markets, the price moves to the equilibrium point where supply equals demand.

The only real difference is that as a savvy investor, you're on both the demand and supply side of the market. If the price of Nike stock is low enough, you'll conclude that it's such a good deal that you'll want to buy it, while if the price is high enough, you'll want to sell it, making you a supplier.

This pushes the question one level deeper: What determines the price at which investors are willing to buy or sell stock? Let's explore some of the different approaches used to value financial assets, including stocks.

fundamental analysis A framework for assessing an asset's fundamental value.

fundamental value The present value of the future profits that a company will earn.

Fundamental value is the present value of future profits. The goal of **fundamental analysis** is to assess an asset's fundamental value. The starting point comes from recognizing that the benefit of owning stock is that it entitles you to a share of a company's future profits. As such, the **fundamental value** of a business is the present value of the future profits it will earn. The fundamental value of a firm determines the fundamental value of stock in that firm. A stock is a good deal when its price is below its fundamental value.

Assessing a business's fundamental value is a four-step process.

Step 1: Forecast future profits. Analysts typically build sophisticated spreadsheet models that project the business's revenues and costs in each of the next 5–10 years. The difference between revenues and costs is the business's expected profits for that year. Beyond that time horizon, analysts usually make their projections by assuming that profits will continue to grow at some constant rate, perhaps reflecting the broader growth rate of the industry.

Step 2: Discount these profits. The opportunity cost principle reminds you that tying up your money comes with an opportunity cost. The opportunity cost of buying a stock is the answer to the "Or what?" question: What else would you do with your money? Perhaps you would buy stock in another company. Each stock will represent a part ownership of a company over its entire lifetime. To compare the two stocks, and thus to consider the opportunity cost of buying any individual stock, you should convert each year's profits into their *present values* to account for this opportunity cost using the discounting formula we introduced in the last chapter. When you're evaluating a risky stock, make sure to use a higher discount rate because the opportunity cost is investing in another risky stock, and riskier stocks typically earn a higher return.

Step 3: Add up the sum of those discounted future profits. The sum of the present value of all of Nike's future profits is your estimate of Nike's fundamental value.

Step 4: Divide the company's fundamental value by the total number of shares. There are 1,600,000,000 Nike shares and each has a claim on Nike's future profits. So the fundamental value of a single Nike stock is 1/1,600,000,000 of the company's fundamental value.

> How to assess a business's fundamental value:
> 1. Forecast future profits
> 2. Discount these profits
> 3. Add up the sum of those discounted future profits
> 4. Divide the company's fundamental value by the total number of shares

If you find Nike stock cheaper than this, then the cost-benefit principle says you should buy the stock. If you're right, and the stock price heads toward its fundamental value, you'll be able to sell the stock for a profit. But even if the market never corrects itself, you can hold that Nike stock, and your calculations suggest that over the long term you'll enjoy a stream of dividends that's more valuable than the price you paid for it.

Here's the big caveat: This investment strategy will succeed only if your estimate of Nike's fundamental value is more accurate than the stock price. If it's not, you may think you're buying an underpriced stock, but actually end up buying an overpriced one.

Relative valuation relies on comparable businesses. An alternative approach, called **relative valuation,** assesses the value of an asset by comparing it to similar assets. In the simplest form of relative valuation, you assess the price of something by comparing it with an almost identical "twin." For example, relative valuation says that if a two-bedroom fourth-floor apartment sold for $120,000, then the value of the almost identical apartment across the hallway is also $120,000. Of course, this only makes sense if the first apartment was sold at an appropriate price.

> **relative valuation** An assessment of the value of an asset by comparing it to similar assets.

Relative valuation gets a bit more difficult when you can't find an identical twin. For instance, no company is anywhere near to being Nike's twin — Nike is more than twice the size of its nearest competitor, Adidas (and is 10 times larger than Under Armour). To get around the problem of comparable size, you can look at *financial ratios* that abstract from each firm's size. Two of the relative-valuation ratios used by Wall Street analysts are:

- *Price-to-book ratio,* which measures a firm's stock price relative to the *book value* per share, which is a measure of the business's net assets per share (calculated as total assets less liabilities). If Nike uses its assets to generate profits at a similar rate as Adidas, then both Nike and Adidas should have a similar price-to-book ratio.

- *Price-to-earnings ratio,* which measures a firm's stock price, relative to last year's profits, measured as *earnings per share*. The idea is that a company with twice the earnings of Adidas should be worth twice as much. If this is true, then Nike and Adidas should have a similar price-to-earnings ratio.

Do the Economics

Use relative valuation to price Nike's stock.

Figure 7 contains some key 2021 financial data for Adidas, one of Nike's key competitors. We're going to use these numbers to estimate Nike's value.

a. Calculate the price-to-book ratio for Adidas stock.

$$\text{Adidas' price-to-book ratio is } \frac{\text{Price per share}}{\text{Book value per share}} = \frac{\$144}{\$23.90} = 6.03$$

b. Calculate the price-to-earnings ratio for Adidas stock.

$$\text{Adidas' price-to-earnings ratio is } \frac{\text{Price per share}}{\text{Earnings per share}} = \frac{\$144}{\$6.45} = 22.3$$

Okay, let's use your calculations to value Nike's stock.

c. If Nike can produce the same price-to-book ratio as Adidas, what's the value of Nike stock? Note that Nike's book value per share was $9.49.

$$\frac{\text{Price per share}_{\text{Nike}}}{\text{Book value per share}_{\text{Nike}}} = 6.03$$

$$\text{Rearranging: Price per share}_{\text{Nike}} = 6.03 \times \text{Book value per}$$
$$\text{share}_{\text{Nike}} = 6.03 \times \$9.49 = \$57$$

Figure 7 | Sneakers, by the Numbers

Measure	adidas	NIKE
Stock price per share	$144	$119
Earnings per share	$6.45	$3.75
Book value per share	$23.90	$9.49

Data from: Adidas, Nike.

d. Let's try another approach. If Nike had the same price-to-earnings ratio as Adidas, what is the value of Nike stock? Note that Nike's earnings per share was $3.75.

$$\frac{\text{Price per share}_{\text{Nike}}}{\text{Earnings per share}_{\text{Nike}}} = 22.3$$

Re-arranging: Price per share$_{\text{Nike}}$ = $22.3 \times$ Earnings per share$_{\text{Nike}}$ = $22.3 \times \$3.75 = \$84$

Okay, we've used two relative-valuation techniques, and they give different values. One says that Nike stock was worth $57, while the other says it was worth $84. In reality, Nike's stock price was at a much higher level of $118. But our analysis suggested that this was overvalued, and indeed, the stock fell back to around $100 by mid-2022. ■

The key to getting a relative valuation right is to make sure that you're comparing companies that are otherwise quite similar. This means that you should compare Nike only to companies with similar risk, growth prospects, and funding needs. But this doesn't mean just comparing Nike to other sporting goods companies. Some analysts have argued that Nike should also be compared with other shoe companies, such as Crocs, clothing companies, such as Champion, or luxury brands, such as Coach.

EVERYDAY Economics   **How much should you pay for that house?**

What's a good price for this tiny house?

You can apply the same principles you use to value stocks to value real estate. When the time comes for you to buy your first home, they can help you decide how much you're willing to pay for a house or condo.

Just as the *fundamental value* of a business derives from the profits it delivers each year, the fundamental value of a home derives from the "profit" you make from not having to pay rent each year. And just as you can figure out how much a stock is worth by adding up the present value of these future profits, you can figure out how much a home is worth by adding up the future value of this implicit rent. Once you purchase a home, your opportunity cost of living in it is the rent you could earn if you rented it to someone else instead.

You can also use *relative valuation* to value a home. If you can't find a twin for the home that you're buying, focus instead on a relative-valuation ratio. The most common ratio investors use when valuing housing is the price-to-size ratio. As with all relative-valuation techniques, it's important to compare like with like, and in this case, it means comparing houses of a similar quality in a similar neighborhood. If similar-quality homes in your neighborhood typically sell at a price-to-size ratio of around $100 per square foot, then this approach says that a 2,000-square-foot house will sell for around $200,000. It also says that a 400-square-foot tiny house will sell for $40,000. ■

The Efficient Markets Hypothesis

Nike's stock price is determined by supply and demand. Demand to buy Nike stock comes from people who believe that Nike's fundamental value is higher than its stock price. Supply of Nike stock comes from investors who want to sell it because they believe its fundamental value is lower than the price. In equilibrium, demand equals supply, which means that Nike's stock price moves to the exact point where there are as many bets placed that it is overpriced as there are that it is underpriced. This perspective suggests that a stock price represents the market's collective judgment about a company's fundamental value.

Stock prices reflect all publicly available information about a company's fundamental value. When an analyst discovers some good news for Nike — perhaps the cost of rubber used to make sneakers will be a little lower — it leads them to upgrade their assessment of Nike's value. As a result, the fund that they manage will buy more stock in Nike, and this extra demand will nudge the price up. Another analyst discovers some bad news — sales are slow in Malaysia! — leading their fund to sell the stock, which nudges the price down.

As thousands of analysts dig into the details, Nike's stock price will come to reflect all of this information. That's the idea behind the **efficient markets hypothesis,** which holds that at any point in time, financial prices reflect all publicly available information.

It's tough to beat the market.
The efficient markets hypothesis doesn't mean that a stock's price is always exactly equal to its fundamental value. Rather, it says that it's impossible to predict whether it is under- or overpriced based on publicly available information.

This explains why it's so hard to make money buying and selling stocks. You're looking to buy a stock whose fundamental value is higher than its price. But the efficient markets hypothesis says that it's impossible to tell whether a stock is under- or overpriced — or at least, it's impossible unless you have information that is not known by other people. Information that isn't publicly known is called inside information, trading on inside information is illegal (that's called insider trading). The market includes many traders, each of whom diligently look for an edge. If any information indicated that Nike was underpriced, all these traders would have already snapped up the underpriced Nike stock, thereby bidding the price back up to its fundamental value.

The same idea applies to other financial markets, too. Billions of dollars' worth of bonds and foreign currencies are traded every day, with thousands of analysts and traders looking for every little edge. As such, it's nearly impossible to identify a bond or foreign currency that is undervalued.

Some markets are less competitive. For example, the market for houses, Picassos, and baseball cards may not be perfectly efficient. But even so, there are enough smart cookies trading these assets that even sophisticated finance professionals find it very difficult to identify undervalued assets. That's why people digging through flea markets — or scrolling through eBay — looking for undervalued antiques typically end up with little to show for their efforts.

Financial prices move unpredictably.
The logic of the efficient markets hypothesis also suggests that it will be impossible to predict whether stock prices will rise or fall over the next minute, hour, day, week, or year. After all, if there's information suggesting that the stock price should rise next Friday, then some trader will figure out that they can make money by buying the stock on Thursday to sell on Friday afternoon. You could beat them to it by buying the stock on Wednesday instead, but some smarty might jump ahead of you and buy stock on Tuesday. Follow this logic far enough, and you'll see that people buy and sell stock today based on news about the future, and they'll do this to the point that they eliminate any predictable future stock price changes.

If forward-looking traders eliminate all predictable stock price changes, all that's left will be unpredictable changes. This logic suggests that stock price *changes* are unpredictable. This is really just an application of the idea that stock prices already reflect all publicly available information — in this case, it says that the stock price already reflects the information that would otherwise cause the stock price to rise or fall in the future. When a price moves in an unpredictable way, we say it follows a **random walk,** which means that it follows an unpredictable path.

Technical analysis looks for patterns—even where none exist.
All this means that *technical analysis* — studying graphs of financial prices over time, finding patterns, and trying to use those patterns to predict the future — doesn't really work. You can't make money predicting the unpredictable. This can be hard for people to believe. Humans have an instinctive need to try to find order among chaos, and that instinct can easily lead you to believe that you can spot patterns even where none exist.

A random walk doesn't mean that stock prices move in any crazy old way. Good news still means that a stock price will rise, but the stock price will rise as soon as traders get

efficient markets hypothesis The theory that at any point in time, stock prices reflect all publicly available information.

Everyone at the flea market is hoping they'll find an underpriced treasure.

random walk When a price follows an unpredictable path.

wind of it, which may even be before the positive outcome occurs. For example, the stock of a pharmaceutical company will rise as soon as word gets out that the company has developed an effective new treatment for Covid-19. And it will rise again when they learn that the new drug has been approved by the FDA. By the time the company actually shows a profit from selling the new Covid-19 treatment, all those profits are already expected by stockholders and thus are reflected in the stock price.

Do the Economics

Can you predict stock price movements?

Let's test out this random walk idea. Can you predict whether stock market prices will rise or fall? Figure 8 shows stock price data for a random month for each of 99 leading stocks. If you think the stock rose the next day, mark it with a ✓, but if you think it fell, mark it with a ✗.

Figure 8 | **Can You Predict Whether These Stocks Will Rise or Fall Next?**

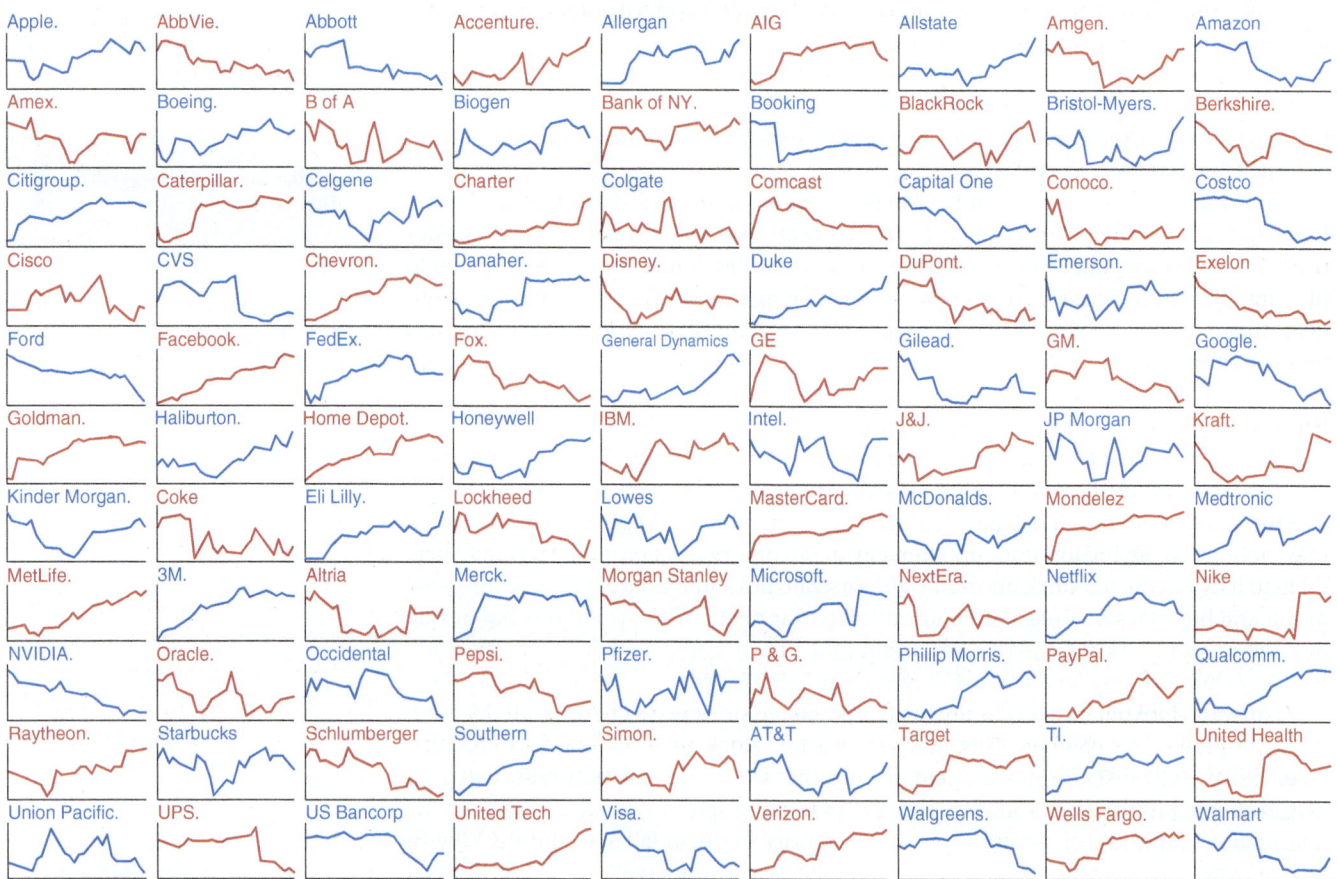

Data from: Bloomberg.

<u>Answer:</u> Hey, make sure you've finished making your predictions before you look up the answer! Seriously. Finish it first.

Okay, so now you're really done? If there's a period at the end of a stock's name, that means the stock rose the next day.

How did you do? Most students get roughly as many right as they get wrong — somewhere between 44 and 55 out of 99 — which is just what the random walk theory suggests. Occasionally there's a student who gets a few more right than wrong, but the margin is still small enough that it could be luck. ∎

The Value of Expert Advice

A few years back, an English newspaper ran a stock-picking contest pitting a leading wealth manager, a stockbroker, and a fund manager against a ginger cat called Orlando. The pros did what pros normally do, crunching reams of data to find what they considered the best stocks to buy. By contrast, Orlando threw his favorite toy mouse onto a grid representing different stocks. At the end of the year, Orlando had beaten the pros.

That's nuts, right? Wouldn't you figure that knowing nothing about stocks — or being a cat — would be a severe handicap in a stock-picking contest?

Not so fast, says the efficient markets hypothesis. If it's impossible — or at least really difficult — to beat the market, then it must also be really hard to do worse than the market. After all, if Orlando really were a worse stock picker on average, then you could make money just by doing the opposite of whatever he did. It follows that if the efficient markets hypothesis is right, Orlando is as good at picking stocks as any professional. (And in this case, he got a bit lucky and beat them.) This is the logic that once led an economist to claim that "a blindfolded monkey throwing darts at a newspaper's financial pages could select a portfolio that would do just as well as one carefully selected by the experts."

Thousands of researchers — including both university professors and Wall Street analysts — have conducted careful studies trying to assess whether they can predict where stocks are going. The conclusion tends to be that it's incredibly hard to predict stock prices, although it may not be impossible. You've probably heard of Warren Buffett — he's made billions by seeking out businesses that he thinks are undervalued. But while everyone wants to be like Buffett, few have been able to mimic his success.

Orlando wasn't quite purrfect, but he beat three pros.

Not even experts can beat the market consistently. Here's the surprising truth about financial analysts: While some make money, even more lose money, relative to a strategy of just buying a small chunk of each company. So what keeps these analysts going? The short answer is that the money they're losing belongs to investors like you, and people like you keep hoping that they've found the right financial expert who will allow them to beat the market. But hope isn't reality, and you probably haven't found one of the handful of financial whizzes who can beat the market.

To see this, let's consider how the typical person invests in the stock market. Most people who hold stocks do so through **mutual funds,** which buy a portfolio of stocks (and sometimes bonds) on their behalf. Your employer's retirement plan will probably allow you to choose from a list of different mutual funds into which you can put your savings. There are two types of mutual funds:

mutual fund A fund that buys a portfolio of stocks (and sometimes bonds) on your behalf.

- **Actively managed** mutual funds pay handsome salaries to expert stock pickers who put your money in the stocks that they think are likely to do particularly well.

- **Index funds** don't pay for any fancy stock pickers; instead, they just program a computer to automatically buy every stock that is in the S&P 500 or some other broad market index.

actively managed When a fund is managed by stock pickers.

index fund A mutual fund that consists of a broad market index.

If you're ever tempted to put your money in an actively managed mutual fund, think again. Over the past 20 years, the average actively managed mutual fund earned an annual return of 8.14%. By contrast, Figure 9 shows that putting your money a comparable stock index called the S&P 500 — which is what index funds do and involves no expertise at all — earned an average return of 9.68%. That difference might sound small, but it adds up. An $100,000 investment in the S&P 500 would have grown to $635,000 over this period, while the actively managed funds would have yielded $478,000. You would have netted an extra $157,000 by *not* hiring an expert stock picker.

Figure 9 | **It's Hard to Beat the Stock Market**

Average annual investment returns from 2001-2021

S&P 500	9.68%
Actively managed mutual funds	8.14%

Data from: SPIVA U.S. Scorecard.

What explains this? It's not that professional stock pickers are particularly bad at picking stocks. Rather, they're not particularly good. The stocks they pick rise roughly in line with the S&P 500, but they charge you a lot of money for their "expertise." These high fees make them a bad bet.

Past performance is no guarantee of future performance. In my experience, nearly every stock picker will tell you that they're going to do well in the next few years. Many of them will tout their track records, telling you that they've beaten the market in the past. But these same claims always have an asterisk[*] next to them directing you to the fine print:

> *Past performance is no guarantee of future performance.

Did you see the fine print? It actually understates the case. It should say this instead:

> *Past performance is almost completely unrelated to future performance.

Careful studies have shown that a fund's performance in the past year does not help predict how well the fund will do in the future. Researchers studying decades of returns have found no positive correlation between past and future performance of mutual funds over the past 40 years. In fact, they found that in recent years you could actually have done a little worse by relying on past performance, as the top performers tend to do slightly worse than their competitors.

Whatever made a stock picker do well in the past didn't help them much in the future. It's the sort of pattern that suggests that none of them are better than the market all the time, but some of them get lucky some of the time.

Remember Warren Buffett? A few years ago he offered to bet that the S&P 500 stock index would outperform the most actively managed funds — known as hedge funds — over 10 years. Buffett said that he waited expectantly for "a parade of fund managers . . . to come forth and defend their occupation." After all, he said, if they were so confident in their ability, why wouldn't they put a little of their own money on the line? Well, there was a good reason that only one person took the bet: That person lost. The loser conceded, stating, "Passive investing is all the rage today." Why? Because the difficulty of beating the market means that your portfolio will grow faster if you put your money in well-diversified, low-fee index funds.

EVERYDAY Economics   How to save like an economist

Figure 10 | Investment Advice from Leading Economists

"*In general, absent any inside information, an equity investor can expect to do better by holding a well-diversified, low-fee, passive index fund than by holding a few stocks.*"

Responses of leading economists:

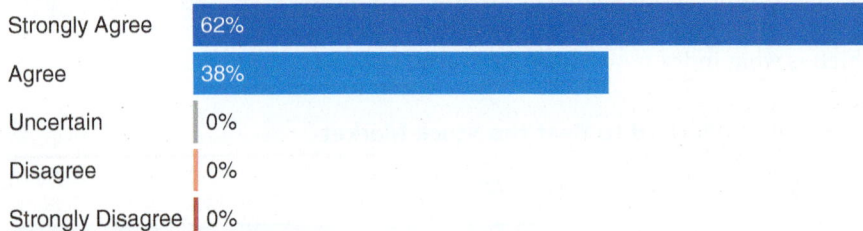

Strongly Agree	62%
Agree	38%
Uncertain	0%
Disagree	0%
Strongly Disagree	0%

Data from: IGM Economic Experts Panel.

What do economists do with their own money? Given the evidence so far, you won't be surprised to hear that most of them put their savings into well-diversified index funds. Figure 10 shows the results of a survey that asked an expert panel of economists whether a person does better in the stock market by picking a few stocks or by choosing a well-diversified, low-cost index fund. An index fund doesn't pay for any fancy stock pickers, which helps them keep their fees really low. The best of these funds are so lean that they have very few expenses — about 0.2% of the money they're handling for you, compared to a number closer to 1% or sometimes as much as 2% for an actively managed mutual fund. An index fund also ensures that you have a well-diversified portfolio. Economists ignore past stock-picking performance because it doesn't predict future performance. The only indicator they focus on is the fees that are charged, which are sometimes called expense ratios. They focus on fees because they're the best predictor of a fund's returns. After all, even if it's hard to predict good stocks, it's easy to predict that paying high fees will make you poorer. While saving a fraction of a percentage point on fees each year doesn't sound like a big deal, it is. If you put $100,000 in an index fund for 30 years and let it compound, you could end up saving around $120,000 in fees if you choose the lowest-cost option. ■

The efficient markets hypothesis teaches you the value of modesty.

There's so much money to be made by whoever can figure out how to predict which stocks will rise, and when, that it remains a hot area of research. For now, it's probably best to say the debate is between those who think that the efficient markets hypothesis is right most of the time, versus those who think it's right nearly all of the time. If you can be first to bring new information to the market, you can probably profit from it, but realize that new information gets incorporated so quickly that you might only have milliseconds to react.

More importantly, even if you don't believe the efficient markets hypothesis is exactly right, it sounds an important warning that you should always bear in mind: Be modest about your ability to pick stocks, or indeed any financial asset. Before you trade, you should ask yourself: Is it likely that the market has overlooked the information you're relying on? Is it likely that your analysis is smarter than the collective wisdom of thousands of traders who spend their lives studying that stock? Always remember that if a stock's price doesn't align with your valuation, there's a good chance that it's your valuation that's wrong, rather than the stock price.

The stock market can help predict economic changes. Experts find it hard to beat the stock market because market prices already embed so much expertise and information. But this also means that stock prices reflect what people think will happen to individual companies and the economy overall. If stocks in many companies are rising, that's a signal that traders are expecting good times ahead, and if stocks are falling, that's a signal that perhaps there's bad news ahead. As Figure 11 shows, the S&P 500 — which is a broad indicator of stock prices — tends to rise in anticipation of a strong economy, and fall in anticipation of an economic downturn. In February 2020, stock prices fell as news of the potential impact of the Covid pandemic spread. And stock prices fell in 2022 as fears of a recession grew.

Figure 11 | Stock Price Movements Predict GDP Growth

Percent change over the past year
GDP Stock prices (S&P 500)

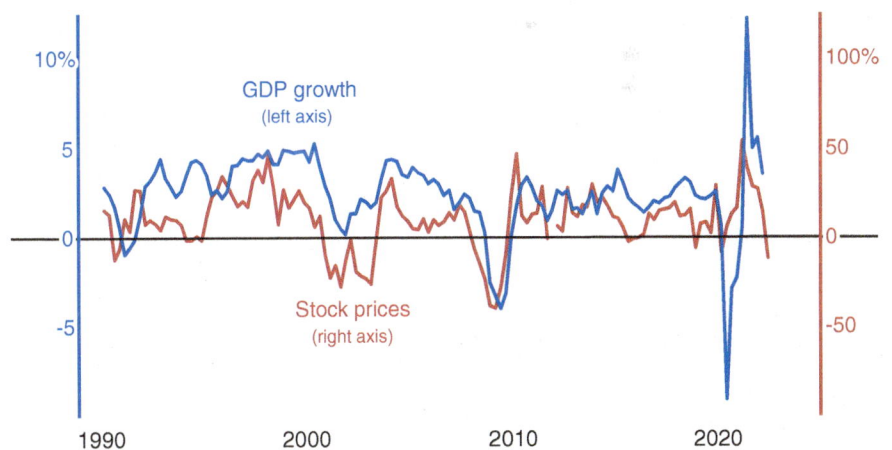

Data from: BEA and S&P.

As a result, stock prices are a closely watched macroeconomic indicator. That said, stock prices are extremely volatile, and not every blip translates into changing economic conditions. In fact, sometimes stock prices do some pretty puzzling things, which brings us to our next topic: stock market bubbles.

Financial Bubbles

As the internet economy started to blossom in the late 1990s, Silicon Valley was an extraordinary, almost magical place. New companies sprang up nearly every day, and many enjoyed explosive growth. The internet was the Wild West, and young programmers

Figure 12 | Mania Surrounding the Dot-com Boom Led to a Bubble in Tech Stocks. . . Until It Burst

NASDAQ composite index, a measure of the price of tech-industry stocks

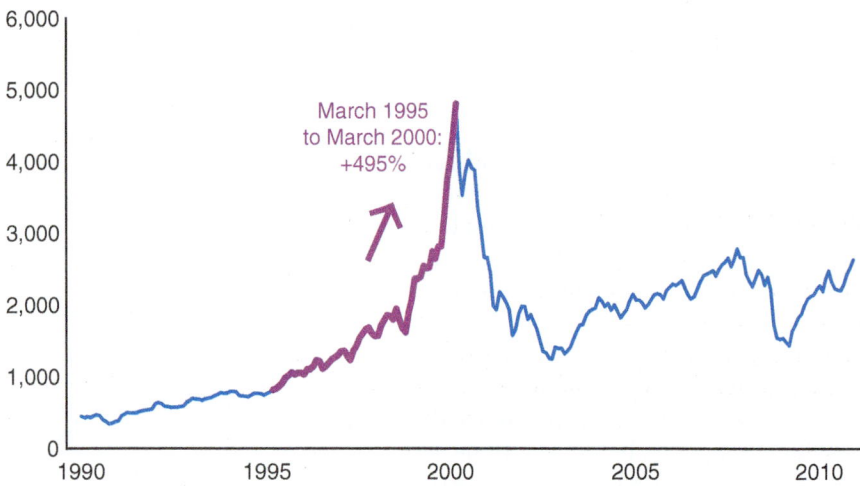

March 1995 to March 2000: +495%

Data from: NASDAQ.

speculative bubble When the price of an asset rises above what appears to be its fundamental value.

Not worth $6 billion.

"greater fool" theory The idea that people buy an investment because they expect other people to buy it from them at a higher price.

were the settlers making their fortune as they explored the new frontier. Amazon, eBay, and Google were born, and their founders became incredibly rich. It seemed like anyone with a good idea, and some with a bad idea, could get funding with a snappy-sounding pitch to hungry investors.

Investors were excited for a piece of the action, paying increasingly higher and higher prices for stock in these young companies. By March 2000, this building excitement had led the price of the NASDAQ index — a basket of mainly tech-related stocks — to rise by 495%, as shown in Figure 12. Some companies that had never made a profit were priced as if they were worth billions. For instance, stock in a grocery delivery service called Webvan rose so high that the company was valued as if it were worth $6 billion, even though it had less than $5 million in revenue at the time and was operating at a loss. The price of many of these technology stocks was disconnected from their future profits.

When the price of an asset — like a stock — rises above what appears to be its fundamental value, we call it a **speculative bubble** because prices are highly inflated. And just like a bubble, it can keep inflating for a while, until — POP! — it bursts. In March 2000, the dot-com bubble did just that, and the value of many of these stocks plummeted. Webvan's stock price fell from $25.44 to $0.06, before it went bust, along with dozens of other dot-com hopefuls. If you had invested $1,000 in the NASDAQ in March 2000, it was worth only $260 two-and-a-half years later.

What could possibly lead to a bubble like this? To answer that, we'll have to talk about cute puppies.

The stock market is like a puppy beauty contest. One view of the stock market is that it's like a puppy beauty contest. Here's how: In a puppy beauty contest, there are photos of a bunch of puppies, and if you correctly guess which is most popular — that is, the one that most people guess to be cutest — then you're eligible for a prize.

It's your choice now:

Which puppy would you pick?

(Hint: If you're thinking, "Which puppy is cutest?" think again.)

The best strategy isn't to pick the cutest puppy. It's to pick the puppy that you think *others* will think is cutest. Or go a step further: You want to pick the puppy that you think others are most likely to think that others will pick. And so it goes on. Keep thinking this way, and soon enough, you won't be thinking about which puppy is cute at all, but rather you'll focus on other people's expectations about other people's expectations.

How does this relate to stocks? Stock-buying behavior can resemble a puppy beauty contest because what a stock is worth is what someone else will pay for it. So, instead of picking the stock that will yield the best return, you might pick the stock that you think others will soon bid up. This idea, that people buy an asset because they expect other people to buy it from them at a higher price, is called the **"greater fool" theory** because it means that you'll buy a stock (like Webvan) at five times what it is really worth, as long as you think there's some greater fool out there who will be willing to pay 10 times what it is worth next week. If everyone believes that everyone else believes that tech stocks will keep rising, then everyone will keep buying tech stocks in hopes of selling them later at an even higher price. And that's how a bubble keeps getting inflated.

This is not a strategy that I recommend. While it will work for a while — as long as the bubble keeps inflating — all bubbles eventually burst, and one day you'll wake up to discover that you can't find a "greater fool" willing to overpay for your overpriced stock. This happened to tech stocks in 2000, and when the market crashed, it wiped out many people's life savings.

Even if it's a bubble, it might not be about to burst. Our analysis of stock market bubbles is not quite complete. There's one remaining mystery: Why aren't speculative bubbles stopped by other investors taking the opposite position? There are three key reasons why bubbles persist.

Reason 1: It can be hard to spot a speculative bubble. The internet was new and exciting, and no one really knew how much it would transform the global economy. You might suspect that Webvan is overvalued, but in the excitement over the internet, you convince yourself that it might be the next generation's Walmart.

Reason 2: Even if you spot a speculative bubble, it can be hard to bet against it. Okay, you think Webvan stock is overpriced. Now what? You won't buy it, but beyond that, if there's no easy way to bet that a stock will go down, the price won't reflect your opinion.

Reason 3: You don't know when the bubble will burst. Tony Dye was a British money manager who understood that dot-com stocks were in a bubble. He sold all his tech stocks and warned his clients to stay out. Eventually, he was proven to be correct. But not for a few years. Meanwhile, his clients watched unhappily as their friends got rich buying dot-coms. Tech stocks kept rising, leading newspapers to ridicule Dye. As his clients abandoned his firm, Dye took "early retirement," which probably meant he was forced out.

The problem is that a bubble can outlast you. For Tony Dye, the bubble lasted longer than he could keep his job. For those betting that stocks will fall, the bubble can last longer than your savings. So even when you're right about it being a bubble, it's really difficult to predict when it will burst.

EVERYDAY Economics | **What do housing, tulips, and alpacas have in common with the stock market?**

Speculative bubbles don't just drive occasional bouts of stock market exuberance — they're also important in many other markets, too.

Perhaps the most consequential bubble to hit a large number of American families occurred in the early 2000s. Home loans were easy to get, and house prices always seemed to rise. Together, these trends made homeownership seem both accessible and profitable. Some folks bought houses to live in, while others bought them with an eye to making a few quick improvements, and then selling (or "flipping") them at a higher price. For a while, it worked, and house prices more than doubled in Miami, Tampa, Las Vegas, and Phoenix, as you can see in Figure 13. Then the housing market bubble burst, and house prices fell by half or more.

Figure 13 | A Bubble Led to Inflated House Prices . . . Until It Burst

Change in house prices since January 2000

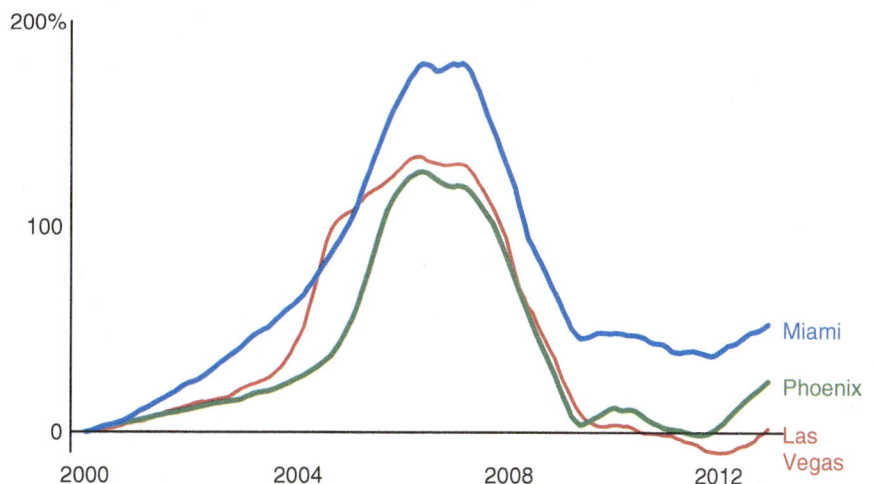

Data from: S&P/Case-Shiller Indices.

Catherine Hood/EyeEm/Getty Images

What is this alpaca worth?

The decline in house prices left many people with debts they could not repay. This was the first domino to fall in a chain of financial market problems that eventually caused the financial sector to freeze up in 2008, and brought on a global recession.

Perhaps the strangest ever bubble occurred in seventeenth-century Holland, when the Dutch became enamored with tulips. They saw tulips as valuable because a single tulip could be used to breed more tulips, which could be sold to others who saw tulips as valuable. At the peak of the bubble, the price of a single tulip bulb rose to the value of a luxury house. You can guess what happened next: The bubble burst, and tulip prices fell by over 95%.

A similar story happened with alpacas, the cute South American animals with llama-like long necks and long eyelashes. In the 1990s and 2000s, farmers in the United States became gripped by an alpaca craze, paying top dollar for alpacas, in hopes of breeding more alpacas that other farmers might pay top dollar for. For a while, it worked, and prices spiraled as high as half a million dollars for a top breeder. But then the bubble burst, and prices plummeted, forcing many investors into bankruptcy. Some were forced to sell their herd for $100 per head or less. ■

15.5 Personal Finance

Learning Objective *Make better decisions in financial markets.*

Our final task to conclude our tour of the financial sector is to bring together the major lessons for managing your personal finances. There are six important lessons I want you to apply to your financial life.

Lesson 1: Harness the power of compound interest. In the previous chapter on investment, you learned about the magic of compound interest. The power of compound interest depends a lot on the interest rate you get. Between 1925 and 2021, the average real annual return from buying government treasury bills was only 0.5%, corporate bonds yielded 3.0%, stocks in large companies yielded 6.9%, and riskier stocks in small companies yielded 8.8%. While past performance is no guarantee of the future, let's take a look at how different financial assets would have fared over that 90-year period. Recall that the compounding formula is

$$\text{Future value in } t \text{ years} = \text{Present value} \times (1 + r)^t$$

Calculate the real future value of $1,000 of savings put in each of these alternatives:

	Average annual real return	Real future value of $1,000 investment in 90 years
Treasury bills	0.5%	$1,000 \times (1 + 0.005)^{90} = \$1,567$
Corporate bonds	3.0%	$1,000 \times (1 + 0.03)^{90} = \$14,300$
Large-company stocks	6.9%	$1,000 \times (1 + 0.069)^{90} = \$405,502$
Small-company stocks	8.8%	$1,000 \times (1 + 0.088)^{90} = \$1.98$ million!

If you're surprised by how much a small amount of money can grow over time, you're not alone. There's a (possibly apocryphal) story that Albert Einstein once declared "the power of compound interest the most powerful force in the universe."

While compounding happens automatically with bank deposits — the interest you earn is deposited into your savings account where it too earns interest — the same principle applies to bonds and stocks. If you reinvest what you earn, your little nest egg will grow into a secure retirement fund. That's why you should start saving early and save your gains. Over the past century, stocks have had a much larger average annual return than bonds, which means effectively more compound interest if you use your dividend payments to buy more stocks. So you may end up with a larger nest egg with stocks than with bonds — but remember that stocks are riskier.

Lesson 2: Don't pick individual stocks. If you do want to put your money in stocks, it's best not to try to pick winners and losers in the stock market. Even if the efficient markets hypothesis is not perfectly right, it is *mostly* right. So while it may not be completely impossible to beat the market, it's still really, really, hard to do. Here's a sad truth: Research shows that many investors are overconfident, believing that they have the ability to beat the collective wisdom of the market, even though most of them actually can't. So don't bother trying to pick individual stocks that will outperform the market. Remember, Orlando the cat might do a better job.

Lesson 3: Diversify your portfolio to reduce risk. If you put your money into just a few big things, you run the risk of losing it all. It's far better to put small amounts of money into lots of different assets. This diversification will reduce how much your wealth will move up and down each year, making it less risky. The easiest way to diversify your stock holdings is to buy index funds, which do all the work of buying a basket of many different stocks for you.

Lesson 4: Past performance is no guarantee of future performance. Instead of picking stocks, some people pick stock pickers, putting their money into actively managed mutual funds. Some of these stock pickers have done well in the past. Not only is past performance no guarantee of future performance; they're almost unrelated. Don't believe professional stock pickers who promise you that they'll beat the market.

Lesson 5: Minimize fees. One easy way to ensure you still get a better return is to minimize the fees you pay. Don't buy and sell stock a lot — that will cost you brokerage fees, and the stock you're buying probably won't be any better than the stock you're selling. Avoid actively managed mutual funds that charge hefty fees for their useless "expertise." And if you're looking at passively managed indexed funds, shop around to find the fund that charges the lowest fees.

Lesson 6: Follow all five rules with low-cost index funds. The easiest way to follow all of these lessons is to put your savings in low-cost index funds. It's what most economists do with their money!

> Financial lessons:
> 1. Harness the power of compound interest.
> 2. Don't pick individual stocks.
> 3. Diversify your portfolio to reduce risk.
> 4. Past performance is no guarantee of future performance.
> 5. Minimize paying fees.
> 6. Follow all five rules with low-cost index funds.

15.6 Tying It Together

Four Functions—and One Big Risk—of the Financial Sector

The financial system performs several important functions in modern economies, without which existing businesses would find it difficult to expand and new businesses would find it hard to get started. That means that economies would struggle to grow, which means lower living standards for people. In short, we all benefit when the financial system works. And it works by serving four key functions.

Function 1: It reallocates resources from savers to borrowers. The financial sector facilitates the growth of businesses by moving resources to where they can best be used. You can think of it as a *bridge* that connects savers who have spare resources with borrowers who need more resources than they currently have. When savers put their money in the bank, buy bonds, or buy stock, the financial sector trucks moves the money so that potential borrowers can access the funds. This funding enables people to make investments — in a college education, a family home, or launching or expanding their business — when they wouldn't otherwise be able to pay for those investments up front.

Function 2: It shifts resources through time. You can also think of the financial sector as a *time machine* that can move your money through time. This is particularly important for investments that involve a big up-front cost today that'll generate ample returns in the future. The financial sector makes it possible to spend money today that you'll only earn in the future. It effectively gives you the means to zap money from the future to the present — by borrowing from a bank, issuing stock, or issuing bonds. Alternatively, if you want to zap money from the present into the future, you just need to deposit that money in the bank, or alternatively put it in stocks or bonds. In the future, when you need that money, you can make a bank withdrawal or sell those stocks or bonds. Voila! Your money just traveled through time to meet Future You. And hopefully it grew a bit along the way.

Function 3: It reallocates, spreads, and reduces risk. The financial sector does more than move money around, it also plays a protective role, *reallocating, spreading, and diversifying risks*. The financial sector helps people reduce risk by slicing it into smaller pieces that can then be bought and sold. It lets you buy a small amount of many different stocks and a small amount of bonds issued by many different companies, and lets your bank loan your savings to many different borrowers. The result is that you'll hold a diversified portfolio, which is a lot less risky than one big bet. As people buy and sell these risks, the risks will be reallocated to the people best positioned to bear them. The result of all this diversification and reallocation is that each of us faces less risk, which means you can sleep easier, knowing your savings will still be there tomorrow.

Function 4: It creates liquidity. The financial sector also creates *liquidity*, which means that you can quickly and easily convert your investments into cash, with little or no loss in value. As a partial owner of Nike, you'll always have access to your money because you can easily sell your stock on the stock market whenever you want to. Likewise, buying a 10-year bond doesn't commit your money for 10 years because you can sell that bond on the bond market. And you can turn your bank balance into cash simply by going to the ATM to make a withdrawal. All of this liquidity is a good thing: It means that you can make long-term investments, but you'll still be able to access your money if you need it.

One big risk: It creates interdependence. However, the usefulness of financial markets comes with an important warning. The interdependence principle plays a big role in the financial sector, and all this interdependence can make the economy more vulnerable to financial shocks. The value of a stock or a bond depends on what other people are willing to pay for it, which depends on what they think others are willing to pay for it. This raises the possibility of speculative bubbles, which can burst savagely, destabilizing the economy. When your money is used to fund other financial investments that can be used to fund other financial investments, a chain of interdependence is created, which can cause one bad investment to have ripple effects. If no one knows which other financial institutions are exposed to those losses, then these ripple effects can create a wave of fear, as no one knows whose money is safe.

The point is that even though the financial sector does a lot to make the economy work better — reallocating resources from savers to investors, shifting money through time, spreading and reducing risk, and creating liquidity — it also makes the economy more vulnerable to manias, panics, and crashes.

Chapter 15 Review
Chapter at a Glance

Banks	The Bond Market	The Stock Market

What they are:

Banks	The Bond Market	The Stock Market
A **bank** borrows money from savers and lends it out in an effort to earn itself a profit.	A **bond** is an IOU. Specifically, a promise to pay back a loan with interest.	A **stock** represents partial ownership in a firm that may pay uncertain future dividends.
Shadow banks are financial firms that are similar to banks, but are not regulated like banks.	The **bond market** is where companies and governments can borrow large sums of money.	The **stock market** is the market where people buy and sell existing stocks.

What they do:

1. Reallocate resources from savers to borrowers

Banks	The Bond Market	The Stock Market
A saver deposits money in the bank which the bank lends to others helping fund their investments.	A saver buys bonds, funding company or government investments.	A saver buys shares in a company, funding company investment.

2. Shift resources through time

Banks	The Bond Market	The Stock Market
Money deposited today can be withdrawn in the future. Money borrowed today is repaid in the future.	Bonds bought today can be sold in the future. Bonds sold by companies or governments today must be repaid in the future.	Stocks bought today can be sold in the future. A company selling shares today gives up a share of its profits in the future.

3. Reallocate, spread, and reduce risk

Banks	The Bond Market	The Stock Market
Savings are lent out to multiple borrowers.	Bonds can be bought in multiple companies or governments.	Stock can be bought in multiple companies.

4. Create liquidity

Banks	The Bond Market	The Stock Market
Savers can always withdraw their savings. Borrowers get long-term loans.	Bondholders can sell their bonds. The issuer repays whoever owns the bond on maturity.	Shareholders can sell their stock. The investment remains with the company forever.

5. One big risk: They create interdependencies

Banks	The Bond Market	The Stock Market
Bank runs	Default risk, term risk, and liquidity risk	Speculative bubbles

Other functions

Banks	The Bond Market	The Stock Market
Solve information problems Provide payment services	Fund government debt	Reallocate control

What is:

Liquidity:	The ability to quickly and easily convert your savings into cash, with little or no loss in value.
Speculative bubble:	When the price of an asset rises above what appears to be its fundamental value.
Bank run:	When many bank customers try to withdraw their savings at the same time.
Efficient market hypothesis:	The theory that at any point in time, stock prices reflect all publically available information.

Key Terms

actively managed, 393	fundamental value, 388	random walk, 391
bank run, 378	"greater fool" theory, 396	relative valuation, 389
bond, 381	index funds, 393	retained earnings, 384
default risk, 383	initial public offering, 385	shadow banks, 380
deposit insurance, 379	liquidity, 382	speculative bubble, 396
dividends, 384	liquidity risk, 383	stock market, 385
efficient markets hypothesis, 391	maturity transformation, 378	term risk, 383
fundamental analysis, 388	mutual funds, 393	

Study Problems

Learning Objective 15.1 *Assess the role that banks play in funneling money from savers to investors.*

1. You deposit money into a bank account. Explain what happens to that money and how the bank makes a profit.

2. Do you have a checking or savings account? Why or why not? Would you still have an account if you earned no interest on your deposits? What if you had to pay fees?

3. How does maturity transformation impact long-term investment spending? What are some risks a bank can face trying to balance the tension that maturity transformation creates?

4. Bank runs are often called manias, or panics, but are individual people acting irrationally when they participate in a bank run? Explain your reasoning.

5. For each situation, explain why seeking out an individual saver to borrow money from is not ideal. Then, identify which function of banks eliminates the problem.

    Hint: Banks serve five functions. Read all the scenarios, then determine which function best addresses each situation. A function will be used only once.

    a. As a first-year student, you need to borrow $20,000 for school. You intend to repay this loan over time after you graduate.

    b. You are starting a business in a new industry and need $300 million for your initial investment.

    c. You need to take out a $15,000 loan to purchase a new car. No one who knows you personally has the money to lend.

    d. You want to be able to pay your bills online instead of paying for everything using cash.

6. When the Federal Deposit Insurance Corporation (FDIC) created deposit insurance after the Great Depression, what effect did this have on the occurrence of bank runs? Did the introduction of deposit insurance have the same effect on other financial markets, such as the stock or bond market? Explain.

Learning Objective 15.2 *Understand how companies and governments raise money by issuing bonds.*

7. Explain the differences between a company issuing a bond versus taking a loan from a bank. How are they similar, and how are they different?

8. Your parents are thinking about purchasing bonds with a 25-year term, but they are a little worried that they might need the money before the 25-year term is up. How would they go about accessing the money if they needed it before the end of the term?

9. Around $500 billion in U.S. Treasuries are traded each day and many countries hold U.S. Treasuries, as they are considered very safe. For example, as of May 2022, Japan held $1,213 billion in U.S. Treasuries, and Ireland held $289 billion. Use the three types of bond risks to explain why U.S. government bonds are considered a safe place to put your savings. What is the trade-off that accompanies this low risk?

Learning Objective 15.3 *Learn how companies raise money by issuing stock.*

10. You get a large bonus at the end of the year that you don't plan on spending anytime soon. Should you put your money in stocks, in bonds, or in the bank as savings? What factors inform your decision? Explain.

11. You are discussing buying stocks with a friend and mention that you want to buy a few shares of Amazon stock. Your friend says that's a terrible idea because Amazon has never paid dividends to its shareholders, so you would never receive any of Amazon's profits or make any money off the stock. Is your friend right or wrong? Explain your answer.

12. For each part, determine whether you should put your savings in stocks or bonds. Explain your reasoning.

    a. You want a high return and are not concerned about risk.

    b. You would like to participate in how the companies you invest in are managed.

    c. You are worried about losing money if a company declares bankruptcy.

    d. You want a guaranteed, regular payment from your investment.

13. Stitch Fix offers a subscription that provides users with a personal stylist and shopper, who ships clothes to the subscriber's door. Use the stock market snapshot from Google Finance to interpret the questions about Stitch Fix.

Market Summary > Stitch Fix Inc
NASDAQ: SFIX

30.90 USD -0.50 (1.59%) ↓
Closed: Jul 3, 1:39 PM EDT · Disclaimer
After hours 30.90 -0.000099 (0.00032%)

+ Follow

| 1 day | 5 days | 1 month | 6 months | YTD | 1 year | 5 years | Max |

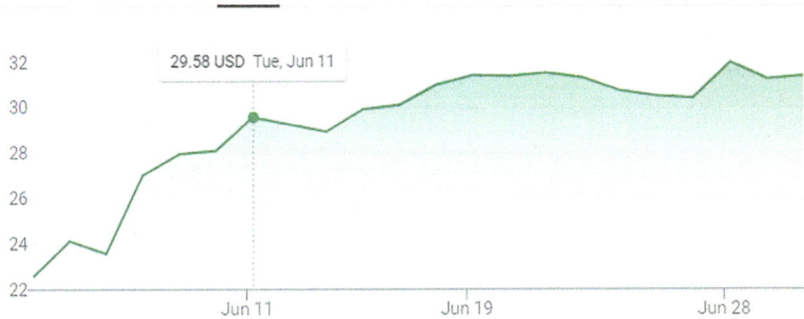

29.58 USD Tue, Jun 11

Open	31.41		Div yield	-
High	31.65		Prev close	31.40
Low	30.71		52-wk high	52.44
Mkt cap	3.12B		52-wk low	16.05
P/E ratio	67.20			

a. How much was a share of Stitch Fix worth at the time of the snapshot?

b. What is the market capitalization? What does that mean?

c. Assess the level of risk associated with investing in Stitch Fix Inc.

Learning Objective 15.4 *Discover what drives financial prices.*

14. Search online to find a company that issues stock on the New York Stock Exchange. Describe how you can assess the company's fundamental value and how you could use that information to decide to purchase the stock or not.

15. Do changes in stock prices precede economic downturns and expansions, or do they follow changes in economic activity? Are stock market prices a cause or an effect of changes in the macroeconomy?

16. The following graph shows the price of Bitcoin — an online cryptocurrency — over time.

Price ($ per bitcoin)

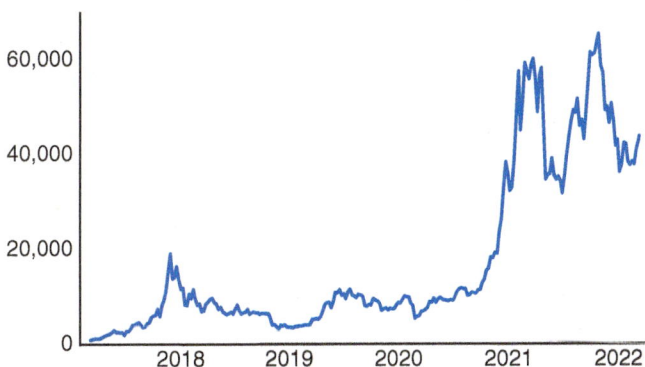

Do you think Bitcoin experienced a speculative bubble? Explain why someone acting rationally would purchase Bitcoin even at a price so much higher than its historical level.

17. Use the following data for Nordstrom to estimate the values for a comparable department store, Macy's. Nordstrom:

Stock price per share (July 2022)	$23.50
Earnings per share (quarter ending July 2022)	$0.13
Book value per share (quarter ending July 2022)	$3.67

a. Macy's book value per share was $19.27. If Macy's produces the same price-to-book ratio as Nordstrom, what is the value of Macy's stock?

b. Macy's earnings per share was $0.54. If Macy's has the same price-to-earnings ratio as Nordstrom, what is the value of Macy's stock?

c. The actual price of Macy's stock as of July 2018 was $36.54. What does this tell us about our valuation technique? What issues (if any) may be leading to any differences?

18. Your friend just received a promotion and wants to save the extra annual income from their raise. They tell you that they're thinking of hiring a fund manager to help decide where to put their savings, saying: "The fee is only

1.1%, and this stock picker has a great track record!" What advice would you give your friend?

19. On March 16, 2020, the stock market fell almost 13%. How can we reconcile these kinds of huge losses in the stock market with the efficient market hypothesis?

Learning Objective 15.5 *Make better decisions in financial markets.*

20. You just opened an online stock trading account. A friend that you trust advises you to put all your money in the stock of one certain company. "It's done really well in the past," she states. "The stock price is only going to go up. If you go all in now, you'll make a ton of money later." Which lessons did you learn from the chapter that will help you analyze your friend's advice?

21. Why do people value liquidity? What are the different ways that banks, the bond market, and the stock market create liquidity?

22. The 1990s was a period of rapid economic growth and a robust stock market that yielded an average annual return of 18.6%!

   a. If you started with $1,000 in stocks at the beginning of the decade, and you reinvested the returns you earned every year, calculate the value of your stocks at the end of the decade.

   b. Did this high rate of return continue into the 2000s and beyond? Look online at stock charts for the S&P 500 to figure out what happened. Use what you learned in the chapter to explain why.

International Finance and the Exchange Rate

In 1893, the Mathison family started a small farm in Washington State, producing enough to feed their family. Over time, the farm grew, and they began selling their crops at local markets. By the 1950s, they were selling in markets outside of Washington, but they were struggling. They would load ripe, freshly harvested cherries onto trains packed with ice and hope they would still be good when they made it to their destination. If their fruit made it to New York with little spoilage, they were nearly guaranteed robust demand from the large population of New Yorkers. But if it got

Family farm, global market.

Courtesy of Stemilt Growers

hot, spoilage rates were punishingly high. In 1958, they made a mere $88 after producing 100 tons of fruit because most of it rotted en route.

To succeed, the Mathisons needed to solve the problem of spoilage. Over the next decade, they worked to improve their packing and transportation methods. By the 1970s, they had succeeded in building a fruit packing, storage, and shipping facility that kept their fruit cold enough to survive a trip across the United States. This innovation not only gave them access to markets as far away as New York, but it also laid the foundation for exporting their fruit around the world. By the 1980s, they were exporting apples and cherries to a handful of countries. They have continued to grow their business by entering new foreign markets. Today, the Mathisons export fruit to 26 countries.

All of this has required the Mathisons to become conversant in exchange rates and international finance. Those are the skills you'll be building in this chapter. We'll analyze what determines how competitive the Mathisons will be in the global market, and whether it makes sense to sell their produce abroad. International transactions often involve foreign currencies, and so we'll dive into how exchange rates are determined, how they respond to changing economic conditions, and how they'll affect the Mathisons' business. Along the way, we'll see how developments in the global economy affect the prices you'll pay as you seek goods, services, customers, investments, and investors from around the world. As you read this chapter, keep your eye on the broader theme, which is that increasingly all business is international business, and so the fates of businesses, communities, and countries around the world are becoming increasingly interdependent.

Chapter Objective

Understand the linkages between the exchange rate, imports, exports, and international financial flows.

16.1 International Trade and Global Financial Flows
See the connections between the domestic economy and the global economy.

16.2 Exchange Rates
Analyze prices that are quoted in different currencies.

16.3 Supply and Demand of Currencies
Analyze the market for currencies and forecast the nominal exchange rate.

16.4 The Real Exchange Rate and Net Exports
Assess how exchange rates and relative prices affect exports and imports.

16.5 The Balance of Payments
Track how money flows around the world using the current account and the financial account.

🎙 Podcast

Think Like an Economist
Exchange Rates and International Finance—The Flow of Currencies Around the World

International Trade and Global Financial Flows

Learning Objective *See the connections between the domestic economy and the global economy.*

Carrying more—and carrying it further.

The story of the Mathisons is the story of millions of businesses that are becoming more tightly integrated into the global economy. We explored the logic of international trade in Chapter 9, where we noted that trade is driven by the idea of comparative advantage — by focusing on those tasks that we can do at the lowest opportunity cost, we can all get more done. Comparative advantage explains why a family in Washington, whose river valleys are the perfect climate for apple growing, might focus on growing apples. And their customers might include a couple in Japan who spend their workdays applying advanced Japanese management techniques to make Toyota's automobile production lines run more efficiently. Therefore, comparative advantage explains why the United States exports apples and imports Toyotas.

Our goal in this chapter is to explore the macroeconomic implications of international trade. The interdependence principle will take center stage as we examine the links between the United States and other countries and the overall global economy. We'll begin by exploring how international trade links the U.S. economy to the rest of the world, and then turn to analyzing the linkages that occur through global financial flows.

International Trade

exports Goods or services produced domestically and purchased by foreign buyers.

imports Goods or services produced in a foreign country and purchased by domestic buyers.

Let's start with international trade, which occurs when people buy or sell goods and services across national borders. **Exports** are goods and services produced domestically and purchased by foreign buyers. **Imports** are goods and services produced in a foreign country and purchased by domestic buyers. Remember that it's not just goods like apples and cars that are traded, but a wide range of services such as tourism, education, entertainment, health care, and business services. You may not have considered yourself an importer of services if you've ever visited a foreign city. But when you spend your money in another country, the host country is "exporting" restaurant meals, hotel stays, and museum visits to you. Similarly, if you decide to spend a term studying abroad, you'll be importing educational services from the host country (who is exporting educational services to you). If you've watched *Squid Game* on Netflix, you were importing from South Korea. And you'll likely find yourself on Zoom at some point in your career talking to clients in another country — business services provided by U.S. companies to international clients are an important part of U.S. exports.

Global trade is a large share of worldwide consumption and production. *Globalization* describes the increasing global integration of economies, cultures, political institutions, and ideas.

Sharp reductions in the cost of international transport and communication have led to explosive growth in trade over the past several decades. The largest cargo ships carry 100 times more cargo than half a century ago. Air transport has become cheaper, enabling more trade in perishable items. Modern computer networks zap vast amounts of data around the world nearly instantly, which has boosted trade in services. And governments in nearly every country have tried to take advantage of these new opportunities by negotiating trade deals that give their citizens (both consumers and businesses) better access to foreign markets.

As Figure 1 shows, these changes led global exports to rise from around 13% of global output in 1970 to 29% in 2021. Trade flows slowed in 2020 as the Covid pandemic disrupted the ability to produce goods and services and to transport them around the globe. The biggest hit to global trade in 2020 and 2021 was the large decline in international tourism, as many countries closed their borders.

However, it's a good bet that globalization will continue its relentless march throughout your life, and so the global economy will play an even larger role in your life and career.

Imports and exports have grown rapidly in the United States. The United States has followed the world trend. Both imports and exports have more than doubled as a share of the economy over the past 50 years. Major U.S. exports include capital goods, such as airplanes and semiconductors, and industrial supplies such as chemicals and refined petroleum. A third of our exports are services.

You probably recognize many imported goods when you're shopping for clothes, household appliances, or cars. But it's important to think beyond consumer goods, as more than half of all imports are intermediate goods or raw materials that are used as inputs by U.S. businesses. Indeed, our imports and exports are closely linked due to global supply chains that connect businesses around the world. For instance, we import crude oil, and then U.S. businesses refine it and ship some of it out as exports of refined petroleum.

Figure 2 shows that imports have exceeded exports since the mid-1970s, which means that **net exports**—the difference between spending on exports and spending on imports—have been negative. The *trade balance* is another name for net exports, and so negative net exports are sometimes called a *trade deficit*.

The United States trades with nearly every country. The United States trades with nearly every country in the world. Figure 3 shows our top seven trading partners, who together account for 58% of our total trade. Our top three trading partners are Mexico, Canada, and China. We also trade a lot with Europe, and when you add up all of our imports and exports with European Union countries, it ends up being our most important trading partner.

Figure 1 | Globalization Has Led to Rising World Trade

Total world exports (which equals total world imports) as a share of world GDP

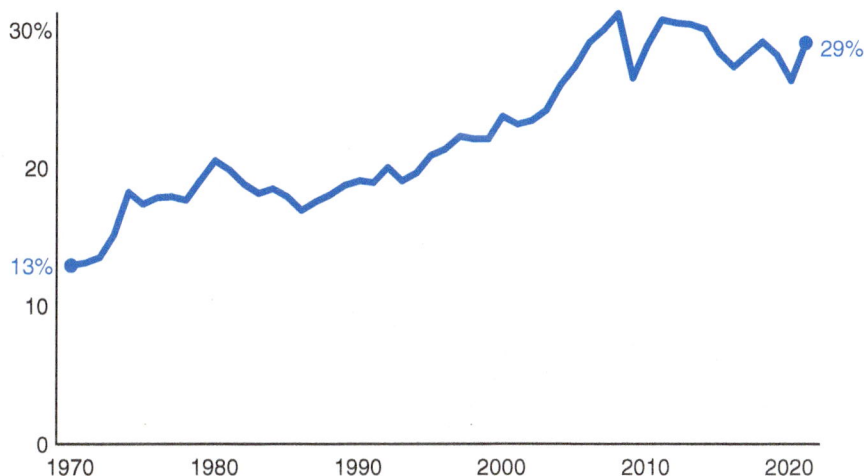

Data from: World Bank.

Figure 2 | Imports to and Exports from the United States

As a share of GDP

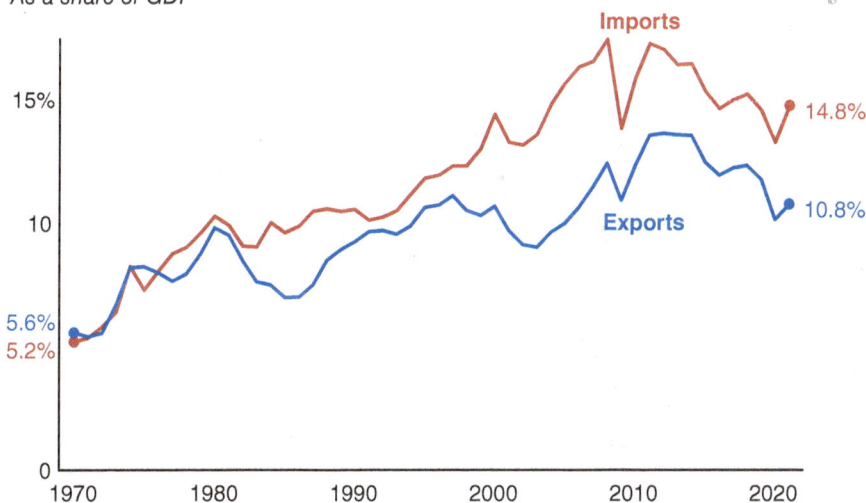

Data from: Bureau of Economic Analysis.

net exports Spending on exports minus spending on imports; also referred to as the trade balance.

Figure 3 | **Major Trading Partners of the United States**

Share of total goods trade with the United States, including imports and exports

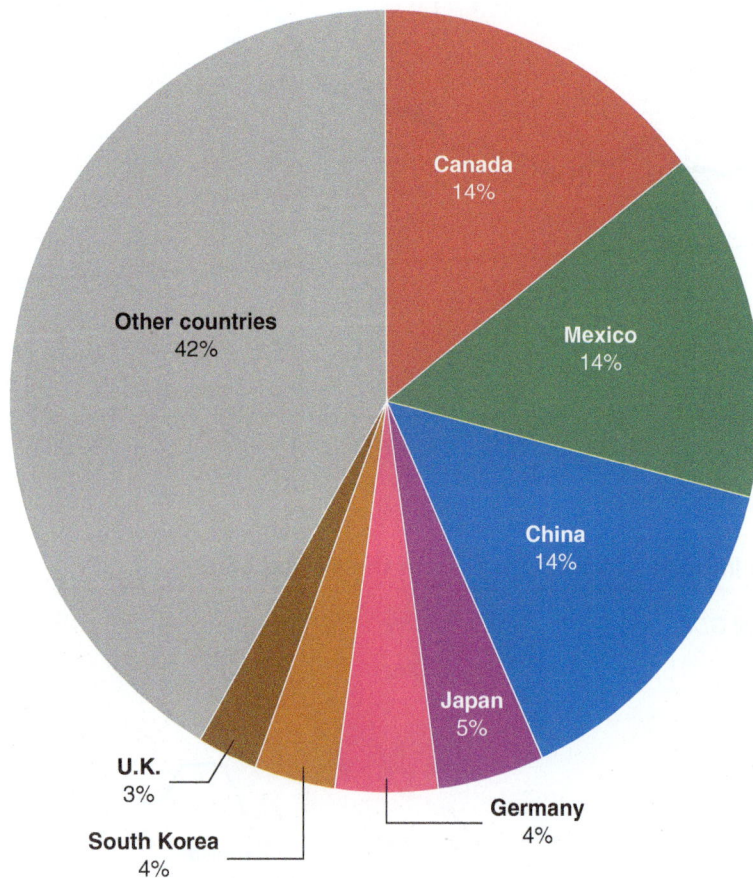

Data from: 2021 Data from Census Bureau.

Figure 4 | **International Trade Is a Smaller Share of the U.S. Economy Than in Many Other Countries**

Imports and exports as a share of GDP

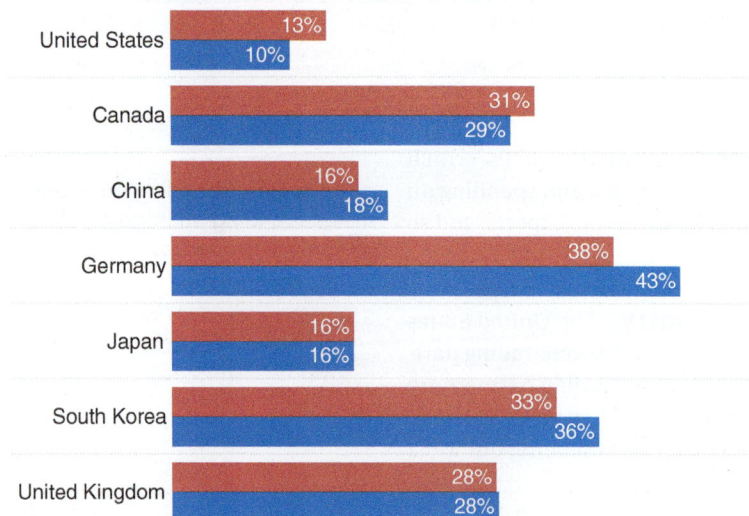

Data from: 2020 Data from World Bank.

The remaining slice of our trade is spread across dozens of countries. But even if these are not major trading partners for the United States, the U.S. market is so big that it's still the most important destination for the exports of many of these other countries. For instance, half of what Nicaragua exports and four-fifths of what Haiti exports go to the United States, yet neither of these flows accounts for more than a fraction of a percent of goods coming into the United States.

Many countries import and export more than the United States. This is partly because the U.S. economy is so large, and so a lot of commerce occurs across state rather than national boundaries. For instance, when an Ohio grocery store purchases orange juice from citrus groves that are a thousand miles south in Florida, it is interstate rather than international trade. But when a Parisian grocery store purchases orange juice from citrus groves that are a bit less than a thousand miles south, it is an import from Spain.

Even though international trade is a big part of the U.S. economy, it plays a bigger role in most other countries. Figure 4 shows that compared to our major trading partners, the United States both exports a smaller share of its output and relies on imports for a smaller share of its spending. In fact, almost every country in the world — apart from a handful of tiny war-torn nations — exports a larger share of what they produce than the United States.

Global Financial Flows

It's not just goods and services that are flying around the world. So too are investment dollars, looking for the most profitable investments. These financial flows reflect investors buying and selling assets in a global capital market. **Financial inflows** refer to foreigners investing in the United States. They're called *in*flows, because their funds flow *in* to the United States. **Financial outflows** describe Americans investing their money in other countries. They're *out*flows, because these funds flow *out* of the United States.

Financial flows are large and include investment in foreign physical assets, financial assets, and loans. These financial flows take three main forms. When foreigners invest in physical assets in the United States — such as when Toyota built a new auto plant in Alabama — it's called *foreign direct investment.* This auto plant hires American workers, but its profits will return to its Japanese owners. When foreigners buy American stocks or bonds, it's called *portfolio investment,* and while American businesses might use these funds to invest in new equipment, foreign investors will receive future payments in return. And when foreigners lend money to Americans, it falls in a final category of *deposits and loans.* This includes both loans made directly to Americans, as well as foreign deposits in American banks, which are then used to fund domestic loans. In each case, these financial inflows help fund investment in new capital assets within the United States. In return, foreigners enjoy the profits, dividends, or interest that their investments generate.

financial inflows Investments by foreigners in the United States.

financial outflows Investments by Americans in foreign countries.

All told, financial inflows added up to an eye-popping $2 trillion in 2021, which is roughly $6,000 per person in the United States. But that's not the whole story, as Americans also invest their funds abroad, creating financial outflows. These financial outflows are also large, and they collectively added up to $1.3 trillion in 2021, or roughly $4,000 per person in the United States. Just as financial inflows can be categorized into foreign direct investment, portfolio investment, and deposits and loans, so too can financial outflows.

Financial linkages are becoming more important over time.

Financial flows between the United States and the rest of the world have risen sharply over the past 50 years, a trend sometimes called *financial globalization.* As Figure 5 shows, financial flows started rising in the 1970s and 1980s as many countries removed *capital controls,* which were rules designed to limit the flow of money across borders. *Deregulation* of the financial sector, both in the United States and elsewhere, also led to new opportunities for money to roam the world looking for better returns. Large *institutional investors* such as pension funds and mutual funds have become more important over time, and they're more likely to look abroad to diversify their portfolios. And *technology* has led to more rapid transmission of information, making investors more comfortable sending their money overseas. *Financial innovation* has created sophisticated new ways for investors to take advantage of new opportunities to diversify and hedge their risks in foreign markets. The result is that both financial inflows and outflows have grown. The global financial crisis that began in 2008 reversed some of this momentum. But the Covid recession did little to slow financial inflows and outflows to the United States, and financial flows are likely to continue to play a large role in the global economy.

Foreign ownership is becoming more common.

As a result of these financial inflows, foreigners have acquired a rising stock of assets in the United States, as shown by the blue line in Figure 6. Some of these are physical assets like Toyota's new auto plant in Alabama, some

Figure 5 | Financial Outflows from and Financial Inflows to the United States

As a share of GDP

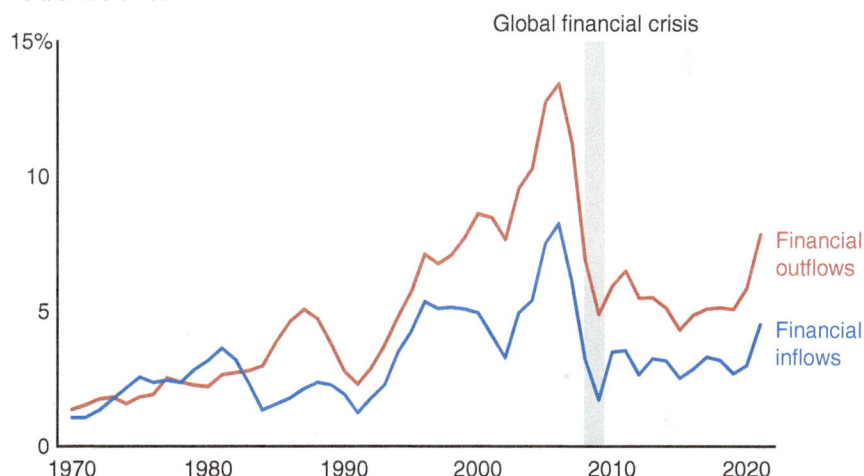

*3-year moving average

Data from: Bureau of Economic Analysis.

Figure 6 | Ownership of Foreign Assets Is Growing

As a share of GDP

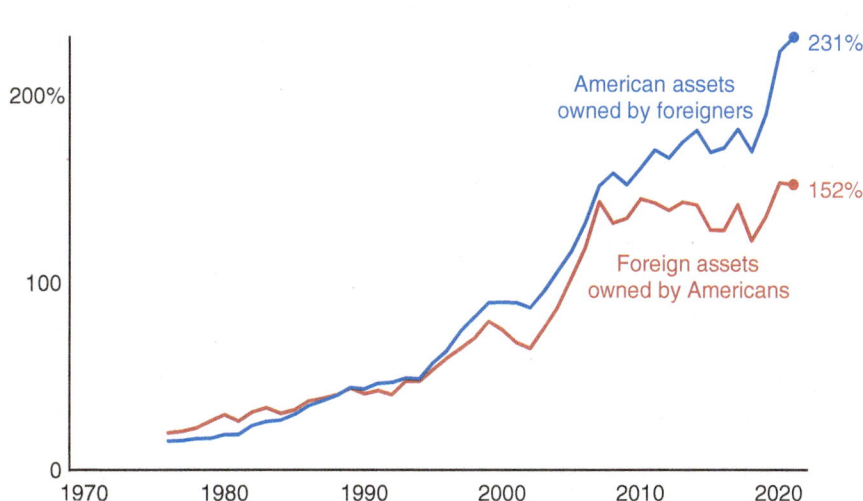

Data from: Bureau of Economic Analysis.

are ownership shares like Ford stock owned by the Japanese financial firm Sumitomo Mitsui, and some are financial assets like U.S. government bonds held by foreign investors. The stock of foreign assets owned by Americans — shown by the red line — has also risen dramatically. This reflects U.S. businesses like Ford setting up production lines in other countries, Americans buying stock in companies like Toyota, or your bank lending money to foreigners. Whether you're aware of it or not, it's likely that if you have any savings, some of it is invested overseas. Indeed, the average American held more than $100,000 in foreign assets in 2021.

Financial linkages help diversify risk across the world. This rise in cross-border ownership means that the U.S. economy is more tightly linked to developments in the global economy than ever. From a *macroeconomic perspective,* it means that disruptions in foreign markets — such as a sudden fall in the Japanese stock market — have an immediate effect reducing the wealth of Americans. Similarly, when the U.S. economy falters, much of the effect is felt overseas.

From a *risk management* perspective, this rising cross-border ownership is a good thing for everyone. Greater diversification reduces the total risk that both Americans and foreigners face. For example, when your retirement account is partly invested in foreign assets, you don't need to worry as much that a domestic downturn will wipe you out.

Just about all business is international. The linkages between the U.S. economy and the global economy — through both international trade and global financial flows — have become more important over time, and they'll likely become even more important over the course of your career. This makes it a good bet that you'll engage in at least some international transactions, in which you'll need to compare prices measured in dollars with prices measured in other currencies. To do that, you'll need to learn about exchange rates.

nominal exchange rate The price of a country's currency, in terms of another country's currency.

How expensive are apples in New York compared to Japan?

Richard Levine/Alamy Stock Photo

Robert Alexander/Archive Photos/Getty Images

16.2 Exchange Rates

Learning Objective *Analyze prices that are quoted in different currencies.*

When the Mathisons sell their apples for $20 a bushel to a grocery store in New York, they get paid $20. (To be extra clear, we'll write this as "US$20," which should be read as "twenty U.S. dollars.") But if a Japanese customer offers to pay them ¥2,400 per bushel, they have to decide whether that's a better deal. (¥ is the symbol for yen which is the currency used in Japan, just as US$ is the symbol for U.S. dollars.) When the Mathisons are comparing prices in different currencies, they're going to need to find a way to — you guessed it — make an apples-to-apples comparison. So they have to figure out the value of a dollar relative to the yen.

Exchanging U.S. Dollars for Foreign Currencies

The price of a country's currency in terms of another country's currency is called the **nominal exchange rate.** The word "nominal" often gets dropped, so when you hear someone talk about the "exchange rate," they typically mean the nominal exchange rate.

Use the nominal exchange rate formula to find the price of a country's currency. We'll focus on the price of a U.S. dollar, since that's the currency that matters most to you. If the price of a U.S. dollar is 120 yen, then the nominal exchange rate is 120 yen per U.S. dollar. This means that you can buy one U.S. dollar for ¥120. You can exchange yen for dollars, or dollars for yen, so this also means that with one U.S. dollar you can buy ¥120.

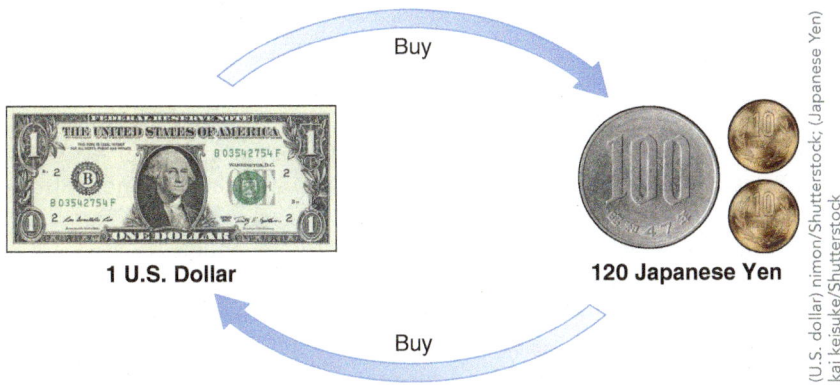

1 U.S. Dollar   **120 Japanese Yen**

Buy

Buy

(U.S. dollar) nimon/Shutterstock; (Japanese Yen)
kai keisuke/Shutterstock

Just as you can exchange ¥120 for US$1, you can also exchange ¥240 for US$2, ¥360 for US$3, and so on. The nominal exchange rate defines the ratio at which you exchange units of a foreign currency like yen for U.S. dollars. This gives us the **nominal exchange rate formula:**

$$\underbrace{\text{Nominal exchange rate}}_{\text{Price of a dollar (in yen)}} = \frac{\text{Number of yen}}{\text{Number of dollars}}$$

nominal exchange rate formula

$$\text{Nominal exchange rate} = \frac{\text{Number of units of a foreign currency}}{\text{Number of dollars}}$$

Rearrange the nominal exchange rate formula to convert dollars into yen. If the Mathisons are selling a bushel of apples for US$20, a Japanese grocery store owner needs to figure out how many yen it will cost them. You can rearrange the nominal exchange rate formula to tell them how many yen they'll pay:

$$\text{Number of yen} = \text{Number of dollars} \times \text{Nominal exchange rate}$$

Let's try this out. If the exchange rate is ¥120 per U.S. dollar, then the price of a US$20 bushel of apples in yen is:

$$\text{Number of yen} = \underbrace{\text{US\$20}}_{\text{Number of dollars}} \times \underbrace{120 \text{ yen per dollar}}_{\text{Nominal exchange rate}} = ¥2,400$$

Rearrange the nominal exchange rate formula to convert yen into dollars. A potential Japanese client might suggest to the Mathisons that they'll buy their apples if they beat the current supplier's price, which is ¥1,800 per bushel. To figure out whether they can beat this price, the Mathisons need to convert this sum back into U.S. dollars. This time, they rearrange the nominal exchange rate formula to tell them how many dollars this is worth:

$$\text{Number of dollars} = \frac{\text{Number of yen}}{\text{Nominal exchange rate}}$$

So if the Mathisons have been offered a price of ¥1,800, and the exchange rate is ¥120 per dollar, then the number of dollars per bushel they've been offered is:

$$\text{Number of dollars} = \frac{\overbrace{¥1,800}^{\text{Number of yen}}}{\underbrace{120 \text{ yen per dollar}}_{\text{Nominal exchange rate}}} = \text{US\$15}$$

Don't accidentally get the exchange rate backward. So far, we've focused on the *price of a dollar,* which is the number of units of foreign currency you can buy with a dollar. You can also think about the *price of a yen,* which describes how many dollars it costs to buy one yen. Instead of saying that one dollar costs 120 yen, you can say that one yen costs 1/120 of a dollar, or US$0.0083. Both are correct; they're just different perspectives.

When you look up an exchange rate, make sure to pay attention to whether you're learning the price of a dollar (which is measured in yen), or the price of a yen (measured in fractions of a dollar). Getting this wrong could lead to some costly mistakes!

Country	Currency	Symbol
United States	Dollar	US$
19 European Union countries (inc.: Germany, France, Italy, Spain)	Euro	€
Australia	Dollar	A$
Brazil	Real	R$
Canada	Dollar	C$
China	Yuan	元
Mexico	Peso	Mex$
India	Rupee	₹
Japan	Yen	¥
Russia	Ruble	₽
South Korea	Won	₩
United Kingdom	Pound sterling	£

How expensive are apples in Germany?

Answers: a. Number of euros = Number of dollars × Nominal exchange rate = US$20 × €0.90 per dollar = €18. b. Number of dollars = Number of euros/Nominal exchange rate = €900/€0.90 per dollar = US$1,000. c. Number of dollars = Number of pounds/Nominal exchange rate = £600/£0.75 per dollar = US$800, which is a better deal.

EVERYDAY Economics   A tour of world currencies

The United States calls its currency the dollar. But it's not the only dollar. A bunch of other former British colonies — including Australia, Canada, and New Zealand — also call their currencies "dollar." These dollars all have different values, and so it's common to put the country's initials before the dollar symbol to keep them straight. (So the U.S. dollar is called the US$, and the Aussie dollar is the A$.) Pay attention when you visit a country that uses "dollars," because some countries — Ecuador and El Salvador, for example — gave up on their own currencies and use actual U.S. dollars.

Peso is also a common name for a currency. Mexico, Argentina, Chile, Colombia, and Cuba all also have pesos (which have different values). Eight countries have rupees including India, Pakistan, and Indonesia. Japan has the yen. China has the renminbi, which is the official name of the currency and means "the people's currency." But renminbi are measured in yuan. The British call their currency the pound sterling, or pound for short. While most countries have their own currency, many European nations gave up their individual currencies in 2002 and adopted a new European currency called the euro whose symbol, €, looks like the first letter of "€urope." As of 2022, 19 countries that are part of the European Union use the euro, although some European Union members don't use it. Several other (mostly small) countries also use the euro. This new super-currency is now the second-most traded currency in the world, behind the U.S. dollar. ■

Remember the three uses of the nominal exchange rate formula. Let's recap. The nominal exchange rate formula is incredibly versatile, because it serves three purposes:

It defines the nominal exchange rate:

$$\underbrace{\text{Nominal exchange rate}}_{\text{Price of a dollar (in yen)}} = \frac{\text{Number of yen}}{\text{Number of dollars}}$$

You can rearrange it to convert dollars into yen:

$$\text{Number of yen} = \text{Number of dollars} \times \text{Nominal exchange rate}$$

You can rearrange it to convert yen into dollars:

$$\text{Number of dollars} = \frac{\text{Number of yen}}{\text{Nominal exchange rate}}$$

Of course, you can apply this formula to any other country. Just replace the word "yen" with "peso," "yuan," "euro," or whatever currency you're using to measure the price of a U.S. dollar. Let's try it out.

Do the Economics

a. The Mathisons are trying to make a deal to sell apples in Germany. If they charge US$20 a bushel, how many euros will a bushel of apples cost a German grocery store if the nominal exchange rate is 0.90 euros per U.S. dollar?

b. The Mathisons have to pay a local logistics company €900 to help them with some customs paperwork. How much is this in U.S. dollars?

c. A British logistics company has offered to do this paperwork for £600 instead. If the nominal exchange rate is £0.75 per U.S. dollar, which is a better deal? ■

Exchange Rates and the Price of Foreign Goods

Exchange rates are among the most important prices in the economy because when an exchange rate changes, it will automatically affect how much it costs to buy millions of imported or exported goods.

Currencies *appreciate* when they become more expensive and *depreciate* when they become less expensive. Be careful, as it's easy to get confused when you're describing exchange rate movements. For instance, when the rate at which you exchange yen for dollars *rises* from ¥100 per dollar to ¥120, then the rate at which you exchange dollars for yen *falls* from US$0.010 per yen, to US$0.008: Rather than argue about whether to describe this as a rise or a fall, economists use different words altogether.

When the number of yen you're charged to buy one dollar goes up — that is, the price of a dollar rises — we describe this as an **appreciation** of the dollar. We say it appreciates because a dollar is now worth more yen (and anyone holding dollars would appreciate that!). Figure 7 shows that the dollar appreciated against the yen for much of 2013 through 2015.

Conversely, when the number of yen that are needed to buy a dollar goes down — that is, the price of the dollar falls — we describe this as a **depreciation** of the dollar. The dollar is like a used car, because when it depreciates, it's worth less. Figure 7 shows that the dollar depreciated against the yen for much of 2007 through 2011.

Figure 7 | Japan/U.S. Nominal Exchange Rate

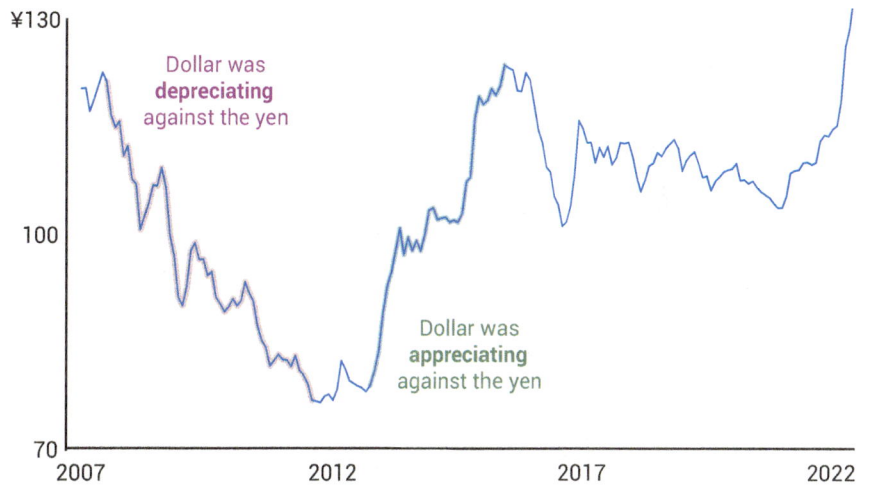

Data from: Federal Reserve Board.

An appreciating dollar makes imports cheaper and exports more expensive. When the dollar appreciates, the goods we import from other countries become less expensive in U.S. dollars. For instance, importing a ¥48,000 Nikon camera costs US$480 when the exchange rate is 100 yen per dollar, but that falls to US$400 when the price of a dollar appreciates to 120 yen. Some people describe an appreciation as leading to a *stronger* dollar; it's stronger because it buys more foreign goods and services.

While an appreciation in the dollar is good news for importers, it's bad news for exporters. For instance, the Mathisons sell their apples at US$20 per bushel, which translates to ¥2,000 per bushel for their Japanese customers when the exchange rate is 100 yen per dollar, but that price rises to ¥2,400 per bushel when the price of a dollar rises to 120 yen. As a result, an appreciation of the dollar causes American exports — like the Mathisons' apples — to become more expensive for foreign buyers. The problem is that while Japanese customers pay more in Japanese yen, the Mathisons don't get any more dollars per bushel.

appreciation When the price of a currency rises.

depreciation When the price of a currency falls.

A depreciating dollar makes imports more expensive and exports cheaper. When the dollar depreciates, the goods we import from other countries become more expensive in terms of U.S. dollars. Some people refer to a depreciation as leading to a *weaker* dollar because it buys fewer foreign goods. While a depreciation is bad news for importers, it's good news for American exporters. Even if they don't adjust the price they charge in U.S. dollars, foreign buyers will find that they now pay less in their currency, leading them to buy more of our exports. Figure 8 summarizes these different ways of describing changes in the exchange rate, and what they mean.

Figure 8 | Different Ways to Describe a . . .

Higher price of a dollar	Lower price of a dollar
• An appreciation of the dollar	• A depreciation of the dollar
• A depreciation of the other currency	• An appreciation of the other currency
• Stronger dollar	• Weaker dollar
• Higher exchange rate	• Lower exchange rate
• Imports are cheaper	• Imports are more expensive
• Exports are more expensive for foreign buyers	• Exports are cheaper for foreign buyers

Figure 9 | Track the Value of the U.S. Dollar Relative to Our Trading Partners Using the Trade-Weighted Index

Index: January 2006 = 100

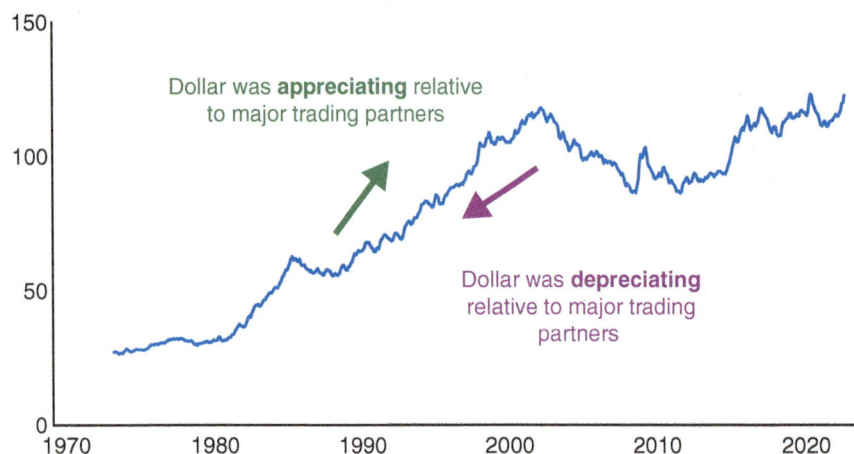

Dollar was **appreciating** relative to major trading partners

Dollar was **depreciating** relative to major trading partners

Data from: Federal Reserve Board.

On any given day, the dollar trades against many different currencies. It might appreciate against the yen, depreciate against the euro, not change against the yuan, and also rise or fall relative to each of dozens of other currencies.

To keep track of the overall strength of the dollar, economists have compiled a summary measure of the value of the U.S. dollar called the *trade-weighted index.* Think of this as being the price of U.S. dollars in terms of a basket of currencies, with each country's weight in that basket reflecting their importance as a trading partner. It effectively averages many different exchange rates into a single index that describes the international value of U.S. dollars. Figure 9 shows this index, which describes whether, on average, the U.S. dollar has appreciated or depreciated over time. You can check out the latest value by looking it up here: https://fred.stlouisfed.org/series/TWEXBGSMTH ∎

16.3   Supply and Demand of Currencies

Learning Objective *Analyze the market for currencies and forecast the nominal exchange rate.*

When the Mathisons sell apples to a grocery store chain in Tokyo, they need to get paid in dollars. But a Japanese grocery store does business in yen. Thus, international trade is possible only if there's a market where they can exchange one currency for another. That market is the **foreign exchange market.** It's the market in which currencies like the U.S. dollar and the Japanese yen are bought and sold.

foreign exchange market The market in which currencies are bought and sold.

The Market for U.S. Dollars

The market for currencies is like any other competitive market, where the forces of supply and demand determine the equilibrium price and quantity. In the foreign exchange market, the products are currencies like the U.S. dollar. Demanders are those, like a Japanese grocery store, looking to buy U.S. dollars in order to purchase U.S. apples. The Japanese grocery store buys U.S. dollars with Japanese yen. Suppliers are folks who are looking to sell their U.S. dollars in return for Japanese yen. For instance, an American camera shop that imports Nikon cameras will supply U.S. dollars in exchange for yen so that it can pay its Japanese wholesaler. The price in this market is the price of a U.S. dollar, which the nominal exchange rate measures as the number of yen you have to pay to buy one U.S. dollar.

There are two main types of international transactions that lead people to demand or supply dollars. First, there are *trade flows,* such as exports of apples and imports of Nikon cameras. Second, there are *financial flows,* such as when Toyota invests in

Made in America, with help from foreign investment.

Daniel Patmore/AP Photo

building a new factory in the United States, or American investors buy stock in Japanese companies.

The demand for dollars reflects foreigners buying U.S. exports and investing in the United States.

When Japanese consumers want to buy American products — that is, exports from the United States — they need to pay with U.S. dollars. This means that every dollar of exports from the United States creates a demand in the foreign exchange market for one U.S. dollar. Similarly, when Japanese investors want to buy American assets, they need U.S. dollars. For example, when Toyota buys or builds a factory in the United States, it needs to buy U.S. dollars to pay for it. Thus, every dollar of financial inflows creates a demand for a U.S. dollar.

The demand curve for U.S. dollars illustrates how the quantity of U.S. dollars demanded varies with the price of U.S. dollars (which is the exchange rate). This downward-sloping demand curve shows that a lower price for U.S. dollars leads to a larger quantity of dollars demanded. It's downward sloping because when the price of the U.S. dollar is low, U.S. dollars cost fewer yen. It follows that it costs fewer yen to buy American products. From the perspective of Japanese buyers, it's like goods exported from the United States are on sale, so they buy more of them. They'll need more U.S. dollars to pay for these American exports, and so a lower price for the U.S. dollar leads them to demand a larger quantity of dollars.

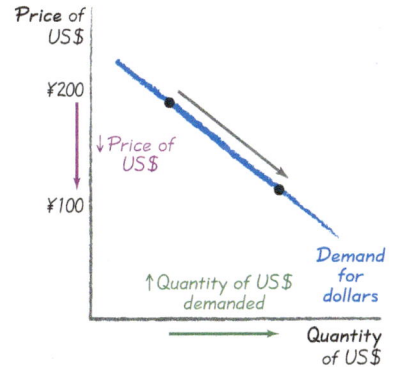

↓ Price of US$ ⟶ ↓ Price in yen of U.S. exports to Japan ⟶ ↑ U.S. exports to Japan ⟶ ↑ Quantity of US$ demanded

The supply of dollars reflects Americans buying imports and investing abroad.

When American buyers pay for Japanese goods — that is, imports into the United States — they need to pay with Japanese yen. They'll supply U.S. dollars to obtain yen in return. This means that every dollar of imports creates a supply in foreign exchange markets of one U.S. dollar. Likewise, when American investors want to invest abroad, perhaps buying stock in Toyota, they'll need Japanese yen to do so. Thus, each dollar of financial outflows creates a supply of one U.S. dollar.

The supply curve for U.S. dollars illustrates how the quantity of U.S. dollars supplied varies with the price of U.S. dollars (which is the exchange rate). This upward-sloping supply curve shows that a higher price of U.S. dollars leads a larger quantity of dollars to be supplied. It's upward-sloping because when the price of U.S. dollars is high, you'll get a lot of yen in exchange for your dollars. This means that Japanese stuff is cheaper in terms of U.S. dollars, and so from the perspective of American buyers, it's like Japanese imports are on sale, and so they'll buy more of them. If the value of U.S. imports from Japan rises, then Americans will need to exchange more dollars into yen to pay for them. As a result, the higher the price of the U.S. dollar, the higher the quantity of dollars supplied.

↑ Price of US$ ⟶ ↓ Price in US$ of imports from Japan ⟶ ↑ U.S. imports from Japan ⟶ ↑ Quantity of US$ supplied

(There's a subtle issue here: A higher price for the U.S. dollar causes Americans to buy a larger *quantity* of imports, but the number of dollars required to buy each imported item falls. As a result, the total number of U.S. dollars spent on imports — and hence the supply of dollars — will rise only if the quantity of imports increases enough to offset the decline in price. In reality, that's what typically occurs, which is why the supply curve is upward-sloping.)

The exchange rate is determined by supply and demand.

The foreign exchange market operates much like any other competitive market, with the forces of supply and demand determining the equilibrium price and quantity. The vertical axis in Figure 10 shows the price of a U.S. dollar, and the horizontal axis shows the quantity of dollars exchanged for yen. The price of a U.S. dollar describes how many yen a buyer has to pay to get one U.S. dollar. The higher the exchange rate, the more expensive the dollar is in terms of yen.

Figure 10 | **The Market for U.S. Dollars**

The price of the U.S. dollar is determined by the supply and demand of dollars.

Ⓐ The **supply of U.S. dollars** is upward-sloping because as the dollar appreciates, it buys more yen, and so imports of Japanese goods become cheaper for Americans. This leads them to spend more on imports, which they can pay for only by supplying more dollars to exchange for yen.

Ⓑ The **demand for U.S. dollars** is downward-sloping because as the dollar depreciates, exports of U.S. goods become cheaper for Japanese people. This leads them to buy more exports, which they can pay for only by demanding more dollars in exchange for yen.

Ⓒ The **equilibrium exchange rate** occurs at the point where **demand is equal to supply**, setting the price of a U.S. dollar at 120 yen.

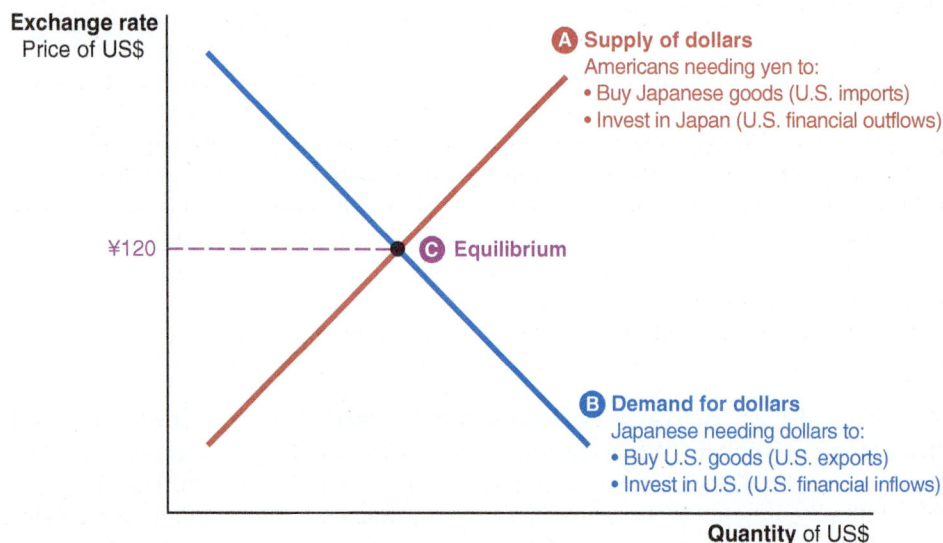

Equilibrium occurs at the point where the supply and demand curves cross, and this determines the price of U.S. dollars. Consequently, the equilibrium exchange rate reflects the balance between the forces of supply and demand, which means that it reflects the influence of U.S. imports and financial outflows on one side, and U.S. exports and financial inflows on the other.

EVERYDAY Economics | **How to keep exchange rates straight**

You've learned that the supply of U.S. dollars comes from Americans looking to exchange their dollars for yen. But if you were studying economics in Japan, you'd learn that Americans looking to exchange their dollars for yen create the demand for yen. Similarly, you've learned the demand for U.S. dollars comes from Japanese folks who are looking to exchange their yen for dollars. But in Japan, you'd learn that this creates the supply of yen. These dual identities arise because the market for U.S. dollars (paid for with yen) is also the market for yen (paid for in U.S. dollars). These are just two sides of the same, umm. . . coin. So, to keep straight which side is up, always:

- *Clarify which market you're analyzing.* Don't just say that you're analyzing the foreign exchange rate market; describe it as the market for U.S. dollars, paid for with Japanese yen.

- *Specify what price you're evaluating.* If you're assessing the market for U.S. dollars, be clear that you're analyzing the price of a U.S. dollar, which we describe as the number of yen needed to buy one dollar. If you're forecasting the price of the yen, the relevant price is the number of U.S. dollars needed to buy one yen.

- *State the origins and destinations.* Don't just say "exports"; say "exports from the United States to Japan."

Follow these three pieces of advice, and you'll avoid *a lot of* confusion. ∎

The exchange rate will change when macroeconomic conditions change. You'll find this framework to be particularly useful for forecasting how the exchange rate will change in response to changing macroeconomic conditions. Our next task is to analyze shifts in the demand for dollars, and we'll then turn to shifts in supply. But before we dive in, remember that in any supply-and-demand analysis, a change in the price — which in this case is a change in the exchange rate — will not shift either the demand or supply curve.

Shifts in Currency Demand

An increase in demand for U.S. dollars shifts the demand curve to the right. As the left panel of Figure 11 shows, an increase in demand causes the price of the U.S. dollar to rise, which is an exchange rate appreciation. The demand curve for U.S. dollars shifts right whenever people want to buy more dollars at any given exchange rate. By contrast, the right panel shows that a decrease in demand for U.S. dollars shifts the demand curve to the left. A decrease in demand causes the price of the U.S. dollar to fall, which is an exchange rate depreciation. The demand curve shifts left whenever people want to buy fewer dollars at any given exchange rate.

Figure 11 | The Demand for Dollars

An Increase in the Demand for Dollars

Ⓐ An increase in exports or financial inflows causes an **increase in demand** for U.S. dollars, shifting the demand curve to the **right**.

Ⓑ This leads the **price of the U.S. dollar to rise**, an exchange rate **appreciation**.

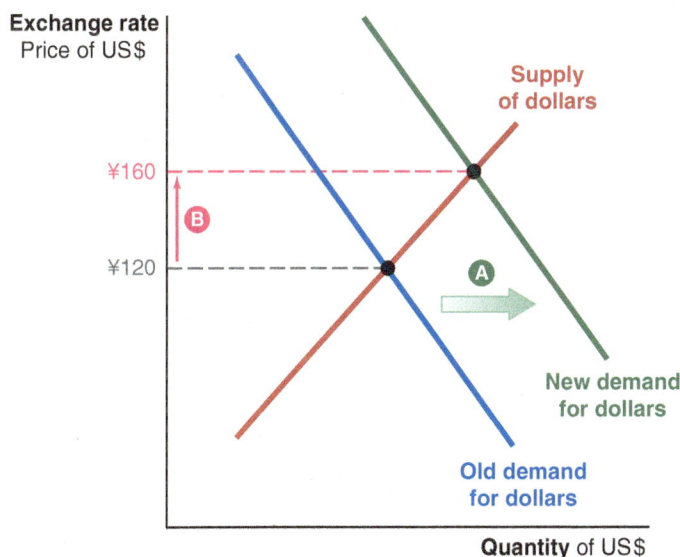

A Decrease in the Demand for Dollars

Ⓒ A decrease in exports or financial inflows causes a **decrease in demand** for U.S. dollars, shifting the demand curve to the **left**.

Ⓓ This leads the **price of the U.S. dollar to fall**, an exchange rate **depreciation**.

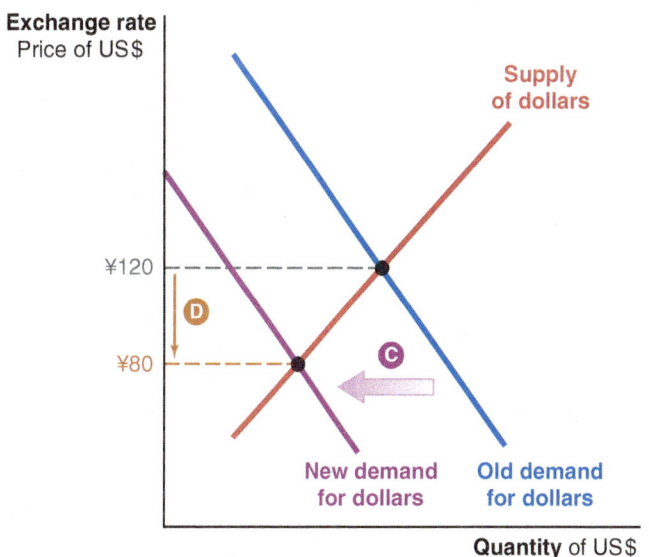

Recall that demand for U.S. dollars comes from foreigners who either need dollars in order to buy U.S. exports or to invest in the United States. The **interdependence principle** reminds us that their decisions depend on developments in other markets and in other countries. As a result, anything — besides the exchange rate — that shifts either how much foreigners spend on exports, or how much they invest in the United States (that is, financial inflows), will shift the demand for dollars. Let's evaluate each of these shifters in turn.

Demand shifter 1: Exports from the United States. Any factor that shifts the dollar value of exports at a given exchange rate will shift the demand for dollars. As a result, exports from the United States — and hence the demand for dollars — shift in response to the following factors:

- *Strength of the global economy:* An increase in the GDP of our major trading partners usually causes an increase in U.S. exports, shifting the demand for U.S. dollars to the right. For instance, an economic recovery in Japan will increase the income of Japanese consumers, and they'll spend some of this extra income on the Mathisons' apples and other American goods and services.

- *Barriers to trade in foreign market:* When foreign governments provide easier access to their markets, exports will increase, shifting the demand for U.S. dollars to the right. For instance, Japanese officials used to require American apples be quarantined before they could be sold, causing high spoilage rates. When this trade barrier was scrapped, the Mathisons started exporting apples to Japan.

- *Domestic innovation and marketing:* Successful innovation and marketing of U.S. goods and services to foreign customers will increase exports, shifting the demand curve for U.S. dollars to the right. For example, the Mathisons have developed new storage and packaging technologies that make their fruit more attractive to foreign customers.

- *Foreign prices:* When foreign prices are higher than their U.S. counterparts, foreign customers switch to buying the American-made goods instead. This increased demand for U.S. exports will shift the demand curve for U.S. dollars to the right. For example, if Japanese apple farmers raise their prices, then some Japanese consumers will switch to American-grown apples, increasing the demand for U.S. dollars. Or if the price of apples from a third country — say, New Zealand — were to rise, some Japanese consumers will switch from New Zealand to American-grown apples.

- *Domestic prices:* When American sellers cut their prices, it leads to a large increase in exports, thereby increasing the demand for dollars. For example, if the Mathisons cut the price of their apples, foreigners will buy more of them. This is where it gets a bit tricky: While this means that the Mathisons will export more apples, each apple costs fewer dollars. Therefore, the total number of dollars that foreigners spend on apples could either rise or fall. In practice, lower domestic prices tend to lead to such a large increase in exports that the demand for dollars will increase.

In each of these cases, you've seen what happens if exports were to increase at a given exchange rate. These same influences also operate in reverse: A *decrease* in exports would lead to a *decrease* in the demand for dollars, which causes the exchange rate to *depreciate*.

Demand shifter 2: Financial inflows into the United States. Foreign investors are usually seeking a combination of a healthy return on their investment, and relatively low risk. This means that financial inflows — and hence demand for dollars — change in response to the following factors:

- *Interest rate differentials:* Foreign investors are sensitive to the **opportunity cost principle**, and the opportunity cost of investing in the United States is investing in either their home country or some other country. As a result, financial inflows are driven by the difference between American interest rates and foreign interest rates. A higher interest rate differential — due to either higher interest rates in the United States or lower interest rates in a foreign country — will increase financial inflows, shifting the demand curve for dollars to the right.

- *Business profitability:* The more opportunities there are for profitable investments in the United States relative to such opportunities in other countries, the larger financial inflows will be. As a result, financial inflows are sensitive to factors like taxes, wage rates, and demand that affect business profitability. Any change that creates a more profitable business climate in the United States will lead to more financial inflows, shifting the demand curve for dollars to the right.

- *Political risk:* The United States is often called a "safe haven" for investing, making it an attractive destination for foreign investors worried about political risks in their own country. Whenever foreign risks rise relative to political risk in the United States — such as the risk of a foreign government coup or seizure of assets — financial inflows into the United States increase, and thus so does the demand for U.S. dollars, shifting the demand curve to the right.

- *Expected exchange rate movements:* Right now, thousands of foreign exchange speculators are evaluating how changing economic conditions are likely to shift the price of the U.S. dollar. Any news that might cause the dollar to rise in the future has an immediate impact, as speculators rush to buy dollars in anticipation of those dollars later rising in value. Increased demand for U.S. dollars by speculators shifts the demand curve for U.S. dollars to the right.

In each of these cases, you've seen what happens if these factors lead financial inflows to increase at a given exchange rate. These same influences also operate in reverse: A *decrease* in financial inflows would lead to a *decrease* in the demand for dollars, which causes the exchange rate to *depreciate*.

Shifts in Currency Supply

Okay, we know what factors shift the demand for U.S. dollars. But what about shifts in the supply of dollars? An increase in the supply of U.S. dollars at any given exchange rate shifts the supply curve to the right. As the left panel of Figure 12 shows, an increase in supply will cause the price of the U.S. dollar to decline, which is an exchange rate *depreciation*. By contrast, the right panel of Figure 12 shows that a decrease in supply at any given exchange rate shifts the supply curve to the left, leading to a new equilibrium in which the price of the U.S. dollar rises, an exchange rate *appreciation*.

> Demand for U.S. dollars:
> 1. Shifts in response to shifts in exports from the United States
> 2. Shifts in response to shifts in financial inflows into the United States
> 3. Does not shift in response to changes in the exchange rate.

Figure 12 | The Supply of Dollars

An Increase in the Supply of Dollars

Ⓐ An increase in imports or financial outflows causes an **increase in supply** of U.S. dollars, shifting the supply curve to the **right**.

Ⓑ This leads the **price of the U.S. dollar to fall**, an exchange rate **depreciation**.

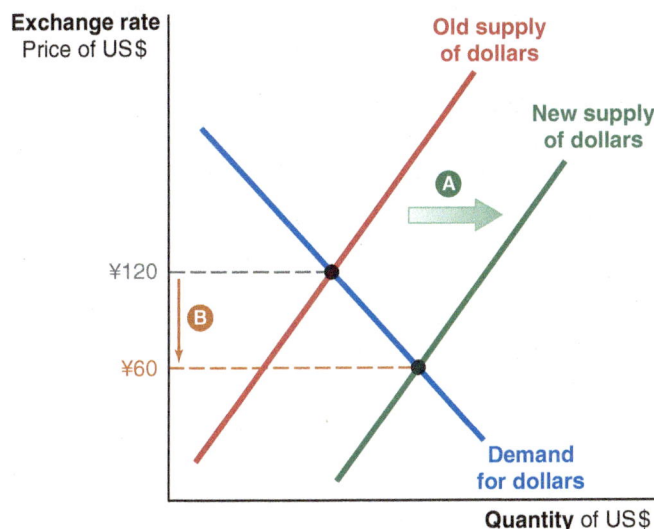

A Decrease in the Supply of Dollars

Ⓒ A decrease in imports or financial outflows causes a **decrease in supply** for U.S. dollars, shifting the supply curve to the **left**.

Ⓓ This leads the **price of the U.S. dollar to rise**, an exchange rate **appreciation**.

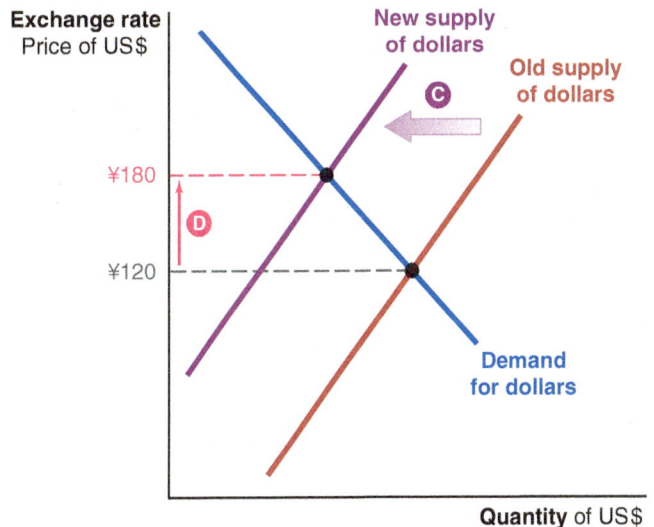

As with the demand for dollars, the supply for dollars reflects the **interdependence principle** at work. The supply of U.S. dollars comes from Americans who need to exchange their dollars for foreign currency, so that they can buy imports or invest their savings abroad, and those decisions depend on developments in other markets. As a result, anything — besides the exchange rate — that shifts either how much people spend on imports, or how much they invest abroad (that is, financial outflows), will shift the supply of dollars. Let's evaluate each of these shifters in turn.

Supply shifter 1: Imports into the United States. Any factor that shifts how much Americans spend on imports will shift the supply of dollars. As a result, imports — and hence the supply of dollars — shift in response to the following factors:

- *Strength of the domestic economy:* An increase in U.S. GDP means that Americans have more income to spend, including on imported goods like Japanese electronics. Thus, an increase in American incomes means more imports, shifting the supply of U.S. dollars to the right.

- *Trade barriers protecting domestic producers:* When the United States reduces tariffs and other barriers that make it difficult for foreign companies to sell their goods to Americans, demand for imports will increase and thus so will the supply of U.S. dollars. For example, when China joined the World Trade Organization, Americans purchased more Chinese imports, which shifted the supply of U.S. dollars to the right.

- *Foreign innovation and marketing:* Innovation in foreign products and better marketing of foreign products to Americans will lead to an increase in American demand for imports. For example, Japanese innovation disrupted the camera industry, shifting demand from American companies such as Kodak to Japanese companies such as Nikon. The result was an increase in imports, which shifted the supply of dollars to the right.

- *Domestic prices:* If American producers raise their prices relative to foreign alternatives, American buyers will switch from buying domestically produced goods and services to buying more imported ones. The result is an increase in imports, which shifts the supply of U.S. dollars to the right.

- *Foreign prices:* Similarly, if foreign producers cut their prices, American buyers will buy more imported goods, increasing the quantity of imports. Typically, demand for imports is very price sensitive, and so lower foreign prices usually lead to an increase in the quantity of dollars supplied, shifting the supply of U.S. dollars to the right.

In each of these cases, you've seen what happens if the quantity of imports were to increase at a given exchange rate. These same influences also operate in reverse: A *decrease* in imports leads to a *decrease* in the supply of dollars, shifting the supply of dollars to the left, which causes the exchange rate to *appreciate*.

Supply shifter 2: Financial outflows from the United States. Remember that when Americans invest abroad, they'll need foreign currency to do so. And so any factor that shifts financial outflows at a given exchange rate will also shift the supply of dollars. The decisions that American investors make about whether to invest their funds abroad or at home lead financial outflows — and hence the supply of dollars — to respond to:

- *Interest rate differentials:* A lower interest rate differential — due to either lower interest rates in the United States or higher interest rates in a foreign country — will increase financial outflows as Americans seek better investment opportunities outside of the United States, shifting the supply curve for dollars to the right.

- *Business profitability:* The fewer opportunities there are for profitable investments in the United States, the larger financial outflows will be. Any change that creates a less investment-friendly business climate in the United States will lead to more financial outflows, shifting the supply curve for dollars to the right.

- *Political risk:* Whenever foreign political risks decline, U.S. investors are more interested in investing abroad, increasing the supply of U.S. dollars, shifting the supply curve to the right.

- *Expected exchange rate movements:* Any news that might cause the dollar to fall in the future has an immediate impact, as speculators rush to sell dollars in

Imports increase thereby increasing the supply of dollars due to:

- ↑ U.S. GDP
- ↓ Barriers protecting domestic producers
- ↑ Foreign innovation and marketing
- ↑ Domestic prices
- ↓ Foreign prices

Financial outflows increase thereby increasing the supply of dollars due to:

- ↓ U.S. interest rates relative to foreign interest rates
- ↓ U.S. business profitability relative to foreign businesses
- ↓ Foreign political risk relative to U.S. political risk
- ↓ Expected future value of the dollar

An increase in financial outflows often accompanies a decrease in financial inflows

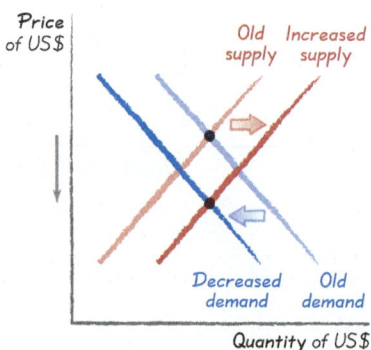

anticipation of those dollars later falling in value. Increased supply of U.S. dollars by speculators shifts the supply curve for U.S. dollars to the right.

Look closely, and you'll notice that this list of factors that shift financial outflows is the mirror image of the list of factors that shift financial inflows, and hence the demand for dollars. This symmetry arises because American and foreign investors are in the same business of scouring the world looking for good investment opportunities, and so they'll respond to similar factors. When investing abroad becomes a better bet, American investors invest less here and more abroad, *increasing* financial *outflows.* When foreigners follow suit and also invest less here and more abroad, the result is a *decrease* in financial *inflows.*

This can make it tricky to analyze financial flows, as nearly any factor that shifts financial outflows, and hence the supply of dollars, in one direction will shift financial inflows and the demand of dollars in the opposite direction. Ultimately these effects will reinforce each other, as an increase in the supply of dollars and a decrease in the demand for dollars will both cause a depreciation. Likewise, a decrease in the supply of dollars and an increase in the demand for dollars will both cause an appreciation.

Okay, that's it — we've analyzed the set of factors that might cause the demand or supply of dollars to shift, and I've summarized them for you in Figure 13. But remember: There's one factor that won't shift either the demand or supply curves, and that's the exchange rate.

> Supply of U.S. dollars:
> 1. Shifts in response to shifts in imports into the United States
> 2. Shifts in response to shifts in financial outflows from the United States
> 3. Does not shift in response to changes in the exchange rate.

Figure 13 | Factors That Shift the Demand and Supply of Dollars

Shifter	Graphically	Examples
↑**Exports** increase the **demand** for dollars		• ↑ World GDP • ↓ Barriers to foreign markets • ↑ Domestic innovation and marketing • ↑ Foreign prices • ↓ Domestic price
↑**Financial inflows** increase the **demand** for dollars		• ↑ U.S. interest rates • ↓ Foreign interest rates • ↑ Business profitability in the U.S. • ↓ Business profitability in foreign countries • ↑ Foreign political risk • ↓ U.S. political risk • ↑ Expected future value of the dollar
↑**Imports** increase the **supply** of dollars		• ↑ U.S. GDP • ↓ Barriers protecting domestic producers • ↑ Foreign innovation and marketing • ↑ Domestic prices • ↓ Foreign prices
↑**Financial outflows** increase the **supply** of dollars		• ↓ U.S. interest rates • ↑ Foreign interest rates • ↓ Business profitability in the U.S. • ↑ Business profitability in foreign countries • ↑ U.S. political risk • ↓ Foreign political risk • ↓ Expected future value of the dollar

Forecasting Exchange Rate Movements

You're now ready to apply these tools to forecast how the exchange rate will respond to changing economic conditions. Simply apply the same three-step recipe you use to predict the results of any supply-and-demand analysis:

Step 1: *Is the supply or demand curve shifting (or both)?*

Will this shift exports or financial inflows into the United States — in which case it shifts the demand curve? Or will it shift imports or financial outflows abroad — which will shift the supply curve?

Step 2: *Is this an increase that will shift the curve to the right, or a decrease that will shift the curve to the left?*

Increases in any international transactions — in imports, exports, financial inflows, or financial outflows — will shift the relevant curve to the right. And decreases in these transactions will shift it to the left.

Step 3: *How will the price — that is, the exchange rate — change in equilibrium?*

Remember, the new equilibrium occurs where the new demand and supply curves cross.

Do the Economics

Think you're ready to try your hand at this? Try working through the following examples.

A "Buy American" campaign leads millions to buy American-made goods instead of imports.

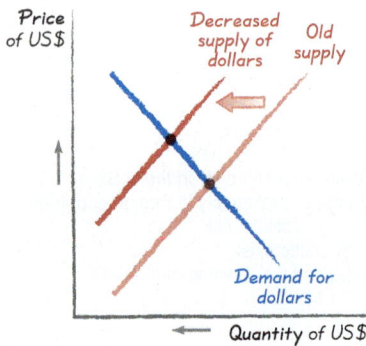

Decreased imports to the United States → Decreased supply of US$.

Result: US$ appreciates

Germany imposes a 30% tariff on U.S. cars.

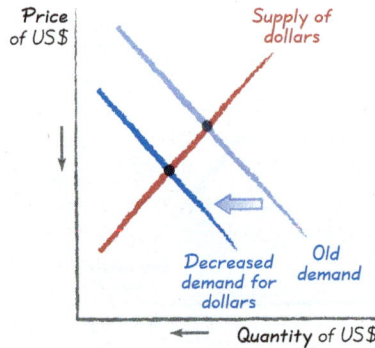

Decreased exports from the United States → Decreased demand for US$.

Result: US$ depreciates

People in China are traveling more, so Chinese airlines are buying more American-made Boeing aircraft.

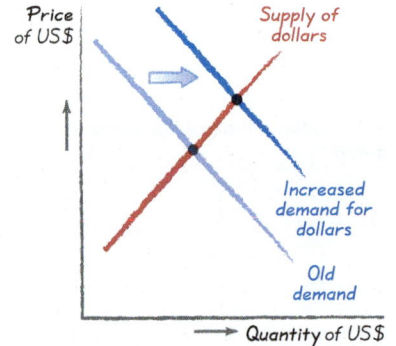

Increased exports from the United States → Increased demand for US$.

Result: US$ appreciates

A strong U.S. economy leads Americans to buy more imports.

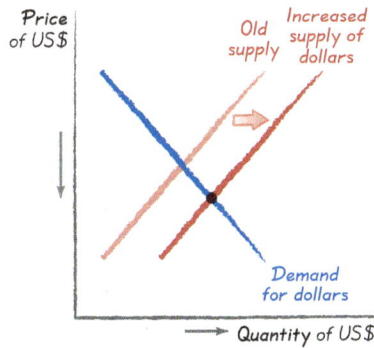

Increased imports to the United States → Increased supply of US$.

Result: US$ depreciates

The Federal Reserve unexpectedly raises U.S. interest rates.

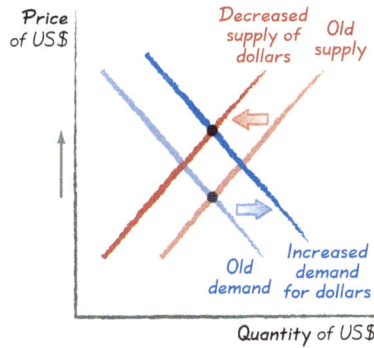

Increased financial inflows and decreased financial outflows
→ Decreased supply of US$ and increased demand for US$.

Result: US$ appreciates

Political turmoil in the United States leads investors to question whether it really is a safe haven.

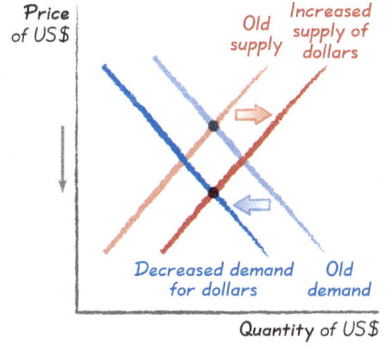

Increased financial outflows and decreased financial inflows
→ Increased supply of US$ and decreased demand for US$.

Result: US$ depreciates ∎

Government Intervention in Foreign Exchange Markets

So far we've described the foreign exchange market as determined purely by the forces of supply and demand. This type of system is called a *floating exchange rate*.

Most countries have a floating exchange rate. The U.S. dollar and the euro are both examples of floating exchange rates and, as a result, the U.S. dollar/euro exchange rate rises and falls as macroeconomic conditions change.

Some countries fix their exchange rate. A *fixed exchange rate* is one where the government effectively sets the price of the currency. For instance, Hong Kong maintains a fixed exchange rate with the United States, and for several decades the price of a Hong Kong dollar has not budged from US$0.13. Hong Kong's central bank achieves this by buying or selling as much currency as needed to prevent the price from moving. When the demand for its currency exceeds supply, it sells Hong Kong dollars, and when there's more supply than demand, it buys Hong Kong dollars. Fixed exchange rates were more common in the decades following World War II.

Some countries operate between these extremes, in what's called a *managed exchange rate* (or a "dirty" float). China is an important example of a country that manages its exchange rate. It officially abandoned its fixed exchange rate in 2005. But in an effort to boost the competitiveness of China's exporters, China held the value of its currency artificially low for much of the next decade, by selling trillions of yuan (and buying trillions of dollars). This cheap yuan policy led to frictions. It meant low prices for American consumers, but it also helped Chinese exporters win business from American companies. China appears to have abandoned this policy sometime around 2015. It still continues to manage its exchange rate, but to a lesser degree.

A floating exchange rate: The euro
Price of a Euro

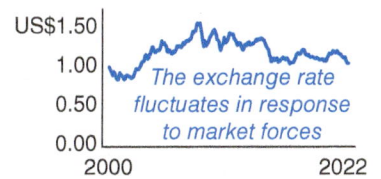

Data from: Federal Reserve Board.

A fixed exchange rate: Hong Kong
Price of a Hong Kong Dollar

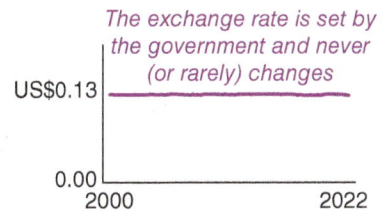

Data from: Federal Reserve Board.

A managed exchange rate: China
Price of a Chinese Yuan

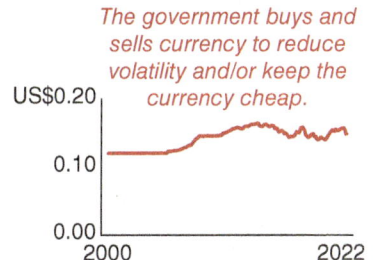

Data from: Federal Reserve Board.

16.4

The Real Exchange Rate and Net Exports

Learning Objective *Assess how exchange rates and relative prices affect exports and imports.*

The Mathisons are engaged in a fierce battle to win over price-sensitive customers in a global marketplace. The more internationally competitive they are, the more apples they can export. Greater international competitiveness will also help the Mathisons persuade American consumers to buy their homegrown apples rather than imported apples from Japan. In short, a company's international competitiveness determines its foreign and domestic sales. And for a country, the international competitiveness of its businesses is a major factor in determining how much it imports and exports.

Real Exchange Rate and Competitiveness

To assess the relative competitiveness of U.S. apple farmers, put yourself in the shoes of a buyer trying to choose whether to buy American apples or those of a foreign rival. You'll compare how much it will cost you to buy American apples to how much it will cost you to buy foreign apples. The lower this ratio, the more likely you are to buy American.

real exchange rate The domestic price divided by the foreign price, expressed in the domestic currency. Calculated as:

$$\frac{\text{Domestic price}}{\text{Foreign price/Nominal exchange rate}}$$

The real exchange rate is the ratio of domestic to foreign prices, measured in the same currency. That's the idea behind the **real exchange rate,** which is the domestic price of a product divided by the foreign price (after converting that price into domestic currency):

$$\text{Real exchange rate} = \frac{\text{Domestic price in dollars}}{\text{Foreign price converted into dollars}}$$

In practice, the price charged by foreign producers is typically quoted in foreign currency — the price of a bushel of Japanese apples is ¥3,000 — and so we'll need to convert it into dollars to make it comparable. The nominal exchange rate formula is helpful here: It says that you can convert a foreign price into dollars simply by dividing by the nominal exchange rate (and so a foreign price of ¥3,000 when the nominal exchange rate is ¥120 per U.S. dollar converts into 3,000/120 = US$25 per bushel). As such we calculate the real exchange rate as:

$$\text{Real exchange rate} = \frac{\text{Domestic price in dollars}}{\underbrace{\text{Foreign price in foreign currency/Nominal exchange rate}}_{\text{Foreign price converted into dollars}}}$$

Do the Economics

If the domestic price of American apples is US$20 per bushel, the nominal exchange rate is 120 yen per dollar, and the foreign price of apples is ¥3,000 per bushel, what's the real exchange rate?

The real exchange rate is:

$$\frac{\text{Domestic price}}{\text{Foreign price/Nominal exchange rate}} = \frac{\text{US\$20}}{\text{¥3,000/¥120 per dollar}} = \frac{\text{US\$20}}{\text{US\$25}} = \frac{4}{5}$$

This says that after converting both prices into the same currency, the price of American apples is four-fifths that of Japanese apples. Given this lower price, the Mathisons can expect to export a lot of apples. (As an exercise, confirm that if you converted both prices into yen instead of dollars, you would get the same answer.) ∎

The real exchange rate measures the (un)competitiveness of U.S. products. A low real exchange rate means that American goods are cheap relative to their foreign rivals — which means that they're internationally competitive. This is why the real exchange rate is often described as a measure of *international competitiveness.* Be careful, though: You might be better off thinking about it as a measure of international *uncompetitiveness,* because a *higher* real exchange rate means that you're *less* competitive.

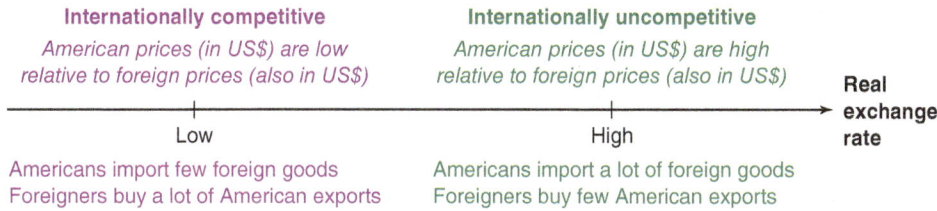

Internationally competitive
American prices (in US$) are low relative to foreign prices (also in US$)

Internationally uncompetitive
American prices (in US$) are high relative to foreign prices (also in US$)

Real exchange rate

Low   High

Americans import few foreign goods
Foreigners buy a lot of American exports

Americans import a lot of foreign goods
Foreigners buy few American exports

A real exchange rate depreciation leads to fewer imports and more exports. Economists find the real exchange rate to be particularly useful because it summarizes the key prices — the domestic price, the foreign price, and the nominal exchange rate — that jointly determine both imports and exports. For instance, a lower real exchange rate means that American apples have become cheaper relative to their foreign counterparts, and this will:

- *Decrease imports*: American buyers switch toward buying the relatively cheaper local goods rather than imported foreign goods.
- *Increase exports*: Foreign buyers will switch to buying the relatively cheaper goods exported from America, rather than their foreign alternative.

The same logic also operates in reverse, implying that a higher real exchange rate will lead to an increase in imports and a decrease in exports.

The real exchange rate is the exchange rate for output. So far we've described the real exchange rate as measuring the price of domestic goods relative to their foreign competitors. By this interpretation, a real exchange rate of 4/5 tells you that domestic producers charge a price that's four-fifths that of foreign producers. There's an alternative interpretation: The real exchange rate is the rate at which you can exchange American goods for foreign goods. Think of it as an apples-to-apples exchange rate: A real exchange rate of 4/5 tells you that each American apple effectively buys you four-fifths of a Japanese apple. By this view, the real exchange rate is the rate at which you can exchange one country's output for another country's output. It's the exchange rate for real goods and services, while the nominal exchange rate is the rate at which you can exchange one country's currency for another's.

The Real Exchange Rate Determines Net Exports

All of these ideas scale up from thinking just about apples to thinking about the whole economy. If the price of American products, on average, were to become cheaper relative to the U.S. dollar price of goods produced overseas, then it follows that American businesses, on average, have become more internationally competitive. Consequently, an economy-wide *real depreciation* will lead total exports to increase, and total imports to decrease. (And a *real appreciation* will decrease total exports and increase total imports.)

An economy-wide real exchange rate reflects broad changes in competitiveness. The economy-wide version of the real exchange rate compares the price of a typical basket of goods and services in each country by comparing movements in the consumer price index in each country after adjusting for changes due to the nominal exchange rate:

$$\text{Real exchange rate} = \frac{\text{Domestic price index}}{\text{Foreign price index/Nominal exchange rate}}$$

The trade-weighted real exchange rate shown in Figure 14 — the *real trade-weighted index* — broadens this idea so that it evaluates U.S. competitiveness relative to a weighted average of dozens of our most important trading partners. You can track the value of this index here: https://fred.stlouisfed.org/series/RTWEXBGS

Figure 14 | When the Real Exchange Rate Rises, Net Exports Fall

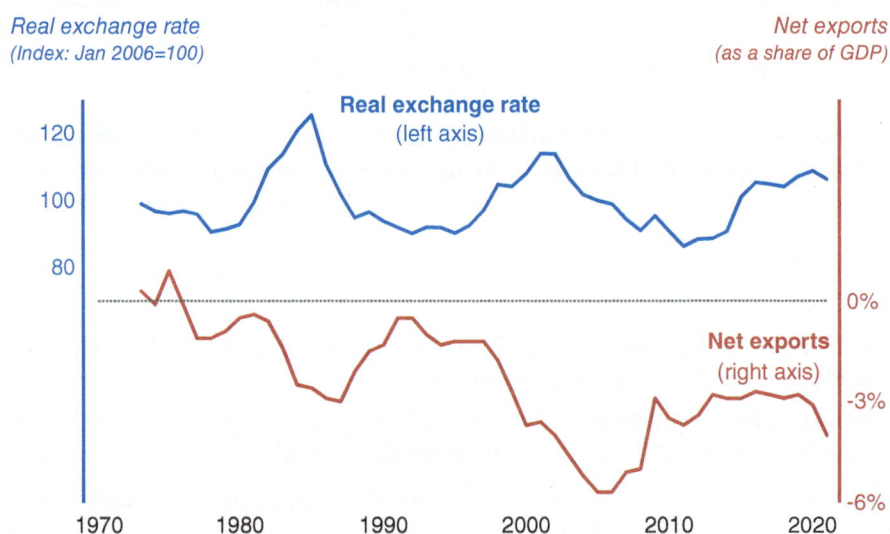

Data from: BEA and Federal Reserve.

The real exchange rate drives imports and exports. This broad measure of the real exchange rate is useful because it summarizes changes in the average competitiveness of American businesses, and whether they're caused by changes in the prices charged by domestic or foreign producers or by changes in the exchange rates of dozens of our trading partners.

The real exchange rate is a key factor driving net exports. After all, if American businesses have become more competitive, they'll be able to outcompete foreign firms in foreign markets, and so they'll export more. They'll also do a better job competing with the foreign businesses that Americans import from, leading to fewer imports into the United States. Figure 14 illustrates that this insight is borne out by real-world data, as movements in the real exchange rate do a good job of predicting changes in net exports.

16.5 The Balance of Payments

Learning Objective *Track how money flows around the world using the current account and the financial account.*

It's time to draw together the threads of this chapter. We began by noting that the American economy is linked to the global economy through international trade and global financial flows. We then explored the role that these play in shaping the supply and demand for U.S. dollars, and analyzed how the real exchange rate also affects imports and exports. Our final task is to describe how to keep track of all of this using the *balance of payments*, which summarize a country's transactions with the rest of the world.

The Current Account and the Financial Account

The balance of payments tracks two important sets of transactions. The *current account* tracks how much income crosses national borders each year, while the *financial account* tallies up financial flows across borders.

The current account tallies up income flows into and out of a country. The **current account balance** measures the difference between the income that Americans receive from abroad and the income that Americans pay to people abroad. The current account tracks all income flows with the rest of the world, and so it's a broader measure than net exports, which only tracks the income earned from exports less the income paid for imports.

The blue bar in Figure 15 shows the income that Americans receive from abroad. The largest source of income from abroad comes from selling exports, such as the income the Mathisons earn from selling their apples to Japanese buyers. The next most important source of income is the investment income that Americans earn on their foreign assets.

current account balance
Measures the difference between the income that Americans receive from abroad and the income that Americans pay to people abroad.

Figure 15 | **The Current Account Tracks Income Received from and Paid to Those Abroad**

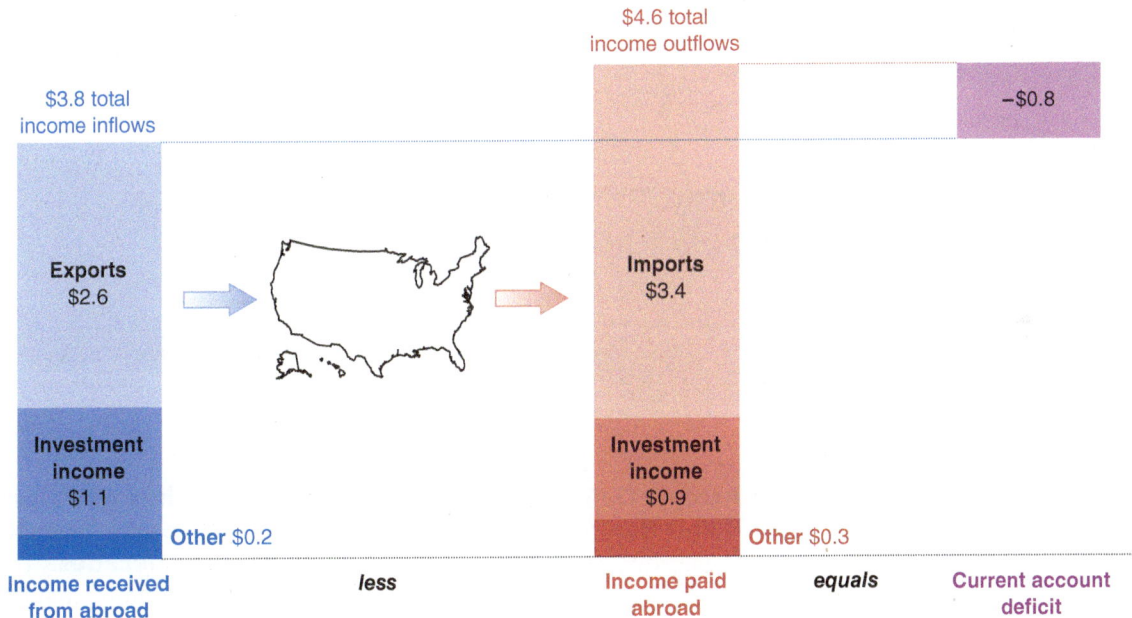

Cross-border income, in trillions of dollars

Data from: Bureau of Economic Analysis.

The red bar in Figure 15 shows the income that Americans pay to people abroad. The largest source of this income is the money that Americans spend buying imports from abroad. Investment income that foreigners earn on the assets they own in the United States is the next largest source. This includes the profit that Toyota's American factories generate for their Japanese owners, the annual interest that American borrowers pay to foreign banks that have loaned them money, and the dividends that American companies pay to their foreign shareholders. In addition, there are some other smaller income flows.

All told, in 2021, Americans received $3.8 trillion in income from abroad, and made $4.6 trillion in income payments to foreigners. As a result, the United States ran a current account deficit of $0.8 trillion. To put this in more human terms, on average, each American received roughly $2,500 less income from abroad than they paid to foreigners.

Notice that the current account doesn't count the sale of assets as income. That's because when you sell $10,000 of your stock in Ford to a foreigner, you're not really generating any income: You're sending someone a financial asset worth $10,000 (your stock certificate), and in return, they're sending you a financial asset worth $10,000 (the cash they hand over). A transfer of existing assets doesn't generate any new income, which is why it's not part of the current account. However, these financial flows are important because they reflect the changing international ownership of assets, and so our next task is to see how we keep track of them.

financial account balance The difference between financial inflows and financial outflows.

The financial account tallies up changes in the ownership of assets. The financial account tracks incoming and outgoing foreign investments. The **financial account balance** measures the difference between financial inflows and financial outflows. Figure 16 shows that in 2020, financial inflows totaled $1.6 trillion, while financial outflows were $1.2 trillion. This yields a financial account balance of a $0.4 trillion surplus, which means that foreigners invested $0.4 trillion more in the United States than Americans invested abroad. In other words, foreigners bought $0.4 trillion more American assets than Americans bought foreign assets.

Figure 16 | The Financial Account Tracks Financial Flows and Hence Changes in Ownership

Financial flows, in trillions of dollars

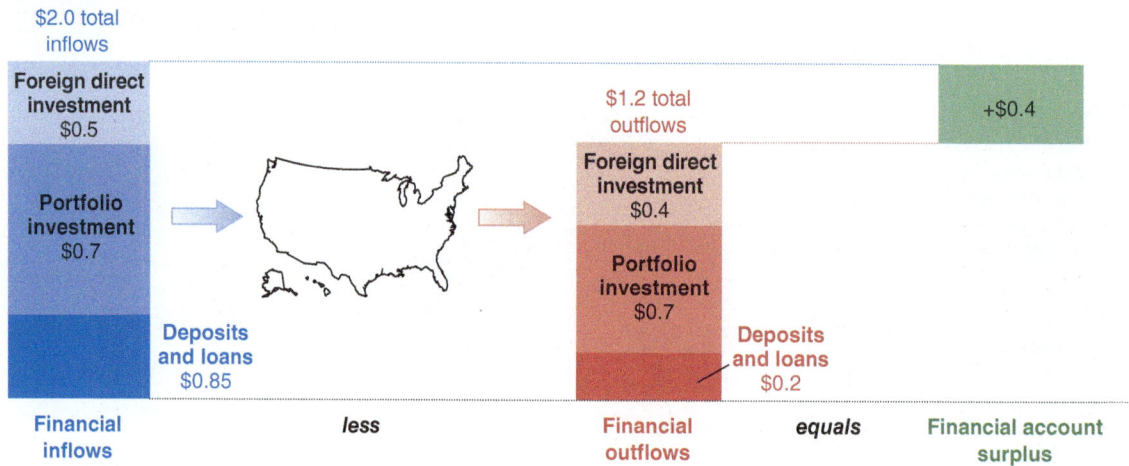

Data from: Bureau of Economic Analysis.

Figure 17 | The United States Has Run a Current Account Deficit for Many Decades . . . Which Implies That It Has Run an Offsetting Financial Account Surplus

As a share of GDP

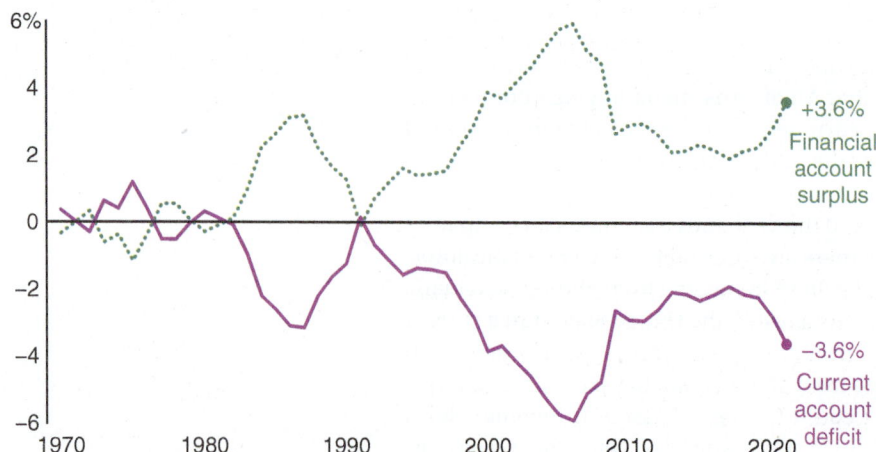

Data from: Bureau of Economic Analysis.

The United States has run a current account deficit and financial account surplus for decades. The purple line in Figure 17 shows that the United States has run a persistent current account deficit since the early 1990s. This deficit means that the income that Americans have paid foreigners has exceeded the income that Americans have earned from abroad. The green line shows that through this same period, the United States has also consistently run a financial account surplus, meaning that each year more funds have been invested in the United States from abroad than Americans have invested overseas.

Put these two pieces together, and the current account deficit describes a net outflow of funds that is exactly offset by the net inflow of funds from the financial account surplus. This connection is not a coincidence: You can think about the current account deficit as the gap between the income and the expenditure of Americans. The financial account is how we pay for it.

Inflows of dollars must equal outflows of dollars. This close connection between the current account and the financial account balance reflects a deeper truth: You can buy a dollar only if someone sells it to you, just as you can sell a dollar only if someone buys it from you. And so inflows of dollars from abroad (which requires buying dollars) must be equal to the outflow of dollars (which requires selling them).

Figure 18 shows that the total inflow of dollars (which reflects both financial inflows and income received from abroad) must be equal to the total outflow of dollars (which reflects both financial outflows and income paid abroad). So it follows that:

Figure 18 | Inflows Equal Outflows

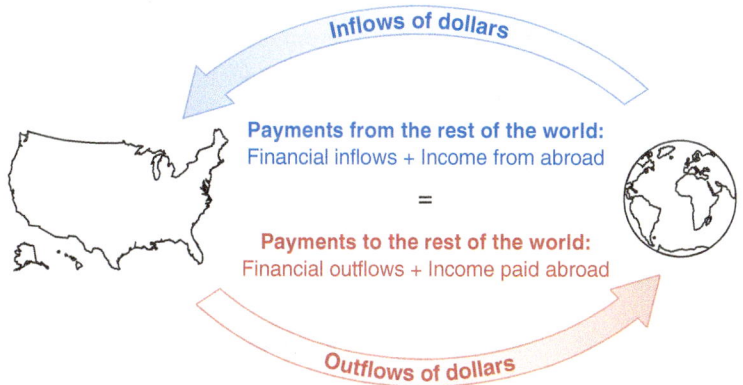

Inflows of dollars

Payments from the rest of the world:
Financial inflows + Income from abroad

=

Payments to the rest of the world:
Financial outflows + Income paid abroad

Outflows of dollars

$$\underbrace{\text{Financial inflows} + \text{Income from abroad}}_{\text{Total inflow of dollars}} = \underbrace{\text{Financial outflows} + \text{Income paid abroad}}_{\text{Total outflow of dollars}}$$

Equality between inflows and outflows implies equality between the current and financial accounts. If we take this inflows-equals-outflows equation and do a quick bit of rearranging, we get the following insight:

$$\underbrace{\text{Income paid abroad} - \text{Income from abroad}}_{\text{Current account deficit}} = \underbrace{\text{Financial inflows} - \text{Financial outflows}}_{\text{Financial account surplus}}$$

The left-hand side of this equation is the current account deficit, while the right-hand side is the financial account surplus. It says that the current account deficit must *always* be matched by an equal financial account surplus. It follows from a simple idea: The uses of cash must be equal to the sources of cash — and the current account describes the uses of cash, while the financial account describes its sources.

EVERYDAY Economics   The global consequences of buying a kimono

For every international action, there's an equal and opposite reaction that ensures the current account deficit and financial account surplus remain equal. To see this, let's track a $100 bill after you spent it buying imports. Perhaps you logged on to Etsy and paid a Japanese artisan US$100 to make you a kimono. Because your new kimono is an import, it added $100 to the current account deficit. What's the equal and opposite reaction?

It depends on what the Japanese artisan does with your $100 bill. They really only have three possibilities:

- They might invest it, buying $100 worth of American assets, which would boost U.S. financial inflows by $100. In this scenario your initial purchase, which added $100 to the U.S. current account deficit, is exactly offset by a foreign investment which adds $100 to the U.S. financial account surplus, maintaining their equality.
- They might buy $100 of American goods and services. In this case, your initial purchase boosted U.S. imports by $100, and their purchase boosted U.S. exports by $100, and in total, the U.S. current account deficit is unchanged.
- They might trade that US$100 on the foreign exchange market to a third person. This just transfers the question of what to do with that US$100 to that third person,

The US$100 you send to pay for this kimono will eventually return to the United States.

who faces the same choices about whether to invest it in the United States, spend it on goods exported from the United States, or trade it to another person. Whichever choice that third person makes, it will ensure that the current account deficit and financial account surplus continue to be equal.

The travels of this $100 bill highlight a deeper truth: every dollar that's spent overseas eventually returns to be spent in the United States, and this truth ensures that the current account deficit is equal to the financial account surplus. ∎

Saving, Investment, and the Current Account

There's another perspective on all this that's worth considering. Recall that the total output of the U.S. economy is measured as:

$$Y = C + I + G + NX$$

A current account deficit arises when we spend more than we earn. In order to simplify things, let's abstract away from investment income, so that the current account deficit is determined purely by net exports. We can rearrange the expression above to make the current account deficit the focus (remembering that the current account deficit $= -NX$):

$$\text{Current account deficit} = \underbrace{C + I + G}_{\substack{\text{Total} \\ \text{spending}}} - \underbrace{Y}_{\substack{\text{Total} \\ \text{income}}}$$

This says that the United States has a current account deficit because total spending exceeds total income. Just as with your own finances, if you're spending more than you're earning, then you'll need a cash infusion to pay for it. In the balance of payments, the excess spending is called the current account deficit, and the cash infusion is called the financial account surplus.

The current account deficit reflects the imbalance between saving and investment. Another important perspective on the current account focuses on the role of saving. If we add and subtract tax revenues (abbreviated as T) on the right-hand side of the previous equation:

$$\text{Current account deficit} = C + I + G + (T - T) - Y$$

And then rearrange this expression, we get:

$$\text{Current account deficit} = I - \underbrace{(Y - C - T)}_{\substack{\text{Private} \\ \text{saving}}} - \underbrace{(T - G)}_{\substack{\text{Government} \\ \text{saving}}} = I - \underbrace{S}_{\substack{\text{National} \\ \text{saving}}}$$

The first expression in parentheses is *personal saving*, which comes from households who save whatever income they don't either spend or pay in taxes. The second expression in parentheses is *government saving*, which is the tax revenues less government spending. (When it runs a budget deficit, government saving is negative.) All told, this says that the current account deficit arises because investment exceeds total national saving (which is the sum of private and government saving, and we denote as S).

When you observe the current account deficit (or alternatively, the trade deficit), you might be tempted to focus on the tradeable sector of the economy to see if there's a problem. This alternative perspective suggests that it's worth focusing on what's driving saving and investment decisions, instead.

Investment is funded by a combination of domestic saving and savings from abroad. Another way to see the link between domestic investment and saving decisions and the balance of payments is to focus on the financial account balance. Recall that a country's current account deficit must be equal to its financial account surplus (so current account deficit = financial account surplus), and rearrange the previous expression to make investment the focus:

$$I = S + \text{Financial account surplus}$$

All investment spending needs to be funded somehow. The right-hand side of this equation illustrates that investment is funded from some combination of national savings and the savings of foreigners. By this view, financial inflows from abroad are useful because they help fund investment.

Current Account Controversies

The current account deficit — and its mirror-image twin, the financial account surplus — are both politically polarizing and poorly understood. And so it's worth asking: Should the United States be worried about its current account deficit?

A current account deficit can reflect people living beyond their means. Some people bemoan the "international imbalances" that lead to current account deficits. They note that as Americans spend more than they earn, they fund the gap by selling assets and borrowing from overseas. As a result foreigners are increasingly taking ownership of American factories and equipment, and Americans are going into debt to foreigners. This might be a signal of a country living beyond its means, especially if the spending is wasteful, and if people borrowing money have no idea how they'll ever pay it back. Even the possibility that the borrowing is unsustainable can cause trouble, as it might lead foreign investors to lose confidence that they'll be repaid, and suddenly stop making loans. While such *sudden stops* are more common in developing countries, the consequences can be severe, as a rapid decline in financial inflows requires difficult adjustments that in many cases lead the economy to tank.

A current account deficit can reflect valuable investments in the future. Others argue that the U.S. current account deficit might best be thought of as a sign of economic health. The flip side of the U.S. current account deficit is a financial account surplus, and this inflow of funding from foreign investors has increased the supply of loanable funds, and spurred more investment. In an economy that's ripe with opportunity, spending more than your current income can be a really good idea, particularly if that spending is directed to high-quality investments that will boost your future income. Under these conditions, reducing the current account deficit (and hence the financial account surplus) would do more harm than good, preventing businesses from making valuable investments that could be the foundation of future economic growth.

And so we're left with the difficult conclusion that a current account deficit might be a symptom of future economic trouble, or it might be a signal of future economic strength. It really depends on how sound the millions of decisions that make up that deficit are.

Don't worry about bilateral trade balances. One thing nearly all economists agree on is that you shouldn't worry about **bilateral trade balances** — how much we buy from one specific country compared to how much they buy from us. For instance, Americans import more from China than they export to China, and so the United States has a bilateral trade deficit with China. But from a macroeconomic perspective, this is largely irrelevant. What matters is whether the totality of U.S. international transactions are sustainable, not just the part related to China.

The question you should ask when you're trading is whether you're getting a good deal, not whether the other side is buying as much from you as you are from them. As one economist memorably put it, "I have a chronic deficit with my barber, who doesn't buy a darned thing from me."

bilateral trade balance How much we buy from a specific country compared to how much they buy from us.

16.6 Tying It Together

Welcome to Youville

Let's revisit the themes in this chapter by studying the most interesting economy in the world: That's the nation of Youville, population one. It was formed when you — and only you — seceded from the United States. Not much changed — you still live at your current address and go about your regular life. But now anything that enters or exits your home counts as an international transaction. The economy of Youville will help illustrate what we can learn from a country's balance of payments.

Let's start by considering Youville's imports, the most obvious of which are the food and clothes you import from stores beyond your national borders. Youville also imports services, the most important of which is the big tuition bill you pay each year for imported educational services. As for Youville's exports, if you hold a part-time job — perhaps you do data entry for a local business — then you're exporting clerical services. If you're at all like most students, the money you send "abroad" to pay for food, clothing, and tuition exceeds the income you're receiving, and so Youville is running a current account deficit.

If you're spending more than you're earning, how do you pay the bills? Most folks in college rely on student loans. These count as financial inflows into Youville, and so Youville runs a financial account surplus. Your current account deficit must be equal to your financial account surplus, because you can spend more than your income only if you have financing coming in to pay those bills.

Should Youville be worried about its current account deficit? It depends. If you're cutting class and loading up on debt so that you can party now without worrying about the money you'll have to pay back later, you're making a mistake. In this case, the current account deficit is a signal that Youville could face economic trouble when those bills come due.

But if you're studying hard, and improving your skills, you'll be well-placed to get a higher-paying job later. Remember, over their lifetime a typical college graduate will outearn a typical high school graduate by more than a million dollars. In this case, there's no reason to worry about Youville's current account deficit, as repaying those debts won't be too difficult. Indeed, the current account deficit is simply a side effect of using "foreign" financing to help fund productive investments that will underpin Youville's future economic growth.

Finally, Youville illustrates a much broader trend. It's a nation that's fully integrated into the world's economy. The population in Youville specialized in a few tasks (clerical services), and it relies on the global economy beyond its borders for most things. It's like globalization on steroids. It's unlikely that the U.S. economy will ever become this integrated into the global economy. But you can bet that through your lifetime, the United States is going to become more like Youville, and international trade and global financial flows will become even more important. And that in turn, means that the material you've learned in this chapter will only become even more valuable.

Chapter 16 Review

Chapter at a Glance

Trade balance = Net exports = Exports sold to foreign buyers − Imports bought from foreign sellers

Exchange Rates

Nominal exchange rate: The price of a country's currency (in terms of another country's currency).

Convert U.S. dollars to yen:

Number of yen = Number of dollars × Nominal exchange rate

$$\text{Nominal exchange rate} = \frac{\text{Number of yen}}{\text{Number of dollars}}$$

U.S. Dollar → Yen

Appreciation
Become more
expensive

Depreciation
Become
cheaper

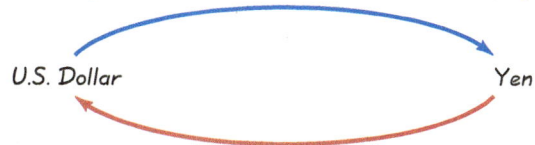

Convert yen to U.S. dollars:

$$\text{Number of dollars} = \frac{\text{Number of yen}}{\text{Nominal exchange rate}}$$

Foreign Exchange Market

A market where you can exchange one currency for another.

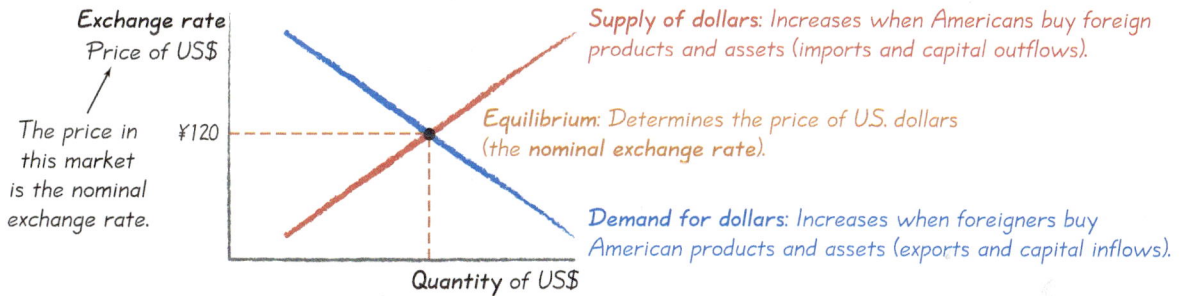

Exchange rate
Price of US$

The price in this market is the nominal exchange rate.

¥120

Quantity of US$

Supply of dollars: Increases when Americans buy foreign products and assets (imports and capital outflows).

Equilibrium: Determines the price of U.S. dollars (the nominal exchange rate).

Demand for dollars: Increases when foreigners buy American products and assets (exports and capital inflows).

Real Exchange Rates and Net Exports

Internationally competitive
American prices (in US$) are low relative to foreign prices (also in US$)

Internationally uncompetitive
American prices (in US$) are high relative to foreign prices (also in US$)

Low ——— High

Americans import few foreign goods
Foreigners buy a lot of American exports

Americans import a lot of foreign goods
Foreigners buy few American exports

$$\text{Real exchange rate} = \frac{\text{Domestic price in dollars}}{\text{Foreign price converted to dollars}}$$

$$= \frac{\text{Domestic price in dollars}}{\text{Foreign price in foreign currency/Nominal exchange rate}}$$

The Balance of Payments

Current account balance = Income from abroad − Income paid abroad
Financial account balance = Financial inflows − Financial outflows

Inflows
= Income from abroad + Financial inflows

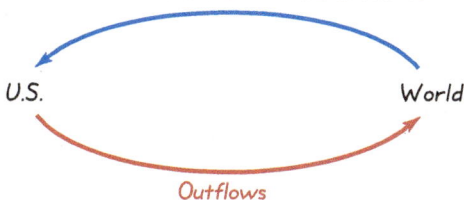

U.S. → World

Outflows
= Income paid abroad + Financial outflows

Inflows = Outflows
Income from abroad + Financial inflows = Income paid abroad + Financial outflows
Financial inflows − Financial outflows = Income paid abroad − Income from abroad

Financial account surplus   Current account deficit

Key Terms

appreciation, 413

bilateral trade balance, 431

current account balance, 427

depreciation, 413

exports, 406

financial account balance, 428

financial inflows, 409

financial outflows, 409

foreign exchange market, 414

imports, 406

net exports, 407

nominal exchange rate, 410

nominal exchange rate formula, 411

real exchange rate, 424

Study Problems

Learning Objective 16.1 *See the connections between the domestic economy and the global economy.*

1. What are the factors that led international trade and global financial flows to rise over recent decades? Do you expect international trade and global financial flows to continue to grow? Why or why not?

2. Americans own almost three times as many foreign assets as they did four decades ago. Some people worry that this makes Americans more vulnerable to the ups and downs in the economies of other countries, while others argue that Americans are more protected against risks. Assess which of these arguments you find more persuasive. (*Hint:* Consider the macroeconomic perspective and the risk management perspective.)

3. The following graph depicts Japanese imports and exports.

Imports to and exports from Japan

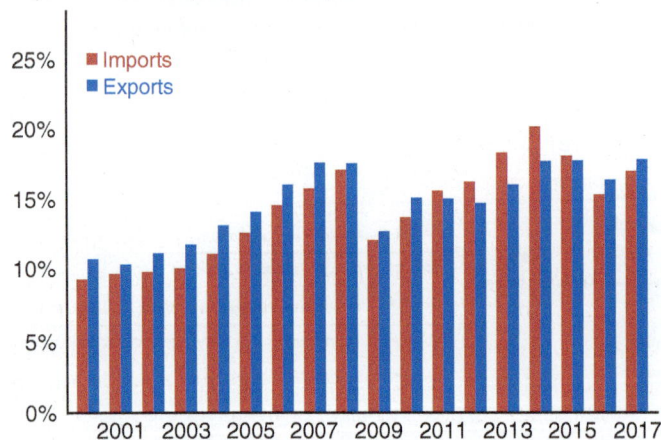

Data from: World Bank.

   a. Describe the general trend in imports and exports for Japan since 2000.

   b. In which years did Japan run a trade surplus? A trade deficit?

4. Determine whether each of the following is an example of an import, export, financial inflow, or financial outflow.

If it is a financial flow, is it an example of foreign direct investment or of portfolio investment?

   a. Tesla began building a factory dedicated to large-scale production of batteries in Shanghai.

   b. A German business pays an American consultant for financial advice.

   c. A U.S. family spends $2,000 on hotels and meals while taking a vacation in London.

   d. U.S. oil refineries purchased US$53 billion of crude petroleum from Canadian oil companies.

   e. You sell a hand-knitted scarf on Etsy to a woman who lives in France.

   f. A saver in Mexico purchases $100 in U.S. government bonds.

Learning Objective 16.2 *Analyze prices that are quoted in different currencies.*

5. Think about your favorite country, and search online for its exchange rate. What is its nominal exchange rate — that is, the price of its currency in terms of U.S. dollars? Has the currency appreciated or depreciated relative to the U.S. dollar over the course of the past year? Are imports to this country more or less expensive than a year ago? Explain your reasoning.

6. Theresa, who lives in the United States, finds a jacket she really wants to buy, but it is only available from Amazon UK, where it is selling for £65. Luckily the seller is willing to ship internationally for an additional £10. If the exchange rate is US$1 for £0.75, how much does the jacket cost in U.S. dollars?

7. You just spent two weeks in Guatemala on vacation. Your trip is over, and you realize that you overestimated how much local cash you would need while in Guatemala. Now you want to convert your remaining 1,500 Guatemalan quetzal (GTQ) back to U.S. dollars. The exchange rate is US$1 for 7.5 GTQ. How many U.S. dollars will you receive?

8. Consider the following graph of the U.S./euro nominal exchange rate.

U.S./Euro exchange rate
Price of a Euro

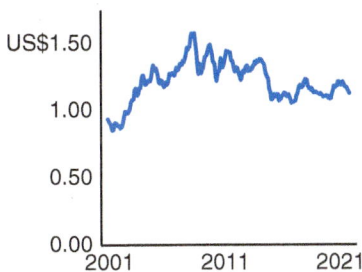

Data from: Federal Reserve Bank of St. Louis.

a. If you traveled to Europe in 2013 and converted US$1,000 to euros, how many euros would you get? What if you were traveling in 2016?

b. Did the U.S. dollar appreciate or depreciate relative to the euro between 2013 and 2016?

Learning Objective 16.3 *Analyze the market for currencies and forecast the nominal exchange rate.*

9. In 2019, the United States enacted trade barriers to restrict imports from China. Use the three-step recipe for forecasting exchange rate movements to explain how you expect the price of the U.S. dollar in yuan to respond to these trade barriers. Chinese policymakers responded by enacting tariffs against U.S. exports to China. How do you think this response affected the price of the U.S. dollar in yuan?

10. What happens to the amount Americans pay for imported goods if the price of the U.S. dollar depreciates? Will Americans import more or fewer goods if the U.S. dollar depreciates?

11. How does a recession in Japan affect the market for U.S. dollars? What do you expect will happen to the price of a U.S. dollar in yen? Illustrate your answer with a graph.

12. If the U.S. Federal Reserve unexpectedly cuts the interest rate, what effect do you expect this will have on the U.S. dollar?

Learning Objective 16.4 *Assess how exchange rates and relative prices affect exports and imports.*

13. Technology-driven improvements in farm productivity led the cost of growing soybeans in the United States to fall, leading U.S. farmers to cut their prices. If the nominal exchange rate is unchanged, what will this mean for the U.S. real exchange rate?

14. You and your friend decide to backpack around Europe. You've been debating whether Europe or the United States is more expensive. They spy a McDonald's and

say that they can prove that Europe is more expensive by comparing the price of a Big Mac in Paris with what it costs in your college town of Madison, Wisconsin. How would you go about comparing these two prices? Why would this information help inform your debate?

15. You are a purchasing manager for General Electric and need to decide whether you should buy stainless steel from a supplier in China or source it from a foundry in Pittsburgh. If you buy it from the Pittsburgh foundry, you'll pay $3,000 per metric ton. If you buy from China, you'll pay 14,000 yuan per metric ton. Both prices include transportation costs. The nominal exchange rate is US$1 for 7 yuan.

a. Calculate the real exchange rate — the price of domestic steel in dollars, relative to the price of imported steel converted into dollars — and use this to decide whether you should buy the domestic or imported steel.

b. A rise in the cost of Chinese labor leads to a rise in the price of Chinese steel to 28,000 yuan per metric ton. The nominal exchange rate is still US$1 for 7 yuan. What has happened to the real exchange rate? Does this make it more or less likely that General Electric purchases steel from the foundry in Pittsburgh?

Learning Objective 16.5 *Track how money flows around the world using the current account and the financial account.*

16. At a family gathering, one of your cousins says, "We spend so much more on imports than other countries spend on our exports. It isn't fair and we should raise tariffs on imports to reduce how much we buy from other countries." How would you explain to your cousin that current account deficits aren't necessarily a sign of economic troubles to come? Think of the best way to describe this intuitively to someone who may not have taken an economics course before. What effect would their policy suggestion — raising tariffs on imports — have on the current account and the financial account? What would happen if our trading partners retaliated by then raising tariffs on goods exported from the United States?

17. In 2021, Germany had the world's second largest current account surplus of US$266 billion. Using this one piece of information, answer the following questions.

a. Which was greater, the income Germans earned from abroad or incomes paid abroad from Germany?

b. What is Germany's financial account balance? Is it a surplus or a deficit?

c. Were financial inflows or financial outflows greater for Germany?

d. Was total spending or total income greater in Germany in 2018?

PART V:
The Business Cycle

Think of the macroeconomy as if it were a concert, with musicians on stage playing different roles. Instead of a singer, guitarist, drummer, keyboard player, and bassist, the players are consumers, investors, importers, exporters, and government policymakers. The interactions of all these players create the harmony and melody that we call the business cycle.

You can enjoy a concert from different vantage points. A seat that's up high and to the west of the stage gives a different perspective on how the music is made than one that's over on the east side of the stage. Both seats provide a good view of the show—it's largely a matter of opinion about which perspective reveals more about the music you're hearing. So it is with macroeconomics: The facts of the economy don't change, but you can observe them from different angles.

This brings us to a decision: Where will you sit for this concert? The next set of chapters offers the opportunity to examine business cycles from one of two different vantage points; your instructor will choose the perspective they judge best suits your needs. Each perspective gives you a good view of the stage—and if you choose to continue your study of economics beyond this course, you will explore them both in time.

The first option is what we call **The Fed View.** Think of this as the view from backstage. Just as government policymakers do, we'll use an *IS* curve to track the real economy, an *MP* curve to illustrate the Federal Reserve Board's interest rate decisions, and a Phillips curve to analyze inflation.

The second option is **The *AD-AS* View**, short for aggregate demand and aggregate supply. It's a perspective that instructors often find useful when teaching first-time economics students. Think of this as a center seat in the mezzanine, from which you can clearly see the interplay between output and the price level.

The roadmaps ahead present an overview of each path through this material. Either path will get you to the same place, which is a clear understanding of business cycles. And they both prepare you for the final part of our journey in Part VI, on economic policy, where we'll use what we've learned about business cycles to see how policymakers can help counter the ups and downs of the business cycle. We'll explore how the Fed adjusts interest rates as part of its monetary policy. And then we'll turn to how the government adjusts its spending and taxation as part of its fiscal policy.

Part V: The Business Cycle (Option 1)

The Fed View

In this pathway, we'll start with a broad overview of **business cycles.** You'll learn to distinguish between short-term fluctuations and longer-term trends, to recognize some common characteristics of business cycles, and to use some key macroeconomic indicators to assess where the economy is and where it might be going.

From there, we'll take our seats at the concert and learn to find the **macroeconomic equilibrium** using the *IS-MP* framework. If the economy were a concert, you might think of this as the view from the Federal Reserve because it's the perspective government policymakers use to assess the economy. We'll start with a brief introduction to **aggregate expenditure** and how it responds to changes in the interest rate, before learning how to use the *IS* curve and the *MP* curve to build a framework for forecasting macroeconomic outcomes.

Continuing down this path, you'll learn to use the **Phillips curve** to forecast inflation, taking account of the role of inflation expectations, the output gap, and supply shocks.

If you want to bring all the pieces together—to truly see the show the same way the Fed does—then we bring together real interest rates, the output gap, and inflation in a brief capstone chapter on the **Fed model.**

---

17 Tracking the Business Cycle

Learn how to track the ups and downs of the economy.

- What are business cycles? What happens during recessions and expansions?
- How do the ups and downs of the business cycle affect you?
- What economic indicators should you follow?
- How can you use these indicators to track the economy?

---

18 Linking Interest Rates and Output Using *IS-MP* Analysis

Analyze the links between spending, interest rates, financial markets, and output that shape the business cycle.

- What causes business cycles?
- Why does the real interest rate shape spending?
- How do financial markets and the Fed affect interest rates?
- What can policymakers do to counter the ups and downs of business cycles?
- How can you forecast where the economy is going?

---

19 The Phillips Curve and Inflation

Assess the causes of inflation.

- What causes inflation?
- How can expectations of inflation actually cause inflation?
- How do economy-wide changes in demand affect inflation?
- How do changes in suppliers' production costs affect inflation?
- Can you forecast where inflation's going next?

---

20 The Fed Model: Putting the Pieces Together

Put the pieces together into a complete model of business cycles.

- How do real-world policymakers view the economy?
- What are the links between the demand and supply sides of the macroeconomy?
- What types of shocks can hit the economy, and what effects will they have?
- How do real-world economists diagnose the causes of economic fluctuations?

Part V: The Business Cycle (Option 2)

Tracking the Business Cycle   **17**

Learn how to track the ups and downs of the economy.

- What are business cycles? What happens during recessions and expansions?
- How do the ups and downs of the business cycle affect you?
- What economic indicators should you follow?
- How can you use these indicators to track the economy?

Aggregate Demand and Aggregate Supply   **21**

Analyze how aggregate demand and aggregate supply determine macroeconomic outcomes.

- How are the tools that microeconomists use to analyze individual markets similar to those that macroeconomists use to analyze the whole economy?
- What determines the total quantity of output that people want to buy?
- What determines the total quantity of output that businesses want to supply?
- How can you forecast the economy's total level of output and average price level?
- How will the economy respond to changing business conditions?
- How does this response vary as the economy has more time to adjust?

A Closer Look at Aggregate Expenditure and the Multiplier   **A**

Explore the influence of aggregate expenditure and the multiplier on the business cycle.

- Why does spending rise and fall, and why does it matter?
- What happens when spending and production get out of sync?
- How can an economy get stuck in a recession or a depression?
- Why do changes in government spending have a multiplied effect on the broader economy?

The *AD-AS* View

This alternative perspective for analyzing business cycles provides you with a different but equally useful view of the economy. We begin once again with a broad overview of **business cycles.** You'll learn to distinguish between short-term fluctuations and longer-term trends, to recognize some common characteristics of business cycles, and to use some key macroeconomic indicators to assess where the economy is and where it might be going.

From there, you'll skip ahead to Chapter 21, to explore the **aggregate demand and aggregate supply framework.** This perspective provides a familiar view of the economy. You'll see how the tools of supply and demand can be effectively scaled up to demonstrate how **aggregate demand and aggregate supply** determine **macroeconomic equilibrium.** You'll learn to use this framework to forecast how the economy will respond to a variety of economic shocks.

Appendix (Optional)

Depending on the path you take, Chapter 18 or Chapter 21 provided a brief introduction to two key concepts in economics: **aggregate expenditure** and **the multiplier.** For a deeper dive into these topics, dig into the more thorough treatment in this fully developed appendix.

Tracking the Business Cycle

Before Ford Motor Company fires up its production lines to churn out more Mustangs, Explorers, and F-150s, it turns to its chief economist, Emily Kolinski Morris. She's in charge of making sure that Ford is well informed about the economy. Her team pores over spreadsheets containing thousands of pieces of economic data. When the government releases a new data point, like the most recent jobs numbers, Morris gets a new piece of the puzzle and quickly incorporates it into her analysis.

Her assessment of the current and future strength of the economy is actionable information that will help her colleagues adjust their

She keeps her eye on the economy so that Ford knows how many cars to produce.

Charlotte Bodak/Ford Motor Co.

production, hiring, and purchasing plans. Ford's production team needs to know how many cars to make and that depends on the state of the economy. In a boom, lots of people will be in the market for a new car. If Ford needs to ramp up production, then it will need to buy more components and hire more workers. In a recession, however, people tend to postpone big purchases like cars. If Morris is worried that the economy is about to slow down, she might advise Ford to suspend hiring or postpone investing in new production lines until it can be more confident about its sales in the coming years.

Morris is talking not about trends from decade to decade, but rather about how the economy will perform over the next year or two. This brings us to our next topic. So far, we've been taking a long-term view of the economy. Now we're going to turn to short-run analysis and look at the economy's year-to-year fluctuations. Sometimes the economy is doing well; sometimes it's not. But it always has a major impact on businesses and people's lives. First, we will examine what business cycles are, next we will identify common patterns across business cycles, and then we will introduce you to tools that you can use to track how the economy is doing. By the end of this chapter, you will be able to read and understand the ups and downs of the business cycle and, just like Emily Kolinski Morris, you will have gathered the info you need to make better decisions.

Chapter Objective

Learn how to track the ups and downs of the economy.

17.1 Macroeconomic Trends and Cycles

Distinguish between long-run economic trends and short-run fluctuations.

17.2 Common Characteristics of Business Cycles

Describe the common features of business cycles.

17.3 Analyzing Macroeconomic Data

Learn to use macroeconomic data to track the economy.

🎙 Podcast

Think Like an Economist

The Boom and Bust of Business Cycles

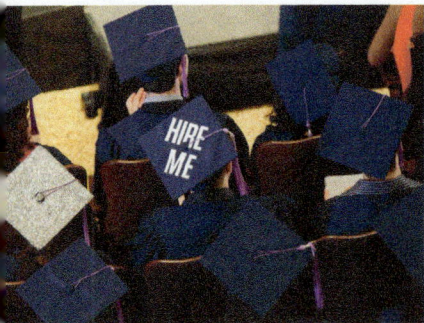

Nicolaus Czarnecki/ZUMAPRESS.com/Alamy Stock Photo

The economy affects the job prospects of college graduates.

business cycle Short-term fluctuations in economic activity.

potential output The level of output that occurs when all resources are fully employed.

17.1 Macroeconomic Trends and Cycles

Learning Objective *Distinguish between long-run economic trends and short-run fluctuations.*

I remember looking forward to graduation, excited to join a world that seemed to be teeming with opportunity. The economy was strong, the stock market was booming, and jobs were plentiful. But by the time I started my job, all that had changed. The economy had stalled, the stock market had tanked, and unemployment had risen: The economy was in a recession. I had secured a job before all this happened, but I was lucky to hold onto it. Friends had their offers rescinded, employers were firing recent hires, and nerves were fraying. It's a familiar story that repeated itself in the wake of the Covid recession.

Hopefully you won't face tough economic times when you graduate, but at some point you will experience both dramatic downturns and periods of calm prosperity. The sharp reversal of fortune that my classmates and I experienced is an example of the sometimes brutal short-term economic fluctuations that we call the **business cycle.**

Trend Growth and the Output Gap

The factors that determine the economy's long-term trajectory likely differ from those that cause the short-term fluctuations that make up the business cycle. That's why it's important to separate the economy's long-run trend from the short-term ups and downs of the business cycle.

Figure 1 shows that the long-run trend in the United States has been for GDP per person to grow at an average rate of 2% per year, and this rate has persisted for more than a century. Long-run economic growth reflects growth in an economy's **potential output** — which is the level of output that occurs when all resources are fully employed. As in ordinary usage, the word "potential" reflects what is possible: Potential output is what we can sustainably produce given our current resources. It reflects the quantity and quality of our inputs to production — the number of workers, their skills, and how much capital they have to work with, as well as all the ideas we have about how to combine those inputs. You learned about the long-run determinants of potential output in Chapter 10.

But in the short run, the economy may fail to meet its potential. Sometimes GDP is higher than potential output, and sometimes it's lower. It's these short-term deviations from potential output that we call the business cycle.

Figure 1 | Real GDP per Person Has Followed a Steady Long-Run Trend for Over a Century

Shown on a log or ratio scale

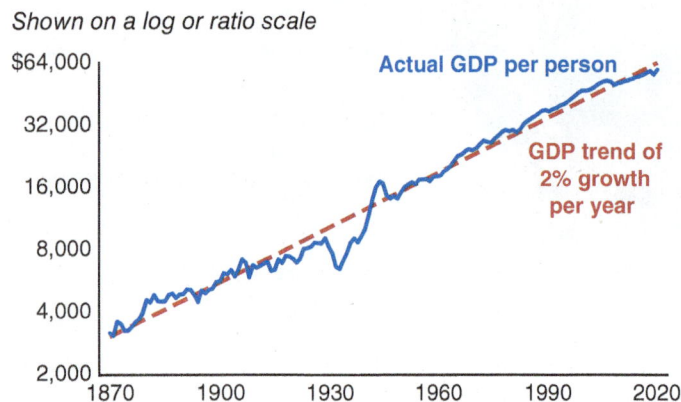

Data from: Historical Statistics of the United States and BEA.

Figure 2 | The Unemployment Rate Fluctuates Over the Business Cycle

Unemployment as a share of the labor force

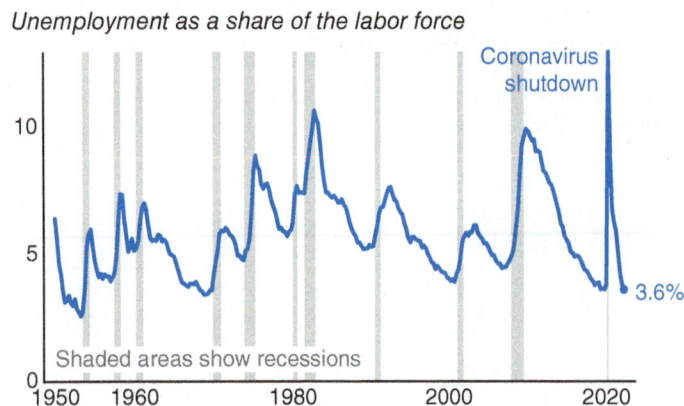

Data from: Bureau of Labor Statistics.

The ups and downs of the business cycle are very disruptive. In a typical recession, GDP may decline by a few percentage points. This may seem small, and indeed, the business cycles in Figure 1 look small compared to the long-run trend. But when you're in the midst of a downturn, it can feel ferocious as businesses fail, workers lose their jobs, and the lives of your friends and family are uprooted.

Figure 2 shows that the business cycle causes the unemployment rate to rise and fall sharply. It shows that the unemployment rate begins to rise in a recession — marked by gray bars — and often continues rising for a few years after the recession officially ends before it slowly declines. Folks who lose their jobs often struggle to find new jobs, and it can take years for the unemployment rate to fall back to where it was prior to the recession. Many people are forced to take lower-paying jobs that don't make full use of their skills. Businesses that otherwise might have succeeded may not be able to weather the storm of a recession and will permanently shut their doors.

Recessions usually don't last long, but they have a lasting impact on people's careers. Researchers have found that even decades later, folks who graduated in a recession tend to earn less than those who graduated in better economic times.

The output gap measures how far GDP is from its potential. The business cycle reflects the tendency for economies to deviate — sometimes for years at a time — from potential output. We measure this deviation using the **output gap,** which is the difference between actual and potential output, measured as a percentage of potential output:

$$\text{Output gap} = \frac{\text{Actual output} - \text{Potential output}}{\text{Potential output}} \times 100$$

A negative output gap means the economy is producing less than it can. A negative output gap means there are idle resources: Workers can't find jobs, equipment lies unused, and storefronts are shuttered. A negative output gap typically corresponds with high unemployment.

A positive output gap means that the economy is producing more than its potential. Producing more than potential output is possible, but only for a while. It means that the economy is using its resources with an unsustainable intensity: People are working extra shifts, factories are putting off repairs, and prices start to rise. This can't continue forever because eventually repairs need to be made and workers will refuse extra shifts. A positive output gap is a bit like life in the few days leading up to exams. You might get too little sleep, postpone doing your laundry, and ignore your friends and family. For those few days your actual output is higher than your sustainable output, but eventually, you'll need a good night's rest, clean clothes, and a social life.

Business cycles cause actual output to deviate from potential output. Figure 3 shows the evolution of output over time as a blue line, contrasting it with potential output shown as a dashed red line. The difference between them, shown in the shaded areas, is a measure of how the economy is performing relative to its potential at each point in time. The figure shows that the economy alternates between periods of undershooting and overshooting its potential.

Figure 4 shows these deviations as measured by the output gap. A **boom** refers to a period when the economy is operating above its potential, and so corresponds with a positive output gap. A positive output gap of +2% means that actual GDP is running 2% above potential GDP. A **bust** occurs when the economy is underperforming its potential, and so corresponds with a negative output gap. A negative output gap of −5% means that actual GDP is running 5% below potential GDP. An output gap of zero means that actual output equals potential output, so the economy is producing at its maximum sustainable level. Goldilocks would declare an output gap of zero to be "just right." Output that's higher is too hot because it's unsustainable. And output that's below potential is too cold because goods and services are being underproduced relative to the economy's potential.

Producing above potential will eventually catch up with you.

output gap The difference between actual and potential output, measured as a percentage of potential output.

boom When the economy is operating above its sustainable potential.

bust When the economy is operating below its sustainable potential.

Figure 3 | Actual Output Fluctuates Around Potential Output

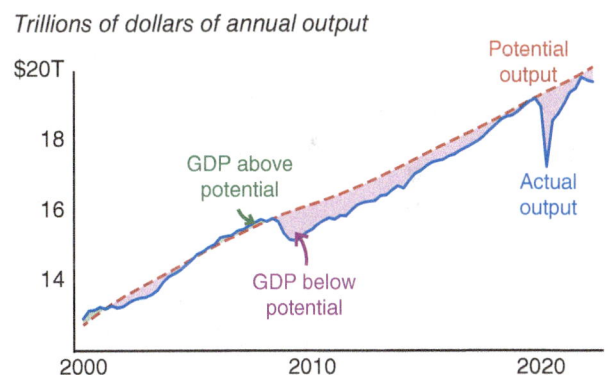

Trillions of dollars of annual output

Data from: Bureau of Economic Analysis and CBO.

Figure 4 | The Output Gap Shows the Gap Between Actual Output and Potential Output

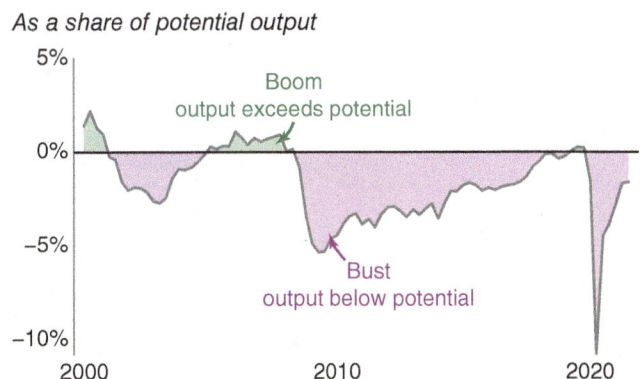

As a share of potential output

Data from: Bureau of Economic Analysis and CBO.

peak A high point in economic activity.

trough A low point in economic activity.

recession A period of falling economic activity.

expansion A period of rising economic activity.

You can see that the economy rarely produces exactly at its potential. Equally, the output gap is often quite small, meaning that the economy is producing near its potential. Figure 4 also shows how deep and rapid the 2020 coronavirus recession was compared to the shallower and more sustained negative output gap that followed the 2008 financial crisis and earlier recessions.

A business cycle runs from a peak, through a recession, to a trough, then into an expansion. Let's take a closer look at the typical stages of a business cycle. A **peak** is a high point in economic activity. Its opposite is a **trough,** which is a low point in economic activity. The period during which economic activity declines — that is, between the peak and the trough — is called a **recession.** The purple-shaded region in Figure 5 shows the 2020 Covid recession. Recessions are sometimes called "contractions" because the economy shrinks or contracts. If it's a particularly bad recession, we might call it a depression.

Figure 5 shows the economy subsequently hit a trough, and then economic activity started rising. A period of rising economic activity is called an **expansion,** and it runs from the trough to the subsequent peak. Economic expansions tend to have a lot of momentum, continuing until some shock — such as a sudden crash in financial markets, a collapse in consumer confidence, a reduction in global trade, a pandemic, or a spike in oil prices — halts further growth, and the economy hits another peak.

Sometimes people forecast that a recession might be due soon when an expansion has continued for several years. But the truth is that expansions don't die of old age after a certain period of time. Instead, they keep going until they're killed by an adverse shock. (Ask 2020.)

Figure 5 | Stages of the Business Cycle

*A **recession** is a period of declining economic activity, so runs from peak to trough*

*An **expansion** is a period of rising economic activity, so runs from trough to peak*

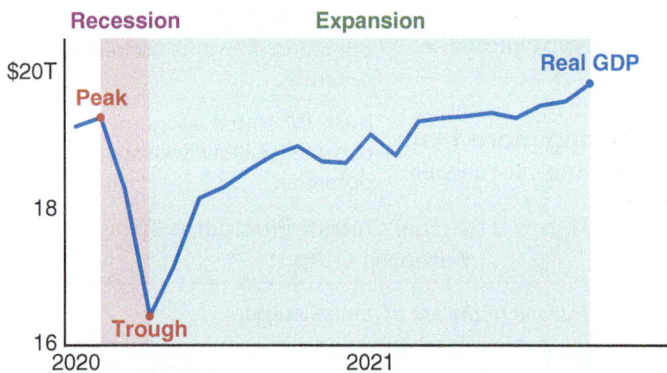

Data from: Monthly GDP estimates from IHS Markit.

Levels tell you where the economy is; changes tell you where it is going. GDP measures the *level* of output, and the output gap presents this level another way by scaling GDP relative to the level of potential output. By contrast, GDP growth rates are about *changes,* describing the rate at which the size of the economy is expanding or contracting.

As you work through this chapter, keep the difference between *levels* and *changes* in mind. Business cycle peaks and troughs describe *levels* — the recent high and low in the level of GDP. Booms and busts are also about levels, and specifically whether GDP is above or below potential output. But whether an economy is in an expansion or a recession is not about levels; it's about *change* — whether economic activity is rising or falling. So when the economy begins expanding, there is positive change, and the recession ends. However, the output gap doesn't close until actual output has grown fast enough and long enough to catch up to potential output. It can take many years of an expansion to emerge from an economic bust.

Interpreting the DATA   Recessions create a lot of unhappiness

Your happiness is intimately tied to the business cycle. How do we know this? Social scientists run large surveys every year or so asking people how happy they are. Most people say they're "very happy" or "pretty happy," with only roughly 10% to 15% stating that they are unhappy. While many things affect the share who say they are unhappy, Figure 6 shows that when the unemployment rate rises, the share of people who describe themselves as unhappy rises. The share who describe themselves as very happy also falls.

This pattern suggests that recessions cause a lot of unhappiness. Indeed, the effect is bigger than what you'd expect just based on the income that's lost due to unemployment. And recessions cause misery beyond those who are directly affected, as the happiness of employed folks falls, too. Researchers have also linked recessions with a rise in divorce, suicide, homicide, mental health difficulties, and a range of other social problems.

This is a key reason business cycles matter: If you can reduce the influence of recessions on economic life, you'll reduce a lot of unhappiness, too. ◾

Business Cycles Are Not Cycles

Business cycle is an important term, but it's a somewhat misleading choice of words. The word *cycle* makes it sound like the economy rises and falls at regular intervals, like a seagull bobbing up and down on a wave, or like a mathematical sine curve. But the economy's fluctuations are anything but rhythmic, reliable, or predictable. Figure 7 shows that some expansions have lasted for only a year, while others have lasted for up to a decade.

Recall that an economic expansion ends because of some adverse shock. And there is no rule of thumb about how long that will take. Recessions aren't an inevitable law of nature — the economy can keep growing as long as nothing goes wrong. Unfortunately, things often do go wrong, whether it's due to a pandemic, a financial crisis, a policy mistake, or other economic havoc. That's what makes it likely that you'll experience a number of recessions during your lifetime. But just because an expansion has gone on for a while doesn't mean that a recession is just around the corner. In fact, in recent decades, expansions have lasted longer than they did in the past. The expansion that began following the 2008 recession is the longest expansion on record in the United States, and it might have continued much longer were it not killed by the coronavirus.

Figure 6 | Unhappiness Rises with Unemployment

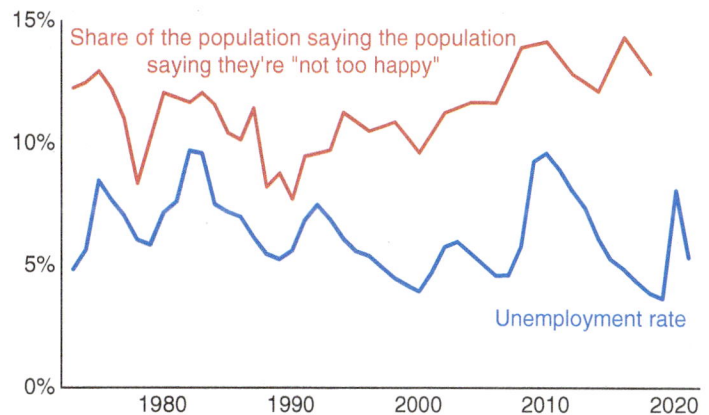

Data from: Bureau of Labor Statistics and General Social Survey.

Figure 7 | Economic Expansions Vary in Their Duration

Year expansion began and the length of the expansion

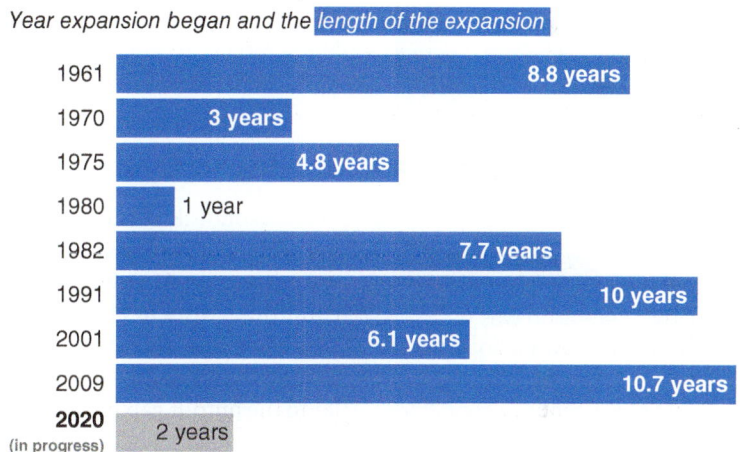

Year	Length
1961	8.8 years
1970	3 years
1975	4.8 years
1980	1 year
1982	7.7 years
1991	10 years
2001	6.1 years
2009	10.7 years
2020 (in progress)	2 years

2020 expansion is 2 years and counting as of April 2022

Data from: National Bureau of Economic Research.

17.2 Common Characteristics of Business Cycles

Learning Objective *Describe the common features of business cycles.*

The novel *Anna Karenina* opens with the observation that "every unhappy family is unhappy in its own way." The observation applies to unhappy economies too, as each recession is unique. Recessions vary in their causes, their duration, and their depth. The same thing is true of expansions. As a result, no two business cycles are ever the same.

While each business cycle is unique, they also tend to have some common features. Let's take a look at what they are.

Figure 8 | Business Cycles Typically Involve Short and Sharp Recessions Followed by Long and Gradual Expansions

Output gap

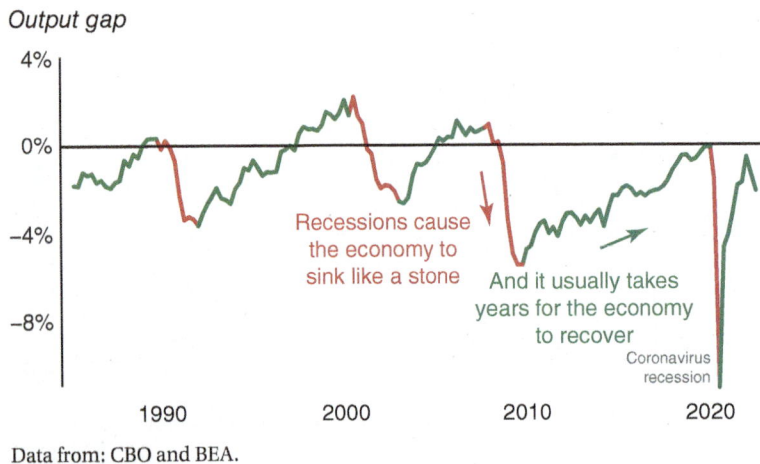

Recessions cause the economy to sink like a stone

And it usually takes years for the economy to recover

Coronavirus recession

Data from: CBO and BEA.

The Covid recession was miserable in its own unique way.

Sean Gardner/Getty Images

persistence Economic conditions today are closely related to those in the near future.

Recessions Are Short and Sharp; Expansions Are Long and Gradual

As you can see in Figure 8, a typical business cycle involves a *short and sharp recession*, followed by a *long and gradual expansion*. Since World War II, the average recession has lasted only one year, while the average economic expansion has lasted five years. Recessions strike quickly, causing sharp declines in output and a rapid rise in unemployment. Expansions tend to be more gradual as the economy slowly recovers and grows. It can take years for the economy to heal and return to normal after a recession, although the rapid bounce-back that followed the coronavirus shutdowns is a notable exception (indeed, this was an unusual business cycle in many ways).

The disruptions that cause an economy to go into recession are varied and have included slowing productivity, oil price hikes, credit controls, high interest rates, banking crises, overvaluation of technology stocks, a housing market meltdown, a financial crisis, and, most recently, a global pandemic.

Business Cycles Are Persistent

Macroeconomic conditions show **persistence,** which means that the state of the economy this year is closely related to conditions next year. Figure 9 illustrates this, plotting the output gap in a given year against the output gap in the following year. If this year's conditions were to always repeat themselves the next year, each dot would lie on the 45-degree line and the output gap would never change. Most of the dots are clustered around the 45-degree line, implying that the output gap in any one year is typically similar to the output gap the next year.

Figure 9 | Business Cycles Are Persistent

The output gap next year is closely related to the output gap this year

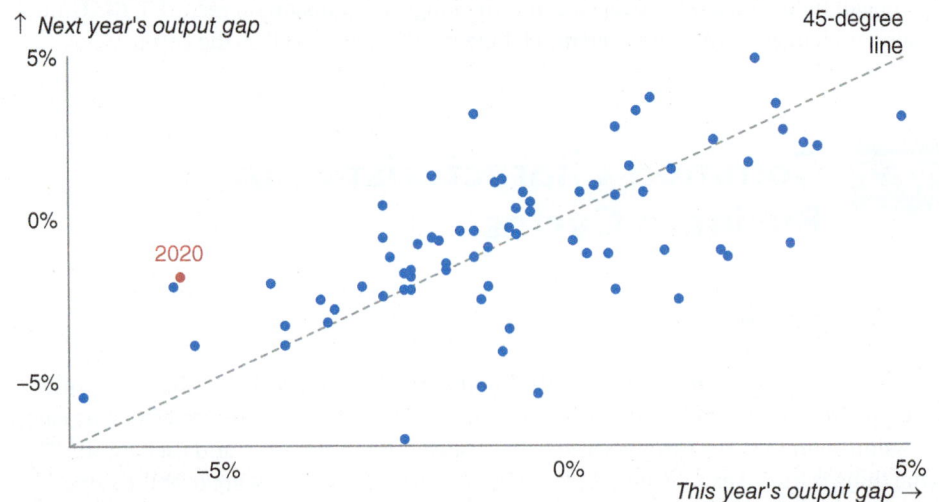

Data from: BEA and CBO.

This tendency for current conditions to persist makes predicting the short term a lot easier! Many forecasters begin with an assumption that whatever happened this year is the best starting point for figuring out what will happen next year. That often proves to be a useful starting point, although occasionally — such as during a pandemic — economic conditions can change quite dramatically.

The Business Cycle Impacts Many Parts of the Economy

The interdependence principle reminds us that the many different parts of the economy are interconnected. That's why many economic variables move up and down together over the business cycle, which is known as **comovement**. This means that if one part of the economy is doing well, then other parts of the economy are probably also doing well. Likewise, if one part of the economy is doing badly, it's likely that the same is true for other parts of the economy. Let's see how.

comovement The tendency for economic variables to rise and fall together.

Different states rise and fall together. The business cycle also affects economic conditions in just about every state in the country, as shown in Figure 10.

Figure 10 | State Unemployment Rates Rise and Fall Together

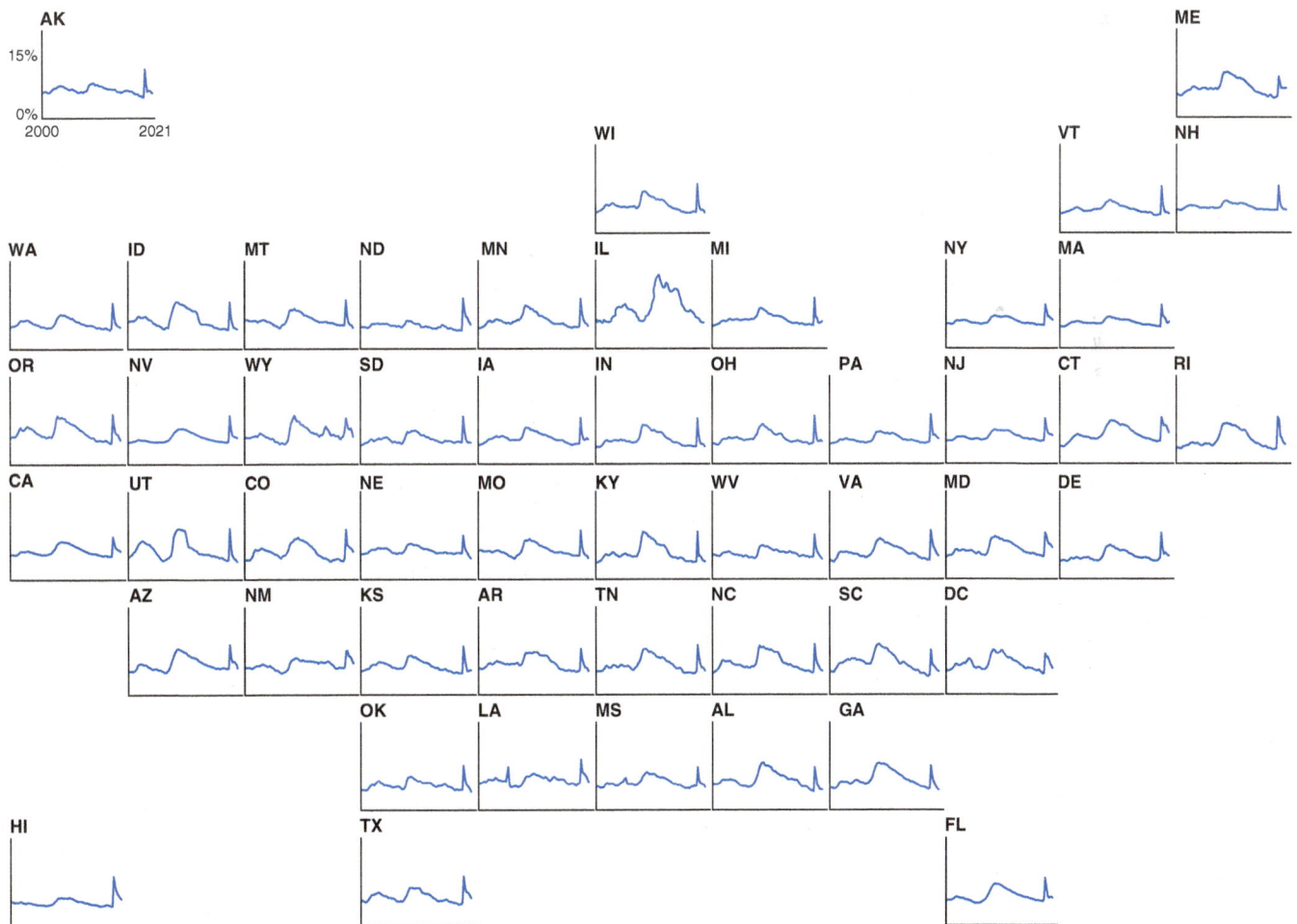

Data from: Bureau of Labor Statistics.

When a recession hits, the effects ripple across the country, as Ford produces fewer cars in Michigan, banks in New York make fewer loans, and families in Texas reduce their spending. And when there's an economic expansion, it also affects every state. Find your state in Figure 10 and compare its unemployment rate with that in nearby states and the rest of the country. While there are some differences across states, no state is immune from the business cycle.

Figure 11 | Many Economic Indicators Rise and Fall Together

Growth over the past year

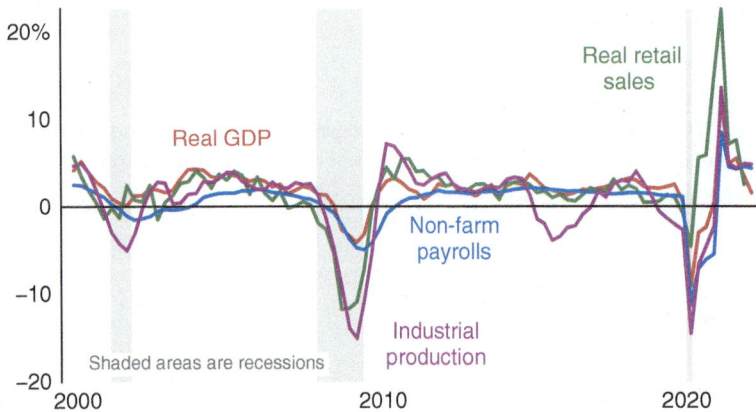

Data from: BEA; BLS; Federal Reserve and Census.

Figure 12 | Goods-Producing and Private Service-Providing Industries Rise and Fall Together, Though Goods-Producing Industries Are Usually More Sensitive to the Business Cycle

Employment growth over the past year

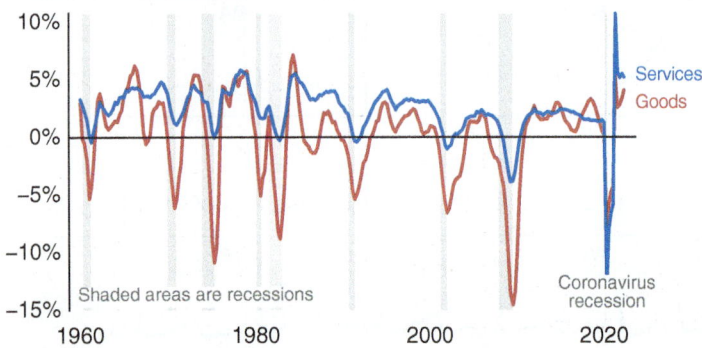

Data from: Bureau of Labor Statistics.

Different economic indicators rise and fall together. There are many different indicators that track economic activity, and they also tend to move together. Figure 11 shows that if GDP is rising, then it's also likely that industrial production is rising, retail sales are rising, and non-farm payrolls are rising. And it's not just these indicators — the creation of new businesses, housing construction, automobile sales, imports from overseas, new investment projects, business profits, workers' real wages, stock prices, inflation and interest rates — all tend to rise and fall together over the business cycle.

Different sectors rise and fall together. The business cycle also affects just about every sector of the economy. Figure 12 shows that the production of goods rises and falls in sync with the production of services. Even within these sectors, most subsectors tend to rise and fall together. So whatever industry you're in, a recession is usually bad for business, while an expansion is good for business. There's an exception to this rule, and it's not shown on the chart: The business cycle is really about the *private sector*, while the *public sector* often follows a different pattern. That's because the output of the public sector is determined by the political process rather than market conditions. In addition, the demand for some government services tends to rise when the rest of the economy falls.

Figure 12 also shows that the production of goods tends to be more sensitive to the state of the business cycle than the production of services. That's because spending on goods — and particularly durable goods like new houses or new cars — can be put off when times are bad. But look closely at Figure 12 and you'll spot one episode where the service sector played the leading role: The 2020 Covid recession led people to shy away from in-person interactions, and so it led to an especially sharp reduction in the use of services like gyms, restaurants, and travel.

leading indicators Variables that tend to predict the future path of the economy.

Some variables lead the cycle, while others lag. **Leading indicators** are variables that tend to predict the future path of the economy. Important leading indicators include business confidence, consumer confidence, and the stock market. Leading indicators help you get a better sense of where the economy is headed because they tend to change first. For example, consumers lose confidence in the economy before they start to substantially cut back their consumption.

lagging indicators Variables that follow the business cycle with a delay.

Lagging indicators are variables that tend to follow business cycle movements with a bit of a delay. Unemployment tends to be a lagging indicator because managers who have invested in developing their staff are reluctant to make cutbacks until they're convinced they're really necessary.

Okun's Rule of Thumb Links the Output Gap and the Unemployment Rate

Economic activity starts to increase at the end of a recession, but the economy will continue to have unused resources until the output gap is closed. One of those resources is workers, and so the unemployment rate moves in sync with the output gap. Figure 13 illustrates this relationship, showing that when output is below potential, unemployment tends to be high, and when output is above potential, unemployment tends to be low.

Figure 13 | Okun's Rule of Thumb Links the Output Gap and Unemployment

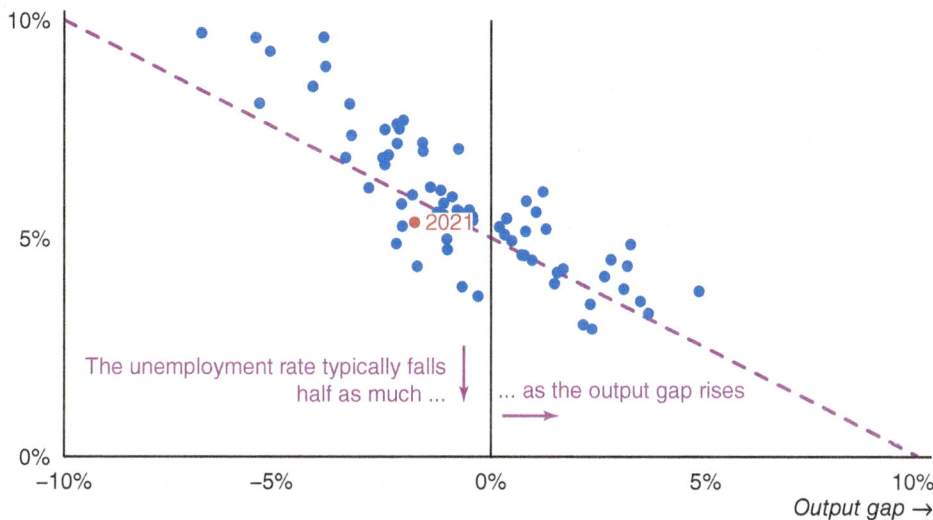

Each dot shows a year's unemployment rate and output gap

↑ **Unemployment rate**

The unemployment rate typically falls half as much ... ... as the output gap rises

Output gap →

Data from: BEA; CBO and BLS.

When output is at potential, the unemployment rate is equal to the *equilibrium unemployment rate*. You learned in Chapter 11 that the equilibrium unemployment rate is the unemployment rate that the economy tends to return to over time, and it occurs when the economy is operating at potential. The equilibrium unemployment rate isn't zero because of both frictional and structural causes of unemployment. Indeed, over the past century the equilibrium unemployment rate in the United States has averaged around 5%.

Okun's rule of thumb quantifies the relationship between output and the unemployment rate. It says that for every percentage point that actual output is less than potential output, the unemployment rate will be around half a percentage point higher. For instance, if you project the output gap will decline from zero to –2%, the unemployment rate will likely rise by about 1 percentage point, from, say, 5% to 6%.

Okun's rule of thumb For every percentage point that the output gap rises, the unemployment rate tends to fall by half a percentage point.

17.3 | Analyzing Macroeconomic Data

Learning Objective *Learn to use macroeconomic data to track the economy.*

The business cycle influences just about every aspect of your life. It's something you'll need to factor in when figuring out whether to spend big because you expect smooth economic sailing, or whether to tighten your belt so you can withstand a coming economic storm. It influences whether you're likely to succeed in finding a better job or whether you need to worry about unemployment. It will determine whether it's a good time to start a business, whether you'll be able to find qualified workers, and whether your input costs are likely to rise.

And so our next task is to figure out how best to analyze macroeconomic data and learn how to read the top indicators that most economists follow. You can look the numbers up for yourself by getting familiar with my friend FRED — which stands for *Federal Reserve Economic Data*. It's a website that graphs just about all the macroeconomic data you might ever want to see, and it is available at: https://fred.stlouisfed.org/. We're going to pull all these ideas together to create a dashboard for tracking the economy. But first, I want to give you some time to get familiar with FRED. Go and do it now. I'll wait.

The Basics of Macroeconomic Data

When you log onto the FRED database to look up the latest economic statistics, one of the first things you might notice is that there are a lot of choices. Real or nominal? Seasonally adjusted or not? Quarterly or annual? Let's start by sorting out what these choices are all about, and which data will best suit your purposes.

Figure 14 | Ice Cream Production Has a Regular Seasonal Cycle, Peaking at the Start of Summer and Hitting a Trough at the Start of Winter

Index, 2017 = 100

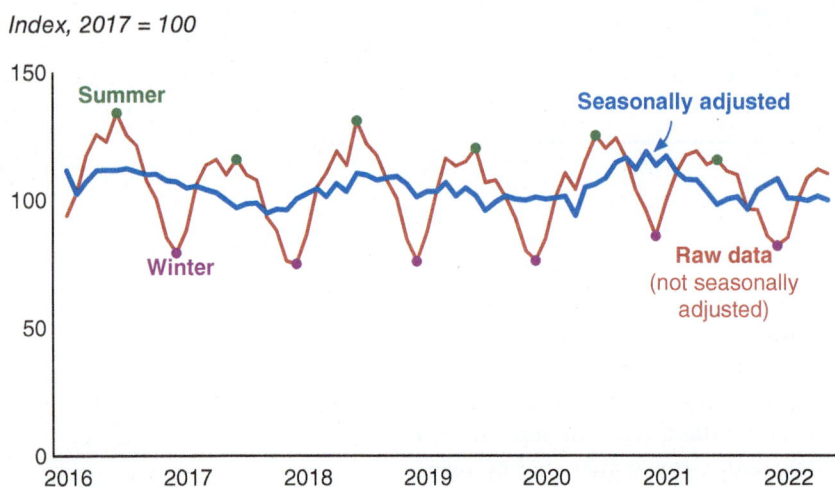

Data from: Federal Reserve Board.

seasonally adjusted Data stripped of predictable seasonal patterns.

annualized rate Data converted to the rate that would occur if the current rate had continued throughout the year.

Seasonally adjusted data take out seasonal patterns. For lots of data series you need to choose between "seasonally adjusted" and "not seasonally adjusted." This choice reflects a reality of economic life: There are strong seasonal patterns in many of the things that we do. For instance, Figure 14 shows that ice cream production spikes in the summer and plummets in the winter. It's not just ice cream, though. Seasonal patterns are evident in most domains of economic life, such as teen employment (which spikes when school ends), retail sales (which rise before the holidays), and construction (which slows during the winter). In each case, **seasonally adjusted** data remove these predictable seasonal influences. The reason to do this is so that you can spot the changes in the underlying trends. Figure 14 shows that ice cream sales have been pretty stable once you take out the seasonal pattern.

If you're trying to assess the underlying strength of the economy, you're usually better off focusing on the seasonally adjusted numbers.

The frequency of different data series varies, but you can compare annualized rates. Most data that you'll want to follow won't be collected annually — they will be collected weekly, monthly, or quarterly (every three months). But you'll sometimes see an option to choose what's called "annualized" data. These data are from a time period of less than a year converted into an **annualized rate** — that is, as if the same rate occurred throughout the year. This makes it easier to compare growth rates measured across different time periods.

You typically want to focus on real data. You'll also run into the words "real" and "nominal" quite a bit. As you learned in Chapter 12, real variables adjust for inflation so that you're comparing quantities, holding prices constant. Nominal variables are expressed in the prices of the year of the data — so nominal GDP in 2010 reflects GDP measured in 2010 prices and nominal GDP in 2020 reflects GDP measured in 2020 prices. The problem with nominal data is that it's hard to tell whether an increase reflects rising prices or rising quantities, which is why you'll typically use real data, such as real GDP, to track the economy's performance over time. Real data series will typically be described as being measured in something like "chained 2012 dollars."

Pay attention to data revisions. Some data are frequently revised, so when you look up data, realize that it might be different from the last time you looked at it. Updates to earlier estimates are called **revisions,** and they can be quite substantial because initial estimates can be based on incomplete data. For instance, in 2021 the speed with which the labor market recovered from the Covid recession was consistently understated by initial data that suggested the economy was creating a bit more than 400,000 jobs per month. Later revisions revealed the reality that more than 500,000 jobs were created each month, which explained why workers were increasingly difficult to find. Let this be a reminder that just because you've seen the data doesn't mean that you have seen the final word.

revisions Updates to earlier estimates.

Top Ten Economic Indicators

Okay, now that you know something about how to analyze macroeconomic data, let's take a look at some key macroeconomic indicators. I often get asked what's the one indicator that I follow to know how the economy is doing. My response? You shouldn't look at only one indicator if you really want to know what's happening! That's partly because different types of data tell you different things, and partly because each indicator is imperfectly measured. Let's take a look at the top ten economic indicators that professional economists, government policy wonks, and financial whizzes tend to follow.

Indicator 1: Real GDP is the broadest measure of economic activity. Real GDP measures the total size of the economy. It's the broadest measure of economic activity since it measures total production, total spending, and total income across the whole economy. It's typically calculated by adding up all spending in the economy — you know, $Y = C + I + G + NX$. (See Chapter 9 for a refresher.) You should focus on GDP growth to see how fast the economy is growing. But keep in mind that GDP data are very incomplete when they're first released.

Top Ten Economic Indicators:
1. Real GDP
2. Real GDI
3. Nonfarm payrolls
4. Unemployment rate
5. Initial unemployment claims
6. Business confidence
7. Consumer confidence
8. Inflation
9. Employment cost index
10. The stock market

Indicator 2: Real GDI provides a useful cross-check on GDP. There's another closely related measure of the economy's total output. An alternative measure called Gross Domestic Income (or GDI, for short) is calculated by adding up total income. Because every dollar of spending is also a dollar of income for whomever received it, GDP and GDI should be equal. In practice, these measurements can differ because they're each constructed using different data sources with different shortcomings. Early reports of the income data are often more reliable than the spending data, and so GDI often flashes warning signs for the economy sooner than GDP does. In fact, many countries combine income and expenditure measurements to create their primary GDP statistic. The United States doesn't do this, so it's worth tracking both measures.

Indicator 3: Nonfarm payrolls tell you if the labor market is improving. Nonfarm payrolls track how many jobs are created each month. It's called "nonfarm payrolls" because it tracks the number of workers on businesses' payrolls. Don't worry about the fact it misses farm jobs; they're only a small fraction of the economy. This indicator is one of the most important because it's released soon after the end of each month, and so it provides an early and quite reliable look at how quickly the economy is creating jobs.

Indicator 4: The unemployment rate is an indicator of excess capacity. The unemployment rate tells you the share of the labor force that wants a

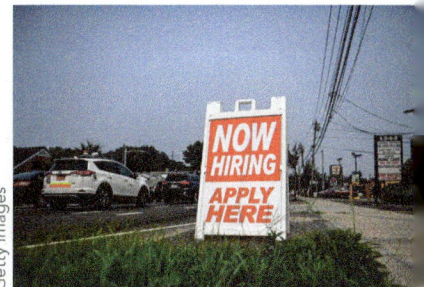

A sign of an improving labor market.

job and hasn't been able to find one. It's a snapshot of how strong the labor market is and how easy it is to find a job. It's important both as an economic indicator — a measure of excess capacity — and also because unemployment is a major source of misery for many people.

Indicator 5: Initial unemployment claims provide a timely indicator. Initial unemployment claims tell you how many people lost their jobs and applied for unemployment insurance during the previous week. These numbers often bounce around a lot, but they're valuable because they're available quickly and offer timely insight into what was happening as recently as last week.

Business confidence tells you what managers are planning.

Jean-Christophe Bott/Keystone/AP Photo

Indicator 6: Business confidence tells you what managers are planning. Business confidence surveys ask managers about their plans over the next few months or years. Business confidence is a leading indicator, and when it starts to fall, a recession might be on the horizon. The most closely watched data series is the Institute for Supply Management's Purchasing Managers' Index. It surveys business executives to find out if they're planning to increase or decrease production, hiring, prices, and more. They are also asked whether the pace of change will slow down or quicken. Sadly, this is the only one of our top ten indicators that you can't download from FRED.

Indicator 7: Consumer confidence tells you what consumers are thinking. Consumer confidence surveys ask regular people how optimistic they are about the economy, which provides useful information about how much they're likely to spend in coming months. The consumer confidence index rises when consumers become more upbeat about the economy, signaling that they're likely to spend more, particularly on big-ticket items like cars or consumer durables. Like business confidence, consumer confidence is a leading indicator. There are a few surveys of consumer confidence, the most frequently cited of which is the University of Michigan's Consumer Sentiment Index.

Indicator 8: The rate of inflation tells you what's happening with prices. Economists pay close attention to the consumer price index because it provides a sense of how much economy-wide prices are growing. For example, if businesses find that sales are booming so much that they're hitting capacity constraints, they may raise their prices faster or more often than they usually do, boosting inflation. As such, rising inflation may indicate that the economy is producing above potential, while falling inflation suggests there remains unused resources.

Inflation tells you about price changes.

CHARLIE VARLEY/Sipa Press/Newscom

Indicator 9: The employment cost index tells you what's happening with wages. The employment cost index tells you how fast wages and benefits are rising. Rising compensation is a sign of a healthy economy, and higher wages often translate into more spending. While there are several measures of wages, this is the only index that accounts for changes in the composition of the workforce. Importantly, it accounts for both wages and benefits, and so it measures the rise in labor costs experienced by businesses. Because higher costs often lead to higher prices, this index is a leading indicator of inflationary pressure.

Indicator 10: The stock market tells you about the future expected profits of businesses. Traders bid up or down individual stocks based on their estimate of each business's future profits. Through this process, stock prices come to reflect investors' expectations about the future strength of corporate profits. A strong overall stock market suggests that traders are optimistic about the future of business profitability, and so it often signals a vote of confidence in the economy more generally. If the stock market is falling, there's reason to be worried.

The S&P 500 is a stock market index that tracks the value of 500 large publicly traded companies. It provides a useful summary of the state of the stock market. Stock prices are often the first sign of either a strengthening or weakening economy, although it's also been known to send false signals. It's worth following, but don't obsess over every blip. As one economist cheekily said, "The stock market has predicted nine out of the last five recessions."

Interpreting the DATA

Why do financial markets sometimes rise after good economic data, and other times fall?

Sometimes when new data come out showing the economy is strong, stock prices fall in response. That sounds crazy, right? Aren't strong economic numbers good for the stock market? Of course they are.

But the stock market is forward-looking, and today's stock prices already incorporate investors' expectations about the future path of the economy. Thus, what matters to investors is whether the latest numbers show the economy is strong or weak *relative to their expectations.* For instance, if stock prices already reflect expectations that the economy is growing very strongly, and the latest numbers show that it's only growing somewhat strongly, then investors will be disappointed by this news. They'll revise their expectations about economic conditions downward, leading the stock market to fall.

To predict how financial markets respond to new economic data, focus on the difference between *outcomes* and *expectations.* ∎

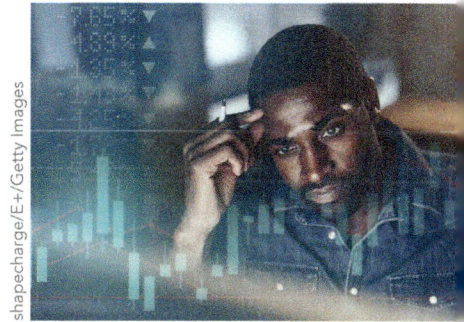

He's evaluating whether the latest numbers beat expectations.

Put ten indicators together in a dashboard. Figure 15 puts the ten indicators together to form a "dashboard" that will help you track the economy. It shows

Figure 15 | A Dashboard for Tracking the Economy

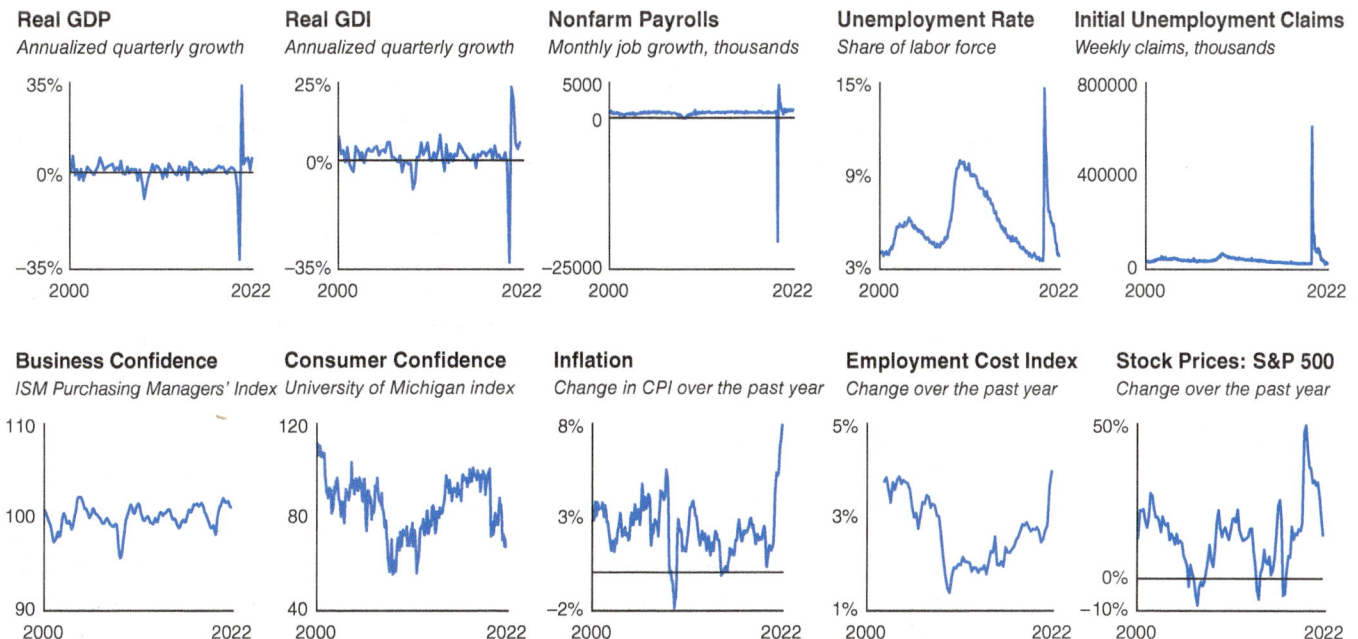

Real GDP
Annualized quarterly growth

Real GDI
Annualized quarterly growth

Nonfarm Payrolls
Monthly job growth, thousands

Unemployment Rate
Share of labor force

Initial Unemployment Claims
Weekly claims, thousands

Business Confidence
ISM Purchasing Managers' Index

Consumer Confidence
University of Michigan index

Inflation
Change in CPI over the past year

Employment Cost Index
Change over the past year

Stock Prices: S&P 500
Change over the past year

Data from: Federal Reserve Bank of St. Louis.

how the economy has evolved since 2000. If you want to see the latest numbers (except for business confidence), the dashboard is online at: https://research.stlouisfed.org /dashboard/17183.

Interpreting the DATA   **Just how unusual was the 2020 Covid recession?**

You recently lived through an economic disruption unlike any other business cycle in history. It wasn't caused by economic dysfunction, but rather a virus. In early 2020, the pandemic led huge swaths of the economy to shut down: Offices sent workers home, schools closed, storefronts were shuttered, and factories ground to a halt. In some cities, this was the result of mandatory stay-at-home orders aimed at slowing the virus's spread, while in others, it reflected people choosing to withdraw from economic life rather than risk their health.

The recession that began in February 2020 was truly global in scope. It was the deepest since the Great Depression, and it caused the largest quarterly decline in output ever recorded. It was also a downturn of astonishing speed and ferocity. In a typical recession, it takes months or even years for job losses to pile up, but in this recession, it took only a few weeks for the unemployment rate to more than triple. The 2020 recession was extraordinary in four respects: It's noneconomic catalyst, its global impact, its depth, and its speed.

The havoc wrought by the Covid recession was so severe that it broke most economic charts. Take a look at the economic dashboard in Figure 15, and you'll see that in many cases the data are so extreme as to be — quite literally — off the charts. (That's why some areas are grayed out — to highlight the missing data.) To give you a sense of the scale and speed of this downturn — and the subsequent recovery! — Figure 16 redraws those same charts, but this time adjusts the axes to make sure that the most extreme changes are visible. You'll notice that this approach leads nearly all of the previous shift in economic conditions to — quite literally! — fade into the background.

It's unlikely that the economy will undergo such wrenching change again during your lifetime (knock on wood), and so the dashboard in Figure 15 arguably provides the more useful baseline against which to compare future economic data. But to answer the more specific question of how extraordinary the Covid recession was, the charts in Figure 16 make the case that the answer is: Quite. Quite extraordinary. ∎

Do the Economics

Head over to the St. Louis Fed's FRED database and look up the latest numbers for our top ten economic indicators, and use these to come to your own judgment about the current state of the economy. Let me help: In the final column of Figure 16, I've included the codes you'll need to look up each indicator. You can get a sense of a "typical" outcome by looking at the second column, which shows the median for each indicator over the past 20 years. Underneath the median, you'll also find the band that the data points are typically within half the time (economists call this the interquartile range), so you can get a sense of which numbers are roughly typical. Numbers outside that band bear watching because they might suggest the economy is either particularly weak or strong.

Your task is to look up the latest data and fill in the final column, then come to a judgment about the current state of the economy. What's your assessment: Is the economy doing well or poorly?

Figure 16 | Compare the Latest Economic Indicators with Their Typical Values

Typical outcomes for the ten key economic indicators

Look up the latest data and compare it to recent history to assess the state of the economy.

Indicator	Median (and interquartile range)	History from 2000–2021	Latest data
Real GDP growth *(quarterly growth at an annualized rate)*	2.3% *(1.1%–3.4%)*		FRED code: GDPC1
Real GDI growth *(quarterly growth at an annualized rate)*	2.4% *(0.5%–3.9%)*	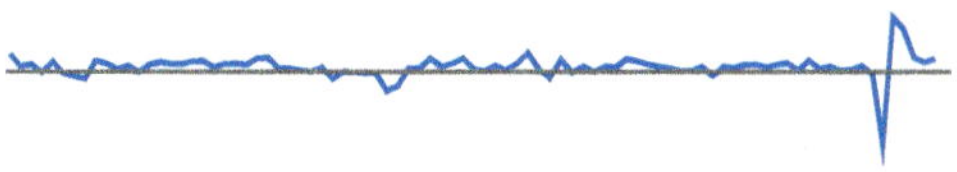	FRED code: A261RX1Q020SBEA
Change in nonfarm payrolls *(monthly change)*	156,000 *(11,500–236,500)*		FRED code: PAYEMS
Unemployment rate *(percent of the labor force)*	5.4% *(4.6%–6.9%)*		FRED code: UNRATE
Initial unemployment claims *(thousands)*	340 *(285–406)*		FRED code: ICSA
Business confidence *(ISM Purchasing Managers Index)*	53 *(50.3–56.6)*		Not on FRED
Consumer confidence *(University of Michigan index)*	87.4 *(76.1–94.2)*		FRED code: UMCSENT
Inflation *(annual percent change in consumer price index)*	2.1% *(1.5%–3.1%)*	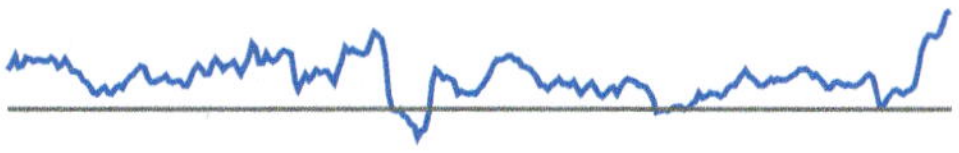	FRED code: CPIAUSCSL
Employment cost index *(annual percent change)*	2.7% *(2.0%–3.3%)*		FRED code: ECIALLCIV
S&P 500 *(percent change over the year)*	9.8% *(0%–16%)*	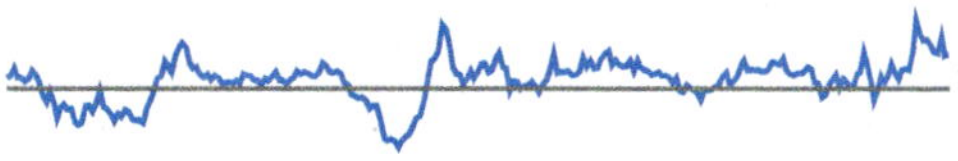	FRED code: SP500

Data from: FRED database. ■

An Economy Watcher's Guide

Now that you understand macroeconomic data and know the main economic indicators to look out for, let's put all of it together. Here are five tips for tracking the economy.

Tip 1: Track many indicators. I've given you a list of ten key economic indicators for a reason: It's best to track many economic indicators, not just one. Our measures of the economy are still imperfect, and the U.S. economy is large and complex, so it's best to follow many different indicators to get a full view of the economy.

As you grow more sophisticated, you may want to add other data series to your dashboard, particularly given how fast new data is becoming available. We're in the midst of a data revolution that is transforming our understanding of the economy. Just about everything you buy is tracked by credit cards, supermarket scanners, and customer loyalty cards. Your feelings about the day are reflected in your Google searches and social media posts. And your weekly pay is tracked by your employer, their payroll company, and the tax authorities. This enormous stream of data — sometimes called "big data" (there's a lot of it!) — is becoming an increasingly important source of new economic indicators. Economists analyze daily data on online prices to help track inflation, credit card purchases to track spending, counts of Google searches for "file for unemployment" to track job losses, and electricity use to track economic activity.

Tip 2: Broad indicators beat narrow indicators. Some indicators are a better reflection of the economy than others, and you should give more weight to indicators that account for a greater share of the economy. For instance, we have lots of data about the industrial sector because it's easy to measure what rolls off a factory production line. But only about a seventh of the economy is in the industrial sector, and so you might be learning about sector-specific factors rather than broader trends.

Tip 3: Seek just-in-time data and distinguish between leading and lagging indicators. Some indicators are published several months after the fact, while others are published only a few days later. To stay up to date, it's best to give more weight to indicators that are published quickly. For instance, you only have to wait four days to learn about the number of initial unemployment claims last week. Nonfarm payroll numbers also come out only a few weeks after they are collected. And the stock market incorporates information in real time. These are timely indicators, telling you about current trends.

In contrast, reliable GDP data are not released until nearly two months after the end of each quarter, which means that in late May you're reading about how the economy performed from January through March. To keep on top of the latest trends, you'll need to be more up to date than that!

But while you want to pay attention to just-in-time data, also remember that some indicators lead the business cycle, while others lag it.

Figure 17 | **Find the Signal by Averaging Over Recent Data Points**

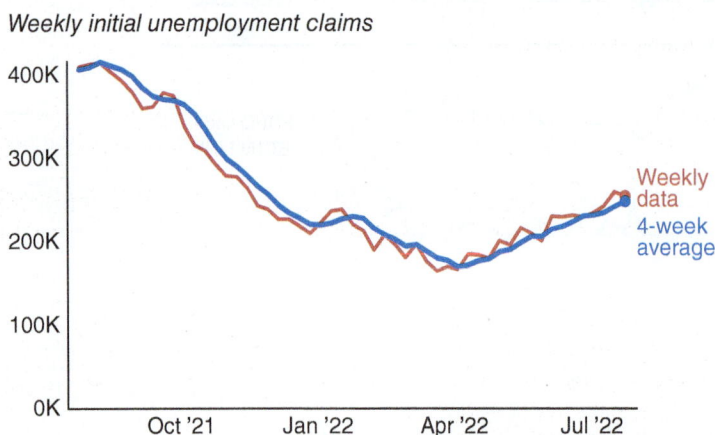

Weekly initial unemployment claims

Weekly data
4-week average

Data from: Department of Labor.

Tip 4: Find the signal amid the noise. Macroeconomic data are often rough estimates based on incomplete samples. This means they contain a lot of *noise,* jumping up and down for reasons unrelated to the underlying trends. That noise makes it harder to discern the *signal* about where the economy is going.

Averaging over the past few data points can help you minimize the influence of this noise, allowing a clearer picture to emerge. Figure 17 shows that the number of people filing for unemployment bounces around a lot from week to week. But if you take an average over the past four weeks, the signal emerges from this noise. To calculate a four-week moving average, simply add up the past four weekly observations and then divide by four.

Another strategy for finding the signal in the noise is to *look past volatile components* of the data so the trend can shine through. For instance, food prices often rise and fall due to the weather, while oil prices partially reflect geopolitical developments in oil-producing countries. Neither gives a useful signal of the underlying inflation rate. Figure 18 shows core inflation, which excludes the influence of food and energy prices, along with a measure of inflation that includes those volatile components. The two measures follow the same long-run patterns, but in the short run core inflation is less volatile and hence is more predictive of long-run inflation trends.

Tip 5: Adjust your outlook when data differ from expectations. An indicator that suggests strong economic growth when you already expected strong economic growth shouldn't change your outlook. What really matters is whether that indicator came in stronger or weaker than expected. When the data matches your expectations, there isn't much news there. But if the data show that the economy is stronger or weaker than you expected, then that's news, and you'll need to adjust your outlook.

Figure 18 | **Find the Signal by Ignoring the Volatile Elements**

Inflation rate over the past year

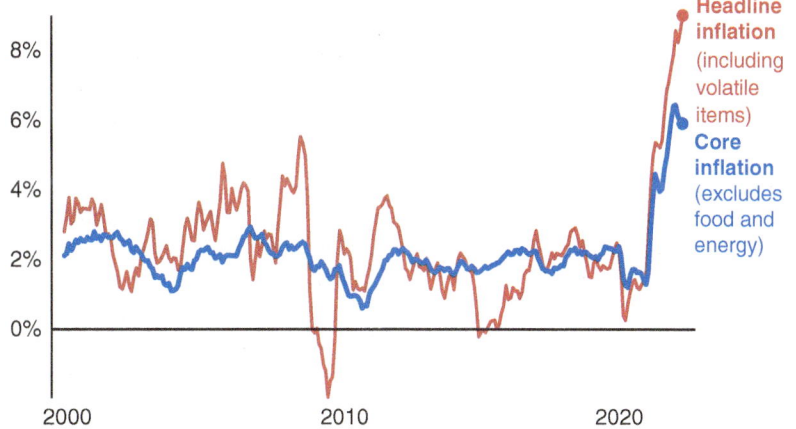

Data from: Bureau of Labor Statistics.

EVERYDAY Economics How to better understand your favorite company, your GPA, and your health

These five tips aren't just about how to better track the economy. They apply to tracking just about anything: the performance of your favorite company, your performance in college, and even your health. In each case, you'll do better if you:

Track many indicators: An analyst tracking Apple follows its revenues, costs, prices, inputs, and so on. A good student tracks their study time, their performance on homework, and their grades on quizzes and exams. And your doctor will track your health by following a "dashboard" of data like your blood pressure, heart rate, and lab tests.

Look at broader indicators that are more representative of Apple's performance, your learning, or your health. For example, while you might own a scale and therefore can easily track your weight, it's not a very broad indicator of overall health. Your resting heart rate or blood pressure is a broader indicator.

Seek just-in-time data, and in particular, the latest news about your company, your academic performance, and your health. Pay particular attention to news that might be a leading indicator of change. Have there been leaks about the next iPhone? Are you keeping up with your class reading? Have you been exercising?

Look through the noise: Don't let an unusual result shape your views too much. Look beyond one particularly good earnings report, an in-class quiz that you took while sleep-deprived, or that unlucky fall that broke a bone to form a better understanding of the true state of your company, your GPA, and your health.

Adjust your outlook when outcomes differ from what you expect: When Apple's sales are up 6%, whether it's good news or bad news depends on what you were expecting. If you thought that the latest iPhone was going to lead to a 10% increase in sales, then the paltry 6% might be bad news. Similarly, if you go into an exam fully prepared and expecting to ace it, a B might be a negative surprise; that same grade might be good news if it was a class in which you had been struggling. Finally, your doctor telling you that you have moderately high blood pressure is good news if you expected it to be very high, but it's bad news if you expected it to be normal. ■

Apple can track your health, and you can track Apple's?

EVERYDAY Economics **How you can put hundreds of Fed economists to work for you**

Whether you're the owner of a small business or the CEO of a huge empire, you can't make good decisions without good information about where the economy is headed. But if you're like most business leaders, you're overworked and short on time, and haven't got the bandwidth to track the economy closely. How are you going to get the information you need about where the economy's headed?

Before you answer, let me add one important fact: The forecasts put together by the Federal Reserve Board have been shown to typically be more accurate than those compiled by professional forecasters, sophisticated statistical models, or Wall Street investors. Fed economists don't get every call right, but they get fewer wrong than anyone else.

It's no surprise: No one devotes more resources to studying the U.S. economy than the Fed. It's home to hundreds of bright economists who spend their careers poring over economic data. They receive private intel and occasional briefings from the federal government, banks, and large corporations. Fed economists also know better than most what's going to happen to interest rates in the future.

All of this means that if you want to figure out where the economy's going, your best bet may be just to follow the Fed's economists. That has gotten a lot easier since the Fed started to publish its forecasts. You can find its latest Summary of Economic Projections here: https://www.federalreserve.gov/monetarypolicy/fomccalendars.htm. This means that a simple mouse click can give you more accurate guidance than you'll get from trying any other approach or paying any other self-proclaimed expert. ∎

17.4 Tying It Together

Long-Run Trends and Short-Run Fluctuations

Economists tend to keep short-run and long-run analyses separate. In the long run — as in Chapter 10 — we focus on how to increase potential output, which is determined by supply-side factors like the number of available workers and the quantity of physical and human capital, as well as the technology for combining them. Generally, long-run analysis is useful for predicting economic changes over decades.

In contrast, when we look at business cycles, we turn to short-run analysis, which focuses on fluctuations around potential output that typically only last for a few years. In the next few chapters, we'll dig more into the drivers of these short-term fluctuations. You'll see that this typically involves paying greater attention to demand-side factors, meaning that we'll focus more on how much people want to spend rather than how much can be produced.

This division of macroeconomic analysis into long-run versus short-run analysis is based on the implicit assumption that the ups and downs of the business cycle have no long-term repercussions. It's an assumption that's helpful because it allows us to separate our analyses of supply-side factors and demand-side factors. It's also an assumption that's probably not quite right.

It's not quite right because "short-run" changes can have long-lasting effects. A recession that throws millions of people out of work is temporary in the sense that the recession will eventually end, and most of the newly unemployed people will find work again when the economy recovers. But it won't undo the damage that people incur from having spent months or sometimes even years without work. The experience they could have gained during that jobless spell is forever lost. Their knowledge of the specifics of working for their former employer will never be useful again. Their next job may not use their skills as

Put the long view and the short view together for a more complete picture of the economy.

effectively. Many people lose skills and valuable work habits, and in some cases, they lose hope. Folks who are pushed to retire early never return, and a long jobless spell can make it hard for some people to ever fully reconnect with the world of work.

There are other lasting losses. Managers typically cut back on investment during a recession, and it can take years before they've fully caught up. The investment in new ideas that drives long-term growth may be put on hold, and it's hard to know if those missing ideas will be generated during the subsequent economic expansion. Valuable relationships are destroyed when businesses stop working together. Even years after the Covid recession, you can still see its effects around you, in businesses that never reopened, or friends who never went back to work.

The possibility that business cycle fluctuations have longer-run implications makes the task of understanding the business cycle all the more important. We've taken a first step in this chapter by learning how to track the business cycle. The next few chapters dig deeper, providing you with a framework for understanding what drives business cycles, so that you can better forecast how market conditions are likely to evolve and assess possible policy responses.

Organizational note: As discussed in this part's opener, different economists analyze business cycles from slightly different perspectives. Much like viewing a concert, you can see things differently depending on where you sit. Now that you've been introduced to business cycles, it's time for you—or more likely, your instructor—to choose your seat for the macroeconomic show. If your instructor wants you to see the economy from the same perspective as the Fed does, they'll direct you to head on to read Chapters 18 and 19 (perhaps with Chapter 20 as a capstone). If your instructor recommends a more traditional view, then they'll have you read Chapter 21. And if they want you to really appreciate the role of aggregate expenditure, they might recommend you start with the appendix. Remember that you'll still be able to see the whole show, no matter where you sit.

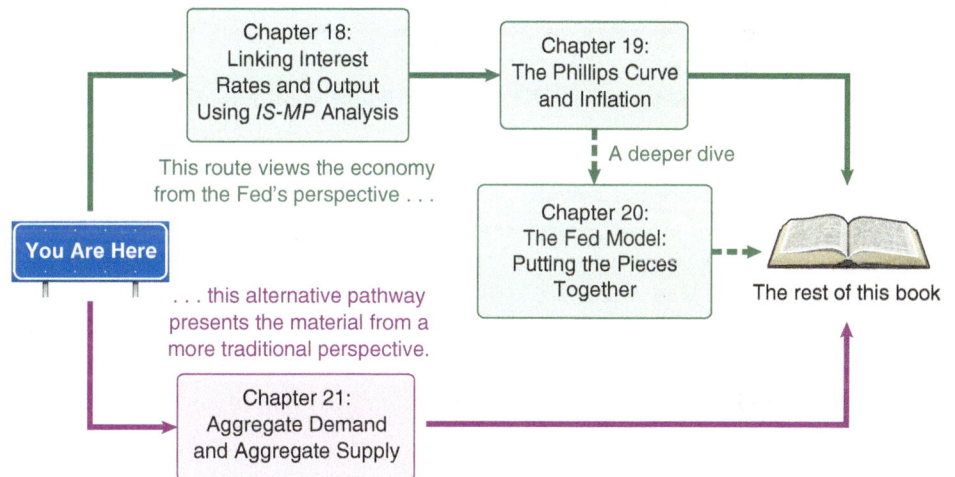

Chapter 17 Review

Chapter at a Glance

Business cycle: Short-term fluctuations in economic activity. The business cycle reflects the tendency for *actual output* to deviate from *potential output*. This deviation is measured using the *output gap*.

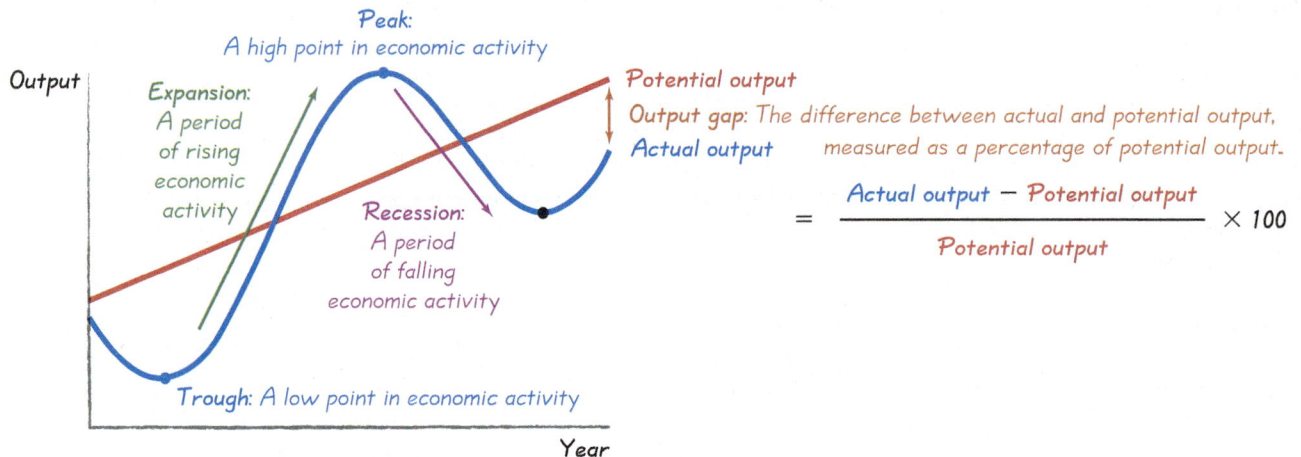

Peak: A high point in economic activity

Expansion: A period of rising economic activity

Recession: A period of falling economic activity

Trough: A low point in economic activity

Potential output

Actual output

Output gap: The difference between actual and potential output, measured as a percentage of potential output.

$$= \frac{\text{Actual output} - \text{Potential output}}{\text{Potential output}} \times 100$$

Distinguish between **levels** (GDP measures the level of output) and **changes** (GDP growth is about changes).

Features of Business Cycles

1. Business cycles are **not cycles**.
2. Recessions **vary** in their causes, their duration, and their depth.
3. Some variables **lead** recessions, while others **lag**.
4. The business cycle is **persistent**.
5. A typical business cycle involves a **short, sharp recession**, followed by a **long and gradual expansion**.
6. Many economic variables **co-move** up and down together over the business cycle.

Okun's rule of thumb: For every percentage point that the output gap rises, the unemployment rate tends to fall by half a percentage point.

Using Macroeconomic Data

Seasonally adjusted: Data stripped of predictable seasonal patterns.
Annualized rate: Data converted to the rate that would occur if the same rate had continued throughout the year.
Nominal variables: Variables expressed in dollars, using the prices of that year's data.
Real variables: Variables adjusted for inflation so you're comparing quantities, holding prices constant.
Leading indicators: Variables that tend to predict the future path of the economy.
Lagging indicators: Variables that follow the business cycle with a delay.
Revisions: Updates to earlier estimates.

Top Ten Economic Indications

- Real GDP growth
- Real GDI growth
- Change in nonfarm payrolls
- Unemployment rate
- Initial unemployment claims
- Business confidence
- Consumer confidence
- Inflation rate
- Employment cost index
- Stock market

Five Rules to Track the Economy

1. Track many indicators
2. Broad indicators beat narrow indicators
3. Seek just-in-time data
4. Find the signal amid the noise
5. Adjust your outlook when data differ from expectations

Key Terms

annualized rate, 450

boom, 443

business cycle, 442

bust, 443

comovement, 447

expansion, 444

lagging indicators, 448

leading indicators, 448

Okun's rule of thumb, 449

output gap, 443

peak, 444

persistence, 446

potential output, 442

recession, 444

revisions, 451

seasonally adjusted, 450

trough, 444

Study Problems

Learning Objective 17.1 *Distinguish between long-run economic trends and short-run fluctuations.*

1. A politician makes the following comment: "The fundamentals of our economy are very strong. According to market economists, we are producing more than anyone expected and even beyond what they call our potential output. My goal is to guarantee that we continue to produce more than our potential output throughout the next few decades." In the long run, do you think the politician could achieve this goal? Explain your reasoning.

2. What do economists mean when they say that business cycles are not cycles?

3. Use the graph to answer the following questions.

Real GDP in Germany

Annual percent change in output

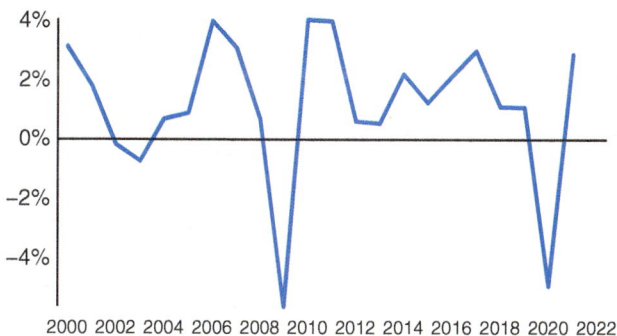

Data from: Eurostat.

a. In what year(s) did Germany experience a recession? Explain your reasoning.

b. What likely happened to unemployment during the recessions?

4. Use the accompanying table to answer the following questions.

Actual and potential output in the United States

Year	Real GDP (trillions)	Potential Output (trillions)
2016	$17.68	$18.02
2017	$18.08	$18.32
2018	$18.61	$18.65
2019	$19.03	$19.02
2020	$18.38	$19.38
2021	$19.43	$19.78

a. Calculate the output gap for each year.

b. What does it mean when the output gap is negative? What does it mean when it is positive?

c. For each year, calculate how much the output gap changed. Compare this to the growth rate of actual output that year, less the growth rate of potential output.

Learning Objective 17.2 *Describe the common features of business cycles.*

5. In the second quarter of 2022, the output gap in the United States was −2.1%. Make a prediction about what you think the output gap will be in a year's time. Explain your reasoning.

6. Explain how you can use consumer and business confidence indices to make predictions about the future state of the economy. For example, how would you expect consumer spending to change over the next year if consumer confidence indices have been falling for several months?

7. Describe some of the historical similarities and differences between recessions. For example, do they always have the same duration and severity? What about expansions?

8. What does it mean if a macroeconomic variable is a leading indicator? A lagging indicator? Give some examples of both leading and lagging indicators.

9. If actual output falls from being equal to potential output to being 5 percentage points below potential output, how would you expect the unemployment rate to change? (Hint: Use Okun's rule of thumb.)

Learning Objective 17.3 *Learn to use macroeconomic data to track the economy.*

10. Explain how you would use the five tips to track the economy to form an outlook of the economy and job market you are hoping to enter after finishing your education. Go online to find data that will help inform your outlook. Hint: bls.gov has excellent information on the outlook of various jobs, and FRED has lots of data on economy-wide indicators.

11. For each of the following, should you use seasonally adjusted data? Why or why not?

   a. You are trying to look at economic growth over the past few quarters and you want to figure out the trend so that you can predict growth over the next year.

   b. You are starting a retail business and want to know how consumer spending changes over the course of the year so that you can hire the appropriate number of staff.

12. What indicators should you use to track each of the following, and why?

   a. The overall size of the economy

   b. Labor market performance

   c. The future trajectory of economic activity

   d. Wages and benefits

13. The S&P 500 has been increasing steadily over the past few months. What does this signal about how investors view future profits? Explain your reasoning.

14. What do you expect to happen to the S&P 500 if it is announced that GDP grew at an annual rate of 2% last quarter but economists were expecting it to grow at an annual rate of 3%?

Linking Interest Rates and Output Using *IS-MP* Analysis

Picture yourself in a few years: You've graduated and landed a great job, and you're looking for a place to live. Maybe you'll rent a studio in a newly renovated building, or a loft in a recently converted warehouse, or a newly constructed house with roommates.

Long before you sign a lease, Marvin Ellison has been thinking about all of these possibilities. As CEO of Lowe's Home Improvement, Ellison is laser focused on the construction and housing

Jessica A. Stewart/The St. Joseph News-Press/AP Photo

Marvin Ellison knows that when interest rates are low, home construction booms.

sectors. His company sells lumber, flooring, and just about everything else that goes into new construction. And whether you rent or buy, chances are you'll spend some money at Lowe's to furnish your new home. The more that people and companies invest in building or renovating homes, the better things look for Lowe's.

That's why Ellison keeps a close eye on interest rates. While his office in Mooresville, North Carolina, might appear to be a long way from Federal Reserve policymakers in Washington, D.C., or the financial whizzes on Wall Street in New York, they're all closely tied through a web of macroeconomic interdependence.

When the Federal Reserve cuts interest rates, Wall Street computers light up as orders to buy and sell flood in. In due course, mortgages and home improvement loans become more affordable. The effects ripple out to Main Street, as sales at Lowe's rise, furniture stores boom, and the job prospects of construction workers improve. Suddenly, folks are earning more, and spending more: The workwear shop sells more boots, the deli sells more sandwiches, and the accountant has more tax returns to process. All along Main Street, you'll see the reverberations of financial changes on Wall Street.

This chapter develops a framework you can use to analyze the spending and production decisions on Main Street, and how they're linked to the financial decisions made by the Fed and Wall Street traders. We'll start by exploring how spending and production respond to the interest rate. Then we'll explore how interest rates are determined. Finally, we'll put the pieces together to forecast how changing market conditions affect total output.

By the end, you'll have a useful framework—called *IS-MP* analysis—to analyze the ups and downs of the business cycle, just as CEOs like Marvin Ellison do. This framework is the real deal: It's the approach that folks in industry, think tanks, government, and the Fed use. Let's make like a Lowe's shovel, and dig in.

Chapter Objective

Analyze the links between spending, interest rates, financial markets, and output that shape the business cycle.

18.1 **Aggregate Expenditure**
Assess the role of aggregate expenditure in driving short-run fluctuations in output.

18.2 **The *IS* Curve: Output and the Real Interest Rate**
Use the *IS* curve to analyze the relationship between the real interest rate and output.

18.3 **The *MP* Curve: What Determines the Interest Rate**
Use the *MP* curve to summarize how the real interest rate is determined.

18.4 **The *IS-MP* Framework**
Forecast economic conditions and how they'll respond to monetary and fiscal policy.

18.5 **Macroeconomic Shocks**
Use the *IS-MP* framework to forecast the effects of macroeconomic shocks.

🎙 **Podcast**
Think Like an Economist
Connecting Interest Rates and Output

A Note for Instructors

If you were expecting to see the *IS-LM* framework here, don't worry! You're still in the right place! This chapter covers the same *IS* curve that economics classes always have, but we'll marry it with a modern treatment of monetary policy that updates the *LM* curve of an earlier generation into an *MP* curve (for monetary policy) that reflects the modern reality that the Fed sets interest rates, rather than the money supply.

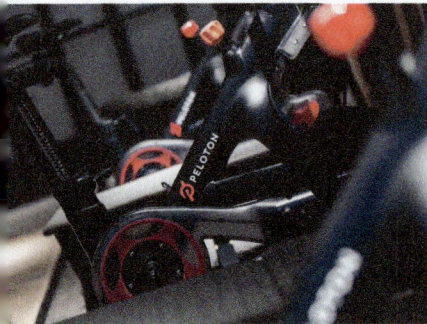

Peloton was spinning its wheels.

aggregate expenditure The total amount of goods and services that people want to buy across the whole economy

= *Consumption*
+ *Planned investment*
+ *Government purchases*
+ *Net exports*

Some abbreviations:
AE: Aggregate Expenditure
C: Consumption
I: Planned Investment
G: Government purchases
NX: Net exports
Y: Output, as measured by GDP

macroeconomic equilibrium
Occurs when the quantity of output that buyers collectively want to purchase is equal to the quantity of output that suppliers collectively produce.

18.1 Aggregate Expenditure

Learning Objective *Assess the role of aggregate expenditure in driving short-run fluctuations in output.*

Peloton was a rising corporate star during the pandemic. Stay-at-home orders and public health concerns had led millions of people to abandon their gym memberships in favor of working out at home using Peloton's connected exercise bikes and treadmills. The company's stock soared as sales rose to previously unimaginable heights. But then its executives made a critical error. They had become so focused on ramping up supply that they badly misjudged demand for their pricey equipment. As the threat of Covid receded, so did demand for Peloton equipment. The company was left with thousands of bikes and treadmills stashed away in warehouses or on cargo ships. It was a costly mistake, tying up around $1.5 billion in unsold inventory without generating any revenue. As a savvy industry analyst, you could have used this mismatch between output and spending to predict — correctly, as it turned out — that Peloton would cut its production, reducing its output to better match demand.

Aggregate Expenditure and Short-Run Fluctuations

The same dynamics play out across the whole economy as executives in millions of businesses adjust their production plans to keep pace with the ebb and flow of demand. This suggests that — at least in the short run — changes in demand drive changes in output. In turn, that implies that you'll do a good job forecasting short-run fluctuations in output if you can predict what's happening to demand.

Aggregate expenditure is the sum of everyone's spending plans. That's why our analysis of business cycles will start by focusing on the demand side of the economy. In particular, we'll focus on **aggregate expenditure,** which refers to the total amount of goods and services that people want to buy across the whole economy — the sum of consumption, planned investment, government purchases, and net exports.

Aggregate expenditure is the sum of four components:

- = *Consumption:* When households buy goods and services
- + *Planned investment:* When businesses purchase new capital
- + *Government purchases:* When the government buys goods and services
- + *Net exports:* Spending by foreigners on American-made exports, less spending by Americans on foreign-made imports.

Economists often use abbreviations to simplify things, and so you might find it easier to write it this way:

$$\underbrace{AE}_{\text{Aggregate expenditure}} = \underbrace{C}_{\text{Consumption}} + \underbrace{I}_{\text{Planned investment}} + \underbrace{G}_{\text{Government purchases}} + \underbrace{NX}_{\text{Net exports}}$$

When you're trying to assess economy-wide demand, you want to focus on how much people (including businesses) want to buy, not the unsold inventories that suppliers accumulate. That's why the measure of investment that's counted in aggregate expenditure is *planned investment,* which includes all the spending on new capital that businesses do but excludes unplanned changes in inventories.

Output adjusts to meet aggregate expenditure. The key idea here is that when the total quantity of output exceeds aggregate expenditure, businesses will cut back their production. And when output is less than aggregate expenditure, businesses will ramp up production, so as not to miss out on making profitable sales.

An equilibrium describes a stable situation with no tendency to change, and so **macroeconomic equilibrium** occurs when the quantity of output that suppliers collectively produce is equal to the quantity of output that buyers collectively want to purchase. As such, macroeconomic equilibrium occurs when the total production of output (measured by GDP) equals aggregate expenditure (which measures the total demand for output):

$$\underbrace{Y}_{\text{Output}} = \underbrace{C + I + G + NX}_{\text{Aggregate expenditure}}$$

This equation simply states that across the whole economy, businesses will adjust their production so that total output matches total spending. And this implies that—at least in the short run—demand conditions determine output. In this context, *short run* refers to the year-to-year ups and downs of the business cycle.

Businesses adjust production in response to unplanned inventory changes. If people purchase less than businesses produce, the extra output will be stored as inventories. But that's not an equilibrium because managers will respond by cutting back production. Likewise, aggregate expenditure might be greater than production for a short while, as businesses make sales with delayed delivery dates or sell their existing inventories. But managers will respond by ramping up production so they don't lose profitable sales. These adjustments will push the economy toward the macroeconomic equilibrium where total output is equal to aggregate expenditure.

If you want to dig deeper into how businesses adjust production so that total output equals aggregate expenditure, then you should turn to the appendix, "A Closer Look at Aggregate Expenditure and the Multiplier." Spoiler alert: It all boils down to one big idea, which is that output adjusts to meet aggregate expenditure. And that in turn means that forecasting output is all about forecasting what will happen to aggregate expenditure.

The Demand-Driven Short Run and the Supply-Driven Long Run

Our focus in this chapter on the demand side of the economy—on aggregate expenditure and its components—is quite different from our analysis in Chapter 10 of long-run economic growth. In long-run analysis—relevant to a period of say, a decade or more—economists focus on the supply side of the economy, analyzing the available supply of labor, physical capital, and human capital, plus the production function that summarizes the state of technological progress. That supply-driven long-run analysis explains the economy's *potential output*. (A reminder: Potential output is the level at which all resources are fully employed; it's the economy's maximum sustainable level of output.) But our focus in this chapter is on the short run and explaining year-to-year fluctuations in *actual output*. And that's where the demand side really matters.

In the short run, actual output may fail to meet potential. If people don't want to buy all that businesses are capable of producing, then companies like Peloton decide they're better off producing less than their potential. And so weak aggregate expenditure can lead the economy to adjust to an equilibrium in which *actual output* falls short of *potential output*, as shown in Figure 1. Even though companies like Peloton could produce more, there's no point if there's no demand for more output. This can lead to an equilibrium in which output is less than potential—an unhappy outcome in which production lines sit empty and workers are left unemployed. An economic slump can be an equilibrium because businesses don't want to produce output that people won't buy, and people don't want to spend more because the economy is weak.

Figure 1 | Actual Output Fluctuates Around Potential Output

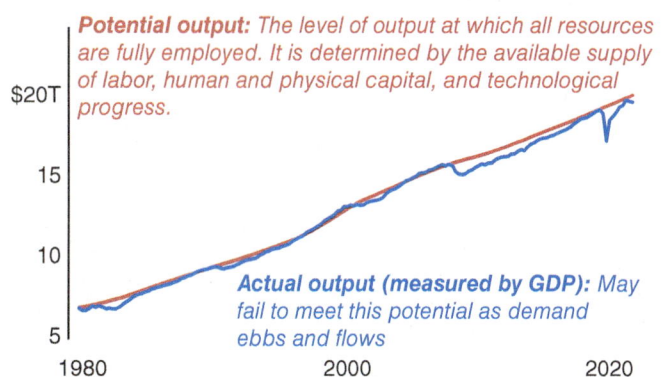

Potential output: The level of output at which all resources are fully employed. It is determined by the available supply of labor, human and physical capital, and technological progress.

Actual output (measured by GDP): May fail to meet this potential as demand ebbs and flows

Data from: Bureau of Economic Analysis and Congressional Budget Office.

Actual output can exceed the economy's potential, but this is not sustainable. Output can exceed potential only if available resources are more than fully employed. This is possible — at least for a short while — if suppliers defer maintenance, run extra overnight shifts, and pay their workers overtime. But it isn't sustainable. Eventually, something has to give, and — as we'll discuss in the next chapter — these pressures can spark inflation.

Whether it's porridge or GDP, aim for "just right."

The output gap focuses on the balance between the short-run demand for and long-run supply of output. This suggests we take a "Goldilocks" approach to evaluating the state of the economy. Potential output describes the economy's maximum sustainable rate of output. When output is below potential, the economy is running too cold. When output exceeds potential, it is too hot and risks overheating. Only when output is equal to potential output will Goldilocks declare that business cycle conditions are "just right."

This chapter is about analyzing short-run fluctuations, so we'll focus on the *output gap,* which measures the gap between actual and potential output, as a percentage of potential output:

$$\text{Output gap} = \frac{\text{Actual output} - \text{Potential output}}{\text{Potential output}} \times 100$$

When actual output is greater than potential, the output gap is a positive number. And when the economy is producing less than potential, the output gap is a negative number. Be careful when you're describing changes in the output gap. For instance, when output falls from being 2% below potential to being 3% below potential, some people say the output gap has gotten smaller (because it's now −3% which is less than −2%), while others say it has gotten bigger (because the size of the gap is now 3% rather than 2%). You're better off avoiding words like bigger and smaller altogether. Instead, when output fails to rise as much as potential (pushing the output gap from −2% to −3%, or from +4% to +3%), you should say the result is a *more negative* output gap. And when output rises more than potential (pushing the output gap up from +3% to +4%, or from −3% to −2%), you should say the result is a *more positive* output gap.

Focusing on the output gap is helpful because it provides a way to disentangle the roles of the demand- and supply-side determinants of output. The supply side of the economy — the supply of labor, human and physical capital, and the state of technological progress — determines potential output. The supply of these inputs grows smoothly over time, which is why Figure 1 shows that potential output typically grows smoothly over time. But actual output moves in fits and starts, suggesting that demand-side factors can drive it to deviate quite substantially from potential output. This is why Figure 2 shows that the output gap fluctuates widely. Our task in this chapter is to explain these fluctuations.

Figure 2 | **The Output Gap Fluctuates Widely**

Difference between actual and potential output, as a percent of potential output

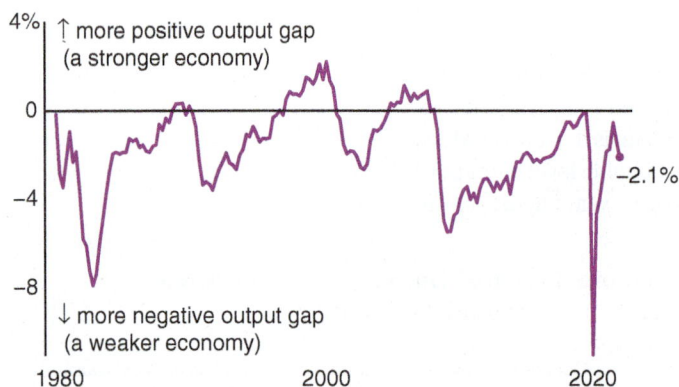

Data from: Bureau of Economic Analysis and Congressional Budget Office.

Be careful not to confuse equilibrium output with potential output. *Equilibrium output* describes the level of output at the point of macroeconomic equilibrium (where the economy will come to rest). We've discovered that equilibrium output is determined by aggregate expenditure. *Potential output* is a different concept: It's the economy's highest sustainable level of production, which is determined by available inputs. Equilibrium and potential output are different because the economy can get stuck producing at output levels far below its potential.

The clearest example of this comes from the Great Depression. During the entire decade of the 1930s, output remained, on average, more than 20% below potential output. Indeed, if it were not for the massive ramp-up in spending associated with World War II, that slump might have persisted much longer. This wrenching episode — which caused tremendous suffering — led to the birth of modern macroeconomics, which is built upon a recognition that equilibrium output can differ from potential output.

To summarize: Equilibrium output describes the economy's resting point; potential output is where Goldilocks wishes it would rest. Bear that in mind as we explore the drivers of aggregate expenditure.

18.2 The *IS* Curve: Output and the Real Interest Rate

Learning Objective *Use the* IS *curve to analyze the relationship between the real interest rate and output.*

The real interest rate may be the most important price in the economy. That's because it represents the opportunity cost of spending. Whenever you're considering a purchase, the opportunity cost principle reminds you to ask, "Or what?" You can spend money now, *or* you can save it, earn interest, and buy even more in the future. The real interest rate, denoted by *r*, tells you how large this opportunity cost is — how much more stuff you'll be able to buy if you wait until next year. So, the real interest rate (which is the nominal interest rate adjusted for inflation) is the price that determines this year's aggregate expenditure.

The real interest rate is also critical because it's one of the levers policymakers adjust to influence the economy. The Federal Reserve raises the interest rate — which increases the opportunity cost of spending — when it wants to induce people to spend less. And when the Fed wants to stimulate more spending, it cuts the interest rate, which reduces the opportunity cost of spending money today. As such, careful adjustments to the real interest rate can help offset booms and busts.

These insights inform the road ahead. We're going to develop a framework for analyzing how interest rates affect spending and hence output, and why interest rates rise and fall. Our goal is to link what's happening on Main Street with what's happening on Wall Street. That means proceeding in two steps. We'll start on Main Street, exploring the market for goods and services. We'll analyze how much people want to spend, and how much businesses decide to produce. The result is a relationship that we'll call the *IS* curve, which illustrates how total spending and output depend on the real interest rate. Then we'll head to Wall Street to analyze how financial markets determine the real interest rate. We'll summarize our findings in a line we'll call the *MP* curve.

Putting these curves together yields a framework that describes what happens when both the goods and services market and financial market are in equilibrium. It takes the interdependence principle seriously, accounting for the ways in which the buying decisions made on Main Street both shape and are shaped by the financial decisions made on Wall Street. You're going to learn to use this framework to analyze the consequences of just about any economic change. (And if you're wondering how these two curves got their names, don't worry; we'll also get to that.)

The most important price in the economy.

Lower Interest Rates Boost Aggregate Expenditure

Let's start our journey on Main Street, analyzing how the real interest rate affects aggregate expenditure. We'll do this by separately exploring how the real interest rate shapes each component of aggregate expenditure, asking how it affects consumption, planned investment, government purchases, and net exports. (We explored some of these themes in greater detail in Chapters 13–16, so we'll just hit the key ideas here.)

Consumption

Real
interest
rate

4%

2%

0%

$\downarrow r \rightarrow \uparrow C$

Consumption

Investment

Real
interest
rate

4%

2%

0%

$\downarrow r \rightarrow \uparrow I$

Investment

Government Purchases

Real
interest
rate

4%

2%

0%

$\downarrow r \rightarrow \uparrow G$

Government purchases

Net Exports

Real
interest
rate

4%

2%

0%

$\downarrow r \rightarrow \downarrow U.S.\ dollar \rightarrow \uparrow NX$

Net exports

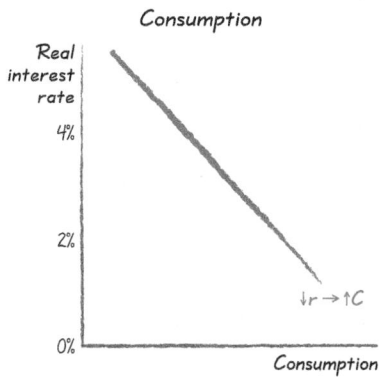

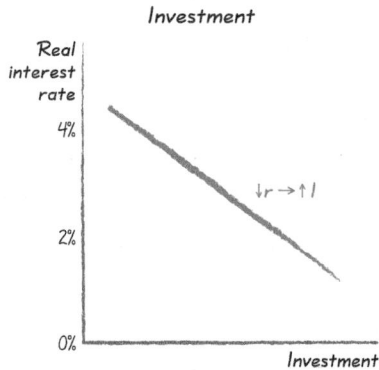

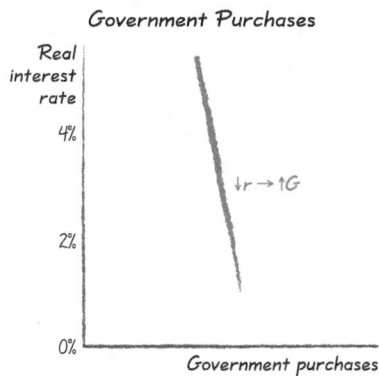

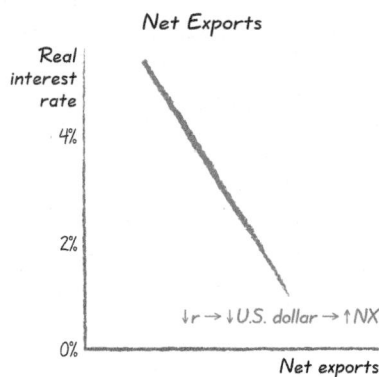

Lower interest rates boost consumption. Your spending decisions depend on the real interest rate because of the opportunity cost principle: The opportunity cost of spending money today is saving that money and earning interest. The lower the real interest rate is, the lower this opportunity cost. And if you're borrowing money to buy new kitchen appliances, a car, or some other big-ticket item, a lower interest rate translates directly into lower monthly payments. As such, a lower real interest rate leads you to substitute toward consumption and away from saving (which is why this mechanism is called a substitution effect).

There's also an income effect, and it depends on whether you're a net saver or borrower. For savers, lower interest rates reduce their interest income, leading them to reduce their consumption. But for borrowers, lower interest rates reduce their repayments, leaving them with more money to spend on other things. On net, these income effects are relatively small, and the substitution effect is the key reason why lower interest rates boost consumption.

Lower interest rates boost investment. For businesses considering capital investments, the real interest rate is important, again because of the opportunity cost principle: Money you spend on new equipment or structures is money that is not in the bank earning interest. That's why the opportunity cost of investing in new capital is lower when real interest rates are lower. As a result, low real interest rates lead to more investment spending. Indeed, a low enough interest rate can be the difference that makes billions of dollars of investment projects worth pursuing, which is why investment is particularly sensitive to the real interest rate.

Lower interest rates boost government purchases. Low interest rates reduce the interest payments the government has to make on its debts. These interest payments don't directly affect aggregate expenditure because they merely transfer money from the government to the folks it borrowed from. But low interest payments mean that there's more money left in the government budget for spending on roads, bridges, and other forms of aggregate expenditure. As a result, lower interest rates can lead to an increase in government purchases, particularly for state governments, which are often required by law to balance their budgets. Low interest rates don't always spur more government purchases, though, because governments might use their extra funds to pay down their debt instead.

Lower interest rates boost net exports. Net exports also depend on the real interest rate, but through an indirect mechanism: Low interest rates make the U.S. dollar cheaper, and this increases net exports (which is exports less imports). Let's take each of these steps in turn.

A low real interest rate in the United States leads international money managers to send their funds to other countries that offer better returns. This means foreign investors will demand fewer U.S. dollars and American investors will supply more U.S. dollars. Both of these shifts lead the dollar to become cheaper. So the initial effect of a lower interest rate is that it takes fewer yen, euros, or yuan (the currencies of Japan, many European countries, and China) to buy an American dollar.

This cheaper dollar increases exports and reduces imports. Start by considering exports: An American-made car that costs US$30,000 ("US$" means "in U.S. dollars") now sells for fewer yen, euros, or yuan than it did before. This effective price cut for foreigners leads them to buy more of our exports. As a result, spending on our exports rises. Next, consider imports: A cheaper dollar means that it now takes more U.S. dollars to buy a €30,000 car (the € sign means "euros"). This effective price rise for Americans leads them to buy fewer imports. If the quantity of imports declines by enough to offset the higher prices, then total spending by Americans on imported goods will also fall. Put these effects together, and lower real interest rates lead to a cheaper U.S. dollar, causing exports to rise and imports to fall. The end result is higher net exports.

The *IS* Curve Describes the Link Between the Real Interest Rate and the Output Gap

Let's summarize what we've found so far. We discovered that a lower real interest rate leads to a rise in every component of aggregate expenditure, boosting consumption, planned investment, possibly government purchases, and net exports.

The real interest rate is the opportunity cost of spending money this year (rather than saving it).

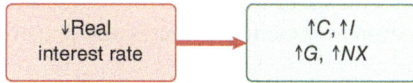

↓Real interest rate	→	↑C, ↑I ↑G, ↑NX

The boost to investment is usually the most important of these effects because investment in machinery and housing tends to be especially sensitive to the interest rate.

Lower interest rates boost aggregate expenditure. The top row of Figure 3 shows that consumption, planned investment, government purchases, and net exports are each higher when the real interest rate is lower. The bottom row simply adds these up to illustrate that aggregate expenditure — which is the sum of each of these forms of spending — is higher when the real interest rate is lower.

Figure 3 | The Real Interest Rate and Aggregate Expenditure

Lower real interest rates yield more consumption, investment, government purchases, and net exports,

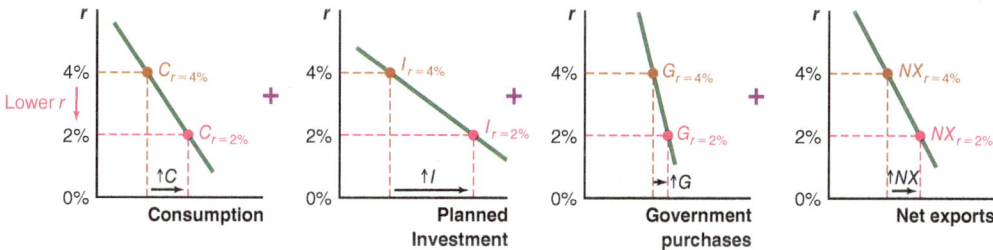

*which implies that lower real interest rates yield higher **aggregate expenditure**.*

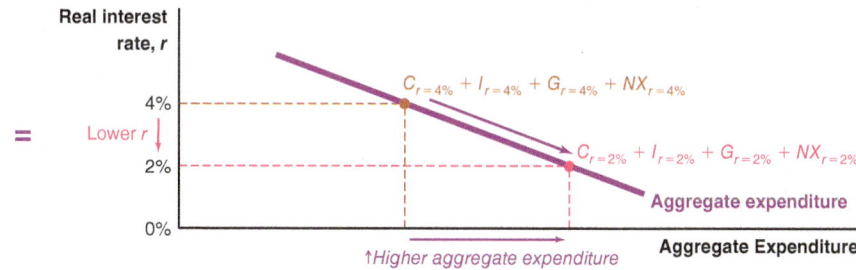

This insight — that a lower real interest rate will boost aggregate expenditure — is central to the framework we're developing. We summarize this finding as:

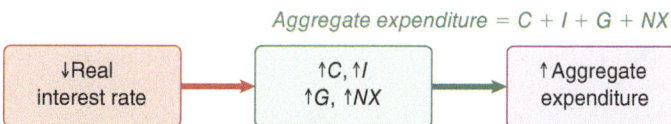

Aggregate expenditure = C + I + G + NX

↓Real interest rate	→	↑C, ↑I ↑G, ↑NX	→	↑Aggregate expenditure

A rise in aggregate expenditure is matched by a rise in output. Recall our previous finding that businesses adjust their output to meet demand, so that output adjusts until it's equal to aggregate expenditure. As a result, a lower real interest rate that boosts aggregate expenditure will lead to a higher level of output:

Businesses adjust output to meet demand so in equilibrium: Output = Aggregate expenditure

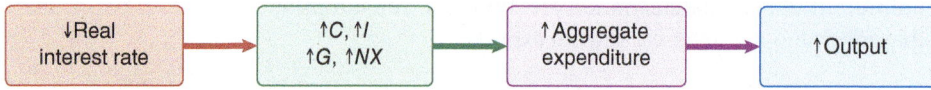

| ↓Real interest rate | → | ↑C, ↑I ↑G, ↑NX | → | ↑Aggregate expenditure | → | ↑Output |

Higher output translates to a more positive output gap. A reminder: Potential output is determined by long-run factors, and so it's unaffected by these business cycle changes. Thus, when actual output rises even as potential output is unchanged, the output gap becomes more positive.

Potential output is unchanged so changes in actual output translate to changes in the output gap

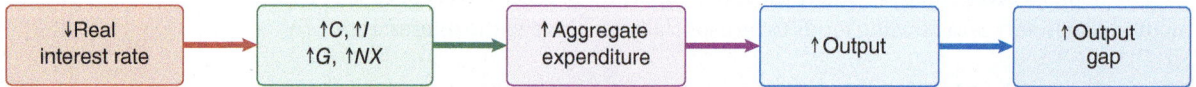

| ↓Real interest rate | → | ↑C, ↑I ↑G, ↑NX | → | ↑Aggregate expenditure | → | ↑Output | → | ↑Output gap |

The *IS* curve illustrates the link between interest rates, output, and the output gap. That's it! We've uncovered how lower real interest rates affect spending and output decisions on Main Street: Lower rates lead to more spending, higher output, and a more positive output gap.

The IS curve shows that lower real interest rates lead to higher output and hence a more positive output gap

| ↓Real interest rate | ———————————————————→ | ↑Output gap |

IS curve Illustrates how lower real interest rates raise spending and hence output, leading to a more positive output gap.

Figure 4 shows this relationship by graphing the **IS curve,** which illustrates how lower real interest rates lead to a more positive output gap. It's called the *IS* curve because it describes *I*nvestment and *S*pending decisions. And it illustrates the *I*nterest *S*ensitivity

Figure 4 | The *IS* Curve

The IS curve illustrates that a lower real interest rate leads to a higher level of output and hence a more positive output gap.

Ⓐ The **real interest rate** is on the vertical axis.

Ⓑ The **output gap**, which goes on the horizontal axis, measures output relative to potential output.

Ⓒ The ***IS* curve** is downward-sloping because **lower real interest rates** boost aggregate expenditure, which leads to a higher level of output, and hence a **more positive output gap**.

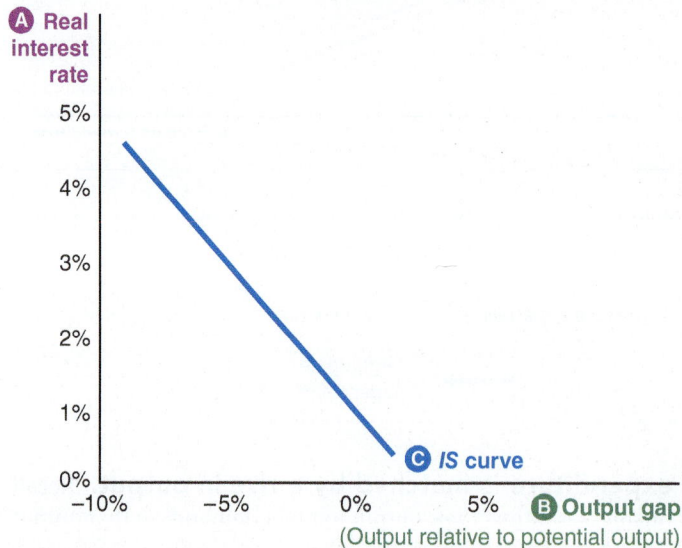

of output. (Historically, it was called the *IS* curve because <u>I</u>nvestment is the key form of interest-sensitive spending, and <u>S</u>aving is used to fund investment.)

The *IS* curve is like a macroeconomic demand curve. You are probably used to thinking about a demand curve as showing this year's demand for a specific product, like gas. In many ways, the *IS* curve is similar — it shows this year's demand for *all* types of output, and so you can think of it as showing the macroeconomic demand for output.

As with a demand curve, the vertical axis shows a price — in this case, that price is the real interest rate, which is the opportunity cost of spending money this year rather than saving it. And the horizontal axis shows the corresponding quantity — the output gap — which is the total quantity of goods and services purchased across the whole economy, relative to potential output.

The *IS* curve is downward-sloping, like a typical demand curve. That's because a lower real interest rate decreases the opportunity cost of making purchases this year, leading people across the whole economy to respond by buying more goods and services. Or you can say this the other way: The higher the real interest rate is, the greater the opportunity cost of buying stuff this year (rather than next), and so the quantity of stuff people demand this year is smaller. And while we call the *IS* curve a curve, as Figure 4 illustrates, it could also be a straight line.

How to Use the *IS* Curve

The *IS* curve is a valuable tool for forecasting economic conditions. For instance, can you forecast what the output gap will be if the real interest is 3%?

Figure 5 illustrates how to figure this out. First, locate the 3% real interest rate on the vertical axis. Then look across until you find the *IS* curve. Now look down to discover that the corresponding level of GDP is 5% *below* its potential level. That's it; you've now got your forecast.

If other things change, so should your forecast. Of course, this is your forecast, holding other things constant. If other factors change, then so should your forecast. This points to another way the *IS* curve can be helpful: You can use it to forecast the consequences of changing economic conditions.

A change in the real interest rate leads to a movement along the *IS* curve. In Figure 5, you started by looking at point A, where the real interest rate is 3%. Now consider what happens if policymakers cut the real interest rate to 1%. Locate the new 1% real interest rate on the vertical axis, and look across until you hit the *IS* curve. Look down, and you'll see that it corresponds to an output gap of 0%, which means that the economy is in that happy place where output equals potential output. And so you can conclude that reducing the real interest rate from 3% to 1% will cause the output gap to change from −5% to 0%.

Notice that this change in the real interest rate led the economy to move from one point on the *IS* curve to another point on the same curve. This makes sense: The point of the *IS* curve is to illustrate how the output gap responds to changes in the real interest rate, and so changes in the real interest rate lead to *a movement along* the *IS* curve.

The IS Curve: Graphing Conventions

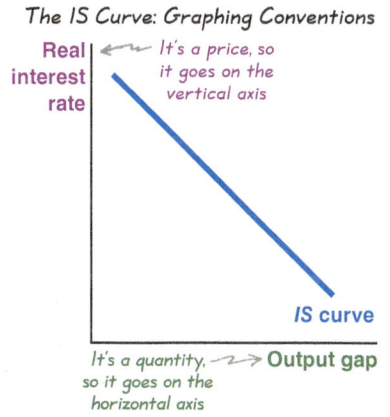

The IS Curve Is Downward-Sloping

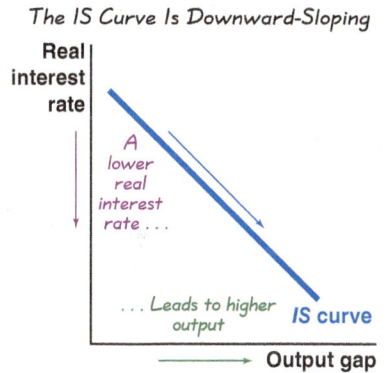

Figure 5 | Changing Interest Rates Leads to a Movement Along the *IS* Curve

Ⓐ When the **real interest rate is 3%**, the **output gap is −5%**.

Ⓑ When the **real interest rate is 1%**, the **output gap is 0%**.

Ⓒ Changes in the real interest rate lead to a **movement along a fixed *IS* curve**.

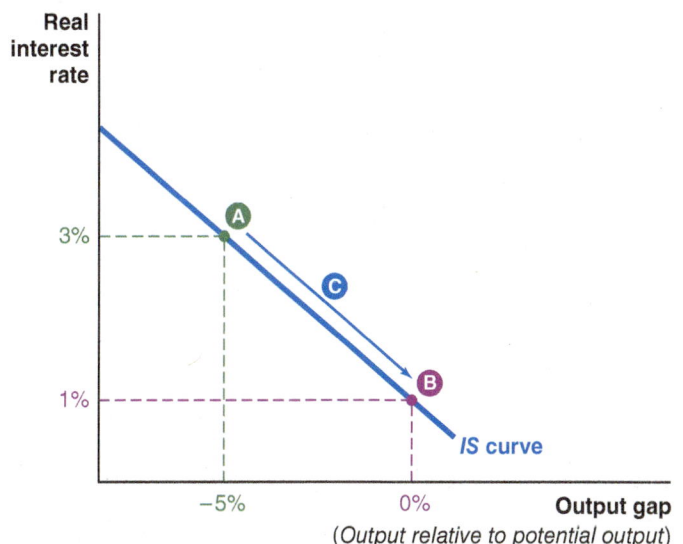

This is where it's important that you distinguish between:

- *Changes in the real interest rate:* which cause a *movement along* the *IS* curve
- *Changes in other factors* that change aggregate expenditure at a given interest rate: which cause the *IS* curve to *shift*

Later in the chapter, we'll look at the changes in other factors that can shift the *IS* curve.

Interpreting the DATA **A lesson from the 1980s: High real interest rates can cause a recession**

Builders got creative when it came to lobbying for lower interest rates in the 1970s.

Back in the late 1970s, Americans were being hammered by double-digit inflation. At the end of the decade, newly appointed Federal Reserve Chair Paul Volcker pledged to do something about it. He figured that if he engineered an economic slump, inflation would fall, as businesses rarely raise their prices when the economy is weak.

To create this slowdown, the Federal Reserve jacked up the interest rate. At its peak, the nominal interest rate was 20%, and the real interest rate was as high as 10%. Just as our analysis suggests, a high real interest rate led businesses to sharply curtail investment spending, households to cut back on consumption, and it caused the U.S. dollar to rise, leading net exports to fall. Aggregate expenditure fell, causing output to decline.

The recession deepened, and protests mounted. Indebted farmers blockaded the Federal Reserve building with their tractors, construction workers mailed their complaints on pieces of lumber, and car dealers sent the Fed coffins containing the keys of unsold cars. One Texas congressman threatened to impeach Volcker.

High real interest rates ended up being too successful at slowing the economy. Output fell to be far below potential output, creating the deepest slump since the Great Depression. The unemployment rate rose from under 6% in 1979 to a peak of nearly 11% in 1982.

This episode settled any remaining debate about the importance of the real interest rate in shaping the business cycle. It vividly demonstrated the relevance of the *IS* curve, as this bout of high interest rates led to lower levels of aggregate expenditure, lower output, and a sharply negative output gap. ∎

At this point, you've got a good handle on the *IS* curve: It tells you what the output gap will be at each real interest rate. But what determines the real interest rate, and what could cause it to change? Answering that requires a trip to Washington, D.C., and then on to Wall Street.

18.3 The *MP* Curve: What Determines the Interest Rate

Learning Objective *Use the* MP *curve to summarize how the real interest rate is determined.*

Our next stop is the financial markets, where interest rates are determined. We'll start by analyzing the role of the Federal Reserve because it's the 800-pound gorilla in financial markets. We'll then incorporate the rest of the financial system to see how other market factors — including the price of risk — shape the real interest rate. We're digging into the factors determining interest rates because the *IS* curve tells us that they have major economic consequences. Our goal is to bring these insights together in a few pages into a compact and useful framework.

The Federal Reserve Sets the Risk-Free Interest Rate

Eight times a year, policymakers meet at the Federal Reserve in Washington, D.C., to decide how high (or low) to set the interest rate. Over two days of meetings, they pore over binders full of data about how the economy is doing, discuss what trends they're seeing in different sectors, debate the implications, and talk through likely scenarios. As policymakers discuss where to set the interest rate, they consult their estimates of the *IS* curve in order to assess the implications of each possible choice.

At the end of this meeting, the Federal Reserve issues a statement detailing how it plans to adjust the interest rate. This process of setting interest rates to influence economic conditions is called **monetary policy.** It's so important that we'll devote all of Chapter 22 to studying it. We'll focus on the big picture now, leaving the details for later.

Atlanta Fed president Raphael Bostic, pondering the *IS* curve.

The Fed sets the nominal interest rate to influence the real interest rate. When the Federal Reserve announces that it's setting the interest rate at 3%, it's actually setting the *nominal* interest rate. But just as this chapter has focused on the real interest rate because that's the rate that people respond to, so does the Fed. If inflation is 2%, then it's just as accurate to say that the Fed set the nominal interest rate at 3% as it is to say that it set the real interest rate at 1%. And so we'll describe the Federal Reserve as setting the *real* interest rate, because in practical terms, that's what it is doing.

monetary policy The process of setting interest rates in an effort to influence economic conditions.

The Fed's decisions percolate throughout the whole economy. The Fed doesn't set every interest rate in the economy. Rather, its policy tool is a specific interest rate called the *federal funds rate,* which is the interest rate on a set of overnight loans that are almost certain to be repaid the next day. There's no such thing as a loan with zero risk, but these overnight loans come pretty close — so close, in fact, that for our purposes you can think of the Federal Reserve as effectively setting the **risk-free interest rate.**

Changes in the risk-free interest rate then percolate through the rest of the economy, affecting the interest rate you're paid on your savings, the interest rate at which you can borrow money for a house or car, the interest rate on your credit card, and the interest rate at which businesses can borrow to fund their investments. But the Fed is not the only force that affects interest rates.

risk-free interest rate The interest rate on a loan that involves no risk.

risk premium The extra interest that lenders charge to account for the risk of loaning money.

The Financial Sector Adds a Risk Premium

There's another critical factor that affects interest rates: risk. Whenever you lend someone money, there are risks involved. You might not get paid back, you might set the interest rate too low, or you might end up needing those funds yourself.

The interest rate on any loan reflects the risk-free rate plus a risk premium. Banks and other lenders demand to be paid extra for taking on these risks. The extra interest that they charge to account for risk is called the **risk premium.** As Figure 6 shows, the risk premium is the reason that the interest rate you pay on your credit card, car loan, housing mortgage, or a business loan is typically higher than the risk-free interest rate set by the Federal Reserve.

Figure 6 | The Interest Rate That Banks Charge Is Higher Than the Risk-Free Rate Set by the Fed, Because Banks Charge a Risk Premium for Risky Loans

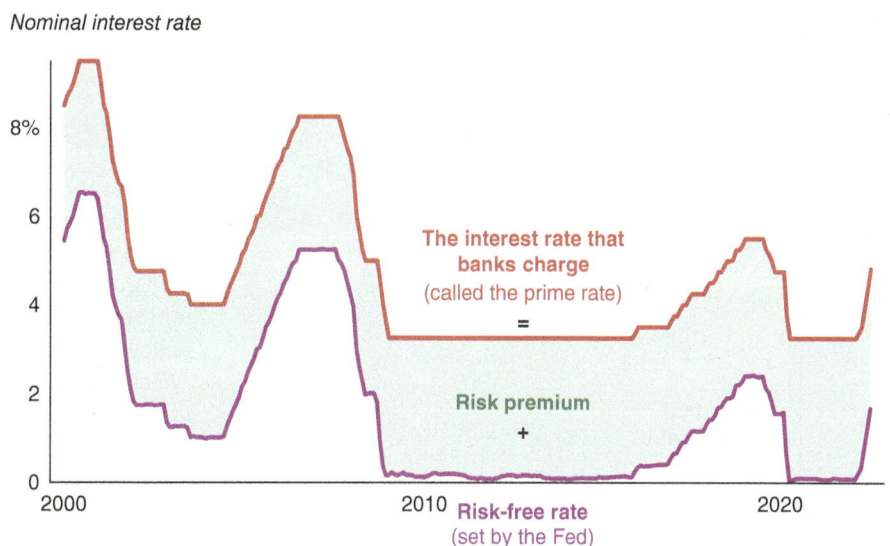

Nominal interest rate

The interest rate that banks charge (called the prime rate)

=

Risk premium

+

Risk-free rate (set by the Fed)

Data from: Federal Reserve Board.

MP curve Illustrates the current real interest rate, which is shaped by monetary policy and the risk premium.

This is where risk is traded.

If you can't make your payments, you can't keep the car.

While riskier borrowers and riskier types of loans might get charged a higher risk premium, for now we'll simply focus on the risk premium that banks charge to folks with good credit.

As a result, the real interest rate that's relevant to the typical borrower — and hence is relevant for our analysis — reflects two influences: It's the risk-free rate (set by the Fed), plus the risk premium, which is determined by financial markets.

$$\text{Real interest rate} = \text{Risk-free real interest rate} + \text{Risk premium}$$

The risk premium is determined in financial markets. This is where Wall Street comes in. That's where the buyers and sellers of risk — mainly big banks and other financial institutions — meet to trade risk. They do this by buying and selling complicated financial contracts that allow them to reallocate the risks in their portfolios — including the risks associated with the money they have loaned you. You can think of the market for risk as being like other markets: There are many buyers and sellers, and just as a buyer of T-shirts has to pay $10 to induce a supplier to produce one, a borrower has to pay their bank a risk premium to induce it to make a risky loan. Seen this way, the risk premium is a price — the price at which lenders are willing to bear the risk associated with lending you money. This price is determined by the forces of supply and demand, and so it reflects changing financial conditions and sentiments in financial markets.

EVERYDAY Economics Why you pay different interest rates on different loans

Macroeconomic analysis focuses on the typical risk premium faced by a typical borrower with good credit. But in your own life, you'll confront different risk premiums on different types of loans, leading you to pay different interest rates.

The riskier the loan, the higher the interest rate you'll end up paying. For instance, a family member might be willing to lend you money at a lower rate than a bank because they'll trust that you'll repay them. (And unlike a bank, they might have other ways of making you pay.) When you take out a car loan, the lender (usually a bank) can repossess your car if you fall behind on your repayments. That makes a car loan less risky than a personal loan, which is why banks offer lower interest rates on car loans than they do on personal loans. Try to borrow money at a payday lending shop, and you'll discover outrageously high interest rates. That's partly because these are risky loans. And it's partly because the only people who aren't driven away by those high rates are usually in some kind of financial pickle, making them riskier still. ∎

Figure 7 | The *MP* Curve

The MP *curve describes the real interest rate, which reflects both the risk-free interest rate set by the Federal Reserve, and the risk premium.*

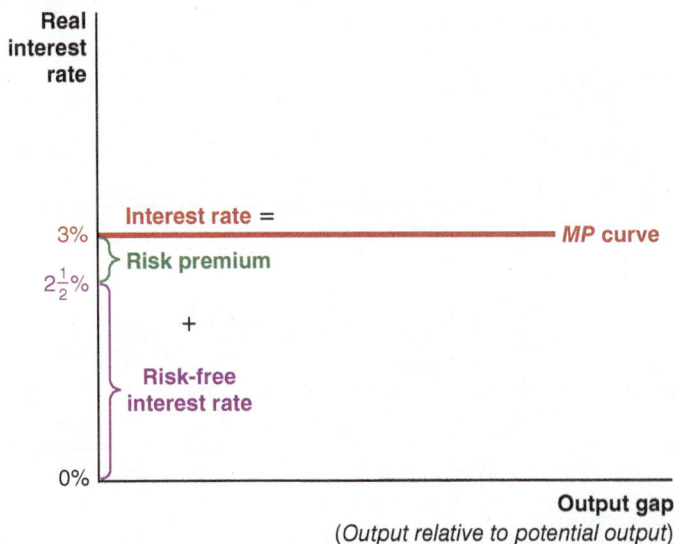

The *MP* Curve

It's time to integrate our analysis of the Fed and financial markets into the broader framework we're developing. We do this by adding a new curve, the **MP curve,** which stands for "**M**onetary **P**olicy," because we use it to illustrate the current real interest rate, which is largely shaped by monetary policy. The name is a bit misleading, because we also use the *MP* curve to illustrate how changes in the risk premium affect the real interest rate.

The *MP* curve illustrates the real interest rate. As Figure 7 shows, if the Federal Reserve sets the real interest rate at $2\frac{1}{2}$%, and the risk premium is $\frac{1}{2}$%, then the *MP* curve is a horizontal line at 3%. We draw the

MP curve as a horizontal line to illustrate that 3% is the real interest rate, no matter what the output gap is.

The *MP* curve illustrates the current real interest rate. If the interest rate changes — either because the Fed changes monetary policy, or changes in financial markets shift the risk premium — the *MP* curve will shift to illustrate this.

You can measure the risk premium using interest rate spreads. Here's a simple trick you can use to track the risk premium: Calculate the difference between the interest rate at which you can borrow and the risk-free interest rate (and make sure you're comparing loans of the same duration). This difference, which is called an *interest rate spread,* is an estimate of the risk premium.

A useful proxy for the risk-free interest rate is the interest rate on loans to the U.S. government, because the U.S. government is almost certainly going to pay its debts. And so you can calculate the risk premium as the difference between the interest rate at which you can borrow and the interest rate on a similar duration loan to the U.S. government.

Interpreting the DATA   How to measure financial risk

The TED spread is an important interest rate spread that economists monitor to track the health of the banking system. Ignore the name — it's an obscure financial acronym — and focus instead on what it is: the difference between the interest rate at which banks lend to each other for a three-month period, and the interest rate at which the U.S. government can borrow for three months. As such, it's a measure of the perceived riskiness of the banking system. Figure 8 shows that the TED spread is usually low and stable, but it spikes during periods of financial stress. For instance, when the global financial crisis emerged in 2008, the TED spread rose sharply, indicating a higher risk premium, which shifted the *MP* curve upward. The TED spread also rose during the early days of the Covid recession — at a time when everything felt uncertain — but it quickly fell as it became clear that this crisis was not going to infect the financial sector. ■

Figure 8 | A Higher TED Spread Signals Greater Risk in the Banking System

The interest rate on 3-month loans to **banks** *less the interest rate on 3-month loans to* **the U.S. government**

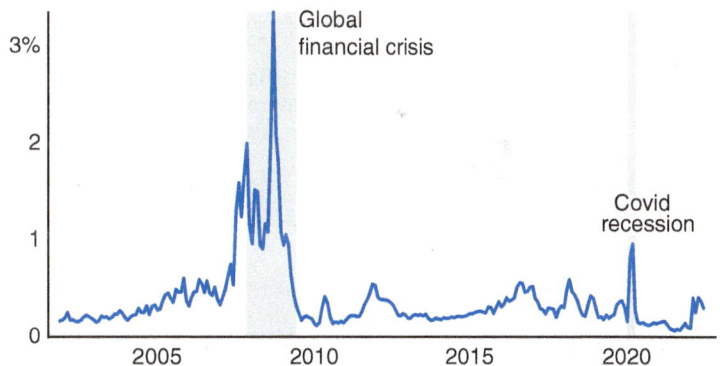

Data from: Federal Reserve and Ameribor.

The *MP* curve is simple because monetary policy is simple. Before we continue, a historical note. You'll notice that the *MP* curve is pretty simple — you just draw a horizontal line to show whatever the current real interest rate is. That's because the Federal Reserve simply announces where it wants to set the interest rate, and the *MP* curve reflects that (plus the risk premium).

It wasn't always so simple. Several decades ago, the Federal Reserve implemented monetary policy by announcing changes in the money supply instead. Figuring out how this affected the economy required a careful analysis of <u>L</u>iquidity and <u>M</u>oney, which is why some economics textbooks describe a more complicated *LM* curve, instead of the *MP* curve. So if you come across a reference to *IS-LM* analysis, they're describing similar ideas, but analyzing an older approach to monetary policy.

You've now developed two powerful tools for understanding the business cycle — the *IS* curve and the *MP* curve. Our next task is to bring them together, into an integrated *IS-MP* framework. Just as businesses, investors, and policymakers do, you'll be able to use this framework to forecast changing economic conditions.

18.4 **The *IS-MP* Framework**

Learning Objective *Forecast economic conditions and how they'll respond to monetary and fiscal policy.*

Okay, let's put it all together. The *IS* curve illustrates how the output gap depends on the real interest rate. And the *MP* curve tells you what the real interest rate will be. Put them together, and you'll have a complete story of what determines the state of the economy. As a manager and as an investor, you'll be able to use this framework to interpret economic news and forecast how it will affect your future.

IS-MP Equilibrium

We bring the *IS* and *MP* curves together in Figure 9. As you know, the *IS* curve shows you the level of the output gap that corresponds with each possible value of the real interest rate. The *MP* curve tells you what the real interest rate is. Their intersection determines the macroeconomic equilibrium. In this example, the risk-free interest rate plus the risk premium sets the real interest rate at 3%, which yields an output gap of –5%.

Figure 9 | The *IS-MP* Framework

The state of the economy is determined by the intersection of the IS *curve and the* MP *curve.*

Ⓐ The ***IS* curve** describes the output gap associated with each real interest rate.

Ⓑ The ***MP* curve** describes the **real interest rate** set by monetary policy and financial markets.

Ⓒ The economy moves to the point of **macroeconomic equilibrium** where the two curves intersect.

Ⓓ This occurs when the **real interest rate** is 3% and the **equilibrium output gap** is –5% (which means that output is 5% below potential output).

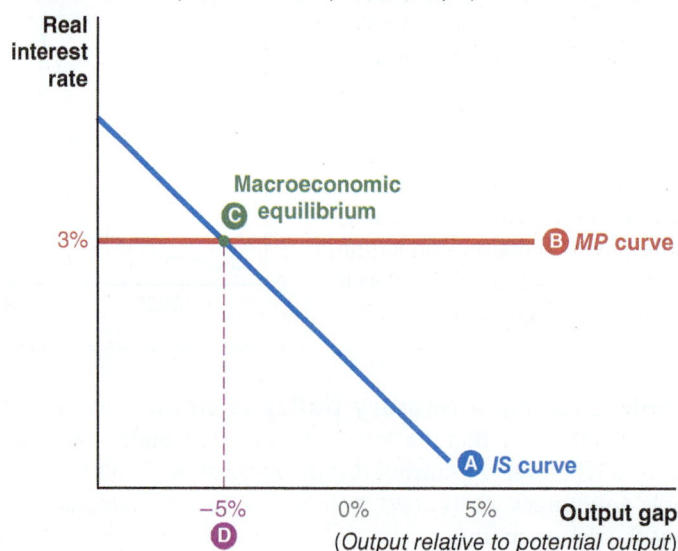

That's it — you've got your forecast for economic conditions. More than that, you've now put together a comprehensive framework for understanding business cycles. This isn't just a textbook exercise — it's the framework that guides the macroeconomic forecasts produced by many government policymakers, think tanks, Wall Street investors, business analysts, and the press.

Fluctuating Demand and Business Cycles

Our analysis of the *IS* curve highlights the central role that aggregate expenditure plays in determining macroeconomic outcomes. This suggests that we can interpret recessions and depressions as reflecting weak or declining aggregate expenditure. By this view, the booms and busts of the business cycle reflect the economy shifting between periods of strong and weak demand. We explore this idea in Figure 10, which illustrates two alternative macroeconomic equilibria.

Strong aggregate expenditure leads to an economic boom and full employment. One possibility is that people are optimistic about the future. Students who are optimistic that they'll get a good job after graduation will spend more money at any given interest rate, as will workers who are optimistic about promotions and pay raises, and so will entrepreneurs who are confident about their business success. These optimistic spending plans are illustrated by the blue *IS* curve in Figure 10, which shows high levels of aggregate expenditure at each level of the real interest rate. This leads to a macroeconomic equilibrium that Goldilocks would declare "just right," because output is at its highest sustainable level. In this happy state of affairs, output is high, unemployment is low, and the economic outlook is sunny enough that continued economic optimism is warranted. Think of this as the macroeconomic equilibrium in good times. With enough optimism, the economy can even hit an equilibrium in which output exceeds potential.

Figure 10 | Booms and Busts

Bouts of optimism and pessimism can drive the economy into booms and busts.

A The **optimistic *IS* curve** describes spending plans in good times when people are optimistic about their economic future.

B It leads to a **boom** where output is at potential, validating people's optimism.

C But if people become **pessimistic** about the future, they'll cut back on how much they plan to spend at any given interest rate, and businesses will respond by cutting production. This decrease in output at any given real interest rate **shifts the *IS* curve to the left**.

D The economy shifts to a **bust,** where output declines to be less than potential output. Because this economic bust is an equilibrium, it will persist if nothing changes.

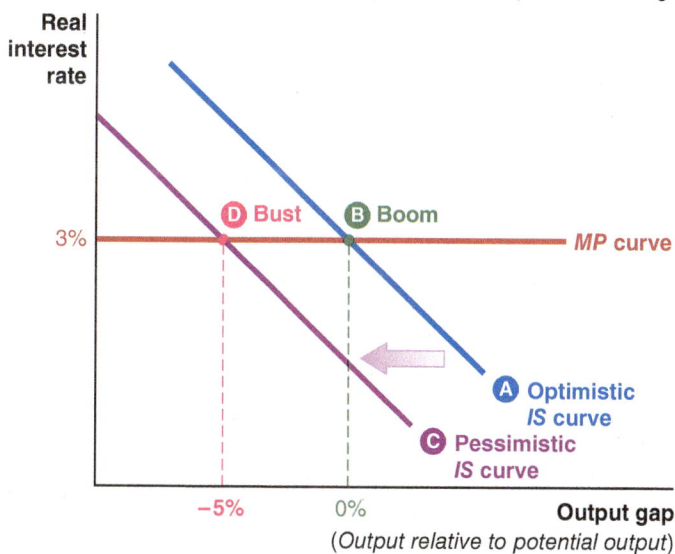

Insufficient spending can lead to an economic bust and unemployment. There's also the possibility that a wave of pessimism hits. Pessimism about future economic conditions might lead consumers to cut back on their spending, or businesses to cut back on their investment plans. In each case, the result is a decrease in aggregate expenditure at any given real interest rate and level of income. This decrease in spending causes the *IS* curve to shift left to the purple line.

This lower level of aggregate expenditure yields a new macroeconomic equilibrium at a much lower level of output. The output gap is now negative, which means that the economy is producing below its potential. Because businesses are producing less, they need fewer workers. The result is an economic bust, in which people have lower incomes and unemployment is widespread. In this unhappy equilibrium, the pessimism that caused the downturn now appears to be warranted. Pessimism about an economic bust has caused an economic bust. Think of this as the equilibrium during the Great Depression, or in any of the sustained downturns since.

Changes in aggregate expenditures create macroeconomic fluctuations. In this analysis, the economy shifts from periods of boom to bust — and points in between — due to changes in aggregate expenditure shifting the *IS* curve. While we've focused on what happens when spending changes due to bouts of optimism or pessimism, similar booms and busts will follow in response to any factor that causes aggregate expenditure to shift at a given interest rate. The broader lesson is that many of the ups and downs of the business cycle reflect shifts in aggregate expenditure.

Interpreting the DATA How to track waves of optimism and pessimism

Figure 11 | **Measures of Business Confidence and Consumer Confidence Track Waves of Optimism and Pessimism**

Index: average value = 100

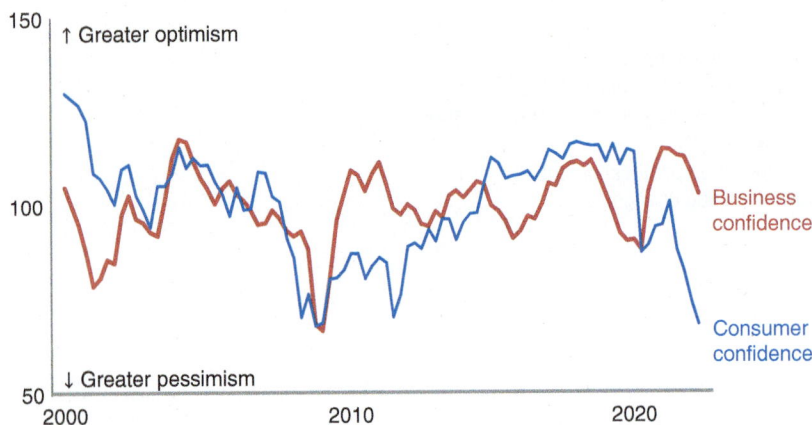

Data from: University of Michigan Index of Consumer Sentiment and ISM Purchasing Managers Index.

By this view, the key to understanding changing business conditions is to keep track of changing spending patterns. If your business sells mainly to consumers, then surveys of consumer confidence can help you keep track of changing consumption plans. If your business sells machinery and investment goods to other companies, then surveys of business confidence can help you keep track of their spending plans. As Figure 11 shows, the economy does indeed appear to experience periods of optimism and pessimism. ■

Recessions can be individually rational and collectively terrible. Many of these ideas about the possibility of deficient demand causing recessions were first put forward (in somewhat different terms) by economist John Maynard Keynes in the wake of the Great Depression, the worst economic slump in modern memory. The Depression shook the faith of many economists, leaving them wondering how it's possible for the economy to perform so poorly as to leave millions of people unemployed. Amid this deep and prolonged downturn, Keynes argued that the economy can be in macroeconomic equilibrium even when output is far below its potential and unemployment is widespread. In doing so, he argued that unless the government intervened, an economic slump could persist for years.

The economic bust you explored in Figure 10 illustrates the modern form of his argument. It illustrates a macroeconomic equilibrium in which the economy produces less than its potential. If nothing changes, the economy will get stuck in this rut. That's because the economy is in a bust, and unfortunately, this unhappy outcome is also an equilibrium. And it's an equilibrium that is unlikely to change; in this scenario, businesses are cutting back on production because people are spending less, and people spend less because they're worried that they might lose their jobs as businesses cut production. These negative beliefs reinforce each other, creating a vicious cycle that leads the slump to persist.

This highlights the paradox of recessions: Each person is individually making the best decision they can, but those decisions add up to a collectively terrible outcome in which the economy is stuck producing less than potential — and less than required to employ everyone. The depressing lesson is that there's no guarantee that businesses will produce enough to keep everyone employed.

How the economy is just like a concert

To understand how recessions happen, think of the U.S. economy as a concert. In a concert economy, your butt is an employer, and your seat is a worker. If you sit down, your seat is fully employed, but if you stand up, your seat is unemployed. How do you decide what to do? The **interdependence principle** dictates that your best choice depends on what others do. At the concert, you'll stay seated if all your neighbors are sitting down. In this equilibrium, every seat is fully employed. But if your neighbors stand up, you're better off standing too, because that's the only way you'll be able to see. When you stand, then others might also have to stand. The result is an equilibrium in which many seats are unemployed. I bet you've been at a concert that switches between the equilibrium in which all seats are employed, to one in which thousands are unemployed.

The same thing happens in the economy: You'll employ plenty of workers at your business if there are plenty of customers willing to buy your products. But the number of customers willing to buy your products depends on how many workers other companies employ. Just as you'll be forced to stand at a concert if others stand, you might be forced to fire some workers if your customers lose their jobs as other companies cut their payrolls. The concert economy can quickly shift from an equilibrium in which every seat is employed by someone to a different equilibrium in which many seats are unemployed, and so too the macroeconomy can shift from the good equilibrium in which every worker has a job, to a bad equilibrium in which millions of workers are unemployed.

Importantly, neither unemployed seats nor unemployed workers are inevitable. When you're at a concert and everyone else is persuaded to sit down, then you'll also sit down, and the seats will be fully employed again. Likewise, in the economy, if people can be persuaded to spend money again, then businesses will increase their production to keep up, and they'll hire the unemployed workers. In fact, as we'll explore shortly, this is precisely how policymakers try to kick-start the economy out of recession. ■

Let's now see how you can use this framework to understand the effects of macroeconomic policy.

It's just like widespread unemployment.

Analyzing Monetary Policy

You probably remember early 2020 as the start of a public health crisis, as Covid spread around an unsuspecting world. But it was also a pivotal moment for economic policymakers, as the health of the U.S. economy was also in danger. Stay-at-home orders had shuttered businesses, international trade ground to a halt, and millions of people were told not to report to work. Stocks tanked, and financial markets threatened to seize up. The economy was in free fall, and no one knew how bad things might get. Google searches for "Great Depression" hit an all-time high, reflecting a widespread fear that a repeat episode was in the cards.

The pressure to avert an economic calamity was intense. Economists met with members of Congress and Federal Reserve officials, often in last-minute Zoom meetings that ran late into the night. They worked from home on kitchen tables hastily repurposed into new offices, while their kids scuttled around underfoot because schools were closed. Some economists crunched numbers on what was happening, while others diagrammed new theories about how the economy works during a pandemic. The goal was to diagnose what was going wrong so they could propose a cure, or at least some way of slowing the spread of economic ill-health.

Within just a few weeks, unemployment had risen from its lowest level in 50 years to its highest level in 50 years. The economy was cratering at a speed unmatched in American history.

The numbers the economists were poring over aren't abstract statistics. They summarize a landscape littered with dormant factories, millions of jobless workers fearful about their livelihood, and families doing without.

Yet another meeting, as the situation worsens.

Figure 12 | Changes in Monetary Policy Shift the *MP* Curve

When the Federal Reserve cuts real interest rates, it stimulates an increase in equilibrium GDP.

(A) In the **recessionary equilibrium**, GDP is less than potential GDP.

(B) Cutting the real interest rate causes the **MP curve to shift down**.

(C) This leads the economy to shift to a **new equilibrium, with higher output**, eliminating the negative output gap.

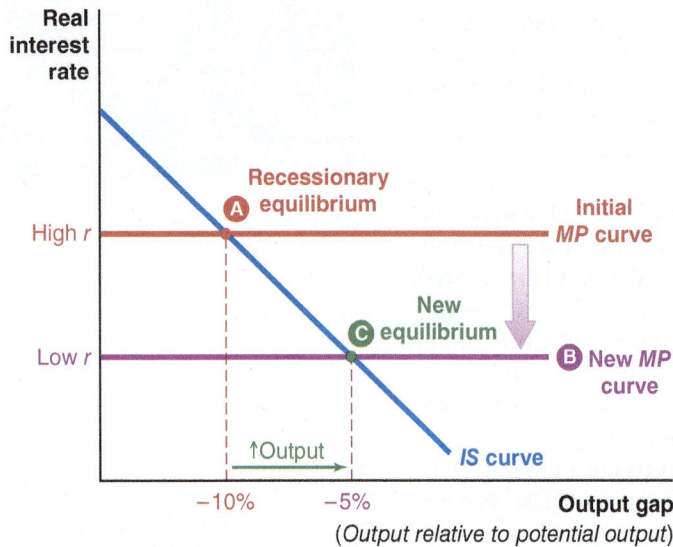

fiscal policy The government's use of spending and tax policies to influence economic conditions.

Figure 13 | Changes in Fiscal Policy Shift the *IS* Curve

When the government increases spending, it stimulates an increase in equilibrium GDP.

(A) Increased government spending causes the *IS* **curve to shift right**. It has a multiplied effect, and so shifts by **ΔG × Multiplier**.

(B) This leads the economy to shift to a **new equilibrium**.

(C) This new equilibrium involves **higher output** and an unchanged interest rate.

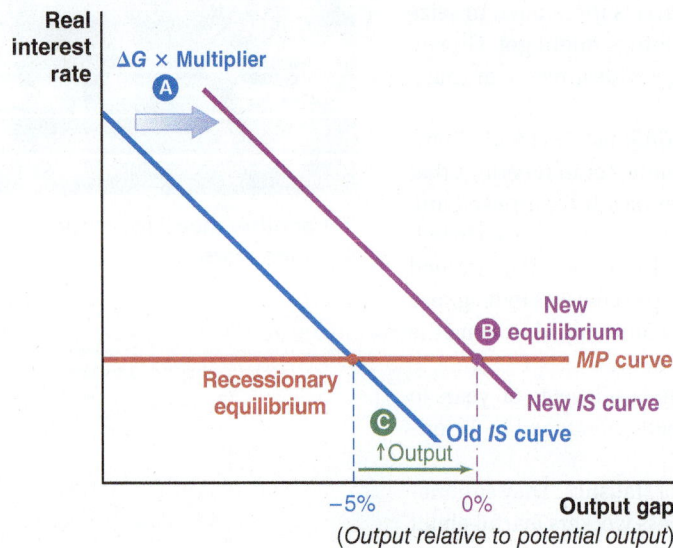

If you were a member of the Federal Reserve or the president's economic team and you faced this wrenching downturn, what would you do?

Monetary policy shifts the *MP* curve. Policymakers at the Federal Reserve responded quickly and decisively, cutting its benchmark interest rate to zero percent in a series of emergency meetings. They also had to solve another problem: The rash of business failures led lenders to worry that their loans might not be repaid, and as a result, the risk premium spiked. To counter this, the Fed provided backstops that reassured lenders that their money would be safe. This restored confidence in financial markets, leading the risk premium to quickly fall back to earlier levels. The net effect of the Fed's actions was to sharply reduce the interest rate.

It's rare to see the Fed act this boldly. What did this mean for the economy, and for businesses? Fortunately, you can use the *IS-MP* framework to figure this out.

When the Fed changes the real interest rate, it shifts the *MP* curve. Cutting the real interest rate shifts the *MP* curve down. Figure 12 shows that this leads to a new equilibrium with higher GDP at a lower real interest rate. Armed with this analysis, savvy managers understood that they should work on reopening plans, because there would likely be at least some demand for their products, albeit less than they might hope for.

The economy largely followed this script suggested by our *IS-MP* analysis, and the Fed's decisive actions calmed financial markets and helped avoid a depression. Even so, the economy was still underperforming. But because the Fed had cut interest rates to zero, it couldn't cut rates any further. (When the nominal interest rate turns negative, banks are better off storing money in their vaults rather than lending it to businesses for a loss.) Despite this constraint, it was clear that more action was required to restore the economy to full health.

Analyzing Fiscal Policy and the Multiplier

Fortunately, the government can also influence the economy through **fiscal policy,** adjusting its own spending and tax policies. Expansionary fiscal policy typically involves direct government purchases (such as building roads and bridges), as well as tax cuts. But the pandemic caused a different kind of recession, forcing businesses to temporarily close, and people to stay home. And so fiscal policy during the pandemic focused on providing income support so that people could resume spending as soon as it was safe to do so.

The main elements of the government's fiscal response provided support to businesses, direct payments to households, expanded and more generous unemployment benefits, support for state and local governments, and measures to counter the virus. All told, the federal government added around $5.8 trillion in emergency measures, which adds up to around $17,500 per American. This was the largest peacetime stimulus ever.

Since government purchases is one of the four components of aggregate expenditure, adjustments in fiscal policy cause the *IS* curve to shift. Greater spending shifts the *IS* curve to the right, while reduced spending shifts it to the left. The income support provided by this stimulus induced people to spend more, boosting aggregate expenditure. As such, it shifted the *IS* curve to the right. Figure 13 shows that this expansionary fiscal policy led to a rise in output, eliminating the output gap.

An increase in spending has a multiplied effect on aggregate expenditure. An initial burst of spending will have repercussions throughout the economy. Consider the money that the government spent improving school ventilation systems. It had a direct effect on factories producing fans, filters, and ductwork, and those factories had to hire new workers to keep up with this extra demand. There are also important ripple effects. For instance, a newly hired worker who spends some of their earnings on a new exercise bike boosts the incomes of Peloton workers and shareholders. There are also second-round ripple effects. As Peloton sells more bikes, it'll hire more production workers, who might buy lunch at a local Subway, leading the franchise owner to hire more sandwich artists. There are third-round effects, too. If some of those new Subway staff members enroll their children in day care, the local child care providers also receive a boost to their income. And so it continues.

As this initial boost in spending reverberates through the economy, it illustrates the importance of the interdependence principle for understanding macroeconomic developments. This interdependence arises because one person's spending is another person's income. It means that extra spending on schools stimulates extra spending in the fitness, food, and child care industries. As the initial burst of government purchases ripples through the economy, it has a multiplied effect, leading to an even larger boost to aggregate expenditure.

An initial boost in spending reverberates through the economy.

The multiplier summarizes the effect of an initial burst of spending on output. You can summarize the consequences of a rise in spending—including both the direct impact and the many rounds of subsequent ripple effects—with a single number called the multiplier. The **multiplier** measures how much GDP changes as a result of both the direct and indirect effects flowing from each extra dollar of spending. For instance, if the multiplier is 2, then an initial $1 boost to spending will generate a total of $2 in additional spending and hence output. When people have a greater propensity to spend any additional income they receive, the ripple effects of an initial burst of spending will be larger, leading the multiplier to be larger.

multiplier A measure of how much GDP changes as a result of both the direct and indirect effects flowing from each extra dollar of spending.

The multiplier is useful, because you can use it to forecast the effects of changes in spending as follows:

$$\Delta GDP = \Delta Spending \times Multiplier$$

Do the Economics

The Covid relief bills set aside around $190 billion in new funding to help schools reopen and stay open during the pandemic. How much will GDP rise after this burst of education spending, if the multiplier is two?

$$\Delta GDP = \underbrace{\$190 \text{ billion}}_{\Delta Spending} \times \underbrace{2}_{Multiplier} = \$380 \text{ billion} \blacksquare$$

If you want to dig more deeply into the logic (and math) of the multiplier, turn to the appendix titled "A Closer Look at Aggregate Expenditure and the Multiplier."

The multiplier determines how far the *IS* curve shifts. The multiplier is relevant to our *IS-MP* analysis because it determines how far the *IS* curve shifts following an initial burst of spending. The new *IS* curve shifts to reflect the new level of aggregate expenditure, and so it needs to account for both the direct effect of new spending and its ripple effects stimulating yet more spending. As a result, Figure 13 illustrates the *IS* curve shifting by an amount equal to the initial change in spending times the multiplier. This shift in the *IS* curve leads to a new equilibrium, which involves higher GDP, but no change in the real interest rate.

This analysis tells you that fiscal stimulus will help the economy grow, and so managers should get ready to increase production. In fact, the economy largely followed this forecast, as the very large fiscal stimulus was central to the economy's strong rebound during the pandemic. Indeed, some economists criticized this stimulus as being too large, arguing that it drove output beyond potential, to an unsustainably high level.

18.5 Macroeconomic Shocks

Learning Objective *Use the* IS-MP *framework to forecast the effects of macroeconomic shocks.*

So far, you've used the *IS-MP* framework to analyze how fiscal and monetary policy affect the economy. You can also use it to assess the likely consequences of other changes in economic conditions like changes in consumer spending or investment. Let's start by identifying the shocks that shift the *IS* curve, and then we'll turn to the shocks that shift the *MP* curve.

Figure 14 | Changes in Spending Shift the *IS* Curve

When spending rises, it stimulates an increase in output.

A Increased spending causes the *IS* curve to shift right. It has a multiplied effect, and so shifts by Δ **Spending** × **Multiplier**.

B This leads the economy to shift to a **new equilibrium**.

C This new equilibrium involves **higher output**, and an unchanged real interest rate.

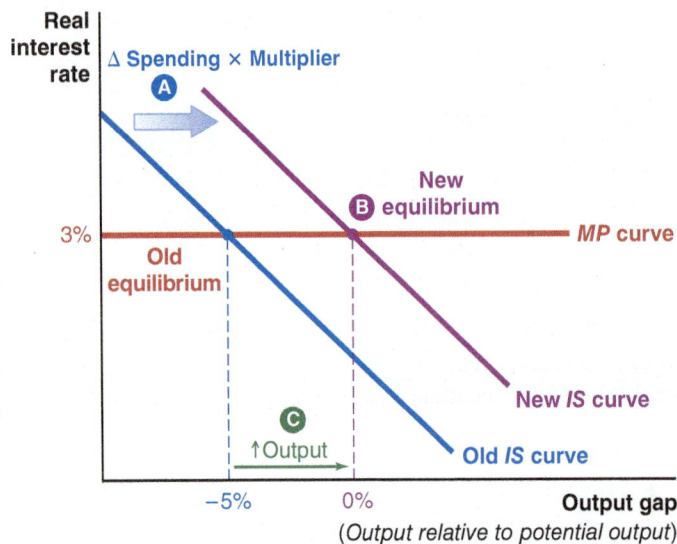

Spending Shocks Shift the *IS* Curve

Recall that the *IS* curve reflects aggregate expenditure at each real interest rate. This means that at a given real interest rate and level of income, *any change in spending will shift the IS curve.* As Figure 14 illustrates, this has a multiplied effect, and the resulting increase in aggregate expenditure will shift the economy to a new equilibrium with a higher level of output and hence a more positive output gap.

The same dynamic operates in reverse — a decrease in spending shifts the *IS* curve to the left. The multiplier also applies to spending cuts, because less spending by one person means less income for another, which leads them to cut their spending. As these cutbacks ripple through the economy, the net result is a multiplied decrease in aggregate expenditure shifting the *IS* curve further to the left. This shifts the economy to a new equilibrium with a lower level of output and hence a more negative output gap.

Shifts in the *IS* curve are driven by **spending shocks,** which change the level of aggregate expenditure associated with a given real interest rate and level of income. As you think through the possible sources of spending shocks, consider each component of aggregate expenditure: consumption, planned investment, government purchases, and net exports.

spending shocks Any change in aggregate expenditure at a given real interest rate and level of income. Spending shocks shift the *IS* curve.

Spending shock 1: Consumption increases when people feel more prosperous. People typically increase their spending when they have more money to spend, or are confident that they soon will. Thus, any development that makes people feel more prosperous — or more confident that they will soon be prosperous — leads to an increase in consumption. (Conversely, anything that makes people feel less prosperous will decrease consumption.) This means that consumption will shift in response to changes in the following factors:

Wealth When the stock market booms, or house prices rise, stockholders and homeowners feel more prosperous because their wealth has increased. As those lucky stockholders and homeowners spend some of their newfound wealth, consumption will increase.

Consumer confidence The interdependence principle reminds you that the decisions you make today depend on your expectations about what's going to happen in the future. And when you feel confident that your income will grow in the future, you might ramp up your spending in advance. As a result, consumption increases when an improved economic outlook boosts consumer confidence.

Taxes and government assistance When the government cuts taxes, or when it increases government assistance payments like unemployment insurance, people have more disposable income that they can use to buy stuff. And so consumption increases when government policy puts more money in people's pockets.

Inequality People with low incomes tend to spend a larger share of their income than do those with higher incomes. It follows that redistributing income from those with higher incomes to those with lower incomes — including through government transfer payments and changes in the tax system — tends to increase consumption.

> *Consumption* increases when people feel more prosperous:
> ↑ Wealth
> ↑ Consumer confidence
> ↑ Government assistance
> ↓ Taxes
> ↓ Inequality

Interpreting the DATA   How a virus is like a tax

Figure 15 shows that the pandemic led consumers to dramatically cut their spending. Partly, this decline in consumption reflects a decrease in wealth as the stock market crashed, but that can't be the whole story, because stocks quickly recovered. And partly it's because consumer confidence fell, though it didn't fall by enough to explain the entire decline in consumption. You need to think creatively to get the other important factor. Think of the coronavirus as effectively imposing a tax on spending. The virus is like a tax, because it makes buying stuff more costly, although that extra cost is not measured in dollars, but rather the health risk associated with going shopping.

Just as our approach suggests, this "tax hike" led people to sharply cut their consumption spending in 2020. Moreover, this insight predicted — correctly! — that people would cut back more on services (like restaurants, concerts, and travel) because they involved a larger "Covid tax." It also explains why spending on goods rebounded quickly, as stores adopted curbside pickup and online ordering. Thinking this way would also have led you to predict — again, correctly! — that consumption would be much stronger in 2021 when vaccines became available. That's because vaccines are like a stimulatory tax cut, as they reduce the health risk associated with purchasing many goods and services (like restaurants and travel). ■

Figure 15 | Consumption Spending Plummeted During the Panademic

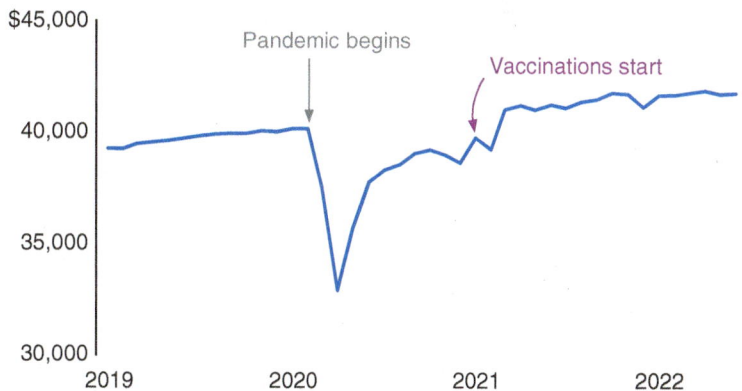

Real consumption spending per person (2012 dollars, at an annual rate)

Data from: Bureau of Economic Analysis.

Spending shock 2: Investment increases when it's profitable for businesses to expand. As a manager, you'll invest in new machinery when you believe that it will be profitable to expand your production. The cost-benefit principle reminds you to consider both the benefits of the extra revenue you'll earn from adding to your production capacity, and the cost of making that investment. As a result, planned investment will shift in response to changes in the following factors:

An expanding economy When the economy is expanding, so is the demand for your products. In order to produce more, managers need to expand their production capacity. As a result, investment in new equipment increases when the economy is expanding more rapidly.

Business confidence Because capital investments tend to last for years, or even decades, your assessments about whether to buy new equipment should depend not only on today's profits, but also on your expectations about future profitability. That's why investment increases when managers are more confident about their long-term profitability.

Corporate taxes Lower corporate taxes increase the after-tax profits that your company will earn from investing in new equipment. As a result, investment falls in response to higher corporate taxes. Conversely, investment rises in response to targeted investment tax credits that reduce the after-tax cost of buying new equipment.

Lending standards and cash reserves If your business finds it hard to borrow money at a reasonable interest rate, you can invest in new equipment only if your company has the cash on hand to do so. It follows that investment tends to increase when loans are easier to get, or businesses have large cash reserves. Cash reserves are particularly important when the financial system is not working well.

Uncertainty If you're uncertain about the economic outlook — it could be great, it could be terrible — remember that you usually have the option to postpone breaking ground on major investment projects until the outlook is a bit clearer. Lower uncertainty leads managers to restart these shelved projects, leading to an increase in investment.

Spending shock 3: Government purchases increase when policymakers decide to spend more on goods and services. For example, Congress may pass legislation to spend more on roads and bridges, invest in pandemic preparedness, or purchase new military equipment. In addition, some government programs — known as *automatic stabilizers* — automatically increase spending when the economy is weak.

Remember that government spending only directly increases aggregate expenditure — and hence shifts the *IS* curve — when the government purchases goods and services. By contrast, many government programs — such as unemployment insurance, or Social Security — simply transfer money from one bank account (the government's) to another (the recipient's), and so they don't *directly* increase aggregate expenditure. However, there's an indirect effect, as redistributing money to people who are more likely to spend it will increase consumption.

Spending shock 4: Net exports increase due to global factors. Net exports rise when people in other countries want to buy a lot of American-made goods and services. It's the interdependence principle at work, as net exports link the U.S. economy with economies around the world. Net exports shift in response to changes in the following factors:

Global economic growth When the economies in other countries do well, their consumers and businesses have more money to spend, and so they buy more goods, including more American-made goods, leading net exports to rise.

The exchange rate When the U.S. dollar becomes cheaper, our goods become cheaper to foreign buyers, leading exports to rise. A cheaper U.S. dollar also means that foreign goods become more expensive (in dollars) for American buyers, leading imports to fall. Both forces — rising exports and falling imports — cause net exports to increase.

Trade barriers Exports increase when there are fewer barriers preventing American businesses from selling their goods in foreign markets, while imports increase when there are fewer barriers preventing foreign businesses from selling to buyers in the United States. Because trade agreements typically reduce barriers preventing both imports and exports, their effect on net exports (which is exports less imports) is unclear. Likewise, trade wars — in which higher trade barriers preventing imports lead other countries to retaliate by raising barriers that prevent foreigners from buying American exports — will reduce both imports and exports, yielding an unclear effect on net exports.

Anything that shifts any component of aggregate expenditure shifts the *IS* curve. At this point, this list of spending shocks that can shift the *IS* curve might seem a bit exhausting. I've put it all together for you in Figure 16.

Figure 16 | Spending Shocks Shift the *IS* Curve

IS Curve Shifters	Examples*
Consumption *rises if people feel more prosperous*	↑Wealth, ↑Consumer confidence, ↑Government assistance, ↓Taxes, ↓Inequality
Investment *rises if it's profitable to expand production*	↑Output growth, ↑Business confidence, ↑Investment tax credits, ↓Corporate taxes, ↑Easier lending standards and more cash reserves, ↓Uncertainty
Government purchases *rise when the government buys more goods and services*	Spending bills, Automatic stabilizers . . . but not transfer payments (at least not directly)
Net exports *rise in response to global factors*	↑Global output growth, ↓U.S. dollar, ↓Trade barriers in foreign markets, ↑Trade barriers to U.S. market

* These examples all cause an increase in aggregate expenditure, which shifts the *IS* curve to the right. Reverse the sign of any arrow and you'll get a change that decreases aggregate expenditure, shifting the *IS* curve to the left.

While this looks like a big table, it all comes down to one idea: The *IS* curve shifts in response to an increase in any component of aggregate expenditure. That's the easy way to remember this list: It's just *C, I, G,* and *NX*.

Okay, with the *IS* curve behind us, what causes the *MP* curve to shift?

Financial Shocks Shift the *MP* Curve

Let's start with the mechanics of shifts in the *MP* curve. As Figure 17 illustrates, these are pretty straightforward. An increase in the real interest rate shifts the *MP* curve up. This leads to a new equilibrium with lower output and hence a more negative output gap. Conversely, a decrease in the real interest rate shifts the *MP* curve down, which leads to a new equilibrium with higher output and a more positive output gap.

When the Federal Reserve adjusts the risk-free real interest rate, or shifts in financial markets change the risk premium, the real interest rate will shift, leading the *MP* curve to shift. We call these changes in borrowing conditions that shift the *MP* curve **financial shocks.**

Financial shock 1: Changes in monetary policy. The Federal Reserve can raise (or lower) the risk-free interest rate, which in turn will shift the *MP* curve. It can do so through two main channels. When the Federal

financial shocks Any change in borrowing conditions that affects the real interest rate at which people can borrow. Financial shocks shift the *MP* curve.

Figure 17 | Shifting the *MP* Curve

The MP *curve shifts due to changes in monetary policy or the risk premium.*

Ⓐ At the **initial equilibrium**, output is equal to potential output.

Ⓑ An **increase in the real interest rate** causes the *MP* curve to **shift up**, leading to a new equilibrium with **lower output** and a **higher interest rate**.

Ⓒ A **decrease in the real interest rate** causes the *MP* curve to **shift down**, leading to a new equilibrium with **higher output** and a **lower interest rate**.

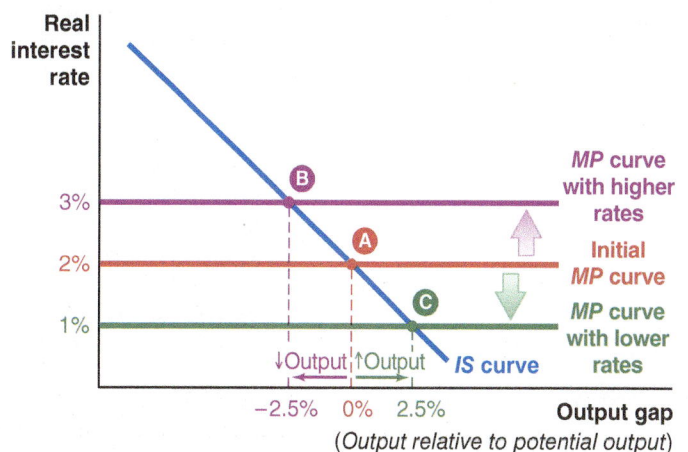

Reserve decides to raise its benchmark interest rate, its decision percolates through financial markets, eventually raising interest rates through the rest of the economy. This higher real interest rate shifts the *MP* curve up. Likewise, when the Fed cuts the real interest rate, it shifts the *MP* curve down.

But that's not the only way the Fed can shift the *MP* curve. Longer-term interest rates are based partly on the current short-term interest rate, and partly on *expectations* about how that interest rate will evolve over the coming months and years. The Fed will often try to influence these expectations. A signal that it expects to raise interest rates in the future is often enough to increase the long-term interest rate, thereby shifting the *MP* curve up.

It's also worth remembering that not every interest rate change that the Fed announces alters the real interest rate. The interest rate the Federal Reserve directly sets is a nominal interest rate, and so if inflation rises by 1%, the Fed will need to raise the nominal interest rate by 1% simply to keep the real interest rate unchanged.

Financial shock 2: Financial market risks shift the risk premium. The *MP* curve also shifts when the risk premium changes. The mechanics here are the same as those following a change caused by the Federal Reserve: A rise in the risk premium raises the real interest rate, which shifts the *MP* curve up. And a decline in the risk premium lowers the real interest rate, which shifts the *MP* curve down.

The risk premium will shift in response to changes in the following risk factors.

Default risk When there's an increased risk that borrowers will *default* — that they won't repay their debts or won't repay in a timely fashion — lenders demand a larger risk premium, which leads the *MP* curve to shift upward.

Liquidity risk When banks need cash — that is, *liquidity* — they can usually get it by selling some of their loans to other lenders. Liquidity risk arises when disruptions in financial markets make it hard to find buyers willing to pay a reasonable price. A rise in liquidity risk increases the risk premium, which shifts the *MP* curve upward.

Interest rate risk Lending someone money at a fixed interest rate for a long time, as in a 30-year mortgage, raises another risk: The long-term interest rate you offer today might turn out to be a bad deal if future interest rates or inflation are unexpectedly higher. And so greater uncertainty about future interest rates or inflation raises interest rate risk, which increases the risk premium, shifting the *MP* curve up.

Risk aversion When lenders become more reluctant to take on risk — that is, when they become more *risk averse* — they'll be willing to make a loan only if they can charge a higher risk premium. Thus, swings in market sentiment that make lenders more risk averse will shift the *MP* curve up.

Any change in the real interest rate shifts the *MP* curve. Let's sum up. The *MP* curve shifts whenever the real interest rate shifts. As Figure 18 shows, the real interest rate reflects the influence of the Fed on the risk-free rate, and changes that lead financial markets to adjust the risk premium.

Monetary policy can raise interest rates either by:

↑ Risk-free rate

↑ Expected future interest rates

Simon Belcher/Alamy Stock Photo

Those rising risks will shift the risk premium.

A higher risk premium will raise interest rates due to:

↑ Default risk

↑ Liquidity risk

↑ Interest rate risk

↑ Risk aversion

Figure 18 | Financial Shocks Shift the *MP* Curve

MP Curve Shifters	Examples
The risk-free rate *rises in response to monetary policy*	↑Risk-free rate, ↑Expected future interest rates
The risk premium *rises if lending becomes riskier*	↑Default risk, ↑Liquidity risk, ↑Interest rate risk, ↑Risk aversion

Forecasting Macroeconomic Outcomes

Okay, let's put all of this together into a simple recipe so that you can forecast how changing economic conditions will shape your market. To assess the likely effects of any change in economic conditions, ask yourself:

Step 1: Is there a *spending shock* (which shifts the *IS* curve), or a *financial shock* (which shifts the *MP* curve)?

Step 2: In which direction, and how far does this shift the *IS* or *MP* curve?

Step 3: What happens to output (and hence the output gap), as well as the real interest rate in the new equilibrium?

Let's take this framework for a test drive, analyzing some of the dramatic shifts that occurred during the Covid recession and subsequent recovery. Along the way, you'll see just how useful this tool was for analyzing and forecasting how the economy responded.

The Fed reads the tea leaves. *On March 3, 2020, there were only 12 Covid cases recorded in the United States, but even that was enough for the Fed to recognize that "the coronavirus poses evolving risks to economic activity," so it cut the interest rate by $\frac{1}{2}$ a percentage point at an emergency meeting, and cut it to effectively zero percent at a follow-up emergency meeting 12 days later.*

Step 1: The Fed's interest rate cut is a financial shock.

Step 2: This shock shifted the *MP* curve down.

Step 3: This shift led to a lower real interest rate and pushed output higher than it would otherwise have been, partly cushioning the blow of the downturn that many felt was coming.

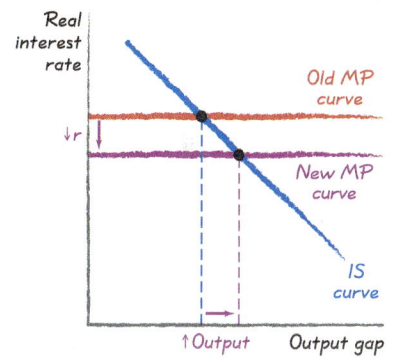

Consumers cut their spending. *On March 13, 2020, the federal government declared a national emergency. Consumers feared that this public health crisis was also going to threaten their economic futures, and they responded by drastically cutting their spending.*

Step 1: A decrease in consumption causes a decrease in aggregate expenditure, which is a negative spending shock.

Step 2: This shock shifted the *IS* curve left.

Step 3: This shift led to sharply lower output creating a large negative output gap at an unchanged real interest rate.

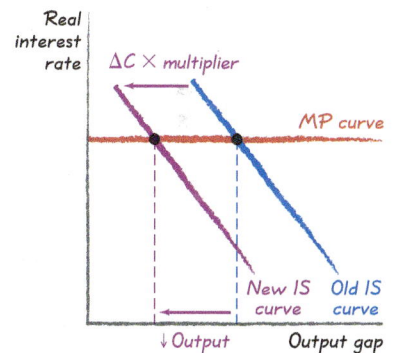

Fear grips Wall Street. *On March 18, 2020, one billionaire called into CNBC and declared "hell is coming." It was clear this downturn would cause massive bankruptcies. The problem on Wall Street was that no one knew who was facing financial strife, and so lending to anyone seemed risky.*

Step 1: Even though the Federal Reserve didn't change its benchmark interest rate, it was now perceived to be much riskier to lend anyone money. As a result, the risk premium rose, leading to higher real interest rates. This is a financial shock.

Step 2: This shock shifted the *MP* curve up.

Step 3: This shift led to a higher real interest rate and lower output, and hence a more negative output gap.

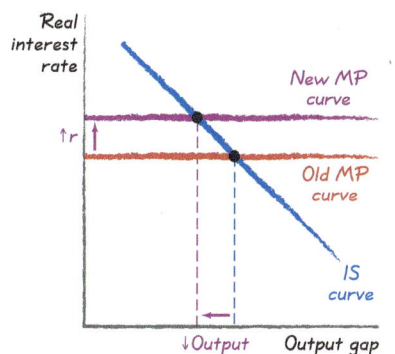

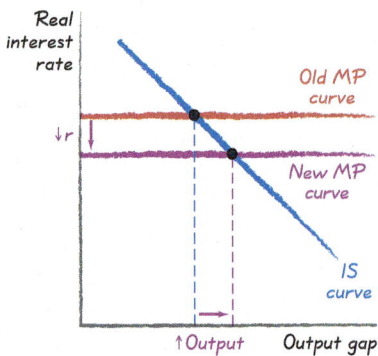

The Fed calms financial markets.

The Fed chair recalled his thinking in the wake of the financial panic gripping Wall Street: "O.K. We have a four-or-five-day chance to really get our act together and get ahead of this. We're gonna try to get ahead of this." On March 23, the Fed responded aggressively, providing backstops that assured lenders their money would be safe.

Step 1: The Fed's backstops worked at reducing this fear, cutting the risk premium. This is a financial shock.

Step 2: This shock shifted the *MP* curve down.

Step 3: This shift led to a lower real interest rate, leading output to be higher than it would otherwise have been.

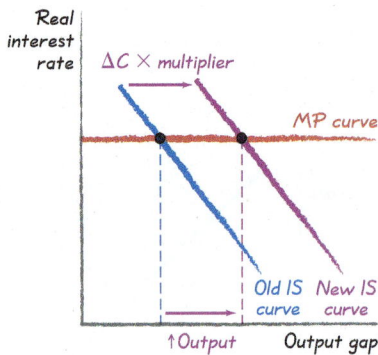

The government sends income support payments.

On March 27, 2020, the government passed the CARES Act that focused on supporting people's incomes. The goal was to ensure people had the means to resume spending when it was safe to do so. This bill included direct payments to households, it made more people eligible for unemployment benefits, and those benefits were made more generous.

Step 1: These income support programs aren't directly counted as government purchases because the government is transferring money, but not buying anything. But these checks meant that people — and particularly low-income folks — had healthier bank balances than before the pandemic. They spent some of this extra income, and this boost to consumption caused aggregate expenditure to rise, which is a positive spending shock.

Step 2: This shock shifted the *IS* curve right.

Step 3: This shift led to a boosted output creating a less negative output gap, but it had no effect on the real interest rate.

Do the Economics

Think you've got this framework all figured out? Here's your chance to practice as you work through nearly a dozen more examples. These aren't contrived textbook examples, but rather some of the shocks that hit the economy during the Covid recession and subsequent stop-start recovery.

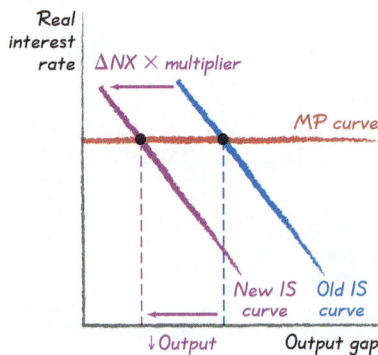

Economic growth slows around the world.

Just as Covid had led the U.S. economy to slow, it caused recessions all around the world, reducing the incomes of many key trading partners.

Step 1: A decrease in net exports reduces aggregate expenditure, which is a negative spending shock.

Step 2: The *IS* curve shifts left.

Step 3: The result is lower output at an unchanged real interest rate.

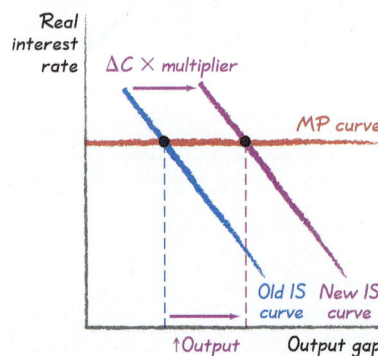

Income inequality declines.

Wages rose more for low-income jobs than others, and the government's income support programs also raised millions of people out of poverty. As a result, income inequality fell.

Step 1: People with lower incomes spend more of their income than those with higher incomes, and so consumption rose, which is a positive spending shock.

Step 2: The *IS* curve shifts right.

Step 3: The result is higher output at an unchanged real interest rate.

Business cashflows improve. *The government launched the Paycheck Protection Program that provided forgivable loans to businesses. This program ensured that businesses had cash on hand.*

Step 1: Greater cashflow leads to greater investment, which is a positive spending shock.

Step 2: The *IS* curve shifts right.

Step 3: The result is higher output at an unchanged real interest rate.

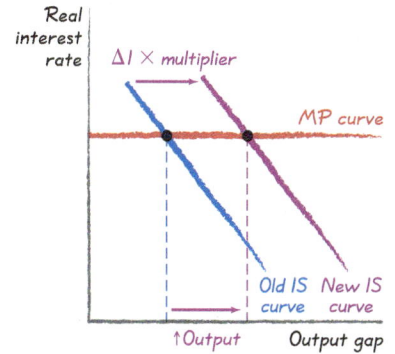

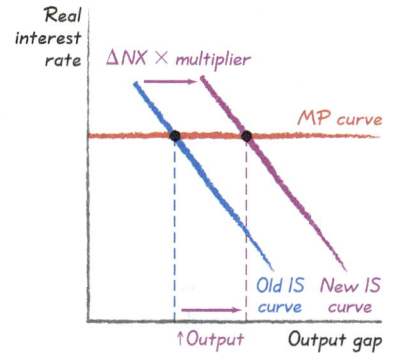

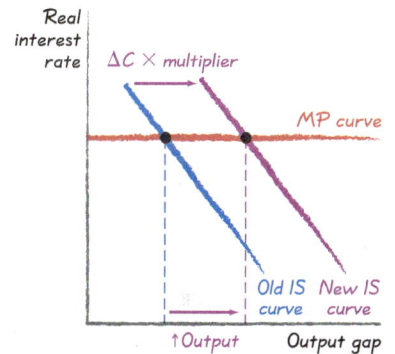

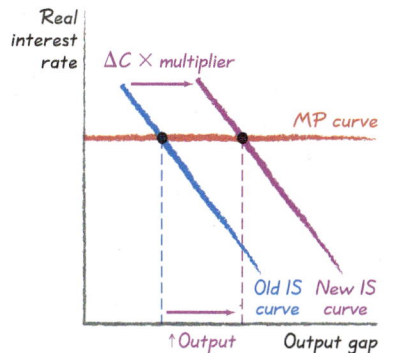

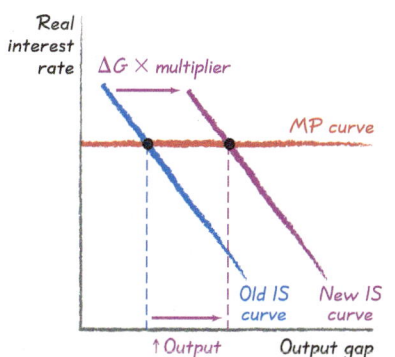

The U.S. dollar depreciates. *Investors became less willing to buy U.S. dollars when the Federal Reserve promised to keep U.S. interest rates low. This reduced demand for dollars caused the value of the dollar to decline.*

Step 1: A cheaper dollar makes U.S. exports cheaper to foreign buyers, boosting net exports, which is a positive spending shock.

Step 2: The *IS* curve shifts right.

Step 3: The result is higher output at an unchanged real interest rate.

House prices rise sharply. *Long lockdowns, and the risk of working from home led people to demand larger houses. The supply of these houses is relatively fixed, so house prices rose sharply.*

Step 1: Higher house prices boost the wealth of homeowners, leading them to spend more, which is a positive spending shock.

Step 2: The *IS* curve shifts right.

Step 3: The result is higher output at an unchanged real interest rate.

Vaccines become available. *As vaccinations became more widespread, people became more comfortable with activities that involved other people, like going shopping, eating at restaurants, and traveling.*

Step 1: Higher consumption boosts aggregate expenditure, and so is a positive spending shock.

Step 2: The *IS* curve shifts right.

Step 3: The result is higher output at an unchanged real interest rate.

Another round of fiscal stimulus. *A second major fiscal stimulus bill, called the American Rescue Plan, is passed. This bill includes funding for schools to safely reopen.*

Step 1: An increase in government expenditures boosts aggregate expenditure, and so is a positive spending shock.

Step 2: The *IS* curve shifts right.

Step 3: The result is higher output at an unchanged real interest rate.

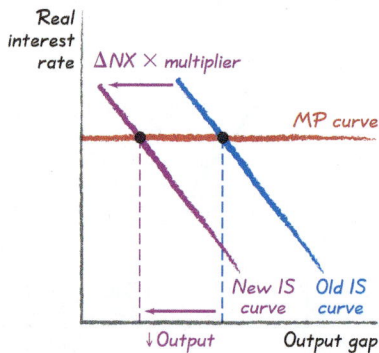

New Covid variants emerge. *The arrival of the highly contagious Delta and Omicron variants wreak havoc in countries with low vaccination rates, causing their economic recoveries to stall.*

Step 1: Weaker economies among U.S. trading partners mean they'll purchase fewer exports from the United States, reducing net exports and hence aggregate expenditure. This is a negative spending shock.

Step 2: The *IS* curve shifts left.

Step 3: The result is lower output at an unchanged real interest rate.

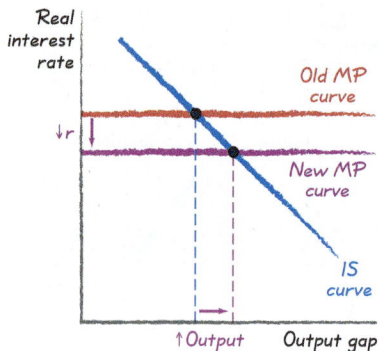

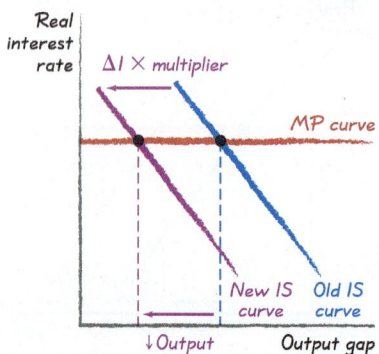

Higher inflation cuts the real interest rate. *While the Fed kept nominal interest rates near zero, rising inflation meant that it effectively allowed the real interest rate (which is the nominal interest rate less inflation) to decline.*

Step 1: The Fed's inaction in the face of rising inflation is a conscious choice to allow the real interest rate to decline. This is a financial shock.

Step 2: The *MP* curve shifts down.

Step 3: The result is higher output at a lower real interest rate.

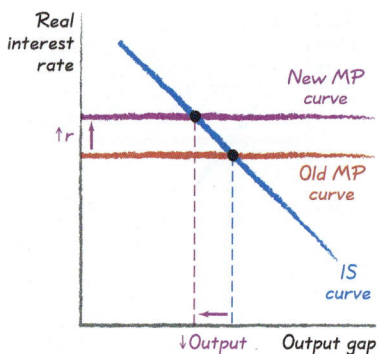

The Fed starts to raise rates. *Concerns that higher inflation may persist led the Fed to begin raising its benchmark interest rate.*

Step 1: The Fed's decision to raise the interest rate is a financial shock.

Step 2: The *MP* curve shifts up.

Step 3: The result is lower output at a higher real interest rate.

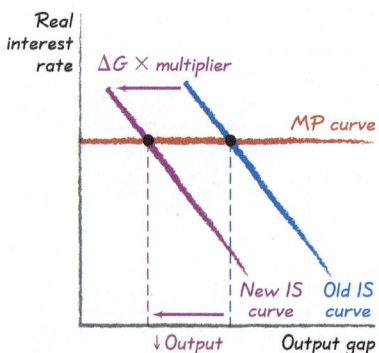

The government's fiscal stimulus programs end. *The end of a fiscal stimulus creates a fiscal contraction as government expenditures decline from their previously higher levels to more normal levels.*

Step 1: This decline in government expenditures causes aggregate expenditure to decline, which is a negative spending shock.

Step 2: The *IS* curve shifts left.

Step 3: The result is lower output at an unchanged real interest rate.

Russia invades Ukraine. *Geopolitical uncertainty rises as many executives wonder what will come next. This heightened economic uncertainty leads businesses to delay investment.*

Step 1: A decrease in investment reduces aggregate expenditure, which is a negative spending shock.

Step 2: The *IS* curve shifts left.

Step 3: The result is lower output at an unchanged real interest rate. ■

18.6 Tying It Together

A Macro Model Is Like a Map

The *IS-MP* framework is the real deal: It's the tool that governments, the Fed, and private-sector forecasters use to organize their thoughts about the economy. It's a framework for understanding how the interplay of aggregate expenditure and interest rate changes drives the ups and downs of the business cycle, and how fiscal and monetary policy can be used to counter these fluctuations. It's essential for business because it tells you how broader macroeconomic changes will buffet your industry.

The *IS* curve reflects the influence of real interest rates on aggregate expenditure. The *MP* curve brings in the financial system, and it illustrates how monetary policy and changes in financial conditions are important influences. Together, they provide a flexible framework that you can use to assess the consequences of changing economic conditions. You can use the *IS-MP* framework to make sense of the constant flow of economic news — about fiscal policy and monetary policy; consumer confidence and business sentiment; developments in Japan, Europe, and China; movements in the exchange rate; and shocks to the financial system.

A word of caution: If you take this framework too literally, it might make the task of managing the economy look a bit too simple. It seems to suggest that you can achieve any level of the output gap just by finding the corresponding real interest rate on the *IS* curve.

Reality is messier. The actual *IS* curve isn't a fixed chart in a textbook that real-world economists just look up. The truth is, the *IS* curve is constantly shifting, which means that the policy that was appropriate yesterday might not be appropriate today. And we don't know the slope of the *IS* curve. Instead, we have to rely on statistical estimates based on how the economy has responded to different interest rates in the past. Who knows if it will respond the same way in the future?

Moreover, the *MP* curve seems to suggest that there's only one interest rate, and it's controlled by the Federal Reserve. That's a useful simplification, but in reality, there are many different interest rates for different types of loans, and while the Federal Reserve has some influence on each of them, it doesn't control them with any precision. And while our analysis tells you what will happen if the *IS* or *MP* curve shifts — which is useful! — it doesn't say much about how quickly those effects will play out.

Even though our simplified frameworks never fully capture the messiness of the world, they're still incredibly helpful. It might help if you think of the *IS-MP* framework the same way you think about Google maps. A map presents a simplified version of reality that sketches the big picture but omits the minor details. It equips you with enough detail to navigate from here to there. And a map is more useful when it's constantly updated to account for changing conditions, as traffic, road conditions, and weather are constantly shifting. Just like that map, the *IS-MP* framework focuses your attention on the most important forces. It omits details, but it gets the big picture right.

And your macroeconomic map is more useful when you update your analysis to account for changing economic conditions. Policymakers use the *IS-MP* framework to help them steer the economy from where it is to where they want it to go. And when they hit economic traffic, they consult that map to see how changing direction might lead to a different destination. This map also guides the decisions made by millions of households, businesses, and investors who need to figure out where we're going, and if there's a faster way there.

Now that you've developed an accurate and useful macroeconomic map, your job is to take it with you on the great open road that's your future career, and use it to navigate to a destination that brings you joy.

Chapter 18 Review

Chapter at a Glance

IS Curve: *Illustrates how lower real interest rates raise spending and hence output, leading to a more positive output gap*

$$\downarrow r \Rightarrow \uparrow C, \uparrow I, \uparrow G \text{ or } \uparrow NX \Rightarrow \uparrow GDP \Rightarrow \uparrow \text{Output gap}$$

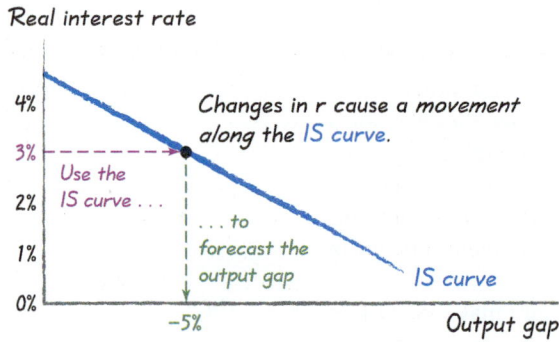

Real interest rate

Changes in r cause a *movement along the* IS curve.

Use the IS curve . . .

. . . to forecast the output gap

IS curve

−5%

Output gap

MP Curve: *Illustrates the current real interest rate, which is shaped by monetary policy and the risk premium.*

Interest rate = Risk-free interest rate + Risk premium
↑ *Monetary policy*   ↑ *Financial markets*

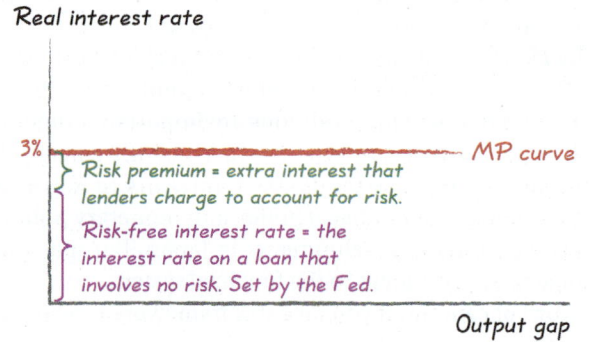

Real interest rate

3%   MP curve

Risk premium = extra interest that lenders charge to account for risk.

Risk-free interest rate = the interest rate on a loan that involves no risk. Set by the Fed.

Output gap

IS-MP Framework

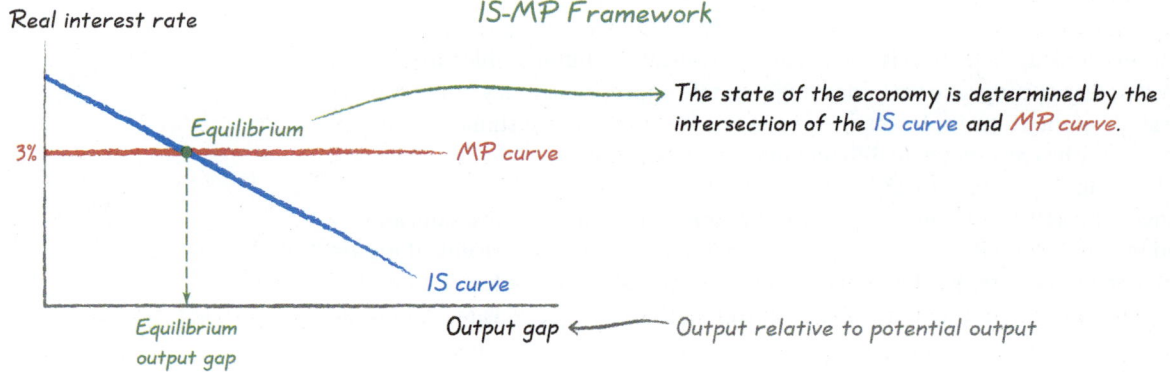

Real interest rate

Equilibrium

3%   MP curve

IS curve

Equilibrium output gap   Output gap

The state of the economy is determined by the intersection of the IS curve and MP curve.

Output relative to potential output

Effects of Macroeconomic Shocks

1. Is there a spending shock (which shifts the IS curve), or a financial shock (which shifts the MP curve)?
2. In which direction, and how far does this shift the IS curve or MP curve?
3. What happens to output in the new equilibrium?

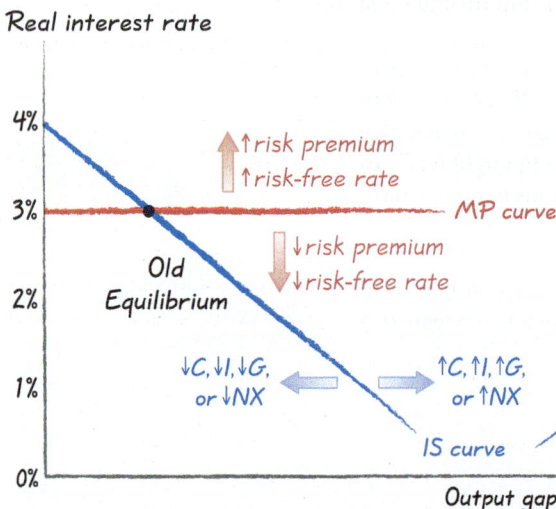

Real interest rate

4%

↑risk premium
↑risk-free rate

3%   MP curve

↓risk premium
↓risk-free rate

Old Equilibrium

2%

↓C,↓I,↓G, or ↓NX   ↑C,↑I,↑G, or ↑NX

1%

IS curve

0%

Output gap

Shifts MP Curve

The risk-free rate rises in response to monetary policy
The risk premium rises if lending becomes riskier

Shifts IS Curve (by ΔSpending × Multiplier)

Consumption (C) rises if people feel more prosperous
Planned investment (I) rises if it's profitable to expand production
Government spending (G) rises in response to expansionary fiscal policy
Net exports (NX) rise in response to global factors.

Key Terms

aggregate expenditure, 464

financial shocks, 485

fiscal policy, 480

IS curve, 470

macroeconomic equilibrium, 464

monetary policy, 473

MP curve, 474

multiplier, 481

risk premium, 473

risk-free interest rate, 473

spending shocks, 482

Study Problems

Learning Objective 18.1 *Assess the role of aggregate expenditure in driving short-run fluctuations in output.*

1. Javier is a department manager at a big box store. Over the last month sales have slumped and he has lots of inventory going unsold. Now it's time to put in his orders to restock for next month. How should he adjust his order for new products and why? How will this decision impact his suppliers?

    Most other businesses are experiencing a similar decline in sales, which has lasted for several months. What does this tell you about aggregate expenditure and output in the economy?

2. How is macroeconomic equilibrium related to equilibrium output? How does equilibrium output differ from potential output?

3. How will businesses adjust their production in response to each of the following changes to aggregate expenditure?

    a. Consumers become more confident in the economic outlook and increase their consumption spending.

    b. Congress passes a new budget that decreases overall government purchases by 0.5% of GDP.

4. In 2017, potential output was $18.17 trillion and output was $18.05 trillion. In 2018, potential output was $18.51 trillion and output was $18.56 trillion. Calculate the output gap for each year. How did the output gap change between 2017 and 2018? Did it become more positive or more negative?

Learning Objective 18.2 *Use the IS curve to analyze the relationship between the real interest rate and output.*

5. Provide an example of how your own consumption would change as the real interest rate changes. Specifically, describe how your opportunity costs change. If other consumers made similar changes, how would that affect aggregate expenditure?

6. Pick a product that you typically buy and draw the demand curve for it. Then draw the *IS* curve for the economy. Compare and contrast the two. What are the prices and quantities for each?

7. The following graph depicts an *IS* curve for the economy.

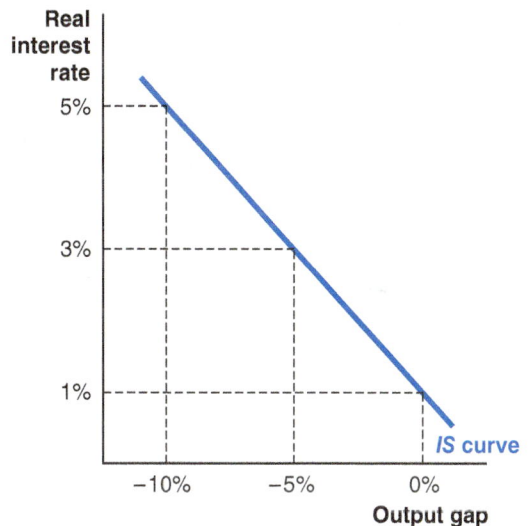

    a. How does the output gap change if the real interest rate rises from 1% to 3%?

    b. Explain the process by which the output gap changed. How did the change in the real interest rate affect aggregate expenditure?

    c. How do actual output and potential output change?

8. For each of the following, illustrate how the *IS* curve will change with a graph.

    a. Poor numbers from several leading economic indicators cause businesses to become pessimistic about the future of the economy.

    b. The real interest rate falls, which causes consumption spending to rise.

Learning Objective 18.3 *Use the MP curve to summarize how the real interest rate is determined.*

9. What determines the risk premium, and how does it affect the real interest rate and *MP* curve?

10. The federal funds rate set by the Fed is 4%, and inflation is 3%. The real interest rate that people can borrow money at is 1.5%.

    a. Draw an *MP* curve.

b. Determine the risk premium. Label it and the risk-free interest rate on your graph.

c. Illustrate how the *MP* curve will change if the risk premium increases.

Learning Objective 18.4 *Forecast economic conditions and how they'll respond to monetary and fiscal policy.*

11. The economy is experiencing an output gap of −3%. Discuss how monetary policy or fiscal policy could be used to raise actual output toward potential output. Could monetary policy and fiscal policy be used together? If so, how?

12. Explain how prolonged recessions can occur and how an economy can become stuck in a slump with actual output falling short of potential output even if both buyers and sellers are making the best decisions they can. How can the economy become unstuck?

13. Draw an *IS-MP* graph where the macroeconomic equilibrium is at a real interest rate of 6% and actual output is 10% below potential GDP. Use this graph to answer the following questions.

a. You're a financial analyst at a regional bank. In a weekly staff meeting, your department head asks your opinion on how Fed policy is going to change in the coming months. If the Fed wishes to close the output gap, how would it change the federal funds rate? Explain your reasoning using the graph.

b. Another analyst in the meeting argues that it's time for the government to cut government purchases in an effort to increase GDP. Would this fiscal policy suggestion cause the output gap to close? Explain using your graph.

14. To combat a recession, the Indian government enacts expansionary fiscal policy, which increases government spending by 2 trillion rupees. In response, GDP rises by 6 trillion rupees.

a. What is the multiplier?

b. The policy pushes India from producing 3% below potential output to now producing 2% above potential output. Illustrate this change in an *IS-MP* graph assuming the real interest rate is constant at 4%.

c. If the Indian government wants to target the highest sustainable level of output, should it continue to increase government spending or pull back? Explain your reasoning.

Learning Objective 18.5 *Use the* IS-MP *framework to forecast the effects of macroeconomic shocks.*

15. Recent releases of leading economic indicators have been a mixed bag: Some of them indicate stable economic growth, while others indicate a looming recession. Explain how businesses will adjust their investment spending as a result of the increased uncertainty. Predict the effect on output.

16. How can the Federal Reserve influence long-term interest rates, and shift the *MP* curve, without changing the current risk-free interest rate?

17. In 2018 and 2019, the United States enacted tariffs on imports from China. In retaliation, China enacted tariffs on goods exported from the United States. How will the output gap change in response to this trade war? Explain your reasoning.

18. Classify each of the following as an example of either a spending shock or a financial shock. Determine how the macroeconomic equilibrium will change by illustrating this shift in an *IS-MP* graph.

a. Lenders become less risk averse and cut the risk premium they charge when making risky loans.

b. The federal government ends a tax cut for families with small children.

c. Congress passes a new tax law that decreases corporate taxes by 10%.

d. Due to signals from the Fed, businesses expect interest rates to rise in the next few weeks.

e. Electric power providers become more confident in the ability for wind farms to meet electricity demand. This leads to a boom in building and producing wind farms across the country.

19. Housing prices in the United States decline dramatically and remain depressed for several months. Using an *IS-MP* graph, explain what happens to the macroeconomic equilibrium in the United States. Using a separate *IS-MP* graph, explain the impact of this housing market crash on the Canadian economy, one of the United States' largest trading partners.

The Phillips Curve and Inflation

The Bloomin' Onion is a softball-sized onion that's cut to resemble a flower, then battered, deep-fried, and served with dipping sauce. It weighs in at 1,950 calories, and it's absolutely delicious. It's the signature dish at Outback Steakhouse, the Australian-themed American restaurant chain with hundreds of locations across the United States.

It's also a microcosm of the American economy. The price of a Bloomin' Onion has risen over time—from $4.95 in 1993, to $6.99 in 2008, and to $9.49 in 2022. Most other goods have followed a similar trajectory, reflecting the macroeconomic trend of rising prices known as inflation. And just as the price of the Bloomin' Onion has risen in fits and starts, the broader inflation rate has fluctuated, rising and falling as economic conditions have changed.

A microcosm of the American economy.

Brent Hofacker/Shutterstock

Restaurant industry executives expect rising costs of their inputs (primarily food and wages) to pose a major challenge they must manage to succeed. They're not alone. *Expectations* of ongoing inflation play a central role in pricing decisions across the whole economy. Expected inflation is a key reason that prices for the Bloomin' Onion—and many other goods—will likely continue to rise over time.

Overall *demand* across the economy also influences inflation. The coronavirus pandemic hit the restaurant business especially hard. Outback Steakhouse and the other restaurants owned by Bloomin' Brands found that many customers avoided restaurants in 2020 and 2021, even after pandemic restrictions were lifted. Outback Steakhouse had dealt with decreased demand before: When the economy tanked in 2008, for example, Bloomin' Brands lowered prices in order to lure diners to their half-empty restaurants. In 2020, they had to be even more creative, lowering some prices and expanding pickup and delivery options.

It's not just demand that influences prices. The rising prices for ingredients were what ultimately led to higher prices at Outback in 2022. These *supply shocks* increased production costs. Indeed, across the whole economy, higher production costs generated higher-than-normal inflation in 2021 and 2022.

We analyzed the consequences of inflation in Chapter 12; our task in this chapter is to understand what causes it. As the Bloomin' Onion illustrates, the rate of change of prices is driven by three key factors: inflation expectations, demand, and supply shocks. In this chapter, we'll develop the framework that top forecasters, executives, and government officials use to analyze inflation, assessing each of these factors separately. Crikey, mate, it's time to get fair dinkum and dig in.

Chapter Objective

Assess the causes of inflation.

19.1 Three Inflationary Forces
Identify the three causes of inflation: inflation expectations, demand-pull inflation, and supply shocks.

19.2 Inflation Expectations
Explore how inflation expectations lead to inflation.

19.3 The Phillips Curve
Analyze the link between the output gap and inflation.

19.4 Supply Shocks Shift the Phillips Curve
Assess how shocks to production costs shift the Phillips curve.

🎙 Podcast
Think Like an Economist
Inflation and the Phillips Curve

19.1 Three Inflationary Forces

Learning Objective *Identify the three causes of inflation: inflation expectations, demand-pull inflation, and supply shocks.*

Let's begin with a brief sketch of the road ahead. Our goal is to understand what drives inflation, and how it responds to economic conditions. That will require understanding the three causes of inflation. I'll introduce those causes to you here, and then we'll dig deeper into each of them in the following sections.

Inflationary Force 1: Inflation Expectations

inflation expectations The rate at which average prices are anticipated to rise next year.

Before Outback Steakhouse prints its new menus, its executives have to decide whether to raise their prices for next year, and if so, by how much. This is where **inflation expectations** — the rate at which average prices are anticipated to rise next year — become relevant. If Outback's top managers expect inflation to be 2% next year, then they'll probably follow suit and raise next year's prices by 2% to keep up. After all, if average prices across the whole economy will rise by 2%, then it's likely that the prices of their key inputs — beef, energy, and rent — will also rise by 2%. The only way for Outback to maintain its profit margin will be to raise prices in line with this rate of expected inflation. But don't just take it from me — read it in their annual report: "the performance of our restaurant depends on our ability to anticipate and react to changes in the price . . . of food."

When other managers across the economy make similar calculations, they'll make similar choices, each raising their prices in line with their inflation expectations. As a result, inflation expectations create inflation. We'll return to this inflationary force in greater detail later in this chapter in the section called "Inflation Expectations."

Inflationary Force 2: Demand-Pull Inflation

When business is good, it can take over an hour to get a table at some Outback Steakhouse locations, as the demand for Aussie "tucker" (that's Aussie-speak for food) outstrips the restaurant's capacity. In the long run, this will lead Outback's managers to consider opening new restaurants. But in the short run, Outback can't increase its supply of meals, so its best bet is to raise its prices.

When there's a line of people waiting, it's time to raise your prices.

demand-pull inflation Inflation resulting from excess demand.

Now consider what happens when the whole economy booms, so that actual output exceeds potential output. During a boom, millions of businesses are in the same situation as Outback Steakhouse, with demand outstripping their productive capacity. Just as Outback raises its prices when demand surges, so do other businesses. These widespread price increases create **demand-pull inflation,** which arises when demand exceeds the economy's productive capacity, pulling prices up. Alternatively, when demand falls short of productive capacity so that the output gap is negative, businesses are likely to moderate their price increases, leading to lower inflation. We'll dig deeper into this link between the output gap and inflation when we introduce a framework for analyzing it called the Phillips curve.

Inflationary Force 3: Supply Shocks and Cost-Push Inflation

The **interdependence principle** emphasizes the importance of linkages between markets, and it's especially relevant to understanding how the Russian invasion of Ukraine pushed up the price of Aussie tucker in the United States. Those tensions led to reductions in oil supply because of sanctions against Russia, which pushed up oil prices, setting off a chain reaction. Initially, products made from oil — like gasoline, heating oil, and propane — became more expensive. These higher energy prices raised the production costs of many businesses, including Aussie-themed restaurants. It cost more to truck ingredients across the country; it was more expensive to heat a restaurant;

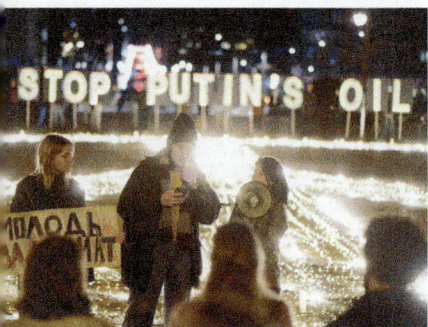

When oil stops flowing, inflation starts rising.

and the energy costs required to run a commercial kitchen rose. Eventually, these higher marginal costs forced Outback Steakhouse to raise its prices.

A similar story plays out across many sectors of the economy, as higher oil prices lead to higher prices for a range of oil-based inputs — including plastics, fertilizers, and rubber. Just as higher marginal costs will lead Outback Steakhouse to raise its prices, millions of other businesses raise their prices when their marginal costs rise. These widespread price increases create inflation. This is an example of **cost-push inflation,** which occurs when prices rise in response to an unexpected rise in production costs. The original catalyst of all this was a *supply shock,* which is why we'll analyze cost-push inflation in more detail under the heading "Supply Shocks."

cost-push inflation Inflation that results from an unexpected rise in production costs.

Understanding Inflation

Put all the pieces together, and we've sketched out the three causes of inflation (and given you a preview of the chapter ahead): It's the result of expected inflation, demand-pull inflation, and cost-push inflation:

Inflation = Expected inflation + Demand-pull inflation + Cost-push inflation

$\uparrow$*Inflation expectations* $\rightarrow$ $\uparrow$*Inflation* $\uparrow$*Output gap* $\rightarrow$ $\uparrow$*Inflation* $\uparrow$*Production costs* $\rightarrow$ $\uparrow$*Inflation*

Okay, that's our brief sketch. We'll spend the rest of this chapter digging into each of these inflationary forces in more detail. Let's start with inflation expectations.

19.2 Inflation Expectations

Learning Objective *Explore how inflation expectations lead to inflation.*

Put yourself in the shoes of the executives at Outback Steakhouse as they decide what prices to set for next year. You've got a sophisticated information system at your fingertips, tracking every detail of your business. It tells you that the food and beverage costs for a typical meal add up to about $7 per person. Detailed supplier data break this down further into the cost of beef, produce, dairy, bread, pasta, and so on. These details help you figure out specific costs per menu item. Labor costs — which include both front-of-the-house waitstaff and back-of-the-house cooks — add another $6.30 per customer, on average. Then other operating costs, including utilities, advertising, and rent, add an extra $5. There's also overhead, such as insurance, lawyers, and the managers at the head office. The restaurant business is a tough one, and profit margins are razor thin.

You need to make sure that your prices remain competitive, which is why Outback monitors the prices charged by other steakhouse chains, fast-casual restaurants, and even the growing competition from meal-delivery services.

As you work your way through reams of spreadsheets, you realize that these data can only tell you what's happened in the past. But you want to know what's going to happen in the future, so that you can ensure your prices are appropriate for whatever the months ahead might hold. That's why your expectations matter.

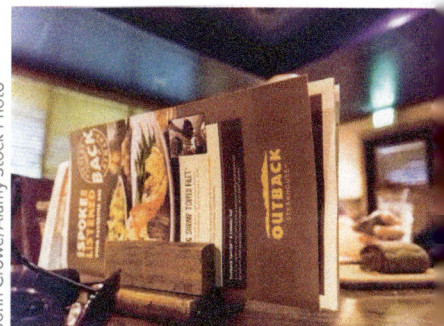

You're about to print thousands of these menus. Better get the prices right.

Why Inflation Expectations Matter

Your inflation expectations describe the rate at which you expect prices to rise, on average, across the whole economy over the next year. They're important to your business because you'll set your prices with an eye to what you expect will happen in the months ahead. And they're important for the economy because inflation expectations are the key driver of inflation in the long run.

Changes in restaurant prices track broad trends in inflation

Percent change over the past year

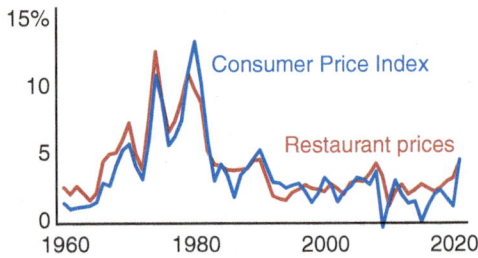

Data from: Bureau of Labor Statistics.

Two key factors for setting prices:
1. Your marginal costs
2. Your competitors' prices

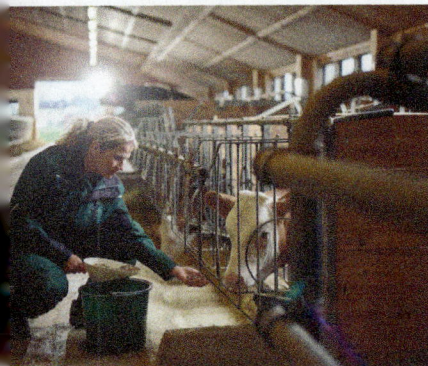

If she's paying more to feed her cattle, you'll pay more for steak.

Set your prices to take account of inflation expectations. Two key factors drive most pricing decisions, and your inflation expectations are relevant to both of them.

First, there's your *marginal costs*. Outback Steakhouse deals with dozens of suppliers who tend to raise their prices in line with the overall inflation rate. Labor costs also often rise with inflation. In some locations, state laws require that minimum wages rise each year with inflation. All of these factors mean that if you expect inflation to be 2% next year, then it's likely that the price of your inputs will typically rise by around 2%. (Some prices will rise a bit more, and some a bit less.) If you want to maintain your profit margin, you'll have to charge higher prices to make up for the higher marginal costs you expect to pay.

Second, consider your *competitors' prices*: If most prices in the economy are rising by 2%, then it's reasonable to expect that your competitors will also raise their prices by around 2% on average. They'll do so partly because their costs are also rising by 2%, and partly because they expect their competitors to respond to rising input costs by raising their prices by 2%. Raising your prices by the same percentage that you expect your competitors to raise their prices will maintain your competitive positioning. The reason you can reasonably expect your competitors to raise their prices is because restaurants generally raise their prices in line with overall inflation, as seen in the figure.

Each of these factors suggests that — at least as a starting point — you should raise next year's prices in line with your inflation expectations. This logic gives a powerful role to expectations, suggesting that you should raise your prices for next year because you expect other businesses — both your suppliers and competitors — to raise their prices. This logic isn't specific to Outback Steakhouse; it applies to just about any business.

Inflation expectations create inflation. There are millions of managers across the country making similar calculations, and in each case, their inflation expectations are central to how they set next year's prices. Each manager figures that if they expect their costs to rise by 2%, and they expect the prices their competitors charge to rise by 2%, their best response is to also raise their prices by 2%. Some managers might expect inflation to be a bit higher and raise their prices a bit more; others might expect slightly lower price increases, leading them to raise their prices by less. But when millions of managers have average inflation expectations of 2%, they'll raise their prices by an average of 2%. Inflation expectations lead to inflation.

That is, *inflation occurs because we expect inflation.*

As we push this logic a bit further, you'll see how important inflation expectations really are. We've seen that expected inflation of 2% leads managers to raise their prices by 2%. The same logic says that if managers expect next year's inflation to be 3%, they should go ahead and raise their prices by 3%. And if managers expect next year's inflation to be 6%, they'll raise their prices by 6%.

We've isolated the first major cause of inflation, so let's summarize:

> **Inflationary Force 1: Inflation Expectations**
> Higher inflation expectations create higher inflation.
> ↑*Inflation expectations* → ↑*Inflation*

Inflation expectations create a self-fulfilling prophecy. There's something pretty extraordinary about this logic. It says that whatever rate of inflation managers expect, they'll end up raising their prices by that amount. It's a *self-fulfilling prophecy:* The widespread expectation of any particular inflation rate is enough to push suppliers to raise their prices so that they'll create that inflation.

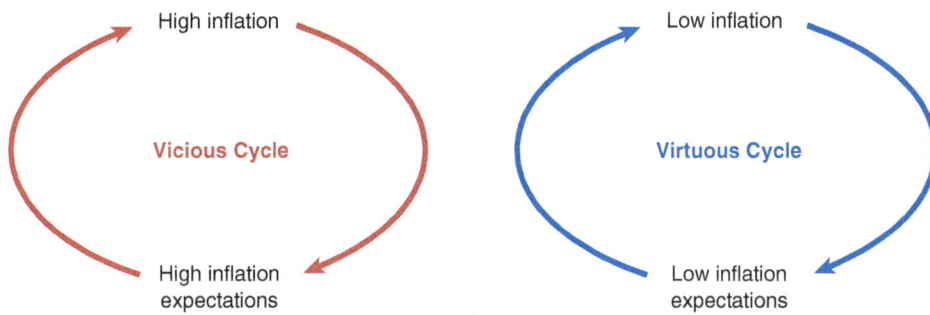

If people expect low inflation, they'll get low inflation. And if people expect high inflation, they'll get high inflation. This means that any inflation rate can become a long-run equilibrium because the inflation rate that people expect ultimately determines the price rises that suppliers set.

Monetary policy tries to shape inflation expectations. These cycles explain why — as Figure 1 shows — some countries have persistently high inflation while others have persistently low inflation. The high-inflation countries are stuck in a vicious cycle where people expect high inflation, which leads to high inflation . . . which leads people to expect high inflation. By contrast, low-inflation countries enjoy a virtuous cycle where people expect low inflation, which leads to low inflation, which leads people to expect low inflation.

This points to an important idea for policymakers: In the long run, the key to achieving persistently low inflation is to convince people that inflation is going to be low. Once you get them to believe it, it will turn out to be true. The challenge is that inflation can occur because of demand or supply factors, and potentially shape expectations about future inflation. Outback faced higher input prices in 2021, which led them to anticipate further price increases in 2022. Policymakers aim to keep expectations for future inflation low even when businesses are experiencing a temporary rise in inflation. We'll analyze the strategies that policymakers use to help the public to expect low inflation in Chapter 22 on monetary policy.

Figure 1 | Inflation Rates Vary Across Countries

Average annual rise in the consumer price index, 2011-2021

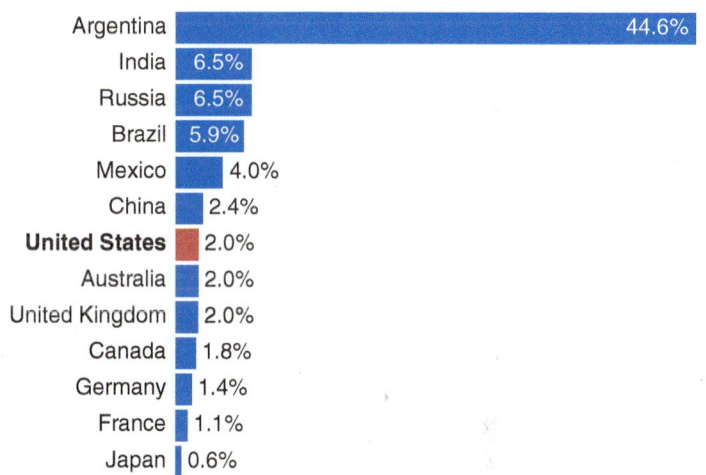

Argentina	44.6%
India	6.5%
Russia	6.5%
Brazil	5.9%
Mexico	4.0%
China	2.4%
United States	2.0%
Australia	2.0%
United Kingdom	2.0%
Canada	1.8%
Germany	1.4%
France	1.1%
Japan	0.6%

*Limited Data for Argentina

Data from: OECD.

Interpreting the DATA | Inflation expectations lead to actual inflation

Our analysis so far suggests that inflation expectations play a central role in determining inflation. One way to assess this claim is to compare how actual inflation tracks expected inflation. Figure 2 shows survey data in which American consumers are asked about their expectations for future inflation. These inflation expectations are plotted along with the actual inflation rate. The figure shows that actual inflation moves around more than the expected inflation rate. But if you look carefully, you'll see that when people expect inflation to rise, it subsequently does rise. This is consistent with the idea that inflation expectations are a key driver of inflation, even though other factors also shape inflation. ■

Figure 2 | Inflation Expectations Lead and Actual Inflation Follows

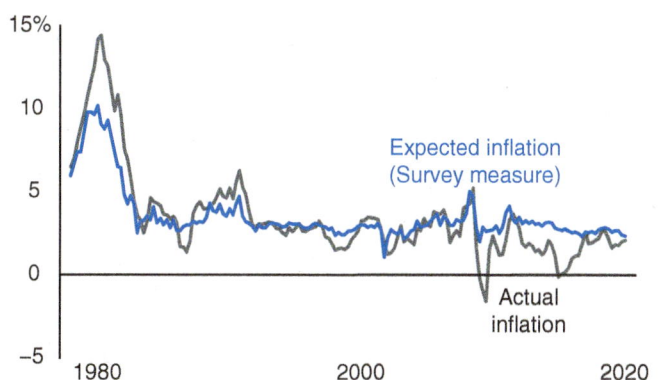

Data from: University of Michigan and Bureau of Labor Statistics.

Measuring Inflation Expectations

Because inflation expectations are a key driver of future inflation, it's important to track inflation expectations over time. There are three ways you can do this: by analyzing surveys, by poring over economic forecasts, and by looking at financial markets.

Figure 3 | Surveys Reveal the Inflation Expectations of Consumers

Expected inflation rate

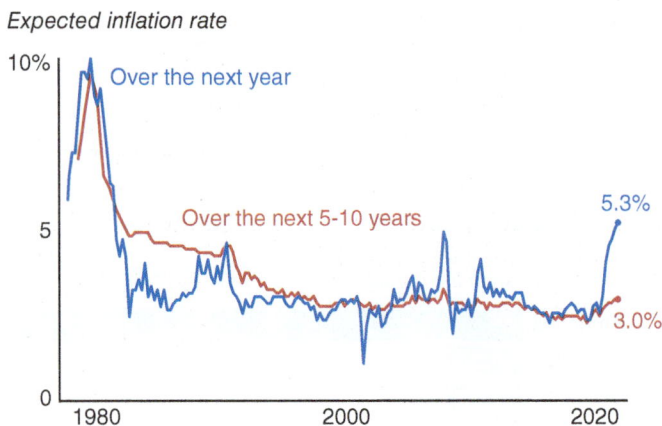

Data from: University of Michigan.

Surveys ask people about their inflation expectations. The simplest way to find out average inflation expectations is to survey a representative group of people. Figure 3 shows inflation expectations over time from an ongoing University of Michigan survey that asks people about their inflation expectations. The blue line illustrates the typical response when people are asked how much inflation they expect over the next year. It's a guide to what people are thinking as they set their prices for next year.

A follow-up question asks people what they expect inflation to be over the next five to ten years. This is helpful for assessing whether people believe the Federal Reserve's promise to keep inflation low and stable. The red line reveals a remarkable transformation in inflation expectations: In the late 1970s, people expected high inflation to persist for many more years. But in the decades since the mid-1980s, people have come to expect low inflation, and they maintain this conviction even when there are short bursts of higher or lower inflation. In mid-2022, inflation in the United States was 9% — high enough that it pushed expectations for inflation over the next few years a little higher. Yet most people still expected inflation to return to its long-run low rate within the next five years.

Figure 4 | Economists' Forecasts Reveal Their Inflation Expectations

Median inflation forecast from surveys of professional economic forecasters

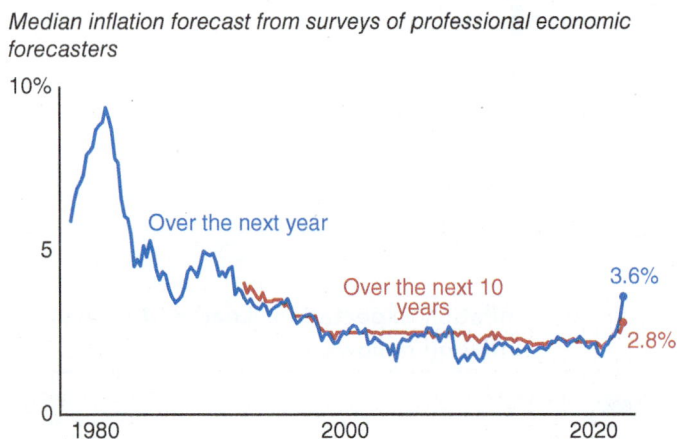

Data from: Survey of Professional Forecasters.

Inflation forecasts reveal the inflation expectations of economists. Another indicator of inflation expectations relies on the inflation forecasts that professional economists publish. Figure 4 illustrates the median inflation forecast from an ongoing survey of professional economists. It shows their inflation expectations when asked to project inflation both over the next year and over the next decade. The blue line shows what they expect inflation to be next year, while the red line shows long-term inflation expectations. Notice that there is somewhat more movement in expectations for the next year than the next decade. Prior to the pandemic, most economist expected annual inflation to average around 2%. An inflationary surge coming out of the pandemic led many to update their inflation expectations to 2.5 to 3%, reflecting their belief that inflation would remain high for a few years before returning to the long-run average of 2%.

Financial markets bet on the future path of inflation. An alternative measure of inflation expectations comes from analyzing financial market data. The Federal Reserve publishes a 10-year break-even rate, which tells you how much you need to earn in interest to be able to buy the same amount of stuff in 10 years with your savings. That rate reflects the behavior of investors who can choose to buy Treasury bonds that give you back the amount you put into savings in nominal terms or who can choose to buy Treasury bonds that protect against inflation. Treasury Inflation-Protected Securities (known as "TIPS") provide protection against inflation because you get the amount of your savings back adjusted for inflation. As you can see in Figure 5, in mid-2022, the 10-year break-even rate was 2.4%, suggesting that investors expected inflation to average 2.4% over the next 10 years. It's an informative measure because it summarizes the collective wisdom of many sophisticated financial traders. Economists also like to track these numbers to see how these market prices respond in real time to changing economic conditions and the actions of the Federal Reserve. The downside of these market-based measures is that they're an imperfect measure of inflation expectations because traders may bid the price of bonds higher or lower, depending on how risky they're perceived to be.

Inflation expectations might be adaptive, anchored, rational, or sticky.

If inflation depends on inflation expectations, then you might ask: What determines people's inflation expectations? Economists focus on four different ways people might form their expectations.

- **Adaptive Expectations:** Some managers might expect recent levels of inflation to continue, which means they have *adaptive expectations*.

- **Anchored Expectations:** Those who might believe that the Federal Reserve will deliver on its promise to ensure that inflation will be around 2% have *anchored expectations,* anchored to the Federal Reserve's inflation target.

- **Rational Expectations:** Those who use all available data and a deep understanding of macroeconomic relationships to come up with the most accurate forecast possible with available data, so that they have *rational expectations*.

- **Sticky Expectations:** There is also evidence that people revisit their views about inflation only irregularly, and so they stick with their previous views for long periods of time, which means they have *sticky expectations*.

For most people, it's probably some combination of all of these factors. If you're a manager, the important thing is not to figure out precisely how inflation expectations are formed, but rather to form the most accurate expectations you can. Fortunately, there's a trick that will help you with this.

Figure 5 | Financial Market Prices Provide a Market-based Measure of Inflation Expectations

Expected inflation over the next ten years

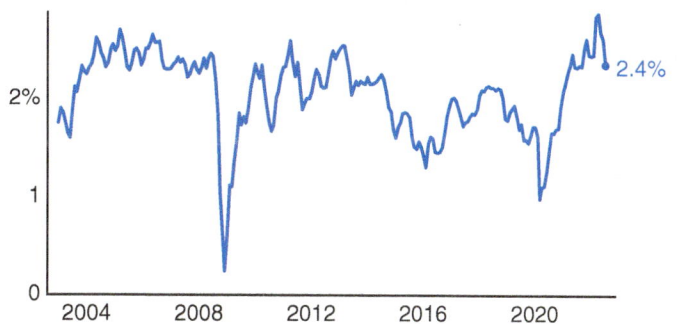

Calculated as:
Expected inflation = Nominal interest rate on a 10-year bond less yield on a 10-year inflation-indexed bond.

Data from: Federal Reserve Bank of St. Louis.

EVERYDAY Economics | To form inflation expectations, turn to the wisdom of a crowd of economists

Many managers rely on their own intuitions to guide their inflation expectations. Think about the benefits of specialization, and you'll realize that doesn't make much sense. As with most things in life, you'll probably get better results if you depend on a specialist, which in this case would mean relying on a professional economic forecaster. Indeed, professional economists typically have more accurate expectations than either managers or the general public. That's why some managers simply call their bank's economist to ask what they predict next year's inflation rate to be.

But there's an easy way to do even better: Studies show that the most accurate forecasts come from taking the average inflation forecast across many different professional economists. (If it's a pride of lions and a gaggle of geese, then I propose we call them a *surplus* of economists.) Indeed, the average of many forecasts is typically more accurate than the forecast of any individual Wall Street whiz.

Point your browser to the Survey of Professional Forecasters from the Philadelphia Federal Reserve. There, you'll find the average inflation expectation across many leading economists. Rely on the average forecast of many professional economists, and you'll have access to the best inflation forecast of all. Even better, it's free! ■

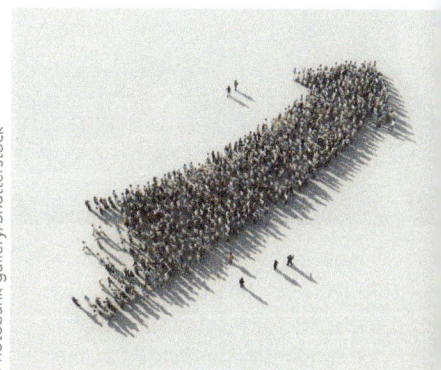

Want to know if inflation will rise or fall? Don't ask one economist . . . ask a crowd of economists.

That's it. We've now identified the key long-run force driving inflation: inflation expectations. But, while inflation expectations are important, they're not the whole story. In the short run, the ups and downs that drive the business cycle might drive inflation higher or lower. That's our next topic.

19.3 The Phillips Curve

Learning Objective *Analyze the link between the output gap and inflation.*

A strong economy has created a rather pleasant dilemma for you and your fellow executives at Outback Steakhouse. Folks have healthy incomes, and so millions more people are willing to splurge to enjoy a steak dinner. But it's a dilemma because Outback Steakhouses are already overflowing, and in many cases, customers are forced to wait for over an hour for a table. Some customers give up waiting and leave. Outback Steakhouse faces **excess demand** given its limited seating capacity, as the quantity demanded at the prevailing price exceeds the quantity that it can supply.

In the long run, if business continues to boom, it's worth building more restaurants. But in the short run, you're stuck with your existing capacity. In this situation, what advice would you give your fellow executives?

excess demand When the quantity demanded at the prevailing price exceeds the quantity supplied.

Demand-Pull Inflation

When demand for your product exceeds your capacity, it's time to think about raising your prices. After all, there's no point in having more customers than you can serve. Outback can raise its prices — and hence its profit margin — and still fill its restaurants. If inflation expectations would normally lead you to raise your prices by 2%, the fact that you're also facing excess demand is a reason to raise your prices a bit more. Similarly, if a tough economy has left you with empty tables, you might want to contemplate cutting prices. In fact, this is precisely what Outback's management has typically done, raising its prices a bit faster when its restaurants face excess demand and lowering them during economic downturns.

Should you raise prices?

Excess demand leads inflation to rise above inflation expectations. A strong economy puts millions of businesses in a similar situation to Outback Steakhouse, with customer demand exceeding what producers can supply. Each of these businesses will respond to their excess demand much as Outback did, by raising their prices by a bit more than required just to keep pace with expected inflation. The result is *demand-pull inflation*, which occurs when excess demand pulls inflation up, so that it rises above expected inflation.

Insufficient demand leads inflation to fall below inflation expectations. Demand-pull inflation can also pull inflation below inflation expectations when demand is unexpectedly weak. To see why, let's return to the dark days following the start of the coronavirus pandemic. In summer 2020, restaurants had reopened to in-person dining, but most people were still uncomfortable with the risk of indoor dining. For Outback Steakhouse, that meant that traffic to their restaurants fell 18% compared to 2019.

How can you bring in the crowds?

insufficient demand When the quantity demanded at the prevailing price is below what's supplied.

Outback was facing a problem of **insufficient demand,** as the quantity of restaurant meals demanded at the prevailing price was far below the quantity that Outback wished to supply. In response, in August 2020, Outback released a new menu with lower prices and larger portions, including cutting the price of the Bloomin' Onion to $7.99. These lower prices helped Outback return to profitability in 2021. It was profitable because sales increased and the marginal cost of serving these extra meals was particularly low as Outback's staff barely had enough customers to stay busy.

In a weak economy, millions of businesses face insufficient demand. Like Outback, most will find that their marginal costs are low when they're producing well below their capacity. They'll follow the same logic Outback used and respond to insufficient demand with price restraint, either raising their prices by a bit less than they otherwise would or in some cases cutting them. Across the whole economy, the result is widespread price restraint that pulls inflation below expected inflation. That is, insufficient demand leads inflation to fall below expected inflation.

When the economy is operating at full capacity, inflation equals inflation expectations. Notice that demand-pull inflation is a separate force that operates in addition to inflation expectations. When there's excess demand, it pulls inflation to rise above inflation expectations, and when there's insufficient demand, it pulls inflation to fall below inflation expectations.

Between these two cases — of excess demand and insufficient demand — is the case where demand matches the economy's productive capacity. In this case there's no demand-pull inflation and hence no pressure for prices to rise faster or slower than expected. And so when the economy is operating at full capacity, inflation is equal to inflation expectations.

The output gap measures the imbalance between output and productive capacity. In all of this, the driver of demand-pull inflation is the imbalance between buyers' demand for output versus the productive capacity of suppliers. This suggests that demand-pull inflation is driven by the *output gap,* which measures actual output relative to potential output.

The Phillips Curve Framework

Putting these pieces together yields two key observations that form the basis of the framework we're building to analyze inflation.

Observation 1: Demand-pull inflation is driven by the output gap. When output exceeds potential output — meaning the output gap is positive — there is excess demand. The more positive the output gap is, the greater the degree of excess demand, and hence the greater the pressure to raise prices. By contrast, when output falls short of potential output — meaning the output gap is negative — there is insufficient demand. The more negative the output gap is, the greater the degree of insufficient demand, and hence the greater the pressure for price restraint.

Observation 2: Demand-pull inflation leads inflation to diverge from inflation expectations. Demand-pull inflation occurs in addition to inflation expectations, meaning that demand-pull factors cause inflation to either rise above inflation expectations (when there's excess demand), or fall below inflation expectations (when there's insufficient demand). That is, it drives **unexpected inflation,** which is the difference between inflation and inflation expectations:

unexpected inflation The difference between inflation and inflation expectations = Inflation − Inflation expectations

Unexpected inflation = Inflation − Inflation expectations

The Phillips curve describes how the output gap is linked to unexpected inflation. Put these two observations together, and we conclude that *the output gap causes inflation to rise above, or fall below, inflation expectations.* We can summarize this as follows:

> **Inflationary Force 2: Demand-Pull Inflation**
> The output gap drives inflation to rise above or fall below inflation expectations.
> ↑Output gap → ↑Inflation (relative to inflation expectations)

Phillips curve A curve illustrating the link between the output gap and unexpected inflation.

Demand-pull inflation creates a link between the output gap and unexpected inflation (the gap between inflation and inflation expectations). When you graph this link, the result is known as the **Phillips curve.** Figure 6 shows the Phillips curve, illustrating how the output gap affects unexpected inflation.

Figure 6 | **The Phillips Curve**

The output gap drives inflation to rise above or fall below inflation expectations.

Ⓐ When **output exceeds potential output,** *excess demand* leads managers to raise prices more, causing **inflation to rise above expected inflation**.

Ⓑ When **output is equal to potential output,** the absence of demand-pull inflation means that **inflation will be equal to expected inflation**.

Ⓒ When **output is less than potential output,** *insufficient demand* leads to price restraint, causing **inflation to fall below expected inflation**.

Unexpected inflation
(Inflation − Inflation expectations)

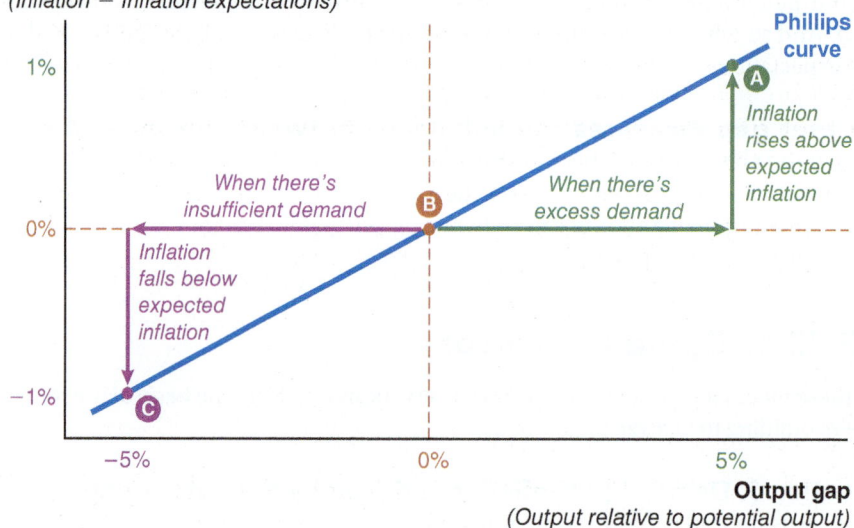

The Phillips curve is named after Bill Phillips, who first discovered the relationship between the output gap and unexpected inflation. He was a bit of a character — a crocodile hunter, adventurer, and war hero, who once jerry-rigged a secret miniature radio while captured in a prisoner-of-war camp. While he passed his economic principles class by only a single point, he went on to make a major mark on the field by showing that excess demand generates inflationary pressure. His analysis of historical data unearthed the importance of demand-pull inflation.

Let's explore this graph in a bit more detail.

Unexpected inflation goes on the vertical axis, and the output gap goes on the horizontal axis. By now, you're pretty familiar with the graphing convention in economics of using the horizontal axis to show what's going on with quantities and the vertical axis to show what's going on with prices. The same conventions apply to the Phillips curve, so make sure you put the output gap (which is about quantities) on the horizontal axis, and unexpected inflation (which is about prices) on the vertical axis. And don't forget that the Phillips curve describes inflation above and beyond that caused by inflation expectations, which is why the vertical axis measures unexpected inflation (which is inflation less inflation expectations).

One more graphing tip: Both the output gap and unexpected inflation can be either positive or negative, so it's usually a good idea to extend both axes into negative territory. That means you draw the axes so that zero is pretty much in the middle. (This may seem unusual at first — it means the axes no longer rise from zero — but you'll see that the curve still makes sense when you draw it.)

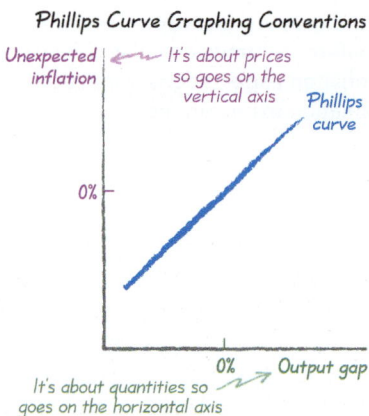

Phillips Curve Graphing Conventions

The Phillips curve is upward-sloping. The Phillips curve is upward-sloping because higher output relative to potential output — a more positive output gap — leads to greater inflationary pressure, causing inflation to rise above inflation expectations. It illustrates the idea that:

$$\uparrow \text{Output gap} \rightarrow \uparrow \text{Unexpected inflation}$$

When output is equal to potential output, then inflation is equal to expected inflation. The Phillips curve passes through the origin, which is the point at which the output gap is zero and unexpected inflation is zero. At this point, output is equal to potential output, and so the absence of demand-pull inflation means that inflation is pulled neither above nor below inflation expectations. As a result, when actual output is equal to potential output, actual inflation is equal to expected inflation.

The Phillips curve predicts how far inflation will diverge from expected inflation. Notice that the vertical axis of the Phillips curve suggests that unexpected inflation can be either positive or negative. This doesn't mean that actual inflation is likely to be negative (that can also happen, but it's rare). Rather, the Phillips curve is all about *unexpected inflation*. When it says that unexpected inflation will be negative, this simply means that actual inflation will be less than expected inflation. And positive rates of unexpected inflation tell you that actual inflation will be greater than expected inflation. Indeed, the Phillips curve is useful because it tells you by how much actual inflation will be above or below expected inflation.

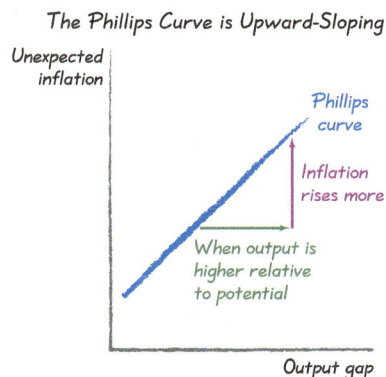

The Phillips Curve is Upward-Sloping

Unexpected inflation / Output gap

Phillips curve
Inflation rises more
When output is higher relative to potential

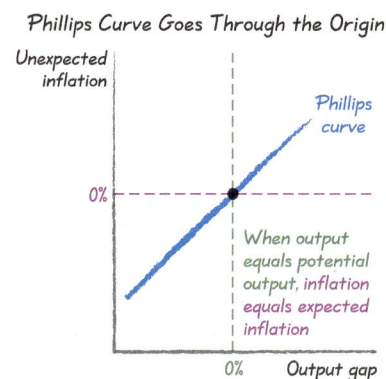

Phillips Curve Goes Through the Origin

Unexpected inflation / Output gap

Phillips curve
0%
When output equals potential output, *inflation equals expected inflation*
0%

EVERYDAY Economics   How Uber is like the Phillips curve

As the concert ends late on a rainy Saturday night, you head outside, pull out your phone, and tap on the Uber app, hoping to summon a ride home. But the app responds that a ride that would normally cost $10 will now cost $30. You look around at the hundreds of other concert-goers nearby, and your inner Bill Phillips explains what's just happened: There are more concert-goers trying to get a ride home than available Uber drivers, so there's excess demand.

Uber's surge-pricing algorithm has kicked in. It's like a turbo-charged Phillips curve, programmed to respond to excess demand by raising prices immediately. We say it's turbo-charged because it usually takes other businesses months rather than minutes to change their prices in response to a surge in demand. That's why the Phillips curve typically describes inflation rising or falling over a period of months.

There's one important difference. During that brief postconcert surge, most other prices — the price of taxis, of buses, or even of rental cars — are unchanged. As such, Uber's surge pricing is best viewed as a change in *relative prices* — it raises the price of taking an Uber relative to taking the bus. By contrast, the Phillips curve describes how a surge in demand across the whole economy leads many businesses to raise their prices, and these widespread price rises create inflation. ∎

It's like the Phillips curve.

The Phillips Curve in the United States

Bill Phillips once described his curve as a "wet weekend's bit of work." He discovered it by plotting historical data for the United Kingdom covering the period from 1861 through 1957. It's time for us to update his plots with an eye to discovering the modern Phillips curve for the United States.

Discover the Phillips curve for the United States. We begin by compiling the relevant historical data. To construct our measure of unexpected inflation, we need to collect data on both the actual inflation rate each year and expected inflation (and here, I'm relying on the measure based on forecasts of professional economists). We calculate unexpected inflation simply as actual inflation less expected inflation. Next, we plot unexpected inflation in each year against the corresponding output gap.

Figure 7 | Discover the Phillips Curve for the United States

Unexpected inflation is higher when the output gap is more positive

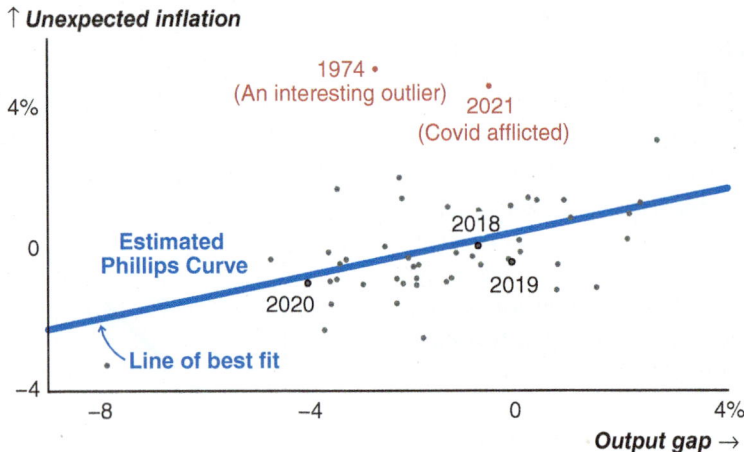

Data from: Survey of Professional Forecasters, BLS and BEA.

Figure 7 plots these data, showing the shape of the Phillips curve for the United States. You'll see that these data roughly bear out the predictions of our analysis: When the output gap is positive so that GDP is high relative to potential GDP, inflation has *typically* risen higher than inflation expectations. And when the output gap is negative so that GDP is low relative to potential GDP, inflation has typically fallen lower than inflation expectations. The upward slope of this curve reveals that the more positive the output gap, the more unexpected inflation there is.

The Phillips curve is an imprecise relationship. The data reveal that the Phillips curve prediction isn't always right. Even so, it remains an important tool because accounting for the output gap leads to more accurate inflation forecasts. The fact that the data do not lie exactly along this Phillips curve suggests that other factors also play a role. For example, the dot for 1974 (in the top left) is nowhere near the Phillips curve. That was a year in which oil prices unexpectedly rose sharply, and we'll come back to explaining why that boosted inflation shortly. Similarly, prices rose sharply in 2021, as demand recovered more quickly than supply could in the wake of the pandemic.

When economists try to figure out what the Phillips curve looks like, they compile data like this and compute a line that best fits the data. The line of best fit in Figure 7 is an example of this sort of analysis. You could do this with a pencil, a ruler, and a bit of judgment, but in the example shown here, I've computed the line of best fit using a spreadsheet. (If you've taken a statistics class, you'll recognize this as a regression line; if you haven't, all you need to know is that this line best describes the relationship on average.)

A more complete analysis would also take account of other factors that might affect inflation, such as changes in oil prices, productivity, or the exchange rate. For now, be patient—we'll incorporate these supply-side factors shortly.

Figure 8 | Use the Phillips Curve to Forecast Inflation

For any given output gap, look up until you hit the Phillips curve, then look across to forecast unexpected inflation.

Ⓐ Locate the **output gap** on the horizontal axis, and look up until you hit the Phillips curve.

Ⓑ Then look across to find your forecast of **unexpected inflation**.

Ⓒ Inflation = **Unexpected inflation** + Inflation expectations.

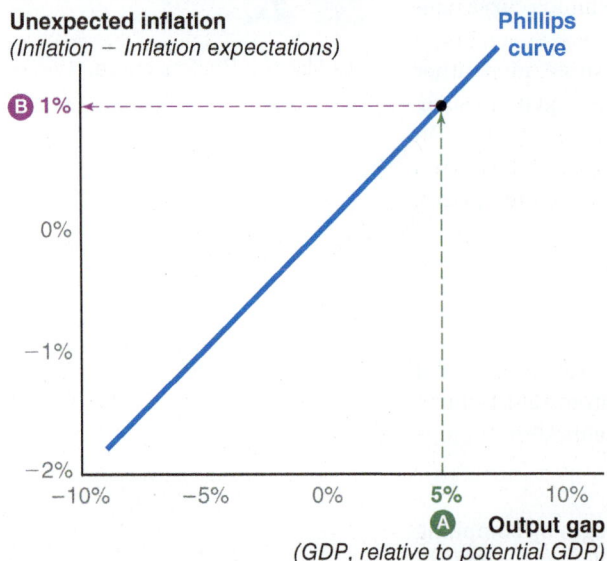

Use the Phillips curve to forecast future inflation.
Investment banks, businesses, and government economists forecast inflation by using estimates of the Phillips curve that are similar to our line of best fit.

It's a two-step process:

Step 1: Assess inflation expectations. You can measure inflation expectations by analyzing surveys of inflation expectations, surveys of economists, or financial market-based measures.

Step 2: Forecast unexpected inflation. This is where the Phillips curve is useful. Start with your estimate of what the output gap will be, look up to the corresponding point on the Phillips curve, and then look across to find your forecast for unexpected inflation. For instance, Figure 8 shows that an output gap of +5% corresponds with unexpected inflation of 1%.

Your inflation forecast, of course, should be the sum of your forecasts for expected inflation and unexpected inflation. So if inflation expectations are running at 2% and you're also forecasting demand-pull inflation to add another 1%, your forecast for inflation should be 3%.

Do the Economics

1. You're about to negotiate your salary for next year, and want to make sure that it adjusts for likely changes in the cost of living. The economy is doing well, and you expect output to be 5% above potential output. Inflation expectations are currently 2%.

   a. Using the Phillips curve in Figure 8, how much of a pay raise will you need to request to be able to buy the same stuff you currently buy?

   b. What if output is 2.5% below potential instead?

   c. What if output is exactly equal to potential output? ∎

Answers: a. Inflation = expected inflation + unexpected inflation = 2% + 1% = 3%. b. If the output gap is –2.5%, the Phillips curve shows unexpected inflation will be –0.5%, so inflation will be 1.5%. c. A 0% output gap corresponds with unexpected inflation of 0%, so inflation will be 2%.

An Alternative Illustration: The Labor Market Phillips Curve

So far, we've described the Phillips curve as the relationship between unexpected inflation and the output gap. We focused on the output gap because it's a measure of output relative to the economy's productive capacity, and so it describes the extent to which managers are dealing with excess demand (which leads them to raise their prices a bit more) or insufficient demand (which leads them to show price restraint). The Federal Reserve has used the output gap and the Phillips curve to forecast inflation since at least the mid-1980s.

But historically, the Phillips curve was drawn a little differently — partly because Phillips's insights pre-dated modern methods for measuring the output gap. This alternative version represents the same ideas — it was just sketched a little differently. Some economists even prefer this alternative version, so it's worth becoming familiar with it.

The labor market Phillips curve links unexpected inflation to the unemployment rate. This alternative approach focuses on the labor market. The idea is that unemployed workers are an unused resource, and so the *unemployment rate* — which is the share of the labor force without a job — provides an alternative measure of whether the economy is producing above or below its productive capacity. If unemployment is high, that means that there are lots of workers who could be hired to help increase output. When unemployment is really low, it can be hard to hire new workers, which in turn makes it hard to raise output to meet demand. Indeed, in Chapter 17, we saw that *Okun's rule of thumb* describes a close link between the output gap and the unemployment rate. It says that a high unemployment rate corresponds with a negative output gap (where output is below potential output, and so insufficient demand is a problem). It also says that an especially low unemployment rate corresponds with a positive output gap (where output exceeds potential output, and so excess demand arises).

It follows that there's an alternative version of the Phillips curve that links low unemployment to higher demand-pull inflation. We can summarize it as saying:

↓ Unemployment rate → ↑ Unexpected inflation

Both versions of the Phillips curve tell the same story. This alternative version of the Phillips curve, which is illustrated in Figure 9, links inflation to unemployment. In order to keep the concepts clear, we'll call this version the **labor market Phillips curve.** It summarizes the *exact* same ideas as the Phillips curve, but it relies on a different measure of excess demand. The most obvious difference — that the curves slope in different directions — is

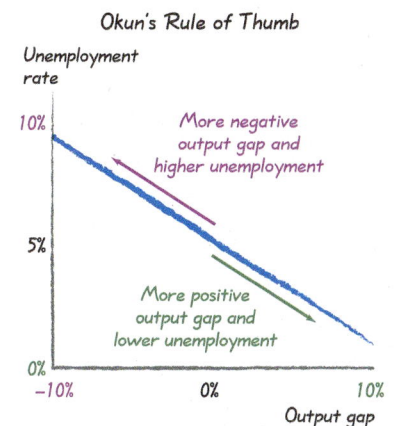

Okun's Rule of Thumb

labor market Phillips curve
A Phillips curve linking unexpected inflation to the unemployment rate.

Figure 9 | **The Labor Market Phillips Curve**

The unemployment rate determines how much inflation will rise above or fall below inflation expectations.

Ⓐ The **unemployment rate** is an alternative indicator of **insufficient or excess demand**.

Ⓑ The **labor market Phillips curve** shows that **higher unemployment leads to lower unexpected inflation**, and **lower unemployment leads to higher unexpected inflation**.

Ⓒ At the **equilibrium unemployment rate, unexpected inflation is zero**, so inflation is equal to inflation expectations.

Unexpected inflation
(Inflation − Inflation expectations)

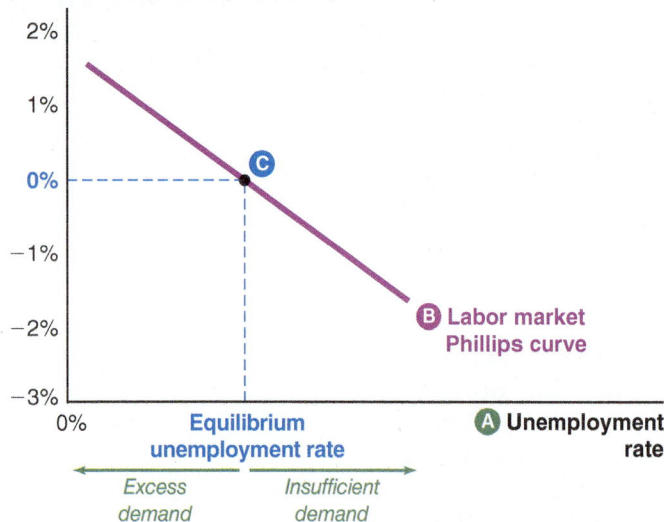

[Figure: graph with vertical axis "Unexpected inflation" ranging from −3% to 2%, horizontal axis "Unemployment rate". A downward-sloping purple line labeled Ⓑ "Labor market Phillips curve". Point Ⓒ where the line crosses 0% unexpected inflation, with dashed lines down to "Equilibrium unemployment rate" on the horizontal axis. To the left of equilibrium is "Excess demand" and to the right is "Insufficient demand". The horizontal axis is labeled Ⓐ "Unemployment rate".]

purely cosmetic. It arises only because excess demand corresponds with a *high* level of output relative to potential output, but a *low* unemployment rate. Both versions of the Phillips curve suggest that excess demand leads to higher inflation.

Inflation is stable at the equilibrium unemployment rate. The inflation rate will be stable only when inflation is equal to inflation expectations, and this occurs at the point where unexpected inflation is 0%. The corresponding unemployment rate is called the *equilibrium unemployment rate*. (You may also hear it called the "natural rate" or the NAIRU, which stands for the "non-accelerating inflation rate of unemployment" — a bit of a mouthful that's trying to say it's the only unemployment rate that will nudge inflation neither higher nor lower.) This is the only unemployment rate that's consistent with stable inflation. The equilibrium unemployment rate is not zero because there remain potential workers who are facing frictional or structural barriers to unemployment. (Remember that we discussed why the equilibrium unemployment rate is not zero, in Chapter 11.) When unemployment is lower than the equilibrium unemployment rate, inflation starts to creep up. It's hard to know with any precision what the equilibrium unemployment rate is — economists debate the matter endlessly — and so rather than emphasizing a particular number, it's probably safer to say that it lies somewhere between 3% and 6%.

Demand-pull inflation is driven by too much demand. We started this chapter by analyzing inflation expectations. We've now also analyzed the demand side of the economy, finding that excess demand creates demand-pull inflation, which causes inflation to rise above inflation expectations. (And insufficient demand causes inflation to fall below inflation expectations.)

While we've analyzed the role of demand in driving price changes, we've yet to explore the role of supply. Let's fix that. As we turn to analyzing how changing supply conditions can produce inflation, we'll discover that supply-side shocks shift the Phillips curve. But to see why, we'll have to explore the link between Outback Steakhouse, global health, and geopolitics.

19.4 Supply Shocks Shift the Phillips Curve

Learning Objective *Assess how shocks to production costs shift the Phillips curve.*

In summer 2021, the pandemic finally seemed to be receding, and executives at Outback Steakhouse breathed a sigh of relief. It had been a rough few years, but they had successfully navigated not only the public health threat but also a deep recession. Their business was intact, and customers were returning to their Australian-themed restaurants (and I can just imagine the shouts of "you bewdy mate!"). The economic recovery meant these customers also had more to spend. Given the improving economy, Outback announced plans to raise its prices by 3%.

But just a few months later, Outback's executives knew they had to revisit those plans. The problem was that Outback's costs were rising. The cost of labor had risen sharply, the global price of beef was up, as was the cost of electricity. Energy prices rose following

Disruptions in one part of the supply chain can ripple out across the globe.

Justin Sullivan/Getty Images

sanctions against Russia, and the price of bread rose amidst concerns that war would destroy Ukraine's wheat crop. Strained supply lines across many sectors led the price of almost every input that Outback relies on to rise.

Ultimately, Outback decided to raise its prices by 5%, which was more than originally planned. Similar pressures led to price rises at the Cheesecake Factory, Cracker Barrel, Chipotle, and many other restaurants. Indeed, higher labor, energy, commodity, and transportation costs affect businesses in nearly every sector. And so the same forces that led Outback to raise its prices by more than they planned also led many other companies to follow suit.

How Supply Shocks Shift the Phillips Curve

This was an example of *cost-push inflation,* where an unexpected boost to production costs pushed sellers to raise their prices.

Rising production costs create an additional reason to raise prices, above and beyond existing inflation expectations and demand-pull pressures. This means that cost-push inflation leads to more inflation at any given level of the output gap, and for any given level of inflation expectations. As Figure 10 illustrates, cost-push inflation causes the Phillips curve to shift.

Rising production costs shift the Phillips curve up. Indeed, *any factor that leads to an unexpected rise in production costs will cause the Phillips curve to shift upward.* The reverse is also true: An unexpected decline in production costs will cause the Phillips curve to shift down as sellers respond by cutting prices (or raising them less). The more that an input price changes, and the more important that input is in the costs of a typical firm, the more it will shift the Phillips curve.

This brings us to our third key insight about the causes of inflation:

Figure 10 | Rising Costs Shift the Phillips Curve

Ⓐ Rising production costs lead to **rising prices** at any given output gap, **shifting the Phillips curve up**.

Ⓑ The result can be that **inflation exceeds inflation expectations**, even when output is below potential output, as at the point shown.

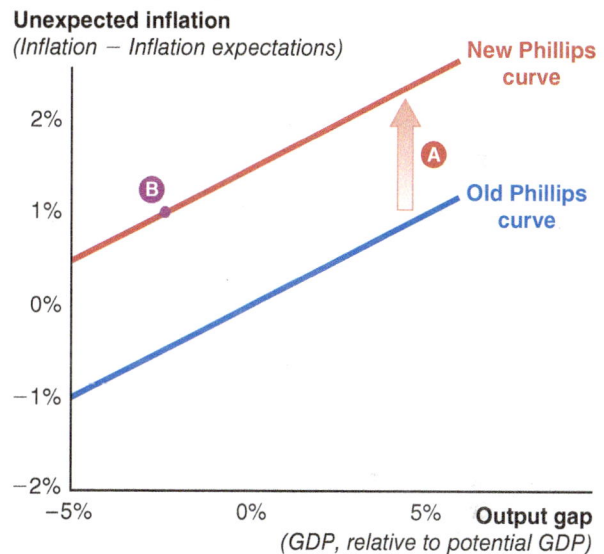

Inflationary Force 3: Cost-Push Inflation
An unexpected rise in production costs will cause higher inflation.
↑ *Production costs* → ↑ *Inflation*

Three causes of supply shocks shift the Phillips curve. This third inflationary force reflects the influence of unexpected changes in production costs, which is why it's called *cost-push inflation.* And because changes in costs shift producers' supply curves, an unexpected change in production costs that shifts the Phillips curve is called a **supply shock.**

There are three causes of supply shocks, and each shifts the Phillips curve: shifts in input prices, shifts in productivity, and shifts in exchange rates. In each case we focus on an *unexpected* change in costs because anticipated rises or falls in input prices will have already been factored into inflation expectations. Let's explore each in turn.

supply shocks Any change in production costs that leads suppliers to change the prices they charge at any given level of output. Supply shocks shift the Phillips curve.

Phillips Curve Shifter 1: Input Prices

Any time the price of your inputs rises, so will your marginal costs, and higher marginal costs lead sellers to raise their prices. Thus, rising input prices lead to rising prices, and because this boosts inflation at any given level of the output gap, it shifts the Phillips curve up. The same forces also operate in reverse, and declining input prices shift the Phillips curve down. The more that an input price changes, and the more important that input is in the costs of a typical firm, the more it will shift the Phillips curve.

The Phillips curve shifts in response to changes in:
1. Input prices
2. Productivity
3. Exchange rates

Input Prices Shift the Phillips Curve

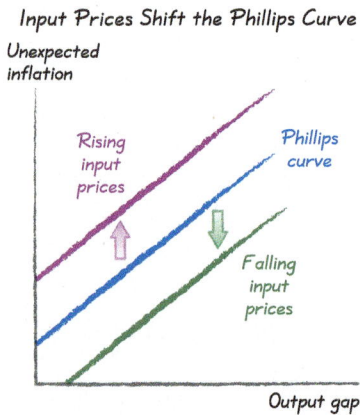

Oil and commodity prices are important input prices. Oil is a major input in many sectors of the economy, and so the changing price of oil has frequently been an important source of cost-push inflation. Oil is important because it can be burned to generate electricity, refined into gasoline or diesel fuel, or synthesized into fertilizer (some of which might be used to grow onions for Outback). A rise in the price of oil has ripple effects throughout the economy, leading to higher electric and heating bills, higher gasoline prices, which lead to higher transportation prices, which raise the prices of nearly everything at your local supermarket. The oil price also bears watching because it has historically been volatile, rising and falling in response to embargoes, wars, and political instability in oil-rich regions, as well as unpredictable discoveries of new energy sources.

Sharp changes in the price of other commodities — including agricultural goods in particular — can also create supply shocks, particularly when severe weather disrupts harvests. It's something that managers at Outback Steakhouse plan for, and indeed, its managers have said that "in most cases increased commodity prices could be passed through to our customers through increases in menu prices." When other companies follow suit, commodity price shocks will generate widespread cost-push inflation.

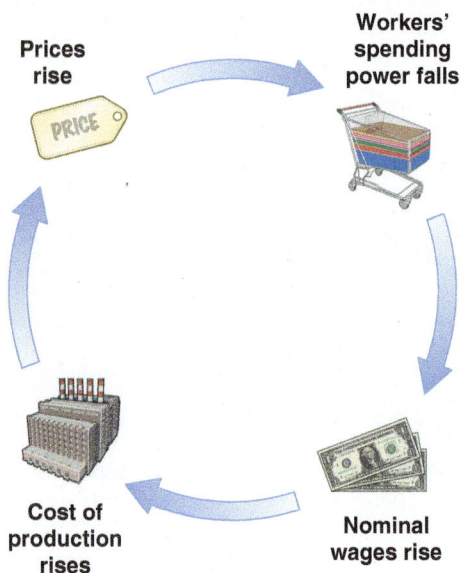

Rising wages can cause a wage-price spiral. Perhaps the most important input price is the price of labor, otherwise known as the hourly wage. A sharp rise in the wages you have to pay to attract quality workers will raise your company's marginal costs, causing many managers to raise their prices. Indeed, in the past, executives at Outback Steakhouse have reported that higher wages "have increased our labor costs . . . To the extent permitted by competition and the economy, we have mitigated increased costs by increasing menu prices." Once again, as other companies follow suit, higher wages will quickly generate cost-push inflation.

Wages are particularly important because they can amplify the effects of a temporary inflation shock and make it persistent. This is because a **wage-price spiral** can take hold, in which workers respond to inflation by demanding higher nominal wages to maintain their spending power, leading businesses to respond to higher wages by raising prices. Thus, an initial inflationary impulse can cause workers to seek higher nominal wages, which causes businesses to further raise their prices, which causes workers to seek higher nominal wages, and so it continues as wages chase prices, and prices chase wages. The result is higher inflation that persists long after the initial inflationary impetus has receded.

wage-price spiral A cycle where higher prices lead to higher nominal wages, which leads to higher prices.

Phillips Curve Shifter 2: Productivity

Your company's productivity also changes your production costs, as a more productive firm needs less of each input to produce the same output. It follows that faster-than-expected productivity growth lowers your marginal costs, leading to greater price restraint at any given output gap. As a result, stronger productivity growth shifts the Phillips curve down — a form of negative cost-push inflation.

It also works the other way. Productivity growth through the 1960s had been quite rapid, and many businesses had gotten in the habit of giving their employees large nominal wage raises without it causing their per-unit costs to rise. But in the mid-1970s, productivity growth slowed even as wages continued to grow rapidly. The result was rising per-unit production costs that led to cost-push inflation. And so weaker productivity growth shifted the Phillips curve up.

Productivity Growth Shifts the Phillips Curve

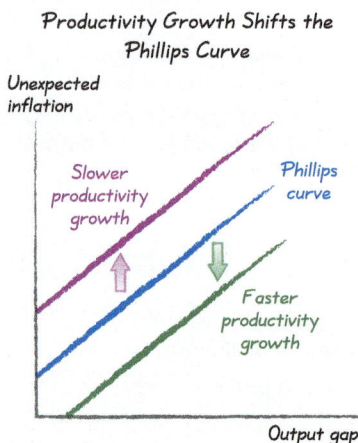

Phillips Curve Shifter 3: Exchange Rates

The nominal exchange rate also creates cost-push inflation, thereby shifting the Phillips curve. There's both a direct effect on the price of goods made overseas and an indirect effect due to the changing prices of foreign goods putting pressure on the prices of domestically produced goods.

Direct effect: When the U.S. dollar depreciates, foreign goods are more expensive. A reminder: The *exchange rate* is the price of a U.S. dollar. For instance, when the exchange rate is 120 Japanese yen per dollar, that means that one U.S. dollar costs 120 Japanese yen. We say that the U.S. dollar *depreciates* when the price of a U.S. dollar falls, say to 100 yen. It means the U.S. dollar becomes cheaper for foreigners to buy; it also means that foreign currency is more expensive for Americans to buy because it will cost more dollars to buy a specific quantity of yen.

This is relevant because you'll need foreign currency to buy goods from foreigners. When the U.S. dollar depreciates, then each U.S. dollar buys less foreign currency. In turn, that means it will take more U.S. dollars to pay for imported goods. And so a depreciating U.S. dollar directly increases the price of foreign-made goods, boosting inflation.

Indirect effects: More expensive foreign goods lead to higher prices on domestic goods. There are also indirect effects that lead American producers to raise their prices:

- *For businesses that rely on imported inputs*: A depreciating U.S. dollar raises the cost (in U.S. dollars) of their imported inputs, and these higher marginal costs lead them to raise their prices.
- *For businesses that compete with imported products*: A depreciating U.S. dollar raises the price (in dollars) of goods made by foreign competitors. This weakens the competitive pressure on domestic businesses, leading some of them to raise their prices.
- *For businesses that export their products*: A depreciating U.S. dollar means that their foreign customers are now willing to pay more (in dollars) for their products. This increased demand from foreign customers may lead some companies to raise the prices they charge their customers in the United States.

A depreciating U.S. dollar shifts the Phillips curve up; an appreciating U.S. dollar shifts the Phillips curve down. Together, these direct and indirect effects mean that a depreciating U.S. dollar boosts inflation at any level of the output gap, thereby shifting the Phillips curve up. When the same forces operate in reverse, a rising value of the U.S. dollar — which we call an *appreciation* of the exchange rate — lowers inflation at any given output gap, shifting the Phillips curve down.

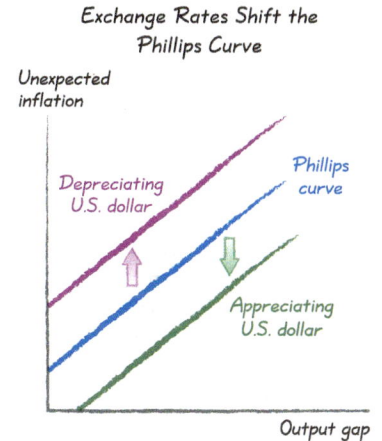

Exchange Rates Shift the Phillips Curve

Shifts versus Movements Along the Phillips Curve

We've covered a lot of ground, so before we conclude, let's recap. We'll do so in a way that clarifies the difference between factors that cause a movement along the Phillips curve, and factors that cause a shift in the Phillips curve.

Demand-pull inflation leads to movement along the Phillips curve. The Phillips curve illustrates the impact of demand-pull factors, showing how inflation changes in response to the output gap. Thus, booms and busts — which lead to changes in the output gap — represent movements *along* the Phillips curve.

Cost-push inflation leads to a shift in the Phillips curve. In contrast, any other factor that changes producers' pricing decisions for a given output gap leads to a shift in the Phillips curve. A shift in your production costs creates pressure to shift your prices, and this occurs whatever the output gap is. We call these shifts supply shocks.

Rising production costs lead to higher marginal costs, causing businesses to raise their prices. The result will be higher inflation at any level of the output gap. Thus, rising production costs shift the Phillips curve up. On the flip side, falling production costs lead businesses to raise their prices by a bit less, or even cut them. The result will be lower inflation at any level of the output gap. Thus, falling production costs shift the Phillips curve down.

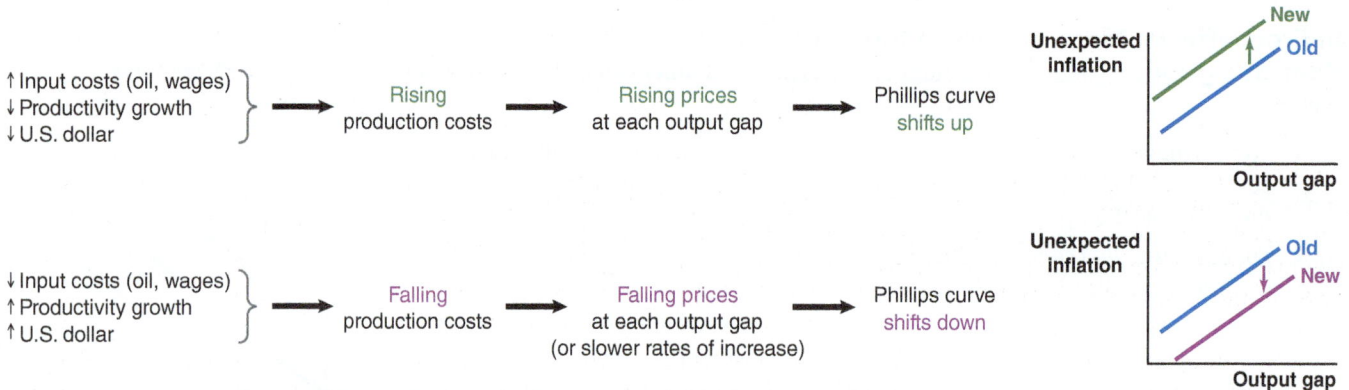

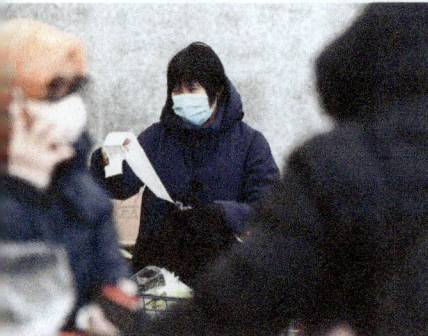

The Phillips curve is about short-run trade-offs, while inflation expectations remain relevant in the long run. We began this chapter by describing inflation expectations as the key long-run cause of inflation. Inflation expectations neither shift the Phillips curve nor cause a movement along it, but they still play an important role in driving inflation. Recall that total inflation is the sum of expected inflation and unexpected inflation. The Phillips curve focuses on the short run in which inflation deviates from inflation expectations, and so it explains *unexpected inflation*. By contrast, rising inflation expectations lead to a rise in *expected inflation*. Thus, changes in inflation expectations are an important long-run factor determining overall inflation at any given level of the output gap and for any given constellation of input costs.

If you expect prices to rise, they probably will.

Is it a demand shock or a supply shock? You can use this framework to better understand why inflation is occurring and whether high or low inflation is likely to continue.

- Demand-pull inflation always leads the output gap and unexpected inflation to move in the same direction: More output leads to higher inflation (for a given level of inflation expectations), while less output leads to less inflation (again, for a given level of inflation expectations). This means that if you see rising demand and rising inflation, you can infer that at least some of the increase in inflation is due to rising demand. This also happened in 2021, particularly late in the year as consumer demand rose sharply and outpaced the productive capacity of the economy.

- Supply shocks can lead to higher inflation, even when output has declined. This means that if you see the double-whammy of higher unexpected inflation and lower output, you can infer that there has been a supply shock. This is what happened in late 2020 and 2021, when output had yet to recover to pre-pandemic output but prices began to rise because of an uptick in global shipping costs and other supply constraints.

- Finally, if inflation rises in line with measures of inflation expectations, then you can infer that inflation expectations have shifted.

19.5 | Tying It Together

In the Long Run, Expectations Are All That Matter

It's time to pan back to take in the big picture. The Phillips curve is central to macroeconomics because it links developments in the real economy — like the output gap or the unemployment rate — with their implications for purely nominal variables, like inflation. But that link has very different implications in the short run versus the long run, and so our final task is to spell those differences out.

Let's start with the *short run,* by which I mean the year-to-year economic fluctuations over the course of a business cycle. In the short run, the Phillips curve illustrates how developments in the real economy shape nominal variables like inflation. For instance, when output is temporarily above potential output, higher inflation will result. Likewise, it suggests that nominal variables affect the real economy. For instance, policymakers can achieve temporarily higher output by allowing inflation to temporarily rise. But this is only a short-run trade-off.

In the *long run* — over periods measured in decades rather than years — the determinants of inflation are very different. Over the long run, the ups and downs of the output gap will average out. (Sometimes the output gap will be positive, and sometimes it will be negative, but on average, it will be close to zero.) The ups and downs of supply shocks will also average out. So neither demand-pull nor cost-push factors matter much over the long run.

This means that in the long run, *inflation expectations* determine inflation. That's a big deal. It means that in the long run, nominal variables like inflation are *not* determined by real variables like output or unemployment. And real variables like output or unemployment are not determined by nominal variables like inflation. This implies that real and nominal variables are unrelated in the long run, an insight sometimes called the **classical dichotomy** because it was first articulated by the early classical economists. This is the idea that in the long run, adding an extra zero at the end of every price tag (including wage rates, bank balances, and currency) wouldn't change how much stuff gets made, how many people work, or indeed, any real variable.

classical dichotomy A purely nominal change — like a change in the average price level — won't have any effect on real variables in the long run.

This distinction between the short- and long-run determinants of inflation lies at the heart of one of the most consequential misinterpretations of the Phillips curve. It's tempting to read the Phillips curve as presenting a trade-off between more output and higher inflation. It appears to suggest that policymakers can choose either more output paired with high inflation, or less output paired with low inflation. Indeed, for a while in the 1960s, some policymakers seemed to believe just that: They read the Phillips curve as if it were a menu of options and their job was just to choose the best macroeconomic meal — their preferred combination of inflation and output. Indeed, they often thought that a little bit of inflation wasn't too high a price to pay for a stronger economy that would raise output and lower unemployment.

It's a tempting inference to draw, but it's also mistaken. Just because high inflation is a common *consequence* of high levels of output doesn't mean that allowing high inflation will lead to sustainably higher output. The problem is that high inflation eventually feeds through to create high inflation expectations.

When policymakers push output above potential output, the immediate impact — illustrated by the Phillips curve — is to push inflation above inflation expectations. Over time, higher inflation leads to higher inflation expectations. If policymakers persist in trying to keep output above potential, the Phillips curve says that a positive output gap will cause inflation to exceed these higher inflation expectations. In turn, this higher inflation leads to even higher inflation expectations. The result is that keeping output above potential leads to ever-rising rates of inflation. As Nobel Prize–winning economist Milton Friedman noted in 1968:

> There is always a temporary trade-off between inflation and unemployment; there is no permanent trade-off. The temporary trade-off comes not from inflation per se, but from unanticipated inflation, which generally means, from a rising rate of inflation.

Figure 11 | **During the "Great Inflation" Rising Inflation Led to Rising Inflation Expectations**

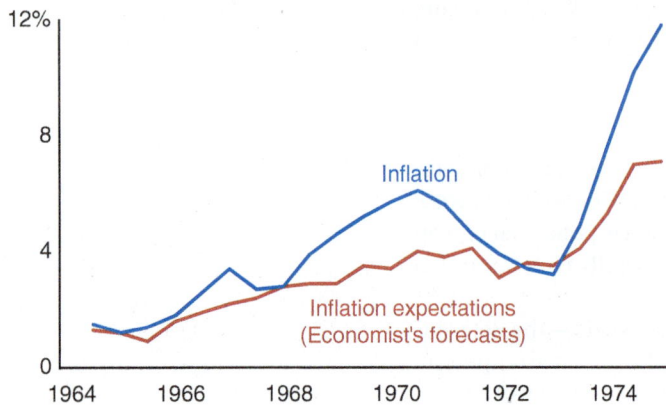

Data from: Livingston Survey and BLS.

Policymakers ended up learning this lesson the hard way. Throughout the late 1960s and 1970s the government made successive attempts to boost the economy by passing tax cuts, increasing government spending, and lowering interest rates. These led to higher inflation, as shown in Figure 11, but no lasting effect on output. The result was a period known as the "Great Inflation," in which inflation rose sharply, and Americans got used to double-digit inflation. The problem was that once policymakers signaled that they were willing to tolerate somewhat higher inflation, people began to expect higher inflation. And so we got the self-fulfilling prophecy of higher inflation due to higher inflation expectations, but no lasting improvements in output.

It was a painful lesson, and it led to a rethinking of the Phillips curve. Today, policymakers understand that the Phillips curve is a useful tool for predicting how inflation will respond to the ups and downs of the business cycle, but it shouldn't be read as a menu of options. We now know that there's no long-run trade-off between inflation and output.

Chapter 19 Review

Chapter at a Glance

Inflation **=** Expected inflation **+** Demand-pull inflation **+** Cost-push inflation

↑Inflation expectations →↑Inflation   ↑Output gap →↑Inflation   ↑Production costs →↑Inflation

The Three Causes of Inflation

Cause #1. Inflation expectations: *Higher inflation expectations create higher inflation.*
↑Inflation expectations ⟶ ↑Inflation

Inflation expectations (the rate at which you expect prices to rise, on average, across the whole economy over the next year) are a key driver of long-run inflation.
• Three ways to track inflation expectations: surveys, economists' forecasts, and financial markets.
• Monetary policy tries to shape inflation expectations.

Cause #2. Demand-pull inflation: *The output gap drives inflation to rise above or fall below inflation expectations.*
↑Output gap ⟶ ↑Inflation (relative to inflation expectations)

Unexpected inflation
(Inflation − Inflation expectations)

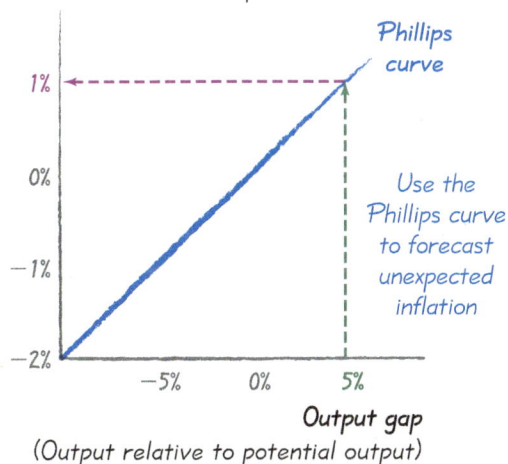

Output gap
(Output relative to potential output)

Demand-pull inflation is driven by the output gap (which measures actual output relative to potential output). It leads inflation to diverge from inflation expectations.

• **Excess demand** (when output > potential output)
  => inflation rises above expected inflation.
• **Insufficient demand** (when output < potential output)
  => inflation falls below expected inflation.
• When output is equal to potential output
  => inflation = inflation expectations.

Demand-pull inflation creates a link between the output gap and unexpected inflation. When you graph this link, the result is known as the Phillips curve.

Cause #3. Cost-push inflation: *An unexpected rise in production costs will cause higher inflation.*
↑Production costs ⟶ ↑Inflation

Unexpected inflation
(Inflation − Inflation expectations)

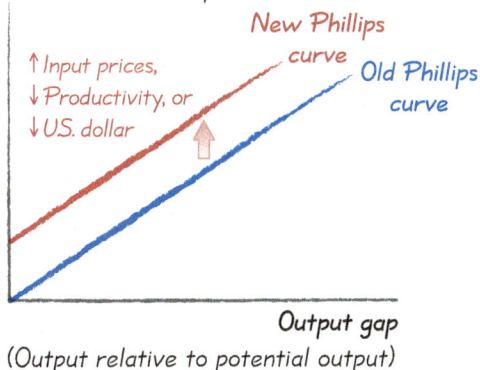

Output gap
(Output relative to potential output)

Rising production costs lead to more inflation at any given level of the output gap, and for any given level of inflation expectations.

Cost-push inflation causes the Phillips curve to shift.

Three types of supply shocks shift the Phillips curve

1. Input prices
2. Productivity
3. Exchange rates

Key Terms

classical dichotomy, 513

cost-push inflation, 497

demand-pull inflation, 496

excess demand, 502

inflation expectations, 496

insufficient demand, 502

labor market Phillips curve, 507

Phillips curve, 504

supply shock, 509

unexpected inflation, 503

wage-price spiral, 510

Study Problems

Learning Objective 19.1 *Identify the three causes of inflation: inflation expectations, demand-pull inflation, and supply shocks.*

1. Rare earth metals are used in the production of many of the personal electronic devices you use every day. Use the interdependence principle to discuss the impact of an unexpected increase in the price of rare earth metals on inflation.

2. You've been invited to help a foreign affiliate of your company set next year's prices. Inflation last year was 5%, the unemployment rate dropped to record lows, and GDP skyrocketed. In addition, geopolitical tensions led the price of crude oil to rise by 50%. Given these circumstances, what do you think annual inflation will be next year, and how will this affect your advice? Explain your reasoning.

3. For each of the following, determine whether inflation expectations, demand-pull inflation, or cost-push inflation — and hence inflation overall — will change.

   a. A rapid influx of foreign investment causes the output gap to become more positive.

   b. The president unexpectedly announces a tariff on aluminum and steel.

Learning Objective 19.2 *Explore how inflation expectations lead to inflation.*

4. Explain how inflation expectations are like a self-fulfilling prophecy.

5. In June 2019, the average price for a cup of coffee in Venezuela was 6,500 bolivars; in June 2018 the average price was just 8 bolivars. This represents an 81,150% increase in a cup of coffee for Venezuelans, who have seen similarly dramatic increases in the prices of everything they buy. Discuss how this experience impacted the inflation expectations of the average Venezuelan during that time, and how those expectations can impact actual inflation.

6. In January 2019, inflation expectations in the United Kingdom fell from 2.9% to 2.6%. What effect will this have on inflation in the United Kingdom if nothing else changes in the economy? Explain your reasoning.

7. Seana owns a small pet shop and expects inflation to be 3% next year. By how much does Seana expect her marginal costs to change? By how much does she expect her competitor's prices to change?

8. You're a pricing analyst for a manufacturing firm. You are tasked with predicting how average prices will change over the next quarter to help your manager decide how to change her prices. How would you find the best estimate of the likely inflation rate? What do you tell your manager, and why?

Learning Objective 19.3 *Analyze the link between the output gap and inflation.*

9. Explain the difference between expected inflation and unexpected inflation.

10. Draw an example of a Phillips curve and a labor market Phillips curve. Explain how they summarize the exact same idea while using different measures of excess demand.

11. You're a junior consultant at a management consulting company and your team has been hired to help guide a struggling regional retailer. You do some research and find that the output gap is currently zero, and inflation is 4%. In an effort to boost output before the next election, the government announces an unexpected stimulus package that you expect will increase next year's output to be 5% above potential.

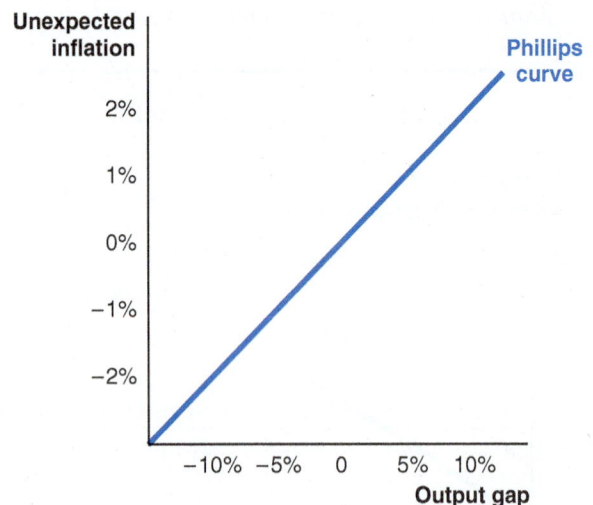

   a. Use the Phillips curve to estimate unexpected inflation after the stimulus.

b. What is your forecast for actual inflation after the stimulus?

c. How do you advise the retailer when they ask you how they should change prices next year, given that the stimulus will have boosted output?

12. Take the Phillips curve from the previous question and illustrate the corresponding labor market Phillips curve where the initial unemployment rate was $7\frac{1}{2}\%$ and the final unemployment rate is $2\frac{1}{2}\%$. What is the equilibrium unemployment rate in the economy?

Learning Objective 19.4 *Assess how shocks to production costs shift the Phillips curve.*

13. If Congress levies a new $1,000 per car tax on car manufacturers to pay for expanded Social Security benefits, how do you think this will impact unexpected inflation?

14. The adoption of vehicle automation has exploded over the last few years: Automated tractors are already in use harvesting produce on farms, while self-driving vehicles are used to move cargo around shipping yards and warehouses. Use a Phillips curve to help explain how this technological change impacts inflation.

15. Recently, policymakers have debated whether an increase in the federal minimum wage (currently $7.25 an hour) would be good for the economy. Use a Phillips curve to explain how inflation would change for the following scenarios. Assume that the output gap does not change.

a. Policymakers announce that effective next week the federal minimum wage will be $15 an hour.

b. Policymakers announce that the federal minimum wage will increase to $15 an hour over the course of the next 10 years by annual increases of $0.78.

c. Explain how the initial increase in the federal minimum wage for low-wage earners could lead to a wage-price spiral throughout the economy.

16. Since 2010, the U.S. dollar has appreciated relative to the Mexican peso. What are the direct and indirect effects on inflation? Explain.

17. Identify whether the following will represent a shift in the Phillips curve or a movement along the Phillips curve. Illustrate with a graph.

a. Consumer confidence increases unexpectedly and causes the output gap to become more positive.

b. Inflation last year was far greater than even the best forecaster expected even though the output gap was zero.

c. A devastating late-spring freeze destroys crops across the eastern United States, which causes the output gap to become more negative.

The Fed Model: Putting the Pieces Together

It's about the size of an old refrigerator, and runs on water. The motor, scavenged from an old military plane, pumps pink-dyed water through a series of transparent plastic tubes and into a variety of tanks, at a rate determined by finely tuned valves. Built in the 1940s by New Zealand economist Bill Phillips, the Monetary National Income Analog Computer, or MONIAC for short, was the most ambitious attempt of its time to account for all the moving parts within the economy.

The MONIAC provided a creative solution to the central challenge of macroeconomics: tracking the many forms of interdependence that make the field so interesting. The water represents flows of income. The valves are calibrated to regulate the flow of water in a way that resembles the economic relationships that determine the flow of income. The valves that determine the rate at which water flows into tanks have neat labels explaining that they represent consumption, investment, government purchases, imports, and exports.

An analog model of the economy.

Want to forecast what will happen if businesses invest more? Tweak the right valve, let the water flow, and see what happens. Paper spools atop the machine and four pens connected to floats within different tanks trace the model economy's ups and downs. Let the water run long enough, and you'll discover where it settles in equilibrium. One Cambridge professor described it as "a thing of wonder and joy." Versions of this liquid economy were used to teach economics at universities around the world, and the Ford Motor Company bought one. If you ever visit the Science Museum in London, you can see it for yourself.

Fortunately, economics has progressed since Phillips's time, so our models no longer look like Rube Goldberg contraptions. But the challenge of how to piece together our partial understanding of economic relationships in a way that accounts for their interdependencies remains central to macroeconomics. And so in this chapter, we're going to do with simple graphs the same thing that the MONIAC tried to do with water: We'll combine key economic relationships to see how they interact to determine macroeconomic outcomes. Think of this chapter as a capstone that draws the various threads of our study of business cycles together. The result will look less like Phillips's liquid data, and more like the sorts of analyses that power government policy decisions, Wall Street investments, and the strategic choices of big businesses.

Chapter Objective

Put the pieces together into a complete model of business cycles.

20.1 The Fed Model
Analyze the Fed model, which puts together the *IS* curve, the *MP* curve, and the Phillips curve.

20.2 Analyzing Macroeconomic Shocks
Use the Fed model to analyze the consequences of financial shocks, spending shocks, and supply shocks.

20.3 Diagnosing the Causes of Macroeconomic Changes
Use the Fed model to diagnose the causes of economic fluctuations.

🎙 Podcast
Think Like an Economist
The Fed Model—Predicting What Will Happen to the Economy

What happens when we put the pieces together?

Fed model The framework that uses the *IS* curve, the *MP* curve, and the Phillips curve to link interest rates, the output gap, and inflation.

20.1 The Fed Model

Learning Objective *Analyze the Fed model, which puts together the IS curve, the MP curve, and the Phillips curve.*

Over the past two chapters you've done something pretty extraordinary: You've developed all of the components necessary to construct a complete model of business cycles. You can draw links from monetary policy and financial markets to interest rates using the *MP* curve, then from the real interest rate through spending decisions to output using the *IS* curve, and then from the consequences for the output gap through to the resulting inflationary pressure using the Phillips curve.

In this chapter, we'll put these components together. The result isn't just a textbook tool — it's the actual framework that businesses, economists, and policymakers use to understand the ups and downs of the business cycle. We call it the **Fed model,** because it's the framework that policymakers at the Federal Reserve use to analyze, forecast, and tweak the economy. They use it because it represents the state of the art model for understanding business cycles.

The Fed Model Combines the *IS*, *MP*, and Phillips Curves

All that remains is to put each of the pieces of our analysis together into this whole. In Chapter 18, you analyzed how the intersection of the *IS* and *MP* curves determines the output gap. And in Chapter 19, you explored the Phillips curve, which illustrates how the output gap shapes inflation. Put the pieces from these two chapters together, and you'll be able to forecast interest rates, the output gap, and inflation.

You can see the connections as follows:

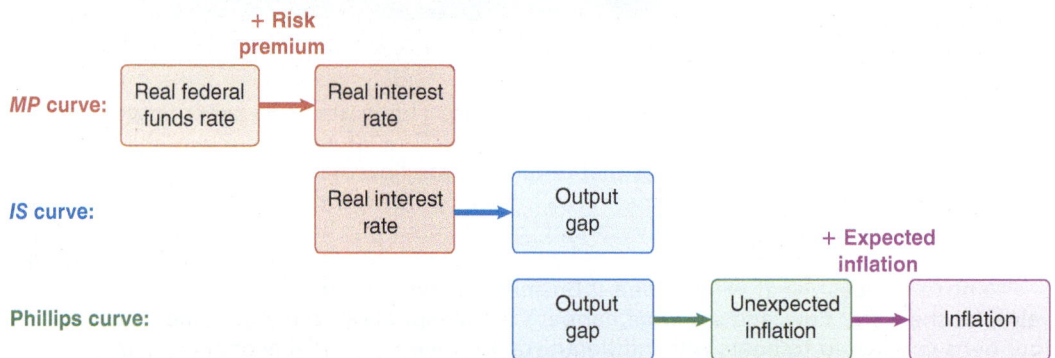

MP curve: Real federal funds rate → **+ Risk premium** → Real interest rate

IS curve: Real interest rate → Output gap

Phillips curve: Output gap → Unexpected inflation → **+ Expected inflation** → Inflation

The Fed model isn't a distinct mode of analysis. Rather, it puts together the pieces you've already developed. That's why it's sometimes also called *IS-MP-PC analysis,* because it combines *IS-MP* analysis with the Phillips curve (or "PC" to its friends):

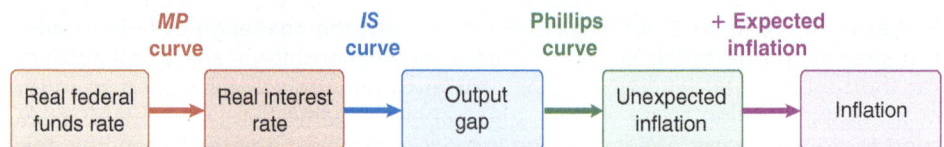

Real federal funds rate → **MP curve** → Real interest rate → **IS curve** → Output gap → **Phillips curve** → Unexpected inflation → **+ Expected inflation** → Inflation

Forecasting Economic Outcomes

Putting these pieces together requires stepping through each of the basic tools we've developed in the past two chapters, in turn.

Start by finding the output gap. Begin your analysis with the *IS-MP* framework, which determines the output gap. We do this in the top panel of Figure 1, which reproduces a familiar chart from Chapter 18. Remember that the vertical axis is the real interest rate and the horizontal axis is the output gap. The *MP* curve is a horizontal line illustrating the current real interest rate, and the *IS* curve is a downward-sloping line illustrating how a lower real interest rate stimulates more spending and output.

Figure 1 | **The Fed Model**

Use the IS-MP framework to find the output gap and the Phillips curve to forecast unexpected inflation.

Start by finding the output gap

Ⓐ Find equilibrium at the point where the **IS curve** intersects the **MP curve**.

Ⓑ Look to the left at the vertical axis to find the **real interest rate**, which is **3%**.

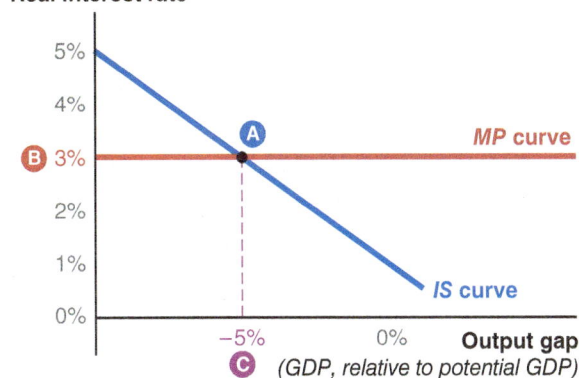

Ⓒ Then look down at the horizontal axis to find **the output gap**, which is **−5%**.

Next, assess inflation

Ⓓ Trace the **output gap** down to the lower graph.

Ⓔ Find the point on the **Phillips curve** with the **same output gap**.

Ⓕ Look to the left at the vertical axis to find **unexpected inflation**, which is **−1%**.

Ⓖ Calculate **Actual inflation** = **Unexpected inflation** + **Expected inflation**.

Importantly, macroeconomic equilibrium occurs where the *MP* curve cuts the *IS* curve. You can look down from the point where the curves cross to find the resulting output gap. In the example shown in Figure 1, you would forecast an output gap of −5%.

Next, assess inflation. Use the Phillips curve to figure out the inflationary implications of this output gap. I've stacked the Phillips curve directly under the *IS-MP* curves in Figure 1, so you can trace the output gap down from the top panel to the lower panel until you hit the Phillips curve. Once you've found the Phillips curve, you just need to look across to find out what will happen to inflation. Recall that the vertical axis of the Phillips curve tells you what will happen to *unexpected* inflation, and you also need to consider the influence of inflation expectations. So to forecast actual inflation, you'll add this forecast of unexpected inflation to the latest reading of inflation expectations.

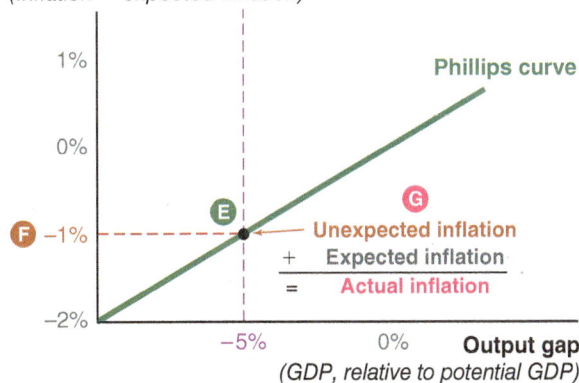

In this example, an output gap of −5% leads to unexpected inflation of −1%, which means that actual inflation will be 1% below expected inflation. If inflation expectations are 2%, this says inflation will be 1%.

You can see why Fed economists like this style of analysis — it delivers a complete set of forecasts: the real interest rate will be 3%, the output gap will be −5%, and unexpected inflation will be −1%, and so if expected inflation is 2%, inflation will be 1%.

But what will happen if economic conditions change? That's where the Fed model really shines. So let's read on.

Warning: Potential shocks ahead.

financial shocks Any change in borrowing conditions that changes the real interest rate at which people can borrow. Financial shocks shift the *MP* curve.

spending shocks Any change in aggregate expenditure at a given real interest rate and level of income. Spending shocks shift the *IS* curve.

supply shocks Any change in production costs that leads suppliers to change the prices they charge at any given level of output. Supply shocks shift the Phillips curve.

Types of shocks:
- Financial
- Spending
- Supply

Three Types of Macroeconomic Shocks

There are dozens of shocks that might hit the economy. You can just imagine the headlines: Stocks crater! Productivity surges! Banks fail! Confidence soars! Exports wither! Dollar skyrockets! Fed raises rates! Pandemic worsens! Oil prices rise! Supply chains snarl! Wages boom! And so on . . . (So! Many! Exclamation! Points!)

There are financial shocks, spending shocks, and supply shocks. Fortunately, the Fed model categorizes each of these many possibilities into one of three types of shocks, each of which is familiar from the past two chapters.

- **Financial shocks:** Any change in *borrowing conditions* that affects the real interest rate — whether due to the Federal Reserve shifting the federal funds rate, or changes in financial markets shifting the risk premium — will shift the *MP* curve.

- **Spending shocks:** Any change in *aggregate expenditure* at a given real interest rate and level of income — whether due to consumption, planned investment, government expenditure, or net exports — will shift the *IS* curve.

- **Supply shocks:** Any change in *production costs* that leads suppliers to change the prices they charge at any given level of output will shift the Phillips curve. Common supply shocks include changes in input prices, import prices, productivity, and the exchange rate.

The Fed model brings together three curves, which are shifted by the three kinds of shocks. Thus, we can summarize our complete framework — which includes the *IS, MP,* and Phillips curves, as well as the economic shocks that cause each of them to shift — as follows:

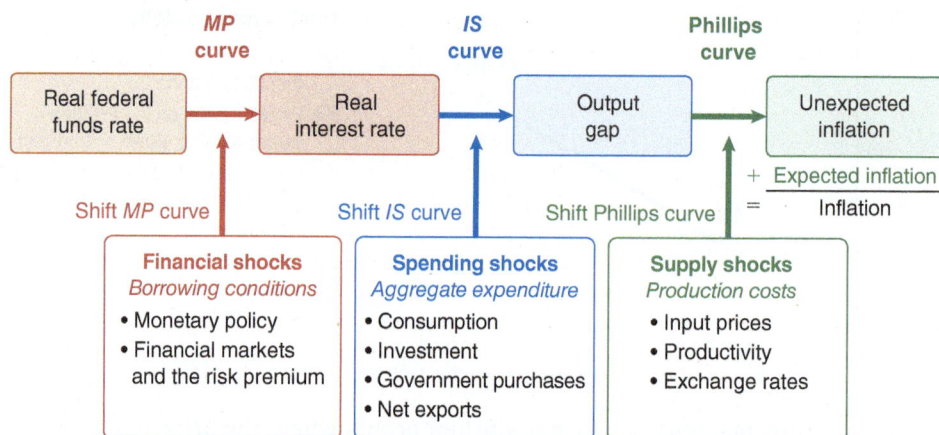

This taxonomy is tremendously helpful because it means that forecasting the consequences of whichever of the zillion things that might happen next to the economy — a disruption in financial markets, plummeting consumer confidence, or rising oil prices — doesn't require a zillion different kinds of analysis. Rather, you simply need to figure out if you're dealing with a financial shock (such as when disruptions in financial markets lead the risk premium to rise), a spending shock (such as when plummeting consumer confidence leads to a decrease in consumption), or a supply shock (such as when oil prices skyrocket). Then it's simply a matter of exploring how that type of shock will affect the economy.

20.2 Analyzing Macroeconomic Shocks

Learning Objective *Use the Fed model to analyze the consequences of financial shocks, spending shocks, and supply shocks.*

One of the most important uses of a macroeconomic framework like the Fed model is to forecast how the economy will respond if a macroeconomic shock knocks it off its current path. That's going to be our next task.

Viorika/E+/Getty Images

A Three-Step Recipe for Analyzing Macroeconomic Shocks

Three steps for analyzing macroeconomic shocks:
1. Identify the shock to determine which curve to shift (and where)
2. Find the output gap
3. Assess inflation

This task is all about exploring the consequences of a shift in the *IS*, *MP*, and Phillips curves. And it'll be a lot simpler if you follow this simple three-step recipe:

Step 1: Identify the shock to determine which curve to shift in which direction. The first thing you need to do is to identify the shock, so you can shift the relevant curve in the appropriate direction. Is this a change in borrowing conditions (a *financial* shock, which shifts the *MP* curve), a change in aggregate expenditure (a *spending* shock, which shifts the *IS* curve), or a change in production costs (a *supply* shock, which shifts the Phillips curve)?

As you assess which direction you should shift the curve, remember the key lessons of the past two chapters:

Financial Shocks Shift the *MP* Curve
An increase in interest rates shifts the *MP* curve up, while a decrease shifts it down.

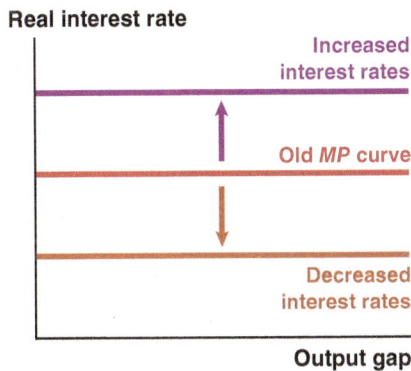

Spending Shocks Shift the *IS* Curve
An increase in aggregate expenditure shifts the *IS* curve to the right, while a decrease shifts it to the left.

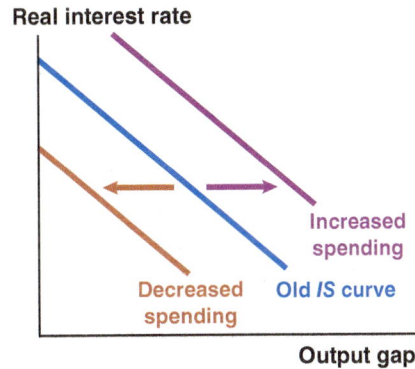

Supply Shocks Shift the Phillips Curve
Rising production costs shift the Phillips curve up, while falling production costs shift it down.

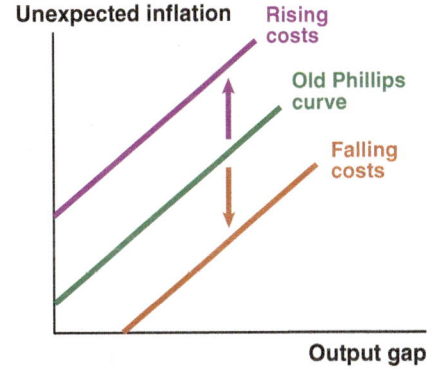

Step 2: Find the output gap. Once you've shifted the appropriate curve in the appropriate direction — or multiple curves if there are multiple shocks — the rest of this process is about analyzing the new equilibrium. And so the second step is familiar: Look at the intersection of the (new) *IS* and *MP* curves to find the equilibrium output gap and real interest rate.

Step 3: Assess inflation. Finally, trace the output gap down from the *IS-MP* graph to the (potentially shifted) Phillips curve to find the inflationary implications of this output gap. Remember, the Phillips curve is all about *unexpected* inflation, and so to forecast actual inflation, you'll add this forecast of unexpected inflation to the latest reading of inflation expectations.

We'll use this three-step recipe to explore the likely consequences of each of the three kinds of shocks: financial shocks, then spending shocks, and finally, supply shocks.

In each of the examples that follow, we'll start with an economy at rest with an output gap of zero and with unexpected inflation of zero (so inflation equals expected inflation). Then we'll forecast how the economy will respond to a shock. Economists are often a pessimistic group, and so in each case we'll analyze adverse shocks that make economic conditions worse. To figure out the effects of a positive shock, simply move the corresponding curve in the opposite direction.

Analyzing Financial Shocks

A financial shock occurs whenever borrowing conditions change the real interest rate at which you can borrow money, thereby shifting the *MP* curve. An increase in the real interest rate will shift the *MP* curve up, while a decrease will shift it down.

Changing borrowing conditions in financial markets shift the *MP* curve.

The *MP* curve shifts in response to monetary policy and financial market risks. The real interest rate is the sum of the risk-free interest rate set by the Federal Reserve and the risk premium determined in financial markets. This means that the *MP* curve will shift in response to changes in:

- *Monetary policy:* When the Federal Reserve raises or lowers the risk-free real interest rate, the rate borrowers pay also changes, shifting the *MP* curve.

- *Financial market risks:* Any change that makes banks more reluctant to lend money at a given interest rate will raise the risk premium, raising the interest rate that borrowers pay, and shifting the *MP* curve. This could arise due to concerns that borrowers may not be able to repay their debt, concerns about liquidity, uncertainty about future interest rates, or rising risk aversion.

(If you feel a bit rusty on this, take a moment to review "Financial Shocks Shift the *MP* Curve" in Chapter 18.)

Higher interest rates lead to lower output and lower inflation. Okay, now it's time to figure out the consequences of an adverse financial shock that raises the real interest rate from 1% to 3%. To figure out the consequences, we'll work through our three-step recipe in Figure 2.

Figure 2 | **Financial Shocks Shift the *MP* Curve**

An upward shift of the MP *curve leads to a decrease in output and lower inflation.*

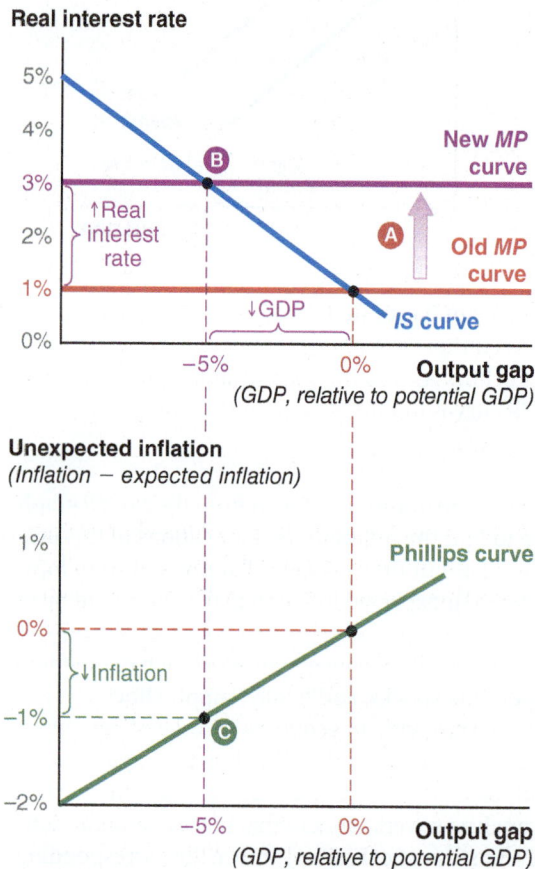

Step 1: Shift the curve

Ⓐ A financial shock shifts the **MP curve** up to the **new real interest rate**.

Look left to find the new real interest rate has risen to **3%**.

Step 2: Find the output gap

Ⓑ Find the new equilibrium where the **IS curve** intersects with the **new MP curve**.

Look down to find that output has fallen and the new output gap is **−5%**.

Step 3: Assess inflation

Ⓒ Look down to find the point on the **Phillips curve** with the same output gap.

Look left to find the new unexpected inflation rate has fallen to **−1%**.

If inflation expectations are unchanged, the actual inflation rate will be 1% lower.

Step 1: *Shift the curve.* Higher real interest rates shift the *MP* curve up by 2 percentage points to a real interest rate of 3%.

Step 2: *Find the output gap.* The new equilibrium occurs where this *new MP* curve crosses the *IS* curve. In this example, this occurs when output shrinks to be 5% below potential output.

Step 3: *Assess inflation.* Trace this output gap down onto the Phillips curve to assess the inflationary consequences. In this case, an output gap of –5% will cause unexpected inflation to decline to –1%. Thus, if expected inflation is unchanged at 2%, actual inflation will fall to be one percentage point lower, at 1%.

You can track the effects as follows:

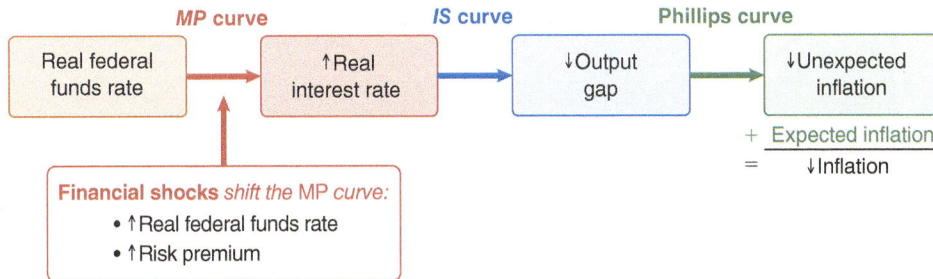

All told, we conclude that a financial shock that leads to higher real interest rates will also lead to lower output and lower inflation. Let's now turn to the effects of spending shocks.

Analyzing Spending Shocks

Spending shocks occur whenever there's been a change in spending — in any element of aggregate expenditure — at a given real interest rate and level of income. An increase in spending will shift the *IS* curve to the right, while a decrease will shift it to the left.

The *IS* curve shifts in response to changes in aggregate expenditure. Total spending is the sum of consumption, planned investment, government purchases, and net exports. This means that the *IS* curve will shift in response to changes in:

- *Consumption,* which may be driven by changes in wealth, consumer confidence, government assistance, taxes, or inequality.
- *Planned investment,* which changes in response to changes in future economic growth, business confidence, investment tax credits, corporate taxes, lending standards, cash reserves, or uncertainty.
- *Government spending,* which reflects the government's fiscal policy, and the operation of automatic stabilizers.
- *Net exports,* which are driven by economic growth among our trading partners, trade policy, and exchange rates.

If any of this is unclear, take a moment to review the section "Spending Shocks Shift the *IS* Curve" in Chapter 18. You don't need to memorize a long list of these factors; rather, make sure you recognize the types of shocks that will lead to changes in spending and hence shift the *IS* curve. You're looking for any shock that will lead to a change in spending at a given real interest rate.

The *IS* curve shifts by the change in spending times the multiplier. Let's evaluate the consequences of an economic shock that reduces aggregate expenditure at any given real interest rate by $625 billion. If the multiplier is two, then this spending shock will set off a chain reaction that will lead aggregate expenditure to decline by a total of 2 × $625 billion = $1.25 trillion. As a result, it will shift the *IS* curve to the left by $1.25 trillion, which is 5% of potential output (because potential output is roughly $25 trillion).

Decreased aggregate expenditure leads to lower output and lower inflation. We can now work through the three-step recipe in Figure 3:

Step 1: *Shift the curve.* We've established that a $1 trillion reduction in aggregate expenditure will shift the *IS* curve to the left by 5% of potential output.

Sandy Huffaker/Getty Images

They're shifting the *IS* curve.

A Spending Shock Shifts the *IS* Curve

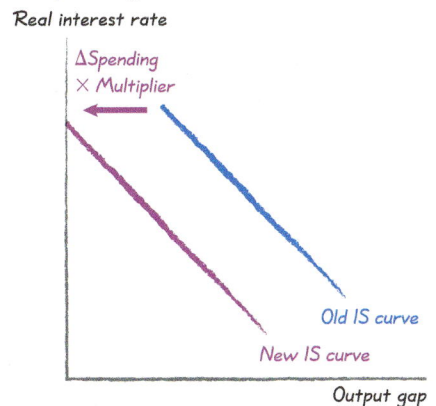

Figure 3 | Spending Shocks Shift the IS Curve

A leftward shift of the IS curve leads to a decrease in GDP and lower inflation.

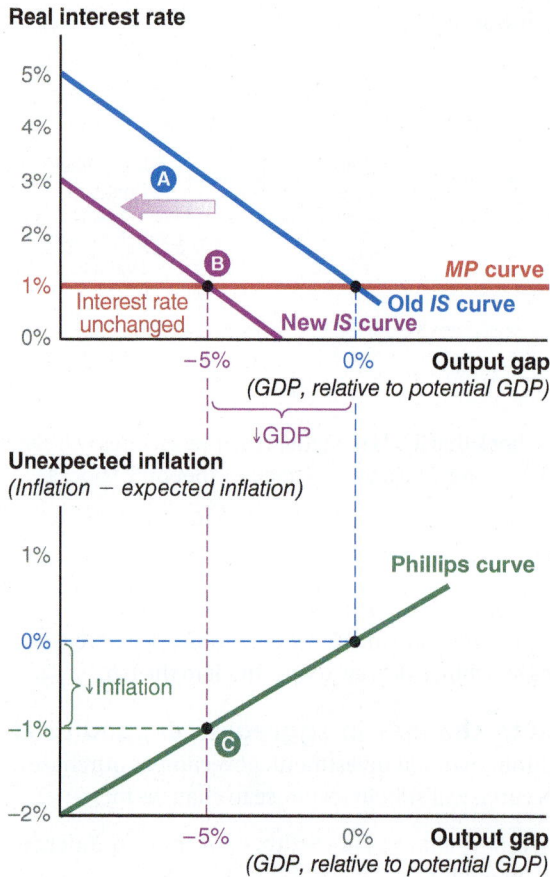

Real interest rate

Step 1: Shift the curve

Ⓐ A decrease in aggregate expenditure shifts the **IS curve** to the left. It moves left by: Δ**Spending** × **Multiplier**.

Step 2: Find the output gap

Ⓑ Find the new equilibrium where the new **IS curve** intersects with the **MP curve**.

Look down to find the new output gap has fallen to **−5%**.

Interest rate unchanged — **MP curve**, **Old IS curve**, **New IS curve**

Output gap (GDP, relative to potential GDP)

↓GDP

Unexpected inflation (Inflation − expected inflation)

Step 3: Assess inflation

Ⓒ Look down to find the point on the **Phillips curve** with the same output gap.

Look left to find the new unexpected inflation rate has fallen to **−1%**.

If inflation expectations are unchanged the actual inflation rate will be 1% lower.

Phillips curve

↓Inflation

Output gap (GDP, relative to potential GDP)

Step 2: *Find the output gap.* Analyze where this *new IS* curve crosses the *MP* curve. In this example, this occurs when output shrinks to be 5% below potential output.

Step 3: *Assess inflation.* Trace this output gap down onto the Phillips curve to assess the inflationary consequences. In this case, an output gap of −5% will cause unexpected inflation to decline to −1%. Thus, if expected inflation is 2%, actual inflation will fall to be one percentage point lower, at 1%.

We can represent this chain of events as follows:

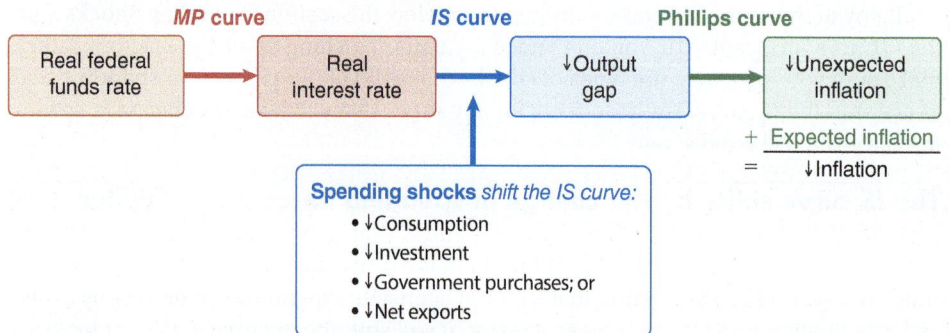

MP curve → **IS curve** → **Phillips curve**

| Real federal funds rate | → | Real interest rate | → | ↓Output gap | → | ↓Unexpected inflation |

+ Expected inflation
= ↓Inflation

Spending shocks *shift the IS curve:*
• ↓Consumption
• ↓Investment
• ↓Government purchases; or
• ↓Net exports

All told, we conclude that a negative spending shock will result in lower output, lower inflation, and no effect on the real interest rate.

Analyzing Supply Shocks

Supply shocks occur whenever there's an unexpected change in sellers' production costs that will lead to price changes at a given output gap. An increase in production costs will shift the Phillips curve up, while a decrease in production costs will shift the Phillips curve down.

The Phillips curve shifts in response to changes in production costs. Production costs drive the pricing decisions of businesses, and hence will change the inflation rate at any given output gap. In turn, production costs shift in response to:

- *Input prices:* When the price of important inputs — such as oil and labor — rise, so will production costs, shifting the Phillips curve up.
- *Import prices:* Higher import prices both directly feed through into higher prices for American consumers, and also affect the price of imported inputs available to domestic producers. The price that Americans pay for imports is a key channel by which shocks in other countries affect inflation in the United States. Rising import prices cause the prices that Americans pay to rise, shifting the Phillips curve up.
- *Productivity:* Faster productivity growth leads to more rapid declines in production costs, shifting the Phillips curve down. When productivity growth is weaker than expected, production costs will rise more quickly than expected, shifting the Phillips curve up.
- *Exchange rates:* Top executives watch the value of the U.S. dollar closely, because it influences the price that Americans pay for imported goods (including imported inputs). The value of the dollar also affects the pressure that global competition puts on the pricing decisions of U.S. businesses. A depreciating U.S. dollar leads imported inputs to become more expensive and makes foreign competitors less competitive, both of which lead domestic prices to rise, shifting the Phillips curve up. An appreciating dollar will shift the Phillips curve down.

(You can review any of this by rereading the section in Chapter 19 on "Supply Shocks Shift the Phillips Curve.")

Rising production costs lead to rising prices and inflation, shifting the Phillips curve.

Increased production costs lead to higher inflation and no change in output. Okay, now it's time to figure out the broader consequences of a supply shock — a rise in production costs that shifts the Phillips curve up. We'll work through the three-step recipe in Figure 4:

Figure 4 | Supply Shocks Shift the Phillips Curve

An upward shift of the Phillips curve leads to a rise in unexpected inflation.

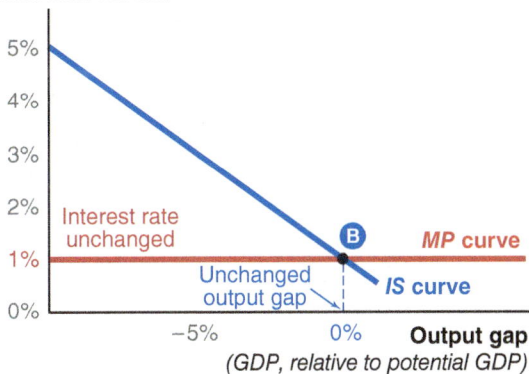

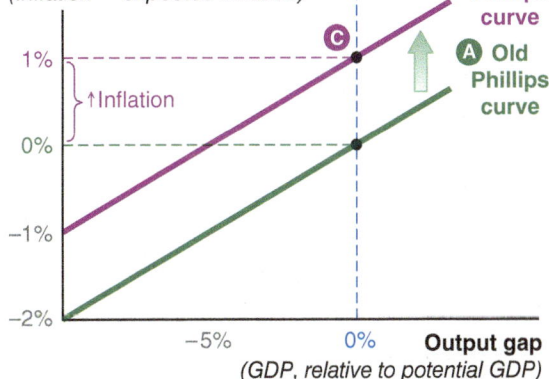

Step 1: Shift the curve

Ⓐ An increase in production costs shifts the **Phillips curve** up.

Step 2: Find the output gap

Ⓑ The output gap is determined by the intersection of the (unchanged) **IS curve** with the (unchanged) **MP curve**.

Look down to find the output gap is unchanged at **0%**.

Step 3: Assess inflation

Ⓒ Look down to find the point on the **new Phillips curve** with the same output gap.

Look left to find the unexpected inflation rate has risen to **+1%**.

If inflation expectations are unchanged, the actual inflation rate will be 1% higher.

Step 1: *Shift the curve.* We've established that higher production costs will shift the Phillips curve upward.

Step 2: *Find the output gap.* The output gap is determined by the intersection of the *IS* and *MP* curves. Because a supply shock shifts neither of these curves, the output gap remains unchanged.

Step 3: *Assess inflation.* Trace this output gap down to the *new* Phillips curve to assess the inflationary consequences. In this case, the unchanged output gap corresponds with higher unexpected inflation of +1%. Thus, if expected inflation is unchanged at 2%, actual inflation will rise to be one percentage point higher, at 3%.

You can summarize this chain of events as follows:

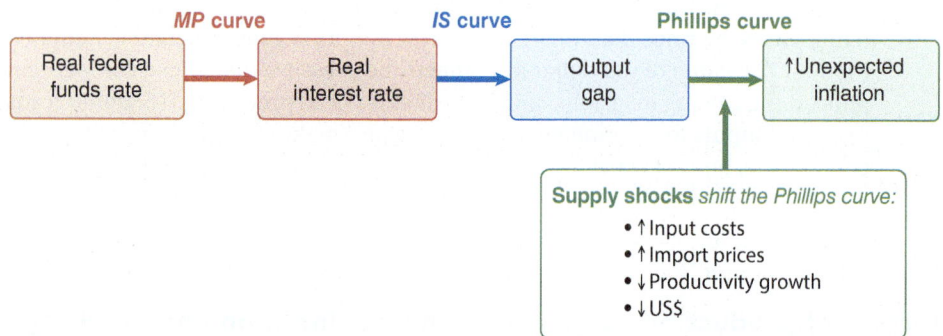

The bottom line of our analysis is that a supply shock leads to higher inflation, with no effect on the real interest rate, or the output gap.

A caveat: A supply shock can cause output to decline. In addition to their effect on inflation, supply shocks can disrupt both actual output and potential output. These effects are important, but because our framework focuses on the output gap (which is the difference between actual and potential output), they didn't show up in Figure 4.

To see how supply shocks can reduce both actual and potential output, consider what would happen if oil prices were to double tomorrow. Over time, businesses would shift from being energy intensive to become more energy efficient. We'd need more hybrid cars and fewer SUVs, and we'd shift from energy-intensive manufacturing toward more energy-efficient services. Given the change in supply conditions, this transition makes long-run sense. But in the short run, this transition creates severe disruptions, as existing factories that were profitable when oil prices were low are rendered unprofitable once they're high. When these factories close, both actual and potential output fall. And so the initial effect is lower output (matched by lower potential output). Production will return to its earlier levels only once more energy-efficient factories have been built.

As a result, a supply shock can cause not only higher inflation, but also short-run stagnation, as output declines. This combination of economic *stag*nation and high in*flation* is called **stagflation.** It's a reminder that when you account for the effects of a supply shock, realize that the shock can lower output by lowering potential output even if the output gap remains unaffected.

stagflation A combination of economic stagnation—or falling output—combined with high inflation.

Interpreting the DATA

How global supply chains strangled the world

In late 2021, the Wood family set out to complete what should have been a pretty straight-forward task: replace their 1995 Chevrolet with a newer model car. They started with nearby dealerships in Seattle, but none had a new Silverado that met their needs. They expanded their search to Idaho, South Dakota, and Texas, but these dealers were also sold out. "I went around and around with dealerships, then branched out to F-150, Ram, Sierra, and Tundra and found either no stock available or crazy markups," Ed Wood said. Eventually, they settled for a Nissan Titan.

This story is a microcosm of the supply shock that caused inflation to rise sharply, to rates not seen in a generation. Most families have a similar story to tell, even if your family's details differ as you confronted home appliance backorders, shortages of building materials, or hard-to-find repair parts. Each of these stories is about a supply shock that shifted the Phillips curve.

Covid revealed a fragility in global supply chains. The production of individual products — like a Silverado — has become an increasingly international endeavor, with each stage of production occurring in different countries, and components sourced from around the world. These complex supply chains are designed for efficiency, but they're not robust to the sort of intermittent global outages that a pandemic might cause. A surge in Covid cases in Malaysia, for instance, might lead a chip factory to pause production, leaving dozens of other factories around the world — including Chevrolet assembly plants — short of vital inputs.

Worse, this fragility was revealed during an extraordinary shift in spending patterns. The pandemic led people to shift from buying services — which typically involve closer interpersonal contact and hence the risk of contagion — to buying goods. This led to a very unbalanced recovery, in which the service sector struggled at the same time as the goods sector was overwhelmed with new orders.

Put these two pieces together, and a wave of global demand met an unstable and input-starved supply side. In the car industry, even though most of the supply chain was healthy, a global chip shortage made it impossible to boost production. The result was mayhem, delayed deliveries, and sharp price rises. The details were different in other industries, but the overall story was similar.

These problems were compounded by chaos on global shipping routes, as the transportation industry was asked to move more goods to more places than ever before. The influx of ships overwhelmed some docks, and the cost of shipping a container from Shanghai to Los Angeles rose from around $2,000 to $25,000. Trading routes that were meant to be international highways became gridlocked. The result was more delays, rising shipping costs, and skyrocketing prices. The Woods eventually settled for a Nissan Titan. Many Americans were forced to settle for higher inflation. ■

Shipping snarls shifted supply.

Justin Tallis/AFP/Getty Images

Do the Economics

Now it's your turn to practice using the Fed model to forecast how the economy will respond as conditions change. Each of the following scenarios is inspired by a real economic shock that hit the U.S. economy in recent decades. In each case, your task is to forecast how real interest rates, the output gap, and inflation will respond.

Scenario 1: *Consumer confidence rises sharply following the election of a populist government.*

Analysis: Higher consumption is a *positive spending shock* that shifts the *IS* curve to the right.

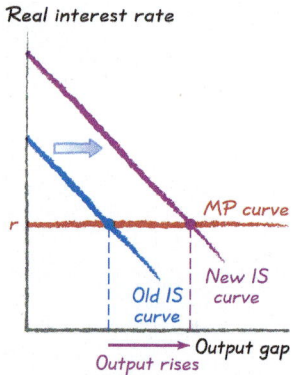

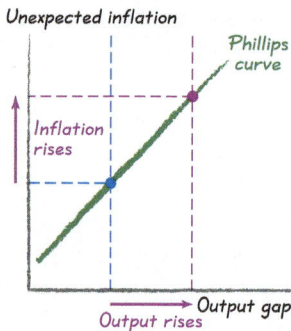

Scenario 2: *Concern that the economy is underperforming leads the Fed to cut interest rates sharply.*

Analysis: Cutting real interest rates is a *financial shock* that shifts the *MP* curve down.

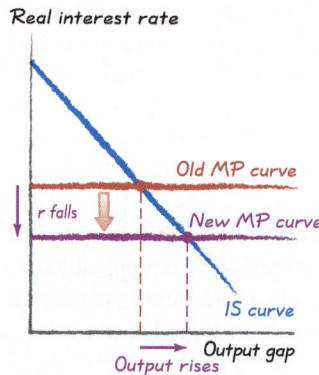

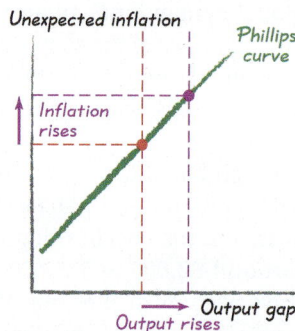

Scenario 3: *Russia's invasion of Ukraine led many countries to impose sanctions. Banning Russian producers from the market decreases the supply of oil, causing the price of oil to spike.*

Analysis: Higher oil prices are an *adverse supply shock*, shifting the Phillips curve up.

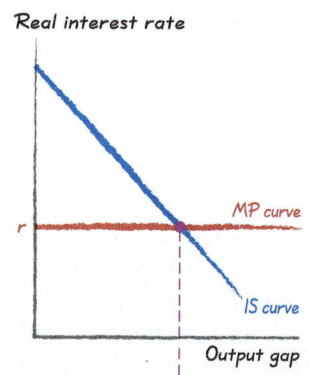

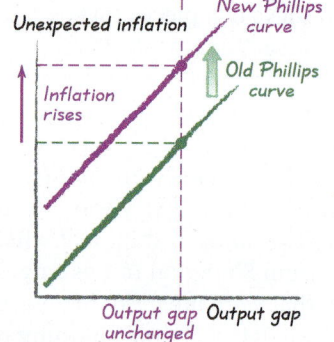

Forecasts:

Real interest rate –

Output ↑

Inflation ↑

Forecasts:

Real interest rate ↓

Output ↑

Inflation ↑

Forecasts:

Real interest rate –

Output –

Inflation ↑

Scenario 4: *Rapid productivity growth due to new technology leads to falling production costs.*

Analysis: Higher productivity growth is a *positive supply shock* that shifts the Phillips curve down.

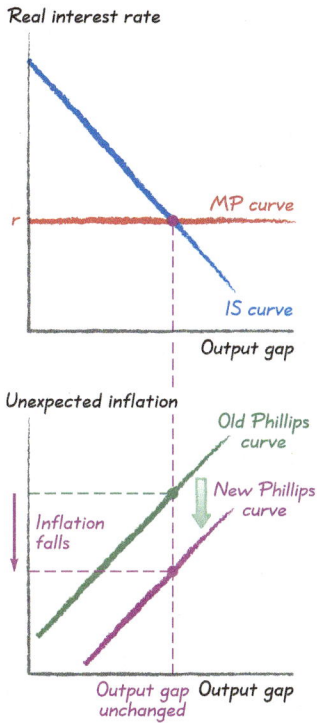

Scenario 5: *An end to the tech boom leads many businesses to rethink their investment in new technology.*

Analysis: A decrease in investment is a *negative spending shock* that shifts the *IS* curve to the left.

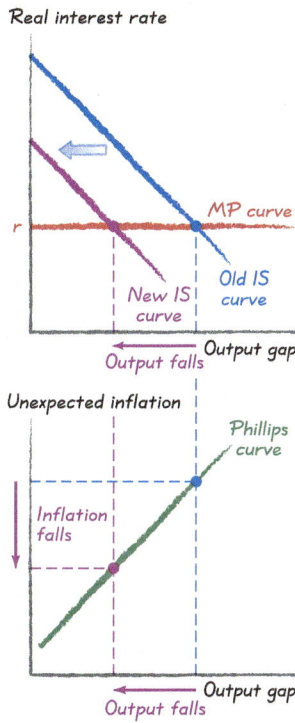

Scenario 6: *Rapidly falling home prices make it difficult for many homeowners to repay their mortgages. The risk of default leads banks to charge a higher risk premium on new loans.*

Analysis: A higher risk premium is a *financial shock* that shifts the *MP* curve up.

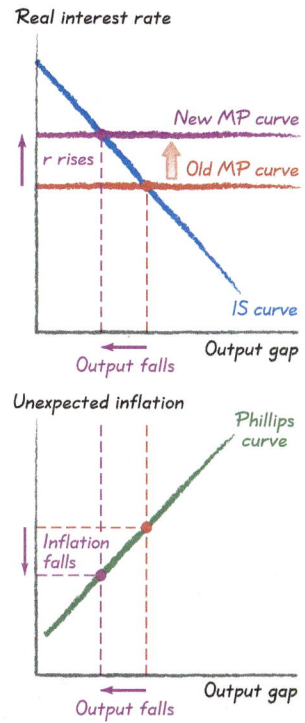

Forecasts:

Real interest rate –

Output –

Inflation ↓

Forecasts:

Real interest rate –

Output ↓

Inflation ↓

Forecasts:

Real interest rate ↑

Output ↓

Inflation ↓

Scenario 7: *Two years after the recession that precipitated it, the government's fiscal stimulus is coming to an end. As a result, government spending is on track to decline to its earlier pre-recession levels.*

Analysis: A decrease in government purchases is an *adverse spending shock* that shifts the *IS* curve to the left.

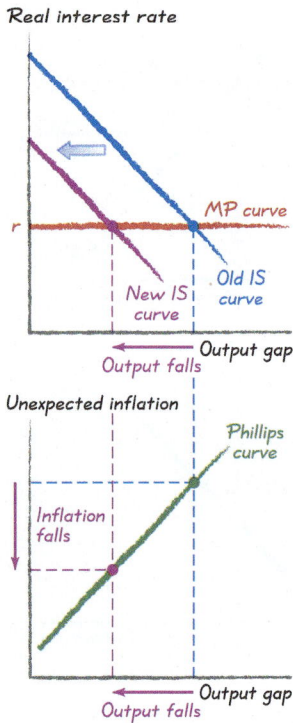

Scenario 8: *The Fed's efforts to restore confidence in the financial system appear to be working, and so banks are cutting the risk premium they charge on new loans.*

Analysis: A lower risk premium is a *financial shock* that shifts the *MP* curve down.

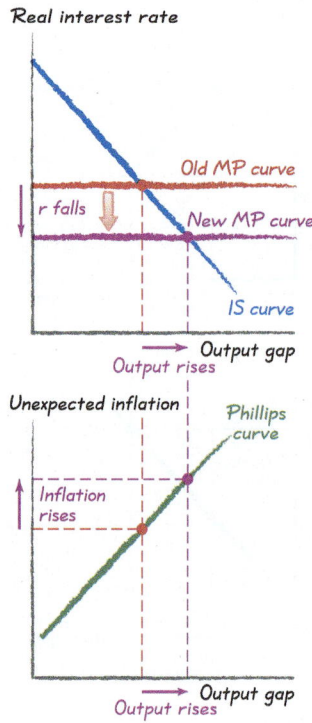

Scenario 9: *The reorganization of work following the pandemic appears to be causing an unexpected surge in productivity growth.*

Analysis: Higher productivity growth is a *positive supply shock* that shifts the Phillips curve down.

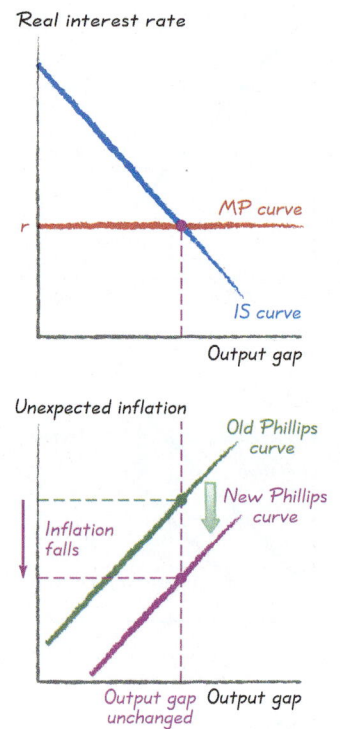

Forecasts:

Real interest rate –

Output ↓

Inflation ↓

Forecasts:

Real interest rate ↓

Output ↑

Inflation ↑

Forecasts:

Real interest rate –

Output –

Inflation ↓

Scenario 10: *Rapid economic growth in China leads to an increase in demand for American-made goods.*

Analysis: Higher net exports is a *positive spending shock* that shifts the *IS* curve to the right.

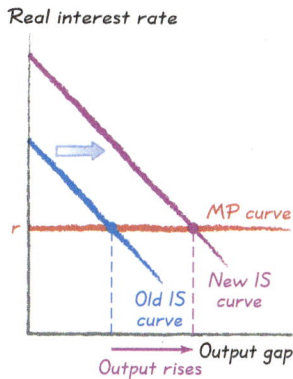

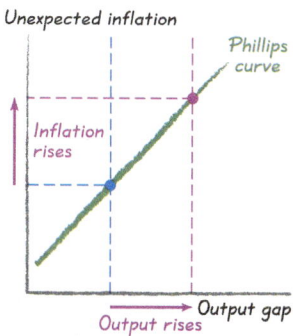

Scenario 11: *A decline in bargaining power is leading nominal wages to rise by less than expected.*

Analysis: Lower than expected input prices is a *positive supply shock* that shifts the Phillips curve down.

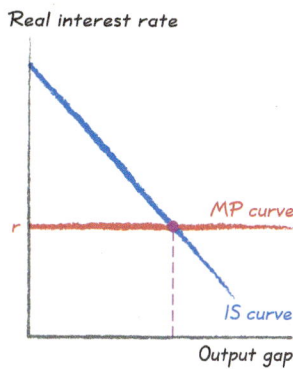

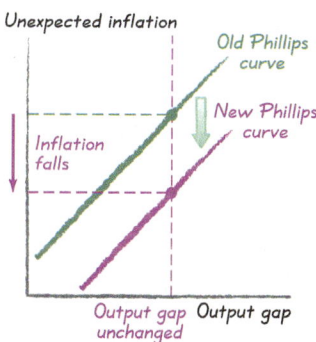

Scenario 12: *A new Federal Reserve chair raises the federal funds rate sharply.*

Analysis: A higher federal funds rate is a *financial shock* that shifts the *MP* curve up.

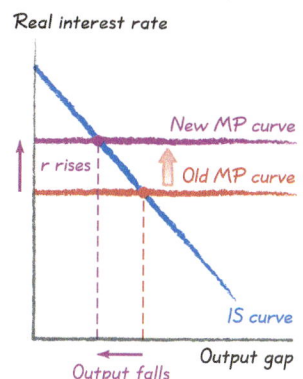

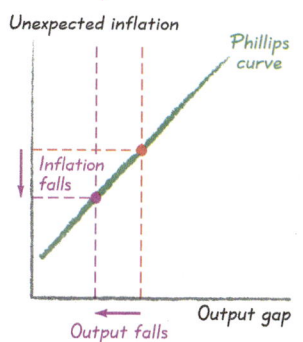

Forecasts:

Real interest rate –

Output ↑

Inflation ↑

Forecasts:

Real interest rate –

Output –

Inflation ↓

Forecasts:

Real interest rate ↑

Output ↓

Inflation ↓ ■

EVERYDAY Economics   Putting macroeconomic models to work

You might be wondering: Is all this curve shifting really what macroeconomists do? If you're working as a macroeconomist — perhaps at the Fed, at the Treasury, in state or local government, at a large corporation, a consulting firm, or a major investment bank — your job will likely include generating economic forecasts. And just as the Fed model suggests, you'll likely rely on the *IS, MP,* and Phillips curves to assess what's likely to happen. But your job will extend beyond saying whether output, inflation, or interest rates will rise or fall. You'll have to be more precise, and say by how much. That's a task much better suited to a computer than a pencil and paper. And so you might code the relationships that each of these curves represent into a spreadsheet, or use a statistical program to create a fully computerized model of the economy.

Still, it's not unusual to see a top economist poring over tables of output from their computerized model, while sketching *IS, MP,* and Phillips curves in the margin, to try to make sense of it all. They're using these graphs as an "intuition pump" to help them explain and understand the somewhat opaque output of their computerized models.

There are better tools for making economic forecasts.

Busà Photography/Moment/Getty Images

Most forecasters have a line at the bottom of their spreadsheet that says "add factor." (The more honest ones label it "fudge factor.") It's a hack. When their computer model disagrees with the intuition they've sketched in the margins, they'll use this line to add a bit to their computer-generated forecast to make it better match their curve-driven intuition. ■

20.3 Diagnosing the Causes of Macroeconomic Changes

Learning Objective *Use the Fed model to diagnose the causes of economic fluctuations.*

So far we've used the Fed model to *predict* the consequences of macroeconomic shocks. But there's another use for it. Economic conditions can sometimes shift sharply, and the economy — unlike a textbook — doesn't come with a big heading telling you whether that shift was caused by a financial, spending, or supply shock. And so you can use what we've learned in this chapter to *diagnose* the causes of macroeconomic fluctuations. It's an important job because the first step to solving a country's macroeconomic ills is diagnosing their cause.

A Brief Recap

Let's draw the threads of our analysis together. Figure 5 summarizes the findings from our analysis of financial, spending, and supply shocks.

Figure 5 | The Consequences of Different Shocks

	Step one	Step two		Step three
	Shift the curve	**Real interest rate**	**Find the output gap**	**Assess inflation**
Financial shocks				
↑ Real interest rates	MP curve shifts up	↑	↓	↓
↓ Real interest rates	MP curve shifts down	↓	↑	↑
Spending shocks				
↑ Spending	IS curve shifts right	No change	↑	↑
↓ Spending	IS curve shifts left	No change	↓	↓
Supply shocks				
↑ Production costs	Phillips curve shifts up	No change	No change	↑
↓ Production costs	Phillips curve shifts down	No change	No change	↓

A Diagnosis Tool

As we've worked to predict economic outcomes, we've read this table from left to right — observing which curves shift, and then tracing out the implications for what that will mean for the real interest rate, the output gap, and inflation. But now, we want to work in reverse: Given what we've observed has happened to these economic indicators, what can we infer about the shocks that have hit the economy?

Look closely at this table, and you'll notice that financial, spending, and supply shocks each leave behind a different pattern of footprints. We can use these differences to diagnose the cause of any recent macroeconomic change. In particular, notice:

1. If the real interest rate changes, that's evidence that the economy has been hit by a *financial shock*.

2. If the output gap has shifted without much movement in the real interest rate, it suggests that there's been a *spending shock*.

3. If inflation rises in a weak economy, or if it falls in a strong economy, that points to a *supply shock* as the cause.

Armed with these rules, let's work through some examples of how this can help you make sense of changing economic conditions.

Do the Economics

In each of the following examples, use your diagnostic tools to assess what economic shock hit the economy:

a. "This makes no sense," said a Wall Street economist, "why is inflation rising even though the economy remains weak? The Phillips curve teaches us that inflation rises when the economy is strong."

If inflation rises while the economy remains weak, you can infer that the Phillips curve has shifted up and the economy is experiencing the sort of adverse supply shock that raises production costs, leading to higher inflation at any given output gap.

b. At a meeting of the Federal Reserve, policymakers were puzzled. "For some reason output is booming, despite the fact that we haven't cut interest rates at all."

If output is rising but interest rates are unchanged, the economy has likely received a positive spending shock, where higher aggregate expenditure at a given real interest rate has shifted the IS curve to the right.

c. "Our sales are falling as is output throughout the economy," noted Ford's chief economist. She noted that she might attribute this to higher interest rates on auto loans but added that these higher interest rates were somewhat puzzling given that the Fed hadn't changed its benchmark interest rate.

Interest rates reflect both actions by the Federal Reserve and the risk premium determined in financial markets. It sounds like these higher interest rates are due to a rising risk premium. When output declines following a rise in interest rates, you can infer the economy has suffered a financial shock that has shifted the MP curve up. ■

20.4 Tying It Together

It's All Connected

Each chapter of this book has focused on one part of the economy, uncovering the key economic forces at work. As we've progressed, I bet you've noticed that the relationships described in any one chapter depend on other economic variables, whose determinants are described in some other chapter. This is the **interdependence principle** in action, and macroeconomics is all about understanding these interdependencies.

Our crowning achievement in this chapter is uncovering how these disparate elements fit together into a coherent whole. The result is a complete model of the macroeconomy that you can use to track the full macroeconomic implications of any change in market conditions. You can use it to forecast how economic conditions are likely to change, what the major threats are to your forecast, and how policymakers can respond.

A model is particularly valuable when you can ask it "what if" questions. And you can use the Fed model to ask: *What if* the global economy craters? *What if* the stock market booms? *What if* productivity growth takes off? Policymakers use the Fed model to ask "what if" questions that directly affect economic policy. At the Fed, they

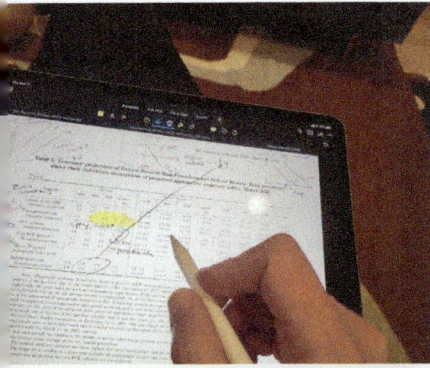

Justin Wolfers

simonkr/Getty Images

You don't need a meteorologist to know which way the wind blows . . . but you do need an economic model.

ask: What if we raise interest rates? What if we lower interest rates? They use a computerized version of the Fed model to figure out what sorts of economic outcomes will result from each interest rate setting, and then choose the policy that corresponds with what they judge to be the best set of outcomes. At the White House and the Treasury, they use similar models to ask: What if we raise government spending? What if we cut taxes? These analyses help guide fiscal policy. And businesses around the country use related models to game out the likely consequences of whatever economic shocks their executives see on the horizon.

The framework you've learned in this chapter puts you remarkably close to the cutting edge of how economists — both those at policy institutions like the Fed, as well as leaders in the financial sector — analyze the economy. And it has a number of features that make it particularly useful.

The Fed model is *dynamic*. You have used this framework to analyze shifts over time from one equilibrium (say, when the real interest rate is low) to another equilibrium (say, after the interest rate has risen). By forecasting changes over time, your analysis is *dynamic*. An even richer analysis would also project the pace at which these changes will occur. These dynamics play an important role in economic forecasting, and they're an important feature of the more complicated computerized versions of the Fed model used in Washington and on Wall Street.

The Fed model is *stochastic*. A key strength of the Fed model is that it provides a coherent way to trace out the consequences of the many random (that is, *stochastic*) shocks that hit the economy. It provides a framework for analyzing virtually any spending, financial, or supply shock, and an understanding of how the size and frequency of these shocks — and how policy responds — will shape the economy's volatility.

The Fed model takes a *general equilibrium* approach. Rather than analyzing individual markets or variables separately, you've learned to analyze all of them jointly, paying careful attention to the ways in which choices in one domain affect those in others. In general equilibrium, everything can depend on everything else, and it's your job to sort out what will happen. The Fed model applies this approach to business cycles, jointly considering consumption, investment, government purchasing, and importing and exporting decisions; it evaluates spending decisions together with production choices; it explores the relationship between the financial sector and the broader economy; and it explores the connections between output and pricing decisions, and hence inflation. It provides a useful framework for analyzing the key economy-wide prices — like the real interest rate, inflation, the exchange rate, wages, and stock prices — which can transmit shocks from one market to another.

But perhaps the real value of the Fed model is that, unlike MONIAC, you can do all of this without getting wet.

Chapter 20 Review

Chapter at a Glance

The Fed Model (IS-MP-PC): A complete model of business cycles that puts together the IS curve, the MP curve, and the Phillips curve. Use it to analyze macroeconomic shocks using a **three-step recipe**:

Step 1—Identify the shock, and shift the relevant curve:

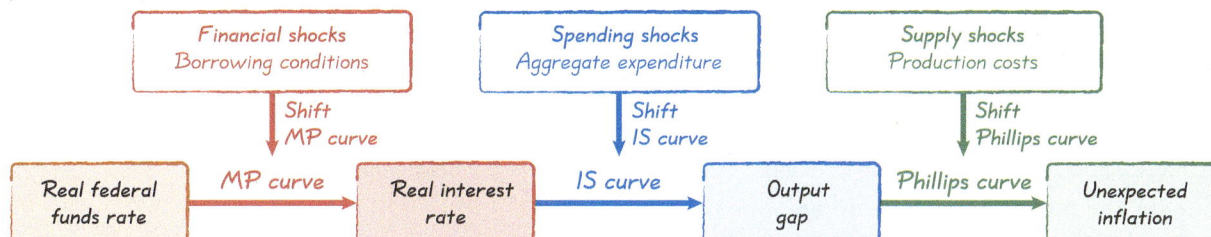

Financial shocks	Spending shocks	Supply shocks
Borrowing conditions	Aggregate expenditure	Production costs

Shift MP curve → Real federal funds rate → MP curve → Real interest rate

Shift IS curve → IS curve → Output gap

Shift Phillips curve → Phillips curve → Unexpected inflation

Step 2—Find the output gap:
Look at the intersection of the IS and MP curves to the find the equilibrium output gap and real interest rate.

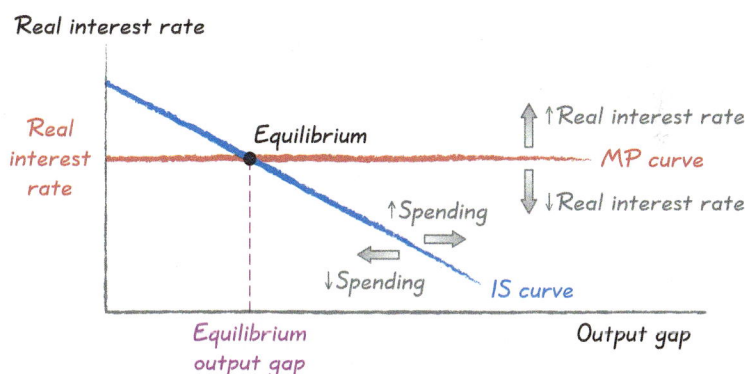

Real interest rate

Real interest rate — Equilibrium — MP curve

↑ ↑Real interest rate
↓ ↓Real interest rate

↑Spending
↓Spending

IS curve

Equilibrium output gap — Output gap

Step 3—Assess inflation:
Use the Phillips curve to find the inflationary implications of this output gap.

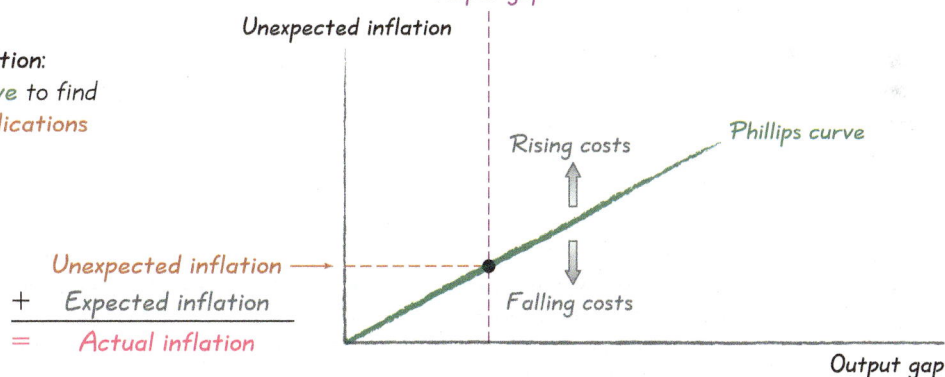

Unexpected inflation

Rising costs — Phillips curve

Unexpected inflation →
+ Expected inflation
= Actual inflation

Falling costs

Output gap

Predicting and Diagnosing the Effects of Economic Shocks

Macroeconomic shock	① Shift the curve	Real interest rate	② Find the output gap	③ Assess inflation
Financial shocks				
↑ Real interest rates	MP curve shifts up	↑	↓	↓
↓ Real interest rates	MP curve shifts down	↓	↑	↑
Spending shocks				
↑ Spending	IS curve shifts right	No change	↑	↑
↓ Spending	IS curve shifts left	No change	↓	↓
Supply shocks				
↑ Production costs	Phillips curve shifts up	No change	No change	↑
↓ Production costs	Phillips curve shifts down	No change	No change	↓

Key Terms

Fed model, 520

financial shocks, 522

spending shocks, 522

stagflation, 528

supply shocks, 522

Study Problems

Learning Objective 20.1 *Analyze the Fed model, which puts together the IS curve, the MP curve, and the Phillips curve.*

1. The interdependence principle says that what happens in one part of the economy will affect other parts. Use the Fed model to explain the interdependence between the real interest rate, the output gap, and inflation.

2. Compare and contrast the three different economic shocks using the Fed model, and explain which curve shifts for each type of shock.

3. Determine if the following changes to the economy are examples of financial, spending, or supply shocks. For each case, explain whether the *IS, MP,* or Phillips curve will shift, and in what direction.

   a. The Chinese government eliminates the tariffs it charges on goods exported from the United States.

   b. The implementation of artificial intelligence in manufacturing has led to faster-than-expected productivity growth, which results in decreasing production costs.

   c. A financial crisis makes banks extremely reluctant to take on risky loans without charging an extremely high risk premium.

   d. Businesses' confidence about the future of the economy falls, which leads them to scrap planned investment projects.

   e. The Federal Reserve raises the federal funds rate from 4% to 5%.

   f. The federal government cuts the corporate tax rate, a move applauded by business executives who say that it will make more investment opportunities profitable.

Learning Objective 20.2 *Use the Fed model to analyze the consequences of financial shocks, spending shocks, and supply shocks.*

4. The economy is experiencing a recession. The output gap is hovering at −7%, causing higher-than-normal unemployment. Using the Fed model, compare and contrast how monetary policy and fiscal policy can impact the economy. What can the Federal Reserve do to stimulate greater output and hence employment? What can the federal government do? What happens if both monetary and fiscal policy are used?

5. You open the newspaper and read that Europe is headed for a recession. Use the Fed model to forecast what you expect to happen to the U.S. economy. Use the three-step recipe for analyzing macroeconomic shocks to explain your answer.

6. The following graph summarizes the state of the economy. Your boss asks you how you think the Federal Reserve should respond to these economic conditions.

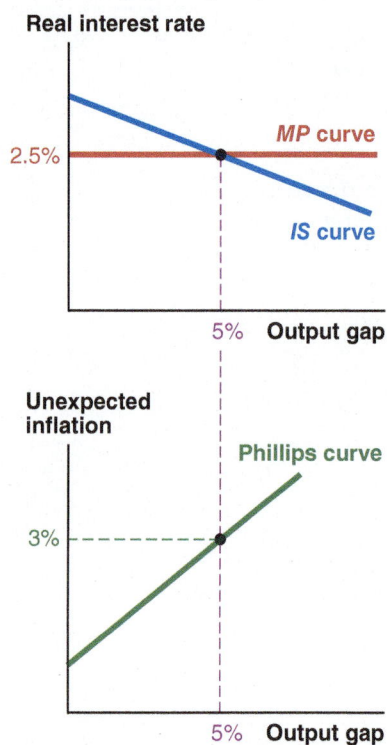

a. Would you recommend that the Fed try to increase, decrease, or not change the real interest rate? Explain your reasoning.

b. What type of shock will your policy change cause?

c. Which curve in the Fed model will shift?

d. Predict what will happen to real interest rates, output, and inflation.

7. For each of the following scenarios, use the Fed model to forecast how output, the real interest rate, and inflation will change. In each case, start with an economy with an output gap of zero and with no unexpected inflation, and illustrate how economic conditions will change.

   a. A breakthrough in solar power technology decreases the price of energy.

   b. The election of a new president leads households to become more hopeful about their future economic prospects, which leads them to increase their consumption.

   c. In response to concerns about rising national debt, the federal government passes a new bill that dramatically reduces government spending on education and the military.

   d. In a shock to financial markets, the Federal Reserve announces that it will decrease the federal funds rate from 3% to 1.5%.

8. Now go back to Study Problem 3 and predict how each change that it lists will impact output, inflation, and the real interest rate. Illustrate your answers.

Learning Objective 20.3 *Use the Fed model to diagnose the causes of economic fluctuations.*

9. Consider the three types of economic shocks: financial shocks, spending shocks, and supply shocks. Discuss how each one affects the real interest rate, output gap, and the inflation rate.

10. Use your answer to the previous question to help you diagnose what kinds of shocks have hit the economy. If the real interest rate changes, what type of shock can you conclude must have occurred? Alternatively, if the output gap has shifted without much movement in the real interest rate, what does this tell you must have happened? Or, what if you find that inflation has risen despite a weak economy, or inflation has fallen despite a strong economy?

11. For each of the following, diagnose which type of economic shock has hit the economy:

   a. You hear a radio report noting that the recession appears to have ended. It says that while output remains less than potential, the output gap has improved from −7% to −5%. The host is interviewing an economist who states, "The change in GDP isn't terribly surprising, as the Federal Reserve continues to cut the real interest rate."

   b. The latest inflation report indicates an unexpected uptick in inflation even though output remains below potential output.

   c. The real interest rate has been stable over the past few quarters, yet output has grown rapidly, leading to a more positive output gap.

Aggregate Demand and Aggregate Supply

Not so long ago, economist Philip Jefferson stood in front of his class, sketching out the sort of macroeconomic curves that you're about to explore. At the time he was an economics professor, teaching introductory economics students who are likely a lot like you: bright, curious, and wondering how to fit all the pieces of the macroeconomy together. Jefferson hasn't just taught students how macroeconomic conditions can change — he has studied what those changes mean for them and their families.

Philip Jefferson showed that the economy looks different for different people.

Sifting through years of data on business cycles and the conditions of people's lives, Jefferson found that poverty and business cycles were more closely linked than many realized. While the abstract models he taught represented policymakers as shifting curves, in reality, they were shaping the livelihoods of millions of low-income people.

That research caught the eye of President Joe Biden, who in 2022 tapped Jefferson to become a Federal Reserve governor. The position offered Jefferson the opportunity to draw together the macroeconomic frameworks he had spent years studying, with the opportunity to really make a difference.

As one of the seven members of the Board of Governors, Jefferson is charged with overseeing one of the most powerful economic institutions in the world. The decisions the Board makes affect all of us. Jefferson and his colleagues spend their days poring over economic data and evaluating forecasts. There's a continuity in Jefferson's story, as the computer models that his staff run to simulate the economy rely on the same ideas and models that Jefferson had both taught his students and used in his own research.

So, as you read this chapter, realize that you're learning not only the ideas that economists like Jefferson (and *your* instructor!) teach to econ students, but also the ideas that power some of the most consequential decisions an economist can ever be asked to make.

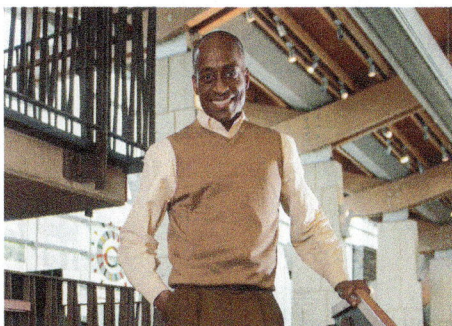

Chapter Objective

Analyze how aggregate demand and aggregate supply determine macroeconomic outcomes.

21.1 The *AD-AS* Framework
Understand how aggregate demand and aggregate supply determine macroeconomic equilibrium.

21.2 Aggregate Demand
Assess the total quantity of goods and services that purchasers want to buy.

21.3 Aggregate Supply
Evaluate the total quantity of goods and services that businesses want to supply.

21.4 Macroeconomic Shocks and Countercyclical Policy
Forecast how the economy will respond to changing conditions.

21.5 Aggregate Supply in the Short Run and the Long Run
Distinguish between the immediate effects, short-run effects, medium-run effects, and long-run consequences of economic shocks.

🎙 **Podcast**

Think Like an Economist
Aggregate Demand and Aggregate Supply

Organizational note: The last three chapters presented one framework for analyzing business cycles, and this chapter presents a different, but closely related, framework. These aren't competing views, but rather alternative perspectives from which to analyze the same economic forces. Your time is valuable, so you should read either Chapters 18–20, or this chapter.

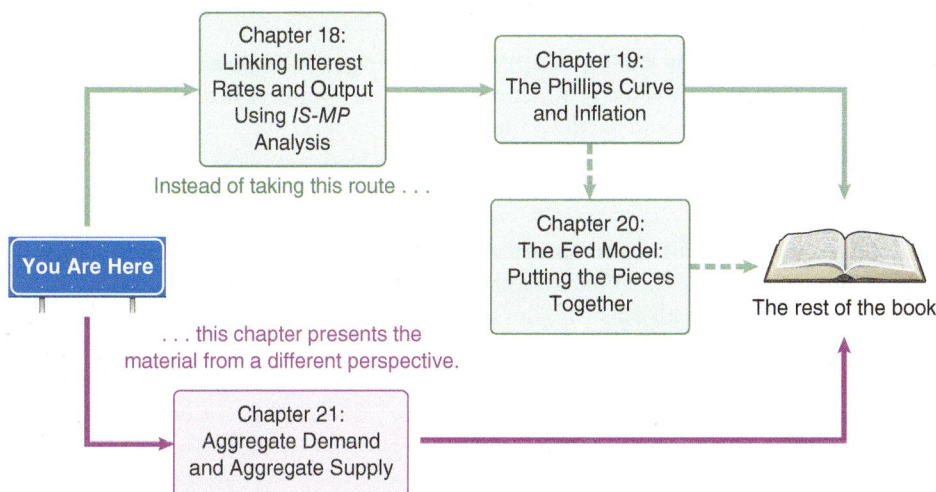

Chapter 18:
Linking Interest Rates and Output Using *IS-MP* Analysis

Chapter 19:
The Phillips Curve and Inflation

Instead of taking this route . . .

You Are Here

. . . this chapter presents the material from a different perspective.

Chapter 20:
The Fed Model: Putting the Pieces Together

The rest of the book

Chapter 21:
Aggregate Demand and Aggregate Supply

541

21.1 The *AD-AS* Framework

Learning Objective *Understand how aggregate demand and aggregate supply determine macroeconomic equilibrium.*

As you think about whether it's a good time to buy a car; get ahead repaying your student loans; look for a new job; or pursue a graduate degree, your answers will likely depend — at least to some extent — on where you think the economy is going. That's why our task in this chapter is to develop a framework that you can use to forecast where the economy is headed.

Introducing Aggregate Demand and Aggregate Supply

Much of this framework will feel familiar from your earlier analysis of how the microeconomic forces of demand and supply determine outcomes in individual markets, like the market for gasoline, coffee, or haircuts. We're going to supersize these concepts and introduce you to their macroeconomic cousins, *aggregate demand* and *aggregate supply,* which describe the forces that determine *aggregate* outcomes such as total output and average prices across the economy as a whole.

Use the *AD-AS* framework to forecast output and the average price level. This supersized version is called the *AD-AS* framework (that's short for A̲ggregate D̲emand and A̲ggregate S̲upply), and it focuses on two key macroeconomic outcomes:

- The *quantity* of output produced across the economy as a whole, which is measured by real GDP; and
- The *price* of that output, which is measured by the GDP deflator. Think of this as the price of a basket containing the many goods and services we produce.

We'll follow the usual convention in economics of plotting price on the vertical axis and quantity on the horizontal axis. Even if this seems familiar, there's an important difference: This supersized framework isn't about explaining the price and quantity of any individual good, but rather what's happening to *total output* and *average prices* across the economy as a whole. Think of it as if people are buying and selling baskets of goods and services, and you're tracking the number of baskets sold, and the price of baskets.

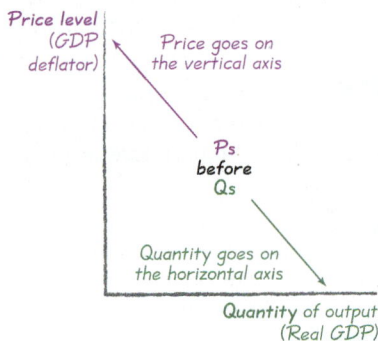

The aggregate demand curve is downward-sloping. The **aggregate demand curve** (or "*AD* curve" to its friends) summarizes the purchasing plans of all buyers throughout the economy. It shows the relationship between the average price level and the total quantity of output that all buyers — consumers, businesses, the government, and overseas customers — collectively plan to purchase. A lower average price level leads buyers to demand a larger quantity of output, which means that the aggregate demand curve is downward-sloping.

The aggregate supply curve is upward-sloping. The **aggregate supply curve** (or "*AS* curve") summarizes the production plans of all suppliers throughout the economy. It shows the relationship between the average price level and the quantity of output that suppliers collectively produce. A higher price level leads suppliers to produce a larger quantity of output, which means that the aggregate supply curve is upward-sloping.

Macroeconomic equilibrium occurs where the curves cross. Scientists describe an equilibrium as a stable situation, with no tendency to change, because opposing forces are in balance. The same idea also applies to the economy as a whole: A **macroeconomic equilibrium** occurs when the quantity of output that buyers collectively want to purchase is equal to the quantity of output that suppliers collectively produce. The economy will be stable at this point because no one wants to buy or sell more or less than they are. As Figure 1 shows, macroeconomic equilibrium occurs at the point where the two curves cross.

aggregate demand curve Shows the relationship between the price level and the total quantity of output that buyers collectively plan to purchase.

aggregate supply curve Shows the relationship between the price level and the total quantity of output that suppliers collectively produce.

macroeconomic equilibrium Occurs when the quantity of output that buyers collectively want to purchase is equal to the quantity of output that suppliers collectively produce.

Figure 1 | The *AD-AS* Framework

The state of the economy is determined by the intersection of the aggregate demand and aggregate supply curves.

(A) The **aggregate demand** curve shows that the quantity of output that buyers collectively plan to purchase falls as the average price level rises.

(B) The **aggregate supply curve** shows that the quantity of output that suppliers collectively produce rises as the average price level rises.

(C) The economy will move to the point of **macroeconomic equilibrium** where the two curves intersect. This is the only point where the quantity of output demanded is equal to the quantity supplied.

(D) This determines the level of **equilibrium GDP**, which in this case is $20 trillion.

(E) It also determines the average **price level**.

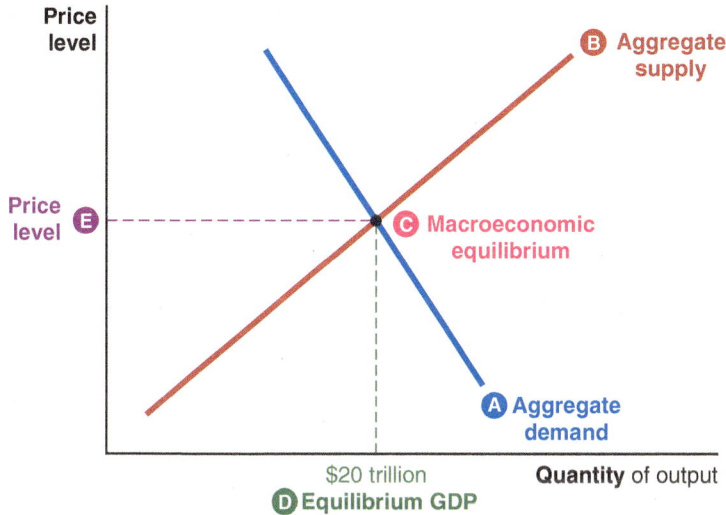

That's it! You now have a powerful framework for forecasting both the level of GDP and the average price level in the economy. As we'll discover, this framework is particularly useful for analyzing the year-to-year fluctuations that make up the business cycle.

Macroeconomic versus Microeconomic Forces

All that remains is to dig deeper into understanding the macroeconomic forces that underlie the aggregate demand and aggregate supply curves and to figure out when changing market conditions lead them to shift. That's our agenda for the rest of this chapter.

The *AD-AS* framework looks a lot like the microeconomic supply-equals-demand framework. This approach should feel familiar from the microeconomic supply-equals-demand framework that you use to analyze individual markets. It's familiar because in micro, as in macro, equilibrium occurs where the curves cross. And when market conditions change, you'll forecast what will happen next by shifting the curves and finding the new equilibrium.

But the *AD-AS* framework summarizes a different set of macroeconomic forces. The micro- and macroeconomic curves summarize different trade-offs. In a microeconomic context, the key opportunity cost of buying gasoline is that you could otherwise spend your money on something else. But in a macroeconomic context, we're focused on spending on *all* goods and services, and so the relevant opportunity cost of buying output *today* is that you could otherwise save your money in order to buy more output in the *future*. In micro, the key trade-offs are across *products,* while in macro, the key trade-offs are across *time*.

Because the forces that shape these macroeconomic trade-offs are so different, it's important that you label the curves in Figure 1 "aggregate demand" (or simply "AD") and "aggregate supply" (or "AS") rather than just "demand" or "supply." The modifier

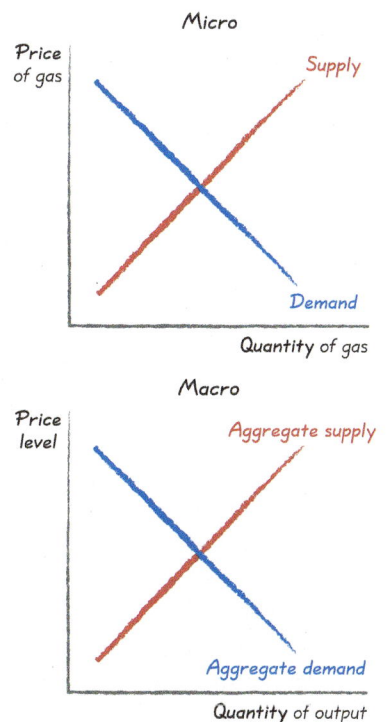

"aggregate" is there to remind you to think about the macroeconomic (or "aggregate") forces. What are those forces? Glad you asked. That's what we're going to analyze next.

21.2 Aggregate Demand

Learning Objective *Assess the total quantity of goods and services that purchasers want to buy.*

The aggregate demand curve summarizes the purchasing plans of all buyers throughout the economy, at each possible price level. It describes the effect that the average price level has on the demand for output. To understand why the aggregate demand curve is downward-sloping, we need to dig into the forces that shape the total demand for output in the economy.

Aggregate Expenditure

aggregate expenditure The total amount of goods and services that people want to buy across the whole economy.
= *Consumption*
+ *Planned investment*
+ *Government purchases*
+ *Net exports*

Aggregate expenditure refers to the total amount of goods and services that people want to buy across the whole economy—the sum of consumption, planned investment, government purchases, and net exports.

Aggregate expenditure is the sum of four components:

- = *Consumption:* When households buy goods and services
- + *Planned investment:* When businesses purchase new physical capital
- + *Government purchases:* When the government buys goods and services
- + *Net exports:* Spending by foreigners on American-made exports, less spending by Americans on foreign-made imports.

Economists often use abbreviations to simplify things, and so you might find it easier to write it this way:

$$\underbrace{AE}_{\substack{\text{Aggregate} \\ \text{expenditure}}} = \underbrace{C}_{\text{Consumption}} + \underbrace{I}_{\substack{\text{Planned} \\ \text{investment}}} + \underbrace{G}_{\substack{\text{Government} \\ \text{purchases}}} + \underbrace{NX}_{\substack{\text{Net} \\ \text{exports}}}$$

When you're trying to assess economy-wide demand, you need to focus on how much people (including businesses) want to buy, not the unsold inventories that suppliers accumulate. That's why the measure of investment that's counted in aggregate expenditure is *planned investment,* which includes all the spending on new capital by businesses, but excludes unplanned changes in inventories.

The aggregate demand curve illustrates the level of aggregate expenditure associated with different values of the average price level. To see why this curve is downward-sloping, we'll need to visit Washington, D.C., to sit in on one of the most economically consequential meetings on the planet.

Why Aggregate Demand Is Downward-Sloping

Eight times a year, policymakers meet at the Federal Reserve — or "the Fed" — in Washington, D.C. Over two days of meetings, they pore over binders full of data about how the economy is doing, discuss trends they're seeing in different sectors, debate the implications, and talk through likely scenarios. When the meeting ends, the Fed announces its new setting for the interest rate.

This is important because the real interest rate shapes aggregate expenditure and hence *aggregate demand.* Importantly, the Fed sets that interest rate based at least partly on what's happening to the *price level.* As such, the Fed is a central player shaping the relationship between the price level and aggregate expenditure, and hence the aggregate demand curve. To see how, let's step through each of the links in the chain connecting a higher price level to the quantity of output demanded.

Some abbreviations
AE: Aggregate Expenditure
C: Consumption
I: Planned Investment
G: Government purchases
NX: Net exports

A higher price level leads to a higher inflation rate. The first link follows from a definition: The inflation rate measures — in percentage terms — how much higher this year's price level is than last year's. Given that last year's price level is set in stone, the higher this year's price level is, the higher this year's inflation rate will be.

Inflation is the rate of change of the price level, and last year's prices can't change. So this year's higher price level translates to a higher inflation rate.

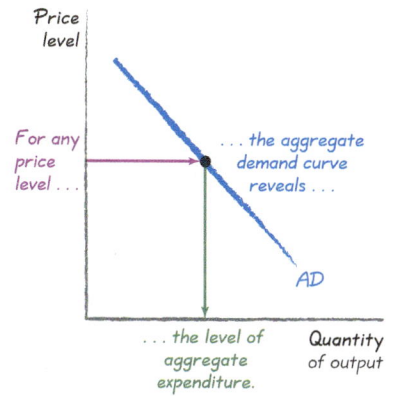

↑Price level ⟶ ↑Inflation

Higher inflation leads the Fed to raise the real interest rate. Here's where the Fed comes in: The Federal Reserve tries to keep the inflation rate stable at its target level. When the inflation rate is either too high or too low, the Federal Reserve will adjust the real interest rate to bring inflation back toward its target level. Specifically, higher inflation leads the Fed to raise the real interest rate, while lower inflation leads it to cut the real interest rate. Thus, we have the next link in the chain:

The Fed responds to higher inflation by raising the real interest rate.

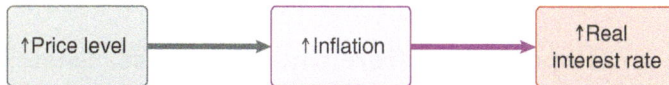

↑Price level ⟶ ↑Inflation ⟶ ↑Real interest rate

The process by which the Fed decides when to adjust interest rates and how it makes those changes, is so important that we'll devote all of Chapter 22, on monetary policy, to understanding how it does this. For now, it's sufficient to note that the Fed responds to higher inflation by setting a higher real interest rate. A rough rule of thumb suggests that when the inflation rate is one percentage point higher, the Fed responds by setting the real interest rate half a percentage point higher.

A higher real interest rate leads to lower aggregate expenditure. A reminder: The real interest rate is the nominal interest rate adjusted for inflation. It matters because it represents the opportunity cost of spending. The **opportunity cost principle** tells you that before spending money, you should ask, "Or what?" You can spend money now, *or* you can save it, earn interest, and buy even more in the future. The real interest rate tells you how much more stuff you'll be able to buy if you wait until next year.

Because a higher real interest rate corresponds to a higher opportunity cost of spending money this year, it leads to less spending and so reduces aggregate expenditure. This is particularly true for investment because a higher real interest rate means that fewer investment projects will be profitable enough to offset the opportunity cost of keeping your money in the bank to earn interest. A higher real interest rate also reduces consumption partly because it raises the cost of borrowing to fund big-ticket items like a car. It can also cause net exports to decline through an *exchange rate effect,* in which inflows of foreign savings cause the U.S. dollar to appreciate, making American exports more expensive for foreigners. Finally, a higher real interest rate raises how much the government must pay in interest on its own debt, which can lead to a decline in government purchases simply because there is less money left over in the budget. Together, these observations tell you that high real interest rates reduce aggregate expenditure, and hence the aggregate demand for output. They're the final link in our chain connecting a higher price level to a lower demand for output:

Higher real interest rates raise the opportunity cost of spending, reducing aggregate expenditure.

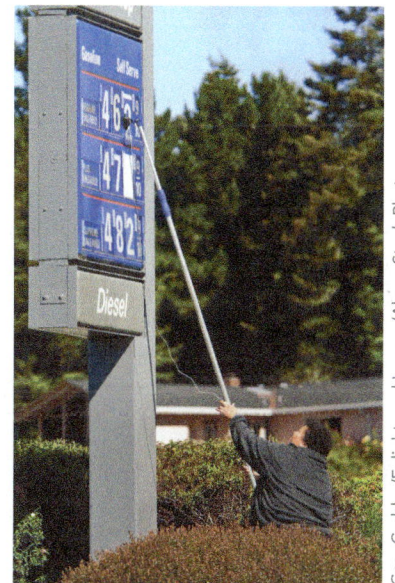

↑Price level ⟶ ↑Inflation ⟶ ↑Real interest rate ⟶ ↓Aggregate demand

Price level

For any price level . . .

. . . the aggregate demand curve reveals . . .

AD

Quantity of output

. . . the level of aggregate expenditure.

The larger the price rise, the higher this year's inflation rate.

Gary Crabbe/Enlightened Images/Alamy Stock Photo

The opportunity cost of buying stuff today is earning interest and buying even more stuff in the future.

Jason Hetherington/The Image Bank/Getty Images

Aggregate Demand Curve

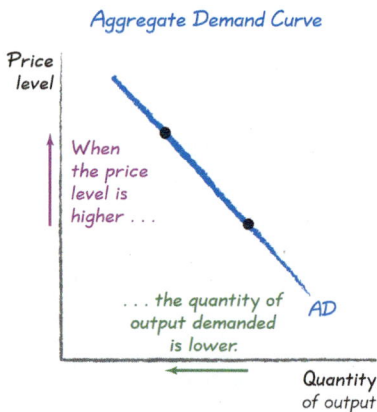

Price level

When the price level is higher . . .

. . . the quantity of output demanded is lower.

AD

Quantity of output

The aggregate demand curve is downward-sloping because a higher price level leads to less aggregate demand. Put the links together, and you've explained why the aggregate demand curve is downward-sloping: The higher this year's average price level, the higher the inflation rate; the Fed responds to inflation by raising the real interest rate; and this higher interest rate leads to lower levels of spending, and hence less aggregate demand.

The aggregate demand curve summarizes this logic, showing that a higher price level ultimately leads buyers to demand a lower quantity of output. The same forces also operate in reverse, and so they also explain why a lower price level leads buyers to demand a higher quantity of output. Because the Fed plays an important role in this process, this is sometimes called the *Fed channel.*

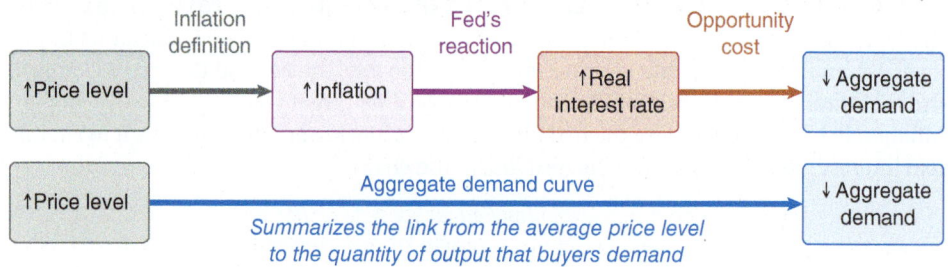

The Fed channel operated differently in the past. Earlier economists described the Fed channel somewhat differently, calling it instead an *interest rate effect.* This is because back in the 1970s the Fed didn't set interest rates directly; instead it focused on hitting pre-announced targets for the nominal money supply, which is the quantity of money in circulation. If the price level rose, then the real money supply — that is, the quantity of money measured in terms of its purchasing power — would mechanically fall. A decrease in the real money supply has the effect of pushing the real interest rate up, which in turn reduces output. The underlying insight of the interest rate effect — that a higher price level can lead to a higher real interest rate which reduces output — remains relevant. The only difference is that today, the Fed sets the interest rate directly, rather than setting the nominal money supply and passively allowing the interest rate to respond. The Fed channel describes the modern version of this dynamic, but in terms that reflect the modern reality that the Fed directly raises the interest rate in response to inflationary price rises.

There are other economic forces that also lead the aggregate demand curve to be downward-sloping. In addition to the *Fed channel,* there's an *international trade effect,* in which a higher price level in the United States leads American-made products to become more expensive relative to foreign goods. Thus, a higher price level reduces net exports, and hence aggregate expenditure. Because net exports is a small component of aggregate expenditure, this effect tends to be small.

There's also a *wealth effect,* in which a higher price level reduces real wealth by reducing the purchasing power of assets whose values are fixed in nominal dollars — like the cash in your wallet. Lower real wealth leads people to spend less. This effect is likely small because changes in wealth tend to lead to relatively small changes in spending. The wealth effect is also partly countered by an offsetting *debt effect* in which a higher price level reduces the real value of people's nominal debts, leading them to spend more.

Analyzing Aggregate Demand

The aggregate demand curve is useful because you can use it to forecast the consequences of changing market conditions. As you do so, be sure to distinguish between the effects of a change in the price level — which will cause a movement along the aggregate demand curve — from shifts in other factors, which shift the curve.

Changes in the price level lead to movements along the aggregate demand curve. The aggregate demand curve illustrates how different price levels lead to differences in the quantity of output demanded. It's useful because when the price level changes, you can simply consult this curve to figure out the new quantity of output demanded. The green arrow in Figure 2 illustrates how a higher price level leads to a movement along the aggregate demand curve to a new point that corresponds to a lower quantity of output demanded. The purple arrow shows that a lower price level leads to a movement along the aggregate demand curve, but this time to a point where there's a higher quantity of output demanded.

Other changes in spending shift the aggregate demand curve. The aggregate demand curve shows the level of aggregate expenditure at each price level. Any other factor — that is, any factor other than a change in the price level — that causes consumers, investors, the government, or foreigners to change their spending plans will shift aggregate expenditure, causing the aggregate demand curve to shift.

Higher spending increases aggregate demand, shifting the curve to the right. The new equilibrium will occur where this new aggregate demand curve intersects the aggregate supply curve. As Panel A on the left of Figure 3 shows, an increase in aggregate demand causes the economy to move to a new equilibrium with higher output and a higher price level. That means that increasing aggregate demand leads to a period of rising output (which we call an expansion) and rising prices (which you should recognize as inflation).

Figure 2 | The Aggregate Demand Curve

Changes in the price level lead to movements along the aggregate demand curve.

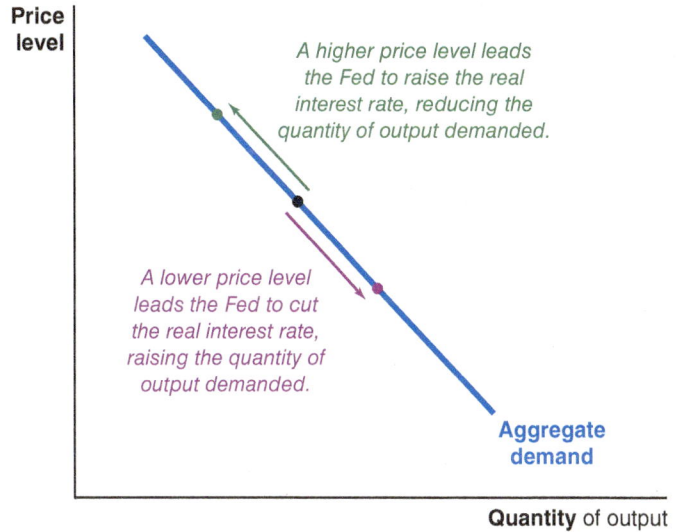

A higher price level leads the Fed to raise the real interest rate, reducing the quantity of output demanded.

A lower price level leads the Fed to cut the real interest rate, raising the quantity of output demanded.

Aggregate demand

Quantity of output

Figure 3 | Shifts in Aggregate Demand

The aggregate demand curve shifts due to changes in aggregate expenditure (at a given price level).

Panel A: An Increase in Aggregate Demand

- **A** An **increase in aggregate expenditure** at any price level causes the **aggregate demand curve to shift to the right**.
- **B** This leads the economy to move to a **new equilibrium**.
- **C** Leading to a **rise in output** (and hence an *economic expansion*).
- **D** It also leads to a **rise in prices** (and hence a burst of *inflation*).

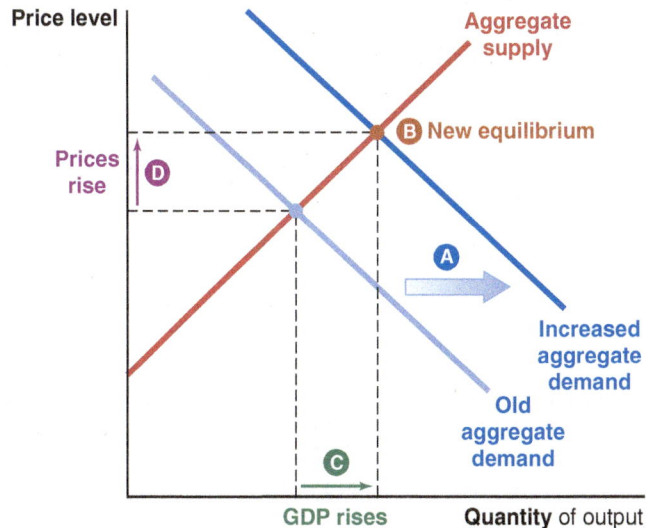

Panel B: A Decrease in Aggregate Demand

- **A** A **decrease in aggregate expenditure** at any price level causes the **aggregate demand curve to shift to the left**.
- **B** This leads the economy to move to a **new equilibrium**.
- **C** Leading to a **fall in output** (and hence a *recession*).
- **D** It also leads to a **fall in prices** (and hence a burst of *deflation*, or perhaps *lower inflation*).

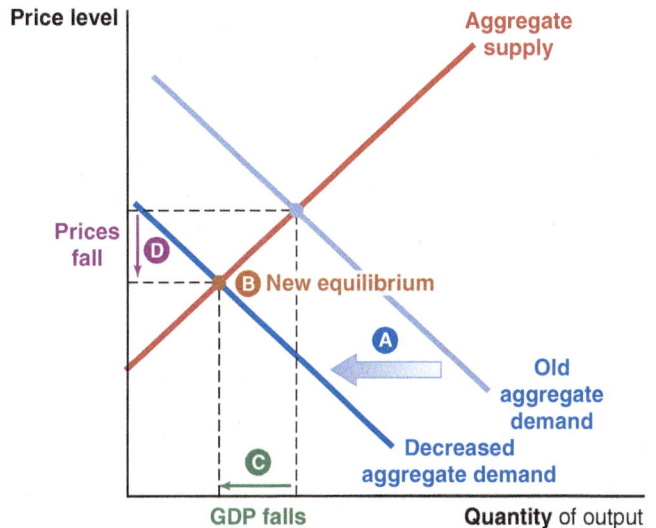

Lower spending decreases aggregate demand, shifting the curve to the left. Panel B on the right of Figure 3 shows that a decrease in aggregate demand shifts the economy to a new equilibrium with lower output and a lower price level. It follows that decreasing aggregate demand leads to a recession (a period of declining economic activity), and deflation (in which the price level is falling). In reality, many economies experience ongoing inflation for other reasons, and so a decrease in aggregate demand might lead to lower inflation, rather than outright deflation.

Aggregate Demand Shifters

So far we've seen that shifts in aggregate demand have an important influence on business cycle conditions. Our next task is to identify the sorts of changes that might catalyze a shift in aggregate expenditure and hence the aggregate demand curve. Remember, *Aggregate expenditure* $= C + I + G + NX$. It follows that aggregate demand will increase in response to an increase in consumption, investment, government spending, or net exports.

Demand shifter 1: Consumption increases when people feel more prosperous. People typically spend more when they have more money to spend, or are confident that they soon will. Thus, any development that makes people feel more prosperous — or more confident that they will soon be prosperous — leads to an increase in consumption, thereby increasing aggregate demand. This means that consumption will shift in response to:

Wealth When the stock market booms or house prices rise, stockholders and homeowners feel more prosperous because their wealth has increased. As those lucky stockholders and homeowners spend some of their newfound wealth, consumption will increase.

Consumer confidence The interdependence principle reminds you that the decisions you make today depend on your expectations about what's going to happen in the future. And when you feel confident that your income will grow in the future, you might ramp up your spending in advance. As a result, consumption increases when an improved economic outlook boosts consumer confidence.

Taxes and government assistance When the government cuts taxes, or when it increases government assistance payments like unemployment insurance, people have more disposable income that they can use to buy stuff. And so consumption increases when government policy puts more money in people's pockets.

Inequality People with low incomes tend to spend a larger share of their income than do those with higher incomes. It follows that redistributing income from those with higher incomes to those with lower incomes — including through government transfer payments and changes in the tax system — tends to increase consumption.

They're shifting the aggregate demand curve.

Sarah Casillas/DigitalVision/Getty Images

Consumption increases if people feel more prosperous:
↑ Wealth
↑ Consumer confidence
↑ Government assistance
↓ Taxes
↓ Inequality

Interpreting the DATA   How a virus is like a tax

Figure 4 shows that the pandemic led consumers to dramatically cut their spending. Partly, this decline in consumption reflects a decrease in wealth as the stock market crashed; but that can't be the whole story, because stocks quickly recovered. And partly it's because consumer confidence fell, though it didn't fall by enough to explain the entire decline in consumption. You need to think creatively to get the other important factor. Think of the coronavirus as effectively imposing a tax on spending. The virus is like a tax, because it makes buying stuff more costly, although that extra cost is measured not in dollars, but rather in the health risk associated with going shopping.

Just as our approach suggests, this "tax hike" led people to sharply cut their consumption spending in 2020. Moreover, this insight predicted — correctly! — that people would cut back more on services (like restaurants, concerts, and travel) because they involve greater health risk and so impose a larger "Covid tax." It also explains why spending on goods rebounded quickly, as stores adopted curbside pickup and online ordering. Thinking this way would also have led you to predict — again, correctly! — that consumption would be much stronger in 2021 when vaccines became available. That's because vaccines are like a stimulatory tax cut, as they reduce the health risk associated with shopping. ∎

Figure 4 | Consumption Spending Plummeted During the Pandemic

Real consumption spending per person (2012 dollars, at an annual rate)

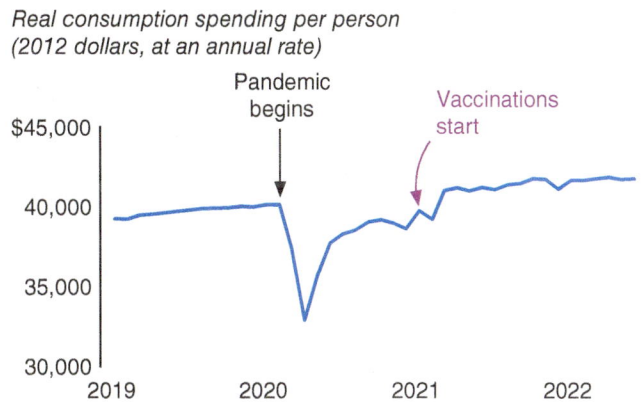

Data from: Bureau of Economic Analysis.

Demand shifter 2: Investment increases when it's profitable for businesses to expand. As a manager, you'll invest in new machinery when you believe that it will be profitable to expand your production. The cost-benefit principle reminds you to consider both the benefits of the extra revenue you'll earn from adding to your production capacity, and the cost of making that investment. As a result, aggregate demand will shift when investment changes in response to:

An expanding economy When the economy is expanding, so is the demand for goods and services. In order to produce more, managers will need to expand their production capacity, and entrepreneurs will see an opportunity to start new businesses. As a result, investment in new equipment increases when the economy is expanding more rapidly.

Business confidence Because physical capital investments tend to last for years, or even decades, your assessments about whether to buy new equipment should depend not only on today's profits, but also on your expectations about future profitability. That's why investment increases when managers are more confident about their future profitability.

Corporate taxes Lower corporate taxes increase the after-tax profits that your company will earn from investing in new equipment. As a result, investment increases in response to a cut in corporate tax rates. Investment also increases in response to targeted investment tax credits that reduce the after-tax cost of buying new equipment.

Lending standards and cash reserves If your business finds it hard to borrow money at a reasonable interest rate, you can only invest if your company has the cash on hand to do so. It follows that investment tends to increase when loans are easier to get, or businesses have large cash reserves. Cash reserves are particularly important when the financial system is not working well.

Uncertainty If you're uncertain about the economic outlook — it could be great, it could be terrible — remember that you usually have the option to postpone breaking ground on major investment projects until the outlook is a bit clearer. Lower uncertainty leads managers to restart these shelved projects, leading to an increase in investment.

It's only a worthwhile investment if the opportunity cost isn't too high.

Demand shifter 3: Government purchases increase when policymakers decide to spend more on goods and services. For example, Congress may pass legislation to spend more on roads and bridges, invest in pandemic preparedness, or purchase military equipment. In some cases, these spending bills have the explicit goal of stimulating an increase in aggregate demand. In addition, some government programs — known as *automatic stabilizers* — automatically increase spending when the economy is weak.

Remember that government spending directly increases aggregate expenditure — and hence shifts the aggregate demand curve — only when the government purchases goods and services. By contrast, many government programs — such as unemployment insurance or Social Security — simply transfer money from one bank account (the government's) to another (the recipient's), and so they don't *directly* increase aggregate

Investment increases if it's profitable to expand production:
↑ GDP growth
↑ Business confidence
↑ Investment tax credits
↓ Corporate taxes
↑ Easier lending standards and more cash reserves
↓ Uncertainty

Government purchases increase in response to:
- Spending bills
- Automatic stabilizers

. . . but not transfer payments (at least not directly)

Net exports increase in response to global factors:
↑ Global GDP growth
↓ U.S. dollar
↓ Trade barriers in foreign markets
↑ Trade barriers to U.S. market

Global factors determine net exports.

Shifts in Aggregate Demand

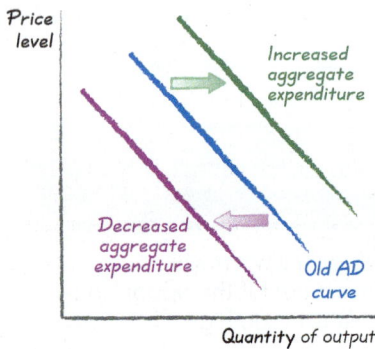

expenditure. However there is an *indirect* effect, as redistributing money to people who are more likely to spend it will increase consumption, and hence aggregate expenditure.

Demand shifter 4: Net exports increase due to global factors. Net exports rise when people in other countries want to buy more American-made goods and services. It's the interdependence principle at work, as net exports link the U.S. economy with economies around the world. Aggregate demand will shift when net exports rise or fall in response to:

Global economic growth When the economies of our trading partners do well, their consumers and businesses have more money to spend, and so they buy more goods, including more American-made goods, leading net exports to increase.

The exchange rate When the U.S. dollar becomes cheaper, our goods become cheaper to foreign buyers, leading exports to rise. A cheaper U.S. dollar also means that foreign goods become more expensive (in dollars) for U.S. buyers, leading imports to fall. Both forces—rising exports and falling imports—cause net exports to increase.

Trade barriers Exports increase when there are fewer barriers preventing U.S. businesses from selling their goods in other countries, while imports increase when there are fewer barriers preventing foreign businesses from selling to buyers in the United States. Because trade agreements typically reduce barriers to both imports and exports, their effect on net exports (which is exports less imports) is unclear. Likewise, trade wars—in which higher trade barriers preventing imports lead other countries to retaliate by raising barriers that prevent foreigners from buying American exports—will reduce both imports and exports, yielding an unclear effect on net exports.

Anything that shifts any component of aggregate expenditure shifts the aggregate demand curve. At this point, this list of changes that can shift the aggregate demand curve might seem a bit exhausting. I've put it all together for you in Figure 5. But you don't need to memorize this whole list, because it's all about just one idea: The aggregate demand curve shifts in response to a change in any component of aggregate expenditure. That's the easy way to remember this list: It's just *C, I, G,* and *NX.*

Figure 5 | Spending Shocks Shift the Aggregate Demand Curve

Aggregate demand curve shifters	Examples that *increase* aggregate demand *(shifting the curve to the right)*
Consumption *rises if people feel more prosperous*	↑Wealth, ↑Consumer confidence, ↑Government assistance, ↓Taxes, ↓Inequality
Investment *rises if it's profitable to expand production*	↑Output growth, ↑Business confidence, ↑Investment tax credits, ↓Corporate taxes, ↑Easier lending standards and more cash reserves, ↓Uncertainty
Government purchases *rise when the government buys more goods and services*	Spending bills, Automatic stabilizers . . . but not transfer payments (at least not directly)
Net exports *rise in response to global factors*	↑Global Output growth, ↓U.S. dollar, ↓Trade barriers in foreign markets, ↑Trade barriers to U.S. market

Note that **interest rates** are not listed, because only some interest rate changes shift the *AD* curve.

*These examples all cause an increase in aggregate expenditure, which shifts the *AD* curve to the right. Reverse the sign of any arrow, and you'll get a change that decreases aggregate expenditure, shifting the *AD* curve to the left.

But interest rate changes don't always shift the aggregate demand curve. The real interest rate matters because it can lead to changes in aggregate expenditure, particularly investment. But it won't always lead the aggregate demand curve to shift. Why? Remember that the aggregate demand curve already reflects the changes in aggregate expenditure due to the Fed adjusting interest rates in response to inflation. We'll dig into when and how changing interest rates shift aggregate demand in a few pages when we analyze monetary policy. To preview: We'll discover that some interest rate changes lead to a movement along the aggregate demand curve, while others cause the curve to shift.

EVERYDAY Economics   How a recession is like a bad night's sleep

It's the night before a major exam, a big interview, or an important recital, and your mind races as you think about how important it is that you sleep well. Perhaps you're lucky, and you fall asleep right away. But if you don't, you might start to worry that you're not yet asleep, which stresses you out . . . making it impossible to fall asleep. Essentially, your anxiety about not sleeping causes you not to sleep. I bet you know the feeling.

The thing is, if you can quiet your fear of not sleeping, you'll find it easier to fall asleep. If you believe you can fall asleep, you probably will. It's a self-fulfilling prophecy. The same kind of self-fulfilling prophecy that prevents you from getting to sleep can cause an economic boom or bust. If you fear that a recession's looming, you might spend less. The problem is that if lots of people fear that a recession is looming, then lots of people will spend less, and aggregate demand will decrease, causing a recession. So if people fear a recession, there will probably be a recession. Pessimistic beliefs about the economy can create a pessimistic reality. President Franklin D. Roosevelt summarized this logic during the Great Depression, famously telling Americans that "the only thing we have to fear is fear itself."

His speech was intended to help switch the economy from an equilibrium of self-fulfilling pessimism to one of self-fulfilling optimism. Roosevelt knew that if he could convince people that the economy would recover, then they would spend more. And if they spent more, the increase in aggregate demand would lead output to rise and the economy to recover. A more optimistic expectation can also create a more optimistic reality. Remember FDR's lesson next time you're struggling to sleep: You have nothing to fear but fear itself. ∎

You have nothing to fear but fear itself.

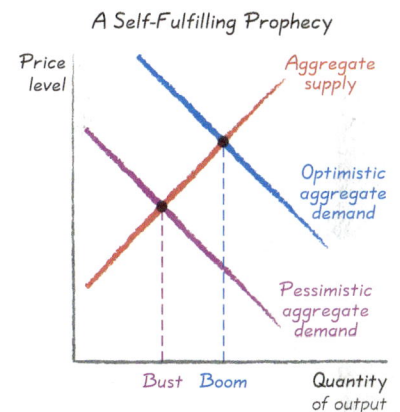
A Self-Fulfilling Prophecy

21.3 Aggregate Supply

Learning Objective *Evaluate the total quantity of goods and services that businesses want to supply.*

The aggregate supply curve describes the production and pricing decisions that suppliers make, and how they respond as macroeconomic conditions change. It's a topic so beefy that we'll need to start with a visit to Outback Steakhouse, the Australian-themed, American-owned chain restaurant.

Why Aggregate Supply Is Upward-Sloping

More precisely, we'll visit corporate headquarters. Put yourself in the shoes of the executives who have to decide what prices to print on next year's menus — what price to charge for the "Bloomin' Onion" (yum), "Kookaburra Wings" (they're really chicken), or a "Chocolate Thunder from Down Under" (just think of the jokes the poor wait staff must endure). At Outback Steakhouse, like almost any other business, pricing decisions depend on the state of the economy.

Higher output leads to higher prices. A strong economy with high GDP is good news for Outback Steakhouse because when incomes are high, your customers are more willing to splurge on a steak dinner. When the economy is doing particularly well, you'll find your restaurants overflowing with customers, and you'll need to pay your staff

What price will Outback charge for a Bloomin' Onion next year?

Aggregate Supply Curve

Price level

AS

B. Leads to higher prices

A. Higher output

Quantity of output

Aggregate Supply Curve

Price level

AS

B. Leads to lower prices

A. Lower output

Quantity of output

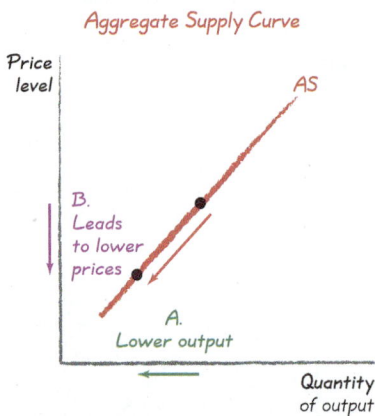

Lower GDP leads to lower prices.

overtime to keep up. Even then, you might not be able to keep up, and some of your customers might leave rather than wait two hours for a table.

A strong economy can lead to *excess demand* given your limited seating capacity. In the long run, if business continues to boom, it's worth building more restaurants. But that takes years; in the short run, you're stuck with your existing seating capacity, which means it's time to raise your prices. After all, even with higher prices, you can still fill your restaurant. And those higher prices will help cover your overtime bill.

The aggregate supply curve describes what happens, on average, across the millions of businesses that make up the U.S. economy. Outback's story is relevant, because when output is high, millions of businesses are in a similar situation to Outback Steakhouse. Many of these businesses will respond to their excess demand much as Outback did, by raising their prices a bit. The result is that in periods of high output, the average price level will be a bit higher than it would otherwise be.

Lower output leads to lower prices. On the other hand, a weaker economy will typically lead to lower prices. To see why, let's return to the early days of the coronavirus pandemic. While many restaurants closed, Outback kept most of its restaurants open. But fear of the virus still kept many customers away. This dramatic decline in restaurant dining caused revenue to crater, leading Outback to incur large losses. These losses reflect the reality that half-empty restaurants are rarely profitable.

Outback was facing a problem of *insufficient demand,* as the quantity of restaurant meals demanded at the prevailing price was far below the quantity that Outback wanted to supply. Management responded by revising the menu to cut the price of several popular dishes. Daniella Vona, Outback's chief marketing officer, said this was driven by a recognition that "value is important to our guests," and in a nod to the economic downturn, she added, "especially now." Outback even cut the price of its Bloomin' Onion. These price cuts made sense because the restaurant's staff barely had enough customers to stay busy, and so the marginal cost of serving extra meals was particularly low.

When GDP is low, millions of businesses face insufficient demand. Like Outback, most will find that their marginal costs are low when they're producing well below their capacity. They'll follow the same logic as Outback and respond to insufficient demand with lower prices. The result is that in periods of low GDP, the average price level across the whole economy will tend to be a bit lower than it would otherwise be.

The aggregate supply curve is upward-sloping because higher output leads to a higher price level. So far you've determined that lower output levels are associated with a lower average price level and higher output levels are associated with a higher average price level. Put the pieces together, and you've constructed an upward-sloping aggregate supply curve that illustrates the rule that the average price level rises with the quantity of output supplied.

Analyzing Aggregate Supply

You'll find the aggregate supply curve to be helpful because you can use it to forecast how economic conditions will change. As you do so, make sure to distinguish between a change in the price level (or a change in output), which causes a movement along the aggregate supply curve, from shifts in other factors that cause the aggregate supply curve to shift.

Changes in the price level lead to movements along the aggregate supply curve. The aggregate supply curve illustrates the price level associated with suppliers producing different quantities of output. You can use it to assess how the price level will respond to changes in output (or equivalently, you can use it to assess how output will respond to changes in the price level). The green arrow in Figure 6 illustrates how a movement along the aggregate supply curve to a higher price level is also associated with suppliers producing a higher quantity of output. (Alternatively phrased, it shows that higher output leads suppliers to push the price level higher.) The purple arrow shows that a lower price level leads to a movement along the aggregate supply curve, but this time to producing a lower quantity of output. (Or, to say it the other way, it shows that lower output leads suppliers to nudge the price level lower.)

What causes the aggregate supply curve to shift? I'm glad you asked . . .

Changes in production costs shift the aggregate supply curve.
The costs of production are central to pricing decisions. And that matters because changing production costs cause suppliers to change the prices they'll charge at any given level of output, thereby causing the aggregate supply curve to shift.

Lower production costs lead businesses to charge lower prices.
As a result, lower production costs reduce the average price level across the whole economy (at any given level of output), thereby shifting the aggregate supply curve downward or to the right. Because this shift leads to an increase in the quantity of output associated with any given price, we say that *lower production costs* lead to an *increase* in aggregate supply. This increase arises because lower production costs boost the profitability of producing stuff, leading suppliers to increase the quantity of output they'll produce at any given price level.

Any factor that decreases production costs will shift the aggregate supply curve down (or to the right), leading to a new equilibrium with both higher output and a lower price level (as shown in Panel A, on the left of Figure 7). The result is an economic expansion, accompanied by deflation. (In reality there are often other factors driving inflation, and so this might lead to a decrease in inflation rather than outright deflation.)

Figure 6 | **The Aggregate Supply Curve**

The relationship between the quantity of output supplied and the average price level.

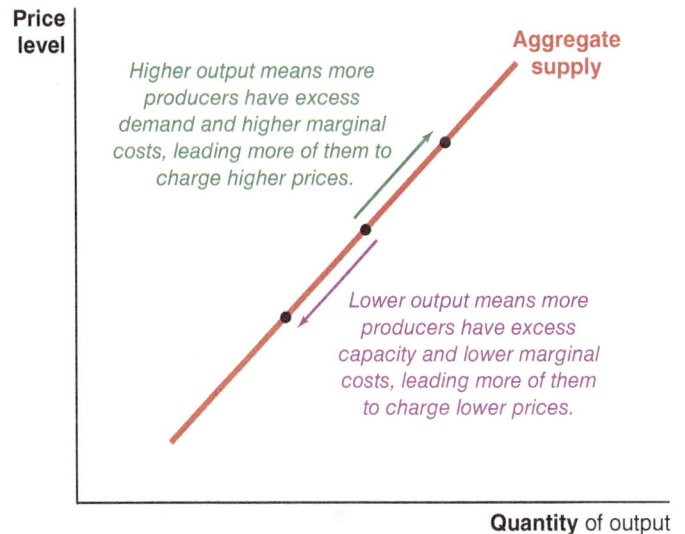

Figure 7 | **Shifts in Aggregate Supply**

The aggregate supply curve shifts due to changes in production costs.

Panel A: Lower Costs Cause an Increase in the Aggregate Supply

Ⓐ A **fall in production costs** causes the **aggregate supply curve to shift to the right (or downward)**.
Ⓑ This leads the economy to move to a **new equilibrium**.
Ⓒ Leading to a **rise in output** (and hence an *economic expansion*).
Ⓓ It also leads to a **fall in prices** (and hence a burst of *deflation*, or perhaps *lower inflation*).

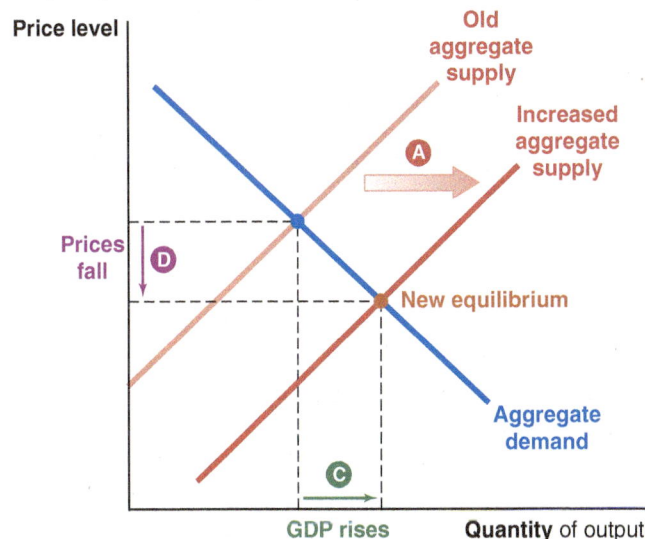

Panel B: Higher Costs Cause a Decrease in the Aggregate Supply

Ⓐ A **rise in production costs** causes the **aggregate supply curve to shift to the left (or upward)**.
Ⓑ This leads the economy to move to a **new equilibrium**.
Ⓒ Leading to a **fall in output** (and hence a *recession*).
Ⓓ It also leads to a **rise in prices** (and hence a burst of *inflation*).

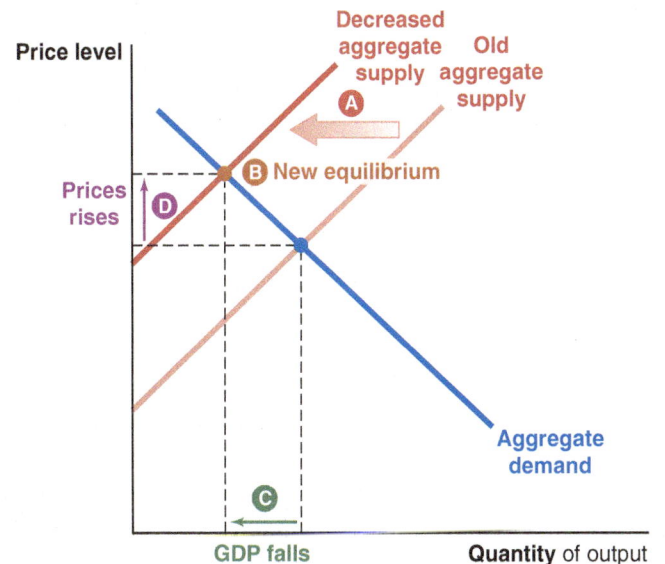

Higher production costs lead businesses to charge higher prices. The resulting rise in the average price level (at any given level of output) shifts the aggregate supply curve upward or to the left. Because this decreases the quantity of output associated with any given price, we say that *higher production costs* lead to a *decrease* in aggregate supply.

Any factor that increases production costs will shift the aggregate supply curve up (or to the left), leading to a new equilibrium with both lower output and a higher price level (as shown in Panel B, on the right of Figure 7). This combination of declining GDP (and hence economic stagnation) and rising prices (and hence inflation) is sometimes called *stagflation*.

A hint: It might be simpler to describe production costs as shifting the aggregate supply curve up or down. While we usually describe curves as shifting left or right, it's just as accurate to describe them as shifting up or down. And in this case it's more intuitive, because *higher* production costs lead businesses to charge *higher prices*, which will shift the aggregate supply curve up (to a *higher* position). And *lower* production costs lead businesses to charge *lower prices*, which will shift the curve down (to a *lower* position).

Shifts in Aggregate Supply

There are four key factors that shift production costs and hence the aggregate supply curve: shifts in input prices, import prices, productivity, and the exchange rate. Let's explore each in turn.

Supply shifter 1: Higher input prices raise production costs. The interdependence principle emphasizes the importance of linkages between markets, and it's especially relevant to aggregate supply. Any time the price of your inputs rises, so will your marginal costs, and higher marginal costs lead sellers to raise their prices, shifting the aggregate supply curve upward (or, equivalently, to the left). The same forces also operate in reverse, and declining input prices shift the aggregate supply curve down (or to the right).

Most businesses rate labor as their most important input, and so changes in wages and other labor costs can cause the aggregate supply curve to shift. Indeed, Outback Steakhouse cited rising labor costs as a key reason for its recent price rises. More generally, higher wages raise a seller's marginal costs, leading them to raise prices at any given level of output. That's why a sharp rise in labor costs causes the aggregate supply curve to shift upward (and to the left).

Economists also keep a close eye on the price of oil because it's used as an input in many sectors, and its price sometimes changes dramatically. Higher oil prices set off a chain reaction. Initially, higher oil prices lead products that are made from oil—like gasoline, heating oil, and propane—to become more expensive. In turn, this raises the cost of heating restaurants, factories, and offices. It also makes operating large equipment, running farms, and trucking goods across the country more expensive. The price of plastics, fertilizer, and rubber—which are also produced using oil—also rise, increasing the marginal costs of businesses that use these products as inputs. Eventually, these higher production costs lead businesses across an array of sectors to raise their prices, shifting the aggregate supply curve upward (or to the left). Other commodity prices—including agricultural goods in particular—can create supply shocks, particularly when severe weather disrupts harvests.

Supply shifter 2: Higher import prices reflect international shocks. When American consumers pay higher prices for imported cars, clothes, or computers, these higher import prices directly raise the average price level in the United States, shifting the aggregate supply curve upward. Higher prices for imported raw materials and intermediate inputs also raise the input costs of American producers, leading them to raise their prices. And even when producers rely on American-made commodities—like

Higher energy prices make everything more expensive.

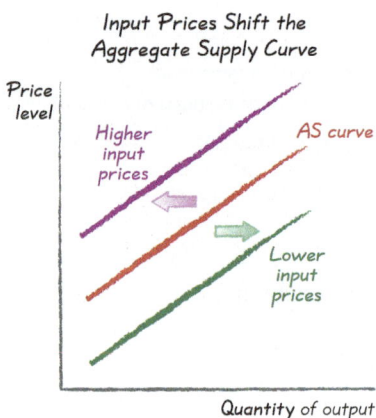

Input Prices Shift the Aggregate Supply Curve

Price level

Higher input prices

AS curve

Lower input prices

Quantity of output

Kansas-grown wheat — their price is effectively set on global markets and so rises and falls in response to global developments. In addition, all imported goods must be transported to the United States, and so changes in shipping costs — which rose dramatically during the pandemic — also shift import prices, and hence production costs.

This means that higher import prices shift the aggregate supply curve upward (or to the left), while lower import prices shift the curve downward (or to the right). More broadly, trade links tie the aggregate supply curve in the United States to supply conditions around the world. Indeed, because goods are often produced in complex global production chains — passing through different stages of production in different countries — aggregate supply is affected by developments not only with America's direct trading partners, but also with countries involved in the earlier stages of production chains. These global interdependencies can be efficient — allocating each task in the production process according to comparative advantage — but they also expose American producers to supply shocks from an array of foreign influences. As a result, import prices — and hence aggregate supply — rise and fall in response to foreign droughts, natural disasters, geopolitical tensions, wars, and trade disputes.

Supply shifter 3: Weaker productivity raises production costs. *Productivity* refers to the quantity of output a business produces per unit of input. Higher productivity means doing more, with less. Conversely, when businesses are relatively unproductive, they have to buy more inputs to produce the same output, and so their production costs are higher. While it's rare for productivity to decline, it can happen. For instance, public health precautions during the pandemic reduced the productivity of many businesses. Outback Steakhouse reduced the seating capacity in many of its restaurants. Other producers had to purchase more inputs, such as hand sanitizer, cleaning supplies, and Plexiglass shields, just to maintain their output. Some precautions — like deep cleaning — required more staff time but yielded no measurable increase in output. A widespread decrease in productivity raises production costs, shifting the aggregate supply curve upward (and to the left).

It also works the other way. Some economists are optimistic that many of the cost-saving investments that companies made during the pandemic — the move to online ordering, fewer meetings, less office space, and new ways of organizing work — will boost productivity over the next few years. If they're right, production costs will fall, shifting the aggregate supply curve downward (and to the right).

Supply shifter 4: A depreciating U.S. dollar raises production costs and reduces competition from abroad. Changes in the nominal exchange rate also shift pricing decisions and hence aggregate supply. Remember, the *exchange rate* is the price of a U.S. dollar in another currency. For instance, when the exchange rate is 120 Japanese yen per dollar, that means that one U.S. dollar costs 120 Japanese yen. We say that the U.S. dollar depreciates when it becomes cheaper for foreigners to buy (say, if the price of a dollar fell to 100 yen). A depreciation also means that foreign currency is more expensive for Americans to buy because it'll cost more dollars to buy a specific quantity of yen.

This really matters for businesses that rely on imported inputs, because a depreciating U.S. dollar raises the cost of their imported inputs. For example, when an Outback Steakhouse offers Wagyu beef imported from Japan, a depreciating U.S. dollar means that it will cost Outback more dollars to import the same quantity of Japanese beef. These higher marginal costs lead Outback's executives to raise their prices. The exchange rate also matters to businesses such as Ford or General Motors that compete with imported products, because a depreciating U.S. dollar raises the price (in dollars) of goods made by foreign competitors like Toyota. This weaker competitive pressure might lead domestic producers to raise their prices. Alternatively, if your business exports its output, a depreciating U.S. dollar makes American goods more competitive with foreign goods, leading foreign customers to be willing to pay more (in dollars) for your products. This increased pressure from foreign customers will lead many American exporters to raise the prices they charge their American customers.

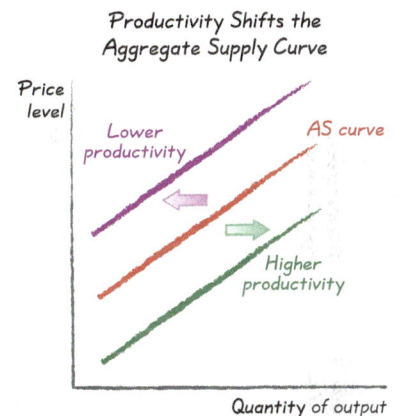

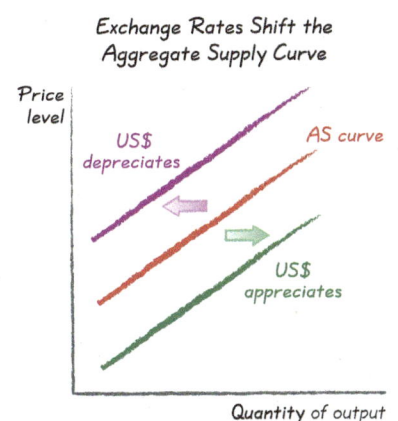

Productivity Shifts the Aggregate Supply Curve

Price level

Lower productivity

AS curve

Higher productivity

Quantity of output

Exchange Rates Shift the Aggregate Supply Curve

Price level

US$ depreciates

AS curve

US$ appreciates

Quantity of output

Consequently, a depreciation in the U.S. dollar leads suppliers to set higher prices at any level of output, shifting the aggregate supply curve upward (or to the left). By contrast, an appreciation of the dollar leads suppliers to set lower prices at any level of output, shifting the curve downward (or to the right).

Interpreting the DATA **How snarled supply chains shifted the aggregate supply curve**

The pandemic revealed a previously hidden fragility in global supply chains. Manufacturing has become an increasingly international endeavor, with each stage of production occurring in different countries, and components sourced from around the world. These complex supply chains are designed for efficiency, but they're not robust to the sort of intermittent global outages that a highly contagious and dangerous virus might cause. A surge in Covid cases in Malaysia, for instance, might lead a chip factory to pause production, leaving dozens of other factories around the world short of vital inputs. Indeed, many car production lines in the United States stood idle because of a global shortage of the computer chips that power the circuitry of modern cars. Similar stories played out in scores of other industries, as missing inputs stalled production lines.

These problems were compounded by chaos on global shipping routes. The pandemic led consumers to cut back on services like restaurant meals, travel, and entertainment, and they shifted to buying goods instead. But remember, goods are produced in these global supply chains that involve a lot of shipping. This burst of spending on goods quickly led global shipping routes to become overwhelmed. Ports became gridlocked, and the cost of shipping a container from Shanghai to Los Angeles rose from around $2,000 to $25,000, even as delays rose. Problems cascaded, as ships that couldn't dock were forced to wait offshore rather than steam back across the ocean with return deliveries. The shift from shopping in person (which required delivery to stores) to shopping online (requiring delivery to individual houses) added further pressure to the logistics industry as warehouses near major population centers soon became overstuffed. The result was mayhem, delayed deliveries, and higher prices. Or, in the language of the *AD-AS* framework, the result was a decrease in aggregate supply, which caused the price level to rise, and output to fall. ■

Shipping snarls shifted supply.

ROBYN BECK/AFP/Getty Images

Aggregate supply shifts in response to changes in production costs, which can be caused by shifts in:

1. Input prices
2. Import prices
3. Productivity
4. The exchange rate

Anything that shifts production costs shifts the AS curve. The point of this analysis isn't to memorize a long list of factors that might shift the aggregate supply curve. Rather, focus on the bigger picture, which is that the aggregate supply curve shifts in response to changes in production costs, and we've identified three four shifters: input prices, import prices, productivity, and the exchange rate.

We're now going to explore how the tools of macroeconomic policy fit in to all of this. And that's going to require a brief visit into one of the most hair-raising periods in modern economic history: the arrival not just of the coronavirus, but also its associated economic ills.

Greatly depressed.

Michael Nagle/Bloomberg/Getty Images

21.4 Macroeconomic Shocks and Countercyclical Policy

Learning Objective *Forecast how the economy will respond to changing conditions.*

You probably remember early 2020 as the start of a public health crisis, as the coronavirus spread around an unsuspecting world. But it was also a pivotal moment for economic policymakers, as the health of the U.S. economy was also in danger. Stay-at-home orders had shuttered businesses, international trade ground to a halt, and millions of people were told not to report to work. Stocks tanked, and financial markets threatened to seize up. The economy was in free fall, and no one knew how bad things might get. Google searches for "Great Depression" hit an all-time high, reflecting a widespread fear that a repeat episode was in the cards.

The pressure to avert an economic calamity was intense. Economists met with members of Congress and Federal Reserve officials, often in last-minute Zoom meetings that ran late into the night. They worked from home on kitchen tables hastily repurposed into home offices, while their kids scuttled around underfoot because schools were closed. Some economists crunched numbers on what was happening, others diagrammed new theories about how the economy works during a pandemic. The goal was to diagnose what was going wrong so they could propose a cure, or at least some way of slowing the spread of economic ill-health.

Within just a few weeks, unemployment had risen from its lowest level in 50 years to its highest level in 50 years. The economy was cratering at a speed unmatched in American history.

The numbers the economists were poring over weren't abstract statistics; they summarized a landscape littered with dormant factories, millions of jobless workers fearful about their livelihoods, and families doing without.

If you were a member of the Federal Reserve or the president's economic team and you faced this wrenching downturn, what would you do?

Monetary Policy

Policymakers at the Federal Reserve responded to the crisis quickly and decisively, cutting its benchmark interest rate to zero percent in a series of emergency meetings. They also rolled out new programs that encouraged banks and others to loan money at relatively low rates. They did so with the hope that lower interest rates would lead people to spend more, and this boost to aggregate expenditure would kick-start a recovery.

The Fed cuts interest rates in response to both low inflation and weak output. This process of the Fed setting and adjusting interest rates in an effort to influence economic conditions is called **monetary policy.** It's worth distinguishing between the two reasons that might lead Fed policymakers to cut interest rates:

- **An inflation-induced response:** Throughout 2020, widespread price cutting — which was especially strong in Covid-sensitive sectors like restaurants, hotels, and airlines — led the price level to be lower than it otherwise would be, and inflation fell sharply. When the Fed is worried that inflation is too low, it responds by cutting the real interest rate. We call this an *inflation-induced* response.

- **An output-induced response:** A year later, the Fed faced a different dilemma. Inflation rose sharply during 2021 to uncomfortably high rates. Instead of raising interest rates to tame this inflationary surge, the Fed kept its benchmark interest rate at zero percent throughout the entire year. Fed officials said they did this to advance a different objective: promoting maximal employment and hence output. The Fed kept the real interest rate lower for longer in an effort to combat the decline in output. We call this an *output-induced* response.

An inflation-induced change in interest rates does not shift the aggregate demand curve. This distinction matters because we evaluate them differently. An inflation-induced response by the Fed is caused by a *change in the price level,* and you should recall that a change in the price level leads to a movement along the aggregate demand curve but not a shift. The Fed's inflation-induced responses are important, and they affect the economy. But their effects are already reflected in the aggregate demand curve whose downward slope illustrates how lower prices induce the Fed to cut the real interest rate, which boosts the quantity of output demanded. As a result, a

monetary policy The process of setting interest rates in an effort to influence economic conditions.

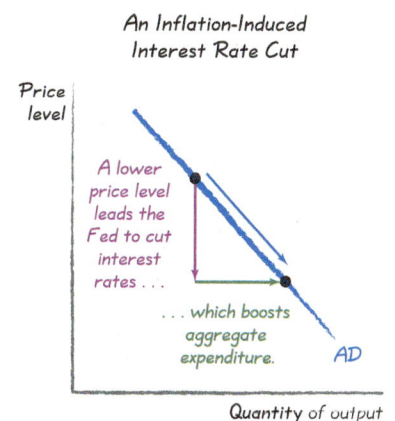

An Inflation-Induced Interest Rate Cut

A lower price level leads the Fed to cut interest rates . . .

. . . which boosts aggregate expenditure.

AD

Price level

Quantity of output

An Output-Induced Interest Rate Cut

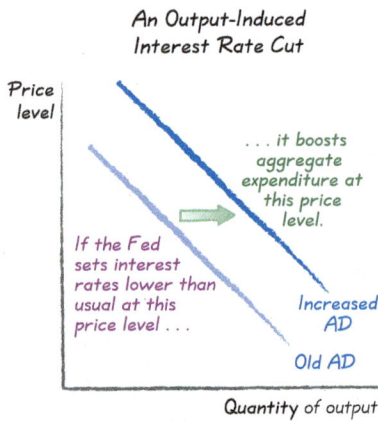

change in the interest rate that's caused by the Fed's typical response to inflation — that is, an inflation-induced response — won't shift the aggregate demand curve.

Any other change in the real interest rate shifts the aggregate demand curve. By contrast, an output-induced cut in the real interest rate reduces the real interest rate at the prevailing price level. It will stimulate greater aggregate expenditure at the current price level, thereby shifting the aggregate demand curve to the right. More generally, any change in the real interest rate — other than the Fed's systematic inflation-induced response to changes in the price level — will change the amount of aggregate expenditure at a given price level, thereby shifting the aggregate demand curve.

Lower real interest rates are expansionary. The Fed is said to be pursuing an *expansionary* monetary policy when it reduces the real interest rate lower than would be expected given its usual response to inflation. An expansionary monetary policy — like that pursued through 2021 — leads to an increase in aggregate demand. As Figure 8 shows, it shifts the aggregate demand curve to the right, leading to a new equilibrium with a higher level of output and higher prices.

Higher real interest rates are contractionary. If the Fed set a higher interest rate than would be expected given its usual response to inflation, it would be described as pursuing a *contractionary* monetary policy. Contractionary monetary policy leads to less spending at any given price level. This shifts the aggregate demand curve to the left, leading to a lower level of output and lower prices.

There's a constraint on interest rates. In the wake of the pandemic, the Fed pursued an expansionary monetary policy, with the goal of kick-starting the economy. But it quickly hit a troubling constraint: Once the Fed has cut the nominal interest rate to zero, further cuts won't work. The problem is that a negative nominal interest rate leads banks to keep money in their vaults (earning zero interest), rather than lending it out and earning negative interest. This constraint prevented the Fed from doing more to juice the recovery. The economy needed more help than monetary policy alone could provide.

Figure 8 | Monetary and Fiscal Policy

Expansionary fiscal or monetary policy shift the aggregate demand curve to the right.

Ⓐ An output-induced interest rate cut, or a boost to government purchases, will **shift the aggregate demand curve to the right**.

Ⓑ In response, the **quantity of output** rises.

Ⓒ And so does the **price level**.

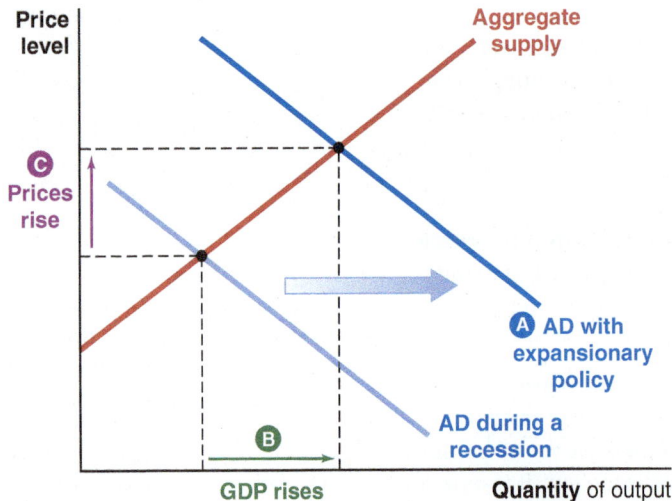

Fiscal Policy and the Multiplier

fiscal policy The government's use of spending and tax policies to influence economic conditions.

Fortunately, the government can also influence the economy by adjusting its own spending and tax policies — that is, through **fiscal policy.** Expansionary fiscal policy typically involves direct government purchases (such as building roads and bridges), as well as tax cuts. The pandemic caused a different kind of recession, forcing businesses to temporarily close, and people to stay home. And so the government's fiscal response focused instead on providing income support. It provided support to businesses, direct payments to households, expanded and more generous unemployment benefits, support for state and local governments, and measures to counter the virus. All told, the federal government added around $5.8 trillion in emergency measures, which adds up to around $17,500 per American. This was the largest peacetime stimulus ever.

The goal of this expansionary fiscal policy was to give people the means to resume spending when it became safe to do so. This spending boost would shift the aggregate demand curve to the right, raising output. To assess how much output might rise in response, we'll need to explore an idea called the multiplier.

An increase in spending has a multiplied effect on aggregate expenditure. An initial burst of spending will have repercussions throughout the economy. Consider the money the government spent improving school ventilation systems. It had a direct effect on factories producing fans, filters, and ductwork, which had to hire new workers to keep up with this extra demand. There are also important ripple effects. For instance, a worker who spends their new paycheck buying an exercise bike boosts the incomes of Peloton workers and shareholders. There are also second-round ripple effects. As Peloton sells more bikes, it will hire more production workers, who might buy lunch at a local Subway, leading the franchise owner to hire more sandwich artists. There are third-round effects, too. If some of those new Subway staff members enroll their children in day care, the local child care providers also receive a boost to their income. And so it continues.

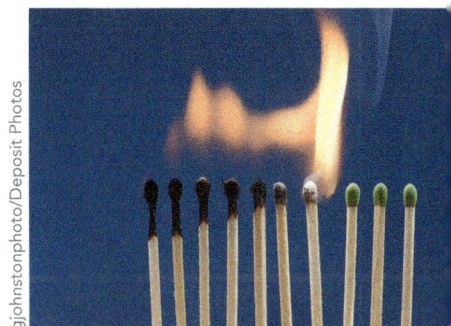

An initial stimulus can spark a lot of subsequent activity.

As this initial boost in spending reverberates through the economy, it illustrates the importance of the interdependence principle for understanding macroeconomic developments. This interdependence arises because one person's spending is another person's income. It means that extra spending by the government stimulates extra spending by construction workers, which stimulates extra spending in the fitness, food, and child care industries. As the initial burst of government purchases ripples through the economy, it has a *multiplier effect,* leading to an even larger boost to aggregate expenditure.

A burst of government spending will crowd out some private spending. There's another dynamic, however, and it tempers this multiplier effect. As spending boosts the demand for output, some businesses will run into capacity constraints. When the demand for their output exceeds their ability to supply it, they'll raise their prices, and the resulting boost to inflation might lead the Fed to raise the real interest rate. These higher interest rates reduce private-sector spending (especially investment). Thus, a burst of government spending might end up *crowding out* some private spending. The overall effect on output depends on how much of the multiplier effect is dampened by crowding out.

The multiplier summarizes the effect of an initial burst of spending on output. You can summarize the consequences of a rise in spending — including the direct impact, subsequent multiplier effects, and crowding out — with a single number called the multiplier. The **multiplier** measures how much GDP changes as a result of both the direct and indirect effects flowing from each extra dollar of spending. For instance, if the multiplier is 2, then an initial $1 boost to spending will generate a total of $2 in additional spending and hence output. When people have a greater propensity to spend additional income they receive, the ripple effects of an initial burst of spending will be larger, leading the multiplier to be larger. It is also larger when the absence of capacity constraints limits the extent of crowding out.

multiplier A measure of how much GDP changes as a result of both the direct and indirect effects flowing from each extra dollar of spending.

The multiplier is useful because you can use it to forecast the effects of changes in spending, as follows:

$$\Delta\text{GDP} = \Delta\text{Spending} \times \text{Multiplier}$$

Do the Economics

The Covid relief bills set aside around $190 billion in new funding to help schools reopen and stay open during the pandemic. How much will GDP rise after this burst of education spending, if the multiplier is two?

$$\Delta\text{GDP} = \underbrace{\$190\text{ billion}}_{\Delta\text{Spending}} \times \underbrace{2}_{\text{Multiplier}} = \$380\text{ billion} \ \blacksquare$$

If you want to dig more deeply into the logic (and math) of the multiplier, read the appendix, "Aggregate Expenditure and the Multiplier."

Forecasting Macroeconomic Outcomes

It's time to pull the threads of this chapter together so that you can use what you now know about aggregate demand and aggregate supply to forecast how the economy will respond to changing market conditions.

Apply the three-step recipe to forecast macroeconomic outcomes.
You'll find forecasting easiest if you work your way through the following three-step recipe. To assess the likely consequences of any change in economic conditions, ask yourself:

Step 1: *Is this a shift in aggregate demand or aggregate supply?*

Remember that the aggregate demand curve shifts in response to changes in any element of aggregate expenditure at the current price level, whether it's due to *C, I, G,* or *NX*. By contrast, the aggregate supply curve shifts in response to changes in production costs.

Step 2: *Is that shift an increase, shifting the curve to the right? Or is it a decrease, shifting the curve to the left?*

Higher aggregate expenditure will shift the aggregate demand curve to the right, while lower aggregate expenditure will shift it to the left. And higher production costs will shift the aggregate supply curve to the left (which might be more intuitively described as an upward shift), while lower production costs will shift aggregate supply to the right (or, equivalently, downward).

Step 3: *How will the price level and quantity of output change in the new equilibrium?*

Compare the old equilibrium with the new equilibrium.

Forecast how the economy responds to macroeconomic shocks.   Let's take this framework for a test drive, analyzing some of the dramatic shifts that occurred during the Covid recession and subsequent recovery. Along the way, you'll see just how useful this tool has proven to be at forecasting the economy's actual response.

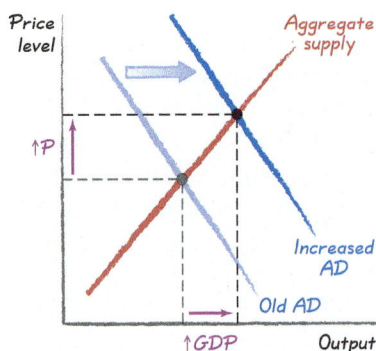

The Fed reads the tea leaves.   *On March 3, 2020, there were only 12 Covid cases recorded in the United States, but even that was enough for the Fed to recognize that "the coronavirus poses evolving risks to economic activity," so it cut the interest rate by $\frac{1}{2}$ of a percentage point at an emergency meeting, and cut it to effectively zero percent at a follow-up emergency meeting 12 days later.*

Step 1: A change in the real interest rate will affect how much people and businesses spend, which *shifts the aggregate demand curve.* (Note that this is an output-induced change.)

Step 2: A lower real interest rate will *increase* aggregate expenditure, *shifting the aggregate demand curve to the right.*

Step 3: This leads both *output and the price level to rise.*

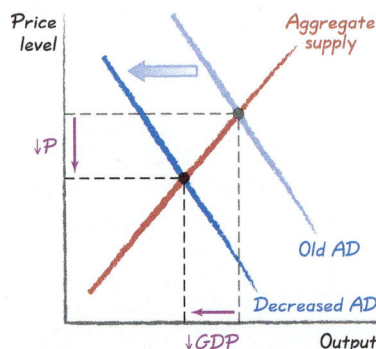

Consumers cut their spending: *On March 13, 2020, the federal government declared a national emergency. Consumers feared that this public health crisis was also going to threaten their economic futures, and they responded by drastically cutting their spending.*

Step 1: A decrease in consumption is a decrease in spending, which *shifts the aggregate demand curve.*

Step 2: A *decrease* in aggregate expenditure will *shift the aggregate demand curve to the left.*

Step 3: This leads both *output and the price level to fall.*

Businesses shut down. *On March 16, 2020, California issued stay-at-home orders, New York followed three days later, and most states followed suit in subsequent weeks. These orders forced many nonessential businesses to temporarily close their doors. Even when the mandates were lifted, many businesses were cautious about reopening. In their judgment, the costs of remaining open were too great.*

Step 1: Businesses that are closed produce less output, which *shifts the aggregate supply curve.*

Step 2: This *decrease* in production (which you can think of as an increase in production costs associated with any level of output) will *shift the aggregate supply curve up and to the left.*

Step 3: This leads *output to fall* and the *price level to rise.*

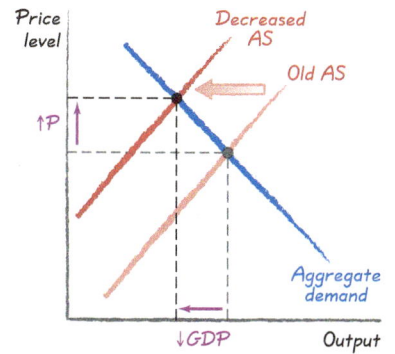

Income support payments: *On March 27, 2020, the government passed the CARES Act which focused on supporting people's incomes. The goal was to ensure people had the means to resume spending when it was safe to do so. This bill included direct payments to households, it made more people eligible for unemployment benefits, and those benefits were made more generous.*

Step 1: These income support programs aren't directly counted as government purchases because the government is transferring money, but not buying anything. But these checks led people to increase their spending, which *shifts the aggregate demand curve.*

Step 2: An *increase* in aggregate expenditure will *shift the aggregate demand curve to the right.*

Step 3: This leads both *output and the price level to rise.*

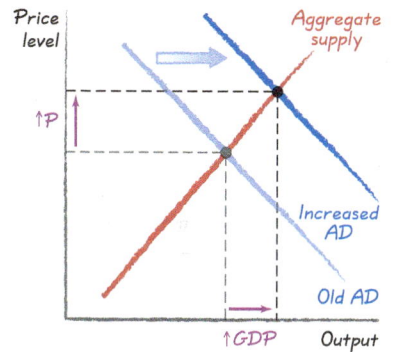

Do the Economics

Think you've got this framework all figured out? Here's your chance to practice as you work through 10 more scenarios. These aren't contrived textbook examples, but rather some of the shocks that hit the economy during the Covid recession and subsequent stop-start recovery:

Economic growth slows around the world. *Just as Covid had led the U.S. economy to slow, it caused recessions all around the world, reducing the incomes of many key trading partners.*

Step 1: A decrease in the incomes of a trading partner leads them to buy fewer American goods, which leads to a decrease in net exports, and thus s*hifts the aggregate demand curve.*

Step 2: A *decrease* in aggregate expenditure will *shift the aggregate demand curve to the left.*

Step 3: This leads both *output and the price level to fall.*

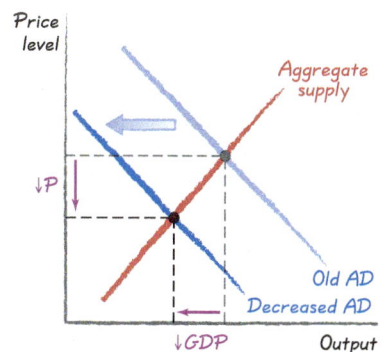

Income inequality declines. *Wages rose more for low-income jobs than for others, and the government's income support programs also raised millions of people out of poverty. As a result, income inequality actually fell.*

Step 1: People with lower incomes spend more of their income than those with higher incomes, and so consumption will rise. Higher aggregate expenditure *shifts the aggregate demand curve.*

Step 2: An *increase* in aggregate expenditure will *shift the aggregate demand curve to the right.*

Step 3: This leads both *output and the price level to rise.*

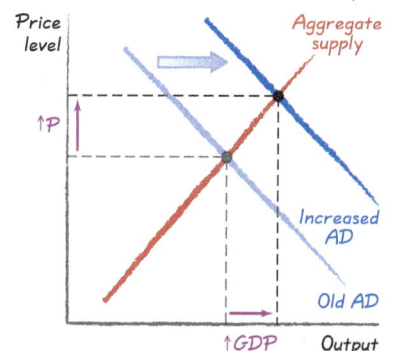

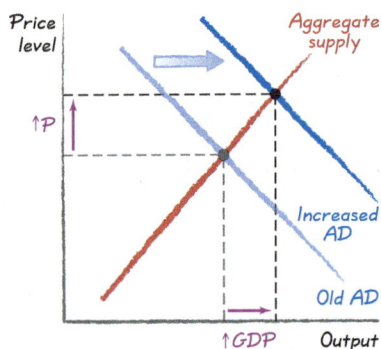

Business cashflows improve. *The government launched the Paycheck Protection Program, which provided forgivable loans to businesses. This program ensured that businesses had cash on hand.*

Step 1: Greater cashflow leads to greater investment, which *shifts the aggregate demand curve.*

Step 2: An *increase* in aggregate expenditure will *shift the aggregate demand curve to the right.*

Step 3: This leads both *output and the price level to rise.*

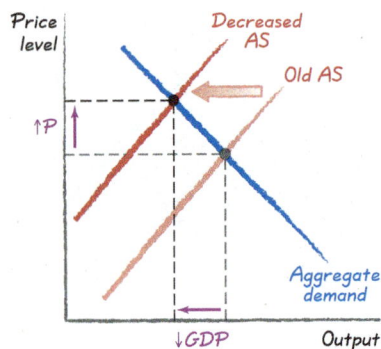

Labor supply shortages emerge. *Older workers became reluctant to return to the workplace while Covid case rates were high. This reduced labor supply led to labor shortages which caused wages to rise.*

Step 1: Higher wages raise input prices and hence production costs, which *shifts aggregate supply.*

Step 2: An increase in production costs *shifts aggregate supply up and to the left.*

Step 3: This leads *output to fall* and the *price level to rise.*

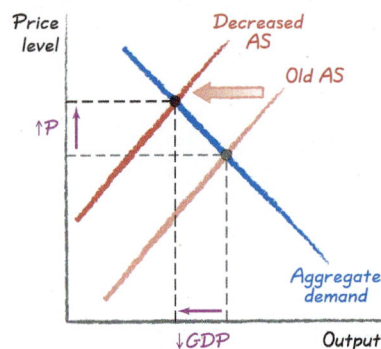

Supply chains got snarled. *Global supply chains were thrown into turmoil, and shipping became expensive and unreliable. The result was long delays and higher prices for many inputs like computer chips.*

Step 1: Higher input prices raise production costs, which *shifts aggregate supply.*

Step 2: An increase in production costs *shifts aggregate supply up and to the left.*

Step 3: This leads *output to fall* and the *price level to rise.*

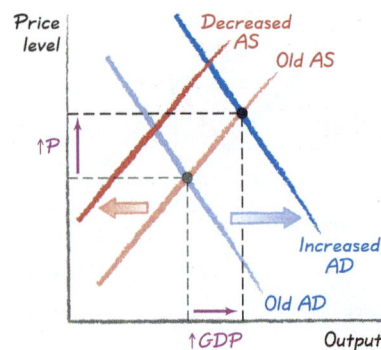

The U.S. dollar depreciates. *Investors became less willing to buy U.S. dollars when the Federal Reserve promised to keep U.S. interest rates low. This reduced demand for dollars caused the value of the dollar to decline.*

Step 1: A cheaper dollar makes U.S. exports cheaper to foreign buyers, boosting net exports, which *shifts the aggregate demand curve.* A cheaper dollar also raises import prices and hence production costs, which *shifts aggregate supply.*

Step 2: The boost to net exports will *shift aggregate demand to the right,* while higher import prices will *shift aggregate supply up and to the left.*

Step 3: This leads the *price level to rise,* while the effect on the *quantity of output produced is indeterminate.*

Vaccines become available. *As vaccinations became more widespread, people became more comfortable with activities that involve other people. This includes not only spending money at stores, but also returning to work.*

Step 1: Higher consumption boosts aggregate expenditure, which *shifts the aggregate demand curve.* Increased labor supply leads wages to fall, *which shifts aggregate supply.*

Step 2: The boost to consumption will *shift aggregate demand to the right,* while lower wages decrease production costs, *shifting aggregate supply down and to the right.*

Step 3: This leads *output to rise,* and the effect on the *price level is indeterminate.*

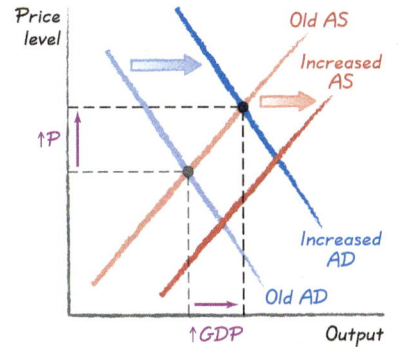

Higher inflation leads the Fed to raise interest rates. *Concern about higher inflation leads the Fed to raise its benchmark interest rate.*

Step 1: An inflation-induced interest rate change *does not shift the aggregate demand curve.* (The pathway by which higher prices lead to a higher real interest rate is already accounted for by the slope of the aggregate demand curve.)

Step 2: Neither curve shifts.

Step 3: This leads to *no change in output or the price level.*

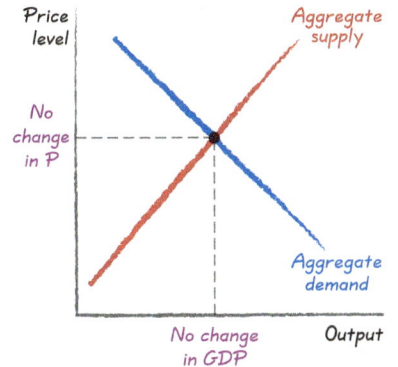

The government's fiscal stimulus programs ended. *The end of a fiscal stimulus created a fiscal contraction as government expenditures declined from their previously higher levels to more normal levels.*

Step 1: This decline in government expenditures causes aggregate expenditure to decline, which *shifts the aggregate demand curve.*

Step 2: A *decrease* in aggregate expenditure *shifts the aggregate demand curve to the left.*

Step 3: This leads both *output and the price level to decline.*

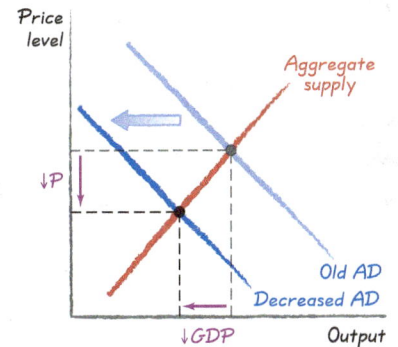

Russia invaded Ukraine. *The United States and its allies imposed sanctions against Russia, which is a major producer of oil. The reduced supply of oil to world markets raised the price of oil.*

Step 1: Oil is an important input, and so this change in input prices affects production costs, which *shifts the aggregate supply curve.*

Step 2: An increase in production costs *shifts aggregate supply up and to the left.*

Step 3: This leads *output to fall* and the *price level to rise.* ■

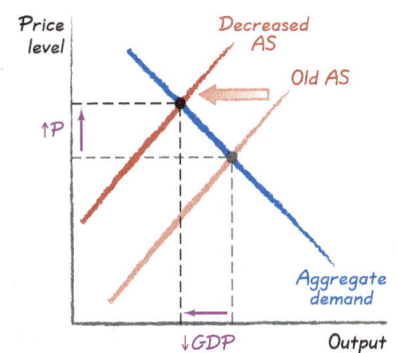

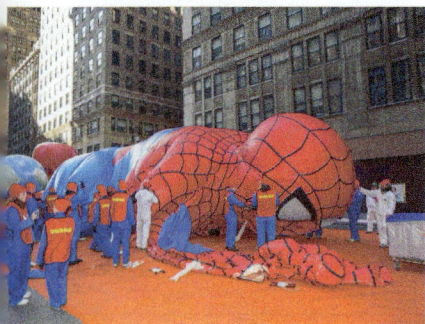
Deflation is rare.

Inflation will be lower when you forecast that the price level will be lower than it otherwise would be. In many of these cases, the *AD-AS* framework led us to predict that the average price level would fall, causing an episode of deflation. Don't take this too literally. In reality, deflation is rare. It's rare because inflation often has its own momentum, and so prices are often rising for other reasons. Think of your forecast as suggesting that this year's price level will be lower than it otherwise would be. When you conclude that this year's price level will be lower than it otherwise would be, you'll often be more accurate if you describe your forecast as a lower rate of inflation, rather than outright deflation.

Summarizing the effects of different macroeconomic shocks. The *AD-AS* framework is useful because it means that forecasting the consequences of whichever of the zillion things that might happen next to the economy — a disruption in financial markets, plummeting consumer confidence, geopolitical turmoil, or snarled global supply chains — doesn't require a zillion different kinds of analysis. Rather, you need to figure out if you're dealing with an aggregate demand shock (such as when consumers freak out), or an aggregate supply shock (like supply chain disruptions). Then it's simply a matter of shifting that curve and exploring how that type of shock will affect the economy.

Figure 9 draws the threads of our analysis together, summarizing our findings about the consequences of each of these types of shocks.

Figure 9 | Consequences of Macroeconomic Shifts

Shock	Effect on output	Effect on price level
Increase in aggregate demand *Spending rises; AD shifts right*	↑	↑
Decrease in aggregate demand *Spending falls; AD shifts left*	↓	↓
Increase in aggregate supply *Production costs fall; AS shifts down/right*	↑	↓
Decrease in aggregate supply *Production costs rise; AS shifts up/left*	↓	↑

My advice is not to memorize this table, but rather to always be ready to use your three-step recipe to figure out for yourself what's going to happen next. But presenting our findings this way highlights two key insights that you're about to find useful:

- Aggregate demand shocks lead output and prices to move in the same direction.
- Aggregate supply shocks lead output and prices to move in opposite directions.

Diagnosing the Causes of Macroeconomic Shifts

So far we've used the *AD-AS* framework to *predict* the consequences of different kinds of macroeconomic shocks. But there's another use for it. Economic conditions can sometimes shift sharply, and the economy — unlike a textbook — doesn't come with a big heading telling you whether the shift was caused by an aggregate demand or aggregate supply shock. But you can use what you've learned in this chapter to *diagnose* the causes of macroeconomic shifts. It's an important job because the first step in curing a country's macroeconomic ills is diagnosing its cause.

In fact, you've already developed this diagnostic tool:

- If output and prices move in the same direction, you can infer that aggregate demand shifted.
- If output and prices move in opposite directions, you can infer that aggregate supply shifted.

Figure 10 essentially starts with the previous figure, and rearranges it to show how you can use what is happening to output and prices to diagnose the underlying cause.

Figure 10 | Diagnosing the Cause of Business Cycle Fluctuations

Observe what is happening to output and prices, to diagnose the cause of economic fluctuations

	Output is rising *(an expansion)*	**Output is falling** *(a recession)*
Prices are rising *(inflation)*	**Aggregate demand increased** (Spending rose)	**Aggregate supply decreased** (Production costs rose)
Prices are falling—or rising less quickly *(deflation or disinflation)*	**Aggregate supply increased** (Production costs fell)	**Aggregate demand decreased** (Spending fell)

Armed with these insights, let's work through some examples of how this can help you make sense of changing economic conditions.

Do the Economics

In each of the following examples, use your diagnostic tools to assess what kind of shock hit the economy:

a. Analysts were puzzled to observe inflation rising even as the economy slid into a recession.

Rising prices and falling output occur when aggregate supply decreases, such as when production costs rise.

b. As the pandemic hit, basically everything closed down, and so analysts were unsure whether to think about this as a shock to aggregate demand or aggregate supply. In those first few months, output fell, as did the average price level.

Falling prices and falling output occur when aggregate demand decreases, due to a decline in spending.

c. As the recovery resumed momentum, output rose rapidly, as did inflation.

The combination of rising output and rising prices suggests that aggregate demand increased. ∎

21.5 Aggregate Supply in the Short Run and the Long Run

Learning Objective *Distinguish between the immediate effects, short-run effects, medium-run effects, and long-run consequences of economic shocks.*

As a forward-looking manager, you'll want to be able to forecast where the economy is going not only over the next few weeks and months, but also the ensuing few years, and even in the longer term beyond that. Changes in aggregate demand often have a fairly immediate effect. But because businesses take a while to change the prices they charge and the wages they pay, supply-side responses can take a while to play out. This can really matter because when suppliers have yet to adjust their prices, they often adjust the quantity of their output instead. And so the initial impact of a macroeconomic shock may be quite different from the longer-term effect. That's why our final task in this chapter is to

A long run.

Would adding zeros to all these price tags change anything?

classical dichotomy A purely nominal change—like a change in the average price level—won't have any effect on real variables in the long run.

adapt our analysis of the aggregate supply curve so that it can generate useful forecasts over many different time horizons.

We'll begin by analyzing two extreme cases: We'll start with the long run, in which all prices have adjusted, and then turn to the opposite extreme of the very short run, in which no prices have adjusted. These two cases will yield useful intuitions that will help us analyze the full set of responses over time.

Aggregate Supply in the Long Run with Flexible Prices

Let's start with the *long run,* which in this context means a period of time long enough that all businesses have had a chance to adjust the prices they charge, to tweak the wages they pay, and to adapt to any price changes from their suppliers, their rivals, and other businesses. Long-run analysis is relevant over time periods long enough for this process of adjustment to be complete — typically several years or longer. Over this time horizon you can think of all prices as responding flexibly to changing conditions.

In the long run, a change in the average price level has no effect on real variables. The question that the aggregate supply curve seeks to answer, is: How will suppliers change the quantity of output they'll produce at different average price levels? In the long run, the answer is: Not at all.

That might seem surprising, but a thought experiment might help explain why. Imagine that you go to sleep tonight, and you wake up a decade later to discover that every price in the economy is ten times higher. This future economy looks just like the present, except every price tag in the economy has grown an extra zero on the end of it. The price of your output is ten times higher, as is the price charged by each of your competitors. The price of your raw materials is ten times higher, as is the price of your electricity and the price of your monthly rent. And because the wage is ten times higher, your customers also have ten times as much income. After getting a quick breakfast (a decade is a long time to sleep!), you have to figure out what quantity of goods your factory should produce. Think about it for a while, and you'll realize that this future economy has a lot more zeros in it, but apart from that, nothing has changed. And if nothing has changed, there's no reason for you to change the quantity of output you produce. Indeed, no one will change the physical quantities of the stuff they buy, sell, produce, or do. In the long run, a change in the price level has no effect on the quantity of goods produced.

This insight reflects an idea called the **classical dichotomy,** and it informs how economists think about the long-run effects of changes in purely nominal variables, like the price level. The *dichotomy* is that what's happening in the real economy — like the quantity of output that businesses produce — can be analyzed separately from purely nominal variables like the average price level. And it's *classical* because it comes from the classical economists whose insights best apply to the long run.

The long-run aggregate supply curve is vertical. This thought experiment reveals that in the long run, the quantity of output that businesses supply will be the same whether the average price level stays at today's level or it rises by a factor of ten. The same logic says that the quantity of output supplied will be the same whether the average price level rises by a lot, a little, or indeed, if it falls. It follows that in the long run the aggregate supply curve must be vertical, as shown in Figure 11.

Figure 11 | The Long-Run Aggregate Supply Curve

In the long run when all prices are flexible, shifts in aggregate demand affect the price level but not output.

A In the long run, the quantity of output supplied is unaffected by the average price level, yielding a **vertical long-run aggregate supply curve**.

B C In both the equilibrium with **strong aggregate demand** and **weak aggregate demand**, output is the same.

D Changes in aggregate demand have **no effect on output**.

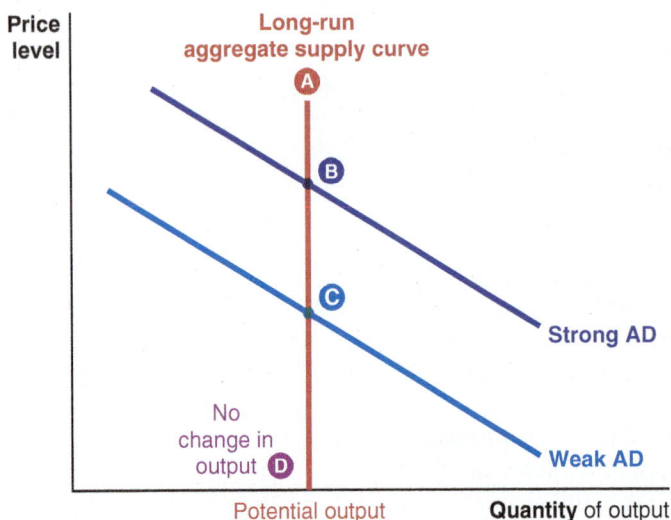

This vertical **long-run aggregate supply curve** illustrates the idea that over time, the economy will return to producing its potential output — the level of output that's produced when all resources are fully employed. The economy gravitates toward its potential output because market prices adjust to ensure that the demand for labor, capital, and raw materials will be equal to the supply.

Aggregate demand is irrelevant to long-run output. Figure 11 illustrates two alternative scenarios — one in which aggregate demand is weak and another in which it is strong. In both cases, the equilibrium level of output is identical (though the price level differs). This suggests that in the long run, aggregate demand is irrelevant in determining output. This insight is the reason that most economic analyses of the long-run determinants of output — like that we conducted in Chapter 10 on economic growth — focus on supply-side factors such as the quantities of physical capital, labor, and human capital that are available, and the technology that producers use to combine them.

long-run aggregate supply curve The aggregate supply curve that applies to the long run when prices have fully adjusted. Because the economy will return to producing its potential output, this curve is vertical.

Aggregate Supply in the Very Short Run with Fixed Prices

Now let's turn to the opposite extreme, and consider how the economy responds to an aggregate demand shock in the *very short run* — that is, over a period of time so brief that no business has had a chance to change its price. In the very short run, all prices are effectively fixed, which means that the aggregate supply curve must be horizontal, as shown in Figure 12.

The very-short-run aggregate supply curve is horizontal. This **very-short-run aggregate supply curve** illustrates the idea that in the immediate aftermath of an economic shock — before managers are able to adjust their prices — the only way that businesses can respond to changing conditions is to adjust the quantity of output they produce. In this context, the very short run might be a period of several weeks. If people feel they can no longer afford a meal at Outback Steakhouse and aggregate demand suddenly collapses, then Outback's restaurants will sit half-empty and its output will decline. (This actually happened in the early days of the pandemic.) And if higher incomes boost aggregate demand and lead people to eat out more, then Outback's output will rise sharply as it sells more meals each week. (This also happened, as the economy later recovered.) Figure 12 illustrates the economy-wide implications, in which changes in aggregate demand will — in the very short run — lead to large changes in output.

very-short-run aggregate supply curve The aggregate supply curve that applies to the very short run, in which no prices have changed. Because prices are effectively fixed, this curve is horizontal.

The response of suppliers depends on the time horizon you're analyzing. Our analysis so far yields a stark contrast: Shifts in aggregate demand lead to large changes in output in the very short run, but no change in output in the long run. These findings might sound contradictory, but they're not. Both Figure 11 and Figure 12 illustrate the response of the same economy with the same suppliers to the same economic shock, but they're showing effects over different time horizons. The immediate (very-short-run) effect of an increase in aggregate demand is that suppliers produce a lot more output, and in the longer run, that effect dissipates and there's no lasting effect on output.

These different responses over different time horizons arise because in the very short run, prices don't adjust at all, leaving the burden of adjustment to quantities; while in the

Figure 12 | The Very-Short-Run Aggregate Supply Curve

In the very short run when prices are fixed, aggregate demand shifts affect output, but not the price level.

A In the very short run, prices are yet to change and so the **very-short-run aggregate supply curve is horizontal**.
B If **aggregate demand is weak**, output will be low.
C If **aggregate demand is strong**, output will be high.
D Shifts in aggregate demand have a **big effect on output**.

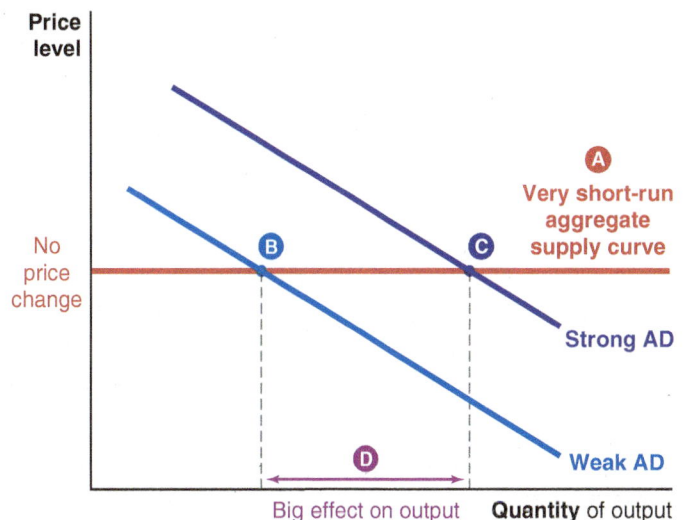

long run, prices fully adjust, leaving none of the burden of adjustment to quantities. Let's now explore what happens in between — over the months or years that are relevant to analyzing the ups and downs of the business cycle.

Aggregate Supply in the Short Run and Medium Run with Sticky Prices

If you ask the managers at Outback Steakhouse why they don't immediately adjust their prices whenever economic conditions change, they'll tell you that changing prices is costly, requiring them to reprint their menus, amend their advertising, and risk antagonizing customers.

sticky prices Prices that adjust sporadically and sluggishly to changes in market conditions.

The **cost-benefit principle** says that it's only worth adjusting your prices if the benefits of doing so exceed these *menu costs*. This logic leads Outback Steakhouse — like many businesses — to have **sticky prices,** which they adjust only sporadically. As a result prices respond only sluggishly to changes in market conditions. Indeed, many businesses — including Outback — update their most important prices only once or twice per year. This really matters for assessing how aggregate supply will respond in the *short run*, which in this context means a period of a few months.

Figure 13 | The Short-Run Aggregate Supply Curve

Some suppliers adjust their prices in the short run.

A In the **very short run**, the **price level is stuck** at its preexisting level. **But as time passes . . .**

B If the economy is experiencing **insufficient demand**, some sellers will **cut prices**.

C If the economy is experiencing **excess demand**, some sellers will **raise prices**.

D The result is an upward-sloping **short-run aggregate supply curve.**

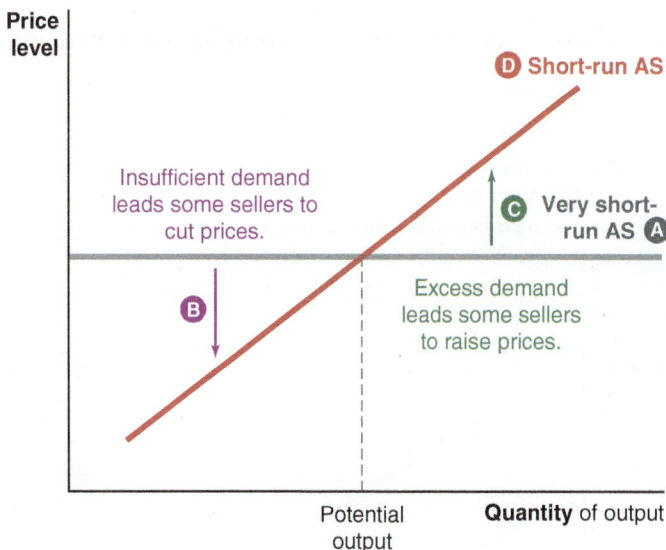

short-run aggregate supply curve The aggregate supply curve that applies over a period when prices are neither fully fixed nor fully flexible. As a result, the short run aggregate supply curve is upward-sloping.

Sticky prices explain why the short-run aggregate supply curve is upward-sloping. Consider how different restaurants might respond to a few months of insufficient demand. Their restaurants will sit half empty, and because their wait staff are underworked, their marginal costs will be low. Outback's executives might consider cutting their prices, but decide not to, figuring it's not worth incurring the cost of reprinting their menus at this time. But a rival like Chili's might have been about to reprint its menu anyway, and so will take the opportunity to cut its prices. Across the whole economy, some businesses are like Chili's — ready to change their prices now — while others are like Outback Steakhouse, and will decide not to change their prices for now. As the purple arrow in Figure 13 shows, when output is below potential, sporadic price cutting in response to insufficient demand leads to a somewhat lower average price level.

Similar dynamics apply to periods of excess demand, but in reverse: Faced with more customers than they can serve, and higher marginal costs due to a rising overtime bill, some suppliers will raise their prices, but others will not. As the green arrow in Figure 13 shows, when output exceeds potential, sporadic price rises in response to excess demand will lead to a somewhat higher price level.

As a result of this partial-but-incomplete adjustment of prices, the **short-run aggregate supply curve** is upward-sloping. Indeed, the upward-sloping aggregate supply curve we've analyzed throughout this chapter is sometimes called the short-run aggregate supply curve.

The aggregate supply curve is steeper in the medium run. Let's now fast forward a year or two to see what changes. We'll call this the *medium run*. The passage of time gives a bunch more restaurants the opportunity to reprint their menus and change their prices. Managers are also more likely to think it's worth paying the menu cost to change their prices in response to insufficient or excess demand that persists for a year or two, rather than just a few months. As a result, in the medium run, prices are less sticky as more sellers adjust their prices to economic conditions.

If output is below potential output, the bold purple arrows in Figure 14 show that these extra sellers cutting their prices will push the average price level down further. Alternatively, if output exceeds potential output, the bold green arrows in Figure 14 show that the extra sellers raising their prices will push the average price level up further. As a result, the medium-run aggregate supply curve is steeper than the short-run aggregate supply curve. More generally, the longer the time horizon you're analyzing, the steeper the relevant aggregate supply curve will be.

Getting from the Very Short Run to the Long Run

We now have all the tools we need to map out the effects of an aggregate demand shock *over time*. The slope of the aggregate supply curve varies, depending on whether you're looking at the shorter- or longer-term response of suppliers. The longer the time period you're analyzing, the more time that managers have had a chance to adjust their prices. Consequently over longer time periods, price adjustments will bear more of the burden of adjustment, leading to an increasingly vertical aggregate supply curve.

Let's explore what this means for how the economy responds to a decrease in aggregate demand. You can forecast the effect of this shift over time, by evaluating this shift relative to the economy's aggregate supply curve in the very short run, short run, medium run, and long run, as follows:

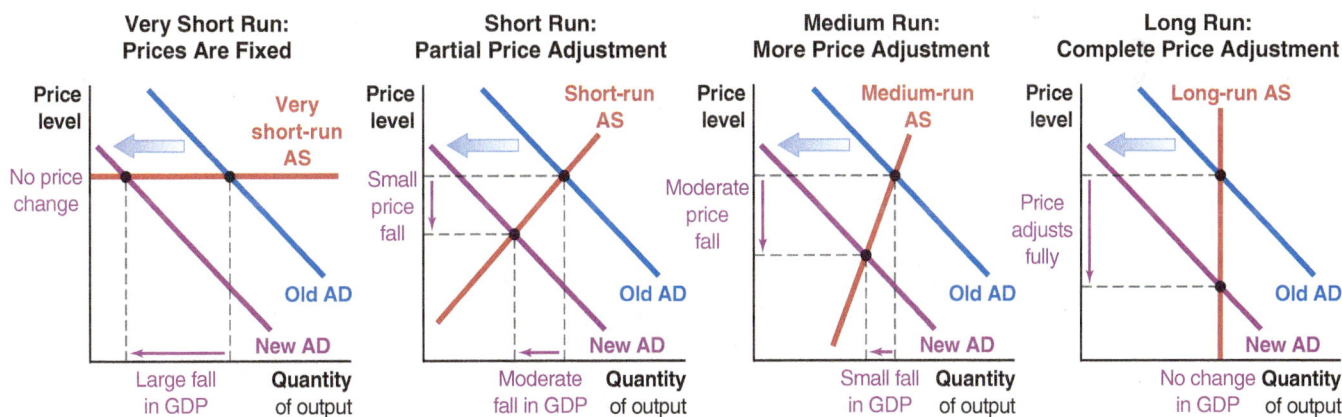

Figure 14 | The Medium-Run Aggregate Supply Curve

More suppliers adjust their prices in the medium run.

Ⓐ In the **short run**, some suppliers have adjusted their prices in response to the state of demand.

But as time passes . . .

Ⓑ **Insufficient demand** will lead **more** sellers to **cut prices**.

Ⓒ **Excess demand** will lead **more** sellers to **raise prices**.

Ⓓ The result is an even steeper **medium-run aggregate supply curve**.

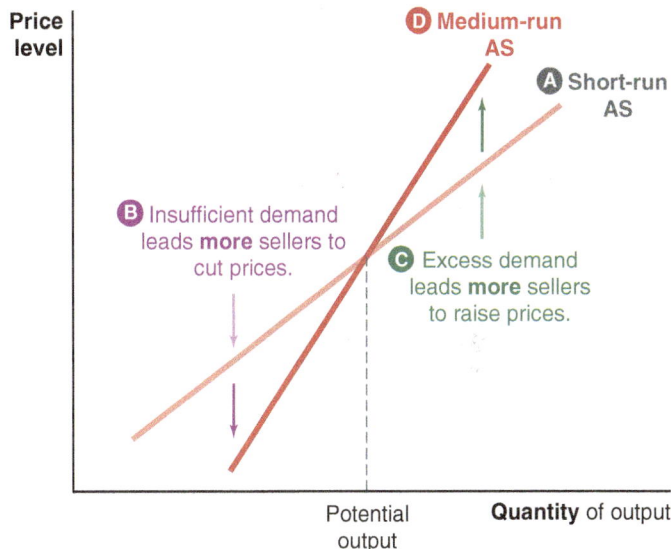

Over the first few weeks hardly any businesses will have had a chance to change their prices, and so our very-short-run analysis is relevant. It suggests the immediate effect will be a recession as output falls sharply. Over the subsequent months, the short-run aggregate supply curve becomes more relevant. It suggests that a few months later the price level will be a bit lower, and the initial decline in output will moderate. In the first year or two following this shock — that is, in the medium run — more businesses will cut their prices, and output will recover somewhat to only be a bit below its pre-recession levels. After a period of several years or more — that is, in the long run — all prices eventually adjust to restore the economy to producing at its potential.

Okay, so how well does this style of analysis work in reality?

The 2008 recession provides a useful testing ground, because it was caused by a sharp decrease in aggregate demand. Most analysts argue that the aggregate demand

Figure 15 | Output Fell Dramatically, During the 2008 Recession, Then Slowly Recovered

Real gross domestic product in trillions of dollars

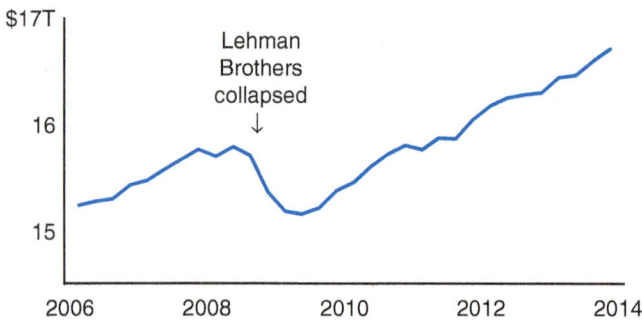

Data from: Bureau of Economic Analysis.

Figure 16 | Prices Slowly Fell, Relative to the Previous Trend

Level of GDP deflator, relative to 2006–2007 trend

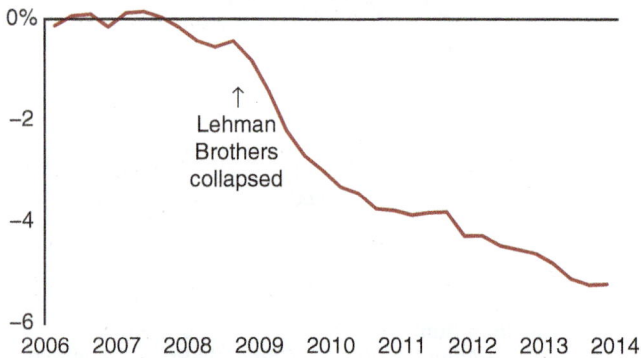

Data from: Bureau of Economic Analysis.

shock happened in the second half of 2008, following the collapse of the investment firm Lehman Brothers. Our very-short-run analysis suggests that this decrease in aggregate expenditure would lead to a large fall in output. Indeed, Figure 15 shows that real GDP declined by more than 3% in the final two quarters of 2008. Our short-run and medium-run analysis forecasts that over the subsequent months and years, this decline in output would dissipate. While output would remain below its earlier levels, the output gap would narrow as the recovery proceeded. And indeed, Figure 15 shows that output started growing again in the middle of 2009. Our long-run analysis suggests that it would take the economy several years or more to return to producing at its full capacity, which again is confirmed by Figure 15.

Our analysis also suggests that part of the reason output fell so sharply is that sticky prices failed to adjust — at least initially. Indeed, as shown in Figure 16, even as output cratered in 2008, the price level remained at levels roughly consistent with its previous trend. Our short- and medium-run analysis suggested that over the subsequent months and years, price adjustments would bear more of the burden of adjustment, and the red line in Figure 16 shows that the price level fell relative to its previous trend for several years. Consistent with our long-run analysis, which had suggested that the lower price level would persist even after the recession was over, the price level appears to have remained permanently lower as a result of this recession.

It's a testament to the value of our *AD-AS* framework that you've just learned that if you had drawn a few aggregate demand and aggregate supply curves back in 2008, you might have been able to predict much of the dramatic economic change that ensued.

21.6 Tying It Together

The Debate Between Classical and Keynesian Economists

You now have all the tools you need to join the discussion of one of the most fiercely debated questions in all of macroeconomics: What role should the government play in countering the ups and downs of the business cycle?

One argument — historically associated with the classical economists, and more recently with new-classical economists — says that the economy is self-correcting, and so there's not much reason for the government to get involved. This argument is based on our long-run analysis, which suggests that the aggregate supply curve is vertical. If the economy is going to return to potential output anyway, they argue, then it may not be worth taking the risk that monetary or fiscal policy will cause other problems.

The counterargument is most closely associated with economist John Maynard Keynes and collaborators including Joan Robinson, who wrote in the wake of the Great Depression, the worst economic slump in modern memory. The Depression shook the faith of many economists, leaving them wondering how it was possible for the economy to perform so poorly as to leave millions of people unemployed. This experience led Keynes to argue that either the economy is not self-correcting as the classical economists had supposed, or the process of adjustment to the long run is too slow and costly to be relevant. According to this perspective, monetary and fiscal policy may be the only way to push the economy back toward full employment in a reasonable fashion.

And while this debate began more than a hundred of years ago, it continues to this day. Keynesian economists count the decade-long recovery from the 2008 global financial crisis as a point in their favor. The Classicals counter that the economy rebounded very quickly following the more recent Covid recession. Keynesians have argued that was due to the dramatic fiscal and monetary policies that they had prescribed, while Classicals respond that the post-pandemic recovery was even faster than the Keynesians had predicted. It's a sure bet that next time the economy goes into a recession, some folks will argue that the government needs to pass a major stimulus, while others will argue that the government should do nothing because the economy will recover faster on its own. Now that you are equipped to join this debate, what's your view?

Chapter 21 Review
Chapter at a Glance

The AD-AS Framework

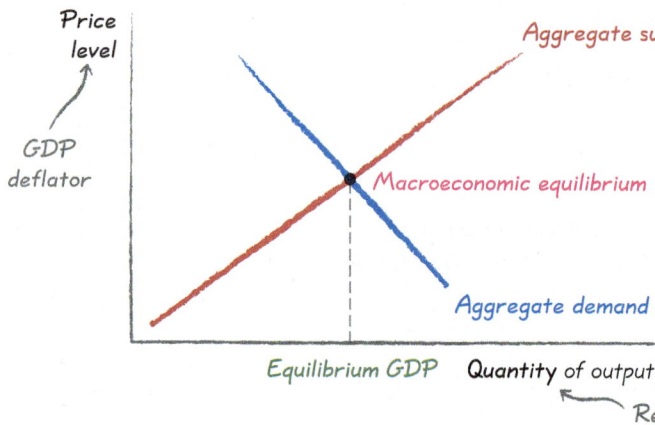

Aggregate supply . . . shows the quantity of output that sellers collectively produce rises as the average price level rises.

Macroeconomic equilibrium . . . where the two curves intersect. It's where the economy is headed.

Aggregate demand . . . shows the quantity of output that buyers collectively plan to purchase falls as the average price level rises.

Forecasting Macroeconomic Outcomes

1. Is there a shift in aggregate demand or aggregate supply?
2. Is that shift an **increase**, shifting the curve to the right? Or is it a **decrease**, shifting the curve to the left?
3. How will the **price level** and **quantity of output** change in new equilibrium?

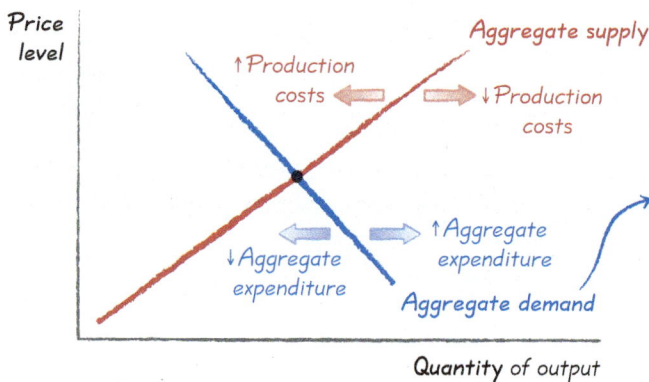

. . . shifts in response to changes in production costs:
1. Input prices
2. Import prices
3. Productivity
4. The exchange rate

. . . shifts in response to changes in aggregate expenditure:
1. Consumption (C)
2. Planned investment (I)
3. Government purchases (G)
4. Net exports (NX)

Monetary and Fiscal Policy

Expansionary **fiscal** or **monetary policy** shifts the **AD curve** to the right.
The **quantity of output** rises and so does the **price level**.
*An inflation-induced cut in interest rates will not shift aggregate demand. Other interest rate cuts will.

Multiplier effect: An initial burst of spending will ripple through the economy, leading to an even larger boost to output.

From the Very Short Run to the Long Run

Very Short Run (a few weeks) → **Short Run** (a few months) → **Medium Run** (a year or two) → **Long Run** (several years or more)

Prices are fixed | Partial price adjustment | More price adjustment | Complete price adjustment

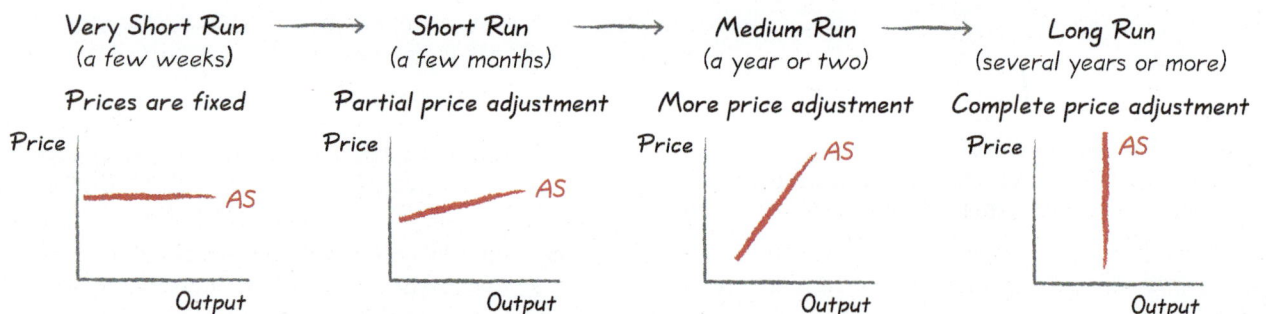

Key Terms

aggregate demand curve, 542

aggregate expenditure, 544

aggregate supply curve, 542

classical dichotomy, 566

fiscal policy, 558

long-run aggregate supply curve, 567

macroeconomic equilibrium, 542

monetary policy, 557

multiplier, 559

short-run aggregate supply curve, 568

sticky prices, 568

very-short-run aggregate supply curve, 567

Study Problems

Learning Objective 21.1 *Understand how aggregate demand and aggregate supply determine macroeconomic equilibrium.*

1. Compare and contrast the microeconomic forces of demand and supply with the macroeconomic forces of aggregate demand and aggregate supply. How do the opportunity costs of buyers in the micro context of a single market (for example, for buyers of gasoline) compare to the opportunity costs of buyers of baskets of "output" in the macro context of aggregate demand?

2. Draw aggregate demand and aggregate supply curves where macroeconomic equilibrium occurs at an output of $20 trillion. On your graph, indicate the equilibrium price level, but don't worry about assigning it an exact value. Indicate on the graph where macroeconomic equilibrium occurs. Make sure to label each part of the graph.

Learning Objective 21.2 *Assess the total quantity of goods and services that purchasers want to buy.*

3. Explain how the Federal Reserve plays a central role in determining the slope of the aggregate demand curve. For example, if a lower price level leads inflation to be below the Fed's target rate, how will the Fed likely react, and how will its actions eventually impact the quantity of goods and services people want to buy?

4. What changes to the economy will lead the aggregate demand curve to shift? What changes will lead to a movement along the aggregate demand curve? Provide a few examples to illustrate your answer.

5. For each of the following, use a graph to show the shift in aggregate demand.

   a. Poor numbers from several leading economic indicators cause businesses to become pessimistic about the future of the economy.

   b. Congress passes a new budget that increases government purchases by 3%.

   c. Housing prices have been declining in recent years, leading homeowners to feel less prosperous.

   d. The Chinese government eliminates the tariffs it charges on goods exported from the United States.

   e. Banks become complacent and begin taking on riskier business loans at lower interest rates.

   f. A rise in the price level leads the Fed to increase the real interest rate.

Learning Objective 21.3 *Evaluate the total quantity of goods and services that businesses want to supply.*

6. How do businesses change their prices at different levels of output, and how does this lead to an upward-sloping aggregate supply curve?

7. What changes to the economy will lead the aggregate supply curve to shift? What changes will lead to a movement along the aggregate supply curve? Provide a few examples to illustrate your answer.

8. Illustrate how each of the following will affect aggregate supply and explain your reasoning.

   a. The implementation of artificial intelligence in manufacturing has led to faster-than-expected productivity growth.

   b. Low levels of output across the entire economy leave many businesses with excess capacity, leading them to lower their prices by 3%.

   c. A bill is passed in Congress that increases the federal minimum wage from $7.25 an hour to $15 an hour.

   d. The U.S. dollar depreciates relative to the Chinese yuan.

Learning Objective 21.4 *Forecast how the economy will respond to changing conditions.*

9. Explain how — depending on the circumstances — the Fed changing the real interest rate can lead either to a movement along the aggregate demand curve or to a shift of the aggregate demand curve. Be sure to consider the two types of responses from the Fed.

10. Illustrate in separate *AD-AS* graphs how the macroeconomic equilibrium will change when the Federal Reserve pursues an expansionary monetary policy (with the goal of raising output) and when it pursues a contractionary monetary policy (with the goal of reducing output). What macroeconomic problems might an expansionary

monetary policy solve? What about a contractionary monetary policy?

11. Explain how an initial increase in government purchases can increase GDP by a greater amount than the increase in government spending.

12. Think of at least one example of a change to the economy that will lead to the following outcomes and illustrate your answers with an *AD-AS* graph.

   a. Output increases and the price level increases.

   b. Output increases and the price level decreases.

   c. Output decreases and the price level decreases.

   d. Output decreases and the price level increases.

13. To combat a recession, the Indian government enacts expansionary fiscal policy, which increases government spending by 2 trillion rupees. In response, GDP increases by 6 trillion rupees.

   a. What is the multiplier?

   b. Illustrate the impact of this expansionary fiscal policy on the Indian economy using an *AD-AS* graph.

   c. How will the average price level change?

14. For each of the following, forecast how prices and output will change by drawing an *AD-AS* graph, and explain your answers using the three-step recipe to forecast macroeconomic outcomes.

   a. The Fed decreases interest rates amid concerns of a looming recession.

   b. The latest data on consumer confidence indicate that consumers have become pessimistic about the future of the economy and are therefore spending less.

   c. Innovations in solar cell technology cause energy prices to decline across the country.

   d. The federal government passes a new bill that dramatically increases government spending on education and the military.

   e. The Mexican government eliminates the tariffs it charges on goods exported from the United States.

   f. Top executives report that they're quite uncertain about the future, as trade deals with the country's largest trading partners are being renegotiated and remain in flux.

   g. Overcrowded ports have created chaos and significantly increased transportation costs for businesses across the country.

Learning Objective 21.5 *Distinguish between the immediate effects, short-run effects, medium-run effects, and long-run consequences of economic shocks.*

15. Explain why, in the long run, a change in average prices has no impact on output. What impact does aggregate demand have in determining output in the long run?

16. One common argument against expansionary fiscal or monetary policy goes like this, "Since the economy returns to potential output in the long run, we should not react to the short-term fluctuations in the economy. If we do nothing, the economy will fix itself." Formulate a counterargument. Which argument do you agree with and why?

17. Why does aggregate supply analysis require looking at specific time horizons to predict macroeconomic outcomes?

18. In an effort to boost output, the government passes a large fiscal stimulus that raises government purchases by $1 trillion. Use the *AD-AS* framework to predict how prices and output change in the very short run, in the short run, in the medium run, and in the long run.

19. For each of the following scenarios, predict how the price level and output will change over time from the very short run to the long run. In each case, consider an economy that was initially producing at its level of potential output.

   a. The government passes legislation that increases corporate taxes by 25%.

   b. Economies around the globe are experiencing rising prosperity and, as a result, demand for U.S. exports increases.

PART VI:
Macroeconomic Policy

Part VI: Macroeconomic Policy

The Big Picture

Everything you've learned so far comes together in our final two chapters, where we'll explore how the government uses its policy tools to try to manage the economy. You'll learn to make sense of the economic news you hear during your daily commute: What's happening with interest rates? Can policymakers prevent a looming recession? Should you worry about government debt? Along the way, we'll learn how to interpret the promises that politicians make when courting your vote.

We'll start by stepping inside a **Federal Reserve** meeting to learn how it sets **monetary policy.** We'll explore the Fed's goals, its targets, and the tools it uses to keep the economy and financial system running smoothly. Along the way, we'll discuss how you should respond to monetary policy when managing your business and personal finances.

Next, we'll take a look at how the government shapes economic outcomes through its **spending and taxing decisions.** We'll uncover what the government spends money on and where it gets the money. Then we'll consider how it can use **fiscal policy** to smooth out business cycles. Finally, we'll take a long, hard look at **government deficits and debt,** and what they mean for you now, and for the economy in the long run.

22 Monetary Policy

Understand how the Federal Reserve makes and implements monetary policy.

- What happens behind closed doors at a Federal Reserve meeting?
- How do the Fed's decisions affect you?
- Can you predict what the Fed will do next?
- Why does the Fed target inflation when it also cares about unemployment?
- How does the Fed implement monetary policy?
- What can the Fed do when it can't lower the interest rate any further?

23 Government Spending, Taxes, and Fiscal Policy

Learn about government spending, revenue, and debt.

- What does the government spend money on (and where does it get the money)?
- What do federal, state, and local governments do?
- What is fiscal policy and how can it help smooth business cycles?
- Why do governments run deficits?
- Should you worry about growing government debt?

Monetary Policy

One of the most important meetings in the world happens every six weeks in Washington, D.C. Nope, it's not at the White House. In fact, the president isn't even invited. The meeting happens at the headquarters of the Federal Reserve — our nation's central bank, called the Fed for short. The attendees are the Federal Reserve governors and the presidents of the regional Federal Reserve Banks.

The Federal Reserve is run by the Fed chair, who is often called the second most powerful person in the world. When the Fed acts to raise interest rates, it sets off a chain of events — borrowing becomes more expensive, which encourages consumers to save today instead of spending and discourages businesses from investing. Higher U.S. interest rates usually also raise the value of the dollar, which makes U.S. exports more expensive and imports to the United States cheaper. All of these changes mean that business decisions all over the world respond to the Fed's decisions. For you, it can mean higher interest rates on your student loans and credit cards.

The Fed raises (or lowers) interest rates for a reason. You've already learned how interest rates affect spending and hence output and unemployment, which filters through to affect prices and inflation. The Fed adjusts interest rates to keep inflation stable and unemployment low. So while you'll pay more in interest when the Fed raises interest rates, its actions mean that prices won't rise as much as they otherwise would.

In this chapter, we'll dig into how the Fed makes and implements monetary policy decisions. You'll learn about the current policy issues surrounding how the Fed makes decisions and the tools it uses. Let's get started!

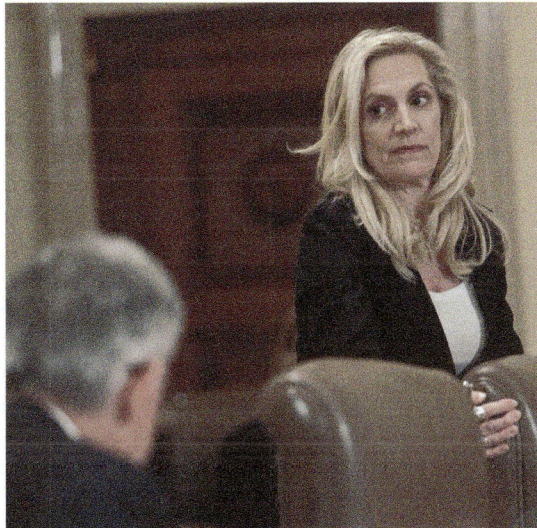

Federal Reserve governor Lael Brainard takes her seat at the most economically consequential meeting on the planet.

Andrew Harrer/Bloomberg/Getty Images

Chapter Objective

Understand how the Federal Reserve makes and implements monetary policy.

22.1 The Federal Reserve
Learn how the Federal Reserve makes monetary policy decisions.

22.2 The Fed's Policy Goals and Decision-Making Framework
Discover how the Federal Reserve assesses its goals and makes interest rate choices.

22.3 How the Fed Sets Interest Rates
Understand how the Federal Reserve implements monetary policy decisions.

22.4 Alternative Tools the Fed Uses to Meet Its Dual Mandate
Learn about some additional tools the Federal Reserve uses to ensure maximum employment and stable prices.

🎙 **Podcast**

Think Like an Economist
Monetary Policy — The Financial Levers that Tame Business Cycles

22.1 # The Federal Reserve

Learning Objective *Learn how the Federal Reserve makes monetary policy decisions.*

monetary policy The process of setting interest rates in an effort to influence economic conditions.

The Federal Reserve's headquarters in Washington, D.C.

Central banks determine a country's **monetary policy,** which is the process of setting interest rates in an effort to influence economic conditions. In the United States, the Federal Reserve is our central bank. It was created by Congress, which gave it instructions to "promote effectively the goals of maximum employment, stable prices, and moderate long-term interest rates." The Fed interprets Congress's instructions as a dual mandate to promote maximum employment while keeping inflation low and stable.

The Fed can't change inflation or employment directly. Instead, it uses interest rates as a tool to influence the economy. Interest rates determine the *opportunity cost* of spending money today. For borrowers, higher interest rates mean a higher cost of credit. For savers, higher interest rates mean forgoing more interest in order to spend money today. Thus, the Fed uses the interest rate to nudge people and businesses to spend more or less today, which in turn affects output, and therefore both employment and inflation.

The Fed's dual mandate leads it to attempt to smooth business cycles. The maximum sustainable level of employment occurs when the economy's output is equal to its potential output, so the Fed will need to pay a lot of attention to GDP even though output is not in its formal mandate.

Their task is difficult because of the imprecision of data and the difficulty of forecasting the future. In practice, this means the Fed balances risks: The risk of setting a too-high interest rate that leads the economy to produce at a level below potential, leaving some people without jobs versus the risk of setting a too-low interest rate that causes output to exceed the economy's potential output, thereby sparking inflation.

Let's explore the Federal Reserve System and the process by which the Fed gathers information, weighs the risks, makes decisions, and then communicates its analysis and decisions to the public.

The Federal Reserve System

Congress created the Federal Reserve System in 1913 in the wake of chaotic bank runs that led many banks to go bankrupt, wreaking havoc on the U.S. economy. The goal was to create a system that would provide greater stability in the banking sector and thus in the macroeconomy. At the time, nearly everyone agreed that a central bank was necessary, but there was disagreement about how centralized its power should be, and how a central bank should balance the needs of the banks with the broader needs of the public.

The result was a central bank with many checks and balances. The Federal Reserve System is comprised of the Board of Governors in Washington, D.C., and 12 Federal Reserve district banks scattered across the country. The Board of Governors is an independent government agency that guides the operation of the Federal Reserve System. It ensures that monetary policy fulfills the instructions given by Congress. The Board of Governors also oversees the operations of the Federal Reserve district banks.

The Federal Reserve system is regionally diverse. The district banks were designed to avoid concentrating too much control in one part of the country. Even though monetary policy decisions reflect national economic conditions, there are differences across the country, and each of the 12 district bank presidents brings information from their district to policy discussions. The Federal Reserve bank in your district is the eyes and ears for your community. A local board of directors, comprised of business leaders and other local community members, chooses the Fed bank president for each district, with oversight from the Board of Governors.

Commercial banks — the banks you use every day because they offer services like checking accounts to the general public — play an important role in the Federal Reserve

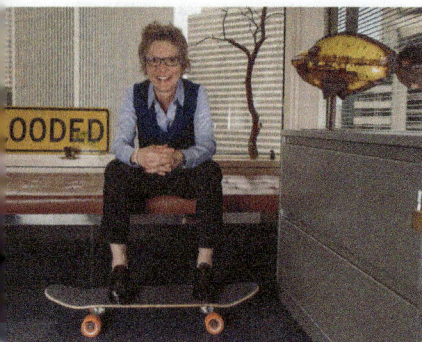

San Francisco Fed President Mary Daly prefers smooth pavement . . . and smooth business cycles.

System. They hold stock in their district's reserve bank and help elect some of its directors. But commercial banks can't profit from their stock in the district reserve banks, nor can they sell it. Ownership of a certain amount of stock is simply a requirement by law of membership in the Federal Reserve System. The unique structure of the district Federal Reserve Banks came out of the desire to solve the problem of instability in the banking system. Making financial institutions an integral part of the system ensures clear and frequent communication between the banking system and the Federal Reserve System.

Central bank independence is important for macroeconomic stability. The Federal Reserve Board of Governors is at the helm of the Federal Reserve System, and it's an independent government agency. It's independent for a reason: Politicians often think too much about the short run — the next election. So, they might overweigh the benefit of a short-run output boost relative to its long-run inflationary cost. For example, President Trump pressured the Fed to lower interest rates in the run-up to the 2020 election. A problem with political pressure is that policymakers can achieve temporarily higher output by overheating the economy, which might unleash future inflation. But this short-run choice to allow higher inflation will eventually lead to higher inflation expectations, which causes higher inflation that persists long after the temporary blip in output dissipates. In the long run, output won't be any higher, but inflation will be. Federal Reserve independence is also important because it creates a system of checks and balances on potentially inflationary fiscal policy. A politician that wants to temporarily boost the economy by mailing checks to people might find that the Federal Reserve will react by raising interest rates.

Research shows that countries that give their central banks more independence have lower inflation rates on average. That means that if you reduce independence, you should expect higher inflation. And, as you learned in Chapter 12, higher inflation is costly.

There is a lot of government oversight of the Fed. Just because the Fed is independent, you shouldn't think that there isn't government oversight. The governors are selected by the president of the United States. The U.S. Senate must confirm the president's nominations. There are seven governors of the Federal Reserve and they each serve a term of up to 14 years. The president, with confirmation by the Senate, selects one of the governors to serve a four-year term as the Fed chair.

The Fed's governors are chosen for their knowledge of monetary policy and their specific perspectives or areas of expertise, all of which shape their assessments. For instance, one governor, Michelle Bowman, had spent her earlier career overseeing banks in Kansas. Another governor, Lael Brainard, spent her career working on international economic issues.

The Fed is also audited by the Government Accountability Office (the GAO), which reviews the Fed's finances and activities. By law, the Federal Reserve board chair must testify before Congress at least twice a year. As Fed Chair Jerome Powell said once when testifying before Congress, "Transparency is the foundation for our accountability." Because the Fed is transparent about both its actions and its interpretations of economic data, anyone can evaluate the Fed's decisions. All of the materials from monetary policy meetings are released within five years of the meeting.

Federal Open Market Committee (FOMC) The Federal Reserve committee that decides on U.S. interest rates. It consists of the Fed governors and district Fed bank presidents.

The conversations around this table will shape the world economy.

The Federal Open Market Committee

The Fed governors and the district Fed presidents form the **Federal Open Market Committee (FOMC),** whose purpose is to decide on U.S. interest rates. They all participate, but only the Fed governors, the New York Fed bank president, and a rotating group of four district Fed presidents vote on policy decisions. The Fed chair runs the FOMC and is the most important spokesperson for the Fed. The FOMC meeting is that meeting mentioned at the start of the chapter — the one that's one of the most important meetings in the world — so let's take a look inside it.

Monetary policy is no longer a boys' club.

Step into the meeting. When you walk into an FOMC meeting, you'll see a big table with the members and participants seated around it. The Fed chair sits in the middle and decides who's going to speak and in what order. These decisions sound minor, but they can have a big impact on outcomes. Former Fed chair Alan Greenspan used to tell everyone what he thought the right monetary policy decision was first, making it awkward for other members to discuss alternatives.

When Ben Bernanke took over as Fed chair in 2006, he took a more democratic approach. In order to foster debate, he waited to share his views until he'd heard everyone else speak. His successors, Janet Yellen and Jerome Powell, followed a similar approach, resulting in a wider range of views and data being brought into the discussion.

Research also shows that greater gender and racial diversity in meetings can improve decision making, and the Fed and Congress have made progress in bringing greater diversity to the FOMC in recent years. In 2017, Raphael Bostic became the Atlanta Fed's 15th president and first Black regional bank president. Five years later, Susan Collins became the first Black female regional bank president. In 2022, the addition of Lisa Cook and Philip Jefferson to the Board of Governors made it the most diverse set of Governors yet.

So now that you know who's at the meeting, let's turn to what they talk about. To decide monetary policy, each member must be prepared to answer three questions:

1. What are your forecasts for the U.S. economy?
2. What are the right policy choices given the economic outlook?
3. How should the Fed communicate its plans effectively to the public?

Each member prepares their answers to these questions in advance, and they'll often arrive at the meeting with quite different views. The meeting is a time for them to discuss their answers to these three questions, develop a consensus view, and make a decision. Let's see how.

FOMC members prepare answers to three questions:

1. What are your forecasts for the U.S. economy?
2. What are the right policy choices given the economic outlook?
3. How should the Fed communicate its plans effectively to the public?

Question 1: What are your forecasts for the U.S. economy? The Fed chair asks everyone to share their views on current economic conditions and their short- and medium-term forecasts for the economy. Each member brings different information, perspectives, and backgrounds. They've each been prepared with reams of data and analysis of that data by expert economists on their staff. The Fed bank presidents also talk to businesses and financial institutions in their districts to get a better sense of their local economic conditions. And each participant brings unique knowledge about the various factors that influence the U.S. economy, from conditions in other countries to stability in the financial sector. The Fed tracks literally thousands of variables, each of which provides clues about the future path of inflation and employment. To measure maximum sustainable employment, the Fed will track unemployment rates because it's a good indicator of how many people without a job are currently willing to work. The Fed also seeks out other labor market indicators to assess whether it's possible to have more people sustainably employed. For example, labor force participation rates indicate how many people might be enticed to seek work. People arrive at the meeting with different forecasts reflecting their unique knowledge, different readings of noisy data, and what they expect to happen if their preferred monetary policy decision is implemented.

Interpreting the DATA How good are the Fed's forecasts?

Let's take a look at some of the forecasts that FOMC members bring into an FOMC meeting. Figure 1 shows their forecasts of economic growth, unemployment, and inflation in each of the next few years, as well as what they expect will occur, on average, in the longer run. These forecasts were prepared for the June 2022 meeting. The top number in each cell is the median forecast, meaning half expect something higher and half expect something lower. The range of forecasts is shown in parentheses.

Figure 1 | FOMC Members' Projections for the U.S. Economy

FOMC Members' Projections for:	Median forecast, released June 2022 (Lowest and highest forecasts in parentheses)			
	2022	2023	2024	Longer run
Change in real GDP	1.7% (1.0%–2.0%)	1.7% (0.8%–2.5%)	1.9% (1.0%–2.2%)	1.8%
Unemployment rate	3.7% (3.5%–4.2%)	3.9% (3.2%–4.0%)	4.1% (3.2%–4.5%)	4.0%
Inflation rate (PCE inflation rate)	5.2% (4.8%–6.2%)	2.6% (2.3%–4.0%)	2.2% 2.0–3.0	2.0%

Data from: Federal Reserve.

Notice that the Fed produces forecasts for the next three years. That's because it wants to identify and counter economic problems before they emerge. If the Fed forecasts trouble in a year or two, then it wants to take action today.

Even the most careful forecasts are often wrong, so if you want to find out if these Fed forecasts were right, use the FRED database to look up what the economic growth rate, the unemployment rate, and the inflation rate really were in each of these years. ■

Question 2: What are the right policy choices given the economic outlook?
Once the committee has debated projections for the economy, it's time to turn the discussion to what they should do about it. The FOMC's primary tool is to influence the real interest rate. Recall that the real interest rate is the opportunity cost of spending, and it tells you how much more you'll be able to buy if you spend your money next year, instead of this year. Similarly, businesses care about the real interest rate because it represents the opportunity cost of making an investment. That's why the real interest rate is effectively the price that determines this year's aggregate expenditure.

The FOMC will raise the real interest rate when it wants to induce people to spend less today and save more for later. It will do this because reducing spending today reduces output, which lowers inflationary pressure. And the FOMC will lower the real interest rate when it wants to stimulate greater spending, which will lead to higher output and higher employment. In the long run, stable inflation and maximum sustainable employment are both achieved when output is equal to potential output.

When recessions hit, the FOMC has to determine whether to lower interest rates, and by how much. This isn't a decision that happens in just one meeting. Rather, it's an ongoing process in which the FOMC constantly assesses (and re-assesses) whether it has taken sufficient action and should keep interest rates where they are, or whether even lower rates are warranted. Similarly, as the economy recovers, the FOMC will gradually return interest rates to normal, attempting to steer the economy back to maximum employment without unduly risking higher inflation. So discussion at most meetings focuses on where the economy appears to be relative to where it was at the previous meeting, and assessing outcomes of the decisions that were made in previous meetings. Had they raised rates enough? Not enough? Too fast or too slow?

Once the members have debated the options and assessed the risks associated with each possible action, the Fed chair typically recommends a course of action, and the FOMC votes on it. Not all of the Fed bank presidents get to vote, but they've all participated equally in the discussion. The New York Federal Reserve Bank president always votes, but the other 11 bank presidents take turns rotating on and off as voting members.

Question 3: How should the Fed communicate effectively to the public?
A former Fed chair once made an offhand comment about interest rates at a

Alan Greenspan: "If I turn out to be particularly clear, you've probably misunderstood what I've said."

Janet Yellen: "We've made a commitment . . . that we would do our best to communicate as clearly as we could."

party. Unfortunately, he was talking to a CNBC anchor. When she told her viewers his comment the next afternoon, stock prices plunged, and bond yields rose to a four-year high. He learned an important lesson: Even offhand comments by a Fed official can move markets. There are billions of dollars to be made from correctly guessing before anyone else when interest rates are going to change. These financial stakes lead those working in financial markets to hang on to utterance coming out of the Fed. But the Fed doesn't want to create excess volatility through misinterpretations of loose party talk.

So what should the Fed say? For much of its history, the Fed took pride in *Fedspeak*, a communication style that relied on intentionally vague and bureaucratic language. The idea was that vagueness would reduce market reactions to anything a Fed official said because no one could be sure what it meant. (Fed Chair Alan Greenspan was so accustomed to Fedspeak that he had to propose to his wife, news anchor Andrea Mitchell, twice because she failed to understand what he was saying the first time.)

Over the past few decades, the Fed has changed its communication policy to move away from Fedspeak and to aim for much greater transparency. Today, the Fed strives to clearly communicate its analysis, decisions, and objectives. This transparency is crucial for accountability. If you disagree with the Fed's policy decisions, you can pinpoint exactly what you are disagreeing with, if you understand why it made those choices.

After each meeting, the Fed issues a statement and the Fed chair holds a press conference announcing and explaining its decisions. After every other meeting, it publishes its forecasts. In between meetings, Fed officials give speeches that often explain their thinking. And twice a year the Fed chair testifies before Congress to explain the Fed's monetary policy actions and plans.

These communication choices reflect strategic decisions: The Fed wants to convince people that it will follow through and achieve its goals. Businesses will be more likely to hire if they believe the Fed will deliver a strong economy, and they're more likely to restrain their price increases if they believe the Fed will meet its goal of price stability. Expectations are an important factor shaping economic decisions, and the Fed is trying to shape those expectations. If the Fed can convince people to expect maximum employment and stable prices, then those outcomes become more likely.

dual mandate The Fed's two goals of stable prices and maximum sustainable employment.

inflation target A publicly stated goal for the inflation rate.

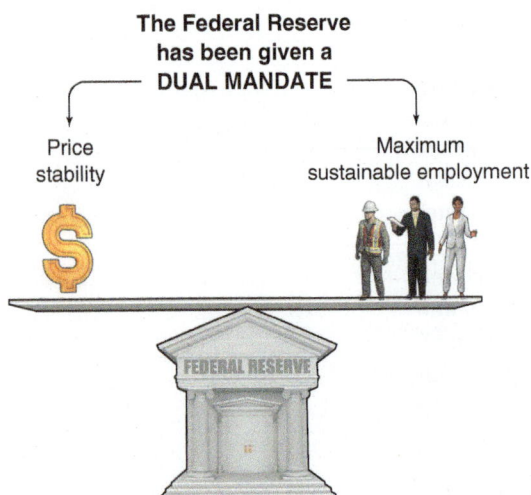

22.2 The Fed's Policy Goals and Decision-Making Framework

Learning Objective *Discover how the Federal Reserve assesses its goals and makes interest rate choices.*

You've now learned what happens during the FOMC meeting, so let's dig into how the Fed assesses its goals and determines its policy choices. The Fed's two goals of stable prices and maximum sustainable employment are known as the Fed's **dual mandate** because it cares about both. Let's start with the Fed's goals and then turn to its policy options.

The Fed's Dual Mandate: Stable Prices and Maximum Sustainable Employment

Central bankers consider prices to be stable when the inflation rate is low and predictable enough that it doesn't play much of a role in people's decisions. If inflation is low enough not to influence or distort people's choices, it has few costs. Low and stable inflation has a precise meaning for the Fed — it means that inflation is close to its **inflation target,** a publicly stated goal for the inflation rate. Let's now turn to analyzing this inflation target.

Price stability means inflation that is near or at the Fed's inflation target. The Fed has an inflation target of 2%. In the late 1990s, FOMC members had agreed somewhat informally to aim for an inflation rate of 2%. But they didn't announce a formal inflation target until 2012, when the Fed changed to a more transparent communication strategy. Each year since then the Fed has continuously reiterated that inflation of 2% over the longer run is most consistent with its mandate for maximum employment and price stability. The pursuit of price stability through an inflation target of 2% is used in many countries around the world. For example, the Bank of Japan (the central bank of Japan), the Bank of England (the central bank of the UK), and the European Central Bank all target 2% inflation.

By setting an inflation target and telling the public what it is, central banks hope to convince price-setters that inflation will be stable at its announced low rate. It's trying to set in motion a virtuous cycle: If people believe that inflation will be low and stable, then price increases will be small, ensuring that inflation in fact remains low and stable. Thus, the more credible the Fed's commitment to low and stable inflation is, the easier it will be to achieve.

Interpreting the DATA | Has the Fed succeeded in meeting its inflation target?

Take a look at actual inflation compared to the Fed's target inflation rate of 2% in Figure 2. Do you think that the Fed has succeeded in ensuring that inflation did not run persistently above or below its target of 2%?

The graph makes it clear that monetary policy isn't an exact science. When the Fed sets the interest rate to try to achieve 2% inflation, actual inflation may turn out to be a bit higher or a bit lower.

Critics argued that in the years following the initial 2012 commitment to a 2% inflation target the Fed treated the inflation target more like a ceiling — making sure that inflation didn't go above 2% instead of aiming for inflation to average 2%. These critics argued that unemployment was too slow to recover coming out of the 2008 recession partially because the Fed didn't keep interest rates low enough for long enough. They argued that if the Fed had used monetary policy more aggressively between 2012 and 2018, employment would have risen more quickly to its maximum sustainable level.

The Fed then announced in 2021 that it would only aim to achieve 2% inflation on average, and that it would allow higher inflation as the economy recovered from the coronavirus pandemic. However, many economists argued that this was risky because inflation can rapidly re-emerge, as it did in the 1970s. And indeed, through early 2021, inflation rose above 6%. I'm writing this sentence in mid-2022, and the Fed still says that it expects inflation to fall back toward its target, and it's projecting inflation of 2.6% by the end of 2023. You can now look up the facts: Did the Fed get this right? ■

Figure 2 | Has the Fed Delivered Inflation Rates Consistent with Its Inflation Target?

Annual change in the price index for personal consumption expenditures

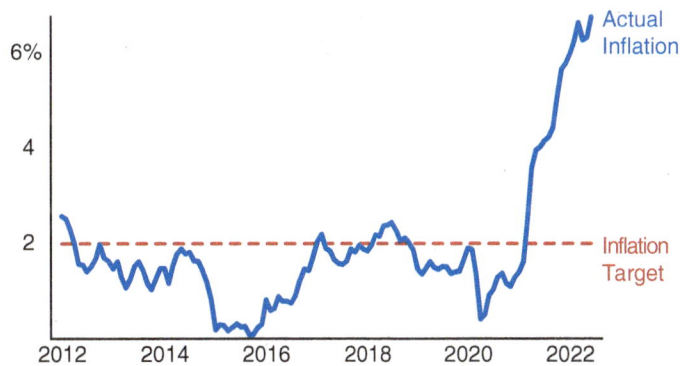

Data from: BEA and Federal Reserve.

Hitting the inflation target promotes maximum sustainable employment.
You might be wondering: Why is the Fed targeting inflation instead of targeting employment? After all, it has a dual mandate — it's supposed to care about both stable prices and employment.

There are two answers to this question. The first is that the inflation rate over the long run is primarily determined by monetary policy, and so it's easily targeted by monetary

The Fed targets inflation to manage the economy.

policy. By contrast, maximum sustainable employment is the amount of employment that occurs when the economy is operating at potential. But employment can change as people decide to work more or less for reasons that have nothing to do with monetary policy (for example, retirement). That's why the Fed pays more attention to the unemployment rate than to total employment. But even the unemployment rate is influenced by factors unrelated to monetary policy. Frictional unemployment is determined by the time it takes for workers and employers to find each other, while structural unemployment is determined by structural barriers in the labor market such as minimum wage laws, unions, labor market regulations, and employers' desire to pay efficiency wages. These factors can change, and when they do, the equilibrium unemployment rate will change. Thus, a Fed target for the unemployment rate would need to change as those factors change.

The second reason that the Fed targets inflation instead of unemployment is due to the interdependence principle: Inflation and unemployment are interdependent. Keeping inflation low and stable at its target also requires keeping the unemployment rate near its lowest sustainable level. When unemployment is higher than this, the economy is operating with excess capacity, leading the inflation rate to decline below the Fed's target. And if unemployment is lower than this, capacity constraints will lead inflation to rise above the Fed's target. So targeting low and stable inflation is consistent with targeting the lowest sustainable unemployment rate. Alternatively phrased, there is no long-run trade-off between price stability and employment stability. That's not to say that the Fed can ignore the unemployment rate when targeting inflation. The Fed needs to look at all of the data available, including the unemployment rate, because each piece of data helps paint the overall picture of the state of the economy.

Why not target zero inflation?
If the Fed's goal is price stability, why doesn't it aim for 0% inflation? There are four reasons not to aim for zero:

Reason 1: Inflation greases the wheels of the labor market. Employers often find it difficult to cut nominal wages, even when real wage cuts are needed to save jobs. But with 2% inflation, they can do it quietly, because failing to give someone a nominal raise this year effectively cuts their real wages by 2%. If inflation were 0%, they would have to cut nominal wages by 2% in order to achieve the same real wage cut. In theory, these are the same. In practice, workers dislike nominal wage cuts much more than they dislike real wage cuts achieved through inflation. So, in order to avoid creating friction with their workers, many employers are reluctant to cut their nominal wages. This means that if inflation is zero, they'll rarely cut real wages — even during a recession. You might be thinking: That sounds great! But recessions cause a decrease in labor demand, and when employers can't cut real wages, they lay off more workers than they otherwise would. This suggests that a 0% inflation target will lead unemployment to rise more during recessions.

Reason 2: The Fed can lower real interest rates by more when inflation is above zero. The Fed faces an important constraint: It effectively can't set nominal interest rates below zero. Economists refer to this as the **zero lower bound.** If the Fed set a negative nominal interest rate, then savers would have to pay to keep their money in the bank. So a –1% interest rate would mean that if you put $100 in the bank, a year later you'd have $99. Why do that when you can put the money in a safe and still have $100 at the end of the year? That's why pushing the nominal interest rate below 0% doesn't actually do much — people can earn 0% by avoiding banks altogether.

This zero lower bound on the nominal interest rate constrains how low the Fed can set the real interest rate (which is what really matters). For instance, if inflation is 2%, then setting the nominal interest rate at the zero lower bound results in a real interest rate of –2%. But if inflation were 0%, this would be impossible, and the lowest the Fed could set the real interest rate would be 0%. In the 2008 recession, the Fed was unable to cut rates as much as needed to fight the recession. This is one explanation for the slow economic recovery and led the Fed to keep nominal interest rates close to 0% for seven years. If not for this constraint, the Fed would likely have set a lower interest rate, which would have

---

Four reasons why the Fed doesn't target zero inflation:

1. Inflation greases the wheels of the labor market.
2. The Fed can lower real interest rates by more when inflation is above zero.
3. A 0% inflation target runs the risk of deflation.
4. Measured inflation may be overstated.

zero lower bound The constraint that nominal interest rates cannot be effectively set below zero.

provided a bigger economic boost. More generally, a lower inflation rate makes it more likely that the Fed will be unable to deliver sufficiently low real interest rates to stimulate a rapid recovery from a recession.

Reason 3: A 0% inflation rate target runs the risk of deflation. If the Fed set a 0% target, it would risk inflation sometimes being below 0%. **Deflation** occurs when prices are falling on average, so that the inflation rate is negative. Deflation sounds great — things are getting cheaper! But it can cause problems because falling prices lead people to delay spending today, in favor of buying stuff in the future when prices are even lower. This decrease in aggregate expenditure will reduce output, which leads prices to fall further, setting off a vicious cycle of deflation, reducing spending, which creates yet more deflation. Worse, this cycle of deflation might lead the inflation rate to become more negative, which raises the real interest rate (which is the nominal interest rate less this negative inflation rate), which further depresses spending.

deflation A generalized decrease in the overall level of prices.

Reason 4: Measured inflation may be overstated. Many economists believe that the measured inflation rate overstates the actual inflation rate. This occurs because the measured inflation rate fails to account for reductions in the cost of living due to unmeasured quality improvements and the introduction of new products. Consequently, a measured inflation rate of zero may actually mean deflation. While the Fed targets a measure of inflation that adjusts for substitution bias, there's still likely upward bias in the measure of inflation it uses. Some estimates of these biases suggest that if the Fed were to target measured inflation of 0%, it would be delivering an actual inflation rate of around −1%, a mild deflation.

Not all economists agree on the optimal inflation target. Some point out that even low inflation erodes the value of a dollar and has costs, and they'd prefer the inflation rate to be zero. Others have argued for a slightly higher target, such as 4%, to create more room for the Fed to cut rates to counter recessions before hitting the zero lower bound. Regardless of this disagreement about the exact target, most economists agree that the Fed should aim to keep inflation low and stable near a publicly announced target rate. This agreement reflects a belief that *inflation targeting* will help the Fed keep inflation low, while keeping employment close to its highest sustainable level.

How the Fed Chooses the Interest Rate

Let's take stock. You know that the Fed is trying to keep inflation at 2%. You also know that the Fed examines lots of data to come up with forecasts for inflation, unemployment, and economic growth. Finally, you know that the Fed lowers the real interest rate when inflation is too low and unemployment is too high. It also raises interest rates when inflation is too high and unemployment is unsustainably low. Because inflation and unemployment are linked to output, the Fed looks for evidence of gaps between expected future output and potential output, and gaps between the current or forecasted inflation rate and its inflation target. In response to such gaps, the Fed can either lower or raise interest rates to try to steer the economy back to its inflation target and potential output.

Let's take a look at the four factors that shape the Fed's policy choices.

Four factors that shape Fed policy:
- The neutral real interest rate
- The nominal interest rate
- The difference between actual inflation and targeted inflation
- The output gap

Factor 1: The Fed starts with the neutral real interest rate. The **neutral real interest rate** is the real interest rate that operates when the economy is in neutral — producing neither above nor below its potential. The neutral real interest rate is important because it tells policymakers what real interest rate will ensure both that the economy doesn't underperform its potential, and that it won't overheat from running ahead of its capacity. Setting the real interest rate higher than the neutral real interest rate will push actual output below potential output. And setting the real interest rate lower than the neutral real interest rate will push actual output above potential output.

Many economists used to think of the neutral real interest rate as being roughly stable at around 2%. The neutral real interest rate is determined by the global supply of and

neutral real interest rate The real interest rate at which real GDP is equal to potential GDP, and hence the output gap is zero.

demand for savings, which is usually pretty stable over time. However, over the last couple of decades, economists have begun to suspect that the neutral real interest rate has fallen. The Fed currently believes that the neutral real interest rate is 0.5%. This decline in the neutral rate is the result of a trend sometimes called *secular stagnation.*

Factor 2: The Fed targets the nominal interest rate when trying to influence the real interest rate.

The real interest rate is the opportunity cost that the Fed is trying to shift in order to steer people's spending and businesses' investment decisions. But in practice, the Fed controls a nominal interest rate. Recall that the nominal interest rate is roughly equal to the real interest rate plus inflation. So once the Fed has decided on a real interest rate it wants to hit, it needs to add in the inflation rate to find the corresponding nominal interest rate.

federal funds rate The interest rate that the Fed uses as its policy tool, which is the nominal interest rate that banks pay to borrow from each other overnight in the federal funds market.

The interest rate that the Fed focuses on is the **federal funds rate,** which is the nominal interest rate that banks pay to borrow from each other overnight in the federal funds market. In the next section, we'll dig into why banks lend to each other overnight, how this market works, and how it affects the broader economy. But for now, we'll simply focus on the Fed adjusting this nominal interest rate.

Factor 3: The Fed compares inflation with its inflation target.

When inflation is higher than the Fed's inflation target, that signals to the Fed that it should set real interest rates higher than the neutral real interest rate in order to encourage consumers and investors to spend less, which will reduce excess demand and hence inflationary pressure. When inflation is lower than the Fed's inflation target, setting real interest rates lower than the neutral real interest rate will encourage consumers and investors to spend more, which boosts demand and hence inflation. The key idea here is that the Fed looks at the *gap between inflation and the inflation rate target,* and uses that difference as a guideline for how much to change the real interest rate.

Fed policymakers don't just look at today's inflation, they also look ahead to forecasts of inflation. If they forecast that inflation is likely to rise or fall above or below their inflation target at some future date, they'll consider changing real interest rates today to get ahead of the problem.

Factor 4: The Fed looks at the output gap.

The output gap is the difference between actual and potential output, measured as a share of potential output. It is zero — or as Goldilocks would say, "just right" — when actual output is equal to potential output. The output gap is important to the Fed because an overheating economy can cause inflation. When the output gap is positive, output exceeds potential output. That can continue for a while — as people work overtime and factories run extra shifts and defer maintenance — but it's not sustainable. Eventually, businesses will respond to this excess demand by raising their prices, sparking higher inflation.

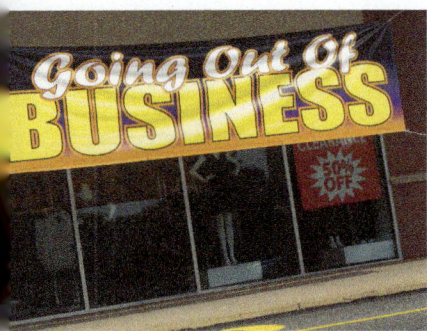

The Fed pays attention to signs like this.

Conversely, if the output gap is negative so that the economy is operating below potential, then employment is likely below its maximum sustainable level, and insufficient demand will cause businesses to cut their prices (or raise them by less), which causes inflation to decline.

So the output gap hints at the future path of two variables the Fed cares a lot about: inflation and employment. A positive output gap occurs when unemployment is below its lowest sustainable level and it will likely spark higher inflation. That's why the Fed responds to a positive output gap by setting the real interest rate above the neutral real interest rate in an attempt to cool the economy and reduce inflationary pressure. A negative output gap corresponds to high unemployment and lower inflation. That will lead the Fed to respond by setting the real interest rate below the neutral real interest rate, so as to stimulate greater spending and output, which will reduce unemployment. The Fed also looks at forecasts of the future output gap so that it can get ahead of any looming problems.

Fed rule-of-thumb The recipe that describes how the Fed often sets the interest rate:

Federal funds rate − Inflation = Neutral real interest rate + ½ × (Inflation − 2%) + Output gap

Putting it all together: The Fed rule-of-thumb approximates what the Fed does.

There isn't really a recipe for monetary policy, but Fed decision making does seem to follow a standard pattern. The **Fed rule-of-thumb** shows how the Fed combines the neutral real interest rate and estimates of inflation and output in deciding how to adjust the interest rate. The Fed influences the economy by changing the real interest rate, but it sets nominal rates. So it evaluates the (nominal) federal funds rate by subtracting its estimate of the inflation rate so as to focus on the real interest rate. It then sets that real rate equal to the neutral real rate plus adjustments for deviations of inflation from its target and output from potential output. This formula shows the Fed rule-of-thumb:

This is the *nominal* interest rate the Fed controls

The real interest rate that would keep the economy neutral

Raise rates by the gap between actual and potential output

$$\text{Federal funds rate} - \text{Inflation} = \text{Neutral real interest rate} + \frac{1}{2} \times (\text{Inflation} - 2\%) + \text{Output gap}$$

The *real* interest rate is what the Fed really cares about so it adjusts for inflation

Raise rates by one half of . . .

. . . the gap between inflation and the Fed's 2% target

The Fed adjust the real interest rate in response to two economic forces:

- **Inflation:** The Fed responds to inflation by raising or lowering the real interest rate by an amount equal to one-half of the difference between inflation and the target rate of 2%. So if the inflation rate is 3% — putting it 1 percentage point above the Fed's inflation target — it will set the real interest rate half a percentage point higher.

- **Output:** The Fed responds to the output gap by raising or lowering the real interest rate by 1 percentage point for each percentage point that actual output deviates from potential output. So if the output gap is +1% — meaning output exceeds potential output by 1% — then the Fed will set the real interest rate to be 1 percentage point higher than it otherwise would be.

Do the Economics

It's your turn to play Federal Reserve governor. Or perhaps you're a bond trader, trying to predict the Fed's next move. The neutral real interest rate is 0.5%, inflation is 4%, and the output gap is 1% — meaning that output is 1% above its potential. What does the Fed rule-of-thumb suggest is an appropriate setting for the federal funds rate?

$$\text{Federal funds rate} - \text{Inflation} = 0.5\% + \frac{1}{2} \times (4\% - 2\%) + 1\%$$
$$= 2.5\%$$

$$\text{Federal funds rate} = 2.5\% + \text{Inflation} = 2.5\% + 4\% = 6.5\% \blacksquare$$

Monetary policy choices are systematic but not automatic. The Fed rule-of-thumb provides a pretty good prediction of the Fed's actual interest rate decisions. Figure 3 shows the actual federal funds rate compared to the Fed rule-of-thumb using a neutral interest rate of 0.5%. The Fed rule-of-thumb is also known as a *Taylor Rule*, named after the economist who demonstrated that the rule did a good job of describing past monetary policy actions.

The fact that the Fed rule-of-thumb is a good predictor of the actual federal funds rate doesn't mean that the Fed follows the rule-of-thumb like a recipe, and it certainly isn't an argument to allow computers to set interest rates using a formula like the Fed rule-of-thumb. You've already seen that FOMC members pore over a range of measures of excess

Figure 3 | The Fed Rule-of-Thumb Tracks How It Has Set the Actual Federal Funds Rate Pretty Closely

(Or at least it did until Covid arrived.)
Nominal interest rate

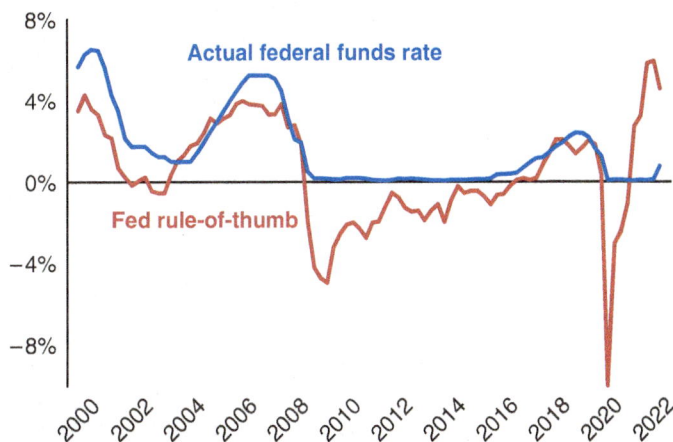

Note that the largest divergence between the *rule-of-thumb* and the *actual federal funds rate* occurs because the Fed can't (or won't) cut the interest rate below zero.

Data from: Federal Reserve, BEA, and CBO.

capacity in the economy to assess the output gap, as well as a range of measures of price changes to assess inflation. They also assess ways in which deeper forces — such as globalization, automation, demographics, market power, inequality, technological change, and financial interconnectedness — might change the structure of the economy.

Fed decisions are *systematic* — meaning that the Fed responds in a reliable fashion to the state of the economy. But they are not *automatic* — meaning that they aren't simply an application of a single rule over time. Fed officials argue that their decisions depart from the rule-of-thumb when their superior information, economic insights, and decision-making abilities suggest that a different choice will help it better meet its dual-mandate of price stability and maximum employment. So even though the Fed rule-of-thumb is a formula that closely tracks Fed decisions, a lot of judgment goes into actual Fed decisions.

The case for rules versus discretion. Some economists worry that the Fed might be tempted to lower interest rates to create a short-term economic boom. If it were to give in to this temptation, it would risk overheating the economy, which could spark higher inflation. Even the perception that the Fed might be tempted to do this can be problematic because it might lead people to expect higher inflation, which leads managers to raise their prices, thereby causing higher inflation.

That's why some economists have suggested that the Fed should follow a strict rule when setting interest rates, arguing that it would effectively remove this temptation, and so might result in lower and more stable inflation. In addition, it would make monetary policy more predictable.

However, strict adherence to a rule has some significant downsides. Most notably, the Fed can't reduce rates below zero even when that is what the Fed rule-of-thumb would suggest. Figure 3 shows how in 2008 and in early 2020, sharply negative interest rates were called for by the Fed rule-of-thumb. Many Fed officials have argued that the prospect of being close to the zero lower bound or the possibility of financial instability means that they sometimes need to take stronger action than the Fed rule-of-thumb suggests. In the recovery from the pandemic, the Fed kept interest rates low even as the Fed rule-of-thumb suggested they should significantly raise interest rates. The pandemic had many unique implications for output, employment, and inflation. Given these unique features, the Fed argued that it was appropriate to let rates stay low even as inflation rose higher than their target.

More generally, discretion risks the folly of humans, but it also allows them to use their judgment to come to better decisions based on all available data. That's why many monetary policy discussions begin with a look at what the Fed rule-of-thumb predicts, and then proceed to assessing how officials might use their discretion to try to make a better policy choice. This approach means that you can usually predict where interest rates are going by consulting the Fed rule-of-thumb, and listening closely to speeches by Fed officials for hints about how they might diverge from it.

22.3 How the Fed Sets Interest Rates

Learning Objective *Understand how the Federal Reserve implements monetary policy decisions.*

When the FOMC announces that it will raise or lower interest rates, it's announcing a new level for a specific interest rate called the *federal funds rate*. But it doesn't directly set the federal funds rate, which you'll recall is the rate that banks charge each other for overnight loans in the federal funds market. Only banks and certain other financial entities can borrow and lend in this market. So in order to implement its new monetary policy decision to shift this interest rate, the FOMC needs to create incentives for banks that shift the supply or demand for loans in this market. Let's explore how it does this.

The Overnight Market for Interbank Loans

We'll begin by thinking through why banks sometimes need to borrow from each other overnight. When you deposit your paycheck in a checking account, the money doesn't just sit as cash in the vault. Banks make money by lending out the funds you've deposited. But when you write a check to your landlord to pay your rent, you expect the bank to give that money to your landlord. Banks must keep cash on hand — known as **reserves** — so that they can make those payments. So banks face a trade-off: If they loan more of their money out, they make more revenue from borrowers paying them interest on those loans, but they also risk not having enough cash available to make payments like the one to your landlord. When they don't have enough cash on hand, they'll need to borrow money to make those payments.

Sometimes banks don't have enough ready cash to make payments on a given day. As a result, they have a demand for funds, which they can meet by borrowing money overnight from another bank in the federal funds market. Other banks may have more cash than they need. These banks are willing to supply funds, lending their spare cash overnight to those who need it. The forces of supply and demand determine the price in this market, which is the interest rate charged on these overnight loans. But these forces are also shaped by the Fed, which uses its tools to shape demand and supply for funds in this market. The interest rate is called the federal funds rate because the Fed gets involved in helping to determine what the rate will be. Let's take a look at how it shapes this market.

The Fed uses a number of tools to encourage banks to hold more or less in reserves. These tools effectively shift the supply or demand of overnight loans to achieve the goal of changing the equilibrium interest rate in the federal funds market. These tools work well: Figure 4 shows that the actual interest rate — called the *effective federal funds rate* — is usually incredibly close to the Fed's target for the federal funds rate. (Notice that the Fed used to set a specific target for the interest rate, but since late 2008, it has set a target range.) Let's explore the tools the Fed uses to hit these interest rate targets.

reserves The cash that banks need to keep on hand to make payments.

> Tools the Fed uses to influence the federal funds rate:
> 1. Pays interest to banks on reserves
> 2. Borrows money overnight from financial institutions
> 3. Lends directly through the discount window
> 4. Buys and sells government bonds

Figure 4 | **The Fed Borrows and Lends to Push the Effective Federal Funds Rate (Which Is the Actual Rate) Close to the Fed's Target for That Interest Rate**

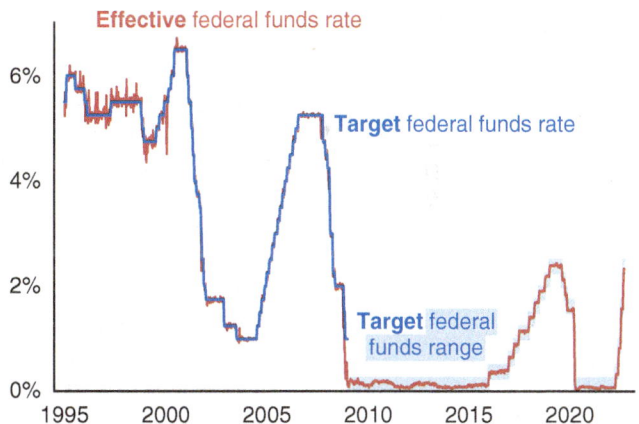

Data from: Federal Reserve.

Tool 1: The Fed pays interest to banks on their reserves.
In order to influence the federal funds rate, the Fed pays interest to banks on reserve balances. This effectively creates a minimum interest rate that a bank will charge before loaning its funds out to anyone, including to other banks, overnight.

If you can just leave your extra cash in your own reserve account and earn a 1% return with no risk of losing your money, you'll take it out of your account and lend it to someone else only if they offer a rate higher than 1%. As a result, the **interest rate on reserves** effectively serves as a floor on the interest rate at which banks will loan their funds. The higher this interest rate, the greater the incentive for banks to hold reserves and the lower the incentive to loan reserves to other banks. Thus, the higher the interest rate on reserves, the higher the interest rate on overnight loans. And so when the Fed wants to increase or decrease the federal funds rate, it raises or lowers the interest rate it pays on reserves.

The Fed used to simply tell banks how much they had to hold in reserves. Reserve requirements were a minimum amount of reserves that each bank had to hold by law. This regulatory approach ensured that each bank would hold at least the minimum amount of reserves that was required. The Fed would then try to influence the federal funds rate by changing the reserve requirement. If the Fed raised the reserve requirement, the supply of funds available in the federal funds market would decrease as banks were required to keep more funds in reserve and thus had less available for lending. This decrease in the supply of funds would raise the federal funds rate.

interest rate on reserves The interest rate the Fed pays to banks on reserves.

The Fed discontinued the reserve requirement in March 2020. Instead, the Fed now pays interest on reserves. However, not all institutions in the federal funds market are eligible to receive interest payments on their reserves. So the Fed must use another tool to set an effective floor for the federal funds rate at those institutions. Let's turn to that tool now.

Tool 2: The Fed borrows money overnight from financial institutions.

The Fed has another way of establishing a floor for the price of borrowing money: It can borrow from financial institutions and pay them interest on the loan. By engaging in overnight borrowing, the Fed increases the demand for overnight loans, which leads to higher interest rates. When it reduces such borrowing, it decreases the demand for overnight loans, which lowers rates. It does this primarily to have a tool to set an effective floor for the federal funds rate at financial institutions that aren't banks.

Let's see how this tool works. The **Open Market Trading Desk,** informally known as **the Desk,** is a trading desk at the Federal Reserve Bank of New York; traders at the Desk buy and sell government bonds. Government bonds are IOUs from the government, saying that the government promises to pay back a certain amount by a certain date at a particular rate of interest. The Fed isn't borrowing money itself, it's simply trading government bonds just like you might buy or sell government bonds (if you have a retirement account, you've probably bought government bonds, albeit indirectly). The difference is that the Fed is trading these bonds in order to influence interest rates. The Desk engages in these trades in order to carry out the directions of the FOMC to influence the federal funds rate. The Desk is called the "open market" desk because it's required to buy and sell in the competitive open market.

The Desk sells a government bond to a bank or other financial institution overnight, with an agreement to buy it back the next day at a higher price. These sales are called **overnight reverse repurchase agreements.** This might sound complicated, but the idea is actually pretty simple: If I sell you a piece of paper today and agree to buy it back at a higher price tomorrow, you're giving me your cash today and I'm promising to give you more cash tomorrow. Effectively then, I'm borrowing your money overnight, and the difference between the cash you give me today and the cash I'll pay you tomorrow is the interest I'm paying you. That's what these agreements do — they set an interest rate at which the Fed is willing to borrow money. These loans effectively set a floor for the federal funds rate — because why would a financial institution lend its money to someone else for less if it could lend to the Fed and make more in interest?

Both paying interest on reserves and the rate of return on overnight reverse repurchase agreements put a lower bound on the federal funds rate. Together, this method of implementing Fed policy for the federal funds rate is known as the **floor framework** because it effectively sets a floor on how low of an interest rate a financial institution will be willing to lend to another.

Essentially, the Fed raises the opportunity cost of lending in the federal funds market. Since no bank should want to lend at a rate lower than its opportunity cost, the alternative options the Fed provides for banks and other financial institutions to earn interest puts a lower bound on how low the federal funds rate will go.

Tool 3: The Fed lends to banks directly through the discount window.

There's another way the Fed can influence the amount of reserves that banks hold. It can lend directly to banks through the *discount window*. It's called that because in the old days, there was an actual window at each of the district reserve banks, where banks sold their loans to the Fed at a discount and later bought them back. Essentially, it was a pawn shop for banks. It doesn't work quite the same way anymore, but the name has stuck. And the main idea is the same — banks offer collateral (something they'll lose if they don't pay back the loan) and get a loan from the Fed that helps them meet their reserve requirements.

The interest rate that the Fed offers through the discount window is called the **discount rate,** and it's typically set higher than the federal funds rate. It's primarily thought of as a backup source for banks that need liquidity but are unable, for some

Open Market Trading Desk (the Desk) A trading desk at the New York Federal Reserve Bank where the Fed buys and sells government bonds.

overnight reverse repurchase agreements When the Desk sells a government bond to a financial institution, with an agreement to buy it back the next day at a higher price.

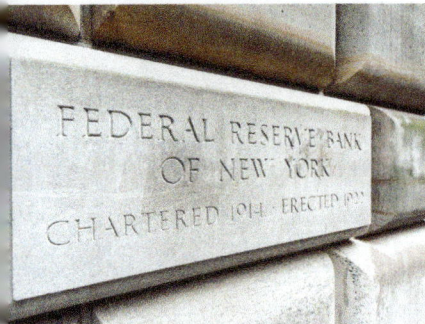

The Desk is housed at the New York Federal Reserve Bank.

Andriy Blokhin/Alamy Stock Photo

floor framework The Fed's approach of setting other interest rates to put a lower bound on how low the federal funds rate will go.

discount rate The interest rate on loans that the Fed offers to banks through the discount window.

reason, to get a loan from another bank at the federal funds rate. It creates an upper bound for the federal funds rate. Banks prefer to borrow from each other at the federal funds rate, but if the federal funds rate goes above the discount rate, they can just borrow from the Fed at the discount rate. Banks tend to use the discount window more during times of economic crisis. During normal times, it is rare for a bank to find itself in a situation in which it neither has enough reserves on hand nor is able to borrow what it needs from another bank. This means that the Fed doesn't use the discount window as a primary tool to impact interest rates. Rather, it uses it more as a backup system to help ensure stability in the financial system.

Tool 4: The Fed buys and sells government bonds. Prior to 2007, rather than trying to influence the federal funds rate by setting an interest rate floor and ceiling, the Fed would buy and sell bonds until it achieved the desired interest rate in the federal funds market. If the Fed wanted to raise rates, it would tell the Desk at the New York Federal Reserve Bank that it should sell bonds. When a bank buys a bond from the Fed, the money it pays is taken from its reserves. With fewer reserves, the bank is more likely to need to borrow reserves and less likely to be able to supply them to other banks. By selling bonds, the Fed increases demand for overnight loans and decreases supply. The net result is that the Fed's bond sales push the federal funds rate up.

When the Fed wanted to lower rates, it bought bonds. The money the Fed paid for the bond added to banks' available reserves. Because banks had more reserves, they'd be less likely to need to borrow from another bank overnight and more likely to be able to lend. By purchasing bonds, the Fed decreases the demand for overnight loans and increases the supply. Therefore, the Fed's bond purchases push the federal funds rate down.

Open market operations refer to the Fed buying and selling government bonds. Overnight reverse repurchase agreements are a form of open market operations. But historically, open market operations through buying and selling bonds were the primary way that the Fed implemented monetary policy decisions.

open market operations The Federal Reserve's buying and selling of government bonds to influence the federal funds rate.

In the 2000s, Fed officials began looking for alternative approaches to move interest rates because buying and selling bonds through standard open market operations didn't always achieve their desired federal funds rate. The 2008 financial crisis sped up some of those changes. Today the Fed uses a floor framework plus the use of an effective price ceiling through the discount rate. By setting the relevant prices — that is, a floor and ceiling for interest rates — and letting market quantities adjust, the Fed can precisely target the federal funds rate without having to indirectly try to influence this price by changing the quantity of bonds traded in the market.

The Impact of Changing the Federal Funds Rate on the Rest of the Economy

OK, so now you know how the Fed adjusts its main tool — the federal funds rate. But how does that affect you? Once the Fed has succeeded in moving the federal funds rate, the effects ripple throughout the economy. Banks adjust many of their interest rates such as those on credit cards, business loans, mortgages, student loans, savings accounts, and auto loans. Those interest rate changes then have broader macroeconomic effects. A lower real interest rate leads to more consumption and investment, an exchange rate depreciation, and higher net exports. This rise in aggregate expenditure leads managers to expand production, which requires them to hire more workers. Higher output leads more businesses to experience capacity constraints, leading them to raise their prices more frequently and by larger amounts, boosting higher inflation. People follow the Fed's decisions closely because they eventually affect nearly every corner of the economy, both in the United States and abroad. Let's see how all of this happens.

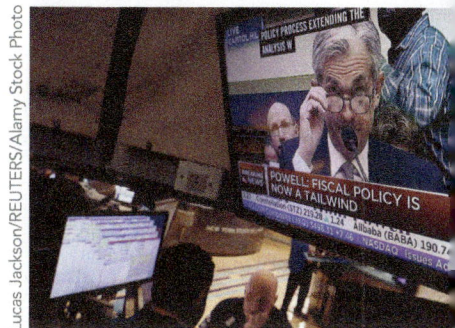

Lucas Jackson/REUTERS/Alamy Stock Photo

The Fed's decisions ripple out and affect every part of the economy.

A change in the federal funds rate percolates through to other interest rates. When the federal funds rate changes, banks reset the rate they charge borrowers because the marginal costs and benefits of making loans has changed. The marginal benefit to your bank of loaning money to you is the interest you pay. Its marginal cost is the opportunity cost — the interest it could earn by leaving the money in its reserves instead. When a lower federal funds rate leads this opportunity cost to fall, the **cost-benefit principle** tells banks to make more loans at any given interest rate. This increase in the supply of loans causes the interest rate that banks charge folks like you to fall.

The federal funds rate directly impacts short-term and variable interest rates. Many variable interest rates — such as the rates on most credit cards — move directly with the federal funds rate. Some private student loans also have a variable rate. Your savings account may have a variable rate that adjusts with the federal funds rate.

Changes in short-term interest rates also percolate through to longer-term loans. To understand why, realize that a longer-term loan can be thought of as a series of short-term loans. So when you pay a fixed interest rate on a five-year car loan, the bank can think of adding up the different interest rates it would charge over each month of the five years. Since the opportunity cost for the bank of making you a five-year loan is not making a series of short-term loans, it will only do so if the interest it earns is at least as great as what it could expect to earn on a series of short-term loans. As a result, long-term interest rates move when the federal funds rate changes, and how much they move depends on how long banks expect the federal funds rate to be at its new rate. Long-term rates will even start moving when banks expect the federal funds rate to be higher in the future if that future period overlaps with the duration of the loan it is issuing.

Interest rates change the value of consuming today versus consuming tomorrow. For consumers and businesses, consumption and investment change with the interest rate because of the **opportunity cost principle**. When the Fed changes the federal funds rate, the effects filter through to change the interest rates you face on things like your savings account and credit cards, which affects your choices about how much to save or borrow. Similarly, the return on savings for businesses changes, as does the cost of borrowing. Likewise, interest rates change how much the government pays to borrow, therefore potentially affecting how much the government has available to spend on other things.

Interest rates change the value of the U.S. dollar. Investors are global actors, seeking the highest risk-adjusted returns they can find. When U.S. interest rates fall, investing in the United States becomes less attractive. With fewer foreign investors trying to buy U.S. dollars so that they can invest in America, the value of the dollar falls. This depreciation means that it takes fewer yen, euros, or yuan (the currencies of Japan, Europe, and China) to buy an American dollar.

When it takes fewer yen to buy a dollar, Japanese consumers can buy American-made goods more cheaply. If you're exporting apples to Japan, you'll get the same number of dollars, but it costs your Japanese customers fewer yen. And that increases demand for your exported apples. Indeed, when the dollar depreciates, people around the world will discover that American goods will be cheaper in terms of their own currency, leading them to buy more goods exported from the United States.

The flip side is that it takes more dollars to buy goods priced in other currencies. In order for a Japanese auto manufacturer to receive the same number of yen, you must pay more U.S. dollars for a Japanese car. That price rise leads to a decline in the quantity of imported goods that Americans demand. If the quantity of imports declines by enough to offset the higher prices, then total spending by Americans on imported goods will also fall.

All this means that low interest rates lead to a cheaper U.S. dollar, causing exports to rise and imports to fall, thereby increasing net exports. The opposite happens when interest rates rise: The value of the dollar rises, making U.S. goods more expensive and foreign goods cheaper, and this leads to a decrease in net exports.

The Fed's decisions, therefore, percolate through the entire global economy because of their impact on global financial flows, exchange rates, and international trade. To summarize, a change in the federal funds rate changes real interest rates throughout the economy, which in turn changes consumption, investment, government spending, and net exports.

Fed decisions affect the U.S. dollar, which affects Japan and the rest of the world.

fotoVoyager/iStock Unreleased/Getty Images

The Fed just lowered interest rates. Is it a good time to borrow?

When the Fed lowers the federal funds rate, other interest rates will follow. You'll likely be able to take out an auto loan for less as a result. So does this make it a good time to buy a car? The Fed hopes you think so — after all, it's trying to boost spending with the lower rates. But whether this is a good decision depends on your personal situation. In particular, it's important to realize that the Fed lowers rates when it sees the economy weakening. That means that you should factor in the chance that you might lose your job. If that were to happen, would you still be able to make payments? Typically, young people are the most vulnerable to high rates of unemployment during an economic downturn. So be extra careful with your budget when you see the Fed lowering rates, and perhaps hold off on that car purchase until you're sure you could support yourself (and the car payment) if you lose your job. ∎

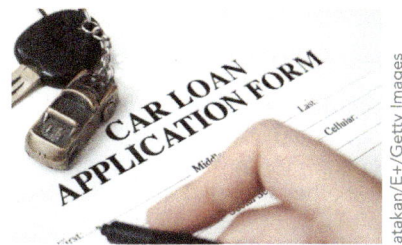

The Fed just lowered rates. Should you take out a car loan?

22.4 Alternative Tools the Fed Uses to Meet Its Dual Mandate

Learning Objective *Learn about some additional tools the Federal Reserve uses to ensure maximum employment and stable prices.*

The Fed's primary tool for affecting the economy is the federal funds rate, but this is not its only tool. The Fed's other tools are particularly relevant when it needs to encourage spending even after it has lowered the federal funds rate to zero. Additionally, the Fed has a responsibility to ensure stability in the financial system. Let's explore some of these tools.

Monetary Policy Choices When Nominal Interest Rates Are Zero

In order to fight the deepest recession since the Great Depression, the FOMC lowered its target for the federal funds rate essentially to zero in 2008. It faced the same decision with an even deeper recession in 2020, once again cutting rates to essentially zero. The zero lower bound meant that the Fed thought it could not push the federal funds rate any lower, so it had to start exploring other instruments that might encourage additional spending. The two main approaches both reflect the same goal — to push longer-term interest rates down. In normal times, the Fed sets a short-term interest rate — recall that the federal funds rate is an interest rate on overnight loans. (That's pretty short term!) But when this rate has hit the lower bound, and the economy is still below potential, the Fed can still push longer-term rates even lower to encourage people and businesses to take out more long-term loans to fund more spending today.

Things were desperate in 2020.

Forward guidance helps push down longer-term interest rates. Communication is an important tool for the Fed because it helps to shape expectations for the future path of interest rates. This can be particularly useful when the federal funds rate is near zero, since the Fed can use communication to commit to low rates in the future. This strategy of providing information about the future course of monetary policy in order to influence market expectations of future interest rates is called **forward guidance**.

The way it works is that the Fed promises that rates will stay low in the future. This pushes down longer-term interest rates because the Fed is promising that people can count on low interest rates for longer. From a bank's perspective, it means the bank can lower the interest rate they charge for longer-term loans. Thus, forward guidance can help

forward guidance Providing information about the future course of monetary policy in order to influence market expectations of future interest rates.

push down the interest rates on longer-term loans, like home mortgages, five-year car loans, and longer-term business loans, and these lower rates will lead more people to buy houses and cars, and make business investments.

For forward guidance to work, it's crucial that people believe that the Fed is committed to keeping rates low for a while, because it's those beliefs that push down the interest rate on long-term loans, spurring more spending.

quantitative easing (QE)
Purchasing large quantities of longer-term government bonds and other securities in an effort to lower long-term interest rates.

Quantitative easing aims to push interest rates below zero. **Quantitative easing,** or QE, is the name given to the Fed's strategy of purchasing large quantities of longer-term government bonds and other securities in an effort to put downward pressure on long-term interest rates, including mortgage rates.

The Fed used quantitative easing to help recover from the 2008 recession, purchasing trillions of dollars of longer-term government bonds and securities between 2009 and 2014. The Fed was in the process of selling these assets when the coronavirus pandemic began. On March 15, 2020, the Fed not only cut interest rates to zero, but it also announced that it would purchase $700 billion in assets. It later announced that it would buy what was needed to meet its goals.

Quantitative easing involves the Fed buying assets, but it isn't exactly spending trillions of dollars through quantitative easing. Instead, it buys government bonds from savers like you. By buying long-term bonds, the Fed is reducing the amount of government debt available for savers to purchase. This encourages savers to supply their savings to other long-term borrowers such as business and homeowners who need mortgages. This increase in the supply of long-term loans to nongovernment borrowers pushes down interest rates. Quantitative easing allows businesses to borrow at lower rates and also pushes down interest rates on mortgages.

Quantitative easing works a lot like open market operations, but instead of buying *short-term* government bonds in order to influence short-term interest rates, the Fed buys *long-term* bonds in order to try to lower long-term interest rates. This reduction in long-term interest rates also helps the Fed convince banks that it's committed to keeping rates low for a long period.

Lender of Last Resort

The sharp economic contraction that occurred in March 2020 combined with the heightened uncertainty in the early days of the pandemic was a potential threat to the financial system. Not only did the Fed deploy all of its tools to lower both short- and long-term interest rates, but it also acted as a source of borrowing more broadly. The Fed plays a key role in ensuring stability in the U.S. financial system. One way it does this is to act as a

lender of last resort The Fed's role as the lender that financial institutions turn to when they're having trouble getting loans.

lender of last resort, meaning it is the lender that banks or other institutions turn to when they need cash right away, but they're having trouble getting a loan elsewhere.

The Fed deployed five key lending programs to ensure small and large companies and city, local, and state governments could access emergency loans. While the details of all of these various programs differed, they had a shared purpose: prevent widespread bank runs, business failures, and general financial panic. A lender of last resort is what it sounds like — someone who gives you a loan when no one else will.

The lender of last resort can prevent a financial crisis. To understand why the Fed acts as a lender of last resort, consider the Fed's failure to act during the Great Depression: The Fed had the capacity to bail out banks, but it opted not to help. If a handful of banks were to go bust, it probably wouldn't pose much of a problem to a huge economy like that of the United States. But bank runs tend to be contagious because the failure of one bank prompts savers at other banks to worry that their bank might be next; those savers race to withdraw their money, and the trouble spreads. Indeed, more than 5,000 banks failed during the early 1930s, contributing to the severity and length of the Great Depression. In 2008 and 2020, the Fed was determined to avoid a replay, which is why it provided hundreds of billions of dollars in loans to prevent banks and other financial institutions from going bust.

The Fed can lose money when it acts as a lender of last resort. When the Fed acts as a lender of last resort, it takes on some of the borrower's risk. After all, if that borrower can't repay its loan, then it's the Fed — and hence taxpayers — who stand to lose money. Some people argue that the Fed should not use public money to prop up private, for-profit companies. For example, during the 2008 financial crisis, loans from the Fed (together with help from the U.S. Treasury) helped prevent AIG, an American multinational insurance company, from going bust. These actions benefited AIG's shareholders, even as they also prevented broader financial chaos, which arguably benefits the taxpayers who were putting their money on the line.

Ultimately, the Fed was fully paid back (with interest) for all the loans it made in its capacity as a lender of last resort during the 2008 financial crisis. But while these bailouts worked well — the American taxpayers made money and helped save some financial institutions — there were real risks involved. The Fed, with the help of the U.S. Treasury, made even more loans during the pandemic. While it's too soon to evaluate how costly the Fed's lending during the Covid recession will ultimately be to the taxpayer, it's clear that these loans helped the economy recover quickly from its steep collapse and preserved many businesses that may have otherwise had to permanently close.

The Fed's willingness to be a lender of last resort can lead borrowers to take bigger risks. There's an old joke that says that if you owe the bank $100, that's your problem, but if you owe your bank $100 million, that's the bank's problem. The Fed faces a similar problem when it acts as lender of last resort to the largest and most interconnected financial institutions. If any big financial firm were to fail, it would create widespread economic chaos, which the Fed was set up to prevent. The problem is that these financial institutions understand that — from the Fed's perspective — they're *too big to fail*. That creates incentives for these financial institutions to take on extra risk. After all, if their financial bets don't pay off, the Fed has little choice but to help them. This suggests that even though the Fed can often soften the flow of a financial crisis by acting as lender of last resort, it may also make future financial crises more likely.

In response, during the 2008 financial crisis, Congress passed legislation known as Dodd-Frank that requires banks to stand on a sounder financial footing, so that they're less likely to need to rely on the Fed to act as lender of last resort during the next crisis. This new law also placed restrictions on the Fed's ability to act as a lender of last resort, in the hope that financial institutions will be a bit more cautious, knowing that the Fed can't bail them out quite so easily.

22.5 | Tying It Together

The Fed Adapts and So Should You

The Federal Reserve is charged with steering the economy into smooth waters, avoiding costly inflation and helping foster a labor market in which unemployment is at its lowest sustainable rate. It's not an easy job, and the Fed hasn't always gotten it right. In the 1970s, the Fed let inflation run too high without taking enough action. It took a period of high interest rates that caused a painful recession with high unemployment in the early 1980s to bring the inflation rate back down. Some of the Fed's critics argue that low interest rates of the 2000s caused the financial crisis that ensued in 2007 and 2008, which led to the Great Recession. Yet, the Fed was seen by many as failing to do enough to push down interest rates (and thus unemployment) during the Great Recession. In the wake of the Covid recession, inflation spiked and the Fed was criticized for not raising rates fast enough to prevent inflation from emerging, or whether these higher rates might cause economic growth to falter.

You learned how the Fed approaches these problems, the questions it asks, the information it uses, and how it makes decisions. The real interest rate is the opportunity cost

Their conversations will shape the world economy.

of consuming today versus saving for tomorrow, and the Fed shapes it to influence the behavior of everyone in the economy.

The Fed's actions highlight just how important the interdependence principle is. The Fed can set one interest rate — the interest rate it pays on reserves — and that sets off a chain reaction throughout the economy by shifting the cost-benefit calculations of nearly everyone in the world. The Fed raises interest rates, and you might see a higher rate on your student loan, leading you to cut back your spending. Foreign investors push up the value of the dollar, since higher interest rates in the United States increase demand to invest in the United States. As you cut back your spending and look for discounts, you find more of them as the price of imports falls and businesses react to the decline in spending by lowering prices. Yet in China, a mother notices that the price of pork has risen because China imports a lot of pork from the United States. So she switches to chicken, which is produced in China, meaning that the Chinese chicken producers see an increase in sales. And so it continues, as the Fed's decision sets off a chain of interdependent decisions.

So now you know why the Fed is so powerful, how it does what it does, and what you can do to make good decisions when the Fed makes a change. My final tip: Now that we've studied business cycles and the Fed, combine your ability to track the economy with your new understanding of where interest rates might be headed. With this information, you'll be better prepared to figure out where the economy is going, which will help you make better decisions in your own life.

Chapter 22 Review

Chapter at a Glance

The Federal Reserve (the Fed): the U.S. central bank. Central banks determine a country's monetary policy (the process of setting interest rates in an effort to influence economic conditions).

Dual mandate: The Fed's two key goals

Maximum sustainable employment

Price stability

Inflation target: A publicly stated goal for the inflation rate. The Fed has an inflation target of 2%.

Why doesn't the Fed target 0% inflation?

- Inflation greases the wheels of the labor market
- The Fed can lower real interest rates by more when inflation is above zero
- The risk of deflation
- Measured inflation may be overstated

Federal funds rate: The interest rate that the Fed uses as its policy tool, which is the nominal interest rate that banks pay to borrow from each other overnight in the federal funds market.

Starts with the *neutral real interest rate* → Targets the *nominal interest rate* in order to influence the *real interest rate* → Compares *inflation* to its *inflation target* → Looks at the *output gap*

A Fed rule-of-thumb approximates what it does:

This is the **nominal** interest rate the Fed controls

The real interest rate that would keep the economy neutral

Raise rates by the gap between actual and potential output

$$\text{Federal funds rate} - \textit{Inflation} = \textit{Neutral real interest rate} + \frac{1}{2} \times (\textit{Inflation} - 2\%) + \textit{Output gap}$$

The *real* interest rate is what the Fed really cares about so it adjusts for inflation

Raise rates by one half of . . .

. . . the gap between inflation and the Fed's 2% target

Tools the Fed uses to influence the federal funds rate:

Sets a floor on the federal funds rate
{ 1. Pays interest to banks on excess reserves
  2. Borrows money overnight from financial institutions

3. Lends directly through the discount window — Sets a ceiling
4. Buys and sells government bonds — What it used to do

Monetary policy choices when nominal interest rates **are zero:**

Forward guidance	Providing information about the future course of monetary policy in order to influence market expectations of future interest rates.
Quantitative easing (QE)	Purchasing large amounts of longer-term government bonds and other securities in an effort to put downward pressure on longer-term interest rates.

Key Terms

deflation, 585

discount rate, 590

dual mandate, 582

Fed rule-of-thumb, 586

federal funds rate, 586

Federal Open Market Committee
(FOMC), 579

floor framework, 590

forward guidance, 593

inflation target, 582

interest rate on reserves, 589

lender of last resort, 594

monetary policy, 578

neutral real interest rate, 585

open market operations, 591

Open Market Trading Desk, 590

overnight reverse repurchase
agreements, 590

quantitative easing (QE), 594

reserves, 589

zero lower bound, 584

Study Problems

Learning Objective 22.1 *Learn how the Federal Reserve makes monetary policy decisions.*

1. Use the opportunity cost principle to explain why the Fed uses interest rates to influence the economy. How do interest rates impact the opportunity cost of spending money today?

2. Why does the Fed pay such close attention to GDP if its mandate is to promote maximum employment while keeping prices stable?

3. Explain why countries with central banks independent from the government have lower inflation on average.

4. For each of the following misconceptions about the Fed, identify what is wrong with the statement and why.

   a. The Federal Reserve lacks accountability because no one audits the Fed. There's no way to know what really goes on behind the scenes.

   b. The Federal Reserve just prints more money when the economy needs it and gives it to banks.

   c. A government agency should not have so much control over the economy because politicians are always just going to do anything to win the next election.

5. In recent decades, the Federal Reserve has transitioned from an intentionally vague and bureaucratic communication style to a more direct and transparent approach. What is the impact on inflation expectations of each of these communication styles?

Learning Objective 22.2 *Discover how the Federal Reserve assesses its goals and makes interest rate choices.*

6. Explain why the Fed targets inflation rather than employment even though both are part of its dual mandate. Use the interdependence principle to help answer the question.

7. What are the pros and cons of targeting a 0% inflation rate? Do you believe the Fed should target 0% inflation, its current 2% inflation target, or some other value? Explain your reasoning.

8. With the advent of big data and increased computing power, some people have advocated for monetary policy by algorithm. Basically, real-time data is fed into a computer program, which then determines monetary policy decisions. Discuss the benefits and potential problems with such an approach.

9. You are working at the campus bookstore earning $15 per hour. Your manager tells you that in the upcoming year you will get a 2% raise. How does your real wage change if inflation next year is 1%, 2%, or 3%? What flexibility does inflation provide employers, especially during an economic downturn?

10. Predict how the Fed would likely respond if the output gap became more positive, so that output moved from being 0.1% above potential output to being 3% above potential output, and inflation rose above its 2% target rate. How would you expect unemployment to change over the next year or two in response to the Fed's actions?

11. Use the Fed rule-of-thumb to predict how the Fed would want to change the federal funds rate and the real interest rate targets for each of the following scenarios if its estimate of the neutral real interest rate is 2%.

    a. A recession hits the economy, leading output to be 0.75% below potential output and inflation to fall to 1%.

    b. An increase in consumer and business confidence pushes the economy to produce output at 2% above potential output, while inflation rises to 3.5%.

Learning Objective 22.3 *Understand how the Federal Reserve implements monetary policy decisions.*

12. Explain how the Fed creates a lower and upper bound for the federal funds rate and the incentives that drive financial institutions to move the federal funds market to that target.

13. Explain how the average American is affected by monetary policy. How does a change in the federal funds rate percolate from Wall Street to Main Street?

14. You are the managing director of a small local bank. The Fed announces that it is moving its federal funds rate target from 2.25% up to 3.0%. How does this impact the interest rates on the business lines of credit and personal

loans you make? What would have to happen for you to also change the interest rate you charge on longer-term loans such as mortgages or business loans?

15. The FOMC is presented with data and analysis that indicates the output gap has changed from being close to 0 to now being large and negative. Additionally, inflation is 1.2% instead of the target of 2%. Predict how the FOMC is likely to change its interest rate target by changing: (1) the floor framework and (2) the discount rate. Explain how altering these rates can help close the output gap.

16. The FOMC increases real interest rates. Explain how each component of GDP—consumption, investment, government spending, and net exports—changes in response, and why. What happens to output, inflation, and unemployment? What would have led the FOMC to increase interest rates?

Learning Objective 22.4 *Learn about some additional tools the Federal Reserve uses to ensure maximum employment and stable prices.*

17. Compare and contrast how changes in the federal funds rate and quantitative easing affect interest rates and the broader economy.

18. Do you think that the Fed's role as a lender of last resort leads financial institutions to make riskier investments? What problem might the economy face if these institutions were left to fail?

19. The Fed has decreased the federal funds rate—a nominal short-term interest rate—to 0%, and yet the economy is still struggling. Explain what tools it still has at its disposal to help spur the economy, and how it could use them.

Government Spending, Taxes, and Fiscal Policy

Every year, typically in early February, the president of the United States releases a proposed budget. In print, it stands nearly as tall as a toddler. Thousands of detailed tables outline actual and proposed spending on everything that is—or might be—funded with federal government dollars.

To budget is to fight over money. And to fight over money is to fight over priorities. What's most important to you: increasing funding for the military, education, or health care? Another aircraft carrier to make us just a little bit safer? More education spending to pay for more teachers, better buildings, and fresher teaching materials that increase student learning? More vaccines to reduce the spread of contagious diseases? Each of these decisions involves opportunity costs—if you spend a dollar on one thing, you're not spending it on another. Your sense of the relative benefits of buying another aircraft carrier versus spending more on education or health care depends on your values, preferences, and beliefs. In other words, the slew of numbers that makes up the budget lays out a vision for society.

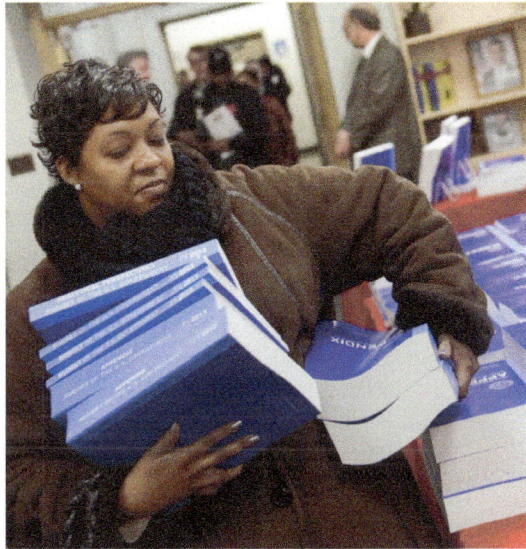

Your economics textbook is light reading compared to the multivolume federal budget.

In the United States, the budget is created with the input of each agency across the federal government. Career government workers spend months developing spending proposals in conjunction with the Office of Management and Budget. As the budget is prepared, vicious fights can break out—even among colleagues who normally consider themselves to be friends—as they struggle to get a share of the limited funding for their preferred programs.

The president's budget doesn't just lay out a vision for our country; it also tells Congress what the administration thinks will happen to the U.S. economy and what role government spending and taxation will play in influencing that outcome. That means the budget is also a plan of attack for smoothing business cycles and helping the economy operate closer to its potential. Ultimately, Congress decides how much will be spent by the federal government and which programs will receive funding each year. Congress passes the budget and asks the president to sign it into law.

In this chapter, we'll take a close look at what the U.S. government spends money on, how it raises revenue, and what happens when it spends more than it raises in revenue. We'll examine how governments use spending and taxation to stabilize the economy, and how government debt affects private investment and the economy. Let's get started!

Chapter Objective

Analyze government spending, revenue, deficits, and debt.

23.1 The Government Sector
Assess the size and scope of the government.

23.2 Fiscal Policy
Discover how fiscal policy can smooth business cycles.

23.3 Government Deficits and Debt
Understand why governments run deficits and the implications of government debt.

🎙 Podcast
Think Like an Economist
Fiscal Policy—Government Spending and Taxes

social insurance Insurance provided by the government against bad outcomes such as unemployment, illness, disability, or outliving your savings.

23.1 # The Government Sector

Learning Objective *Assess the size and scope of the government.*

The government plays a big role in your life. The college you're attending probably gets funding from the federal government. If you're at a state university or community college, your school also receives state or local government support. You might be paying for college with government-funded student loans, grants, or scholarships. Your school might require that you get vaccines that were developed with government-funded research. You likely drive on roads that are built, maintained, and patrolled using federal, state, or local government dollars. And chances are that you or someone in your family has relied on unemployment insurance, food assistance, or government-provided health care at some point.

Together, the spending by federal, state, and local governments adds up to nearly two-fifths of GDP. Let's explore what they spend the money on, and how they raise the money they spend.

Government Spending

The federal government spends more money than state and local governments combined. Figure 1 shows that in 2020 the federal government spent $6.9 trillion, state governments spent another $2.0 trillion, and local governments spent $1.7 trillion.

That adds up to $28,000 for each man, woman, and child in the United States. It's a lot of money, so let's look at what it gets spent on. Because federal, state, and local governments have different responsibilities, we'll look at each separately.

Figure 1 | Total Government Spending

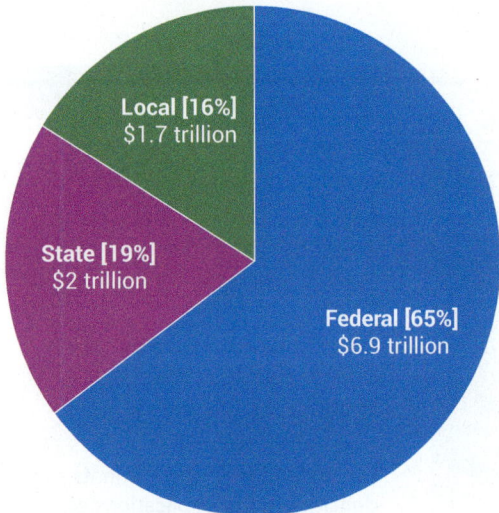

Data from: Latest data from BEA.

"The federal government is an insurance company with a military." This old saying is an exaggeration, but it highlights the reality that the federal government spends most of its money on social insurance programs and the military. **Social insurance** refers to government-provided insurance against bad outcomes such as unemployment, illness, disability, or outliving your savings. Figure 2 shows that social insurance programs — which fall mostly in the slices for Social Security, unemployment, and labor, or Medicare and health — are some of the biggest slices of the federal spending pie. In 2020, social insurance was expanded further to assist people during the pandemic, with money to help businesses stay afloat and extra funding for the unemployed. Taken together, these social insurance programs plus spending on the military and veterans' benefits account for roughly three-quarters of federal government spending. So saying that the federal government is an insurance company with a military may not be exactly right, but it's about three-quarters accurate.

Figure 2 | Federal Government Spending

*Social insurance + military (shown in blue) accounts for over **three-quarters** of federal government spending*

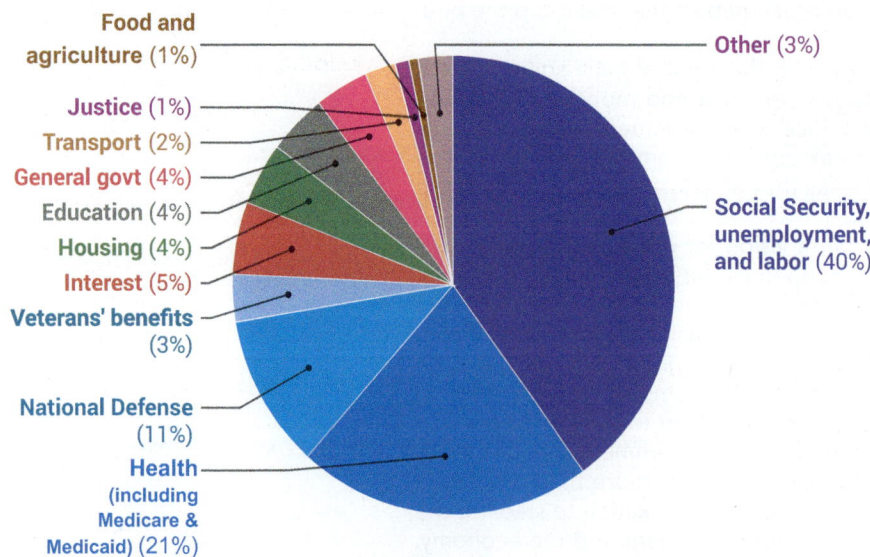

2021 Data from: Office of Management and Budget.

The rest of the pie gets divided into very small slices. Interest on government debt takes a further 5% of the overall budget, leaving just one-fifth of the budget to pay for everything else. That remaining money gets spread pretty thinly across programs such as Pell grants, student loans and all other education spending, school lunch and other food support programs, highways and transportation, housing, science, energy, the environment, and international affairs and foreign aid. Many people think that the government spends a lot more than it actually does on these small slivers of the federal budget.

Four out of every ten dollars the federal government spends goes to the elderly or disabled. This is largely because the government provides a basic income and also pays for health care for almost all Americans over the age of 65. Few of us under age 65 get access to those benefits. The generous support for the elderly partly reflects the social programs set up in the wake of the Great Depression, when poverty among the elderly was a significant problem and people didn't live as long as they do now. It also reflects the different responsibilities of federal, state, and local government.

States provide employment and income support, education, and health care. While there are differences across states, Figure 3 shows that on average, roughly half of state government spending goes toward employment and income support. This spending includes state contributions to Medicaid, unemployment insurance, employment services, and pensions for state employees. You might recall that the federal government also spends money on Medicaid and unemployment insurance. Federal and state governments jointly fund these programs.

States spend nearly a fifth of their budget on education, most of which goes to higher education. (Elementary and secondary education is primarily

Figure 3 | State Government Spending

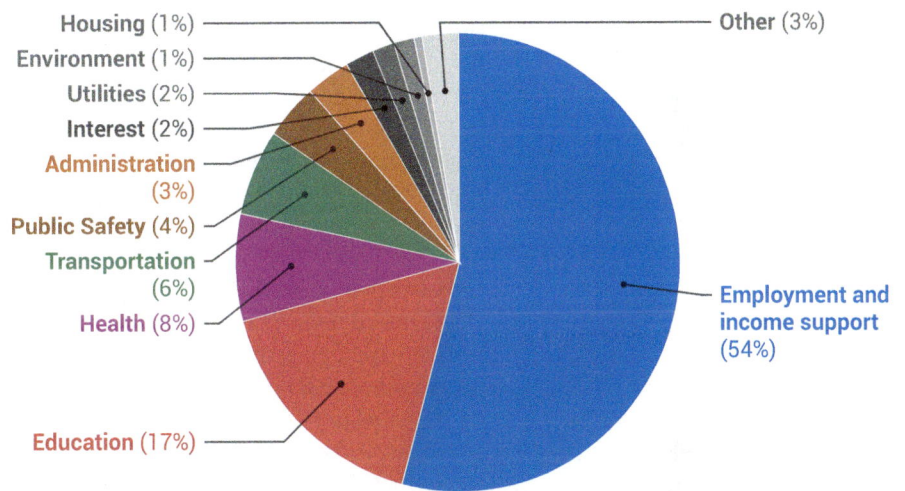

Housing (1%)
Environment (1%)
Utilities (2%)
Interest (2%)
Administration (3%)
Public Safety (4%)
Transportation (6%)
Health (8%)
Education (17%)
Other (3%)
Employment and income support (54%)

2020 Data from: U.S. Census Bureau.

funded and run by local governments.) Your state government also provides services like public hospitals and other costs related to providing health care, state police, prisons, highways, and parks.

Local government provides most of the government services you've interacted with so far in your life. Figure 4 shows that education is the biggest chunk of local government spending, and your local government provides the public primary and secondary schools in your neighborhood. Your local government also provides the community services your family might rely on — bus services, water, sewer lines, local parks and playgrounds, trash and recycling collection, firefighters, police, and emergency services.

Evaluate government spending as a share of available resources. When you express government spending as a percentage of GDP rather than in dollars, you can make comparisons over time and across countries. Government spending as a share of

Figure 4 | Local Government Spending

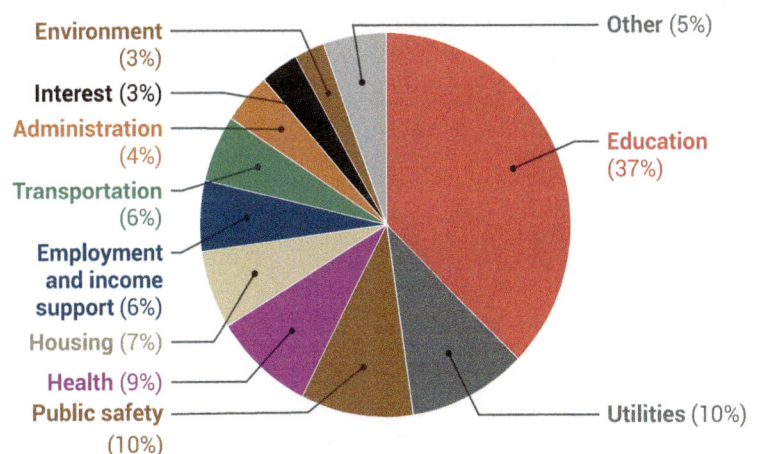

Environment (3%)
Interest (3%)
Administration (4%)
Transportation (6%)
Employment and income support (6%)
Housing (7%)
Health (9%)
Public safety (10%)
Other (5%)
Education (37%)
Utilities (10%)

2020 Data from: U.S. Census Bureau.

a country's GDP adjusts for both price differences and differences in the size of the economy, putting all countries on the same scale.

The federal government has expanded over time. While the federal government spends more than state and local government combined, it hasn't always been this way. State and local government provided most government services throughout the 1800s and early 1900s. The federal government played a much smaller role, focused on national defense and delivering mail.

The federal government had a smaller role partly because it didn't have an easy way to raise revenue. The federal government collected income tax to offset the costs of the Civil War, but ended that tax after a decade. In 1894, Congress passed a 2 percent income tax on the richest Americans, but the U.S. Supreme Court ruled that it was unconstitutional. After that, the federal government was forced to rely mostly on tariffs for revenue. In 1913, the Sixteenth Amendment was passed, giving Congress the power to levy an income tax. This gave the federal government the revenue source it would later need in order to expand.

Federal government spending remained low for the first few decades of the twentieth century, and it was only 3% of GDP when the Great Depression hit in 1929. To counter and cushion the impact of this dramatic slump, President Franklin D. Roosevelt proposed the New Deal in 1933. The New Deal created public works programs, regulatory bodies like the Securities and Exchange Commission, and social insurance programs like Social Security and unemployment insurance. By 1941, federal government spending had risen to 17% of GDP. In the years that followed, federal spending soared even higher to pay for the expenses associated with World War II, but quickly fell after the war ended. However, the spending programs initiated by the New Deal permanently raised federal government spending to roughly the share of GDP spent today.

Government social insurance spending has grown over time. The New Deal created many of our largest social insurance programs; however, there have been a few key expansions since then. In 1965, the federal government created Medicare, which provides health insurance to all those aged 65 or older. It also created Medicaid, which helps states provide health insurance for their poorest residents. In 1997, the federal government created the Children's Health Insurance Program (sometimes known by its acronym, CHIP) to provide health insurance to children whose families earn too much to qualify for Medicaid, but too little to afford private insurance. In 2003, Congress expanded Medicare to provide additional coverage for prescription drugs. And in 2009, Congress passed the Affordable Care Act, which expanded funding for Medicaid and created health insurance subsidies for some low- and middle-income people.

Figure 5 shows that spending on social insurance has grown as a share of GDP, while spending on the military has declined. However, since 1960 real GDP has grown more than fivefold, so even though military spending is lower as a share of GDP, we still spent roughly 1.6 times as much on the military in 2021 as we did in 1960 (after adjusting for inflation).

Much of future federal government spending is already determined. Most social insurance programs entitle you to a certain amount of spending if you meet certain eligibility criteria, which is why they're often called *entitlement programs*. Social Security guarantees to retirees payments that are a function of their past earnings for as long as they live. Medicare guarantees health care for these retirees for as long as they live, regardless of the health problems they might develop.

Figure 5 | Government Spending on Social Insurance Has Risen Over Time, as Military Spending Has Declined

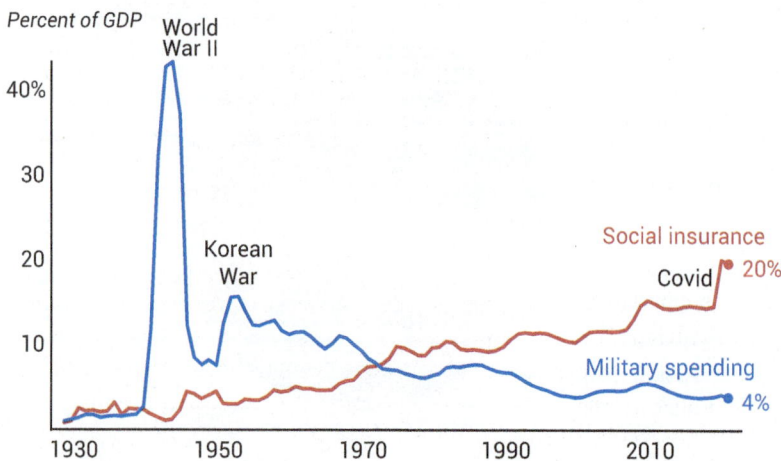

Data from: Bureau of Economic Analysis and the Office of Management and Budget.

It would be hard to plan for retirement if these programs changed much from year to year. That's why both programs are part of the federal budget called **mandatory spending,** which means that the terms of the spending are written into the legislation that created the program. Anything can become mandatory spending if Congress passes legislation mandating it. For example, legislation that's informally known as the farm bill spells out spending on farm subsidies and food stamps. Mandatory spending can be cut only if Congress repeals or amends this earlier legislation.

In contrast, funding for federal agencies and most government programs is **discretionary spending.** This is spending that Congress annually *appropriates* — that is, it provides funds for each specific purpose. By law, the government can spend only money that Congress has appropriated. If it fails to appropriate the funds in time, the government shuts down.

Discretionary spending is what you most often hear about when the government fights over spending. That's because Congress has to decide on discretionary spending each year. Yet discretionary spending is only 30% of federal government spending — and about half of it is spending on the military. The rest is on the smaller slices of the federal budget, such as education, housing, science, energy, the environment, and international affairs.

While Congress fights over discretionary spending, most of the growth in federal spending comes from mandatory spending obligations and interest on the debt. The aging of the baby boomer population and growing life expectancy are increasing spending on mandatory programs for retirees like Social Security and Medicare. In addition, the government's debt is growing, which is leading to higher annual interest payments.

mandatory spending Spending on programs that does not get determined annually; instead, it is set in law.

discretionary spending Spending that Congress appropriates annually.

Government spending is lower in the United States than in other rich countries.
The combination of federal, state, and local spending in the United States added up to 40% of GDP on average across the 2010 to 2020 period. Figure 6 shows that this is a bit lower than in many other developed countries, some of which devote half or more of their GDP to government spending.

Why are other countries spending so much more? It's because their governments tend to publicly provide things that we privately pay for in the United States. For example, most developed countries provide greater access to publicly funded health care; low-cost or free higher education; and paid parental leave. They also offer more support to low-income families.

Government Revenue

Now that you've seen how much the government spends, a natural question is: Where does all the money come from to pay for it? The federal government primarily collects revenue by taxing people's incomes, while state and local governments focus more on taxing people's spending. Let's see how it breaks down.

Federal government tax revenue comes primarily from income and payroll taxes.
Overall, roughly four-fifths of the federal government's revenue comes from either payroll taxes or income taxes. The rest comes from corporate taxes and other taxes, as shown in Figure 7. When you get your paycheck, you'll notice that both payroll taxes and income taxes have been withheld. They sound similar, but there are some important differences.

Figure 6 | Government Spending Is Lower in the United States Than Other Rich Countries

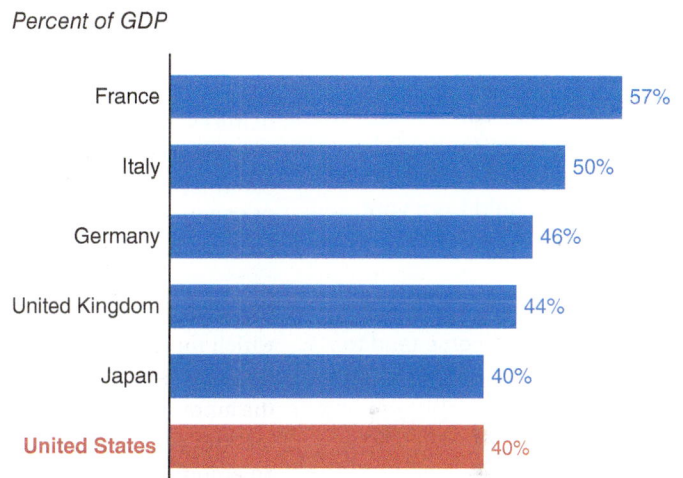

Percent of GDP

France 57%
Italy 50%
Germany 46%
United Kingdom 44%
Japan 40%
United States 40%

Data from: OECD average data for 2010–2020.

Figure 7 | Federal Government Revenue

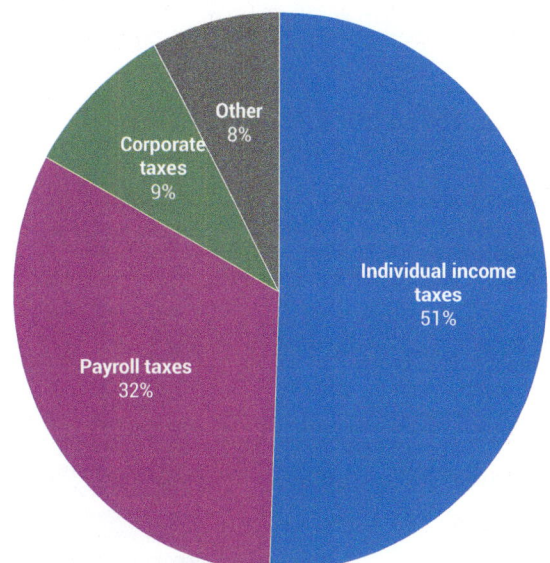

Other 8%
Corporate taxes 9%
Individual income taxes 51%
Payroll taxes 32%

2021 Data from: CBO.

income taxes Taxes collected on all income, regardless of its source.

You pay income taxes on *all* income. Income taxes are taxes collected on *all* income, regardless of its source. Income includes both the income you earn from working and unearned income such as investment income, pensions, capital gains, and inheritance or gift income. *Income* is all the money that you receive in a year, from all sources. Don't confuse this with *wealth,* which is your stock of savings and assets.

payroll taxes Taxes on earned income.

earned income Wages from an employer, or net earnings from self-employment.

Payroll taxes are used to fund social insurance. While income taxes apply to all income, **payroll taxes** apply only to earned income. Your **earned income** includes both wages from an employer and net earnings from self-employment. It also includes bonuses, commissions, and other payments from your employer. Payroll taxes are used to fund social insurance programs like Social Security and Medicare.

Payroll taxes are levied as a fixed percentage of your earned income, and your employer typically withholds them from your wages. You've probably seen these taken out of your paycheck, including 6.2% in payroll taxes for Social Security (sometimes referred to as FICA or OASDI on your pay stub) and 2.9% withheld for Medicare. These payroll taxes add up to 9.1%, so if your employer owes you $100, it will withhold $9.10 to give to the government to cover your payroll taxes, and give you only $90.90. While you see the $9.10 taken out of your paycheck, you may not realize that your employer also has to contribute an additional amount for you as well. It will pay the government another $9.10, meaning that your work cost your employer $109.10, even though you see only $100 on your paycheck and receive only $90.90 after payroll taxes are withheld. (And you'll take home even less after your estimated federal and state income tax is withheld).

Everyone who works pays payroll taxes. However, there's a cap on how much workers must contribute to Social Security: In 2022, for every dollar someone earns above $147,000, no further Social Security taxes are owed. There's no limit on the 2.9% Medicare tax, and in fact, there's an additional payroll tax of 0.9% on earnings over $200,000.

Taxes are withheld from your paycheck.

progressive tax A tax where those with more income tend to pay a higher share of their income in taxes.

Income taxes are progressive. The U.S. federal income tax is a **progressive tax,** which means that those with more income tend to pay a higher share of their income in tax. A tax is progressive when the tax rate you pay increases with your income. That's why the amount you'll actually have to pay in federal income taxes will depend on how much income you receive throughout the year. So even though your employer might withhold an amount for payment of federal income taxes from your paycheck, unlike payroll taxes, this withholding is just a guess at how much you might owe.

taxable income The amount of your income that you pay taxes on.

marginal tax rate The tax rate you pay if you earn another dollar.

Figure 8 shows you the federal income tax rate schedule for single people in 2022. The tax rate you face depends on your **taxable income,** which is the amount of your income you pay tax on. The way it works is that your first $10,275 in taxable income faces a tax rate of 10%. This means that if your taxable income is $5,000, then you'll owe $500 in taxes. If your taxable income is $30,000, then you would pay 10% on your first $10,275 of income and 12% on the remaining $19,725.

The tax rate you pay if you earn another dollar is your **marginal tax rate.** If your taxable income is $30,000, your marginal tax rate is 12%. If your taxable income is $45,000, then the marginal tax rate on the next dollar is 22%. The highest marginal tax rate is 37%, and it applies to every dollar of taxable income over $539,901 per year.

Figure 8 highlights the progressivity of the tax system — as you earn more, your marginal tax rate increases, which ensures that those with higher incomes will end up paying a larger share of their income in taxes.

It may sound simple, but your *taxable income* is not the same thing as the total income you receive. You can subtract many possible deductions from your actual income in calculating your taxable income. To start with, almost everyone gets to subtract what's called the *standard deduction.* In 2022, this was $12,950, which means that if your job paid you $40,000, your taxable income would have been $40,000 – $12,950 = $27,050 (or less if you qualified for other deductions). We'll go over some of these deductions later, but for now realize that when calculating each year's taxable

Figure 8 | The 2022 Federal Income Tax Rate Schedule

For taxable income over . . .	. . . but not over . . .	. . . the marginal tax rate is:
$0	$10,275	10%
$10,275	$41,775	12%
$41,775	$89,075	22%
$89,075	$170,050	24%
$170,050	$215,950	32%
$215,950	$539,900	35%
$539,900	–	37%

income, most people subtract thousands of dollars off of what they actually earn. (You may be starting to understand why people complain about doing their taxes; they spend a lot of time searching for — or worrying that they missed — things to subtract from their income.)

Do the Economics

You currently have a job in which you earn an annual income of $54,950 a year. You take the standard deduction, so your taxable income is $42,000. A competitor wants to hire you and is willing to pay you $3,000 more. The job is similar, but you would no longer be able to walk to work each day.

Given your current taxable income, what's your marginal tax rate?

With a taxable income of $42,000, the tax rate on the next dollar you earn is 22%.

Calculate how much you'll owe in additional federal income taxes if you accept the higher-paying job.

$$0.22 \times \$3,000 = \$660$$

Remember that you'll also owe payroll taxes — 6.2% for Social Security and 2.9% for Medicare — on the additional income. How much more in payroll taxes will you pay?

$$0.062 \times \$3,000 + 0.029 \times \$3,000 = \$273$$

The competitor's job is across town, which will require that you spend $120 a month on bus fare. How much more will you make each year after taxes and transportation costs if you take the new job?

$$\underbrace{\$3,000}_{\text{Extra income}} - \underbrace{\$660}_{\substack{\text{Extra income} \\ \text{tax}}} - \underbrace{\$273}_{\substack{\text{Extra payroll} \\ \text{tax}}} - \underbrace{12 \times \$120}_{\text{New expenses}} = \$627$$

Much of that $3,000 raise got eaten up with your new expenses and taxes (and we've yet to add in any additional state and local taxes you might owe). Bottom line: It's worth doing the math before you pick among jobs because the differences in the take-home pay might not be as big as you first think. ∎

Corporate taxes are paid by people. Six percent of federal taxes are collected from corporations. But what does it mean for a corporation to pay a tax? All taxes require someone to forgo some income. The people who ultimately pay most of the corporate taxes are the owners of the corporations. For publicly held companies, the owners are the shareholders — the people who've invested their money and bought stock in the company. You'll likely be a shareholder one day if you aren't already, since most people hold stock in their retirement accounts.

Workers also bear some of the burden of corporate taxes. As taxes rise, businesses buy less capital, which makes their workers less productive. And when workers are less productive, employers aren't willing to pay them as much. Studies of the effect of corporate taxes on workers' wages vary, but the Congressional Budget Office estimates that for every dollar of corporate tax, workers lose about 25 cents, and shareholders lose 75 cents.

State and local governments collect sales, property, and income taxes. A **sales tax** is a tax on purchases, and it's typically a percentage of the purchase price of goods and services. For example, when you buy a T-shirt in Michigan, you'll pay a 6% sales tax, which is why a $10 T-shirt will cost you $10.60 at the register.

An **excise tax** is a tax on a specific product, such as gas, cigarettes, or alcohol. Unlike a regular sales tax, excise taxes are usually levied based on the quantity you buy, not the price you pay. For example, the federal excise tax on gas is 18.4 cents per gallon, and the state excise tax varies from 8.95 cents per gallon in Alaska to 57.6 cents in Pennsylvania.

sales tax A tax on purchases that's typically a percentage of the purchase price of goods and services.

excise tax A tax on a specific product.

Figure 9 | State and Local Government Tax Revenue

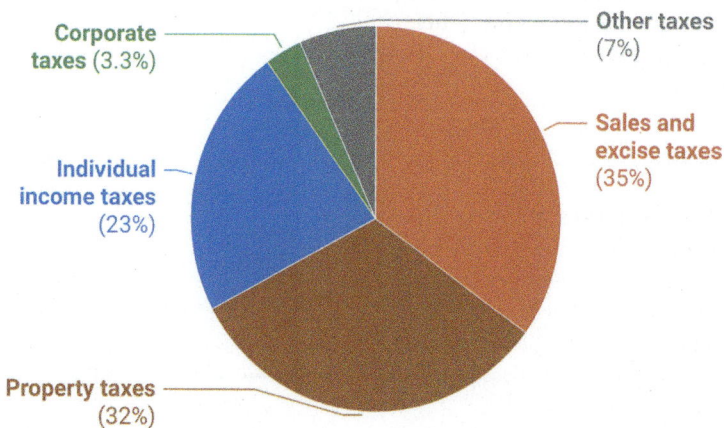

Corporate taxes (3.3%)

Individual income taxes (23%)

Property taxes (32%)

Other taxes (7%)

Sales and excise taxes (35%)

2020 Data from: U.S. Census Bureau.

property tax A tax on the value of property, usually real estate.

regressive tax A tax where those with less income tend to pay a higher share of their income on the tax.

tax expenditures Special deductions, exemptions, or credits that lower your tax obligations, to encourage you to engage in certain kinds of activities.

Congress is eager to hide spending in the tax code.

Figure 9 shows that, collectively, state and local governments raise 35% of their tax revenue through sales and excise taxes. These taxes are the largest source of revenue for state and local governments on average.

Property taxes, which are a type of wealth tax based on the value of property (usually real estate) provide roughly a third of state and local government revenue. Income taxes account for less than a quarter of state and local revenue. Few local governments levy income taxes, and while most states impose their own state income taxes, there are some that do not. Florida, Texas, and Washington rely almost exclusively on sales and property taxes to raise revenue.

A **regressive tax** is one in which those with less income tend to pay a higher share of their income in taxes. Excise, property, and sales taxes tend to be regressive because lower-income households spend a higher share of their income on things like gas, housing, groceries, and clothing. This means that they also spend a higher share of their income on taxes on these items. Because most state and local governments rely heavily on regressive taxes, state and local taxes tend to be overall regressive.

Hidden Government Spending: Tax Expenditures

The U.S. Congress (and governments in most other countries, too) often try to implement desired programs by changing the tax code, rather than directly increasing government spending. **Tax expenditures** describe the special deductions, exemptions, or credits that lower your tax obligations, and hence reduce government revenue. You may have also heard them be called write-offs, loopholes, or tax breaks.

Tax expenditures are a hidden form of government spending. To see how they're equivalent to government spending, let's consider a tax expenditure that's probably pretty important to you and your family—the American Opportunity Tax Credit. The idea that led to this tax expenditure was a desire to have the federal government help more students afford college. The way it works is that you or your parents might be able to subtract a portion of what you've paid in tuition (up to $2,500 a year) from your tax bill.

Congress could have passed this program as a spending program—simply mailing each qualifying student or family a $2,500 check each year. Instead, it implemented this program as a tax credit, and so this tax expenditure subtracts $2,500 from your family's federal income tax bill. For many students and their families, these are equivalent—you end up $2,500 better off whether you get a $2,500 check from the government or you pay $2,500 less in tax. And the government has $2,500 less, either way. But these otherwise-identical alternatives look quite different in the government's budget because a direct-spending program shows up as government spending, while a tax expenditure simply means there's less government revenue than there otherwise would be.

Tax expenditures have a lower political cost. Money that never shows up in the government's coffers is harder to trace than money it spends by sending out checks. Some politicians implement their preferred programs as tax expenditures, rather than as increased government spending, arguing that they're letting people keep their own hard-earned money, rather than raising taxes to pay for more government spending. (Pause for a moment: How convincing do you find this argument?)

Importantly, because tax expenditures are part of the tax code, they don't need to be renewed or evaluated each year as part of the budget process. In a typical year, the federal government "spends" as much through tax expenditures as it does on discretionary spending. And yet, tax expenditures are not part of the annual fight over what to include in the discretionary budget. This lack of review has led the Government Accountability Office to repeatedly urge Congress (to little effect) to scrutinize tax expenditures more closely, rather than allowing them to persist through continued inaction.

Tax expenditures encourage spending on certain goods and services.

Some of the largest tax expenditures include tax breaks offered on employer-provided health insurance, retirement plans, and owner-occupied housing. These tax breaks are the government's way of encouraging you to purchase health insurance, save for retirement, and buy your own home.

The government subsidizes the purchase of health insurance when you buy it through your employer by excluding your insurance premiums (and any premiums paid directly by your employer) from your taxable income. So if you spend $3,000 per year on health insurance through an employer, that $3,000 doesn't count as taxable income. If your marginal tax rate is 22%, that could save you $660 in taxes each year. And if your employer also contributes $2,000 per year toward the cost of your health insurance, that $2,000 also doesn't count as taxable income. (In contrast, if your employer paid $2,000 for life insurance, that payment would be counted as taxable income.)

Congress has also created a number of savings programs that can reduce how much tax you pay when you stash money away for retirement. These tax breaks provide strong incentives to save for retirement.

Finally, the government offers two important tax breaks for buying your own home. The first is that you'll get a tax deduction if you get a mortgage to finance your purchase. The second is more subtle. When you rent your house, your landlord typically has to pay income tax on the rent you pay them. But when you buy the house and become your own landlord, you don't have to pay income tax on the rent you effectively pay yourself. This tax break — not having to pay tax on the rental value of owner-occupied housing — is one of the biggest benefits of homeownership.

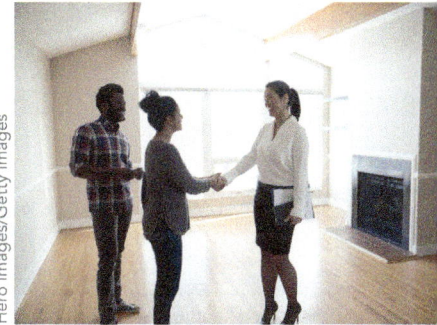

There's a big tax incentive to become a homeowner.

EVERYDAY Economics How much is that employment benefit worth?

When negotiating a salary, it's worth keeping the tax system in mind. Let's say you've got two job offers. One of the jobs offers you a salary of $43,000, along with an employer-provided health insurance plan, for which you'll have to contribute $3,000 per year in premium payments. The other job offers a salary of $45,000, but no health insurance. Shopping around, you learn that you can buy similar health insurance without your employer's help for around $5,000 per year. So which is the better-paying job?

At first, it might sound like the jobs are equivalent if you plan to buy health insurance, because either way you'll have $40,000 after you've paid your health insurance premiums.

Not so fast! You need to consider your taxable income. When you buy health insurance through your employer, you get to subtract the amount you spend on premiums from your taxable income, and so spending $3,000 on employer-provided health insurance reduces your taxable income from $43,000 to $40,000. But you don't get this tax break if your employer doesn't offer health insurance. And so if you spend $5,000 of your $45,000 salary buying health insurance on your own, your taxable income remains $45,000.

All of this means that the higher-wage no-benefit job involves more taxable income, and hence a higher tax bill. In this example, once you've accounted for both the cost of health insurance and the effect on your tax bill, you'll take home more money if you accept the lower-wage job that comes with benefits. More generally, when you're comparing multiple job offers you should consider not only the benefits, but also how they're taxed. It's not unusual to find seemingly lower-paying jobs that offer benefits to be the better deal because some benefits qualify for tax breaks. Indeed, that's one reason that many employers offer benefits. ■

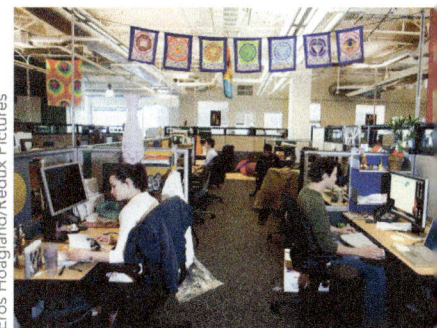

Employer benefits add up!

Figure 10 | Tax Expenditures Strongly Favor the Rich

Share of tax expenditure benefits, by income group

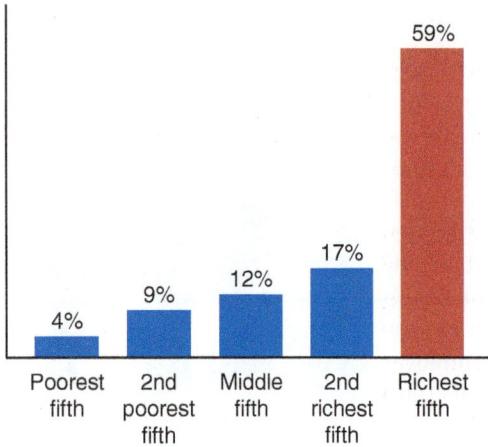

Income group	Share
Poorest fifth	4%
2nd poorest fifth	9%
Middle fifth	12%
2nd richest fifth	17%
Richest fifth	59%

Income quintile

2019 Data from: Tax Policy Center.

Three reasons why tax expenditures primarily benefit the wealthy:

1. The value of tax exclusions and deductions is higher when your income tax rate is higher.
2. Higher-income people tend to buy more tax-preferred goods and services.
3. Most tax expenditures don't provide much help if your income tax bill is zero.

Tax expenditures primarily benefit those with high incomes. Figure 10 shows that more than half of tax expenditures go to the highest-income quintile. There are three reasons for this disparity:

Reason 1: The value of tax exclusions and deductions is higher when your income tax rate is higher. Every dollar you spend on interest for a home mortgage reduces your taxable income by a dollar. If you're one of the richest Americans, your marginal income tax rate is 37%, and so this means that every $100 you spend paying mortgage interest reduces your taxes by $37. By contrast, if you're from a middle-income family with a marginal income tax rate of 12%, every $100 you spend on mortgage interest reduces your taxes by only $12. Nearly half of Americans pay no federal income taxes (although they still pay other taxes like payroll, excise, and sales taxes), so they receive no benefit at all from this deduction. This means that if a high-income person, a middle-income person, and a low-income person each purchase identical houses financed by identical mortgages, the government gives the largest tax cut to the highest-income person, a much smaller tax cut to the middle-income person, and nothing to the low-income person.

Reason 2: Higher-income people tend to buy more tax-preferred goods and services. Of course, high-, middle-, and low-income people don't tend to purchase identical homes. Instead, the more income you have, the more you tend to spend on your house (or save for retirement, or spend on health care — all of which involve tax breaks). And the more you spend on your house, the bigger your mortgage will likely be, and the larger the tax cut you'll get. When you put the higher value of the tax benefit together with the proportionately larger spending on tax-preferred goods, you start to see why tax expenditures go primarily to high-earning families. For instance, a well-off family with a million dollar house might pay $30,000 per year in mortgage interest, and if their marginal tax rate is 37%, this deduction reduces their tax bill by $11,100. A middle-income family might buy a house that's only half as expensive, and because they'll need a mortgage that's only half as big, they'll get a tax deduction that's only half as big. Moreover, if their marginal tax rate is only 12%, then this deduction reduces their tax bill by only $1,800. And a low-income family might get no tax break at all, for reasons we're about to analyze.

The family that bought this house might have received an extra $11,100 back from the government.

But the family that bought this house probably got a lot less.

Reason 3: Most tax expenditures don't provide much help if your federal income tax bill is zero. If your family income is modest, you might not benefit at all from tax expenditures. That's because most tax breaks reduce only your taxable income, but reducing your taxable income below zero does nothing to reduce your tax bill. In practice, after the standard deduction and other credits, a large share of low-income households already have a taxable income of zero.

A **refundable tax credit** tries to solve this problem by providing benefits even to those folks whose taxable income is zero (or less). We say it's *refundable* because you can get a tax refund even if you don't pay any taxes. For example, remember the American Opportunity Tax Credit, which could allow you or your family to get up to $2,500 per year to help with your tuition expenses? It's a partially refundable tax credit, which means that while it doesn't give the full benefit to lower-income families, it gives a *partial* amount of the benefit. Your family can receive up to $1,000 to help with tuition costs through this program even if they don't owe federal income taxes.

refundable tax credit A tax credit for which receiving the credit doesn't depend on owing income taxes.

Tax expenditures are often inefficient, poorly targeted, and persistent. Economists and policy wonks on both sides of the political aisle tend to oppose many (although not all!) of these tax expenditures. Many of those opposed think that there are good reasons for the government to subsidize health insurance, retirement, or housing. However, they oppose the use of tax expenditures — at least as they are currently implemented — because they are poorly targeted and rarely evaluated for effectiveness. The problem is that the budgetary cost of tax expenditures is opaque, and obscures how inefficient some programs are.

Regulation

You've already seen how the government can disguise spending as tax breaks. It can also disguise spending by getting someone else to do it.

Regulation allows the government to require spending, while others pay the bill. Governments often make laws or regulations requiring people or businesses to pay for things directly. For instance, if the government decided that all workers are entitled to paid parental leave, it could pay for parental leave directly through a social insurance program that would be part of its budget. Alternatively, it could require employers to provide parental leave to all workers. Making employers pay for it sounds cheaper — after all, the government doesn't pay a penny for it. But asking employers to pay for it doesn't change the cost, it merely shifts who pays from taxpayers to employers. It's also likely that employers will pass some of the costs on to workers in the form of lower wages. So the cost doesn't disappear; it's just that someone else is paying the bill.

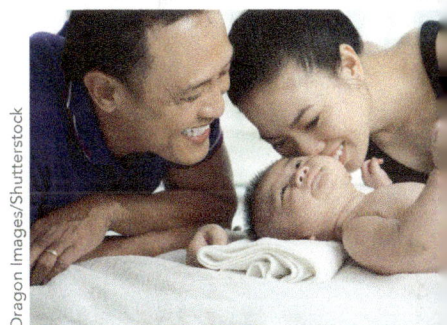

The government could pay for or mandate parental leave, but either way, it costs money.

Regulation changes incentives. Almost any government policy could be set up as a direct-spending program, a tax expenditure, or a regulation. When policy wonks try to figure out the best way to design a policy, they pay careful attention to how people might adjust their behavior in response to the policy. For instance, a regulation that requires employers to pay for parental leave may lead some employers to try to avoid the cost by not hiring workers that they suspect might become parents.

23.2 Fiscal Policy

Learning Objective *Discover how fiscal policy can smooth business cycles.*

Now that you have a good understanding of what the U.S. government spends its money on and how it raises revenue, let's turn to examining the macroeconomic consequences of government choices. We'll focus now on how these decisions affect the year-to-year fluctuations that make up the business cycle, and then we'll conclude this chapter by studying the long-term consequences.

A Countercyclical Force

fiscal policy The government's use of spending and tax policies to attempt to stabilize the economy.

Fiscal policy refers to the government's use of spending and tax policies to attempt to stabilize the economy. It involves the government adjusting its taxes and spending in an effort to reduce output fluctuations and keep actual GDP close to potential output.

expansionary fiscal policy Higher government spending and/or lower taxes to increase aggregate expenditure in response to output below potential.

Higher spending and lower taxes will boost output. Typically, the government responds to weak output with an **expansionary fiscal policy** that involves some combination of higher government spending and lower taxes. Increased government purchases directly increase aggregate expenditure. Lower taxes boost people's after-tax incomes, spurring increased consumption. And because corporate tax cuts both make new investments more profitable and provide the extra cash necessary to fund these new projects, they spur greater investment. The resulting boost to aggregate expenditure increases the demand for output, leading businesses to ramp up production, which raises GDP.

contractionary fiscal policy Lower government purchases and/or higher taxes to decrease aggregate expenditure in response to output above potential.

Lower spending and higher taxes will reduce output. On the flip side, the government can counter an overheating economy with a **contractionary fiscal policy** that involves lower government purchases and higher taxes. The same mechanisms operate in reverse as lower spending or higher taxes decrease aggregate expenditure, and hence output. That's why the government will consider contractionary fiscal policy when it is worried that output in excess of potential output might spark inflationary price rises.

Government spending can add to GDP directly and indirectly. It's worth distinguishing between two types of government spending. The first is *government purchases,* in which the government directly purchases goods and services such as schools, military equipment, vaccine development, and highways. The second is *transfer payments* — money that's taken from the government's coffers and sent to individual households. This distinction matters: Government purchases are counted directly in GDP, but transfer payments don't directly add to GDP because nothing is purchased or produced. However, when the people who receive transfer payments spend that money, they boost aggregate expenditure and hence GDP.

The multiplier effect makes fiscal policy more potent. The interdependence principle reminds us that in addition to these first-round effects of expansionary fiscal policy in boosting aggregate expenditure, there will be ripple effects. That's because one person's spending is another's income, and so an initial burst of spending will cause some people's incomes to rise, which may lead them to boost their spending, which in turn boosts the incomes of others, causing them to spend more also. The *multiplier effect* describes the possibility that an initial boost in spending will set off ripple effects that ultimately lead to a larger rise in GDP. The same effects also operate in reverse, and an initial decrease in aggregate expenditure due to a contractionary fiscal policy can also have a multiplied effect that leads to a larger decline in GDP.

The government purchased the Covid vaccine that you might have received.

There's a microeconomic rationale for countercyclical fiscal policy. So far, we've focused on the potential for fiscal policy to affect macroeconomic outcomes. But there's an alternative microeconomic argument for countercyclical government spending that applies whenever the government can choose *when* to embark on a new project, such as building a new highway, bridge, or airport. The opportunity cost principle suggests an investment is best done during an economic slump. That's because when unemployment is high, the next best use of a construction worker's time might be worth less, as their next best alternative might be working in a job that doesn't use their skills, or perhaps unemployment. Moreover, because real wages tend to be lower during a slump, these projects can be completed more cheaply. Similarly, capital equipment may be idle during a recession, which means a lower opportunity cost of putting machines to work on government investment projects.

Interpreting the DATA | Can a one-time government payment to households boost spending during a recession?

When the financial crisis hit in late 2007 and early 2008, one of the government's first responses was to send payments to taxpayers of up to $600 per person. The thinking behind this expansionary fiscal policy was that higher income leads to higher consumption, and so these one-time payments would stimulate greater aggregate expenditure and hence output. But some economists were skeptical it would work. They noted that this income boost was temporary, and so people might save, rather than spend, their rebate check. Indeed, if you were worried about a looming recession, would you advise your friends to spend this windfall, or save it for a rainy day?

In total, the government mailed out $100 billion in rebates. Careful studies showed that within the first three months, people had spent somewhere between $50 billion and $90 billion of this money. This estimate covers a wide range, but it tells us two things. First, people spent much of this money, and definitely more of it than more skeptical economists expected, suggesting that even a temporary boost to income can stimulate an immediate boost in consumption. Second, people spent less than if the government had spent the money directly on goods and services. After all, when the government spends a dollar, the whole dollar is spent, but when it mailed a dollar to people, they only spent 50 to 90 cents of it.

During the 2020 recession, the government was convinced that sending people money would not only help people keep a roof over their head and food on the table, but it would support the overall economy by increasing spending. The Covid recession was even shaper than the 2008 recession, so they sent a lot more money. For example, a family of four could have been eligible to receive up to $11,400 in payments from the federal government.

Figure 11 shows that people spent less than half of the payments they received. While those with lower incomes or greater income loss spent a greater portion of the money they received. However, many people were able to work remotely without income loss. And unlike other recessions, the pandemic changed people's spending patterns due to health concerns, not just income loss. With closed restaurants, limited travel, and work/study pajama days at home, the marginal propensity to consume out of an additional dollar was unusually low.

Figure 11 | People Saved More of Their 2020 Stimulus Payments Than They Spent

*Overall **58%** of all stimulus payments went into **saving** — either new saving or paying off debt. Only **42%** of these stimulus payments were **spent**.*

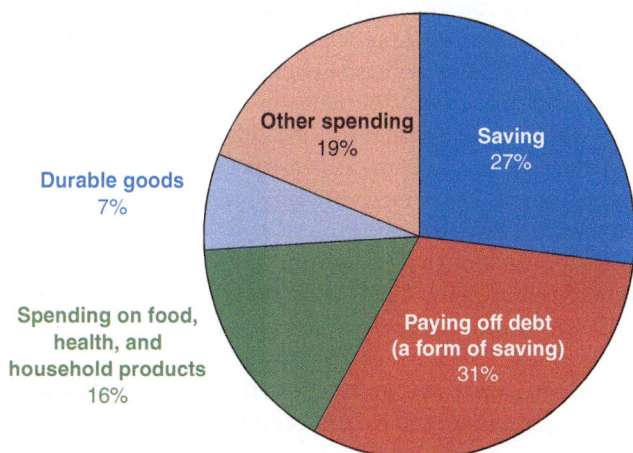

Results from a survey asking Americans what they did with government CARES Act payments (of $1,200 per qualifying adult and $500 per child).

Data from: Coibion, Gorodnichenko & Weber (2020). ■

discretionary fiscal policy Policy that temporarily changes government spending or taxes to boost or slow the economy.

Expansionary fiscal policy in action.

Discretionary government spending can involve substantial time lags. If the economy starts slipping into a recession, Congress may consider passing legislation to temporarily increase spending or cut taxes, with an eye toward boosting the economy. This is called **discretionary fiscal policy** because Congress has to use its discretion and decide to take action. Similarly, the government may use discretionary fiscal policy to cut spending or raise taxes when output is above potential. One of the biggest challenges with discretionary fiscal policy is getting the timing right, because there are delays at every step of the process.

The first step of discretionary fiscal policy is recognizing that it's needed. Macroeconomic data are imperfect and often send conflicting signals, and so it can take months for policymakers to recognize that the economy has stalled or is overheating. This was the case in the 2008 recession, which began slowly and only became apparent over time; even months later the data understated the severity of the recession. In contrast, in 2020, policymakers knew that the novel coronavirus spreading across the country would not only make people sick, but it would also result in a sharp economic slowdown. In March 2020, some state governors began ordering people to stay at home. But even in states that allowed businesses to continue to operate, customers chose to stay away. This clear evidence that an economic downturn was imminent meant that policymakers could act before signs of the recession had appeared in the data.

Once policymakers realize that the economy needs help, they have to formulate a plan. This second step can be the source of lengthy delays, as Congress must come up with a plan and pass legislation authorizing it. The more politically contentious a tax or spending idea is, the more difficult it can be to get rapid political agreement.

The third step is to actually spend the money, and with complex infrastructure projects, this can take months, or even years. The government tries to maintain a pipeline of "shovel-ready projects" — projects for which much of the planning and engineering work have been done in advance — so that an increase in funding can lead to an immediate increase in spending. In practice, shovel-ready projects are hard to find.

The delays involved in discretionary fiscal policy mean that during short downturns, it's unlikely that Congress will be able to act quickly enough to boost aggregate expenditure when it's needed. When it acts too late, the boost might arrive after the economy has already recovered. At worst, this can mean that discretionary fiscal policies become procyclical instead of countercyclical, which would destabilize the economy.

Interpreting the DATA   Did discretionary fiscal policy work in the 2007–2009 recession?

In response to the deepening recession through 2009, Congress decided a more expansionary fiscal policy was needed and it passed the American Recovery and Reinvestment Act. This bill included tax cuts and a temporary increase in both government purchases and transfer payments. All told, it pumped an extra $787 billion into the economy.

It also provided an interesting laboratory for economists to study the effects of discretionary fiscal policy. Several important studies analyzed what happened when idiosyncrasies in federal funding formulas led some states to receive more spending than otherwise comparable states. They found that those states that received more spending typically experienced more robust recoveries. Even though it took some time to spend the money, this recession was so deep and long-lasting that the Recovery Act was still timely enough to have saved millions of jobs, albeit at a cost of billions of dollars. ∎

Fiscal policy works best when it's timely, targeted, and temporary.
Fiscal policy works best when it is implemented before economic conditions have severely worsened, when it targets those parts of the economy that are most affected, and when it's used for only as long as it's needed. This leads to the three *T*s of fiscal policy: It must be timely, targeted, and temporary. *Timely* refers to the idea that policymakers must act quickly, getting ahead of looming problems. *Targeted* refers to the idea that fiscal policy — unlike monetary policy — can focus on the specific regions, industries, and

Fiscal policy works best when it's:

1. Timely
2. Targeted
3. Temporary

groups of workers who need the most help. Fiscal stimulus is more likely to be effective when it's targeted in a way that gets money in the hands of those who are more likely to spend it. By contrast, sending money to people who are going to save it or pay off existing debt won't raise spending and hence won't boost GDP. Finally, *temporary* refers to the idea that extra spending is no longer required when the economy has recovered. Indeed, as we're about to see, if a rise in government spending were to persist, it risks reducing private investment.

Government spending can crowd out investment spending. Sometimes a rise in expansionary fiscal policy will lead to a decline in private spending, and particularly investment — an effect known as **crowding out.** It's as if the government enters an already crowded store and cuts in front of some of the customers. More precisely, crowding out occurs when expansionary fiscal policy leads to a higher real interest rate, which reduces private spending. Because investment is particularly sensitive to the real interest rate, the main impact will be to reduce investment. The extent of crowding out depends on the time period being analyzed and the state of the economy. Let's see why.

In the short run, expansionary fiscal policy will boost output, and (as we discussed in Chapter 22) the Fed typically responds to a more positive output gap — and the possibility that it will spark inflation — by raising the real interest rate, which reduces investment. The extent of crowding out depends on how aggressively the Fed responds to the output gap, and that in turn depends on how much excess capacity the economy has. During a deep recession — when there's a lot of excess capacity — both fiscal and monetary policy are likely working in concert, and so the Fed is unlikely to raise the real interest rate in response to an expansionary fiscal policy. As a result, there won't be much crowding out. But a politician might be tempted to pass a fiscal stimulus when the economy is already operating close to potential (perhaps in the hope of creating a boom that will make them more popular with voters in the next election). In that case, the Fed will likely counter by raising rates, and these higher rates will lead to substantial crowding out.

In the long run, the neutral real interest rate — the rate that ensures that output is equal to potential — is determined by the supply and demand of loanable funds (we analyzed this market in Chapter 14). Expansionary fiscal policy involves the government dissaving, which decreases the supply of loanable funds. This decrease in supply will raise the neutral real interest rate, and these higher rates will deter investment. (You could alternatively think about the government's borrowing as increasing the demand for loanable funds, which has the same effect of raising the neutral real interest rate.)

Remember that in the long run, output cannot sustainably exceed potential output, which is determined by the supply of available labor, human and physical capital, and technological progress. Because increased government spending doesn't affect potential output, it won't affect the long-run level of output. By this view, in the long run every extra dollar of government spending will crowd out a dollar of private spending, and so fiscal stimulus can have only temporary effects on output.

Automatic Stabilizers

An **automatic stabilizer** is a fiscal policy that adjusts as the economy expands and contracts without policymakers taking any deliberate action. It's *automatic* because no policymaker has to take any action — the adjustments are built into current law. And it's *stabilizing* because these adjustments are countercyclical, boosting output during recessions and reducing it during expansions. Automatic stabilizers are built into both tax and spending programs. Let's dig into each, in turn.

Government revenue automatically adjusts during business cycles. Almost everything about a recession is bad: Business profits fall, some workers lose their jobs, others have their hours cut, and average wages decline. As a result, incomes fall. But there's a silver lining to this loss of income: You'll pay less in taxes. This automatic stabilizer helps support after-tax incomes, ensuring that spending — and hence output — won't decline by as much as it otherwise might.

crowding out The decline in private spending — and particularly investment — that follows from a rise in government borrowing.

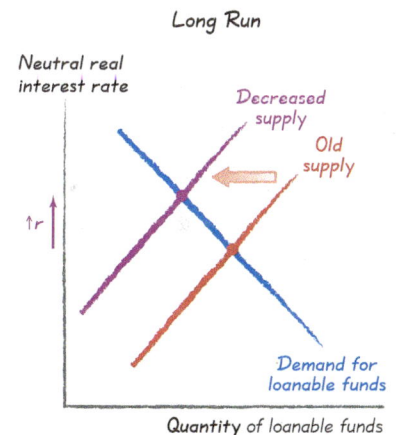

Long Run

Neutral real interest rate

Decreased supply

Old supply

↑r

Demand for loanable funds

Quantity of loanable funds

automatic stabilizers Spending and tax programs that adjust as the economy expands and contracts, without policymakers taking any deliberate action.

Steve Helber/AP Photo

During recessions, some workers get fewer shifts.

When incomes fall, tax payments fall for two reasons. The first one is probably obvious: You pay income taxes on your income, so if you earn less income, you have less to pay taxes on, so you'll pay less tax. The second is subtle. Because income taxes are progressive — meaning that tax rates are higher when you earn more — as your income falls, so does your tax rate. As a result, if a recession halves your pre-tax income, the amount of tax you'll pay will fall by more than half, meaning that your after-tax income falls by less than half. Progressive taxes cushion the blow of a recession.

As a result, the government takes in less tax revenue during a recession. This keeps more money in the hands of businesses and consumers, who might spend it, boosting aggregate expenditure, and hence output.

A similar dynamic operates — in reverse — during an economic boom. As income rises, taxes automatically start to rise, both because there's more income to tax overall, and because as people earn more, they are bumped into higher tax brackets. As a result, federal tax revenues rise. Money that the government collects in taxes is money that people can't spend, so this reduces aggregate expenditure and hence output. As such, the tax system acts to counter both booms and busts, smoothing out business cycle fluctuations.

Government spending automatically adjusts during business cycles. Government spending also rises automatically during a recession. When income falls, more people qualify for government benefits, such as supplemental nutrition (SNAP, also known as food stamps), Pell grants and other student financial aid, and Medicaid, for which eligibility is based at least partially on income. As more people lose their jobs due to a downturn, more people become eligible to receive unemployment insurance. And if your state is experiencing particularly high unemployment, the period of time for which you can claim unemployment benefits may automatically rise. These additional payments support aggregate expenditure by allowing those receiving support to spend more than they would have otherwise been able to.

The reverse happens during a boom: When people earn more, they're less likely to qualify for government support programs. As a result, government spending on these programs falls automatically as the economy recovers. And so this inbuilt tendency for government spending to rise during recessions and then fall during expansions works to counter the business cycle.

Automatic stabilizers are timely, targeted, and temporary. These automatic changes in taxes and spending are *timely* because they're automatically triggered whenever people's incomes decline. They're also well *targeted* because taxes decline only for those whose income has fallen, and eligibility for income support payments depends on each person's financial or employment status. And they're *temporary* because they automatically reverse course as the economy reverses course.

This makes them quite effective, and the Congressional Budget Office estimates that automatic stabilizers have historically added around 0.4% to GDP for every percentage point that GDP falls below potential GDP. As such, even many economists who are wary of discretionary fiscal policy often argue in favor of creating more automatic stabilizers. With a bit of imagination, the amount of spending on almost any government program could be tied to the state of the economy. Yet politicians often prefer discretion, because it allows them to steer tax and spending changes to benefit their preferred constituencies, and they can claim political credit for these changes.

Fiscal Policy and Monetary Policy Interactions

When the threat of a recession looms, policymakers have two main ways to respond. The Fed can adopt an *expansionary monetary policy* by lowering interest rates, which will encourage more spending. In addition — or instead — the government can adopt an *expansionary fiscal policy* by increasing government purchases and cutting taxes. In many respects these policy tools are quite similar — they each operate by boosting aggregate expenditure and hence output. So when will one tool be more effective than the other?

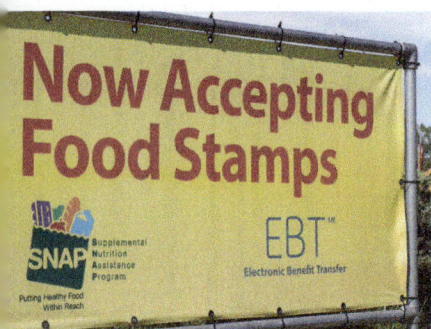

More people receive government benefits during recessions.

Jonathan Weiss/Alamy Stock Photo

Monetary policy is more nimble. The Fed is constantly assessing the state of the economy, ready to act as soon as it senses an impending problem. A decision to lower interest rates can be implemented by the end of the afternoon. And so the advantage of monetary policy is that it can be implemented quickly. The disadvantage is that changes in interest rates don't immediately boost spending, and it can take a year or more before lower interest rates stimulate more spending. That's why fiscal policy through automatic stabilizers can work in concert with monetary policy to more quickly steer the economy back to potential output.

Fiscal policy can be more targeted. An oil price shock can cause a boom in the oilfields of Texas and a recession in Michigan as auto sales plummet. Fiscal policy can target support to Michigan or any other region of the country that is struggling, just as it can target the auto sector, or other specific industries. And so while fiscal policy can be tailored to local economic conditions, monetary policy imposes a one-size-fits-all solution on the whole economy.

Fiscal policy is particularly important at the zero lower bound. When the Fed can't cut short-term nominal rates any further — and its capacity to cut long-term rates is limited — discretionary fiscal policy might be the only effective tool left to stabilize the economy. When policymakers are worried about this possibility, fiscal policy and monetary policy can work in concert to reinforce each other. That's why the Fed initially responded to the pandemic by cutting nominal interest rates to zero, and then the federal government passed discretionary fiscal policy to further stimulate the economy.

Both fiscal and monetary policy helped end the 2008–2009 recession.

23.3 Government Deficits and Debt

Learning Objective *Understand why governments run deficits and the implications of government debt.*

Now you know what the government spends money on, how it raises revenue, and how it uses spending and tax policy to stabilize the economy. It's time to talk about the longer-run implications of the government's budget.

🎙 Podcast
Think Like an Economist
Budget Deficits and Government Debt

Government Budget Deficits

The federal government rarely brings in enough revenue to pay for all its spending, and so it borrows a lot of money. In those years in which government spending exceeds government revenue, the government runs a **budget deficit,** and it must borrow money to fund this shortfall. On those seemingly rare occasions when government revenue exceeds spending, the result is a **budget surplus.** While budget surpluses are quite rare in the United States, they're relatively common in many other countries.

The government's *debt* is the total accumulated amount of money that it owes. Its budget *deficit* in a given year adds to the total debt, while a budget *surplus* can be used to repay its debt. The deficit measures the *flow* of new borrowing over a year, while the debt measures the accumulated *stock* of borrowing at a point in time.

If you're taking out student loans, you're probably familiar with this distinction between deficits and debt: Your personal deficit is the amount you borrow each year when your spending exceeds your income; your student loan debt is the total amount you've borrowed since becoming a student. When you graduate, get a job, and start paying off your student loans, you won't be running at a deficit anymore. But you will probably have student loan debt for many more years.

budget deficit The difference between spending and revenue in a year in which spending exceeds revenue.

budget surplus The difference between spending and revenue in a year in which revenue exceeds spending.

Figure 12 | Federal Government Spending and Revenue Determine the Budget Deficit or Surplus

as a percent of GDP

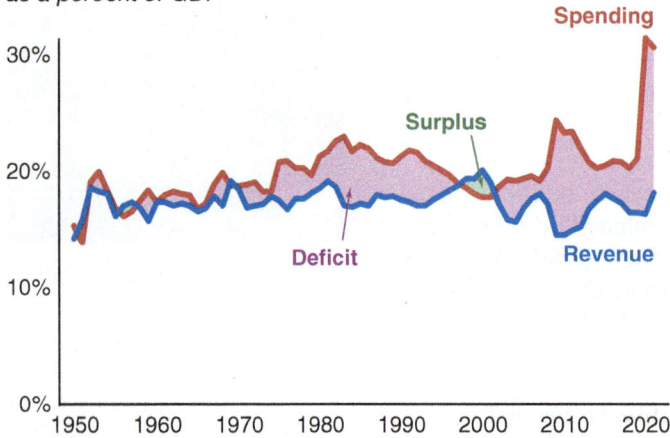

The Federal Budget Has Frequently Been in Deficit and Only Occasionally in Surplus

as a percent of GDP

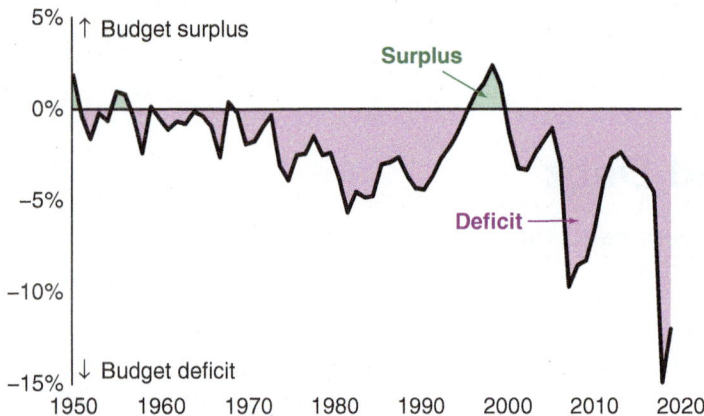

Data from: Office of Management and Budget.

The federal government runs deficits. There are four things to notice about federal government spending and revenue:

1. *The federal government typically runs budget deficits.* The purple areas in Figure 12 show budget deficits, and the green areas show surpluses. You'll notice that there isn't much green in the graph.

2. *Persistent large budget deficits are a relatively recent phenomenon.* For most of U.S. history, peacetime deficits were typically quite small. However, this appears to have changed in recent decades, and since the 1980s, large annual deficits have become a persistent feature of the U.S. federal government, with the exception of 1998 to 2001.

3. *Wars and pandemics require a sudden surge of spending that results in budget deficits.* The government ran its biggest deficits in the 1940s and the 2020s. In the 1940s, borrowing was done to support the military during World War II. Spending in 2020 and 2021 was needed to fight the coronavirus pandemic. Both wars and pandemics require a quick surge in spending. Borrowing money effectively means asking future generations to pay some of the cost, which makes sense given that the benefits of winning the war or beating the pandemic last for generations.

4. *Business cycles create budget deficit cycles.* The federal government's budget deficit tends to rise during recessions and fall during expansions. Partly, this is due to the use of expansionary fiscal policy as Congress tends to temporarily boost spending and cut tax rates to counter recessions. In addition, the size of the deficit or surplus reflects the influence of automatic stabilizers. During a slump, the government both takes in less tax revenue and spends more on income-support programs, raising the deficit. Likewise, a boom creates more tax revenue and reduces the number of people relying on government programs. This reduces the deficit and occasionally produces a surplus such as in the late 1990s.

Four facts about government spending and revenue:
1. The federal government typically runs budget deficits.
2. Persistent large budget deficits are a relatively recent phenomenon.
3. Wars and pandemics require a sudden surge of spending that results in budget deficits.
4. Business cycles create budget deficit cycles.

When should the government run deficits? The usual way that people think about budget deficits is that they reflect a mismatch between *how much* the government spends and *how much* revenue it takes in. But an alternative perspective is that they reflect a mismatch between *when* the government spends money and *when* it takes in the revenue to pay for this spending. This framing suggests that deficits (or surpluses) often make sense because there's no reason to expect the pattern of when it's best to spend money to match the pattern of when it's best to raise revenue.

When the government spends on infrastructure like roads, highways, airports, internet connectivity, and research, the benefits of that spending will last for decades. So why should it pay for it all upfront? Just as many people borrow money to purchase a house and then pay it off over time, the government can borrow to make investments and pay for those investments over time. Moreover, government investments help spur GDP growth, making it easier for the government to subsequently repay those debts.

A related argument for deficit spending is that whenever there is a need for a surge in spending — like during a pandemic — it's inefficient to collect all the revenue at once.

Raising taxes a lot in one year and lowering them the next creates distortions, leading people to shift income from one year to the other. People tend to change their behavior more to avoid taxes when tax rates are higher. So smoothing taxes over time reduces economic distortions. It also reduces the burden of taxes because people prefer to smooth their consumption.

Just as you're starting to get comfortable with the government running budget deficits, it's time to discuss the problems — many of which come from the costs to the economy when the government accumulates large amounts of debt. We'll turn to the problems of government debt shortly. But for now, let's consider the political problem.

Budget deficits may reflect short-run political incentives. Spending programs are popular with voters, but raising taxes to pay for those programs is not. That's why election-minded politicians like to spend money on programs that make voters happy, but they don't like raising taxes to pay for them. These unbalanced incentives might explain why the federal government typically runs budget deficits.

But it's not just that deficits reflect short-run political incentives; such incentives might also lead to a bigger and more inefficient government. The problem is that if politicians can get the political benefit of spending without facing the cost, they're likely to approve more spending than they otherwise would. And so the ability to run deficits may also lead to more government spending — even on programs whose costs exceed their benefits. One proposal that is often suggested to fix these unbalanced incentives is to require the government to balance its budget. This would force politicians to consider not only the benefits of new spending programs, but also the costs of raising the revenue to pay for them.

Requiring a balanced budget would make business cycles worse. A *balanced budget rule* requires a government to balance its budget each and every year. Such a rule for the federal government would cause another set of problems because it would not be able to use fiscal policy to counteract business cycles. Indeed, balancing the budget each year would require it to implement a fiscal policy that would exacerbate economic fluctuations.

Remember, a downturn leads to lower tax revenues. A balanced budget rule would force the government to raise tax rates or cut spending (or both) in the midst of a downturn. Further, government spending automatically rises during downturns as more people qualify for benefits. To maintain an annually balanced budget, such programs would need to be scaled back at exactly the time when more people need them. This would not only hurt those who've lost their jobs or seen their incomes decline — it would also worsen the broader economic slump. That is, balancing the budget during a recession would lead to a contractionary fiscal policy, which would reduce aggregate expenditure, causing output to decline even more.

This is in fact what happened in many states during the 2007–2009 recession. State governments that faced balanced budget requirements saw their revenues decline. In response, they raised tax rates and cut spending, which exacerbated the downturn. Roughly half a million municipal workers, including teachers, firefighters, police, and other emergency responders, were cut from city payrolls during the 2007–2009 recession and its aftermath. These reductions increased unemployment and depressed aggregate expenditure. During the 2020 recession, the federal government acted swiftly to provide funding to states to help offset declines in their tax revenues and reduce the chances that state and local cutbacks would exacerbate and extend the length of the recession.

Deficit debates reflect both economic forces and value judgments. The value judgment is whether the next generation should help pay for the spending priorities of the current generation. You might think, "No way!" But consider how much richer you are than your grandparents were at your age. Real personal incomes — meaning incomes adjusted for inflation — have more than doubled over the past four decades. That means that you can buy twice as much stuff as your grandparents could back then. In economic

freedomnaruk/Shutterstock

Serge Racoon/Alamy Stock Photo

Investments in infrastructure benefit many generations.

skipperchong/iStock/Getty Images

Many state legislatures are required by law to balance the budget each year.

terms, the sacrifice from having you pay an extra dollar in taxes is likely much smaller than it would have been if your grandparents had footed the bill. The onward march of innovation that allows us to more quickly address challenges like the spread of new diseases means that future generations will likely continue to be better off than the ones who came before. If so, the sacrifice they will need to make to pay a bit more in taxes is even smaller still. And if today's spending is what allows the next generation to be even richer than the current generation — by investing to address climate change, for example — then the next generation may be the biggest beneficiaries of the spending. Debates about economic forces reflect concern about debt's impact on the economy. Those concerns are what we're going to turn to now.

Government Debt

Government debt is the total amount the government owes. It reflects the long history of both past borrowing to fund budget deficits, and past repayments from occasional surpluses. The government borrows by selling *government bonds* to savers in both the United States and abroad. Government bonds are effectively IOUs from the government, promising to repay the amount it borrowed, plus interest. When you buy a government bond, you're loaning the government money. You'll probably invest some portion of your future retirement savings in government bonds, making you one of these lenders.

gross government debt The total accumulated amount of money the government owes.

    The total debts of the federal government — called the **gross government debt** — added up to $31 trillion in 2022. But about $6.5 trillion of this debt is money that one part of the federal government owes another part of the federal government. What really matters is the debt that the federal government owes to others — to individuals, businesses, and other governments both here and abroad. This is called the **net government debt,** and it amounts to nearly $25 trillion. (Net government debt is sometimes called "debt held by the public" and it's recalculated every day, down to the penny. Just for fun, look up today's numbers at https://fiscaldata.treasury.gov/datasets/debt-to-the-penny /debt-to-the-penny.)

net government debt The debt that the government owes to individuals, businesses, and other governments both here and abroad.

Evaluate a country's debt relative to a country's GDP. Numbers measured in the trillions can be hard to make sense of, so let's try to develop a sense of scale. It makes sense to think about a country's debt relative to its capacity to repay it. That's why economists typically focus on the ratio of a country's government debt to its annual GDP, which is a measure of the resources available to make repayments. In the United States, this *debt-to-GDP ratio* in 2021 was 97%. This says the net government debt is equivalent to what we currently produce in 97% of a year.

Government debt is currently high, relative to our history. Figure 13 shows the debt-to-GDP ratio since the federal government was formed. It shows that government debt tends to rise sharply in times of war or severe economic downturns. The debt-to-GDP ratio roughly doubled between 2008 and 2013, as the government increased spending to fight the recession. The debt-to-GDP ratio grew more stable in the ensuing years, before shooting up in 2020 and 2021, as government spending rose by unprecedented amounts to tackle the pandemic. As GDP recovered, the debt-to-GDP ratio came down, but as of 2022, it remained substantially higher than prior to the pandemic.

Figure 13 | Net Government Debt Rises Sharply During Wars and Major Recessions

As a percent of GDP

Data from: CBO and OMB.

U.S. government debt is comparable to that of other advanced countries. Figure 14 compares the net government debt of the United States (as a share of GDP) to that of other large advanced economies. As this figure illustrates, governments get by with a variety of debt levels, and the United States is in the middle of the pack. And while all of the countries shown in this figure have a net government debt, a small number of countries — including Finland and Norway — both have a negative debt, which means that they've put aside a stockpile of money for the future. At the opposite extreme, Japan has the highest debt-to-GDP ratio of any country in the world, much of it due to successive attempts to use expansionary fiscal policy to revive its economy, which has struggled since the 1990s. The United States government debt is currently well below Japan's, which has the highest debt to GDP ratio of any advanced economy. But it may not stay that way for long.

Government debt is expected to grow rapidly over coming decades. Figure 15 shows recent projections from the Congressional Budget Office, which suggest that if the government maintains its current course, the debt-to-GDP ratio is expected to grow to nearly 200% of GDP by 2050.

We have a fairly clear idea about where the debt is headed because much of the federal budget — and much of its rise — reflects promises the government has made about future payments. In particular, spending on Social Security and Medicare is projected to grow rapidly as more of the population reaches the ages at which they'll be eligible to draw benefits. These benefits are an **unfunded liability** — a commitment to incur expenses in the future without a plan to pay for them. The federal government has a lot of unfunded liabilities, and they're projected to be the primary driver of rising deficits and debt over coming decades.

They're also intimately tied to the other key driver of government debt, which is interest payments. The more the government borrows, the more interest it pays. As unfunded liabilities push the debt higher, the government will have to make increasingly larger annual interest payments, which in turn will also push deficits and debt higher still. In 2021, the federal government spent 5% of its budget paying interest on the debt, but that's expected to double within the next decade and to continue to grow after that. Interest rates were at historic lows for much of the twenty-first century, but they are expected to rise in the coming years. However, it's impossible to predict interest rates in the future. The risk is that as interest rates increase, the debt becomes more expensive, and a growing share of the federal budget will go to paying interest on the debt. High interest rates can lead to a lot of government spending on interest on government debt, crowding out other government spending priorities.

All of this raises the question: How worried should you be about government debt? I have good news and bad news. The good news is that in the next few pages, I'll tell you about some reasons not to be so worried. But the bad news is that the following few pages give you some reasons to be more concerned. At the end, it will be up to you to figure out where you stand.

Figure 14 | Net Government Debt in the United States Is Comparable to Other Advanced Economies

Percent of GDP

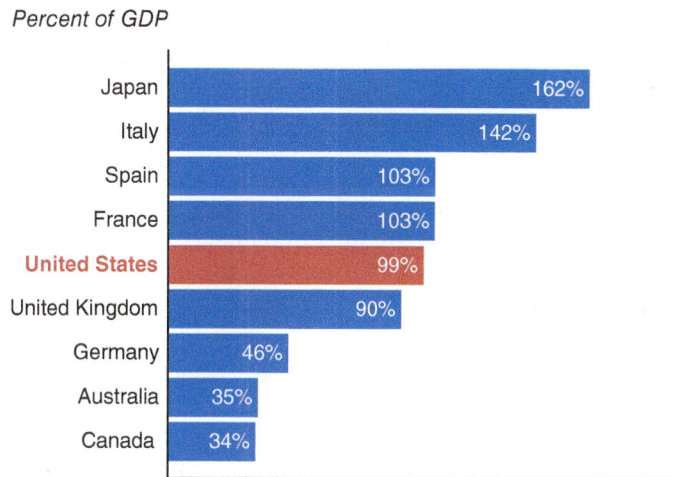

2020 Data from: IMF.

unfunded liability A commitment to incur expenses in the future without a plan to pay for those expenses.

Figure 15 | The Federal Government's Net Debt Is Projected to Continue Growing

Debt as a percent of GDP

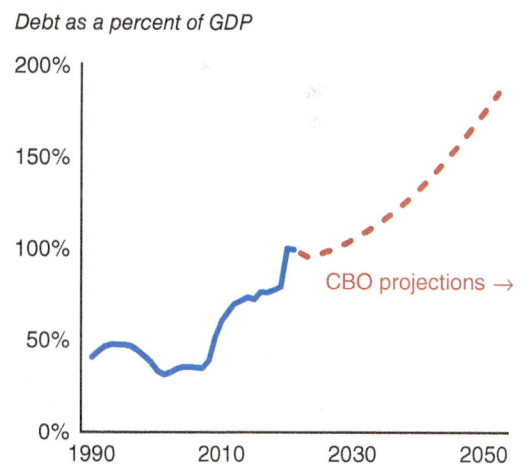

Data from: Congressional Budget Office.

Reasons Not to Worry About the Debt

People who want to stoke alarm about government debt often divide the size of the debt by the size of the population to argue that each of us owes a lot of money. Scaling big numbers is a good idea, and when you divide the net government debt of around $25 trillion by the total population of 330 million, you get roughly $75,000 per person. That sounds like a lot (and it might sound even worse when you add it to your student loan debt!).

But you do not owe anybody $75,000. Don't make the mistake of thinking about government debt as if it's your personal household debt. Understanding why the government's finances are not like a family's finances yields five reasons not to worry so much about the government's debt.

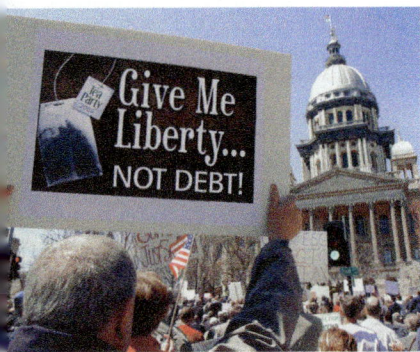

Don't let people scare you about the debt!

Reasons not to worry about government debt:

1. Most of our government debt is money owed by Americans to Americans.
2. Future generations can help repay the debt.
3. It wouldn't take a big adjustment to repay the debt.
4. The government never really needs to repay the debt.
5. The government has options that you don't.

The government can print money. You can't.

Reason 1: Most of our government debt is money owed by Americans to Americans. When a family is in debt, the problem is that it owes money to someone else. But the government debt is different. To a large degree, it's money that we owe ourselves. More than half of the debt is held by U.S. investors. These investors are mostly people who are simply saving for retirement by putting their money in what is considered a safe asset, since U.S. Treasury bills come with the full faith and credit of the U.S. government. And so while the American people owe the debt, they are also owed much of the debt.

Reason 2: Future generations can help repay the debt. It's also important to remember that the government — unlike a household — can repay its debt over many generations. And so that means that the burden of repaying $25 trillion in debt can be spread over not only the current population of 330 million, but also hundreds of millions of people in future generations. That might even be fairer. After all, much of this debt reflects major investments by past generations building infrastructure, creating a well-functioning economy, and defending the country from military threats. These are investments that future generations will continue to enjoy, so why not ask them to chip in to help pay the costs, too? When there are many more than 330 million Americans repaying the debt, your personal "share" is much less than $75,000.

Reason 3: It wouldn't take a big adjustment to repay the debt. Even if the current cohort of Americans decides it should repay the entire debt, the burden may not be as bad as you fear. Here's why. Recall that the government spends $30,000 a year per person. So over your lifetime the government will likely spend well over a million dollars on you. Your current "share" of the debt is small relative to this. It follows that if the government decides to repay the debt, it wouldn't have to cut much of the spending it plans to do over your lifetime. So even if your generation alone had to pay back the entire debt, it might not be as bad as you think if it pays it back slowly — like over the course of your life.

Reason 4: The government never really needs to repay the debt. The U.S. government has been in debt more or less continuously since its formation. Yet that hasn't proven to be a problem. That's because government debt doesn't have to be fully repaid to be sustainable. What matters is whether the government has the means to make the required payments. That's why economists focus on the debt-to-GDP ratio, which measures our current debt relative to our capacity to pay. However, the U.S. government debt has been rising over the past two decades as a share of GDP, which concerns many economists. But notice that returning to a sustainable outcome requires getting the debt to be a stable share of GDP, not eliminating the debt. And that's a much easier task.

Reason 5: The government has options that you don't. People get into trouble with debt when their monthly paycheck can't cover their monthly payments. Their problem is that it's really hard to increase the amount of revenue coming into a household to cover the rising interest payments going out. But the federal government can pretty easily raise more revenue — it just has to raise taxes. Indeed, raising tax rates by a few percentage points would be enough to stabilize the debt-to-GDP ratio. Remember, the federal government can tap a rather extraordinary resource that individual households cannot — the combined incomes and wealth of 330 million people (and their descendants).

The government has one more option that households don't: It can literally print money, and use that money to repay its debt. But as seductive as this seems, it's rarely a good idea. Printing more money to chase the same quantity of goods and services leads to inflation, and in some cases, it has led to chaotic hyperinflation. And lenders aren't happy because even if the government repays the nominal value of their debt, it's paying them dollars that are worth a lot less. When a government inflates away its debt like this, lenders are very reluctant to ever lend to them again.

EVERYDAY Economics   Can you count on Social Security?

The premise behind Social Security is that if you contribute to the program through payroll taxes during your working years, it will provide you with a reasonable income in retirement. But roughly half of young Americans worry that Social Security will not be able to pay them benefits when they retire. Don't give in to the alarmism — Social Security will likely still be around when you retire!

The naysayers are right to be concerned that Social Security in its current form appears poised for financial difficulties. The problem is that it's paying out more in benefits than it's raising in revenue. That can't continue forever. But it can continue until the program spends the last of its existing stockpiles of cash, which is projected to occur around 2033.

What happens when the stockpiles run out? Social Security won't suddenly stop paying benefits. Let me repeat that: Social Security won't suddenly stop paying benefits. Rather, it will have to make sure that it pays out no more than it takes in through payroll taxes. Projections suggest that around 2075 — when many of today's college students will stop working — retirees will still get roughly 70% of what's been promised, even if no action is taken by the government to prevent benefit cuts. That's less than you've been promised, but the point is that even the worst-case scenario involves you getting a large chunk of the Social Security benefits promised.

If the economy grows a bit faster, or wage growth is more rapid, or if increased immigration or a higher birth rate boosts the number of workers, there will be more revenue from payroll taxes available to pay even more. And at some point Congress might get around to restructuring the program to put it on a sounder financial footing.

My advice: Don't panic about Social Security because it will at least partially be there for you. But on the other hand, don't be rash — you should also plan to save enough that you'll get by even if Social Security doesn't deliver quite as much as promised. ■

They are worried that Social Security won't be there for them.

Reasons to Worry About Government Debt

Just as you're starting to feel comfortable with government debt, it's time to turn the tables, and dig into some of the reasons you should be concerned.

Reason 1: Slower economic growth. High and rising debt risks slower economic growth. The problem is that the government borrows funds that might otherwise be used to finance investments in productive capital, like new machinery. Without this funding, the private sector invests in less capital, which makes workers less productive, meaning they produce less output. Indeed, the Congressional Budget Office has estimated that average per-person income could be about $5,000 higher by 2050 if the federal government were to reduce its debt-to-GDP ratio to its historical average.

Reason 2: Future fiscal choices are constrained. Higher government debt makes it harder to borrow more when the government needs funds. It won't be able to easily borrow during national emergencies, such as wars, recessions, natural disasters, or pandemics. It will also find it harder to borrow for important national investments that will yield benefits for generations, such as infrastructure.

Reason 3: The risk of a crisis of confidence. The U.S. government pays just about the lowest interest rates of anyone, anywhere in the world. That's because investors are confident that when they loan the U.S. government money, they'll be repaid in full and in a timely manner. That confidence is a valuable asset, saving the government billions of dollars in lower interest payments each year.

That confidence is also fragile. Consider the possibility that at some point investors become concerned that the government's debt is unsustainable. Perhaps they're worried

Reasons to worry about government debt:
1. Slower economic growth
2. Future fiscal choices are constrained
3. The risk of a crisis of confidence
4. A debt crisis becomes more likely

that the government will miss its next scheduled loan repayment. If, for example, Congress decided not to allow the United States to take on any more debt, then the United States would find it hard to pay off existing debt that was coming due — because it regularly pays off one creditor and borrows from another. A perceived risk of not getting paid would lead lenders to charge the government a higher interest rate. The problem for a government that has borrowed a lot of money is that even a small rise in the interest rate will lead to a large rise in its annual interest bill. If its interest bill gets too large, it won't be able to make those loan repayments. And so the perception that the government debt is unsustainable can lead lenders to charge higher interest rates, and those higher interest rates create the reality that the government's debt is unsustainable. Even worse, this kind of *crisis of confidence* — where investors' fears spark a vicious cycle of higher interest rates and less sustainable debt — can happen in the blink of an eye.

Think of this as a self-fulfilling prophecy, with either a good or a bad outcome. The good outcome occurs when lenders think that the government will repay them, leading them to charge low interest rates, and because interest rates are low, the government easily makes its scheduled repayments. The bad outcome occurs when lenders think the government won't make its payments, so they charge higher interest rates. This crippling interest burden may even lead the government to miss its scheduled payments. And so the observation that the United States is currently enjoying the good outcome is no guarantee that things won't change tomorrow.

Take a look at Greece, where in 2009, investors suddenly became concerned that the government might not repay its debt. The interest rate that lenders charged the Greek government rose from 5% in 2009 to over 25% in 2012. What had been a difficult fiscal situation became untenable, as it became virtually impossible for Greece to meet its annual interest payments. Ultimately, the European Union and the IMF stepped in with emergency loans and a recovery program. But along the way, this crisis led to a modern-day depression in Greece.

Reason 4: A debt crisis becomes more likely. At its worst, high government debt can lead to a *debt crisis* in which the government simply can't repay its loans. The government stops making payments on its debt, and so investors abruptly refuse to lend it any more money. When a government can't borrow money, it must immediately balance its budget by raising taxes or cutting spending (or both). When this occurred in many Latin American countries in the early 1980s, the abrupt shift to a contractionary fiscal policy plunged many of these countries into sharp recessions. The more recent crisis of confidence that led the interest rates Greece faced to soar also plunged it into a debt crisis in which it simply couldn't repay its loans.

Greece faced a debt crisis starting in 2009.

23.4 Tying It Together

Previous Generations Have Made Your Choices Harder

An idealized view of how government works is that a smart population will vote for smart policies and a responsive government will deliver what people most value. By this idealized view, those values will determine the government's taxing and spending priorities, how it uses fiscal policy to actively fight recessions, and how it will manage its debts to ensure that your generation pays its fair share, but no more.

Perhaps that was once a more reasonable description for some government programs in the first half of the last century. Back then, the federal government's only real tasks were national defense and delivering the mail. Unemployment insurance, Social Security, Medicare, and Medicaid are all programs that built the American safety net of the twentieth century. Today, they take up a large and growing share of government spending, and these commitments constrain what government can do. It means that your generation has inherited a mature government with a long history of passing mandatory spending and tax bills in which future plans for government taxing and spending priorities are already largely spelled out.

Our past decisions can be changed if we decide that our priorities for government taxing and spending have shifted. The challenge is that it's harder to enact change when you have to scrap the choices made by previous generations. Eliminating or even reducing promised spending (and tax expenditures) is politically difficult, even when we all agree that there are better ways to spend our money. The task of shaping the government to serve your generation has been made even harder because past generations made spending plans without accompanying plans to raise enough revenue to pay for them. At the start of 2020, the federal government planned to spend $4.75 trillion, but expected revenue of only $3.64 trillion. The reality was an even larger deficit, as American families and businesses needed help from the federal government to survive the Covid pandemic. Actual spending soared to $6.6 trillion, while revenue was $3.4 trillion. The result of the government spending was a quick economic recovery and reduced hardship. But debt also soared, and there is no plan to bring debt down.

There are decades of planned spending ahead with no plan for how to cover the cost. Some people argue that these unfunded liabilities mean that your generation faces a constrained choice about the type of government you can have. But the reality is that you have to confront the current fiscal realities to make change. And while it might take more effort to enact change than was required by previous generations, if you have the political will, you can help shape government spending and tax choices to reflect your generation's priorities.

Chapter 23 Review
Chapter at a Glance

The Government Sector: Government spending has grown over time as the role of the government in providing social insurance and education has expanded.

Social insurance: Government-provided insurance against bad outcomes such as unemployment, illness, disability, or outliving your savings.

Federal Spending
- Social insurance programs
- Military

State Spending
- Social insurance programs
- Education

Local Spending
- Education
- Community services

Federal government revenue sources:
- Payroll taxes
- Income taxes
- Corporate taxes

State and local government revenue sources:
- Sales and excise taxes
- Property taxes
- Income taxes

Hidden Government Spending: The government has other ways to effectively spend money without any spending showing up on their books. These are not counted as government spending but they have the same effect.

1. **Tax expenditures**: Congress can implement programs through the tax code. These are special deductions, exemptions, or credits that lower your tax obligations to encourage you to engage in certain kinds of activities.
2. **Government regulation**: The government can mandate that citizens or businesses engage in certain behavior that costs money.

Fiscal Policy: The government's use of spending and tax policies to attempt to stabilize the economy. Fiscal policy is more important at the zero lower bound and works best when it's timely, targeted, and temporary.

Discretionary fiscal policy: Policy that temporarily changes spending or taxes to boost or slow the economy.

Automatic stabilizers: Spending and tax programs that adjust as the economy expands and contracts, without policy makers taking any deliberate action.

Budget Deficits

Budget deficit: The difference between spending and revenue when spending exceeds revenue over a year.

Budget surplus: The difference between spending and revenue when revenue exceeds spending over a year.

Four facts about government budget deficits:
1. The federal government typically runs budget deficits.
2. Persistent large budget deficits are a relatively recent phenomenon.
3. Wars and pandemics require a sudden surge of spending that results in budget deficits.
4. Business cycles create government budget deficit cycles.

Government Debt

Gross government debt: The total accumulated amount of money the government owes.

Net government debt: The debt that the government owes to individuals, businesses, and other governments both here and abroad.

Reasons not to worry about government debt
1. Most of our government debt is money owed by Americans to Americans.
2. Future generations can help repay the debt.
3. It wouldn't take a big adjustment to repay the debt.
4. The government never really needs to repay the debt.
5. The government has options that you don't.

Reasons to worry about government debt
1. Slower economic growth.
2. Future fiscal choices are constrained.
3. The risk of a crisis of confidence.
4. A debt crisis becomes more likely.

Key Terms

automatic stabilizers, 615

budget deficit, 617

budget surplus, 617

contractionary fiscal policy, 612

crowding out, 615

discretionary fiscal policy, 614

discretionary spending, 605

earned income, 606

excise tax, 607

expansionary fiscal policy, 612

fiscal policy, 612

gross government debt, 620

income taxes, 606

mandatory spending, 605

marginal tax rate, 606

net government debt, 620

payroll taxes, 606

progressive tax, 606

property taxes, 608

refundable tax credit, 611

regressive tax, 608

sales tax, 607

social insurance, 602

tax expenditures, 608

taxable income, 606

unfunded liability, 621

Study Problems

Learning Objective 23.1 *Assess the size and scope of the government.*

1. Explain how the saying, "The federal government is an insurance company with a military," while exaggerating a bit, does generally describe U.S. federal government spending.

2. What is mandatory spending, and how does it differ from discretionary spending?

3. How do federal, state, and local government spending differ in focus?

4. How is a tax expenditure similar to government spending? How is it different?

5. You're working as a staffer for a representative of Congress from your state. The representative is looking to co-sponsor a bill to provide assistance to low-wage workers who want to pursue higher education. The representative asks you to brief them on how they might implement it as (a) a direct-spending program, (b) a tax expenditure, or (c) using regulation. Describe the implications, as well as some of the pros and cons of each approach.

6. A friend of yours argues that federal government spending is out of control and significant cuts in spending are needed to reduce the size of the government. Your friend tells you that if we cut federal government spending on science and international affairs, it will really reduce the size of the government. Do you agree? Why or why not?

7. Spending on Medicare and Social Security is expected to grow over the next few decades as the share of the population who are elderly grows. Explain why an aging population increases government spending on these programs. How might future spending change if Medicare and Social Security were discretionary spending programs instead?

8. Marissa just got hired at a new job for an annual salary of $112,950. After the standard deduction, her taxable income will be $100,000. Use the marginal tax rates shown in Figure 9 to calculate how much she will owe in income taxes if she has no other income and no additional deductions. What share of her income would she be paying in taxes?

9. In an effort to encourage people to purchase electric cars, the federal government passes a tax credit of $2,500 for each new electric car that is bought in the United States. Who do you think will benefit from this tax expenditure? What do you think the government's goal is with such a tax expenditure? Do you think that the tax expenditure is likely to achieve this goal?

10. A politician says, "We could help low-wage workers by offering them tax credits like the earned income tax credit. However, it would be cheaper to help them by raising the minimum wage because that would cost the government nothing." Evaluate this argument.

Learning Objective 23.2 *Discover how fiscal policy can smooth business cycles.*

11. Use the three *T*s of fiscal policy to explain the challenges of using discretionary fiscal policy to counter a recession.

12. Explain how different types of government spending add to GDP directly and indirectly, and how a rise in government spending can have a multiplied effect on GDP.

13. Explain how increases in government spending can crowd out investment spending. Is crowding out a major concern when the economy's output is below its potential?

14. Describe how automatic stabilizers respond when output is above potential output. Assess the extent to which these responses are timely, targeted, and temporary.

15. The Fed has conducted expansionary monetary policy to combat a recession but is running up against the zero lower bound, and the economy is still not recovering. What other steps could the government take in order to try to stabilize the economy?

16. Which of the following are examples of expansionary fiscal policy, and which are examples of automatic stabilizers?

a. The government paid an extra $25 million in unemployment insurance claims last month.

b. New legislation temporarily extends unemployment benefits for an additional 26 weeks.

c. The IRS collected $50 billion more in taxes last year, even though tax rates were unchanged.

d. Congress appropriates an additional $125 million in funds to help states pay teachers during a recession.

17. If the economy slides into a recession next year, and Congress does nothing to adjust existing tax and spending programs, how will government spending and government revenue change? Do any of these adjustments help stabilize the economy?

18. Now consider what happens if the federal government introduces new government spending to combat the recession. How will this affect the economy in the short run? As the economy recovers, political pressures lead the government to keep this spending in place. What are some possible long-run consequences of making the increased government spending permanent?

Learning Objective 23.3 *Understand why governments run deficits and the implications of government debt.*

19. Explain why requiring the federal government to balance its budget each year would limit its ability to respond to an economic downturn. Many states do require balanced budgets. Why might this policy exacerbate an economic downturn in a state?

20. How is government debt different from personal debt?

21. In 2022, the federal government spent $5.9 trillion and brought in revenue of $4.4 trillion.

    a. Is this a budget deficit or surplus, and what is its size?

    b. If net government debt in 2022 was $24.5 trillion, what will it be in 2013?

    c. GDP was $25.4 trillion in 2022 and $26.8 trillion in 2023. How has the debt-to-GDP ratio changed from 2022 to 2023?

22. A political candidate has written an op-ed piece in which they claim that the U.S. government debt has continually grown and is out of control. The candidate includes the following graph as evidence.

Gross federal government debt

Trillions of dollars

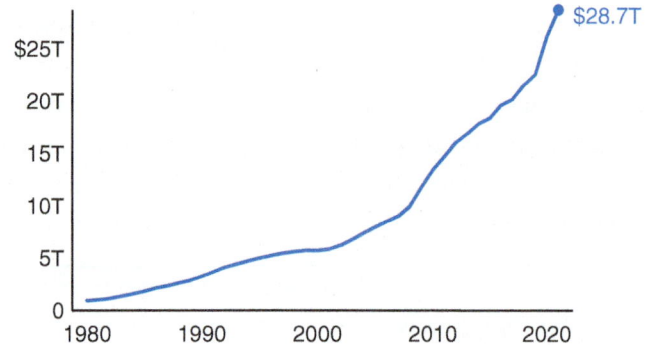

Data from: U.S. Treasury.

The candidate further argues that there is no way the government can sustain this level of debt by comparing it to a person who is constantly spending more than they make and racking up large amounts of consumer debt.

a. This graph shows gross government debt of $29 trillion in 2021, but you've read that net government debt is $22.5 trillion. What explains the difference?

b. Do you think the candidate's presentation of the data speaks to whether the debt is sustainable or not? How might you give greater context?

c. Is the candidate's argument about personal debt being similar to government debt a valid argument? Why or why not?

23. The president has just signed a new budget that drastically cuts taxes without decreasing government spending. When asked about the dramatic increase in deficits that will occur due to the tax cuts, the president responds, "We're going to see some amazing economic growth because of this new policy, so much growth that we're going to grow our way out of any short-term increases to government debt." If this extra economic growth doesn't materialize, what are some of the risks to the U.S. economy?

A Closer Look at Aggregate Expenditure and the Multiplier

Stocks tanked. A typical investment in the stock market worth $100 just a few years prior quickly fell to be worth only $13. Bankruptcies soared and more than a third of all banks failed, erasing families' savings. The economy shrank by nearly 30%, and roughly one in four people who wanted to work couldn't find jobs. The Great Depression began in 1929 and launched a dark decade in U.S. history. It didn't just reshape the American economy, it reshaped society. Poverty and malnourishment rose. Evictions led to widespread homelessness. The birth rate fell and the suicide rate spiked.

This extraordinary episode also changed economics forever. It exposed the mistakes of an earlier generation of economic thinkers who had argued that the economy would quickly repair itself. This period saw the introduction of the term macroeconomics, and it led to the development of a new approach to understanding broad economic trends. John Maynard Keynes and colleagues such as Joan Robinson created a macroeconomic framework that explains the painful reality that recessions and depressions can be common, costly, and persistent.

This chapter outlines the framework they built. We'll start by analyzing the central role that spending decisions play in determining economic outcomes. Then we'll explore how it's possible for the economy to get stuck in a bad equilibrium in which joblessness and misery can persist. Finally, we'll investigate the possibility that changes in spending can have a multiplied effect on the broader economy.

Together, these insights suggest that a determined government can halt an economic slump by boosting spending. This prescription was tested as the government scrambled to counter the Great Depression. President Roosevelt's New Deal boosted government spending and appeared—at least for a while—to halt the economic decline. As Hitler rose to power in Europe, nervous investors sent their funds to the United States, which lowered interest rates and stimulated greater spending. The U.S. government's heavy investment in the war effort also helped to boost spending. Ultimately, economic growth resumed, the Depression ended, and this new field of macroeconomics had proved its worth. The insights we'll explore in this chapter have since been built into the foundations of modern macroeconomics.

Photographer Dorothea Lange documented the dire circumstances of the Depression.

Library of Congress, Prints & Photographs Division

Objective

Explore the influence of aggregate expenditure and the multiplier on the business cycle.

A.1 Aggregate Expenditure and Income
Measure aggregate expenditure and analyze how it varies with income.

A.2 Macroeconomic Equilibrium and the Keynesian Cross
Find the macroeconomic equilibrium and analyze how it changes as economic conditions change.

A.3 The Multiplier
Analyze how moderate changes in spending can have bigger consequences through the multiplier effect.

A.1 # Aggregate Expenditure and Income

Learning Objective *Measure aggregate expenditure and analyze how it varies with income.*

When businesses assess how macroeconomic conditions are likely to shape the demand for their products, they focus on the total amount of goods and services that people want to buy. That is, they focus on **aggregate expenditure,** which refers to the total amount of goods and services that people want to buy across the whole economy. Let's dig a little deeper into aggregate expenditure to better understand how it is measured.

Aggregate Expenditure

Aggregate expenditure is the sum of four components:

- = *Consumption:* When households buy goods and services
- + *Planned investment:* When businesses purchase new capital
- + *Government purchases:* When the government buys goods and services
- + *Net exports:* Spending by foreigners on American-made exports, less total spending by Americans on foreign-made imports

Aggregate Expenditure = $C + I + G + NX$. Economists often use abbreviations to simplify things, and so you might find it easier to write the equation this way:

$$\underset{\substack{\text{Aggregate} \\ \text{expenditure}}}{AE} = \underset{\text{Consumption}}{C} + \underset{\substack{\text{Planned} \\ \text{investment}}}{I} + \underset{\substack{\text{Government} \\ \text{purchases}}}{G} + \underset{\substack{\text{Net} \\ \text{exports}}}{NX}$$

Whichever way you write it, the point is simply that aggregate expenditure is the sum of spending on American-made goods by all economic actors: consumers, businesses, governments, and those engaged in international trade.

Aggregate expenditure includes planned investment, but excludes inventories. Notice that aggregate expenditure depends on *planned investment,* rather than *total investment.* Let me explain the distinction. **Planned investment** refers to the investments that a business intentionally makes when it buys capital goods such as buildings, machinery, and software. We use the modifier "planned" to distinguish this from *total investment,* which — because of an accounting convention — also includes unplanned changes in inventories.

When Ford buys equipment to open a new production line, that's a planned investment, and it counts as aggregate expenditure. But when Ford can't sell all the cars it produces, it stockpiles the extra cars as inventories. While accountants classify this increase in inventories as investment, they're not a planned investment, and hence we don't count them in aggregate expenditure. That's because when you're trying to assess economy-wide demand, you want to focus on the stuff that consumers, businesses, and governments purchase, not the unsold inventories they accumulate. Unsold inventories are also the key to seeing the difference between GDP (which measures total production of *output* including unplanned investment) and aggregate expenditure (which measures total *spending*).

Now that you know how to measure aggregate expenditure, let's analyze its key determinant: income.

Aggregate Expenditure Rises with Income

When business analysts forecast aggregate expenditure, they pay special attention to income because it plays an important role in shaping people's spending decisions. We're going to follow their lead.

---

aggregate expenditure The total amount of goods and services that people want to buy across the whole economy.
= Consumption
+ Planned investment
+ Government purchases
+ Net exports

Some abbreviations
AE: Aggregate Expenditure
C: Consumption
I: Planned Investment
G: Government purchases
NX: Net exports

planned investment Business spending on new capital such as machinery, software, and buildings. Unlike total investment, it excludes changes in inventories.

A planned investment.

An unplanned investment.

Higher income leads to higher consumption and hence higher aggregate expenditure. To see why income matters, let's focus on consumers (like you!). Most people tell me that if their income were higher, they would spend more. If so, then higher individual income leads to higher individual consumption. And because millions of people respond this way, when income across the whole economy is higher — that is, when GDP is higher — then total consumption also tends to be higher.

Figure 1 summarizes this idea with the **consumption function,** a line plotting the level of consumption associated with each level of income. It illustrates the insight that higher GDP leads to higher total consumption. (You might recognize this idea from Chapter 13 on consumption.)

The marginal propensity to consume determines how much consumption rises when income rises. Typically, when your income rises, you'll spend a fraction of it and save the rest. The fraction of each extra dollar of income that a typical household spends is called the **marginal propensity to consume** (or "*MPC*" for short). You can measure the fraction of each dollar someone spends as the ratio of the change in consumption to the change in income. Most people don't immediately spend all of the extra income they get, suggesting that the marginal propensity to consume is less than one. The slope of the consumption function (remember, slope is "rise over run") is the ratio of the change in consumption to the change in income. That is, the slope is equal to the marginal propensity to consume.

The marginal propensity to consume is useful because it tells you how much consumption — and hence aggregate expenditure — rises with income. For instance, if the marginal propensity to consume is 0.5, then each extra dollar of income will lead to 50 cents of extra spending this year. It tells the government that if it were to send each American a $100 check in an effort to stimulate the economy, this year's spending will rise by $50 per person. At the level of the whole economy, it says that if income were to rise by $100 billion, you should forecast that consumption will rise by $50 billion.

The aggregate expenditure line shows how aggregate expenditure rises with income. We now have all the pieces we need to graph the relationship between aggregate expenditure and total income. Let's start with consumption and build up from there. The lower line in Figure 2 is the consumption function, which illustrates the tendency for consumption to rise with income (or, equivalently, it shows how consumption rises with GDP).

Aggregate expenditure is consumption plus planned investment, government purchases, and net exports. As a result, the aggregate expenditure line lies above the consumption function, and the distance between them is equal to the sum of these other components. If these other components of spending are unaffected by income, then the aggregate expenditure line lies a fixed distance above the consumption function. This means that the slope of the aggregate expenditure line is the same as the slope of the consumption function, and is equal to the marginal propensity to consume. For now, we're holding planned investment, government purchases, and net exports constant, but in a few pages, we'll see what happens when they shift.

Figure 1 | **The Consumption Function**

Ⓐ The consumption function shows how consumption rises with the level of income (GDP).

Ⓑ The slope of the consumption function is equal to the **marginal propensity to consume**, which describes the **extra consumption** that arises from each dollar of **extra income**.

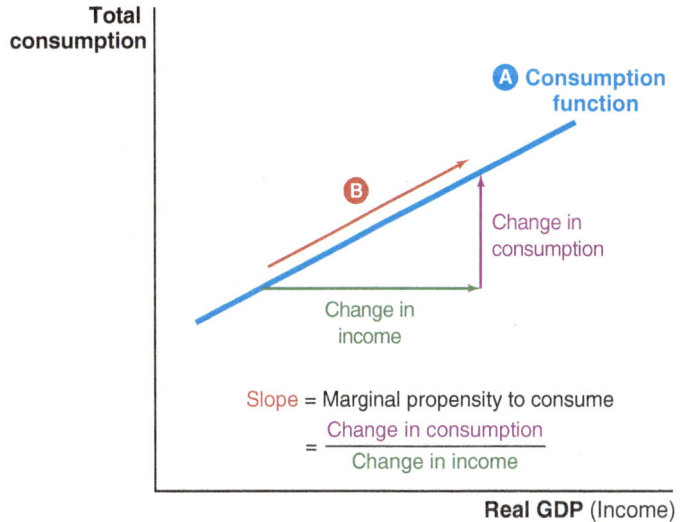

Slope = Marginal propensity to consume

$$= \frac{\text{Change in consumption}}{\text{Change in income}}$$

consumption function A line plotting the level of consumption associated with each level of income.

marginal propensity to consume The fraction of each extra dollar of income that households spend on consumption.

What fraction do you spend?

JoeFox Liverpool/Radharc Images/ Alamy Stock Photo

Figure 2 | Aggregate Expenditure Rises with Income

Aggregate expenditure is the sum of consumption, planned investment, government purchases, and net exports.

A Higher income leads people to spend more, and so consumption rises with GDP.

B Aggregate expenditure also includes planned investment, government purchases, and net exports, and so it lies above the consumption function.

C As a result, aggregate expenditure rises with income (even if planned investment, government purchases, and net exports don't change).

D The aggregate expenditure line has the same slope as the consumption function: Its slope is the marginal propensity to consume.

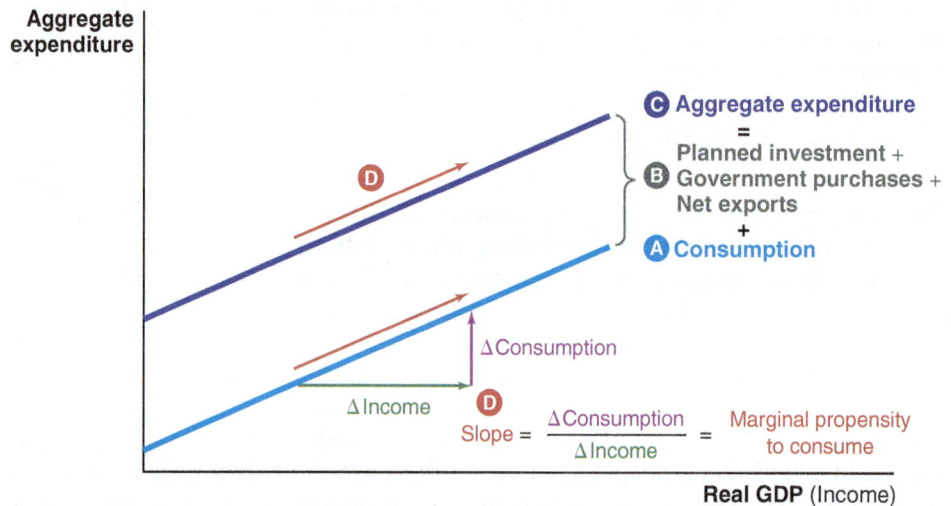

Figure 3 | Use the Aggregate Expenditure Line to Forecast Spending

A Locate the level of GDP on the horizontal axis, and look up until you hit the aggregate expenditure line.

B Then look left to find the level of aggregate expenditure associated with this level of GDP.

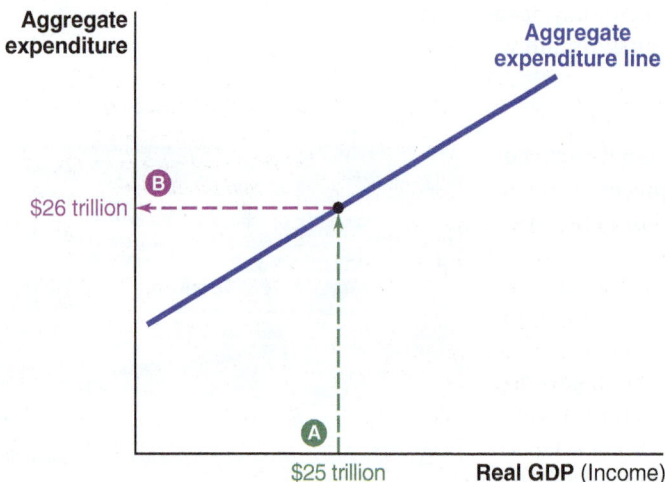

How to Use the Aggregate Expenditure Line

The aggregate expenditure line is a valuable tool for managers, and you can use it to assess how robust spending is likely to be next year. For instance, you can forecast what aggregate expenditure will be if total income — that is, GDP — is $25 trillion next year. Figure 3 illustrates how to figure this out. First, locate your GDP forecast on the horizontal axis, then look up until you hit the aggregate expenditure line. Now look across to discover that the corresponding level of aggregate expenditure is $26 trillion.

If other things change, so should your forecast. Economists often talk about their forecasts as holding other things constant. If other factors change, then so should your forecast. You can use the aggregate expenditure line to forecast the consequences of changing economic conditions. As you do so, it's important to distinguish between:

- *Changes in income,* which cause a *movement along* the aggregate expenditure line; and

- *Changes in other factors that change aggregate expenditure at any given income level,* which cause the aggregate expenditure line to *shift*.

Let's see how this works in practice.

A change in income leads to a movement along the aggregate expenditure line. What happens when income changes? For instance, what will aggregate expenditure be if GDP rises to $29 trillion?

In Figure 4, locate this new income level on the horizontal axis, and look up until you hit the aggregate expenditure line. Look left, and you'll see that it corresponds to aggregate expenditure of $28 trillion. You can conclude that increasing income by $4 trillion will lead aggregate expenditure to rise by $2 trillion.

Notice that this change in income led spending to move from one point on the aggregate expenditure line to another point on the same line. This makes sense: This line shows how aggregate expenditure responds to a change in income, and so therefore changes in income do not shift this line. Instead, *a change in income leads to a movement along the aggregate expenditure line.*

Figure 4 | **A Change in Income Causes Movement Along the Aggregate Expenditure Line**

Ⓐ When GDP is $25 trillion, aggregate expenditure is $26 trillion.
Ⓑ When GDP is $29 trillion, aggregate expenditure is $28 trillion.
Ⓒ Changes in income lead to movement along the aggregate expenditure line.

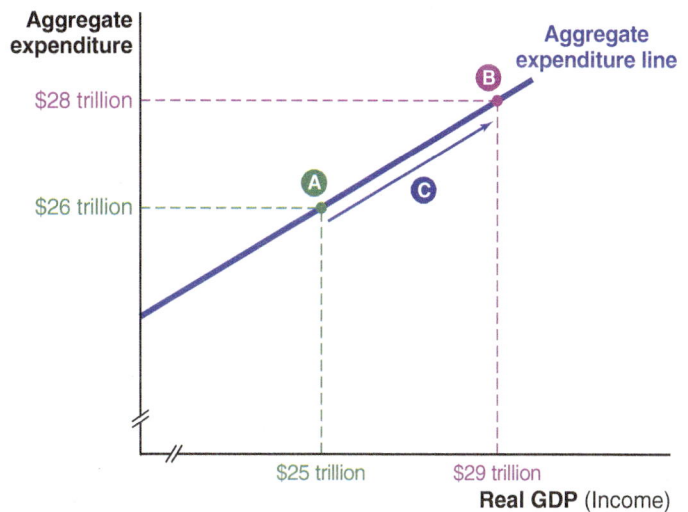

A.2 Macroeconomic Equilibrium and the Keynesian Cross

Learning Objective *Find the macroeconomic equilibrium and analyze how it changes as economic conditions change.*

Ask a business owner how much they plan on producing, and they'll say that it depends on how much people plan on spending. Ask people how much they plan to spend, and they'll say it depends on how much income they expect to earn. Ask them how much income they expect to earn, and they'll tell you it depends on how much work they have, which depends on how much businesses produce.

If this all feels a bit circular, that's because it is. As Figure 5 shows, spending depends on income, income depends on production, and production depends on spending. This is the interdependence principle at work, and it arises because one person's spending creates a demand for others to produce more output, which boosts their income. When those folks spend that extra income, they'll kick-start further cycles of interdependence as their spending stimulates greater production, more income, and yet more spending.

Figure 5 | **Macroeconomic Interdependence**

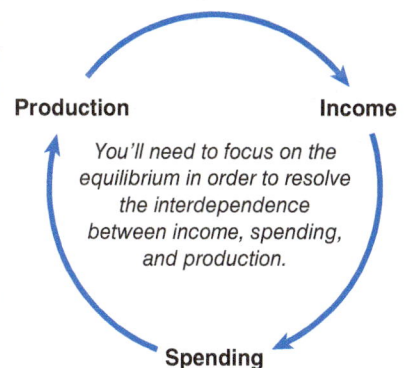

Aggregate Expenditure in Macroeconomic Equilibrium

This interdependence makes macroeconomics seem harder than it really is. The secret to resolving this apparent circularity is to look for the equilibrium that results from the interaction of income, spending, and production.

Scientists describe an equilibrium as a stable situation with no tendency to change. In microeconomics, an individual market has a tendency to move to the equilibrium where the quantity of a product that's supplied is equal to the quantity demanded. The idea of macroeconomic equilibrium is similar, but rather than analyzing an individual market, it involves thinking about the economy as a whole.

Macroeconomic equilibrium occurs when aggregate expenditure matches total production. Macroeconomic equilibrium is the point at which the total quantity of output that buyers collectively want to purchase is equal to the total quantity of output that suppliers collectively produce. As such, it happens when aggregate expenditure (a measure of the total demand for stuff) equals GDP (a measure of total production, or the total supply of stuff):

$$\text{Aggregate expenditure} = \text{GDP}$$

macroeconomic equilibrium Occurs when the quantity of output that buyers collectively want to purchase is equal to the quantity of output that suppliers collectively produce.

When total spending and total production are in balance, there's no tendency for total output to change. That's why you can forecast that an economy that's in macroeconomic equilibrium is likely to stay there—at least until something else intervenes.

Macroeconomic equilibrium doesn't mean that every single market for each individual product is in supply-equals-demand equilibrium. Supply might exceed demand in some markets (leading those suppliers to cut back on production), while in others, demand might exceed supply (leading those suppliers to expand production). In a macroeconomic equilibrium, these effects offset and, across the economy as a whole, businesses are producing as much stuff as people are willing to buy. As a result, there's no reason for *total* production to either increase or decrease.

Figure 6 | Macroeconomic Equilibrium Occurs on the 45-Degree Line

Equilibrium occurs when: *Aggregate expenditure = GDP*.
The 45-degree line shows all possible points of macroeconomic equilibrium.

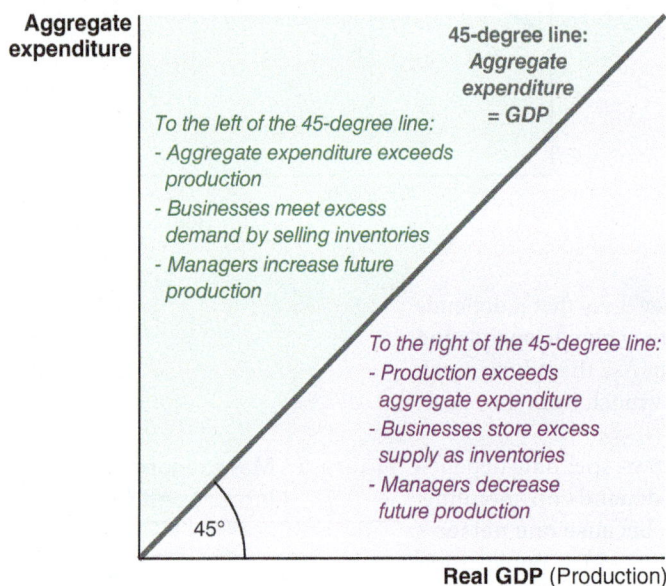

Aggregate expenditure

45-degree line:
Aggregate expenditure
= GDP

To the left of the 45-degree line:
- Aggregate expenditure exceeds production
- Businesses meet excess demand by selling inventories
- Managers increase future production

To the right of the 45-degree line:
- Production exceeds aggregate expenditure
- Businesses store excess supply as inventories
- Managers decrease future production

45°

Real GDP (Production)

Macroeconomic equilibrium occurs on the 45-degree line. Figure 6 illustrates a simple graphical trick to find all the points that are consistent with a potential macroeconomic equilibrium: When you graph aggregate expenditure against GDP, the set of points where the two are equal is simply the 45-degree line. That's because a 45-degree line shows all the points where the value on the vertical axis (that is, aggregate expenditure) is equal to the value on the horizontal axis (which is GDP). Thus, the 45-degree line illustrates all the possible points of macroeconomic equilibrium.

Production will adjust toward the 45-degree line. At points to the right of the 45-degree line, GDP exceeds aggregate expenditure, which is not an equilibrium. At these points—shown in purple—suppliers are producing more than people want to buy. Initially, they'll store this excess supply as inventories. But producers don't want to keep accumulating warehouses full of unsold inventories, and so eventually they'll adjust by cutting production. This tendency to cut production when it exceeds aggregate expenditure will push the level of output back toward a macroeconomic equilibrium where aggregate expenditure and production are in balance—which occurs on the 45-degree line.

Alternatively, at points to the left of the 45-degree line, GDP is less than aggregate expenditure, which also is not an equilibrium. At these points—shown in green—suppliers are producing less than people want to buy. Initially, they'll meet this excess demand by selling inventories, but that can't continue forever. Rather than risk forgoing profitable sales if their inventories run out, they'll ramp up production. This tendency to raise production when it's less than aggregate expenditure will push the level of output back toward macroeconomic equilibrium, once again bringing them into balance along the 45-degree line.

All of this says that as managers adjust their production levels to better match aggregate expenditure, they'll push GDP back toward macroeconomic equilibrium and the 45-degree line. It follows that any point along the 45-degree line can be a macroeconomic equilibrium.

Equilibrium occurs where aggregate expenditure crosses the 45-degree line. Okay, so the 45-degree line illustrates the many possible points of macroeconomic equilibrium where GDP could come into balance with aggregate expenditure. To figure out which of these possible outcomes will be next year's actual outcome, you'll need to figure out which one coincides with next year's actual level of aggregate expenditure. And so it's time to bring the aggregate expenditure line back into our analysis.

Macroeconomic equilibrium occurs at the point where the aggregate expenditure line meets the 45-degree line. As Figure 7 illustrates, at this point the level of aggregate expenditure is equal to GDP.

Figure 7 | **Macroeconomic Equilibrium**

Equilibrium occurs where the aggregate expenditure line meets the 45-degree line.

Ⓐ The **45-degree line** shows the set of possible equilibria where *aggregate expenditure = GDP*.

Ⓑ The **aggregate expenditure line** shows how total spending varies with the level of GDP.

Ⓒ **Macroeconomic equilibrium** occurs where the **aggregate expenditure line** crosses the **45-degree line**, ensuring that spending and production plans are consistent with each other.

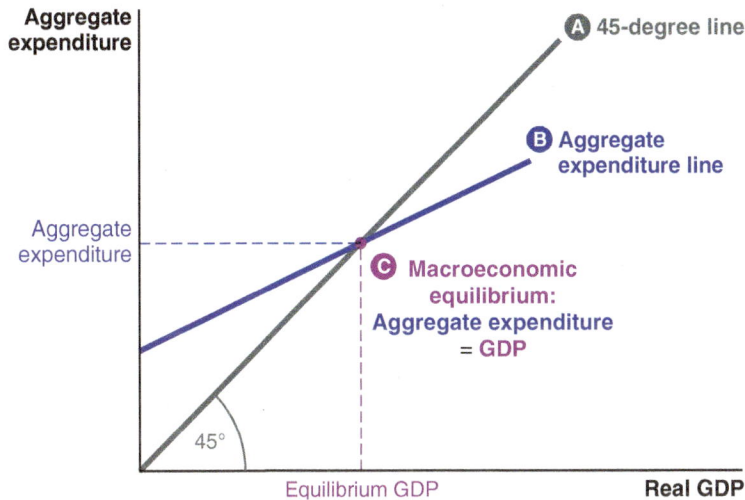

That's it! Now you know how to find the point of macroeconomic equilibrium: It occurs where the aggregate expenditure line crosses the 45-degree line. This framework is often called the *Keynesian cross*, and you can probably see why. It's a *cross* because it suggests that the economy will move to the level of output where the two lines cross. And it's *Keynesian* because it illustrates the central insight of John Maynard Keynes, that spending plays a key role in determining macroeconomic outcomes.

Equilibrium GDP can fall short of potential output. A macroeconomic equilibrium describes where we expect the economy to come to rest. But that doesn't necessarily mean that it's a good outcome — merely that it's a stable one. Just as you can come to rest in a good place or a bad one, so can the economy. A macroeconomic equilibrium can occur at a high level of GDP or at a low one — it really depends on the position of the aggregate expenditure line. For instance, during the Great Depression, equilibrium GDP was far below potential output.

A low-GDP equilibrium.

Luke Sharrett/Bloomberg Creative Photos/Getty Images

Shifts in Aggregate Expenditure

So far we've focused mainly on the effects of changes in *income,* which lead to *movement along the aggregate expenditure line.* Let's now expand our analysis to also include factors that might cause a change in aggregate expenditure *at any given income level* causing a *shift in the aggregate expenditure line.*

It's important to distinguish between two forces that change spending: income and everything else. As you evaluate changes in spending, simply ask yourself: What caused this change? If it's a change in income, the aggregate expenditure line won't shift. But if it's any other factor, then it shifts the aggregate expenditure line. As we're about to see, any shift in the aggregate expenditure line leads to a new level of equilibrium GDP.

A decrease in spending will shift the aggregate expenditure line down. Let's start by considering the effects of a decrease in aggregate expenditure. This would occur if consumers cut back on their spending, businesses reduce planned investment in new equipment, governments reduce their purchases, foreigners spend less on our exports, or Americans import more of their purchases from abroad. Any factor that leads to a decrease in aggregate expenditure *at any given income level*—whether due to a change in *C, I, G,* or *NX*—will shift the aggregate expenditure line downward, as shown by the purple line in Panel A on the left of Figure 8.

Figure 8 | Shifts in Aggregate Expenditure Can Cause Recessions and Expansions

Panel A: A Decrease in Spending

Ⓐ A **decrease in aggregate expenditure** at any given level of income causes the **aggregate expenditure line to shift down**.

Ⓑ This leads the economy to move to a **new equilibrium**, with a lower level of GDP, and hence lower income and employment.

Ⓒ Because **GDP decreases**, it follows that a decrease in aggregate expenditure causes a **recession**.

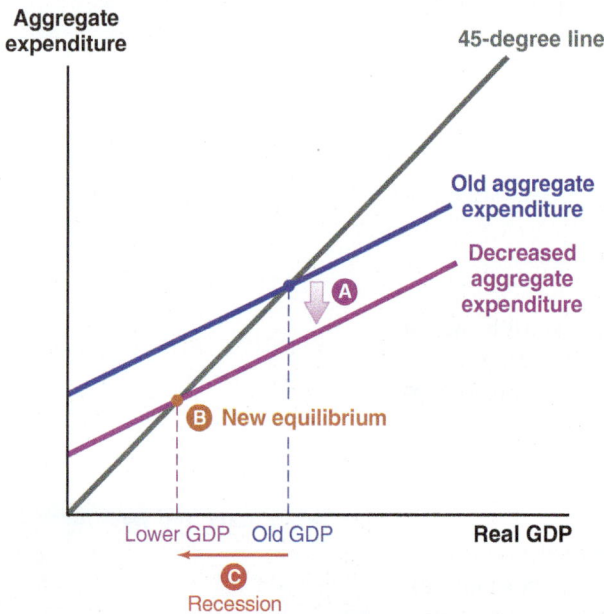

Panel B: An Increase in Spending

Ⓐ An **increase in aggregate expenditure** at any given level of income causes the **aggregate expenditure line to shift up**.

Ⓑ This leads the economy to move to a **new equilibrium**, with a higher level of GDP, and hence higher income and employment.

Ⓒ Because **GDP increases**, it follows that an increase in aggregate expenditure causes an economic **expansion**.

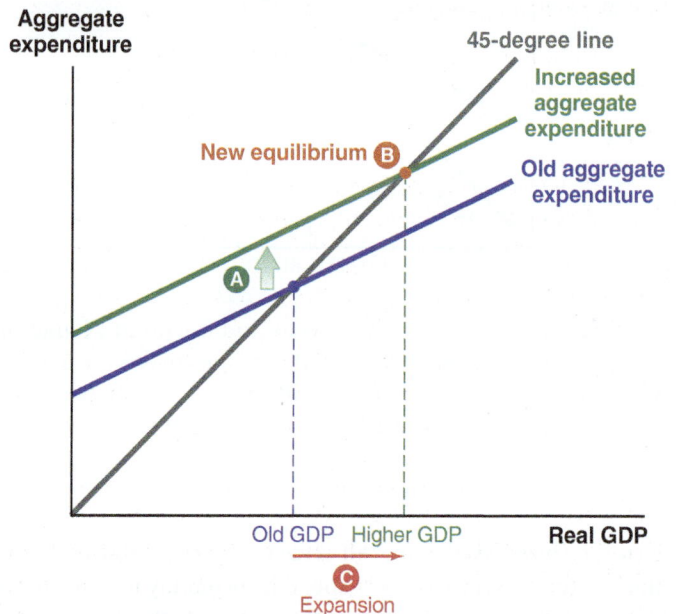

This lower level of aggregate expenditure yields a new macroeconomic equilibrium at a lower level of GDP. As the economy adjusts to this new equilibrium, GDP declines, causing a recession or, in a severe case, a depression. In this new equilibrium, output is much lower, and so businesses need fewer workers. As a result, this low-GDP equilibrium corresponds with widespread unemployment. Think of this as the equilibrium during the latest recession, or perhaps the Great Depression. Even worse: Because this economic slump is a macroeconomic equilibrium, it's likely to persist until something else causes it to change.

A positive spending shock will shift the aggregate expenditure line up. Following similar logic in the opposite direction suggests that an increase in aggregate expenditure can spark an economic boom. This increase in spending could reflect a rise in *C, I, G,* or *NX*. Whatever the cause, any factor that leads to an increase in aggregate expenditure *at any given income level* will shift the aggregate expenditure line upward, as shown by the green line in Panel B on the right of Figure 8.

This boost to spending yields a new macroeconomic equilibrium at a higher level of GDP. As the economy adjusts to this new equilibrium, GDP rises, causing an economic expansion. In this new equilibrium, output is much higher, and so businesses need more workers. As a result, this high-GDP equilibrium corresponds with low unemployment. Think of this as the equilibrium during an economic boom.

Predicting the State of the Economy

Congratulations! You've now developed a framework that you can use to forecast how the economy will respond to changing economic conditions.

Follow the three-step recipe to forecast how the economy will respond. All you need to do is answer the three questions:

Step 1: *Have spending plans changed?*

The question here is whether aggregate expenditure will change at any given income level. That means asking whether consumers will alter their spending, businesses will change how much they plan to invest, policymakers will adjust government purchases, foreigners will shift their spending on exports from the United States, or Americans will change whether they make their purchases from abroad. (Make sure you remember to think about each of the components of aggregate expenditure—including C, I, G, and NX.)

Step 2: *Shift the aggregate expenditure line.*

Is this an *increase* in spending at any given income level (shifting the aggregate expenditure line upward) or a *decrease* (shifting it down)?

Step 3: *Analyze the new equilibrium.*

How does the equilibrium level of GDP change in the new equilibrium? And how does it compare to potential output, which is the level of GDP at which all resources are fully employed?

Let's practice using this framework to forecast where the economy is going.

Example 1: *The government passes a fiscal stimulus bill that raises the level of government purchases by $1 trillion. How will this affect GDP?*

Let's follow our three-step recipe:

Step 1: This fiscal stimulus bill leads to an increase in government purchases—and hence aggregate expenditure—at any given income level.

Step 2: This increase in government purchases will increase aggregate expenditure, thereby shifting the aggregate expenditure line up by $1 trillion.

Step 3: As the figure illustrates, the new equilibrium level of GDP is higher than the previous level.

Example 2: *The Federal Reserve raises interest rates.*

Let's follow our three-step recipe:

Step 1: An increase in real interest rates leads households to consume less and businesses to invest less at any given income level.

Step 2: This decrease in consumption and investment will decrease aggregate expenditure, thereby shifting the aggregate expenditure line down.

Step 3: As the figure illustrates, this leads to a new equilibrium level of GDP that's lower than the previous level.

Do the Economics

Think you've got this business of economic forecasting all figured out? Here are a half-dozen more examples—ripped from the headlines of the Covid recession and subsequent recovery—for you to work through.

She's looking into the future.

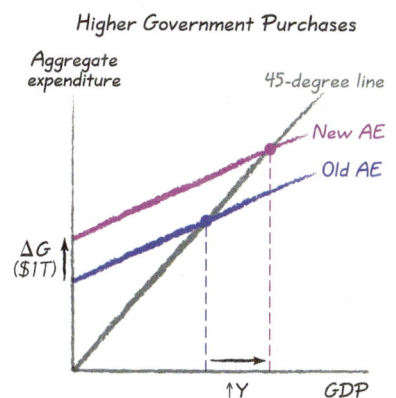
Higher Government Purchases

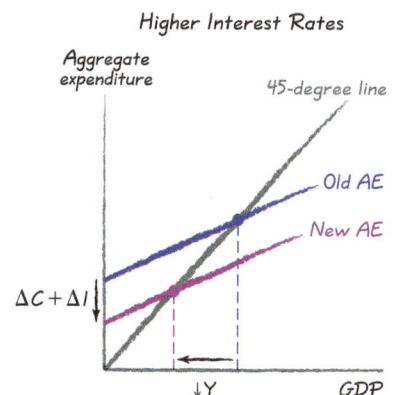
Higher Interest Rates

Scenario 1: *Fear and anxiety led consumers to cut back on their spending.*

Step 1: A decrease in consumption decreases aggregate expenditure.

Step 2: A decrease in aggregate expenditure shifts the aggregate expenditure line down.

Step 3: Spending cuts lead to lower GDP.

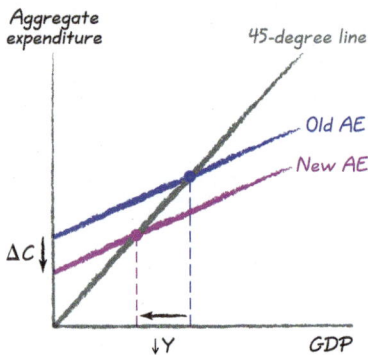

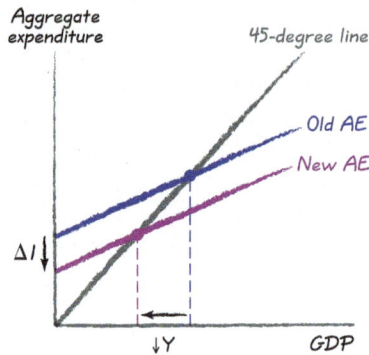

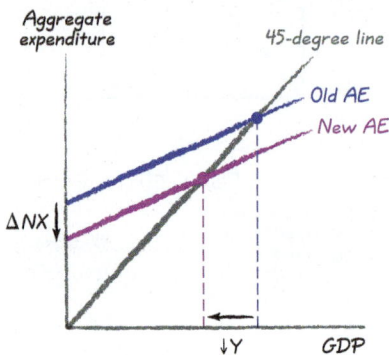

Scenario 2: *When financial markets froze up, businesses found it hard to get a loan to fund their investments.*

Step 1: A decrease in investment decreases aggregate expenditure.

Step 2: A decrease in aggregate expenditure shifts the aggregate expenditure line down.

Step 3: Spending cuts lead to lower GDP.

Scenario 3: *The Federal Reserve was worried about the impact of Covid on the economy, so it cut the interest rate to zero.*

Step 1: An increase in consumption and investment (and possibly also net exports) increases aggregate expenditure.

Step 2: An increase in aggregate expenditure shifts the aggregate expenditure line up.

Step 3: Higher spending leads to higher GDP.

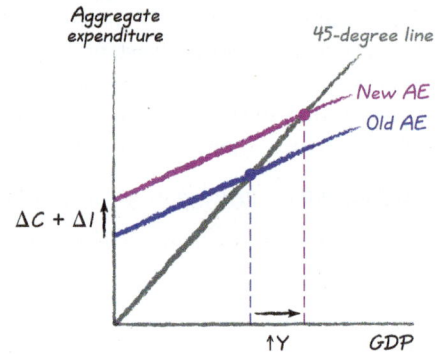

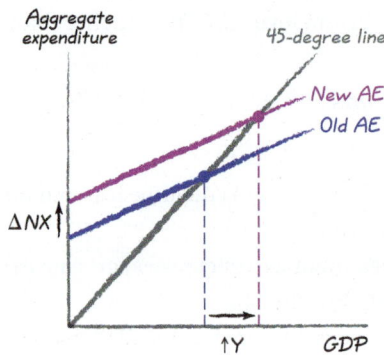

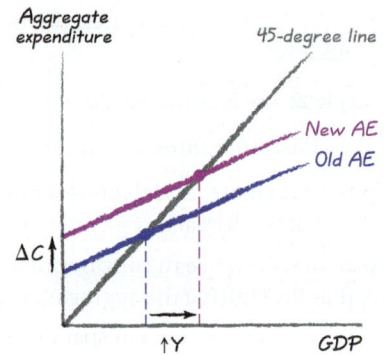

Scenario 4: *When Europe entered a recession, it cut back on purchases of American exports.*

Step 1: A decrease in net exports decreases aggregate expenditure.

Step 2: A decrease in aggregate expenditure shifts the aggregate expenditure line down.

Step 3: Spending cuts lead to lower GDP.

Scenario 5: *A decrease in the value of the U.S. dollar made American exports more attractive to foreigners.*

Step 1: An increase in net exports increases aggregate expenditure.

Step 2: An increase in aggregate expenditure shifts the aggregate expenditure line up.

Step 3: Higher spending leads to higher GDP.

Scenario 6: *The government sent checks of $1,200, then $600, then another $1,400 to most taxpayers, and consumers responded by spending more.*

Step 1: An increase in consumption increases aggregate expenditure.

Step 2: An increase in aggregate expenditure shifts the aggregate expenditure line up.

Step 3: Higher spending leads to higher GDP.

Moderate changes in spending can have large effects on output. There's one final point to notice, and it's evident in each of the examples you've just worked through: The shift in the aggregate expenditure line (the change in spending noted along the vertical axis) is small relative to the resulting change in real GDP (the shift along the horizontal axis). This suggests that even small or moderate changes in aggregate expenditure can have quite large effects — effectively multiplied effects — on GDP. These multiplied effects further reinforce the idea that moderate shifts in aggregate expenditure can drive the large changes in output that occur over the business cycle. This insight also suggests that government policy can have a sizable effect on GDP, as moderate changes in government purchases can have a multiplied effect on output. Let's dig deeper into understanding how these multiplier effects work.

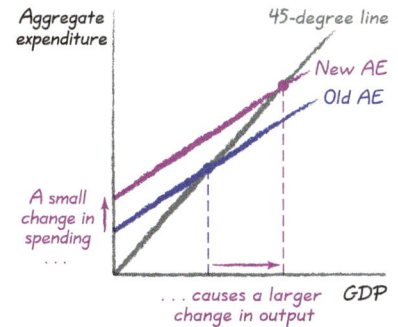

A.3 The Multiplier

Learning Objective *Analyze how moderate changes in spending can have bigger consequences through the multiplier effect.*

The arrival of the coronavirus plunged the economy into a wrenching recession. The immediate cause was a combination of stay-at-home orders, fear, and anxiety, which led to a dramatic decline in spending. The problem is that when spending falls, businesses cut back on production, which causes job losses, leading consumers to cut back even further on spending. Economists warned of the need to break this vicious cycle.

In response, the government passed a series of new stimulus bills. Some of this was direct government expenditures, such as the money spent to improve school ventilation systems. Much of this emergency spending took the form of income support — checks for households, forgivable loans for small businesses that kept workers on payroll, and expanded unemployment benefits. The goal of this income support was to give people the means to resume spending when it was safe to do so. A boost to consumption would shift the aggregate expenditure line upward, stimulating higher output and an economic recovery. It was the largest fiscal stimulus in memory, leading managers to ask: How will this affect my business?

The Multiplier Effect

Caroline owns a major HVAC supplier in Atlanta, and she asked her top analysts to evaluate the likely effects of the stimulus for her business. Digging into the details, they noted that the government planned to spend billions of dollars on ventilation and Covid preparedness projects. Caroline immediately directed her staff to look for the best contracts to bid on and to make plans to hire extra workers to work on those projects. Think of this boost as the direct effect of the stimulus.

An initial increase in spending boosts incomes, leading to more spending. There are also ripple effects. Even though the stimulus contained almost no direct spending on cars, economists at Ford still projected it would boost their sales. By their thinking, some of the workers Caroline hired would spend some of their new earnings on new cars. There are also second-round ripple effects. For instance, when Ford hires workers so that it can expand production, some of those new workers will buy lunch at a nearby Subway, leading the franchise owner to hire more sandwich artists. And there are third-round effects, too. If the newly hired sandwich artists spend some of their pay on child care, then local day-care providers will also see higher incomes. And so it continues, showing the power of the interdependence principle, as an initial burst of spending in the HVAC sector reverberates through the auto, food prep, and child care sectors, and out to the broader economy.

Add up the ripple effects to find the total effect on GDP. How far does this process go, and how much does an extra dollar of spending raise GDP? Let's zoom in and track a single dollar of extra spending as it percolates through the economy.

Initially, the government spends a dollar, perhaps on an upgraded ventilation system. Then the ripple effects begin. In the first round, the government's extra spending also counts as extra income for Caroline, and she'll spend some of it. If her marginal propensity to consume is 0.5, she'll increase her spending by $0.5 \times \$1 = 50$ cents. There's a second-round effect: Caroline's extra spending raises someone else's income by 50 cents, and they'll spend a fraction of this extra income. If the typical marginal propensity to consume is 0.5, then Caroline's spending generates an additional 0.5×50 cents $= 25$ cents of spending. The third-round effects follow the same pattern, with the folks whose income just rose by 25 cents deciding to spend an extra 0.5×25 cents $= 12.5$ cents. And so it goes on, with each further round of ripple effects yielding yet another boost to spending, although these ripples are successively smaller.

Beyond the initial impact, there are ripple effects.

$1.00 → $0.50 → $0.25 → $0.125 → ...

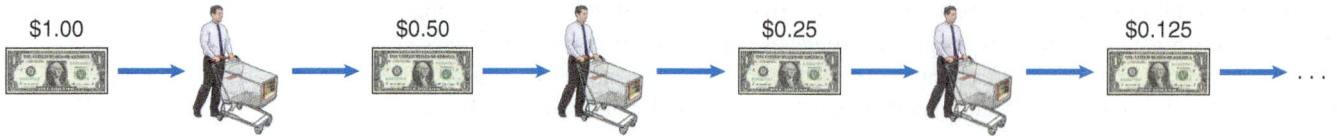

Add it all up, and you'll discover that the initial $1 r: $1 + $0.5 + $0.25 + $0.125 + $0.063 + $0.031 + $0.016 + $0.008 + ⋯ = $2.00.

Don't get too wrapped up in the math for now (we'll come back to it). Focus on the bigger picture, and you'll see that a one-dollar increase in aggregate expenditure has a larger effect — a multiplied effect — on GDP. This is a pretty extraordinary insight because it suggests that moderate changes in spending can have much larger macroeconomic effects. This *multiplier effect* is the reason that many economists believe that the governments can counter large swings in GDP by making moderate adjustments to government purchases.

The Size of the Multiplier

multiplier A measure of how much GDP changes as a result of both the direct and indirect effects flowing from each extra dollar of spending.

You can summarize the consequences of a rise in spending — including both the direct impact and the many rounds of subsequent ripple effects — with a single number called the multiplier. The **multiplier** measures how much GDP changes as a result of both the direct and ripple effects flowing from each extra dollar of spending. In our simple example, the multiplier is 2 because a $1 boost to spending generated a total of $2 in extra GDP.

The multiplier is useful because you can use it to forecast the effects of changes in aggregate expenditure, as follows:

$$\Delta GDP = \Delta Spending \times Multiplier$$

Do the Economics

How much will GDP rise after a new program of renewable energy credits — effectively an incentive for businesses to invest in renewable energy — leads to an additional $100 billion increase in investment in the sector, if the multiplier is 2?

$$\Delta GDP = \underbrace{\$100\ billion}_{\Delta Spending} \times \underbrace{2}_{Multiplier} = \$200\ billion\ \blacksquare$$

The multiplier is larger when the marginal propensity to consume is larger. How big is the multiplier in practice? As you're about to see, it all depends on the marginal propensity to consume (*MPC*), which you'll recall is the fraction of each dollar of extra income that gets spent. The marginal propensity to consume matters because the size of each subsequent ripple effect depends on the extent to which extra income translates into extra spending.

To see this, let's work through the implications of a rise in spending in Figure 9. The initial rise in spending is $\Delta Spending$. In the first-round ripple effect, the recipient of that spending will increase their spending by $\Delta Spending \times MPC$. In the second round, the recipient of that extra spending will spend a proportion of it, yielding a further increase in spending of $(\Delta Spending \times MPC) \times MPC$. In the third round, the recipient of that extra income will increase their spending by $(\Delta Spending \times MPC \times MPC) \times MPC$, and so it goes on.

Figure 9 | Multiplier Effects

Initial change	$= \Delta Spending$
First-round ripple effect	$= \Delta Spending \times MPC$
Second-round ripple effect	$= \Delta Spending \times MPC \times MPC$
Third-round ripple effect	$= \Delta Spending \times MPC \times MPC \times MPC$
. . .	. . .
Total change in GDP	$= \Delta Spending \times \underbrace{(1 + MPC + MPC^2 + MPC^3 + \cdots)}_{Multiplier}$

Add it all up, and you'll find that the total effect of a rise in spending on GDP is: $\Delta Spending \times (1 + MPC + MPC^2 + MPC^3 + \cdots)$, where the expression in parentheses is the multiplier. The expression in parentheses is the sum of a geometric series, and the beautiful thing is that it all adds up to $1/(1 - MPC)$. That's it. As a result, the multiplier is equal to:

$$\text{Multiplier} = \frac{1}{1 - MPC}$$

For instance, when the marginal propensity to consume is 0.5, then the multiplier is $1/(1 - MPC) = 2$. More generally, the larger the marginal propensity to consume, the larger the ripple effects from an initial boost to spending, and hence the larger the multiplier.

EVERYDAY Economics   Beware of developers bearing economic impact studies

The multiplier effect is an important part of macroeconomic analysis, but beware, because it's often misused in microeconomic studies. For instance, every few years a major sports team approaches their city or state government, asking for large subsidies to build a new stadium. They'll bring with them architectural drawings, and an "economic impact analysis," in which their highly paid consultants detail the extra spending the stadium will bring. They'll usually describe massive multiplier effects that suggest the effect on local businesses will be enormous. For instance, when the former Oakland Raiders proposed moving to Las Vegas, they estimated that a new football stadium would stimulate an extra $472 million in annual spending that — due to multiplier effects — would boost output by $786 million per year. The team's owners used these numbers to convince local legislators to kick in $750 million of taxpayer money to help fund their stadium.

Does the multiplier justify using public money to build private stadiums?

But these analyses often don't tell the whole story. The first problem is that a new stadium may not boost aggregate expenditure much at all — even if the stadium typically sells out. If you spend $60 more on football tickets, I bet you'll pay for it partly by spending less on other forms of entertainment. So, spending more on football tickets means less spending on other forms of entertainment. The point is the total boost to aggregate expenditure (which is what matters for total output) is smaller than the boost to the team's revenue. The second problem is that the multiplier for a city is typically quite small because spending spills across city borders. For instance, when the newly employed folks at the Las Vegas Raiders football stadium spend their earnings on food, movies, and technology, they'll boost the economy of California (where lots of agricultural products, movies, and software are produced) more than Nevada (where the income was earned). Together, these ideas explain why economists have found that stadiums rarely provide much of a boost to the local economy. ■

The multiplier applies to all increases in spending. There's one final thing to note: While we've focused on the effects of an increase in government purchases, the multiplier applies with equal force to any increase or decrease in aggregate expenditure. Just as increasing government purchases will have ripple effects, so, too, will changes in consumption, investment, or net exports.

Interpreting the DATA   How big is the multiplier?

Economists have conducted hundreds of studies attempting to answer the question: How big is the multiplier? In most cases they try to assess how effectively fiscal policy — changes in government spending and taxes — can stimulate a weak economy.

This turns out to be a surprisingly difficult question to answer. The problem is that the relationship between government purchases and output reflects (at least) three different forces. The first is the *multiplier effect,* in which greater government purchases boost future output. The second is called the *fiscal policy reaction function,* which reflects the reality that policymakers implement fiscal stimulus — increasing government purchases — when they anticipate weaker future output. The third is the *monetary policy reaction function,* which describes the Federal Reserve's tendency to cut interest rates when it anticipates weak future output. The multiplier effect creates a link from higher government purchases to higher future output. The fiscal policy reaction function creates a link from lower future output to higher government purchases. And the monetary policy reaction function creates a link from lower future output to lower interest rates, which boosts aggregate expenditure. All of this means that the correlation between government purchases and future output reflects a mishmash of these three forces.

In response, researchers have devised some ingenious studies to measure the multiplier effect. They first isolate and then track the effects of changes in government purchases that aren't caused by the state of the economy (and hence don't reflect the fiscal policy reaction function), and that don't cause the Fed to respond (and hence don't reflect the monetary policy reaction function). Some studies examine changes in government spending on the military caused by geopolitical tensions, finding that these lead to higher output. Others examine the historical record, finding that declines in tax rates, which were motivated by long-run considerations unrelated to the business cycle, also subsequently boost output. Still others have examined how the funding formulas used in stimulus programs have led to a bigger increase in government purchases in some states than in others, finding that those states that received a bigger increase in government spending subsequently enjoyed a more robust economic recovery.

So, you might ask, what is the multiplier? Figure 10 illustrates an attempt by nonpartisan economists at the Congressional Budget Office to synthesize the available studies. It illustrates three key findings:

- The central estimate — shown in red — is that the multiplier is about 1.5.

- The ripple effects that create the multiplier effect *play out over time* and may take over a year to become fully evident.

- There is *tremendous uncertainty* about the multiplier. The top gray line shows the "high estimate," which is that the multiplier is 2.5. The lower gray line shows the "low estimate," which is that the multiplier is 0.5. (If you're wondering how the multiplier could be less than one, realize that businesses and consumers can partly counteract a rise in government purchases by cutting back on their consumption and investment spending.) In between these high and low estimates is a vast gray expanse, which illustrates that even today, economists don't think they know the size of the multiplier with any certainty. ■

Figure 10 | Estimates of the Multiplier Effect

The effect on GDP of a $1 boost to aggregate expenditure

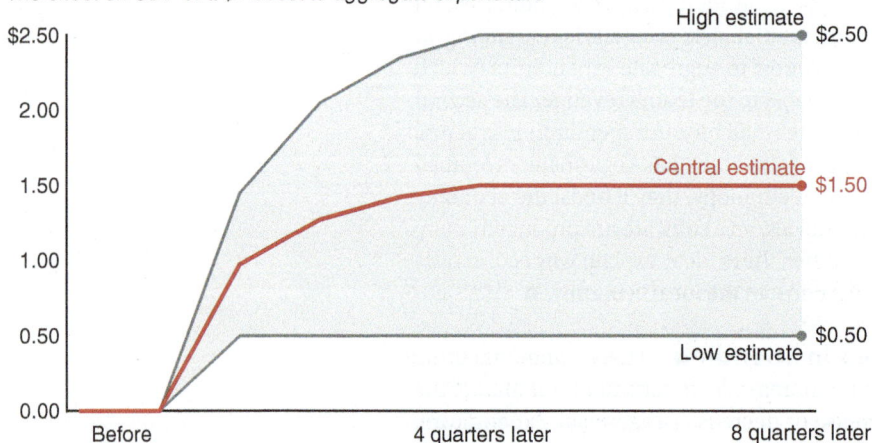

Estimates apply when the Fed does not respond by changing interest rates.

Data from: Congressional Budget Office.

A.4   Tying It Together

Aggregate Expenditure Is Important, but It's Not the Whole Story

Our analysis in this appendix is all about one big idea: Aggregate expenditure is a major factor shaping macroeconomic outcomes. It matters because if people don't want to buy much stuff, then businesses won't produce much stuff. As a result, the economy can get stuck in the sort of depressed, low-spending, low-output equilibrium that led to the Great Depression.

Fortunately, there's also a happier outcome in which people buy a lot of stuff, and so businesses produce a lot of stuff, leading to a high-spending, high-output equilibrium in which there are jobs for everyone. There are also many other possible outcomes between these extremes of depression and full employment.

The more stuff people demand, the more stuff the economy will produce . . . and deliver.

Aggregate expenditure focuses on the demand side of the economy.
The key lesson of our analysis is that the demand side of the economy — that is, aggregate expenditure — really matters. Moreover, the multiplier effect reinforces this point. When the effects of any change in consumption, planned investment, government purchases, or net exports have multiplied effects on GDP, the economy is susceptible to being knocked off course. As a result, even modest changes in aggregate expenditure can lead to economic booms and busts. The same insights suggest that government policy really matters because changes in government purchases can help push the economy back on course.

These ideas are all important. Indeed, each of them has been built into the foundations of the modern frameworks economists use to understand the economy. Equally, it's worth emphasizing that our analysis of aggregate expenditure doesn't yield a complete account of the macroeconomy. Income is not the only driver of aggregate expenditure — interest rates also play a major role. That, in turn, suggests the need for a more complete analysis to also account for the role of the financial sector in shaping interest rates and therefore spending decisions. (We went there in Chapters 18 or 21.)

The supply side is important when the economy is close to capacity.
Our focus on the role that buyers and the demand side of the economy play means that we've yet to say much about the sellers and the supply side of the economy. Implicitly, we've been assuming that when the demand for stuff rises, businesses are willing to supply more of that stuff at the current price. This is why extra spending translates into extra production, rather than shortages or higher prices.

But when the economy is close to full capacity, businesses cannot easily increase production, or they wouldn't want to do so without raising their prices. Perhaps their production lines are already overloaded, or maybe key inputs like skilled workers are hard to come by. When these supply-side constraints are binding — which can occur when output exceeds potential output — it's no longer appropriate to assume that extra spending will translate into extra production. Rather, it may spark higher prices and inflation. This suggests that it's important to integrate this appendix's demand-side emphasis on aggregate expenditure with an understanding of how supply constraints can lead inflation to emerge. (We dug into this in Chapter 19 or the second half of Chapter 21.)

Economists emphasize demand in the short run and supply in the long run.
Finally, this distinction between demand- and supply-side analysis can help you integrate your understanding of the determinants of the state of the economy in the short and long run. In Chapter 10, we analyzed the long-run determinants of the level of potential output, emphasizing that it reflects the number of workers, their skill levels, the number of machines they have to work with, and the technology for combining them. This emphasis on the supply side — the quantity and quality of inputs to production — is appropriate for analyzing the economy's potential output, which is the level that occurs when all resources are fully employed.

But in the short run, the economy may fail to meet this potential. Indeed, a shortfall in aggregate expenditure will lead the economy to produce below its full-employment potential. This explains why economists tend to emphasize demand factors in the short run and supply factors in the long run. Fluctuations in demand are the source of many of the short-run disruptions that make up the business cycle, while supply factors determine the economy's long-run potential. Of course, in the real world, distinctions are never quite as sharp as in textbooks. Sometimes, changes on the supply side can also cause short-run disruptions. And sometimes, short-run demand disruptions — like the Great Depression, or many of the recessions since — last for so long and do so much damage that they have long-run consequences.

Appendix A Review

Appendix at a Glance

Aggregate expenditure	=	C	+	I	+	G	+	NX
The total amount of goods and services people want to buy across the whole economy.		Consumption		Planned investment		Government purchases		Net exports

Aggregate expenditure rises with income (and hence real GDP), since consumption rises with income.

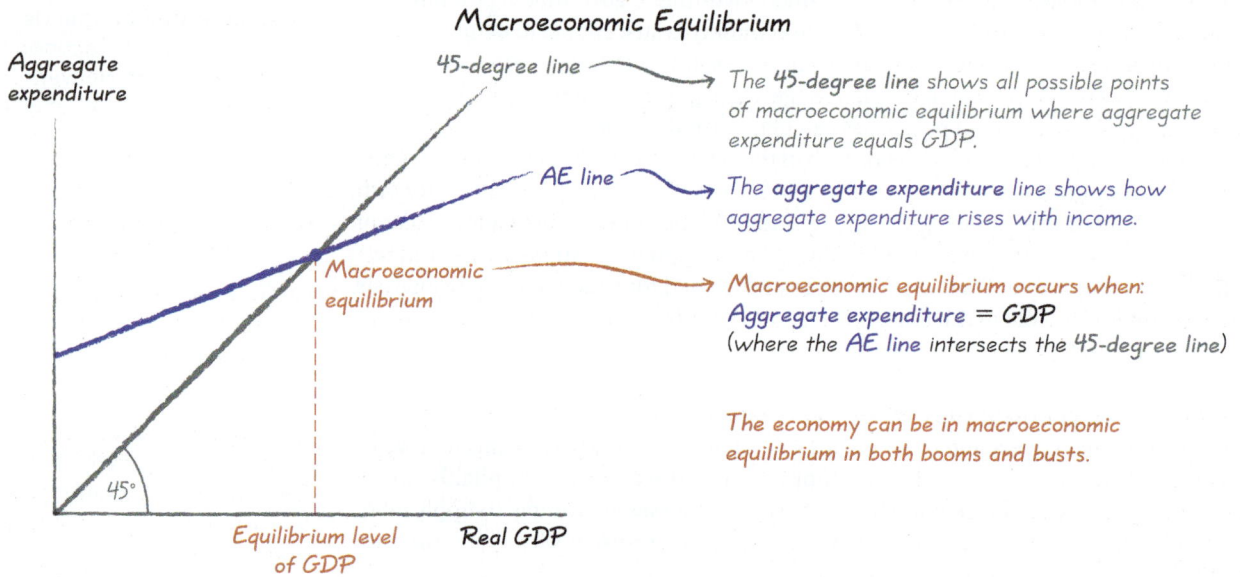

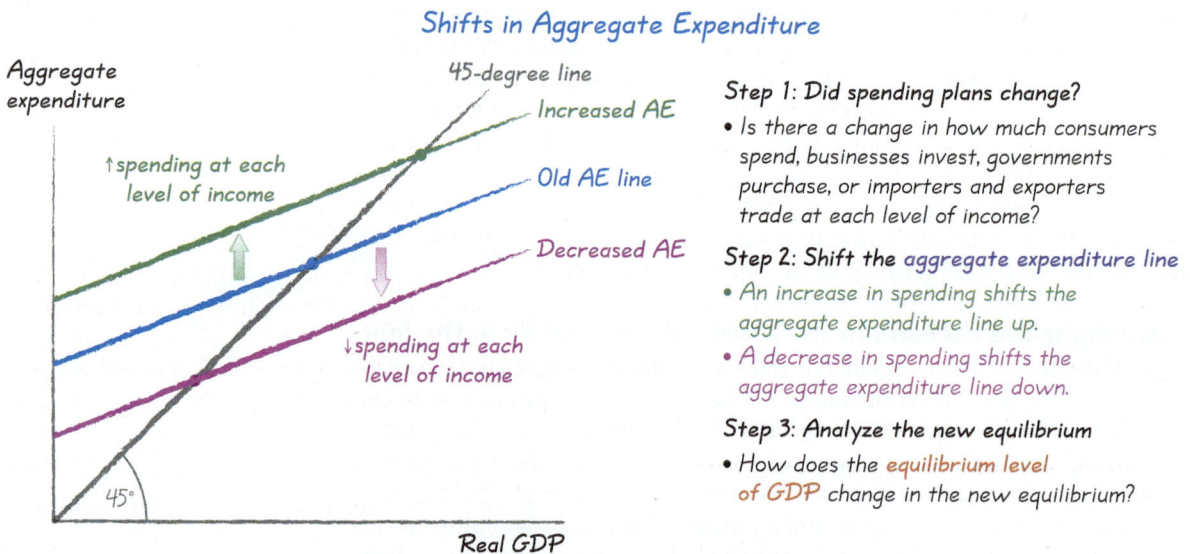

Macroeconomic Equilibrium

Aggregate expenditure

45-degree line → The **45-degree line** shows all possible points of macroeconomic equilibrium where aggregate expenditure equals GDP.

AE line → The **aggregate expenditure** line shows how aggregate expenditure rises with income.

Macroeconomic equilibrium → Macroeconomic equilibrium occurs when: **Aggregate expenditure = GDP** (where the AE line intersects the 45-degree line)

The economy can be in macroeconomic equilibrium in both booms and busts.

45°

Equilibrium level of GDP   Real GDP

Shifts in Aggregate Expenditure

Aggregate expenditure

45-degree line

Increased AE

↑spending at each level of income

Old AE line

Decreased AE

↓spending at each level of income

45°

Real GDP

Step 1: Did spending plans change?
• Is there a change in how much consumers spend, businesses invest, governments purchase, or importers and exporters trade at each level of income?

Step 2: Shift the aggregate expenditure line
• An increase in spending shifts the aggregate expenditure line up.
• A decrease in spending shifts the aggregate expenditure line down.

Step 3: Analyze the new equilibrium
• How does the equilibrium level of GDP change in the new equilibrium?

The Marginal Propensity to Consume (MPC) and the Multiplier

Marginal propensity to consume	Multiplier	Total change in GDP
The fraction of each extra dollar of income that you spend.	A measure of how much GDP changes as a result of both the direct and indirect effects flowing from each extra dollar of spending.	The larger the multiplier, the more GDP increases when spending increases.
$MPC = \dfrac{\Delta Consumption}{\Delta Income} < 1$	$Multiplier = \dfrac{1}{1 - MPC}$	$\Delta GDP = \Delta Spending \times Multiplier$

Key Terms

aggregate expenditure, A-2

consumption function, A-3

macroeconomic equilibrium, A-5

marginal propensity to consume, A-3

multiplier, A-12

planned investment, A-2

Study Problems

Learning Objective A.1 *Measure aggregate expenditure and analyze how it varies with income.*

1. Explain why unplanned inventory changes are not considered part of aggregate expenditure.

2. You receive $1,000. How much of it will you spend this year, and how much of it will you save? What is your marginal propensity to consume?

3. In 2019, real GDP in the United States increased by $426 billion and consumption spending increased by $281 billion.

   a. What do these data suggest was the marginal propensity to consume?

   b. If real income increases by $500 billion in 2023, use this estimate of the marginal propensity to consume to predict how consumption spending will change in 2023.

4. Use the graph to answer the following questions.

Aggregate expenditure and consumption
(trillions of $)

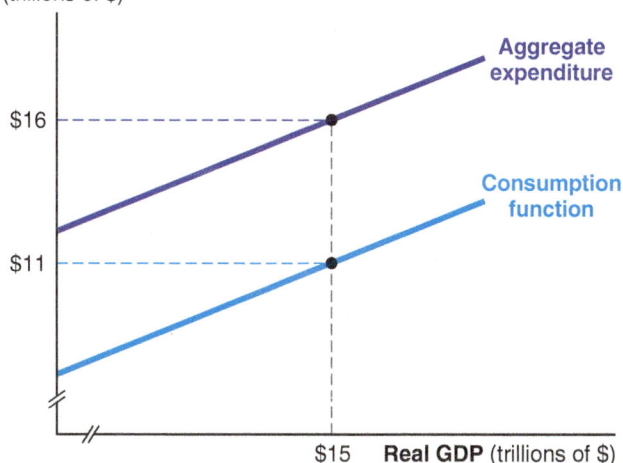

a. What is consumption spending if income is $15 trillion?

b. What is aggregate expenditure if income is $15 trillion?

c. What is the sum of planned investment, government purchases, and net exports when income is $15 trillion?

d. If income rises, will consumption rise, fall, or stay the same? Will this cause the consumption function to shift? Explain your reasoning.

e. If income falls, will aggregate expenditure rise, fall, or stay the same? Will this cause the aggregate expenditure line to shift? Explain your reasoning.

Learning Objective A.2 *Find the macroeconomic equilibrium and analyze how it changes as economic conditions change.*

5. Spending depends on income, income depends on production, and production depends on spending. Explain how this circular interdependence is resolved at the macroeconomic equilibrium.

6. Explain why the 45-degree line represents all the possible points of macroeconomic equilibrium. Why would production tend to change if it is to the left or right of the 45-degree line?

7. Use the Keynesian cross to illustrate how changes in aggregate expenditure can lead to changes in output. Provide an example of something that would lead to a recession and something that would lead to an expansion. Illustrate each example with a small graph showing the shift in aggregate expenditure and the subsequent change in output.

8. If aggregate expenditure in Thailand this year is on track to be $500 billion and output is $450 billion, is the economy currently at a macroeconomic equilibrium? Predict how unplanned inventories will change. How will producers respond to this imbalance? Do you anticipate GDP will rise or fall in response?

9. Draw an aggregate expenditure graph and label the macroeconomic equilibrium on it occurring when real GDP is $20 trillion. Then illustrate how a decrease in aggregate expenditure will lead the economy to experience a recession as it shifts to a new macroeconomic equilibrium where real GDP is $18 trillion.

10. Forecast how aggregate expenditure and real GDP will change in each of the following scenarios. Indicate which component of aggregate expenditure changes and illustrate your answers with a graph.

    a. A sharp uptick in stock prices increases consumer wealth and makes consumers willing to spend more at each level of income.

    b. The European Union imposes tariffs on all goods imported from the United States, which causes U.S. exports to fall.

    c. Congress passes a new tax law that removes a business investment tax credit. In response to this change, businesses spend $500 billion less on new machinery and building projects.

d. Congress passes a fiscal stimulus package that devotes $1 trillion to improving infrastructure across the country.

e. Bolstered by reassurances from the Fed, businesses become confident that historically low interest rates will continue for the foreseeable future and begin to plan large investment projects.

Learning Objective A.3 *Analyze how moderate changes in spending can have bigger consequences through the multiplier effect.*

11. If everyone has the same marginal propensity to consume as you indicated in your answer to Question 2, determine the multiplier. Explain why the marginal propensity to consume determines the multiplier.

12. Your state legislators and governor are debating whether they should use state funds to encourage motion picture studios to shoot and produce films in your state. The governor's office issues a report that includes the following statement:

"The average budget for a movie is $70 million, but our consultants estimate that this will have broader ripple effects across many industries and will boost state output by about $210 million."

What multiplier is the governor's office using to come to this conclusion? Do you think the multiplier is realistic for this scenario?

13. In response to a $240 billion increase in government purchases, GDP increased by $360 billion.

a. What is the multiplier?

b. Use this estimate to predict how GDP will change if businesses invest an additional $100 billion in capital investment projects.

c. What is the marginal propensity to consume?

14. The federal government is expected to pass a new spending bill that increases government purchases by $50 billion. Predict how GDP will change if the multiplier is 1.2. Explain why the change in GDP is not exactly equal to the change in government spending.

Glossary

A

absolute advantage The ability to do a task using fewer inputs.

absolute poverty A measure of the adequacy of resources relative to an absolute standard of living.

actively managed When a fund is managed by stock pickers.

aggregate demand curve Shows the relationship between the price level and the total quantity of output that buyers collectively plan to purchase.

aggregate expenditure The total amount of goods and services that people want to buy across the whole economy; Consumption + Planned investment + Government purchases + Net exports.

aggregate supply curve Shows the relationship between the price level and the total quantity of output that suppliers collectively produce.

annualized rate Data converted to the rate that would occur if the current rate had continued throughout the year.

appreciation When the price of a currency rises.

automatic stabilizers Spending and tax programs that adjust as the economy expands and contracts, without policymakers taking any deliberate action.

B

bank run When many bank customers try to withdraw their savings at the same time.

bilateral trade balance How much we buy from a specific country compared to how much they buy from us.

bond An IOU. Specifically, a promise to pay back a loan with interest.

boom When the economy is operating above its sustainable potential.

budget deficit The difference between spending and revenue in a year in which spending exceeds revenue.

budget surplus The difference between spending and revenue in a year in which revenue exceeds spending.

business cycle Short-term fluctuations in economic activity.

bust When the economy is operating below its sustainable potential.

C

capital Assets such as equipment, structures, and intellectual property that are used repeatedly to produce output.

capital stock The total quantity of physical capital that can be used in the production of goods and services.

catch-up growth The rapid growth that occurs when a relatively poor country invests in its physical capital.

change in the quantity demanded The change in quantity associated with movement along a fixed demand curve.

change in the quantity supplied The change in quantity associated with movement along a fixed supply curve.

circular flow diagram A simple model of the economy that illustrates how households and businesses are linked.

classical dichotomy A purely nominal change — like a change in the average price level — won't have any effect on real variables in the long run.

comovement The tendency for economic variables to rise and fall together.

comparative advantage The ability to do a task at a lower opportunity cost.

complementary goods Goods that go together. Your demand for a good will decrease if the price of a complementary good rises and will increase if the price of a complementary good falls.

complements-in-production Goods that are made together. Your supply of a good will increase if the price of a complement-in-production rises.

compounding formula Future value in t years = Present value $\times (1 + r)^t$

compounding The accumulation of money over time, as you earn interest on both your principal and accrued interest.

congestion effect When a good becomes less valuable because other people use it. If more people buy such a product, your demand for it will decrease.

constant returns to scale Increasing all inputs by some proportion will cause output to rise by the same proportion.

consumer price index (CPI) An index that tracks the average price consumers pay over time for a representative "basket" of goods and services.

consumer surplus The economic surplus you get from buying something. Consumer surplus = Marginal benefit – Price.

consumption function A curve plotting the level of consumption associated with each level of income.

consumption Household spending on final goods and services.

consumption smoothing Maintaining a steady or smooth path for your consumption spending over time.

contractionary fiscal policy Lower government purchases and/or higher taxes to decrease aggregate expenditure in response to output above potential.

cost-benefit principle Costs and benefits are the incentives that shape decisions. You should evaluate the full set of costs and benefits of any choice, and pursue only those whose benefits are at least as large as their costs.

cost-push inflation Inflation that results from an unexpected rise in production costs.

credit constraints Limits on how much you can borrow.

crowding out The decline in private spending — and particularly investment — that follows from a rise in government borrowing.

current account balance Measures the difference between the income that Americans receive from abroad and the income that Americans pay to people abroad.

cyclical unemployment Unemployment that is due to a temporary downturn in the economy.

D

deadweight loss How far economic surplus falls below the efficient outcome; Deadweight loss = Economic surplus at the efficient quantity – Actual economic surplus.

decrease in demand A shift of the demand curve to the left.

decrease in supply A shift of the supply curve to the left.

default risk The risk that your loan won't be repaid.

deflation A generalized decrease in the overall level of prices.

demand-pull inflation Inflation resulting from excess demand.

deposit insurance A guarantee that you won't lose the money you deposit in the bank.

depreciation rate The proportion of an investment's remaining productive capacity you lose each year due to depreciation.

depreciation The decline in capital due to wear and tear, obsolescence, accidental damage, and aging; when the price of a currency falls.

diminishing marginal benefit Each additional unit yields a smaller marginal benefit than the previous unit.

diminishing marginal product The marginal product of an input declines as you use more of that input.

diminishing marginal utility Each additional dollar yields a smaller boost to your utility—that is, less marginal utility—than the previous dollar.

discounting Converting *future values* into their equivalent *present values*.

discounting formula Present value = Future value in t years $\div (1 + r)^t$

discount rate The interest rate on loans that the Fed offers to banks through the discount window.

discretionary fiscal policy Policy that temporarily changes government spending or taxes to boost or slow the economy.

discretionary spending Spending that Congress appropriates annually.

disposable income Your after-tax income.

dissaving The excess amount you consume above your income in a given period that you therefore must pay for by either withdrawing money from your savings or borrowing money.

distributional consequences Who gets what.

dividends A share of profits that a company pays to its shareholders.

domestic demand curve Shows the quantity of a product that all domestic consumers added together plan to buy, at each price.

domestic supply curve Shows the quantity of a product that all domestic suppliers added together plan to sell, at each price.

dual mandate The Fed's two goals of stable prices and maximum sustainable employment.

E

earned income Wages from an employer, or net earnings from self-employment.

economic efficiency An outcome is more economically efficient if it yields more economic surplus.

economic surplus The total benefits minus total costs flowing from a decision; it measures how much a decision has improved your well-being.

effective marginal tax rate The amount of each extra dollar you earn that you lose to higher taxes and lower government benefits.

efficiency wage A higher wage paid to encourage greater worker productivity.

efficient allocation Allocating goods to create the largest economic surplus, which requires that each good goes to the person who'll get the highest marginal benefit from it.

efficient markets hypothesis The theory that at any point in time, stock prices reflect all publicly available information.

efficient outcome The efficient outcome yields the largest possible economic surplus.

efficient production Producing a given quantity of output at the lowest possible cost, which requires producing each good at the lowest marginal cost.

efficient quantity The quantity that produces the largest possible economic surplus.

employed Working-age people who are working.

equilibrium price The price at which the market is in equilibrium.

equilibrium quantity The quantity demanded and supplied when the market is in equilibrium.

equilibrium The point at which there is no tendency for change. A market is in equilibrium when the quantity supplied equals the quantity demanded.

equilibrium unemployment rate The long-run unemployment rate to which the economy tends to return.

equity A measure of fairness. An outcome yields greater equity if it results in a fairer distribution of economic benefits.

excess demand When the quantity demanded at the prevailing price exceeds the quantity supplied.

excise tax A tax on a specific product.

expansion A period of rising economic activity.

expansionary fiscal policy Higher government spending and/or lower taxes to increase aggregate expenditure in response to output below potential.

exports Goods or services produced domestically and purchased by foreign buyers.

export To sell goods or services to foreign buyers.

F

federal funds rate The interest rate that the Fed uses as its policy tool, which is the nominal interest rate that banks pay to borrow from each other overnight in the federal funds market.

Federal Open Market Committee (FOMC) The Federal Reserve committee that decides on U.S. interest rates. It consists of the Fed governors and district Fed bank presidents.

Fed model The framework that uses the *IS* curve, the *MP* curve, and the Phillips curve to link interest rates, the output gap, and inflation.

Fed rule-of-thumb The recipe that describes how the Fed often sets the interest rate:

Federal funds rate – Inflation = Neutral real interest rate + ½ × (Inflation – 2%) + Output gap

final goods and services Finished goods or services.

financial account balance The difference between financial inflows and financial outflows.

financial inflows Investments by foreigners in the United States.

financial outflows Investments by Americans in foreign countries.

financial shocks Any change in borrowing conditions that affects the real interest rate at which people can borrow. Financial shocks shift the *MP* curve.

fiscal policy The government's use of spending and tax policies to attempt to stabilize the economy.

fixed cost Those costs that don't vary when you change the quantity of output you produce.

floor framework The Fed's approach of setting other interest rates to put a lower bound on how low the federal funds rate will go.

foreign exchange market The market in which currencies are bought and sold.

forward guidance Providing information about the future course of monetary policy in order to influence market expectations of future interest rates.

framing effect When a decision is affected by how a choice is described, or framed. You should avoid framing effects altering your own decisions.

frictional unemployment Unemployment due to the time it takes for employers to search for workers and for workers to search for jobs.

fundamental analysis A framework for assessing an asset's fundamental value.

fundamental value The present value of the future profits that a company will earn.

future value The amount that your money will grow into by a specific future date, as a result of accumulating interest.

G

gains from trade The benefits that come from reallocating resources, goods, and services to better uses.

GDP deflator A price index that tracks the price of all goods and services produced domestically.

GDP per person Total GDP divided by the population; also referred to as *GDP per capita*.

globalization The increasing economic, political, and cultural integration of different countries.

government failure When government policies lead to worse outcomes.

government purchases Government purchases of goods and services.

"greater fool" theory The idea that people buy an investment because they expect other people to buy it from them at a higher price.

gross domestic product (GDP) The market value of all final goods and services produced within a country in a year.

gross government debt The total accumulated amount of money the government owes.

H

"holding other things constant" A commonly used qualifier noting that your conclusions may change if some factor that you haven't analyzed changes. (In Latin, it's *ceteris paribus*.)

human capital The accumulated knowledge and skills that make a worker more productive.

hyperinflation Extremely high rates of inflation.

hysteresis When a period of high unemployment leads to a higher equilibrium unemployment rate.

I

import quota A limit on the quantity of a good that can be imported.

imports Goods or services produced in a foreign country and purchased by domestic buyers.

import To buy goods or services from foreign sellers.

income taxes Taxes collected on all income, regardless of its source.

increase in demand A shift of the demand curve to the right.

increase in supply A shift of the supply curve to the right.

indexation Automatically adjusting wages, benefits, tax brackets, and the like to compensate for inflation.

index fund A mutual fund that consists of a broad market index.

individual demand curve A graph that plots the quantity of an item that an individual buyer plans to purchase at each price.

individual supply curve A graph plotting the quantity of an item that a business plans to sell at each price.

inferior good A good for which higher income causes a decrease in demand.

inflation A generalized rise in the overall level of prices.

inflation expectations The rate at which average prices are anticipated to rise next year.

inflation fallacy The mistaken belief that inflation destroys purchasing power.

inflation rate The annual percentage increase in the average price level.

inflation target A publicly stated goal for the inflation rate.

initial public offering When a company first sells stock directly to the public.

insufficient demand When the quantity demanded at the prevailing price is below what's supplied.

interdependence principle Your best choice depends on your other choices, the choices others make, developments in other markets, and expectations about the future. When any of these factors changes, your best choice might change.

interest rate on reserves The interest rate the Fed pays to banks on reserves.

intergenerational mobility The extent to which the economic status of children is independent of the economic status of their parents.

intermediate goods and services Goods or services used as inputs in the production of other products.

internal markets Markets within a company to buy and sell scarce resources.

investment line The line that shows how lower real interest rates lead to higher levels of investment.

investment Spending on new capital assets that increase the economy's productive capacity.

involuntarily part time Someone who wants full-time work and is working part time because they haven't found a full-time job.

IS **curve** Illustrates how lower real interest rates raise spending and hence output, leading to a more positive output gap.

K

knowledge problem When knowledge needed to make a good decision is not available to the decision maker.

L

labor force participation rate The percentage of the working-age population that is either employed or unemployed.

labor force The employed plus the unemployed.

labor market Phillips curve A Phillips curve linking unexpected inflation to the unemployment rate.

labor productivity The quantity of goods and services that each person produces per hour of work.

lagging indicators Variables that follow the business cycle with a delay.

law of demand The tendency for quantity demanded to be higher when the price is lower.

law of diminishing returns When one input is held constant, increases in the other inputs will, at some point, begin to yield smaller and smaller increases in output.

law of supply The tendency for the quantity supplied to be higher when the price is higher.

leading indicators Variables that tend to predict the future path of the economy.

lender of last resort The Fed's role as the lender that financial institutions turn to when they're having trouble getting loans.

liquidity risk The risk that if you need to sell an asset quickly, you may not be able to get a good price for it.

liquidity The ability to quickly and easily convert your investments into cash, with little or no loss in value.

long-run aggregate supply curve The aggregate supply curve that applies to the long run when prices have fully adjusted. Because the economy will return to producing its potential output, this curve is vertical.

long-term unemployed People who have been unemployed for six consecutive months or longer.

M

macroeconomic equilibrium Occurs when the quantity of output that buyers collectively want to purchase is equal to the quantity of output that suppliers collectively produce.

mandatory spending Spending on programs that does not get determined annually; instead, it is set in law.

marginal benefit The extra benefit from one extra unit (of goods purchased, hours studied, etc.).

marginal cost The extra cost from one extra unit.

marginally attached Someone who wants a job and who has looked for a job within the past year, but who isn't counted as unemployed because they aren't currently searching for work.

marginal principle Decisions about quantities are best made incrementally. You should break "how many" questions into a series of smaller, or marginal decisions, weighing marginal benefits and marginal costs.

marginal product The increase in output that arises from an additional unit of an input, like labor.

marginal propensity to consume The fraction of each extra dollar of income that households spend on consumption.

marginal tax rate The tax rate you pay if you earn another dollar.

marginal utility The additional utility you get from one more dollar.

market A setting bringing together potential buyers and sellers.

market demand curve A graph plotting the total quantity of an item demanded by the entire market, at each price.

market economy Each individual makes their own production and consumption decisions, buying and selling in markets.

market failure When the forces of supply and demand lead to an inefficient outcome.

market for loanable funds The market for the funds used to buy, rent, or build capital.

market supply curve A graph plotting the total quantity of an item supplied by the entire market, at each price.

maturity transformation Using short-term loans to make long-term loans.

means-tested programs Programs for which eligibility is based on income and sometimes wealth.

menu costs The marginal cost of adjusting prices.

monetary policy The process of setting interest rates in an effort to influence economic conditions.

money Any asset regularly used in transactions.

money illusion The (mistaken) tendency to focus on nominal dollar amounts instead of inflation-adjusted amounts.

movement along the demand curve A price change causes movement from one point on a fixed demand curve to another point on the same curve.

movement along the supply curve A price change causes movement from one point on a fixed supply curve to another point on the same curve.

MP curve Illustrates the current real interest rate, which is shaped by monetary policy and the risk premium.

multiplier A measure of how much GDP changes as a result of both the direct and indirect effects flowing from each extra dollar of spending.

mutual fund A fund that buys a portfolio of stocks (and sometimes bonds) on your behalf.

N

net exports Spending on exports minus spending on imports; also referred to as the trade balance.

net government debt The debt that the government owes to individuals, businesses, and other governments both here and abroad.

net wealth The amount by which your assets exceed your debts.

network effect When a good becomes more useful because other people use it. If more people buy such a good, your demand for it will also increase.

neutral real interest rate The interest rate that operates when the economy is in neutral—producing neither above nor below its potential; the real interest rate at which real GDP is equal to potential GDP, and hence the output gap is zero.

neutral real interest rate The real interest rate at which real GDP is equal to potential GDP, and hence the output gap is zero.

nominal exchange rate The price of a country's currency, in terms of another country's currency.

nominal exchange rate formula

Nominal exchange rate =

$$\frac{\text{Number of units of a foreign currency}}{\text{Number of dollars}}$$

nominal GDP GDP measured in today's prices.

nominal interest rate The stated interest rate without a correction for the effects of inflation.

nominal variable A variable measured in dollars (whose value may fluctuate over time).

nominal wage rigidity Reluctance to cut nominal wages.

normal good A good for which higher income causes an increase in demand.

normative analysis Prescribes what *should* happen, which involves value judgments.

not in the labor force Those in the working-age population who are neither employed nor unemployed.

O

Okun's rule of thumb For every percentage point that the output gap rises, the unemployment rate tends to fall by half a percentage point.

open market operations The Federal Reserve's buying and selling of government bonds to influence the federal funds rate.

Open Market Trading Desk (the Desk) A trading desk at the New York Federal Reserve Bank where the Fed buys and sells government bonds.

opportunity cost The true cost of something is the next best alternative you have to give up to get it.

output gap The difference between actual and potential output, measured as a percentage of potential output.

overnight reverse repurchase agreements When the Desk sells a government bond to a financial institution, with an agreement to buy it back the next day at a higher price.

P

payroll taxes Taxes on earned income.

peak A high point in economic activity.

perfect competition Markets in which (1) all firms in an industry sell an identical good; and (2) there are many buyers and sellers, each of whom is small relative to the size of the market.

permanent income hypothesis The idea that consumption is driven by permanent income rather than current income.

permanent income Your best estimate of your long-term average income.

persistence Economic conditions today are closely related to those in the near future.

Phillips curve A curve illustrating the link between the output gap and unexpected inflation.

physical capital The tools, machinery, and structures that are inputs in the production process.

planned economy Centralized decisions are made about what and how goods and services are produced and allocated.

planned investment Business spending on new capital such as machinery, software, and buildings. Unlike total investment, it excludes changes in inventories.

positive analysis Describes what *is* happening, explaining why, or predicting what will happen.

potential output The level of output that occurs when all resources are fully employed.

poverty line An income level set by the government below which a family is defined to be in poverty; also called a poverty threshold.

poverty rate The percentage of people whose family income is below the poverty line.

precautionary saving Saving to be prepared for a financial emergency.

prediction markets Markets whose payoffs are linked to whether an uncertain event occurs.

present value The amount of money that you would need to invest today in order to produce a specific benefit in the future.

price-taker Someone who decides to charge the prevailing price and whose actions do not affect the prevailing price.

producer price index (PPI) A price index that tracks the prices of inputs into the production process.

producer surplus The economic surplus you get from selling something. Producer surplus = Price – Marginal cost.

production function The methods by which inputs are transformed into output which determines the total production that's possible with a given set of ingredients.

production possibility frontier Shows the different sets of output that are attainable with your scarce resources.

progressive tax A tax where those with more income tend to pay a higher share of their income in taxes.

property rights Control over a tangible or intangible resource.

property tax A tax on the value of property, usually real estate.

Q

quantitative easing (QE) Purchasing large quantities of longer-term government bonds and other securities in an effort to lower long-term interest rates.

R

random walk When a price follows an unpredictable path.

Rational Rule for Buyers Buy more of an item if the marginal benefit of one more is greater than or equal to the price.

Rational Rule for Consumers Consume more today if the marginal benefit of a dollar of consumption today is greater than (or equal to) the marginal benefit of spending a dollar plus interest in the future.

Rational Rule for Investors Pursue an investment opportunity if the present value of future profits is greater than (or perhaps equal to) the up-front cost.

Rational Rule for Markets Produce more of a good if its marginal benefit is greater than (or equal to) the marginal cost.

Rational Rule for Sellers in Competitive Markets Sell one more unit if the price is greater than (or is equal to) the marginal cost.

Rational Rule If something is worth doing, keep doing it until your marginal benefits equal your marginal costs.

real exchange rate The domestic price divided by the foreign price, expressed in the domestic currency. Calculated as:

$$\frac{\text{Domestic price}}{\text{Foreign price/Nominal exchange rate}}$$

real GDP GDP measured in constant prices.

real interest rate The interest rate in terms of changes in your purchasing power; ≈ Nominal interest rate – Inflation rate

real variable A variable that has been adjusted to account for inflation.

recession A period of falling economic activity.

refundable tax credit A tax credit for which receiving the credit doesn't depend on owing income taxes.

regressive tax A tax where those with less income tend to pay a higher share of their income on the tax.

relative poverty A measure of the adequacy of resources relative to the material living standards of your contemporary society.

relative valuation An assessment of the value of an asset by comparing it to similar assets.

reserves The cash that banks need to keep on hand to make payments.

retained earnings The profits that a company chooses not to give as dividends to shareholders.

revisions Updates to earlier estimates.

risk-free interest rate The interest rate on a loan that involves no risk.

risk premium The extra interest that lenders charge to account for the risk of loaning money.

Rule of 70 Divide 70 by the annual growth rate to approximately get the number of years until the original amount doubles.

S

sales tax A tax on purchases that's typically a percentage of the purchase price of goods and services.

saving The portion of income that you don't spend in a given period.

scarcity Resources are limited, therefore any resource you spend pursuing one activity leaves fewer resources to pursue others. Scarcity implies that you always face a trade-off.

seasonally adjusted Data stripped of predictable seasonal patterns.

shadow banks Financial firms that act like banks but, since they are not actually banks, do not have to follow the same rules as banks.

shift in the demand curve A movement of the demand curve itself.

shift in the supply curve A movement of the supply curve itself.

shoe-leather costs The costs incurred trying to avoid holding cash.

shortage When the quantity demanded exceeds the quantity supplied.

short-run aggregate supply curve The aggregate supply curve that applies over a period when prices are neither fully fixed nor fully flexible. As a result, the short run aggregate supply curve is upward-sloping.

social insurance Government-provided insurance against bad outcomes such as unemployment, illness, disability, or outliving your savings.

someone else's shoes technique Imagine yourself in someone else's position in order to understand their objectives and constraints, and forecast the decisions they will make.

specialization Focusing on specific tasks.

speculative bubble When the price of an asset rises above what appears to be its fundamental value.

spending shocks Any change in aggregate expenditure at a given real interest rate and level of income. Spending shocks shift the *IS* curve.

stagflation A combination of economic stagnation — or falling output — combined with high inflation.

sticky prices Prices that adjust sporadically and sluggishly to changes in market conditions.

stock market The market where people buy and sell existing stocks.

structural unemployment Unemployment that occurs because wages don't fall to bring labor demand and supply into equilibrium.

substitute goods Goods that replace each other. Your demand for a good will increase if the price of a substitute good rises, and it will fall if the price of a substitute good falls.

substitutes-in-production Alternative uses of your resources. Your supply of a good will decrease if the price of a substitute-in-production rises.

substitution bias The overestimate of the cost of living that occurs because people substitute toward goods whose prices rise by less.

sunk cost A cost that has been incurred and cannot be reversed. A sunk cost exists in whatever choice you make, and hence it is not an opportunity cost. Good decisions ignore sunk costs.

supply shocks Any change in production costs that leads suppliers to change the prices they charge at any given level of output. Supply shocks shift the Phillips curve.

surplus When the quantity demanded is less than the quantity supplied.

T

tariff A tax on imported products.

taxable income The amount of your income that you pay taxes on.

tax expenditures Special deductions, exemptions, or credits that lower your tax obligations, to encourage you to engage in certain kinds of activities.

technological progress New methods for using existing resources.

term risk The risk that arises from uncertainty about future interest rates.

trade costs The extra costs incurred as a result of buying or selling internationally, rather than domestically.

transfer payments Payments that transfer income from one person to another.

trough A low point in economic activity.

U

underemployed Someone who has some work but wants more hours, or whose job isn't adequately using their skills.

unemployed Working-age people without jobs who are trying to get jobs.

unemployment rate The percentage of the labor force that is unemployed.

unexpected inflation The difference between inflation and inflation expectations
= Inflation – Inflation expectations

unfunded liability A commitment to incur expenses in the future without a plan to pay for those expenses.

user cost of capital The extra cost associated with using one more machine next year $= (r + d) \times C$

utilitarianism The political philosophy that government should try to maximize total utility in society.

utility A measure of well-being.

V

valuation formula Present value of an ongoing stream of payments
$$= \frac{\text{Next year's profit}}{r + d}$$

value added The amount by which the value of an item is increased at each stage of production.
= Total sales – Cost of intermediate inputs

variable costs Those costs — like labor and raw materials — that vary with the quantity of output you produce.

very-short-run aggregate supply curve The aggregate supply curve that applies to the very short run, in which no prices have changed. Because prices are effectively fixed, this curve is horizontal.

voluntary exchange Buyers and sellers exchange money for goods only if they both want to.

W

wage-price spiral A cycle where higher prices lead to higher nominal wages, which leads to higher prices.

wealth All the assets — including savings, cars, a home — that you currently have.

willingness to pay The maximum amount a buyer would be willing to pay for something. To convert costs or benefits into their monetary equivalent, ask yourself: "What is the most I am willing to pay to get this benefit (or avoid that cost)?"

working-age population Those age 16 or older who are not in the military or institutionalized.

world price The price that a product sells for in the global market.

Z

zero lower bound The constraint that nominal interest rates cannot be effectively set below zero.

Index